D1823094

Register of Educational Research in the United Kingdom

Volume 8: 1989-91

National Foundation for Educational Research
in England and Wales

THE LIBRARY
NATIONAL FOUNDATION FOR
EDUCATIONAL RESEARCH
IN ENGLAND & WALES
THE MERE, UPTON PARK
SLOUGH, BERKS. SL1 2DQ

DATE: 15·11·91

CLASS: 2A, J

AUTHOR: Register of
Educational Research

NFER-NELSON

B 4 252527 6

British Library Cataloguing in Publication data
Register of educational research in the United Kingdom
    Vol. 8, 1989-91
    1. Education, Research by British educational institutions
    I. National Foundation for Educational Research in the United Kingdom
    370',7'8041

ISBN 0-7005-1271-3

Published by The NFER-NELSON Publishing Company Ltd., Darville House, 2 Oxford Road East, Windsor, Berkshire SL4 1DF, England

First published 1991
© 1991, National Foundation for Educational Research in England and Wales

ISBN 0 7005 1271 3
Code 8094 02 4

All rights reserved, including translation. No part of this publication may be reproduced or transmitted in any form or by any means, electronic or mechanical, including photocopying, recording or duplication in any information storage or retrieval system, without permission in writing from the publishers.

Phototypeset by Hybert Design & Type · Maidenhead · Berkshire
Printed by Antony Rowe Ltd, Chippenham, Wiltshire

How to use the Register

The Register entries are arranged alphabetically according to the name of the institution at which the research was carried out; within each institution, the entries are arranged alphabetically by department and within the department by researcher. The entries are also consecutively numbered.

Name and subject indexes appear at the back of the volume. The subject index is based on keywords which have been selected from the EUDISED Multilingual Thesaurus and those suggested by the researchers. Each entry is listed against all of its keywords.

Although every effort has been made to check that the details of the entries supplied by the researchers are correct, there may be some errors and inconsistencies, for which we apologise.

The details of the research projects contained in this Register are stored on an IBM microcomputer at the National Foundation for Educational Research (NFER) and entries are continuously updated and new material is added as it is received. Therefore, it is possible to provide Register users with printouts of more up-to-date information. A modest charge is made for this service, which is available from:

Register of Educational Research in the UK
National Foundation for Educational Research
The Mere
Upton Park
Slough
SL1 2DQ
Berkshire
Telephone: (0753) 874123

Contents

Aberdeen University

8/0001

University Teaching Centre,
Kings College, Aberdeen AB9 2UB
0224 480241
Grays School of Art
Garthdene Road, Aberdeen AB2 2QD
0224 33247 ext 41
Gray, C.A. Ms; *Supervisor:* McAleese, W.R. Dr

Teaching styles and creativity in higher art education: 'adaptivity' as style

Abstract: The research aims to improve teaching methods and examines the style of teaching which complements and encourages creativity and the mechanics and outcomes of this activity. Within the researchers's own college, teaching staff have been interviewed concerning their approaches to teaching etc. There are plans to interview/questionnaire students, and to undertake observation/case studies (hopefully in other colleges as well). The researcher is in the process of developing 3D models which help lecturers to exteriorize their styles, identifying and making explicit what is normally considered an intuitive process.

Source of Grant: Robert Gordon's Institute of Technology, Aberdeen: £365 per year
Date of Research: 1984-1989
KEYWORDS: art education; creativity; higher education; teaching method; teaching technique

8/0002

Language Centre, Regent Walk, Aberdeen AB9 2UB
0224 485449
Farrington, B. Mr

LITTRE Translation Learning System

Abstract: The aim of this research is to further the development, in the light of extended piloting with teachers and learners, of the LITTRE system. LITTRE is a set of CALL (Computer Assisted Language Learning) programs which uses the principle of the Expert System to give practice in translation. LITTRE is unusual among materials in that (i) it works at a relatively high level of linguistic sophistication, that is to say approximately A-level, and (ii) it is not a straight forward tutoring system, does not contain any 'right' answers, and is designed for a consultative rather than tutorial use. It is in fact a semi-intelligent tutoring system: intelligent because of the considerable flexibility of its responses, and semi-intelligent in so far as building the complex tree of predictable and possible translations for a given sentence is work that, given the level of language being processed, must be done by hand. At present a version of LITTRE, running on Acorn BBC microcomputers is in use in a number of educational establishments for teaching French. An authoring package, which facilitates greatly the construction of the data tree has been produced. However the increasingly general use of 16-bit IBM-compatible computers is opening up new possibilities, and work has started on the development of a much more sophisticated version of the system. This will be much more powerful than the present version and will be able to run on a variety of different computer systems.

Published Material: FARRINGTON, B.F. (1986). LITTRE, 'An expert system for checking translation at sentence level'. In: FOX, J. (1986). Computer assisted language learning. UEA Papers in Linguistics. University of East Anglia, Norwich, pp.57-74.; FARRINGTON, B.F. (1986). Un Mini Systeme Expert pur Apprendre la Traduction, Les Amis de Sevres. CIEP Paris, pp.108-116.; FARRINGTON, B.F. (1986). 'Triangular Mode Working: The LITTRE project in the field', System, Vol 14, No 2, pp.199-204.
Source of Grant: No funding
Date of Research: 1984 – continuing
KEYWORDS: computer assisted instruction; french language; language teaching; teaching aids; translation

8/0003

Department of Education
King's College, Aberdeen AB9 2UB
0224 272729
Nisbet, J.D. Prof.

International review of the teaching of thinking

Abstract: Research on the teaching of thinking has attracted interest worldwide in recent years, especially in the USA where many schools and colleges offer courses on problem solving and thinking skills. There are over 100 programmes which claim to improve thinking, and academic courses alert students to the thinking skills at the heart of their subjects. The aims of this review are to provide a comprehensive bibliography of books and programmes on the teaching of thinking, to build a conceptual structure for different approaches, to analyze underlying assumptions, and to identify key concepts and issues. Teaching methods for improving thinking skills will also be reviewed; in particular the use of metacognitive strategies for monitoring and managing thinking processes.

Published Material: NISBET, J. & SHUCKSMITH, J. (1986). Learning strategies. London: Routledge
Source of Grant: Spencer Foundation (Chicago)
Date of Research: 1989-1990
KEYWORDS: cognitive development; problem solving; teaching method; thinking

8/0004

Department of Education
Taylor Building, Kings College, Old Aberdeen AB9 2UB
0224 272729
Hendry, L.B. Prof.; Shucksmith, J. Ms; Philip, K. Ms; Jones, L. Ms

Young people, drug misuse and HIV in the Grampian region

Abstract: This study aims to investigate the sources of knowledge about drug use held by young people aged 10 – 22 in the Grampian region of Scotland. Knowledge about links between illicit drug taking, sexual behaviour and HIV (Human Immunodeficiency Virus) will be explored, and the lay beliefs of young people themselves will be examined as they may be influential in interpreting health education messages. Young people's perceptions of the relevance of health education materials on drug use and HIV currently in use within the region will also be looked at. An assessment will be made, not just of the materials themselves, but also of styles of delivery, in order to answer questions about how effectively such packages are targeted and how appropriate and effective they might be. The training needs of professionals working with young people in these areas will also be addressed. Other studies, however, have shown great differences between knowledge about health and the way in which that knowledge is mediated through context to influence behaviour. Thus, routes into drug use will be investigated; parental behaviours, peer influences, substance availability, and socio-economic background may all be factors predisposing young people to drug misuse. Similarly, gaps between knowledge about health beahviours and actions will be explored in relation to sexual activity. Access to, and availability of contraception and safer sex advice are typical of the sorts of issues these interviews will need to raise. The sensitivity of this issue in relation to young people is recognized and is addressed in the methodology. Thus the study will use in depth methods to gauge the variety of contexts in which young people operate. A study of prevalence of adolescent drug misuse and HIV incidence lies within the scope of this project, but evidence will be gathered from secondary sources and from the perceptions of involved professionals as to the levels and distribution patterns of illicit drug use. Ultimately, it is hoped that the results of this study will enable health educators to target their work effectively, with the promotion of ideas which have appeal and relevance to this age group.

Source of Grant: Grampian Health Board: £52,000
Date of Research: 1990 – continuing
KEYWORDS: acquired immune deficiency syndrome

8/0005

Department of Education
Aberdeen AB9 1FX
0224 27279
Stewart, C. Fr; *Supervisor:* Darling, J. Dr

Deschooling as found in the theorists of the sixties and seventies and the relevance of this writing to contemporary Western society

Abstract: The deschooling theory suggests that schools cannot be significantly improved. The school system is in terminal decline because it is an inappropriate response to the needs of children and young people as well as imposing intolerable strains on teachers. Youth are among the new dispossessed, and as such, their needs may be illuminated through the insights of liberation theology. This research will attempt to examine these theories and relate them to contemporary Western society.

Source of Grant: No funding
Date of Research: 1989 – continuing
KEYWORDS: deschooling

8/0006

Department of Education
King's College, Aberdeen AB9 2UB
0224 272729
Duthie, S. Mrs; *Supervisor:* Hendry, L.B. Prof.

Marketing further education: evaluation of a tripartite partnership
Abstract: The aim is to invesigate whether further education colleges 'market' or 'sell' their product (courses), and to investigate the feasibility of marketing further education by setting up a tripartite partnership between further education, industry and students. Primary and secondary research will be done by questionnaire, interviews, and desk research into the needs of students and the needs of industry. The problem of identifying needs of customers will be looked into, and whether further education can or cannot market to meet its customer needs.
Source of Grant: No funding
Date of Research: 1990 – continuing
KEYWORDS: *college of further education; industry further education relationship; marketing; student need*

8/0007

Department of Education
King's College, Aberdeen AB9 2UB
0224 272729
Hendry, L.B. Prof.; Craik, I. Mr; Mack, J. Mr

Measuring the benefits of youth work
Abstract: The main objective of the research project is to formulate an initial set of criteria which, by application on a national basis, will allow comparisons both within and across various categories of youth work. It will focus on assessing the benefits of youth work as it applies to young people and for wider society. It is also intended that these 'performance indicators' will assist in the development of self evaluation in the youth work field. Following the development of an initial set of categorizations of youth work a general questionnaire survey of young people and youth workers will be undertaken. Thereafter five or six 'typical' youth work settings will be chosen for more detailed examination and analysis. The survey and in depth interview process will also be applied to a group of young people who are non-youth work participants. It is intended that this youth work project will benefit from association with a major longitudinal nationwide research programme covering young people's leisure and lifestyles (1985-91) housed within the Department of Education. Thus research personnal appointed to the youth work project will be able to collaborate with an experienced group of research colleagues.
Source of Grant: Scottish Education Department
Date of Research: 1990 – continuing
KEYWORDS: *youth service*

8/0008

Department of Education
King's College, Aberdeen AB9 2UB
0224 272729
Watt, J. Dr

Evaluation of part week provision of nursery education in the Grampian region
Abstract: This research is evaluating the Grampian region's five pilot projects in nursery education in which children are offered 1-4 part day sessions per week instead of the traditional 5 sessions offered elsewhere in the Region. Two projects are based in rural areas and staff travel between centres. The aim of the project is to identify parents' and staff perceptions of the advantages and disadvantages of the provision for children, parents and staff and its implications for existing under fives provision in each area. The fieldwork comprises interviews with all staff in nursery units, a cross section of regional administrators, up to 300 questionnaires from parents, 40 to 60 parent interviews, and informal observation groups.
Source of Grant: Grampian Region Under Fives Committee
Date of Research: 1990 – continuing
KEYWORDS: *early childhood education; nursery school; pre-school education*

8/0009

Department of Education
King's College, Aberdeen AB9 2UB
0224 272729
Hendry, L.B. Prof.; Shucksmith, J. Ms; Welsh, J. Dr

Lifestyles and leisure interests of pupils in a residential school for young people with emotional, social and behavioural difficulties
Abstract: This project is a collaborative study designed to evaluate the development of pupils' lifeskills; teacher-pupil relationships; the leisure curriculum and school-community links in a local residential school for young people with emotional, social and behavioural difficulties. Thus the research can be seen as a set of case studies of a small number of pupils embedded in a wider study of the school's social and leisure programme. The methods employed are a mixture of interview and interpretative techniques with young people including those developed within our large-scale study (Young Peoples' Leisure and Lifestyles in Modern Scotland) discussions with staff; observations of staff meetings, staff-pupil interactions and young people's peer groupings. Thus the project can be seen as a set of case studies embedded in a wider study of the school's social/leisure programme. The sample includes a small number (perhaps no more than 8) of selected young people in the age range 14-16 years. In addition, pupils who have left the school within the last two years, their parents, teachers and social workers are to be surveyed in order to gain a wider picture of young peoples' social development and continuing leisure interests.
Source of Grant: Scottish Education Department: £7,500
Date of Research: 1986-1989
KEYWORDS: *leisure education; maladjusted deviant behaviour; school-community relation; teacher-pupil relation; youth*

8/0010

Department of Education
Aberdeen AB9 2UB
0224 272729
Seed, P. Dr

Social aspects of integration
Abstract: This project is a study of the integration of hanndicapped children with complex learning difficulties into mainstream schooling. Four different kinds of school provision are compared, ranging from the totally integrated to the totally segregated.
Source of Grant: Scottish Education Department: £5,000
Date of Research: 1988-1989
KEYWORDS: *handicapped; integration; learning difficulty; special education*

8/0011

Department of Education
King's College, Aberdeen AB2 2UB
0224 272729
Shucksmith, J. Ms; Hendry, L.B. Prof.; *Supervisor:* Morrison, S.A. Miss

The differential socialization and psychological factors associated with pre-adolescents demonstrating differing degrees of sociability in their leisure activites
Abstract: The development of social behaviour, within the context of play, has been mapped out through a variety of stages, e.g. Piaget (1951), Gesell (1949), Sutton-Smith (1955). However, such structural approaches fail to take individual differences into account. This study aims to isolate a number of children who show distinct patterns of interaction in terms of their leisure pursuits. The interaction patterns studied are solitary, dyadic and social patterns. These children are then examined for related psychological and socialization factors, such as social class, popularity, self-esteem, conformity and achievement motivation. The methods used include an adaption of Pacala's Social Interaction Preference Inventory, diaries, interviews, established psychological tests, and retrospective leisure profiles. The results will provide overall pictures of children with preferences for different interaction patterns, the possible causes of these different patterns and the psychological effects which may have resulted from the different socialization patterns.
Source of Grant: Economic and Social Research Council: £2,975
Date of Research: 1988-1990
KEYWORDS: *child; interaction; leisure; socialization*

8/0012

Department of Education
University Teaching Centre, Aberdeen AB9 2UB
0224 272189
Batley, S.A. Miss; *Supervisor:* McAleese, W.R. Dr

Visual information retrieval: browsing through pictorial databases on videodisc
Abstract: This research is concerned with the retrieval of pictorial information from a database on videodisc. Traditional database access is via keywords, but this may be inappropriate if the information sought is pictorial. An alternative means of retrieval is being

explored – browsing. A videodisc database of 950 photographs has been created for the research. A program in the authoring language microtext provides access to this database. The program allows for three search types: serendipitous browsing, specific browsing, and keyword search. Four visual information types have been identified, which correspond to the different information needs which may be satisfied by a picture: specific, general/nameable, general/abstract, general/subjective. 41 subjects took part in an experiment designed to examine visual information search strategies. These 41 subjects fall into four distinct user groups: school-children, postgraduate students, undergraduate students (librarianship) and librarians. Users were given eight tasks (searched) to perform (two of each of the visual information types). Users selected one of the three search types for each task, retrieved and stored a record of an appropriate image. Five factors affecting picture retrieval were explored: the nature of the information (i.e. pictures rather than text), the database structure, the task or information need, the user, the interface. Preliminary findings indicate that the search strategies adopted by users are largely dependent upon two factors: the nature of the task or information need, and individual user characteristics (e.g. personality and existing knowledge). A second experiment designed to examine browsing strategies in greater detail is now in the final stages of development.
Published Material: Videodisc browsing and the retrieval of visual resources. In: Proceedings of the fifth international conference on technology and education, Edinburgh. March 1988. CED Consultants, 1988, pp.117-120.
Source of Grant: Economic and Social Research Council
Date of Research: 1985-1989
KEYWORDS: database; information retrieval; photograph; picture; videodisc

8/0013
Department of Education
King's College, Aberdeen AB9 2UB
0224 272729
Morrison, S.A. Miss; *Supervisor:* Hendry, L.B. Prof.; Shucksmith, J. Ms
Peers, pals and preferences: the effects of peer status and social needs on the self-concept of pre-adolescent children
Abstract: This study examines the effects of individual social needs (i.e. preference for solitary, dyadic or group interaction) on the relationship between the social self-concepts and peer status of pre adolescent children. In addition, the psychological characteristics and social cognitions associated with different self-concepts, peer status and social needs were examined. A combination of cross-sectioned and qualitative techniques were employed, therefore the results are partly empirical and partly inferential.
Source of Grant: Economic and Social Research Council: £2,860 per annum
Date of Research: 1988 – continuing
KEYWORDS: achievement; child; leisure; play; sex difference; social class

8/0014
Department of Education
Old Aberdeen AB9 2UB
0224 272000
Chessell, G.S.J. Mrs; *Supervisor:* Nisbet, J.D. Prof.
The role and function of learning resources in higher education
Abstract: The role and function of learning resources in higher education is being considered (i) in the context of its historical background and (ii) by studying resource development at various levels of education in the UK and abroad. The issues to be studied fall into three main catagories; (1) the control of learning resources; (2) the management and organization – the tension between competing professions (3) the purposes of resource development – service/research/innovation/initiative. It is hoped to reveal the factors affecting resource development and allow a framework for analyzing these factors to be constructed.
Source of Grant: No funding
Date of Research: 1987-1990
KEYWORDS: administration of education; educational policy; higher education; learning resources

8/0015
Department of Education
King's College, Aberdeen AB9 2UB
0224 272729
Sanders, D. Mr; *Supervisor:* Hendry, L.B. Prof

A study of the approach of Grampian mainstream schools to discipline and the nature of alternative provision for pupils with severe behavioural problems
Abstract: The main thrust of the research programme is to develop a better knowledge and understanding of factors that lead to pupils becoming disruptive. It is hoped that through this knowledge 'pupils at risk' may be identified at an earlier stage and more appropriate education be provided, through which, benefit may be derived for the pupils, the parents, the teachers and the school generally. Thus far the research has included returns from the head teacher/staff of all primary, secondary and special schools in Aberdeen. Secondly, P7 and S2 pupils are being surveyed by questionnaire (approximately 4000 in total). The returns from schools concentrate on school prospectus, discipline and sanctions policies, and views on the approaches made to resolve pupils with behavioural problems. The pupil questionnaire is designed to gain a better insight in to pupil attitudes to family, school and themselves and to match this to the opinions of the pupils' teacher. The results of this will guide the future programme, but additionally, it is anticipated that some case studies of 'excluded' pupils and the value of alternative provision, will be explored.
Source of Grant: Grampian Regional Council: fees
Date of Research: 1987-1990
KEYWORDS: attitude; discipline; disruptive behaviour; misconduct; pupil

8/0016
Department of Language
Aberdeen AB9 2UB
0224 485449
Farrington, B. Mr
Computer assisted learning materials for translation
Abstract: The aim of this research is to investigate the potentiality of semi-intelligent tutoring systems for teaching translation. This is a development and extension of work done on the Scottish Computer Based French Learning Project, the report on which was published in 1984. That project produced the first version of LITTRE, which is a knowledge-based system for learning LI to L2 translation, running on microcomputers. Later versions of LITTRE are very much more powerful, though still running on very small micros, and are in use in a number of institutions. Current activity is centred first on producing a compiled version of the system capable of running on a wide variety of 16-bit computers in which the power and flexibility of the expert-system approach can be fully exploited, and second, on developing a version of the system which can give training in L2 to L1 translation, an activity in which, up to now, computer assisted learning has played no part.
Published Material: FARRINGTON, B. (1986). 'Triangular mode working: the LITTRE project in the field', SYSTEM, Vol 14, No 2, pp.199-204.; FARRINGTON, B. (1988). 'The intelligent artefact is a rotten teacher'. In: AGER, D. (Ed). Written skills in the undergraduate curriculum. London: CILT.; FARRINGTON, B. (1988). 'AI 'grandeur' or 'servitude''? In: CAMERON, K. (Ed). Program structure and principles in computer assisted language learning. London: Intellect.; A complete list of publications is available from the researcher
Source of Grant: No funding
Date of Research: 1984 – continuing
KEYWORDS: computer assisted instruction; french language; language teaching; translation

8/0017
Department of Psychology
Kings College, Aberdeen AB9 2UB
0224 272240
Pont, H.B. Mr
Cognitive assessment of maladjusted children
Abstract: A cognitive social learning approach to assessment is based on the belief that social behaviour is determined by the individuals expectations and beliefs about a situation, and is under the control of mediating processes such as self control or reflective ability. The need therefore is to focus on what a person constructs in specific situations rather than to infer general explanatory traits as merely to describe behaviour. Within the terms of the above approach several areas of cognitive social functioning were identified as being of particular significance in the study of behaviourally and/or emotionally disturbed children, eg. self perception, perception of problem behaviour, perception of others and interpersonal problem-solving skills. The present study includes an in depth assessment of the population (c40 children) of a residential special school

for emotionally/behaviourally disturbed children in the above areas together with a full professional and current behaviour assessment. Performance of the target group is compared with normal controls and a group of problem behaviour controls from a List D setting to identify differences in functioning.
Source of Grant: No funding
Date of Research: 1985-1990
KEYWORDS: assessment; child; cognitive process; maladjusted; social behaviour

8/0018
Departmetnt of Psychology
Psychology Building, Aberdeen AB9 2UB
0224 272190
Duncan, E. Mrs; *Supervisor:* McAleese, W.R. Dr
Intelligent interface for integrated knowledge systems
Abstract: The aim of the research is to collaborate with industrial partners in producing a computer based authoring system linked to videodisc. Cognitive issues concerned with knowledge elicitation and representation are being explored. These will involve experimentation with graphical representations using a window-environment workstation to enable authors to write computer based learning materials using different media.
Source of Grant: Science and Engineering Research Council: £179,000
Date of Research: 1986-1989
KEYWORDS: author; computer; computer assisted instruction; interactive video; knowledge; teaching aids

Accrington & Rossendale College

8/0019
Department of Science & Technology
Sandy Lane, Accrington BB5 2AW
0254 393521
Jones, F. Mr; *Supervisor:* Tyas, D. Mr
Youth access
Abstract: The general aim of the project is to provide an innovative and alternative method of access to training and education for young people with latent ability to study successfully at an advanced level and develop high level skills. The intention is to secure a route to higher education or employment of young people not traditionally attracted to further study. A modular course of study is to be created, in which the curriculum is industry led and which leads ultimately to a higher education course, or employment at technician level. A completely flexible approach is ensured by including a broad range of vocational areas (although based on the footwear industry) within the course and by producing a curriculum which can be negotiated with the individual young person in consultation with the sponsoring employer.
Source of Grant: Training Enterprise Education Division
Date of Research: 1989-1990
KEYWORDS: access to education; course; transition from school to work; vocational education; youth

Anglia Business School

8/0020
Sawyers Hall Lane, Brentwood CM15 9BT
0277 216971
Curran, C.A. Mr
An investigation into aspects of the management of secondary schools
Abstract: The aim of this research is to identify current management practices in secondary schools of a London Borough with special reference to mechanisms of resource allocation and their underlying values. The methodology comprises a questionnaire and follow-up semi-structured interviews of governors, heads of department and 'other ranks'. The target group is all 20 secondary schools in an outer London Borough.
Source of Grant: Essex Institute of Higher Education: £2,000
Date of Research: 1988-1989

KEYWORDS: administration of education; resource allocation; secondary education

8/0021
Centre for Higher Education Management, Danbury Park
Conference Centre, Danbury
Park, Chelmsford CM3 4AT
0245 354491
Anglia Business School
Victoria Road South, Chelmsford
0245 412141
Kells, H.R. Prof.
Models and theories of self-regulation: a multi-national study
Abstract: A multi-stage, fifteen year project to describe, understand and improve higher education self-regulation processes. Earlier stages were empirical, later stages qualitative and theory building. Focus was on North America and Western Europe. In the early stages, retrospective descriptive and correlational studies of self-evaluation processes were employed in North America. In the middle stages, qualitative case analyses, propositional in nature, were conducted in Holland and North America.
Published Material: KELLS, H.R. & KIRKWOOD, R.J. (1979). 'Institutional self-evaluation processes', Educational Record, pp.25-45.; KELLS, H.R. (1988). Self-study processes. New York and London: Macmillan.; KELLS, H.R. & van VUGHT, F.A. (1988). 'Theoretical and practical aspects of a self-regulation and quality control system for Dutch higher education', Tijdschrift Voor Hoger Onderwijs, Vol 6, No 1, pp.15-20. February.; KELLS, H.R. (1990). 'The inadequacy of performance indicators', Higher Education Management', November.; KELLS, H.R. (1990). 'Purposes and means in higher education evaluation', paper presented at the General Conference of the Organization for Economic Co-operation and Developments Institute on Management of Higher Education, Paris, September. Higher Education Management Journal.; KELLS, H.R. (1990). 'The use of incentives in program review and planned change', paper given at European Association for Institutional Research, Lyon, September. Higher Education Management Journal.
Source of Grant: No funding
Date of Research: 1990 – continuing
KEYWORDS: institutional evaluation

Anglia College of Higher Education

8/0022
Sawyers Hall Lane, Brentwood, Essex CM15 8BT
0277 264504
Nickson, M.T. Dr
A study of the culture of the mathematics classroom
Abstract: The project consists of an exploration of current research in this area and the implications for effective teaching and learning of mathematics with a view to inclusion in project on evaluation of children's mathematical learning.
Source of Grant: No funding
Date of Research: 1988-1989
KEYWORDS: classroom; culture; learning; mathematics

8/0023
Sawyers Hall Lane, Brentwood, Essex CM15 9BT
0277 216971
Sussex University
Department of Education
Falmer, Brighton BN1 9RH
0273 606755
Turner, M.A. Mr; *Supervisor:* West, N. Mr; Cooper, B. Dr
The management of probation and induction of teachers in primary schools
Abstract: The pilot and main study investigated approaches to the management of probation and induction in five LEAs, chosen to represent rural, suburban and urban perspectives. Overall, 11 schools were used and interviews were conducted with all participants within them of the management of probation and induction on five occasions during a year (Head, Deputy, designated support teachers, probationers). The methodology was of partially structured but open ended interviews which were recorded by the

interviewer, and transcribed and analyzed for key factors. The research analysis is proceeding in an attempt to identify significant patterns and models in the management of probation and induction.
Source of Grant: No funding
Date of Research: 1987 – continuing
KEYWORDS: induction; primary education; probationary teacher; teacher education

Anglia Higher Education College

8/0024
    Educational Research Centre, Sawyers Hall Lane, Brentwood CM15 9BT
    0277 216971
    Best, R.E. Dr
The place of information skills in initial teacher education
Abstract: There is a growing body of research to suggest that pupils in primary and secondary schools are not encouraged to use the library, nor provided with much opportunity to do so. References to libraries and resource centres as the 'hub' of the curriculum appear to have largely a rhetorical force. The teaching of study-skills, library skills and the handling of information generally seems to be given low priority in many schools. The research reported here begins with the hypothesis that these deficiencies are at least partly the result of the way teachers are trained. Using interviews, observation and questionnaires, the report explores the place of the library and of information handling skills in the BEd courses offered in four teacher-training institutions. The attitudes and practices of tutors, students and librarians are described and a number of distinct perspectives are established. Perceptions of user-education, course requirements, student competence in information-handling, and the strategies students adopt to 'play the system' are discussed at some length. Attention is focused on the important issues of assessment, the integration of study-skills, library use and course content, and the impact of emotional factors on library use, and some examples of good practice are offered. The report concludes with an agenda of issues for debate by all those involved in the review and development of teacher training courses.
Published Material: BEST, R., ABBOTT, F. & TAYLOR, M. 'Teaching skills for learning', British Library, 'Library and Information Research Report' series, (forthcoming).; BEST, R. 'Library use and teacher training', Education Libraries Journal, (forthcoming).
Source of Grant: British Library Research and Development Department: £25,150
Date of Research: 1987-1990
KEYWORDS: information skills; library; teacher education

Arts Council

8/0025
    Department of Dance and Mime
    105 Piccadilly, London W1V OAU
    071 629 9495
    Bedford College of Higher Education
    37 Lansdowne Road, Bedford MK40 2BZ
    0234 51966
    Rae, P. Ms; *Supervisor:* Hoyle, S. Ms
Young people dancing
Abstract: This research was carried out in West Yorkshire, Devon and Cornwall in order to evaluate current dance provision for young people. It is based on discussions, interviews and questionnaires and draws on documentation.
Published Material: HOYLE, S. (Ed). (1990). Young people dancing. London: Arts Council of Great Britain, Department of Dance & Mime.
Source of Grant: Arts Council: £2,500 plus expenses
Date of Research: 1988-1989
KEYWORDS: dance; educational provision; youth

8/0026
    Department of Dance & Mime
    105 Piccadilly, London W1V OAU
    071 629 9495
    Bedford College of Higher Education
    37 Lansdowne Road, Bedford MK40 2BZ
    0234 51966
    Burns, S. Ms; *Supervisor:* Hoyle, S. Ms
South Asian dance in education
Abstract: This project will evaluate South Asian dance in education. It aims to (i) plan and monitor a 10 week residency at Bedford College by South Asian dance artists. This is a pilot project, the findings of which will be disseminated nationally. (ii) Develop an awareness of South Asian dance styles amongst teachers and trainee teachers and assist them in using South Asian dance in their teaching programmes. (iii) Develop the understanding and appreciation of South Asian dance amongst schools and community groups in Bedford and the surrounding area. (iv) Prepare resource materials and guidelines for use in education. (v) Produce a written evaluation of the work currently being done by South Asian dance artists in education, and make recommendations to the Arts Council and Eastern Arts for further development.
Published Material: HOYLE, S. (1990). South Asian dance in education: an example of current practice. London: Arts Council of Great Britain, Department of Dance & Mime.
Source of Grant: Arts Council, Eastern Arts, Bedfordshire Education Authority; Bedford College of Higher Education; £3,500 plus expenses and project budget
Date of Research: 1988-1989
KEYWORDS: Asia; dance; evaluation

Associated Examining Board

8/0027
    Stag Hill House, Guildford GU2 5XJ
    0483 506506
    Cresswell, M.J. Mr; Ward, M.A.G. Mr; Wilmut, J. Mr; *Supervisor:* Houston, J.G. Dr.
Examinations research programme
Abstract: The Research and Statistics Division carries out research into fundamental problems associated with educational measurement together with work on specific syllabuses. The Division is also involved in collaborative studies with the other GCSE (General Certificate of Secondary Education) Boards to ensure that the examinations of all Boards are set and marked to comparable standards. Particular general areas of study presently being pursued are: (a) reliability of marking; (b) the weighting of examination components; (c) profile reporting of examination results; (d) differentiated assessment; and (e) the assessment of modular schemes. The Division is also concerned with development work for GCSE (General Certificate of Secondary Education) examinations within the Southern Examining Group, of which the Board is a part.
Published Material: CRESSWELL, M.J. (1984). 'Estimating the effects of reducing the number of papers in an examination', Educational Studies, Vol 10, No 1.; WILMUT, J. & BODDINGTON, A.J. (1984). 'The development of a common 16 + examination for the Schools Council History 13-16 project', Teaching History, Vol 40, pp.22-25.; CRESSWELL, M.J. (1986). 'Examination grades – how many should there be?', British Educational Research Journal, Vol 12, No 1, pp.37-54.; CRESSWELL, M.J. (1986). 'A review of borderline reviewing', Educational Studies, Vol 12, No 2, pp.175-190.
Date of Research: 1983 – continuing
KEYWORDS: evaluation; examination; measurement technique; standard

Aston University

8/0028
    Aston Business School, Aston Triangle, Birmingham B4 7ET
    021 359 3011
    Lee, G. Dr
Developments in distance learning in management education

Abstract: A review of developments in the use of distance learning techniques in MBAs (Master of Business Administration) and other management development programmes with special reference to their implications for management learning.
Source of Grant: No funding
Date of Research: 1986 – continuing
KEYWORDS: distance study; management education; video recording

8/0029
Department of Modern Languages
Aston Triangle, Birmingham B4 7ET
021 359 3611
Kolinsky, E. Dr
The treatment of contemporary history in school textbooks, with special reference to the treatment of the holocaust in West German textbooks
Abstract: This study focuses on the analysis of school textbooks published since 1972 with a special focus on history teaching. It is a follow-up study of an earlier analysis published in Yad Vashem studies in 1976. The study draws on quantitative contents analyses of school books and draws on recent historiography to evaluate the balance between information and interpretation in history presentations for secondary school teaching. Special emphasis is given to an evaluation of primary source usage and of personal accounts in school history.
Source of Grant: Georg Eckert Institute: Fellowship £700
Date of Research: 1988-1989
KEYWORDS: history; secondary education; textbook

8/0030
Department of Modern Languages
The Triangle, Birmingham B4 7ET
021 359 3611 ext 4217
Hantrais, L. Prof.; Crompton, R. Ms; Walters, P. Ms
Women in professional occupations in France and Britain
Abstract: The research aims to examine two policy issues. The shortage of qualified workers in Britain is generating concern about retaining well qualified women in the workforce. The prospect of freedom of movement for workers within the European Community after 1992 is provoking interest in the transferability and equivalence of national qualifications. The relationship between qualifications and occupations in two European countries is being investigated, by conducting research in Britain and France on women's entry into pharmacy, banking, accountancy and law and on their career progression in these professional occupations. Another important focus of the research is the relationship between the State, educational institutions and professional associations in organizing qualifications and determing the structure of occupations in the two societies. The study is based on secondary analysis of available data on women in the four occupational areas combined with in depth interviews of fifteen qualified women in each of the occupations in the two countries. The material about career patterns, commitment and achivement are being analyzed within the context of information about social institutions in an effort to explain national variations in the structure of occupations according to gender.
Published Material: CROMPTON, R., HANTRAIS, L. & WALTERS, P. (1990). 'Gender relations and employment', British Journal of Sociology, Vol 41, No 3, pp.329-339.
Source of Grant: Economic and Social Research Council: £22,400 European Commission for Equal Opportunities Unit; supplementary award: £5,985
Date of Research: 1989 – continuing
KEYWORDS: career ladder; comparative education; EEC; labour shortage; women's profession; women's employment

8/0031
Department of Modern Languages
The Triangle, Birmingham B4 7ET
021 359 3611 ext 4217
Hantrais, L. Prof.
Education, training and labour markets in Europe
Abstract: The aim of the current series of research seminars is to examine the implications of 1992 for social policy in Europe. The seminars provide a forum for researchers in comparative social science to discuss the theoretical, methodological, managerial and practical problems involved in cross-national collaborative projects from a multi-disciplinary perspective. The participants in the seminars come from a wide range of social science institutions through-out Europe and are well known for their international work. The themes being examined in the seminar on Education, Training and Labour Markets in Europe and the subsequent publication cover the relationship between education, training, socialization and employment in the EC Member States. Issues concerned with the changing structure of qualifications, the impact of new technologies and the deployment of skills in manufacturing are investigated, and the effects of national variations in credentials on labour mobility are highlighted.
Published Material: HANTRAIS, L., MANGEN, S. & O'BRIEN, M. (1991). (Eds). 'Training and labour markets in Europe', Cross-National Research Papers, Vol 4, No 2.
Source of Grant: Training Enterprise Education Division: approximately £800-£1,000
Date of Research: 1990 – continuing
KEYWORDS: comparative education; education; EEC; Europe; labour market; qualification; skill; technological change; training

8/0032
Department of Modern Languages
The Triangle, Birmingham B4 7ET
021 359 3611 ext 4217
Hantrais, L. Prof.
Managing professional and family life
Abstract: This comparative study of the education, employment and family life of well qualified women in two European Community member states examines the process whereby women in Britain and France who have undergone higher education seek to maximize returns on the time and effort invested while also often raising a family. In addition to investigating the place of women in the educational system, and particularly in higher education, their entry into the labour market, and their family and employment patterns, explanations are sought for the differences observed in terms of the wider social, political and economic environments. Secondary analysis of the available national data is combined with comparisons of the social systems and of relevant policies in the two countries. The results from a new qualitative study based on a matched sample of well qualified British and French women (100 in each country) are introduced in order to compare and contrast the ways in which women manage their professional and family lives. The research deals with the accountability of higher education, changing patterns of female employment and the strategies adopted for combining paid work with childraising. The impact of European Community legislation on individual member states and the mobility of labour within the Community are also considered, as well as the possible impact of national and European policy on social behaviour. The study demonstrates that British women may not be benefiting from their education as much as their French counterparts but it also suggests that current employment patterns, and in particular the British phenomenon of the career break should not be considered inevitable.
Published Material: HANTRAIS, L. (1990). Managing professional and family life: a comparative study of British and French women. Aldershot; Vermont: Gower (Dartmouth Series).; HANTRAIS, L. (1989). 'Higher education in Britain and France: the relevance of comparisons for an understanding of European integration', Integration, Vol 3, No 1, pp.129-151.
Source of Grant: ESRC/CNRS (Economic and Social Research Council/Cross National Research Group) Franco-British Programme The French Embassy, London Aston University, Department of Modern Languages: joint support for travel and publications
Date of Research: 1987-1990
KEYWORDS: comparative education; family life; France; higher education; United Kingdom; women's education; women's employment

8/0033
Department of Modern Languages
Aston Triangle, Birmingham B4 7ET
021 359 3611
Fletcher, J.M. Dr; Upton, C.A. Dr
Transcription and analysis of the domestic accounts of Merton College, Oxford, for the Tudor period
Abstract: College domestic accounts remain as one of the last largely unexplored sources of university academic, social, political and economic history for the Tudor period. Those of Merton College are particularly full for this century. The project will transcribe and publish these accounts. At the same time, a series of articles will describe and evaluate the material they contain and, where possi-

ble, link it with that available from other similar educational institutions. The work is expected to show in detail the various problems that Oxford colleges met at this period in their relations with secular and ecclesiastical authorities and to provide some insight into the management of college finance. Since Merton College was an establishment of middle size, with a stable position and well established links with the outside world, this study will also throw light on the role of the educated elite in Tudor society and the reactions of that society to problems of the provision and control of higher education in a world affected by changes of the Renaissance and Reformation.
Published Material: FLETCHER, J.M. and UPTON, C.A. (1983). 'Destruction, repair and removal: an Oxford college chapel during the Reformation', Oxoniensia, No 48, pp.199-30.; FLETCHER, J.M. & UPTON, C.A. (1984). 'A short description of the sixteenth century domestic accounts of Merton College, Oxford'. In: Die Geschichte der Universitaten un ihre Erforschung, Leipzig, pp.54-67.; FLETCHER, J.M. & UPTON, C.A. (1987). 'Monastic enclave' or 'open society'? A consideration of the role of women in the life of an Oxford college community in the early tudor period', History of Education, No 16, pp.1-9.
Source of Grant: Economic and Social Research Council, Merton College and the British Academy: jointly £5,000
Date of Research: 1980 – continuing
KEYWORDS: *administration of education; financial resources; higher education; history of education; university*

8/0034
Department of Modern Languages
Gosta Green, Birmingham B4 7ET
021 359 3611
Carroll, T.C. Ms; *Supervisor:* Ager, D.E. Prof.
Attitudes to language: a cross cultural study
Abstract: The study is concerned with attitudes to language in the United Kingdom, France and Japan. 'Attitudes to language' comprises: (i) Attitudes to the mother tongue; (ii) attitudes to foreign languages; and (iii) attitudes towards foreigners learning and speaking one's mother tongue. The attitudes of three target groups (exchange students/recent graduates; business people working abroad; a group more representative of the general population without experience of living abroad) from the three countries will be compared and contrasted against a background of more generalized attitudes and official policy on language in the United Kingdom, France and Japan.
Source of Grant: University of Aston studentship
Date of Research: 1984 – continuing
KEYWORDS: *foreign languages; France; Japan; language teaching; mother tongue; United Kingdom*

8/0035
Department of Modern Languages
Aston Triangle, Birmingham B4 7ET
021 359 3611
Upward, C. Mr
The reform of English spelling by omission of redundant letters
Abstract: Proposals for rationalizing English orthography date back to the sixteenth century. Modern proposals have assumed that reform merely required consistent representation of Received Pronunciation, but they took little account of the psychological and administrative practicalities of introducing a visually revolutionary system. One such proposal, the Simplified Spelling Society's 'New Spelling' (1948), formed the basis for Sir James Pitman's 'Initial Teaching Alphabet', which proved the educational benefits of regularized spelling, but was unsuited for a general reform of written English. In 1982, Valerie Yule published on the concept of 'Cut Spelling', which meant reform by omitting redundant letters rather than introducing new letters to words. The aim of the project is to systematize the concept of Cut Spelling, explore its linguistic implications, and develop a coherent reform proposal based on it. The concept of Cut Spelling has been reduced to 3 main rules: (1) Omission of letters irrelevant to pronunciation; (2) extended use of syllabographic ⟨L, m, n, r⟩ in post-accentual syllables, with morphophonemic regularization of inflections; (3) simplification of doubled consonants. The implications of such a system have been explored under a number of headings: (i) degree of visual disruption resulting from different kinds of spelling change; (ii) reduction of grapheme-variety; (iii) avoidance of spelling error; (iv) economy of representation; (v) homophones and homographs; (vi) phonographic and graphotactic innovation; (vii) diachronic tendencies towards Cut Spelling in English and other European lan-

guages. In conclusion, Cut Spelling offers a practicable new approach to the modernization of English spelling, combining compatibility with traditional orthography, enhanced regularity, and significant economy in use.
Published Material: UPWARD, C. (1989). 'Conflicting eficiency criteria in cut speling-2', Journal of the Simplified Spelling Society, Vol 3, No 1, pp.21-29.; UPWARD, C. (1989). 'The initial teaching alphapbet and spelling reform', UK i.t.a. Federation Newsletter, Spring, pp.13-18.; UPWARD, C. (1989). 'Recent developments in 're-regulating' written German', Journal of the Simplified Spelling Society, Vol 3, No 1, pp.15-17.; UPWARD, C. & GREGERSEN, E. (1989). 'Morfemes and cut spelling', Journal of the Simplified Spelling Society, Vol 3, No 1, pp.25-29.; UPWARD, C. (1990). 'Rule of thum', Times Educational Supplement, No 3882, November 23, pp.R16.; UPWARD, C. (1991). approximately 40 articles in, The Oxford Companion to the English Language. Oxford: Oxford University Press. (forthcoming). A complete list of publications is available from the researcher.
Source of Grant: from Department of Modern Languages and Simplified Spelling Society: minor costs
Date of Research: 1982 – continuing
KEYWORDS: *English language; literacy; reading; spelling*

Banstead Mobility Centre

8/0036
Park Road, Banstead, Surrey SM7 3EE
0737 351674
North London School of Physiotherapy, 10 Highgate Hill, London N19
071 272 1659
Ponsford, A-S. Mrs; *Supervisor:* Cornwell, B. Mrs; Simms, B. Mrs; French, S. Miss
The cerebral palsy driver
Abstract: Banstead Mobility Centre, part of the Queen Elizabeth's foundation for the Disabled, was established in May 1982 to assist disabled people to achieve an optimum level of outdoor mobility which would enrich the quality of their working and social life. A team consisting of medical consultant, orthoptist, educational psychologist, physiotherapist and driving consultant do a full day' assessment on the disabled client's ability to learn to drive or return to driving. There is a need to find out more about the cerebral palsy group in order to make more accurate predictions regarding this group's ability to learn to drive. A Department of Transport funded three year research project 'Disabled drivers, the outcome of assessment tuition and training' was started in 1986. A follow-up questionnaire has been sent out to clients one year after their assessment and then at six monthly intervals for those still learning. The returned questionnaires provide information on how many driving lessons were taken, who was used as a teacher, what adaptations the car had and what problems were experienced during the tuition period. In addition to analysing these questionnaires from ex-clients who have cerebral palsy, 20 of this group under 30 years of age who have cerebral palsy and are either learner drivers or novice drivers will be interviewed and observed while driving. The aim is to find out the extent to which impaired motor control has been safely overcome and the manner in which this has been achieved. These results would be helpful to future learner drivers with cerebral palsy.
Published Material: PONSFORD, A-S. Mrs (1989). 'The man nobody believed could drive', Therapy Weekly, 27 April 1989.
Source of Grant: Spastics Society: £974100
Date of Research: 1989 – continuing
KEYWORDS: *cerebral palsy; driver education; motor disorder; physical handicap*

Barnsley Local Education Authority

8/0037
Berneslai Close, Barnsley S7R 2HS
0226 733252
Further Education Unit

Grove House, 2-6 Orange Street, London WC2H 7WE
071 321 0433
McCoy, S. Mr; *Supervisor:* Croll, D. Mr

Education audit as a basis for tertiary reorganization

Abstract: This research has arisen out of the need for improvement in post-16 participation and attainment in Barnsley local education authority which is below the national average. Institutions are also having to come to terms witht the 16 + demographic downturn, an economic recession and changes to the local occupational structure. A tertiary plan for the authority, based on a single institution has been agreed by the Education Committee, and will be implemented from September 1990. Using FEU guidance there will be a Barnsley Education Audit. It will include an analysis of curriculum quality and equity, and will also place the results of the audit within the context of the authority's curriculum entitlement policy. This will provide an opportunity to confirm that an audit exercise and an entitlement policy are complimentary. The audit will also allow the framework to be applied to non FEU establishments. A project team will be established and will comprise staff from participating institutions and its activities will include planning a project strategy, developing an inventory, design and construct audit instruments, collect relevant data using questionnaires, interviews and documentary sources, carry out performance evaluation, analyze data, and develop an appropriate action plan. There will be four phases to the project. Phase 1: January 1990, planning and audit design. Phase 2: from April 1990, collection of data. Phase 3: from September 1990, collection, recording and analysis of data. Phase 4: from January 1991, evaluation, reporting and action planning. Outcomes will include a collaborative model for an LEA post- 16 audit, a tested audit framework and instruments, a report of the exercise, and a LEA post- 16 action plan.

Source of Grant: Further Education Unit
Date of Research: 1990 – continuing
KEYWORDS: education audit; sixteen to nineteen education; tertiary education

Bath College of Higher Education

8/0038

Department of Education
Newton Park, Newton St Loe, Bath BA2 9BN
0255 873701
Eden, C.E. Mrs

The development of gender roles in young people

Abstract: Twenty students on a YTS (Youth Training Scheme) were interviewed during 1986-1988. The focus of questions concerned experiences of family and schooling leading to stereotypical occupational choices. Such choices ran counter to claims made by proponents of the YTS that gender stereotypes would be challenged within the scheme. The research points to the continuing power of gendered environments and cultural definitions of gender roles.

Published Material: EDEN, C. & AUBREY, K. (1988). 'YTS and gender – continuity or challenge'. In: COLES, B. (Ed). Young careers. Buckingham: Open University Press.
Source of Grant: No funding
Date of Research: 1987-1990
KEYWORDS: sex difference; sex role; stereotype; youth training scheme

8/0039

Department of Education
Newton Park, Newton St Loe, Bath BA2 9BN
0255 873701
Cush, D. Ms

Buddhists and Christians in Britain today

Abstract: The aim of the research is to produce materials to support the teaching of Buddhism and Christianity at GCSE (General Certificate of Secondary Education) and A level. For 'Buddhists in Britain today' twelve individuals were interviewed at length about their beliefs and values and how they affect their lives. For 'Christians in Britain today' fifteen individuals were interviewed. A major aim was to show the rich diversity of both traditions and to take a sample that fairly represented the different sub-traditions, male and female perspectives, and the perspectives of different age groups and ethnic groups.

Published Material: CUSH, D. (1986). 'Teaching Buddhism for A level and other public examinations', British Journal of Religious Education, Autumn 1986.; CUSH, D. (1990). Buddhists in Britain today. Sevenoaks: Hodder & Stoughton. (forthcoming); CUSH, D. (1990). Christians in Britain today. Sevenoaks: Hodder & Stoughton. (forthcoming)
Source of Grant: No funding
Date of Research: 1980-1990
KEYWORDS: Buddhism; Christian education; Christianity; General Certificate of Secondary Education; secondary education; sixth form; teaching aids

8/0040

Department of Education
Newton Park, Newton St Looe, Bath BA2 9BN
0225 3701
Barnes, S.J. Mr

Investigation into the use, range and structure of topic work at the lower junior school level

Abstract: This investigation has arisen as a result of concern over the lack of direction and isolation of topic work in the curriculum as a whole. The aims are: (1) to examine the range and use of topic work; (2) to discover the main topics taught at lower junior level; and (3) to relate topic concepts to developmental levels of pupils. The main purpose is to impose some overall structure on topic work which allows for progression, evaluation and assimilation into the curriculum. The details of method, range and research have not yet been finalized.

Source of Grant: No funding
Date of Research: 1986 – continuing
KEYWORDS: curriculum; junior school; project work

Bath University

8/0041

Department for the Study of Organizational Change and Development
Claverton Down, Bath BA2 7AY
0225 826826
Carberry, H. Ms; *Supervisor:* Reason, P. Dr

Person-centred learning in management education: a systems perspective

Abstract: Enabling people to take responsibility for their own learning is an aim few would dispute as ideal, yet moves in that direction seem barely visible. Using co-operative inquiry as a research philosophy, the environments/systems within which person-centred learning does or does not exist will be investigated. Management education in higher education establishments is the focus of the inquiry.

Source of Grant: Employer assists with tuition fees
Date of Research: 1987-1990
KEYWORDS: higher education; learning conditions; management education; self-instruction

8/0042

Department of Education
Claverton Down, Bath BA2 7AY
0225 826826
Calderhead, J. Dr; Robson, M. Dr

Images of teaching and learning in student teachers' professional development

Abstract: The project aims to examine the nature of student primary teachers' conceptions of teaching and learning, how these influence what students abstract from their experiences in college and school, and how their early conceptions shape the growth of their own classroom practice. 24 student teachers, divided between two primary pre-service training courses in England and Australia, are being followed through their teacher training careers. The students are being interviewed at regular intervals. In order to tap their more tacit understandings of classrooms, videotapes of teaching are shown to students who are invited to comment on what they observe; students are also asked to write accounts of lessons in the form of scripts as a means of making explicit their assumptions about teaching and learning.

Published Material: CALDERHEAD, J. (Ed). (1988). Teachers' professional learning. Lewes: Falmer Press.; CALDERHEAD, J. (1991). Images of teaching: Student teachers early conception of

classroom practice. Teacher and Teacher Education, January.
Source of Grant: Internally supported
Date of Research: 1987 – continuing
KEYWORDS: *primary education; professional development; student teacher; teacher education*

8/0043
Department of Education
Claverton Down, Bath BA2 7AY
0225 826826
National Institute for Careers Education and Counselling
Sheraton House, Gloucester Street, Castle Park, Cambridge
CB3 0AX
0223 460277
Jamieson, I. Prof.; Watts, A. Mr; Miller, A. Mr
Re-working work experience
Abstract: An action research based study of work experience for students up to the age of 18 in full time education in England and Wales. The research also draws on comparative material beyond the United Kingdom. The research investigates current practice in England and Wales form an administrative, oranizational and curriculum point of view and attempts to develop new models for examining the concept of work experience.
Published Material: MILLER, A., JAMIESON, I.M. & WATTS, A.C. (1989). 'Reviewing work experience: a national perspective', London: Schools/Curriculum Industry Partnership/National Curriculum Council.; WATTS, A.C., JAMIESON, I.M. & MILLER, A. (1989). 'Testing the world of work', Education, Vol 173, No 25.
Source of Grant: DES (Department of Education & Science): £2,000
Project Trident: £2,000
Date of Research: 1987-1990
KEYWORDS: *comparative education; experiential learning; industry education work experience*

8/0044
Department of Education
Claverton Down, Bath BA2 7AY
0225 826826
Oulton, C.R. Mr; *Supervisor:* Selmes, C. Dr
Theory through practice? An investigation into the role of educational theory in initial teacher education
Abstract: The relationship between theory and practice in initial teacher education remains a contentious issue. The research programme consists of an investigation into the relationship between theory and practice espoused in one PGCE (Postgraduate Certificate in Education) course. The researcher is a methods tutor on the PGCE course programme. The research methodology consists of a series of in depth interviews with tutors to establish their perception of the relationship between theory and practice and how they believe the course develops the students understanding of that relationship. These perceptions will be compared with those of a group of students who will be interviewed at key stages during the course. A key issue in the research is an individual student's conception of how they think they are going to learn to teach. The research attempts to test the hypothesis that a student's conception of how they think they are going to learn to teach may make it difficult for them to make sense of the course. Where such blocks to learning are identified attempts will be made to help the students to reconstruct their conception. This remedial action will be undertaken, where necessary, within a group of six students who are in the researcher's method group. This group will be compared with a group of students who do not work with the researcher.
Source of Grant: No funding
Date of Research: 1988 – continuing
KEYWORDS: *teacher education; theory practice relationship*

8/0045
Department of Education
Claverton Down, Bath BA2 7AY
0225 826826
Nash, R. Mr; *Supervisor:* Jamieson, I.M. Prof.
An examination of pupil learning experiences in enterprise education
Abstract: There has been a growing interest in enterprise education in all types of schools during the past five years which in turn has led to a growing number of Mini-Enterprise and Young Enterprise companies being established (Durowse & Elliot, 1988). There appears to be an implicit belief by advocates of such schemes that the experiential teaching methods used enable pupils to learn more effectively than a didactic approach (Jamieson, Miller & Watts, 1988). There is, however, little hard evidence at present to support

this assumption. The aim of the project is to establish what knowledge, skills and attitudes are gained by pupils participating in enterprise activities, and to establish what factors contribute to the learning process that takes place during enterprise activities. The research will be in three stages. Firstly to establish the knowledge, skills and attitudes gained by pupils participating in an enterprise activity, to investigate the effectiveness of experiential learning during enterprise activities and how this contributes to the development of pupils' understanding of economic concepts, and to establish the strength/weaknesses of the various enterprise education models.
Source of Grant: No funding
Date of Research: 1988 – continuing
KEYWORDS: *enterprise education; experiential learning; learning process*

8/0046
Department of Education
Claverton Down, Bath BA2 7AY
0225 826826
Cleves, I.M. Mr; *Supervisor:* Jamieson, I.M. Prof.
Practical maths project
Abstract: In England for some years teaching material has been produced for use in schools which is based on the workplace. Among this has been material for mathematics teaching. However, it is questioned as to how well this material has been received by maths teachers. The project aims to examine the reaction of mathematics teachers (secondary) to this material, such as awareness, takeup, and perceived value and to this concept. It is also intended to develop process models for development and dissemination of such materials. The data for the project is being obtained by postal survey of teachers, interviews with teachers, advisers and others involved in maths education, interviews with pupils and industrialists', group evaluation of materials by practising teachers, and collection and analysis of case studies of activity in this field. Teachers in the state system, in secondary schools, in England and others related are being surveyed, as an opportunity sample. The models for dissemination will involve groups of established teachers and ITE (Initial Teacher Education) and will involve both prepared materials, and the development of materials. It is intended to produce materials which will assist teachers in incorporating such materials into their classrooms if they wish.
Source of Grant: British Petroleum Education: £100,000
Date of Research: 1988 – continuing
KEYWORDS: *industry; mathematics; simulation; teacher response; teaching aids*

8/0047
Department of Education
Claverton Down, Bath BA2 7AY
0225 826826
McNiff, J. Miss; *Supervisor:* Whitehead, A.J. Mr
An explanation for an individual's educational development through the dialectic of action research
Abstract: The purpose of the text is to analyze the eduational development of a reflective practitioner. It contains two analytic frameworks. The inner framework considers the origin, constitution, and use of values in education. Within this framework the researcher examines the dominant assumptions of the literature of values education, and that of other related disciplines, and concludes that they are not adequate as a basis for generating an explanation for her own educational development. The outer framework analyzes the researchers own educational development in terms of an educational theory which can account for this development as both a generative and transformatory process. The presentation is designed to show the origin, constitution and use of a critical eduational science in which educational research can be shown to be both intrinsically educational and a proper base for teaching.
Published Material: McNIFF, J. (1988). Action research: principles and practice. London: MacMillan.
Source of Grant: No funding
Date of Research: 1981-1990
KEYWORDS: *action research; educational research; individual development; philosophy of education; values education*

8/0048
Department of Education
Claverton Down, Bath BA2 7AY
0225 826826
Elsiddig, M.O. Mr; *Supervisor:* Jamieson, I.M. Prof.

Expanding higher education and the Open University – the case of the Sudan as an example for developing countries
Abstract: The purpose of this study is to examine critically the demand and opportunity for higher education in the developing countries in general and the Sudan in particular, and to see to what extent expansion in the system could be achieved. The study then goes beyond that and considers a national institution of distance and open learning at university level in terms of needs, purposes, and in terms of the possibility in practice in the Sudan. The study will be based on three sources. Firstly, historical documents and literature reviews of the reasons for higher education demand, higher education system, distance and open learning system, and open universities. In addition, literature and administrative reports on general and higher education in the Sudan are to be analyzed. Interviews will be held with the leading figures in education in the Sudan and related organizations, into the possibility of higher education expansion and the formation of an open learning institution. An in depth observation of the ISETI (Inservice Educational Training Institute), which adopts a distance learning approach will also be used. From this part of the study will emerge generalizations concerning the appropriateness of distance learning in the Sudan.
Source of Grant: Sudan Government
Date of Research: 1986-1990
KEYWORDS: *developing country; distance study; higher education; open learning; Sudan*

8/0049
Department of Education
Claverton Down, Bath BA2 7AY
0225 826826
The Royal Society for the Arts
8 John Adam Street,
London WC2N 6EZ
071 930 5115
English, T. Mrs; *Supervisor:* Chapman, C. Mr
The home – school contract of partnership. A joint initiative between the National Association of Headteachers and Education for Capability
Abstract: This is a joint initiative between NAHT (National Association of Headteachers) and Education for Capability to encourage home/school links which meet the criteria of the home/school contract of partnership. There will be a nationwide project to select schools to pilot a funded scheme designed to strengthen existing house/school links and to develop new strategies. Questionnaires will be sent to 60 representative primary and secondary schools in Avon, Gloucestershire, Somerset and Wiltshire. Follow up visits will be made to schools with interesting practice. A final report of findings with recommendation for selection of school/schools for a pilot project will be presented to the Royal Society for the Arts in mid-December 1989.
Source of Grant: Royal Society for the Arts: £1,500
Date of Research: 1989-1989
KEYWORDS: *home school relationship; parent participation; parent-school relation*

8/0050
Department of Education
Claverton Down,
Bath BA2 7AY
0225 826826
Harris, A. Ms; *Supervisor:* Jamieson, I.M. Prof.
An investigation into teaching approaches in enterprise education
Abstract: This project aims to investigate the teaching approaches adopted by teachers involved in enterprise work. It intends to provide information about the teaching approaches used by teachers in an enterprise teaching context and to compare these approaches with those used in other lessons. Using each teacher as his or her own control, the research will adopt a triangulation of methods including classroom observation, questionnaire and interview. The sample has been chosen from all teachers involved in enterprise work within GCSE (General Certificate of Secondary Education) and incorporates a diverse cross section of schools. The study will involve in depth observation of ten to twelve teachers over several terms and will include pupil questionnaires and interview.
Source of Grant: No funding
Date of Research: 1988 – continuing
KEYWORDS: *enterprise; enterprise education; General Certificate of Secondary Education; teaching method*

8/0051
Department of Education
Claverton Down, Bath BA2 7AY
0225 826826
Blandford, S. Miss; *Supervisor:* Harvey, T.J. Dr
Integrated arts: The study, development and evaluation of a scheme for third year secondary school pupils
Abstract: The Wiltshire LEA (local education authority) has an inter-arts programme currently practised under the auspices of the Manpower Services TVEI (Technical and Vocational Education Initiative) scheme. Although this is limited to one area of the county, the programme has implications for further curriculum development in the integration of the arts. This study seeks to investigate the present position of the arts in schools, to review the philosophies on the integration of the arts, and to develop and evaluate a 1-term integrated arts programme for 3/4th year pupils. There will be a survey of secondary schools in Wiltshire and Avon which will involve four local schools in implementing an integrated arts programme. A critical review of the philosophies of integration of the arts will be carried out. This will include a study of the work of Ross, Wilkins and Reimer; Gulbenkein and Burdett. A survey by questionnaire will also be carried out to ascertain the present arts teaching situation in Wiltshire and Avon; and to assess the degree of integration. The production of a teaching/resource package for a third/fourth year integrated arts course. A trial of the above in four local schools, to be taught by a music, a dance, a drama and an art teacher. Finally to evaluate the above in the four schools. The evaluation will include classroom observation and discussions with teachers, pupils and advisers.
Source of Grant: No funding
Date of Research: 1985-1990
KEYWORDS: *arts education; integrated curriculum; secondary education*

8/0052
Department of Education
Claverton Down, Bath BA2 7AY
0225 826826
Cleves, I.M. Mr; *Supervisor:* Richards, P. Dr
An examination of factors affecting the adoption of workplace-related materials in the secondary mathematics classroom
Abstract: English teachers of mathematics use a variety of resources and other materials as vehicles for teaching their subject. There has been pressure for some of these materials to be workplace related for a variety of reasons. Some teachers embrace this willingly, others with great reluctance. The aim is to explore factors which make teachers of mathematics feel more or less willing to use this type of resource. This is being done by using the following approaches: firstly, a postal survey of teachers to establish usage of these resources, awareness of these resources, perceptions of this area, perceptions of pupils feelings, as well as data on variables which may affect these perceptions. There will also be a literature survey. Secondly, there will be a triangulation of these perceptions by interviews with teachers, pupils, advisers, industrialists and others involved in mathematics education. At this stage there will be a further study of literature. Teachers from LEAs (local education authorities) throughout England have been surveyed in an opportunity sample structured, in so far as possible, to give a range of environmental factors and teacher types.
Source of Grant: British Petroleum: £100,000
Date of Research: 1988 – continuing
KEYWORDS: *industry; mathematics; simulation; teacher response; teaching aids*

8/0053
Department of Education
Claverton Down, Bath BA2 7AY
0225 826826
Whitehead, A.J. Mr
A dialectical/living form of educational theory
Abstract: The research is aimed at replacing the discredited disciplines approach to educational theory with an alternative which is grounded in the descriptions and explanations that individual learners give for their own educational development. The creation of such a living educational theory is being attempted by a group of practitioner researchers who are conducting action enquiries into their own professional practice. The research has moved through four distinct phases. Initially (1972-78) the main concerns focused on methodology, particularly the development of an action research approach for investigating questions of the kind, 'How do I improve

my practice?. The work then moved on to epistemological questions concerning the nature of the claims to educational knowledge which could be generated through using an action research methodology. This phase of the enquiry focused on the unit of appraisal, the standards of judgement and the dialectical logic of such claims to educational knowledge. The third phase of the enquiry focused on questions concerning the power relations surrounding attempts to gain academic legitimacy for a dialectical approach to educational theory. Recent enquiries have focused on a description and explanation of the researchers own educational development who supports the good order and power truth within a university. The collaborative nature of the research can be seen in an extending network of practitioner researchers, associated with the School of Education at Bath University, who are producing descriptions and explanations for their own educational development as learners in their professional practice.
Published Material: WHITEHEAD, A.J. (1989). 'How do we improve research based professionalism in eduation? – a question which includes action research, educational theory and the politics of educational knowledge', British Educational Research Journal, Vol 15, No 1. A full list of publications is available from the researcher.
Source of Grant: No funding
Date of Research: 1972 – continuing
KEYWORDS: educational research; philosophy of education; professional development; theory of education

8/0054
Department of Education
Claverton Down, Bath BA2 7AY
0225 826826
Austwick, K. Prof.
Teacher education research project
Abstract: Students may enter teaching via the postgraduate certificate course, the BEd degree, or by concurrent degree and certificate courses. All of these are provided in one or both of the University and College of Higher Education in Bath. The project will study the academic and geographical background of incoming students, their attitudes, opinions and academic progress whilst in College/University, and the career patterns they follow afterwards in teaching. Academic and other data about students is already available in the Registry. Questionnaires on opinions and attitudes will be given to selected groups on entry and departure. Academic data are also available from College/University records. Procedures will be developed for following up students in their later careers.
Published Material: AUSTWICK, K. & CARTER, K.A. (1978). 'Concerning the PGCE student', British Journal of Teacher Education, Vol 4, No 3, pp.223.
Source of Grant: University Research Fund
Date of Research: 1976 – continuing
KEYWORDS: achievement; attitude; career; student; teacher education

8/0055
Department of Education
Claverton Down, Bath BA2 7AY
0225 826826
Southampton University
Department of Education
Southampton SO9 5NH
0703 595000
Bloomer, R.G. Mr; Scott, W.A.H. Dr; Fenner, R. Mr; *Supervisor:* Thompson, J.J. Prof.; Kelly, P.J. Prof.
Industry-related work within initial teacher education
Abstract: The aim of this project is to build up as comprehensive a picture as possible of current industry-related activities in initial teacher education, of planned future developments and of tutors' developmental needs. All primary and secondary courses in the United Kingdom leading to BEd and concurrent degrees and to postgraduate certificates in education were surveyed. Both educational studies and methods courses across the whole curriculum were examined with personal enquiries being directed to those responsible for industry-related work in institutions. Questionnaires were also administered to education studies and to methods tutors. Foci of enquiry included aims and organizations of courses, numbers of students involved, involvement of people from outside teacher education, methodologies and resources employed, benefits to students, staff development activities, the impact of Circular 3/84 and future plans and needs. The survey has shown a considerable increase in the provision of such activities since a similar survey of 1985, the development of greater consensus on the aims of industry-related work and a particular concentration on aims linked closely with student's teaching in schools.
Source of Grant: Department of Education & Science
Date of Research: 1988-1989
KEYWORDS: industry; teacher education

8/0056
Department of Education
Claverton Down, Bath BA2 7AY
0225 826826
Sunderland Polytechnic
Hammerton Hall, Gray Road, Sunderland SR2 7EE
091 515 2351
Hufton, N.R. Mr; *Supervisor:* Calderhead, J. Prof.
Modelling the professional learning process of teachers: an analysis of research and theory
Abstract: The research examines past accounts of teacher learning and current research into teacher thinking, learning and development. These sources are theoretically highly eclectic. The aim is to find a common language and theory for reconciling accounts developed within different reference frames, to supply and critique and to make suggestions for a reliable modelling of teacher professional learning, at least at a level of general description.
Source of Grant: Institutional support for costs and fees
Date of Research: 1989 – continuing
KEYWORDS: learning process; professional development; teacher education

8/0057
Department of Education
Claverton Down, Bath BA2 7AY
0225 826826
Hones, G.H. Dr
Geography 16-19
Abstract: Originally set up in 1976, the Project's development phase was completed in 1985 when funding ceased. By that time new Project courses had been established, including one at 'A' level. It was not possible to obtain funding for a much needed 'aftercare' system in 1985 but BP has now agreed to support this for a 3 year period (1987-90). The major tasks are seen as: (1) disseminating the Project's ideas, courses and resources; (2) supporting the rapidly increasing number of teachers involved in such courses as the new 'A' level (offered through the University of London School examinations Board); (3) developing new initiatives (CPVE, TVEI, AS level); (4) evaluating the effect of Project courses, with special reference to the reaction of (a) teachers and pupils to the syllabus style, enquiry learning approach and models of assessment, (b) tutors in higher education to the students who have followed such courses.
Published Material: NAISH, M. (1978). 'Progress and Planning in the Geography 16-19 Project, Classroom Geographer', Focus on Geography 16-19, Bulletin of Environmental Education, No. 126, November. This issue contains a resume of the project work.; NAISH, M. (1985). 'Geography 16-19'. In: BOARDMAN, D. (Ed). New directions in geographical education. Lewes: Falmer Press
Source of Grant: British Petroleum: £43,000 over 3 years
Date of Research: 1987-1990
KEYWORDS: curriculum development; geography; secondary education

8/0058
Department of Social Science
Centre for the Analysis of Social Policy, Claverton Down, Bath BA2 7AY
0225 826826 ext 5249
Lee, T. Mr
Social disadvantage and LEA resource allocation to schools
Abstract: This is a two year study of resource allocation in education prompted by the introduction of LMS (Local Management of Schools) in 1990. The specific focus is the process by which schools receive money for social disadvantage or special educational needs. At the national level, the project compares the methods which LEAs have adopted for measuring social disadvantage and/or special educational needs and analyzes the implications of different methods. This forms a continuation of research which began with a collection of LMS submsissions in Autumn 1989. The study will continue to trace and report on the evolution of LMS and formula funding where it relates to special needs, analyzing the origins and

impacts of demands made by central and local government, schools, professional staff and parents. At the local level, between four and eight education authorities will be examined over the two years as case studies of policy making and implementation. Particular attention is paid to the reasons why these LEAs have incorporated a special needs factor in their funding formula for allocating budgets to schools. This involves investigating the definitions of 'social disadvantage' or 'special educational needs' employed by the authority and the way these definitions are translated into policy, i.e. choice of social indicators and resource allocation practice. The confidentiality of information received from these case study authorities will be strictly observed.
Source of Grant: Economic and Social Research Council: £35,780
Date of Research: 1990 – continuing
KEYWORDS: *budgetary control; financing; resource allocation; school; socially handicapped; special education*

8/0059
>Department of Social Sciences
>Claverton Down, Bath BA2 7AY
>0225 826826
>Nobes, G. Mr; *Supervisor:* Haste, H. Dr

Young childrens understanding of social rules and game rules: their conceptions of rules they invent themselves
Abstract: Groups of 3 five to seven year olds were observed playing with unfamiliar materials. Their discourse and activity were analyzed using a coding scheme designed for this research. Interest has focused on the tendency of certain children to claim knowledge or expertize about what should be done with the play materials, or what the children must do, despite there being no actual requirement to do so. These claims to knowledge and expertize usually, though not always, concern what the speaker has done, or seen done, before. These findings relate to two areas of interest in children's social development. Firstly, they show examples of strategies by which young children control others. However the 'expert' conceives of her 'expertize', these claims to knowing what must be done are efficient strategies in children's attempts to be socially effective. Secondly, these findings have important implications for our understanding of children's conceptions of rules. Unlike the children observed and interviewed by Piaget, these children invent their own games and ways of building with the materials. They invent their own rules and regulations. Yet they still appear to treat these rules as if they were necessary and unalterable. The implications for Piagetian and Vygotskian theory are discussed.
Source of Grant: Economic & Social Research Council: £2,800 per annum for 3 years
Date of Research: 1984-1990
KEYWORDS: *child; game; play; social development*

Bedford College of Higher Education

8/0060
>Polhill Avenue, Bedford MK41 9EA
>0234 51671
>Franklin, M.

The role of play in the language development of second language learners in primary classrooms
Abstract: Second language learners with limited English are inevitably disadvantaged in learning in all areas of the curriculum. The aim of this research is to use targeted role play for primary children with limited English and explore the way it affects their performance in mainstream classrooms. Data will be collected by participant observation using radio microphone and video. The data will be evaluated using ethnographic techniques as well as linguistic analysis. As well as the linguistic and sociological implications of play, the effect on mathematical development will be studied by one researcher. A particular feature of this research is the expected involvement of a mother tongue research assistant to relate the mother tongue conversations which intermingle with English during the play sessions.
Date of Research: 1987-1990
KEYWORDS: *English (second language); language development; mathematics; play; primary education*

8/0061
>37 Lansdowne Road, Bedford MK40 2B2
>0234 51966
>Smith, J.H. Mrs

Interactive video project: design and authoring of laser disc IV for use in schools and colleges in teaching dance
Abstract: This research project at Bedford College of Higher Education has been hailed as a breakthrough and a major advance in bringing together technology and an art form for the purpose of enhancing teaching and learning of dance performance. A pilot disc was produced in February 1989 and was in use in test schools and colleges from March to June 1989. A report is being prepared for December 1989. This disc demonstrates a GCSE contemporary dance study performed by a professional dancer. In the LEARNING mode the dance may be optionally accompanied by dance notation and there is facility to freeze frame, move backward, forward or in slow motion over and over again at the press of a single button. In the ARTISTIC performance mode different perspectives of the dancer (e.g. overhead shot, close-up of feet or arms) may be shown simultaneously with an inset of the audience's view of the dancer and a second sound track of spoken teaching points is an option too. A menu of options is on screen for easy reference in addition to a temporal gauge and spatial placement grid. These graphics with bar counts to provide very simple means of reference to the data which is laser read and access is also extremely simple through brilliantly conceived computer programming. The final report will be of interest for those concerned with teaching dance as an art form. It aims to show how interactive video can be of great value as a resource for all in a dance studio.
Source of Grant: Digital Equipment Co.; computing equipment: £27,000 Calouste Gulbenkian Foundation: £15,000 Arts Council: £1,000 Bedford Physical Education Old Students Association (salary for research assistant): £20,000 Bedford College; secondments: £8,000 Television Fund: £5,000
Date of Research: 1987-1989
KEYWORDS: *dance; interactive video; secondary education*

8/0062
>37 Lansdowne Road, Bedford MK40 2BZ
>0234 51966
>Capel, S.A. Dr

Longitudinal study of stress and burnout in middle and upper school teachers
Abstract: The purpose of this study is to (1) determine factors causing stress and burnout in British teachers (both predictive and concurrent), (2) compare factors causing burnout in physical education teachers, teachers of other subjects and headteachers, and (3) determine changes in levels of burnout at different times during the school year. This study is needed to contribute to data about factors causing stress and burnout in teachers. More importantly, very few longitudinal studies of burnout have been conducted (e.g. to look at whether individuals increase, decrease or maintain the same level of burnout over the course of a year, if elements of burnout change at different times, and if different factors are related to burnout at different times of the year), therefore this study adds valuable new information here. The sample consisted of teachers from 80 Bedfordshire schools working with children ages 9 to 18 years who were sent questionnaires in September, 1987, February, 1988, and June, 1988. Analyses include analyses of variance, regression analyses and multivariate multiple regression with follow-up canonical correlation analyses, where appropriate, to determine the effect of selected variables included in each of the three questionnaires on burnout. They also include correlational and profile analyses to determine any changes in levels of burnout over time, and at different stages of the school year.
Published Material: CAPEL, S.A. (1987). 'The incidence of and influences on stress and burnout in secondary school teachers', British Journal of Educational Psychology, Vol 57, No 3, November, pp.279-288.; CAPEL, S.A. (1989). 'Stress and burnout in secondary school teachers: some causal factors'. In: COLE, M. and WALKER, S. (1989). Teaching and stress. Milton Keynes: Open University Press.; CAPEL, S.A. (1988) 'Teacher stress and burnout', Scottish Learning Difficulties Association (Lothian Branch) Newsletter, Spring.; CAPEL, S.A. 'Stress and burnout in teachers', British Journal of Educational Psychology. (Paper sent for review, October 1989).; CAPEL, S.A. 'A longitudinal study of burnout in teachers', British Journal of Educational Psychology. (Paper sent for review October 1989).
Source of Grant: No funding
Date of Research: 1987-1989

KEYWORDS: head teacher; physical education; stress; teacher behaviour

8/0063
37 Lansdowne Road,
Bedford MK40 2BZ
0234 51966
Whitehead, J. Dr
Achievement orientations and persistence in adolescent sport
Abstract: The purpose of this study was to discover whether the Sport Motivation questionnaire could predict subsequent drop out in adolescent sport. It extends the work of Ewing who identified three achievement orientations (ability, task mastery and social approval) and found them to discriminate between adolescents categorized according to their current status as sport competitors, dropouts, or non-participants. The SMQ identifies 2 additional achievement orientations (teamwork and breakthrough) and redefines ability as superiority. It was employed to test the predictive validity, rather than concurrent validity, of the achievement orientations as indicators of sport persistence. 71 rugby players and 65 athletes aged 9 to 19 years completed the SMQ and were followed up for a year. A MANOVA showed that subsequent dropouts differed from continuing competitors in their original achievement orientations. Three of the 5 orientations entered a significant discriminant function: superiority, teamwork and breakthrough. Dropouts were characterized by high superiority and low teamwork orientations. Further exploration showed that rugby dropouts showed lower initial teamwork orientations than continuing players, and athletics dropouts had higher superiority orientations than continuing competitors. The results were discussed in relation to the influence of goal type and sport context on achievement behaviour.
Source of Grant: National Coaching Foundation: £3,190 Bedford College of Higher Education
Date of Research: 1985-1989
KEYWORDS: achievement; adolescent; dropout; motivation; sport

8/0064
37 Lansdowne Road,
Bedford MK40 2BZ
0234 51966
Bott, J. Mrs; *Supervisor:* Smith, J. Ms
Interactive video: rhythmic gymnastics
Abstract: Initial preparation towards the idea of producing an interactive video disc on rhythmic gymnastics was carried out during the spring/summer of 1989. A syllabus was formatted and approved by the Midland Examining Board for the introduction of a GCSE examination, to commence in 1990. The content material was set out, and a linear video recording of the first steps was made for reference purposes.
Published Material: BOTT, J. (1989). Rhythmic gymnastics – the skills of the game. Swindon: Crowood Press.
Source of Grant: Bedford College of Higher Education (expenses): £200
Date of Research: 1989 – continuing
KEYWORDS: gymnastics; interactive video; physical education

8/0065
Polhill Avenue,
Bedford MK41 9EA
0234 51671
Grugeon, E. Mrs; Franklin, M. Miss
The role of play in the language development of second language learners in primary classrooms
Abstract: Second language learners with limited English are inevitably disadvantaged in learning in all areas of the curriculum. The aim of this research is to use targeted role play for primary children with limited English and explore the way it affects their performance in mainstream classrooms. Data will be collected by participant observation using radio microphone and video. The data will be evaluated using ethnographic techniques as well as linguistic analysis. As well as the linguistic and sociological implications of play, the effect on mathematical development will be studied by one researcher. A particular feature of this research is the expected involvement of a mother-tongue research assistant to relate the mother-tongue conversations which intermingle with English during the play sessions.
Date of Research: 1988-1990
KEYWORDS: ethnic minority; language development; play; primary education

Berkshire County Council

8/0066
Research and Intelligence Unit, Chief Executive's Office, Shire Hall, Shinfield Park, Reading RG2 9XD
0734 875444 ext 3028
Feltbower, P. Mrs; Newsome, I.M.
Analysis of sixth form courses
Abstract: Annual 100% survey of sixth form provision in the county's schools over a period when most sixth forms have been declining in size. For each set of pupils pursuing an examination course, the schools are asked to complete one line of the survey form concerning subject code, number of 1st, 2nd and 3rd year sixth form students, planned duration of course, taught periods per week inside and outside normal school hours and any sharing arrangements. A number of analyses are produced as routine, mainly for the use of the Advisers, covering such topics as the distribution of set size and subjects offered. They now form a useful time series of detailed information which has been utilized in, among other things, discussions on school mergers and closures. More recently, work has been directed towards producing more compact analyses and 'profiles' of each school in terms of a few simple measures, to improve both the feedback to the schools and the accessibility of management information.
Published Material: Background papers are available on request.
Source of Grant: County Council budgets
Date of Research: 1981 – continuing
KEYWORDS: administration of education; main subject; number of pupils; secondary education; sixth form

8/0067
Research and Intelligence Unit, Chief Executive's Office, Shire Hall, Shinfield Park, Reading RG2 9XD
0734 875444 ext 3022
Cross, W.P.
Careers service analyses
Abstract: Monthly analyses of the file are undertaken to monitor the performance of the service and its effectiveness in helping young people. A cohort study is made annually to study the experiences of young people in finding employment and to provide information about their career preferences and outcomes. This is now in its third year.
Published Material: Background papers may be copied if required.
Source of Grant: Berkshire County Council
Date of Research: 1984 – continuing
KEYWORDS: careers guidance; Careers Service; employment opportunities; transition from school to work

8/0068
Research and Intelligence Unit, Chief Executive Office, Shire Hall, Shinfield Park, Reading RG2 9XD
0734 875444 ext 3022
Cross, W.P.
Analysis of examination results
Abstract: Information is received from NICER (National Consortium for Examination Results) and examination results are analyzed by subject, sex and school and a combination of the three. These are in the form of detailed tabulations, summary measures of performance and 'profiles' for schools. Results for exams taken at different times are matched together to produce overall summaries of attainment.
Published Material: Background papers may be copied if required.
Source of Grant: Berkshire County Council
Date of Research: 1981 – continuing
KEYWORDS: achievement measurement; examination; performance; school

8/0069
Research and Intelligence Unit, Chief Executive's Office, Shire Hall, Shinfield Park, Reading RG2 9XD
0734 875444 ext 3022
Feltbower, P. Mrs
Monitoring the work of the School Psychological Service
Abstract: A snapshot survey has been introduced to record the characteristics of children receiving attention and the work with which officers are involved. Each survey consists of 10 randomly chosen snapshots in a single week, for two weeks each term, with all staff of the service completing a form. Cross-tabulations are produced at appropriate intervals using the SPSS package.

Published Material: Background papers may be copied if required
Source of Grant: Berkshire County Council
Date of Research: 1986 – continuing
KEYWORDS: child psychology; survey

8/0070

Research and Intelligence Unit,
Chief Executive's Office,
Shire Hall, Shinfield Park, Reading RG2 9XD
0734 875444 ext 3022
Bounds, T. Mr
Berkshire school pupil forecasting system
Abstract: The objective of the Berkshire school pupil forecasting system is to predict the numbers of pupils of each age group in every Berkshire school, for up to 10 years ahead. The basic approach in forecasting is the 'cohort trend' method, where changes observed to cohorts of pupils over previous years are applied in the future. Recent enhancements to the system include: (1) the prediction of primary school entry (i.e. 5 year old) age pupils by relating intakes to the past and predicted resident population of the school catchment area, using data from the Research and Intelligence Unit's Population Estimation and Projection Models; and (2) prediction of intakes to secondary schools by using data from the Education Department's computerized Secondary School Allocation System. Forecasts are produced twice yearly; a preliminary forecast using pupil numbers at September, and the main forecast using pupil numbers in January.
Published Material: Background papers are available on request.
Source of Grant: Berkshire County Council
Date of Research: 1976 – continuing
KEYWORDS: forecasting; number of pupils; school

8/0071

Research and Intelligence Unit,
Chief Executive's Office,
Shire Hall, Shinfield Park, Reading RG2 9XD
0734 875444 ext 3028
Feltbower, P. Mrs
Survey of recruitment and staffing difficulties in secondary schools
Abstract: The need to form a full picture of the staffing problems in schools has prompted the development of a systematic monitoring of the recruitment process and the resulting teaching force. A system is in pilot for incorporating the collection of information on attempts to recruit into the routine of administration. A survey of the level of qualifications of secondary teachers in post (in the subjects they are actually teaching) first carried out in 1986, has been repeated in 1988, with the intention that is should be annual from now on.
Source of Grant: Berkshire County Council
Date of Research: 1986 – continuing
KEYWORDS: recruitment; secondary education; teacher

8/0072

Research and Intelligence Unit,
Chief Executive's Office,
Shire Hall, Shinfield Park, Reading RG2 9XD
0734 875444 ext 3022
Bourne, T.S.
Literacy screening analyses
Abstract: Each year a survey of the literacy capabilities of children in the 7+ and 9+ year groups is undertaken: (1) to identify those children in need of particular help; and (2) to use the results at school level as an index of educational needs in the school. This index is combined with indices of social needs, based on census variables and free school meals, to give a score for the school. This is used to help allocate discretionary teaching resources.
Published Material: Background papers may be copied if required.
Source of Grant: Berkshire County Council
Date of Research: 1986 – continuing
KEYWORDS: educational need; literacy; resource allocation

Birmingham Polytechnic

8/0073

North Centre, Perry Barr, Birmingham B42 2SU
021 331 5000
Green, D. Dr

Assessing quality in higher education
Abstract: The project aims to investigate the feasibility of developing an agreed definition of quality in higher education and a framework within which various methodologies for systematically assessing quality might be tested. The first phase comprises the search for and documentation of examples of good practice in quality assessment in higher education in the UK and overseas. The second phase will focus on the development of the framework and the testing of an agreed 'tool kit' of methodologies. These might include measurement of value added, educational audit; quality management techniques such as British Standard 5750; and student satisfaction.
Source of Grant: No funding at present
Date of Research: 1991 – continuing
KEYWORDS: assessment; higher education; quality of education

8/0074

North Centre, Perry Barr, Birmingham B42 2SU
021 331 5000
Green, D. Dr; Brannigan, C. Mr
Evaluating satisfaction with educational experience among part-time students: preliminary research into input indicators derived from students' perception of quality
Abstract: The Student Satisfaction project explores how quality measurement might be improved by incorporating customer-determined parameters. Specifically it set out to devise a methodology for evaluating student satisfaction (a proxy for quality), and to develop a 'tool kit' of student centred research methods which could be used systematically to evaluate the quality of education provision from the users' viewpoint, and monitor changes in that quality over time. The first stage (1988-89) focused on part-time students. Since then the research has been extended to cover the educational experience of both full and part-time students.
Published Material: GREEN, D., O'SHEA, J. & THOMAS, K. (1989). 'Evaluating satisfaction with educational experience among part-time students: a report to CNAA'. Birmingham: Birmingham Polytechnic.; GREEN, D. (1990). 'Evaluating students' views of their educational experience', (CNAA (Council for National Academic Awards) Briefing Paper 24, July).; GREEN, D. (1990). 'User survey of library services at Birmingham Polytechnic, Final Report'. Birmingham: Birmingham Polytechnic.; GREEN, D. (1990). 'Student satisfaction: assessing quality in higher education from the customer's view', Paper presented at the International Conference on Assessing Quality in Higher Education, St Andrews, Scotland. July. (To be published as part of the proceedings of the conference by the University of Tennessee).; GREEN, D. (1990). 'Student Satisfaction project: Report on the 1990 Student Satisfaction Survey' November. Birmingham: Birmingham Polytechnic.
Source of Grant: Birmingham Polytechnic: £95,000
Date of Research: 1988 – continuing
KEYWORDS: part-time student

8/0075

National Centre for Down's Syndrome, Westbourne Road, Edgbaston, Birmingham B15 3TN
021 454 3126
Cherrington, D.H. Prof.; Brinkworth, R. Mr; Hon, Y.C. Mrs; *Supervisor:* Cherrington, D.H. Prof.; Brinkworth, R. Mr
The development of the 3-5 year old Down's Syndrome children
Abstract: The study aims to extend the range of support materials for parents during the difficult pre-school period of 3-5 years. As a programme, it will build upon the substantial body of research completed by Mr Brinkworth on the Down's Syndrome child of 0-2 years of age and the work already done at the Centre for Advanced Studies in Education on the pre-school child. Parents who come to the National Centre for advice, find a substantial body of materials there to support them in the first 2 years of their child's life. The materials are presented in the form of parent guides and these are supplemented by clinical advice during interviews with National Centre staff. This early support has done much to improve the general condition of young Down's Syndrome children and has enhanced their general level of activity and capacity for learning. Consequently, many parents are in urgent need of carefully structured supplementary materials for that very active and important period in their child's development. It is intended, by drawing on the skills of a range of specialists like physiotherapists, speech therapists, child and educational psychologists, to bring together the existing material on the development of the Down's Syndrome child aged 3-5. This in turn will be set against those materials which exist

for the normal child. The intention will then be to make selections and adaptations based on practical work with Down's Syndrome children which will form a collection of special materials and activity guides for parents. The guides themselves will be supplemented by parent training sessions, films and video presentations of these programmes in action.
Published Material: BRINKWORTH, R. (1984). 'Down's Children's Association Parent Guides: 1.0 to 6 months; 2.6 months to 3 years; 3 years to 5 years. London: DCA (revised edition).
Source of Grant: Independent Order of Odd Fellows, Manchester: £10,000
Date of Research: 1983-1990
KEYWORDS: Down's Syndrome; parent education; pre-school child; teaching aids

8/0076
Institute of Art and Design,
Margaret Street,
Birmingham B3 3BX
021 331 5968
Swift, J. Dr; Seed, J. Dr; *Supervisor:* Hartnell, R. Mr
Art and civic culture in Birmingham 1870-1914
Abstract: A descriptive and analytical historical study of art and art education in Birmingham in the last quarter of the nineteenth century, including prominent individual and institutions, and the interaction of this art and art education with the contemporary civic culture of municipal socialism, and the contemporary artistic culture of fine art and the arts and crafts movement.
Source of Grant: Birmingham Polytechnic: fees John Ruskin Prize of the Guild of St George: £350
Date of Research: 1986 – continuing
KEYWORDS: art education; history of art

8/0077
Department of Education
Centre for Advanced Studies in Education,
Westbourne Road,
Edgbaston,
Birmingham B15 3TN
021 331 6020
Franklin, W.L. Mr; *Supervisor:* Hannan, A. Dr;
Hall, E. Ms
The multicultural curriculum in further education: a case study
Abstract: The project aims to investigate the manner in which wider social definitions and aspects of social structure are reproduced in the further education curriculum in relation to the influence of 'multiculturalism' upon that curriculum. It will also study how perceptions of 'multiculturalism' influence curriculum content, transmission and impact; the extent to which career or professional interests affect innovations in the curriculum in this area and the way in which one curriculum innovation is influenced by others taking place simultaneously in further education.
Source of Grant: No funding
Date of Research: 1985 – continuing
KEYWORDS: curriculum; further education; multicultural education

8/0078
Department of Education
Perry Barr,
Birmingham B42 2SU
021 331 5473
Jackson, H. Dr; Cherrington, D.H. Prof.; *Supervisor:* Duncan, D. Ms
Second language development in Asian under-fives, with special reference to semantic syntax and lexis
Abstract: Language development can be studied in terms of syntax, semantics, lexis, pragmatics and phonology. It is thought that the most productive line of investigation of L2 English development would be to look at the development of semantic syntax, and lexis, in production rather than comprehension. The aims of the investigation will be to: (a) analyze the data; (b) compare the L2 English from the L1 Punjabi subjects with that from the L2 Bengali subjects; (c) compare the L2 English data/analysis with L1 English data/analysis; (d) derive a clinical assessment procedure.
Source of Grant: No funding
Date of Research: 1986-1990
KEYWORDS: bilingualism; language development; pre-school child; semantics

Birmingham University

8/0079
Foundation for Conductive Education, Edgbaston, Birmingham B15 2TT
021 414 4947/8
Birmingham Institute for Conductive Education
Bell Hill, Northfield, Birmingham B31 1LD
021 477 0801
Sutton, A.; Lambert, M.
Evaluation of conductive education
Abstract: Conductive Education is a system for teaching motor-disordered children and adults to function independently, their underlying condition notwithstanding. It has been developed in Hungary in the years since the Second World War and now constitutes the regular provision for children with relevant disorders in the Hungarian education system. It is currently exciting enormous interest around the world because of the apparent advantages that it incurs in motor independence, mental and personal development and parental satisfaction. A collaborative study has been established with the Peto Institute in Budapest where this system was developed to train British conductors (specialist teachers) and set up the system in the UK, initially for cerebrally palsied children and adults with Parkinson's disease. Training will be in the hands of Hungarian specialists, curriculum development a British responsibility.
Published Material: COTTAM, P. and SUTTON, A. (1985). Conductive Education: a system for overcoming motor disorders. London: Croom Helm.; SUTTON, A. (1986). 'Learning to function despite a handicap', The Listener, No 115, (2954), pp.16-17.; AUBREY, C. & SUTTON, A. (1986). 'Handwriting: one measure of orthofunction in Conductive Education', British Journal of Special Education, Vol 13, pp.110-114.; SUTTON, A. (1987). 'Conductive education: hope for motor-disordered', Health at School, Vol 2, pp.166-168.; SUTTON, A. (1988). 'Conductive education', Archives of Disease in Childhood, Vol 63, pp.214-217.; SUTTON, A. 'The impact of Conductive Education'. In: JONES, N. (Ed) Special Needs Handbook, No 2, (in press).
Source of Grant: Charitable funding
Date of Research: 1987 – continuing
KEYWORDS: conductive education; motor disorder; special education

8/0080
Department for Cultural Studies
Birmingham B15 2TT
021 414 3344
Green, A. Dr
Education and state formation: the social origins of national education systems
Abstract: Education and State Formation examines the social origins of national education systems in 19th Century Prussia, France, England and the U.S.A. The study analyzes significant differences in the timing and forms of national education and assesses the validity of various explanatory theories. Using comparative analysis of the differential structures of schooling, a new interpretation explains the rise of national systems in terms of the process of state formation. Nationalism, the search for bureaucratic, economic and military efficiency, and the need for the dominant classes to secure hegemony over subordinate groups, are all seen as important factors in the early development of national systems. Drawing on Gramscian theory the case studies show how marked differences in the relations between state and civil society and the forms of hegemony in each country produced significant differences in educational provision, from the centralized, etatist systems of continental Europe, to the decentralized U.S. systems and the laissez-faire arrangements of the English voluntary system. Particular attention is given to the reasons for the relative underdevelopment of English education and the effects of the peculiar legacy of the 19th century educational voluntarism on present day schooling and the debates surrounding it.
Published Material: GREEN, A. (1986). 'Lesson in standards', Marxism Today, January 1986.; GREEN, A. (forthcoming). Educational and state formation. London: Mcmillan.
Source of Grant: Economic and Social Research Council: 1 year's grant
Date of Research: 1984-1989
KEYWORDS: history of education; national planning; system of education

8/0081

Department of Curriculum and Teaching Studies
Centre for Religious Education Development and Research,
Edgbaston, Birmingham B15 2TT
021 414 4808
Grove, J.E. Mrs; Spencer, L. Miss; *Supervisor:* Hull, J.M.
Prof.

Religious education artefact project
Abstract: The object of REAP (Religious Education Artefacts Project) is to prepare boxes of sacred objects (artefacts) from several world religions together with notes intended for children of reading ages 8 to 10 years together with teaching notes. Boxes are available on free loan to schools in the Birmingham area from the City of Birmingham Central Library. Collections so far deal with Hinduism, Islam, the Sikh faith and Judaism.
Published Material: British Journal of Religious Education editorials, Summer and Autumn, (1986). pp.125-7, 191 and pp.1-3.
Source of Grant: Industry and charitable trusts: jointly £7,761
Date of Research: 1985-1990
KEYWORDS: *audio-visual aids; multicultural education; primary education; religious education; teaching aids*

8/0082

Department of Curriculum and Teaching Studies
Edgbaston, Birmingham B15 2TT
021 414 4827
University College of Swansea
Department of Education, Hendrefoilan, Swansea SAZ 7NB
0792 201231
Sanders, S.E. Ms; *Supervisor:* Wynne-Willson, W.S. Dr;
Taylor, P. Prof.

A study of maths teachers perceptions of mathematics
Abstract: This is a study of how teachers perceive mathematics, and how this affects teaching styles, content of lessons, perception of pupil achievement and pupils achievement in identified mathematical areas, by an in depth study of a small number of teachers of each type identified, in order to investigate how their perception colours their teaching, by observation in the classroom and by written testing of their pupils.
Source of Grant: No funding
Date of Research: 1987 – continuing
KEYWORDS: *achievements; mathematics; teacher behaviour; teaching technique*

8/0083

Department of Education
Centre for Education Management and Policy Studies, PO Box 363, Birmingham B15 2TT
021 414 3344
Ranson, S. Prof.

A new system of government for education
Abstract: The research aims to develop knowledge and understanding about the new system of government for education following the 1988 Education Reform Act and how the system develops over time. In particular, it will examine the tension within the system between its principal characteristics of (central) administrative regulation and (local) public choice and accountability. Further aims are to develop theoretical analysis of choice and constraint in the creation of educational systems of government and to develop a longitudinal research methodology which periodises study of system development.
Published Material: RANSON, S. & THOMAS, H. (1989). 'Education reform consumer democracy'. In: STEWART, J. & STOKER, G. (Eds), The future of local government. London: Macmillan.
Source of Grant: Economic & Social Research Council: £50,381
Date of Research: 1989 – continuing
KEYWORDS: *administration of education; educational policy; system of education*

8/0084

Department of Educational Psychology
Centre for Child Study, Edgbaston, Birmingham B15 2TT
021 472 1301
Merrett, F. Dr; *Supervisor:* Wheldall, K. Dr

Behavioural approach to teaching project
Abstract: Observational research has been applied to determine the kinds of behaviours that teachers find most troublesome and the sort of responses they commonly give to such behaviours. Empirical research has been employed to investigate the effectiveness of certain behavioural techniques (e.g. rules, praise and ignoring, RPI) and packages to be used for teaching teachers classroom behaviour management skills have been developed based upon this research. The packages have been applied in INSET (Inservice Education and Training of Teachers) and the results have been evaluated through questionnaire and by objective (before and after) observation.
Published Material: A list of publications can be obtained from the NFER on request. WHELDALL, K. & MERRETT, F. (1985). The behavioural approach to teaching package (BATPACK) for use in Primary and Middle schools. Birmingham: Positive Products.; MERRETT, F. & WHELDALL, K. (1988). The behavioural approach to teaching secondary aged children (BATSAC). Birmingham: Positive Products.; WHELDALL, K. & GLYNN, T. (1989). Effective classroom learning. Oxford: Basil Blackwell.
Source of Grant: No funding
Date of Research: 1980 – continuing
KEYWORDS: *class management; inservice education and training of teachers; misconduct; teacher behaviour*

8/0085

Department of Educational Psychology
School of Education, P.O. Box 363, Birmingham B15 2TT
021 414 3344
Faulkner, J.R. Miss; *Supervisor:* Doherty, J. Dr

Attitudes to high academic achievement in girls: a comparative study of the attitudes of second, third and fourth year pupils attending mixed-sex and single-sexed comprehensive schools
Abstract: The main aim of this study was to investigate the effect the type of school pupils attended (mixed or single-sex) had on the development of their attitudes to high academic achievement in girls. The influence of three further independent variables: school background (middle class ex grammar or working class ex-secondary modern), year group (2nd, 3rd or 4th), and the sex of the respondents was also examined. The research was carried out among 1,823 Birmingham secondary school children aged between 12 and 15 years. Of these, 409 took part in the pilot study and 1,414 were involved in the main investigation. The main study pupils attended 6 city comprehensive schools: 2 girls-only schools, 2 boys-only schools and 2 mixed-sex (co-educational) schools. Pupils' responses were analyzed using both the analysis of co-variance and the analysis of variance statistical techniques, and a correlation analysis was also carried out. It was expected that no significant differences would emerge between the respective groups on the basis of school type, but significant effects in favour of single-sex schools were produced on the scales designed to measure pupils' attitudes to high academic achievement in girls. No significant effects emerged on the basis of school background. Girls from all-girls schools also showed less traditional attitudes towards women's rights and their roles in contemporary society than their counterparts in mixed-sex schools, and they possessed significantly higher levels of self-esteem. All boys, however, regardless of age, or the type of background of schools attended, tended to hold more traditional attitudes than girls towards the rights of women in general. It was concluded, therefore, that the type of school attended was the major factor influencing pupils' responses, and although it cannot be said with certainty that the single-sex schools were fostering a clearly positive attitude towards high academic achievement in girls, they certainly appeared to make the development of a clearly negative one significantly less likely.
Source of Grant: City of Birmingham: Local Education Authority
Date of Research: 1985-1989
KEYWORDS: *achievement; attitude; co-education; girls' education; secondary education; sex difference; single sex schools*

8/0086

Department of Educational Psychology
School of Education, Birmingham B15 2TT
021 414 3344
Coates, E.A. Mrs; *Supervisor:* Clark, M. Prof.

A study of young children's use of language in peer group and peer/adult group discussion
Abstract: This research examines infant-age children's use of language in peer group and peer/adult group discussion. This involves an analysis of their language levels in order to ascertain how they differ in the two situations. The relationship between the levels of language used in oral and written work is also examined. Two samples were involved. Sample one consisted of 44 five year old children, 17 of whom were studied again at the age of seven. Sample

two consisted of 16 four year old children, 12 of whom were studied again at the age of five.
Published Material: COATES, E. (1985). 'An examination of the nature of young children's discussions, both in peer groups and with an adult, and the implications of these for the development of linguistic skills in the infant classroom'. In: CLARK, M. (ed). (1985). 'Helping communication in early education'. Educational Review, Occasional Publications, No 11.
Source of Grant: No funding
Date of Research: 1984-1989
KEYWORDS: *discussion; language development; primary education; verbal interaction*

8/0087
Department of Psychology
Edgbaston, Birmingham B15 2TT
021 472 1301 ext 2269
Robinson, E.J. Dr
Children's understanding of their knowledge or ignorance of utterance meanings
Abstract: During the early stages of mastery over language, children interpret verbal messages despite their ignorance of the meaning of many of the units and stuctures of the language used. The use of strategies to interpret problematic utterances appears to be incompatible with coming to understand that a verbal message may not provide adequate clues to the speaker's intended meaning. The researcher plans to examine some of the circumstances under which younger and older children are prepared to abandon the implicit working assumption that the speaker's intended meaning can be identified on the basis of the message given. In particular, investigations will be made into the importance of children's increasing awareness that they do or do not know the referential boundaries of particular words.
Published Material: ROBINSON, E.J. & WHITTAKER, S.J. (1987). 'Children's conceptions of relations between messages, meanings and reality', British Journal of Developmental Psychology, No 5, pp.81-90.; ROBINSON, E.J. & WHITTAKER, S.J. (1986). 'Children's conceptions of meaning-message relationships', Cognition, No 22, pp.41-60.
Source of Grant: Economic and Social Research Council: £64,334
Date of Research: 1985-1990
KEYWORDS: *child; communication; language development; meaning; verbal communication*

8/0088
Department of Psychology
Edgbaston, Birmingham B15 2TT
021 472 1301/0300
Stones, E. Prof.
Psychology and pedagogy: investigations into the relationships between principles of psychology of human learning and practical teaching and the supervision of practical teaching in teacher training
Abstract: The work comprises a variety of investigations by experienced teachers into different aspects of pedagogy and employing different approaches. Qualitative as well quantitative data are sought for. Surveys of current practice are complemented by empirical work exploring the effects of theory based practical pedagogical intervention into the teaching of a wide variety of subjects. Experiments are predominantly naturalistic, clinical, learning based and outcome-oriented case studies involving small groups of teachers or student teachers and their pupils.
Source of Grant: No funding
Date of Research: 1983 – continuing
KEYWORDS: *psychology of education; teacher education; teaching practice; theory of education*

8/0089
Department of Social and Administrative Studies
Edgbaston, Birmingham B15 2TT
021 472 1301
Szreter, R. Dr
Women in English universities through the Twentieth Century
Abstract: Phase I of the research involves the investigation of the long-term trends in the women's share in the prestigious 'key profession' of university teaching, based on 5 university institutions of different types at 10-year intervals, 1920-1980, using data from published records and a questionnaire. Phase II involves an extended and more sophisticated version of the period covering 1921-1970 is being prepared. Phase III studies the impact in the English universities on the participation and standing of women as teachers and girls as students of the fall in the number of corresponding males during 1940-1945, and their mass return as ex-servicemen in the late 1940s. University records and some questionnaire data provide the evidence, plus some relevant publications of the period. Work on the boundary of the social history of higher education and sociology of womanhood.
Published Material: SZRETER, R. (1983). 'Opportunities for women as university teachers in England since the Robbins Report of 1963', Studies in Higher Education, Vol 8, No 2, pp.139-150.; SRETZER, R. (1985). 'Women as university teachers in England, 1921-1970', International Standing Conference for th History of Education, Higher Education and Society, Vol II, pp.678-687.; SZRETER, R. 'Concerns of women teachers as reflected in the Journal of the Women's Education Union, 1873-1881', 10th International Standing Conference for the History of Education. The Social Role and Evolution of the Teaching Profession in Historical Context, Vol 5, pp.196-203.
Source of Grant: No funding
Date of Research: 1978 – continuing
KEYWORDS: *history of education; sociology of education; twentieth century history; university; woman teacher*

8/0090
Department of Social and Administrative Studies in Education
Edgbaston, Birmingham B15 2TT
021 472 1301
Thomas, H.R. Mr
Financial delegation in schools
Abstract: The aim of the research is to explain the priorities of financial delegation and to compare this with the stated aims of the scheme: (1) to examine structures of management and decision-making; (2) to test hypotheses about patterns of virement against actual budgetary allocations; (3) to explain the nature of choices underlying budgetary decisions. The method will be: (i) Interviews with personnel in schools and LEA (Local Education Authority) offices; and (ii) quantitatim analysis of budget and expenditure statements.
Published Material: HEWLETT, M.W. & THOMAS, H.R. (1983). 'The Effects of Granting Financial Autonomy to an LEA maintained School', CORE (Collected Original Resources in Education) Fiche LD03, Vol 7, No 1.; HUMPHREY, C. & THOMAS, H. (1983). 'Making efficient use of scarce resources', Education, Vol 162, No 7, pp.125-126, 12 August.; HUMPHREY, C. & THOMAS, H. (1983). 'Counting the cost of an experimental scheme', Education, Vol 162, No 8, pp.145-146, 19 August.; HUMPHREY, C. & THOMAS, H. (1985). 'Giving schools the money', Education, Vol 165, No 19, pp.419-420, 10 May.; THOMAS, H. (1987). 'Efficiency an opportunity in school finance autonomy'. In: THOMAS, H. & SIMKINS, T. (Eds). Economics and education management: emerging themes. Lewes: Falmer Press.
Source of Grant: No funding
Date of Research: 1981 – continuing
KEYWORDS: *budgetary control; financial resources; school*

8/0091
Department of Special Education
Research Centre for the Education of the Visually Handicapped, Selly Wick House, 59 Selly Wick Road, Birmingham B29 7JE
021 471 1303
Tobin, M.J. Dr
Longitudinal investigation of cognitive development and educational achievement in blind and partially sighted children
Abstract: This investigation, begun in 1973, aims to monitor aspects of the psychological and educational development of blind and partially sighted children attending special schools for the visually handicapped in England and Wales. The sample of 120 is estimated as constituting some 47 per cent of the age group, the visual acuities of the children ranging upwards from nil to 4/36 plus (as measured on the Snellen chart). The subjects are tested at least once every year by the researcher and his assistants. Among the major variables being measured are: (1) print and Braille reading; (2) mathematics attainment; (3) short-term memory; (4) verbal and non-verbal reasoning; (5) speed of information processing; (6) various 'Piagetian' constructs; (7) personality and self-concept. Degree of residual vision, cause of visual defect, age of onset and social class constitute some of the major independent variables.
Published Material: TOBIN, M.J. (1979). 'A longitudinal study of blind and partially sighted children in special schools in England

and Wales', Insight, Vol 1, No 1, Summer.; TOBIN, M.J. (1987). 'Visually handicapped teenagers' opinions about special and mainstream schooling', The New Beacon, January.
Source of Grant: Birmingham University Royal National Institute for the Blind
Date of Research: 1973 – continuing
KEYWORDS: achievement; blind; cognitive development; performance; special visually handicapped

8/0092

Department of Special Education
Research Centre for the Education of the Visually Handicapped, Selly Wick House, 59 Selly Wick Road, Birmingham B29 7ET
021 471 1303
Tobin, M.J. Dr
Reading by the blind: Braille and Moon
Abstract: A series of experiments are being undertaken on various aspects of tactile reading by blind children and adults. Experimental comparisons are being made among alternative letter shapes with the aim of producing a more legible tactile code for older adults and for those with poor tactual ability. For Braille, measurements are being made of Braille reading speed, accuracy, and comprehension among blind school children; experimental comparisons are also being made to evaluate alternative 'papers' on to which Braille can be embossed. Trials are also being conducted on methods to enable sighted adult volunteers to teach reading and writing of Moon-type to newly-blinded adults.
Published Material: COOPER, A., DAVIES, B.T., LAWSON-WILLIAMS, N. & TOBIN, M.J. (1985). 'An examination of natural and synthetic papers for embossing Braille', The New Beacon, Vol LXIX, No 823, pp.325-328, November.; TOBIN, M.J., BURTON, P., DAVIES, B.T & GUGGENHEIM, J. (1986). 'An experimental investigation of the effects of cell size and spacing in Braille – with some possible implications for the newly-blind adult learner', The New Beacon, Vol LXX, No 829, pp.133-135. May; TOBIN, M.J. & HILL, E.W. (1989). 'Harnessing the community: Moonscript, the Moon-writer and sighted volunteers', British Journal of Visual Impairment, Vol VII, No 1, pp.3-5.
Source of Grant: Birmingham University Royal National Institute for the Blind
Date of Research: 1985 – continuing
KEYWORDS: Braille; blind; reading; visually handicapped

8/0093

Department of Special Education
Research Centre for the Education of the Visually Handicapped, Selly Wick House, 59 Selly Wick Road, Birmingham B29 7ET
021 471 1303
Birmingham University
Department of Special Education
Edgbaston, Birmingham B15 2TT
021 471 1301
Tobin, M.J. Dr; Mason, H. Ms
Speed of visual information processing
Abstract: The aim is to measure the speed of visual information processing of partially sighted pupils on tasks similar to those used with their fully sighted peers. Preliminary findings have indicated a large discrepancy between the average performances of the partially sighted and the published norms for the fully sighted. Further work is now being undertaken with a larger sample of partially sighted children with a view to reducing normative data for the population of partially sighted pupils. Trials are also being conducted on a test to measure speed of tactile information processing.
Published Material: TOBIN, M.J. & MASON, H. (1986). 'Speed of information processing and the visually handicapped child', British Journal of Special Education, Vol 13, No 2, pp.69-70, June (Research Supplement)
Source of Grant: Birmingham University Royal National Institute for the Blind
Date of Research: 1985 – continuing
KEYWORDS: blind; information processing; learning pace; performance; visually

8/0094

Department of Special Education
Research Centre for the Education of the Visually Handicapped, Selly Wick House, 59 Selly Wick Road, Birmingham B29 7JE

021 471 1303
Spencer, S. Mr; Ross, M. Mr; *Supervisor:* Tobin, M.J. Dr
Development of microcomputer software for educational and vocational applications (for blind and partially sighted persons)
Abstract: The Research Centre has a programme of individual research and development projects concerned with using and adapting microcomputer technology to allow visually handicapped children and adults to have access to databases, educational materials, and word processing systems. Software has been developed so that output can be produced in Braille, large print, computer graphics and synthetic speech. Details of software are provided by means of regular newsletters, information sheets, and software documentation, all of which is available on request from the Research Centre.
Published Material: HAWLEY, A. et al (1987). 'Electronic publishing and visually handicapped learners', The New Beacon, Vol LXXI, No 844, pp.253-255.; SPENCER, S. (1987). 'Centre computer base for visually handicapped children, students and adults', British Journal of Visual Impairment, Vol 2, pp.67-69.; SPENCER, S. & ROSS, M. (1988). 'Visual stimulation using microcomputers', European Journal of Special Needs Education, Vol 3, No 3, pp.173-176.; SPENCER, S. & ROSS, M. (1988). 'Visual stimulation using microcomputers', European Journal of Special Needs Education, Vol 3, No 3, pp.173-176.; SPENCER, S. & ROSS, M. (1989). 'Closing the gap, facilitating integration: microcomputer technology and the handicapped learner', Special Children, Vol 28, pp.20-21.; SPENCER, S. & ROSS, M. (1989). 'Assessing functional vision using micrcomputers', British Journal of Special Education, Vol 16, No 2, Research Suppplement, pp.68-70.; SPENCER, S. & ROSS, M. (1989). 'Software packages for the young visually handicapped', Special Children, No 31, pp.20-21.
Source of Grant: Royal National Institute for the Blind: (part of annual grant which also covers other work)
Date of Research: 1983 – continuing
KEYWORDS: blind; computer assisted instruction; microcomputer; software; teaching aids; visually handicapped

8/0095

Department of Special Education
School of Education, PO Box 363, Birmingham B15 2TT
021 414 3344
Birmingham Polytechnic
Westbourne Road, Birmingham B15 3TN
021 454 5106
Upton, G. Prof.; Stengelhofen, J. Mr
A distance-taught course for teachers of children with language difficulties
Abstract: The aim of the project is to develop a distance taught course for teachers of children with speech and language disorders.
Source of Grant: Department of Education and Science: £76,421
Date of Research: 1989-1990
KEYWORDS: distance study; language impairment; speech handicapped; teacher education

8/0096

Departmetn of Psychology
South West Campus, Edgbaston, Birmingham B15 2TT
021 414 4906
Cochrane, R. Prof; *Supervisor:* Bairstow, P. Dr
An evaluation of conductive education
Abstract: The Foundation for Conductive Education in conjunction with the Peto Institute in Budapest has set up a pilot project to bring the Hungarian system for treating children with cerebral palsy to Britain. An Institute has been set up in Birmingham which will take a limited number of children and trainee Conductors and expose them to Conductive Education from 1 January 1988. Adults will also be included in the project in years 3 and 4. An evaluation of the effectiveness of Conductive Education in improving motor abilities, intellectual functioning and social functioning is being undertaken at the same time. Three main questions will be adhered; (1) what are the key principals underlying Conductive Education?; (2) does the Birmingham Project faithfully replicate the original Hungarian scheme of Conductive Education?; does Conductive Education produce more benefits for the disabled than traditional therapies?.
Source of Grant: Department of Education and Science: £343,000 over 5 years
Date of Research: 1987 – continuing
KEYWORDS: cerebral palsy; conductive education; motor disorder; special education

8/0097
School of Education
PO Box 363, Birmingham B15 2TT
021 472 1301
Cox, P. Ms; Taylor, P. Mr
Primary school science and the National Curriculum
Abstract: This study of science education in primary schools is a contribution to the debate about the kind of science education that should be undertaken by primary school teachers. It is a contribution based upon the ways in which some primary school teachers think about science, both as a subject and as an activity; about the objectives of science education and about the conditions under which it should be taught. A broad methodology has been used; questionnaires, interviews and classroom observations. Fifteen fairly typical primary schools participated; 94 teachers completed the questionnaire of which 9 were interviewed in depth; 3 classes observed and the science guidelines of 5 schools analyzed.
Published Material: COX, P. & TAYLOR, P. (1989). Primary school science and the National Curriculum. Primary schools Research and Development Group.; CLARE, J. (1989). 'Primary school survey fails staff on science. Daily Telegraph', July 10 1989, pp.4.
Source of Grant: Primary Schools Research and Development Group
Date of Research: 1988-1989
KEYWORDS: primary education; science education

8/0098
School of Education
Edgbaston, Birmingham B15 2TT
021 414 3344
Harber, C.R. Dr
Political Education in Africa
Abstract: A study of the role of the school in the inculcation of political knowledge and values in sub-saharan Africa. Various research techniques (questionnaires, content analysis, participant observation) were used to examine the school's role in transmitting a range of political orientations including those towards national unity, socialism and national development.
Published Material: HARBER, C.R. (1989). Politics in African education. London: MacMillan Press.
Source of Grant: Internal funding from Birmingham University
Date of Research: 1977-1989
KEYWORDS: Africa; political education; political socialization; role; school

8/0099
School of Education
Edgbaston, Birmingham B15 2TT
021 414 3344
Lowe, R.A. Dr
A social history of English education 1964-1987
Abstract: This is an analysis of social change and formal education in post-war Britain. Focus will be on demographic influences, the impact of suburbanization, changes in affluence and economic structure and in the nature of the media.
Published Material: LOWE, R. (1988). Education in the post-war years: a social history. London: Routledge.
Source of Grant: No funding
Date of Research: 1988 – continuing
KEYWORDS: demography; economic conditions; history of education; sociology of education

8/0100
School of Education
Edgbaston, Birmingham B15 2TT
021 414 3344
Harber, C. Dr; Meighan, R. Dr
Democratic learning in teacher education
Abstract: This is a study of democratic and co-operative learning methods in initial teacher training. This is based on participant observation of a social studies methods group over the last decade. The average size of a group is 12-15 students. Students decide their own timetable and plan, organize and execute sessions with tutors acting as facilitators.
Published Material: MEIGHAN, R. & HARBER, C. (1986). 'Democratic learning in teacher education: a review of experience at one institution', Journal of Education for Teaching, Vol 12, No 2, pp.163-72.; MEIGHAN, R. & HARBER, C. (1986). 'A case study of democratic learning in teacher education', Educational

Review, Vol 38, No 3, pp.273-282.
Source of Grant: No funding
Date of Research: 1986 – continuing
KEYWORDS: democratic learning; teacher education; teaching method

8/0101
School of Education
Edgbaston, Birmingham B15 2TT
021 414 3344
Harber, C. Dr
Politics and education in Africa
Abstract: This is a study of the relationship between the political system and the educational system in Africa. The broad influence of ideology on the education system, as well as the contradictions between official policy and the reality of schooling, have been examined in a series of case studies – Nigeria, Kenya, Tanzania and Zimbabwe.
Published Material: HARBER, C. (1989). Politics in African Education. London: MacMillan.
Source of Grant: No funding
Date of Research: 1977 – continuing
KEYWORDS: Africa; government policy; politics; system of education

8/0102
School of Education
Edgbaston, Birmingham B15 2TT
021 414 3344
Harber, C. Dr
Political education in Britain
Abstract: This is a study of the nature of provision of political education in Britain, with particular reference to the 14-16 age group, the broad subject area of social studies and to education for democracy.
Published Material: HARBER, C. (1987). Political Education in Britain. Lewes: Falmer Press.
Source of Grant: No funding
Date of Research: 1986 – continuing
KEYWORDS: political education; secondary education; social studies

8/0103
School of Education
Centre for Child Studies, PO Box 363, Birmingham B15 2TT
021 414 3344
Upton, G. Prof.; Wheldall, K. Dr; Merrett, F. Dr; Houghton, S. Dr; Smith, C. Mr
Dealing with disruptive behaviour in secondary schools: an action research approach to the development of a two stage cascade model of inservice training
Abstract: The aim of this research programme is to create a cadre of well trained teaching professionals equipped with the expertize to deal effectively with disruptive pupil behaviour in secondary schools, who would subsequently be able to advise, support and train colleagues experiencing difficulties. The proposal INSET programme will provide teachers with the necessary counselling and pastoral skills which will enable them to offer constructive, sympathetic but essentially practical advice on how to cope with, for example, disruption-induced stress. In addition, they will be able to assist in the development of staff-training packages on how to deal with disruptive behaviour based on research already completed and expertize already in existence.
Source of Grant: University Grants Committee
Date of Research: 1989-1990
KEYWORDS: disruptive behaviour; inservice education and training of teachers; pupil; secondary education

8/0104
School of Education
PO Box 363, Birmingham B15 2TT
021 414 3344
Miller, C.J. Ms; *Supervisor:* Fraser, B. Mr; Stackhouse, J. Dr
A distance learning course for teachers of children with speech and language disorders
Abstract: The project aims to investigate the needs of teachers of children with language disorders and to develop a distance-learning course based on the identified needs. The needs are investigated via a survey of special schools and units. The syllabus is designed

and will be presented via prepared materials, summer schools, and locally based tutor groups.
Source of Grant: Department of Education and Science: £76,421
Date of Research: 1989-1990
KEYWORDS: distance study; language impairments; special school; speech handicapped; teacher education

8/0105

School of Education
Centre for Religious Education Development and Research, PO Box 363, Birmingham B15 2TT
021 414 3344
Grimmitt, M.H. Dr; Grove, J.E. Mrs; Hull, J.M. Prof.; Spencer, L. Miss
Religion in the Service of the Child (RiSC)
Abstract: The project builds upon the earlier 'Religious Education in the Early Years' project 1987/9, to test and further extend the pedagogy and the range of materials so far created. Observational and interview methods to record educational effectiveness of direct encounter between child and explicit world religion materials. This project is associated with the teacher training programme.
Published Material: GRIMMITT, M., GROVE, J., HULL, J.M. & SPENCER, L. (1991). A gift to the child, Religious Education in the primary school. Hemel Hempstead: Simon & Schuster. *Source of Grant:* Church related charitable trusts and industry: £42,053
Date of Research: 1989 – continuing
KEYWORDS: early childhood education; multicultural education; religious education; teaching aids

8/0106

School of Education
Centre for Education Managemnt and Policy Studies, PO Box 363, Birmingham B15 2TT
021 414 3344
Thomas, H. Dr
The funding of schools after the 1988 Reform Act
Abstract: The research aims to describe and analyze the patterns of resource distributions in LEAs as embodied within their funding formulae and their rules regarding those activities which will either be retained centrally or, alternatively, delegated to schools. In addition, it will: (a) examine the change in priorities as the system moves from the existing method of funding to another; (b) investigate the relationship between the resource allocation priorities of LEAs and to those schools; (c) inquire into the rationale of resource decisions within schools and the processes which underlie them.
Published Material: THOMAS, H. et al (1989). Financial delegation and the local management of schools. London: Cassells.
Source of Grant: Leverhulme Trust: £41,550
Date of Research: 1989 – continuing
KEYWORDS: administration of education; financial resources; local education authority; resource allocation; school

8/0107

School of Education
Centre for Religious Education Development and Research, Edgbaston, Birmingham B15 2TT
021 414 4820
Hull, J.M. Prof; Reeve, J. Miss
Cathedrals through touch and hearing
Abstract: The aim of the project is to explore the problems of presenting architecture to visually handicapped people. Cathedrals in England are being equipped with special facilities including wooden models, ground plans, tactile illustrations, cassette recordings and braille guides. The project is mainly confined to West Midlands cathedrals during 1988/9 but it will work in more than 20 cathedrals nationwide during the following years. The work is sponsored by the Archbishop of York.
Published Material: HULL, J.M. (1990). Touching the rock: an experience of blindness. London: SPCK (Society for the Promotion of Christian Knowledge).; HULL, J.M. (1990). 'On being a whole body seer: an epistemic condition for the education of the blind', British Journal of Visual Impairment, Summer, pp.62-63.; HULL, J.M. (1990). 'The God of the blind', The New Beacon, Vol 74, No 877, pp.200-204. June.
Source of Grant: Industrial and charitable sources: £162,179
Date of Research: 1986 – continuing
KEYWORDS: audio visual aids; blind; religious education; special education; teaching aids; visually handicapped

8/0108

School of Education
Examination and Assessment Research Unit, Edgbaston, Birmingham B15 2TT
021 414 3344
Riding, R.J. Dr; Buckle, C.F. Mr; *Supervisor:* Thompson, S. Dr
The computer determination of learning styles as an aid to individualized instruction
Abstract: The research is directed towards developing a computer based test of 'propensity to think verbally/visually'. This propensity will be measured in two ways, by relative response times to yes/no decisions about objectively visual or verbal aspects of pairs of words and by the relative effect on these times of the inclusion of pairs of items which do not satisy the question criterion but which would normally be seen together in one 'visual frame'. The expectation is that such items will facilitate decision making by visualizers whilst inhibiting that of verbalizers. The validity of the test will be investigated through correlations of the test scores with relative performance on a variety of visual and verbal tasks, and with personality as measured by the Junior Eynsenck Personality Inventory. A computer based adaption of existing tests of field/dependance independance will also be produced. British Gas training packages will be evaluated and designed in the light of existing learning theory, of the advent of CD ROM, and of their possible adaption to learning styles, identified by the computer based tests, which may be suggested by any functional correlations found.
Source of Grant: Training Agency (now Training Enterprise Education Division): £68,261
Date of Research: 1988-1989
KEYWORDS: computer assisted instruction; learning strategy; learning test; verbal learning; visual learning

8/0109

School of Education
Edgbaston, Birmingham B15 2TT
021 414 3344
Tall, G.E. Dr
The management of Curriculum Change with particular reference to the introduction of active learning in the pastoral curriculum
Abstract: The aim of the research is to evaluate how different schools have introduced Active Tutorial Work in their schools. The research is eclectic in origin. The contact with the school is invariably via a teacher who teaches at the school and who has come to the University to study for a degree. The emphasis is in confidentiality (schools are not named) and on eclecticism. Whilst the major methods used are teacher questionnaires, to provide a broad picture, and semi-structured individual interviews, to provide detail, one of the evaluators can provide a participant's overview. The results and conclusions are that: it is very evident that poor management and inadequate inservice training has created very poor teacher attitudes towards the introduction of active tutorial work. Teaching staff must be committed to a development, given support and, probably, the latitude and freedom to adjust the teaching approach to fit the age of their pupils. Older pupils seem less willing to use ATW.
Published Material: TALL, G.E. (1985). 'An evaluation of the introduction of active tutorial work in a Birmingham Comprehensive School', Pastoral Care Vol 1, No 3, pp.24-32.; TALL, G.E. et al (1986). 'A long-term management initiated approach to improve a school's pastoral system and an evaluation of the introduction of active tutorial work', Pastoral Care, Vol 1, No 4, pp.38-43.; TALL, G.E. et al (1988). 'Pastoral education, evaluation and GRIST', Pastoral Care, Vol 2, No 6, pp.17-22.
Source of Grant: No funding
Date of Research: 1983 – continuing
KEYWORDS: curriculum development; learning strategy; secondary education; teaching method; tutorial

8/0110

School of Education
Edgbaston, Birmingham B15 2TT
021 414 3344
Meighan, R. Dr
Analysis of home-based education as practised by members of Education Otherwise and the implications of more flexible forms of education system, i.e. Flexischooling
Abstract: A neglected perspective in education has been that of parents, in particular their activity as educators. This theme was taken up in the late seventies as a case study of Education Otherwise and

its constituent parents who were educating their children at home. This is now extending into more general enquiries into the activities of parents as educators and the implication for more flexible forms of educational institutions e.g. Flexischooling.
Published Material: MEIGHAN, R. (1986). A sociology of educating; 2nd Edition. London: Cassell, Chapters 5 and 33.; HARBER, C., MEIGHAN, R. & ROBERTS, B. (1984). Alternative educational futures, Chapter 12. London: Holt Rinehart & Winston.; TOOGOOD, P., MEIGHAN, R. et al. (1987). Flexischooling. A Dialogue Publication.; MEIGHAN, R. (1988). 'Flexischooling: Education for tomorrow, starting Yesterday'. Education Now Publishing Co-operative. A full list of publications is available from the researchers.
Source of Grant: No funding
Date of Research: 1977 – continuing
KEYWORDS: home education; parent role

8/0111
> School of Education
> Centre for Religious Education Development and Research,
> Edgbaston, Birmingham B15 2TT
> 021 414 4836
> Hull, J.M. Prof.

The education of the church and the pleasures of capitalism
Abstract: The project has to do with the education of the religious consciousness of adults under the conditions of industrial modernity and late capitalism. The approach is multi-disciplinary, drawing particularly upon sociology, social psychology and theology to create an understanding of the barriers to religious maturity for modern adults. Special emphasis is placed upon ideology and false consciousness, and resources are being drawn from Marxist and Freudian theory (critical theory).
Published Material: HULL, J.M. (1983). What prevents christian adults from learning?. London: SCM Press.
Source of Grant: No funding
Date of Research: 1985 – continuing
KEYWORDS: adult education; christianity; religious education

Bradford University

8/0112
> Management Centre,
> Emm Lane, Heaton,
> Bradford BD9 4JL
> 0274 542299 ext 258
> Gray, C.L.N. Mr

The development of an operational gestalt for a 'hot' networked business game
Abstract: 'BUSGAM' is a business game developed at the Bradford University Management Centre, for under-graduate, post-graduate and post-experience courses. The game gives participants practice in making top level management decisions under time pressure. It helps to integrate the functional business disciplines such as marketing, finance, production and organizational behaviour. It is primarily for the teaching of business policy, although it has benefits which make it suitable for use in other contexts, for example, business induction training for engineers. The game incorporates the innovative mechanism of the 'hot' environment supported by database and graphics software on distributed microcomputer system. Dynamic interaction between teams and the simulation environment is inherent; the algorithm iteration is pseudo-continuous. Current research centres on incorporating the game into 'enterprise' teaching and developing supporting materials, for instance case studies.
Published Material: GRAY, C. & HOPE, R. (1989). The development of a 'hot' business management game'. In: Perspectives on gaming and simulation. London: Sagset.; GRAY, C. (1989). 'The development of a hot business game', British Journal of Educational Technology, Vol 20, No 1, pp.66-67.; GRAY, C. (1988). 'The development of a 'hot' business game'. University of Bradford Vice-Chancellor's Annual Report. pp.33.
Source of Grant: Computers in Teaching Initiative (CTI); 1987-1989: £100,000 1989: salary only
Date of Research: 1987 – continuing
KEYWORDS: business education

8/0113
> Management Centre, Emm Lane, Heaton,
> Bradford BD9 4JL
> 0274 542299
> Buckley, P.J. Prof.; Mirza, H.N. Mr

The European teaching of international business
Abstract: An investigation of methods of teaching of international business in higher education institutions in the European Community. An assessment and evaluation of content, level and methods. An investigation of the possibility of international exchange and collaboration.
Published Material: BUCKLEY, P.J. & MIRZA, M.N. (1989). 'The European teaching of international business: prospects for collaboration and exchange'. Report submitted to the Erasmus Bureau of the European Commission. pp.23. Brussels: Erasmus Bureau of the European Commission.
Source of Grant: European Community Erasmus Bureau: 2,800 ECU
Date of Research: 1989 – continuing
KEYWORDS: business education

8/0114
> Management Centre, Emm Lane, Bradford BD9 4JL
> 0274 542299
> Oakland, J.S. Prof.; Porter, L.J. Dr

Development of teaching materials and modules for total quality management
Abstract: The research will involve the development of new teaching materials and modules in the area of Total Quality Management. It will involve training needs analysis in participating organizations, questionnaires, in-company interviews, and case study development. The materials will be used throughout Europe by a University-Enterprise Training Partnership, set up with the European Foundation for Quality Management in Eindhoven. The work will involve several universities throughout Europe.
Published Material: OAKLAND, J.S. (1989). Quality management. Oxford: Heinemann.
Source of Grant: European Economic Community Commett II programme for 3 years Universities Funding Council/Pickup programme for 1 year
Date of Research: 1990 – continuing
KEYWORDS: higher education; management of education; teaching materials

8/0115
> Research in Education Unit, Bradford BD7 1DP
> 0274 733466
> Crawford, K. Mr; *Supervisor:* Hitch, P.J. Dr; Hearn, J. Dr

The professional socialisation of student teachers: A study of attitudinal change during school practice
Abstract: The aim of this research is to examine the changes which take place in the attitudes and behaviour concerning teaching of student teachers during teaching practice. The sample will be of student teachers on teaching practice in a local authority middle school. Methods will consist of the following: (1) before-and-after administration of a standardized instrument measuring orientations to teaching and the teaching profession; (2) semi-structured interviews on perceived changes, and socialization agents (staff and pupils); and (3) observations of classroom interaction (to be used as material for interview content).
Source of Grant: No funding
Date of Research: 1986-1989
KEYWORDS: attitude change; student teacher; teacher behaviour; teacher role; teaching practice; work attitude

8/0116
> Continuing Education Unit, Richmond Road, Bradford,
> West Yorkshire BD7 1DP
> 0274 733466
> Leeds University
> Department of Adult and Continuing Education
> Leeds LS2 9JT
> 0532 334527
> Geale, J.C. Mr; Taylor, R. Dr

To develop wider access to Leeds and Bradford Universities for mature students
Abstract: The project aims: (a) to explore within both universities ways in which mature students' access to existing full-time degrees can be facilitated; (b) to develop modular programmes designed to attract mature students; (c) to develop 'open studies programmes'

to enable individuals to attend part of internal full-time or part-time courses with a view to credit accumulation; (d) to develop access routes for mature students in both arts/social studies and science/engineering areas; (e) to develop co-operation with other higher education institutions in West Yorkshire on credit accumulation and transfer joint marketing, etc.; (f) in these ways to increase substantially the flow of mature students into both universities; (g) to monitor and assess the developments and produce a report on the successes and failures which will be of value to other universities.
Source of Grant: Department of Education and Science: £65,000
Date of Research: 1988-1990
KEYWORDS: *access to education; continuing education; higher education; mature student*

8/0117
Department of Social and Economic Studies
Research in Education Unit, Bradford BD7 1DP
0274 733466 ext 6268
Walker, R.E. Mr; *Supervisor:* Macey, M. Ms
The role of employment interests in the governance of further education institutions
Abstract: The study investigates the impact of the 1988 Education Reform Act, Section 152 on the government of Further Education institutions by evaluating the outcomes of the increased participation of relevant employment-related interests. The selection and recruitment of representative governors will be followed to ascertain how and by whom 'relevant' employment interests are determined. The composition of the new governing bodies will be analyzed. The employer governors' commitment to their duties, their attitude to policy issues and their relationship with other governors will be studied. The proposed overview of developments is being supported by comparative case studies of twelve colleges, selected to represent a cross-section of local education authorities in terms of size, geographical location, political control and administrative structure. The relevant literature is being reviewed and an in depth analysis of official documentation and other current source material is being undertaken. In addition, interviews, questionnaires and observations of meetings are being used to determine the relationships between governors, the roles they adopt and the location of power in the new system of FE governance. The identification of different decision-making styles is intended to produce models for employer participation through the practical application of appropriate organization theory.
Source of Grant: Bolton Institute of Higher Education: fees
Date of Research: 1988 – continuing
KEYWORDS: *administration of education; college of further education; employer; governing body; participation*

8/0118
Department of Social and Economic Studies
Richmond Road, Bradford BD7 1DP
0274 733466
Measham, F.C. Ms; Truman, C.A. Ms; *Supervisor:* Allen, S. Prof.
Comparison of the employment experiences of male and female graduates at Bradford University in courses not traditionally undertaken by women
Abstract: A study is being conducted of male and female graduates from Bradford to assess their experiences in the labour market and how they see their future employment prospects. The study focuses on women who have followed traditionally 'male-orientated' courses and compares their experiences with male and female contemporaries. A postal questionnaire of 300 graduates received a 29% response rate. Preliminary analysis suggests 44% of women experience discrimination at work (which can be positive or negative). Men and women feel on an equal career footing up to management level but have noticed few women in senior management positions. Respondents were asked how they view their future career prospects and if they had plans to combine a career and family. The majority of respondents considered it would pose problems for women but felt that it is a woman's responsibility and her choice to have a family. Women who took non-traditional courses and went on to non-traditional employment such as engineering felt that their career was evidence of equal opportunities and changing attitudes. Some women, however, who graduated in traditionally 'male' subjects then veered back into 'female' careers such as teaching or personnel. Initial conclusions suggest despite increasing numbers of women on courses not traditionally taken by women and widening career possibilities, women still face barriers to equal opportunities at work.

Source of Grant: Department of Social and Economic Studies: £500
Date of Research: 1987-1990
KEYWORDS: *career; employment; graduate; labour market; women's employment*

8/0119
Department of Studies in Psychology
Bradford BD1 7DP
0274 733466
Sherrard, C.A. Dr
Problem-solution pairs in learning to use a word-processing programme: a single case study
Abstract: This is a single case study of an adult learning to use an advanced word-processing programme. The aim is to analyze a substantial body of concurrent self-report (seven 30-minute sessions) from the subject on problems encountered during learning, and strategies for their solution. Content analysis, discourse analysis, and conversation analysis will be applied to identify learning problems, the subjects' strategies of solution, and possibly the interaction of speech characteristics (hesitation, disfluency etc.) with the subject's own identification and accounts of problems. The conclusion will include recommendations for more accurate identification and explanation of learning problems, and for improved design of instructional materials.
Source of Grant: No funding
Date of Research: 1988-1989
KEYWORDS: *adult eduction; computer assisted instruction; learning strategy; word processing*

Brighton Polytechnic

8/0120
Chelsea School of Human Movement,
Eastbourne BN20 7SP
0323 21400
Thomond College of Education
Limerick, Ireland
Standeven, J.B. Dr; Duffy, P.; Grobe, C. Dr; Thompson, B. Prof.; Wilcox, R. Dr
A four country comparative study of education for leisure in high schools and teacher preparation programmes
Abstract: This study undertook a systematic comparative analysis of leisure education across four countries, (Canada, England, Ireland and the United States of America). Within each of the four countries studied, four sub-populations were identified: high school students, high school education personnel, college? university personnel and graduating college students. The main focus was placed upon international comparisons on selected dimensions related to education and education for leisure. The sample consisted of 1,700 high school students, 100 high school teachers, 35 university personnel and 39 graduating students. Specially developed survey instruments were administered within regions of each country. Analysis of variance was employed to establish if there were statistically significant differences between countries. Findings indicated that there is rhetoric on both sides of the Atlantic, but there is a tendency to 'do' more in North America on a less conclusive rationale, and to 'think' more in England and Ireland but with a failure to implement effective programmes.
Published Material: DUFFY, P. et al. (1989). 'Methodological bases for a cross national comparative study of education for leisure'. In: FU, F., NG, M.L., SPEAK, M. (Eds). (1989). Comparative physical edcuation and sport, Volume 6. The Chinese University, Hong Kong, P.E. Unit.; GROBE, C. et al. (1989). 'The leisure perceptions, preferences and patterns of high school students: a comparison across four countries'. In: FU, F., NG, M.L., SPEAK, M. (Eds). (1989). Comparative Physical Education and Sport, Volume 6. The Chinese University, Hong Kong, P.E. Unit.; THOMPSON, G.B. et al. (1989). 'Education for leisure: a four country comparison of perceptions and attitudes of teachers in high schools and teacher perception Institutions'. In: FU, F., NG, M.L., SPEAK, M. (Eds). (1989). Comparative Physical Education and Sport, Volume 6. The Chinese University, Hong Kong, P.E. Unit.; STANDEVEN, J. et al. (1989). 'Education for leisure: a comparison across four countries'. In: FU, F., NG, M.L., SPEAK, M. (Eds). (1989). Comparative Physical Education and sSport, Volume 6. The Chinese University, Hong Kong, P.E. Unit.; STANDEVEN, J. (1989). 'Education for lesiure: domain assumptions and problems

for cross cultural research'. In: MURPHY, W. (Ed). (1989). Children, schooling and education for leisure: leisure, labour and lifestyles, Vol 5. London: Leisure Studies Association, U.K.
Source of Grant: International Council of Sports Science and Physical Education: £500 The British Council: travel support University of New Brunswick, Department of Education: computing support
Date of Research: 1986-1990
KEYWORDS: comparative education; leisure education; physical education

8/0121
> Department of Education
> Countryside Research Unit, Falmer, Brighton BN1 9PH
> 0273 606622
> Merrist Wood College of Agriculture & Horticulture
> Worplesdon, Guildford GU3 3PE
> 0483 232424
> Lukehirst, C.T. Dr; Brazier, J. Mr; Hood, J.M. Mr

Farm woodland training project
Abstract: The Woodland Training Project will enable farmers and landowners to utilize and regenerate existing farm woodland and to plan and manage new woodland based enterprises involving free training, flexible access and local provision, the project should prove very attractive to farmers and landowners. The principal objectives of the Woodland Training Project are: to create new jobs and the chance of redeployment for existing workers, to provide opportunities for income generating alternative enterprises leading to integrated rural development and to provide scope (with European Commission assistance) to regenerate some of the declining and/or threatened rural communities. Training will be provided by highly experienced forestry/arboricultural staff in the specialist colleges of Holme Lacy, Hereford and Merrist Wood, Surrey. Managed by the European Farm Development Group (EFDG), a consortium comprising Brighton Polytechnic, Holme Lacy and Merrist Wood colleges, the project will train farmers in the basic craft and new technological skills needed to take on woodland management as part of a farming system. Management level training in environmental impact assessment of planting, the establishment of wood or timber processing, sports, recreation, field laboratories, value added wood-working crafts, and wildlife and landscape conservation and enhancement will be included. Training will encourage the creation of new jobs for existing farmworkers and/or for self-employed workers who are seeking woodlands to set up small businesses under such schemes as the Enterprise Allowance Scheme. Farmers in the south east, Welsh borders and Wales (36FTE) will volunteer to take part in the project. This sample will provide the basis for comparative studies in farmers attitudes to retraining and test a variety of approaches to methods and content within the context of adjusting to the demands of adapting to changes in the Common Agricultural Policy. During the second year the approach of other Member States of the European Community will be examined and the results evaluated vis-a-vis existing approaches to Adult Farm Education.
Published Material: LUKEHURST, C.T. (1986). 'The management and conservation of farm woodland', Quarterly Journal of Forestry, Vol 78, No 4, pp.105-114.
Source of Grant: European social fund: £245,836 Matched funding: £245,836
Date of Research: 1988 – continuing
KEYWORDS: agricultural training; teaching method

8/0122
> Department of Education
> Falmer, Brighton BN1 9PH
> 0273 606622
> Lorac, C.

Communication and social skills project concerned with audio visual language and learning: the concept of an audio language; pupil use of this language and its effects on their learning
Abstract: The primary concern of the Communication and Social Skills Project concentrates on the development of a concept of audio visual language and learning and its relation to the development of communicative competence, social sensitivity and learning across the curriculum. The initial study covered: (1) The feasibility of introducing audio visual language and learning methods in the current climate; (2) the effects on the pupils in terms of increased opportunities for developing communication; (3) social skills; (4) the contribution it would have in general subject learning. Stage 2 extended the research to more teachers to show the technical proce-

dure which can be translated into practical activities for teachers and pupils developing audio visual language skills through producing their own audio visual statements. They also provide teachers with guidelines on the principles of communication and social skills development. Material including packs, teacher's handbook and video tapes have been produced. The Communication and Social Skills Project is endeavouring to extend its research to intercultural education, using the audio visual methods it has developed to promote cross-cultural awareness, understanding and tolerance amongst those of different race, community, idealogical persuasion and geographical situation.
Published Material: LORAC, C. & WEISS, (1981). 'Communication and Learning'. Wheaton/Pergamon.; LORAC, C. & WEISS, (1985). 'Communication and social skills; hands on: a complete course in audio visual production'. Cardiff: Drake Educational Associates Ltd.; LORAC, C. (1985). 'Communication and social skills; seeing the process: audio visual language and learning'. Cardiff: Drake Educational Associates Ltd.; LORAC, C. & WEISS. 'Communication and social skills; hello Europe: European cultural and language audio visual exchange project', (forthcoming).
Source of Grant: Schools Council: Commission of European Communities: European Cultural Foundation: Gulbenkian Foundation: School Curriculum Committee
Date of Research: 1976 – continuing
KEYWORDS: audio-visual method; communication; language development; social skills

8/0123
> Department of Education
> Falmer, Brighton BN1 9PH
> 0273 606622
> White, M. Dr; *Supervisor:* Owen, J.C. Mrs

Telsoft interactive video education centre
Abstract: The Telsoft Interactive Video Education centre is (a) raising awareness into the use of IV (Interactive Video) in Education, and (b) developing IV packages for INSET (inservice education and training of teachers) in Business Education. Raising awareness is effected by means of workshops, demonstrations and conferences held on site or in school, most of which include significant hands-on experience. All courses are tailored to suit the requirements of the participants. Interactive video packages in Business Education are designed for use by teachers in schools which are considering the introduction of Business Education cross-curricular themes. Thus the first package is an introduction to Economic Awareness, the second raises issues which are often met when Economic Awareness is taught across the curriculum. Other titles in preparation include school-industry links, design and technology and an overview of Business Education. Associated development work includes extension to Archimedes and IBM formats.
Published Material: A full list of published IV packages is available from the researcher
Source of Grant: Training Enterprise Education Division, Teacher Support Unit, TVEI Unit: £300,000 over 3 years
Date of Research: 1988 – continuing
KEYWORDS: audiovisual aids; business education; educational technology; inservice education and training of teachers; interactive video

8/0124
> Department of Education
> Falmer, Brighton BN2 4AT
> 0273 693655
> Mares, C. Ms

Tidy Britain group schools project
Abstract: The project has been involved in developing, pilot-testing and publishing teaching materials, teachers' handbooks and other classroom resources covering all stages of compulsory education and, more recently, initial teacher training. The principle aim of the project is to create educational materials which can be used to support work in many subjects but which add an element of environmental awareness and encourage children to develop a sense of ownership and responsibility for, place. All materials are developed and pilot-tested with teachers, advisers and others in education. Industry, government departments, local government and environmental organizations all provide advice and assistance.
Published Material: A full list of published materials is available from the researcher
Source of Grant: Tidy Britain Group: £55,000
Date of Research: 1988 – continuing
KEYWORDS: environmental study; teaching aids

8/0125

Department of Primary Education
Faculty of Education, Falmer, Brighton BN1 9PH
0273 606622
Mitchell, H. Ms; Supervisor: Dombey, H. Dr
A naturalistic study of early literacy
Abstract: This research focuses on the development as readers of
12 young children, and the supporting strategies provided for them
at home and at school. The subjects are children in three schools,
with a close focus on one child in each school. There is a considerable amount of taped data collected at home and school for each
of the three children. All the schools are using the psycholinguistic approach to the teaching of reading, and the children's parents
are closely involved in a home/school dialogue, and read with their
children regularly. Weekly observations of the children have been
carried out throughout the year, and the children's teachers have
contributed their own observations on a regular basis. Parents have
also been interviewed about their views of the school's approach
to reading and their attitudes towards literacy. Analysis of the data
will be carried out by a number of methods in order to establish
a model of parent/child interaction and teacher/child interaction
in psycholinguistic readings. The purpose of this study is to create
a model of the reading process undertaken by the child in the home
situation, and a similar model of the process in the school enabling
a deeper understanding of the nature of literacy as perceived by
child, parent and teacher. The intention is to clarify how teachers
using the psycholinguistic approach can most profitably build on
what parents perceive as their role, and further, how the dialogue
between parents and teachers can be extended.
Source of Grant: Brighton Polytechnic
Date of Research: 1988 – continuing
KEYWORDS: literacy; parent participation; psycholinguistics;
reading

8/0126

Department of Primary Education
Falmer, Brighton BN1 9PH
0273 606622 ext 278
Bell, A.J. Ms; Supervisor: Homan, R. Dr; Lister, I. Prof.
**Education in and for peace: an investigation of the relationship
between school ethos and the aggressive attitudes and behaviours
of pupils**
Abstract: The aim of the research is: (1) to identify the constituent
parts of school ethos; (2) to use examples of school practice where
policy has been established; and (3) to examine the nature of that
policy and its effects on pupils' attitudes and behaviours. A pur-
posive sample of 6 schools is being used, each from different counties throughout England. Methods of data collection include: (i)
Both participant and non-participant observation; (ii) interviewing staff and pupils; and (iii) group discussions. It is hoped that
we can identify a typology of school ethos and particularly create
a model of a 'peaceful' ethos. Attitudes towards school, self-esteem,
and aggressive behaviour will be examined fully if research proceeds to PhD status.
Source of Grant: East Sussex County Council
Date of Research: 1985-1989
KEYWORDS: peace studies; school life; social development; student behaviour

8/0127

Department of Primary Education
Falmer, Brighton BN1 9PH
0273 606622 ext 219
Homan, R. Dr; Tomlinson, S. Prof.; Supervisor: Jungkunz,
T.J. Ms
The implementation of multicultural education in all white areas
Abstract: The project is undertaken in the wake of the Swann
Report on multicultural education, 'Education for All', (March
1985), which stressed the need for multicultural education to permeate all schools, not only those in ethnically mixed areas. The investigation will involve a case study examination of the progress of
multicultural innovations within primary schools in three all white
counties in the South East. The focus will be on the relationship
between local education authority multicultural initiatives and their
effects on individual school policy, practice and curriculum content. The researcher will document (a) the nature of intervention;
which are the most appropriate strategies, methods and approaches
for use in all white schools; (b) the nature of resistance; reasons
for lack of permeation.
Source of Grant: No funding

Date of Research: 1988-1990
KEYWORDS: educational innovation; educational policy; multicultural education; primary education; race relations

Bristol Polytechnic

8/0128

Department of Education
Redland Hill, Bristol BS6 6U2
0272 656261
Crypt School
Podsmead, Gloucester G12 6AE
0452 24371
Croll, P. Mr; Holmes, M. Mr
Time spent on homework and academic achievement
Abstract: As part of a wider study of the relationship between home
and school factors and academic achievement in a local authority
grammar school an investigation was made of the relationship
between the pupils' self-report of the time they spent on homework
and their levels of achievemnt in school examinations. Pupils varied
considerably in the amounts of time they reported spending on their
homework, and levels of time on homework had a fairly strong
positive association with academic achievement. This association
was maintained when verbal reasoning scores at entry to the school
and parental class and education were controlled. However, the
association between time on homework and performance was considerably stronger for pupils from working-class backgrounds and
pupils whose parents had not themselves had experience of a selective school than for other pupils. Parental social class and education were only weakly related to the amount of time their children
spent on homework and part-time employment and the amount
of time spent watching television were not related to time on homework. The variable with the strongest relationship with time on
homework was how regularly parents signed their child's homework diary.
Published Material: HOLMES, M. & CROLL P. (1989). 'Time
spent on homework and academic achievement', Educational
Research, Vol 31, No 1, February.
Source of Grant: No funding
Date of Research: 1981-1988
KEYWORDS: achievement; homework; secondary education

8/0129

Department of Education
Redland Hill, Bristol BS6 6UZ
0272 741251
Bristol Polytechnic
Department of Nursing, Health and Applied Social Studies
Redland Hill, Bristol BS6 6UZ
0272 741251
Aggleton, P.J. Dr
Young people's health knowledge and AIDS
Abstract: This project has used ethnographic research methods to
explore young people's health knowledge in relation to HIV infection and AIDS (Acquired Immune Deficiency Syndrome). A series
of semi-structured informal interviews have been carried out with
gay and non-gay young people in an attempt to explore their present
understanding of AIDS as well as the behaviours which they believe
may minimize personal risk of infection. Preliminary research findings indicate that young people operate with a variety of lay health
beliefs in 'making sense' of HIV infection and AIDS. There is strong
evidence to support the existence of miasmatic, endogenous and
serendipitous lay theories of causation operating with respect to
the factors perceived as likely to result in HIV infection and AIDS.
This in depth enquiry is now being followed up by a regional survey
of 1,000 young people aged between 16-19.
Published Material: AGGLETON, P., HOMANS, H. & WAR-
WICK, I. (1987). 'Health Education, Sexuality and AIDS', Paper
presented at the International Sociology of Education Conference,
Birmingham, January.; HOMANS H., AGGLETON, P. & WAR-
WICK, I. (1987). Learning about AIDS – participatory health edu-
cation strategies. London: Health Education Council.; WARWICK,
I., AGGLETON, P.J. & HOMANS, H. (1988). 'Young people's
belief about AIDS'. In: AGGLETON, P.J. & HOMANS, H. (Eds).
Social aspects of AIDS – papers given at the first UK conference
on social aspects of AIDS. Basingstoke: Falmer Press.; AGGLE-
TON, P.J. WARWICK, I. & HOMANS, H. (1988). 'Young people,

sexuality education and AIDS', Youth and Policy, Vol 23, pp.5-13.; AGGLETON, P.J., MOJSA, J. & WARWICK, I. (1988). 'Shaping up to the syndrome', Youth in Society, May, pp.10-13.; WARWICK, I. (et al) (1988). 'Young people's health beliefs and AIDS', Revue Francaise de Civilisation Britannique, Vol 5, pp.59-76.; WARWICK, I. & AGGLETON, P.J. (1988). 'AIDS education and youthwork involving young people', Youth Clubs, Vol 48, pp.4-7.; WARWICK, I., AGGLETON, P.J. & HOMANS, H. (1988). 'Construction and commonsense – young people's beliefs about AIDS', Sociology of Health and Illness, Vol 10, No 3, pp.213-232.
Source of Grant: Bristol Polytechnic Research Committee: £27,000 over 3 years
Date of Research: 1986-1989
KEYWORDS: Acquired Immune Deficiency Syndrome (AIDS); health education; youth

8/0130
Department of Education
Redland Hill, Bristol BS6 6UZ
0272 656261
Bristol University
Department of Education
35 Berkeley Square, Bristol BS8 1JA
0272 303030
Broadfoot, P. Dr; Pollard, A. Dr; Croll, P. Mr; Osborn, M. Mrs; Abbott, D. Mrs
Primary assessment, curriculum and experience: a study of educational change under the National Curriculum
Abstract: The aims of the research are to examine the implementation of the National Curriculum in infant schools, to analyze the responses of heads, teachers and children and to evaluate assessment procedures and materials. A mixture of qualitative and quantitative approaches to data collection will be used. Data will be collected by interviews with heads and teachers in an initial sample of fifty schools and by detailed classroom studies in a sub-sample of ten of the schools. Interviews will be conducted early in the study and repeated two years later. Heads, or department heads, and other teachers, will discuss their experiences of National Curriculum requirements and their effect on the life of the school and on their own work. Among other areas of concern will be heads' experience of change, their strategies for providing for this and its perceived effects on school ethos and on relations among staff and with outside bodies, including parents. Teachers will be asked to consider the impact of the National Curriculum and its assessment procedures on the curriculum and pedagogy of schools and on their own classrooms, changes in curriculum content, assessment and record-keeping and perceived changes in pupils' attitudes to schooling and in their learning. Classroom studies will involve observation and discussion with teachers and children and will include periods of time when standard assessment tasks are being completed.
Source of Grant: Economic and Social Research Council: £150,000
Date of Research: 1989 – continuing
KEYWORDS: assessment; curriculum; educational change; primary education; reform of education

8/0131
Department of Education
Redland Hill, Bristol BS6 6U2
0272 734483
Brockington, D. Mr
Equal opportunities in the Youth Training Scheme
Abstract: The project seeks to develop good practice in the field of equal opportunity in respect of race and gender. The field team work with Youth Training Scheme managers and staff in a coaching and consultancy role, in order to foster the progress of good practice in the recruitment, induction, supervision and training of young people. The field team manager has written a short 'trainers guide' based on the experience of the work.
Source of Grant: Manpower Services Commission: £15,000
Date of Research: 1987 – continuing
KEYWORDS: equal opportunity; youth employment; youth training scheme

8/0132
Department of Education
Redland Hill, Bristol BS6 6UZ
0272 656261
Brockington, D. Mr; Seward, R. Mr
Training access points

Abstract: This project is one of twenty national pilot projects which are developing a database of training and other learning opportunities. Research work is taking place in refining the programme; in evaluating the individual user's needs for guidance and counselling; and in consulting with industry and commerce to discover the most efficient methods of using the database to increase awareness and take up training.
Source of Grant: Manpower Services Commission: £180,000
Date of Research: 1987 – continuing
KEYWORDS: course; database; information technology; training

8/0133
Department of Education
Redland Hill, Bristol BS6 6UZ
0272 741251
Pollard, A. Dr
Young pupils' learning
Abstract: This programme of research is primarily concerned with the learning stances and strategies which children adopt in school. The researcher will monitor the infant-school careers of two small cohorts of children using a variety of ethnographic methods. In respect of the social factors which influence the children's approaches to learning, the study will focus on three particular social groups – the children's parents, teachers and peers. The aims of the research are: (1) to investigate social factors influencing the learning stance and strategies adopted by young children in two schools serving contrasting socio-economic communities; (2) to trace the development of young children's learning stances and strategies through their infant-school careers; (3) to explore the analytic potential of social constructivist models of learning when combined with symbolic interactionist approaches to the study of classroom processes; (4) to develop ways of conducting collaborative research with teachers, parents and children; (5) to consider the implications of the research for classroom, school and national policies regarding teaching and the curriculum.
Published Material: POLLARD, A. (Ed). (1987). Children and their primary schools: a new perspective. Lewes: Falmer Press
Source of Grant: No funding
Date of Research: 1987 – continuing
KEYWORDS: learning strategy; primary education; social environment

8/0134
Department of Education
Redland Hill, Bristol BS6 6U2
0272 741251
Power, S. Ms; *Supervisor:* Whitty, G.J. Prof.; Barton, L. Mr
Pastoral care and the curriculum
Abstract: The investigation aims to relate curricular organization to wider issues of cultural reproduction and social inequality. The development of 'pastoral care' as a distinct area of secondary school organization will be researched to assess the extent to which the construction and maintenance of curricular boundaries act as significant factors in structuring educational experience, legitimating the differentiation of staff and pupils, and perpetuating inequalities.
Source of Grant: Economic and Social Research Council
Date of Research: 1987-1990
KEYWORDS: care; curriculum; guidance; secondary education; social inequality

8/0135
Department of Education
Redland Hill, Bristol BS6 6U2
0272 741251
Welch, G. Dr
Musical concepts and mental imagery in the congenitally blind
Abstract: Procedures have been devised by which blind people can describe their mental representations of musical stimuli. A large scale survey of people who have been blind from birth is being conducted to provide data on these representations and to compare them with those of sighted people. The results will make it possible to investigate a number of aspects of understandings of music.
Published Material: WELCH, G. (1987). 'Musical potential and behaviour in visually handicapped children', Journal of Blind Welfare, LXXI, pp.838.
Source of Grant: Bristol Polytechnic
Date of Research: 1985 – continuing
KEYWORDS: blind; cognitive process; music education

8/0136

Department of Education
Redland Hill, Bristol BS6 6U2
0272 741251
Harnett, P. Mrs

Children's observations in the classroom

Abstract: The project aims to examine the quality of young children's observations, focusing especially on their means of interpreting and communicating findings and knowledge. Gardner (1984) suggests the means for acquiring and communicating information might be developed through a variety of symbolic processes which are linked with specific areas of the brain and intelligences and this provides some theoretical perspective for making observations of children in the classroom. In particular the project is involved in investigating the hypothesis that linguistic communication might be inadequate representation of symbolic understanding in a non-verbal domain. Consequently, if there is freedom to communicate experiences in a variety of ways does this (a) represent a truer picture of children's understanding? (b) facilitate greater efficiency in the verbal communication of understanding? Classroom studies are being developed from this perspective.
Source of Grant: No funding
Date of Research: 1987-1989
KEYWORDS: *communication; comprehension; primary education*

8/0137

Department of Education
Redland Hill, Bristol BS6 6UZ
0272 741251
Whitty, G. Prof.; Barton, L. Mr; Pollard, A. Dr

The reform of teacher education in six countries

Abstract: The research focuses upon reform programmes in teacher education in Australia, Great Britain, Iceland, Spain, Sweden and the United States. It involves a systematic consideration of the history of recent reforms in each nation. These specific national studies explore both the contexts of policy formulation and the contexts of its implemetation. A comparative method is being used to identify general structural developments that underlie the reform proposals and to investigate how those developments are being mediated by the particular social conditions in the various nations. This juxtaposition of the historically specific with structural concerns permits a comparison that has theoretical implications for the broader understanding of social and educational policy in contemporary Western societies.
Published Material: WHITTY, G., BARTON, L. & POLLARD, A. (1987). 'Ideology and control in teacher education'. In: POPKEWITZ, T. (Ed). Critical Studies in Teacher Education. Lewes: Falmer Press.
Source of Grant: Icelandic Research Trust Rockefeller Foundation Johnson Foundation – support for conference
Date of Research: 1985-1989
KEYWORDS: *comparative education; educational policy; reform of education; education*

Bristol University

8/0138

Department of Education
22 Berkeley Square, Bristol BS8 1HP
0272 303030
Open University
Department of Education
Walton Hall, Milton Keynes MK7 6AA
0908 274066
Broadfoot, P. Dr; Nuttall, D. Prof.

Report of the National Evaluation of Extension Work in Record of Achievement Schemes

Abstract: This report describes the evaluation of the Records of Achievement (RoA) pilot schemes extension from April 1988 to March 1990, funded through Education Support Grant. Seven themes provided the focus for the evaluation and the main findings are described in the report in the context of each theme. These findings are reviewed in part two of the report, which is followed by an appendix summarising evidence about RoA and pupils with special educational needs and for pupils in primary schools which the project was also able to collect. The seven themes are: the relationship of RoA and other comparable initiatives within schools and their combined effect on the curriculum and organization of schools; RoA for 16-19 year olds in schools and the uses made by post-19 institutions; the relationship between RoA and subsequent profiles in FE (further education and YTS (Youth Training Scheme) schemes; the use of IT (Information Technology) computer support in the production of records; recording achievement through the full age-range of a school; the resource implications of replicating RoA schemes and maintaining them once established; dissemination of schemes from pilot schools to a wider range of schools within an authority. In reviewing the seven themes collectively, part two of the report identifies the need for coherence in RoA practice across institutions, initiatives and age groups as the most important requirement for continuing growth. Overall the report provides a unique source of evidence and insight about current issues in relation to RoA which should be of interest to all those involved in education.
Published Material: BROADFOOT, P., GRANT, M., JAMES, M., NUTTALL, D., STIERER, B. (1989). Interim Report of the National Evaluation of Extension Work in Records of Achievement Schemes. London: HMSO.
Source of Grant: Department of Education and Science: £109,226
Date of Research: 1988-1990
KEYWORDS: *assessment; evaluation; profile; record of achievement; student record*

8/0139

Department of Education
Centre for Assessment Studies, 22 Berkeley Square, Clifton, Bristol BS8 1HP
0272 303030 ext 388
Squirrel, G. Ms; *Supervisor:* Broadfoot, P.M. Dr

An evaluation of the use of Records of Achievement and action planning

Abstract: A number of Youth Development Projects (YDPs) funded by the Training Enterprise Education Division are looking at action planning. At school level, action planning, whether used with pupils or school leavers, builds on the Records of Achievement process. Pupils or leavers are asked to consider personal, academic, training and vocational goals in consultation with an adult, be it a teacher or other, eg. a school counsellor or a careers officer. The pupil can then explore future goals and desired lifestyle, think about current interests, prior learning and past achievements. In gathering this information and making use of the adult as a 'sounding board' it is hoped that the pupil/leaver will be able to plan future goals and to reach understanding of the possible routes in training, or higher education employment which might be most personally suitable. The research undertaken by two fieldworkers seeks through intensive interview and particpant observation to understand the process of action planning within the various YDP contexts. Planning may vary according to the differing social, economic, ability and age backgrounds of pupils/leavers or according to the goals of the action plan, be it for career development or tied to a more specific in-school task, such as the Youth Awards Scheme.
Source of Grant: Training Enterprise Education Division
Date of Research: 1989 – continuing
KEYWORDS: *action planning; occupational choice; planning; transition from school to work; youth*

8/0140

Department of Education
35 Berkeley Square, Bristol BS8 1JA
0272 303030
Acker, S. Dr; Hill, T. Dr; Black, E. Ms

Students, supervisors and the social science research training process

Abstract: This project is one of four qualitative studies funded by the Economic and Social Research Council to investigate the experiences of research students in social science departments. The project's theoretical contributions will be to greater understanding of the social science research student supervision process, through collecting data on policies, practices, experiences and expectations from both students and supervisors. The supervisor-student relationship is conceptualized as a teaching-learning interaction embedded in a framework of contextual factors, including structures and cultures of departments and disciplines. An additional anticipated outcome is a practical contribution to academic staff development. In the British model of social science graduate education the supervisor plays a key role, yet training for supervisors is minimal. This project will help discover from experienced supervisors what, in their opinion, is 'good practice' and from less experienced ones, what they would like to learn. The main part

of the study will consist of in depth interviews with a sample of supervisors and research students in eight or nine departments. A particular focus will be upon the disciplines of psychology and education, although several other subjects will also be represented. The approach is qualitative; the data will be combed for themes with the aid of a suitable micromputer and software package.
Source of Grant: Economic and Social Research Council: £36,972
Date of Research: 1990 – continuing
KEYWORDS: higher education; post-graduate; research; social sciences; staff development; supervision

8/0141
    Department of Education
    35 Berkeley Square, Bristol BS8 1JA
    0272 303030
    Acker, S. Dr
Primary school teachers' work and cultures
Abstract: It is the aim of this study to extend knowledge of teachers' work and culture through intensive study of two primary schools. Like other social worlds, the primary school is in certain respects a closed culture. Each school evolves a distinctive set of cultural understandings about what is required of a teacher to be seen as a competent member of the group. To investigate these concerns, an ethnographic approach was chosen, drawing upon participant observation, in depth interviews and documentary evidence. The main school, where work began in April 1987, is an inner city primary school of 200 children. All teachers and the head were observed and interviewed. A comparison school, a junior school with a middle-class intake and 360 children, was added to the study in April 1988. 'Change' has emerged as a particular, although not exclusive, theme. Paradoxically, it is one of the constants in school: it comes from all directions, from the individual teacher, from colleagues, from the head, from the local education authority, from central government. Another theme is 'stereotypes and reality': how far do popular or sociological stereotypes accord with the difficult, stressful daily reality?
Published Material: ACKER, S. (1990). 'Managing the drama: the headteacher's work in an urban primary school', Sociological Review, 1990, forthcoming.; ACKER, S. (1990). 'Teachers' culture in an English primary school: continuity and change', British Journal of Sociology of Education, Vol 11, No 3, 1990, pp.257-275.
Source of Grant: No funding
Date of Research: 1987-1990
KEYWORDS: culture; primary education; teacher

8/0142
    Department of Education
    National Development Centre for School Management
    Training, 35 Berkeley Square, Bristol BS8 1JA
    0272 303030 ext M283
    Wallace, M. Dr; *Supervisor:* Bolam, R. Dr
Managing multiple innovations in schools
Abstract: The programme of education reforms currently being introduced by the British Government requires all state maintained schools to introduce more or less simultaneously several major innovations, together with any changes initiated by LEAs and by the schools, while attempting to maintain the quality of their ongoing work. This initial exploratory study aims to identify how schools cope with the introduction of several innovations at once, to develop theory on the management of planned change, and to develop methods of monitoring the processes involved in managing multiple innovations. A case study will be undertaken of one primary and one secondary school in the same LEA, focusing mainly on the work of the headteacher, senior staff and other teachers in planning, preparing for and introducing the changes. In addition several of the LEA personnel involved in supporting the schools will be interviewed. A second primary and secondary school will be studied to see whether the findings from the case study schools apply to schools elsewhere. Research methods will include interviews, a survey of relevant documents, a questionnaire and limited observation.
Source of Grant: Economic & Social Research Council: £10,390
Date of Research: 1989-1990
KEYWORDS: administration of education; educational change; educational innovation; reform of education

8/0143
    Department of Education
    National Development Centre for School Management
    Training, 35 Berkeley Square, Bristol BS8 1JA

0272 303030
Oldroyd, D. Mr; *Supervisor:* Bolam, R. Dr
Management development in TVEI National Development Project in curriculum delivery
Abstract: The overall aim of the project is to identify and develop effective collaborative practice in TVEI(E) (Technical and Vocational Education Initiative Extension) between LEAs, institutions, groups and individuals with particular reference to curriculum delivery. TVEI(E) in particular offers opportunities for sharing resources and decision-making at a time when other pressures are forcing schools into competition and rivalry. The project would focus on the new kinds of relationships arising from TVEI(E) and other educational changes that stress the value of collaboration, co-operation and partnership in working on common problems and, ultimately, enhancing pupil learning. It is intended to develop training packages or teams of experts in collaborative skills and to assist LEAs in integrating training for collaborations in TVEI (with particular reference to curriculum delivery) into their overall management development programme.
Source of Grant: Training Enterprise Education Division, Department of Employment: £100,000
Date of Research: 1989 – continuing
KEYWORDS: administration of education; co-operation; curriculum; local education authority; management development; Technical and Vocational Education Initiative

8/0144
    Department of Education
    National Development Centre for School Management
    Training, 35 Berekeley Square, Bristol BS8 1JA
    0272 303030 ext M283
    McMahon, A. Ms; *Supervisor:* Bolam, R. Dr
National co-ordination of the school teacher appraisal pilot schemes
Abstract: The aim of this project has been to co-ordinate the pilot work on school teacher appraisal in six LEAs (Croydon, Cumbria, Newcastle, Salford, Somerset and Suffolk. The major outcome will be policy recommendations to the Secretary of State for Education for a national framework for school teacher appraisal. The co-ordination strategy has five broad strands: (a) workshop conferences for consortium representatives; (b) interviews with teachers and LEA advisers/officers in the pilot LEAs; (c) development of guideline material on appraisal; (d) writing policy issue papers on various aspects of appraisal for the National Steering Group; (e) national dissemination through publications and conferences. The co-ordination team intend to produce three books on appraisal in primary and secondary schools and LEAs.
Published Material: MCMAHON, A. (1989). 'School teacher appraisal schemes in England: the pilot scheme experience', In: WILSON, J. et al (Eds) (1989). Assessment for teacher development. Sussex: Falmer Press
Source of Grant: Department of Education and Science: £300,000
Date of Research: 1987-1990
KEYWORDS: evaluation; teacher appraisal

8/0145
    Department of Education
    22 Berkeley Square, Bristol BS8 1HP
    0272 303030
    Baines, B. Ms; *Supervisor:* Broadfoot, P.M. Dr; Nuttall, D.L. Prof.
Profiling in TVEI (Technical and Vocational Education Initiative): a research and development study
Abstract: The project was designed first to elicit examples of profiling within TVEI (Technical and Vocational Education Initiative), and having described a variety of approaches, to construct a set of criteria with which to organize the variety of practice currently prevailing. A number of models of practice from this preliminary 'mapping exercise' were chosen for detailed case study and dissemination. The focus of the research is on 'action research' involving working with teachers in the chosen institutions and on seeking to disseminate good practice to other schools and teachers. The research is being conducted in relation to the national evaluations of TVEI and of PRAISE (Pilot Records of Achievement in Schools) and the broader implications will be investigated. For 1988-1989 the major focus of the work has been on disseminating the results of the project through national and local dissemination activities. A final report on the project is now available.
Source of Grant: Manpower Services Commission (MSC): £88,535
Training Agency: (1989) £39,000
Date of Research: 1986-1989

KEYWORDS: achievement measurement; action research; profile; Technical and Education Initiative (TVEI)

British Association for Commercial and Industrial Education

8/0146

Department of Education
Helen Wodehouse Building,
35 Berkeley Square,
Bristol BS8 1JA
0272 303030
Bristol Polytechnic
Department of Education
Redland Hill,
Bristol BS6 6U2
0272 656261
Stevens, L. Mrs; *Supervisor:* Satterley, D. Dr

Validation of the Bristol scale of language development
Abstract: The research attempted follows on from the research work produced by G. Wells whilst at Bristol University. From the longitudinal language data he acquired, he and his fellow researchers produced a developmental language assessment scale incorporating syntax, semantics and pragmatics. The scale is called the Bristol Scale of Language Development. The scale is expected to be used by nursery teachers and speech therapists. The research attempted was intended to: (a) see if it was possible to replicate the range of developmental language achieved by Dr Wells from naturalistic settings in controlled language sampling situations (b) see if the language sample achieved was the same across different children from different home/school backgrounds. (c) see if there was scorer agreement across and between samples and if it was feasible to be used by the aforementioned professionals. Two nursery settings of 3 year olds were selected, home and school samples were taken, school samples in 3 contexts i.e. looking at books, creative play and non directed chat. Home samples were in 3 contexts but no researchers were involved. 6 children from each school were matched for age and sex and recorded in the 3 contexts over 3 monthly intervals. Transcripts were produced and scored and compared. Results are being analyzed currently.
Source of Grant: No funding
Date of Research: 1983-1989
KEYWORDS: early childhood education; language development; measurement technique

8/0147

Department of Psychology
8-10 Berkeley Square,
Bristol BS8 1HH
0272 303030
Southgate, P. Mr; Hewstone, M. Dr

Schools liaison evaluation
Abstract: This research evaluated whether Police-Schools Liaison, as practiced by the Avon and Somerset Constabulary, has any measureable impact on young people's attitudes to the police and offending. A questionnaire study based on 1,245 secondary school pupils, tested on two occasions, one year apart compared views of the police in schools with ('Target') and without ('Control') a Schools Liaison Officer (SLO). It offered no statistical support for the hypothesis that Police-Schools Liaison engenders more positive orientations to the police. Although attitudes to the police were marginally positive, they became less positive over time in both 'Target' and 'Control' schools. There was no evidence that Liaison input into the 'Target' schools slowed this decline. Although reported face-to-face contact was low, pupils judged their SLO as distinct from the 'Police in general' and viewed him more positively than the 'Police in general', but as rather atypical. Two smaller studies on pupils' perceptions of their SLOs followed up this question. The first showed how pupils classified their SLO in terms of other 'authority figures' and professionals. The SLO was seen as sharing features with a set of 'caring and welfare' professionals, and differing from other sorts of police officers and authority figures. The second study showed, via interviews, that the pupils did not view their SLO as typical of the police, or their interactions with him as typical of (rather negative) police-youth encounters. It was concluded that Police-Schools Liaison, as presently practised in Avon, does not lead to any generalized change of attitude towards the police.
Source of Grant: Home Office: £36,000
Date of Research: 1987-1989
KEYWORDS: police; police-school relationship; youth attitude

British Association for Commercial and Industrial Education

8/0148

16 Park Crescent, London W1N 4AP
071 636 5351
Strickland, C. Ms

BACIE (British Association for Commercial and Industrial Education) local collaborative project information dissemination service
Abstract: The local collaborative project (LCP) programme is designed to encourage collaboration between training providers and local industry, in order to effectively meet local training needs. The aim of the information dissemination project was to investigate and meet the information needs of those involved in LCP's. The LCP information dissemination service is a result of these investigations information on LCP activity is entered onto a database and relevant data can be generated according to need. The information service supplies relevant information to LCP managers on a regular and automatic basis. Queries are also received from a wider audience, anyone interested in provision of training, and information is supplied free of charge.
Source of Grant: Department of Education and Science: £52,650
Date of Research: 1986 – continuing
KEYWORDS: co-operation; industry; information dissemination; training

Brunel University

8/0149

Runnymede Campus, Cooper Hill Lane, Englefield Green, Egham TW20 OJZ
0784 431341
Thornton, A.S.; *Supervisor:* Down, B.K. Dr

A follow up study of the physically handicapped children who were educated in different environments
Abstract: This is a follow up study of a group of young people who were pupils, or former pupils, of a special school for physically handicapped children. The thirty two members of the study group used for this research were chosen from the sample of fifty three, who were the core group of the earlier piece of work, and who have since then been educated in a variety of environments, including integrated educational situations. Particular attention is paid to the social consequences of physical disability and factors which seem to ameliorate or exacerbate the resultant impediments. A qualitative approach is used within the framework of a multiple case study format. However, because of the comparatively long time span from which material is available, in the case of many subjects, periods in excess of twenty years, it is possible to utilize a longitudinal perspective throughout most of the work. This is adopted in an effort to arrive at a holistic view of the situation of the young people involved. Their current situation is examined and the apparent effect on their life chances of the diverse settings in which they were educated is noted.
Source of Grant: No funding
Date of Research: 1987-1990
KEYWORDS: case study; deviance; physically handicapped; social adjustment; special school

8/0150

Department of Education
Research Centre, Runnymede Campus, Coopers Hill Lane, Egham TW20 OJZ
0784 31341
Abu, M.S. Mr; *Supervisor:* Harris, N.D.C. Prof.

An exploratory study of mathematical difficulties of pre-university students at University Technology Malaysia and the relation to the dimensions of mathematical ability
Abstract: The study described in this thesis arose in response to the concern regarding the disappointing performance in mathematics demonstrated by undergraduates at Universiti Teknologi Malaysia (UTM). Specifically, the aim of the study is to investigate these mathematical difficulties and their relationship to the structure of mathematical ability. The methodological

problems and the procedure regarding the study relate to the lack of relevant resources in Malaysia. The design of the research instruments had to be started ab initio. Methods for developing a measure of general ability g are presented for use within the Malaysian context. The sample of the study is taken from UTM. Two tests are described in this thesis, namely the Mathematics Diagnostic Test and the transformed Primary Mental Abilities (PMA) Battery. The latter was generated by translating the Thurstone PMA Batter for Grades 9-12. The methods of investigation regarding the mathematical difficulties were (a) item analysis of students' responses, (b) the examination of students' written work, (c) a case study of students' routes to solutions, (d) a questionnaire method to check the mis-match between lecturers' expectation and students' actual performance on the test. For the transformed PMA battery, the raw data on each sub-test are first factor analyzed to establish the essential 'factors'. The summed (factor) scores derived from the first analysis are then factor analyzed in order suggest a way in which the data could be used in the exploration of the structure of mathematical ability. The data obtained from the mathematics test are first analyzed to examine the students' mathematical difficulties. The data are then mapped into a test space containing the transformed PMA variables and several academic attainments. A factor analysis is then performed using an inter-item correlation matrix. The factorial structure is compared with the two-factor structure as proposed by Furneaux and Rees (1978). The main finding is that for the mathematics tested, there appear to be two main determinants of mathematical ability. Such a structure seems to agree with the two-factor structure model of ability in terms of 'mathematics' only but not with the existence of a group factor over and above the general ability g.
Source of Grant: University of technology, Malaysia
Date of Research: 1987-1990
KEYWORDS: ability; assessment; mathematics; undergraduate; Malaysia

8/0151

Department of Education and Design
Runnymede Campus, Egham TW20 OJZ
0784 31341
Lancaster, A.R. Mr; *Supervisor:* Harris, N. Prof.
The provision of on-line graphic materials for the NERIS database
Abstract: Up until October 1987 the National Educational Resources Information Service provided a database of materials to schools which could be down loaded in part or in its entirety in a text form via a microcomputer and modern link to the Open University computer where the database is held. In the last year Brunel University has assisted in the development of the mechanism by which graphic images may also be retrieved, enabling a wider range of resources to be obtained on-line. The work has included a review and choice of suitable software to process the graphic images and the establishment of a procedure by which the initial drawings are taken through to the stage where they are available on the database.
Source of Grant: National Educational Resources Information Service: £9,000
Date of Research: 1987-1989
KEYWORDS: audiovisual aids; database; information retrieval; information service; teaching aids

8/0152

Department of Education and Design
Runnymede Campus, Englefield Green, Egham TW20 OJZ
0784 31341
Thornton, A. Mr; *Supervisor:* Down, B. Dr
A follow-up study of physically handicapped children who were educated in different environments
Abstract: This is a follow-up study of a group of young people who were pupils, or former pupils, of a special school for physically handicapped children. The thirty two members of the study group used for this research were chosen from the sample of fifty three, who were the core group of the earlier piece of work, who have since then been educated in a variety of environments, including integrated educational situations. Particular attention is paid to the social consequences of physical disability and factors which seem to ameliorate or exacerbate the resultant impediments. A qualitative approach is used within the framework of a multiple case study format. However, because of the comparatively long time span from which material is available, in the case of many subjects, periods of in excess if twenty years, it is possible to utilize a longitudinal perspective throughout most of the work. This

is adopted in an effort to arrive at a holistic view of the situation of the young people involved. Their current situation is examined and the apparent effect on their life chances of the diverse settings in which they were educated is noted.
Source of Grant: No funding
Date of Research: 1987-1990
KEYWORDS: physically handicapped; social handicap; social status

8/0153

Department of Education and Design
Runnymede Campus, Englefield Green, Egham TW20 OJZ
0784 431341
Reid, J. Mrs; *Supervisor:* Thomas, J.D. Mr; Down, B. Dr
The effectiveness of implementing a multicultural and antiracist education
Abstract: The research reviews the effective changes in school practices of the LEAs (local education authorities) policies. It traces the changing trends and concerns regarding the amount of take-up, the process and impact of which are qualitatively and quantitatively assessed. The research objectives are threefold. Firstly, to establish what is recognized as multicultural and antiracist education in local education authorities and schools. To establish whether there are differences in provisions between the LEAs and schools and whether multicultural and antiracist education practices at the primary level help the performances/achievements at secondary level. The introductory section, a historical perspective, discusses the rise of multicultural and antiracist education awareness. Issues on prejudices and institutional racism are included. A survey of the literature and a review of other researches are undertaken in order to base the similarities and differences of this research. The investigation is three dimensional, analyzing the LEAs policies, the primary and secondary schools policies and comparing/contrasting the schools objectives according to needs. The methodologies are ethnographic – the 'involved' observer, questionnaires and interviews. The implications of the Education Reform Act 1988 are also discussed, particularly equal opportunity and education for all in relation to cross-curricular dimensions – is it a policy which will permeate an education for a multicultural society? The results are assessed, the outcomes discussed and summarized according to the underlying hypothesis – have LEAs and schools policies affected positive changes?
Source of Grant: No funding
Date of Research: 1988 – continuing
KEYWORDS: antiracism education; multicultural education

8/0154

Department of Education and Design
Runnymede Campus, Egham TW20 OJZ
0895 74000
Jonietz, P. Mrs; *Supervisor:* Harris, N.D.C. Prof.
International education in international schools: developing a consensus of opinion
Abstract: This research explores how international schools appear diverse in location, size, population, funding and governing body, but are similar in goals, objectives, and curricula. It will then enquire whether teachers, administrators, and parents can reach consensus on the thesis that international schools establish an educational system because they are similar to each other and different from national systems. Schools in Frankfurt, London, and Washington, D.C. each serve as research sites. This is because they each have a well established community base, an experienced multinational faculty, a multinational, multicultural student body, English as the language of instruction, and European Council of International Schools accreditation. They have also adopted the International Baccalaureate diploma to cut across cultures and boundaries. The research employs triangulation through archive review, interviews, and questionnaires to demonstrate consensus on how these international schools are related to traditional definitions of international education, as well as to a larger organizational system of international education.
Source of Grant: No funding
Date of Research: 1987-1990
KEYWORDS: curriculum; international school; system of education

8/0155

Department of Education and Design
Faculty of Education and Design, Englefield Green, Egham TW20 OJZ

67 74000
Guy's Hospital, Division of General Practice,
London Bridge, London SE1 9RT
071 407 7600 ext 2155
Walker, M. Mr
An evaluation of the patient care/trainer's course
Abstract: South East Thames Area Health Authority promotes a
one year part-time course run by Guy's Hospital. The course is
designed (i) to improve G.P. (General Practitioner) consultation
skills; (ii) to enable G.P.s to become trainers (i.e. take on a trainee
G.P.). About 20 G.P.s per year take the course. The investigation
is to determine the effectiveness of the course and will use a combination of structures and ethnographic techniques. Methods
include observation, diaries, recorded loose structured interviews,
recorded consultations and questionnaires. There will be two control groups, one drawn from partners of the course members, and
another from G.P.s from another region. Comparisons will be made
between the organizers aims, course members aims, course members consultations and those of the control groups before and after
the course. During the course, ethnographic techniques will be used
to gain greater understanding of the processes involved on the
course.
Published Material: RIDSDALE, L. & WALKER, M. (1990). 'Continuing medical education at a university: evaluation of an MSc
in general practice', Journal of the Royal Society of Medicine',
No 83.; WALKER, M. (1990). 'Altering attitudes, neglecting skills;
a case study in the education of GP trainers', Qualitative Health
Research, (USA).
Source of Grant: Department of Health and Social Security: £10,000
Date of Research: 1988-1989
KEYWORDS: consultation; course; doctor; inservice training;
trainer

Department of Education and Design
Runnymede Campus, Englefield Green, Egham TW20 0JZ
60 31341
Sweet, A.J.E. Mr; *Supervisor:* Smith, F.S. Mr; Down, B. Dr
**An enquiry into the examination procedures used to assess students
qualifying for associate membership of professional institutes in
business and finance, with particular reference to the Chartered
Institute of Bankers**
Abstract: The examinatios set by the business professions are notable for pass rates which are generally between 25% and 50%. The
low pass rates can be seen as a deliberate means of restricting entry
to the professions by setting very high standards. The research is
an exploratory exercise to consider whether the high failure rates
are caused by difficult examinations or other factors. Academic
research interest has been mainly confined to school or university
examinations with little interest in professional institutes' examinations. Therefore a wide literature survey is undertaken to set the
context in which the professional examinations can be studied.
Other examinations have norm-referencing purposes but the professional examinations are essentially pass/fail examinations although
set in a norm-referencing framework. They may be described as
criterion-referenced but they fail to specify what an examinee's performance means in relation to the workplace. The syllabuses and
examination schemes of seven professions are analyzed and it is
found that there is not systematic approach to syllabus presentation. Question papers set by seven professional associations are analyzed to determine the levels of cognitive ability required and it
is found that the tests are mainly of knowledge and application
of principles with little need for professional judgement. Therefore the high failure rates are not caused by extreme difficulty.
Closer investigation of the Chartered Institute of Bankers shows
that examiners are willing to award high marks and there is no policy
to ensure low pass rates. Weaknesses are found in the quality of
some marking but the major reason for high failure rates seems
to be the lack of basic textbook knowledge by candidates.
Source of Grant: No funding
Date of Research: 1983-1990
KEYWORDS: assessment; examination; profession; vocational
education

Department of Education and Design
Runnymede Campus, Englefield Green, Egham TW20 0JZ
0784 31341
Barr, G.V. Mr; *Supervisor:* Rees, R.M. Dr
**The development and application of a Mathematics Curriculum
Framework for students aged 14 +**
Abstract: This thesis describes the rationale, development and application of a non-contextual mathematics curriculum framework for
students aged 14 +. This development arose out of the work carried out on the difficulties that students of all ages experience in
learning mathematics and studies of the structure of mathematical ability. The development includes as part of its background a
study of the history of mathematics curriculum development,
together with a survey of the relevant assessment theory in the context of mathematics education. The construction of the Mathematics
Curriculum Framework (MCF) resulted from the desire of the City
and Guilds of London Institute to have a coherent and flexible structure for the mathematical content of pre-vocational and vocational
schemes and examinations. The author was requested to devise this
structure. The MCF is designed as a spiral curriculum, emphasis-
ing the development of conceptual structures in hierarchical system
of levels, making use of the 'bottom up' strategy of curriculum
development. The levels have been designed to provide achievable
concepts and skills, based on diagnostic studies, so that each level
demands more inference as the conceptual structures are developed.
The framework has been designed to be a tool for curriculum
developers. The thesis describes two curriculum developments of
the MCF made by the author. The first development discussed is
the City and Guilds Numeracy scheme. This application was concerned with the development of syllabi and assessment procedures.
The second application was for the Joint Board for Pre-Vocational
Education; it involved the development of a syllabus, assessment
procedures and materials for the Numeracy content of the Certificate of Pre-Vocational Education.
Source of Grant: No funding
Date of Research: 1983 – continuing
KEYWORDS: assessment; curriculum development; examination;
mathematics; performance

Department of Education and Design
Runnymede Campus, Englefield Green, Egham TW20 0JZ
0784 31341
Mothersole, B.I. Mrs; *Supervisor:* Morris, J. Dr
Female philanthropy and women novelists of 1840-1870
Abstract: Many women writers between 1840 and 1870 were producing a particular form of social or 'social protest' novel which is
identified here as a 'philanthropic novel', a form distinguishable
in content and tone from social novels written by men of the same
period. The philanthropic novel is a work which has as its main
protagonist a philanthropic heroine who is modelled – perhaps
more covertly than overtly but significantly so – on the great
revolutionary female philanthropists and social campaigners of the
day, such as Elizabeth Fry, Florence Nightingale and Josephine
Butler. Despite the social and economic constraints imposed on
women, the middle years of the nineteenth century saw an
unprecedented upsurge of both women novelists and women philanthropists. A high proportion of women writers, including Elizabeth
Gaskell and Charlotte Yonge, were philanthropists themselves;
others, like Charlotte Bronte and George Eliot, admired the activities of eminent philanthropists. Although the majority of women
novelists lacked the wider experience of politics, the law and commerce which was available to male writers, they now had available
to them this new experience of philanthropy to draw upon for their
novels. Notably, philanthropic heroines created by male authors,
such as Charles Dickens, Benjamin Disraeli and Charles Kingsley,
were more commonly depicted along conventional stereotyped lines
as 'ministering angels': the male authors were less inclined to rely
on actual women philanthropists as models even though they were
personally acquainted with many of these revolutionary women.
This analytical and psychological enquiry into the social history
and novels of the period, reveals that the philanthropic novel not
only played a crucial part in the developing literary tradition of
women; it also led to a new, freer consciousness for women which
assisted in reappraisal of themselves and their worth to the wider
community.
Source of Grant: No funding
Date of Research: 1982-1990
KEYWORDS: history; literature; novel; sex difference; social role;
woman

Department of Government
Uxbridge UB8 3PH
0895 56461

Kogan, M. Prof.; Becher, R.A. Prof.
Process and structure in higher education
Abstract: The aim of this research has been to produce a conspectus of contemporary British higher education set in a framework of a synoptic model of the system. The model and the analysis are based on a revised, extended and updated version of the material contained in the earlier study, 'Process and Structure in Higher Education', (Heinemann, 1980). It marks off four distinct levels of the system and two complementary modes of working, the normative and the operational. The data sources for the current study have been multiple. The relevant published literature over the period from 1978 has been systematically studied and analyzed. In depth and open-ended interviews have been held with 15 key decision makers in the both the university and polytechnic sectors, based on a set of issues derived from recent research writings and from major policy themes of current concern. The revised model, with tentative conclusions drawn from the literature and interviews, was exposed to the critical scrutiny of an international group of leading higher education scholars at a three day conference held in London in September 1989. Finally, the full analysis as then developed, was submitted for critical review to four readers who offered independent appraisals of the literature. This was thus an iterative process by which the account was built up progressively from the initial literature review to the final critique of the draft text. The main conclusion is that while the essential academic values and the socio-technology of higher education in Britain remains surprisingly resilient to outside intervention, the system has nonetheless accommodated itself to the values of the system planners, the advocates of an external market, and the demands of the public at large.
Published Material: KOGAN, M. & BECHER, R.A. (1980). Process and structure in higher education. London: Heinemann.; KOGAN, M. & BECHER, R.A. (1991). Structure and process in higher education. London: Routledge. (forthcoming).
Source of Grant: Economic and Social Research Council: £16,258
Date of Research: 1988-1989
KEYWORDS: administration of education; educational policy; higher education; sociology of education; system of education

8/0160
Department of Government
Uxbridge UB8 3PH
0895 56461
Sussex University
Department of Continuing and Professional Education
Falmer, Brighton BN1 9RG
0273 506157
Kogan, M. Prof.; Becher, R.A. Prof.; Henkel, M. Ms
Graduate education in the UK
Abstract: The research concerns developments in British higher education at two levels. The recent history of the policy of graduate education is reviewed with a view to creating a policy analysis in which the conflicting objectives of graduate education are analyzed; the governmental machinery for generating policy in graduate education described; the relationship between graduate education and staffing of higher education put under scrutiny. This part of the study leads to the critique of existing policies and proposals for its improvement. The second level of the study is that of micro-analyses of graduate education in different disciplinary areas. The analysis includes a summation of the essential characteristics of the discipline concerned, the way in which it recruits its students, the extent to which there is pre-requisite structured training before research is undertaken; the expectations within the discipline, and the relationship between graduate training and recruitment for higher education staffing and cognate professions. The methods involved are a study of secondary sources and interviews at both levels. The research is a continuation of material to be published in R. Burton Clark's comparative study of graduate education in the UK, France, West Germany, Japan and the USA. The researchers have contributed two chapters on the lines described above. It is intended to update and greatly expand the material contained in those chapters. The disciplines studied will be: bio-medical studies; economics; history; modern languages; physics and sociology.
Published Material: CLARK, R.B. (1991). The research foundations of graduate education. Los Angeles: University of California Press.
Source of Grant: Funding being sought
Date of Research: 1991 – continuing
KEYWORDS: educational policy; graduate study; higher education; recruitment; United Kingdom

8/0161
Department of Government
Uxbridge UB8 3AS
0895 56461
Open University
Department of Education
Walton Hall, Milton Keynes MK7 6AA
0908 652048
Bennett, N.D. Mr; *Supervisor:* Kogan, M. Prof.
The implementation of LEA curriculum policies in two Metropolitan authorities
Abstract: This is an examination of the impact of local education authority (LEA) curriculum policies on teachers' practice in two Metropolitan LEAs, in the context of literature on policy-making and implementation, curriculum theory, organization theory and school improvement. Sixty teachers in six schools, three in each LEA, are discussing in extended semi-structured interviews the influences they take into account, or are aware of being influenced by, when preparing work or working in the classroom. Headteachers are also interviewed. The sample is stratified by seniority and subject area, and matched across schools so far as possible. The schools are comparable between LEAs for size and character. First indications show the weakness of these LEAs' policies as influences on practice, and an attempt will be made to map the pattern of influences perceived by the teachers on their work, to compare the perceived strength of impact, and to relate these to structural and affective influences.
Source of Grant: No funding: employers have paid fees prior to 1988
Date of Research: 1984 – continuing
KEYWORDS: curriculum development; educational policy; influence; local education authority; teaching method

8/0162
Department of Human Sciences
Uxbridge UB8 3PH
0895 56461
Richardson, J.T.E. Dr
Cognitive processes in student learning
Abstract: Over the last 20 years, cognitive psychologists have made considerable advances in the development of theories of human learning and memory. Nevertheless, it is commonplace that such models cannot easily encompass the sort of learning that occurs in real life situations. During the same period, researchers into higher education have carefully investigated the knowledge and skills relevant to a variety of academic disciplines. Their findings have major implications for policy and practice in higher education, but they need to be interpreted within clearly articulated models of the cognitive processes underlying student learning. This research attempts to integrate these two areas of investigation. It will provide cognitive psychologists with a rich and qualitatively different body of evidence against which to evaluate the validity and generality of their theories of human learning and development; it will provide researchers into higher education with sophisticated theoretical descriptions of the strategies and processes employed in academic contexts; and it will provide teachers in higher education with statements of the practical applications of this research.
Published Material: RICHARDSON, J.T.E. (1983). 'Student learning in higher education', Educational Psychology, Vol 3, Nos 3 & 4, pp.305-331.; RICHARDSON, J.T.E., EYSENCK, M.W. & PIPER, W.D. (Eds). (1987). 'Student learning: research in education and cognitive psychology', Guildford: SRHE & Open University Press.
Source of Grant: No funding
Date of Research: 1983 – continuing
KEYWORDS: cognitive process; higher education; learning process

8/0163
Department of Sociology
Kingston Lane, Uxbridge UB8 3PH
0895 56461
Marsland, D. Prof.; Day, M. Mr; Bradford, S. Mr
Social education of young people
Abstract: The general aim of the programme is to research the informal social education of young people, particularly the social educational work of the Youth Service. This aspect of education has been little researched, compared with formal education, despite its increasing importance in the light of weaknesses in the schools and the impact of unemployment. Since this is a programme, rather than a single project, it is not possible to specify design and method

criteria. Projects have included both local and national studies of young people, youth work and youth workers; use of rigorous attitude towards measurement instruments, mail and self-complete quantitative surveys, and in depth interviews and observation; analysis also ranges widely from highly statistical computer based techniques to qualitative assessment. The researchers are committed to strengthening the rigour of research on youth and social education, which tends to be dangerously small-scale and soft. These issues are taken up in Marsland, D. 'Research on youth work', to be published by NYB (National Youth Bureau) as an Occasional Paper in May 1985.
Published Material: MARSLAND, D. (1978). 'Sociological explorations in the service of youth'. Leicester: National Youth Bureau.; DAY, M. & MARSLAND, D. (Eds). (1979). 'Black kids, white kids: what hope?' Leicester: National Youth Bureau.; MARSLAND, D. (1984). 'Work to be done', Youth Call.; MARSLAND, D. (1982). 'The sociology of adolescence and youth'. In: HARTNETT, A. The social sciences in educational studies. Oxford: Heinemann.; MARSLAND, D. (1982). 'It's my life: young people's leisure', Leisure studies, Vol 1, No 3.; MARSLAND, D. (1983). 'Dreams or strategies: the future of the Youth Service', Youth and Policy, Vol 1, No 4.; MARSLAND, D. (1985). 'Playing seriously: young people and leisure', Youth in Society, March.
Source of Grant: Baseline support from consortium of LEAs to pay for salaries and back-up on a continuing basis, plus awards from: Social Science Research Council (SSRC); Department of Education & Science (DES); Council for Racial Equality (CRE); Gulbenkian Foundation; Carnegie Trust, etc.
Date of Research: 1973 – continuing
KEYWORDS: community education; socialization; youth welfare

Cambridge Institute of Education

8/0164
Shaftesbury Road, Cambridge CB2 2BX
0223 69631
Bradley, H.W. Mr
Evaluation of head teacher and teacher appraisal in Cambridgeshire
Abstract: Two separate schemes are being evaluated; one for the introduction of appraisal into schools, all of them primary, and another for the appraisal of primary and secondary school headteachers. Data is being collected by means of interviews with a sample of participants and also by correspondence with some of the headteacher group. The work is concentrating upon participants' experiences during the process and their opinions about the various facets of appraisal.
Source of Grant: Cambridgeshire Local Education Authority: £4,000
Date of Research: 1990 – continuing
KEYWORDS: evaluation; head teacher; teacher appraisal

8/0165
Shaftesbury Road, Cambridge CB2 2BX
0223 69631
Bradley, H.W. Mr
Evaluation of the Teacher Appraisal Pilot Project Phase II
Abstract: At the beginning of the research period, most of the schools in the project had completed their experience of the first phase (TAPP 1) and were about to begin the second (TAPP 2). The circumstances of the development of the project mean that this evaluation is limited to the work of lower and nursery schools. Evaluation visits were grouped into two periods. In the first period all schools were visited that had completed TAPP 1 and were preparing for TAPP 2. In the second period, all except one of the schools was revisited, plus the two schools new to the project. In the total of seven days visits, as well as interviewing some members of the LEA staff involved in the project and maintaining a regular dialogue with the TAPP co-ordinator, 35 teachers in 8 schools were interviewed individually, some once and some twice. The interviews concentrated on teachers' and headteachers' experience during the process and upon their opinions and feelings about it. They also sought to clarify how each school had interpreted the freedoms open to it within the original brief. The evidence of this evaluation is that in TAPP 2, Bedfordshire has the basis of a successful system of appraisal, provided that the resource base can be expanded to maintain support at the level enjoyed by the pilot schools. There is considerable enthusiasm for it in the lower schools where it has been piloted and in the best examples it is already making an impact on school development. The evidence of TAPP suggests that people 'grow into' appraisal along a phased development, and this evidence needs to be considered in plans for future extension and for training.
Published Material: BRADLEY, H.W. (1990). Evaluation of the Teacher Appraisal Pilot Project Phase II. Cambridge: Cambridge Institute of Education.
Source of Grant: Bedfordshire Local Education Authority: £2,500
Date of Research: 1989-1990
KEYWORDS: evaluation; teacher appraisal

8/0166
Shaftesbury Road, Cambridge CB2 2BX
0223 69631
Nias, J. Dr; Southworth, G.W. Mr; Campbell, P. Ms
Whole school curriculum development and staff relationships in primary schools
Abstract: Previous research undertaken for the Primary School Staff Relationships Project established that in some primary schools of medium size, staff shared curricular goals and worked productively together to implement them, while in others good working relationships existed among teachers with different aims. Further, social cohesion appeared to lead in some schools, but not in others, to curricular growth. There appears therefore, to be no unambiguous connection between positive staff relationships and whole school curricular development. Yet, teachers have increasingly to collaborate and co-operate in the formulation and implementation of whole school curricular activities and the adoption of school development plans and a national curriculum makes this an imperative. These obsrvations raised 3 questions which this research addressed: (1) where productive working relationships co-exist with an explicit commitment to whole school curricular planning and development, what aspects of school organization and adult relationships appear to make this possible? (2) does the adoption of whole school curricular policies modify practice? (3) given the relationship between curricular and teacher development, what impact does membership of such schools have upon their teaching and nonteaching staff? In addressing these questions the project illuminated such issues as school leadership, collegiality and curriculum coordination. Case studies of 5 medium sized primary schools were constructed following part-time participant observation over the course of one year's fieldwork and the cleared case studies then provided the basis for subsequent analysis and identification issues. The research identified and studied the formal and informal ways in which curricular decisions are reached, and implemented; the location and nature of curricular and social leadership; examined whether agreement to implement specific curricular policies has any effect on pupils' learning experiences; analyzed collegiality and examined job satisfaction and motivation of staff.
Source of Grant: Economic and Social Research Council: £87,930
Date of Research: 1988-1990
KEYWORDS: curriculum development; interpersonal relations; primary education

8/0167
Shaftesbury road, Cambridge CB2 2BX
0223 69631
Sebba, J. Ms
The National Curriculum development team (severe learning difficulties)
Abstract: A team of eight seconded teachers from the Eastern Region are developing materials for National Curriculum Key Stage 1. They will be piloting these with teachers of pupils with severe learning difficulties. The materials will be revised on the basis of the pilot work and then made available through publication. The work is focusing on assessment, record-keeping, topic/thematic approaches and developing routes to learning within Key Stage 1. The purpose of this project is to assist access to the National Curriculum of all pupils.
Source of Grant: No funding
Date of Research: 1990 – continuing
KEYWORDS: learning difficulty; special education; teaching

8/0168
Shaftesbury Road, Cambridge CB2 2BX
0223 69631
Rouse, M.D. Mr; Balshaw, M. Ms

Special educational needs, collaborative staff development for teachers: a joint initiative between the Cambridge Institute of Education and Cambridge Local Education Authority
Abstract: The aim of the research is to examine the issues involved in setting up a collaborative initiative between a local education authority and a school of graduate studies education with a focus of meeting special educational needs in mainstream schools. It arose out of the drawbacks and limitations of traditional approaches to teacher development in special education, the problems associated with changing teachers but not their institutions, the development of whole school approaches to special educational needs, linking the professional development of teachers with the development of their institutions, and collaboration as a key to progress. The researchers will be following up three years cohorts by questionnaire and interviews and case studies to illuminate the particular. The researchers will produce interim results of the research hopefully in 1990. The recommendations will be based on findings to date and will have a heavy emphasis on multilevel collaboration.
Published Material: ROUSE, M. (1991). 'Collaborative INSET and special educational needs'. In: UPTON, G. (Ed). (1991). Staff training and Special Educational Needs. London: Fulton.
Source of Grant: No funding
Date of Research: 1989-1990
KEYWORDS: further education of teachers; inservice teacher education; mainstreaming; special education; teacher development

8/0169
Shaftesbury Road, Cambridge CB2 2BX
0222 69631
West, M. Mr; Howard, J. Ms
Management development in TVEI (Technical and Vocational Education Initiative)
Abstract: The Cambridge Institute of Education in collaboration with Bedfordshire, Cambridgeshire, Norfolk and Suffolk TVEI (Technical and Vocational Education Initiative) projects will produce a distance learning management development package. The participants in the development, and subsequently the target group, will be from secondary schools across the four LEAs (local education authorities). The involvement of staff in schools will be to identify needs and in the first instance they would be mainly sources of information. Therefore the project would not be obtrusive of individual teacher's time. The package will support the development of the project management skills of the institutional TVEI manager. The package will also enable these key management personnel to engage in curriculum analysis and planning activities related to TVEI extension. Although the project focus targets the institutional TVEI manager, it is envisaged a wider potential use by those with management roles both in LEAs and in schools. During the programme the developers of the management package will draw upon the experience of TVEI-related staff in LEAs and schools. The data gathered will be analyzed to establish needs and priorities associated with the management of TVEI as a specifically funded project. Methods of helping staff to develop the necessary management skills will be investigated, and trial materials prepared for use within a sample of schools across the LEAs. During the trialling process the project team will evaluate the extent to which the materials are considered helpful/effective by users (both individuals and schools). The materials will be modified and redrafted as appropriate in the light of this evaluative data before the final package is prepared.
Published Material: HOWARD, J. & WEST, M. (1991). The coordinator role in schools. Sheffield: Training Enterprise Education Division. (forthcoming).; WEST, M. & HOWARD, J. (1991). Co-ordination in schools: a critically annotated bibliography. Sheffield: Training Enterprise Education Division. (forthcoming).; WEST, M. & HOWARD, J. (1991). Management Development. Sheffield: Training Enterprise Education Division. (forthcoming).
Source of Grant: Local Education Authorities: £19,650
Date of Research: 1990 – continuing
KEYWORDS: distance study; further education of teachers; inservice teacher education; management development; technical education; vocational education

8/0170
Shaftesbury Road, Cambridge CB2 2BX
0223 69631
London University
King's College London, 552 Kings Road, London SW10 0UA
071 836 5454
Walsh, A. Ms; *Supervisor:* Brown, M. Dr

The calculator as a catalyst for change – children and number
Abstract: Although the electronic calculator is well accepted as a tool in society and with young children, very little is known about the possible potential of the effective use of a calculator to support the learning of number within mathematics for children in the primary years, and thus also its possible potential as a catalyst for change. This research study uses an ethnographic methodology to follow the development of four schools in their attempts to integrate the calculator into the teaching and learning of number with children from 6- to 7- years upwards, which began as part of the work of the Primary Initiatives in Mathematics Education project in which the researcher played a leading development. Some evidence presented to date calls into question the general perception of how and when children acquire particular number concepts and skills and their ability to deal with them. The research study involves a detailed analysis of these findings with particular reference to the development of place value and further research focusing on the children's understanding of and ability to use and apply number. It is intended to address issues related to implications for teaching.
Source of Grant: No funding
Date of Research: 1987 – continuing
KEYWORDS: arithmetic; calculator; curriculum development; number; primary education

8/0171
Shaftesbury Road, Cambridge CB2 2BX
0223 69631
Howard, J. Ms; Hopkins, D. Dr
Information skills in GCSE (General Certificate of Secondary Education) and the role of the librarian
Abstract: The GCSE national criteria which lay down assessment objectives, have a similar content for each subject. They call for each pupil, in each subject, to learn how to learn, how to use what they have learnt and how to communicate this to others. Pupils need to be able to use books and other human and media resources to define a problem, select the facts they require, analyze them, look at alternative solutions, evaluate their chosen solution and present it. This project is designed to examine the role of information skills within GCSE. Curriculum developments such as TVEI (Technical Vocational Education Initiative) have promoted a radical rethink of teaching/learning style and GCSE is building on such earlier initiatives. The project will carry out a nationwide survey and analysis of current provision based partially on an analysis of GCSE documentation and information skills currently being completed at the University of Loughborough. On the basis of these findings, development work will be facilitated by the series of examples of interesting practice, workshop sessions and discussion documents.
Published Material: HOWARD, J. (1991). 'Information skills and the secondary curriculum: some practical approaches'. British Library & Information Research Report No 84.
Source of Grant: British Library: £39,300
Date of Research: 1989-1990
KEYWORDS: General Certificate of Secondary Education; information skills; librarian; role

8/0172
Shaftesbury Road, Cambridge CB2 2BX
0223 69631
Bristol University
Department of Education
22 Berkeley Square, Bristol BS8 1MP
0272 303030
James, M. Ms; Broadfoot, P. Dr
Pilot records of achievement in schools evaluation
Abstract: The PRAISE (Pilot Records of Achievement in Schools Evaluation) was established by the DES (Department of Education and Science) and the Welsh Office to evaluate the experience of pilot projects in order to inform the work of the RANSC (Records of Achievement National Steering Group). PRAISE reported to RANSC in July 1988. PRAISE was then extended to report on outstanding issues. Further development work in pilot schemes was focused on the relationship of ROA (Records of Achievement) and other comparable initiatives within schools and their combined effect on the curriculum and organization of schools, ROA for 16-19 year olds in schools and the uses made by post-19 institutions, the relationship between ROA and subsequent profiles in FE (further education) and YTS (Youth Training Schemes) schemes, the use of information technology/computer support in the production of records, recording achievement

through the full age range of a school, the resource implications of replicating ROA schemes and maintaining them once established, and dissemination of schemes from pilot schools to a wider range of schools within an authority. Each scheme was required to set up an independent local evaluation to address its experience on each of the themes for which it was funded. The PRAISE national team now based at Bristol and Cambridge Institute of Education, has dovetailed its evaluation so that it worked closely with each local evaluator in a complementary fashion. An interim report on extension work was published in 1989 and the final report will be available in summer 1990.
Published Material: BROADFOOT, P. et al (1988). Report of the national evaluation of pilot schemes. London: HMSO.; BROADFOOT, P. et al (1989). Interim report of the national evaluation of extension work in Records of Achievement Schemes. Open University and Bristol University, and Department of Education and Science.; BROADFOOT, P. et al (1991). 'Records of Achievement: Report of the national evaluation of extension work in pilot schemes'. London: HMSO.
Source of Grant: Department of Education and Science Welsh Office: Main phase 1985-1988 £239,000 Extension phase 1988-1990 £108,000
Date of Research: 1985-1990
KEYWORDS: achievement; assessment; evaluation; profile; student record

8/0173
Shaftesbury Road, Cambridge CB2 2BX
0223 69631
Drummond, M.J. Ms
Bedfordshire expansion of early years education project 1989-1990
Abstract: In the summer of 1989, Bedfordshire Education Committee initiated the opening of 20 units in primary and lower schools for 4-year olds. This major expansion is accompanied by a research and development project run jointly by Bedforshire LEA (local education authority) and the Cambridge Institute of Education. The project comprises inservice programmes for teachers, nursery nurses, and headteachers involved, classroom observations and interviews conducted by the research team. The collection of further observational data by the teachers participating in the project together with interviews, will provide the basis for assessing and evaluating the quality of the provision in the new 4 + units.
Source of Grant: Bedfordshire Local Education Authority: £8,800
Date of Research: 1989-1990
KEYWORDS: early childhood education; pre-school education; primary education

8/0174
Shaftesbury Road, Cambridge CB2 2BX
0223 69631
Cambridge University
Department of Education
17 Trumpington Street, Cambridge CB2 1QA
0223 332878
Hargreaves, D.H. Prof.; Hopkins, D. Dr; Leask, M. Ms
School development plans project
Abstract: School development plans, in their simplest form are a set of curriculum and organizational targets with implementation plans and have lines set by the school on an annual basis within the context of local and national aims. The plans are usually based on a three to five year cycle with details for the first year and broad intentions for subsequent years. They may or may not include details of specific performance indicators, staff development plus INSET (Inservice Training of Teachers) plans and resource (both human and financial) implications. The project is designed to produce a systematic analysis of school development plans at both school and LEA (local education authority) levels. On the basis of this analysis the project team will provide practical guidance for schools, LEAs and governors on the most effective means of preparing, implementing and evaluating school development plans. The project will produce for the DES (Department of Education and Science) two booklets of practical guidance for schools and LEAs. The first will be distributed to schools/LEAs in Autumn 1989. A second and more detailed guidance document, wth greater emphasis on the implementation of school development plans and based on intensive case study research will be prepared for distribution to schools/LEAs in September 1990.
Published Material: HARGREAVES, D.H. et al (1989). Planning for school development. London: Department of Education and Science.; HARGREAVES, D.H., HOPKINS, D. & LEASK, M.

(1990). The management of developing planning. London: Department of Education and Science.; HARGREAVES, D.H. & HOPKINS, D. (1990). 'Not just another initiative', Times Educational Supplement, 16 February.; HOPKINS, D. (1991). 'Changing school culture through development planning'. In: BROWN, S. & RIDDELL, S. (Eds). School effectiveness: an account of research findings for senior management in schools. London: HMSO.; HARGREAVES, D.H. & HOPKINS, D. (1991). The empowered school. London: Cassell.
Source of Grant: Department of Education and Science: £121,000
Date of Research: 1989-1990
KEYWORDS: educational development; plan; planning of education; school

8/0175
Shaftesbury Road, Cambridge CB2 2BX
0223 69631
Rouse, M. Mr; Ainscow, M. Mr; Sebba, J. Ms
Special needs support for the development of Key Stage 3 Standard Assessment Tasks in technology
Abstract: The Cambridge Institute of Education is providing special needs support and consultancy to the Midlands Examination Group (MEG) and Middlesex Polytechnic Technology Centre in their work in developinng key stage 3 standard assessment tasks (SATs) in technology on behalf of the Schools Examination and Assessment Council (SEAC). The Institute's involvement is help in considering issues and developing strategies relating to the assessment of all pupils in technology at the age of 14. Key questions include: is it possible to devise common assessment tasks which are capable of being carried out by all pupils in a meaningful way? How might it be possible to produce non-discriminatory assessment tasks? What, if any, adaptations or amendments will be necessary to ensure that pupils with disabilities and/or special educational needs are assessed fairly.
Source of Grant: Schools Examination & Assessment Council via Midlands Examination Group and the University of Cambridge Local Examinations Syndicate: £10,000 per annum
Date of Research: 1989 – continuing
KEYWORDS: assessment; physically handicapped; special education; standardized test

8/0176
Shaftesbury Road, Cambridge CB2 2BX
0223 69631
Sebba, J. Ms
The National Curriculum development team (severe learning difficulties)
Abstract: The National Curriculum Development Team (Severe Learning Difficulties) currently consists of eight seconded teachers, six of whom are from the local education authorities in the eastern region, one from the Autistic Society and one from Meldreth Manor School (Spastic Society). Two additional teachers will be joining the team. These teachers have been working together since January 1990 to promote good practice for pupils with severe learning difficulties within the National Curriculum. The team is concerned with establishing methods of accessing National Curriculum to all pupils. To this end, they are supporting teachers through school based development work, developing and evaluating resources for classroom and INSET (Inservice Education and Training of Teachers) use and collating and disseminating existing good practice nationally. It is intended to produce written guidelines for teachers covering principles and examples on the development and differentiation of Programmes of Study at Key Stage 1. In addition, staff development resources will be produced.
Published Material: BYERS, R. (1990). 'From myths to objectives', British Journal of Special Education, Vol 17, No 3, pp.109.; SEBBA, J. & CLARKE, J. 'Meeting the needs of pupils with severe learning difficulties within National Curriculum history and geography'. In: ASHDOWN, R., CARPENTER, B. & BOVAIR, K. (Eds). The curriculum challenge: pupils with severe learning difficulties and the National Curriculum. London: Falmer.; SEBBA, J. & FERGUSSON, A. (1991). 'Reducing the marginalization of pupils with severe learning difficulties through curricular initiatives'. In: AINSCOW, M. (Ed). Effective schools for all. London: Fulton.; ROSE, R. (1991). 'Promoting group work in schools for children with severe learning difficulties', British Journal of Special Education, (in press).
Source of Grant: National Curriculum Council Local Education Authority; 8 seconded teachers: jointly £140,000
Date of Research: 1989 – continuing

KEYWORDS: *National Curriculum; severe learning difficulty; special education*

8/0177

Shaftesbury Road, Cambridge CB2 2BX
0223 69631
Hopkins, D. Dr; Howard, J. Ms

Inservice training needs of chartered school librarians

Abstract: School libraries are being bombarded with curriculum initiatives, and are increasingly expected to play a key role in curriculum development, and to work with teachers in supporting and extending pupil learning. During the work on 'Information Skills in GCSE and the role of the librarian' it became obvious that school librarians would welcome some research on establishing professional development needs in fulfilling this role. The research has investigated ways of enhancing the professional development of school librarians in order for them to be a more effective resource in the use of information skills within the secondary school. In particular it focused on those skills needed to take an active part in curriculum development, working with others, and strategies for supporting teachers and learning. A final report, and recommendations for action, have been drawn up for those working at the school, the LEA, Institutions of Higher Education and at DES (Department of Education and Science) level.

Published Material: HOWARD, J. & HOPKINS, D. (1990). Crossing the great divide: with support the school librarian can enhance pupils' learning. London: The British Library. (The British Library Report 6014).
Source of Grant: The British Library: £4,510
Date of Research: 1990-1990
KEYWORDS: *curriculum development; information skills; librarian; library role; professional development; school library*

8/0178

Shaftesbury Road, Cambridge CB2 2BX
0223 69631
Bradley H.W. Mr; Howard, J. Ms

Patterns of employment and development of teachers after long INSET courses

Abstract: The main hypotheses to be explored are that long award bearing INSET (Inservice Education and Training of Teachers) should be protected because of its value to the profession and the education system, and that such INSET develops the future leaders of the profession. A number of higher education institutions will be asked to identify a representative cross-section of teachers who have completed longer INSET activities in 1980, 1985 and 1988. A target total of 100 teachers will be sought in each cohort. These teachers will be asked to provide information on; the development of their careers since commencing the activity, ways in which their local education authorities have used the knowledge and skills developed during the activity, and ways in which their schools have benefited directly from the knowledge and skills developed during the activity. Information will also be sought from their LEAs about how they were selected and how their skills have been used.

Source of Grant: Department of Education and Science: £24,896
Date of Research: 1990 – continuing
KEYWORDS: *further education of teachers; inservice teacher education*

Cambridgeshire Institute of Education

8/0179

Shaftesbury Road, Cambridge CB2 2BX
0223 69631
Cole, R.A. Mr; *Supervisor:* Conner, C. Dr

To investigate the use of distance learning application, in particular interactive video, in the service training of primary school teachers

Abstract: This research uses the Primary Interactive Video Inservice Teacher Training Disc, 'Missing the Obvious', to evaluate the use and influence of this disc and the design of other discs for distance learning on classroom teaching. A number of teachers were selected for study in schools used for piloting and trialling the use of interactive video in Education Project under the direction of the N.I.V.E. (National Interactive Video Centre) in London.

Source of Grant: No funding
Date of Research: 1988 – continuing
KEYWORDS: *inservice education and training of teachers; interactive video; primary education; teacher education*

Cambridge University

8/0180

Centre of English as an International Language, Keynes House, Trumpington Street, Cambridge CB2 1QA
0223 332340
Brown, G. Prof.; Williams, J. Dr; Malmkjaer, K. Dr; Rossner, R. Mr

Processing meaning change in extended texts: effects of comprehension skill

Abstract: In any text the correct interpretation of a word is a function of the meaning of the word and its text environment. Very often texts require the initial interpretation of a word to be changed as the text proceeds. The aim is to see whether readers of different levels of ability are sensitive to such changes as they read short stories. Comparisons will be made among good and poor readers at secondary school, and learners of English as a second language. The research examines situations in which an adjective changes its connotation (e.g. reliable comes to mean boring), the referent of a noun is radically transformed (e.g. a car is turned into a bundle of scrap metal), and the text implies a more specific instantiation of a general term (e.g. the text implies that someone described as a criminal is an arsonist). Comprehension of these changes often requires following a referential chain through the text, from the first mention of a critical word, through a sequence of pronouns to a second mention of the critical word. Comprehension of the second mention of the critical word is assessed at the moment of reading using on-line probe techniques adapted from psycholinguistic research. Preliminary data from university students show good comprehension of changes of state of concrete nouns and of instantiations of category terms, although the data for change of connotation of adjectives is equivocal.

Source of Grant: No funding
Date of Research: 1989-1990
KEYWORDS: *comprehension; meaning; reading; reading skills; word study skills*

8/0181

Centre of English as an International Language, Keynes House, Trumpington Street, Cambridge CB2 1QA
0223 332338
Birmingham University
Department of Education
Edgbaston, Birmingham B15 2TT
021 414 5696
Knowles, G.M. Mr; Malmkjaer, K.S. Dr

Fairytales and fantasy: telling, writing and translating

Abstract: H.C. Andersen's fairytales exhibit consistency in certain lexical and syntactic choices. The impact of this consistency is discussed and the originals compared to translations into English, from different periods. The translations rarely retain the originals' consistency. The translations are compared to British children's literature of their respective periods. Their 'failure' to match the originals is shown to be motivated by the same concerns which ensure consistency of linguistic choices in other literature from the same periods, partly, if not exclusively directed at children. A comparison is made between authored and collected fairytales; while linguistic consistency is achievable in both written and oral literature, it is easily lost in the process of preparing collections of oral literature for publication. The reasons for this are in some ways similar to those which may cause particular differences between original writings and their translations. The lexicalization of magic and fantasy fiction for children and adults (including books based on current television series) is examined with a view to showing how they bear on contemporary culture. Conclusions relate to stylistics, critical linguistics and translation studies and comparative literature.

Published Material: KNOWLES, M. & MALMKJAER, K. (1989). 'Translating ideology: language, power and the world of the tin soldier', English Language Research Journal, Vol 3.
Source of Grant: No funding
Date of Research: 1989 – continuing

KEYWORDS: children's liteature; fairy tale; literary criticism; style; translation

8/0182

Centre of English as an International Language, Keynes House, Trumpington Street, Cambridge CB2 1QA
0223 332338
Brown, G. Prof.
English in Ghana
Abstract: This is an investigation of the variability of English usage by educated Ghanaians with a view to identifying what could serve as a realistic model of the English language for pedagogical and professional purposes in Ghana. It is now generally agreed that there are several 'standard Englishes' throughout the English-speaking world, each of which is as legitimate as another. Teachers are baffled by this notion as none of these 'varieties' has defined standards acceptable to the educational ministries and government institutions in the countries concerned. Furthermore, an obvious requirement for any teacher of English must be a thorough grasp of what it is that is to be taught. The research focuses on three issues. Firstly, how acceptable are the forms which are described in the literature as characteristics of 'Ghanaian English'. How acceptable are these forms to the native speaker of English. Finally, how far, if at all, is 'Ghanaian English' understandably different from 'Nigerian English' or 'Indian English'.
Source of Grant: Overseas research student award: £2,358 per annum Overseas student bursary: £4,000 per annum Pembroke College bursary: £4,652 per annum
Date of Research: 1989 – continuing
KEYWORDS: English language; Ghana; language policy; language standardization

8/0183

Centre of English as an International Language, Keynes House, Trumpington Street, Cambridge CB2 1QL
0223 332340
Brown, G. Prof.; Malmkjaer, K. Dr; Williams, J. Dr; *Supervisor:* Brown, G. Prof.
Trading lexical interpretation in extended prose
Abstract: The project will investigate the ability of subjects to identify subtle changes of sense in the use of a word as a text progresses and the word is repeated several times. The range of subjects to be compared will include academically able native speakers, academically unsuccessful native speakers, and non-native speakers of English. A range of methods will be used to investigate the phenomena including on-line probe recognition tasks, protocol questionnaires, and the analysis of extended discussion of the texts by subjects working in pairs.
Source of Grant: Endowment
Date of Research: 1990 – continuing
KEYWORDS: discourse analysis; lexicology; morphology; word recognition

8/0184

Department of Education
17 Trumpington Street, Cambridge CB2 1QA
0223 332888
Fenn, G. Dr; Wattles, B. Mrs; Pechey, A.M.; Davis, C. Mrs; Smith, S.J. Miss; *Supervisor:* Bruce, D.J. Dr
General programme concerned with psycholinguistic development
Abstract: This research is a variety of aims and approaches in the field of language and its interrelations with cognition, and currently includes the following PhD programmes: DAVIS, C. 'The understanding of television formats and the processes involved in the acquisition of media literacy skills'; PECHEY, A.M. 'The effects on memory of textural and pictorial modes of presentation'; SMITH, S.J. 'Language learning in children'; SLEE, N.M. Miss, 'Religious language in childhood and adolescence'.
Published Material: BRUCE, D.J. 'Features of attempted speech reading by deafened adults'. In: AILA 81 proceedings 1 (Eds. BENGT SIGURD and JAN SUARTVIK), Lund, Sweden.
Source of Grant: Department of Health & Social Security (speech reading); Department of Education & Science (follow-up study of backwardness in reading)
Date of Research: 1983 – continuing
KEYWORDS: cognition; language development; psycholinguistics

8/0185

Department of Experimental Psychology
Downing Street, Cambridge CB2 3EB

0223 332200
Goswami, U.C. Dr
Phonological and orthographic knowledge and reading development
Abstract: The aim of the research is to discover whether there is a link between a child's phonological awareness and that child's reading strategies. There will be two experiments with 24 and 30 6- year olds respectively. Children were taught to read a 'clue' word containing a consonant blend e.g. TRip and wiNK and test words with shared consonant blends e.g. TRot, taNK. Phonological awareness of intra-syllabic units which predicts TRIP – TROT is easier than WINK – TANK. The research showed that there was transfer in TRIP-TROT condition only, and concluded that phonological awareness does effect learning about letter sequences.
Published Material: GOSWAMI, U.C. 'Learning about spelling sequences: the role of onsets and rimes in analogies in reading', Child Development, (forthcoming).
Source of Grant: Spencer Foundation, USA: £3,429
Date of Research: 1989-1990
KEYWORDS: letters (alphabet); orthographic symbols

8/0186

Department of Experimental Psychology
Downing Street, Cambridge CB2 3EB
0223 333553
Russell, J. Dr
Young childrens' acquisition of 'non-natural' concepts
Abstract: The proposed research would employ the technique of 'learnability' to investigate the extent to which young children are naturally inclined to acquire some kinds of concept rather than others. The initial assumption is that there are at least two kinds of concept that do not feature in our conceptual system: (1) those that straddle different ontological categories (e.g. one word covering both a kind of artifact and a kind of animal); (2) those that are disjunctive rather than conjunctive (e.g. a word for things that are either blue or square). The question is whether young children have predispositions against the kind of concepts that can be called 'non-natural'. Type (1) are 'ontologically non-natural' and type (2) are 'disjunctively non-natural'. The researcher aims to study the learnability of ontologically non-natural concepts by means of short narratives followed by memory tasks, and the learnability of disjunctive concepts by means of sorting tasks and discrimination learning tasks. Because the children will already have had extensive experience with natural concepts it will not be surprising if the natural concepts prove easier to acquire. For this reason the research will investigate the relative difficulty of non-natural versus natural concepts across age.
Source of Grant: Economic and Social Research Fund: £26,228
Date of Research: 1988 – continuing
KEYWORDS: cognition; concept analysis; concept formulation; early learning; learning process

8/0187

Department of Experimental Psychology
Visual Development Unit,
Downing Street, Cambridge CB2 3EB
0223 332200
Atkinson, J. Dr; Braddick, O. Dr; Wattam-Bell, J. Mr
Normal and abnormal development of human vision; prediction and prevention of strabismus and amblyopia in infants detected by photorefractive screening
Abstract: The programme will study the development of cortical pattern processing, binocular function, refraction and visual attention during infancy, in association with studies of impaired development. Clinical applications of new tests in these areas will be devised to provide an integrated visual assessment programme. Behavioural and VEP methods will be used to study the developing mechanisms underlying orientation and directionality, sensitivity, and texture perception, and their integration for object perception. Follow-up will continue of children detected with refractive errors in our photorefractive infant screening programme (project award) with investigation of the links between pre-school visual deficits and learning disability in school. This will include studies of visual crowding in pre-school children and dyslexics to discover possible precursors of visual dyslexia.
Source of Grant: Medical Research Council Project Grant Award (1983-1987) MRC Programme Grant Award (1981-1991)
Date of Research: 1976 – continuing
KEYWORDS: child development; learning difficulty; pre-school child; vision

8/0188

Department of Experimental Psychology
Downing Street, Cambridge CB2 3EB
0223 332200
Mackintosh, N. Prof.; Mascie-Taylor, C.G.N. Dr; West, A.M. Dr

Cognitive and educational attainment in different ethnic groups

Abstract: The researchers have completed educational and cognitive testing of some 1,200 children aged 7 to 15 in three towns in the south-east Midlands, in an attempt to compare the attainments of different ethnic groups. The most consistent finding of the study was that at most ages, children of Pakistani or Bangladeshi origin obtained lower scores on most tests than did those of any other group, and that Indian and West Indian children, although scoring below whites, did reasonably well. In the initial, cross-sectional study, there was relatively little evidence of any systematic changes across different age levels. The researchers have recently been able to supplement these data with a longitudinal follow-up of some of the younger children. When analyzed (in 1990) these new data should provide more definitive evidence on the performance of these children as they progress through school.

Published Material: MACKINTOSH, N.J. & MASCIE-TAYLOR, C.G.N. (1985). 'The IQ Question'. In: Report of a Committee of Inquiry into the Education of Children from Ethnic Minorities. London: HMSO.; MACKINTOSH, N.J. (1986). 'The biology of intelligence?', British Journal of Psychology, Vol 77, No 1, pp.1-18, February.; MACKINTOSH, N.J., MASCIE-TAYLOR, C.G.N. & WEST, A.M. (1988). 'West Indian and Asian children's educational attainment: issues and outcomes in multicultural education'. In: VERMA, G. & PUMFREY, P. (Eds). Part 2. London: Falmer Press.

Source of Grant: Economic and Social Research Council: £19,440
Date of Research: 1986-1990
KEYWORDS: *achievement test; cognitive development; economic conditions; ethnic minority; family environment; social environment*

8/0189

Department of Social and Political Sciences
Sociological Research Group,
Free School Lane, Cambridge CB2 3RQ
0223 337733
Blackburn, R.M. Dr; Marsh, C. Dr

Matching marginals: a new approach to studying changes in class inequalities

Abstract: When studying changes in access to advantaged forms of education over time, formidable interpretive difficulties appear. Before changes in class inequalities can be assessed it would be necessary to take into account overall changes in the number of places available, the number of people competing for these places and the distribution of social classes. The researchers have devised a method of genuinely holding the effects of the class distribution constant, and have been able to re-interpret some major debates about changing class access as a consequence.

Published Material: BLACKBURN, R.M. & MARSH, C. (1990). 'Education and social class: revisiting the 1944 Education Act with fixed marginals', British Journal of Sociology, (forthcoming).; BLACKBURN, R.M., PRANDY, K., SILTANEN, J. & MARSH, C. (1990). 'Matching marginals: a new approach to studying changing inequality', Paper presented to 1990 British Sociological Association Annual Conference.; BLACKBURN, R.M., MARSH, C., PRANDY, K. & SILTANEN, J. (1990). 'A new approach to studying changing equality', Working Paper 2, Cambridge: Sociological Research Group.; MARSH, C. & BLACKBURN, R.M. (1991). 'Class differences in access to higher education'. In: BURROWS, R. & MARSH, C. Consumption and class: division and change. London: Macmillan (forthcoming).

Source of Grant: No funding
Date of Research: 1988-1990
KEYWORDS: *access to education; equal education; equal opportunity*

Canterbury College of Technology

8/0190

New Dover Road, Canterbury CT1 3AJ

0227 66081
Christchurch College
North Holmes Road, Canterbury CT1 1QU
0227 762444
Price, T.K. Mr; *Supervisor:* Bounds, C. Dr

Impact of Training Enterprise Education Division funding on curriculum change in further education

Abstract: This research seeks to assess the impact of TEED (Training Enterprise Education Division) funding on the process of curriculum change in FE (further education) colleges in England and Wales. The research has its origin in the Government's White Paper 'A new training initiative: a programme for action'. Its main objectives were to develop skill training including apprenticeship, in such a way as to enable young people entering at different ages with different educational attainments to acquire agreed standards of skill appropriate to jobs available, and to provide them with a basis for progress through further learning. Also anticipated is a move towards a position where all young people under the age of 18 have the opportunity of entering a period of planned work experience combined with work related training and education. Finally, to open widespread opportunities to adults whether employed or returning to work to acquire, increase or update their skills and knowledge during the course of their working lives. Their objectives provided the focus of much of the TEED activity during the period of this research 1985-1990. The research has been concerned with four TEED programmes; namely the Youth Training Scheme, The Adult Training Strategy, Work-Related Further Education, and the Technical and Vocational Education Initiative, and it is the impact of these programmes on further FE colleges in England and Wales which is the focus of this research. The thesis attempts to show that a relatively low level of investment by the Government through TEED in FE colleges has resulted in a high level of curriculum change.

Source of Grant: No funding
Date of Research: 1985-1990
KEYWORDS: *curriculum development; educational policy; financing; further education; government policy*

Cargenbridge Resource Centre

8/0191

Department of Education
Cargenbridge, Dumfries
0387 61234
Scottish Council for Educational Technology
Dowanhill, 74 Victoria Crescent Road,
Glasgow G12 9JN
031 334 9134
Gilmour, T. Mr; Bowman, M. Dr

The use of a local area network in a primary school

Abstract: The research will investigate the effect on teaching methods and learning processes of having access to a network system from each class base in a primary school. It will also assess potential benefits from having an appropriate range of software packages readily available at appropriate workstations. The innovative uses of software such as teletext emulators and desk-top publishing over a network in a primary school will be researched and an investigation into the possible adminstrative uses of the network in a primary school will be carried out.

Source of Grant: Scottish Council for Educational Technology: £24,639
Date of Research: 1988 – continuing
KEYWORDS: *computer assisted instruction; computer network; educational software; learning process; local area network; primary school; teaching method*

Central London Polytechnic

8/0192

London Management Centre, 35 Marylebone Road, London
NW1 5LS
071 486 5811 ext 225/231
Stanworth, M.J.K. Prof.

A longitudinal study of the influence of training on small business success.

Abstract: The prime element of the proposed work will be a 3-year longitudinal examination of a sample of small businesses in three separate geographical locations: the South East, the East Midlands and the North East of England. The study will focus upon the influence of training on success, assessed in terms of growth and other parameters of business efficiency and effectiveness. In each geographical location the samples will be equally divided into 2 separate groupings. One of these will act as a 'control' illustrating the manner in which firms employing between 5 and 20 employees currently manage their learning. The other will be studies using an 'action research' strategy using comparative interventions in key areas to ascertain the impact of training on the performance of these firms compared to the control group.
Source of Grant: Department of Education and Science (PICKUP): £120,000
Date of Research: 1988 – continuing
KEYWORDS: *business education; small business; success; training*

Centre for International Studies

8/0193

Meadowlea House, Littleham Road, Exmouth, Devon EX8 2QT
0395 264902
Morgan, R. Dr; Tyacke, A. Dr
An examination of course work being undertaken at initial training level on international issues in the United Kingdom
Abstract: The research aims to identify personnel and courses which promote an international dimension, including a European dimension in the initial training of teachers in the United Kingdom. Course objectives, content, resourcing and evaluation, form level and duration are being examined together with personnel training and qualification.
Source of Grant: European Community Mini Grants Scheme
Date of Research: 1990-1990
KEYWORDS: *international studies; teacher education*

Cheltenham and Gloucester College of Higher Education

8/0194

The Park Campus, Cheltenham GL50 2QF
0242 513836
Gemie, S. Dr
The State and women's schooling in France, 1815-1914
Abstract: This research will test recent theoretical models of the State and of women's relationships to public power structures by reference to the experience of schoolmistresses and schoolgirls in nineteenth century France. To assess the effects of the presentation of official role models of ideal feminine types on female students at teacher training colleges. To further understanding of the effects of limited entry into public positions on women's mentalities and to analyze women's ability to re-formulate official ideas in the light of their experience – in particular, their relationship to feminist, anarchist and socialist sub-cultures following their entries into the teaching profession. The research sample was based on archive research in Lyon, Caen, Bordeaux, Lille and Paris, and may involve reference to a data base of the careers of some 200 schoolmistresses. Methods involved social and cultural historical investigation, with some guidance from recent works by feminist and critical theorists.
Published Material: GEMIE, S. 'The schoolmistress's revenge: secular schoolmistresses, academic authority and village conflicts in France, 1815 to 1848', History of Education. (forthcoming).
Source of Grant: Cheltenham and Gloucester College of Higher Education: £1,500
Date of Research: 1988 – continuing
KEYWORDS: *feminism*

8/0195

Oxtalls Campus, Oxtall Lane, Gloucester GL2 9HN
0242 426700
Bray, S.A. Mrs

An investigation of current insurance qualifications in the European Community
Abstract: The aims and objectives of this research are to investigate the various insurance qualifications within the European Community, their level, the recognition they receive within individual member states and how they compare with the insurance qualifications elsewhere in the European Community. It is also intended to enquire how transferable these qualifications are in the light of 1992, how can qualifications which have been gained in the United Kingdom be applied to jobs in the European community and the implications for business studies/language courses. How applicable are qualifications which have been gained in other European countries to work in the UK insurance industry. The investigation will be carried out in European countries where insurance features most prominantly. Methodology will include desk research, data collection, contacting professional bodies from each country, insurance companies, Chamber of Commerce and The National Council for Vocational Qualifications (NCVQ). No definite conclusions have yet been drawn.
Source of Grant: College Research Fund: £900
Date of Research: 1990 – continuing
KEYWORDS: *EEC; insurance; qualification*

8/0196

Business Development Centre, Oxstalls Campus, Oxstalls Lane, Gloucester GL2 9HV
0242 513836
Further Education Unit
Information Centre, Grove House, 2-6 Orange Street, London WC2H 7WE
071 321 0433
Meeke, N.H.J. Dr
Information engineering: implications for further education/higher education
Abstract: This research arises out of parallel developments in hardware, software and communication systems and most particularly because of the integration of all three elements. Now the computer generalist will have to be knowledgeable and skilled in all three elements. It aims to determine the need for a triple approach to information engineering in the 1990's integrating hardware, software and communications into a single course to determine the weighting given to current specialists to achieve the best integrative mix. Also to review current curricula for evidence of such integration and established examples of good practice. Finally to make recommendations with regard to a framework of curriculum content and structure, provide exemplars suited ot the curriculum framework for illustrative purpose and make recommendations with regard to staff development issues arising. An investigation will be undertaken through structured discussions with interested parties including examining and validating bodies, professional institutions, government departments, industry and commerce, and relevant trades unions. College staff would provide exemplars of the curriculum content and structure framework recommended. A steering committee will be established to include representatives of a selection of interested parties. A report will be put forward for consideration for publication by the FEU which outlines the aims, methodology and findings of the project.
Source of Grant: Further Education Unit
Date of Research: 1990 – continuing
KEYWORDS: *computer engineering; curriculum; further education; higher education; information science*

8/0197

The Park Campus, Cheltenham GL50 2QF
0242 513836
Bristol University
Department of Education
Helen Wodehouse Building, 35 Berkeley Square, Bristol BS8 1JA
0272 303030
Ross, K.A. Dr; *Supervisor:* Garratt, R. Dr
A cross-cultural study of people's understanding of the functioning of fuels and the process of burning
Abstract: The research contributes to the growing understanding being gained, of the way people conceptualize their environment. It studied people's conceptions of the origin and fate of the matter of energy in organic fuel-oxygen systems when they burn, and their appreciation of the way ecosystems are driven by the decay of solar engergy. Over 150, mainly scientifically literate, adults, and over 200 children were involved in the study. It used a range of research

techniques. The major part involved the development of a questionnaire for adults which probed their understanding of the functioning of three fuels: wood, petrol and food. Some data were collected by interviews. The range of alternative frameworks that people used represent in themselves a substantial part of the findings. The aim, however, was to develop concept profiles which summarise these beliefs, in a form suitable for use by teachers. Concept profiles are presented which show the range of beliefs in five concept areas: matter energy, burn, fuel and food. The research looked at the roots of language and the influence that mother-tongue (English and four African languages) might play on the way people conceptualize the functioning of fuels. The results were analyzed according to the formal science background, and other background variables of the sample, which included, for example, a group of firemen, and science teachers from Africa. The results for burning are the most dramatic. Less than a third of those with chemistry 'A' level and beyond saw flame-burning as the building up of oxides. The rest of them saw the energy as being in fuels, to be released as bonds broke open. Oxygen was simply a helper. The implications for teaching are that we should spend far more time in bringing children's own conceptions out into the open. Only then can these beliefs be challenged.
Published Material: ROSS, K.A. (1988). 'Matter scatter and energy anarchy', School Science Review, Vol 69, No 248, pp.438-445, March.; ROSS, K.A. (1991). 'Burning – a constructive process', School Science Review.
Source of Grant: No funding
Date of Research: 1984-1990
KEYWORDS: adult; concept formation; cross-cultural research; earth sciences; fuel; misconception; scientific concepts

8/0198

The Park, Cheltenham GL50 2AF
0242 532700
More, C.R.V. Dr
History of Cheltenham Training College 1847-1947
Abstract: This research will trace the history of Cheltenham Training College (later the separate colleges of St Paul and St Mary) which was the largest Evangelical training college and at times the largest college in the country. The history will focus on eight areas: the foundation of the College; its management over the succeeding century in the light of national changes in the educational and religious framework; the qualifications, pay and conditions of staff; the origins and destinations of students; the syllabus; the expectations of students while training, and the formation and characteristics of the student ethos; sport and physical exercise; and the relationship between old students and the College. The study will use a full range of sources: e.g. annual reports, governors minute books, inspectors' reports, staff and student registers, student magazines, reminiscences and photographs.
Source of Grant: Cheltenham and Gloucester College of Higher Education: £24,000
Date of Research: 1990 – continuing
KEYWORDS: college of education; history of education; teacher education; United Kingdom

8/0199

Department of Education and Health
The Park, Cheltenham GL50 2QG
0242 513836
Charlton, A.D. Dr; Jones, K. Ms; Leo, E. Ms; Indoe, D. Mr; James, J. Ms
Evaluating of a teacher training package designed to enhance pupils' self-image
Abstract: The research involves an evaluation of an inservice teacher training package constructed by the researchers. The package – EASI Teaching Package (Enhancement Approaches with the Self-Image) – is designed to assist teachers improve the self-image of their pupils. Evaluation will incorporate a pre-/post treatment of design. Seventy two teachers (drawn from nine primary schools) are to constitute the Treatment group. They will receive the EASI Teaching Programme (four one hour meetings) over a four week period. A comparison group (similar size/type to the Treatment group) will receive no special treatment. Pre-/post evaluations will utilize indices of pupils' self-image reports and behavioural functioning.
Source of Grant: No funding
Date of Research: 1990 – continuing
KEYWORDS: inservice teacher education

8/0200

Department of Education and Health
The Park, Cheltenham GL50 2QF
0242 513856
Davidson, J. Ms; *Supervisor:* Terrell, C. Dr; Noyes, P. Dr
Computer assisted learning in the teaching of reading
Abstract: This research will develop and evaluate a computer aided learning system for the teaching of reading incorporating recent advances in digitised speech output. This simulates the usual reading instruction process where the teacher provides individual assistance to the learner by spoken prompts. Scanning techniques now enable pages of reading books already in use in primary classrooms to be displayed on a microcomputer and a child's voice is recorded, digitised and used to provide the speech. These prompts are issued when the child highlights words or whole pages with which they may be having difficulty. This system has the advantage of providing additional reading practice with an infinitely patient non-judgmental listener and avoids the humiliation that some children experience when seen to fail in front of a skilled reader. The initial reaction from pupils and teachers has been favourable, largely due to the clarity of the voice and the fact that teachers can use books which are already used in their schools and do not therefore need to change dramatically their approach to reading. The results of initial trials undertaken in Gloucestershire primary schools comparing groups of children using the system with control groups have shown the system to be of benefit in the teaching of reading. These comparisons are made by recording improved performance in standardized reading tests and measurements of sight vocabulary. The improvement goes beyond the immediate situation and evidence suggests it influences general reading attainment. Work has now started in the area of helping children who have had difficulty in learning to read.
Source of Grant: No funding
Date of Research: 1988 – continuing
KEYWORDS: computer assisted instruction; reading

8/0201

Department of Education and Health
The Park, Cheltenham GL50 2QF
0242 532714
Noyes, P. Dr
A survey of student expectations and perceptions of higher education
Abstract: This research aims to identify the nature of student expectations of the college. The major source of these expectations will be discovered, and an investigation into how they change will be conducted. Especially at the time of most impact, i.e. the first two weeks at college, and after one year at college. Areas where the college fall short of student expectation will be identified. Issues for further research and areas of college practice which may need to be adapted will be recommended. Links will be established with the quality assurance study of the induction process. The link between expectations, academic performance and satisfaction will be investigated. There will also be a contribution to the debate on the efficacy of expectation theory in explaining human behaviour. All students entering the college in September 1990 will be surveyed by questionnaire. Firstly, before they arrive at college to monitor initial expectations. Secondly, immediately after the induction process to ascertain immediate changes in perceptions after the initial impact of coming to college has been experienced. Thirdly, after a year at college, to measure perceptions of that time. Expectation Theory will be used as a means of examining the process of attitude change that will occur during the year, and outcome measures will be collected by means of satisfaction indices calculated from questionnaire responses and academic performance indicated by college grades.
Source of Grant: College Research Fund
Date of Research: 1990 – continuing
KEYWORDS: expectancy; higher education; perception; student

8/0202

Department of Education and Health
The Park, Cheltenham GL50 2QF
0242 513856
Attilar Joszef University
Department of Sociology
Saeged 6722, Petofi Sandor Str., 30/34, Hungary
010 36 62 21 611
Cowen, H. Mr; Rosie, A. Dr; Gabor, K. Mr

A comparative study of student youth social and political lifestyles in Hungary and England

Abstract: The research project builds upon an international youth study already carried out in Hungary, Germany and the Netherlands. Its focus is on the social profiles, social and political orientation and lifestyles of student youth in localities in Hungary and England, comparing how student youth are living through Europe's economic and political changes. Student bodies in Sopron and Kosseg, Hungary, and Cheltenham and Gloucester, England will be the subject of interviews by questionnaire. Students will selected under three basic categories; older, secondary school students; further education and technical college students and students in higher education. They will be questioned on a series of central issues relating to patterns of social orientation; most important life events; perspectives and attitudes towards personal and societal futures; political interest and participation; group activities and cultural activities. Findings will be compared and then considered in the light of current youth and educational policies in each country.
Source of Grant: Hungarian Academy of Social Science (local study)
Date of Research: 1991 – continuing
KEYWORDS: *economic change; life style*

8/0203

Department of Education and Health
The Park, Cheltenham GL50 2QF
0242 513856
Fahey, W.S. Mr; Cutting, E. Ms

The identification of the needs of lesbian and gay students in higher education

Abstract: From a self selected sample of at least 50 lesbians and gay students currently taking courses in 10 separate institutions of higher education, the authors in this study aim to, examine students' perceptions of their needs, explore the extent to which these needs are currently being met within educational institutions, and develop a strategy to reduce or eliminate inequalities in higher education related to student sexuality. Methodology will include a postal questionnaire followed by a selection of semi-structured interviews with quantitative and qualitative aspects.
Source of Grant: No funding
Date of Research: 1991 – continuing
KEYWORDS: *lesbianism; student needs*

8/0204

Department of Education and Health
The Park, Cheltenham GU50 2QF
0242 513856
Brown, B. Miss; *Supervisor:* Sugden, D.A. Dr

An examination of teaching and learning strategies for children with movement learning difficulties

Abstract: In this research, fifty children aged 2- to 11- years with movement learning difficulties have been examined for six years in a movement learning context whilst they have been engaged in developing rudimentary and fundamental movement abilities. The childrens movement development has been examined in the context of their total development. The teaching considerations surrounding the teachers role, curriculum content, teaching strategy and learning environment have been critically analyzed in the context of the movement learning experience of the children. The children were taught in segregated and integrated settings.
Source of Grant: No funding
Date of Research: 1984 – continuing
KEYWORDS: *movement education*

8/0205

Department of Education and Health
The Park, Cheltenham GL50 2QF
0242 513856
Bown, R. Dr; *Supervisor:* Mungham, G. Mr

Children and popular television: primary school age range

Abstract: This study is concerned with media education in the primary school and has a particular focus on children in the junior school age range and their consumption of popular television. It explores the viewing habits of such children; identifies the types of programmes that they watch; analyzes the nature and content of these programmes; and suggests ways in which schools may, in the pursuit of educational aims, profitably respond to these findings. An initial survey has been conducted involving interviews with 100 children and questionnaires administered to a further 343 children.
Published Material: BOWN, R. (1990). 'The amen team: ideology

violence and religion', Media Education Journal, No 10.; BOWN, R. (1991). 'The significance of popular television: a case study for its use in the classroom'. In: CHARLTON, T. & DAVID, K. (Eds). Behaviour in school: towards a whole school approach. London: McMillan.
Source of Grant: No funding
Date of Research: 1985 – continuing
KEYWORDS: *mass media; primary school; television*

8/0206

Department of Education and Health
The Park, Cheltenham GL50 2QF
0242 513856
Oxford University
Department of Experimental Psychology
Oxford OX1 2JD
0865 270360
Huxford, L.M. Mrs; *Supervisor:* Terrell, C. Dr; Bradley, L. Dr

The relationship between the phonological strategies employed in the early stages of reading and spelling

Abstract: This research comprises longitudinal and intervention studies aimed at examining young children's developing phonological strategies in reading and spelling. It contributes to the growing body of data on the connections between reading and spelling (e.g. Bryant and Bradley, 1980; Cataldo and Ellis 1988. Fifty six children, aged between 3½ and 5½ years, who had satisfied a minimum requirement of phonological ability were included in the sample for the longitudinal study. A combination of standardized tests and tasks specifically devised and refined for the study have been used. A battery of eight tests were constructed to compare reading and spelling, controlling for alphabet and use of visual and contextual strategies. In order to assess children's phonological development against other factors of experience and ability, measures of age, reading, spelling, alphabetical knowledge, intelligence, memory and hearing were taken. The pattern of results from forty three of the children supports the claim that children appear to acquire a phonological strategy in spelling before an equivalent strategy. Forty two children in two experimetnal groups and a control group are taking part in the intervention study. The effects on reading acquisition of two different approaches to writing are being measured.
Published Material: BRYANT, P.E. & BRADLEY, L. (1980). 'Why children sometimes write words which they do not read'. In: FRITH, U. (Ed). Cognitive processes in spelling. London: Academic Press.; CATALDO, S. & ELLIS, N. (1988). 'Interaction in the development of spelling, reading and phonological skills', Journal of Research in Reading, Vol 11, pp.86-109.
Source of Grant: No funding
Date of Research: 1987 – continuing
KEYWORDS: *child; phonology; reading; spelling*

8/0207

Department of Education and Health
The Park, Cheltenham GL50 2QF
0242 513856
Rosie, A.J. Mr; *Supervisor:* Davies, W.B. Prof.

Fractured lives: an ethnographic study of a YTS (Youth Training Scheme) course

Abstract: The study examined the lives of a group of twenty four young people, aged between sixteen and eighteen, who attended a one year vocational scheme in a south Midlands town during 1985/86. The majority of group members had previously attended special schools. The investigation involved observation of the group throughout the year. Data was collected through participant observation, structural interviews, examination of records and sociometric enquiries. The framework for the investigation drew upon both anthropology and sociology with the concepts of symbolic experience, social drama, ritual, being of central importance. Within the sociology of education a theory of differentiation and polarization has been developed over recent years to explore the relationship between pupil responses to school and teacher categorizations of pupils. It was found that this analysis could be extended to the post-school experiences of the observed group. However, the theory of differentiation and polarization was extended through deploying the categories of 'group' and 'grid' elaborated by Mary Douglas. It was found that the group of young people formed three district sub-groups inhabiting different spaces on a grid: group matrix. Movement within the matrix derived from the experiences of differentiation and polarization.

Source of Grant: No funding
Date of Research: 1984-1990
KEYWORDS: ethnography; sociology of education; vocational education

8/0208

Department of Health and Education
The Park, Cheltenham GL50 2QF
0242 532714
Corbett, P.J.S. Mr; Noyes, P. Dr
The development of oracy and literature
Abstract: The Oracy and Literature Research Centre was formed in 1990 to draw together research into language development. Research involved various strands involving college staff, students and teachers. The aim is to research identified aspects of language development, particularly the development of spelling through emergent writing, process writing, reading/writing links, using visits to develop language, the value of process writing in developing literacy skills in children experiencing learning difficulties. Sample sizes vary. Methodology includes observation, tape recording, video, diaries, analysis of samples, survey and questionnaire. Results will be disseminated through conference, journal articles and monographs
Source of Grant: Cheltenham & Gloucester College of Higher Education
Date of Research: 1991 – continuing
KEYWORDS: language development; learning difficulty; literacy; oral expression; reading; special education; spelling; writing

8/0209

Faculty of Education and Health
The Park, Cheltenham GL50 2QF
0242 532714
Noyes, P. Dr
A study of teaching methods in a college of higher education
Abstract: This research will identify the teaching needs of new members of academic staff in the Faculty by means of paired observation and discussion groups. Action research techniques are then being used to develop and monitor teaching methods. Nine academic staff are involved and the direction of the project will depend upon identified needs and decisions reached during discussion.
Source of Grant: Faculty of Education
Date of Research: 1990 – continuing
KEYWORDS: academic staff development; inservice teacher education

Chester College of Higher Education

8/0210

Cheyney Road, Chester CH1 4BJ
0244 375444
Exeter University
Department of Education
St Luke's, Exeter EX1 2LU
0392 76311
Heaney, S. Mrs; *Supervisor:* Golby, M. Dr
Graduates becoming primary teachers: a study of the development of reflective professionalism by graduates following a school-based one year primary course in initial teacher education
Abstract: Case study material will be assembled in order to examine the development of reflective professionalism in graduates following a one year school-based course of initial teacher-training. Work will be done with sequential intakes over 3 or more years of 25 in number.
Source of Grant: Personal and college funding
Date of Research: 1987 – continuing
KEYWORDS: graduate; primary education; professional development; teacher education; teacher socialization

City of London Polytechnic

8/0211

100 Minories, London EC2M 6SQ
071 283 1030

Brunel University
Uxbridge, Middlesex UB8 3PH
0895 74000
Hawkins, A.S. Mrs; Glickman, L. Mr; Jolliffe, F. Mrs
Probablistic intuitions and concepts in statistics
Abstract: The research aims at synthesising existing research in statistics/probability teaching and learning. Various empirical studies have also been carried out to supplement this synthesis e.g. a survey of 350 plus statistics teachers from mathematics and "user"-disciplines. The teachers' training, attitudes towards, and awareness of the changing nature of statistics, their use of technical resourses, and their own and their students' difficulties with statistics and probability were included. The ultimate objective of the project is the production of a handbook for teachers of statistics, incorporating commentaries on relevant research and research methodologies, and guidance concerning teaching methods and materials.
Source of Grant: No funding
Date of Research: 1986-1990
KEYWORDS: statistics; teaching method

City of Sheffield

8/0212

Department of Education
Metropolitan District, PO Box 67, Leopold Street, Sheffield S1 1RJ
0742 735708
Garforth, J.M. Ms
Positive action in areas of social disadvantage
Abstract: Since 1983 Sheffield Local Education Authority has been carrying out a Positive Action Project, whereby an index of net disadvantage is used to identify a small number of schools to receive an additional teacher for the academic year. Each year headteachers are asked to identify the aims for the work of this extra teacher and to monitor and evaluate this work. Particular questions considered include how the benefits pupils receive from extra teacher contact can be made explicit; whether some strategies are more helpful than others; and if it is possible to set up such a project on a one year basis so that benefits will remain when the teacher is withdrawn.
Source of Grant: Local Education Authority (LEA)
Date of Research: 1983 – continuing
KEYWORDS: disadvantaged; positive action; resource allocation; teacher

8/0213

Department of Education
Metropolitan District, PO Box 67, Leopold Street, Sheffield S1 1RS
0742 735708
Aspinwall, K. Ms
Development and evaluation of Sheffield Curriculum Initiative
Abstract: The Sheffield Curriculum Initiative (SCI) is a large scale attempt to develop school centred innovation as the basis for a district-wide strategy of curriculum change. The strategy involved a substantial secondment programme in which teachers spent part of their time working back in their schools on specific aspects of curriculum innovation related to longer term plans of development. SCI is a major collaborative enterprise involving the LEA, its schools and the Sheffield University and Polytechnic Education Departments. The Initiative began in 1986 and a substantial evaluation archive has evolved composed of extensive interview data collected from secondees, other teahcers, university and polytechnic tutors, LEA advisers and officers. The evaluation is now looking at outcomes, eg classroom effects, which teachers attribute at least in part to SCI intervention.
Published Material: FULKER, P., REGAN, P. & THOMPSON, J. (1977). The Sheffield SFS Programme. An evaluation: Management implications for schools and LEAs. Sheffield: City of Sheffield Education Department.; ASPINWALL, K. (1987). Some responses to SFS secondees to this year's programme. Evaluation Report. Sheffield: City of Sheffield Education Department.; ASPINWALL, K. (1987). A climate for change. A report on the first year of Sheffield's School Focused Secondment Initiative. Evaluation Report. Sheffield: City of Sheffield Education Department.; ASPINWALL, K. (1988). A bit of the sun: teacher development

through an LEA curriculum initiative. Sheffield: City of Sheffield Education Department.; GARFORTH, J.M. (1988). Evaluation of the Sheffield Curriculum Initiative in Secondary Schools. Sheffield: City of Sheffield Education Department.; RUDDUCK, J. & WILCOX, B. (1988). 'Issues of ownership and partnership in school-centred innovation: The Sheffield experience', Research Papers in Education, Vol 3, No 3, pp.157-180.
Source of Grant: Local Education Authority (LEA)
Date of Research: 1986 – continuing
KEYWORDS: curriculum development; educational innovation; evaluation

City University

8/0214
Social Statistics Research Unit
(NCDS User Support Group),
Northampton Square,
London EC1V OHB
071 253 4399 ext 4109
Fogelman, K. Mr; Shepherd, P.; *Supervisor:* Fox, A.J. Prof.
National Child Development Study (NCDS) (1958 Cohort)
Abstract: NCDS is a long-term study of the development and circumstances of all the people in this country who were born in the week 3-9 March 1958. Following the original perinatal study, follow-ups have been conducted by the National Children's Bureau at the ages of 7, 11, 16 and 23. At each of the follow-ups during the school years, information was obtained by: (1) Questionnaires completed by schools: (2) attainment tests; (3) parental interviews; (4) medical examinations; and (5) at 11 and 16 only, personal questionnaires. At each of these stages, information was obtained on some 90% of the original births, with the addition of new immigrants born in the same week. At age 23, 76% (N = 12,537) were retraced and interviewed on: (a) post-school education and training; (b) labour market experiences: (c) family formation; (d) health; (e) housing; and (f) leisure. In addition, in 1977/78, schools and other educational institutions provided details of cohort members' public examination entries and results to that date. Among the educational issues which have been explored with these data are: (i) General patterns of attainment and behaviour, and their relationship with social background; (ii) ability-grouping in secondary schools; (iii) selective and non-selective secondary schooling; (iv) special education; (v) school attendance and truancy; (vi) sex differences; (vii) careers guidance; and (viii) sex education. All NCDS data are available through the ESRC (Economic and Social Research Council) Data Archive. Since April 1985, ESRC has funded the User Support Group to promote and facilitate use of these data by other researchers. Plans are now being developed for a further stage of the study, to take place in 1989.
Published Material: A full list of publications can be obtained from the researchers on request
Source of Grant: The User Support Group is funded by the ESRC (Economic and Social Research Council), with related projects funded by the DHSS, ESRC, Department of the Environment and the Alcohol Education Research Council. Past stages of the study were funded by the National Birthday Trust Fund, ESRC, and various government departments.
Date of Research: 1958 – continuing
KEYWORDS: child development; social structure

8/0215
Northampton Square,
London EC1V OBH
071 253 4399 ext 4525
Golombok, S. Dr; Rust, J. Dr
Pre-school activities inventory
Abstract: The Pre-School Activities Inventory is a psychometrically constructed questionnaire for the measurement of sex-role behaviour in children. It is completed by the child's parents, teacher or nursery staff. The questionnaire contains 28 items, and is divided into three areas: toys and games, activities and characteristics. It is currently in the process of validation by comparing parents responses on the questionnaire with teacher's ratings of masculinity and femininity, and vice versa. British norms should be available by mid 1989.
Source of Grant: No funding

Date of Research: 1988 – continuing
KEYWORDS: pre-school child; questionnaire; sexual behaviour

8/0216
Department for Continuing Education
Northampton Square, London EC1V OHB
071 253 4399
Parry, G. Mr; Davies, P.A. Ms
Wider access and the professional engineering institutions
Abstract: A research project carried out during January – May 1989 used questionnaire and interview studies to investigate the place of non-A level and mature entry in the policies and preferences of professional engineering institutions and to examine the principles and procedures governing accreditation and registration. Although they were nominated and authorized bodies of The Engineering Council, the professional institutions were found to differ in their stance on many key issues, especially in their attitudes towards entry routes and standards. Some identified, preferred or required entry qualifications – usually in terms of A level point scores – while others communicated their interest by encouragement rather than prescription. Most professional institutions acknowledged that there was a mismatch between their proclaimed position and that perceived and experienced by some in academic departments of engineering. This appeared to be a function in part of the accreditation process itself which was retrospective and required engineering departments to justify what had been done rather than involve the professional bodies in the planning and recognition of new arrangements. In general, the professional institutions recognized the need to recruit more students into engineering studies but they saw this as essentially a matter for the higher education establishments. Indeed their knowledge, experience and understanding of intiatives to widen access for young and older people was extremely limited.
Published Material: PARRY, G. & DAVIES, P. (1990). Wider access and the professional engineering institutions. London: Council for National Academic Awards.; PARRY, G. & DAVIES, P. (1990). 'The professional engineering institutions: agents of change or closure?' In: PARRY, G. (Ed). Wider entry to engineering higher education. Conference proceedings. London: Engineering Council, Training Enterprise Education Division and Royal Society of Arts.; PARRY, G. & DAVIES, P. (1990). The role of the professional engineering institutions'. In: PARRY, G. (Ed). Engineering fixtures: new audiences and arrangements for engineering higher education. London: Engineering Council.
Source of Grant: British Petroleum and Council for National Academic Awards (CNAA): £8,000
Date of Research: 1989-1989
KEYWORDS: access to education; accreditation; engineering; higher education; professional education

8/0217
Department of Continuing Education
Northampton Square, London EC1V OHB
071 253 4399
Parry, G. Mr; Davies, P. Ms
Evaluation of the introduction of a national framework for the recognition of Access courses to higher education in England and Wales and Northern Ireland
Abstract: This research will be a twenty month study of the introduction of the CNAA/CVCP (Council for National Academic Awards/Committee of Vice Chancellors and Principals) national framework for the recognition of Access courses to higher education. The research project aimed to trace the origin, development and impact of the framework as a means of extending opportunities for adults without conventional qualifications to participate in higher education. The first phase focused on the first round of approvals of authorized validating agencies and involved content analysis of published documents and interview and observational studies of the central body. The extended phase focused on subsequent rounds of approvals and case studies of selected authorized validating agencies to monitor the impact of the framework at local level and in relation to Access course providers and students. The study involved both formative and summative evaluation and results and conclusions were to be disseminated through an interim and final report.
Source of Grant: Training Enterprise Education Division Further Education Unit Department of Education and Science Unit for the Development of Adult Continuing Education: jointly £63,000
Date of Research: 1990 – continuing
KEYWORDS: further education

8/0218

Department of Continuing Education
Northampton Square, London EC1V OHB
071 253 4399
Parry, G. Mr; Thompson, A. Dr

Access co-ordinators in institutions of higher education in the United Kingdom

Abstract: This is a one year research project investigating the role of access co-ordinators in higher education who have responsibility for extending and supporting the participation of mature and non-traditional students. The first phase used a questionnaire to heads of continuing education in all universities, polytechnics and colleges to collect baseline data on patterns of provision and activity. The second phase involved the identification of a small number of institutions for more qualitative and detailed investigation using case study methods. A final report would be made available to responding institutions and to others on request.

Source of Grant: Universities Funding Council: £15,000
Date of Research: 1990 – continuing
KEYWORDS: co-ordinator; mature student; non-traditional education

City University Business School

8/0219

Department for Personnel Research and Enterprise Development, Frobisher Crescent, Barbican Centre, London EC2Y 8HB
071 920 0111
Dobson, P. Mr; *Supervisor:* Williams, A.P.O. Prof.

Development and validation of a management development workshop

Abstract: Assessment Centre (AC) technology is well developed within the context of management selection. This research is aimed at developing a 2 to 3 day workshop which builds on AC technology, but is only concerned with development. To date two workshops have been run on 50 MBA (Master of Business Administration) students. These preliminary trials are enabling improvements to be made in terms of face validity, acceptability and feasibility. The next stage is to develop measures which assess the learning which takes place in the workshop. The final stage of the research is to systematically vary selected variables (e.g. type of simulation exercise), and to measure the effects of these variations on the learning process. The learning/developmental objectives of the workshop are twofold: to help individuals become more aware of their strengths and weaknesses as a manager of people, and to enable them to develop their skills in assessing the behaviour of others and in providing feedback and counselling.

Source of Grant: Supported by City University Business School
Date of Research: 1987-1990
KEYWORDS: assessment; learning strategy; management education

Cleveland County Council

8/0220

Research and Development Unit,
PO Box 17, Melrose House, Melrose Street,
Middlesborough, Cleveland TS1 2YW
0642 248155
Lofthouse, M. Mr

Development of computer applications in school administration

Abstract: This research will involve the development of computer applications in school administration. The first application is for school option block structuring and pupil allocation. The system compiles fourth year option blocks so that as many as possible of the pupils' original subject choices can be satisfied. The system then allocates pupils to classes in such a way as to produce balanced class sizes and prints out class lists and individual pupil information. A second application is for parents evening scheduling. The system produces a schedule of appointments for a parents evening. Each teacher receives an individual print out listing their timeta-ble for the evening. Late starters can be catered for. Finally, allocation of first year pupils to classes. The system generates balanced classes for new first year secondary pupils according to mixing criteria, stipulated by the schools. For example, if required, it will attempt to split boys and girls equally between classes, and at the same time will try to produce mixed ability classes and to split the pupils from each feeder school equally between classes. The system has several optional facilities. It is possible to keep certain groups of pupils together. Particular pupils may be 'forced' into particular classes. Maximum class sizes may be defined. The generated class mixes may be analyzed. It is hoped that the research will produce three systems that run on the Acorn BBC Master and The Acorn BBC Archimedes 3000 microcomputers.

Published Material: LOFTHOUSE, M. & SKIRVING, A. (1987). Users' manual: Allocation of first year pupils to classes. Middlesborough; Cleveland County Council: Research and Intelligence Unit.; LOFTHOUSE, M. (1987). Users' manual: School option block structuring and pupil allocation. Middlesborough; Cleveland County Council: Research and Intelligence Unit.; LOFTHOUSE, M. (1988). Users' manual: Parents evening scheduling. Middlesborough; Cleveland County Council: Research and Intelligence Unit.

Source of Grant: No funding
Date of Research: 1980-1989
KEYWORDS: administration of education; computer; computer uses in education; school organization

College of Ripon and York St John

8/0221

Lord Mayor's Walk, York YO3 7EX
0904 56771
Peskett, R. Dr; *Supervisor:* French, P. Dr

Language and classroom control

Abstract: The project is to provide detailed analysis of interactions used by infant teachers to maintain order and attention by pupils. Specific areas include: (1) methods for gaining and sustaining pupils' attention; (2) methods of pre-empting breakdowns in order; and (3) methods for redressing breakdowns. The project is of particular and practical benefit to student teachers to overcome anxiety concerning classroom management. Student teachers fail to learn by classroom observation of experienced teachers because they do not know what to look for. Experienced teachers tend to respond automatically to a situation without analyzing their actions and are not aware of their routine skills and practices. The project seeks to establish an alternative reliable source of knowledge. Methods include: (1) analysis of classroom video recordings for identification of teachers' methods; (2) recognition of teachers responses; and (3) consideration of descriptions and preparation of examples of methods. The planned outcome of this research is to include: (1) statement of interactional structures and processes through which order and attention are maintained – mainly of interest to academic researchers; and (2) a practical statement for students in training and educators, taking the form of interactional task related units for the use of teacher education courses, with examples of transcribed interaction with edited cassette tapes.

Source of Grant: Nuffield Foundation with support from above
Date of Research: 1984 – continuing
KEYWORDS: class management; classroom discipline; primary education; teacher behaviour; teacher-pupil relation

Coopers & Lybrand Associates

8/0222

Plumtree Court, London EC4 4HT
071 583 5000
Open University
Walton Hall, Milton Keynes MK7 6AA
0908 274066
Thompson, Q. Dr; *Supervisor:* Harland, G.E. Dr

Relative costs of open learning

Abstract: This study examined the relative costs of open learning compared to more traditional forms of training and the reasons companies decided to use open learning, and in particular the importance of costs as a factor in their decision. The research involved a survey of fifty companies which have used OL (open learning), and ten case studies examining the relative costs of open learning to companies. The striking conclusion from the survey is that companies' decisions to use OL were usually not explicitly related to costs, despite the indications from the case studies that OL is often subststantially cheaper. The most frequent reasons for choosing OL were the logistics of training; because trainees were scattered around the country, on shift work, or difficult to release from their job. The implications of the survey are that promotion of OL should emphasise its logistical advantages as least as much as the cost advantages. We have produced a checklist for companies to work through when considering whether to use OL systems which emphasizes these points. The case studies demonstrate that OL can cost substantially less than equivalent conventional training. The main reason is that less trainee time is spent away from productive work. In the cases involving computer based training (CBT) and interactive video (IAV), the training using these technologies took less time overall.
Source of Grant: Training Agency: £60,000 DES (Pickup): £10,000 National Economic Development Office: £5,000
Date of Research: 1988-1989
KEYWORDS: cost; open learning

Coventry Polytechnic

8/0223
>Learning Systems Centre,
>Priory Street, Coventry CV1 5FB
>0203 224166
>Dandy, D. Mrs; Howells, F. Mrs; *Supervisor:* Cox, S. Mr

An open learning package for Spanish at intermediate level
Abstract: The researchers are attempting to produce material (curriculum development) for Open Learning in Spanish; not quite at beginners' level, but rather at the problem point (roughly equivalent to O/A level), when the language becomes difficult. All known methods for language teaching will be considered or even used.
Source of Grant: Coventry Polytechnic: ½ time teaching secondment plus £1,250
Date of Research: 1988-1989
KEYWORDS: curriculum development; language teaching; Spanish language

8/0224
>Priory Street, Coventry CV1 5FB
>0203 224166
>Corness, P. Mr

ALPS – (Automated Language Processing Systems) computer assisted translation system as a language learning tool
Abstract: Computer assisted translation (CAT) systems are being increasingly used in translation departments in business and industry. The department feels it is vitally important to incorporate such advances in information technology into its degree courses. On the recently revised BA Modern Languages Degree scheme, work with ALPS now features in the First Year Approaches to Language Studies, in the Information Technology Option in Second and Final Year and in translation work at all levels. It is hoped to introduce in the near future a Translation Option, which would include more advanced practical application of ALPS. It is also planned to incorporate work with ALPS on the language modules in European Engineering Studies and other degree courses. This is seen as a natural development of the department's successful Computer Assisted Language Learning programme. ALPS was selected from among a number of different systems because of its interactive approach, which makes possible new types of computer assisted language learning activities and text analysis facilities, in addition to familiarising students with up to date tools of the modern practising translator. A member of the department has spoken at international conferences about the language learning applications of ALPS at Coventry Polytechnic, and is Education Representative on the International Alps Users' Group, with the opportunity to keep abreast of CAT developments in the business and industrial world.

Published Material: CORNESS, P. (1986). 'The ALPS computer assisted translation system in an academic environment'. In: PICKEN, C. (Ed) (1986). Translating and the computer, 7. London: Aslib.
Source of Grant: Coventry Polytechnic
Date of Research: 1985 – continuing
KEYWORDS: computer assisted instruction; higher education; information technology; language teaching; translation

8/0225
>Priory Street, Coventry CV1 5FB
>0203 224166
>Jones, D.E. Mr; Orsini Jones, D.M.

Multi-media course in Italian language
Abstract: The aim is to prepare a course for the teaching of Italian language which would be suitable for use in the Polytechnic. It will therefore need to make use of audio and video recording facilities and computer programs as well as written material, and to be usable with limited input from teaching staff. Work is currently progressing on a beginners course, but it is hoped ultimately to produce an integrated course for three years.
Source of Grant: No funding
Date of Research: 1986 – continuing
KEYWORDS: language teaching; Italian language; polytechnic; teaching aids

8/0226
>Priory Street, Coventry CV1 5FB
>0203 24166
>Hocking, B. Dr

Developing teaching materials on the international politics of the environment
Abstract: The aim of this project is to develop teaching materials on the subject of the environment as an issue on the international agenda. These will comprise a bibliography and a course guide which can be used in the context of traditional courses or self-learning environments.
Source of Grant: Coventry Polytechnic; Learning Systems Development Fund
Date of Research: 1990 – continuing
KEYWORDS: environment; teaching aids

8/0227
>Priory Street, Coventry CV1 5FB
>0203 24166
>Hocking, B. Dr

Developing a joint BA Honours Course in international studies and business studies
Abstract: The purpose of this project is to develop a course which focuses on the international context in which modern business operates and, thereby, provides a broader educational experience than is the case with most undergraduate courses in business studies.
Source of Grant: Staff Development Programme
Date of Research: 1990 – continuing
KEYWORDS: business education

8/0228
>Priory Street, Coventry CV1 5FB
>0203 24166
>Taylor, K.

Material for a literature and politics course
Abstract: This research will involve collecting course materials for a new third year undergraduate course on literature and politics, with particular reference to Britain and Europe in the contemporary period, and also to changing ideas and values in view of the rapid changes in East/West Europe.
Source of Grant: Coventry Polytechnic
Date of Research: 1990 – continuing
KEYWORDS: Europe; higher education; literature; politics; social change; teaching aids; undergraduate study

8/0229
>Priory Street, Coventry CV1 5FB
>0203 24166
>Hoskyns, C. Ms; Wilkinson, S. Ms

Introducing women's studies modules in undergraduate degrees in the polytechnic
Abstract: The aim of the project is to develop course materials for core courses in women's studies suitable to be offered in a wide range of BA degree courses in the polytechnic, and to negotiate

their adoption. The courses will be taught on a multi-disciplinary basis.
Source of Grant: Coventry Polytechnic
Date of Research: 1989 – continuing
KEYWORDS: women's studies

8/0230
Department of Art and Design
Gosford Street, Coventry CV1 5RZ
0203 24166
French, D. Mr
Learning from Europe: exchanges and industrial experience
Abstract: This is a study of undergraduate exchanges with other European Community countries in order to establish the extent of provision, the operation of schemes and the various models of organization. The mailed questionnaire produced a near complete return and three main models were identified. In combination with the above, the project examined practices of industry/university links in Communication Studies in France and Belgium. The flexibility in use of professionals as visiting lecturers and of placements of varying lengths were identified as positive features of practice in the countries concerned.
Source of Grant: Council for National Academic Awards: £5,000
Date of Research: 1986-1988
KEYWORDS: communication studies; Europe; exchange visit; higher education; industry; undergraduate

8/0231
Department of Art & Design
Priory Street, Coventry CV1 5FB
0203 838690
Bevan, R. Mr; *Supervisor:* Richards, C.J. Dr
Conceptualization design and orientation in complex multimedia structures
Abstract: The aim of this research is to develop more intuitive and creative methods of designing and representing interlinked information in interactive, non-linear multimedia structures, providing simple and effective means of orientation and navigation within such structures.
Source of Grant: Apple Computer UK Ltd: £23,000 per annum
Date of Research: 1989 – continuing
KEYWORDS: autoinstructional aid; computer assisted instruction; programmed text

8/0232
Department of Geography
Priory Street, Coventry CV1 5FB
0203 224166
Matthews, M.H. Dr
Catchments, schools and the characteristics of teachers
Abstract: This research examines the influence of the neighbourhood on teacher characteristics, with particular reference to comprehensive schools in Coventry. The focus is upon a consideration of whether the characteristics of teachers in the inner city and Social Priority Schools differ from their colleagues in schools in suburban locations and of nonpriority status. It was thought that such an approach would provide an assessment of the efficacy of some aspects of existing spatial policies aimed at alleviating educational disadvantage. A sample of 526 teachers drawn from 8 schools participated in the survey. A questionnaire was used to seek information on demographic, educational, experiential, and attitudinal details. The results suggest that the strong relationship between areas and teachers, recognised in a number of studies conducted in the USA, is little evident in this British case study. Within Coventry there is a lack of inter neighbourhood variation in the compositional makeup of teachers. The policy implications of these findings are to be discussed.
Published Material: MATTHEWS, M.H., AIREY, A. and TACON, L. (1988). 'The influence of the neighbourhood on teacher characteristics: a case study of Coventry', Envirnoment and Planning A, No 20, pp.681-688.; MATTHEWS, M.H., AIREY, A., and TACON, L. (1988). 'Catchments, schools and the characteristics of teachers'. In: BONDI, E. and MATTHEWS, M.H. Education and Society, Chapter 9. pp.257-284.; BONDI, E. and MATTHEWS, M.H. (1988). Education and Society: structures in the politics, sociology and geography of education. London: Routledge
Source of Grant: Nuffield Foundation: £3,000
Date of Research: 1986-1988

KEYWORDS: educational policy; geographical location; teacher behaviour

8/0233
Department of Geogrpahy
Priory Street, Coventry CV1 5FB
0203 224166
Matthews, M.H. Dr
Gender, graphicacy and geography
Abstract: This research investigates the influence of gender-related differences in home range experience upon cognitive mapping ability. The sample constituted 166 children aged between 6 and 11 from a suburban school. Each child was asked to draw a map of their journey to school and home area. Three different methods of stimulus presentation were used; free-recall sketching and the interpretation of either a large scale plan or an aerial photograph. A structured interview with every individual provided information on home range behaviour. The study confirms a growing differential between the activity spaces of boys and girls within their home area during early childhood. Strong positive relationships are found between home range behaviour and information on place and awareness of space. Discernible sex differences are revealed in both the quantitative accretion of environmental knowledge and in the qualitative manner that children are able to externalize their mental imagery. Contrasts first appear around the middle years of early schooling at a time when boys begin to enjoy greater parental granted rights within their locality. By the age of 11 boys were able to draw maps broader in conception and more detailed in content than correspondingly aged girls. In terms of both mapping ability and map accuracy a significantly higher proportion of boys managed to depict places in a spatially coherent manner. Generalization is complicated by the method of stimulus presentation and the nature of the environment. The educational significance of the results are to be discussed.
Published Material: MATTHEWS, M.H. (1986). 'Geography, graphicacy and gender', Educational Review, Vol 38, pp.259-71.; MATTHEWS, M.H. (1986). 'The influence of gender on the environmental cognition of young boys and girls', Journal of Genetic Psychology, Vol.3, pp.295-302.; MATTHEWS, M.H. 'Children as map makers'. Geographical Magazine, March, pp.124-128.; MATTHEWS, M.H. (1987). 'Gender, home range and environmental cognition', Transactions of the Institute of British Geographers, No.1, pp.43-57.; MATTHEWS M.H. (1987). 'Sex differences in spatial competence: the ability of young children to map 'primed' unfamiliar environments', Environmental Psychology, Vol 7, No 2, pp.77-90.; MATTHEWS, M.H. (1988). 'Gender and geography', Geographical Magazine, August, pp.47-50.
Source of Grant: British Academy/Nuffield Foundation: £5,000
Date of Research: 1986 – continuing
KEYWORDS: cognitive process; geography; map; sex difference

8/0234
Department of Languages, Politics and History
Priory Street, Coventry CV1 5FR
0203 224166
May, R.A. Mr; Henderson, I. Dr
The move to corporate status
Abstract: A major change in higher education has occurred with the creation of the Polytechnics and Colleges Funding Council and the move to corporate status of Polytechnics. This project is concerned with the interplay of national, regional and local interests which is a rich area of study for the process of policy-making. There will also be important implications for the quality and type of education.
Source of Grant: Learning Systems Development Fund: £2,200
Date of Research: 1988-1989
KEYWORDS: administration of education; educational policy; higher education; polytechnic

8/0235
Department of Social Science and Policy Studies
Priory Street, Coventry CV1 5FB
0203 631313
Leicester University
Department of Psychology
University Road, Leicester LE1 7RH
0533 522522
Annett, M. Dr; Manning, M. Dr; *Supervisor:* Annett, M. Dr
Laterality, reading and ability in children
Abstract: Previous research has suggested important associations

between human laterality and ability. Left-handers (by definition those individuals with a minimal degree of dependence on their right hands) together with others presenting an over-dependency towards dextrality, were identified as 'high risk' groups for learning difficulties. Evidence indicated that mild to moderately dextral individuals were positively advantaged for ability. The present research aimed to empirically test several hypotheses derived from Annett's (1970; 1985) right shift theory. 353 children (175 females; 175 males) from six state schools in Warwickshire and the West Midlands (1 inner city, 1 rural, 2 suburban, 2 mixed rural and council) were assessed individually by two researchers on psychometric tests and new experimental work. Ages ranged from five to eleven years. Children were seen in order of their classroom register, and not on the basis of either handedness or ability. Results showed that risks for reading difficulties were greatest among children at both extremes of the laterality continuum. The research extended previous work in its identification of three sub-groups of poor readers who differed for laterality. The general characteristics of the three poor reading groups resembled descriptions in the wider literature of specific reading retardates, backward readers and dyslexics (Rutter & Yule 1975) 'specifics' were more likely lacking dextral bias, 'backwards' strongly right-handed and 'dyslexics' more often found to be mild to moderatly dextral.
Published Material: ANNETT, M. & MANNING, M. (1989). 'The disadvantages of dextrality for intelligence', British Journal of Psychology, Vol 80, Pt 2, pp.213-226.; ANNETT, M. & MANNING, M. (1990). 'Arithmetic and laterality', Neuropsychologia, Vol 28, No 1, pp.61-69.; ANNETT, M. & MANNING, M. (1990). 'Reading – a balanced polymorphism with heterozygote advantage', Journal of Child Psychology and Psychiatry, Vol 31, No 4, pp.511-529.
Source of Grant: Medical Research Council: research assistant salary
Date of Research: 1986-1990
KEYWORDS: *abiltiy; dyslexia; laterality; learning difficulty; left-handed; reading*

8/0236

Department of Social Science and Policy Studies
Priory Street, Coventry CV1 5FB
0203 24166
Macey, S.J. Mr; Barlow, J.M. Ms; *Supervisor:* Macey, S.J. Mr
Treatment adherence in ankylosing spondylitis patients
Abstract: The mainstay of treatment for AS (ankylosing spondilitis), a progressive, incurable and disabling form of arthritis, consists of regular performance of an exercise regime designed by physiotherapists. Self help groups for AS have developed in order to educate patients and promote treatment adherence. Preliminary pilot work has suggested the importance of psychosocial variables in explaining self help behaviour in relation to health. The aims of the research are: to evaluate self help exercise treatment, evaluate the efficacy of self help groups in educating patients and promoting treatment adherence, and to identify psychosocial factors associated with self help behaviour. Research will be survey based recruiting patients through rheumatology clinics and the National Ankylosing Spondylitis Society. Estimated number of patients in the sample is 500. Data collection methods include questionnaires, psychological scales and physiological measurements.
Published Material: BARLOW, J.H., MACEY, S.J. & STRUTHERS, G. (1990). 'Health locus of control beliefs and treatment adherence amongst ankylosing spondylitic (AS) patients', Clinical Rheumatology, Vol 9, No 2, pp.32.; BARLOW, J.H., MACEY, S.J. & STRUTHERS, G. 'Health locus of control beliefs amongst arthritic (ankylosing spondylitis) patients', Proceedings of the 4th Annual European Health Psychology Society Conference. (in press).
Source of Grant: Coventry Polytechnic
Date of Research: 1990 – continuing
KEYWORDS: *self help programmes*

Craigie College of Education

8/0237

Ayr KA8 OSR
0292 260321
Silverwood Primary School

Kennedy Drive, Kilmarnock KA3 7SZ
0563 24400
Clark, A.P. Mrs; Bowie, S. Ms
Communication and socialization with profoundly deaf and hearing children
Abstract: The main aim is to develop expression, creativity and inventiveness leading to improved communication and socialization in deaf and hearing children. The subjects are a small group of deaf children and equivalent numbers of hearing children. Work in inventive movement, expressive movement, ethnic dance and games has been undertaken. In all four areas tasks have been set orally and in sign. Whenever possible the children work in pairs, one deaf, one hearing. The tasks necessitate communication between children to provide a movement answer. Each lesson includes a group discussion where all the children are encouraged to participate and increase the mutual vocabulary. It is not possible to offer scientific data at present but speculation is possible. After a series of lessons the deaf children appear less aggresive and more patient in attempting to communicate. The hearing children seem more prepared to try any method, sign, gesture, mime to make themselves understood. As lessons progressed it became more difficult to distinguish the deaf from hearing while moving. In the next series of lessons there will be a parallel programme in a mainstream primary school with a profoundly deaf child in the class.
Source of Grant: Scottish Education Department Craigie College Research Fund
Date of Research: 1986 – continuing
KEYWORDS: *communication; deaf; movement; physcial education; socialization*

8/0238

Department of Expressive Arts
Craigie Way, Ayr KA8 OSR
0292 260321
Livingston, K. Mrs
The motivational aspects of physical education
Abstract: The research is intended to explore the hypothesis that the psychological orientation of children to physical education activity is largely responsible for their physical activity patterns as adults. This is being undertaken a background of concern that physical education programmes generally fail to contribute to children's fitness.
Source of Grant: College funded
Date of Research: 1988 – continuing
KEYWORDS: *fitness; motivation; physical education*

8/0239

Department of Expressive Arts
Craigie Way, Ayr KA OSR
0292 260321
Ross, A. Mr; Kennedy, R. Mrs
The musical development of the nursery child
Abstract: The research is designed to explore the ways in which young children are helped to develop an awareness of sound/music in the nursery setting. It is hoped that materials will be created which will assist the process of music/sound awareness. These materials will be trialled and evaluated.
Source of Grant: College funded
Date of Research: 1989-1990
KEYWORDS: *auditory perception; music education; nursery school; pre-school child*

8/0240

Department of Social Studies
Ayr KA8 OSR
0292 260321
Forbes, D. Mr; *Supervisor:* Forbes, D. Mr
Concepts in environmental studies in the primary school
Abstract: The development of concepts has been emphasized as an important aim for primary school work in environmental studies, (note that in Scotland, environmental studies is usually defined as embracing all work in science, history, geography and health education). Anecdotal evidence suggests that teachers are not entirely clear as to what is meant by concepts and how best to develop them with pupils. Initially this project will investigate the extent to which a problem does exist for teachers and what the nature of the problem is. This will involve sending questionnaires to a sample of 40 schools in Ayrshire to be completed by all teachers in these schools. This will be followed by interviews in selected schools from the sample. The further development of the research will depend on the initial

findings and the availability of funds. The project was 'put on ice' until the situation in schools was resolved but is now underway again. Approximately two-thirds of the schools have returned the questionnaires which are now being analyzed.
Source of Grant: Scottish Education Department: £650
Date of Research: 1985 – continuing
KEYWORDS: *concept formation; environmental study; primary education*

Cranfield Institute of Technology

8/0241

School of Social Policy, Cranfield, Bedfordshire MK43 OAC
0234 751122
Bedford College of Higher Education
Polhill Avenue, Bedford MK41 9EA
0234 51671
Reeves, J. Mrs; *Supervisor:* Fletcher, C. Dr
A study of the process of implementation of the National Curriculum in Science in a Cambridgeshire primary school
Abstract: The overall aim of the project is to make an in depth study of how a Cambridgeshire primary school responds to the new National Curriculum in Science. The principal research method to be used will be participant observation, supplemented by questionnaires and interviews. The initial foci of the study are (i) the anxieties and concerns of teachers in the face of the impending changes. (ii) the continued viability of topic based teaching.
Source of Grant: Bedford College of Higher Education: Staff development programme
Date of Research: 1988 – continuing
KEYWORDS: *curriculum development; primary education; science education*

Crewe and Alsager College of Higher Education

8/0242

Crewe Road, Crewe CW1 1DU
0270 589995
Mountford, B. Mr; Braund, C. Mr
management development profiling in schools
Abstract: This is a survey of literature (UK and abroad) and institutions to determine the extent of use and awareness of management development profiles as a resource for recording the development needs of managers. The survey will review the use of profiles in the education service and in the industrial, commercial and service sectors. An account of the north-west initiative in school management profiling will also be presented.
Source of Grant: Department of Education and Science: £6,000
Date of Research: 1989-1989
KEYWORDS: *administration of education; management education; profile*

8/0243

Education Management Centre,
Alsager, Stoke-on-Trent ST7 2HL
0270 882500
Seymour, R.P. Mr; West-Burnham, J. Mr
Learning styles and education management
Abstract: This research uses the work of Honey and Mumford on learning styles and applies it to the education sector. Ninety-eight senior managers in schools and colleges were investigated to ascertain their preferred learning styles. From this, education management norms were obtained to compare with other management groups in industry and commerce. Links between styles and other personal background information were investigated and applications for education management have been derived. Follow-up work is in progress and a selected group of 48 respondents are being investigated further using the Honey and Mumford Learning Diagnostic Questionnaire.
Published Material: SEYMOUR, R. & WEST-BURNHAM, J.

(1989). 'Learning styles and education management, Part One', International Journal of Educational Management, Vol 3, No 4, December 1989, pp.19-25.
Source of Grant: College sponsored
Date of Research: 1988-1989
KEYWORDS: *administration of education; learning style; management education*

8/0244

Hassall Road, Alsager ST7 2AL
09363 3231
Heathcote, G. Dr; *Supervisor:* Kempa, R.
Health education professional development project
Abstract: The aim is to research and develop teaching/training materials for providers/implementers of Health Education Courses.
Source of Grant: Health Education Authority: £110,000
Date of Research: 1986-1989
KEYWORDS: *health education; teaching aids; teacher education*

8/0245

Hassall Road, Alsager ST7 2AL
09363 3231
Heathcote, G. Dr
Professional development of teachers in health education
Abstract: The aim is to plan, implement and evaluate a postgraduate Diploma for teachers in Health Education using a process related collaborative implementation model.
Source of Grant: Health Education Authority: £30,000
Date of Research: 1990 – continuing
KEYWORDS: *health education; need; teacher*

8/0246

Department of Education
Hassall Road, Alsager ST7 2HL
09363 3231
Hardie, B. Mr
A study of the attitudes, aims and priorities of primary school heads and other teachers towards developing links with industry and the world of work
Abstract: There is a taken for granted assumption that schools-industry links are a good thing. However, little is known about the attitudes of teachers to these links and whether such attitudes would promote or hinder effective links between schools and industry. This project aims to uncover these attitudes using questionnaires and a case study approach.
Source of Grant: Cheshire Local Education Authority
Date of Research: 1987 – continuing
KEYWORDS: *industry; school-community relation; teacher behaviour*

8/0247

Department of Education
Hassall Road, Alsager ST7 2HL
09363 3231
Smith, I.R.M. Mr; *Supervisor:* Cooper, R.J.H. Mr; Robinson, J.F. Mr; Taylor, L. Mr
Evaluating Cheshire local education authorities small schools education support grant project
Abstract: Cheshire LEA investigated an ESG project to develop clusters of small rural primary schools to promote and stimulate experiential learning. The aim of this evaluation is to explore the possibilities and problems of managing this ESG project concentrating on the role of the co-ordinator. Three clusters of 6 schools are involved. Methods focused on interviews, non-participant and participant observation and documentary analysis.
Source of Grant: Cheshire Local Education Authority: £12,000
Date of Research: 1987-1989
KEYWORDS: *learning strategy; primary education; small school; rural school*

Dartington Social Research Unit

8/0248

Foxhole, Dartington Hall, Totnes, Devon TQ9 6EB
0803 862231

Bristol University
Department of Social Policy
40 Berkeley Square, Bristol BS8 1HY
0272 303030
Cleaver, H. Mrs; *Supervisor:* Millham, S. Prof. (Bristol University)

A continued evaluation of 'Catch 'em Young'

Abstract: The study will explore the possible long term benefits for children who were involved in 'Catch 'em Young', a 3 year scheme established to prevent delinquency and behaviour problems in secondary school children. The report submitted to the DES in 1989 scrutinized children's behaviour as they transferred from primary to secondary school. The long term follow up study allows us to focus on the study group of 495 children as they pass through school, make important career decisions and enter the adult world. The previously applied methodology, which used both extensive and intensive dimensions, will be utilized. Thus, we would continue to combine an overview resulting from a survey of the experiences of the study children with insights and perceptions of a small group of children, their teachers and parents. When linked with the earlier research findings, it will provide an opportunity to explore how family, school and peer group influences interact in the transitions of adolescents.

Source of Grant: Department of Education and Science; 'Catch 'em Young' project: £30,000 over five years

Date of Research: 1990 – continuing

KEYWORDS: *adolescence; behaviour disorder; delinquency; occupational pupil; secondary school; transition from school to work; life skills*

Department of Education & Science

8/0249

Room 15/2, Elizabeth House,
York Road, London SE1 7PH
071 934 9148
Illston & Crowcroft
Newton House, Newton St Cyres,
Exeter EX5 5BL
0392 851508
Illston, J.M. Prof.; Crowcroft, R.S. Mr

Monitoring and evaluation of the manufacturing systems engineering programme

Abstract: The Manufacturing Systems Engineering (MSE) programme arose from the acceptance by Government of Engineering Council recommendations calling for more MSE – trained graduates. Funding to strengthen MSE provision has been allocated to 36 higher education institutions. The research programme aims to look at each initiative with a view to: (i) evaluating the influence of the MSE programme quantitatively by comparing outcomes to financial input, the outcomes to include student recruitment, equipment, staff development, course management, new building, sponsorship etc.; (ii) comparing the content of curricula and the approaches to teaching and learning, highlighting examples of innovation and technical merit; (iii) comparing styles of collaboration and the forms of support within and between institutions and with employers; (iv) studying the spectrum of provision within the MSE programme in order to determine main areas of interest and research, future developments, gaps etc.; (v) describing the level of morale, staff enthusiasm, and commitment and motivation surrounding the MSE programme.

Source of Grant: Department of Education & Science: £49,500

Date of Research: 1989 – continuing

KEYWORDS: *engineering; evaluation; higher education; vocational education*

8/0250

Room 15/2, Elizabeth House,
York Road, London SE1 7PH
071 934 9000
Research Services Ltd
Station House, Harrow Road, Wembley HA9 6DE
081 903 1399
Windle, R.E. Mr; *Supervisor:* Dale, H.M. Mr

Student income and expenditure survey

Abstract: The published report presents an analysis of the income and expenditure of all students studying courses that are within the ambit of the mandatory awards scheme. This covers traditional undergraduates studying for first degree as well as mature and sandwich students. The investigation is intended to provide benchmark information against which proposed changes in the funding arrangements for student support can be assessed in future years. The data is based on personal interviews with 1430 students in 60 institutions. The institutions were selected with probability proportional to the number of eligible students. Potential respondents were selected systematically from college/polytechnic/university records. Selected students were invited for interview on campus in February/March, 1989. In the case of students who were married/cohabiting, the spouse/partner was also interviewed. The questionnaire covered all aspects of income and expenditure, the main categories of income being grants/awards, money from parents/other relatives, earnings benefits, loans, dissavings, other income and, on the expenditure side, housing, travel, course-related expenses, entertainment, clothes and other expenditure. Data from the personal interview was supplemented by a seven day diary used to record items of routine day-to-day expenditure. The report gives a detailed breakdown of the income and expenditure of various groups. Shortfalls in income are investigated as well as the nature and extent of borrowing and dependence on state benefits. The extent to which particular groups may be disadvantaged by the present grants system is also studied.

Published Material: Student income and expenditure survey (1989). Wembley: Research Services Ltd.

Source of Grant: Department of Education & Science: £110,000

Date of Research: 1989-1989

KEYWORDS: *expenditures; income; student; undergraduate*

Department of Employment

8/0251

Careers Service Branch, Caxton House, Tothill Street, London SW1H 9NF
071 273 5545
Bedford, F.D.

Careers office management by pupil appraisal system

Abstract: Development of a questionnaire for the screening of fourth and fifth form pupils, and of a computer programme for batch analysis of completed questionnaires. Output from the programme includes the allocation of pupils to categories of need so that their suitability for different levels of careers guidance can be assessed. Questionnaires designed in conjunction with the National Foundation for Educational Research are administered to all fourth year pupils in 7 secondary schools in East Sussex and a further 7 in Essex. Print-outs from computer analysis are returned to careers departments. Developments are made in response to the feedback they provide.

Date of Research: 1986 – continuing

KEYWORDS: *careers guidance; questionnaire*

Department of Environmental Studies

8/0252

Craigie College of Education, Craigie Way, Ayr KA8 OSR
0292 260321
Lockie, J. Mr

Technology from waste

Abstract: This small scale research project is designed to develop pupil resource material in the form of a construction kit which will use/recycle waste materials. The research will investigate whether such a kit will stimulate creative activity in primary school pupils, promote a problem solving approach, provide opportunities to practice and improve experimental design, and encourage the application of scientific principles.

Source of Grant: College funded

Date of Research: 1988-1990

KEYWORDS: *creativity; environmental study; problem solving; teaching aids; waste*

Derbyshire College of Higher Education

8/0253

Western Road, Mickleover, Derby DE3 5GX
0332 514911
Dolan, J. Mr; Roberts, R.J. Dr; *Supervisor:* Littler, G.H.
Industry and work in the primary school
Abstract: This research project results from a dissatisfaction with
the ways in which 'Industry in the Primary School' seemed to be
developing via simulations, visits, etc. It was decided to undertake
a two part research/curriculum development project that would
begin by examining children's perceptions; how these influenced
teachers' choices of curriculum responses and examine concepts
following a period of curriculum development in two selected and
contrasting schools. A questionnaire has been devised, piloted and
used with two J4 classes in different schools. It samples various
aspects of the pupils' views of 'work'. Additionally a small number
were interviewed. A class discussion on the topic was observed and
recorded. These three elements represent the data on childrens' perception. In the light of these, staff in each school and researchers
have devised approximately six one week curriculum development
projects forming a 'Work in School' and 'Work in the Local Community' which is presently ongoing. Preliminary results indicate
that children in the different schools view work in some contrasting ways – particularly with regard to a dimension of 'autonomy
in work' and there are gender differences on a number of dimensions. These appear to be confirmed in the childrens' minds on the
dimension sampling 'The changing nature of work; particularly in
relation to the future. They appear to be questioning the values
underlying the present structure of 'rewards for work' on that
dimension.
Source of Grant: No funding
Date of Research: 1987 – continuing
KEYWORDS: *curriculum development; employment industry; perception; primary education; school-community relation*

8/0254

Western Road, Mickleover, Derby DE3 5GX
0332 514911
Spavold, J. Mrs; Underwood, J. Dr
**Using complex computer programmes: a case study of a local his-
tory database**
Abstract: This project aims to facilitate effective use of a specific
database by naive users; to investigate their problems in accessing
information from a computer database and to provide a research
tool for history in higher education. The objectives are to investigate: (a) users' problems in connection with a specific database
and its documentation; (b) the influence of previous knowledge on
performance with the database; (c) the nature of users' strategies
when interrogating databases, including the development of cognitive maps; (d) the relationship between cognitive maps, search
strategies and pre-knowledge on the use of databases; (e) types of
research strategies employed in interrogating databases. The following will be prepared: (a) a database capable of accommodating material from 16th and 17th century wills and inventories, and
a standard sample datafile; (b) a standard format file for other
users, for comparative research; (c) a package of support material.
A sample datafile will be created and used for testing and checking at all stages, as the first element of the project. It will be subjected to field trials drawing subjects from our own history students
and those at neighbouring institutes, as a population of machine-
naive historians. The control group will be the College's computing students. The research will produce materials suitable for use
in higher education and articles on the study.
Source of Grant: Internal funding
Date of Research: 1987-1989
KEYWORDS: *computer assisted instruction; database; higher education; history; information retrieval; information skills*

8/0255

Western Road, Mickleover, Derby DE3 5GX
0332 514911
Roberts, R.J. Dr; Mckean, R. Mrs; *Supervisor:* Dale, A.;
Littler, G.H.
Evaluation of the BEd (Hon) Initial Degree
Abstract: The aims of this research project are to evaluate the B.Ed
Hons degree at Derbyshire College for a number of different

research perceptions, and in doing so to provide faculty and validating body with data upon which sound judgements could be made
about the standing and future of the degree and provide course
management with data upon which valid course development could
be used. The evaluation is of the experience of the cohort of students and associated staff of the 1987 entry in College and off-
site, in particular in practice schools. The mode of enquiry is
through 'whole college evaluation' and 'research based teaching'
together with independent 'process evaluation' facilitated by the
employment of a research assistant. The case study will cover
approximately 120 students and 30+ staff.
Source of Grant: Supported by Derbyshire College
Date of Research: 1987 – continuing
KEYWORDS: *academic degree; evaluation; higher education;
teacher education*

8/0256

Department of Education, Humanities and Social Science
Western Road, Mickleover, Derby DE3 5GX
0332 514911
Wallace, G. Dr
Professsional collaboration in hostile environments
Abstract: In the context of recent and ongoing 'restructuring' of
state education, what counts as professional practice and professional accountability is being redefined and re-negotiated. Building on the evidence of the demoralising and alienating processes
experienced by middle school teachers between 1979 and 1982
(unpublished PhD thesis), research is continuing into the processes
of professional adaptation to change which are beginning to emerge.
Some of this work is developmental and theoretical and is a re-
working of data gathered for PhD thesis in the context of continuing political initiatives. However, evidence of new collaborative
professional practices is emerging through a critical review of the
literature of professionalism and managerialism, through GCSE
research, through the processes of 'statementing' in relation to children with 'special needs', and through a range of other initiatives
whereby professionals are regrouping to renegotiate their interests
within and across institutions. The research aims to scrutinize these
developments at all levels, including fieldwork using qualitative
methodologies into the way in which professionals are co-operating
across agencies (teachers, social workers, police), in relation to perceived student 'needs' for welfare and counselling.
Published Material: WALLACE, G. (1985). 'Middle schools
through the looking glass'. In: Walford, G. (Ed). Schooling in Tur-
moil, Beckeham: Croom Helm.
Source of Grant: No funding
Date of Research: 1986 – continuing
KEYWORDS: *adjustment; educational innovation; educational
policy; teacher behaviour*

8/0257

Department of Education, Humanities and Social Sciences
Western Road, Mickleover, Derby DE3 5GX
0332 514911
Roberts, R.J. Dr; Rich, C.G. Mrs
**A qualitative evaluation of award-bearing inservice courses for
teachers, with particular reference to inservice BEd.(min) and MEd**
Abstract: An investigation into the perceptions and expectations
of award-bearing inservice courses held by teachers, head teachers,
advisers, administrators, college and university tutors. During
1986/87, it is intended to collect data on the extent to which current award-bearing courses meet the expectations relevant groups
have of them.
Source of Grant: No funding
Date of Research: 1985 – continuing
KEYWORDS: *certificate; course; evaluation; inservice training*

Doncaster Metropolitan Institute of Higher Education

8/0258

Department of Humanities
High Melton, Doncaster DN1 3EX
0709 582427 ext 273
Royal Institute of Public Adminisration
Regents College, Inner Circle, Regents Park,

London NW1 4NS
071 486 8221
Hughes, D.J. Mr; *Supervisor:* Barnes, J. Ms
Managing change: case studies in secondary school management styles

Abstract: This research involves two case studies centering around the management of the current changes in education brought about by recent Government legislation. It is based upon how 2 secondary schools are adapting their management styles and structures to meet the demands of the National Curriculum, TVEI (Technical and Vocational Education Initiative) and local financial management. The study is based on field research being undertaken in a North Midland local authority over the next three years. It is hoped that the case studies will both extend our empirical knowledge about how schools respond to change and provide a check on current theoretical perspectives on this issue. The research will involve interviews, observation, shadowing and document collection in the schools concerned and with relevant outside agencies, ie. feeder primary schools and LEA advisers. To date a pilot scheme of interviews has been undertaken with 11 of the 17 secondary heads in this authority. The intention here was both to choose two case study schools and to generate research questions which could be followed up in subsequent research. The researcher proposes to keep in contact with the other nine schools in this initial pilot scheme through further interviews and questionnaires over the next two years.
Source of Grant: Grant Related Inservice Training (GRIST)
Date of Research: 1988 – continuing
KEYWORDS: *administration of education; educational change; reform of education; secondary education*

Dorset Institute of Higher Education

8/0259

Wallisdown Road, Poole BH12 5BB
0202 524111
Wildey, E.M. Mr
The design, development and implementation of a simulated management information system based on a relational database – an analysis of the process

Abstract: The research starts from the propositions that (1) advances in hardware and software have made possible a coherent strategy for integrating all the information needs of the business within a Management Information System (MIS); and (2) Business education needs to reflect these current developments if it is to provide the environment in which students can develop the vocational and academic skills required of today's business graduates and diplomats and (3) these skills can be developed within an overall framework in which subject lecturers can provide both functional and, in co-operation with others, integrated applications; (4) most lecturers have neither the time nor sufficient computing skills to develop their own model. The research concerns a company simulation and associated MIS, including transaction processing, for teaching/learning purposes. It will be based on the Oracle relational database software. The expected outcomes are: (1) a model which all business disciplines can use to develop realistic teaching/learning applications based on common data and an agreed framework but adaptable to lecturers' own developing objectives; (2) a range of discipline-based and integrated prototype applications to illustrate the potential of the model; (3) an analysis of the research process, including a survey of attitudes and experiences of staff and students involved.
Source of Grant: Internally funded
Date of Research: 1987-1990
KEYWORDS: *business management; commercial education; computer assisted information system; instruction; simulation*

8/0260

Department of Information Systems
Wallisdown Road, Poole BH12 5BB
0202 524111
Pigott, D.E. Mr
The development of an intelligent tutor that uses a business game to evaluate and train students

Abstract: The ultimate test of business students is how well they run a real business. This is how they should be evaluated! So evaluation through business games seems the best approximation. Evaluation also reveals shortcomings and encourages formation and testing of teaching strategies. The research aims to develop a computer program that (i) evaluates student performance and (ii) encourages good performance, as individual students play a computerized mangagement game. This consists of the following stages: develop game, evaluate students, develop analyzer sub-programs, develop tutor, assess whole program and report. The program evaluates the use of some quantitative methods as aids to management decision making by business students. It can also be used to train students before final assessment.
Source of Grant: No funding
Date of Research: 1987-1990
KEYWORDS: *business management; commercial education; computer assisted instruction; evaluation; game*

Dudley Education Authority

8/0261

Dudley Teachers Centre, GRASP Project, Laburnum Road, Kingswinford, Dudley DY6 8EH
0384 293420
Darwood, D. Mr; *Supervisor:* Jones, G.H. Mr
Getting results and solving problems (GRASP)

Abstract: GRASP (Getting Results and Solving Problems) is an action – research project aimed at enhancing the effectiveness of teachers and pupils by the application of a shared perception framework to teaching and learning. The accent of the project is on the 'Getting Results' rather than the solution of problems, by a considered appreciation of what results are wanted and how they are to be achieved. Initially the project involves 12 schools; 4 secondary and 8 feeder primary; including during the first year of the project the 8-14 age range and some 60 teachers, supported by a central advisory team of six: two Project Leaders, three researchers and an administration assistant. During the academic year 1990/91 the project will add a further 20 schools. The project is totally cross-curricular and mixed ability. It is intended to increase the project to include special education. The project works through INSET in practice, method and classroom support.
Source of Grant: Department of Trade and Industry Comino Foundation Training Agency (now Training Enterprise Education Division)
Date of Research: 1987-1990
KEYWORDS: *achievement; aims of education; learning strategy; problem solving; method*

Dundee University

8/0262

Microcomputer Centre, Dundee DD1 4HN
0382 23181 ext 4145
Newell, A.F.Prof.; Arnott, A.L. Dr
A communication system for severely disabled non-speaking people that helps to produce casual and formal conversations

Abstract: Work has begun on a design for a conversation aid that will help a physically disabled non-speaking person to interact with others in a natural manner, and at a rate approaching that of unimpaired speakers. Although only in its initial stages, this work is showing great promise in providing an efficient and effective communication system for the physically disabled. The subject of this research proposal is the continuation of work on the modelling of conversation patterns in a computer, and the implementation of a prototype communication aid for the speech impaired based on this model. This communication aid will allow the user to navigate through conversations by presenting them with a limited number of choices for their next utterance which are automatically selected from a large store of previously prepared text. Thus, unlike current phrase storage devices, the user will not have to remember a large number of codes or mnemonics in order to access the appropriate phrase. This will give a much higher communication rate than is possible using current devices. The project will also involve exploration of methods which enable the user to convey individual personality and current mood (e.g. happy, angry, sad). Although when using this aid the major part of a conversation will be carried out

by pressing a single key, or one of a small number of keys, to produce entire phases, there will also be facilities to make up an entirely new phrase. This facility will be based on 'PAL', a predictive-adaptive-lexicon based typing aid for severely physically disabled people already developed at the Microcomputer Centre. This significantly speeds up the typing of text by predicting words based on general frequency and recent use by the user. As with the other work in the Microcomputer Centre in this field, the design criteria will include speed of operation, ease of operation, and use of commercially available components.
Source of Grant: The Spastics Society: £40,000 over two year period
Date of Research: 1988-1990
KEYWORDS: computer; communication; conversation; physically disabled; speech handicapped

8/0263
> Centre for Medical Education,
> Dundee DD1 4HN
> 0382 23181
> Leiper, J.M. Dr; *Supervisor:* Harden, R.M. Prof.

Assessment of the educational needs of health professionals in terminal care
Abstract: The aim of this project is to provide new methods of teaching terminal care to health professionals (doctors and nurses), and to assess the learning needs of these groups.
Source of Grant: National Society of Cancer Relief
Date of Research: 1986-1990
KEYWORDS: death; educational need; health service personnel; teaching method

8/0264
> Centre for Medical Education,
> Dundee DD1 9SY
> 0382 23181
> Ninewells Hospital and Medical School
> Centre for Medical Education,
> Dundee DD1 9SY
> 0382 60111 ext 2286
> Mulholland, H. Dr

Development of the membership examination of the Royal College of General Practitioners
Abstract: The College Membership Examination is already highly developed but it needs to change to keep pace with different expectations and attitudes to the role of the general practitioner. The research will carry out detailed analysis of the reliability and validity of the existing examination and investigate possible new assessment methods.
Source of Grant: Royal College of General Practitioners: £75,000
Date of Research: 1988-1990
KEYWORDS: assessment; doctor; examination; professional association

8/0265
> Department for Medical Education
> Ninewells Hospital and Medical School,
> Dundee DD1 9SY
> 0382 60111
> Baker, K.L. Miss; *Supervisor:* Harden, R.M. Prof.; Mullholland, M. Dr

Distance learning and the continuing education of general practitioners
Abstract: The need for continuing medical education is generally accepted. However, the effectiveness and efficiency of traditional approaches have been questioned. In the current climate of financial accountability, the potential benefit of new approaches to continuing education need to be investigated. This study uses the CASE (Clinical Assessment for Systematic Education) Programme as an example of distance learning and uses the participants in the Programme in order to assess its effectiveness. The study aims to investigate: (1) attitudes to distance learning programmes; (2) the use of distance learning programmes, (3) changes in practice, knowledge and competence resulting from a distance learning programme, (4) changes in doctors' attitudes to continuing education following participation in a distance learning programme. Methods are based on contemporary educational thinking, persuing an illuminative type of evaluation. Instruments include: telephone interviews, questionnaires, observation and face to face interviews.
Source of Grant: Department of Health and Social Security

Date of Research: 1988-1989
KEYWORDS: continuing education; distance study; doctor

8/0266
> Department for Medical Education
> Ninewells Hospital and Medical School, Dundee DD1 9SY
> 0382 60111
> Harden, R.M. Prof.; Peacock, C. Dr

'If only I had the time'
Abstract: This programme is being developed with the aim of improving the management skills of general medical practitioners (GPs). It comprises a manual containing sections on planning, organising, implementing, and monitoring (collectively known as the management cycle), and on techniques such as time management, delegation, communication, recruitment, teamwork, and conflict resolution. Participants will also receive a series of 18 'Doctor's diaries' in which the activities of a typical general medical practice are described. Management topics arising in the diaries are highlighted, and cross referenced to appropriate sections of the manual. The diaries will be issued monthly, and each will carry a short self-assessment test of the true/false variety. Participants will be encouraged to carry out the test, returning their responses on a pre-printed card sent with the diary. On receipt of the card a personalized commentary on the given responses will be sent to the participant. The programme has been developed by a team of management consultants, GPs, and educationalists. The views of a wide range of GPs are being sought and the results of this research embodied in the programme. There is little material available on management in general practice and this programme is breaking new ground.
Source of Grant: Funding by ICI Pharmaceuticals Ltd. through Royal College of General Practitioners
Date of Research: 1987-1989
KEYWORDS: continuing education; doctor; management education; time

8/0267
> Department of Educational Studies
> Centre for Continuing Education, Dundee DD1 4HN
> 0382 623181
> Hartley, J.D. Dr

Culture and pedagogy in nursery education
Abstract: The study comprises an ethnography of three nursery schools; two in deprived inner city areas and one in a middle class suburb. The study examines how time, space and activities are structured and relates these arrangements to the social composition of the respective catchment areas.
Published Material: HARTLEY, J.D. (1987). 'The time of their lives: the bureaucratisation of time and space in early education'. In: POLLARD, A. (Ed). Children and their primary schools. Lewes: Falmer Press.
Source of Grant: No funding
Date of Research: 1986-1989
KEYWORDS: bureaucracy; culture; ethnology; nursery school; sciences of education; social structure

8/0268
> Department of Educational Studies
> Dundee DD1 4HN
> 0382 23181
> Hartley, D. Dr; Roger, A. Ms

Policy making in Scottish education: a case study
Abstract: The case study concentrated upon recent policy relating to curriculum and assessment for 5- to 14-year olds in Scotland. The study indicates the professions concern about a perceived increase in central control of education.
Published Material: HARTLEY, D. & ROGER, A. (1991). Curriculum and assessment in Scotland: a case study of policy. Edinburgh: Scottish Academic Press.
Source of Grant: No funding
Date of Research: 1987 – continuing
KEYWORDS: assessment; centralization; curriculum; educational policy

8/0269
> Department of Educational Studies
> Dundee DD1 4HN
> 0382 23181
> Roger, A. Ms

Adult educational guidance

Abstract: This is a review of research on policy and practice of adult educational guidance in Scotland in the past three years. The review indicated the need for expansion of current guidance provision; the lack of quality monitoring and the need for resources. Further research is needed into on-course guidance, employers' guidance roles and the quality of guidance provision.
Published Material: ROGER, A. (1990). 'Research on adult educational guidance'. In: Adult learning in Scotland: a review of education and policy. Edinburgh: Scottish Council for Research in Education and Scottish Institute of Adult and Continuing Education.
Source of Grant: No funding
Date of Research: 1989-1990
KEYWORDS: adult education; educational guidance

8/0270

Department of Medical Education
Ninewells Hospital and Medical School, Dundee DD1 9SY
0382 60111 ext 2286/7
Harclen, R.M. Prof.; McKellican, J.F. Dr; Strachan, L.A. Mrs; Laidlaw, J.M. Miss; Fisher, S. Dr
Education of patients with peptic ulcer disease and the role of the general practitioner
Abstract: This programme has been developed to help meet the requirements of two of the recent trends in medical practice. Firstly, that of patients taking a greater responsibility for their own health care and also the need for better patient education. The aims are (1) to improve the health of patients with peptic ulcer disease through an effective patient education programme; (2) to investigate the form and delivery of such a programme: this will include such features as designating a role to the general practitioner, the design of materials which maximize readability, motivation of patients to use the programme, individualization of the materials through interaction and targeting in order to meet a patients individual needs, having an ongoing programme, and recognition of the patient as a family/household member; (3) to collect information about patients with ulcer disease and determine their perceived needs in terms of education. The content of the programme will be determined through interviews with general practitioners, patients, and gastroenterologists. The programme will be designed in three parts. The first booklet will contain introductory information on the disease and introduce the concept of self-help, (General practitioners shall be given additional information in their version of this booklet). A second booklet will give practical advice to patients and finally there will be a questionnaire which will allow the information to be personalized. Evaluation of the programme will make use of the patient responses in the third part and will be followed up with a further questionnaire and interviews with a random sample of patients and general practitioners.
Source of Grant: Glaxo Laboratories Limited: 1st year £120,000
Date of Research: 1987-1990
KEYWORDS: disease; health education; patient

8/0271

Department of Political Science and Social Policy
Perth Road, Dundee DD1 4HN
0382 23181
Kendrick, A.J. Dr; *Supervisor:* Mapstone, E.L.G. Prof.
A study of reviews of children in care in Scotland
Abstract: The first stage of the research will undertake an overview of current policies and structures for reviews of children in care under the provisions of Section 20A of the Social Work (Scotland) Act by means of the analysis of policy documents, guidelines or procedure manuals. This will be supplemented by the collection of information on the structure and practice of reviews from social work managers, Children's Panel Chairs and Regional Reporters. The second stage of the research will focus on two regions and will involve a retrospective study of review minutes for 100 children in each region over a 3 year period. The research will also involve attendance at review meetings for 20 children in each region over an 8 month period and collection of information from the participants in the meetings by questionnaire and/or interview.
Source of Grant: Social Work Services Group: £58,785
Date of Research: 1987-1990
KEYWORDS: casework; childcare; decision making; social work

8/0272

Department of Psychology
Dundee DD1 4HN

0382 23181
Todman, J.B. Dr; Crombie, I.K. Dr
The effect of vitamin and mineral supplementation on verbal and non-verbal reasoning of school children
Abstract: In this research, a randomised controlled trial was carried out to measure vitamin and mineral supplementation for seven months on performance in tests of reasoning in 86 school children aged 11- to 13. A small, non-significant difference between the supplementation and control groups was found in two of the non-verbal tests used. In the main non-verbal test, for which a positive effect had previously been reported (Benton & Roberts, 1988), the net difference in change in scores between the active and placebo groups was 2.4 units (95% CI − 1.5 to 6.3). This direction of effect was not seen with the other tests used. It was concluded that the results did not support the hypothesis that vitamin and mineral supplementation improves the performance of school children in tests of reasoning. The two non-verbal tests which had shown small, positive effects were used in a further study in which changes in non-verbal IQ were recorded following training in non-verbal reasoning. If any variable has a systematic effect on non-verbal IQ, a positive correlation should be found between change scores obtained on different tests of non-verbal reasoning. Individual difference tests of changes in non-verbal IQ associated with vitamin supplementation, and those associated with training were compared. The correlation between change scores for the two non-verbal tests was significant following training but not following vitamin supplementation. The difference between the two correlations was also significant. The results confirmed the original conclusion.
Published Material: CROMBIE, I.K. et al (1990). 'The effect of vitamin and mineral supplementation on verbal and non-verbal reasoning of school children', Lancet, Vol 335, pp.744-747.; McNEIL, G. et al (1991). 'Nutrient intake in school children: some practical considerations'. Conference Proceedings of the Nutrition Society. (forthcoming).; TODMAN, J.B. et al (1990). 'Protracted intrusive research in schools: why us?', Educational Studies, Vol 16, No 2, pp.141-149.; TODMAN, J.B. et al (1990). 'An individual difference test of the effect of vitamin supplementation of non-verbal IQ'. Proceedings of the British Psychological Society Abstracts. Leicester: British Psychological Society.
Source of Grant: Scottish Hospitals Endowment Research Trust: £29,427
Date of Research: 1988-1990
KEYWORDS: dietetics; intelligence quotient; intelligence test; non-verbal test; nutrition; reasoning

8/0273

Department of Psychology
Dundee DD7 4HN
0382 23181
Todman, J. Dr; Alm, N. Dr
Sequential control of prepared conversational units in real time
Abstract: As physically disabled people without speech have great difficulty communicating with others, current computer support systems are unable to faciltate a conversation at anything approaching a normal rate. This study is exploring the feasibility of an approach based on the pre-storing of conversational units organized within a Mackintosh Hypercard system. A prototype is being developed and tested with people simulating disability and using the prototype to carry out conversations via a voice synthesizer. The study opens up the possibility of genuine tutorial interactions for disabled, non-speaking people who wish to pursue educational objectives.
Source of Grant: Dundee University Research Initiatives Grant: £4,004
Date of Research: 1990 − continuing
KEYWORDS: communication; computer assisted instruction; conversation; physically handicapped

8/0274

Department of Psychology
Dundee DD1 4HN
0382 23181
Todman, J.B. Dr; Antram, M. Dr; *Supervisor:* Antram, M. Dr
Social skills, sex and health education for pupils with severe learning difficulties
Abstract: This project aims to assess the needs of pupils with severe learning difficulties attending a special school in the areas of social skills, sex and health education; to evaluate different types of teaching materials and methods; and to set up a program for social skills,

sex and health education which can be implemented at all levels within the school. The information gained from a pilot study will be used to identify the main areas of pupils needs. Proposed materials for topic packs will be tested, initially with the class of pupils used in the pilot study. After each session, pupils will be rated for concentration, participation, and general attitude towards the material. Successful material will then be tried in other classes within the school and adapted to suit different age groups, using feedback from class teachers via checklists and questionnaires. Acquisition of information and skills will be assessed by oral testing and by practical sessions, i.e. pupils will be put in 'problem' situations in a real life setting to see how well they cope. Throughout the project parents will be consulted by means of interviews and questionnaires at regular intervals to provide feedback to the staff.
Source of Grant: Scottish Education Department: £2,950
Date of Research: 1988 – continuing
KEYWORDS: health education; learning difficulty; mental retardation; sex education; social skills; special school

8/0275

Department of Psychology
Dundee DD1 4HN
0382 23181
File, P.E. Dr; Todman, J.B. Dr; *Supervisor:* Todman, J.B. Dr

Teaching basic touch screen skills to 'special needs' children
Abstract: This project is a development from an earlier project on training two way classification skills in moderately mentally retarded children. In that project, touch screen and concept keyboard versions of an educational game were developed. In evaluation trials, teachers were particularly positive about the potential of the touch-screen for use with the least able children. It seemed, however, that specific training of skills involved in using the touch-screen effectively was needed before the full benefits of using the available touch-screen software could be gained. In particular, such basic skills as targeting, single and sequential tracking, leading and anticipating cannot be assumed with mentally handicapped people or with other populations (eg. physically handicapped; pre-school children) for whom the touch-screen offers substantial advantages. The current project is aimed at the development and evaluation of a sequentially related set of program modules designed to facilitate the acquisition of these critical prerequisite skills.
Source of Grant: Scottish Council for Educational Technology: £8,035
Date of Research: 1988-1990
KEYWORDS: computer assisted instruction; mental retardation; microcomputer; special needs

8/0276

Department of Psychology
Dundee DD1 4HN
0382 23181
File, P.E. Dr; Glenday, P. Ms; Todman, J.B. Dr; *Supervisor:* Todman, J.B. Dr

Micro assessment and training of planning skills in special needs youngsters
Abstract: This project aims to develop and evaluate a microcomputer-based diagnostic test of skills. The software will be aimed at 16 to 18 year old 'special needs' youngsters on post-school courses emphasizing independent living skills, though it should also be useful at primary level and with special needs secondary pupils. The diagnostic task will be based on a procedure that has been shown to discriminate between qualitatively different levels of planning ability in young children. The programs will be evaluated against 'real world' planning criteria being developed in conjunction with the Special Needs Section staff where the research is being carried out.
Source of Grant: Scottish Council for Educational Technology: £8,682
Date of Research: 1988-1990
KEYWORDS: diagnostic test; mental retardation; microcomputer; planning; special needs

8/0277

Department of Psychology
Dundee DD1 4HN
0382 23181
Cupolillo, M. Mrs; *Supervisor:* Willatts, P. Dr

Effects of tutoring style on problem solving competence in pre-school children
Abstract: Joint activity between an adult and a child may contribute directly to development. The adult can provide a framework or 'scaffolding' which serves to organize new performance for the child. The aim of this project is to examine the nature of this joint activity or tutoring, and to identify effective tutoring methods for promoting development. The project has two main parts: (1) identification of tutoring methods. Parents and their 4 year old children will be recorded on video as they solve a construction task. Parental tutoring methods will be analyzed according to criteria established in previous research. The aim is to replicate previous findings concerning the effectiveness of different tutoring methods, and to establish whether parents do consistently use only one tutoring method. It is possible that a detailed microanalysis will reveal shifts in methods that have not been revealed in previous studies. (2) Effectiveness of tutoring methods. Tutoring may produce only short-term gains on specific tasks, or may have more wider ranging benefits. This will be investigated in a study of different tutoring methods on problem solving tasks with 4 and 5 year olds. The study will consider whether some tutoring methods lead to long-term retention of problem solving skills and generalization to new problems.
Source of Grant: C.N.Pq Brazil Scholarship
Date of Research: 1986-1989
KEYWORDS: pre-school education; problem solving; tutoring

8/0278

Department of Psychology
Dundee DD1 4HN
0382 23181
Seymour, P.H.K. Dr

Intervention in dyslexia
Abstract: The research will employ a microcomputer based cognitive assessment procedure in order to plot change over time in cognitive systems underlying reading and spelling competence and will seek to assess the cognitive consequences of narrowly defined teaching interventions. A single case approach will be used with samples of normal and dyslexic children.
Published Material: SEYMOUR, P.H.K. & MacGREGOR, C.J. (1984). 'Developmental dyslexia: a cognitive experimental analysis of phonological, morphemic and visual impairments', Cognitive Neuropsychology, Vol 1, pp.43-82.; SEYMOUR, P.H.K. (1986). Cognitive analysis of dyslexia. London: Routledge and Kegan Paul.
Source of Grant: Medical Research Council: £36,900
Date of Research: 1987-1990
KEYWORDS: cognitive development; dyslexia; teacher role

8/0279

Department of Psychology
Dundee DD1 4HN
0382 23181
Edinburgh University
Deparment of Sociology
Buccleuch Place, Edinburgh EH8 9LN
031 667 1011
Abrams, W.D. Dr; Emler, N.P. Dr; *Supervisor:* Emler, N.P. Dr; Jamieson, L. Dr

Economic and political socialization 16-19: a Scottish study
Abstract: An interdisciplinary social (psychology and sociology) longitudinal study. A random sample of the economic and political socialization of 16-19 year olds from the Kirkcaldy district of Fife, Scotland. Two cohorts (800 15-16 year olds and 800 17-18 year olds) of young people respond to a survey questionnaire every year for 3 years. 120 respondents from each cohort are also interviewed. The project explores beliefs, attitudes and participation in different educational, economic, institutional and political systems against a background of career decisions, employment, household composition and resources. Particular emphasis is laid on the density, intensity and frequency of contact within individual's social networks. The relationship between social representations, social identity, social participation and career trajectories is examined and modelled statistically. An intensive ethnological study of small numbers from each cohort is conducted to explore these processes in greater depth. The project is one of 4 conducted around Britain as a part of the '16-19 Initiative'. The survey element is common to all 4 teams, and should provide a representative picture for young people in Britain. Kirkcaldy is economically representative of Scotland as a whole. This Scottish study also researches the impact of national identity upon political socialization.
Source of Grant: Economic and Social Research Council (ESRC):

£67,000 (to Dundee) ESRC: £58,000 (to Edinburgh)
Date of Research: 1987-1990
KEYWORDS: attitude; interpersonal relations; participation; political social interaction; youth

8/0280

Department of Psychology
Dundee DD1 4HN
0382 23181
Todman, J.B. Dr; File, P.E. Dr
Boys and girls use of a menu-driven microprolog relational database resource
Abstract: The general aim of the project is to explore the extent to which a relatively 'intelligent' and 'friendly' educational computing resource finds favour with pupils (especially girls) who are not attracted by what is currently available. A prototype for a menu-driven database resource written in Microprolog has been developed to run a BBC Master microcomputer. Logically identical personal preference and objective data versions have been produced in parallel in order to investigate the suggestion that girls in particular would be more accepting of computers if they were able to adopt a more personal communicative approach. It is intended to run a series of controlled studies with 3 secondary pupils to investigate the variables affecting attractiveness of the relational database resource. The independant variables of interest are: – (1) gender; (2) the nature of the database to be constructed and interrogated (i.e. an emphasis on subjective views, preferences, opinions versus an emphasis on objective facts in relation to a content area; and (3) initial favourableness of attitude to computers. The dependant variables will include elicited pupil evaluations of the resource and change in attitude to computers. The latter will be measured by means of an attitude scale that is being developed for the project. Early results from validation trials using 'known groups' and 'induced change' methodologies suggest that the instrument will be sufficiently sensitive to changes in attitude to serve the purpose.
Source of Grant: University of Dundee Research Initiatives Fund: £3,100
Date of Research: 1987-1989
KEYWORDS: attitude change; database; microcomputer; pupil; sex difference

Durham University

8/0281

Department of Education
Leazes Road, Durham DH1 1TA
0385 64466
Foster, G.; *Supervisor:* Gilliland, J.
An examination of teachers' views of children with special educational needs and the provision of special units attached to primary schools
Abstract: The investigation seeks to examine how far the provision in schools for children with SEN (Special Education Needs) influences the way teachers view a child. Variables could include organization of the unit, number of anciliary staff working with the child, extent of medical involvement, child's level of development. The hypothesis would be that the more 'segregated' or 'specialized' the provision, the more likely the teacher is to hold negative views of the child or his likely response to the learning situation. In other words, it is the way we provide for the child that influences his education just as much as his level of development.
Source of Grant: Cambridgeshire County Council: fees
Date of Research: 1985 – continuing
KEYWORDS: child development; special education; teacher behaviour

8/0282

Department of Education
Durham DH1 1TA
091 3742000
Turner, C.J. Mr; *Supervisor:* Batho, G.R. Prof.; McMurtrie, D.A. Mr
Children with special needs and the GCSE
Abstract: The development of GCSE: (1) Is the examination relevant to the less able? (2) teachers' reactions to the examination; (3) monitoring pupil progress; (4) European studies as a case study

involving pupils from a mixed sex, lower and middle ability range in a comprehensive school; (5) socio-economic variable will also be considered.
Source of Grant: LEA funded
Date of Research: 1986 – continuing
KEYWORDS: ability grouping; comprehensive school; european studies; evaluation; GCSE (General Certificate of Secondary Education); special education

8/0283

Department of Education
Leazes Road, Durham DH1 1TA
091 3742000
Al-Arrayed Shirawi, M.I.; *Supervisor:* Goodings, R.F. Mr
Development of modern education in Bahrain
Abstract: A study of educational development in Bahrain. The research concentrates on the historical growth of the education service in the context of the economic, geographical, demographic and social conditions of the islands. Particular attention is paid to the impact of oil revenues in the 1960s, the current effect of the decline in oil production and the strategies which have been adopted to sustain growth in this situation. Bahrain is clearly located in the Arab-Islamic world but the characteristics which are peculiar to the islands are noted.
Source of Grant: No funding
Date of Research: 1984-1989
KEYWORDS: Bahrain; education; system of education

8/0284

Department of Education
Leazes Road, Durham DH1 1TA
091 374 2000
Gott, R. Dr; Ashman, A. Mr
Issues in the teaching of science
Abstract: The aim of the research project is to investigate science schemes for pupils of age 11-13 in the Durham LEA. To provide an evaluation schedule for use on INSET (Inservice Education and Training of Teachers) courses for heads of science funded under DES 86/1. The research team will include 3 teachers seconded part-time from Durham county schools.
Source of Grant: Durham University Grants Council: £8,500 Durham LEA (Local Education Authority)
Date of Research: 1987-1990
KEYWORDS: curriculum development; evaluation; inservice education and training of science education

8/0285

Department of Education
Leazes Road, Durham DH1 1TA
091 3742000
May, P.R. Mr
The moral effects of language
Abstract: To explore the moral implications and effects of different kinds of speech, e.g. lies, words used in anger, praise, berating, exhorting, encouraging, etc. relating this to biblical teaching in the subjects. Methods include extended interviews of children and teachers plus classroom observation.
Source of Grant: University Research Fund: £125
Date of Research: 1986-1989
KEYWORDS: language; moral education; religious education; spoken language

8/0286

Department of Education
Leazes Road, Durham DH1 1TA
091 3742000
Biselela, T. Mr; *Supervisor:* Byram, M.S. Dr
Bilingualism and TEFL (Teaching English as a Foreign Language): a methodological approach – the case of Zairean French/Tshiluba speakers
Abstract: This project has arisen from the researcher's observation of how English is taught to Zairean Tshilbua (French speakers). The methods used so far to teach these people are the nowadays widely-spread 'direct methods' which are indeed 'direct' only in that they are modelled on how native speakers of a language acquire/learn their mother tongue. If they are appropriate and direct it is only for monolinguals. They are inappropriate for bilinguals. This is so because of the difference in number and kinds of learning strategies and processes these two groups use. The aims of this study are: (1) To investigate the similarities and differences between

monolinguals and bilinguals as far as learning strategies and processes are concerned; and (2) to try to devise a bilingual method to be used to teach English to Tshiluba/French speakers. The population to be studied is that of Tshiluba/French learners of English; teachers of English and inspectors are also to be included. Thus, the sample will be drawn from this population: (1) through simple randomization for the learners; and (2) systematic selection for the teachers and inspectors. Data will be collected by questionnaires, interviews and class observation for analysis by the researcher. As the area on which the target population is scattered is too large, the researcher will select 3 to 4 towns and villages. Schools and their forms and streams will be selected through simple random sampling, and the triangulation approach will be used since the data to be collected are mostly qualitative and therefore complex.
Source of Grant: British Council Scholarship
Date of Research: 1986-1989
KEYWORDS: bilingualism; language teaching; learning process; teaching method

8/0287
Department of Education
Leazes Road, Durham DH1 1TA
091 3742000
Lee, W.O.; *Supervisor:* Goodings, R.F. Mr
A comparative study of educational problems in three modern Asian societies: Japan, Singapore and Hong Kong
Abstract: A comparative study of educational development in 3 contrasting Asian societies. The problems of modernization in the context of strong traditional cultures are analyzed and examined. Particular attention is paid to the response of the schools to the linguistic and economic pressures of the societies. There is detailed discussion of the administration and funding of the educational system, and the principles of democratic control. Points of similarity and difference among the societies are considered and some explanation offered.
Source of Grant: O.R.S. scholarship
Date of Research: 1984-1989
KEYWORDS: comparative education; Hong Kong; Japan; Singapore

8/0288
Department of Education
Leazes Road, Durham DH1 1TA
091 374 2000
Batho, G.R. Prof.
History of the GCSE (General Certificate of Secondary Education)
Abstract: The Historical Association has produced a pamphlet on GCSE History Teaching which is being revised annually. Additionally, the Leverhulme Trust has financed the secondment of history teachers to work on prototypes of GCSE History Projects.
Published Material: Pamphlets for Historical Association
Source of Grant: Leverhulme Trust
Date of Research: 1985-1990
KEYWORDS: curriculum development; general certificate of secondary education; history; secondary education

8/0289
Department of Education
Leazes Road, Durham DH1 1TA
091 374 2000
Vayro, J. Mr
Design related activities and technological problem solving in the primary school
Abstract: To identify a range of tools, equipment, materials and resources for design related activities and technological problem solving in the primary school and to prepare literature which may be useful to both students in initial training courses and to practising teachers. To collate information with regard to suggested policy and actual codes of practice in primary schools, from curriculum documents issued by the advisory service and other professional agencies in the UK.
Source of Grant: No funding
Date of Research: 1987 – continuing
KEYWORDS: craft, design and technology; curriculum development; primary education; teaching aids

8/0290
Department of Education
Leazes Road, Durham DH1 1TA
091 374 2000

Thompson, L.A. Miss
Innovations in teacher education: a collaborative approach to the professional preparation of primary schoolteachers
Abstract: Innovations in teacher education is a pilot study in school-based tutoring. It involves 3 UDE (University Department of Education) tutors, 7 schoolteachers, 22 BEd., 3 students and several primary school children in a collaborative approach to the professional preparation of students in initial teacher education.
Source of Grant: No funding
Date of Research: 1987-1989
KEYWORDS: educational innovation; primary education; teacher education; tutor

8/0291
Department of Education
Leazes Road, Durham DH1 1TA
091 374 2000
Mason, A.E. Mrs
The influence of formal and informal classrooms on the teaching patterns of five year olds
Abstract: This is an observational study of the progress of infant children from ages 5-7 years in formal and informal classrooms. The background to this research is the everlasting debate about the efficacy of 'formal' versus 'informal' methods. The aim is to establish any differences in attitude or achievement shown by children in these different situations. Illuminative evaluation via participant observation techniques will be carried out over a 2 year period. The Bury Infant Check was used as a sample at beginning and end of research time. Two classes of reception infants, 25 children in each class, one class from each school ('formal', 'informal') were used.
Source of Grant: No funding
Date of Research: 1987-1990
KEYWORDS: formal education; informal education; primary education; teaching method

8/0292
Department of Education
Leazes Road, Durham DH1 1TA
091 374 2000
May, P.R. Mr
Teachers' religion and the concept of role
Abstract: This research will be carried out using structured extended interviews of schoolteachers to determine how far teachers' religious connections directly influence their perceptions of teaching role (and their consequent practice).
Source of Grant: School of Education provided £125 for the first interviews
Date of Research: 1986-1990
KEYWORDS: religious affiliation; teacher behaviour

8/0293
Department of Education
Leazes Road, Durham DH1 1TA
091 374 2000
Vayro, J. Mr
Graphicacy, design drawing and visual communication in CDT secondary phase
Abstract: This research looks at how to introduce aspects of the new GCSE design and communication syllabus into selected local comprehensive schools. Examples of design graphics and visual communication techniques produced by both teachers and pupils will be photographically recorded and sets of slides prepared with appropriate text to provide school-based resources.
Source of Grant: No funding
Date of Research: 1984 – continuing
KEYWORDS: craft design and technology; curriculum development; graphic arts; non-verbal communication; secondary education

8/0294
Department of Education
Leazes Road, Durham DH1 1TA
091 374 2000
Cornelius, M.L. Mr
Use of board games in the teaching of mathematics
Abstract: This research is concerned with the history of games and uses in investigational work in teaching of mathematics. The aim of the research is to stimulate pupil investigations in mathematics through the use of board games. Details of board games from a wide range of civilizations and periods have been identified and

described. Mathematical activities based on these games have been devised and piloted with pupils. Methods used included classroom trials with investigations based on games. The results and conclusions, largely contained in book (1988) but classroom work is continuing.
Published Material: BELL, R. & CORNELIUS, M.L. (1988). Board games around the world: a resource book for mathematical investigations. Cambridge: Cambridge University Press
Source of Grant: Research Committee, sabbatical leave fund
Date of Research: 1985-1989
KEYWORDS: game; mathematics; teaching aids

8/0295
Department of Education
Leazes Road, Durham DH1 1TA
091 374 2000
Thompson, L.A. Miss; Byram, M.S. Dr
Ethnic identity and social networks in the transition from home to nursery school
Abstract: This research concerns ethnicity and social networks in the nursery school.
Source of Grant: University of Durham Research Committee and School of Education Research Committee: £870 plus £800
Date of Research: 1987-1989
KEYWORDS: ethnic group; nursery school; social interaction

8/0296
Department of Education
Leazes Road, Durham DH1 1TA
091 374 2000
Thompson, L.A. Miss
Local education authority policy in action
Abstract: Local education authority policy in action is a survey of South Tyneside Local Education Authority's curriculum guidelines for language development in practise in primary schools. A survey is being made of South Tyneside LEA's Language Policy in practise in 64 primary schools. This project is being planned with 2 LEA advisers. The data will be collected and analyzed in collaboration with 2 LEA funded schoolteacher associates.
Source of Grant: South Tyneside Local Education Authority
Date of Research: 1988-1989
KEYWORDS: curriculum development; educational policy; language development; local education authority; primary education

8/0297
Department of Mathematical Sciences
Old Shire Hall, Durham DH1 3HP
0385 64466
Hull University
Department of Education
173 Cottingham Road, Hull HU5 2EH
0482 46311
Tobias, R.K. Dr; *Supervisor:* Armitage, J.V. Dr; Bajpai, A.C. Prof.; Fletcher, T.J. Dr; Vessey, T.M.
Strategies in teaching mathematics at sixth form level
Abstract: The rapid development of new technology and the introduction of the microcomputer enables the 'modern' mathematics of the 1960's to enhance the mathematical experiences of pupils in a practical and comprehensible way, and to prompt a new style of teaching and learning mathematics at sixth-form level. There is a fundamental core of mathematics which must find a place in the secondary mathematics curriculum. Emphasis is on a method of presentation of certain key topics which illustrate the basic pattern of group structure. Former complications of putting plane geometry on a logical footing have to be avoided. The use of complex numbers highlights significant and sometimes rather difficult geometrical ideas. Attempts are made to show how some of these may be presented to extend the basic pattern to that of linear algebra. The use of linear complex algebra presents vividly the symmetries of the platonic solids. The realistic presentation of the aesthetic side of 3-dimensional geometry is anticipated by investigating the uses of the microcomputer in the mathematics classroom. New insights are made into ideas appropriate to senior pupils in schools and existing material often thought to be beyond their scope is being re-written. The work is supported by suggested lesson sequences, transcripts of sound and video recorded presentations and examples of pupils' work. The question of assessment and evaluation at sixth-form level of the proposed new style of teaching mathematics is being addressed.
Published Material: TOBIAS, R.K. (Ed). (1983). 'Mathematics for

the middle years – a spiral development', Mathematics in School, Vol 10, No 2, March 1981, to Vol 12, No 2, March.; TOBIAS, R.K. (Ed). (1982). 'Linearity – its place in the school curriculum', International Journal of Mathematical Education in Science and Technology, Vol 13, No 3 & 4.
Source of Grant: No funding
Date of Research: 1986 – continuing
KEYWORDS: curriculum development; mathematics; microcomputer; secondary education; sixth form; teaching method

8/0298
Department of Psychology
Old Shire Hall, Durham DH1 3HP
0385 3742000
Crook, C.K. Dr
Computer networks and social processes in education
Abstract: The research consists of field studies of practice within two settings where local area computer networks have been established for collaborative work: a primary school and a university teaching department.
Source of Grant: Durham University: £12,000
Date of Research: 1986 – continuing
KEYWORDS: computer network; computer assisted instruction; co-operation; higher education; primary education

8/0299
Department of Sociology and Social Policy
Elvet Riverside II, New Elvet, Durham DH1 3JT
0385 3742000
Ellison, N. Dr
Making sense of equality: labour's education policy since 1945
Abstract: The research is primarily designed to investigate developments in the Labour party's education policy since the second world war. Particular areas to be examined include Labour's attitudes to grammar schools in the late 1940s and early 1950s and the nature of the change in policy from the tripartite system to comprehensive education, particularly the changing ideas in the party that informed it. The success or failure of comprehensive schooling will be analyzed in terms of Labour's own developing ideas about the meaning of education, and particularly about how this relates to changing ideas about 'equality'. Finally, the party's present policies on education need to be evaluated. Continuity in Labour's education policy need to be examined, especially after the party's recent Policy Review. Much of this research will be historical and will thus draw upon archival and library-based resources. However, interviews will be used as a means of collecting material for the more contemporary aspects of the research.
Source of Grant: No funding
Date of Research: 1988-1990
KEYWORDS: comprehensive school; education policy; equal opportunity; political party

8/0300
Department of Theology
Durham DH1 1TA
0385 64466
University of Marburg
D-3550 Marburg an der Lahn, Germany
Minney, R. Mr; *Supervisor:* Roberts, R.H. Dr
The work of Rudolf Otto and its relevance to religious education in Britain at the present time
Abstract: Rudolf Otto in his book 'Das Heilige' has been most influential in the study of religion for nearly 70 years. In particular his treatment of the non-rational in religion marks him out as one of the earliest of the phenomenologists. The researcher intends to investigate the possibility of a continuous development with regard in particular to his use of the category of feeling within the human disposition. This is not fully specified in Otto's work. It will be necessary to establish the precise meaning and use of his key terms, including especially 'Ahnung' and 'Divination', in the context of Otto's method, as a preliminary to investigating the unity and continuity of his thought as a whole, especially his thought on the human disposition. Following from this, there is an apparent problem concerning religious educability in as much as Otto considers that the 'sensus numinis' can be developed through 'Divination', but that this sensitivity cannot be directly communicated or taught. This means that the method of its development remains unclear. Yet in the late 1980s the question of children's spirituality and religious development through education is fast becoming one of the central questions in religious education. The same

experiential dilemma seems to lie at the heart of Otto's work and also of the practice and development of religious education today. Thus the research on Otto should not only serve to clarify and establish Otto's own thought and its level of consistency, but also to cast light on current issues in religious education and education as such in practice and development in Britain today.
Source of Grant: Durham University: £1,500
Date of Research: 1984 – continuing
KEYWORDS: *religion; religious education; theology*

Ealing College of Higher Education

8/0301
St Mary's Road, Ealing, London W5 5RF
081 579 4111
Leeds Polytechnic
Department of Education
Beckett Park, Leeds LS6 3QS
0532 462903/4
Mitchell, P.; Cullen, P.
Long term study of the aspirations of hotel and catering students
Abstract: The research is concerned with the views that potential students on hotel and catering courses have about employment prospects in this industry. The research is also concerned with the skills potential students believe are necessary for a career in hotel and catering. The main research method has been the analysis of questionnaires, administered to applicants before being interviewed, prior to interview at Leeds Polytechnic and Ealing College. Preliminary findings suggest a limited understanding of managerial employment. The data also indicates a changing perception of the reasons for wishing to pursue a high level course in the hotel and catering trade.
Source of Grant: Initial funding from National Advisory Body (NAB) special initiative
Date of Research: 1987 – continuing
KEYWORDS: *career aspiration; employment; hotel and catering education*

8/0302
1 The Grove, London W5 5DX
081 579 4111
Thames Polytechnic
Manresa House, Holybourne Avenue, Roehampton, London SW15 4JF
081 789 6688
Roberts, C. Ms; Kapoor, S. Ms; Garnett, C. Mr
Teaching and learning strategies in multi-ethnic further education classrooms
Abstract: The aim of the project is to establish what teaching and learning strategies contribute to the progress and achievement of ethnic minority students in work-related further education classes and to develop some staff training materials. Four London colleges will be visited on a regular basis and the researchers will work closely with four Business and Technical Education Council (BTEC) lecturers who have agreed to participate in the project as teacher/researchers. Audio and video recordings will be made in the classroom and interviews carried out with lecturers and students. The second part of the project is the development of staff training materials. These will include case studies and a video.
Source of Grant: Training Enterprise Education Division: £47,000
Date of Research: 1989 – continuing
KEYWORDS: *ethnic minority; further education; learning strategy; multicultural education; teaching method*

8/0303
Department of English Language Teaching
Grove House, The Grove, London W5 5DX
081 579 5000
Byram, M. Dr; Roberts, C. Ms
Cultural studies in advanced language learning: the year abroad in under-graduate courses
Abstract: The aim of this research is to develop a more integrated approach to language and culture on 4 year language degree courses. This will be done by introducing principles of ethnography in the second year of the degree. Students will then write ethnographies

of the target culture while abroad, which will then be evaluated. Two language staff will learn ethnographic approaches and their learning will be documented. They will then develop a new course for the language students.
Source of Grant: ESRC (Economic and Social Research Council): £44,000
Date of Research: 1990 – continuing
KEYWORDS: *academic degree; culture; ethnography; languages; language teaching; study method; undergraduate study*

8/0304
Department of English Language Teaching
Grove House, 1 The Grove, London W5 5DX
081 579 5000
Lancaster University
Department of Education, Department of Linguistics, University House, Bailrigg, Lancaster LA1 4YL
0524 65201
Piper, A.J. Ms; *Supervisor:* Allwright, R.L. Mr (University of Lancaster, Dept of Linguistics & Modern English)
Undergraduates writing in English as a second language: using a 'reformulation' approach in the teaching of academic writing
Abstract: The study concerns an academic writing programme for undergraduate learners of English as Second Language studying for a BA in Applied Language Studies at a British college of higher education. The programme extended intermittently over five months and used a 'reformulation' approach, in which the class studied original and teacher-reformulated versions of individual student essays written for a politics course. The research primarily investigates the relationship, if any, between the instruction programme and the development of the students' essay writing. There were eight subjects, each of whom provided data in two forms: academic work and personal information. Each subject wrote four politics essays in first and final draft form over the period. They also attended three two-hour 'reformulation' classes. These were audio-recorded, providing 200 pages of transcribed group and whole class work. The subjects also provided information about themselves through interviews and questionnaires. The analysis of the data is in two parts. Firstly, a coded analysis of transcripts of the three writing classes, which seeks to establish topics and quality of discussion. Secondly, a developmental analysis of the essays written by the students over the period of instruction.
Published Material: PIPER, A.J. (1989). 'Writing instruction and the development of ESL writing skills: is there a relationship?' System, Vol 17, No 2, pp.211-222.
Source of Grant: Support from Ealing College by reduction of teaching hours and part payment of fees until 1989
Date of Research: 1987 – continuing
KEYWORDS: *English (second language); language teaching; undergraduate; writing*

8/0305
Department of Library and Information Studies
St Mary's Road, London W5 5RF
081 579 4111 ext 3329
Roberts, S.A. Dr; Bartle, D.G.
Continuing Education for Library and Information Management (CELIM)
Abstract: The aim of the project was to initiate an evaluated programme of continuing education for library and information service managers. The project has a number of related sub-aims: (1) To establish a viable and relevant curriculum and structure for continuing education in library and information service management; (2) to use an action research mode to explore the relationship between courses offered, professional needs, and the dynamics of the market for continuing education; (3) to explore the way in which this initiative in management education relates to the general structure of professional continuing education, with respect to 2 factors – credit-based, mixed mode, open learning methods and the roles and responsibilities of the professional institutions.
Published Material: ROBERTS, S.A. & BARTLE, D.G. (1985). 'Continuing Education for Library and Information Management: A state of the art report', Report to the British Library R. & D. Department by Ealing College of H.E., School of Library and Information Studies, September 1985.
Source of Grant: College funded Research Assistant: £7,500 approximately
Date of Research: 1985 – continuing
KEYWORDS: *further education; librarian; management education; vocational education*

University of East Anglia

8/0306

Centre for Applied Research in Education,
Norwich NR4 7TJ
0603 56161

Davies, R. Dr; *Supervisor:* Schostak, J. Dr

Alcohol cultures in relation to secondary aged pupils

Abstract: The research consists of a twelve month feasibility venture using case study approaches in order to represent young people's own experiences of their gradual socialization into alcohol use. An important aim of the project relates to curriculum development, whereby materials grounded in young people's own accounts may prove to be more 'authentic' and hence relevant to secondary aged pupils.

Source of Grant: Alcohol Education and Research Council: £22,000
Date of Research: 1989-1989
KEYWORDS: adolescent; alcohol; curriculum development; drinking; health education; personal and social education

8/0307

Department of Education
Norwich NR4 7TJ
0603 56161

Bakopoulos, C. Mr; *Supervisor:* Schostak, J.F. Dr

Learning to write through the medium of word processing

Abstract: This research consists of case studies of the work of young children learning to write using word processing. The research involves the videoing of the children at work to facilitate close textual analysis as children write and revise.

Source of Grant: No funding
Date of Research: 1987-1989
KEYWORDS: microcomputer; primary education; word processing; writing

8/0308

Department of Education
Norwich NR4 7TJ
0603 56161

Schostak J.F. Dr

Early years of listening and talking project

Abstract: This is an action research project which takes a whole school approach to the improvement of teacher-pupil relationships and pupil-pupil relationships. The focus is upon children learning to deal with their own problems through the processes of negotiation. These problems may be personal/emotional, social or academic. The object is to develop strategies by which children become more independent, responsible and articulate. The implication of this is that the relations between teachers and pupils become more democratic. The teachers have supply cover to enable them to record and analyze classroom practice and pupil relationships both in and out of the classroom. The project is already having profound effects on the ways teachers talk about children and children talk to each other, particularly in the resolution of aggression.

Published Material: SCHOSTAK, J.F. (1988). Developing more democratic modes of teacher-pupil relationships: The early years talking and listening project, Conference paper, Third Annual Conference of the Educational Network of Northern Ireland, November 1988.

Source of Grant: LEA GRIST: (Grant-related In-Service Training): £10,000
Date of Research: 1988-1989
KEYWORDS: interpersonal relations; problem solving; socialization; teacher-pupil relation

8/0309

Department of Education
Norwich NR4 7JT
0603 56161

Cheltenham and Gloucester College of Higher Education
Department of Education and Health
The Park, Cheltenham GL50 2QF
0242 513856

Jones, K. Mr; *Supervisor:* Haylock, D.W. Dr

The special oral language needs of low attaining pupils in mathematics

Abstract: The research sets out to develop a theoretical framework to help teachers to understand the relationship between various kinds of verbal activity and learning in mathematics, thereby allowing them to determine, more accurately, the special oral language needs of pupils who experience learning difficulties in this area of the curriculum. This is achieved by examining ways in which researchers have analyzed and described models of talk which predominate in mathematics classrooms; critically analyzing research which claims that other models of talk facilitate learning in mathematics; enquiring, via a generative analysis of pupils' (N = 40) natural language strategies, into the range of verbal activity which appears to promote the breadth of learning intended within recently stated aims of mathematics education. The study also evaluates (via technical action research) the effectiveness of such a framework in allowing teachers, on a principled basis, to plan activities specifically designed to develop children's oral language capabilities in mathematics and, subsequently assess the relative effectiveness of those activities from the point of view of their contribution to the growth of competence in mathematical language performance. The particular focus of the research is the oral language needs of 8- to 10- year old low attaining pupils in numerical problem solving. Whilst supporting the notion that certain forms of discussion might facilitate learning in mathematics, the researcher argues that this is frequently tied to just one aspect of that process, notably the clarification of concepts. Recently stated aims of mathematics education (e.g. National Curriculum Council, 1989) demand a much greater range of learning, each facet of which might, arguably have its own specialized language requirements. The research enquires into the kinds of verbal activity which appear to promote the full range of learning intended throughout the breadth of the mathematics curriculum.

Published Material: JONES, K. & CHARLTON, T. (1988). 'The special oral languaging needs of low attaining children in mathematics', Links, Vol 12, No 2, pp.22-28.

Source of Grant: No funding
Date of Research: 1985 – continuing
KEYWORDS: classroom communication; low attainment

8/0310

Department of Education
Norwich NR4 7TJ
0603 56161

McBride, R. Mr; *Supervisor:* Schostak, J.F. Dr

Study of inservice training

Abstract: This is a qualitative research study of the nature and provision of inservice training by local education authorities.

Published Material: MCBRIDE, R. (Ed). (1989). The inservice training of teachers. Sussex: Falmer Press

Source of Grant: No funding
Date of Research: 1987-1989
KEYWORDS: educational provision; inservice education and training of teachers; local education authority

8/0311

Department of Education
Norwich NR4 7JT
0603 56161

Bell, A. Dr

Support for rural primary schools

Abstract: This research is concerned with tracing the development of schemes to provide additional support to small rural primary schools. It seeks to identify issues and dilemmas within such support mechanisms.

Published Material: BELL, A. & SIGSWORTH, A. (1987). The small rural primary school: a matter of quality. London: Falmer Press.; BELL, A. (1988). 'The Federation: a support system for rural primary schools', Cambridge Journal of Education, Vol 18, No 2.

Source of Grant: Ernest Cook Trust: £12,000 Bernard Matthews plc: £500
Date of Research: 1985-1989
KEYWORDS: primary education; rural school; small school

8/0312

Department of Education
Centre for Applied Research in Education,
Norwich NR4 7TJ
0603 56161

MacDonald, B. Prof.; Schostak, J.F. Dr

Evaluation of the national project on problem solving 5-13

Abstract: The aim of this research is to provide an evaluation of the impact of the National Problem Solving Project's techniques and philosophies on the teaching and learning strategies of teachers

and pupils. The methodology of the project is qualitative in design and seeks to be both formative and summative. It will generate case studies of good practice in a range of schools, covering as far as possible, the 7 LEA's involved in the project. It will generate comparative studies of the impact of the project on a range of schools selected to be representative of the LEA's.
Source of Grant: Standing Conference on Schools Science and Technology (SCSST): £47,000
Date of Research: 1988-1990
KEYWORDS: primary education; problem solving; learning strategy; teaching method

8/0313
Department of Education
Norwich NR4 7TJ
0603 56161
Pound, J.F. Dr
History in the junior/middle school, with special reference to the place of local history and the use of source materials
Abstract: History in the junior/middle school has been critisized for being superficial and lacking a coherent framework, particularly with regard to the structure and sequencing of what is taught; points which have been re-emphasised more recently in the HMI publication: 'History in the primary and secondary years: an HMI view'. The diversity of approach (if any) reflects the uncertainties and lack of expertise of many teachers, and it is significant that a recent survey carried out in Chester, North Cheshire and the Wirral emphasises the importance of having transcripts of documents of local significance made available with suggestions for use in classrooms, as well as having historical source material for children made available in booklet form. The primary objective of the research is to confirm the Cheshire evidence as a prelude to making available a variety of sources for use in the classroom as well as guidance in their use.
Source of Grant: No funding
Date of Research: 1988-1990
KEYWORDS: curriculum development; history; local studies; reference material

8/0314
Department of Education
Norwich NR4 7TJ
0603 56161 ext 2627
Pound, J.F. Dr
Grammar schools and university education in sixteenth/seventeenth century Norfolk, with special reference to Gonville and Caius College, Cambridge
Abstract: This research aims to ascertain the number of school and institutions sending pupils to university in Tudor and Stuart Norfolk, with some impression of their social background. A similar exercise has been carried out concerning grammar school pupils from Bury St. Edumunds and Manchester in eighteenth century England
Published Material: POUND, J.F. (1986). 'The social and geographical origins of the English grammar school pupil: Bury St. Edmunds and Manchester grammar schools in the reign of George II', History of Education Society Bulletin, No 37, Spring 1986, pp.12-19.
Source of Grant: No funding
Date of Research: 1988-1990
KEYWORDS: history of education; social environment; student; university

8/0315
Department of Education
Norwich NR4 7TJ
0603 56161
Salisbury, A.J. Dr
Children's perceptual-spatial abilities through interactive microcomputing
Abstract: Some fundamental questions are posed by the conventional teaching of primary geometry. How can geometry be made more interesting, vital and relevant? How can it be related across the curriculum? Such a curriculum has been constructed using pictures and interactive microcomputing. The computer programme was designed and is now being followed up with children aged 6, 9, and 12. The follow up will be used to provide a formative evaluation of the programme.
Published Material: SALISBURY, A.J. (1983). Projective geometry in the primary school Curriculum; Children's Spatial-perceptual

abilities. Unpublished PhD dissertation, University of London.; SALISBURY, A.J. (1984). 'A Study of children's preferences for projective and other geometric transformations', International Journal of Mathematical Education for Science and Technology, Vol 16, No 4, pp.525-532.; SALISBURY, A.J. (1987). 'Primary School Geometry: some unusual activities', International Journal of Mathematical Education for Science & Technology, Vol 18, No 3, pp.471.
Source of Grant: Department of Education: £500
Date of Research: 1985-1990
KEYWORDS: curriculum development; geometry; perceptual development; primary education; spatial ability

8/0316
Department of Education
Norwich NR4 7TJ
0603 56161
Tickle, L. Mr
The education of new entrants to teaching
Abstract: The aim of this research is to identify the educational experiences of new teachers and develop theories of/for effective induction. So far, a sample of two cohorts of c150 each, has been studied, using questionnaire, participant observation and interview.
Published Material: TICKLE, L. (1988). The inservice education of Norfolk probationary teachers. University of East Anglia.; TICKLE, L. (1988). 'New teachers and the development of professionalism'. In: HOLLY, M. and MCLOUGHLIN, C.S. (Eds). Perspectives on Teacher Professional Development. London: Falmer Press.
Source of Grant: No funding
Date of Research: 1987-1990
KEYWORDS: probationary teacher; student teacher; teacher education

8/0317
Department of Education
Norwich NR4 7TJ
0603 56161
Brown, G. Prof.; Shaw, G. Dr; Whittaker, R. Mr
Characteristics of distractible children
Abstract: Attention disordered/hyperactive high IQ children were matched with a comparison group for age, sex and verbal reasoning. A range of tasks involving perception, focal and peripheral recall, incidental memory, problem solving and creative thinking was given and evidence on laterality and incidence of allergies collected. In comparison with a matched group of non-distractible children the group under investigation displayed a high degree of mixed laterality and a high incidence of allergies. Whilst equal in performance on tasks with high verbal loading, distractible children showed very significantly superior performance in tasks which demanded figural creativity. Replication in the UK and a comparative study in the USA are now under way, and further studies will seek to explain the findings.
Published Material: SHAW, G. & BROWN, G. (1990). 'Laterality and creativity concomitants of attention problems', Developmental Neuropsychology, Vol 6, No 1, pp.39-57.
Source of Grant: University of East Anglia: £500
Date of Research: 1988 – continuing
KEYWORDS: assessment; attention; gifted; hyperactivity; performance

8/0318
Department of Education
Norwich NR4 7TJ
0603 56161
Fororge
Irish Farm Centre, Bluebell, Dublin
Coghlan, J.A. Fr; *Supervisor:* Bell, A. Dr
Fororge: National youth development organization (Republic of Ireland)
Abstract: This research is a history of the development of the National Youth Development Organization in Ireland. It traces the origins, emergence of the structure of the organization and the development of its ideas regarding youth work, community development and volunteerism.
Source of Grant: No funding
Date of Research: 1987 – continuing
KEYWORDS: community development; Ireland; youth organization

8/0319

Department of Education
Norwich NR4 7TJ
0603 56161
Botros, F.L. Ms; *Supervisor:* Brown, G. Prof.
Towards a national system for the teaching of parenting skills in Egypt
Abstract: An extensive survey of child-rearing practices has been undertaken in the Minia region of Egypt. The findings, in conjunction with a survey of "best practice" as exemplified in western literature, and recognizing possible cultural differences, has been employed in constructing a syllabus for educating young Egyptian adults in parenting techniques. A flexible mode of delivery, geared to the present educational system, has been devised, as have mechanisms for evaluating the success of the project.
Source of Grant: Egyptian government
Date of Research: 1984-1989
KEYWORDS: child rearing; Egypt; moral education; parent role

8/0320

Department of Education
Norwich NR4 7TJ
0603 56161
Azevedo, O. Mrs; *Supervisor:* Brown, G. Prof.
The application of metacognitive techniques to the acquisition of comprehension and reading skills
Abstract: The hypotheses are that: (1) metacognitive training will improve 4th grade children's comprehension of expository text as measured by tests; (2) no differences will exist between training done by individualized instruction, group sessions, and class sessions; (3) 8th graders used as tutors will enhance their own comprehension. (Grades relate to Brazilian schools). Experimental work has now been completed in Brazil, and analyses are under way. Early results suggest that, contrary to expectations, the group tutoring technique is markedly superior to other methods on a number of important measured indices.
Source of Grant: Coordenagao de Aperfeicoamento de Pessoal de Nivel Superior; Brazil
Date of Research: 1986-1990
KEYWORDS: Brazil; cognition; comprehension; reading

8/0321

Department of Education
Norwich NR4 7TJ
0603 56161
Turner, T.W. Mr; *Supervisor:* Schostak, J.F. Dr
Discovering meaning; an essay on the creation of meaning
Abstract: The research provides a radical re-appraisal and re-conceptualization of the nature of and processes inherent to education and the teaching of English.
Source of Grant: No funding
Date of Research: 1988 – continuing
KEYWORDS: langauge teaching; philosophy of education

8/0322

Department of Education
Centre for Applied Research in Education,
Norwich NR4 7TJ
0603 56161
MacDonald, B. Prof.; Stronach, I. Mr
Evaluation of the Economic and Social Research Council programme: information technology in education research
Abstract: In 1988 the InTER (Information Technology in Education Research) programme was launched with initial funding of one million pounds allocated to three research consortia, a programme co-ordination centre and an independent policy evaluation. The research centres are funded for three years, the evaluation for four years. Further research centres are planned, up to a total of ten or eleven. The evaluation is designed to be formative rather than summative, responsive rather than pre-ordinate. It will be guided by a set of general aims, which include the encouragement of self-reflection, assisting policy development, improving information-sharing within and beyond the programme and preserving programme learning for future use. Methodologically, the evaluation will be eclectic, but favouring qualitative methods and relying heavily on contextualized judgement. A first report, examining InTER's origins and the selection processes that produced the consortia has been published – 'Making a Start: the origins of a research programme'.
Source of Grant: Economic and Social Research Council: £161,000

Date of Research: 1988 – continuing
KEYWORDS: educational policy; information technology; research

8/0323

Department of Education
Centre for Applied Research in Education,
Norwich NR4 7TJ
0603 56161
Maimunah Syed Zin, S. Miss; *Supervisor:* MacDonald, B. Prof.
Curriculum innovation: case studies of man and the environment in the Malaysian primary school curriculum
Abstract: The exercise is concerned with a national curriculum innovation and its implementation in primary schools in Malaysia. Man and the Environment is a new subject which replaces the traditional disciplines of history, geography, science, health education and civics in the curriculum. Like any other curriculum innovation previously introduced, it brings with it certain changes and demands, in the hope that these will enhance the quality of education offered. Since this is an innovation that affects the entire primary school system, it is important to know how the various people involved have grappled with the challenges and demands created. It is also crucial to know the extent to which the teacher, who is a key determinant of the effectiveness of the programme, has internalized the intended outcomes and how best he can be equipped to enable him to play his expected role. Experience gained in this innovation would have implications for future programmes. The approach to the study is mainly through case studies in four schools, supplemented by data from other sources.
Source of Grant: Ministry of Education, Malaysia: full Malaysian study grant
Date of Research: 1986-1989
KEYWORDS: curriculum development; environmental study; Malaysia; primary education

8/0324

Department of Education
Centre for Applied Research in Education,
Norwich NR4 7TJ
0603 56161
Somekh, B. Ms; *Supervisor:* Elliott, J. Prof.
PALM; pupil autonomy in learning with microcomputers
Abstract: The PALM project involves teachers in approximately 30 schools carrying out research into their use of microcomputers to bring about more autonomous learning in their students. The project schools span the age range 5-18, but it is anticipated that slightly more emphasis will be placed on work in the 11-16 age range. PALM is an action research project in which teachers carry out research with the active participation of their students and support from the team. In each of the local education authorities there is a difference of emphasis: in all cases the teachers themselves decide on the precise focus of their research. PALM is particularly interested in testing the claims made for the role of computers in learning: do they enable students to take more responsibility for their own learning? The project approach is based on a belief that the curriculum depends on what teachers do in classrooms, not on statements of intent, but on practical enactments. It places faith in the professionalism of teachers who are the key figures in curriculum development and therefore, of necessity, must be key figures in research which feeds into the processes of real curriculum change. Within the action research methodology PALM teachers feed the results back into their teaching immediately to enable research into curriculum change. PALM is therefore a project which combines curriculum development, teacher inservice training and research.
Source of Grant: Micro Electronics Education Support Unit (MESU): £16,600 (for two years) Cambridgeshire, Essex and Norfolk County Council: full costs of 3 teachers seconded for two years full time
Date of Research: 1988-1990
KEYWORDS: independent work; computer assisted instruction; microcomputer; development; teaching method

8/0325

Department of Education
Norwich NR4 7TJ
0603 56161
Ahmed, A.A. Mr; *Supervisor:* Smith, W.D. Dr
An investigation into policy and practice in the Egyptian education system in the light of the English experience

Abstract: The research investigates provision and planning within the Egyptian education system and questions whether decision-making within the system accords with the published official pronouncements. The study is based upon existing documentation plus qualitative data for interviews undertaken within Egypt. Those interviewed include officials at the Ministry of Education and officials and teachers in Minia County. To afford a basis of comparison similar investigations are being undertaken within the English system.
Source of Grant: Egyptian Education Bureau
Date of Research: 1984-1989
KEYWORDS: educational policy; Egypt; planning of education

8/0326
Department of Education
Norwich NR4 7TJ
0603 56161
Wright, D.R. Mr
Pupils as evaluators of textbooks
Abstract: Textbooks for pupils are reviewed by teachers, not by pupils. Pupils are encouraged nowadays in school to express opinions and to evaluate evidence. The research seeks to experiment with pupils as reviewers of textbooks and other school books. Pupils in the UK and in Australia are invited to review textbooks and information books. Their written observations are incorporated into articles discussing this new approach. Teachers are involved in evaluating pupils' observations. Results and conclusions will be illuminative, not definitive. Ten provisional conclusions are included in publication (3) below. The findings have implications for teachers and for educational publishers.
Published Material: WRIGHT, D.R. (1987). 'A pupil's perspective on textbooks: issues of motivation and racism', Internationale Schulbuchforschung, Vol 9, No 2, pp.137-142.; WRIGHT, D.R. (1988). 'Applied textbook research in geography'. In: GERBER, R. & LIDSTONE, J. (Eds). Skills in geographical education. International Geographical Union.; WRIGHT, D.R. (1990). 'The role of pupils in textbook evaluation', Internationale Schulbuchforshung, Vol 12, No 4.
Source of Grant: No funding
Date of Research: 1987 – continuing
KEYWORDS: evaluation; pupil; textbook

8/0327
Department of Education
Norwich NR4 7TJ
0603 56161
Brown, G. Prof.; *Supervisor:* Brown, G. Prof.; Azevedo, O. Dr
Intervention study in Brazilian primary schools to enhance comprehension skills
Abstract: The purpose of this study was to investigate the reading and comprehension and metacomprehension ability displayed by forty children attending two intact classes from two Brazilian public primary schools serving a low income community from a large city: either at the beginning of their fourth year of schooling or after they were submitted to twelve forty-five minutes training sessions distributed over two months, or after three months of normal schooling without experimental intervention. Results indicate that the majority of children were not able, at pre- test to produce the main idea of a passage when asked to tell its content nor could they identify it in a paragraph when asked to do so. They also failed to apply strategies such as text reinspection to aid their comprehension or to resolve comprehension problems. After training, the experimental groups differed significnatly from the control group on the identification of the main idea of expository paragraphs. In addition, they showed a tendency to re-read text or portions of it to enhance comprehension or to resolve comprehension problems more often than their counterparts. No apparent difference was found between the Dyadic and the Small group formats. Discussion of these results led to the tentative conclusions that firstly, reading comprehension of expository text can and should be taught; identification of main idea and text reinspection may be the best candidates to begin teaching; and due to the motivating power observed in the small group interaction associated with the lack of evidence of the superiority of the dyadic group format, teaching, involving a group of children may be a good and economical environment for teaching comprehension of reading assignments.
Published Material: de AZEVEDO, O.S.P. (1990). Helping children comprehend expository text: an intervention study in Brazilian

primary schools. Unpublished PhD thesis. University of East Anglia.
Source of Grant: Brazilian Government
Date of Research: 1985-1990
KEYWORDS: Brazil; cognition; comprehension; metacognition; primary school; reading

8/0328
Department of Education
Norwich NR4 7TJ
0603 56161
Ormell, C.P. Mr
Analysis of understanding as an educational aim and ways to detect its achievement
Abstract: The research is aimed at answering the question, 'how can we detect whether a child understands something, using objective behavioural methods'. In most cases, 'understanding x' means 'having a fully assimilated model of x'. The chief assessment method consists of seeing whether children can apply the model swiftly and confidently to new circumstances. The central issue reduces to; how to generate suitable 'new circumstances' in the numbers and variety required. To achieve reliability a lot of testing is needed, but this is only acceptable if the child's assessment experiences are also prime learning experiences. This means that the 'circumstances' used need to meet high standards of relevance, interest and memorability from the child's point of view. A major parameter is the degree to which the curriculum is 'liberal'. The more 'liberal' the curriculum the more distant its topics from the child's immediate experience. This makes it harder to devise appropriate 'new circumstances', but unless this problem can be solved, the production of behavioural tests for understanding will fail.
Published Material: ORMELL, C.P. (1985). An anatomy of understanding. University of East Anglia: Maths Applicable Group.; ORMELL, C.P. (1979). 'On analyzing understanding', Educational Research, Vol 22, No 1, pp.32-38.; ORMELL, C.P. (1980). 'On memorization', Educational Research, Vol 23, No 1, pp.62-64.; ORMELL, C.P. (1988). 'Is there a future for liberal education?', Cambridge Journal of Education, Vol 18, No 2, pp.167-177.
Source of Grant: No funding
Date of Research: 1978 – continuing
KEYWORDS: assessment; behaviour rating scales; comprehension tests; learning

8/0329
Department of Education
Norwich NR4 7TJ
0603 56161
University of Minia
Department of Education
El Minia, Egypt
Ormell, C.P. Mr; Abdel-Ghany, I.M. Dr
Children's 'application readiness with basic maths'
Abstract: 'Application Readiness' is a new idea in mathematics education. It signifies the condition in which a child has assimilated the applicative potency of a new mathematical concept so well that he/she is able spontaneously (without prompting or cueing) and unselfconsciously to recall and apply that concept to a practical situation needing that concept for its solution. The aims of the research are to clarify the idea of application readiness, to produce tests for it and to improve earlier tests: to trial such tests in schools and evaluate the results. Topics covered so far include basic (natural number) arithmetic up to 99 and simple fractions.
Published Material: ABDEL-GHANY, I. & ORMELL, C.P. (1985). Problem solving with basic maths: ten lessons. University of East Anglia: Mathematics Applicable Group.; ORMELL, C.P. (1989). 'Application readiness in mathematics at 10/11'. In: Applications and modelling in learning and teaching mathematics. Chichester: Ellis Horwood.
Source of Grant: Egyptian Bureau, London
Date of Research: 1981 – continuing
KEYWORDS: concept formation; mathematics; test construction

8/0330
Department of Education
Norwich NR4 7TJ
0603 56161
Open University
Walton Hall, Milton Keynes MK7 6AA
0908 274066
Fisher, E. Dr; Elliott, J. Prof.; Mercer, N. Dr

Spoken language and new technology (SLANT)
Abstract: This research aims to contribute to knowledge about the development of children's exploratory and argumentative talk through computer based classroom activities. It is also intended to describe activities which serve this function and the range and quality of exploratory and argumentative talk and to provide information about the role of the teacher in mediating and supporting such activities. It is hoped that this work will make a contribution to educational policy and practice by generating practical suggestions for how computers may be used effectively to stimulate exploratory talk and reasoned arguments in the classroom, with particular reference to the curriculum goals of English and spoken language development across a range of curriuclum areas. This research will adopt a social interactionist approach and will draw on VYGOTSKIAN perspectives.
Source of Grant: Economic and Social Research Council: £90,000
Date of Research: 1990 – continuing
KEYWORDS: *classroom; computer assisted instruction; group work; teacher role; verbal communication*

8/0331
Department of Education
Norwich NR4 7TJ
0603 56161
Walwyn, P.F. Dr
Equal opportunities in education: a philosophical enquiry
Abstract: This is a philosophical enquiry into equal opportunities in education with special reference to gender, race, special needs, religion, class and homosexuality. The aim is to explore the feasibility of operating with egalitarian principles within a comptetitive and commercial ethos.
Source of Grant: No funding
Date of Research: 1989 – continuing
KEYWORDS: *equal opportunity; philosophy of education*

8/0332
Department of Education
Norwich NR4 7TJ
0603 56161
Wilkinson, A.M. Prof.
The development of oracy
Abstract: The researcher's original book 'Spoken English' (1985) introduced the concept and term 'oracy' in education. The present research is to update the work in the light of recent developments. The central thrust constructs a model of assessment for reciprocal utterance on the one hand and extended utterance on the other, in classroom situations. The presentation is also concerned to use discourse and narrative based on novelist techniques as his ways of valid access to the material.
Published Material: WILKINSON, A.M. (1980). 'Our first great conversationalists', In: English in Education, Vol 23, No 2, Summer 1989, pp.12-24.; WILINSON, A.M. et al (1990). Spoken English illuminated. Milton Keynes: Open University Press.
Source of Grant: No funding
Date of Research: 1987-1989
KEYWORDS: *assessment; English language; language development; oral expression*

8/0333
Department of Education
Norwich NR4 7TJ
0603 56161
Baker, R. Dr
Assessment of middle school pupils in science using video recordings
Abstract: The aim is to examine middle school children (8-12 years) in their understanding of science and scientific concepts using video presentations. Presently children in many schools are assessed through written scripts. Through the use of videos children will present their experiments/investigations, film themselves and record their ideas orally.
Source of Grant: Department funding: £1,000
Date of Research: 1989-1990
KEYWORDS: *assessment; primary education; science education; video recording*

8/0334
Department of Education
Centre for Applied Research in Education,
Norwich NR4 7TJ
0603 56161

May, N. Mr; Kushner, D. Dr; Ebbutt, D. Mr; *Supervisor:* Elliott, J. Prof.
Assistance with the development and implementation of changes in Police probationer training
Abstract: The aim of the work will be to contribute towards the national implementation of a new programme of training for police recruits in England and Wales. The University staff will undertake a range of contributory tasks as follows: (1) the formulation and implementation of the modular foundation course and post-foundation course in force probation training; (2) the development and implementation of a case study based learning curriculum; (3) the development and implementation of quality control criteria and procedures; (4) Tutor Constable training and the development of an on the job training curriculum; (5) the development o f pre-course self study programmes.
Published Material: MacDONALD, B., ARGENT, M., ELLIOTT, J., MAY, N., MILLER, P., NAYLOR, T., NORRIS, N. (1987). 'The Final Report of the Stage II Review of Police Probationer Training in England and Wales', London: HMSO.; ELLIOTT, J. (1988). 'Why put case study at the heart of the police training curriculum?' In: SOUTHGATE, P. (Ed). New directions in Police training. London: HMSO.
Source of Grant: Home Office: £90,582
Date of Research: 1988-1989
KEYWORDS: *curriculum development; police; probation period; training; vocational education*

8/0335
Department of Education
Norwich NR4 7TJ
0603 56161
Brown, C.A. Mrs
Sex-related differences in young childrens technological achievements with special reference to the use of construction materials
Abstract: A study by the APU (Assessment of Performance Unit) showed that experience with construction materials was markedly different in boys and girls. The rise in scientific and technological work in the primary curriculum has made this differential background more important. Such knowledge that exists in the considerable literature on play and construction material does not attend to the sex differences referred to by the APU. The investigation therefore attempted to add to that scanty knowledge provided by the APU on the basis of single interviews with children. The current study by Brown follows on from an initial study of 7 year olds in which the gender gap was documented over a period of 12 months during which the quantity and quality of models produced by 16 boys and 16 girls as a result of specific arrangements to facilitate equal access to materials was implemented. Criteria for models made during the year were drawn up to indicate the range of achievement. Results indicating the narrowing but not elimination of the gender gap resulted in a study to investigate the phenomenon in an earlier age group. A subsequent year long study of a class of 4- to 6- year old pupils also showed that a gender gap narrowed but persisted in spite of equal access strategies being implemented over 12 months. The criteria derived from this study were used in a second similar class a year later to support the teacher in not only ensuring equal access to materials but also to structure the work to encourage all children to try to meet the criteria. Structured access was found to narrow the gender gap further than simple equal access, consequently a programme offering it to all the classes in the school was devised. In 1990/91, children who have received such structured opportunities throughout their time in the school are to be monitored to see if their 3 years of equal opportunities together with a structured programme of criteria have affected the gender gap to any greater extent. As a by product of the research a second study has been carried out to determine the extent to which construction sets can contribute to meeting the objectives of the national curriculum throughout the school during 1989/90. Results of that study have led to its continuation for a further year in 1990/91.
Published Material: BROWN, C.A. (1987). 'Using construction kits for model making: some observations of children's technological development', Primary Science Review, No 4, Summer, pp.26-27.; BROWN, C.A. (1989). 'Girls, boys and technology: getting to the roots of the problem: a study of differential achievement in the early years', School Science Review, (Science Education Notes), Vol 71, No 255, pp.138-142. December.; BROWN, C.A. (1990). 'Girls, boys and technology: some observations of general progress and of gender related differences in achievment when using

construction sets in the early years', School Science Review, Vol 71, No 257, pp.33-40. June.
Source of Grant: University of East Anglia: £600(1987)-88; £200 (1988-89)
Date of Research: 1987 – continuing
KEYWORDS: construction; construction set; model technology; primary education; science education; sex difference

8/0336
Department of Education
Norwich NR4 7TJ
0603 56161
Georgetown College
Kentucky, KY 40324, USA
Brown, G. Prof.; Shaw, G.A. Dr
Studies of attention disordered – hyperactive (ADHD) children
Abstract: A series of experiments is in progress to explore the cognitive skills of children with attention disorders and hyperactivity. In particular the research is investigating unusual facets of memory and high levels of non-verbal creativity in ADHD (Attention Disordered Hyperactive Children) children. There is also strong evidence of high levels of mixed laterality, left handedness and allergic conditions. Further work is aimed at improving selection procedures of subjects and refining the specially designed measures.
Published Material: SHAW, G.A. & BROWN, G. (1990). 'Laterality and creativity concomitants of attentional problems', Developmental Neuropsychology, Vol 6, No 1, pp.39-59.
Source of Grant: Partially funded by the University of East Anglia and Georgetown College
Date of Research: 1989 – continuing
KEYWORDS: attention deficit disorder; cognition; creativity; hyperactivity; learning difficulty

8/0337
Department of Education
University Plain, Norwich NR4 7TJ
0603 56161
Williamson, A. Mrs; Norris, N. Dr; *Supervisor:* Shephard, T.F. Dr
A local education authority's financial devolution pilot scheme: one school's involvement
Abstract: This study concerns one school's involvement in a Financial Devolution Pilot Scheme which was introduced in April 1986 to a selected number of schools and colleges in Norfolk. The research was undertaken by the head teachers of one of the participating schools. The pilot scheme had three main thrusts: firstly the devolution of the budget; secondly, the introduction of information systems to support the school based administration and financial management, and finally, the development of a financial model to distribute resources to schools by formulae, in accordance with the County's policies and practices. The formulae addresses all areas of the delegated budget including; staffing, equipment and materials, cleaning and caretaking and the day to day maintenance of buildings. The original intention was for the experiment to run for a three year period, but the pilot scheme had become a rolling programme, providing experience for the schools and colleges involved, and a period of preparation for the officers of the LEA, in anticipation of the introduction of the national Local Management of Schools scheme. The management environment and the financial and accounting systems within the school, appeared to accommodate the introduction of the scheme. The study highlighted several issues which have been addressed. They include, value for money, class size, real and notional salaries. Additionally a survey of LEAs was undertaken to determine the degree to which sections of the budget were commonly distributed to schools in England and Wales. A wide diversity of practice was found with significant differences between Metropolitan, London and County Authorities.
Source of Grant: Norfolk Education Department: fees
Date of Research: 1986-1990
KEYWORDS: budgetary control; decentralization; financial resources

8/0338
Department of European History
School of Modern Languages, Norwich NR4 7TJ
0606 56161
Fox, J.D. Mr; *Supervisor:* Labbett, B.D.C. Mr
Learning languages with computers
Abstract: The project has two aims; an initial enquiry into how best to use computers in second language learning. The thesis includes a historical survey of Computer Assisted Language Learning (CALL) from 1960 to 1990 in relationship with educational theory, computer assisted learning theory, linguistic theory and applied linguistic and language teaching methodology theory. In order to carry out the enquiry, the thesis includes discussion of problems obscuring our understanding of CALL. The thesis concludes with summaries and recommendations for both research and teaching.
Published Material: FOX, J.D., MATTHEWS, A., MATTHEWS, C. & ROPE, A. (Eds). (1990). 'Educational technology in modern language learning', A report for the Training Enterprise Education Division. Sheffield: Training Enterprise Education Division.
Source of Grant: No funding
Date of Research: 1986-1990
KEYWORDS: computer assisted instruction; educational technology; language teaching; second foreign language

East London Polytechnic

8/0339
Centre for Institutional Studies, Manbey Park Road, London E15 1EY
081 590 7722
Locke, M. Mr; Sharma, S. Mr; *Supervisor:* Locke, M. Mr
Mature students in higher education
Abstract: The aim is to investigate how institutions of higher education can improve their services for mature students. The project has collected interview and questionnaire data on the views and experiences of mature students. It is exploring through case studies how institutions are meeting the needs of mature students. It is undertaking pilot staff development projects with non-teaching staff.
Published Material: LOCKE, M. & JOHNSON, C. (1990). 'Mature students and Polytechnic of East London: a report on Phase One of the Mature Students Project'. London: Polytechnic of East London, Centre for Institutional Studies.; JOHNSON, C. & LOCKE, M. (1990). 'Experiences and views of mature students'. London: Polytechnic of East London, Centre for Institutional Studies.; SHARMA, S.W. (1990). 'An investigation of mission statements and their relevance to mature students'. London: Polytechnic of East London, Centre for Institutional Studies.
Source of Grant: East London Polytechnic
Date of Research: 1988 – continuing
KEYWORDS: mature student

Edge Hill College of Higher Education

8/0340
St Helens Road, Ormskirk L39 4QP
0695 75151
Robinson, W.D. Dr
The teaching of effective thinking
Abstract: Research into the teaching of effective thinking and its incorporation in the curriculum. Promotion of unity between practitioners and dissemination of information via newsheet 'Teaching Thinking'.
Source of Grant: Edge Hill College of Higher Education
Date of Research: 1988 – continuing
KEYWORDS: philosophy; secondary education; teaching; thinking

8/0341
St Helens Road, Ormskirk L39 4QP
0695 75171 ext 207
Mottershead, D.N. Dr
An investigation of the relations between geography and science teaching and learning in the secondary curriculum
Abstract: The study will pursue the following lines: (1) investigation of GCSE criteria for geography and science to identify the extent of commonality; (2) investigation of overlap between geography and science syllabuses; (3) investigation of the extent of science qualifications among geography teachers; (4) identification

of good practice in geography/science collaboration in schools from a variety of sources; (5) specific case studies of good practice in geography/science collaboration. National Curriculum developments have focused interst on the geography/science boundary. Future lines of work will investigate delivery and good practice in National Curriculum implementation.
Source of Grant: Geographical Association: £1,500 to date, renewable annually
Date of Research: 1987 – continuing
KEYWORDS: curriculum development; geography; science education; secondary education

8/0342

Department of Inservice Studies
St Helens Road, Ormskirk L39 4QP
0695 75171
Freeman, A. Dr
Evaluation of INSET (Inservice Education and Training of Teachers) in two LEAs (local education authorities)
Abstract: The research project is investigating, in two different LEAs, the provision of INSET, and the process of evaluation of this provision. In one authority, an evaluation has been undertaken of the Teachers' Centres, including a national survey which will be processed and data available in December 1988. In the other authority an in depth survey of INSET is in the process of completion, together with an analysis of how this is evaluated. The possibilities for evaluation methods are being explored. The aim is to produce a process whereby LEAs can evaluate their INSET provision.
Source of Grant: College funding: £800
Date of Research: 1987-1989
KEYWORDS: evaluation; inservice education of teachers and training; local education authority

Edinburgh University

8/0343

Edinburgh Centre for Mathematical Education,
James Clerk Maxwell Building,
The King's Buildings,
Mayfield Road, Edinburgh EH9 3JZ
031 667 1081 ext 2953
Searl, J.W. Dr
Development of teaching/learning materials for 16+ mathematics including computer programs, videotapes, practical activities, investigations, tape/booklets, consolidation exercises, posters
Abstract: This research arises out of the reorganization and reform of math courses in Scottish colleges of further education leading to the development of new teaching and learning approaches. Materials have been developed to support the new approaches, including computer programs, audiotape booklets, posters, videotapes, consolidation exercises, practical activities and investigations. These have been evaluated in Scottish schools and colleges following the illuminative evaluation approach. The study demonstrated that it is possible to develop materials for 16+ mathematics which are appropriate to the needs of all pupils/students and which provide a genuine multimedia approach to the teaching.
Published Material: POTARI, D. & SEARL, J.W. (1989). 'Creating a learning environment for 16+ mathematics', Teaching Mathematics and its Applications, Vol 8, No 2, pp.56-68.
Source of Grant: No funding
Date of Research: 1986-1990
KEYWORDS: colleges of further education; multimedia approach

8/0344

Centre for Educational Sociology,
7 Buccleuch Place, Edinburgh EH8 9LW
031 667 1011
Raffe, D.; Croxford, L.; Howieson, C.; *Supervisor:* McPherson, A.F. Mr
Young people's experience of National Certificate Modules
Abstract: The project will analyze data from the Scottish Young People's Surveys (1985-1989) to ascertain the impact and development of the 16+ proramme among young people. The analyses will cover five broad areas: National Certificate models in context, whether educational, social, occupational or geographical; trends

between the first and third Action Plan year groups; progression into, within and out of the modular system; attitudes to the National Certificate; and modules within schools.
Published Material: a full list of publications are available from the Research Administrator, Joan Hughes at Edinburgh University
Source of Grant: Scottish Education Department: £62,075
Date of Research: 1988 – continuing
KEYWORDS: curriculum; Scotland; secondary education; youth

8/0345

Centre for Educational Sociology,
7 Buccleuch Place, Edinburgh EH8 9LW
031 667 1011
Raffe, D.; Lamb, J.M.; Jones, G.; Brannen, K.; Hughes, J.M.; Lowden, S.; Middleton, L.; *Supervisor:* McPherson, A.F. Mr
Spring 1989 and autumn 1989 Scottish Young People's Surveys
Abstract: This project covers three further postal surveys in the Scottish Young People's Surveys series. A 10% national sample of young people who started in S4 in 1987, and an overlapping 10% of leavers from the 1987/88 session, will be surveyed in spring 1989. The latter will extend the biennial sequence of leavers surveys since 1977. Also, a 10% sample of young people who started in S4 in 1985 will be surveyed in autumn 1989. This will add to existing data on the sample, which was first surveyed in spring 1987.
Published Material: a full list of publications is available from the Research Administrator, Joan Hughes at Edinburgh University
Source of Grant: Scottish Education Department: £270,496
Date of Research: 1988-1990
KEYWORDS: school leaver; Scotland; secondary education; survey; transition from school to work; youth

8/0346

Call Centre (Community Aids for Language & Learning),
4 Buccleuch Place, Edinburgh EH8 9LW
031 667 1011
Sutherland, E. Ms; Joss, A. Mrs; *Supervisor:* Odor, J.P. Mr
Microtechnology and disabled learners
Abstract: The CALL (Communication Aids for Language Learning) Centre in Edinburgh University combines research and development with service to clients with a range of communication difficulties who are assessed to determine if micro technological aid(s) may be useful. Over time, the CALL team has acquired an understanding of the assessment process and now wishes to share that by means of the CALL training materials package. At the heart of the package are the stories of CALL's clients. Through the telling of these stories CALL hopes to enable others to understand the process of assessment more fully. The stories are being told in the form of a stack of cards on a Macintosh computer (using Hypercard). Users navigate their own way through the stack of cards with a set of easy-to-use navigation tools. It is in five sections and includes a glossary and a notepad facility. From the stackware version a traditional linear text based version will be produced. Ultimately the stack will be available on a CD-Rom. CALL's stack will be public domain and free. Optional supplementary support will be available at cost. It has been written with both teachers and therapists in mind and clients of all ages.
Source of Grant: Technical and Vocational Education Initiative (UK)
Date of Research: 1988-1990
KEYWORDS: assessment; communication; educational technology; handicapped; teaching aids; speech handicapped

8/0347

Centre for Educational Sociology,
7 Buccleuch Place, Edinburgh EH8 9LW
031 667 1011
Raffe, D.; Willms, J.D.; *Supervisor:* McPherson, A.F.
Standards, tests and parental choice: preparing for change
Abstract: The aim of this research is to study the implications and consequences of parental choice of secondary schools, particularly in relation to the effectiveness of schooling and the testing of it.
Published Material: A bibliography of published work is available from the Research Administrator
Source of Grant: Nuffield Foundation: £21,295
Date of Research: 1988-1990
KEYWORDS: assessment; parent choice; performance; school effectiveness; secondary education

8/0348
> Godfrey Thomson Unit,
> 24 Buccleuch Place, Edinburgh EH8 9JT
> 031 667 1011
> Normand, B.J. Mrs; *Supervisor:* Pollitt, A. Mr

Profiles in English
Abstract: The purpose of this project is the development of English language assessment materials for use as a classroom resource for primary schools. 'Profiles in English' provides a comprehensive profile of each child's abilities in all of the language modes using contextualised language tasks with authentic communicative purposes.
Source of Grant: Macmillan Education
Date of Research: 1987-1990
KEYWORDS: assessment; English language; primary education; profile; teaching

8/0349
> Research Centre for the Social Sciences,
> 7 Buccleuch Place, Edinburgh EH8 9LW
> 031 667 1011
> Lamb, J.M.; Bechhofer, F.

Design of conceptual model for documentation database and prototype in SIR (School Information Retrieval)
Abstract: The project aims to provide a generalisable conceptual model for a documentation database.
Published Material: A bibliography of published work is available from the Research Administrator
Source of Grant: Economic and Social Research Council: £17,600
Date of Research: 1989-1990
KEYWORDS: computer assisted instruction; database; microcomputer; model

8/0350
> Centre for Educational Sociology,
> 7 Buccleuch Place, Edinburgh EH8 9LW
> 031 667 1011
> Raffe, D.; Howieson, C.; *Supervisor:* McPherson, A.F. Mr

The impact of TVEI: secondary analysis
Abstract: A secondary analysis of existing data is to be carried out in order to evaluate the impact of the Technical and Vocational Education Initiative in Scotland.
Published Material: A bibliography of published work is available from the Research Administrator
Source of Grant: Economic and Social Research Council
Date of Research: 1988-1989
KEYWORDS: Scotland; survey; Technical and Vocational Education Initiative; transition from school to work; vocational education; youth employment

8/0351
> Centre for Educational Sociology,
> 7 Buccleuch Place, Edinburgh EH8 9LW
> 031 667 1011
> Garner, C.L. Mr; *Supervisor:* McPherson, A.F. Mr

The development of a school catchments analysis system
Abstract: The research aims to construct an integrated, user-friendly system which links spatial and social data, providing the capability to produce high quality cartographic output together with spatial and statistical analyses. The system would be generalisable to many local authority/research needs but would be developed and illustrated through its application to the specific problem of changing school catchments.
Published Material: A bibliogoraphy of published work is available from the Research Administrator
Source of Grant: Economic and Social Research Council
Date of Research: 1988-1989
KEYWORDS: catchment areas; geographic location; information system; school distribution

8/0352
> Centre for Educational Sociology,
> 7 Buccleuch Place, Edinburgh EH8 9LW
> 031 667 1011
> Raffe, D.; Croxford, L.; *Supervisor:* McPherson, A.F. Mr

Progress towards a National Curriculum
Abstract: This research aims to address the social, institutional and administrative issues in delivering the National Curriculum, in the context of change over time, and with particular reference to secondary education.
Published Material: A bibliography of published work is available from the Research Administrator
Source of Grant: Economic and Social Research Council
Date of Research: 1988-1989
KEYWORDS: curriculum; educational change; educational policy; secondary education

8/0353
> Centre for Educational Sociology,
> 7 Buccleuch Place, Edinburgh EH8 9LW
> 031 667 1011
> Raffe, D.; Patterson, L.; *Supervisor:* McPherson, A.F. Mr

Economic and Social Research Council Survey link scheme (2)
Abstract: The research examined the problems of the measurement of socio-economic status using hierarchical linear models; missing data and modelling educational attainment.
Published Material: A bibliography of published work is available from the Research Administrator
Source of Grant: Economic and Social Research Council: expenses
Date of Research: 1988-1989
KEYWORDS: achievement; model; performance; school effectiveness; survey

8/0354
> Centre for Educational Sociology,
> 7 Buccleuch Place, Edinburgh EH8 9LW
> 031 667 1011
> Raffe, D.; *Supervisor:* McPherson, A.F. Mr

Scottish Young Peoples Survey: TVEI follow-up
Abstract: The research will use data from the Scottish Young People's Surveys to follow up survey respondents who had been on TVEI courses to study their subsequent careers in education, training or the labour market and to describe their views on the perceived relevance of TVEI to these careers.
Published Material: A bibliography of published work is available from the Research Administrator
Source of Grant: The Training Enterprise Educational Division, Department of Employment
Date of Research: 1988-1990
KEYWORDS: Scotland, survey, Technical and Vocational Education Initiative; transition from school to work; vocational education; youth employment

8/0355
> Centre for Educational Sociology,
> 7 Buccleuch Place, Edinbugh EH8 9LW
> 031 667 1011
> Raffe, D.; Willms, J.D.; *Supervisor:* McPherson, A.F. Mr

A longitudinal study of school effects and their stability
Abstract: The research will be to examine questions on the accuracy to which estimates of schools effects can be made, on whether differences between school in their effects are stable from one year to the next, and on the factors that contribute to stability.
Published Material: A bibliography of published work is available from the Research Administrator
Source of Grant: Economic and Social Research Council
Date of Research: 1988-1989
KEYWORDS: outcomes of education; performance indicators; school effectiveness; secondary education

8/0356
> Centre for Educational Sociology,
> 7 Buccleuch Place, Edinburgh EH8 9LW
> 031 667 1011
> Raffe, D.; Howieson, C.; *Supervisor:* McPherson, A.F. Mr

The impact of TVEI: a survey to measure change and progress
Abstract: This research aims to boost sample numbers in the 1989 Scottish Young People's Survey to cover pupils participating in Technical and Vocational Education Initiative projects, to make comparisons with a 1987 study, and to enable changes over time in the impact of TVEI to be assessed.
Published Material: A bibliography of published work is available from the Research Administrator
Source of Grant: Economic and Social Research Council
Date of Research: 1988-1989
KEYWORDS: Scotland; survey; Technical and Vocational Initiative; transition from school to work; vocational education; youth employment

8/0357

Centre for Educational Sociology,
7 Buccleuch Place, Edinburgh EH8 9LW
031 667 1011
McPherson, A.F. Mr; Raffe, D.; Lamb, J.M.; Jones, G.;
Hughes, J.M.
Continuation of Scottish Young People's Survey
Abstract: The biennial series of surveys of Scottish school leavers
is to be continued.
Published Material: A bibliography of published work is available from the Research Administrator
Source of Grant: Scottish Education Department: £120,000
Date of Research: 1990 – continuing
KEYWORDS: *school leaver; Scotland; secondary education; survey; transition from school to work; youth*

8/0358

Centre for Educational Sociology,
7 Buccleuch Place, Edinburgh EH8 9LW
031 667 1011
McPherson, A.F. Mr; Raffe, D.; Garner, C.; McPherson,
A.F. Mr
Area deprivation study
Abstract: This project aims to study the effects that deprivation
has on school achievement and on the lives of 16 to 19 year olds.
Published Material: A list of publications is available from the
Research Administrator.
Source of Grant: John Watsons Trust: £20,000
Date of Research: 1988-1990
KEYWORDS: *achievement; deprived; secondary education; youth*

8/0359

Centre for Educational Sociology,
7 Buccleuch Place, Edinburgh EH8 9LW
031 667 1011
Raffe, D.; Furlong, A.; Ritchie, P.
Routes of young people into and within the labour market
Abstract: To consider the movements of young people into the
labour market (from school or college) and within the labour
market, (between Youth Training Scheme, employment and unemployment, between occupations and if possible between employers).
The study will draw on the information provided by the Scottish
Young Peoples Survey.
Published Material: A list of publications is available from the
Research Administrator.
Source of Grant: Industry Department of Scotland: £40,000
Date of Research: 1988-1989
KEYWORDS: *labour market; Scotland; transition from school to
work; youth employment*

8/0360

Department of Artificial Intelligence
80 South Bridge, Edinburgh EH1 1HN
031 225 7774
Howe, J.A.M. Prof.; Brna, P. Dr
Computer aided recognition of misconceptions about simple electrical circuits
Abstract: It is desirable to have a more detailed understanding of
how faulty beliefs (misconceptions) arise, how they are maintained,
and how new beliefs effectively replace old ones. The long term
goal is to use this understanding to guide the researchers in the
development of exploratory regimes which can assist students to
improve their grasp of some domain. Consequently, the ability is
needed to recognize that one or more misconceptions are held by
a given student and to characterize this set of beliefs. This project
is concerned with the problem of recognizing misconceptions as
students are in the process of constructing simple electrical circuits.
The method of investigation entails the construction of a number
of student models. These are computational representations of the
beliefs associated with simple electrical circuits. Various interpreters
of these computational models are being constructed. The information obtained from the student's behaviour in constructing a
circuit, the circuit's actual behaviour, and the student's exploratory activity will be the basis for exploring the diagnostic issues.
Source of Grant: Science and Engineering Research Council Economic and Social Research Council Medical Research Council:
jointly £89,380
Date of Research: 1989 – continuing

KEYWORDS: *belief; cognition; computer assisted instruction;
learning process; science education*

8/0361

Department of Artificial Intelligence
80 South Bridge, Edinburgh EH1 1HN
031 225 7774
Cawsey, A.J. Dr
Generating explanatory discourse
Abstract: This research has involved developing a computer model
of explanatory discourse. As computers are increasingly used to
present advice, help or explanations to novice users, it is important to consider how best to structure the resulting discourse. This
involves organizing what to say (depending on the user's knowledge
and the structure of the domain knowledge), and managing any
dialogue (such as interruptions). In a tutorial context, it may also
involve responding to perceived misconceptions, involving the
novice in the explanation and checking their understanding. As the
explanatory dialogue progresses, assumptions about the user's
knowledge must be updated. The model is based on analyses of
human face to face explanations and on related work on tutorial
dialogues, discourse analysis and text generation. It is fully
implemented, and an initial evaluation has been done, suggesting
that it has potential as a practical approach for the computer generation of complex explanations. Recent work has concentrated on
the modelling of communication failure and repair in such dialogues.
Published Material: CAWSEY, A. (1989). 'Explanatory Dialogues',
Interacting with Computers, Vol 1, pp.69-92, March.; CAWSEY,
A. (1989). 'The structure of tutorial discourse'. In: BIERMAN,
D., BREVKER, J. & SANDBERG, J. (Eds). (1989). Artificial Intelligence and Education, Conference Proceedings, pp.47-53. May.
Amsterdam, IOS.; CAWSEY, A. (1990). 'Generating explanatory
discourse'. In: DALE, R., MELLISH, C. & ZOCK, M. (Eds). Current Research in Natural Language Generation. London: Academic
Press.
Source of Grant: Science and Engineering Research Council
Date of Research: 1989 – continuing
KEYWORDS: *artificial intelligence; autoinstructional aid; automatic teaching; computer assisted instruction; dialogue (language);
explanation; teaching machine*

8/0362

Department of Artificial Intelligence
80 South Bridge, Edinburgh EH1 1HN
031 225 7774
Valley, K. Miss; *Supervisor:* Ross, P.M. Dr; Conlon, T. Mr
Applications of artificial intelligence and expert systems technology to education
Abstract: This research describes the design, implementation and
evaluation of an expert system shell for use in education. An initial evaluation was carried out to establish some criteria for the
design of the new shell. This comprised an evaluation of expert
system shells by experienced teachers; an evaluation of several expert
system shells by the author; and a case study visit to a school computer studies department. The teachers were also asked for their
views on the possible uses of shells in the classroom. An expert
system shell was designed and implemented as a result of this evaluation. This has an environment for building knowledge bases; an
environment for consulting knowledge bases; a knowledge representation language allowing separation of domain and problem solving knowledge; and three supplementary tools. The most important
of these is an explanation tool, which allows exploration of the
domain knowledge in a knowledge base. In response to posed questions, the tool can produce domain based explanations using a
domain indpendent generation technique, and each explanation can
be explored further through relevant follow-up questions. This tool
provides a means whereby users can learn about the domain of the
knowledge base being explored. An evaluation of this shell by
teachers with previous experience of expert system shells suggests
that it has the potential for use throughout the school curriculum
as an educationl medium.
Source of Grant: Economic and Social Research Council with
Research Machines Ltd. under Information Technology in Education (ITE) programme
Date of Research: 1986-1990
KEYWORDS: *artificial intelligence; computer assisted instruction;
computer science; microcomputer*

8/0363

Department of Artificial Intelligence
80 South Bridge, Edinburgh EH1 1HN
031 225 7774
Pain, H.G. Dr

A language based tool-kit for use by children with special educational needs

Abstract: Recent research has emphasized writing as a cognitive process, and is open to introspection and control. Pupils need to both develop a general awareness of thought and language and to gain understanding of the processes of writing, of patterns and forms of language and of the relationship between the writer and the audience. In gaining this awareness and understanding, the learner may need the opportunity to explore language and to experiment with it. Research in artificial intelligence – in the area of natural language processing in particular – has provided the possibility of creating 'language exploration environments' for learners to use. Computer based tools may also be used to support the writing process. 'Writers' Assistants' facilitate the generation and organization of ideas; the composing, editing and revision of text; and the provision of feedback and checking of the text. Writing support tools have been used most commonly as word processing packages providing basic text editing facilities. The potential use of these tools, by children with special education needs, has not yet been examined. This proposal relates to the use of a kit of such tools by children with special needs. This involves the identification of existing tools for language exploration and support; the integration of a number of suitable tools into a basic tool-kit; the design and implementation of the tool-kit on a machine suitable for testing purposes in schools. The use of the tools would be monitored over a one year period and the feasibility of its further use considered. Necessary changes would be made to the tool-kit design, informed by observation of its use. It is expected that teaching materials for use in conjunction with the tool-kit would also be produced.
Source of Grant: Scottish Council for Educational Technology, Microelectronics in Education Committee: £76,378
Date of Research: 1987-1990
KEYWORDS: *computer assisted instruction; language development; special education*

8/0364

Department of Education
Centre for Research on Learning and Instruction,
12 Buccleuch Place, Edinburgh EH8 9JT
031 667 1011
Tait, H. Miss; Thompson, S. Mrs; *Supervisor:* Entwistle,
N.J. Prof.

Promoting effective learning

Abstract: Student failure and non-completion represent a waste of scarce resources in higher education. It is therefore important to try to identify the factors that lead to non-completion. This project aims to draw up a checklist which departments could use to try to identify students who are at risk of failing, and to provide a handbook of suggestions for improving teaching which may promote effective learning, based on examples of good practice and innovation gathered from the literature.
Published Material: ENTWISTLE, N.J., KOZEKI, B. & TAIT, H. (1989). 'Pupils' perceptions of school and teachers', British Journal of Educational Psychology, Vol 59, No 3, pp.326-350.; ENTWISTLE, N.J. & TAIT, H. (1990). 'Approaches to learning, evaluations of teaching, and preferences for contrasting academic environments', Higher Education, 1990.
Source of Grant: Scottish Education Department: £40,000
Date of Research: 1990 – continuing
KEYWORDS: *higher education; learning strategy; student; teaching method*

8/0365

Department of Education
Old College, South Bridge, Edinburgh EH8 9YL
031 667 1011
Edinburgh University
Department of Education
10 Buccleuch Place, Edinburgh EH8 9JT
031 337 1011
Macaulay, C. Ms; Wall, D.E. Ms; *Supervisor:* Entwistle,
N.J. Prof.

The transition from school to higher education in Scotland

Abstract: School leavers in Scotland can enter higher education from highers qualifications in the fifth year or from highers/sixth year studies in the sixth year. There are also sizeable numbers of English 'A' level qualified students at certain Scottish institutions. The aims of this project are; (i) to ascertain admissions policies and practices of a sample of higher education institutions (universities and central institutions) with regard to age and qualifications; (ii) to identify differences in performance according to those variables, looking particularly at the match between first year teaching and the level of entry qualification. Patterns and trends have been elicited in the first instance through statistical information. A variety of courses in the arts, social sciences and sciences have been chosen for in depth study. Key personnel involved with first year courses and admissions have been interviewed and students have completed a questionnaire about their transition from school to higher education, in particular about their preparation, qualifications on entry, and experiences of their first year course.
Source of Grant: Scottish Education Department: £64,991
Date of Research: 1988-1990
KEYWORDS: *admission requirements; higher education; performance; school leaver; Scotland*

8/0366

Department of Education
10 Buccleuch Place, Edinburgh EH8 9JT
031 667 1011
Macaulay, C. Ms; Situnayake, G. Ms; Tait, H. Ms;
Supervisor: Entwistle, N.J. Prof.; Hounsell, D. Dr

Performance of technology students in Scottish higher education

Abstract: The purpose of this study is to investigate the performance of students in Scottish higher education who are taking degree or Higher National Diploma (HND) courses in technological subjects. The initial focus has been on students in their first year of Electrical and Electronic Engineering courses. A sample of three central institutions and two universities offering one or both of these courses (5 B.Eng, 2 HND) was selected. The first year students (508) enrolled on these courses completed a questionnaire designed to explore their perceptions of different parts of the course and approaches to study. Detailed interviews with a smaller sample of students (42) explored these relationships in greater depth. These student characteristics will then be compared with levels of examination performance at the end of the first year. It is hoped that by combining this information it will be possible to predict how well future students will perform in the first year of Electronic and Electrical Engineering courses. It is also intended that interviews with course leaders and supporting academic staff will assist in the identification of a range of sources of difficulty in technology courses. It may then be possible to suggest ways of improving the overall level of performance on such courses.
Source of Grant: Scottish Education Department: £65,000
Date of Research: 1987-1989
KEYWORDS: *Scotland; higher education; technology; performance; assessment*

8/0367

Department of Education
10 Buccleuch Place, Edinburgh EH8 9JT
031 667 1011
Entwistle, N. Prof.; Napuk, A. Mrs; Dickie, S. Ms

English language monitoring

Abstract: The main aim is to assess national standards of attainment across the language modes of reading, writing, listening, talking and interaction. A representative national sample will be drawn from P4, P7 and S2 and assessed using appropriate test materials. Some tests used in the 1989 survey will be repeated to provide a basis of comparison.
Source of Grant: Scottish Education Department: £121,000
Date of Research: 1991 – continuing
KEYWORDS: *achievement; assessment; English language*

8/0368

Department of Education
10 Buccleuch Place, Edinburgh EH8 9JT
031 667 1011
Cartmell, C. Dr; *Supervisor:* Steward, T.G. Mr; Hutchinson,
C. Mrs

The assessment of generic aspects of competence in National Certificate modules

Abstract: This project will investigate two areas to be found both within Scottish National Certificate Modules and also within Youth Training Scheme outcomes: personal effectiveness and communi-

cation skills. The major focus of the project is to develop guidelines on the assessment of a behavioural outcomes approach to teaching and learning in further education in Scotland, as seen in the 2,000 or so modules recognised by SCOTVEC (Scottish Vocational Education Council), which have been subjected to a recent revision in the areas of Personal and Social Development and Communications. A new structure to the modules in the PSD group has emerged and will shortly be taken up in college provision. This investigation will develop appropriate tools for classroom observation of the two aspects of competance both in specialist PSD or communication modules as well as across the board in a wide range of vocational modules. Following the piloting of a new personal effectiveness module, the project will attempt to give formative feedback on the module before it becomes more widely available, and this process will contribute to the major aim of developing guidelines for assessment of outcomes in the PSD area. A similar process will be generated in relation to communication modules and it is anticipated that there will be much common ground between both areas of assessment.
Source of Grant: Scottish Education Department: £69,000 over two years
Date of Research: 1987-1989
KEYWORDS: *assessment; communication; further education; personality development; skill*

8/0369

Department of Education
10 Buccleuch Place, Edinburgh EH8 9JT
031 667 1011
Hitt, P.D.P. Mr; *Supervisor:* King, K.J. Dr; Steward, T.G. Mr

Perceptions of management in schools: a study of the perceptions of individual teachers on the issue of management in schools
Abstract: This research has arisen from an interest in management. The researcher is particularly keen to discover how teachers define and understand the topic and what action might be appropriate to develop understanding and ability. The aims of the research are to; (1) investigate teachers' perceptions of management in secondary, primary and independent schools in Lothian; (2) to assess the level of understanding which teachers have of management processes; (3) discover what differences of views, if any, there are between promoted and non promoted staff; (4) to enquire if there is any correlation between subject background and views of management; (5) evaluate what the research indicates about future training needs. The research will be qualitative involving interviews with teachers in a sample of Lothian Region secondary schools and primary schools and a sample of independent schools in Edinburgh. Teachers will be interviewed from all different subject backgrounds and age groupings. There will be approximately 200 teachers interviewed, 90+ from secondary, 70 from primary and 30+ from the independent sector. The interviewees will include all levels of promoted and non promoted staff from head teacher to probationer. The sample will include an appropriate portion from each subject background and age cohort. Each interviewee will be invited to respond to five statistical questions and a qualitative interview schedule − covering ten questions. The interviews will last approximately 45 minutes. A limited number of follow-up in depth interviews may be undertaken.
Source of Grant: Lothian Region: 40% of fees
Date of Research: 1986-1990
KEYWORDS: *administration of education; inservice training; management; perception; staff development; teacher behaviour*

8/0370

Department of Education
10 Buccleuch Place, Edinburgh EH8 9JT
031 667 1011
Balarabe, M. Mr; *Supervisor:* Entwistle, N.J. Prof.; Thomson, G.O.B. Dr

Motivational factors influencing the academic attainments of Nigerian Hausa children
Abstract: The study aims to investigate the motivational factors and approaches to studying influencing the academic attainments of Nigerian children in three states of the federation and the personal and social aspects of home and school related to them. In trying out the instruments before the field work, a pilot study was done using questionnaires developed earlier by N.J.Entwistle and B.Kozeki in their studies with British and Hungarian children. An attributions test was also developed and tried out covering success and failure outcomes in the home and school. Following the pilot

study and factor analysis, the present subscales were decided upon and used with the Nigerian children. Questionnaires were administered with various subscales on home, school and peer aspects of motivation, personality and attitudes to school subjects in mathematics and English. The attributions questionnaire was also included. In addition to questionnaires completed by Nigerian subjects, personal reports made in essay form on their expectations in life; their likes and dislikes in school; and parental and personal views on most important things in life were collected. The total sample size is approximately 500, with the subjects being final year secondary school pupils. The West African Examinations Council results (W.A.E.C.) of the subjects will be used as measures of attainment. A Teachers' ratings of pupils in academic and personality aspects was also obtained. Interviews with teachers and school administrators on the factors influencing the children's performance at school were also carried out.
Source of Grant: Association of Commonwealth Universities, London: £200
Date of Research: 1986-1989
KEYWORDS: *achievement; child; motivation; Nigeria; social environment*

8/0371

Department of Education
Godfrey Thomson Unit,
4 Buccleuch Place, Edinburgh EH8 9LW
031 667 1438
Aitken, S. Dr; Millar, S. Ms; Nisbet, P. Mr; *Supervisor:* Odor, P. Mr

Communication aids for language and learning (CALL)
Abstract: This is a research and development project, including service delivery, offering help in assessing what communication aids or teaching programmes are needed for learners with disabilities. Development work includes investigation of how these aids might be incorporated within, and contribute towards, curriculum development. Research is carried out into a wide range of aspects of communication difficulty and technology, with development of a new microelectronic and computing systems to exploit new technologies. Support is given to clients and carers in tailoring and using the chosen system. Activities cover a Scotland-wide assessment service; information, demonstrations and advice and loan services. Training is offered through the media of seminars, awareness training, short and long term secondments for training of professionals including teachers, psychologists, social workers, programmers and technicians. Specific projects include specialised safe interfaces; toy-environment control boxes; software microworlds; smart wheelchair; software toolkits for communication aids and computer based learning; Public Domain Software (discs and manuals).
Published Material: AITKEN, S. (1987). 'Me and my therapists', The Scottish Child, Winter, pp.16-17.; AITKEN, S. (1988). 'Computer aided instruction with the multiply impaired', Journal of Mental Deficiencey Research, No 32, pp.257-263.; BUULTJENS, M. & AITKEN, S. (1987). 'Assessment of vision in multiply impaired children', British Journal of Special Education, No 14, pp.112-114. A complete list of publications is available from the research office.
Source of Grant: Scottish Education Department: £110,000 per annum
Date of Research: 1986 − continuing
KEYWORDS: *communication; curriculum development; educational technology; handicapped; teaching aids*

8/0372

Department of Education
10 Buccleuch Place, Edinburgh EH8 9JT
031 667 1011 ext 6703
Wu, L.F. Miss; *Supervisor:* Entwistle, N.J. Prof.

An exploratory study on school readiness, with special reference to the school-aged children in Taiwan
Abstract: The aim of the present research is twofold. First, to explore the reality of school readiness in progress, and second to discover the causes for the difference in childrens readiness. The sample comprises thirty six school-age entrants and their parents and four primary 1 teachers in Taiwan. Open-ended interviewing and fieldnote observations are the major methods employed in fieldwork.
Source of Grant: The Republic of China, Ministry of Education
Date of Research: 1986-1990
KEYWORDS: *primary education; school readiness; Taiwan*

8/0373

Department of Education
10 Buccleuch Place, Edinburgh EH8 9JT
031 667 1011
Thomson, G.O.B. Dr; Riddell, S.I. Dr

Post-school placements of children and young people with Records of Needs

Abstract: This research will examine the post-school outcomes of recorded pupils, in particular those for whom Records of Needs have been opened, who have been placed in mainstream settings. Quantitiative, qualitative and case study methods will be used to examine: transition to independent living and employability; the role of future needs assessment in developing appropriate goals for recorded young persons; the wishes of young persons themselves; cost-effectiveness issues attendant on school placements and post-school experience. The expected outcome of the research is that possible indicators for successful post-school placement might be identified in terms of the nature of special educational needs and how these have been met in the school years.

Source of Grant: Scottish Education Department: £60,000
Date of Research: 1989 – continuing
KEYWORDS: handicapped; special needs; transition from school to work; youth

8/0374

Department of Education
Godfrey Thomson Unit,
24 Buccleugh Place, Edinburgh EH8 9LN
031 667 1011
Pollilt, A.B. Mr; Hutchinson, C.J. Mrs; Napuk, A. Mrs; Munro, L. Mrs; Dickie, S. Ms; *Supervisor:* Entwistle, N.J. Prof.

Assessment of achievement programme: English language (second round)

Abstract: The main aim is to assess what national standards of attainment are in reading, writing, listening and speaking and oral interaction skills at primary 4, primary 7 and secondary 2. To do this a nationally representative sample of pupils will be assessed at each stage using appropriate test materials. These will include some of the tests used in the 1984 project in order to provide a basis for comparison.

Source of Grant: Scottish Education Department: £89,935
Date of Research: 1987-1990
KEYWORDS: achievement; assessment; English language; primary education; Scotland; secondary education

8/0375

Department of Education
10 Buccleuch Place, Edinburgh EH8 9JT
031 667 1011
Smith, E.G. Mr; *Supervisor:* King, K. Dr; Hounsell, D. Dr

Teacher perception of staff development

Abstract: The aim of this research is to construct a model of staff development based on an experimental investigation of teacher perceptions. Prior to the experimental work there has been a literature search, a chapter within placing staff development in a historical content and a chapter which explores the models of staff development which arise from the literature. Though the literature is substantial, experimental work has not been common. From the concepts and principles which appear in existing models, a questionnaire will be prepared which will examine teacher opinion. An initial survey of the opinions of eighty teachers, has already been carried out, which has allowed methods to be explored and the results have also pointed to areas where significant differences of policy interest could exist between teacher and national models. The main data collection, by piloted questionnaire, will be carried out nationally from a random sample of teachers. The collection and analysis of results will be followed up by open interviews of twenty five teachers. It is likely that the discussion of results will go beyond simple comparison of models. More sophisticated modelling should be possible which will allow for the consideration of policies which could avoid the conflicts of the past.

Published Material: SMITH, E.G. (1987). Teacher perceptions of staff development. Report to Lothian region (based on initial survey work).; SMITH, E.G. (1986). Staff appraisal in an American High school. Report to the Lothian region and the British Council.
Source of Grant: Lothian region: 40% of fees
Date of Research: 1986 – continuing
KEYWORDS: educational policy; staff development; teacher attitude

Essex Institute of Higher Education

8/0376

Sawyers Hall Lane, Brentwood, Essex Cm15 9BT
0277 216971
Badley, G.F. Mr

An evaluation of the American community college

Abstract: The community college appears to be a unique American institution which combines elements of vocational, technical, further adult and higher education. The research aims to explore and evaluate from the perspective of British further and higher education the central mission and philosophy of the American community college. The research is based on an 'illuminative' approach to evaluation where the primary concern is to describe and interpret rather than measure or predict. Hence it involves a series of visits to appropriate 'sample' colleges, a study of relevant materials and documents, an examination of significant processes and critical features and interviews with important personnel. The visibility, size, accredibility and comprehensiveness of the community college makes it appear to be a post-school educational system in itself. It is uniquely American, congruent with American values of openness, tolerance and liberality, a 'communiversity' which is nevertheless struggling with its sense of mission.

Published Material: BRADLEY, G. (1988). 'Unique, authentic and American: a British view of the community college', Journal of Further and Higher Education, Vol 12, No 2, Summer 1988, pp.72-79.
Source of Grant: Visits to USA colleges: since 1986: Essex LEA £200 Central Bureau: £500 Essex IHE: £1,000
Date of Research: 1986 – continuing
KEYWORDS: community; further education; higher education; system of education; States of America

8/0377

Department of Education
Victoria Road South, Chelmsford CM1 1LL
0245 354491
Cole, A. Ms

Voting registration and take-up amongst people with a mental handicap

Abstract: The right to vote is now enjoyed by all people with mental handicaps in Great Britain, unless they are subject to an order under the Mental Health Act 1983. The aim of this project is to establish indicators as to whether that right is taken up by people with mental handicaps. The underlying hypothesis is that voting take-up amongst people with mental handicaps is low, and that this is a reflection of their lack of knowledge about: – (a) their rights; and (b) the practical tasks of registration and voting. This being the case, it is the intention to develop a training package for staff to use with people who have mental handicaps, and evaluate the effect that this has upon their voting behaviour. The scope of the initial investigation is limited to one country, taking a sample of approximately 200 people with mental handicaps who have well-developed skills in other areas of performance. The investigation will involve: (1) cross referencing with the electoral roll to establish voting registration and take-up during the General Election 1987; (2) interviews with people who have mental handicaps to establish knowledge of right to vote and procedure, (3) questionnaires to staff to establish amount and content of any electoral education prior to the election.

Source of Grant: In house Research Bursary: £662.10
Date of Research: 1987 – continuing
KEYWORDS: election; mentally handicapped; participation

8/0378

Department of Health, Nursing and Social Work
Victoria Road South, Chelmsford CM1 1LL
0245 493131
Surrey University
Department of Educational Studies
Guildford GU2 5XH
0483 571281
Hilton, A. Dr; Jarvis, P. Dr; *Supervisor:* MacKenzie, A. Mrs

The community learning environment: a study of students and practical work teachers in district nursing

Abstract: Documents from the English National Board for Nursing Midwifery and Health Visiting and from the United Kingdom

Central Council indicate that future nurse learners will be required to have considerable community experience in their qualifying courses. Although district nurses, health visitors and others have undertaken courses in the community for many years there has been little research into the learning that takes place in the practice area. Research findings from hospital studies of ward learning show that not all wards provide an environment conducive to learning and raises questions about all learning environments in the workplace, particularly in the patient or client area. The study is based on the grounded theory methodology developed by Glaser and Strauss and has been shown in the pilot study to be a useful means of exploring the learning environments of district nurse students. It involves interviewing and observing students in the practice setting; interviewing practical work teachers; recording and transcribing the interviews; continually monitoring and analyzing the data, and later, relating it to existing theory. In the first year of the main study, district nurse students have been selected from one institution that can offer a wide range of teaching environments from different health authorities and covering different geographical placements. A different institution will be used in the second year of the main study, from which to make a further selection of district nurse students.
Source of Grant: Internal bursary for first year: £770
Date of Research: 1986-1989
KEYWORDS: community; learning conditions; nurse; practical work; vocational education

Essex University

8/0379

Department of Language and Linguistics
Wivenhoe Park, Colchester CO4 3SQ
0206 873333
Sharkey, N.E. Dr
Learning novel words in context
Abstract: The research combines insights from artificial intelligence with the methods of experimental psychology in order to find out how children and adults use textual context to compute the meanings of new words. The types of contexts to be used in the study are knowledge based and goal based. Normative studies have been conducted to obtain the routine actions that adults believe to occur in certain everyday situations. In some of the studies these norms are used to generate very short stories which contain either a blank or a novel word. The substitute for the blank or novel word is predicted from the norms. Developmental differences are being examined. One of the aims of the research is to provide guidelines for a new test measure for the diagnosis of specific deficits in contextual skills.
Source of Grant: The Leverhulme Trust: £38,460
Date of Research: 1987-1989
KEYWORDS: comprehension; meaning; word

8/0380

Department of Sociology
Colchester CO4 3SQ
0206 873044 or 0206 873049
Wolpe, H. Mr; Unterhalte, G. Ms
Economic change, social conflict and education in contemporary South Africa
Abstract: The research examines the sources and organization of competing policies on education in South Africa. It investigates reformist policies (corporate capital), anti-reformist policies (right wing Afrikaaner parties), and popular demands for 'peoples' education' The latter also raises the question of the co-operative analysis of education policies in some Third World Countries e.g. Tanzania, Zimbabwe and Nicaragua. The investigation is by way of documentary and archival research as well as unstructured interviews with key figures in the sphere of education.
Published Material: WOLPE, H. (1988). 'The struggle for education in South Africa'. In: LONSDALE, J. (Ed). South Africa in question. Cambridge: African Studies Centre.
Source of Grant: Ruth First Memorial Trust Fund: Approximately £200,000 over 2 years
Date of Research: 1988-1990
KEYWORDS: educational policy; South Africa

Exeter University

8/0381

HEA Schools Health Education Unit, Wolfson Laboratories, Higher Hoopern Farm, Exeter EX4 4QJ
0392 264722
Regis, D. Mr; *Supervisor:* Balding, J. Mr
Self-concept and conformity in theories of health education
Abstract: An idea at the heart of much health education and personal and social education (PSE) in schools is that good self-concept improves attitude behaviour consistency and resistance to social pressure, but the literature in experimental psychology on this issue is confused. A questionnaire based on Lindsay-Clift's (1986) implementation of the Fishbein-Ajzen framework was given to 800 schoolchildren aged 12-15 regarding their smoking and drinking behaviour. This included measures of belief, attitude and social influence but also of self-esteem and locus of control. Through regression analysis of behavioural intentions the hypothesis was tested that young people with good self-concept have a relatively greater weight of attitude than normative influence upon intention, ie. were more consistent and less conforming. Results indicated the reverse, indicating that those with a better self-concept are less consistent and more conforming, a finding replicated in a smaller follow-up study. The researcher believes this pattern of results appears because behaviour which is in accord with the expectations of others is likely to result in more positive social relations and thus a better self-esteem (and a more internal locus of control). This is in general supported by the body of work on the development of self-concept since Coopersmith (1968). The central idea in PSE that good self-concept can act as an antidote to social influence may be flawed in that harmonious social relations are what maintains good self-concept.
Published Material: REGIS, D. (1988). 'Conformity, consistency and control', Education and Health, Vol 6, No 1, 1988, pp.4-8.; REGIS D. & BALDING, J.W. (1988). 'Smoking and self-esteem', Education and Health, Vol 6, No 3, 1988, pp.61-66.
Source of Grant: ESRC (Economic & Social Research Council) studentship 1986-1989 School of Education Research Committee 1988
Date of Research: 1986-1990
KEYWORDS: adolescent; drinking; health education; self-concept; smoking; behaviour

8/0382

HEA Schools Health Education Unit, Wolfson Laboratories, Higher Hoopern Farm, Exeter EX4 4QJ
0392 264722
Balding, J.W. Mr
Just a tick 'personal development and health education enquiry'
Abstract: The aim is to promote and support effective health education in primary and secondary schools by obtaining reliable information about the views of pupils, parents, governors, school staff, and health-care professionals with respect to the health-related topics that should be included in the curriculum. This survey method, with origins as far back as 1976 and under periodic review and revision since that time, has been widely used throughout the United Kingdom. The groups concerned are pupils (boys and girls aged 8-19), parents (mothers, fathers, or single parents of 5-19 year olds) and governors, teachers (primary, secondary), and health care professionals (doctors, nurses, health visitors, school nurses, health promotion officers etc). The project is based on the use of questionnaires with the specified groups. There are separate sets of questionnaires for use in primary and secondary schools. When a school chooses to use the questionnaires the data is processed and returned to the school. The results form an agenda for debate at meetings held with parents, staff, and governors to examine the outcome. In 1985 there was a national survey using this method which surveyed 11 local education authorities involving 15,770 parents, 1,054 teachers, 449 health care professionals and 10,984 pupils.
Published Material: BALDING, J. (1986). 'The 'Just a Tick' materials and their use in schools', Education and Health, Vol 4, No 1, 1986, pp.5-8.; BALDING, J. (1988). Parents and health education. Exeter: HEA Schools Health Education Unit.; Health Education Priorities for the Primay School Curriculum (1990). Exeter: HEA Schools Health Education Unit.
Source of Grant: HEA (Health Education Authority), 1985-87
Date of Research: 1976 – continuing
KEYWORDS: health education; parental attitude; parent-school relation; school governor; survey

8/0383

HEA Schools Health Education Unit, Wolfson Laboratories, Higher Hoopern Farm, Exeter EX4 4QJ
0392 264722
Balding, J.W. Mr

Health related behaviour in secondary school children

Abstract: The project aims to support curriculum development in health education. If teachers can be reliably informed of the behaviour of young people in areas related to healthy development, courses in health education can be designed or modified to make them more relevant to curriculum needs. The method used is a questionnaire, The Health Related Behaviour Questionnaire, now in its 12th version, and is continually under review. The areas covered are wide-ranging and include dental care, diet, hygiene, medication, money, physical activity, road safety, self-esteem, social activities, personal relationships, drugs (including alcohol and tobacco) and AIDS (Acquired Immune Deficiency Syndrome). A school or group of schools will elect to survey year groups in their school, the results are processed and returned to the school for use in their curriculum planning and with the pupils themselves. Resulting from the hundreds of schools using the questionnaire is a substantial database (for example in 1988 204 schools used the survey – 36,115 pupils). This database is used to examine health related behaviour in more detail.
Published Material: A list of publications is available from the researcher
Source of Grant: HEA (Health Education Authority) Regional Health Authorities Local Health Authorities
Date of Research: 1979 – continuing
KEYWORDS: *behaviour; health education; secondary education; survey*

8/0384

Department of Psychology
Washington Singer Laboratories,
Perry Road, Exeter EX4 4QG
0392 213505
Supervisor: Mitchell, D.C. Dr

Cognitive analysis of fluent reading and learning to read

Abstract: The aim of the research is to determine the cognitive processes underlying fluent reading and learning to read. The methods are experimental and often involve speeded responses and groups of words or sentences presented on a screen under the control of a microcomputer. Specific tasks that have been used include lexical decision tasks, subject paced reading tasks, tachistoscopic recognition tasks and mind-recall tasks. To date the researchers have carried out work on work-recognition, sentence parsing and text integration with particular reference to the influence of context or prior knowledge at all levels. Some of the most recent work concerns the role of lexical and pragmatic effects of parsing. Contributions from PhD students include work on automatic processing of word meaning, the use of script-knowledge in comprehension, the use of plans and goals in comprehension, and individual differences in reading skills.
Published Material: A full list of publications can be obtained from the researcher on request
Source of Grant: No funding
Date of Research: 1984 – continuing
KEYWORDS: *cognitive process; comprehension; reading*

8/0385

Department of Psychology
Washington Singer Laboratories, Exeter EX4 4QG
0392 264626
Griffiths, M.D. Mr; Supervisor: Lea, S.E.G. Dr; Webley, P. Dr

The acquisition, development and maintenance of gambling in children and adolescents

Abstract: The topic of adolescent gambling is attracting growing interest, but there has still been little controlled or systematic research into the area, and much of that which has been written would best be described as 'armchair theorizing'. The literature concerning pre-adult gambling behaviour falls into three general categories – (a) direct and indirect studies concerning adolescent gambling; (b) studies of the economic socialization of children, and (c) consideration of gambling as play and games as pre-cursors to gambling. This research will concentrate on the acquisition and development of gambling behaviour in children and adolescents, by presenting an overview of the area examining each of these categories. In addition preliminary findings obtained during interviews with self confessed addicted adolescent fruit machine gamblers and results of a pilot questionnaire survey on acquisition and development of fruit machine gambling in adolescents will be discussed. Special emphasis will be placed upon the playing of fruit machines as it is this activity which is currently regarded as the biggest problem concerning young gamblers in England. The current program involves investigation of a number of factors including skill perception in the playing of fruit machines, the illusion of control (Langer, 1975) and subjective physiological arousal. The two approaches chosen in the investigation of these factors are (a) the analysis of regular versus non-regular players in a real arcade and (b) complimentary questionnaire to be administered through the various helping organizations (e.g. Parents of Young Gamblers, Gamblers Anonymous etc).
Source of Grant: ESRC (Economic and Social Research Council): £2,859
Date of Research: 1987 – continuing
KEYWORDS: *adolescent; gambling*

8/0386

School of Education
Interactive Technologies Curriculum Centre,
Heavitree Road, Exeter EX1 2LU
0392 264861
Wright, B. Mr; Tearle, P. Ms

Research and development of interactive video materials for teaching classroom control and management on Initial Teacher Training courses

Abstract: This project will compare the effectiveness of three types of interactive video delivery systems in the teaching of classroom control and management in Initial Teacher Training. A single copy of the VHS videotape 'Critical Incidents in the Classroom' has been pressed onto a plastic videodisc. This videodisc provides a set of stimulus scenes which show typical classroom management and control problems together with a number of different possible outcomes. The three different delivery formats to be evaluated will be a Microtext menu-driven programme using the BBC IV system, an IV bar code booklet using the WAVES system, and a menu driven IV tape programme using the Telesoft system. All of these formats will assume a lecturer-controlled environment using the interactive video in its presentational mode.
Published Material: WRIGHT, B. & TEARLE, B. (1990). The solution finds a problem: interactive video and classroom management. London: Council for Educational Technology. (Occassional Paper No.1); WRIGHT, B. & DILLON, P. (1990). 'Some applications of interactive video in Initial Teacher Training', Educational and Training Technology International, Vol 27, No 1, pp.43-50.
Source of Grant: Department of Education and Science: £1,464
Date of Research: 1989-1990
KEYWORDS: *class management; computer assisted instruction; educational technology; interactive video; teacher education*

8/0387

School of Education
St Luke's, Heavitree Road, Exeter EX1 2LU
0392 76311
Travers, P.R. Dr

Anti-smoking health education in schools: an interactive computer based approach using a recording spirometer

Abstract: Testing in schools started in the autumn term of 1984. Since then 3,146 initial tests and 156 re-tests have been carried out. With the exception of one school where whole year groups were taught, form groups of about 30 children have been used. In the first and second years, information was gathered through question and answer and practical projects. Later years are given a more formal lecture. This initial period established the meaning of 'lung function' stressing the positive effects of exercise and the negative ones of inhaling smoke from cigarettes. Following the talk, pupils are asked to fill in a confidential questionnaire concerning the smoking habits of the pupils and their family, and exercise taken. The results of each test are discussed privately with each pupil and questions are encouraged. Smokers are told exactly what their results mean as far as impairment of lung function is concerned. Suggestions are made as to ways of overcoming the problems that they may encounter when trying to stop smoking. Re-test results are discussed, where it is pointed out that the lung function of those who stop smoking improves whereas those who do not, suffer further deterioration. The research has shown that this approach to the problem is most effective. Pupils stop smoking when they are shown immediate effects, not told of effects in the future, and pupil interest

in the tests is high. The research continues and the final report will be submitted to the Research Trust early in 1987.
Source of Grant: Rehabilitation and Medical Research Trust
Date of Research: 1984-1990
KEYWORDS: health education; smoking; teaching aids; teaching technique

8/0388

School of Education
St Luke's, Exeter EX1 2LU
0392 264796
Bennett, S.N. Prof.

Four year old children in infant schools
Abstract: A study of four year old children in infant schools was undertaken during 1987 in three LEA's, each having a different intake policy. The purposes were threefold: to ascertain the attitudes of headteachers and teachers to the education of such children, and the school and classroom organizations appropriate to this; to assess the nature and quality of the learning experiences provided in the classroom; and to identify those aspects of the organization and teaching which best sustain quality learning experiences. Interviews were carried out with head and class teachers in sixty schools, followed up by extensive observations of children in eighteen classes. Analyses concern the nature and quality of the childrens classroom learning experiences and the teaching activities which sustained them.
Source of Grant: Local Education Authority Consortium: £70,000
Department of Education and Science: £23,177
Date of Research: 1989-1989
KEYWORDS: learning; primary education; reception class

8/0389

School of Education
Physical Education Association Research Centre,
Heavitree Road, Exeter EX1 2LU
0392 263263
Balding, J. Mr; Gentle, P. Dr; Kirby, B. Dr

Coronary prevention in children
Abstract: An exhaustive survey is to be carried out of known physiological risk factors, their behavioural antecedents and the psychological and social origins of these behaviours. Several hundred schoolchildren from local secondary schools aged 11-16 are being studied. The research involves comprehensive fitness testing, assessment of habitual physical activity, anthropometry and blood lipid analysis, together with a questionnaire assessing beliefs, attitudes, social pressures and self-reported behaviour in the areas of tobacco and alcohol consumption, diet and exercise. If relative scores on physiological parameters are maintained into adult life then individuals at risk from coronary heart disease can be identified in childhood. Overall activity levels as revealed by pulse rates seemed to be very low. There are strong links between health-related beliefs and behaviours but also between behaviour and social pressures. The data is being examined in detail for educational implications, on the basis of which new interventional materials may be designed.
Published Material: A list of publications is available from the researcher
Source of Grant: Northcott Medical Foundation IBM UK Trust Physical Education Association Oxenham Will Trust Trustee Savings Bank various other business and industrial sources, totalling: £70,000
Date of Research: 1985 – continuing
KEYWORDS: child; fitness; heart disease; prevention

8/0390

School of Education
Centre for Innovation in Mathematics Teaching,
St Luke's, Heavitree Road, Exeter EX1 2LU
0392 217113
Hobbs, D. Mr; *Supervisor:* Burghes, D. Prof.

Alternative mathematics
Abstract: This research is concerned with the development of a full GCSE (General Certificate of Secondary Education) curriculum project in mathematics for years 4 and 5 at secondary school. The proposed development has modules in: (1) science and technology; (2) environment; (3) business and commerce; (4) design; and (5) leisure and recreation. Materials for each module will be developed and assignments for the GCSE assessment will be designed, including extended projects and school based assessment.
Source of Grant: Department of Trade and Industry, Industry Education Unit: £285,000 over 4 years

Date of Research: 1986-1990
KEYWORDS: assessment; curriculum development; examination; mathematics; secondary education

8/0391

School of Education
St Luke's, Heavitree Road, Exeter EX1 2LU
0392 263263
Bennett, S.N. Prof.; Nichol, J.D. Dr; *Supervisor:* Bennett, S.N. Prof; Nichol, J.D. Dr

Group interactive processes and pupil understanding in co-operative groups using PROLOG (PROgramming in LOGic)
Abstract: This study aims to link two current research studies. One concerns the implementation and evaluation of an integrated humanities project, using authoring programs, including expert systems, written in PROLOG, and word processing. The pupils are using authoring packages to write their own programs in the knowledge domains and sub-domains studied. The second project has the aim of gaining a better understanding of processes and their effects when children interact in groups with computers. In this study group composition rules are being systematically manipulated in relation to task difficulty, group interaction processes, pupil understandings and task outcomes. The new study will concentrate on group interactive processes and pupil understandings during the creation of programs in co-operative groups using PROLOG. It will enable the first systematic attempt to evaluate and compare the learning outcomes in the school environment of both conventional CAL (Computer Assisted Learning) and that based on research into artificial intelligence and logic programming. The research techniques necessary for such a study will include the acquisition and analysis of children's discourse, diagnostic interviewing to assess pupil understandings, and experimental studies to assess the impact of differing composition rules.
Source of Grant: Economic and Social Research Council: 3 year research studentship
Date of Research: 1986-1989
KEYWORDS: computer assisted instruction; comprehension; group work; interaction; program

8/0392

School of Education
St Luke's, Heavitree Road, Exeter EX1 2LU
0392 263263
Wragg, E.C. Prof.

Primary teaching skills (continuation of Primary Teachers' Professional Skills Project)
Abstract: This study grows out of the Teacher Education Project. It is a study of teachers' opening explanations of two topics. The teacher is given two topics to introduce in any way he or she chooses. The first is 'insects' and the second is 'The Island of Zarg' – a map of the fictitious island about which the children are to write. The teacher sets up the topic for ten minutes with a group of four (two boys and two girls) above average or four average 8 or 9 year olds, and is observed by one of the researchers. The children then have to complete a test paper on insects and write a creative essay entitled 'My adventure on the Island of Zarg'. Classroom interaction data and children's written responses are then analyzed. Over 128 'explanations' have been collected to-date. The results will be published in their own right as well as used to create teacher training materials.
Source of Grant: Exeter University Research Fund: £5,000 (1984-1986) funding for further 3 years being sought
Date of Research: 1984 – continuing
KEYWORDS: primary education; teacher education; teacher-pupil relation; teaching skill

8/0393

SChool of Education
St Luke's, Heavitree Road, Exeter EX4 4QJ
0392 76311
Bristol Polytechnic
Department of Education
Redland Hill, Bristol BS6 6U2
0272 656261
Frawley, P.A. Mr; *Supervisor:* Hughes, M. Dr

An investigation into the effects of computer program design on the ease of use of the program by junior aged children
Abstract: The project has begun with a pilot investigation which involves the researcher in working with children on two similar computer programs, (GRASS, Newman College, Birmingham and

QUEST, Advisory Unit, Hatfield, Herts.). The children undertake a series of tasks linked to a tutorial session. The work is recorded on video tape (2 cameras – one on the children and the second on the computer screen.) The analysis will attempt to determine the influence of design (i.e. command driven structures versus menu driven programmes), as compared with other factors, such as prior experience, intelligence, personality and cooperative working. The second phase of the project will concentrate upon any of these factors which appear to predominate.
Source of Grant: Funded by Bristol Polytechnic
Date of Research: 1986-1990
KEYWORDS: *assessment; computer assisted instruction; database; performance; pupil; software*

8/0394

School of Education
St Luke's, Heavitree Road, Exeter EX1 2LU
0392 263263
Harvey, C.J. Mr; *Supervisor:* Smith, M. Dr
A study of George Lyward: his ideas and their application to contemporary education
Abstract: George Lyward was a remarkably successful teacher, who worked first in prep, grammar and public schools, and then, after he had recovered from a breakdown, ran an educational establishment – really a therapeutic community – Finchden Manor, Tenterden, from 1935-1973. He had a way with the bright but delinquent or disturbed 14-22 year old boys who were referred to him from state and public schools by psychiatrists and magistrates. The aims of the research are: (1) to study all Lyward wrote, taught and achieved, and then apply his ideas and 'approach' to working in an 11-16 mixed school; (2) to contact as many staff, old pupils, visitors to Finchden, social workers and educationists who knew Lyward; (3) to obtain material by reading, interviewing, questioning, interpreting and elucidating, and by collecting original and unpublished material which is said to exist although scattered and in many hands. Results are not yet known.
Published Material: a full list of publications can be obtained from the researcher on request.
Source of Grant: Somerset Local Education Authority: Fees and monthly travel to Exeter funding is being sought from a St Luke's Trust Fund to cover further expenses
Date of Research: 1986-1990
KEYWORDS: *biography; community education; maladjusted; philosophy of education; school*

Further Education Unit

8/0395

Information Centre,
Grove House, 2-6 Orange Street, London WC2H 7WE
071 321 0433
Bolton, A. Ms
The development of employment led training provision in colleges of further education for those with special educational needs or disabilities
Abstract: This research arises out of the effect of demographic change on the labour market and its implications for people with disabilities or special educational needs who have placed themselves in the workforce. Much FE (further education) provision is based on life skills rather than pre-vocational or vocational training, although work carried out by the National Council for Vocational Qualifications and FEU has suggested that they can carry out a wider range of jobs if adequate training is provided. It will aim to develop and enhance employment led training provision for those with special educational needs or disabilities so that this group can take advantage of new employment opportunities. A project co-ordinator will, with the supervision of FEU, work with a group of colleges and LEAs, and each college/LEA will fund its own staff development activities. Two FEU publications, 'Learning Support' (a staff development resource pack) and 'Enabled to Work', (a study that examines the support needs of young people with disabilities), will be used as key material for initiating and supporting change. Institutions will draw upon their own individual action plans based on a needs analysis carried out in conjunction with the project co-ordinator. Review and evaluation will be built into each institutional plan and into the project as a whole. A handbook will be produced containing guidelines for developing employment led

training. There will be staff development sessions for college staff involved in work with learners with special educational needs or disabilities and the development of models of good practice that link colleges of FE with other agencies. A contribution to developing institutional expertise in the implementation of individual learning programmes will also be included.
Source of Grant: Further Education Unit
Date of Research: 1990 – continuing
KEYWORDS: *employment opportunities; further education; labour market; physically handicapped; special education; vocational training*

8/0396

Information Centre,
Grove House, 2-6 Orange Street, London WC2H 7WE
071 321 0433
Pursaill, J. Mr; *Supervisor:* Granger, M. Mr
Quality assurance in FE: BTEC validated courses
Abstract: This research arises out of recent developments of guidelines for evaluation, and encouraging institutions to take greater responsibility in preparing the re-validation of courses. As NVQs (National Vocational Qualifications) become established, it becomes increasingly important for colleges to concentrate on quality provision. The research aims to identify the relationship between internal course review and evaluation and re-validation by an external body. Also to monitor the effect of review and evaluation and re-validation procedures and the implications for curriculum development; organizational support; and staff development. It will be carried out by a project worker, reporting to a steering committee composed of BTEC (Business and Technician Education Council), CNAA (Council for National Academic Awards), HMI (Her Majesty's Inspectorate) and college senior managers and an advisory group composed mainly of the participating colleges. This will investigate current approaches to review, evaluation and re-validation, select a sample of colleges to represent different approaches to review and, evaluation and re-validation, different vocational sectors, and different client groups. There will be an investigation within the selected sample; of review, evaluation and re-validation procedures, procedures for consequent curriculum development, institutional response, staff development implications of quality assurance procedures, the role of external moderators in review evaluation and re-validation. There will be a series of case studies of review and evaluation in preparation for re-validation and a report on quality assurance procedures for BTEC validated courses identifying the benefits and implications for FE colleges.
Source of Grant: Further Education Unit
Date of Research: 1989-1990
KEYWORDS: *course; evaluation; further education; quality of education; validation*

8/0397

Grove House, 2-6 Orange Street, London WC2H 7WE
071 321 0433
Noble, P. Ms; King, K. Ms; *Supervisor:* Davies, R. Mr; Amner, P. Ms
Computer aided Records of Achievement
Abstract: The research follows up the 1984 Department of Education and Science policy statement that a national system of Records of Achievement should be developed. The advent of NVQs (National Vocational Qualifications), with competence based objectives, and an increased demand for more flexible modes of learning require more sophisticated record keeping systems. Recent changes in institutional systems have led to the development of more sophisticated CMIS (College Management Information Systems). This with the changes in aspects of curriculum development, relates directly to the record keeping systems in FE (further education) colleges. Also technology advances have led to cheaper and more sophisticated hardware and software systems. It will aim to survey existing developments in Computer Aided Records of Achievement and to facilitate these developments. A further aim is to clarify issues relating to Computer Aided Records of Achievement and CMIS. Finally to produce a draft user specification for a Computer Aided Records of Achievement system. A limited survey will be conducted of FE establishments and employment training establishments who are developing or piloting systems. Additional pilots of promising systems will be promoted and supported. An evaluation system for the surveying and piloting of these systems will also be devised, and from this a draft user specification will be derived. Eventually, two bulletins will be published which will outline the systems' features. A seminar for college management will be

organized to clarify issues relating to systems. A report will be produced covering the evaluation results and draft user specification. There will also be involvement in the general debate on the relationship between CMIS, Computer Aided Record of Achievement systems, curriculum development, institutional development and associated staff development.

Source of Grant: Further Education Unit
Date of Research: 1989-1990
KEYWORDS: computer uses in education; electronic data processing; further education; records of achievement; student record

8/0398

Information Centre,
Grove House, 2-6 Orange Street, London WC2H 7WE
071 321 0433
Rawlinson, S. Miss
Post 16 Core Skills
Abstract: The National Curriculum Council's 'Core Skills 16-19' offered recommendations for the implementation of core skills in A/AS levels and vocational courses. SEAC (School Examinations and Assessment Council) are now working on the practicability of implementing the core skills listed in the report, and how attainment might be described, assessed and reported. The NCVQ (National Council for Vocational Qualifications) is also to report on vocational courses in consultation with FEU/SEAC. The FEU has been carrying out a study of core skills in practice in eight colleges in order to create a set of criteria for learning programmes and procedures which foster the acquisition of core skills, and to examine the implications of these for assessment and certification. The present proposal would further develop this work by testing out the criteria in colleges with a view to refining them before recommending their incorporation. An FEU Development Officer will co-ordinate a series of pilot schemes in a cross section of schools and/or colleges. A Regional Development Officer in the appropriate region will work with a project worker in each of the colleges, to co-ordinate the development of core skills. College staff will also be involved by Steering Committee meetings, attendance at Development Workshops on core skills, and will produce reports which may form the basis for publications. Colleges will also be given finance for the manager and project workers to develop procedures, relevant materials and staff development. Overall co-ordination will be carried out by an FEU Development Officer. The eventual aim is to further refine the definition of core skills, the identification of characteristics of learning programmes and recording procedures which foster, recognize and reward attainments in core skills. There will be formative and summative reports and the final report could be used for regional developments.
Source of Grant: Further Education Unit
Date of Research: 1990 – continuing
KEYWORDS: core skill; further education; post-compulsory education; sixteen to nineteen education; vocational education

8/0399

Information Centre,
Grove House, 2-6 Orange Street, London WC2H 7WE
071 321 0433
Clyde, A. Mr
Training in context
Abstract: The Training Enterprise Education Division/FEU project, 'Training for the Future' (1990) involved 12 colleges developing interdisciplinary assignments to assist with the preparation of trainees to meet the current and future demands of industry. An assignment from Halesowen College identified concepts and methodology upon which future research could be based, and which would lead to demonstration materials and processes which will be adaptable for training in industry, colleges and training centres. Another, at Calderdale College, related to the development of a production control and manufacturing unit, and has provided experience in the delivery of integrated training of the type envisaged in the proposed project. The research will develop a curriculum framework that will be appropriate for the development of training, and produce modular learning and training materials which will all be appropriate for a range of levels with any company, education institution (14 +) or training organization. It will also identify appropriate methods of delivery of the curriculum, identify staff development issues and implement a staff development programme. The market research, curriculum development and implementation will be undertaken by staff of Halesowen College (Administration Base), Calderdale College, North Staffordshire Skills Centre and FEU (Further Education Unit) representatives, and other compa-

nies and colleges in the research programmes. This is the first phase of a larger exercise of market research, development of materials, piloting, evaluation and revision of materials, and a second phase of production and dissemination of project materials. This will encompass NCVQ (National Council for Vocational Qualifications) criteria and certification will be raised with national accreditation bodies. The project will report to the Training Enterprise Education Division on each phase. A curriculum framework and learning and training materials which have been evaluated within a variety of organizations and contexts will be cleared. Staff development guidelines will be considered, a number of trainers who have had experience in delivering the project materials, and finally proposals for dissemination of the project materials.
Source of Grant: Training Enterprise Education Division
Date of Research: 1990 – continuing
KEYWORDS: curriculum development; further education; industrial education; resource materials; training

8/0400

Information Centre,
Grove House, 2-6 Orange Street, London WC2H 7WE
071 321 0433
Murdin, M. Ms
The implememtation by colleges of further education of learning (and associated assessment procedures) leading to competence based qualifications for learners with special needs
Abstract: This research arises out of the development of National Vocational Qualifications and in particular the implications for learning with special needs. It aims to develop guidelines, including examples of good practice, for the FE (further education) system to implement competence based vocational qualifications for learners with special needs more effectively. A project co-ordinator will liaise with colleges, control the quality and progress of agreed activities, receive regular reports from the colleges, report to the FEU (Further Education Unit), visit the colleges, produce a final report, disseminate the information produced and attend meetings convened by the FEU/Training Enterprise Education Division. Work on the project will be based at 6 colleges of FE who will undertake development work. A final report will eventually be published. Guidelines will be produced for the FE system to assist in the implementation of competence-led programmes for learners with special needs. Intelligence data to inform the Work Related Further Education Development Fund 'overarching project' (RP 495 Extension) will be stated. Finally, guidelines for staff development; dissemination events including workshops and recommendations to the Training Enterprise Education Division will be produced. A bulletin describing the first phase of the FEU's work in this important area and based on work carried out by the Rathbone Society, supported by Remploy is available from the unit.
Source of Grant: Further Education Unit
Date of Research: 1990-1990
KEYWORDS: further education; National Vocational Qualification; special education; vocational education

8/0401

Information Centre,
Grove House, 2-6 Orange Street, London WC2H 7WE
071 321 0433
Longden, W. Mr
The institutionalisation of competence-led curricula
Abstract: The aim of the research is to develop case studies illustrating examples of good practice, for the FE (further education) system to implement more effectively the institutionalisation of competence-led curricula across all areas of college activity. In the first phase of the project (August to September 1989), a project consultant will be appointed and a consultative group formed to support the work of the co-ordinator. In the second phase (October 1989 to January 1990), the consultant will visit approximately 25 FE colleges to discuss the general implications of NVQ (National Vocational Qualification) developments with the principal/vice-principal senior management team of the college and explore with them how they view the future of the college and mechanisms for change. The final phase (February 1990 to Summer 1990) will involve a sample of the colleges being selected for in depth investigation. Case studies will be developed illustrating how a number of colleges coped with the demands of implementing a competence-led curricula, and reconciled these developments with other pressures on their institutions. The college case studies will form an FEU publication. Intelligence data will be provided to the 'overarching project' (RP 495 Extentsion). Recommendations will be

provided to the Training Enterprise Education Division Work Related Further Education Development Fund. Dissemination events will be offered.
Source of Grant: Further Education Unit
Date of Research: 1989-1990
KEYWORDS: competency based education; curriculum; further education; vocational education

8/0402

Grove House, 2-6 Orange Street, London WC2H 7WE
071 321 0433
Mid Kent College of Higher and Further Education
City Way, Rochester ME1 2AD
0634 830644
Levett, J. Mr

Civil engineering site management

Abstract: A survey of companies in the Kent area has shown there is a shortage of site management skills amongst their staff, and relevant training is required. Although there are training programmes in the building industry to develop such skills, there is no comparable competence based, flexible training programme for civil engineering staff. This research aims to assist with site management training for civil engineers and technicians. College staff will produce modules which will include material for self study and assessment and be supported by tutorials and tutor based assessment. A demand has been established for initial packages in production planning and organization, site surveying, setting out and dimensional control, practical aspects of technology, and project computing. College staff have a wide experience in the construction industry and draft materials will be prepared which will be piloted and evaluated. Comments will be sought for the professional institutions and other parties through a steering committee, and it is anticipated that company support will be forthcoming to support the production of four further training modules. It is planned to produce an evaluated series of modules suitable for training of civil engineers and technicians, and a report to the FEU describing the processes undertaken in the development and implementation of the training materials and an evaluation of their effectiveness
Source of Grant: Further Education Unit
Date of Research: 1990 – continuing
KEYWORDS: further education

8/0403

Elizabeth House, York Road, London SE1 7PH
071 934 9000
Canterbury College of Technology
New Dover Road, Canterbury CT1 3AJ
0227 66081
Price, T.K. Mr; Manser, E.D. Mr; *Supervisor:* Huxley, M. Ms

FEU (Further Education Unit) Project RP335: access of students with special educational needs directly into mainstream provision

Abstract: The aim of this project is to examine some of the curriculum implications of providing opportunities for those with learning difficulties to take part in mainstream provision. The project is divided into 3 phases: (1) to identify a small group of students with special educational needs who wish to seek direct admission to mainstream provision. The students under consideration are likely to have physical or sensory handicaps, in some cases allied to moderate learning difficulties. Identification will take place through: (i) an examination of applications to attend college courses; and (ii) consultations with various agencies in the locality involved in supporting young people with special educational needs. (2) A detailed needs analysis will be involved, focused on a small number of students selected from the group identified in (1). (3) This phase will be concerned with the implications for the institution and for the students seeking to make provision to meet the needs analysis completed in (2). Issues to be considered will include: (a) Appropriate staff development likely to assist changes in approach and attitude via general awareness; (b) raising changes in teaching and learning modes; (c) alternative validation processes; (d) implications for resources to support the learning situation, in particular the enhancement of student and staff support mechanisms; and (e) organizational change needed in response to the curriculum needs expressed through the project. During this phase it is hoped to provide the opportunity for at least one student to take part in a suitable form of existing mainstream provision and to monitor the student's progress and the results of implementing the arrangements determined in the early stages of the project. A final report is being pre-

pared which will be suitable for consideration for publication by FEU covering the following points: (i) it will set out the various elements in the process of curriculum change; (ii) it will assist this and other colleges to understand more fully the implications of extending mainstream provision to students with various forms of special need; and (iii) should provide pointers to the planning of future mainstream provision for this student group.
Source of Grant: Further Education Unit (FEU): £6,000
Date of Research: 1986 – continuing
KEYWORDS: curriculum development; further education; handicapped; integration; learning difficulty; special needs

Glasgow University

8/0404

Department of Psychology
Glasgow G12 8QQ
041 339 8855
Anderson, A.H. Dr; Garrod, S. Dr; Mullin, J. Mr

The development of referential communication skills from 7-15

Abstract: This project is intended to investigate the development over the school years (7-15) of the interactive communication skills needed to support reference. The project revolves around two well established techniques for eliciting dialogues in restricted settings: the map communication task developed by Brown, Anderson, Yule and Shillcock (1983) and the co-operative maze game task developed by Garrod and Mullin. Both techniques yield spontaneous dialogues containing references to locations on a map or a maze. In year 1 of the project we tested pairs of children from primary 4 primary 6 and secondary 2 on both tasks. In year 2 these children will be retested to obtain dialogues from primary 5, primary 7 and secondary 3. This sampling procedure will yield cross-sectional and longitudinal data from the children which will allow us to draw comparisons across skill level and age. The dialogues are transcribed and performances are assessed first in terms of the overall communication success achieved by each pair of subjects and secondly in terms of the interactional strategies that speakers of different ages adopt. The use of two somewhat different techniques increases the chance of finding convergent evidence on the principal interactional skills which children need to develop to become effective communicators.
Published Material: CLARKE, A. & GARROD, S. (1989). 'Semantic negotiation in school children,'. Paper presented at the biennial meeting of the Society for Research in Child Development, April 27-30th 1989, Kansas City, Missouri.; ANDERSON, A.H., CLARK, A. & MULLIN, J. (1989). Paper presented at the 3rd European Conference for Research on Learning & Instruction, September 4-7th, Madrid.
Source of Grant: ESRC (Economic and Social Research Council): £30,000
Date of Research: 1988-1990
KEYWORDS: interaction; language development; verbal communication

8/0405

Department of Psychology
Adam Smith Building, Glasgow G12 IRT
041 339 8855
Anderson, A.M. Dr; Morsbach, G. Dr

The development of reading skills in first and second language readers

Abstract: In this project, the researchers intend to test the development of a wide range of reading skills and sub-skills in pupils at various ages from primary 1 to secondary 4. Their interest lies in comparing the performances of readers whose first language is not English with their monolingual peers. They are interested in describing the relationship between various sub-skills to overall reading skill, particularly in those readers (first and second language readers) who are not developing very effective overall reading skill.
Published Material: MIRZA, Z. & MORSBACH, G. (1985). 'Home background and English language comprehension of Punjabi-speaking primary school children', New Community, Vol 12, pp.430-435.
Source of Grant: Application for funding to Leverhulme Trust
Date of Research: 1987-1990
KEYWORDS: foreign languages; performance; mother tongue; reading

8/0406
Department of Psychology
Adam Smith Building, Glasgow G12 8RT
041 339 8855
Garrod, S. Dr; Anderson, A.H. Dr
The development of spoken communication skills between 5-20 years
Abstract: This project uses techniques for eliciting and analyzing task orientated dialogue which have been developed by the researchers, and by Brown, Anderson and Shadbolt originally for use with adults and adolescents. However, in this case, they are going to be applied to children from 6-18 years, in order to investigate the development of interactive communication skills. Two major aspects of communication will be considered: (1) Ability to establish successful reference; and (2) ability to co-ordinate on a mutually accepted common conception of the dialogue domain and set of interpretation principles for expressions in the language. It is intended to use about 100 subjects in this project.
Published Material: BROWN, R.I.F., ANDERSON, A.H. & SHADBOLT, N. (1985). 'Listening Comprehension'. Report of SED Project JHH/190/1. ANDERSON, A.H. & GARROD, S. (in press). 'The Dynamics of Referential Meaning in Spontaneous Dialogue'. In: REILLY, R. (Ed.) Communication Failure in Dialogue. North-Holland.; ANDERSON, A.H. & GARROD, S. 'The dynamics of referential meaning in spontaneous dialogue'. In: REILLY, R. (Ed). Communication failure in dialogue. Barking: North-Holland. (in press).; GARROD, S. & ANDERSON, A.H. (1985). 'Some observations on the semantics of natural dialogue'. In: SEVREN, WEYTERS & HOPPEN-BROVERS (Eds). Meaning and the lexicon, pp.259-266. UNU Science Press.
Source of Grant: application for funding to ESRC (Economic and Social Research Council)
Date of Research: 1987-1989
KEYWORDS: interaction; language skill; oral expression; spoken language

Gloucestershire College of Arts and Technology (GLOSCAT)

8/0407
73 The Park, Cheltenham GL50 2RR
0242 532024
Whitfield, R. Prof.; Dekker, A. Ms
Completion rates and other performance indicators in educational opportunites for unwaged adults
Abstract: This small project was set up in the wake of the 1987 DES report 'Managing Colleges efficiently'. Its aim was to investigate completion rates and progression routes on educational opportunities for the unemployed, to examine reasons why some people failed to complete their courses, and to examine an appropriate range of performance indicators in this field. A combination of statistical data and qualitative data derived from questionnaires and informal interivews was used to illuminate the research problems. The study, though viewed within a county-wide context, focuses on courses for the unemployed at Gloucestershire College of Arts and Technology, which has sites at both Cheltenham and Gloucester. Gloucestershire LEA gives fee remission for unemployed adults who wish to study for up to 21 hours per week by 'in-filling' onto certain existing courses and onto courses which have been specially targeted for unemployed adults. This scheme operates in all LEA funded colleges in Gloucestershire and is supported by a separate educational guidance service for adults. Information gained in the study was used to examine the extent to which completion and certification rates are appropriate measures of success, and to examine other course performance indicators (such as incidental learning, peer-group contact, and changes in self-esteem) to indicate the value of participation in the educational opportunities available. The findings of the research relate to administrative parameters relevant to student growth (awareness of provision, enrolment and support services), the input profile of students, the educational process (course content, teaching methods and facilities) and outcomes (student progress, achievements and destinations). A range of practical difficulties for students was uncovered. Findings relate to the report 'Managing Colleges Efficiently' so as

to move the debate about performance indicators a small step forward. The project report concludes with a series of recommendations regarding performance indicators, institutional management and supportive policy research.
Published Material: WHITFIELD, R. and DEKKER, A. (1989). Completion rates and other performance indicators in educational opportunities for unwaged adults. Leicester: NIACE
Source of Grant: National Institute of adult continuing education (NIACE): £5,828
Date of Research: 1988-1988
KEYWORDS: adult education; dropout; educational provision; performance indicator; unemployed

8/0408
The Park Campus,
73 The Park, Cheltenham GL50 2RR
0242 532024
Whitfield, R.C. Prof.
Exploration of concerns and values in late adolescence
Abstract: Initially this is intended to be a piece of descriptive research among young people in the 16-21 year old age range. The aim is to ascertain issues of most concern to samples of these young people still in full or part-time study; gender, institutional and home environment relationships with the patterns of concerns are of interest. The main method of data collection is a confidential questionnaire administered under controlled conditions. This lists 27 topics of potential concern and asks questions about home circumstances, the nature of friendship, personal aspirations and help obtained or otherwise on the topic of most interest. The study is related to the investigator's interest in the broad area of preparing young people for adult roles in family life. A sample size of about 600 is being built up.
Source of Grant: No funding
Date of Research: 1986 – continuing
KEYWORDS: adolescence; ambition; family life; role; value; youth attitude

8/0409
Department of Art and Design Studies
Oxstalls Campus,
Oxstalls Lane, Gloucester GL2 9HW
0452 426799
Waddell, G. Mr; Butler, D. Ms; Litchfield, I. Ms; Makirinne-Crofts, P. Ms; Hillman, A. Ms
Computer aided design/computer aided manufacture
Abstract: The study of the latest innovations in computer aided manufacture and pattern design systems for application in different levels of teaching at degree, diploma and higher diploma level. Joint research initially between Gavin Waddell of the School of Fashion and William Bates of Computing, Electronic and Mathematical Studies to look into the future needs of the creative designer and the CAD systems for ACME (Application of Computers to Manufacturing Engineering). The results of this characterization process would help formulate a strategy for further research activities and would assist existing commercial organizations in planning CAD systems that link in with their existing CAM systems.
Date of Research: 1985-1989
KEYWORDS: computer; design; higher education; teaching technique

8/0410
Department of Environmental Studies
The Gloucester Centre for Environmental Education,
Oxstalls Campus,
Oxstalls Lane, Gloucester GL2 9HW
0452 426799
Supervisor: Sawyer, D. Rev.
Research into the natural and built environments of Gloucestershire
Abstract: The Centre is involved in researching and producing packs, booklets, leaflets, exhibitions, statistics and information for use by GLOSCAT (Gloucestershire College of Arts and Technology) departments, county schools and community groups.
Published Material: a full list of publications can be obtained from the researcher on request
Source of Grant: Gloucestershire County Council; Training Enterprise Education Division Community Programme RIBA (Royal Institute of British Architects) Architecture Workshop
Date of Research: 1983 – continuing
KEYWORDS: environmental study; teaching aids

8/0411

Department of Social and Scientific Studies
The Park Campus, 73 The Park, Cheltenham GL50 2RR
0242 532123
Cutting, E. Mrs; Fahey, W.S. Mr
Expectations of the School Health Service. Part I (1986): parental expectations of the Primary School Health Service
Abstract: Given the current emphasis on making 'services more responsible to the consumer' (HMSO Primary Health Care: 'An Agenda for Discussion') and the client-centred approach of the Cumberlege report that 'consumers should have a stronger voice' (J. Cumberlege Neighbourhood Nursing: 'A Focus for Care') the researchers decided to examine the views of a sample of parents rather than professionals in Part I (1986). The School Nursing Course class of 1986 investigated, with the help of the 2 tutors, in 15 different local authority areas of England and Wales. A sample of 160 parents were chosen randomly from primary school registers, but it was not possible to choose the schools themselves randomly. A two-part structured questionnaire was prepared by the tutors, designed to highlight significant variations in the level of parental demand for: (a) school health services; and (b) health education programmes. Parents were asked to indicate their expectations of 12 services and 8 education topics. Findings were correlated with social class, family type, and health or illness of children, etc., and presented via tables and histograms.
Source of Grant: No funding
Date of Research: 1986-1989
KEYWORDS: *expectancy; health education; health service; parental attitude; parent-school relation; primary education*

Harris City Technology College

8/0412

The Dyslexia Centre,
9 Maberley Road, Upper Norwood, London SE19
081 771 2261
Christchurch College
North Holmes Road, Canterbury CT1 1QU
0227 762444
Tod, J. Ms; *Supervisor:* Jones, L. Mr; Abbott, P. Mr
Dyslexia research project
Abstract: A three year research project has been set up at the Dyslexia Centre of the newly formed Harris City Technology College in Upper Norwood, South London. The research body is Harris City Technology College in conjunction with Christchurch College, Canterbury. The aim of the new centre is the development of best practice in the teaching of dyslexic students, the provision of special teacher training in this area of learning difficulty and the undertaking of research and development in the use of technology and materials appropriate to the teaching of dyslexic students. The aims of the project are: to measure the progress over three academic years of a group of pupils entering the Harris CTC in September 1990, diagnosed as having the specific learning difficulty known as dyslexia, using a range of approaches designed to enable these pupils to participate fully and effectively in the CTC curriculum which includes access to the National Curriculum; to devise new approaches and resource materials in order to test their value for pupils in the Harris CTC and to enable the Centre to develop resource materials for a wide use with the CTC age group (11-18); to develop the use of information technolgy and work with dyslexic pupils in the Harris CTC and to disseminate good practice in this respect.
Source of Grant: Department of Education and Science: £250,000 over three years
Date of Research: 1990 – continuing
KEYWORDS: *computer assisted instruction; dyslexia; learning difficulty; teacher education; teaching aids*

Harrow College of Higher Education

8/0413

Northwick Park, Harrow HA1 3TP
081 864 5422
Ward, R. Dr
Tutorial support for part-time students in higher education: problems and opportunities
Abstract: Although mature part-time students in higher education frequently require tutorial guidance and institutions claim to provide it, actual practice is extremely variable. Apart from organizational constraints, both the students and their tutors may have limited expectations of what might be achieved in a tutorial and fail to use the opportunity effectively. The research aims to establish the parameters of good tutorial practice with a view to initiating staff-development programmes. Investigations will take note of: (a) the logistics of providing tutorials; (b) perceptions of students and tutors and of their experiences; (c) the conduct of tutorials, strategies for learning.
Source of Grant: No funding
Date of Research: 1988 – continuing
KEYWORDS: *higher education; part-time student; tutorial*

8/0414

Northwick Park, Harrow HA1 B9P
081 864 5422
Cherrington, R. Ms; *Supervisor:* CROLL, E. DR
Youth and modernisation in contemporary China
Abstract: This research is based on initial observations during a sabatical in China of the various reactions of youth in contemporary China to the recent 'Open Door' and modernisation policies. The very nature and definitions of youth seem to be changing as Chinese society becomes a modern industrial nation. The state, however, still has centralised power over youth and through the use of its propaganda and information departments emit messages of the 'Ideal' young person. Research is to cover the form of this ideal and how youths in real life match up to this. A variety of sociological perspectives need to be considered and their usefulness as a tool for understanding contemporary Chinese youth assessed.
Published Material: CHERRINGTON, R. (1987). 'Student Demonstration in China', Times Educational Supplement, 9th January.; CHERRINGTON, R. (1987). 'Urban change in a small town', China Now, February.
Source of Grant: No funding
Date of Research: 1986 – continuing
KEYWORDS: *china; youth; sociology*

Hatfield Polytechnic

8/0415

Occupational Research Centre,
PO Box 109, College Lane, Hatfield AL10 9AB
07072 79000
Taylor, J.A. Mrs; *Supervisor:* Kirton, M.J. Mr; O'Connor, N. Mr
Investigation of self-reported problems and difficulties of high-IQ secondary school children in relation to their cognitive style and other variables
Abstract: High intelligence is no guarantee of success: while some children of high intellectual ability succeed in school, being well adjusted and performing outstandingly, others, of equally high ability, seem to cause problems for themselves and others, are persistently seen as difficult and abrasive, and sometimes drop out all together. Some of these differences may be explained in terms of Adaption-Innovation theory: adaptors may fit well into systems and make the most use of them, being well adjusted and doing well at school; innovators may experience more problems, even generating them for themselves. Reported difficulties and problems may be different or even exacerbated in those of high intelligence. A critical outcome of the work will be the analysis, in relation to the background variables, of the advantages and disadvantages gifted children have in consequence of their cognitive style, and the ways in which they exploit their advantages and cope with their disadvantages. The Kirton Adaption-Innovation Inventory and a group test of general intelligence will be given to two whole years in two schools. The top 5% in terms of IQ score, and a small non-gifted sample, will be presented with a detailed questionnaire. This will relate directly to the problem of explaining academic success, or lack of it, in terms of A-I theory, e.g., attitudes to school discipline, favoured methods of working, preferred style of teaching, etc. Information concerning ways of managing problems arising from

a combination of cognitive style and intelligence will be ordered to give greater understanding of the relationship between these two concepts.
Source of Grant: Fees, expenses: paid by employer
Date of Research: 1987-1990
KEYWORDS: adjustment; cognition; gifted; performance; secondary education

8/0416
Department of Education
College Lane, Hatfield AL10 9AB
94 79000
Campbell, R. Dr
Hearing children read
Abstract: Now in its second phase, this study aims to explore the effectiveness of various teacher responses to the mistakes of early beginning readers. An in depth case study of two children reading to their teacher throughout a school year has been conducted. Interactions were audio-recorded and subsequently transcribed. Results have suggested that a word cueing strategy was particularly helpful to the reader. However effectiveness needs to be explored at various levels and recent articles have debated this topic.
Published Material: CAMPBELL, R. (1986). 'Social relationships in hearing children read', Reading, Vol 20, No 3, pp.157-167. December.; CAMPBELL, R. (1987). 'Oral reading errors of two beginning readers', Journal of Research in Reading, Vol 10, No 2, pp.144-155, September.; CAMPBELL, R. (1988). 'Is it time for USSR, SSR, SQUIRE, DEAR or ERIC?, Education, Vol 16, No 2, pp.3-13, June.; CAMPBELL, R. (1988). Hearing children read. London: Routledge
Source of Grant: No funding
Date of Research: 1980 – continuing
KEYWORDS: early reading; mistake; reading aloud; teacher-pupil relation; teaching technique

8/0417
Department of Education
Wall Hall Campus, Aldenham, Watford WD2 8AT
9486 852511
Thornton, M.E. Ms; *Supervisor:* Young, M.F.D. Mr
Subject specialization and the primary school curriculum
Abstract: It is intended to critically examine the effects of an increasing centralist emphasis upon subject specialism in the primary school and the implications this might have: (a) for the tradition of generalist class teaching in the primary school sector, (b) for the curriculum as experienced by primary aged pupils, and (c) the teaching methods and organizational features through which it is transmitted. School based investigations will take place in the Autumn of 1988. It is anticipated that the sample will include all infant, junior and JMI (junior mixed infants) schools in one division of a local education authority. In each school curriculum guidelines will be examined, the head teacher and a selection of teaching staff will be interviewed (determined by age of pupils taught e.g. 5-, 7- and 11 years), and classroom observations will be made on the basis of teaching staff interviewed.
Source of Grant: Hatfield Polytechnic: 75% of fees
Date of Research: 1986-1990
KEYWORDS: curriculum development; curriculum subject; primary education; specialization

8/0418
Department of Education
Wall Hall Campus, Aldenham, Watford WD2 8AT
9486 852511
Jackson, A. Dr
Children's early spelling
Abstract: The research is directed at the early stages of literacy acquisition with special emphasis on beginning writing and spelling. The theoretical background rests on the work of Dr Uta Frith, and, in particular her model of how children learn to read and write. (Frith 1986). The model suggests that children should start by spelling 'logographically' before they spell 'alphabetically,' which in turn, is superceded by correct, 'orthographic' spelling. The aim of this project was to collect young children's attempts at spelling to see if they were, in fact, spelling logographically. It was also intended to follow these children over a few months to see if there were any changes as they developed. Five months were spent visiting nursery schools and playgroups during which the drawings and writings of more than 100 children were collected. As their own name is usually the first thing that children learn to write, all chil-

dren were asked to write that. They were also asked to write any other words they knew to get as many examples as possible of their writing. In addition, all children were asked to draw a man (Goodenough: Draw-a-man-test) to get an indication of the child's intellectual maturity. This procedure was repeated on each successive visit. The majority of data has now been collected and analysis will commence soon. In order to assess the children's writing a categorization system has been devised. Preliminary analysis suggests that young children do engage in logographic writing but that there is little relationship between the relative sophistication of children's drawing and writing.
Source of Grant: No funding
Date of Research: 1988-1990
KEYWORDS: early childhood education; spelling; writing

8/0419
Department of Education
Wall Hall Campus, Aldenham, Watford WD2 8AT
09276 2511
Kernohan, H. Mr
Visual memory in children
Abstract: Short-term visual memory tasks involving simultaneously presented data are given to two age groups of profoundly deaf children and the results compared with those of control groups of hearing children. As expected, complexity of task, fast presentation time and increased retention interval adversely affect recall. Examination of the organizational output of the subjects suggests that different recall strategies are employed by the two groups.
Published Material: KERNOHAN, H. (1986). 'Visual memory for simultaneously presented data', Journal of the British Association of Teachers of the Deaf, Vol 10, No 1, pp.4-9.
Source of Grant: No funding
Date of Research: 1985 – continuing
KEYWORDS: deaf; memory; visual perception

8/0420
Department of Education
Wall Hall Campus, Aldenham, Watford WD2 8AT
07072 79000
Jackson, A. Dr
Microcomputer use in the primary school
Abstract: This is an extension of research commenced at postgraduate level (towards a PhD). It investigates some of the psychological variables which influence children's performance during microcomputer based problem solution when working alone or in groups. It also considers the current uses of microcomputers in primary education, and factors which affect use. Previous surveys (see publications) have revealed that microcomputers are primarily used for group rather than individualised instruction in the primary school. This research addresses the question of why, and whether groups of children show superior performance compared to children working alone on a series of mathematical problems. All experiments have been, and will be conducted in primary schools working with 10- to 11- year old children. Performance is examined in terms of (1) time to problem solution, (2) number of moves to solution, (3) types of moves made. Over 300 children have been tested in 5 experiments so far. Initial results indicate that groups of 3 children do show superior on-task decision making to individuals. There was an indication that group interaction could be more beneficial for performance over and above the provision of a software based 'help-facility'. Further investigations will include (1) differences in decision making strategy between groups and individuals, and (2) the conditions under which intragroup discussion is beneficial to performance.
Published Material: JACKSON, A., FLETCHER, B.(C) & MESSER, D.J.(1986) 'A survey of microcomputer use and provision in primary school', Journal of Computer Assisted Learning, Vol 2, No 1, pp 45-55.; JACKSON, A., FLETCHER, B. (C). & MESSER, D.J. (1988). 'Effects of experience on microcomputer use in primary schools: results of a second survey', Journal of Computer Assisted Learning, Vol 4, No 4, pp.214-226, December.; MESSER, D.J., JACKSON, A. & MODHAMEDALI, M. (1987). 'Influences on computer based problem solving: help facilities, intrinsic orientation, gender and home computing', Educational Psychology, Vol 7, No 1, pp.33-46.
Source of Grant: No funding
Date of Research: 1988 – continuing
KEYWORDS: group work; individual work performance; microcomputer; primary education; problem solving

8/0421

Department of Education and Humanities
Wall Hall Campus, Aldenham, Watford WD2 8AT
0923 852511
Miller, L.K. Mrs; *Supervisor:* Campbell, R. Dr; Trendall, C. Dr

The share-a-book project
Abstract: The project has arisen from the growing awareness of insights on learning to read to be gained by observing young children's earliest interactions with print and the increasing recognition of the role of the home environment and parental involvement in promoting early literacy development. A successful initiative in this area has been the introduction of shared reading schemes in primary schools, which recognize the importance of parents reading to and sharing books with their children. The share-a-book scheme will extend into pre-school. The principles embodied in the concept of shared reading schemes could be viewed as a pre-cursor to such a scheme. The research will focus upon the implementation and evaluation of a 'share-a-book' scheme in a community playgroup and will involve a group of 40 experimental group children and their parents with 10 control children and parents. Evaluation will relate to the children's emerging literacy skills and linked parental behaviour. The viability of the scheme will be evaluated for Cambridgeshire library service. Quantitative and qualitative methods of data collection will be used. These will include; (i) recording the number of books loaned and parental comments on these; (ii) a pre/post questionnaire relating to the children's emerging literacy skills and related parental behaviour; (iii) pre and post testing of the children's concepts about print; (iv) tape recordings of parents and children in naturalistic story reading sessions.
Source of Grant: No funding
Date of Research: 1988-1990
KEYWORDS: *early reading; literacy; parent participation; primary education*

8/0422

Department of Humanities and Education
Wall Hall Campus, Aldenham WD2 8AT
0923 852511 ext 3941
Campbell, R. Dr; Scrivens, G. Mrs; Mangan, M. Mr

an investigation of sustained silent reading in the primary school
Abstract: Following the strong recommendations that there should be more emphasis on silent independent reading in primary schools there is limited evidence that the procedure defined as SSR (sustained silent reading) can have a beneficial effect on childrens attitudes to reading and reading achievement when used with a course of reading instruction. The aim of the study is; (i) to identify schools using SSR within the local division and/or county by means of a questionnaire; (ii) to explore and analyze how SSR is organized within some of these schools; (iii) to investigate how the activity is perceived by teachers, children and parents by means of triangulation methods and interviews; (iv) to ascertain any possible gains in reading performance or attitudes to reading assessed within the schools; (v) to discover any particular problems these schools might experience in the use of SSR. If this project is extended it will follow the form of an investigation of an adaption of SSR named 'Book-Time' which would be set up in one or more nursery schools or play groups. There is very little evidence to date of the organizational difficulties which might occur or of the benefits to 3-5 year old children. This study would, therefore, be providing a contribution to knowledge about pedagogical practices.
Published Material: CAMPBELL, R. (1988). 'Is it time for USSR, SSR, Squirt, Dear or Eric?', Education 3-13, Vol 16, No 2, June 1988, pp.22-25.; CAMPBELL, R. (1989). 'The teachers as a role model during sustained silent reading', Reading, Vol 23, No 3, November 1989, pp.179-183.
Source of Grant: No funding
Date of Research: 1988 – continuing
KEYWORDS: *primary education; reading; silent reading*

8/0423

Department of Psychology
College Lane, Hatfield AL10 9AB
07072 79623
Fletcher, B. Dr; *Supervisor:* Messer, D.J.A. Dr

Psychological aspects of microcomputer use in schools
Abstract: The project has a number of major strands, each of which has been investigated in both the primary and secondary school settings: (1) survey of the provision and use of microcomputers in schools, including teacher and headteacher attitudes which may

affect use. (2) The comparative efficacy of group versus individual microcomputer use, and an examination of solid and cognitive factors which affect problem solving performance. (3) Consideration of the role of software-based feedbacks in learning (including informational and motivational feedback, competitive feedback, graphical feedback, software-based 'help', delayed and immediate feedback) In class experimentation/observation is continuing. The projects are primarily concerned with determining those aspects of microcomputers which may have a major impact on childrens learning. To date several hundred children, and around three hundred teachers have participated in the research.
Published Material: FLETCHER, B.(C). (1985). 'Group and individual learning of junior school children on a microcomputer based task', Educational Review, Vol 37, No 3, pp.251-261.; JACKSON, A., FLETCHER, B. (C). & MESSER, D.J.A. (1986). 'Survey of microcomputer use and provision in primary schools', Journal of Computer Assisted Learning, Vol 2, No 1, March/April, pp.45-55.; MOHAMEDALI, M.H., MESSER, D.J.A. & FLETCHER, B. (C). (1987). 'Factors affecting microcomputer and programming ability in secondary school children', Journal of Computer Assisted Learning, Vol 3, No 4, September, pp.224-239.; MESSER, D.J.A., JACKSON, A. & MOHAMEDALI, M. (1987). 'Help facilities, intrinsic orientation, gender and home computing: influences on computer based problem solving', Educational Psychology, Vol 7, No 1, pp.33-46.
Source of Grant: Economic and Social Research Council (ESRC) Hertfordshire County Council
Date of Research: 1984-1990
KEYWORDS: *feedback; groupwork; individual work; microcomputer; problem solving; behaviour*

Heriot-Watt University

8/0424

Department of Business Organization
Chambers Street, Edinburgh EH1 1HX
031 449 5111
Keenan, A.

The recruitment of graduates, with special reference to selection interviews
Abstract: To improve our understanding of graduate processes, particularly psychological factors in selection interviews. The ultimate aim of the research is to improve graduate recruitment from both students' and employers' perspectives.
Published Material: KEENAN, A. (1976). 'Interviewers' evaluations of application characteristics: differences between personnel and non-personnel managers', Journal of Occupational Psychology, Vol 49, pp.223-230.
Date of Research: 1974 – continuing
KEYWORDS: *employment; graduate; interview; selection criterion*

Hotel and Catering Training Board

8/0425

International House, High Street, Ealing, London W5 5DB
081 579 2400
Battersby, D.L.N. Mr; Locke, G. Mrs

Local collaborative project on tourism in London
Abstract: The project has been put together at the request of the Manpower Services Commission and the Department of Education and Science, by the Hotel and Catering Training Board in conjunction with the London Visitor and Convention Bureau. Collaboration has been made with trade and professional bodies, colleges of further education, polytechnics, private and public sector employers and local education authorities. There is currently a skill shortage in the tourism industry with insufficient new employees attracted to the work offered. In addition, existing vocational and training provision is inadequate to meet current and future needs. The overall aim of the project is to assist employers, education and training providers to work together to ensure that the training needed for employment in tourism is available and accessible for adults employed across London, and to define the action needed

to ensure that any training that takes place results in a cost effective investment in terms of greater stability of the workforce. The project is in 5 stages: (1) Definition of the training task. The collaborating providers have formed 3 task groups in the areas of: (a) hotel and catering; (b) tourism and leisure; and (c) travel and transport. Each group will determine the content of tourism training needs by means of up to 200 case studies and will review existing training and education. Overview research will draw together the scope and size of the tourism industry and establish occupational profiles. (2) From the above information will come an analysis of action needed. (3) Stage 3 will be the development of provision including piloting and evaluation. (4) This stage will establish and promote the new provision. (5) Stage 5 will be ongoing throughout the project, strengthening long term collaboration between all parties.
Source of Grant: Department of Education and Science (DES): £100,000 English Tourist Board: £10,000
Date of Research: 1986-1989
KEYWORDS: employment; manpower need; tourism; vocational training

Huddersfield Polytechnic

8/0426

Department of Education
Holly Bank Road,
Lindley,
Huddersfield HD3 3BP
0484 425611
Bennett, Y. Dr; Thorpe, S. Ms
The teaching and learning of computer literacy/information technology on the Youth Training Scheme with reference to gender
Abstract: A multi-method approach was used involving case studies, observations and a questionnaire to 100 trainees (62 girls, 38 boys) on seven sites. The speciific foci of the research were the gender dimensions of the Youth Training Scheme in the context of information technology. The aim was to investigate to what extent the girls' experience of information technology under the Youth Training Scheme was comparable to that of boys. On-the-job training experiences were found to be qualitatively quite different for boys and girls; the boys had access to a variety of work experiences whilst for the girls training was narrowly defined, where it involved the use of computers. The association of computers with other forms of technical knowledge placed computer related activities in the terrain of masculine pursuits. The teaching-learning environment was often embued with practices and coded references that raised gender as a relevant aspect in the learning of computer related skills.
Source of Grant: Kirklees Education Authority: Approximately £20,000
Date of Research: 1983-1988
KEYWORDS: information technology; sex difference; Youth Training Scheme

8/0427

Department of Education
Holly Bank Road,
Huddersfield HD3 3AN
0484 25611
Huddersfield Royal Infirmary
Acre Street,
Huddersfield
0484 22191
Logue, R. Mr; *Supervisor:* Roberts, G.L. Dr; Sheehan, J. Mr; Robson, C. Prof.
The role of the staff nurse
Abstract: Because of dissatisfaction expressed about the initial training of nurses for their later role as staff nurses the aim is to critically analyze the role of the staff nurse with a view to suggesting more appropriate education and training. Non-participant observation at two hospitals (N = 50) and a survey of nurses, doctors and others involved with staff nurses (N = 600) has been carried out at several hospitals. Results are in the process of being analyzed.
Source of Grant: No funding
Date of Research: 1982-1989
KEYWORDS: nurse; vocational education

8/0428

Department of Education
Holly Bank Road, Lindley, Huddersfield HD3 3BP
0484 425611
Atipioko, E. Mr; Benett, Y. Dr; *Supervisor:* Swift, D. Dr
A study of morale in a sample of engineering lecturers in further education
Abstract: The aim of this study was to investigate the meaning and dimensionality of morale amongst engineering lecturers in a sample of colleges of further education in Yorkshire. The field work was in two phases. Phase 1 was a qualitative study intended to elicit lecturers' statements about morale. As a result, 96 statements were selected to characterize the 16 aspects of teaching which the respondents associated with morale. These statements were then incorporated into a questionnaire which was completed by 211 lecturers in five other colleges of further education. In Phase 2, the questionnaire data was analyzed using (a) a principal components analysis, (b) a series of two-way analyses of variance, to measure differences in morale between mechanical engineering lecturers and electronics engineering lecturers. The results showed that there were statistically significant differences with regard to four aspects, namely salaries, teaching equipment, falling rolls, and student behaviour.
Source of Grant: The British Government Technical Co-operation Training Awards: Approximatley £16,000
Date of Research: 1986-1988
KEYWORDS: engineering; further education; morale; teacher

8/0429

Department of Education
Holly Bank Road, Lindley, Huddersfield HD3 3BP
0484 425611
Bennett, Y. Dr; McGoldrick, C. Ms
Open learning in polytechnics and colleges of higher education
Abstract: The project aim was to provide information which would contribute to the expansion of the use of open learning in advanced further education and to the advice given to local education authorities. The research examined how open learning has been implemented in institutions (particularly polytechnics) which provide advanced further education. Ten institutions which are providers of advanced further education were visited over a period of seven weeks. In each institution key informants were interviewed about the institutional policy on open learning, the funding of the open learning provision and the deployment of the staff involved. A semi-structured interview schedule was used. The findings showed that there was a pervasive feeling of marginalisation from the respectable mainstream of full-time and sandwich education. One constraint was that for work at degree level writers of open learning materials need to bring the materials up to date constantly and that this can be costly.
Published Material: Further Education Unit (1987) Implementing open learning in local authority institutions; 2nd ed. London: FEU.
Source of Grant: Further Education Unit, Training Agency: Approximately £10,000
Date of Research: 1987-1988
KEYWORDS: educational policy; higher education; open learning

8/0430

Department of Education
Holly Bank Road, Lindley, Huddersfield HD3 3BP
0484 425611
Benett, Y. Dr; Lee, B. Prof.
The assessment of supervised work experience
Abstract: There is evidence that the benefits of work experience are considerable. However, it is not clear what procedures for learning at the workplace and for assessing the learning outcomes are best. The aim of the research was to identify and describe examples of good practice for the assessment of work. The study has focused on the supervised work experience component of CNAA validated courses in each of four subject areas at the polytechnic (Huddersfield) namely, business, computing, education and engineering. An intensive, comparative, case study approach was used. The data analysis has examined variations within each course and between the four courses. As a result of the study an assessment model for supervised work experience has been developed and the underlying theoretical issues have been clarified.
Source of Grant: Council for National Academic Awards (CNAA); Development Services: Approximately £25,500
Date of Research: 1987-1989
KEYWORDS: assessment; higher education; work experience

Hull University

8/0431
> 173 Cottingham Road, Hull HU5 2EH
> 0482 860806
> Andrews, R.J.; *Supervisor:* Protherough, R. Dr

A study of narrative and argument writing in three Beverley comprehensive schools
Abstract: The aim of the study is to explore the connection between narrative and argument, with particular reference to the teaching of the 'essay' form. The hypothesis is that narrative structures underpin those of the argument and that a clarification of this relationship might well provide a basis for helping students of all ages to write essays more readily. The study will limit itself to writing in all the primary and secondary schools in one town: Beverley in East Yorkshire, where there are 3 large comprehensives. Methods used will include interviews, questionnaires and most importantly, analysis of scripts, as well as observation of teaching methods. The study will draw on the various disciplines of literature, psychology of child development, linguistics and education.
Published Material: ANDRES, R. (1989). Narrative and argument. Buckingham: Open University Press.
Source of Grant: Seedcorn grant from University of Hull: £685
Date of Research: 1987 – continuing
KEYWORDS: argumentation; composition; narration; writing; written expression

8/0432
> Department of Adult and Continuing Education
> Hull HU6 7RX
> 0482 46311
> *Supervisor:* Squires, G. Dr; Bright, B. Dr

Dissatisfaction of religious studies students in church colleges of higher education
Abstract: The problem being investigated is the observed dissatisfaction of some religious studies students who undertake causes in higher education. The study will be concerned to look at attitude formation prior to college and how this may affect the response certain students make to causes in academic theology. The study will try to make some assessment about the motivation which brought these students onto such courses. It is intended to engage in qualitative research by extended (structure) conversations rather than quantative research. The sample will probably be very small and be limited to one or two such institutions. The aim of the study is practical, to consider teaching methods, aims of such causes, student expectations and curriculum design. It is not intended that this research should be anything more than particular to specific institutions, i.e. the church colleges of higher education.
Date of Research: 1987 – continuing
KEYWORDS: higher education; motivation; religious education; student behaviour; theology

8/0433
> Department of Education
> Cottingham Road, Hull HU6 7RX
> 0482 46311
> Wing, F.P. Mr

The development of higher education in a developing city: Hong Kong, 1900-1980
Abstract: The main aim of this study is to trace the development of higher education in Hong Kong in the period 1900 to 1980. From the study, several characteristics of British policy towards the development of the education system in the colony are apparent. During the period from 1843 to 1900, influences emanating from Britain, China and Hong Kong had an effect upon the education system in the colony. In the beginning of the twentieth century, changes in educational thinking led to the expansion of secondary, tertiary and technological provision. Education ceased to be a laissez-faire matter and became a prime object of planning and policy. In the area of higher education, the English speaking University of Hong Kong followed the English tradition and attempted to maintain acceptable academic standards. The University was set up in 1910 with the purpose of meeting local needs, although it had a secondary purpose of serving neighbouring areas, particularly China. It was an elite institution. The Chinese University of Hong Kong, which was founded in 1963 offered degrees of equivalent standard to the University of Hong Kong. The teaching medium was Chinese and it followed the American system of the four-year college. Both universities in the colony, however, had their special mission in building a "cultural link" between the East and West. In 1972, the Hong Kong Polytechnic was founded – as a natural outgrowth of the Technical College. The political status of the colony exerted a great influence in the development of higher education, because it was impractical for her to gain self-government or independence. Unlike other British colonies, the special role of the universities and colleges founded on the Asquith plan was defined by the Asquith Commission essentially within the context of preparation for national self-government. Thus the universities and other institutions of higher education in the colony had to follow their own programme of development. This thesis is an analysis of the progress made.
Source of Grant: No funding
Date of Research: 1986-1988
KEYWORDS: educational policy; higher education; Hong Kong

8/0434
> Department of Education
> Cottingham Road, Hull HU6 7RX
> 0482 46311
> Al-Mosawi, N.H. Mr; *Supervisor:* McClelland, V.A. Dr

An analytical study of the utilization of classroom verbal interaction in social studies teaching in the secondary schools of Bahrain
Abstract: Analyzing Classroom Verbal Interaction (CVI) by means of systematic observation is receiving insufficient attention in Bahrain. The present study aims to establish how far CVI skills are utilized in the teaching of social studies in secondary schools in Bahrain and to help develop such utilization by means of the 'Verbal Interaction Category System' (VICS) of Amidon and Hunter as a systematic observation technique. The study uses two research methods; descriptive and experimental. It is designed to examine four null hypotheses concerning the utilization of CVI skills in connection with: sex, qualification, years of experience and teaching subjects. All social studies teachers in the secondary schools of Bahrain are subjects of the study. A multi-stage field work project has been designed and carried out. It embraces a questionnaire; two observations of CVI performance and a training programme for the experimental group by means of an instructional module along with a pre-test and a post-test. The findings of the first observation (prior to the training programme) indicate: (a) that the lecturing style is still regarded as the favourite teaching method for social studies; (b) the absence of most CVI skills; (c) that CVI generally takes place between the teacher and the pupils rather than between the pupils themselves; and (d) the wide use of narrow questions which mainly require the eliciting of factual information. The findings of the second observation (post-training programme) indicate that the training programme had greatly helped the experimental group teachers to improve and develop their understanding and use of CVI skills. It has been recommended that teacher training programmes include a special topic dealing with CVI by means of the systematic observation technique. It has also been recommended that special attention be given to the use of a variety of teaching strategies, particularly those which create positive verbal interaction in the classroom, and to the formulation and use of a variety of oral questions with an emphasis upon those dealing with high level cognitive processes.
Source of Grant: Bahrain University
Date of Research: 1985-1988
KEYWORDS: Bahrain; history; secondary education; teaching method; verbal interaction

8/0435
> Department of Education
> Cottingham Road, Hull HU6 7RX
> 0482 46311
> Duffy, H. Fr; *Supervisor:* McClelland, V.A. Prof.

The effects of Vatican Council II on the development of theology as an integral part of liberal education
Abstract: This study presents the relationship between liberal education and Catholic theology. To introduce the relationship there are presentations describing: (1) the mutual functions of liberal education and Catholic theology; (2) the ongoing relationship between liberal education and Catholic theology. These presentations are given in the first two chapters. Chapter one sets the stage, explaining the function of the liberal arts and the liberal sciences with respect to theology, and the function of theology with respect to the liberal arts and the liberal sciences. Chapter two offers an historical analysis of the ongoing relationship between liberal education and Catholic theology, showing how liberal education has been responsible for developments in Catholic theology and how Catholic

theology has influenced developments in liberal education. The second chapter focuses on three important periods which represent major shifts in the relationship between liberal education and Catholic theology. These periods are described as The Hellenistic Period, The Scholastic Period, and The Modern Period. The second part of the study deals with the perennial issue of methodology in liberal education and Catholic theology. This latter part of the study describes the transition that took place in liberal education and Catholic theology from a classical methodology to an historico-contemporary method. Chapter three, which begins the second part of the study, deals with method in liberal education and Catholic theology prior to Vatican Council II. Chapter four discusses method in liberal education and Catholic theology after Vatican Council II. The last chapter shows the effects of an historico-contemporary methodology on liberal education and Catholic theology.

Source of Grant: No funding
Date of Research: 1986-1989
KEYWORDS: catholicism; liberal education; theology

8/0436
Department of Education
Cottingham Road, Hull HU6 7RX
0482 46311
9 Eylul Universitesei
Buca Egitim Fakultesi, Buca, Ismir, Turkey
Moore, J.L. Dr; Songun, R. Prof.
A comparative study of students; attitudes to technology education as functions of teacher, pupil, classroom and some social variables in Turkey and the UK
Abstract: This research has been developed from a study of attitudes and classroom practices in secondary school computer education. Classroom environment and technology attitude scales for use with post-secondary students in technology schools and FE colleges in the UK and Turkey will be selected and validated. The instruments will be used to look for relationships between attitudes and classroom variables in groups of students studying on a range of technology-based courses. It is hoped that results can be applied to the design and content of technical teacher training courses.
Source of Grant: No funding
Date of Research: 1989 – continuing
KEYWORDS: attitude; further education; teacher education; technology

8/0437
Department of Education
Cottingham Road, Hull HU6 7RX
0482 46311
Warburton, P. Mr; *Supervisor:* Sleap, M. Mr
National Survey of children's activity patterns
Abstract: Of all man's diseases, statistics show that coronary heart disease is the most serious in terms of premature death and disablement. Evidence now shows that, in addition to cigarette smoking, high blood pressure and high serum cholesterol, lack of physical activity is a major risk factor. Preliminary findings suggest that young children are not active enough to ensure protection from heart disease. This survey aims to provide a detailed analysis of the activity patterns of children aged five to eleven years. Data is being collected by two methods. (a) an activity diary which is completed by the parent or guardian of the child, (b) direct observation of the child during their free time. The survey involves a sample of five thousand children from all regions of England. The main focus of the results will be upon the frequency of vigorous activity displayed by the children. There will also be considerable attention paid to the range and type of activities in which the children engage.
Source of Grant: The Sports Council Children's Play and Recreation Unit: £12,000
Date of Research: 1988-1989
KEYWORDS: child; exercise; health

8/0438
Department of Education
Cottingham Road, Hull HU6 7RX
0482 463111
Warren, J. Mr; *Supervisor:* McClelland, V.A. Prof.
The treatment of moral and intellectual education in (British) radical and denominational periodicals c.1825-1875
Abstract: The 19th Century was obsessed with both education and the periodical. Periodicals were regarded as highly influential on politically significant public opinion. They also offered what Gissing

called 'specialism popularized': the writings of influential thinkers rendered accessible for the educated, but preoccupied, reader. An analysis of the treatment of education in selected periodicals should therefore provide important insights into 19th century attitudes to education through a medium which has not been adequately researched to this time. The following are to be considered: (1) the extent to which the periodicals follow a constant stance on education; (2) the reaction of the periodical writers to important social and political measures. The research concentrates on moral and intellectual education, since these aspects reflect the twin concerns of many 19th century writers on education, who found that division of the topic both meaningful and fruitful.
Source of Grant: No funding
Date of Research: 1987-1990
KEYWORDS: history of education; periodical

8/0439
Department of Education
Cottingham Road, Hull HU6 7RX
0482 46311
Waugh, D.G. Mr; *Supervisor:* Gorwood, B. Dr
Implementing educational changes in primary school with particular reference to small schools
Abstract: the research takes the form of questionnaire and survey work on the methods used, and problems encountered, when primary schools attempt to meet the requirements of the 1988 Education Reform Act. A survey of around 200 schools is being undertaken and a number of case studies will be made. The aim of the research is to determine whether school size affects the ability to implement change. It is hoped that recommendations can be made, which will draw upon examples of 'good practice', to enable schools to fulfil legal requirements in an educationally acceptable way.
Source of Grant: Hull University: fees
Date of Research: 1990 – continuing
KEYWORDS: educational change; educational legislation

8/0440
Department of Education
Cottingham Road, Hull HU17 8SP
0482 46311
Sleap, M. Mr
Happy heart project
Abstract: The Happy Heart project is an initiative which aims to promote active lifestyles among primary school children. After three years of development work and trialling in over one hundred schools, a number of resources have now been produced to help teachers promote active lifestyles. The present phase of the project involves dissemination of project ideas and resources in approximately sixty education authorities. Evaluation will take the form of feedback from teachers regarding the usefulness of project resources and assessment of children's activity levels before and after involvement in Happy Heart work
Published Material: SLEAP, M. & PERCH, J. (1990). Happy heart 1. Surrey: Thomas Nelson.; SLEAP, M. & WARBURTON, P. (1990). Happy heart 2. Surrey: Thomas Nelson.; SLEAP, M. & HICKMAN, J. (1990). PE for life 1. London: Health Education Authority.; SLEAP, M. (1990). PE for life 2. London: Health Education Authority.; SLEAP, M. (1990). 'Health in primary school physical education'. In: ARMSTRONG, N. (Ed). (1990). New directions in PE. Illinois: Human Kinetics Ltd.; SLEAP, M. (1989). 'The happy heart project: promoting active lifestyles amongst primary school children', British Journal of PE, No 20, pp.171-172.; SLEAP, M. (1990). 'With hearts and minds', Child Education, July, pp.34-35.
Source of Grant: Health Education Authority: £260,000
Date of Research: 1987 – continuing
KEYWORDS: heart disease; health education; physical education; primary education

8/0441
Department of Education
Cottingham Road, Hull HU6 7RX
0482 46311
Elliott, G.G. Mr
Monitoring schools and appraising teachers: a study of context, methods and results
Abstract: A survey of 104 local authorities in the United Kingdom by postal questionnaire is to be carried out to ascertain how far they are involved in monitoring the work of schools. This is complemented by in depth studies of six authorities to see how the

process is implemented and how schools are responding. Parallel studies are planned to investigate the context and procedures for appraising teachers. In particular the study will focus on teacher appraisal and the professional development of teachers.
Published Material: ELLIOTT, G.G. (1980). 'Self evaluation and the teacher – a national map', National Association of Inspectors and Educational Advisers Journal, No 14, pp.2-5. Spring.; ELLIOTT, G.G. (1982). 'Self evaluation and the teacher', Journal of Curriculum Studies, Vol 14, Part 1, pp.89-90.; ELLIOTT, G.G. (1982). 'Self evaluation and the teacher', Journal of Curriculum Studies, Vol 14, Part 3, pp.366-370.; ELLIOTT, G.G. (1982). 'Accountability or professional development: alternative modules for teacher and school evaluation', The Journal of Evaluation in Education, No 1, pp.2-5.; ELLIOTT, G.G. (1984). 'Self-evaluation and the teacher: annotated bibliography and report on current practice, parts 1-5, 1980-1984. London: School Curriculum Development Committee.
Source of Grant: University of Hull: 1985; £1,500 Schools Curriculum Development Committee: 1982; £30,150 Schools Council: 1980; £500: 1981; £500 Hull University; (Seedcorn Research Grant): £1,000
Date of Research: 1980-1990
KEYWORDS: evaluation; local education authority; school; teacher

8/0442

Department of Music
Cottingham Road,
Hull,
North Humberside HU6 7RX
0482 46311
Birkinshaw, A.J. Ms; *Supervisor:* Ford, A. Mr
The British composer in society 1945-1990
Abstract: The research consists of a study of the place of composer in society in the latter half of the 20th Century. Although it will include a study of the composer's relation to the performer/conductor of his works, the BBC (British Broadcasting Corporation) and media, and the musical establishment, it will also include a study of the composer and education. This chapter will include a study of the composer's employment in education; educational commissions; the education of the composer and his future audience/performers. Methods used include questionnaires, secondary material, interviews etc.
Source of Grant: No funding
Date of Research: 1988 – continuing
KEYWORDS: composer; education; music

8/0443

Department of Psychology
Hull HU6 7RX
0482 497911
Sewell, D.F. Dr; Rostron, A.B. Dr
Examination of the implications of information technology for cognitive development
Abstract: The Educational Technology Research Group was established in 1979 by Drs Sewell and Rostron to investigate the potential of modern technology in the educational context. Specific aspects of the Group's work include: (a) An investigation of the relationships between information technology, education and cognition. Development of a theoretical framework for the implementation of effective computer aided learning strategies; (b) application of modern technology to the development of cognitive and linguistic skills in the hearing impaired and in children with severe learning difficulties. The production and evaluation of software designed to enhance such skills; (c) implications of instructional design models (e.g. Gagne, Reigeluth, Landa) and cognitive science for the design and evaluation of computer based materials. The Group's particular concern is to bridge the gap between cognitive theory and educational practice in the design and implementation of computer mediated learning experiences. Research on these issues is currently being carried out in primary and special schools.
Published Material: A full list of publications can be obtained from the NFER on request
Source of Grant: support for a research assistant (September 1984-September 1985) currently provided by the Joseph Rowntree Memorial Trust
Date of Research: 1983 – continuing
KEYWORDS: cognitive development; computer assisted instruction; educational technology; information technology; special education

8/0444

Department of Psychology
Cottingham Road, Hull HU6 7RX
0482 46591
Sewell, D.F. Dr
Instructional design theory and the design and evaluation of computer assisted learning
Abstract: The purpose of the work is to examine the implications of instructional design models for the development and evaluation of computerassisted learning. Instructional design is concerned with specifying optimal methods of instruction to bring about desired changes in student behaviour and knowledge. It can be seen as a 'linking science' between conventional learning theories and educational practice; current work by the Educational Technology Group in the Psychology Department is using instructional design theory in: (a) the analysis of simple cognitive skills – cognitive task analysis; and (b) the development of computer based materials for communication-impaired children.
Published Material: ROTHERAY, D.R., SEWELL. D.F., & MORTON, J.R. (1986). 'The design and evaluation of educational software for children with severe learning difficulties', Programmed Learning and Educational Technology, Vol 23, No 2, pp.119-123.
Source of Grant: No funding
Date of Research: 1986 – continuing
KEYWORDS: computer assisted instruction; evaluation; software; teaching aids

8/0445

Department of Social Policy and Professional Studies
Cottingham Road, Hull HU5 2EH
0482 46311
Wiles, M. Mr; *Supervisor:* Alaszewski, A. Dr
New technology: the case of general practice
Abstract: The effective use of new technology will require that doctors become skilled in its use or alternatively that its use be delegated to other staff. Such changes will inevitably affect professional status and the distribution of authority. The researcher is examining how the profession controls and assimilates the new technology, the consequences of possible medical de-skilling and how these changes affect the professional process and professional status. Consideration is being given as to whether the profession, based upon historical/sociological precendents and assessment of present developments, will be able to assimilate and neutralize the effects of new technology. The educational element in this research is provided by the fact of the update of new technology is dependent upon the education of general practitioners in the use of computers and new technology.
Source of Grant: Economic and Social Research Council
Date of Research: 1986-1989
KEYWORDS: computer; doctor; information technology; management; professional status; skill

8/0446

Department of Sociology and Social Anthropology
Hull HU6 7RX
0482 46311
Tovey, P.A. Dr; *Supervisor:* Creighton, C. Dr
Contemporary public schools and the life process: cultural and ideological dimensions of the lived experience
Abstract: The research is an analysis of the 'process of development' of a sample of sixteen subjects who attended 'public school' during the term of office of the present government. The specific methodology of the study was that of the 'life history', in which each subject produced a written account of their life. This was followed by a taped interview which allowed elaboration of issues raised and discussion of aspects of experience not previously covered. Questionnaires were sent to headmasters in order to gauge the specific values of particular schools and to triangulate, where possible, information provided by subjects on the nature of their schooling. The research offers a contribution to sociological discussion at a number of levels. It provides information on the process of elite production and reproduction, and the role in this of 'institutions of influence' and the individual's mediation of the input from these sources; central sociological themes and concepts have been utilized, assessed and developed. Aspects of public school life previously accorded limited or inaccurate attention have been subject to empirical and theoretical analysis. The interaction of class and gender, control and hierarchy, the continued relevance of 'fagging' and the 'old boy' network and crucially the nature of subcultural affiliations are the principal examples. The nature of the

sector's self presentation is outlined. This specific utilization of the life-history technique illuminates its value and potential as a sociological method.
Source of Grant: Economic and Social Research Council; Competition award:
Date of Research: 1986-1990
KEYWORDS: personal narrative; subculture

8/0447
Department of Sociology and Social Anthropology
Hull HU6 7RX
0482 46311
Tovey, P.A. Dr; *Supervisor:* Creighton, C. Dr
Processes involved in the development of attitude and behaviour patterns among pupils in contemporary independent schools
Abstract: This study is an investigation of the developmental process of approximately sixteen ex public school pupils, in their early twenties, from two (or three) very well known educational institutions. By means of written life stories and taped interviews, an understanding of the nature and process of family life, schooling experiences and post school life is sought. In this way it is intended to take an understanding of the relationship between family, school, occupational status and power beyond available statistical data. As such, the research whilst treating developments as an individual mediated process, will analyze it within the context of class society and 'structures' of inequality. Subjects were selected by means of identification of four types; those from 'traditional' public school families, those new to the sector, 'assisted places' pupils and females. This was done in order to reveal developmental processes across the range of pupils. Issues central to the work include: the nature and influence of habitat and cultural capital, the relationship between class and gender, sub-cultural activity, interaction of values between family and school and overall the relationship (complementary or contradictory) between parts of the individuals life and the way these are interpreted and acted upon. The research is currently at the fieldwork stage.
Source of Grant: Economic and Social Research Council Competition Award
Date of Research: 1986-1989
KEYWORDS: family life; occupational success; personality development; private school; pupil; social class

Imperial College

8/0448
53 Prince's Gate, Exhibition Road, London SW7 2PG
071 589 5111
Cox, B.M. Dr; *Supervisor:* Jenkins, J. Mr
Intelligent tutoring systems: the representation and presentation of knowledge for teaching purposes using artificial intelligence techniques, stressing the importance of the explanation and understanding processes
Abstract: The research examined the relationship between explanation and understanding as key concepts in the design of domain-independent ITS (Intelligent Tutoring Systems). The design of current Intelligent Tutoring Systems is, in general, very restricted by being domain dependent and tailored to individual applications. Every specific learning/teaching situation that may arise must be anticipated. To avoid such restrictions, it is desirable to have a design with a more context-independent approach. In order to achieve such an aim the design must focus on user characteristics, instructional content and pedagogic strategies, rather than on specifics of domain in knowledge. The basic issues involved are, therefore, those concerned with the nature of knowledge, communication, learning, teaching and understanding. The purpose of the research is to demonstrate that there are very practical advantages to be derived in focusing the design of ITS on explanation and understanding in terms of freeing the design from domain-specific considerations. The EDUD explanation-driven, understanding directed approach provides an opportunity for a systematic and generic accommodaton of learning/teaching situations in a variety of domains.
Published Material: COX, B., POLLITZER, E. & JENKINS, J. (1988). 'An organization of domain knowledge for tutoring systems', Proceedings of the Third International Symposium on Knowledge Engineering, Madrid, Spain.; COX, B., POLLITZER, E. & JENKINS, J. (1988). An explanation-driven, understanding-

directed user model for intelligent tutoring systems, Institute of Electrical Engineers Colloquium on Intelligent Tutorial Systems, Digest No 1988/69, May.; COX, B., POLLITZER, E. & JENKINS, J. (1988). 'Explaining and understanding engineering problems – an intelligent tutoring approach'. In: GERO, J.S. (1988). Artificial intelligence in engineering: diagnosis and learning. pp.387-401. Elsevier Science Publishers B.V.
Source of Grant: Science and Engineering Research Council
Date of Research: 1986-1989
KEYWORDS: artificial intelligence; autoinstructional aid; computer assisted instruction; teaching machine

8/0449
Humanities Programme, Mechanical Engineering Building, Exhibition Road, London SW7 3BX
071 589 5111 ext 7053
Hughes, J.C. Mr; *Supervisor:* Goodlad, S. Dr
Peer tutoring from colleges to schools
Abstract: The aim of the project is to promote peer tutoring schemes, similar to Imperial Colleges' 'Pimlico Connection', around the United Kingdom. This is when volunteer students from further or higher education act as tutors in local primary and secondary schools in science, maths and technology lessons. The professional teacher uses them as an extra, and valuable teaching resource. The student tutors provide positive role models to the school pupils and in doing so it is hoped to increase the aspiration for them to stay on in education and training beyond 16. There is the possibility of funding for new pilot projects as part of BP's 'Aiming for a College Education' programme.
Published Material: GOODLAD, S. & HIRST, B. (1989). Peer tutoring: a guide to learning by teaching. London: Kogan Page.; GOODLAD, S. & HIRST, B. (1990). Explorations in peer teaching. Oxford: Blackwell.
Source of Grant: British Petroleum: £117,000
Date of Research: 1990 – continuing
KEYWORDS: mathematics; peer group teaching; science education; teaching method

Inner London Education Authority

8/0450
Research and Statistics Branch, Addington Street Annexe, County Hall, London SE1 7UY
081 663 1066
Monitoring equal opportunities in employment
Abstract: The ILEA (Inner London Education Authority) is committed to a policy of equal opportunities and to a programme of action to promote race and sex equality throughout the education service. As part of this policy, the Authority now proposes to introduce a system to collect and keep records on the Authority's employees as a basis for monitoring its equal opportunity employment policies. Information on those registered as disabled and on the sex of employees is already recorded as a matter of routine and can be analyzed to show their position in the work force. The priority is to obtain information on the ethnic composition of the staff. The classification to record ethnic background will be based on the CRE's (Commission for Racial Equality) revised classification. Data collection will be via line managers and all staff will have the right to inspect their entry and, if they wish, to amend it. The ILEA will utilize the Greater London Council's code of practice on confidentiality and security to ensure security of the data.
Date of Research: 1985-1989
KEYWORDS: employment; equal opportunity

Institute for the Study of Drug Dependence

8/0451
1 Hatton Place, London EC1N 8ND
071 430 1991
Dorn, N. Dr

Drug related youth work materials project
Abstract: The project aims to develop materials for use by youth workers, part-time workers and youth service management. The materials will be drafted on the basis of consultations with the field, then amended, published, launched, implemented and monitored.
Source of Grant: Department of Education and Science: £98,300
Date of Research: 1986-1989
KEYWORDS: *drug education; youth service*

Jordanhill College of Education

8/0452
> Department of Primary Education
> Southbrae Drive, Jordanhill, Glasgow G13 1PP
> 041 959 1232
> Pearson, M. Mrs

Music and micros
Abstract: This project will investigate the use of the microcomputer as an aid to developing music as a means of personal expression with children in the Primary 4 to 7 stage of the primary school. The research will be conducted in four schools in Strathclyde Region with teachers who have little specialist knowledge of music. The research will include: (i) classroom observation and interviews with both class teachers and children; (ii) the development of materials for use in the classroom; (iii) pre-test and post-test of the children's musical abilities to determine the success of the strategies used.
Source of Grant: Scottish Council for Educational Technology (SCET): £4,000
Date of Research: 1988-1990
KEYWORDS: *computer assisted instruction; microcomputer; music education; primary education*

Jordanhill College of Education

8/0453
> Southbrae Drive, Glasgow G13 1PP
> 041 959 1232
> Craigie College of Education
> Beechgrove, Ayr KA8 OSR
> 0292 42245
> White, G. Mr; Lockie, J. MR; Storie, M. Miss; Jackson, M. Mrs; McGuinness, R. Mrs; Ward, R.

Learning and teaching in colleges of education: information technology/INSET developments on a post graduate certificate of education (primary) course
Abstract: The project will investigate, through interviews with previous cohorts of students, the strengths and weaknesses of the PGCE (post-graduate certificate in education) course as a preparation for the initial years of teaching. It will also consider the effectiveness of linking specific aspects of preservice training to the inservice training of serving teachers. The experiences of students on school experience block of a teacher education course will be studied in depth and recommendations made about how the demands of the course can be matched more closely to the particular needs of particular classrooms. Finally recommendations will be made for the closer co-operation of teachers in the training of future members of the profession.
Published Material: WHITE, G.R. & MACINTYRE, A. (1989). IT/Inset developments linked to PGCE (Primary) courses. Glasgow: Jordanhill College of Education.
Source of Grant: Standing Committee on Research: £5,700
Date of Research: 1988-1989
KEYWORDS: *inservice education and training of teachers; student teacher; teacher education; teaching practice*

8/0454
> Southbrae Drive, Glasgow G13 1PP
> 041 959 1232
> Robertson, P. Mrs; *Supervisor:* Smith, I.R.M. Mr; Rand, J. Mr

Training of trainers
Abstract: Over the last ten years a 'trainer of trainers' approach has been widely used in educational innovation in Scotland. However, there has been no formal evaluation. In response to this the Scottish Education Department has funded an evaluative study to ascertain the effectiveness of the model within education. The project is designed in three stages. The initial stage will cover a detailed literature survey, a survey of recent and current course provision, research into the pilot School Board Initiative, intensive study of several cases and the forming of hypotheses to be used in consultancy and action research with School Board Initiatives. The second stage consists of consultancy involvement with three major courses and post-course evaluations. Finally there will be post-course follow-ups with participants and others in client relationships with course providers. The methodology consists of illuminative research employing observation, discussions, semi-structured interviews and questionnaires. Stage 2 will have a strong element of action research.
Source of Grant: Scottish Education Department: £58,442
Date of Research: 1988 – continuing
KEYWORDS: *evaluation; inservice education and training of teachers; trainer*

8/0455
> Southbrae Drive, Jordanhill, Glasgow G13 1PP
> 041 959 1232
> Niven, S.M.; Howgego, J.

Staff development for further ecucation college principals: an evaluation
Abstract: The project aims to evaluate the effectiveness of the investigation of further education issues by 5 working groups of further education college principals as a process of staff development.
Source of Grant: Scottish Education Department (SED)
Date of Research: 1989-1989
KEYWORDS: *college of further education; principal; staff development*

8/0456
> Southbrae Drive, Jordanhill, Glasgow G13 1PP
> 041 959 1232
> McCall, J. Dr; Macgregor, J. Mr; Robertson, I.J. Mrs; Weston, R.A.J. Mr; *Supervisor:* Bryce, T.G.K. Dr

Techniques for assessment of practical investigations in biology, chemistry, physics and science (TAPS 3)
Abstract: The proposals for Standard Grade Biology, Chemistry, Physics and Science inlcude 'practical abilities' as a major element to be assessed internally for certification purposes. Experimental and investigative work feature in each of the science subjects. The project will attempt to identify the investigative skills required in these subjects (focusing principally on Standard Grade, levels 1 and 2) and to investigate ways in which 'practical investigations' might be validly and practicably assessed by teachers. The experience gained (and the assessment techniques successfully generated) in the TAPS 1 and TAPS 2 projects form the background to this project, although new problems are posed by any requirements for teacher-assessed investigative work.
Published Material: TAPS Newsletter 9, December 1988, Jordanhill College of Education.; BRYCE, T.G.K. et al (1988). 'Assessing practical investigation', Paper presented at SERA Conference (St Andrews University), September 1988.; BRYCE, T.G.K. & ROBERTSON, I.J. (1988). 'The singer, not the song', Studies in Science Education, Vol 15, pp.135-143.; ROBERTSON, I.J. & BRYCE, T.G.K. 'Practicable practical assessment'. In: BENNETTS, J. (Ed). The assessment and moderation of coursework in school science: the state of the art. Association for Science Education (ASE). (in press). A full list of publications is available from the author.
Source of Grant: Scottish Education Department: £134,814
Date of Research: 1987-1990
KEYWORDS: *assessment; practical work; science education*

8/0457
> Southbrae Drive, Jordanhill, Glasgow G13 1PP
> 041 959 1232
> Mangan, J.A. Dr

Ideology and education: the ancient universities, liberal education and the games ethic
Abstract: The intention of this enquiry is to add to our knowledge of British and Imperial educational ideologies and the social history of the ancient and universities. In the late nineteenth century

'Oxbridge' was the matrix of the hugely influential moralistic ideology of athleticism – disseminated enthusiastically by alumni throughout the public, state and colonial school systems of Motherland and Empire. The ramifications of ethical inspiration were even more widely dispersed. It is far from notional to suggest that the activities characteristic of the rivers and playing fields of the late-nineteenth century Oxford and Cambridge were load-bearing supports under-pinning the moral structure of British and Imperial society. Attitudes, relationships and administrators owed much to the ethical imperatives of the playing fields. The ethos and activities associated with 'athleticism' within the 'Oxbridge' colleges influenced the educational and cultural practices of the empire and inspired the future recreational habits of the entire world. The significance of the ancient universities for a world-wide cultural metamorphosis has still to be appreciated, investigated and evaluated, and this is the major purpose of this investigation. The study will be an intensive and comparative inquiry involving comparison of the varied responses of selected 'Oxbridge' colleges, to the dominant ideology of the secondary system of education in the Victorian and Edwardian eras.
Published Material: MANGAN, J.A. (1986). The games-ethic and imperialism: aspects of the diffusion of an ideal. London: Allen Lane/Penguin.
Source of Grant: Economic and Social Research Council (ESRC): £25,000
Date of Research: 1986 – continuing
KEYWORDS: history of education; ideology; sport; university

8/0458

Arts Department
Southbrae Drive, Jordanhill, Glasgow G13 1PP
041 959 1232
Abernethy, G. Ms; Hart, D. Mr
Human computer interface in art
Abstract: The project aims to establish whether computer systems and software can release the pupils' latent creative ideas and skills in art to the same extent as the word processor is claimed to have done for creative writing in English.
Source of Grant: Jordanhill College: £482
Date of Research: 1989-1990
KEYWORDS: art education; computer assisted instruction; creativity

8/0459

Department of Business Studies
76 Southbrae Drive, Glasgow G13 1PP
041 959 1232
Finlayson, B. Mr
Software information and support
Abstract: The research and development work has, as its aim, the provision of information to business studies and economics teachers regarding the nature of software available to support learning in the subject areas concerned and also the appropriateness of such software. Research will also be undertaken with a view to considering integrated software for business studies and economics use and parts of the proposal will also cover the dissemination of information on 'good practice' with regard to the use of software in specific learning situations related to business studies and economics and also offer suggestions regarding the nature of hardware required and best suited to business studies and economics teachers' needs.
Source of Grant: Scottish Council for Educational Technology, Microelectronics in Education Committee: £12,600
Date of Research: 1987-1990
KEYWORDS: commercial education; economics; microcomputer; secondary education; software

8/0460

Department of Community Education
Southbrae Drive, Jordanhill, Glasgow G13 1PP
041 959 1232
Rowlands, C.J. Mr
Survey of students' employment – community education courses in Scotland
Abstract: The purpose of the research is to investigate the employment situation of Youth and Community Work students who qualified from Jordanhill, Moray House and Northern Colleges of Education. The jobs obtained by students will be studied according to certain criteria i.e. sex, length of course followed and the types of appointment accepted will be investigated..
Published Material: ROWLANDS, C.J.(1989). On appointments

taken up by students completing their full time training in Youth and Community Departments of Jordanhill, Moray House and Northern College of Education in June 1988. Glasgow: Division of Community Education, Jordanhill College.
Source of Grant: No funding
Date of Research: 1988-1990
KEYWORDS: community education; employment; youth service

8/0461

Department of Computing and Business Studies
Southbrae Drive, Jordanhill, Glasgow G13 1PP
041 959 1232
Munro, R.K.
Models for the transfer to software
Abstract: The aims of the project are: (i) identification of factors (particularly cultural) which inhibit the development of software (especially within the social subjects sphere); (ii) creation of educational software which can be used in a number of countries – is language independent yet culturally sensitive; (iii) evaluation of educational software produced; (iv) formulation of models for the development of educational software.
Source of Grant: European Economic Community: 50,000 ECU/Yr
Date of Research: 1987-1989
KEYWORDS: computer assisted instruction; microcomputer; social studies; software

8/0462

Department of Computing & Business Studies
Southbrae Drive, Jordanhill, Glasgow G13 1PP
041 959 1232
Brown, R. Mr
Bank of Scotland Research & Development Fellowship
Abstract: The research will investigate current courses in the Business Subjects area (initially at Standard Grade but ultimately across the range of short courses and modules) and identify appropriate areas of the courses which could be supported by materials on electronic banking. The second phase will involve developing, piloting and evaluating classroom materials (for teachers and pupils) for appropriate banking elements within the following courses: office and information skills, economics, finance and accounting, social and vocational skills, management and information studies. Appropriate short courses and modules in the banking and money management areas will also be developed. Finally production and distribution of the materials to schools and colleges will be organized and inservice courses on the use of the materials will be arranged.
Source of Grant: Bank of Scotland: £50,000
Date of Research: 1988-1990
KEYWORDS: banking; business education; curriculum development

8/0463

Department of Education and Psychology
Southbrae Drive, Glasgow G13 1PP
041 959 1232 ext 316
Christie, D.F.M. Mr
Students' experiences and approaches to learning in the B.Ed Primary Degree
Abstract: The study arises out of a concern to examine the attitudes and approaches of students in a new Primary B.Ed degree programme. Interviews were conducted with a cross section of 41 students from the 4 years of the degree programme. A version of N. Entwistle's "Inventory of Approaches to Study" was prepared and results of a sample of 257 students were analyzed. Small samples of 12 students and 6 staff members completed repertory grids about elements of the course and tutors, in the case of students, and about students in the case of tutors. The main results from interviews were that: students differentiated among elements of the course in terms of "theory" and "practice"; there was stronger vocational commitment among first and fourth year students; the course was seen as demanding but in sheer quantity rather than challenging quality of work; students were generally poor at managing their study time and relied on peer interaction in carrying out assignment work. The responses to the Inventory, comprising 16 subscales, were factor analyzed. The 4 main factors emerging were deep approach; personal insecurity; negative attitudes to study and surface/serialist approach. Cross sectional comparisons of the 4 year groups produced significant differences on 8 subscales. Students in the second and third year of the course showed more negative attitudes, less of a deep approach and less effective study skills by their self-report responses. The results of the repertory grid shed

further light on students' attitudes and the ways in which students are perceived by their tutors.
Published Material: CHRISTIE, D.F.M & St. PAUL, T. (1988). 'Students' experiences and approaches to learning in the B.Ed primary degree'. Glasgow: Jordanhill College; CHRISTIE, D.F.M. (1988). 'Students' approaches to learning in a B.Ed degree programme'. Paper presented at the Annual Conference of the Scottish Educational Research Association, St Andrew's, 1988
Source of Grant: Scottish Education Department; Intercollege standing committee on research: £4,000
Date of Research: 1988-1988
KEYWORDS: academic degree; attitude; learning strategy; motivation for studies; student teacher

8/0464
>   Department of Education and Psychology
>   Southbrae Drive, Glasgow G13 1PP
>   041 959 1232
>   Macbeath, J.E.C. Mr; Woolfson, L. Ms

Learning about teaching
Abstract: The aim of this research is to identify good practice in the pre-service education of secondary teachers from the perspectives of students, tutors and school personnel. A researcher was appointed for a 3 month period to conduct interviews with students, college and school staff asking them to identify specific aspects of effective learning/teaching in the newly validated CNAA (Council for National Academic Awards) course. The research identified aspects of effective organization and tutoring which illustrated (a) the importance of supporting student-centred tutoring and classroom consultancy; (b) the value of collaboration between traditionally separate disciplines; (c) the importance of college-school negotiation and working relationships; (d) the significance of modelling in college-based approaches to teaching and learning.
Published Material: MACBEATH, J.E.C. & WOOLFSON, L. (1988). Learning about teaching. Glasgow: Jordanhill College.
Source of Grant: SCOR (Standing Committee on Research): £5,000
Date of Research: 1988-1988
KEYWORDS: secondary education; teacher education

8/0465
>   Department of Education and Psychology
>   Southbrae Drive, Jordanhill, Glasgow G13 1PP
>   041 959 1232
>   MacBeath, J. Mr; Hough, M. Mr

Inter-professional training needs
Abstract: The project aims to identify issues in inter-professional work and develop appropriate training programmes.
Published Material: HOUGH, M. & MACBEATH, J. (1989). Working together: Report on the Inter-Professional Needs Training Project. Jordanhill College of Education.
Source of Grant: Scottish Education Department (SED): £5,000
Date of Research: 1988-1989
KEYWORDS: profession; training; vocational education

8/0466
>   Department of Further Education
>   Southbrae Drive, Glasgow G13 1PP
>   041 959 1232
>   Stillie, D. Mr

Evaluation of mentor support systems in colleges of further education
Abstract: As recently as two years ago half of the further education teacher training course was put on a distance teaching/learning mode. Experienced and teacher trained FE lecturers were selected and trained to provide support for course members during the college based block. The aim of the project was to investigate and evaluate the mentor support systems operating in colleges of further education in support of lecturers under training. In the investigation fifteen colleges of further education were visited and senior staff, mentors and students interviewed. Questionnaires were issued to one hundred mentors and one hundred lecturers on the training course and over eighty returned by each cohort sample. The questionnaire returns covered every college in Scotland. The findings of the investigation indicate considerable support for mentors for colleagues in training. Mentors are satisfied with their role as outlined by the Training College. A variety of support systems operate in colleges and appear to be effective.
Source of Grant: Standing Committee on Research (SCOR): £2,500
Date of Research: 1988-1988

KEYWORDS: adviser; distance study; further education; teacher education

8/0467
>   Department of Further Education
>   CAST (Curriculum Advice and Support Team),
>   Southbrae Drive, Glasgow G13 1PP
>   041 959 1232
>   Martin, W.J. Mr; Robertson, I. Mr; *Supervisor:* Natusch, I. Mr

National Certificate Guidance Information System
Abstract: This project is located within the School of Further Education, Jordanhill College, and will be conducted in collaboration with SCOTVEC (Scottish Vocational Education Council), Falkirk College of Technology (Central Region), the Dean Education Centre (Lothian Region), and the Anniesland College (Strathclyde Region). The aim is to produce an easily-operable information system which will meet the guidance needs associated with the negotiable curriculum of the National Certificate. It will contain information on modules in the NC catalogue, access, articulation and equivalence programmes: Information will be accessed via a friendly question and answer route which will simulate a typical guidance consultation, or by more direct routes. Such access will enable a wide range of users, such as guidance staff, learners, employers, teachers, training officers, senior educational staff, parents, national and regional development officers, to obtain high quality guidance and resource information from a single comprehensive source. The initial phase of the project will be one of investigation, information gathering, identification and organization of relevant facts, and expertise. This will be followed by construction of a knowledge base of rules, relationships, procedures, and conclusions. Central to this development will be the input from staff at the piloting centres and others to identify goals, define guidance rules and consultation methodology. The national dimension of the project will also be considered, i.e. portability to other unit based systems, e.g. The Engineering Industry Training Board's (EITB) system of module segments; and links with other computerized information systems.
Source of Grant: Scottish Education Department/Training Enterprise Education Division: £99,000
Date of Research: 1988-1990
KEYWORDS: curriculum; guidance; information system; Scotland

8/0468
>   Department of Further Education
>   Southbrae Drive, Jordanhill, Glasgow G13 1PP
>   041 959 1232
>   Stillie, D. Mr; McQueeny, L. Mr; Stirling, M. Mr; Millar, M. Mr

Assessment of work based experience in the employment led curriculum
Abstract: The aim of the project is to investigate the possibility of developing competency based profiles that could be used in the assessment of work based experience.
Source of Grant: National Board for Nursing & Midwifery (Scotland): £3,500
Date of Research: 1989-1990
KEYWORDS: assessment; nurse; profile; vocational education; work experience

8/0469
>   Department of Physical Education
>   Southbrae Drive, Jordanhill, Glasgow G13 1PP
>   041 959 1232
>   Sharp, R. Dr

State and status of physical education in Scotland
Abstract: The research will determine the views of Scottish secondary teachers of physical education about the curriculum, aims and purposes, methods and current developments. The overall aim is to provide a platform for comparison with the British survey and future Scottish surveys.
Source of Grant: Jordanhill College: £850
Date of Research: 1988-1990
KEYWORDS: physical education; Scotland; secondary education

8/0470
>   Department of Primary Education
>   76 Southbrae drive, Glasgow G13 1PP
>   041 959 1232

Scottish Council for Educational Technology
74 Victoria Crescent Road, Glasgow G12 9JN
041 334 9314
McKay, R. Mr
Group interaction in the use of microcomputers
Abstract: This project is entitled Cope Project 6 and will investigate the nature and quality of group interactions involving the
use of the microcomputer. Consideration of the influence of school
policy, school and class organization, teaching styles, teacher/pupil
interaction, pupil/pupil interaction and software used. The project
will involve an examination of the development of discussion skills
and abilities to work co-operatively in a group context.
Source of Grant: Microelectronics in Education Committee: £2,750
Date of Research: 1988-1990
*KEYWORDS: computer assisted instruction; discussion; group
learning; group work; microcomputers; teaching method*

8/0471
Department of Primary Education
Southbrae Drive, Jordanhill, Glasgow G13 1PP
041 959 1232
Andrews, J. Mrs
Three primary school boards: the first years
Abstract: Three case studies will be carried out to establish how
a school and its community perceive their role in the new school
board, and its functions and their feeling of preparedness for par-
ticipation in the boards. How these perceptions alter over the first
year of school boards will also be investigated.
Source of Grant: Jordanhill College: £482
Date of Research: 1989-1990
*KEYWORDS: administration of education; governing body;
primary education; school-community relation; Scotland*

8/0472
Department of Psychology
School of Education,
Southbrae Drive, Jordanhill, Glasgow G13 1PP
041 959 1232
Bryce, T.G.K. Dr; Startk, R. Mrs; Walker, A. Dr; Dalziel,
H. Mrs
Monitoring of achievement in Science: Second Round [MAS 2]
Abstract: This project aims to assess the achievement of Scottish
pupils at the P4, P7 and S2 stages in certain aspects of science.
The approach and methodology will be based on that of the
monitoring exercises undertaken at Jordanhill College between
1985-1988. The exercise will involve a minor revision of the assessment framework; the design and pilot testing of new or amended
assessment materials; the conduct of the main testing programme
in the summer term 1990, marking completed tests, defining analyses to be undertaken; writing the project report for the Scottish
Education Department and preparing draft dissemination materials
for teachers. Advice and assistance on aspects of test design and
data analysis will be provided by the AAP Central Support Unit.
Account will be taken of the 5-14 curriculum and assessment
development programme.
Source of Grant: Scottish Education Department (AAP): £141,000
Date of Research: 1989 – continuing
*KEYWORDS: achievement measurement; assessment; science edu-
cation*

8/0473
Department of Psychology
School of Education,
Southbrae Drive, Jordanhill, Glasgow G13 1PP
051 959 1232
Johnson, A. Mr; Ainsworth, S. Mr
**An examination of the recruitment of minority ethnic students to
Jordanhill College**
Abstract: The project will examine the recruitment patterns in Jor-
danhill College, detail the experiences of black students in teacher
education and provide feedback on recruitment to local black com-
munity members.
Source of Grant: Jordanhill College: £440
Date of Research: 1989-1990
KEYWORDS: ethnic minority; recruitment; teacher education

8/0474
Department of Special Educational Needs
Southbrae Drive, Jordanhill, Glasgow G13 1PP
041 959 1232

MacKay, G. Dr
Conductive education for pupils with complex difficulties
Abstract: The aims of the project are to describe, understand and
evaluate the influence of conductive education on 3 local authority
(Strathclyde Region) day schools for pupils with complex learning
difficulties.
Source of Grant: Scottish Education Department (SED)
Date of Research: 1989-1990
*KEYWORDS: conductive education; learning difficulty; special
education*

8/0475
Inservice Training Department
Southbrae Drive, Jordanhill, Glasgow G13 1PP
041 959 1232
Robertson, A.H. Mr
Development of diagnostic test items for use in P6 mathematics
Abstract: The project will examine how to diagnose difficulties in
mathematics at the P6 stage in the primary school and develop
remedial strategies, both for their own intrinsic value and as an
aid to class teachers in preparing children for national testing.
Source of Grant: Jordanhill College and ICI: £1,000
Date of Research: 1989-1990
KEYWORDS: diagnostic test; mathematics; primary education

8/0476
Inservice Training Department
Southbrae Drive, Jordhanill, Glasgow G13 1PP
041 959 1232
Rand, J. Mr
**TVEI (Technical and Vocational Education Initiative) local
evaluation**
Abstract: The College has been responsible for the local evalua-
tion of former TVEI pilot projects. The format and nature of the
research tasks have varied from project to project, the primary focus
has been to help projects identify development needs.
Source of Grant: Individual Scottish local authorities: £40,000
approx.
Date of Research: 1986 – continuing
*KEYWORDS: evaluation; secondary education; Technical and
Vocational Education Initiative*

Keele University

8/0477
Centre for Social Research in Education, Keele ST5 5BG
0782 621111 ext 3431
Gleeson, D. Mr; *Supervisor:* McLean, M. Mrs; Siggers, T.
Mr
**TVEI(E) (Technical and Vocational Education Initiative (Exten-
sion) Project)**
Abstract: The aim of the study is to evaluate the county wide extension of TVEI (Technical and Vocational Education Initiative) in
Staffordshire and to provide independent and impartial assessment
of a cluster based strategy, how it affects school and college curriculum, organization, community, links with employers and other
support services across the county. The research adopts an action
oriented approach to evaluation, involving formative methods of
reporting.
Published Material: GLEESON, D. (1988). The paradox of training: making progress out of crisis. Milton Keynes: Open Univer-
sity Press.; GLEESON, D. (1990). Training and its alternatives.
Milton Keynes: Open University Press.
Source of Grant: Training Enterprise Education Division and
Staffordshire LEA: £250,000 (including £100,000 INSET package)
Date of Research: 1988 – continuing
*KEYWORDS: evaluation; Technical and Vocational Education
Initiative*

8/0478
Centre for Social Research in Education, Keele, Staffordshire
ST5 5BG
0782 621111
Gleeson, D. Mr; *Supervisor:* Gough, G. Dr
**Ready for Work in the 1990s: A study on young peoples' attitudes
to work, further education and training in North Staffordshire**
Abstract: To study potential employees' (14-15 year olds) percep-

tion of the range of employment opportunities open to them on leaving full-time education. Also to define an approach by which employers and education together can broaden and improve school leavers' understanding of job opportunities thereby ensuring that a wider section of the community consider entering a career in business or industry.
Published Material: Gleeson, D. (1989). A study on young peoples' attitudes to work, further education and training in North Staffordshire. Keele: centre for social research in education, Keele University.
Source of Grant: Training Enterprise Education Division and North Staffordshire local employer network: £6,900
Date of Research: 1989-1989
KEYWORDS: attitude; employment opportunities; school leaver; transition from school to work; youth employment

8/0479
> Centre for Social Research in Education, Keele, Staffordshire ST5 5BG
> 0782 621111 Ext 3431
> Gleeson, D. Mr; *Supervisor:* Burgess, R. Mr

Research and evaluation of Cheshire LEA'S Technical and Vocational Education Initiative (TVEI), Inservice Education and Training of Teachers (INSET) & Education Support Grant (ESG) programmes
Abstract: The aims are to provide up-to-date case study analysis of a small group of Secondary, Primary, Special Schools and a Further Education institution, in order to evaluate the impact of TVEI (Technical and Vocational Education Initiative), INSET (Inservice Education and Training) and ESG (Education Support Grant) initiatives on staff development and teaching/learning processes.
Source of Grant: Cheshire local education authority (LEA): £35,000
Date of Research: 1989 – continuing
KEYWORDS: education support grant; evaluation; inservice education and training of teachers; local education authority; technical and vocational education initiative

8/0480
> Centre for Social Research in Education, Keele, Staffordshire ST5 5BG
> 0782 621111 Ext 3431
> Gleeson, D. Mr; *Supervisor:* Gunn, M. Ms

Evaluation of Staffordshire LEA Inservice Training and Education of Teachers (INSET) Project Local Education Authorities Training Grant Scheme (LEATGS)
Abstract: To evaluate aspects of training in the context of primary feeder schools and their cluster high schools. It is concerned with teacher experience on INSET (Inservice Education and Training) and how LEA (Local Education Authority) provision matches needs of individual schools and teachers.
Source of Grant: Staffordshire local ecucation authority (LEA): £13,500
Date of Research: 1989-1990
KEYWORDS: evaluation; inservice education and training of teachers; local education authority

8/0481
> Department of Applied Social Studies and Social Work
> Keele, Staffordshire ST5 5BG
> 0782 621111
> Ormrod, P. Mrs; *Supervisor:* Bolger, A.W. Mr

Guidance of adult learners
Abstract: A group of adult learners in higher education are being studied in order to determine the routes they used back into education and the sources of any guidance they received.
Source of Grant: No funding
Date of Research: 1987-1990
KEYWORDS: adult education; guidance; higher education

8/0482
> Department of Education
> Keele ST5 5BG
> 0782 621111 ext 3406
> Bale, J.R. Mr

International recruiting of student-athletes by American universities
Abstract: The project seeks to identify the extent of recruitment of foreign student-athletes by U.S. universities and the experience of such recruits while resident in the United States of America.
Published Material: BALE, J.R. (1988). 'The international recruit-

ing game: foreign student athletes in American Universities'. In: BONDI, E. and MATTHEWS, H. (Eds). Educational society: social, political and geographical perspectives. London: Routledge; BALE, J.R. (1987). 'Alien student-athletes in American higher education; locational decision-making and sojourn abroad', Physical Education Review, Vol 10, No 2, pp.81-93.; BALE J.R. (1988). 'Foreign students in NCAA Division 1 Universities; an empirical study of six men's sports', Journal of Comparative Physical Education and Sport, Vol 10, No 1, pp.21-31.
Source of Grant: No funding
Date of Research: 1985 – continuing
KEYWORDS: athletics; foreign student; recruitment; United States of America; university

8/0483
> Department of Education
> Keele ST5 5BG
> 0782 621111
> Parkhouse, P.G.J.T. Mr

Impact of the National Curriculum proposals in science on independent schools
Abstract: The aim of the study is to see whether the National Curriculum for science is likely to produce a divergence in quality of science students leaving maintained schools and independent schools (who will not be constrained to adopt the National Curriculum proposals). The sample consists of 100 independent schools chosen to reflect the spread of such schools viz. for the single sex, mixed, boarding, day, urban, rural and with and without sixth forms. In addition, schools were matched for the spread of sizes found in the independent sector. The research tool is a questionnaire to be followed up with interviews with about 10% of the sample schools. Only INTERIM results are currently available. There is little evidence that independent schools will depart from their single science subject teaching, in which they have considerable expertise. A-levels are prepared for, since the advent of the GCSE (General Certificate of Secondary Education), in ways which maintain the content level of the old GCEs yet incorporating the new assessment techniques. There is virtually no AS level teaching. The evidence points towards the suggestion that independent schools will maintain a traditional output of academically orientated students whereas maintained schools will probably produce a more 'process-orientated' student.
Source of Grant: Department funds: £240
Date of Research: 1988-1990
KEYWORDS: National Curriculum; private school; science education

8/0484
> Department of Education
> Keele ST5 5BG
> 0782 621111
> Parkhouse, P.G.J.T. Mr

The National Science Curriculum proposals: who has actually read it?
Abstract: Anecdotal evidence from visits to school science departments has suggested that not every person teaching science within a school has a copy of the National Curriculum proposals for science and that those who do have not had time to read it, let alone reflect upon it. This small-scale piece of research has taken a sample of schools within a fifty mile radius of the University of Keele containing 300-400 science teachers to whom questionnaires have been issued. It aimed to discover to what extent rank and file members of science departments have acquainted themselves with the National Curriculum and what reaction they had to selected proposals within it.
Source of Grant: Departmental funding
Date of Research: 1988-1989
KEYWORDS: science education; teacher behaviour

8/0485
> Department of Education
> Keele ST5 5BG
> 0782 621111
> Powell, G.W. Mr

The order of knowledge
Abstract: The study will offer a radical re-assessment of the development of education, especially since the Renaissance. It will involve a new interpretation of the significance of Plato's analysis of the classical conceptual system which has dominated our education.
Source of Grant: No funding

Date of Research: 1988 – continuing
KEYWORDS: *history of education; theory of education*

8/0486

Department of Education
Keele ST5 5BG
0782 621111
Corden, R. Mr; *Supervisor:* Evans, T. Mrs
An investigation of the collaborative interaction and talk of children in relation to their perception of teacher audience, task purpose and learning context
Abstract: The study is of task related, or work focused discourse of small groups of 12- to 13- year old pupils working within the naturalistic settings of the classroom. It is concerned with the way in which children engage in a variety of tasks and use language (spoken) to interact and collaborate in the learning process when the teachr is not in a central, authoritative position (physically) and when the discussion has the 'potential' to be negotiable and not dominated by one ommipotent figure. The study will attempt to identify the way in which pupils engage in discussion in relation to their percpetion of teacher audience and the subsequent perceptions of contextual learning conditions and task purpose. The study adopts an ethnographic, or ethnomethodological approach and makes extensive use of audio and video recordings. The use of retrospective analysis and triangulation will be adopted in order to try and encompass the 'whole' group interaction and to be sensitively aware of contextual factors and particularly, the way in which the pupils' perceptions of 'audience' (as projected by the teacher) affects the interactional process and use of language in the learning process.
Source of Grant: No funding
Date of Research: 1987 – continuing
KEYWORDS: *group work; learning process; verbal interaction*

8/0487

Department of Education
Keele ST5 5BG
0782 621111
Gleeson, D. Mr; Carlen, P. Dr; Wardough, J. Mr
Law, education and social control: the case of non school attendance
Abstract: This study looks at the processing of non-school attendance in relation to inter-agency links: education, law and social welfare services.
Source of Grant: Economic and Social Research Council: £65,000
Date of Research: 1988 – continuing
KEYWORDS: *absenteeism; attendance; law; social control*

8/0488

Department of Education
Keele ST5 5BG
0782 621111
Mardle, G.D. Mr; Colclough, P. Mr; Shain, F. Ms; Modiba, M. Ms; *Supervisor:* Mardle, G.D. Mr
Equal opportunites policies in schools and colleges post local management developments from the 1988 Education Act
Abstract: In the past, policy initiation in the education system has in general, been the responsibility of either the Government or the local education authority. Under the 1988 Education Act this has changed. Secondary schools and further education colleges now have control over their budgets and also a far higher degree of control over certain policy initiatives. Within the context of many other pressures this has lead to a degree of inertia in certain areas. Particularly, the development of equal opportunity policies has been one of those affected. The aim of this investigation is to examine, via questionnaire and case study material, the effects of current legislation on the area of equal opportunity policy in schools and colleges. The focus of attention starts with the political aspects of the problem. It then goes on to examine the way in which such policy in the areas of gender, race and disability is seen by the participants, developed in the institutions and the methods deployed in putting it into practice. It is hoped the results and conclusions of the study will enable more institutions to develop and implement such policies.
Source of Grant: No funding
Date of Research: 1991 – continuing
KEYWORDS: *equal education; gender equality*

8/0489

Department of Education
Centre for School Research,
Keele, Staffordshire ST5 5BG
0782 621111
Brighouse, T.R.P. Prof.; Gough, G. Dr; Johnson, M. Mr; Glover, D. Mr
Successful schooling
Abstract: The project aims to establish further information and knowledge about 'successful schooling', by means of questionnaires and in depth interviews in 15-18 core study schools.
Source of Grant: Local Education Authorities: £25,000
Date of Research: 1990 – continuing
KEYWORDS: *evaluation; performance; school effectiveness; success*

8/0490

Department of Education
Keele, Staffordshire ST5 5BG
0782 621111
Mountford, B. Mr; *Supervisor:* Wringe, C.A. Dr
Effectiveness and rationality in the evaluation of educational institutions
Abstract: A conceptual enquiry into the notion of effectiveness in an educational context. Shortcomings in the 'product' view of effectiveness are brought to light and the alternative of effectiveness as rational process is proposed.
Source of Grant: No funding
Date of Research: 1981-1989
KEYWORDS: *administration of education; evaluation; school effectiveness*

8/0491

Department of Education
Keele, Staffordshire ST5 5BG
0782 621111
Marques, L. Mr; *Supervisor:* Thompson, D.B. Mr
Children's alternative ideas about earth-science concepts e.g. continental drift and plate tectronics
Abstract: Children's alternative ideas relating to earth-science concepts have been only modestly researched. Following work on children's ideas of the origin of the earth, the origin of life and the nature and origin of volcanoes, attention has turned to their views of the origin of continents, oceans and the possible wandering of the former. Following a pilot study with pupils and teachers and six in depth interviews with pupils, a questionnaire survey of the views of 400 Portuguese children will be administered. Results and conclusions cannot be forecast but it is conjectured that many garbled ideas will acrue from watching television, reading newspapers and attempting to use ideas drawn from science and geography lessons at school.
Source of Grant: No funding
Date of Research: 1989 – continuing
KEYWORDS: *child; cognition; earth sciences; science education*

8/0492

Department of Education
Keele, Staffordshire ST5 5BG
0782 621111
Thompson, D.B. Mr
The history of geological and earth-science education in the United Kingdom
Abstract: The history of geological and earth science education in the UK reveals the important part geology, geologists and the geological profession played in the early days of the growth of science education 1830-1900 in both schools and vocational courses e.g. of the Department of Science and Arts. The wives of geologists were in the van of women's education and extra mural education. A decline to a nadir in the 1930s has been followed by a steady rise in the growth of interest, culminating in the formation of the Association of Teachers of Geology (1967) (now the Earth Science Teachers' Association (1988)) and the acceptance of Earth Science in the National Science Curriculum (1989).
Source of Grant: No funding
Date of Research: 1970 – continuing
KEYWORDS: *earth sciences; geology; history of education; science education*

8/0493

Department of Education
Keele, Staffordshire ST5 5BG
0782 621111
Thompson, D.B. Mr

Curriculum materials for earth-science teaching in the National Curriculum

Abstract: Earth Science is new to the science curriculum in the United Kingdom. Curriculum materials need to be written, trialled and published quickly. Trials are to be carried out on whole classes of 20-30 pupils. Materials are designed for variety and balance of approach and a concentration on pupil activity including practical experimental work. Publication is via the Earth Science Teachers' Association "Science of the Earth" and "Project Earth".
Published Material: THOMPSON, D.B. (1989). 'SCIENCE OF EARTH, UNIT 14. HOW DO TEMPERATure and pressure change as we go down into the Earth'? Sheffield Earth Science Teachers Association Teachers' Guide 10pp. Students' worksheet.
Source of Grant: No funding
Date of Research: 1988 – continuing
KEYWORDS: curriculum development; earth sciences; science education

8/0494

Department of Education
Keele, Staffordshire ST5 5BG
0782 621111
Wakelin, M. Mrs; *Supervisor:* Brighouse, T.R.P. Prof.;
Wringe, C.A. Dr

The use of performance indicators in the evaluation of educational institutions

Abstract: Current use of performance indicators is to be surveyed and evaluated in relation to currently proposed educational aims. Their validity as a measure of educational effectiveness and their affect on the performance of teachers and institutions will be assessed.
Source of Grant: No funding
Date of Research: 1989 – continuing
KEYWORDS: administration of education; evaluation; performance indicator; school effectiveness

8/0495

Department of Education
Keele ST5 5BG
0782 621111
Toy, K. Mr; *Supervisor:* WRINGE, C.A. DR

Educational management, teacher evaluation and teacher autonomy

Abstract: This is principally a conceptual and library study. Theories of educational management and teacher evaluation are to be explored in relation to a concept of teacher autonomy. Historical and current expectations and practice will be examined in the light of available documentary evidence, and a small number of exemplary case studies may be undertaken.
Source of Grant: No funding
Date of Research: 1986 – continuing
KEYWORDS: administration of education; autonomy; evaluation; teacher role

8/0496

Department of Education
Research & Evaluation Unit, Keele ST5 5BG
0782 621111 ext 391
McLean, M. Ms; *Supervisor:* Gleeson, D. Mr

Local Evaluation of TVEI (Technical and Vocational Education Initiative)/TRIST (TVEI-Related Inservice Training)/GRIST (Grant related INSET)

Abstract: The study looks at the background and development of TVEI (Technical and Vocational Education Initiative) and TRIST (TVEI-Related Inservice Training) in local institutions. The research adopts an action oriented approach to evaluation, involving formative methods of reporting.
Published Material: End of year reports and separate reports to schools and colleges involved in TVEI/TRIST.; GLEESON, D. (1988). TVEI and secondary education. Buckingham: Open University Press.
Source of Grant: Local Education Authority (LEA)/Manpower Services Commission (MSC): £60,000; £150,000; £11,000
Date of Research: 1985 – continuing
KEYWORDS: evaluation; inservice training; TVEI (Technical and Vocational Education Initiative)

8/0497

Department of Education
Keele ST5 5BG
0782 621111
Manchester Polytechnic
Department of Hotel, Catering and Institutional Management
Old Hall Lane, Manchester M14 6HR
061 224 7341
Ineson, E. MRS; *Supervisor:* Kempa, R.F. Prof.

Study of factors affecting students' success and drop-out rates in hotel mangement courses

Abstract: Students' success in hotel management courses is frequently judged by employers in terms of a range of qualities other than academic ones. The research aims at identifying these non-academic qualities and, thereafter, will focus on the extent to which their development can be predicted before or at the commencement of students' courses. Central to the study is the administration of personality and related inventories to students on hotel management training courses. Data obtained in this way will be supplemented by information from interviews.
Source of Grant: No external funding
Date of Research: 1986-1990
KEYWORDS: aptitutde; assessment; employer; management education; student

8/0498

Department of Education
Keele ST5 5BG
0782 621111
Ayob, A. Mrs; *Supervisor:* Kempa, R.F. Prof.

Group work in school science

Abstract: Group work is a common feature in school science courses, especially in the context of practical work in laboratories and in the field. Group work is defined as 'activity in which groups of 2 or more pupils work together in collaboration, either on identical activities or different aspects of the same activity, usually without direct supervision or control by the teacher'. The aim of this study is to obtain a detailed understanding of what actually goes on in group learning settings in science education, of particular interest is the explorations of the nature of the learning interactions as they take place among pupils involved in group work and the influence of these interactions on the achievement of individual pupils and the group as a whole. The overall study is planned to take place in two phases. In the initial one, information will be sought about the current situation as regards group learning in science, and to obtain this 'baseline' information, questionnaire-based enquiries will be sent to schools in the UK and in Malaysia. The second phase of the investigation will involve the study of group work in its natural setting, i.e. the classroom and school laboratory. It will be conducted by means of direct observation as well as through the analysis of audio and video recordings. Arrangements will be made for this kind of observational work to be conducted in UK schools and also in Malaysian schools. The results of this study will be discussed in terms of its implications to practising teachers, with regard to organization and management of group work in science.
Source of Grant: The Malaysian Government: expenses and fees until completion of study
Date of Research: 1986-1990
KEYWORDS: group work; interaction; Malaysia; practical work; science education

8/0499

Department of Education
Keele ST5 5BG
0782 621111
Tolley, J. Ms; *Supervisor:* Wringe, C.A. Dr

The evaluation of foreign language teaching objectives (with particular reference to the teaching of French)

Abstract: An empirical investigation of factors determining the choice of objectives for the teaching of French at school level, including pupil motivation and the communication needs of individual and industry and commerce.
Source of Grant: Staffordshire Local Education Authority: teacher secondment for one year
Date of Research: 1986 – continuing
KEYWORDS: aims of education; french language; language teaching

8/0500

Department of Psychology
Keele ST5 5BG
0782 621111
Newberry-Tarrier, S.J. Mrs; *Supervisor:* Hegarty, J. Dr
Computers to aid decision making by adults who have mental handicaps

Abstract: Research has indicated that mentally handicapped people find problem solving difficult. The aim of this project is to identify areas in everyday living which involve difficult decision making tasks and to develop appropriate computer software which might act as a training aid. Expert systems have already been developed which help people of average intelligence to make better, more informed decisions. This type of system could be developed to help in group homes in decisions about grocery shopping, budgeting and menu planning. During the first year of research a pilot study of shopping in the community highlighted; (1) problems experienced by clients when shopping; (2) the types of decisions they must make; (3) what help and training was provided by their carers. From this work the researchers were able to develop a scheme to aid decision making whilst shopping. The scheme was used in a larger study comparing 3 group homes whilst grocery shopping. Computer software to address some of the difficulties encountered during these studies is now being developed.
Source of Grant: Stallington Hospital, North Staffordshire Health Authority
Date of Research: 1987-1990
KEYWORDS: computer assisted instruction; decision-making; interactive video; mentally handicapped

8/0501

Department of Psychology
Keele, Staffordshire ST5 5BG
0782 621111
Branthwaite, A. Dr; Ross, A. Dr
Use of continuing education by medical practitioners

Abstract: This research was conducted in order to investigate patterns of attendance and non-attendance at continuing education meetings, and examine factors which encourage or inhibit use of such facilities. The characteristics of regular, occasional and non attenders were compared in terms of demographic variables, attitudes to continuing education, attitudes to work and the lifestyle of a General Practitioner. The research used qualitative and summary methods by interviewing initially some 32 GPs followed by a questionnaire to over 600. The findings provide course organizers with a detailed insight into the attitudes and perceptions of frequent and infrequent attenders. The research recommends that the role of the General Practitioner Tutor should be enhanced to provide more direct contact and influence with small groups of doctors.
Published Material: BRANTHWAITE, A., ROSS, A. et al (1988). Continuing education for General Practitioners. London: Royal College of General Practitioners, occasional paper 38.; BRANTHWAITE, A. and ROSS, A. (1988). Satisfaction and job stress in General Practice, Family Practice, 5, pp.83-93.
Source of Grant: West Midlands Regional Health Authority: £16,000
Date of Research: 1985-1989
KEYWORDS: continuing education; doctor; medicine

8/0502

Department of Psychology
School of Human Development, Keele ST5 5BG
0782 621111 ext 4413
Afzalnia, M.R. Mr; *Supervisor:* Hartley, J. Prof.
Television viewing, reading and listening: a study in childrens' cognition

Abstract: This research is concerned with the role of television in children's schooling performance. The literature suggests that viewing television gives children skills that might influence their other cognitive skills. Especially, it is argued, the attentional demands involved in audio and visual processing might create a new skill which might affect other receptive communication skills. This study examines 5 hypotheses, including the assumption that 'there is a positive relationship between the tendency to listen to television and children's verbal receptive (reading and listening) achievement when controlling for IQ'. The term 'tendency to listen' is used to mean listening attention for the uptake of audio information from television programmes as a behaviour and not an intention or willingness to do so. Seventy eight 9- to 10- year olds were selected from a local junior school to take part. A device for measuring children's tendency to listen to television was designed. The results from this device were analyzed whilst children's comprehension of the content was controlled. Other tests of reading, intelligence and listening skills, together with two questionnaires, were used to collect information about the children's abilities and their parents' and teachers' attitudes towards their viewing study and listening habits. The results indicated that the children's reading and listening test scores were highly and significantly correlated with each other. In addition, the relationship between their tendency to use the audio channel of tv and their comprehension of tv was positive and high. However, when their comprehension and IQ was controlled, this relationship with their listening and reading achievement, was not considerable. Further analyses of variance have indicated that those viewing for less time were more advanced in their reading and listening scores but not superior in their audio attention to tv. It is concluded that a closer attention to the audio channel of tv does produce a better understanding of tv; and that this understanding is related to verbal receptive skills. However, mere listening tendency to tv cannot on its own predict children's reading and listening performance.
Source of Grant: No funding
Date of Research: 1988-1990
KEYWORDS: achievement; cognition; communication; listening; reading; television

8/0503

Department of Psychology
Keele, Staffordshire ST5 5BG
0782 621111
City General Hospital
London Road, Newcastle upon Tyne NE4 6BE
091 2738811
Trueman, M.; Hutt, S.J. Prof.; Lynch, A. Dr; Rowley, J. MS; *Supervisor:* Hutt, S.J. Prof.; Campbell, C. Dr; Cooper, R. Dr; Tomlin, P. Dr
The long-term sequelae of febrile convulsions in infancy

Abstract: The investigation examines the effects upon children aged 4 years of a febrile convulsion missing the first three years of life. Eighty four children were compared with 89 control children aged 4 years. The effects of various aspects of aetiology and clinical manifestation of the convulsion on cognitive performance have been examined. The age of onset has a significant effect on performance of females from working class backgrounds. Those girls who suffered convulsions before 13 months performed significantly worse than other girls with febrile convulsions and the control girls. Recurrent convulsions depress the performance of working class males but not other males or any of the female groups. Neither the length, nor if the convulsion is single or multiple, has a reliable effect on cognitive performances. This ongoing study is being developed three-fold: (1) to relate the cognitive findings to other information collected on the neurological and EEG (Electroencephalographic) status of children; (2) to examine how the convulsive children behave in a number of simulated real-life situations; and (3) to examine both convulsive and control children in terms of their educational achievement and social skills in late childhood and early adolescence.
Published Material: LYNCH, A., MITCHELL, L.B., VINCENT, E.M., TRUEMAN, M. & MACDONALD, L. (1982). 'The McCarthy scales of children's abilities: a normative study on English four-year olds', British Journal of Educational Psychology, No 52, pp.133-143.; LYNCH, A., VINCENT, E.M., MITCHELL, L.B. & TRUEMAN, M. (1982). 'How 'flat' are normal ability profiles in 4-year olds?', Child Care, Health & Development, No 8, pp.39-49.; TRUEMAN, M. (1983). 'Febrile convulsions and intellectual development'. University of Keele.; TRUEMAN, M., LYNCH, A. & BRANTHWAITE, A. (1984). 'A factor analytic study of the McCarthy Scales of Children's Abilities', British Journal of Educational Psychology, No 54, pp.331-335.; TRUEMAN, M. & HUTT, S.J. (1985). 'Early brain development and experience'. In: BRANTHWAITE, A. & ROGERS, D. (Eds). Children growing up'. Buckingham: Open University Press.
Source of Grant: Medical Research Council Spastics Society National Fund for Research into Crippling Diseases
Date of Research: 1976 – continuing
KEYWORDS: cognitive development; epilepsy; pre-school child; sex difference

8/0504

Department of Psychology
Computer Applications to Special Education, Keele ST5 5BG

0782 621111
Seale, J. Mrs; Newberry-Tarrier, S.J. Mrs; Topping M.J.
Mr; *Supervisor:* Hegarty, J.R. Dr

Computer applications to special education

Abstract: The aim of the research is to support users of microcomputers in special education, particularly those who work with adults who have severe learning difficulties. The work combines research, development of software and hardware devices, consultancy and staff training. There are three major research projects: (1) Staff development. A detailed study of 11 centres using micros has revealed the dimensions of effective management of the computer as an educational resource. The research has produced a management profile (AMMASE) which can be used to identify weaknesses and strengths in management and create goals. (2) Expert Systems Project. Detailed observational research of adults with a mental handicap whilst shopping for groceries has produced a specification for a computer aid which will help them produce their own shopping lists based on the grocery stocks normally required for their weekly needs. The software is now written for a hand-held microcomputer with integral touch screen and printer which allows clients who cannot read or write to input the current grocery stocks and thus create a shopping list (which is graphical). Evaluation of the system is in progress. (3). A robotic device to allow people to eat unassisted has been developed. This low cost device is now in use and is being evaluated.

Published Material: COLLINS, R. (1989). 'Computers and special education for adults'. In: HARTLEY, J. & BRANTHWAITE, J.A. (Eds). The Applied Psychologist. Buckingham: Open University Press.; TOPPING, J. 'Potential of computerized robot arms as an aid to eating'. In: HARWIN, W.S., GOSINE, R.G. & JACKSON, R.D. Proceedings of the Cambridge Workshop on Rehabilitation Robotics. Cambridge University: Cambridge University Engineering Department. A full list of publications is available from the researchers.

Source of Grant: Various public and charitable sources
Date of Research: 1985 – continuing
KEYWORDS: *microcomputers; expert systems; rehabilitation; robotics; training; severe learning difficulties*

8/0505

Department of Psychology
Keele ST5 5BG
0782 621111
Hartley, J. Prof.

Designing instructional text

Abstract: This research focuses on the design of instructional text – mainly in the form of printed materials – which enables the reader to do or to understand something. The research covers three areas: (i) the layout of such materials; (ii) the language of such materials; and (iii) the use of structural devices which enable people to find their way about a piece of text. Work with layout stresses the importance of using the 'white-space' systematically in order to convey the underlying structure of text. Work with language suggests the importance of simpler wording. Work with 'access structures' indicates how devices such as headings and summaries can aid recall. Recently the research has shifted its focus of interest from work with printed text to work with braille, audio-taped instruction, and electronic text.

Published Material: HARTLEY, J. (1988). 'Using principles of text design to improve the effectiveness of audiotapes', British Journal of Educational Technology, Vol 19, No 1, pp.4-16.; HARTLEY, J. (1989). 'Text design and the setting of Braille', Information Design Journal, Vol 5, pp.183-190.; HARTLEY, J. (1990). 'Textbook design: current status and future directions', International Journal of Educational Research, Vol 14, pp.533-541.; HARTLEY, J. (1990). Author, printer, reader, listener: four sources of confusion when listening to tabular/diagrammatic information', British Journal of Visual Impairment, Vol VIII, pp.51-53.; HARTLEY, J. (1991). 'Tabling information', American Psychologist, (in press).; HARTLEY, J. (Ed). (1991). Technology and writing: readings in the psychology of written communication. London: Jessical Kingsley Ltd (in press).

Source of Grant: No funding
Date of Research: 1970 – continuing
KEYWORDS: *design; teaching aids; textbook; typography; visual perception*

8/0506

Department of Psychology
Keele, Staffordshire ST5 5BG

0782 621111
Trueman, M. Mr

Attitudes towards computers

Abstract: A series of 4 studies have been carried out using the Computer Attitude Scale to measure computer anxiety, computer liking and computer confidence. A study of undergraduate students showed that males had more experience in using computers and liked computers more than females did. However, there was no sex difference in computer anxiety or computer confidence. A second study of undergraduates found that males had more experience of using computers, liked computers more and were more confident with computers than females in the study. This study also showed a correlation between higher neuroticism scores and found that males had more experience with computers and were more likely to have access to a computer than females were. Males were more confident about using computers and they liked computers more than females. The final study looked at the relationship between androgeny (as assessed by the Personal Attributes Questionnaire, Spence & Helmreich, 1978) and the Computer Attitude Scale in a sample of 4th form school children. There were no sex differences in computer anxiety, computer liking or computer confidence. However, androgynous individuals had higher computer liking scores than masculine, feminine or undifferentiated individuals. Also, there were a series of significant sex and androgeny interactions in which androgenous males and masculine females were less anxious, liked computers more and were more confident about computers than the other groups.

Published Material: TRUEMAN, M. (1989). 'Attitudes towards computers'. Paper presented to the 5th Annual Wolverhampton Polytechnic Educational Research Conference. San Antonio, Ibiza.; TRUEMAN, M. (1990). 'The effects of gender and computer experience on attitudes towards computers', CORE (Collected Original Resources in Education), Vol 14, No 3, 1990. (Fr. BO1 on No 1 of 9 microfiches).

Source of Grant: No funding
Date of Research: 1985 – continuing
KEYWORDS: *attitude; computer; sex difference*

8/0507

Department of Psychology
Keele ST5 5BG
0782 621111
Beh-Pajooh, A. Mr; *Supervisor:* Hegarty, J. Dr

Attitude modification and integration of severely mentally handicapped persons

Abstract: In recent years, a great deal of attention has concentrated upon the education, care, welfare and in one word 'lives' of persons with special needs. As a result of this the 'Normalization Principle' has become internationally influential on the human services for mentally handicapped persons. More specifically, 'Integration' of Severely Mentally Handicapped (SMH) persons into mainsteam educational settings (e.g. regular schools and classes) has generated a great deal of research, as well as controversy among different groups of educators, psychologists, and social policy makers. The purpose of this research is to study and assess the variation of attitudes held by parents of non-handicapped children, college teachers and college peers towards SMH children (under seven years old) and adolescents (16-19 years old) as a social outcome of partially integrated programmes. The programmes have been implemented at the nursery class of Merryfields School for children with severe learning difficulties and at the home care unit of Newcastle College of Further Education. The research question asks: are there any significant differences between scores of the following groups of subjects' attitudes towards SMH persons? (a) subjects who have experienced no social contact; (b) subjects who have experienced less social contact; (c) subjects who have experienced more social contact. The hypothesis is that one who has experienced more social contact with SMH persons, has a more positive or favourable attitude in comparison with one who has not or experienced this less. The research method consists of participant observation, structured interview, and questionnaire.

Source of Grant: No funding
Date of Research: 1987-1990
KEYWORDS: *attitude; integration; mentally handicapped; special needs*

8/0508

Department of Psycholoyg
Keele, Staffordshire ST5 5BG
0782 621111

Seale, J.K.; *Supervisor:* Hegarty, J.R. Dr
Microcomputers in special education: the management of an innovation
Abstract: The microcomputer has great potential in special education and promises to be an effective and powerful educational tool. Different managerial practices in implementing the microcomputer, however, can influence its potential effectiveness. The purpose of this research is to investigate effective management strategies for implementing microcomputers into special education centres. The first stage of the research involved studying centres who were using computers in order to assess what is effective and ineffective management of the microcomputer. Two centres were studied, each for a ten week period. These were an occupational therapy unit and a social education centre. Both were attached to residential hospitals. The methods used to study these centres were participant observation, and structured interview. Results from the studies showed that such factors as control over resources, extensive support networks and extensive staff involvement appeared to have a positive influence on microcomputer use. The second stage of the research will develop a checklist which will enable managers to assess the effectiveness of their strategies for implementing microcomputers. These results will be fed back to centres to improve effectiveness.
Source of Grant: Keele University studentship: £2,800 per annum
Date of Research: 1987-1990
KEYWORDS: administration of education; educational innovation; microcomputer; special education

8/0509
Department of Social Anthropology and Social Work
Keele ST5 5BG
0782 621111
Finer, A. Mr; *Supervisor:* Bolger, A.W.
Clumsiness in children
Abstract: A sample of children have been measured for motor control using a modified stableometer. Children assessed as clumsy have experienced training in motor control and their improvement compared to a control group.
Source of Grant: Local Education Authority: fees
Date of Research: 1982-1989
KEYWORDS: measurement; motor development

8/0510
Department of Sociology and Social Anthropology
Keele ST5 5BG
0782 621111
Daher, J. Mr; *Supervisor:* Thomas, J. Ms
Educational television in Iraq
Abstract: The thesis examines the intentions behind, and results of, the introduction of educational television in Iraq. It assesses the advantages and disadvantages of educational television in developing countries generally. It examines the context of the Iraqi policy particularly in terms of the changing role of education, the occupational structure, and State development objectives. It compares ETV (educational television) watching in two schools, one predominantly middle class, one mainly working class. Two hundred children were interviewed and the results analyzed according to class, gender and educational level of parents. Students and teachers attitudes to ETV generally, and to the presentation of particular programmes, were also assessed. In general, the desire of the government to minimise class and gender inequalities through such technological means was shown to be over-optimistic. Both home bacckground and school setting appeared to have an effect on ETV watching and commitment.
Source of Grant: Government of Iraq
Date of Research: 1987-1990
KEYWORDS: developing country; educational policy; educational television; Iraq

8/0511
Department of Sociology, Social Anthropology and Social Work
Keele ST5 5BG
0782 621111
Al-Shani, R, Mr; *Supervisor:* Bolger, A.W.
Counselling and guidance of overseas students in higher education
Abstract: A sample of overseas students from universities in Britain have been surveyed as to their perception of problems they have experienced and the sources of help they have used. Student counsellors have been questioned as to their work with overseas students and their perceptions of the problems involved.
Source of Grant: Iraqi Government
Date of Research: 1986-1989
KEYWORDS: foreign student; guidance; university

Kent University

8/0512
Canterbury CT2 TN2
0227 764000 ext 3374
Rootes, C.A. Mr
The politics of the higher educated in Western Europe
Abstract: This project considers the political consequences of the post-war expansion of higher education. It considers the development of higher education, the changes in the occupational structure associated with the increasing employment of university and college graduates, and the employment experience of those graduates, especially since the dramatic expansion of the 1960s – 1970s. Of special concern are the social and political movements which have been seen as arising from middle-class radicalism, but the more general political attitudes, associations and behaviour of the higher educated are also considered. Particular attention has been paid to the hypothesis that radicalism among the higher educated is a product of actual or incipient unemployment or underemployment but even in the most critical cases (Italy), this thesis is found to be unsupported. Other countries considered are Britain, France, West Germany, Sweden and the Netherlands. The research is conducted under the auspices of the European Consortium for Political Research.
Published Material: ROOTES, C.A. The politics of the higher educated. Melbourne Journal of Politics, 18 (November 1986) pp.184-200.; C.J. LEVY and ROOTES, C.A. Disoccupazione intellectuale e mobilitazione politica. Bibliotecca Della Liberta, Vol.XXII, No. 97, (April-June 1987) pp.139-169.; ROOTES, C.A. The politics of the higher educated in Britain and Italy since 1900. Report to Economic and Social Research Council (on Grant E00232091) July 1986.
Source of Grant: Economic and Social Research Council (1984-6): £20,000 Nuffield Foundation: (1986) £1,000
Date of Research: 1984-1989
KEYWORDS: Europe; graduate; higher education; politics

8/0513
Canterbury CT2 7NZ
0227 764000 ext 3374
Rootes, C.A. Mr
Radical student movements in western societies since 1960
Abstract: This is a continuing project on the causes and consequences of student radicalism in western societies, but with special attention to France and Australia and comparative reference to the US and Western Europe. The research employs a diversity of methods and considers a variety of aspects of student movements but particular attention has been paid to the political context of the development of student radicalism and the subsequent life histories of former student activists. The latter is focused around a longitudinal study of 80 former activists in Queensland, Australia.
Published Material: ROOTES, C.A. (1980). 'Student radicalism: politics of moral protest and legitimation problems of the modern capitalist state', Theory and Society, Vol 9, No 3, pp.473-502. May.; ROOTES, C.A. (1981). 'Students as agents of radical social change', Social Alternatives, Vol 2, No 1, pp.51-56. March.; ROOTES, C.A. (1981). 'On the future of protest politics in western democracies', European Journal of Political Resarch, Vol 9, No 4, pp.421-432. December.; ROOTES, C.A. (1982). 'Student activism in France: 1968 and after'. In: PHILIP G.CERNY (Ed). Social movements and protest in France. London: Frances Pinter.; ROOTES, C.A. (1983). 'Students: are they really so conservative?', Politics, Vol 18, No 1, pp.120-126. May.; ROOTES, C.A. (1988). 'The development of radical student movements and their sequelae', Australian Journal of Politics & History, Vol 34, No 2.
Source of Grant: Social Science Research Council: (1978-9) £4,500 Nuffield Foundation: £2,000
Date of Research: 1969 – continuing
KEYWORDS: Australia; France; student unrest; Western Europe

8/0514
Institute of Social and Applied Psychology, Canterbury,

Kent CT2 7LZ
0227 764000
Forrester, M.A. Dr; Shire, B. Ms

Children's understanding of estimation

Abstract: There is an increasing emphasis in mathematics education on the importance of estimation abilities in children. This study investigates the role of context upon primary-aged children's estimation skills. Children in three age groups (from aged 5-8 years) were asked to carry out a range of estimation tasks involving distance, area and volume measurements. The tasks varied in type and complexity and were either of a 'real world' or 'mathematics task' form. In addition to performance measures the children's answers to questions on how they carried out the estimates were recorded and analyzed. Quantitative and qualitative analyses found significant effects for context and child strategy. Estimates in contexts perceived as mathematical were different, both in that they changed with age and in their error patterns, from contexts involving perceptual-motor skills. The results are discussed within a model of estimating.

Published Material: FORRESTER, M.A., LATHAM, J. & GALLI-PHILLIPS, L. (1989). Exploring young children's understanding of estimation. Proceedings of the Day Conference, British Society for Research into Learning Mathematics, Brighton Polytechnic, May 1989.; SHIRE, B. (1989). Children's understanding of approximations. Proceedings of the Day Conference, British Society for Research into Learning Mathematics, Birmingham University, November 1989.; FORRESTER, M.A., LATHAM, J. & GALLI-PHILLIPS, L. 'Exploring estimation in young primary school children', Educational Studies in Mathematics, American Journal, forthcoming.

Source of Grant: Kent University: £2,000
Date of Research: 1987-1990
KEYWORDS: estimation (mathematics); mathematics; primary education

Kidderminster and District Health Authority

8/0515

The Croft, Sutton Park Road, Kidderminster DY11 6LJ
0562 824711
Alexander Patterson School
Lea Castle Hospital, Cookley, Kidderminster DY10 3PP
0562 850461 ext 302
Mitchell, D. Mr

Educational software for the multiply handicapped child

Abstract: This is an ongoing research and development project using primitive techniques of observation and evaluation. The objective is to improve the quality of currently available software and develop new software for the needs of the multiply handicapped youngster with severe learning difficulties. The client population are those attending the school and other schools associated with the Research Centre for the Education of the Visually Handicapped (RCEVH). Work has focused on enabling efficient access to microtechnology, especially using single line switches, touch screens and other devices. The results of the work are published by RCEVH, both as software and articles, information sheets, etc. A number of peripheral products, and associated information sheets, have resulted.

Published Material: MITCHELL, D. (1984). 'Evaluation of Computer Software for Children with Severe Learning Difficulties', Research Exchange, Vol 3, pp.9. NCSE.; MITCHELL, D. (1985). 'The Scribbler: a report of the use of the Cheyne Scribbler (touch screen)', Alexander Patterson School Information Sheet.; MITCHELL, D. (1986). 'BORIS: Interface box offering 4 in/out lines', Alexander Patterson School Information Sheet.; MITCHELL, D. (1986). 'Buttons Box: Interface to match Buttons software', Alexander Patterson School Information Sheet.; MITCHELL, D. (1986). 'Auditory Scanning Communication Aid: speech synthesis aid developed by REACH (Recreational and Educational Aids to Communication for the Handicapped) (Lea Castle Hospital Communication Aids Team)', Alexander Patterson School Information Sheet.; MITCHELL, D. 'Twelve months with David', RCEVH Computer Assisted Learning for th Visually Handicapped: Newsletter No 9, pp.15.; MITCHELL, D., PAINTER, C. & BLENKHORN, P. (1986). 'The less able, visually handicapped youngster: a resource list for staff using the BBC microcomputer',

RECVH Information Sheet No 7.; MITCHELL, D. (1986). 'Starting Points: a brief set of suggestions to arrange the optimum conditions for a less able, visually handicapped youngster to use a microcomputer and display', RCEVH Information Sheet No 8.

Source of Grant: Kidderminster and District Health Authority; £3,000 Council for Educational Technology: £600 now in conjunction with Research Centre for the Education of the Visually Handicapped (RCEVH) funded from internal sources and small external donations

Date of Research: 1986 – continuing
KEYWORDS: handicapped; learning difficulty; microcomputer; software; visually

King Alfred's College

8/0516

Sparkford Road, Winchester SO22 4NR
0962 841515 ext 265
Rowntree, P. Dr

An evaluation of the Kodaly-style and Silver Burdett music teaching methods in primary schools

Abstract: The study is concerned with (1) children's learning, (ii) teacher response and (iii) children's attitudes in relation to two differing methods of music teaching. The study involves children and staff in some eight primary schools. The methods involve teaching, structured observation and standardized testing.

Source of Grant: No funding
Date of Research: 1988 – continuing
KEYWORDS: music education; primary education

8/0517

Winchester SO22 4NR
0962 841332
Chambers, J.E. Ms; *Supervisor:* Perry, D. Mr

Getting results and solving problems (The GRASP Project)

Abstract: The investigation is seeking to identify ways of enabling individuals to reflect upon the processes by which they 'get results'. It is looking at the development of problem-solving skills in the context of teacher training, industrial management training and professional training more widely. It aims to offer means by which individuals may come to an explicit awareness of the processes by which they pursue their own purposes. It seeks to find ways by which individuals may learn to pursue intentions more effectively. The particular setting in which this work is based is the Department of Design and Technolgy at KAC. Some of the investigation involves the observation of student teachers engaged in technological designing and making, in order: (1) to contribute to an understanding of the design processes involved in such activity; (2) to ascertain whether student teachers transfer the learning which they derive from technolgocial designing and making to other contexts, particularly to their own management of learning in the classroom; (3) to identify ways in which such transfer might be effectively ensured; (4) to suggest strategies by which those responsible for the education and training of teachers could support their students' capacity to achieve results. The investigation also aims to provide findings which are of wider relevance outside teaching by paralleling its work with student teachers with similar work in industry and other professional settings, such as nursing. The project is linked to two others with similar aims, one based in a number of schools in Dudley and the other in the Management Development Unit at Salford University.

Source of Grant: DTI (Department of Trade and Industry) Comino Foundation
Date of Research: 1987-1990
KEYWORDS: design; management education; problem solving; teacher education; technology

8/0518

Sparkford Lane, Winchester SO22 4NR
0703 841515
Southampton University
Department of Education
Highfield, Southampton SO9 5NH
0703 595000
Bunyard, D.M. Mr; *Supervisor:* MEREDITH, M. MR; BRUMFITT, C. PROF.

Microworld and metaphor

Abstract: The research argues for the adoption of a particular definintion of computer based microworlds and develops the theme that metaphorical thinking is a fundamental response, both to the challenge of designing these microworlds and to their use in education. Arising from the definition presented, a self-reflective component is identified that links with the explanatory use of metaphor, analogy, and anecdote, by designers, teachers, and children. The functional correlate to this within the microworld is seen to be a capability for re-programming. This raises the general question of how programmming skills can be fostered within a microworld and a detailed response is provided by focusing on a specific investigation: the attempt to design a microworld that will encourage the use of conditional statements within Logo. Consideration is then given to the pedagogical prespectives implied by the use of these microworlds.
Published Material: BUNYARD, D.M. (1989). 'Why microworlds? part 1', Micromaths, Vol 5, No 2, Summer 1989, pp.33-35.; BUNYARD, D.M. (1989). 'WHY MICROWORLDS? PART 2', MICROMATHS, VOL 5, No 3, Autumn 1989, pp.20-23.; BUNYARD, D.M. (1989). 'A screen microworld with a sensing turtle', Logos, Spring 1989, pp.14-17.
Source of Grant: King Alfred's College: half fees
Date of Research: 1985-1990
KEYWORDS: *computer microworld; computer programming; learning*

King Alfred's College of Higher Education

8/0519

Sparkford Road, Winchester SO22 4NR
0962 841515
Clayton, T. Mr; *Supervisor:* Hackney, A. Dr
Welfare assistance as a resource to help with the education and management of children with special educational needs in ordinary primary schools
Abstract: The research is being carried out by an educational psychologist with responsibility for overseeing County's Assessment Procedures and advising on provision for special needs. The aims are to obtain statistics concerning the deployment of Welfare Assistants; to assess their own expectations of their duties and compare them with those of the schools and to ascertain the difference between expectation and reality. Changes to the current situation will be considered, particularly as regards training. Country-wide survey is via documentation and questionnaires. Results are not yet available.
Source of Grant: Wiltshire Local Education Authority
Date of Research: 1985 – continuing
KEYWORDS: *assistant; class management; integration; primary education; special needs*

Kingston Polytechnic

8/0520

Educational Development Unit, Penrhyn Road, Kingston upon Thames KT1 2EE
081 549 1141
Further Education Unit
Information Centre, Grove House, 2-6 Orange Street, London WC2H 7WE
071 321 0433
Wisdom, J. Mr; *Supervisor:* Godfrey, R.J. Dr
Languages for all: an evaluation of an initiative to provide modern language support for higher education students
Abstract: The aim of this research is to evaluate the 'Languages for All' programme devised by the School of Languages at Kingston Polytechnic. The programme was part of the institutions response to the challenge of the single European market. Now the polytechnic has a policy of making available to all students the opportunity of learning one of the major European languages. The Kingston programme will be compared and contrasted with similar initiatives in other selected institutions. The experience of Kingston will be drawn upon to propose guidelines for FHE (further

and higher education) institutions seeking to update the foreign languages skills of students for whom languages are not the main study discipline, with particular reference to the single European market in 1992. Investigation will be through formal consultation with students using a group interview technique, using a 'pyramid' discussion structure resulting in a written report. The project will be based on the material resulting from this consultation process with a large number of the language classes formed by students and by academic and general staff. There will also be group interviews with year groups to investigate current attitudes to languages, and why some students chose not to take up or dropped out of language options. This consultation process will be carried out between January-Easter 1990. The polytechnic will also carry out a Languages Audit amongst a significant number of the polytechnics staff to discover existing competence. Other elements of the evaluation exercise will cover the relative effectiveness of different forms of language teaching (e.g. language labs, tapes, textbooks) and the benefits and difficulties which result from the use of a number of skill levels and teaching students from different disciplines together. The training programme for part-time staff will also be evaluated. An evaluation report will be produced for publication by the Further Education Unit.
Source of Grant: Further Education Unit
Date of Research: 1990-1990
KEYWORDS: *further education; higher education; language skills; language teaching; modern languages*

8/0521

Department of Education
Gipsy Hill Centre, Kingston Hill, Kingston KT2 7LB
081 549 1141
Montgomery, D.M.L. Ms
Teacher appraisal
Abstract: A pilot study undertaken in 2 schools with 4 secondary teachers found the appraisal system effective in improving performance and creating satisfactory teaching performance in those found seriously wanting. The main study is in progress appraising a range of primary and secondary teachers of all abilities with pre- and post-interaction analysis. Video taped samples will be presented to experienced judges to determine the effectiveness of the 'treatment'. The video taped samples will be randomly selected and presented in a Latin square design. These results and others will be subjected to classical analyses of variance and qualitative analyses.
Published Material: MONTGOMERY, D. (1984). 'Evaluation and enhancement of teaching performance', (Learning Difficulties Project publication), Kingston Polytechnic.; MONTGOMERY, D. (1985). 'The Nubis Credibility', Education, March, pp. 259.; MONTGOMERY, D. (1985). 'Teacher appraisal: a theory and practice for evaluation and enhancement', Inspection and Advice, Vol 21, No 1, pp.16-19.; MONTGOMERY, D. 'Effective teaching and performance enhancement', New Era in Education, Vol 69.; MONTGOMERY, D. & HADFIELD, N. 'Appraisal in the primary school', (Learning Difficulties Project publication), Kingston Polytechnic.; MONTGOMERY, D. & HADFIELD, N. (1989). Practical teacher appraisal. London: Kogan Page.
Source of Grant: Kingston Polytechnic: £24,000
Date of Research: 1983-1989
KEYWORDS: *evaluation; performance; teacher; teaching*

Lancashire Polytechnic

8/0522

Corporation Street, Preston PR1 2TQ
0772 22141
Billingham, S.C. Dr
Perceptions of and attitudes towards higher education among 16-19 year olds in full-time further education
Abstract: This research is intended to include the attitudes towards and perceptions of higher education among 16-19 year olds pursuing a range of full-time courses in further education. The project is being conducted in 5 colleges of further education: Accrington & Rossendale, Blackburn, Burnley, Nelson and Colne College and W.R. Tuson (Preston). Data gathered by a questionnaire (administered to students during tutorial sessions) will be analyzed in respect of a range of variables including age, sex, type of course being studied, year of study, previous qualifications, ethnic origin

and social class. It is hoped that through this data the researchers will be able to give a picture of any systematic variations in attitudes/perceptions of higher education across and between social groups and feed this information into decision making and planning processes in both FE and HE so as to inform future decisions about such issues as course and curriculum development, admissions policies, student support and marketing of educational guidance.
Source of Grant: Lancashire Polytechnic Research Committee: £400
Date of Research: 1988-1989
KEYWORDS: *attitude; further education; higher education; planning of education; social class; student*

8/0523
Computing Services,
Corporation Street, Preston PR1 2TQ
0772 22141
Barnish, R. Mr; *Supervisor:* Smith, E.H. Dr
Establishment of the Further Education Courseware Centre (FECC)
Abstract: In 1987, Education Support Grants were awarded to establish centres for Information Technology (IT) staff development in Further Education (FE) colleges. Many of these centres were charged with the development of computer based teaching and learning materials for a wide range of subject disciplines. This project aims to establish a uniform approach to the review of these courseware materials; review a representative group of the courseware covering the full range of subject disciplines; produce regular newsletters for distribution to the FE community; establish and maintain a nationally accessible database of courseware and reviews; establish links with other courseware review groups and courseware collections and provide a means whereby the FE community can access and/or purchase courseware.
Source of Grant: Department of Education and Science: £50,554
Date of Research: 1989-1990
KEYWORDS: *computer assisted instruction; further education; teaching aids*

8/0524
Combined Studies Programme,
Corporation Street, Preston PR1 2TQ
0772 201201
Mellor-Clark, J. Mr; *Supervisor:* Abramson, M.G. Mr
The Lancashire Integrated Colleges Scheme (LINCS): patterns of recruitment, attainment and progression (1984-89)
Abstract: The research will focus on the five years of operational experience of the Lancashire integrated Colleges Scheme (LINCS). This scheme was the first in the UK to provide 'franchised' level 1 subject components of the honours degree from Lancashire Polytechnic to local colleges of further education. Making full use of the latest SPSS (x) computer package, the research will make a detailed and sophisticated quantitative analysis of LINCS cohorts since 1984, when the scheme started, and draw conclusions on the following issues: (i) socio-economic analysis of LINCS cohorts, (ii) why do they succeed? (iii) Why do they fail? (iv) Why do some LINCS students progress to higher levels of the degree at the Polytechnic and some do not? Quantitative data will be supported later by qualitative research techniques.
Source of Grant: Lancashire Polytechnic Research Committee: £8,500 research assistant salary plus expenses
Date of Research: 1989-1990
KEYWORDS: *adult education; credits; further education; higher education; integration; part-time course*

8/0525
Department of Chemistry
Corporation Street, Preston PR1 2TQ
0772 22141
Brattan, D. Dr
Open learning methods in chemistry
Abstract: Preparation, use of and evaluation of open learning texts in physical and analytical chemistry. The main aims of this research are to evaluate a change to learning rather than teaching methods and to examine ways of increasing access to higher education. Evaluation will be by interview and questionnaire.
Source of Grant: Lancashire Polytechnic: £100 Computer facilites and Open Learning texts – School of Chemistry
Date of Research: 1988 – continuing
KEYWORDS: *chemistry; higher education; open learning*

8/0526
Department of Combined Studies
Corporation Street, Preston PR1 2TQ
0772 22141
Clutton, E. Dr; *Supervisor:* Abramson, M.G. Mr; Grannell, M. Dr
Forging higher education links with an isolated community: West Cumbria College as a case study
Abstract: The research focuses on mature, part-time students on the Access course and the Lancashire Integrated Colleges Scheme (LINCS) courses at West Cumbria College (Workington, Cumbria) which is isolated on the West Coast of Cumbria and approximately 80 miles away from Lancashire Polytechnic. The aim is to explore student's perceptions of higher education (within these new courses) and the construction of formal institutional links between the college and the polytechnic. Lancashire Polytechnic has validated the college's Access course and has 'franchized' Level 1 subject components of the BSc/BA (Hons) Combined Studies Programme to the college since 1986.
Published Material: ABRAMSON, M. (1988). The Lancashire Integrated Colleges Scheme (LINCS): widening access with advanced standing. London: The Royal Society.
Source of Grant: CNAA (Council for National Academic Awards) Small Development Fund: £5,600
Date of Research: 1987-1988
KEYWORDS: *access programme; continuing education; higher education; mature student; part-time course*

8/0527
Department of Community Studies
Corporation Street, Preston PR1 2TQ
0772 22141
Ali, Y.
The experience of black students on social work courses
Abstract: The research is intended to explore the different experiences of black and white students in social work education, with a view to informing future course and curriculum development, admissions policies, student support, placement practices, etc. A sample of 10 students (5 white, 5 black) are undergoing structured in depth interviews on a termly basis for the duration of their 2 year CQSW (Certificate of Qualification in Social Work) course. The research stands within the context of developing qualitative research into black student experience to follow on from the qualification of students on Polytechnic courses by ethnic origin.
Source of Grant: Racial Equality Unit (Lancashire Polytechnic)/Central Council for Education and Training in Social Work: £500 for 1st year of project (to be confirmed)
Date of Research: 1988-1989
KEYWORDS: *course; ethnic minority; polytechnic; social work*

8/0528
Department of Historical and Critical Studies
Corporation Street, Preston PR1 2TQ
0772 22141
Dunn, D. Dr; Timmins, G. Mr
Applications of computerized historical simulations to higher education
Abstract: Nearly all UK and some US manufactured software has been tested. A template has been devised to evaluate any pieces of software likely to have a relevance in higher education. The exercise of undergraduates using the template for evaluating existing software has often proved a useful point of focus for their historical investigations. Equally, as a means of systematizing and standardizing the reviewing and evaluation processes required when appraising new software, the template has been highly successful. However, only one piece of commercially available software (US produced) is thought to have the characteristics of a program suitable to the needs of higher education history students. The researchers note that non-professionally marketed software may fulfil their evaluation criteria, and are aware of programs developed by researchers in other institutions that might rate as 'simulation' software. There is a need for the production of a new type of non-topic specific simulation program that can interact with existing and on-line databases, computerized books and spreadsheet packages. The researchers are investigating the possibility of producing such a piece of software themselves.
Published Material: DUNN, D. (1988). 'Template for evaluating simulation software', Northwest Journal of Historical Studies, Vol 1, No 1, pp.104-111.; DUNN, D. (1989). 'Computerized simula-

tions as teaching tools', Northwest Journal of Historical Studies, Vol 1, No 2.
Source of Grant: Polytechnic 1987/88: £273; 1988/89: £378
Date of Research: 1987 – continuing
KEYWORDS: computer assisted instruction; higher education; history; simulation; software

Lancaster University

8/0529
> Institute for Post-Compulsory Education,
> Bailrigg, Cartmel College, Lancaster LA1 4YL
> 0524 765201
> Ellwood, S. Ms; *Supervisor:* Fulton, O. Dr

Admissions to higher education
Abstract: This is a study of policy and practice in admission to higher education. Methods include interviews with 200 admission tutors and 30 central admissions officers/registrars in 25 institutions (universities, polytechnics, colleges of higher education) plus statistical analysis of data from UCCA and PCAS (Universities Central Council on Admissions/Polytechnic Central Admissions System). The aims are to establish variations in and differences between policy and practice in a range of institutions and disciplines and the process of policy development in the light of demographic and national planning funding changes.
Published Material: FULTON, O. (1989). Admissions to higher education: policy and practice. Sheffield: Training Enterprise Education Division.; FULTON, O. & ELLWOOD, S. (1989). 'Admissions, access and institutional change'. In: FULTON, O. (Ed). Access and institutional change. Buckingham: Open University Press.
Source of Grant: Training Enterprise Education Division: £45,000; 1988/89, followed by further unfunded analysis for full publication.
Date of Research: 1988 – continuing
KEYWORDS: admission; educational policy; higher education

8/0530
> Institute for Research & Development in Post-Compulsory Education, Lancaster LA1 4YW
> 0524 65201
> Barton, D. Dr; Hamilton, M. Dr

Literacy in the community
Abstract: This project will investigate the role of literacy in adult life in contemporary Britain, by means of ethnographic interviews and observation. It will document the everyday practical uses of literacy in the household and in the community and examine how they interface with school and work. The aim is to extend the view of literacy which currently informs educational practice at all levels and to contribute to the debate on levels of literacy in our society. The focus will be on literacy 'practices' or 'events' and on exploring the social meanings of literacy to the people involved.
Published Material: A series of working papers are now available on request from the researcher.
Source of Grant: Economic & Social Research Council: £54,000
Date of Research: 1989 – continuing
KEYWORDS: adult; community; literacy

8/0531
> Institute for Research and Development in Post-Compulsory Education, Lancaster LA1 4YW
> 0524 65201
> Hamilton, M. Dr

The definition and context of school failure in the United Kingdom
Abstract: This project is co-ordinated by Professor Pol-Dupont at the University of Mons, Belgium. It aims to carry out comparative research into school failure in six member states culminating in a conference on School Failure in Europe for September 1989. So far the first phase of the project has been completed, in which representatives from each country have researched the statistical and sociological background to school failure in their own national context.
Published Material: The Macrosociological approach to school failure: a perspective from the United Kingdom (1988) (working paper). Institute for Research and Development in Post-Compulsory Education, University of Lancaster.
Source of Grant: European Economic Community

Date of Research: 1988-1989
KEYWORDS: Europe; failure; school

8/0532
> Institute for Research and Development in Post-Compulsory Education, Cartmel College, Bailrigg, Lancaster LA1 4YL
> 0524 65201
> Saunders, M.S. Dr; Helsby, G. Ms

TVEI (Technical and Vocational Education Initiative) Evaluation Programme
Abstract: The programme (which also includes related projects at this Institute funded by the MSC) is a comprehensive evaluation of TVEI (Technical and Vocational Education Initiative), using quantitative methods – cohort studies of entrants to the programme at different periods, using questionnaires/tests, and of comparison groups of non-entrants – classroom observation, interviews/debriefings of key participants, etc.
Published Material: FULTON, O. (1987). 'The Technical and Vocational Training Initiative: an assessment'. In: Education and training UK 1987, Policy Journals.; HELSBY, G. (1989). 'Central control and grassroots creativity, the paradox at the heart of TVEI'. In: Education and training UK 1989 Policy Journals.; HELSBY, G. (1990). 'TVEI pilots in profile'. In: Hopkins, D. (Ed). TVEI at the change of life. Clevedon, Multilingual Matters.; HELSBY, G. & BAGGULEY, P. (1990). Student outcomes in 12 pilot LEAs. Sheffield: Training Enterprise Education Division.; SAUNDERS, M., HELSBY, G. & FULTON, O. (1991). Changing the curriculum: the TVEI experiement. London: Routledge.; HELSBY, G. & SAUNDERS, M. 'Performance indicators: bureaucratic control or developmental tool?'. Link Magazine, Lancaster University.
Source of Grant: 13 Local Education Authorities using Manpower Service Commission (MSC) funds: £500,000 to date
Date of Research: 1983 – continuing
KEYWORDS: evaluation; Technical and Vocational Education Initiative (TVEI)

8/0533
> Lancaster LA1 4YX
> 0524 65201 ext 4163
> Topham, P. Mr; Binstead, D. Mr

Interactive video and computer based learning for management education and development
Abstract: This is a follow up to a similar project just completed. (Laboratory studies into the use of interactive video for management education and training). The aim is to explore how managers may be helped to learn at a distance, using interactive video (I.V.) technology, or computer based technology (CBT). This will be done by the following steps; (a) to identify an area of learning suitable for management development (e.g. interpersonal skills); (b) make a programme of 1-4 hours duration, (c) test and evaluate this by video recording the learners interacting with the technology and each other; (d) redesign the programme; (e) re-test; (f) write the conclusion.
Source of Grant: Consortium of 10 organisations – total budget: £100,000
Date of Research: 1987-1989
KEYWORDS: computer assisted instruction; distance study; educational technology; interactive video; management education

8/0534
> Centre for Educational Research and Development, Cartmel College, Bailrigg, Lancaster LA1 4YL
> 0524 65201
> Wigan Education Department
> Gateway House, Standishgate, Wigan WN1 1XL
> 0942 44991
> *Supervisor:* O'Hare, E.

Collaborative research projects with Wigan LEA, in particular evaluation of Records of Achievement in the National PRAISE project
Abstract: Within the National PRAISE project, evaluation work is carried out of Records of Achievement (ROA) schemes for local education authorities. Interest is focused on the topics: research implications; Further Education/Youth Training Scheme issues; ROA dissemination; full age-range implications; relationships with other curricular activities in the school. One 1-year full-time teacher secondment is attached to each of these sub-topics. An Interim report is scheduled for March 1989. The final report is due in March 1990.

Source of Grant: Wigan Local Education Authority GRIST budget,
Supervision fee: £500 per term/secondment
Date of Research: 1987-1990
KEYWORDS: achievement; educational policy; student record

8/0535

Department of Education
University House, Cartmel College, Bailrigg,
Lancaster LA1 4YW
0524 65201
Helsby, G.

Overview of the 14-19 curriculum and the impact of new development

Abstract: Concern over the speed and scale of new developments in the 14-19 curriculum led to the establishment in September 1983 of a 14-19 Curriculum Development and Inservice Training Unit. The overall aims of the group were to investigate current developments with a view to identifying 'good practice', to disseminate that information and ultimately to help to clarify inservice (and, by implication, preservice) teacher training needs. In a developing area, and with little previously published material, the main approach adopted was to visit schools and institutions currently involved in curriculum development and to seek information from those actively participating, including senior management, teaching staff and students. Overall planning and policy was also discussed with those at advisory level. As the researchers progressed, it became possible to identify important themes for research (e.g. vocational preparation, staff development, TVEI (Technical and Vocational Education Initiative) profiles and assessment; common threads emerged from the various developments, and it became possible to compare and contrast, and to put individual initiatives into some sort of context. Since the 14-19 field is an area of such rapid change, it seemed imperative that the findings should be disseminated as speedily as possible. The researcher has produced periodic 'bulletins' on the various developments which now have a wide readership in the north-west, and has also been involved in both inservice and preservice teacher training, as well as acting as an informal advice and resource centre for teachers.
Published Material: a number of bulletins have been produced on various aspects of 14-19 curriculum. A full list of publications are available from the researcher on request.
Source of Grant: Lancashire Education Authority: full-time secondment of school teacher fellow
Date of Research: 1983-1990
KEYWORDS: curriculum development; educational innovation; inservice education and training of teachers; secondary education

8/0536

Department of Education
University House, Bailrigg, Lancaster LA1 4YL
0524 65201
Rogers, C. Dr

An evaluation of a new initial teacher education course

Abstract: The project aims to investigate the reactions of students to a new initial teacher education course primarily in terms of perceptions of relevance of course, effect on personal development and motivation and self-esteem. The entire first cohort to experience the course are included in the sample. Data is gathered by questionnaire and interview. Initial results indicate some loss of self-esteem as result of early course attendance. Subject study was not initally seen as relevant to professional development, but it was in terms of personal development.
Source of Grant: Individual institutions: £2,000
Date of Research: 1988-1990
KEYWORDS: course; evaluation; teacher education

8/0537

Department of Educational Research
Cartmel College, Bailrigg, Lancaster LA1 4YL
0524 65201
Serafingos, J. Mr; *Supervisor:* Calderhead, J. Dr

Teachers planning and evaluation of mathematics in Greek high schools

Abstract: This project is an examination of the ways in which a sample of Greek mathematics teachers think about their subject and their teaching, and how these understandings influence the kinds of experiences that are selected and presented to children in the mathematics curriculum. This is of particular interest in Greek education because of the high emphasis that is placed upon high school teachers' subject degree studies and the lack of any signifi-

cant professional training for high school teaching.
Source of Grant: Greek Ministry of Education scholarship
Date of Research: 1988 – continuing
KEYWORDS: Greece; mathematics; secondary education

8/0538

Department of Educational Research
Cartmel College, Bailrigg, Lancaster LA1 4YL
0524 65201
Clare, B. Mr; *Supervisor:* Calderhead, J. Dr

Classroom oracy

Abstract: The research concerns oracy in the secondary school classroom; particularly, at how teachers can facilitate oral interaction by creating a positive climate for talk, and, how pupil perspectives on the teacher and the nature of classroom talk affects their attitudes and responses. It is hoped to establish pupils' views on classroom talk with teachers and the dimensions they perceive to be important for good talk to take place.
Source of Grant: Bolton LEA secondment
Date of Research: 1988 – continuing
KEYWORDS: curriculum development; language development; oral expression; secondary education

8/0539

Department of Educational Research
Cartmel College, Bailrigg, Lancaster LA1 4AY
0524 65201
Gray, H.L. Dr

The marketing of secondary schools

Abstract: Thirty schools where advertising is well developed have been subjected to in depth interviews about their understanding of marketing. Ten non-active schools were researched likewise for comparison of concepts.
Source of Grant: Private sector: £40,000
Date of Research: 1989 – continuing
KEYWORDS: advertising; marketing; secondary education

8/0540

Department of Educational Research
Cartmel College, Bailrigg, Lancaster LA1 4YL
0524 65201
Rogers, G. Dr

Evaluation of inservice education

Abstract: The research seeks to assess student reaction to an innovating B.Ed. programme. The research was carried out by means of questionnaire and interviewer.
Source of Grant: Lancaster University; School of Education and Charlotte Mason College
Date of Research: 1988-1989
KEYWORDS: academic degree; evaluation; teacher education

8/0541

Department of Educational Research
Cartmel College, Bailrigg, Lancaster LA1 4YL
0524 65201
Mortimore, P. Prof.

Leadership in schools

Abstract: Contemporary secondary schooling in the UK, in many European countries and in North America, is considered in many respects problematic. Alleged declining standards of achievement and behaviour and, in the UK, low staying-on rates, are all cited as evidence of 'problems' of secondary schooling. Not all schools, however, manifest these difficulties to the same extent. Reviews of research studies have indicated that 'leadership' is one of the key factors which distinguishes more-effective from less-effective schools. This research will focus on the headteachers and their senior management teams of a stratified random sample of 48 secondary schools drawn from eight local educational authorities (LEAs) in the north west of England. The data will consist of interviews with, and observations of, the headteacher and senior staff as well as information about the school. This information will include measures to indicate effectiveness (intake data, examination results, attendance rates etc). Both qualitative and quantitative methods of data gathering and analysis will be employed. The school-based data on effectiveness will be related to the data collected on the intentions and actions of the headteacher and senior management team. This data will be analyzed to explore whether the intentions and actions of those responsible for the more effective schools differ from those responsible for other schools. In this way, effective leadership should be identified. Participating LEAs, in addition

to agreeing access to schools, will be asked to second two secondary deputy headteachers for one term. These 16 or so deputies will each be trained to carry out interviews and observations in three schools in a neighbouring LEA. The theoretical importance of the research lies in its attempt to assess the extent to which theoretical models of leadership and management are borne out in practice. The findings should also have considerable relevance for the policies and practice of both LEAs and governing bodies which, under the 1986 and 1988 Education Acts, are to be responsible for the appointment and training of headteachers. Finally, the findings should aid identification of indicators of headteacher effectiveness needed in preparation for the programmes of (head teacher) appraisal currently being explored in schools and LEAs.
Published Material: MORTIMORE, P. et al (1988). School matters. Open Books.; RUTTER, M. (1979). Fifteen thousand hours. Open Books.
Date of Research: 1989 – continuing
KEYWORDS: administration of education; head teacher; leadership; quality of education

8/0542

Department of Educational Research
Cartmel College, Bailrigg, Lancaster LA1 4YL
0524 65201
Phillips, P. Mrs; *Supervisor:* Calderhead, J. Dr
The impact of inservice training on classroom teaching
Abstract: Inservice provision is presently characterized by a trend towards short, school-based courses. This project consists of 6 case studies of secondary school English teachers, 3 of whom are engaging in school-based inservice, the other 3 taking courses in English teaching at a local institution of higher education. By examining teachers' expectations before the courses, their experiences of the courses, and their follow-up activities in the classroom, it is intended to describe the various processes at work in influencing teachers' classroom practice.
Source of Grant: No funding
Date of Research: 1987-1990
KEYWORDS: course; influence; inservice education and training of teachers; teaching method

8/0543

Department of Educational Research
Cartmel College, Bailrigg, Lancaster LA1 4YL
0524 65201
Bundy, R. Mr; *Supervisor:* Calderhead, J. Dr
Empowerment in student teachers' professional development
Abstract: The project aims to follow a group of 'early years' postgraduate student teachers through the PGCE (Post-Graduate Certificate in Education) course and into their first year of teaching. This is an ethnographic study investigating the processes of negotiation which enable students and teachers to make their professional experience fulfilling, to demonstrate their competence to others, and to become 'empowered' within their own professional community.
Source of Grant: No funding
Date of Research: 1989 – continuing
KEYWORDS: probationary teacher; professional development; student teacher; teacher education

8/0544

Department of Educational Research
Cartmel College, Bailrigg, Lancaster LA1 4YL
0524 65201
Peatfield, A. Ms; *Supervisor:* Calderhead, J. Dr
Interactive science in the primary school
Abstract: The project aims to evaluate an interactive, 'hands-on' approach to teaching science and technology in a primary school. Systematic classroom observation and interviews are being used to examine teachers' roles in this teaching approach, and to assess children's acquisition of scientific concepts and skills, and to consider the role of language and mathematics in their learning.
Source of Grant: No funding
Date of Research: 1988 – continuing
KEYWORDS: primary education; science education; teaching method

8/0545

Department of Educational Research
Cartmel College, Bailrigg, Lancaster LA1 4YL
0524 65201

Tomlinson, S. Prof.; Galloway, D. Dr; Armstrong, D. Mr
Identifying emotional and behavioural difficulties: participant perspectives
Abstract: The research has three fundamental aims: (a) to elucidate the process of assessment from the perspectives of parents, children, professionals responsible for identifying special needs and administrators responsible for producing Statements; (b) to describe, and provide a theoretical analysis of, sources of conflict and of agreement in the assessment process; (c) to develop a theoretical understanding of the concept of EBD (emotional and behavioural difficulties), from the perspectives of the various people involved in assessment, whether as clients or as professionals. The above aims give rise to policy related objectives which may conveniently be expressed as questions: (a) what criteria do professionals, mainly teachers, use when requesting formal assessment on the grounds that a child has EBD? (b) How do professionals' concepts of EBD influence: (i) their perspectives of their own role in the assessment process: (ii) their choice of procedures to use in identifying a child's special educational needs? (c) how may professionals differ between each other in their perceptions of a child's problems, and how are such differences resolved? (d) how may professionals differ in their perceptions of a child's problems, and how are such differences resolved? (e) How, and in what ways, may assessment affect parents' and children's perceptions of themselves, and of the agencies with which they come into contact? (f) How, and in what ways, may assessment affect a teacher's perception of a child?
Source of Grant: Economic and Social Research Council: £40,370
Date of Research: 1989 – continuing
KEYWORDS: assessment; behaviour disorder; emotional disorder; special needs

8/0546

Department of Educational Research
Cartmel College, Bailrigg, Lancaster LA1 4YL
0524 65201
Lancashire Polytechnic
Department of Combined Studies
Preston PR1 2TQ
0772 221421
Hurst, A. Mr; *Supervisor:* Galloway, D. Dr; Tomlinson, S. Prof.
Higher education and disabled students: individual and institutional perspectives
Abstract: This research considers the experiences of a small number of people with impaired mobility as they attempted to obtain places in higher education in the mid 1980's. The approach is qualitative rather than quantitative. It is based on documentary evidence and on interviews with the students and their tutors. Most of the subjects originate from a specialist college. Following a discussion of the general context of higher education, some specific considerations are highlighted and explored in relation to disabled people. This is followed by a series of case studies following the progress of individual applicants. To balance this there is an examination of how higher education institutions develop policy and provision for disabled students. Again a case study approach is used and is intertwined with some action research. Finally, changes in the structure and financing of higher education and the ways in which these impinge upon disabled students are discussed.
Published Material: HURST, H.A. (1984). 'Adolescence and physical impairment: an interactionist approach'. In: BARTON, L. & TOMLINSON, S. (Eds). Special Education and Social Interests. London: Croom Helm.; HURST, A. (1990). 'Higher education and disabled students'. In: CORBETT, J. (Ed). An uneasy transition: disaffection and discontinuities in post school education and training. London: Falmer Press (forthcoming).
Source of Grant: Lancashire Polytechnic: research fees plus up to £200 travel expenses for four years
Date of Research: 1983-1990
KEYWORDS: access to education; higher education; physically handicapped

8/0547

Department of Educational Research
Cartmel College, Bailrigg, Lancaster LA1 4YL
0526 65201
Summerfield, A.P. Dr
Gender, training and employment: an historical analysis 1939-50
Abstract: This is a study of the relationships between the training and employment of women during the Second World War and the

immediate post-war period. The central research question is whether wartime training altered women's position in the labour market on either a temporary or a permanent basis. In pursuit of answers the research scrutinizes the formualtion and outcomes of training and employment policy in ther period 1939-50.
Published Material: SUMMERFIELD, P. (1989). 'What women learned from the second world war', History of Education, Vol 18, No 3, September 1989, pp.213-230.
Source of Grant: Economic and Social Research Council: £43,000
Date of Research: 1990 – continuing
KEYWORDS: *history of education; labour market; training; women's education; women's employment*

8/0548

Department of Educational Research
Cartmel College,
Bailrigg, Lancaster LA1 4YL
0524 65201 ext 4507
Rogers, C.G. Dr
Pupils' attributions for success and failure in school classrooms
Abstract: The research is based on the attributional theory of achievement motivation developed by B. Weiner. The aim of the study is to explore the range of attributions used by school pupils to explain success and failure in the classroom. In particular the study is designed to identify the effects of age-related development and the effects of curriculum structure and classroom practice. The sample consists of all children in 3 classes from each of 2 primary schools. Data has been gathered by means of open-ended interview. Analysis is still under way. Early results suggest significant effects of classroom practice and age. These results have broad implications for the development of a classroom based theory of achievement motivation.
Published Material: ROGERS, C.G. (1986). 'Sex roles in education'. In: HARGREAVES, D. & COLLEY, A. (Eds). The Psychology of Sex Roles. London: Harper & Row.; ROGERS, C.G. (1986). 'Pupils attributions in the classroom context', Paper presented at BERA Annual Conference, 1986.; ROGERS, C.G. (1987). 'Attribution theory and motivation in school'. In: HASTINGS, N. & SCHWIESO, J. (Eds). New directions in Educational Psychology, Vol 2, Behaviour and Motivation. Sussex: Falmer Press.; ROGERS, C.G. (1988). 'Teachers expectations and pupils achievement'. In: ENTWISTLE, N.J. (Ed). Handbook of educational ideas and practices. London: Croom Helm.; ROGERS, C.G. 'Disaffection in the junior years: a perspective from theories of motivation'. In: DOCKING, J.W. (Ed). Education and alienation in the primary school. Sussex: Falmer Press (in press).; ROGERS, C.G. (1989). 'Expectations and the early years'. In: DESFORGES, C.W. 'Early childhood education', British Journal of Educational Psychology, Special Monograph Series.; ROGERS, C.G. & KUTNICK, P. (Eds). (1989). Readings in the social psychology of the primary school. London: Routledge.
Source of Grant: Lancaster University Social Science Research Fund (unfunded from June 1987)
Date of Research: 1984 – continuing
KEYWORDS: *achievement; failure; motivation; primary education; success*

8/0549

Department of Educational Research
Cartmel College,
Bailrigg, Lancaster LA1 4YL
0524 65201
Goodyear, P. Dr
Computer aided systems modelling
Abstract: The overall project is concerned with developing software to support computer based modelling of environmental systems in educational settings. It uses the language LOGO to construct modelling toolkits, which students can use to develop their understanding of ecosystems and their systems modelling skills. An ESRC-link research student is studying 'Cognitive aspects of environmental systems modelling through novice-expert comparisons'. An intended outcome of this research is an improved knowledge-base from which to construct better computer assisted learning tools.
Published Material: GOODYEAR, P. (1987). 'Clear, foggy and black boxes: Towards an adaptable environment for novice programmers', Aspects of Educational Technology, Vol 20.; GOODYEAR, P. (1987). 'A toolkit approach to computer aided systems modelling'. In: LEWIS, R. & TAGG, E. (Eds). Trends in computer assisted education. Oxford: Blackwell.

Source of Grant: Economic and Social Research Council (ESRC): linked studentship (1986-88)
Date of Research: 1985 – continuing
KEYWORDS: *computer assisted instruction; software; teaching aids*

8/0550

Department of Educational Research
Cartmel College, Bailrigg, Lancaster LA1 4YL
0524 65201
Wen Lin, T.C. Mrs; *Supervisor:* Tomlinson, S. Prof.
A working methodology for evaluating the integration of children with learning difficulties into ordinary schools in the Brazilian education system
Abstract: The aim of this research is to formulate a working methodology for evaluating integration of children with learning difficulties into ordinary schools in the Brazilian educational system. The topic of this research originated from an encounter with co-ordinators of the Board of Special Education of State Secretary of Education of Minas Gerais – Brazil. At this encounter, evaluation of integration process was pinpointed as one of the major areas of weakness needing improvement. For example, in 1985, there were approximately 3,000 children being integrated in Minas Gerais; however, there was no evaluation programme being conducted to monitor those integrations. It was suggested that theoretical support and working methodologies are needed to aid local educational authorities, school educational counsellors, etc., in monitoring and assessing integration processes. The activity programme for this research will follow 4 main stages: (1) the first stage will be (a) an analysis of existing research methodologies of evaluating integration processes and (b) evaluation methodologies used by LEAs (local education authorities) to monitor integration programmes in the UK. Whenever possible, methodologies used in other countries will be included in the analysis. The examination will focus on: (i) aspects evaluated; (ii) relevance of those aspects; (iii) validity of methods used to assess those aspects; and (iv) applicability of the methodology. Literature review and interview with relevant personnel in LEAs will be the two main activities. By the end of this stage, a report may be produced containing a summary of the methodologies, a critical analysis and principles of evaluation. (2) The second stage will consist of the elaboration of the proposed working methodology, taking into consideration the lessons learned from the first stage and the realities of the Brazilian educational system. (3) The third stage will be the application of the methodology in Brazil, in order to test its effectiveness. (4) Finally, the fourth stage will be for improving the methodology and writing up the thesis. It is expected that the end result will provide the educationists involved in the special education with a useful tool, which will help them to provide children with special needs with more adequate educational conditions.
Published Material: WEN LIN, T.C. (1987). 'The development of special education in Brazil', Disability, Handicap and Society, Vol 2, No 3, pp.259-284. Re-printed in the Mental Handicap Bulletin, September 1988.
Source of Grant: Brazilian government: scholarship
Date of Research: 1986-1989
KEYWORDS: *Brazil; evaluation; integration; learning difficulty; methodology; special education*

8/0551

Department of Educational Research
Cartmel College, Bailrigg, Lancaster LA1 4YL
0524 65201
Glenwright, P. Mr; *Supervisor:* Rymaszewski, R.H.; Breen, M.
Modern languages teaching and TEFL (Teaching English as a Foreign Language): a comparative study
Abstract: The research aims to compare practice in modern languages and 'English as a foreign language' classrooms. Practitioners' conceptions of communicative language teaching will be explored with a view to proposing what these 2 traditions may have to offer each other. The research is at an early stage, but surveys, interviews and classroom observation may all play a part in data collection.
Source of Grant: Economic and Social Research Council (ESRC): studentship
Date of Research: 1986-1989
KEYWORDS: *communication; comparative research; foreign languages; language teaching; modern languages*

8/0552

Department of Educational Research
Cartmel College, Bailrigg, Lancaster LA1 4YL
0524 65301 ext 2884
S Martin's College of Higher Education
Department of History
Bowerham Road, Lancaster LA1 3JD
0524 63446 ext 257
Smith, L. Dr; Knight, P. Dr

Primary teachers' conceptions of child development in history learning

Abstract: There is widespread support for two recommendations, that history has an important place in the National Curriculum and that teachers should be sensitive to the developmental needs of children. Yet there has been almost no research into primary school children's developing historical competence. Two studies will be carried out. One study will involve teachers of upper and lower juniors who are skilled at teaching history topics. A variety of techniques will be used to chart their general beliefs about child development, as well as their specific estimates of what children of given ages might normally be expected to achieve in history. A second study will examine lessons which the teachers reckon to embody good practice, first to chart how good, primary school history teaching proceeds, and secondly, to clarify the relationship between the planned and the delivered curriculum, with particular reference to the ways teachers combine the disciplinary demands of teaching history with the need to adapt the discipline to their classroom practice. It is expected that the findings offered to the academic community will be complemented by more descriptive works oriented to trainee and experienced teachers.

Source of Grant: Economic and Social Research Council: £33,000
Date of Research: 1988-1989
KEYWORDS: child development; history; primary education

8/0553

Department of Managment
Centre for the Study of Management Learning,
Lancaster LA1 4YX
0524 65201 ext 4855
Fox, S. Dr; Tanton, M. Ms; Burgoyne, J. Prof.; Easterby-Smith, M. Dr; McLeay, S. Prof.; Fieldsend, S. Ms

Human resource management and corporate performance

Abstract: The aims of this research are to investigate the processes whereby UK senior managers are selected, rewarded, educated and developed. To investigate the coherency of personnel policies, and the degree of integration between HRM (Human Resource Management) strategy and corporate strategy. Methods include field research in 60 large UK companies in several sectors, using semi-structured interview methods and additional documentary sources (eg. company reports) statistical analysis of the 60 UK companies financial structures.

Source of Grant: Economic and Social Research Council: £71,150
Date of Research: 1988-1990
KEYWORDS: management education; personnel management

8/0554

Department of Sociology
Cartmel College, Lancaster LA1 4YL
0524 65201
Walters, R.S. Mr; *Supervisor:* Warde, A. Dr; Hughes, J. Dr

Teachers – a culture under stress

Abstract: The aim of the research is to examine the apparent rise in stress within the social context of the teaching situation. Stress is seen as an endemic feature of teaching. Two aspects of this are of particular concern. Firstly, how different individual teachers respond to cultural expectations about the role of the teacher and the effects that this may have on the stressful features of this work. Secondly, how educational changes, including changes in definitions of the teachers' role stemming from either outside of or within the teachers' culture, can affect the kind of stress in teaching and the availability of coping measures. The empirical work involves an interactionist approach to the study of stress in the work environment of a sample of primary and secondary school teachers in several schools. Qualitative data will be obtained using formal and informal interviews, conversation and observation. Within a general context of cultural analysis the analytic framework derives from several sources – the development of a sociological understanding of the concepts of stress and emotion, including the application of the concepts of emotional labour and feeling rules to teachers and to teaching as a service industry; the development of an occupa-

tional culture of teachers and how such a culture has been affected by recent educational changes. Of particular relevance here are the human and personal costs to the teacher, especially in terms of the potential estrangement from teaching.

Source of Grant: ESRC (Economic and Social Research Council: £5285
Date of Research: 1987 – continuing
KEYWORDS: teacher; mental stress

Learners First

8/0555

13 Morley Square, Bristol BS7 9DW
0272 423504
The Open College
3rd Floor, St James Building, Oxford Street,
Manchester M1 6FQ
061 228 6415
Lewis, R. Mr; Knasel, E. Dr

Open College – National Institute for Careers Education and Counselling (OC-NICEC): careers work open learning course for the Department of Education and Science

Abstract: The Open College is currently adapting a staff resource pack drafted for the DES (Department of Education and Science) by Dr Bill Law of NICEC (National Institute for Careers Education and Counselling). The resulting course will be a flexible open learning package aimed at the professional development of those working in careers education and guidance both in schools and related fields. The course will be text led and supplemented with audio. The contents of the course will be 8 A4 workbooks, each of 32 pages; 1 A4 study guide of 18 pages; 1 A4 project and assignment booklet of 18 pages; 1 A4 consultant's/tutor's notes of 18 pages and a 45-60 minute audio cassette.

Source of Grant: Department of Education and Science: £63,000
Date of Research: 1990 – continuing
KEYWORDS: career education; flexible learning; individualized teaching; open learning; resource materials; vocational guidance

Leeds Polytechnic

8/0556

Carnegie School of Human Movement Studies & Physical Education, Beckett Park Site, Headingley, Leeds LS16 5JP
0532 462903/4
Day, I.G.; *Supervisor:* Scraton, S. Dr; Talbot, M. Prof.; Deem, R. Ms

Masculinity and physical education

Abstract: The aim of the study is to investigate the extent to which boys' physical education reproduces/challenges dominant masculine ideologies. The methodoloy includes: (1) quantitative research methods which will initially be used in the form of an audit of the selected Local Education Authority (Leeds). This will provide general information concerning the programmes and delivery of physical education in 84 schools within the 11-16 age range. These statistical/arithmetical data will illuminate various aspects of the provision of boys' physical education in terms of curriculum (gender specificity), teacher organization, teaching methods and extra curricular provision. (2) Key personnel involved in the implementation of equal opportunity policies and the delivery of physical education will be identified and interviewed. This will include the physical education advisor, equal opportunity personnel and a group interview of heads of physical education departments. This aspect of the research will seek to establish the source and process of policy decision making, how policies are disseminated, evaluated and monitored, and to establish to what extent boys are considered within gender power relations and equal opportunity programmes. (3) Qualitative approaches, including participant observation and in depth interview techniques, will be used to examine how the stated aims, objectives, policies and personal attitudes of the key personnel in physical education are articulated in practice, and the limitations and structures within which physical education functions. Four schools within the research authority will be selected to represent a range of curriculum practices and historical backgrounds (single sex, co-education, working class and middle

class etc.). These schools will provide the opportunity to observe the everyday practices of physical education and to conduct more informal interviews and discussions with those involved in the teaching and organization of boys' physical education, and with the boys at the delivery end.
Source of Grant: No funding
Date of Research: 1989 – continuing
KEYWORDS: boy; equal opportunity; physical education; sex difference

8/0557

Centre for Community Education,
Calverley Street, Leeds LS1 3HE
0532 462730
Bekker, P.C. Dr; *Supervisor:* Shaw, M. Dr
Course evaluation: using students' experience of teaching and learning
Abstract: The purpose of the project was to identify and disseminate methods whereby course teams could use students' experience of learning and teaching in course evaluation as a normal part of course review and development. This part of the project was based on the currently enrolled students (approx. 250) on the part-time B.A. (Hons) Combined Studies Degree Scheme (modular, open access, mature students) in Humanities (art history, literature, history) and Social Sciences (politics, pshychology, sociology). A case study of developing practice is being prepared using records, questionnaires, open discussion over a two-year period.
Source of Grant: Council for National Academic Awards (CNAA) Development Fund
Date of Research: 1988-1989
KEYWORDS: course; evaluation; higher education

8/0558

Department of Education
Beckett Park, Leeds LS6 3QS
0532 759061
McManus, M. Mr; *Supervisor:* Williams, R. Dr; Sugden, D. Dr
Suspension and exclusion from school
Abstract: The research aims to discover the causes and cures of high exclusion rates in some school by means of statistical, multiple regression analysis of data from 50 high schools. It has been concluded that exclusion and associated misbehaviour may be related to identified school policies and teacher practices, skills and attitudes. Inservice 'intervention' has been prepared for teachers across school sectors and age ranges.
Published Material: McMANUS, M. (1987). 'suspension and exclusion from high schools: the association with catchment and school variables', School Organization, Vol 7, No 3 1987, pp.261-271.; McMANUS, M. (1989). Troublesome behaviour in the classroom: a teachers' survival guide. London: Routledge.
Source of Grant: Leeds City Council: £350 per annum 1985/89
Date of Research: 1986-1990
KEYWORDS: discipline; disruptive behaviour; secondary education; suspension

8/0559

Department of Education
Beckett Park, Leeds LS2 3QS
0532 462903/4
Leeds University
Department of Education
Leeds LS2 9JT
0532 334527
Shaw, E.D. Mrs; *Supervisor:* Whalley, G.E. Dr
Records of achievement in the North of England from 1983 to 1990
Abstract: During the period 1983 to 1990, Records of Achievement, which were originally seen as a desirable innovation by individual schools, became the subject of government policy and direction and a means by which the examining boards became involved in the work of the schools. The research involves an investigation into the part played by these several bodies in the development of Records of Achievement over this period, including the use made of their powers and influence, with particular reference to the work going on in schools. Data is being obtained from a number of individual schools, chiefly across the whole of the North of England. Other sources include committee papers, reports and evaluations, both local and national; personal contact and informal interviews with pupils, teachers, heads and deputy headteachers, LEA officers, staff of examining bodies and local and national evaluators.

Source of Grant: Leeds Polytechnic: funding for year 4
Date of Research: 1986-1990
KEYWORDS: achievement; assessment; board of examiners; record of achievement

8/0560

Department of Education
Beckett Park, Leeds LS2 3QS
0532 462903/4
Walsh, S.M.; *Supervisor:* Scarborough, J. Ms
The changing role of home economics in schools: the impact of the design and technology National Curriculum proposals on home economics in local schools
Abstract: The research consists of an evaluation via a questionnaire of the current design and technological capability being fulfilled via home economics. The National Curriculum proposals for design and technology were published in June 1989. Already a great deal of design and technology is occurring in local schools. A survey is being carried out in order to measure what is currently being offered and how this may change in the light of the proposals. It will then be possible to evaluate what resources teachers will require for the implementation of the design and technology curriculum from a home economics perspective.
Source of Grant: National Association of Teachers of Home Economics: £1,000
Date of Research: 1989-1990
KEYWORDS: curriculum development; design; home economics; technology

8/0561

Department of Education
Beckett Park, Leeds LS6 3QS
0532 462903/4
Leeds University
Department of Education
Leeds LS2 9JT
0532 333180
Wood, G.S. Mr; *Supervisor:* Child, D. Prof.
A longitudinal study of the changing relationship between extroversion and achievement in primary and secondary school
Abstract: This study will trace the changing relationship between academic achievement and personality across primary and secondary school years. Some consideration will be given to attributions associated with success and failure. The received view of such studies is that a positive relationship exists between extroversion and achievement at primary school and a negative relationship exists at the secondary level. What has not been clearly demonstrated however, is whether the reversed relationship at secondary school involves the same or different children i.e. do children at primary school adapt their behaviour in secondary school to succeed or do different children succeed in secondary school. A longitudinal study has been initiated to clarify this issue. Children will be studied in different primary age groups and followed through bi-annually at secondary school, where half of the experimental population will be staggered one year to give coverage in every secondary year until a change is detected and satisfactorily demonstrated. Reference will be made to any distinctive changes in style of teaching and rational testing.
Source of Grant: No funding
Date of Research: 1989 – continuing
KEYWORDS: achievement; extroversion; personality; primary education; secondary education

Leeds University

8/0562

Children's Learning in Science Research Group,
Centre for Studies in Science and Mathematics Education,
Leeds LS2 9JT
0532 334675
Squires, A. Mrs; *Supervisor:* Driver, R. Prof.
Leeds National Curriculum science support project
Abstract: This project is designed to develop curriculum support materials for teaching and learning science in Key Stage 3 of the National Curriculum. The project is reviewing the children's alternative conceptions literature and preparing summaries which will provide insights into children's understandings of science across

the range of concept domains of the National Curriculum. In addition, guidance will be offered on teaching strategies which might be employed to enhance conceptual development in each of the domains. The principal outcomes from the project will be a series of booklets for teachers outlining the findings from the research reviews and aimed at informing classroom practice. In essence the project is interpreting the alternative conceptions research literature for practical use by teachers.
Source of Grant: Leeds Education Authority: £203,135
Date of Research: 1989 – continuing
KEYWORDS: comprehension; concept formation; science education; teaching aids

8/0563

Department of Edcucation
Leeds LS2 9JT
0532 431751/334527/334604
Carter, D.C. Mr; *Supervisor:* Orton, A. Dr
Students' understanding of motion in a circular path
Abstract: In a pilot study, carried out during spring term 1988, access was obtained to samples of scripts of candidates for A-level examinations in mathematics set by the University of London School Examinations Board and by the Joint Matriculation Board in June 1987. In particular, responses to questions set on the topic of circular motion were studied. Analysis of the data obtained suggests that there are students within all A-level grade classifications who would appear to hold misconceptions about the cause of motion in a circular path. The origins and extent of these misconceptions need to be revealed; in particular as to the existence of a force MW(2)T and the direction in which it acts. Misconceptions might arise as a result of teaching received, reading textbooks, study in other subject areas (the topic is in most A-level physics syllabuses, and also approached generally in GCSE physics courses), or from the media (there is much evidence from newspaper articles and from popular TV science programmes that explanations of the cause of circular motion are misconceived). It is proposed to take samples of students who are following A-level mathematics and/or physics courses, investigate their understanding of the cause of circular motion, attempt to identify the origins of any misconceptions, and make suggestions for teaching.
Date of Research: 1988 – continuing
KEYWORDS: comprehension; mathematics; mechanics; secondary education

8/0564

Department of Education
Leeds LS2 9JT
0532 334527
Burke, C.S. Mr; *Supervisor:* Orton, A. Dr
A study of spatial understanding in relation to mathematical situation
Abstract: This research concerns the use of diagrams in communicating mathematics. A classification of current usage in terms of the correspondence between the signifying structure of the diagram and the nature of the signified structure which the diagram represents led to a number of experiments with pupils. Analysis of the appropriateness, effectiveness and potential of each kind of representation has involved (1) psycho-spatial pre-requisites for understanding within different age ranges; (2) mathematico-spatial pre-requisites for learning development; (3) the context of use in the classroom; (4) clarity and appeal of design and presentation; (5) time taken for comprehension by different age and ability levels; (6) complexity of information content. Experimental work includes encoding and decoding of both homomorphic and paramorphic representations. The study will end with a guide to good practice for teachers.
Published Material: BURKE, C.S. (1986). 'An uphill struggle or a downhill run?', Mathematics in School, Vol 15, No 2, pp.2-5, March.
Date of Research: 1984-1989
KEYWORDS: diagram; mathematics; space perception; teaching technique

8/0565

Department of Education
Overseas Education Unit, Leeds LS2 9JT
0532 334569
Lancaster University
Department of Linguistics
Lancaster LA1 4YT

0524 65201
Coleman, H. Mr; Allwright, R.L. Mr
Lancaster-Leeds language learning in large classes research project
Abstract: The project is primarily concerned with the learning and teaching of English as a second language or foreign language in the context of large classes. It has four aims. Firstly, to develop links with individuals and institutions concerned with large classes (LCs), to organize meetings and other events for the purpose of discussing current research, undertake and promote research into specific aspects of language learning and teaching in LCs, and to develop and maintain a bibliography. A series of project reports are now being published, and more reports will appear in the future. Colloquia have been organized in Chicago (1988), Warwick (1989), San Antonio (1989), Dublin (1990) and San Francisco (1990). The specific issues being investigated include the following: Firstly, the aetiology of large classes, the definition of a 'large class', patterns of teacher and learner behaviour in large classes, teachers' perceptions of large classes, learners' perceptions of large classes, approaches to the management of large classes; relationship between class size and language acquisition, and teachers' and learners' strategies in large classes.
Published Material: A complete list of publications is available from the researchers.
Source of Grant: The British Council: £1,500 The Bell Educational Trust: £300 The Centre for British Teachers: £500
Date of Research: 1986 – continuing
KEYWORDS: class size; English (second language); first foreign language; teaching

8/0566

Department of Education
Leeds LS2 9JT
0532 431751
Finer, A.R. Mr; *Supervisor:* Child, D. Prof.
The effect of a thinking skills programme on the development of selected performance measures in prelingual deaf students
Abstract: The aim of the present investigation is to utilize a course for deaf students that provides a conceptual framework which underpins the many curricula changes taking place in schools. The course consists of a series of visually based discussion tasks which highlight and develop many essential cross curricular pupil resources. The course addresses a range of overlapping cognitive, linguistic, personal and social issues, all of which are relevant to the specific needs of deaf students. Samples of prelingual deaf students attending resourced mainstream schools will be used at primary and secondary levels. Assessment will be made of intellectual abilities, reading comprehension, social functioning, problem solving ability and educational measures similar to proposed standard attainment tasks in the context of the National Curriculum. Subjects will follow a programme over the period of an academic year and rate and amount of improvement will be measured and comparisons made with control groups. Four schools will be used with experimental and control groups totalling 60 in each at both primary and secondary level. Stepwise regression analysis will be used to identify predictor variables for a number of criterion measures, prior to the use of multiple analysis of co-variance. Teacher and educational interpreter effects will be examined on the development of the criterion measures.
Published Material: FINER, A.R. (1990). 'The effectiveness of a thinking skills programme on the educational attainment of secondary age deaf students', pp.53. In: Proceedings of the 17th International Congress on Education of the Deaf in Rochester, New York. National Technical Institute for the Deaf.
Source of Grant: No funding
Date of Research: 1989 – continuing
KEYWORDS: interdisciplinary approach

8/0567

Department of Education
Leeds LS2 9JT
0532 431751
Anning, A.J.E. Ms; Kicks, G. Mrs
Technology at Key Stages 1 and 2
Abstract: This research has its origins when technology was introduced as a 'new' subject at Key Stages 1 and 2 in September 1990. The NCC (National Curriculum Council) Technology Guidelines were written on the basis of little empirical evidence of what children aged 5-11 can understand, know or do in technology. The start of this small scale research project coincides with the implementation of the Technology Orders. The project seeks to

observe and record the strategies of children engaged in technology activities in years 1 and 3 and to collect evidence of development in their capabilities in design and technology over a period of one year in the first instance; to establish a database of examples of Key Stages 1 and 2 technology in action in classrooms and to compare the data with expectations of pupil performances set out in the NCC Technology curriculum for Key Stages 1 and 2. An initial set of interviews and school visits in 2 LEAs will provide information about: The policies of LEAs and schools on introducing technology into classrooms; attitudes of head teachers and teachers to teaching technology; the kind of resources, both human and physical, available to implement the NCC Technology Orders; the kind of tasks teachers intend to set children in technology and the kind of progression in technology teachers expect of the children in their classes. Detailed observations in 4 classrooms in the 2 LEAs will focus on: the practical strategies children use on technology tasks; evidence of their conceptual grasp of aspects of technology; the dynamics of collaborative work on tasks; boy/girl differences and the match between evidence offered of children's capability in technology and the prescribed NCC technology curriculum.
Source of Grant: Departmental Funds: £14,718
Date of Research: 1990 – continuing
KEYWORDS: curriculum technology; primary education

8/0568
Department of Education
Centre for Studies in Science and Mathematics Education,
Leeds LS2 9JT
0532 431751
Bassett, J.M.; *Supervisor:* Wain, G.T.
Key Stage 1 of the National Curriculum in Mathematics as it relates to infant schools in Huddersfield
Abstract: This research study will investigate the mathematics curriculum of 70 schools engaged in Key Stage 1 of the National Curriculum in Huddersfield. It will cover the background to the setting up of the National Curriculum and the philosophy which underpins it. It will involve looking at infant/firm school models of the curriculum and, in particular, the Mathematics Curriculum and to relate these to the National Curriculum. The content of Key Stage 1 of the National Curriculum will be analyzed and compared with the pre National Curriculum Mathematics Curriculum. Similarly the assessment component will be analyzed in terms of assessment theory and pre National Curriculum assessment procedures in school. The influence of the Standard Assessment Tasks of school internal curriculum assessments and approaches to teaching methods will be ascertained. The results of the first unreported Standard Assessment Tasks and the first reported Standard Assessment Tasks will be analyzed in terms of what they mean in themselves and the affect on schools. The effects of the National Curriculum on the content of the Mathematics Curriculum in Schools, internal assessment, and approaches to mathematics teaching will be assessed by means of a teacher questionnaire. This will be sent to all teachers involved in Key State 1 in 70 Huddersfield schools. A separate questionnaire will be sent to mathematics co-ordinators in the same schools. Selective interviews in a sample of the schools will be used to support the questionnaires. The questionnaires cover teacher opinions on effectiveness of National Curriculum INSET (Inservice Education of Teachers), areas where further training is needed, areas in which teachers feel confident/lacking confidence and resource needs to implement National Curriculum Mathematics.
Source of Grant: No funding
Date of Research: 1989 – continuing
KEYWORDS: National Curriculum

8/0569
Department of Education
Leeds LS2 9JT
0532 334527
Rayner, M.J. Mr; Williams, R.P. Mr
Analysis of content, evidential forms and rhetoric of published HMI reports on schools
Abstract: The study aims to systematically analyze a sample (to be determined) of published reports on schools by Her Majesty's Inspectorate (HMI). It is intended to seek patterns amongst those issues, practices and events which are the subject of positive and negative comment in the reports. The language associated with such evaluations and the nature of the evidence accompanying them will also be examined.

Source of Grant: School of Education Research Funds: £15,000
Date of Research: 1990 – continuing
KEYWORDS: rhetoric

8/0570
Department of Education
Centre for Studies in Science and Mathematics Education,
Leeds LS2 9JT
0532 421751
Johnston, K. Ms; Brook, A. Ms; Holding, B. Dr; Asoko, H. Ms; Needham, R. Mr; Scott, P. Mr; *Supervisor:* Driver, R.H. Dr
Children's learning in science project
Abstract: This project is involved in research into the understanding of selected science concepts by school students. Phase I involved content analysis of pupils' written responses to questions given as part of the National Surveys conducted on behalf of the Assessment of Performance Unit. The analysis of written responses was supplemented with interviews with pupils and teachers. Phase II has been a collaborative exercise involving practising science teachers. Data obtained during the first phase has been used as a basis for developing teaching materials and strategies designed to improve learning in three areas of particular conceptual difficulty: (i) energy; (ii) plant nutrition; and (iii) particulate theory. The focus has been on the development of activities and exercises which encourage the active participation of young people in relating school science to their own experiences, in order that they may develop confidence in using scientific ideas. Phase III involves two main initiatives: (1) further research into conceptual understanding in science, with particular emphasis on the development of ideas across the age range 5-16; (2) an investigation of factors which encourage teachers to their change their thinking and practice, and the development of a series of workshop packs for pre-service and inservice teacher training, focusing on interactive methods of teaching and learning science.
Published Material: SCOTT, P., DYSON, T. and GATER, S. (1987). A constructivist view of learning and teaching in science. University of Leeds; Centre for Studies in Science and Mathematics Education.; NEEDHAM, R. & HILL, P. (1987). Teaching strategies for developing understanding in science. University of Leeds; Centre for Studies in Science and Mathematics Education.
Source of Grant: Department of Education and Science
Date of Research: 1986-1989
KEYWORDS: comprehension; learning strategy; science education; secondary education

8/0571
Department of Education
Centre for Studies in Science and Mathematics Education,
Assessment of Performance Unit – Science, Leeds LS2 9JT
0532 334623
Archenhold, W.F. Mr; Holding, B.; Daniels, S. Mrs; Bell, J.F. Mr
Assessment of Performance Unit – Science
Abstract: The original Assessment of Performance Unit's project (1977) was set up by the Department of Education and Science to carry out five annual surveys of the science performances of 11, 13 and 15 year olds in England, Wales and Northern Ireland. They were intended to be a 'base-line' for a longer term monitoring programme. The team is located at King's College, London and at Leeds University. The former are responsible for question development and survey organization at 11 and 13, while the latter are responsible for both at age 15 as well as data analysis at all three years. Between 1980-84 annual surveys took place and over 500 schools and between 12,000/15,000 pupils took part at each age. Apart from the results of pupil testing, schools were asked about their resources for science, their goals, range of science subjects and uptake of science courses by 15 year olds. A great mass of information has been generated by the surveys. Since 1984 the project has been conducting a series of research studies including secondary analysis of the existing survey data, and a longitudinal study investigating progress in science. With the introduction of the National Curriculum, the science teams have been used as a source of expertise by both the National Curriculum Council (NCC) and the School Examinations and Assessment Council (SEAC). Reports and conference papers have been written on the findings and numerous talks organized to teacher groups and other interested parties, both here and abroad. (See also entry for Assessment of Performance in Science under Leeds University).

Published Material: a full list of publications can be obtained from the researchers on request.
Source of Grant: School Examinations and Assessment Council; Assessment of Performance Unit: £690,996
Date of Research: 1986-1990
KEYWORDS: assessment; science education; secondary education

8/0572

Department of Education
Leeds LS2 9JT
0532 334527
Crowther, C.M. Ms; *Supervisor:* Shorrocks, D. Dr
A psychological analysis of the development of writing abilities in children for whom english is either a first or second language
Abstract: This research aims to examine the development of writing abilities across the age range 7 to 13 and to compare the effects of learning to write in a first and second language. As writing is construed as one particular example of a cognitive skill, the significance of knowledge, strategies and metacognitive factors in the development of writing abilities is assessed, as well as the interrelationship between writing and other higher level cognitive functions such as memory encoding and retrieval, comprehension and problem solving. In addition, the work seeks to examine the Vygotskian postulate that there is a strong association between interpersonal interaction and intrapersonal cognitive functioning.
Source of Grant: No funding
Date of Research: 1985 – continuing
KEYWORDS: cognitive development; language; writing; written expression

8/0573

Department of Education
Leeds LS2 9JT
0532 334569/334571
Lancaster University
Department of Linguistics
Lancaster LA1 4YT
0524 65201
Coleman, H. Mr; Allwright, R.L. Mr (Lancaster University, Dept of Linguistics)
Lancaster-Leeds language learning in large classes research project
Abstract: The project has four objectives: (1) to develop a bibliography on language learning in large classes (LCs); (2) to develop links with individuals and institutions concerned with LCs; (3) to organize occasional meetings for the purpose of discussing recent research and (4) to undertake its own research. The project is primarily concerned with the learning and teaching of English as a foreign language. Work has progressed as follows: (1) the eleventh version of the bibliography was issued in 1989; (2) informal links have been established with several hundred individuals in different parts of the world; particularly in India, Indonesia, Japan, Pakistan and the United States; (3) Five international colloquia have been held: Chicago 1988, San Antonio 1989, Warwick 1989, San Francisco 1990 and Dublin 1990. More meetings are planned for New York, Exeter and Karachi in 1991. (4) questions on which research has already been carried out include the following – what is a 'large class' for language teachers? what makes teaching LCs difficult? what approaches to teaching in LCs are available? More than 700 teachers in manyCs countries have completed two questionnaires. Perceptions of class size are primarily influenced by the size of the LARGEST class currently taught. Responses are being analyzed by country of origin and by type of institution (primary/secondary/tertiary).
Published Material: MCLEOD, N. (1989). What teachers cannot do in large classes. Lancaster/Leeds: Language Learning in Large Classes Project.; PEACHEY, L. (1989). Language Learning in Large Classes: a pilot study of South African Data. Lancaster/Leeds: Language Learning in Large Classes Project.; SABANDAR, J. (1989). Language learning in large classes in Indonesia. Lancaster/Leeds: Language Learning in Large Classes Project.; SARANGI, U. (1989). A consideration of methodological issues in analysing the problems of language teachers in large classes. Lancaster/Leeds: Language Learning in Large Classes Project.; COLEMAN, H. (1989). Approachment to the management of large classes. Lancaster/Leeds: Language Learning in Large Classes Project.; ALLWRIGHT, D. (1989). How important are lessons, anyway? Lancaster/Leeds: Language Learning in Large Classes Project.; A complete list of publications is available from the researcher

Date of Research: 1986 – continuing
KEYWORDS: class size; language teaching;

8/0574

Department of Education
Leeds LS2 9JT
0532 431751
Henry, M. Mr; *Supervisor:* Jenkins, E.W. Mr; Sharp, P.R. Dr
Technical education, 1880-1914, with particular reference to the printing trade
Abstract: The study uses a range of primary sources to examine the origins, nature and development of technical education for the printing industry from 1880 to 1914. The study is placed in the broader context of the technical education movement and addresses the questions concerned with the politics of curriculum design and innovation in the area of vocational education. It also examines the relationship between employers and employees and evaluates the effect of technical education classes upon the education and training of printers.
Published Material: HENRY, M. (1987). 'The nineteenth-century printing apprenticeship: elements of change'. In: MYERS, R. & HARRIS, M. Aspects of printing from 1600, Oxford Polytechnic Press, pp.90-113.
Date of Research: 1986 – continuing
KEYWORDS: history of education; printing; technical education

8/0575

Department of Education
Nurse Selection Project,
153 Woodhouse Lane, Leeds LS2 9JT
0532 354527
Ciechanowsky, A. Ms; Boydon-Jagger, J. Mrs; *Supervisor:* Child, D. Prof.
Validation of the DC (Dennis Child) selection tests into nurse training
Abstract: Having designed an alternative selection device (DC tests) for entry to nurse training which is equivalent to 5 'O' levels, it was felt important to check if those so selected were achieving similarly to those who entered by the 5 'O' level route. The purpose of the DC tests was entirely to do with educational achievement and NOT as a predictor of nurse competence. Therefore, the only valid criterion is academic performance of students in schools and colleges of nurse training. A sample of 350 DC entrants and the same number of 'O' level entrants from all parts of the UK are being monitored for their progress through nurse training. Academic performance is being recorded at suitable intervals. Drop-out rate and any other comments about performance are also being gathered during training.
Published Material: CHILD, D. (1988). The Nurse Selection Project. Interchange, Autumn 1988. pp.16-20.
Source of Grant: General Nursing Council (England and Wales) Trust
Date of Research: 1986-1990
KEYWORDS: achievement test; nurse; selection; student; validity

8/0576

Department of Education
Nurse Selection Project,
153 Woodhouse Lane, Leeds LS2 9JT
0532 334527
Child, D. Prof.; Borrill, C.S. Dr; Ciechanowski, A. Ms; Michaud, A. Mrs
Nurse selection project (UKCC (United Kingdom Central Council for Nursing, Midwifery and Health Visiting))
Abstract: The project is concentrating on two main research areas: monitoring the career choices of adolescents and a validation study of the DC test series, an alternative entry route into nurse training. The study of young people's career choices is cross sectional and longitudinal and is exploring how and why they become interested in nursing as a career, and why it is they change their minds. The insights from this work will be used to make recommendations about how to encourage and keep young people interested in nursing. A sample of 648 school pupils and college students in 3 regions of England are being followed over a period of 4 to 5 years using questionnaires and a subsample of 20% interviewed each year. The validation study of the DC test series is following the progress of 629 entrants to nurse training. The performance of 315 students who entered training with 5 'O' levels or more is being compared with 314 who passed a DC test to enter.

Other researches have been carried out on the test, such as a study of the effect of age on performance and the effect of practice and coaching and coaching on performance. The project also carries out short term research at the request of the funding bodies.
Published Material: CHILD, D. et al (1988). Selection for nurse training; making decisions. University of Leeds Press.; BORRILL, C.S. 'Cultivating an interest in nursing'. Nursing Times, December 14th, 1988, pp.44-45.; BORRILL, C.S. (1989). 'Nursing an ambition'. Nursing Times, Vol 85, No 34.; CHILD, D. et al (1990). Taking the DC test − a guide for candidates. University of Leeds Press.
Source of Grant: United Kingdom Central Council for Nursing, Midwifery and Health Visiting/ Department of Health: jointly £300,000 over 5 years
Date of Research: 1987 − continuing
KEYWORDS: nurse; recruitment; selection; student

8/0577
Department of Education
Leeds LS2 9JT
0532 334527
Manchester Polytechnic
Department of Educational Studies
799 Wilmslow Road, Didsbury, Manchester M20 8RR
Barratt-Pugh, C.; *Supervisor:* Shorrocks, D. Dr; Tough, J. Dr
A study of the development of English as a second language in a classroom context
Abstract: The research aims to explore the development of English as a second language, in the speech of ten children aged between five and seven years, within a classroom context. The development of communicative competence will be traced through an analysis of structural and functional development, within a conversational framework. Evidence from recent research suggests that language development may be facilitated by certain types of conversational interaction, thus the learner's use of conversation strategies will be identified and analyzed in relation to the emergence of particular grammatical structures.
Source of Grant: 75% tuition fees paid by Manchester Polytechnic. 25% tuition fees paid by self
Date of Research: 1982-1990
KEYWORDS: communication; English (second language); language development; primary education

8/0578
Department of Education
Leeds, LS2 9JT
0532 334527
Driver, R.H. Prof.; Medway, P. Dr; Williams, R.
Leeds University TVEI (Technical and Vocational Education Initiative)
Abstract: The purpose of this initiative is to provide a network of support for change agents (mainly advisory teachers) in local education authorities involved in the TVEI Pilot and Extension. This is to be achieved through: (a) collaboration with LEA nominees in investigating methods for enabling professional and curriculum development in key areas of TVEI; (b) the establishment of a resource base of material supporting such professional and curriculum development; (c) the provision of courses and consultation, first locally and then nationally. It is intended that the processes of providing for the professional development of teachers will be monitored, analyzed, and eventually presented in a form suited to publication.
Source of Grant: Training Enterprise Education Division: £150,654
Date of Research: 1988 − continuing
KEYWORDS: curriculum development; professional development; Technical and Vocational Education Initiative (TVEI)

8/0579
Department of Education
Leeds LS2 9JT
0532 431751
Alamina, J. Mrs; *Supervisor:* Archenhold, W.F. Mr; Jenkins, E.W. Mr
A study of children's understanding of aspects of chemical change with particular reference to Nigerian secondary school pupils
Abstract: Chemical change is a concept central to all school chemistry courses. The study explores pupils' own understanding of this concept using structured interviews with a sample of c.200 Nigerian secondary school pupils. Emphasis is placed on eliciting students'

own understanding of chemical change in a variety of laboratory and everyday contexts. The pedagogical implications of the findings will be explored.
Source of Grant: Commonwealth scholarship
Date of Research: 1988 − continuing
KEYWORDS: chemistry; comprehension; Nigeria; secondary education

8/0580
Department of Education
Childrens Learning in Science Research Group CSSME,
Leeds LS2 9JT
0532 334527
Scott, P.; *Supervisor:* Driver, R. Prof.
Science and technology in action
Abstract: The project will evaluate the effectiveness of pedagogical approaches designed to develop secondary students' appreciation of and ability to evaluate the range of factors involved in technolgoical developments and decision making. Action research will be undertaken with a group of secondary school teachers.
Source of Grant: Nuclear Electricity Information Group: £78,000
Date of Research: 1989-1990
KEYWORDS: secondary education; technological change; teaching method

8/0581
Department of Education
Childrens Learning in Science Research Group,
Leeds LS2 9JT
0532 334527
Carmichael, P.; *Supervisor:* Driver, R. Dr
An evaluation of the learning experiences of boys and girls in secondary school science classes involved in a curriculum development project
Abstract: The study is an investigation into the participation of girls and boys in science classes based on differing pedagogical approaches. Pupils' participation in class discussion, the time spent on different activities and learning outcomes are compared for girls and boys in the different classroom environments.
Source of Grant: Economic and Social Research Council linked studentship
Date of Research: 1987-1990
KEYWORDS: sex difference; secondary education; science education; participation; curriculum development

8/0582
Department of Education
Leeds LS2 9JT
0532 334527
Hartley, J.R. Mr; Driver, R. Dr
Information technology in education research programme: conceptual change in science
Abstract: The aim of the research is to understand the process by which students change their conceptions about natural phenomena from everyday intuitive ideas to those taught in school science courses. The research programme will investigate in particular the role that computer software tools can play in promoting such a change.
Published Material: DRIVER, R. & SCANLON, E. (1989). 'Conceptual change in science', Journal of Computer Assisted Learning, Vol 5, No 1, March 1989.
Source of Grant: Economic and Social Research Council INTER Programme: £113,000
Date of Research: 1988 − continuing
KEYWORDS: computer assisted instruction; concept formation; science education; secondary education

8/0583
Department of Education
Leeds LS2 9JT
0532 334527
Spanos, D. Mr; *Supervisor:* Orton, A. Dr
Change of school in Greece and pupils' difficulties with mathematics
Abstract: The motivation for this research is the problem of learning mathematics and the distress caused in pupils by change of school at specific ages with the accompanying change in both syllabus and teaching style. In order to investigate what specifically causes problems a test was devised and set to pupils in the age range 13-15. The main part of the research is based on individual interviewing of 140 pupils and the analysis of the data obtained.

Source of Grant: No funding
Date of Research: 1985-1989
KEYWORDS: Greece; learning strategy; mathematics; teaching method

8/0584

Department of Education
Leeds LS2 9JT
0532 334527
Moncur, D.R.S. Mr; Supervisor: Orton, A. Dr

Students' understanding of literal algebraic equations and formulae
Abstract: This research has been devised to compare the ability of pupils and students to solve numerical and literal equations in order to analyze why many learners find the step from numerical to literal so difficult. A preliminary study based on group testing was carried out using pupils from four schools in different parts of Britain. In some schools the literal equations were placed before the numerical. The main part of the research is based on individual interviews with a large sample of pupils, and transcription of this data is currently taking place.
Source of Grant: No funding
Date of Research: 1987 – continuing
KEYWORDS: algebra; cognitive process; comprehension;

8/0585

Department of Education
Study of Continuing Education Unit, Leeds LS2 9JT
0532 333210/1
Institut fur Erziehungswissenschaft II
Universitat Tubingen, FRG-7400 Tubingen, Germany
Marriott, J.S. Prof.; Coles, J. Mrs

Intercultural influence in adult/popular education: England and Germany 1890-1955
Abstract: The overall project involves a historical investigation of the intercultural 'reception' of ideas and institutional forms in the field of adult education. The present phase deals with reciprocal Anglo-German contacts at the periods: – (1) 1890-1914: emphasis on German interest in the university extension and settlement movements; (2) 1918-1933: – structure and effects of international contact with special reference to pacifism, women's and workers' education; (3) 1945-1955: 'German educational reconstruction' – the contribution of English adult education and adult educators.
Published Material: MARRIOTT, S. (1987). Un role sociale pour les universities? Reactions... In: UEBERSCHLAG, G. & MULLER, F. (eds) (1987). Education Populaire. Presses Universitaires de Lille.; MARRIOTT, S. (1991). Germany and the World Association for Adult Education, 1919-1946. In press.
Source of Grant: Leverhulme Trust: £10,600 (1990-91)
Date of Research: 1988 – continuing
KEYWORDS: adult education; intercultural education; Germany, Federal Republic

8/0586

Department of Education
Leeds LS2 9JT
0532 333217/333227/333210
Ingram, A.D. Mr; Supervisor: Marriott, J. Prof.

Music education for adults in Britain: a critique of provision and policy
Abstract: The research will examine the historical development of music education for adults. It will then seek to establish the philosophy and rationale of present provision, its determining policies, how those policies have developed and how they relate to earlier responses. This will be carried out by means of interviews, questionnaires and examination of documents from local education authorities, music, schools and other providers of music education. Finally, the research will consider the future of music education and making music education for adults a better experience.
Source of Grant: No funding
Date of Research: 1987 – continuing
KEYWORDS: adult education; music education

8/0587

Department of Education
Leeds LS2 9JT
0532 334527
Rusholme, A. Mr; Supervisor: Marriott, S. Prof.

An evaluation of distance learning as a method of management development in selected industries
Abstract: The research is the development of an evaluation mechanism for use by users of open learning, providers of open learning and delivery agents. Long ago it became apparent from preliminary research that no such evaluation mechanism exists. The research will ask a series of questions which have been developed from existing material and experience of open learning and delivery agents/providers of open learning. The end product will be the presentation of a guidelines document for everyone connected with open learning to use. The research is restricted to educationalists and those involved in the health service professions since the author has direct contacts with these two groups. The sample used will be a local one (for the pilot study) and a national one (for the final questionnaire).
Source of Grant: No funding
Date of Research: 1987 – continuing
KEYWORDS: distance study; evaluation; management development; open learning

8/0588

Department of Education
Leeds LS2 9JT
0532 334527
Bradford & Ilkley Community College
Great Horton Road, Bradford BD7 1AY
0274 753166
Robinson, P. Mr; Supervisor: Marriott, S. Prof.

Attitudes towards 'economic course' provision in the public further education sector
Abstract: During the 1980's the Further Education (FE) sector has come under increasing pressure to operate within the context of a 'New Right Market Economy'. The purpose of this research is to enquire into and collect information about people's perceptions of how economic course provision within FE can be developed more effectively. Given a context of increasing comptetitiveness from other public and private agencies, the research aims to examine the attitudes of staff in terms of their willingness to embrace this current entrepreneurial philosophy, as well as to further consider present management and administrative structures in order to assess the degree to which these existing structures may hinder or facilitate flexible responses to commercial demands. The research has an ethnographic base and will aim to interview respondents from four sample areas, college managers and administrators, college staff academic and technical, other local training providers and industrial managers. There will be an initial pilot project which will take place within Bradford & Ilkley Community College during the academic year 1989/90. Five subsequent research projects will be developed during the following 18 months.
Source of Grant: Bradford & Ilkley Community College: fees approx £400 per term
Date of Research: 1989 – continuing
KEYWORDS: course; economics of education; further education

8/0589

Department of Education
Leeds LS2 9JT
0532 334544
Snape, J.M. Mr; Supervisor: Child, D. Prof.

Stress on college lecturers working in the North East of England and its possible effects on student learning
Abstract: This study presents the findings of research into aspects of stress among lecturers working in colleges of further education in the North East of England. The empirical work was carried out over one academic year with 130 lecturers and 213 of their students, all chosen at random, participating in the study. Seven instruments were used, namely: a 'stress' questionnaire; two types of logs, and a personality questionnaire for lecturers; and one 'annoyance' questionnaire and two types of logs for students. The study set out to address the broad question of whether stress among college lecturers affected the teaching process and, in turn, the students' learning. The data highlighted that there were three broad problem areas or sources of stress for the lecturers: the teaching process, relationships, and other factors. These were further divided into the categories: resources, teaching, and the environment; students, staff, and management and aspects external to the college; and administration. The effects of these stressors on the lecturers were demonstrated in feelings and actions which affected the role as a teacher, both inside and outside the classroom. Statistical analysis of all the responses revealed that similar stressors, and sources of annoyance, occurred throughout the academic year in all the colleges sampled. The lecturers with the most class-contact were found to have lower levels of self-esteem and higher levels of anxiety. This aspect

was demonstrated particularly by female respondents, and those new to teaching. There were indications that the teaching process and students' learning were negatively affected by lecturers' stress, as perceived either directly or indirectly, by both students and lecturers. It was the potential learning experience that was seen to be most at risk.
Source of Grant: No funding
Date of Research: 1986 – continuing
KEYWORDS: college of further education; learning process; stress; teacher behaviour; teaching personnel

8/0590
Department of Education
Leeds LS2 9JT
0532 334521
Roper, T. Mr; *Supervisor:* Orton, A. Dr
The historical development of selected principles in mechanics and the relationship with growth of understanding in students
Abstract: The development of the principles of mechanics throughout history has been slow and faltering. The same can be said about the growth of understanding of these principles in students. The study aims to investigate the relationship between the historical development and the growth of understanding.
Source of Grant: No funding
Date of Research: 1989 – continuing
KEYWORDS: comprehension; mechanics;

8/0591
Department of Education
Leeds LS2 9JT
0532 334521
de Medeiros, C.F. Mrs; *Supervisor:* Orton, A. Dr
An investigation into errors made in attempts to solve mathematical problems
Abstract: The study aims to investigate teacher perceptions of pupils' errors in elementary arithmetic with a view to developing teacher training techniques which will enable teachers to improve their teaching methods. Selected groups of young pupils have been tested using simple problems and their errors have been classified by teachers in training, in a preparatory study aimed at clarifying the issues and problems. A further study of pupils' problem solving has yielded data which is currently being analyzed.
Source of Grant: Brazilian Government: university fees
Date of Research: 1988 – continuing
KEYWORDS: arithemetic; error; mathematics; teacher education; teaching method

8/0592
Department of Education
Leeds LS2 9JT
0532 334521
O'Brien, C. Mr; *Supervisor:* Jenkins, E.W. Mr; Medway, P. Dr
A study of technological capability amongst pupils with particular reference to progression
Abstract: The introduction of design and technology into the National Curriculum focuses attention on pupils' technological capabilities and on the way(s) in which these change with age. The study seeks to define aspects of technological capability and to examine the development of one or more of such aspects in pupils between 5-16 years. The study is likely to be based on work with a sample of perhaps 50 pupils and will use both classroom based observation and tests to assess pupils capabilities.
Source of Grant: No funding
Date of Research: 1989 – continuing
KEYWORDS: ability; pupil; technology

8/0593
Department of Education
Leeds LS2 9JT
0532 334545
Williams, R. Mr; Southworth, A. Mrs
Evaluation of the Leeds Local Education Authority Technical and Vocational Education Initiative
Abstract: Leeds Local Education Authority (LEA) introduced the Technical and Vocational Education Initiative (TVEI) into 5 pilot schools in September 1988. A central project team of a director and three assistant directors, together with advisory teachers and coordinators has been established. In 1989-90, TVEI is being introduced into 15 second phase schools and also tertiary involve-

ment is under way. The Leeds TVEI project is an enhancement of the whole curriculum for all students aged 14-18. The external evaluation is formative producing feedback in various forms including written reports on agreed 'mini-contracts' and 'on the hoof' oral feedback. During the first year, in addition to two termly reports and an annual report, several formative reports to specified audiences were produced. Management issues in the project were a major focus including the functioning of the 5 consortium groups of schools and the activities of the various role groups in the central project. During the second year of the evaluation the focus is more on in-school activities with a particular focus on language and communication issues across the curriculum. A full range of data collection techniques are being employed, including interviews, participant observation, questionnaires and documentary analysis.
Source of Grant: Leeds Local Education Authority: £80,000
Date of Research: 1989 – continuing
KEYWORDS: evaluation; local education authority; Technical and Vocational Education Initiative

8/0594
Department of Education
Leeds LS2 9JT
0532 334631
Martin, A. Mr; *Supervisor:* Hartley, J.R. Mr; Foster, E. Dr
Nero is dead: evaluation of a computer based simulation for the teaching of history
Abstract: The research will examine some implications of the use of computer assisted simulations for the teaching and learning of history in secondary schools. The thesis that a computer assisted simulation exercise can both extend significantly the range of methods available for the teaching of history as it is currently practised, and support a reconceptualizing of some of the objectives of history teaching will be examined through the evaluation of the simulation 'Nero is Dead' in school situations.
Published Material: MARTIN, A. (1988). 'Nero is dead: enhancing a classroom simulation through computer support', In: LOVIS, F. & TAGG, E.D. (eds). Computers in Education, Amsterdam Elsevier, pp.279.283.
Source of Grant: No funding
Date of Research: 1988 – continuing
KEYWORDS: computer assisted instruction; history; simulation; teaching aids

8/0595
Department of Education
Leeds LS2 9JT
0532 334521
Lewis, I. Mr; *Supervisor:* Jenkins, E.W. Mr; Donnelly, J.F. Dr
A study of technological capability as manifest in secondary school pupils' project work
Abstract: The study is an exploration of 'the technology project' with particular attention being given to its origination, development and closure. An attempt is made to establish the criteria used by pupils in, for example, choosing one solution/design criteria in preference to another, evaluating/appraising their project as it develops. The work is based on an ethnographic study of pupils in classes in five Sheffield schools. A sample size of about 10 pupils is likely to be involved.
Source of Grant: Leeds University, Department of Education Sheffield Local Education Authority
Date of Research: 1989 – continuing
KEYWORDS: ability; project work; secondary education; technology

8/0596
Department of Education
Leeds LS2 9JT
0532 334544
Child, D. Prof.; Baker, R. Mr
Survey of communication practices in schools for the hearing impaired in the United Kingdom
Abstract: In 1987 a survey was carried out with a number of schools for the hearing impaired in England and Scotland using a total communication approach. When the findings were circulated, suggestions were made by several headteachers for a further study to explore in more details the ways in which different modes of communication are used, demand for resource materials, training of staff and parents in communication skills and the roles of deaf people in the schools. It has subsequently been suggested that a

new survey be carried out to establish exactly what range of approaches are used throughout all the schools at the present time. A questionnaire was designed which asks for communication approaches in use, in order to provide a base of information for planning for future needs. At the same time, it goes more deeply into aspects of practices in schools using a total communication approach, in response to the requests already made by headteachers. The questionnaire has now been circulated and a 100% return obtained. The data are in the process of being analyzed. The findings will be circulated to all participants.
Source of Grant: Northern Counties School for the Deaf: £4,000
Date of Research: 1099 – continuing
KEYWORDS: *communication; deaf; hearing defect; special school*

8/0597

Department of Education
Leeds LS2 9JT
0532 334521
McAuley, J. Mr; *Supervisor:* Orton, A. Dr
Cognitive style and learning mathematics
Abstract: The implications of cognitive styles such as field dependence and field independence in learning mathematics have not been widely investigated. This study aims to focus on such styles and the implications in learning matrices. It is expected that pupils will be assessed and classified on a field dependence – field independence spectrum and the effects of different teaching styles will be measured.
Source of Grant: No funding
Date of Research: 1989 – continuing
KEYWORDS: *cognitive process; learning; mathematics*

8/0598

Department of Education
Leeds LS2 9JT
0532 431751
Austrey C of E First School
St Nicholas Close, Austrey, Atherstone,
Warwickshire CV9 3EQ
Bates, R.G. Mr; *Supervisor:* Shorrocks, D. Dr; Beard, R. Dr
A study of the relationship between oral and written language skills in the early years of schooling
Abstract: The research is aiming to explore some of the interrelationships between activities prior to writing (such as oral work, drawing/illustration, note-making) and children's written products, and to relate these findings to what is known about memory encoding and retrieval processes in children. In particular, the work is to be set against the theoretical background suggested by Vygotsky that memory, as a higher level cognitive function, has its origins in social interactions. The sample is a small group of 6 year old children in the naturalistic setting of a first school curriculum.
Source of Grant: Warwickshire County Council: tuition fees
Date of Research: 1984-1989
KEYWORDS: *language development; language skil; memory; oral expression; primary education; writing*

8/0599

Department of Education
Leeds LS2 9JT
0532 431751
Blow, D.A.R.; *Supervisor:* Whalley, D.G. Dr
A study of the development of skill as a function of teaching and learning in schools, with particular reference to the implications for teacher training
Abstract: This is an attempt to discover what all the parties in the education process understand by the term skill and how this relates to the societal view. The investigation will be conducted by unstructured interviews and the gathering of information from a variety of sources.
Source of Grant: No funding
Date of Research: 1985-1990
KEYWORDS: *learning; skill; teacher education; teaching*

8/0600

Department of Education
Centre for Studies in Science and Mathematics in Education,
Leeds LS2 9JT
0532 431751
Jagger, J.M. Mrs; *Supervisor:* Orton, A. Dr n)
Students' understanding of acceleration as a vector in the context of mechanics

Abstract: This research aims to investigate the growth in students' understanding of acceleration as rate of change in velocity (as distinct from rate of change of speed) in the context of mechanics. Pupils' understanding was investigated by means of questionnaires administered to them three times during their A level mathematics course. A questionnaire was also given to first year Honours mathematics undergraduates. The sample involved included, 120 lower sixth formers who had elected to study mathematics at A-level; 120 upper sixth formers who were studying mathematics at A-level; 60 first year Honours mathematics undergraduates. The school pupils were taken from three comprehensive schools in the north of England. About 40 of them have been followed through from Lower sixth to Upper sixth including an extra questionnaire in March.
Published Material: JAGGER, J.M. (1985). Introducing mechanics – a response. Mathematics in school, Vol 14, No 1, pp.24-26.; JAGGER, J.M. (1985). 'A review of the research into the learning of mathematics'. In: ORTON, A. (Ed). Studies in mechanics learning. Leeds University.; JAGGER, J.M. (1987). 'Students' understanding of acceleration', Mathematics in school, Vol 16, No 4, pp.24-25.
Source of Grant: Economic and Social Research Council – 1 year 1986-87
Date of Research: 1985 – continuing
KEYWORDS: *acceleration; comprehension; higher education; mathematics; mechanics; secondary education*

8/0601

Department of External Studies
Leeds LS2 9JT
0532 334527
Taylor, R.K.S. Dr
Continuing education practice in Canada and the UK: a case study of Calgary and Leeds Universities
Abstract: Continuing education provision in Canada and the UK operates on different models. This research analyzes assumptions, priorities, models, financing, curriculum approaches and outcomes in the two countries, using case study material for Calgary and Leeds.
Source of Grant: Alberta/Leeds Exchange Scheme: £1,800 travelling expenses
Date of Research: 1988 – continuing
KEYWORDS: *comparative education; Canada; continuing education*

8/0602

Department of External Studies
Leeds LS2 9JT
0532 333180
Taylor, R.K.S. Dr; Steele, G.J. Dr
An examination of the inter-relationship between adult education development, Gandhian philosophy, the Congress Party, and the legacy of the British Raj, in India between 1935 and 1955
Abstract: This project concerns the influence of British cultural values, practices and structures on the development of adult education in India in the period 1935 to 1955. British cultural legacy was not homogenous: as with the industrial British society from which it sprang, its imperial strands were diverse and often conflicting. One major theme of this study will be to disentangle these various elements and to match them up both to the empirical development of adult education structures in India, and to the political dimensions of British culture in the UK. An essential concern of this study will be the relationship between Gandhian philosophy and adult education development. Linked to this will be a study of the educational dimension to the emerging Congress Party as the dominant political force in India before, during and after Indian independence.
Source of Grant: Universities Funding Council: £20,000 for 1990-91
Date of Research: 1989 – continuing
KEYWORDS: *adult education; history of education; India*

8/0603

Department of Psychology
Leeds LS2 9JT
0532 334527
Sheppard, B.A. Dr; Sheehy, N.P. Dr; *Supervisor:* Sheppard, B.A. Dr
Educational countermeasures for media violence
Abstract: A partial replication of an intervention study by Huesmann et al was carried out, which aimed to modify aggressive

behaviour in 9 year olds, by educating them about the nature of television violence and raising their awareness of it. It was also predicted that changes to their understanding and attitudes towards television violence would generalize and lead to different perceptions of aggression and violence within their peer groups. One hundred and nine 8- to 9-year olds from schools in the north of England participated in this study. They come from the full range of socio-economic backgrounds. Baseline measures taken included gender, television violence viewing, child aggression, judgement of television reality and reading age. There was a pre-and post-test (intervention) experimental design. The pre- and post-test measures were: peer nominated aggression, picture of television studio, meaning of 'violence', watching and preference for television violence. The findings indicate that a short, limited investment of resources can be applied to bring about substantial changes in children's comprehension and awareness of aggression and violence on television. There was no link between either overall viewing of television or video viewing and aggressive behaviour. The report considers the importance of other factors in the children's lives in appraising the significance of these findings.
Source of Grant: Independent Broadcasting Authority: £30,000
Date of Research: 1987-1989
KEYWORDS: aggression; intervention; mass media effects; television; violence

8/0604

Department of Psychology
Leeds LS2 9JT
0532 334527
Ward, P. Dr; Sheehy, N. Dr
Development of evaluation of a hyper-text tool for teaching functional neuroanatomy
Abstract: This research will involve the design and implementation of a computer based training package for functional neuroanatomy. The package integrates text with high definition images and graphics with a 'hypertext' authoring tool.
Source of Grant: International Business Machines: £80,000
Date of Research: 1989-1990
KEYWORDS: anatomy; autoinstructional aid; automatic teaching; computer assisted instruction; neuroanatomy; neurology

8/0605

Department of Social Policy and Sociology
Leeds LS2 9JT
0532 334406
Bradford & Ilkley Community College
Department of Contemporary Studies
Great Horton Road, Bradford BD7 1AY
0274 753159
Molloy, S. Mr; Carroll, V. Ms; *Supervisor:* Faithorn, R. Mr; Warwick, D. Dr
A transbinary study of the progress and performance of non-standard entrants to higher education and the development of course, institutional and national monitoring systems
Abstract: The project will collate and analyze data relating to approximately 2000 first degree students of Leeds and Bradford Universities, Bradford and Ilkley Community College, and Leeds and Manchester Polytechnics. The data has already been, or will be, collated from initial application forms, and departmental and institutional records. It will be integrated on a single computer file and analyzed with cross-tabular and multivariate statistical techniques available through an SPSS application programme. The data will differentiate between the educational qualifications of NSE's and identify Access entrants from each individual course. The analysis will compare the annual completion rates, pass rates, and degree classifications of: Standard entrants, non-standard entrants, and; non-standard entrants with different entry qualifications; Access entrants from different Access courses; non-standard entrants and Access entrants in university and public sectors; non-standard entrants and Access entrants of different age, sex, and ethnic background. Current literature and preliminary surveys suggest that existing institutional systems provide insufficient, and imperfectly integrated data, and that these lacunae are reflected in national statistics. The validity of current and proposed student record systems, as a resource for the monitoring of NSE's and AE's will be evaluated in the light of these independently produced progress performance profiles. The evaluation exercise aims to advise participating institutions on the development of their information systems in relation to NSE's and AE's and to recommend appropriate development strategies for NSE amd AE monitoring at course,

institutional and national levels. This will be effected through involvement and consultation with course tutors, members of registry staff, and systems development personnel in each institution and a final one-day collaborative seminar. Further dissemination would involve a national one-day conference and publication of final report. Data from postal questionnaires will be analyzed to examine the employment experience of former Access students graduating between 1975 and 1987, with particular reference to comparisons between university and public sector graduates. Data will be made available through publication.
Source of Grant: CNAA: £15,000
Date of Research: 1988-1989
KEYWORDS: access programme; assessment; higher education; information system; mature student; performance

8/0606

Department of Sociology
Leeds LS2 9JT
0532 431751 ext 6420
Fisher, R. Mr; *Supervisor:* Varcoe, I. Dr
An examination of Marxist analyses of education with special reference to the effect of the ideas upon schooling
Abstract: The aim of the project is to review the literature of the sociology of education written by Marxists. The study will summarize the findings under various headings, derived from Marxist theory. Gaps will be identified; the coherence and validity of findings will be assessed. An attempt will be made to assess how far Marxist sociology of education has influenced practice.
Source of Grant: No funding
Date of Research: 1984-1990
KEYWORDS: Marxism; philosophy of education; sociology of education

Leicester Polytechnic

8/0607

Scraptoft Campus, Scraptoft, Leicester LE7 9SU
0533 431011
Bennett, R. Dr; *Supervisor:* Allison, B. Prof.; Denscombe, M. Dr; Huxley, M. Mr
The significance of dance in community based projects
Abstract: Following a broad survey of the national, regional and local policies for the promotion of dance, the research follows a case study approach using a combination of observation, participant observation, and interview techniques to look at the effects of gender, race and class on the take-up of community based dance initiatives.
Source of Grant: Local authority secondment of Dr Bennett
Date of Research: 1987-1990
KEYWORDS: dance; participation; race; sex difference; social class

8/0608

Centre for Postgraduate Teacher Education, Scraptoft, Leicester LE7 9SU
0533 431011
Iwano, M. Miss; *Supervisor:* Mason, R. Dr; Denscombe, M. Dr
Curriculum reform in Japanese art education: the case of multiculturalism
Abstract: This research will investigate, analyse and evaluate Japanese art curriculum at primary, secondary and high school levels. It will explore the possibility of curriculum reform in Japanese art education with reference to theory and practice of multicultural education. Since multicultural education has been applied in non-western societies, the study will aim also to identify key principles which might be taken into account or underpin an international concept and application multicultural education.
Source of Grant: No funding
Date of Research: 1989 – continuing
KEYWORDS: art education; curriculum development; Japan; multicultural education

8/0609

Centre for Postgraduate Teacher Education, Scraptoft Campus, Scraptoft, Leicester LE7 9SU
0533 431011

Kypreou, I. Miss; *Supervisor:* Allison, B. Prof.; Mason, R. Dr

The assessment of art at first degree level: a comparative study of the principles and methods underlying assessment of Fine Art students in Athens and Leicester

Abstract: The study sets out: (a) to determine the role theories of art criticism play in the assessment of Fine Art students at first degree level; (b) to determine whether assessment procedures in two Fine Art institutions (Leicester – documented procedures, Athens – non-documented procedures) can be described relative to major theories of art criticism; and (c) to determine the extent to which the differing procedures of assessment utilised in the two institutions are subject to or are affected by the theoretical positions adopted by individual examiners. Fieldwork (observation, interview and questionnaire) will be carried out in the two institutions.
Source of Grant: No funding
Date of Research: 1988 – continuing
KEYWORDS: art education; assessment; higher education

8/0610

Centre for Postgraduate Teacher Education,
Scraptoft Campus, Scraptoft, Leicester LE7 9SU
0533 431011
Impey, G. Mr

Inservice Training and Education of Teachers (INSET) for the National Curriculum in the primary phase

Abstract: The project will investigate the response of a number of primary schools to the Inservice Training and Education of Teachers (INSET) and staff development demands of the National Curriculum. In depth case studies of selected schools are planned and negotiations and discussions are taking place with a view to starting in April 1989.
Published Material: EVERTON, T. and IMPEY, G. (Eds). (1989). Information Technology-Inservice Training and Education of Teachers (IT-INSET): Partnership in training. London: Fulton David.
Source of Grant: No funding
Date of Research: 1989-1990
KEYWORDS: inservice education and training of teachers; primary education

8/0611

Department of Education
Centre for Postgraduate Studies in Education,
Scraptoft Campus, Scraptoft, Leicester LE7 9SU
0533 431011
Rawding, M.D. Mr; *Supervisor:* Mason, R.M. Dr; Allison, B. Prof.

Relationship between works of literature and works of art with reference to interpretation theory and implications for school curricula

Abstract: The investigation seeks answer to three related questions. Firstly, what is available in art educational literature that relates both to the particular concept of artistic intention and the broader area of controversy which has arisen in connection with the theoretical relationship of art and criticism? Secondly, what insights can the study of the concept of artistic intention provide regarding conceptual issues associated with the theoretical relationship of art and criticism? Thirdly, what steps are required to 'bridge the gap' between philosophy of art (ref. critical theory) and philosophy of education (ref. curriculum theory) in order to translate theoretical materials arising from the study of the concept of artistic intention into a coherent pedagogy of art criticism? It is anticipated that the study will render the nature of controversy in philosophical aesthetics more readily available to the field of education by providing a framework for a theoretically coherent and consistent pedagogy of criticism. Hence the study will conclude with recommendations for the curriculum development that include reference to the synthesis of subject content, methods of teaching and learning and curricular aims and objectives.
Source of Grant: No funding
Date of Research: 1985-1990
KEYWORDS: aesthetics; art education; critical sense; curriculum development

8/0612

Department of Education
Centre for Postgraduate Studies in Education,
Scraptoft Campus, Scraptoft, Leicester LE7 9SU
0533 431011

Tyers, J.M. Mr; *Supervisor:* Allison, B. Prof

The personality and other attributes, qualities, abilities and opinions of 'A' level design students

Abstract: The aims of the investigation are (1) to objectively identify and quantify the differences between the structure and content of the 'A' level design examination course and other 'A' level examination courses; (2) to identify and compare the personality characteristics and other attributes, abilities and opinions of 'A' level design students with those who study other 'A' level design subjects; (3) to identify the relationship and other variables in the personality characteristics of 'A' level design students; (4) to determine the extent to which, if any, the 'A' level design course develops certain personal qualties, attributes, abilities and opinions of those who study the subject; (5) to determine the validity of teacher assessment of personal qualities leading to success in the 'A' level design examination. The subjects include c.200 'A' level design students in a representative group of Leicestershire schools, c.50 other 'A' level students and c.30 'A' level design teachers. Instruments consist of a number of questionnaires and rating scales, the 16PF Personality Factor Questionnaire and AH4 and AH6 general ability tests. Complete data on 'O' and 'A' level results of all subjects. The methods consist of (1) Descriptive and (2) Causal-Comparative studies and (3) a quasi-experimental longitudinal study. It is expected that the study will provide standardized 16PF norms for British students of design and/or 'A' level in general.
Source of Grant: No funding
Date of Research: 1987-1990
KEYWORDS: design education; personality; student

8/0613

Department of Education
Centre for Postgraduate Studies in Education,
Scraptoft Campus, Scraptoft, Leicester LE7 9SU
0533 431011
Elatta, T. Mr; *Supervisor:* Mason, R.M. Dr; Allison, B. Prof.

An investigation into Sudanese visual imagery and its implication for curriculum development in art education

Abstract: The aim of the research is to establish a basis for curriculum planning and reform in art education which reflects the nation's cultural heritage with reference to indigenous imagery. It will be implemented in two parts. Part A will involve fieldwork and focus on the documentation and classification of artefacts. Part B will be in the form of a survey of students' work. The procedures will be (i) a survey and analysis of indigenous Sudanese artefacts surface design; (ii) the development of a taxonomy of imagery for the classification of indigenous surface design to facilitate the identification of art styles of the different regions of the Sudan; (iii) a survey of Sudanese graphic design students' work between 1968 and 1987 to determine whether or not indigenous heritage is apparent; (iv) an analysis of the findings and their implications for curriculum planning in art education in the Sudan.
Source of Grant: Sudanese government
Date of Research: 1987-1990
KEYWORDS: curriculum development; design; graphic arts; Sudan

Leicester University

8/0614

Department of Education
21 University Road, Leicester LE1 7RF
0503 523713
Holt, B.S. Rev.; *Supervisor:* Woodhouse, D. Dr

Values in school: priorities, qualities and perceptions regarded as important by head teachers, teachers and students in a cross-section of seondary schools in Leicestershire.

Abstract: The intention is to enquire into what head teachers, teachers and students in secondary schools think schools are, or should be, about. It is intended to look at what IS rather than at what OUGHT to be; but the IS includes what members of the schools think OUGHT TO BE. The sources of information are as follows: (a) a questionnaire completed by 266 students, 103 teachers and 9 heads from 11 schools, including three 11-16 state schools, three 14-18 state schools, three 11-18 state schools and two 11-18 public schools. The students are all fifth years — as representative of those at the end of the statutory schooling period; (b) Interviews with 11 heads and 38 teachers; (c) literature provided by the schools.

All this is supported by brief visits (so far of one week) spent in each school. It is intended that the results of the questionnaires will be fed back to the individual schools and supplementary questions asked at that time. The hypotheses from which the enquiry has been started are as follows: (1) that the type of school has an influence on the values conveyed; (2) that schools need a clearly worked out and coherent philosophy of the moral (and indeed religious) basis of schooling; but that, in many cases, this is not made explicit or openly clarified; (3) that, nevertheless, it is possible to perceive a pattern of values and priorities in practice in the schools. (4) that there is a lack of clear motivators (or performance indicators) for values education in schools.
Published Material: HOLT, B.S. (1972). Looking for meaning: a book of school assemblies. London: S.C.M. Press.
Date of Research: 1988 – continuing
KEYWORDS: *moral education; priority; secondary education; value system*

8/0615
Department of Education
21 University Road, Leicester LE1 7RF
0533 523713
Thody, A.M. Mrs; Jones, D. Mr
Managing change: the role of chief education officers
Abstract: The aims of this research are to consider the extent to which the roles of chief education officers have altered, and to ascertain the extent of power and influence of directors of education and how their work is organized. The research method will involve: shadowing of 5 Directors of Education over periods of between 3 and 5 days each; recording their activities and analyzing them from managerial and political perspectives. Local Education Authorities selected represented the political spectrum: Labour, Hung and Conservative. This material was compared with historical evidence of previous Directors of Education. The shadowing was completed in 1988 and analysis is proceeding. Data has been extracted on hours worked (very long); types of contacts (e.g. much more political contact in Authorities with a party which has a big majority); and distribution of time amongst activities. Historical data is now being collected.
Source of Grant: University of Leicester Research Committee: £1,000
Date of Research: 1986 – continuing
KEYWORDS: *administration of education; director; history of education*

8/0616
Department of Education
21 University Road, Leicester LE1 7RF
0503 523713
Slater, A.R. Mrs; *Supervisor:* Merry, R. Dr
Encouraging literacy for students with special needs
Abstract: There is much controversy about the ways in which literacy is acquired and consequently much debate about how children should be taught to read and write. The debate can perhaps be broadly represented as 'language experience' approaches versus 'skills-based' approaches. One of the aims of this project is to consider the relevance of this debate to the education of students who have severe learning difficulties. Most of the research takes place in Leicestershire's 7 schools for pupils with severe learning difficulties and mainly involves approximately 30 students aged 11-16 years, who have some understanding of what the written word represents. Analysis of their reading and writing abilities has been carried out, and strategies to aid literacy have been developed, (eg. using word-processing facilities). Consideration has been given to teaching approaches used. A questionnaire was developed and administered to 60+ special school teachers in order to gauge attitudes to aspects of literacy. Teacher interviews have also been employed. In addition, the distinction between specific literacy difficulties and general learning difficulties will be explored. Initial findings suggest that the debate surrounding literacy for mainstream pupils is certainly as relevant for those in special education. Further, the prevalent assumptions that a skills-based approach to teaching literacy is more appropriate to pupils with special needs, are challenged.
Source of Grant: Seconded by LEA with salary
Date of Research: 1987-1990
KEYWORDS: *learning difficulty; literacy; special education; special needs; teaching method*

8/0617
Department of Education

21 University Road, Leicester LE1 7RF
0533 52313
Newman, B.K. Mr; *Supervisor:* Ball, D. Mr
Control technology in the primary school
Abstract: The aim of this research is to investigate the development of control technology in primary schools. Current investigations centre upon the evaluations of the current position in primary schools, the evaluation of the effect of in-service training and the development of an icon control language, as an improved way of introducing icon control. The research will attempt to isolate problems involved with the progress of control technology into schools and hopefully make positive suggestions towards overcoming any problems.
Source of Grant: GRIST (Grant-related Inservice Training) award: £1,200 (approx) over 3 years
Date of Research: 1987-1990
KEYWORDS: *curriculum development; information technology; primary education*

8/0618
Department of Education
University Road, Leicester LE1 7RF
0533 523713
Brown, M.F. Mrs; *Supervisor:* Wright, C. Dr; Foggelman, K. Prof.
Multi-cultural education: images at primary level
Abstract: Is concern about minority pupils a worthy matter or are there more pressing problems in education? What does multi-cultural education mean in terms of actual school practice? Who is referred to when we use the term ethnic minority'? In this study an observational research will be conducted, with the aim of analyzing attitudes and views of teachers and pupils of given primary schools. Three types of schools will be researched. Formal and informal interviews with individuals and groups of teachers and pupils will be conducted. Records and reports will also be assessed in order to discover views on multi-cultural education and to ascertain if school experiences of ethnic-minority pupils in the various schools are similar. It will also be decided whether the internal system of the schools and their teaching methods have differential effects on the pupils of ethnic minority. The three different types of schools examined are: (a) large primary schools in inner city areas (Birmingham and London) where there exists a high percentage of pupils from ethnic minority backgrounds. In these schools multi-cultural educational techniques are used to an extreme to cater for 'supposed needs' especially in the area of language development; (b) primary schools in developing towns (Northampton and Cambridge) where pupils of multi-ethnic backgrounds attend on a smaller scale, and multi-cultural teaching methods and practices are incorporated in the curriculum successfully; (c) rural primary schools where heads and teachers alike believe that multi-cultural education is not needed in their school as no pupils of multi-ethnic backgrounds attend. They find multi-cultural education baffling, misleading and foreign. The study prompts questions in relation to the degree of multi-cultural awareness and practices observed in schools.
Source of Grant: Funded by own business (Independent school)
Date of Research: 1988 – continuing
KEYWORDS: *ethnic minority; multicultural education; primary education*

8/0619
Department of Education
21 University Road, Leicester LE1 7RF
0503 523713
Cortazzi, M. Mr; *Supervisor:* Ashton, P.M.A. Dr
Teachers' anecdotes: access to cultural perspectives through narrative analysis
Abstract: This research proposes that narrative analysis can be used to study occupational or cultural perspectives – in this case, of teachers. Part I examines models of narrative analysis from sociology, sociolinguistics, psychology, structural literature and anthropology. The 'evaluation model' developed by the sociolinguist, W. Labou was selected, enriched and supplemented by other models, to analyze nearly 1000 narratives told by primary teachers in order to examine the tellers' cultural perspectives. There is a major focus on the teachers' perspectives on: outstanding children in the classroom, breakthroughs in pupils' learning, teachers' planning, incidents of disaster and burnout in the classroom and 'awkward' parents. Conclusions are drawn on each of these topics and on primary teachers' perspectives generally.

Source of Grant: No funding
Date of Research: 1980-1989
KEYWORDS: content analysis; narration; primary education;
teacher

Department of Education
21 University Road, Leicester LE1 7RF
0503 523713
Thody, A.M. Mrs; Supervisor: Lofthouse, M. Dr
The contribution of training to school governors' roles

Department of Education
21 University Road,
Leicester LE1 7RF
0533 523713
Abbas, A.K. Mr; Supervisor: Young, G.M.Dr
A contrastive study of adverbial positions in English and Arabic with pedagogical implications

Abstract: The study is concerned with the syntactic order of adverbials in standard English and modern standard Arabic. It is hypothesized that the particular problems which adverbials pose lie in the relative distributional freedom they enjoy in both languages. The major aim of this study was to discuss at length the positions that English and Arabic adverbials readily occupy. Then a comparison was carried out displaying the points of similarity and discrepancy between the two languages in this specific linguistic area. Of the methods of investigation employed, the first was elicitation with many examples from the newspapers or grammar books providing evidence as to the acceptability of adverbial positions. The second was an acceptability technique which utilized the native speakers' reactions towards sentences with different adverbial positions which were distributed in the questionnaires. At the end, the study concluded that 'adverbial positions' remains a disorderly area of grammar which in turn causes more problems to learners of both languages than any other linguistic area. Language learners differ, in most cases, in their judgement of the acceptability of adverbial positions owing to the complex interplay of factors that influence the choice of these positions. However, this study offered a classification according to which adverbial positions have been refined and made easier to detect. So teachers, as well as textbook writers, may utilize the findings of this study when dealing with adverbial positions in English and Arabic.
Source of Grant: Iraqui Government
Date of Research: 1986-1989
KEYWORDS: Arabic; english language; linguistics; syntax

Abstract: The aims are to evaluate the school governor training courses offered by Leicestershire Local Education Authority and the Workers' Educational Association and their relationship to the roles of school governors; to analyze the composition of school governing bodies and the role expectations of governors. All governor training courses in Leicestershire were monitored during the autumn term, 1986, and the spring term 1987; all governors undergoing training (200) and all tutors were questioned; all Leicestershire governors whether trained or not also received questionnaires (6000). The return rate was 33%. Evaluation was completed by spring 1987. The role expectations of governors altered with training. Training courses were well liked but required minor amendments. Social analysis (N.B. relates to governing bodies before the implementation of the 1986 Act) revealed that the occupational composition of governing bodies did not match general expectations. There were about one third with education related backgrounds, one third with industrial/technological occupations and very few housewives, vicars or retired people. Social class composition, as anticipated, was predominantly classes I-II. The research has led to a reconsideration of how governors' roles might be defined and has produced an analysis of their covert roles as legitimators, protectors, supporters.
Published Material: THODY, A. (1987). Training courses for school governors – towards a vocational curriculum. Curriculum, Winter, 1987, Vol 8, No 3, pp.37-42.; THODY, A. (1987). 'The 1986 Act – the more it changes, the more it stays the same', Management in Education Vol 1, No 4.; THODY, A. & WILSON, D. (1988). 'School Governing Bodies and the Pressure group Arena', Local Governing Policy Studies, Vol 15, No 2, September.; Evaluation of Leicestrshire LEAs School Governors' Training 1986-1987 – a report on Leicestershire's use of Education Support Grant Funding. Not published, but copy available in School of Education Library, Leicester University.
Source of Grant: Part funded by Leicestershire LEA: £1,200
Date of Research: 1986-1990
KEYWORDS: administration of education; school governor; training

Department of Education
21 University Road,
Leicester LE1 7RF
0503 523713
Akkoyunlu, B. Miss; Supervisor: Ball, D. Mr
The use of microcomputers in British schools, the implications for their use in Turkish schools and the improvement of computer assisted learning in Turkish schools

Abstract: Computer assisted instruction is a new area for study and practice in Turkey. Research studies are very limited and qualified personnel are scarce. Utilization of computers has a relatively long history, in some countries such as England, the USA, Japan and Holland, and there is a considerable amount of experience and accumulated knowledge in the use of computers for education. By reviewing research studies and investigating practices and the present status of computer assisted instruction in the other countries the study aims to achieve the following objectives: (1) to draw relevant lessons of experience for Turkish computer assisted instruction practices in order to establish a sound ground for implementation and development; (2) to suggest procedures and methods which will fit the Turkish educational system for the development of the use of microcomputers for instruction; (3) to provide criteria and a frame of reference for evaluating the practices of computer assisted instruction in Turkey. The data will be gathered in two ways: (1) by reviewing and analyzing the literature on computer assisted instruction and by drawing implications for the Turkish case, (2) by conducting some case studies in which different approaches are utilized for the implementation of computer assisted or computer based instruction. For data collection, an observation list, questionnaires and interview techniques will be employed. The full design of the study will be completed by collaborative and co-operative work with related members of the School of Education at Leicester University.
Source of Grant: Hacettepe University
Date of Research: 1985 – continuing
KEYWORDS: comparative education; computer assisted instruction; microcomputer; Turkey

Department of Education
21 University Road, Leicester LE1 7RF
0533 5237113
Bishop Grosseteste College
Lincoln LN1 3DY
0522 513579
Whittaker, J. Miss; Supervisor: Ashton, P.M.E. Dr
Evaluating teachers' learning

Abstract: This study is rooted in 'illuminative evaluation' and draws on the reactions and experiences of many teachers and students who have used the 'Curriculum in Action' materials in order to evaluate their practice and classroom curricula. The objective is to help teachers become more effective by examining three key questions: (1) how does the observation, recording and analysis of the curriculum by teachers affect their thinking and learning? (2) what is the nature of their thinking and learning? (3) what are the teachers' perceptions of the effects of their observation, recording and analyses and their subsequent thinking and learning on their classroom practice?. The study has two specific objectives: (1) to see whether it is possible to describe the stages of teachers' professional development, gained through inservice courses and activities. (2) to develop and explore the use of interactive video as a research tool, particularly in its contribution to the examination of the three research questions. The stages of professional development identified to date are: zero learners; diffident pragmatists; inspirers; committed innovators; the undiscerning; rejectors.
Published Material: WHITTAKER, J. (1988). 'Curriculum in action: an approach to evaluation'. In: NIAS, J. & GROUNDWATER-SMITH, S. (1988). The enquiring teacher. London: Falmer.
Source of Grant: No funding
Date of Research: 1984-1989
KEYWORDS: curriculum development; professional development; teaching method; teaching quality

8/0624
Department of Education
21 University Road,
Leicester LE1 7RF
0503 523713
Taylor, D. Mr; *Supervisor:* Jones, D.K. Mr
A study of the development of the curriclum in the elementary schools of Birmingham, Nottingham and Derby, 1870-1933
Abstract: This is a study of the development of the elementary school curriculum in Birmingham, Nottingham and Derby, 1870-1933. This covers the whole of the School Board era and the first thirty years of the Local Education Authority. In essence the thesis attempts to trace the expansion of the elementary school curriculum which, at the beginning of the period, was little more than reading, writing and arithmetic but which, by the end of the period, embraced a large number of subjects. The reasons for this expansion are examined not so much by looking at the central authority role but by examining the role played in this expansion of the curriculum by local personalities elected on to the School Board and Local Authority, and by identifying the educational issues which were widely discussed at the time by these bodies and by a very lively local press. The issues examined include: how many subjects should be taught; whether an expansion of the curriculum threatened the standards in reading, writing and arithmetic; the place of technical and practical education in the curriculum and whether this threatened literary subjects and the place of vocationalism in elementary schools. Thus the study not only enables a comparison between the three areas but also between School Boards and Local Authorities. The bulk of the research material came from local archives and included School Board and Local Authority Minutes, Annual Reports, special investigations etc, the wide coverage given to the above issues in the local press and an examination of elementary school log books 1870-1933.
Source of Grant: No funding
Date of Research: 1984-1989
KEYWORDS: *curriculum development; history of education; primary education*

8/0625
Department of Education
University Road,
Leicester LE1 7RF
0533 523713
Milonas, E. Mrs; *Supervisor:* Annis, P.M. MIss; Lofthouse, M. Dr
A study of an individualized mathematics programme, School Mathematics Project, in selected Greek primary schools.
Abstract: The present study examines the possibilities of applying an individualized programme of mathematics, namely SMP 7-13 in Greek primary schools. The research was prompted by the fact that the changes in the philosophy and practice of primary education as well as the evolution in the theory of mathematics manifested at the outset of the 20th century hardly affected Greek educational matters, whilst they revitalized and transformed the British educational system. The programme extended over three stages; the pre-pilot, the pilot and the main study. The latter was conducted for one year in three schools each one of which accepted children of different social strata. The application of the research exposed a number of difficulties innate either in the individualized programme itself or in the Greek school environment and function. Despite those difficulties, however, and the impediment of the limited sample the present research allowed for certain encouraging implications. An attempt to innovate the content, and moreover the teaching of mathematics is not only imperative but it is also feasible provided, however, that certain conditions are taken into consideration. In relation to the applicability of SMP 7-13 to the current Greek educational system, the aspect adopted by the present study is that it could constitute a valuable supplement to the existing mathematics programme.
Source of Grant: No funding
Date of Research: 1984-1988
KEYWORDS: *Greece; mathematics; primary education*

8/0626
Department of Education
University Road, Leicester LE1 7RF
0533 522522
Wright, C. Dr
Multicultural education images at primary level
Abstract: This research looks at multicultural education. What is it in the practical sense of classroom work and teaching, and how does it function in multi-racial schools?. How does it function in 'all-white schools'?. Are teachers being adequately prepared to teach in a multi-cultural environment or are the teachers training institutions failing or ill-equipping many of its students?. Do we need multi-cultural education in the style which it is often negatively interpreted in schools; as education required in schools where 'black' or 'asian' pupils attend.
Source of Grant: No funding
Date of Research: 1988 – continuing
KEYWORDS: *multicultural eduction*

8/0627
Department of Education
21 University Road,
Leicester LE1 7RF
0553 522522
Hargreaves, L.M. Dr; *Supervisor:* Galton, M.J. Prof.
Study skills in project based assessment at primary level
Abstract: The purpose of the study was to assess childrens' performance in a broader range of curriculum areas than those assessed by standardized tests of reading, mathematics etc. A mini project at two levels of difficulty (8- to 9- year olds; 10- to 11- year olds) was prepared and sent to the 68 small schools participating in the Department of Education and Science funded project 'Curriculum Provision in Small Primary Schools', (PRISMS). The project content was a local study of an imaginary village. Children recorded their own use of resources; books, maps, pictures, friends and teacher help if used. It included a listening-drawing task, a cognitive mapping task and the construction of a graph as well as multiple choice of items, all contributing to an extended story account. The sample size included over 300 children at each level. The main results after factor analysis on both younger and older children's responses suggest that specific topic content and the specific resource used (e.g. picture) are more closely related to performance than are process skills (e.g. observation). The resource dependence may be more pronounced as children get older. Separate factors involving literacy, graphicacy and numeracy emerged. Case studies were used to test the classroom feasibility of the materials.
Published Material: PATRICK, H. & HARGREAVES, L. (1990). 'Small and large schools: some comparisons'. In: GALTON, M. & PATRICK, H. Curriculum provision in the small primary school. London: Routledge.
Source of Grant: Economic and Social Research Council: £6,500
Date of Research: 1984-1990
KEYWORDS: *assessment; learning test; primary education; project method; study skills; teaching aids*

8/0628
Department of Education
21 University Road,
Leicester LE1 7RF
0533 522522
Patrick, H. Mrs; *Supervisor:* Bernbaum, G. Prof.
A study of academic staff in university departments of education
Abstract: The research was conducted as part of the Department of Education and Science (DES) funded project 'The structure and process of initial teacher education in universities in England and Wales'. The aims are to study occupations of university lecturers in education against the background of the occupations of university lecturers and school teachers. A survey of all university lecturers in education in University Departments of Education (UDEs) offering Postgraduate Certificate of Education (PGCE) courses in England and Wales: 1255 lecturers in education; 60 per cent (762) respondents. Methods used were questionnaire and semi-structured interviews. A comparison was made of the occupations of school and university teachers in terms of characteristics of members of the occupation, nature of the work they do, control of the occupations, occupational theoretic and ideology and occupational status. Data on lecturers in education show that on these five factors they differ from both school and university teachers but their close links with school teaching put them on the margin of the mainstream of university teaching.
Published Material: a full list of publication can be obtained from the researcher on request
Source of Grant: Department of Education and Science (DES) (1979-83): £100,000 approximately
Date of Research: 1979-1990
KEYWORDS: *teacher education; teacher role; teaching personnel; university*

8/0629

Department of Education
21 University Road, Leicester LE1 7RF
0533 523706
Liverpool University
Department of Education
Centre for Research in Primary Science and Technology,
126 Mount Pleasant, PO Box 147, Liverpool L69 3BX
051 794 3268
Harlen, W. Prof.; Schilling, M. Dr; Russell, T.J. Mr

Primary Science Teaching Action Research (STAR) Project
Abstract: The research is concerned with developing and evaluating ways of helping to spread good practice in primary school science. Its detailed aims are: (1) To add to the understanding of the nature of effective learning experiences in science for children aged 9 to 11 years; (2) to study the variables of the classroom and teaching which affect children's learning in science at this level, to define criteria for identifying 'good practice' in science teaching and to provide examples of it, (3) to develop training programmes which can improve primary school science practice, to evaluate their impact and make comparison with other teachers within the same school who have not been subjected to the training programmes. 50 schools in four LEA's (Cheshire, Wirral, Leicestershire and Sheffield) are involved. The information is gathered about classroom processes by direct observation and by assessment of pupils through practical and written forms of test. Action research is the main vehicle for bringing about change in the classrooms involved.
Published Material: SCHILLING, M. & RUSSELL, T. (1988). 'The primary science teaching action research project', Primary Science Review, No 8, Autumn, pp.24-26.; RUSSELL, T. & HARLEN, W. (1990). Assessing Science in the primary classroom. London: Paul Chapman Publishing Ltd.; SCHILLING, M. (Ed) (1990). Assessing science in the primary classroom: written tasks. London: Paul Chapman Publishing Ltd.; CAVENDISH, S. (Ed) (1990). Assessing science in the primary classroom: observing activities. London: Paul Chapman Publishing Ltd.
Source of Grant: The Leverhulme Trust: £141,000
Date of Research: 1986-1989
KEYWORDS: inservice education and training of teachers; primary education; science education; teaching aids

8/0630

Department of Education
21 University Road, Leicester LE1 7RF
0533 523688
Galton, M. Prof.; Foggelman, K. Prof.

Rural schools curriculum enhancement national evaluation project
Abstract: The project is a national evaluation of the ESG initiative in support of small rural schools. The project team will compare and contrast the initiative as it has developed locally in 9 local education authorities. Attempts will be made to identify the effectiveness of different strategies used to enhance the curriculum provision in small rural schools. The main research strategy will be case study although both questionnaires and in depth interviews will also be used.
Source of Grant: Department of Education and Science
Date of Research: 1989 – continuing
KEYWORDS: educational provision; rural school; small school

8/0631

Department of Education
21 University Road, Leicester LE1 7RF
0533 522522
Beauchamp College
Oadby, Leicester
0533 715809
Eales, A.G. Mr; *Supervisor:* Everton, T. Mr

Styles of effective Heads of Mathematics in secondary schools
Abstract: Although there is considerable literature about what a Head of Department might do, there is very little known about what it is that makes one Head of Department more effective than another. This research focuses on a number of Heads of Mathematics, considered by a 'panel of judges' to be effective, in the intention of identifying aspects of personal style which contribute to effectiveness. Originally seven Heads of Mathematics were interviewed using a lightly structured schedule and a pen-picture was prepared for each of them. In order to give considerably more depth and validity to such pen-pictures four Heads of Mathematics, including two from the original seven, were each asked to nominate four colleagues who could also be asked about the style of the Head of Mathematics. The resulting pen-pictures which have derived from the interviews with the heads of department and their nominees have proven to be more comprehensive and much longer (about 6000 words each). These pen-pictures were returned to the Heads of Department for comment, both on the pen-pictures themselves and the processes used to construct them. The processes involved bear considerable relevance to appraisal procedures for middle-management in schools; particularly that aspect of appraisal which looks to improve the effectiveness of the appraisee.
Source of Grant: Leicestershire Education Committee: £500 per year until completion
Date of Research: 1986-1990
KEYWORDS: effectiveness; head of department; mathematics; middle management; teacher appraisal

8/0632

Department of Education
21 University Road, Leicester LE1 7RF
0533 523675
Fogelman, K.R. Prof.; Galton, M.J. Prof.; Dowling, S.M. Mrs; Graham, M. Mr

Impairment of motor function at 5 years and cerebral pathology in the neonatal period
Abstract: The research involves the follow-up at 5 years of 150 low birth weight babies (1500 grams) to assess motor impairment and intellectual progress.
Source of Grant: Action research for the crippled child: £45,765
Date of Research: 1989-1990
KEYWORDS: birth; child development; intellectual development; motor disorder

8/0633

Department of Education
21 University Road, Leicester LE1 7RF
0533 523675
Fogelman, K.R. Prof.; Edwards, J.M. Mrs; Ball, D.G. Mr

East Midlands Records of Achievement project
Abstract: The project consists of an evaluation of the applications of information technology to Records of Achievement in Northamptonshire (educational support grant extension). The teachers' reponse to the use of information technology will also be studied. Available sofware will be evaluated.
Source of Grant: Northamptonshire Education Authority: £7,000
Date of Research: 1989-1990
KEYWORDS: administration of education; information technology; Records of Achievement

8/0634

Department of Education
21 University Road, Leicester LE1 7RF
0533 523675
Rogers, L.T. Mr; Barton, R. Mr; Marshall, G. Mr; Bertram, J. Dr

Tools for scientific thinking
Abstract: The aim is to produce hardware, software and curriculum materials which provide teachers and pupils with new practical methods for gaining and understanding of traditionally 'difficult' scientific concepts.
Published Material: ROGERS, L.T. et al (1989). Practical science with microcomputers: Biology (trials material). London: National Council for Educational Technology.
Source of Grant: National Council for Educational Technology: £15,000
Date of Research: 1987-1990
KEYWORDS: computer assisted instruction; concept formation; microcomputer science education; teaching aids

8/0635

Department of Education
21 University Road, Leicester LE1 7RF
0533 523675
Galton, M.J. Prof.; Sutton, J.A. Mr

The evaluation of Technical and Vocational Education Initiative (TVEI)
Abstract: An evaluation is to be carried out of the Technical and Vocational Education Initiative (TVEI) in Leicestershire. The development of evaluation within a curriculum review will be investigated. Specific attention will be paid to performance indicators in the review.

Source of Grant: Leicestershire Education Authority: £15,853
Date of Research: 1989-1990
KEYWORDS: evaluation; performance indicator; Technical and
Vocational Education Initiative

8/0636

Department of Education
21 University Road,
Leicester LE1 7RF
0533 523675
Fogelman, K.R. Prof.; Edwards, J.M. Mrs; Vlaeminke, M.
Dr

Research programme for the Speaker's Commission on Citizenship

Abstract: A review of research evidence on citizenship will be carried out, followed by a qualitative study of active citizenship in
schools in two counties and the planning and writing up of a
national survey of citizenship and volunteering.

Source of Grant: Esso (UK) Speakers' Commission on Citizenship
Northamptonshire Education Authority Leicestershire Education
Authority: jointly £30,000
Date of Research: 1989-1990
KEYWORDS: citizenship education; voluntary work

8/0637

Department of Education
21 University Road,
Leicester LE1 7RF
0533 522522
Mayer, G.S. Mr; Supervisor: Lofthouse, M. Dr

**Designing appraisal procedures in the primary school and the role
of the external consultant in the field of school-based innovation**

Abstract: The Teacher Appraisal Research Project was set up in
Northamptonshire to research ways of studying appraisal procedures' that can be managed in a non threatening, non salary related,
way for improving job performance, job satisfaction, and in turn
assisting career development in consultation and co-operation with
schools and teachers'. While working with five primary schools
the researcher used a Key Issues approach to designing the appraisal
procedures and an Action Research methodology for participation
and information gathering. The work resulted in the schools' designing their own distinct set of appraisal procedures and the more
important conclusions from the research were that: (i) participation in the process of designing the appraisal procedures leads to
a feeling of ownership; (ii) appraisal procedures should be designed
and set up to suit the appraisee; and (iii) some flexibility should
be given to teachers to modify appraisal guidelines so that they can
in some way reflect their school's organizational style. The second
part looks at the increasingly important role of the external consultant now that schools are being encouraged to buy in help they
require to make their school-based inservice training more effective. While this research used a more traditional, academic approach
the schools' headteachers were essential in evaluating the success
of an external consultant. The result or conclusion to this section
is a list of eight 'recommendation or principles for the role of the
External Consultant'.

Source of Grant: Funding by local industry
Date of Research:
KEYWORDS: consultant; educational innovation; primary edu-
cation; teacher appraisal

8/0638

Department of Education
21 University Road,
Leicester LE1 7RH
0533 523699
Yazigy, A. Miss; Supervisor: Cortazzi, M. Mr

Reading and schema theory

Abstract: The aim of the research is to help students at primary
levels, learning English as a second language, to be good readers
(i.e. with a high level of comprehension) using the schema theory.

Source of Grant: Full scholarship by Christian Aid
Date of Research: 1989 – continuing
KEYWORDS: English (second language); language teaching;
primary education; reading

8/0639

Department of Education
21 University Road,
Leicester LE1 7RF
0533 423718

Nene College
Moulton Park, Northampton NN2 7AL
0604 715000
Langley, K.M. Dr; Supervisor: Merry, R. Dr

Evaluation of the 14-16 curriculum project in Northamptonshire

Abstract: The 14-16 Curriculum Project in Northamptonshire was
one of the Lower Achieving Pupils Projects funded by both the
Department of Education and Science and the European Communities Commission. Originally the project involved six pilot schools
with cohorts in the 4th and 5th form of pupils who were not considered suitable for an examination-led curriculum. The Project curriculum inside school was pupil-centred, negotiated and integrated
with outside school activities such as community service, college
link courses, work experience and residentials. Profiles validated
by the City and Guilds recorded pupils' achievements. The evaluation research included a longitudinal study of a 20% sample of
the 1st and 2nd cohorts of pupils (58). The perceptions of people
involved with the pupils in the community, FE (further education)
colleges and on employers premises were collected and triangulated
with views of teachers, head teachers and school governors. The
results of each element of the study were written up by topic for
the local education authority and results compared using cluster
analysis. The approaches developed worked well for pupils when
operated within a suitable, structured, school management framework. Perceptions of the different groups had not changed in the
last twenty years.

Published Material: FURTHER EDUCATION UNIT, (1987).
Evaluation of Northamptonshires 14-16 Curriculum Project.
F.E.U.; LANGLEY, K.M. (1986). Perceptions of school gover-
nors. Northamptonshire County Council. November.; LANGLEY,
K.M. (1987). Perceptions of parents. Northamptonshire County
Council. January; LANGLEY, K.M. (1987). Post-school destina-
tions. Northamptonshire County Council. March; LANGLEY,
K.M. (1987). School-college links. Northamptonshire County Coun-
cil. June; LANGLEY, K.M. (1988). Integration of the Project
within schools. Northamptonshire County Council. July. Reports
are available from the Project Office, Cliftonville Middle School,
Northampton.

Source of Grant: European Economic Community Department of
Education: jointly £5,000 per year
Date of Research: 1984-1990
KEYWORDS: curriculum development; educational innovation;
low attainer; secondary

8/0640

Department of Psychology
University Road,
Leicester LE1 7RH
0533 522522
Annett, M. Dr

**Phonological and visuospatial processing at the left and right of
the laterality distribution**

Abstract: The right shift (RS) theory of handedness has led to the
hypothesis that there are specific risks for cognitive processing,
associated with the rs − − and rs + + genotypes. The genotypes
cannot be identified directly, but are more frequent at the left and
right of the continuum of right minus left (R-L) hand skill. Those
at the left are at risk becaus they lack something which assists the
growth of speech in the left hemisphere. Those at the right are at
risk because they carry a double dose of a factor which appears
to work by handicapping the right hemisphere. Annett and Manning (1990) have shown that reading ability varies with laterality
in normal schoolchildren such that children at both extremes are
likely to be poorer readers than those in the centre. The purpose
of the proposal is to show; that a double dissociation between people
specifically at risk for phonological and visuospatial processing,
associated with the left and right of the R-L hand skill distribution; and that this dissociation is relevant to subtypes of dyslexia.
Among poor readers, error patterns associated with 'phonological' versus 'surface' or dyseidetic' dyslexias could be more prevelant
at the left and the right of the laterality distribution respectively.

Published Material: ANNETT, M. & MANNING, M. (1990).
'Reading and a balanced polymorphism for laterality and ability',
Journal of Child Psychology and Psychiatry, No 31, No 4,
pp.511-529.; ANNETT, M. (1991). 'Phonological processing and
right minus left hand skill, Quarterly Journal of Psychology. (forthcoming).; ANNETT, M. (1991). 'Reading upside down and mirror
text in groups differing for right minus left hand skill, European
Journal of Cognitive Psychology. (forthcoming).

Source of Grant: Wellcome Trust: £50,545
Date of Research: 1991 – continuing
KEYWORDS: *brain hemisphere functions*

8/0641
Department of Psychology
University Road,
Leicester LE1 7RH
0533 522167
Colman, A.M. Dr
Minimal social situation: multi-person generalization
Abstract: This research will investigate the classic minimal social situation of a two person game of incomplete information in which the players are ignorant of their interdependence. The win-stay, lose-change principle, based on the Law of Effect explains why they none the less generally learn to co-operate over trials. In an n-person generalization of the game, the win-stay, lose-change principle surprisingly predicts evolution to co-operation only in even-sized groups depending on the configuration of initial strategy choices. Empirical tests are underway.
Published Material: COLEMAN, A.A., COLMAN, A.M. & THOMAS, R.M. (1990). 'Co-operation without awareness: a multiperson generalization of the minimal social situation', Behavioural Science, Vol 35, pp.115-121.
Source of Grant: No funding
Date of Research: 1988 – continuing
KEYWORDS: *game theory*

8/0642
Department of Psychology
University Road,
Leicester LE1 7RH
0533 522167
Colman, A.M. Dr; Norris, C. Ms; *Supervisor:* Colman, A.M. Dr
Context effects on cognitive processing of television programmes and advertisements
Abstract: This research will involve a series of experiments which focus on the effects of psychological involvement in television programmes on recall and recognition of the programmes and accompanying advertisements. Preliminary results based on experiments with undergraduate subjects have suggested that high involvement is associated with deep processing and superior recall of the programmes and the accompnying advertisements. No support has been found for the contrary hypothesis that involving programmes distract viewers from and yield poorer memory for the accompanying advertisements.
Source of Grant: University scholarship
Date of Research: 1988 – continuing
KEYWORDS: *advertising; cognitive process; memory; television*

8/0643
Department of Psychology
Leicester LE1 7RH
0533 554455
Hargreaves, D.J. Dr; Colman, A.M. Dr
Development and change in everyday likes and dislikes
Abstract: An improved understanding of the sources of everyday likes and dislikes would be of lasting theoretical importance in psychology, and might also have practical applications in education, product design and marketing, broadcasting, and leisure industries. Although experimental aesthetics has been an active field of research in psychology for more than a century, many interesting questions remain unanswered. The aims of the project are to investigate the development of attitudes towards everyday objects, names and tunes, and to discover why liking for such things sometimes increases and sometimes declines when they become more familiar. A new theory linking familiarity, complexity, and liking for two special classes of objects will be tested rigorously for the first time. The research method will be modelled on previous work of members of the Aesthetics Research Group published during the period 1972-82. Laboratory experiments will be used to gauge the reactions of people of various ages and population groups to a variety of visual, verbal and musical items.
Published Material: a full list of publications can be obtained from the researchers on request
Source of Grant: Economic and Social Research Council: £16,720
Date of Research: 1983 – continuing
KEYWORDS: *aesthetics; attitude; psychology*

8/0644
Department of Psychology
Leicester LE1 7RH
0533 554445
Colley, A.M. Dr; Hargreaves, D.J. Dr; *Supervisor:* Colley, A.M. Dr; Hargreaves, D.J. Dr; Hollin, C.R. Dr; Taylor Davies, A. Mrs
Perceptions of work and leisure: The effects of gender roles
Abstract: The research investigates changes in perceptions of work and leisure by males and females across their life span. A questionnaire study has already been conducted of 300 subjects ranging in age from 16-85. The focus is on the interaction between age and sex in affecting perceptions of the importance and enjoyment of work and leisure. This initial explanatory investigation will lead to the formulation of more detailed studies of target subject groups.
Published Material: HARGREAVES, D.J. & COLLEY, A.M. (Eds). (1986). The Psychology of Sex Roles. London: Harper and Row.
Source of Grant: No funding
Date of Research: 1986-1990
KEYWORDS: *leisure; perception; sex difference; work attitude*

8/0645
Department of Psychology
University Road, Leicester LE1 7RH
0533 522522
Hargreaves. D.J. Dr; Galton, M. Prof.
Teaching and learning in the creative arts: assessment of aesthetic development: the DELTA project
Abstract: This is a collaborative research project on teaching and learning in the creative arts and the assessment of aesthetic development in primary school children. It involves collaboration between researchers in psychology and education as well as between researchers, teachers and the local education authority. The project aims to provide a normative data base of children's creative productions in writing, drawing and music and to formulate some preliminary guidelines for an assessment by teachers as well as by children themselves. The project has two main phases. In Phase I, normative samples of children's creative productions in each of the three art forms will be collected from children at the three age levels, 7-, 9- and 11- years. In Phase II teachers will be asked to make open-ended assessments of the data collected in Phase I using a repertory grid-based methodology. This data will be analyzed to reduce the pool to a composite set of primary constructs and these will form the basics for the refined assessment criteria which will be used to evaluate the aesthetic work of primary school children.
Published Material: HARGREAVES, D., GALTON, M. & ROBINSON. S. (1989). 'Developmental psychology and arts education'. In: HARGREAVES, D. (Ed). Children and the arts. Buckingham: Open University Press.
Source of Grant: Economic and Social Research Council: £29,000
Date of Research: 1987 – continuing
KEYWORDS: *aesthetic education; assessment; creativity; primary education*

8/0646
School of Education
21 University Road, Leicester LE1 7RF
0553 523680
Galton, M.J. Prof.; Fogelman, K. Prof.; Hargreaves, L. Dr; Cavendish, S. Dr
Rural schools curriculum enhancement national evaluation (S.C.E.N.E) project
Abstract: The rural S.C.E.N.E. (Schools Curriculum Enhancement National Evaluation) project is evaluating 14 pilot projects using (ESG) education support grants to extend the range or improve the quality of the curriculum in rural primary schools. The various local authority pilot projects have used a range of strategies to achieve this: for example, the use of clustering of schools to share resources and inservice provision; the employment of co-ordinators and advisory teachers with varying duties; the provision of transport to bring children from small schools together into larger peer groupings. The grants were taken for between three or five years. Most of the projects will be complete by 1991. Six case studies of schools in LEAs which have used similar strategies are being conducted. The data collection includes interviews; questionnaires to ESG and non-ESG schools; classroom observation of childrens activities; projective activities for children, major themes which are emerging include the history of school co-operation in an area and the effectiveness of 'working alongside' as an inservice method.

Source of Grant: Department of Education and Science: £90,000
Date of Research: 1989 – continuing
KEYWORDS: *evaluation; primary education; rural school; small school*

Liverpool Institute of Higher Education

8/0647
Woolton Road, Liverpool L16 8ND
051 722 7331
Norton, L. Dr; Armstrong, J. Ms
A longitudinal survey study of special needs of mature students throughout their college life
Abstract: The research is envisaged as a longitudinal survey of a cohort of 150 mature students pursuing an undergraduate degree at Liverpool Institute of Higher Education. It is intended to follow these students through from their first year to graduation. Research methods will include questionnaires at yearly intervals, with in depth interviews of a sample of these students. The aim is to establish whether mature students have special needs in terms of academic difficulties and practical/domestic arrangements. Mature students who fail to obtain a degree will also be followed up in an attempt to understand what practices are involved in successful completion of a degree course.
Source of Grant: Liverpool Institute of Higher Education; Dept of Continuing Education: funding for photocopying and postage
Date of Research: 1988 – continuing
KEYWORDS: *undergraduate; mature student; special needs*

8/0648
Stand Park Road, PO Box 6, Liverpool L16 9JD
051 722 2361 ext 256
Farrell, J.B. Mr
An evaluation of a pilot scheme for recording achievements (N.P.R.A.) for Sefton LEA
Abstract: This is an external evaluation of a pilot scheme for recording achievements. The evaluation began in July 1987 and is centred on three comprehensive schools in Sefton LEA. The sample size is 100 teachers and 194 students. The construction and validation of a likert scale to measure the attitudes of students and teachers has been an important dimension of the evaluation. Interviews with teachers have helped to focus the content of the items used in the scale. The measuring instrument is structured around the four purposes for recording achievements which are set out in the DES Interim Report, 1984 – this yields four sub-scales within the instrument. The results are that significant differences were noted when students in the upper sets were compared with those in the lower sets. Those in lower sets were more in favour of recording achievements. Girls in the sample had a significantly higher mean score on the scale when compared with the boys, – in respect of motivation of personal development (purpose ii) and curriculum and organization (purpose iii). The split-half reliability of the scale is $r = 0.862$ (students) and $r = 0.877$ (teachers).
Source of Grant: Sefton LEA: £4,000 (on completion of the report)
Date of Research: 1987 – continuing
KEYWORDS: *achievement; attitude scale; record of achievement*

Liverpool Polytechnic

8/0649
Department of Combined Studies
C F Mott Campus, Liverpool Road, Prescot,
Merseyside L34 1NP
051 207 3581
Harrop, A. Dr; Daniels, M, Dr; Foulkes, C. Mrs
Methods of observing human behaviour
Abstract: The accuracy of Momentary Time Sampling (MTS) and Partial Interval Recording (PIR) have been investigated as a function of various behavioural and sampling parameters. Computer simulation studies indicate that MTS is, on average, accurate in estimating total duration of behaviour. Although PIR cannot estimate accurately frequency or duration it is more sensitive to

behavioural change than MTS. The extent to which human observers may utilize effectively these observational techniques is presently under investigation, by comparing observer records with videotaped recordings. The validity of various commonly-used methods of assessing inter-observer agreement has also been examined. Problems have been identified with all major indices of observer agreement. It is suggested that researchers should report observers' primary data in published studies.
Published Material: HARROP, A. & DANIELS, M. (1985). 'Momentary time sampling with time series data: A commentary on the paper by Brulle & Repp', British Journal of Psychology, Vol 76, 1985, pp.533-537.; HARROP, A. & DANIELS, M. (1986). 'Methods of time sampling: a reappraisal of momentary time sampling and partial interval recording', Journal of Applied Behaviour Analysis, Vol 19, 1986, pp.73-77.; HARROP, A., FOULKES, C. & DANIELS, M. (1989). 'Observer agreement calculations: the role of primary data in reducing obfuscation' British Journal of Psychology, Vol 80, 1989, pp.181-189.
Source of Grant: National Advisor Body (NAB): £23,000 (1985-1988)
Date of Research: 1984 – continuing
KEYWORDS: *observation; research technique; sample; time*

8/0650
Department of Education
I.M. Marsh Campus, Barkhill Road, Liverpool L17 6BD
051 724 2321
Lloyd, J.M.; *Supervisor:* Leaman, O. Dr
Management leadership and moral education
Abstract: This dissertation is intended to extend the frontiers of leadership studies by being the first to offer an ideal model of leadership for schools – where liberal education is the main aim of the school. The originality of the model lies in its explication of leadership through exercise control. Most writers about leadership advocate leadership control through use of power or participation as a device to gain or maintain control. The aim of this work is not to advocate devices, but to focus attention upon leadership through rational and moral example which may enhance control. In fact, where other writers may be concerned with leadership for the good of an organization alone, one of the aims of this thesis is to offer a model of leadership by the good, for the good of the school. The nature of the thesis is philosophical although it discusses the work not only of philosophers, but also of psychologists, sociologists and management theorists. In fact, there are few philosophers involved in discussion about leadership today. Moreover, this is an area of educational theory often conceptually muddled and confused; an attempt has been made to clarify issues that may otherwise have eluded an understanding of leadership, specifically for secondary schools.
Source of Grant: Local Education Authority: fees
Date of Research: 1988 – continuing
KEYWORDS: *administration of education; leadership; theory of education*

Liverpool University

8/0651
PO Box 147, Liverpool L69 3BX
051 709 6022
Harrop. S. Mrs
History of the University of Liverpool; 1981-1991
Abstract: This project is to update and extend Thomas Kelly's History of Liverpool University 1981 to 1991. The research will be based on documentary sources and oral evidence from past and present staff and students.
Published Material: KELLY, T. (1981). For advancement of learning. Liverpool: Liverpool University Press.
Source of Grant: University of Liverpool
Date of Research: 1989 – continuing
KEYWORDS: *history of education; university*

8/0652
Department of Education
19 Abercromby Square, PO Box 147, Liverpool L69 3BX
051 794 2478
Doubler, S.J. Ms; *Supervisor:* Harlen, W. Prof.
Science teaching: supporting effective teacher change

Abstract: This research is linked with STAR (Science Teaching Action Research) Project. STAR focuses on promoting effective learning and teaching of science in the primary school, while this work is concerned more specifically with the teacher and the teacher's experiences during the STAR project. The main questions addressed by the study are: (1) Does thinking and practice change as a result of project efforts? (2) What are the significant factors in producing or inhibiting change? The study is being conducted in the Boston, Massachusetts area. It involves 10 teachers from six school districts. The key factors in identifying members of the study group were interest, involvement in process-based science and three years participation in the STAR Project. The impact of intervention with teachers is determined by taking into consideration teachers' work situations, education, experience, thinking and current practice. As well as identifying changes within the entire study group, a case study of each teacher identifies individual change and its related causes. Information has been collected through the use of two STAR Project research instruments, as well as other instruments designed specifically for this study. A questionnaire was used to collect baseline data about each teacher's work situation and background. Information about practice and the teacher's perception of change was gathered through the use of interviews, survey, formal student observations and documentation of teacher comments and writing. Observation, interviews and the survey were carried out for three consecutive years.
Source of Grant: University of Liverpool: £90 (travel expenses)
Date of Research: 1987-1990
KEYWORDS: *educational innovation; primary education; science education; teacher behaviour*

8/0653

Department of Education
PO Box 147,
Liverpool L69 3BX
051 794 2478
Blyth, W.A.L. Prof.

Assessment of children's progress in humanities in primary schools and at the age of transfer to secondary education

Abstract: This exploratory and mainly qualitative investigation has been based in a series of schools, primary for the most part, but with some secondary and middle, and in each case it has depended on first-hand interaction with teachers and children in the schools concerned. More recently it has been extended to include a survey of practice in various parts of the country, and this too has been conducted on a basis of personal contact at least by correspondence, and where possible by visit, often in association with a programme of inservice education. Thus the study has come to comprise three main sections: (1) experimentation with various kinds of assessment procedures with children, mostly at the age of 10-11, the nature of the procedures being drawn from the research literature. The outcomes have been treated with rudimentary quantitative methods where appropriate; (2) discussion with teachers and others about how the process of incidental assessment in primary humanities, as well as of more formal testing, is in fact conducted, and how it might be amended; (3) collation of information from schools, LEAs, and institutions of higher education in England (and occasionally elsewhere) about research and innovation in the assessment of primary humanities. Here, an additional emphasis has been placed on assessment of primary industry education. The movement towards the establishment of National Curriculum, with its implications for assessment especially since the recent publication of the Report of the Task Group on Assessment and Testing, has given increased immediacy to the whole study. The provisional outcomes constitute only a prolegomenon to systematic research, but they do point the way towards useful methods of both formative and summative assessment in a part of the primary curriculum in which studies in assessment have hitherto been rather neglected.
Published Material: BLYTH, W.A.L. (1988). 'Appraising and assessing young children's understanding of industry'. In: SMITH, D. (Ed). Industry in the primary school curriculum. Lewes: Falmer Press.; BLYTH, W.A.L. (1987). 'Towards assessment in primary humanities', Journal of Education Policy, Vol 2, No 4, 1987, pp.353-360.; BLYTH, W.A.L. (1989). Making the grade: Assessing humanities in primary schools. Buckingham: Open University Press.
Source of Grant: Schools Council: £500 Dept of Trade & Industry: £200
Date of Research: 1981-1989
KEYWORDS: *assessment; humanities; primary education*

8/0654

Department of Education
19 Abercromby Square, PO Box 147, Liverpool L69 3BX
051 794 2496
Danvers, M. Mr; *Supervisor:* Thomas, D.J. Mr

Case study of TRIST (TVEI-Related Inservice Training) initiatives in one LEA

Abstract: This is a study of the origin and development of TRIST provision within an LEA using illuminative evaluation approaches.
Source of Grant: No funding
Date of Research: 1986-1989
KEYWORDS: *local education authority; inservice education and training of teachers; Technical and Vocational Education Initiative (TVEI)*

8/0655

Department of Education
PO Box 147, Liverpool L69 3BX
051 794 2477
Hall, J.S. Ms.; *Supervisor:* Harlen, W. Prof.

Investigation of the effects of different INSET experiences on teachers' understanding and perception of their role in teaching science at the elementary level (in US schools)

Abstract: Twentyfour elementary school teachers in Vermont, USA, were involved in an extensive summer workshop run by primary science specialists from England in 1987. Eighteen have continued follow-up work consisting of a 13-week series of meetings. Inservice work has been directed at enabling teachers to encourage the use by children of process skills in science activities. Teachers' understanding of these skills and their role in learning has been monitored during the course. Some instruments have also been used with teachers involved in a conventional inservice course in elementary science in the USA and with a group of teachers in England, for comparison.
Date of Research: 1988 – continuing
KEYWORDS: *inservice education and training of teachers; primary education; science education; United States of America*

8/0656

Department of Education
19 Abercromby Square, PO Box 147, Liverpool L69 3BX
051 794 2451
Meakin, D.C. Mr

Philosophy of the curriculum with particular reference to moral, religious, physical education and personal and social education

Abstract: This research has been within the area of the philosophy of the curriculum, with particular reference to moral, religious, aesthetic and physical education. It has mainly been concerned with three questions: (i) how these kinds of education are to be characterized; (ii) how, if at all, they might be justified; (iii) whether any general criteria can by established for including subjects and activities in the school curriculum.
Published Material: MEAKIN, D.C. (1981). 'Physical education: an agency of moral education?', Journal of Philosophy of Education, Vol 15, No 2, 1981, pp.241-253.; MEAKIN, D.C. (1982).'Moral values and physical education', Physical Education Review, Vol 5, No 1, 1982, pp.62-82.; MEAKIN, D.C. & SANDERSON, P. (1983). 'Dance in English secondary schools today', Journal of Aesthetic Education, Vol 17, No 1, 1983, pp.69-83.; MEAKIN, D.C. (1983). 'On the justification of physical education', Momentum, Vol 8, No 3, 1983, pp.10-17.; MEAKIN, D.C. (1986). 'The moral status of competition: an issue of concern to physical educators', Journal of Philosophy of Education, Vol 20, No 1, 1986, pp.59-67.; MEAKIN, D.C. (1988). 'The justification of religious education reconsidered', British Journal of Religious Education, Vol 10, No 2, 1988, pp.92-96.; MEAKIN. D.C. (1989). 'Personal, social and moral education and religious education': the need for conceptual clarity', British Journal of Religious Education, Vol 11, No 1, 1989, pp.15-21.
Source of Grant: No funding
Date of Research: 1973 – continuing
KEYWORDS: *aesthetic education; philosophy of education; curriculum subject; physical education; moral education; religious education;*

8/0657

Department of Education
PO Box 147, Liverpool L69 3BX
051 794 2504
Beattie, N.M. Dr

The Freinet Movement in its international context
Abstract: The aim is to explore the Freinet Movement, which has been central to most 'progressive' developments in French education, over the period 1920 to the present day, and to describe and discuss its cross-national impact. This has been considerable in some areas (e.g. Italy post-1945, Portugal post-1974) and nil in others (e.g. United Kingdom). By placing a very broad movement of opinion and practice in its cultural and historical context, this long-term enquiry should produce some clarification of elusive culture-bound ideas such as 'progressive' and 'international dissemination'.
Date of Research: 1987 – continuing
KEYWORDS: France; international exchange; system of education; theory of education

8/0658

Department of Education
PO Box 147, Liverpool L69 3BX
051 794 2504
Beattie, N.M. Dr
School Improvement Councils in Massachusetts
Abstract: School Improvement Councils are a 1985 innovation to involve parents and teachers more closely in the operation of schools in Massachusetts. The aim of the enquiry is to apply to these changes the model elaborated for Europe in the researcher's earlier study (Beattie, 1985) to see whether it proves illuminating in a United States context, and to draw appropriate policy conclusion for the the USA and Europe. As in the earlier study research methods are based largely on documentation and open-ended interview.
Published Material: BEATTIE, N.M. (1985). Professional parents: parent participation in four Western European countries. Sussex: Falmer Press.; BEATTIE, N.M. (1988). Legislating for dynamism. Duplicated report obtainable from author.; BEATTIE, N.M. (1989). Through the looking glass: a Western European perspective on school improvement in Massachusetts. IRE Report No 16.
Source of Grant: Centre for Educational and Policy Studies, University of Liverpool: £700
Date of Research: 1988-1990
KEYWORDS: administration of education; Europe; parent-teacher participation; parent-teacher relation; United States of America

8/0659

Department of Education
Centre for Research in Primary Science & Technology,
126 Mount Pleasant, Liverpool L69 3BX
051 794 3267
London University
King's College, Centre for Educational Studies,
552 King's Road, London SW10 OUA
071 836 5454
Russell, T, Mr; Osborne, J. Mr; Longden, K. Mr; McGuire, L. Ms; Bell, D. Dr; Wadsworth, P. Mrs; *Supervisor:* Black, P. Prof.; Harlen, W. Prof.
Primary science processes and concept exploration project (Primary SPACE project)
Abstract: The Primary SPACE (Science Processes and Concept Exploration) project is an action research project which aims firstly to explore the ideas primary school children hold in the science concept areas of changes in materials, evaporation/condensation, electricity, growth, forces and their effect on movement, light, living things and their adaptation to their environment, and sound. Information is being collected by teachers and researchers through interview, discussion and analysis of children's written work and drawings. This information is then being used as a starting point for trying to influence the formation and development of children's ideas through application of process skills during classroom work. The study involves forty-two classes in schools representing ILEA, Knowsley and Lancashire LEAs, and covers the entire primary age range. The research is being continued into all areas of the National Curriculum in Science and used as a basis for curriculum material development.
Published Material: HARLEN, W. (1987). What is going on in SPACE. University of Liverpool; Centre for Research in Primary Science & Technology.; WATT, D. (1987). 'Primary SPACE project phase one: an exploration of children's scientific ideas, Primary Science Review, No 4, summer, 1987, pp. 27-28.; Research reports entitled 'Growth', 'Light', 'Evaporation and Condensation' and 'Sound' are available from Liverpool University press.
Source of Grant: Nuffield Foundation 1987-9 Nuffield-Chelsea Curriculum Trust 1989-91
Date of Research: 1987 – continuing

KEYWORDS: concept formation; primary education; science education

8/0660

Department of Education
19 Abercromby Square, PO Box 147, Liverpool L69 3BX
051 794 2507
Ferguson, S.; Strivens, J.
The impact upon pupil learning and classroom interactions when using computer based communications (e-mail) as an international link
Abstract: Electronic mail and its uses in schools has been promoted by the Department of Education and Science, Department of Trade and Industry and private e-mail networks. It is now being used as part of the secondary school IT curriculum and is part of project work in primary and secondary schools where it is used to link schools in the UK and internationally. This research examines the opportunities and problems associated with classroom-based e-mail work and focuses upon classroom interactions and pupil learning in international links.
Published Material: FERGUSON, S. & STRIVENS, J. (1988). The Red Hill/Marion Street E-Mail Projects: an evaluation report the Bromley Education Authority. Liverpool University; Liverpool Evaluation and Assessment Unit (copies available from Bromley LEA, IT Centre).
Source of Grant: No funding
Date of Research: 1988 – continuing
KEYWORDS: curriculum development; electronic mail; international exchange

8/0661

Department of Education
19 Abercromby Square, PO Box 147, Liverpool L69 3BX
051 794 2507
Ferguson, S.
School/Industry Compacts: the translation of an American model to England
Abstract: The Boston Compact has been used as a model for school/industry compacts in the UK and have been promoted by government, industry and local authorities since late 1987. This research builds upon first-hand knowledge of the original Boston Compact to make comments upon the applicability of this American model to the English education setting.
Source of Grant: No funding
Date of Research: 1988 – continuing
KEYWORDS: comparative education; school-industry relation; United States of America

8/0662

Department of Education
126 Mount Pleasant, PO Box 147, Liverpool L69 3BX
051 794 3278
Martland, J.R. Mr; Stewart, R.R. Mr; Walsh, S. Ms
Developing navigational skills in young children
Abstract: The aims of the project are to examine the abilities of children aged 10; (a) to acquire and use two key skills in orienteering and navigation, namely map orientation and direction finding using a protractor compass; (b) to benefit from two different teaching/coaching approaches; (c) to solve a series of navigational problems ranging from simple to complex. The methods use include skills analysis, controlled experimentation and ethnography. Ten teachers and approximately 250 children aged 10 are involved. The teachers receive instruction to enable them to teach the use of a protractor compass; they then teach half of their class using one of the approaches ('serial' and 'conceptual'), and then teach the other half using the alternative approach at a later stage according to a simple cross over design.
Source of Grant: National Coaching Foundation: £10,497 (1989-91)
Date of Research: 1989 – continuing
KEYWORDS: navigation; orienteering; outdoor pursuits

8/0663

Department of Education
PO Box 147, Liverpool L69 3BX
051 794 2551
Taylor, I. Mr; *Supervisor:* Harlen, W. Prof.; Derricott, R. Mr
Evaluation of the programme of appraisal of teaching in the veterinary faculty
Abstract: A programme for evaluating teaching in the veterinary

faculty was introduced in 1988. Two members of the department of education submitted a proposal to evaluate this innovation. The evaluation of the appraisal of teaching focuses on both the processes and the products of appraisal. Data are collected about the operation of teaching appraisal from students, academic staff and from 'official peers' who observe teaching.
Source of Grant: University funding 1988-1989: £25,000 Universities funding counil 1989-1990: £25,000 University funding 1990-1991: £25,000
Date of Research: 1988 – continuing
KEYWORDS: *evaluation; higher education; teacher appraisal; teaching quality medical education*

8/0664

Department of Education
19 Abercromby Square, Liverpool L69 3BX
051 794 2572
Marsden, W.E.
A headteacher dynasty: illuminating the history of education in England and Wales from the 1840s to the 1930s through the biographies of three generations of one teaching family
Abstract: In the course of previous research it has become apparent that a large amount of, albeit widely scattered, archive material is available in a notable headteacher dynasty, the Adams family. The intention is to undertake a longitudinal study of this family, following through three generations of educational experience from the 1840s to the 1930s, a critical hundred years in the history of education in England and Wales. The range of institutions with which the family, at least six members of which were headteachers, was involved cover, including training, a national school; several British and foreign schools; three British Society training colleges; a works school; London Board schools; two universities; army education; 20th-century 'central' secondary schools; and a private school. The range of geographical settings is also wide. The study will explore continuity and change in education over time in England and Wales; a range of educational trends and theories as applied in particular cases; and shifting social contexts and values as they interacted in various rural but mostly urban settings over the period under review.
Published Material: MARSDEN, W.E. (1990). Educating the respectable: a study of Fleet Road Board school, Hampstead, 1879-1903. London: The Woburn Press
Source of Grant: University of Liverpool research fund
Date of Research: 1990 – continuing
KEYWORDS: *head teacher; history of education*

8/0665

Department of Education
19 Abercromby Square, PO Box 147, Liverpool L69 3BX
051 794 2000
Bishop Grosseteste College, Newport, Lincoln LN1 3DT
0522 27347
Hopkins, S.T. Mr; *Supervisor:* Harlen, W. Prof.
An investigation into the interpretative categories used by primary school teachers and by students in initial primary teacher training in conceptualizing and evaluating the teaching and learning of science and technology
Abstract: The research aims to elicit the constructs used by primary school teachers and by students in initial primary teacher training in conceptualizing and evaluating the teaching and learning of science and technology. The research aims to identify a comprehensive set of constructs underlying classroom practice and to generate a typology of categories which can serve as organizers for the constructs of many different teachers and which can be used to devise a model of professional development. Methodly is phenomenographical and elicitation of constructs is being effected by using an instrument which requires respondents to record in writing their reflections on the success and failure of a particular episode of teaching and learning. As a sample, 50 primary school teachers; 120 students in initial primary teacher training (B.Ed., PGCE, Science main stubject and non-science main subject), will be used.
Source of Grant: Bishop Grosseteste College: 50%
Date of Research: 1986-1990
KEYWORDS: *primary education; science education; teacher education; technolgy*

8/0666

Department of Psychology
PO Box 147, Liverpool L69 3BX

051 709 6022
Liverpool Institute of Higher Education, Woolton Road, Liverpool L16 8ND
051 722 7331
Faber, D. Mrs; *Supervisor:* Lovie, A.D. Dr
Binet's work and achievement: the first intelligence scales of 1905
Abstract: The area of this research is the history of psychology. Although Binet is recognized as the pioneer of intelligence testing and his influence has been very great, the genesis of his scales is often misrepresented. The researcher's aim is to explain the achievement of Alfred Binet (1857-1911) with reference to his Intelligence Scales of 1905, the first 'true' tests of intelligence. The research involves identifying Binet's changing conceptions of intelligence and its developmental aspects, and tracing the origins of the test items in his experimental work in the 20 years preceding 1905. This also necessitates an examination of Binet's view of psychology as a science, his conception of a psychological experiment and the nature and role of introspections. The social and cultural contexts are important contributing factors to Binet's achievement, and are explained with reference to testing in other countries. In France political forces and an immediate educational problem led to the Minister of Education's decision to have Paris school children tested or screened for ineducability. Binet's work, particularly that in association with the 'Societe Libre pour l'Etude Psychologique de l'Enfant', was known by the authorities in 1904. The commission was entrusted to Binet; his earlier work and later collaboration with Simon resulted in the finally produced Scales of 1905, amply justifying their trust in the psychological work of Binet.
Source of Grant: Liverpool University: half of fees
Date of Research: 1988 – continuing
KEYWORDS: *history of education; intelligence test; psychology*

8/0667

Department of Sociology
Eleanor Rathbone Building,
Myrtle Street, PO Box 147, Liverpool L69 3BX
051 709 6022 ext 2644
Roberts, K. Mr; Strivens, J. Ms; Derricott, R. Mr
16-19 Initiative: Liverpool
Abstract: Random samples totalling 1600 of 15 and 17 year old cohorts from Liverpool schools are being surveyed by questionnaire in 3 successive sweeps. Interview surveys with sub-samples are also being conducted. The aim is to identify different career trajectories from education into the labour market, and to relate their career paths to economic and political socialization, the development of social representation, social attributions, self-concepts and efficacy.
Source of Grant: Economic and Social Research Council (ESRC): £74,000
Date of Research: 1986 – continuing
KEYWORDS: *socialization; transition from school to work; youth employment; youth unemployment;*

London University

8/0668

School Examinations Board,
Stewart House, 32 Russell Square, London WC1
071 636 8000
Kingdon, M. Dr
Performance matrices in GCSE (General Certificate of Secondary Education) Science
Abstract: In July 1987, the Secondary Examinations Council undertook to fund a number of research projects in science and several other subjects in order to investigate further the viability of criterion referencing. Each of the five examining groups had a working party investigating the possibilities with one of its integrated science syllabuses. These small working parties usually included a Chief Examiner, Moderator and Subject Officer. The jargon by this time had shifted to Performance Matrices rather than Criterion Referencing or Grade Criteria. At the end of 1987 five models had emerged from the examining groups. These reflected the idiosyncracies of particular syllabuses and the divergent 'views of science' in the five working parties. It was generally felt that the operational value of these models could only be tested by piloting. The LEAG (London and East Anglia Group (GCSE Examining Board)) model relates to the syllabus Science Combined for which a suite of four basic

papers and four extension papers is offered. The 1989 basic and extension papers for Science Topics (papers 4 and 5 (iv)) are being constructed so as to meet syllabus specifications and allow normal GCSE grading whilst permitting a research analysis to test the performance matrix model. Other examining groups will be exploring ways in which their models can be piloted. In some cases this may involve materials which help teachers and candidates to focus attention on particular domains and attributes in preparation for examinations. Such ventures will have the financial and moral support of School Examinations and Assessment Council.
Published Material: BENNETTS, J. & MUNDIE, J. (1989). 'Performance matrices in GCSE Science', Education in Science, No 131, January 1989.
Source of Grant: School Examinations and Assessment Council
Date of Research: 1987 – continuing
KEYWORDS: achievement measurement; General Certificate of Secondary Education; science education

8/0669

King's College,
552 King's Road, London SW10 0UA
071 872 3156
Bliss, J. Dr; Ogborn, J. Prof.; Martinand, J-L. Prof.; Jensen, J.A. Prof.

The Esprit project
Abstract: The aim of the research programme is to provide the specifications for explanation facilities intelligible to children within intelligent learning environments. The project was conceived in order to explore ways of closing the gap between recent research in cognitive science and education which construes explanation as a constructive act; and explanation as currently implemented in expert and knowledge based systems. The design of the study is fourfold, firstly to focus on children's and teachers' explanations for a given domain; examine the issues involved in implementing such explanations within an information technology learning environment, evaluate the acceptability of prototype explanation systems to children using microworld and simulation software; and specify the final prototype explanation systems. The working group will fund individual research proposals submitted within these relevant areas. The outcomes will have both theoretical and practical significance. It will be possible to describe the explanations that satisfy children within a given domain and to compare these to those of the expert/teacher. Simultaneously, it will be possible to provide an analysis of the formal and practical problems of implementing explanation systems where explanations match both need and understanding.
Source of Grant: The European Economic Community
Date of Research: 1989 – continuing
KEYWORDS: computer assisted instruction; computer microworld; expert system; information technology

8/0670

Institute of Education,
20 Bedford Way, London WC1H OAL
071 636 1500
Packer, Y. Mrs; *Supervisor:* Swanwick, K. Prof.

Music and the therapeutic education of emotionally and behaviourally disturbed children
Abstract: Research was carried out amongst children with emotional and behavioural difficulties to ascertain whether or not music education could be sustained in such a context and whether it might benefit their personal development of the pupils. Severe limitations were placed on the role of the researcher as a result of the dearth of music education in EBD (Emotional and Behavioural Difficulties) schools and as a result of the nature of the subject. These imitations shape the course of the research which ultimately centred on the researcher's own professional practices as teacher and actively involved generalist teachers in the assessment of pupils' response. The work was carried out concurrently in three EBD schools. During the course of one academic year a wide spectrum approach included interviews, questionnaires, case studies and action research. The central part of the work was the use of an adapted time series observation carried out throughout the second term enabling repeated samples to be taken of the behavioural attitude of children. Throughout the study the roles of teacher and researcher were reversed – the teachers assessing the effectiveness of the work of the researcher. The finding indicate that music education can be successfully incorporated into the curriculum of EBD schools and that it may positively effect the personal development and interpersonal relationships between disturbed children.

Source of Grant: No funding
Date of Research: 1986-1990
KEYWORDS: behaviour disorder; emotional disorder; music education; special school

8/0671

Institute of Education,
20 Bedford Way, London WC1H OAL
071 636 1500
Swanwick, K. Prof.; Jarvis, C. Mrs

The Tower Hamlets String Teaching Project
Abstract: The research sought to understand the dynamics of an internationally recognized programme of string teaching to whole classes, mainly in primary schools in the Tower Hamlets area and other close boroughs in London. Existing documentation was reviewed, including video recordings, publications and papers on file pertaining to the project. This enabled the researchers to determine something of the history, organization and underlying philosophy of the work and to devise an appropriate methodology for the second phase; that of systematically observing the content teaching and learning in the 13 project shools. These observations were carried out over a period of two months and included interviews with project staff, head teachers and others associated with the scheme. The Report gives some insight into a unique educational endeavour and it includes a close analysis of the processes of lessons as well as documenting the context and materials used.
Published Material: University of London, Institute of Education, March 1990. The Tower Hamlets String Teaching Project: A Research Report. London: University of London, Music Department.
Source of Grant: Various sources within the City of London: jointly £15,000
Date of Research: 1989-1990
KEYWORDS: group learning; music education; musical instrument; primary education

8/0672

Institute of Education,
20 Bedford Way, London WC1H OAL
071 636 1500
Delshadian, R. Mrs; *Supervisor:* Gardner, R. Dr

The growth and development of the International Schools within the general educational framework of Iran 1953-80, their demise within the context of the Iranian Revolution
Abstract: The aim of the thesis is to examine the historical background and development of the International Schools in Iran during the reign of Mohammad Reza Shah (1941-1979). The thesis examines the structure and purpose of these schools, and the role they played during this time. The modernization process during this time is also examined. The disintegration of these schools during 1978-1979 is presented. The second half of the thesis is devoted to a number of hypotheses, religious, cultural, and economic, clarifying the reasons for the demise of the International Schools within the context of the advent and take over of a new revolutionary Islamic regime. Finally the case study will be used to focus on the cultural relevance of this type of education within a national framework the conflict aroused, and the necessity of alignment within the existing culture of a country, in this case a country with Shiite Islamic educational and cultural patterns. The thesis is mainly anecdotal using Western orientated and Islamic reference books to maintain a balance of views.
Source of Grant: No funding
Date of Research: 1981 – continuing
KEYWORDS: religion and education

8/0673

Institute of Education,
20 Bedford Way, London WC1H OAL
071 636 1500
Little, A.W. Prof.

Education and change in plantations: the case of Sri Lanka
Abstract: This research represents an exercise in 'reflection practice', the researcher having been involved in a series of development interventions in plantation education in Sri Lanka over the past eight years. The research is based around the experience of change in one plantation school in relation to broader changes in educational, economic and political structures and policies over the past twenty years. Theoretically it draws from literature on educational change, on education and development, and on plantations as institutions. It seeks to work towards a set of propositions about

individual learning and societal development under conditions of economic and social disadvantage. The methods employed for this research include field observation, documentary analysis and interviews.
Published Material: LITTLE, A.W., KEMP, C. & DAVIES, S. (Eds). (1987). 'People in plantations: means or ends?' (special issue). Institute of Development Studies Bulletin, Vol 18, No 2.
Source of Grant: No funding
Date of Research: 1987 – continuing
KEYWORDS: educational change; educational development

8/0674
>   Institute of Education, Thomas Coram Research Unit,
>   41 Brunswick Square, London WC1N 1AZ
>   071 278 2424
>   Blatchford, P. Dr; Burke, J. Ms; Farquhar, C. Ms;
>   *Supervisor:* Tizard, B. Prof.

The contribution of parents and teachers to children's achievement in the infant school
Abstract: This project is concerned with children's learning experience at home and at school both before and throughout the infant school. The aim is to relate their educational achievements to their experiences at school and to their parents' help at home. The sample is composed of the September 1982 entrants to reception classes in 33 ILEA (Inner London Education Authority) infant schools in multi-racial areas. It is balanced for ethnicity and sex, the two major groups being children of white indigenous parents, and children of black parents of West Indian origin. The children are being followed through infant school. The design involves repeated testing of the extent of the children's literacy and numeracy, and classroom information from repeated interviews with parents and teachers. The interviews are with the parents and are concerned with collecting demographic data, and with obtaining a detailed account of parental educational help at home. They are also concerned with the parents' attitude to the school and the teachers, and their contacts with the school. The interviews with the class teachers centre on their parent involvement and multicultural practices and their assessment of the children's behaviour and achievement. The level of work the children are introduced to is also being assessed. A follow-on study is being planned for 1988/89.
Published Material: TIZARD, B. (1984). 'Parents, teachers and the infant school'. ESRC Newsletter, No 52, June, pp.11-13.; BLATCHFORD, P., BURKE, J., FARQUHAR, C., PLEWIS, I. & TIZARD, B. (1985). 'Educational achievement in the infant school: the influence of ethnic origin, gender and home on entry skills', Education Research, Vol 27, No 1 February, pp.52-60.; FARQUHAR, C., BLATCHFORD, P., BURKE, J., PLEWIS, I. & TIZARD, B. (1985). 'A comparison of the views of parents and reception teachers', Education 3-13, Vol 13, No 2, Autumn, pp.17-22.; BLATCHFORD, P., BURKE, J., FARQUHAR, C., PLEWIS, I. & TIZARD, B. (1987). 'Associations between pre-school reading skills and later reading achievement', British Education Research Journal, Vol 13, No 1. A full list of publications is available from the Unit and also from the NFER.
Source of Grant: ESRC (Economic and Social Research Council)
Date of Research: 1982-1989
KEYWORDS: achievement; home education; parent-child relation; parent-school relation; pre-school education; primary education

8/0675
>   Goldsmith's College,
>   Lewisham Way, New Cross, London SE14 6NW
>   081 692 7171
>   Hextall, I.J. Mr

Education and transformations in the labour process
Abstract: The research is focused on the material connections between state education and transformations in the labour process and the division of labour. A particular concentration will be on the implications of youth unemployment and the work of state secondary schools, and includes the responses of state education policies to these developments. The research is designed to utilize historical and contemporary data and materials in connection with specific policy documents formulated by central government departments, semi-autonomous bodies such as the Manpower Services Commission or Schools Council, and local education authorities. No specific sample is used, but much of the analysis focuses on inner-city areas such as Lewisham, and pays particular attention to the segmentation of the labour force on racial and gender lines.
Source of Grant: No funding

Date of Research: 1977 – continuing
KEYWORDS: educational policy; labour market; transition from school to work; youth unemployment

8/0676
>   Institute of Education,
>   20 Bedford Way, London WC1H OAL
>   071 636 1500
>   Dyer, D.H.; Lines, D.R.

Cambridge Business Studies Project
Abstract: This project has six objectives: (1) To foster the development of business education courses at 16+ and 18+ level, giving advice and support to teachers; (2) to develop and disseminate to teachers aids and materials primarily of value for 16+ and 18+ courses; (3) to develop inservice training courses for intending teachers and others wishing to extend their expertise; (4) to liaise with examining bodies and others for appropriate curriculum development; to foster dialogue between teachers and others interested in business education; (5) to liaise with business and industry; and (6) to monitor work and interpret and report as required.
Published Material: A list of teaching materials and syllabuses etc. is available from the researchers.; DYER, D.M. & CHARLES, I. (1987). Business Studies: an introduction. Harlow: Longman.
Source of Grant: Cambridge Business Studies Trust
Date of Research: 1967 – continuing
KEYWORDS: commercial education; curriculum development; inservice education and training of teachers; teaching aids

8/0677
>   Institute of Education, Medical Research Council
>   Developmental Psychology Project,
>   18 Woburn Square, London WC1H ONS
>   071 380 0596
>   *Supervisor:* O'Connor, N. Dr; Hermelin, B. Dr

Memory, intelligence and talent
Abstract: The proposed experiments address questions concerning the nature of the specific talents found among idiots-savants and gifted normal children. One question is the degree to which the cognitive strategies used by such talented people are intelligence independent. A second is the nature of the impressive memory which seems to underlie their frequently surprising performance. Experiments will test whether this memory is predominantly rote or organized and, if the latter, whether organized 'semantically' or according to some 'syntactic' system as for logic or mathematics. In addition, the possible relevance of non-cognitive variables such as obsessive preoccupations will be assessed.
Published Material: HERMELIN, B. & O'CONNOR, N. (1985). 'Logico-affective states and non-verbal language'. In: SCHOPLER, E. & MESIBOV, G. (Eds). Communication Problems in Autism, New York: Plenum Publishing Co.; SLOBODA, J., HERMELIN, B. & O'CONNOR, B. (1985). 'An exceptional musical memory', Music Percpetion, Vol 3, No 2, pp.155-170.; HERMELIN, B. & O'CONNOR, N. (1986). 'Spatial representations in mathematically and in artistically gifted children', British Journal of Educational Psychology, Vol 56, pp.150-157.; HERMELIN, B. & O'CONNOR, N. (1986). 'Idiot-savant calendrical calculators: rules and regularities', Psychological Medicine, Vol 16, pp.885-893.; O'CONNOR, N. & HERMELIN, B. (1986). 'Sensory handicap and cognitive defect'. In: Sensory impairments in mentally handicapped people, London: Croom Helm. San Diego, Calif: College Hill Press Inc.
Source of Grant: Medical Research Council
Date of Research: 1990 – continuing
KEYWORDS: ability; cognition; gifted; intelligence; memory; mental retardation

8/0678
>   Institute of Education,
>   20 Bedford Way, London WCIH OAL
>   071 636 1500
>   Staff College
>   The Work Based Learning Project,
>   Coombe Lodge, Blagdon, Bristol BS18 6RG
>   0272 62503
>   Levy, M. Mrs; *Supervisor:* Lawton, D. Mr; Melling, G. Mr;
>   Fuller, J. Mr; Tinsley, D.

The Work Based Learning Project
Abstract: The Work Based Learning Project continues with the development work put in place during the YTS Core Skills Project (mid 1982 – August 1986) and the first Work Based Learning Project (mid 1986 – August 1988). It is designed to assist the Train-

ing Agency with quality development strategies in regard to policy, implementation and technical work required to encourage and support the take-up of work based learning (WBL) as a new model for Vocational Education and Training (VET) across all three New Training Initiative (NTI) target groups (NTI 1 relating to long-duration training to 16-18 vocational training and NTI 2 relating to 16-18 vocational training and NTI 3 relating to widening opportunities for adults). Work based learning is defined as 'Linking learning to the work role' and having three inter-related components, each of which provides an essential contribution to that learning process: (i) structuring learning in the workplace; (ii) providing appropriate on-job training/learning opportunities; (iii) identifying and providing relevant off-job learning opportunities. The central project team will work with a range of 'satellite' projects around the UK. Each of these is dedicated to developing and implementing, within a national framework, different facets of the design, delivery and accreditation of work based learning. These satellite projects receive separate, additional funding from The Training Agency.
Published Material: LEVY, M. (1986). 'Work based learning: tools for transition', (FESC information Bank Paper No 2220) Coombe Lodge: Further Education Staff College.; LEVY, M. (1987). 'The Core Skills Project and work based learning: an overview of the development of a new model for the design, delivery and accreditation of work based learning', Sheffield: MSC.; Work Based Learning Project Team (1989). 'Achieving quality in employment training: designing and using work based projects', (FESC Information Bank Paper No 2465).; Work Based Learning Project Eam (1989). 'A guide to work based learning terms', Sheffield: Training Agency.
Source of Grant: Department of Employment – The Training Agency: £291,651 over the duration of the project
Date of Research: 1986-1990
KEYWORDS: apprenticeship; curriculum development; inservice training; vocational education; work experience

8/0679
Goldsmith's College,
Lewisham Way, New Cross, London SE14 6NW
081 692 7171
Blenkin. G.M. Ms; Kelly, A.V. Mr
Early childhood education
Abstract: The concern is to explore and analyze developmental approaches to education in the early years. An analysis of this model of education and curriculum planning will be followed by discussions of its implementation in the major areas of the curriculum and of its implications for the education and inservice education of teachers.
Published Material: BLENKIN, G.M. & KELLY, A.V. (1988). (Eds). Early Childhood Education. London: Paul Chapman
Source of Grant: Contract with Harper & Row Ltd
Date of Research: 1987 – continuing
KEYWORDS: curriculum development; early childhood education; inservice training

8/0680
King's College,
Centre for Educational Studies,
Chelsea Campus, 552 King's Road, London SW10 OUA
071 836 5454
West London Institute of Higher Education
Gordon House, 300 St Margaret's Road,
Twickenham TW1 1PT
081 891 0121
Taylor, R.C. Mr; *Supervisor:* Watson, D. Mrs
Programming in schools
Abstract: This is an investigation into the programming of micrcomputers as a classroom activity, with particular reference to claims made for LOGO (with some reference to PROLOG) languages. Action research is favoured at this stage. Interest lies in skills involved and their generalizibility outside the immediate activity of programming. The centrality of the teacher, and of the structured learning situation, are key assumptions and will be investigated. Suspicion of Papertrain, 'automatic learning' ideology is also prominent in this research.
Source of Grant: No grant (75% funding from employing institution)
Date of Research: 1989 – continuing
KEYWORDS: computer programming; learning strategy; microcomputer

8/0681
Goldsmiths College,
Lewisham Way, New Cross, London SE14 6NW
081 692 7171
Adams, T. Ms; *Supervisor:* Bann, S. Prof.
Psychoanalysis and image contruction
Abstract: 'The artist' is a term publicly associated with the professional practice of those who manipulate imagery. Often obscure and apparently unstable, the criteria for identifying artists rely primarily on self-professed definition. Can an artist produce 'non-art' and still be named 'artist', or conversely can a 'non-artist' produce artefacts? The form, 'art' as distinguished from the, 'artist', is here examined within specific educational, clinical and studio contexts. Art therapy, as process, indicates the paradoxical position of the 'non-artist'. If a 'non-artist' produces several paintings in a clinical setting s/he will not readily be identified as an 'artist', but instead be seen as a 'patient producing some art'. Yet, if an individual claiming the role of 'artist' becomes a patient and produces work in the clinical environment, s/he, although seen as an 'artist being a patient' will retain the definition 'artist'. Are there clinical situations in which the 'non-artist' can transcend the role 'patient' and enter the role 'artist'? These issues are presented by: (1) a review of those texts which identify the basis of artistic motivation; and the relationship between 'psychosis' and configuration and historical 'images of the unconscious'; (2) a study of therapists' definitions of art activity; (3) archival material; for example, 'Art Brut', Lausanne; Jungian archive, Zurich; (4) comprehensive profiles of: four contemporary 'established' artists and a number of clinical institutions where the concept of 'art' is therapy, and the concept of 'artist' is subordinate; (5) an overview of education and recruitment policies of 'art therapists' in Britain.
Published Material: ADAMS, T. (1988). 'The risk of creative solitude', Viewpoints, Summer 1988.; ADAMS, T. (1989). 'Freud, sublimation and narcissism', Viewpoints, Autumn 1989.
Source of Grant: No funding
Date of Research: 1984-1990
KEYWORDS: art; therapy

8/0682
Institute of Education,
Sociological Research Unit, 57 Gordon Square,
London WC1H 0NO
071 636 1500
Holland, J Dr; Ramazanogle, C.R. Dr; Sharpe, S.F. Ms; Scott, S.J. Ms; Thomson, R. Ms
Young women, sexuality and the limitation of Acquired Immune Deficiency Syndrome (AIDS)
Abstract: The study is a qualitative exploration of the sexual practices, beliefs and understanding of young women, and the practical implications for the spread of Human Immunodeficiency Virus (HIV) infection. Two groups in inner city areas of London and Manchester are being studied, using a range of research methods. The study will produce a detailed description and analysis of what young women know about sexuality and about AIDS; the ideas which they have about risk, danger and control in sexual encounters, how they behave sexually; why they behave as they do, and what factors are likely to constrain or to encourage change in their behaviour. The practical application of the study is directly relevant to the containment of the AIDS epidemic. The imformation gathered will also be relevant to changing other aspects of health care related to women's sexual behaviour, such as pregnancy, cervical cancer, and sexually transmitted diseases. The work will provide information on the efficacy of current government health programmes and will offer practical recommendations which will have policy implications in the field of health and sex education.
Source of Grant: Economic and Social Research Council (ESRC)
Date of Research: 1988-1990
KEYWORDS: Acquired Immune Deficiency Syndrome (AIDS); health education; sexual behaviour; woman

8/0683
Institute of Education,
20 Bedford Way, London EC1H 0AL
071 636 1500
Birmingham Polytechnic
Margaret Street, Birmingham B3 3BX
021 331 5000
Walkerdine, V. Prof.
Girls and mathematics
Abstract: The Girls and Mathematics Unit carried out nine funded

projects examining girls performance in mathematics from nursery to secondary school. The research used observation, experiments, testing and interviews of children at school and home, parents and teachers.
Published Material: WALDEN, R. & WALKERDINE, V. (1982). Girls and mathematics: the early years. (Bedford Way Papers, No.8) London: University of London, Institute of Education.; WALDEN, R. & WALDERDINE, V. (1985). Girls and mathematics: from primary to secondary schooling. (Bedford Way Papers, No.24) London: University of London, Institute of Education.; WALKERDINE, V. et al (1989). Counting girls out. London: Virago
Source of Grant: Economic and Social Research Council (ESRC): approx £80,000 Leverhulme Trust: approx £80,000 Equal Opportunities Commission: approx £20,000 Nuffield Foundation: approx £13,000
Date of Research: 1980-1989
KEYWORDS: equal opportunity; girl; mathematics; sex difference

8/0684

Centre for Educational Studies,
552 King's Road, London SW10 0UA
071 836 5454 (Project Officer: 071 872 3093)
Murray, R. Dr; Paechter, C. Ms; *Supervisor:* Black, P. Prof.
Cross-curricular assessment through coursework at GCSE (General Certificate of Secondary Education)
Abstract: The project has three main aims: (1) to promote and support work by school and college students in which they tackle realistic problems as part of their learning; (2) to ease the demands that GCSE coursework makes on students by finding ways in which interdisciplinary projects can be used to satisfy the requirements of more than one GCSE subject; (3) in the longer term to collect and disseminate examples of good practice so as to provide schools and LEAs (local education authorities) with models for planning, implementing and assessing cross-curricular work, with a view to encouraging this sort of approach to become part of teacher's normal practice.
Published Material: BLACK, P. & MURRAY, R. (1988). 'GCSE and TVEI: making a match of it', Insight (Journal of TVEI), No 14, Autumn 1988, pp.26.
Source of Grant: Training Enterprise Education Division: £60,000 School Examinations and Assessment Council (SEAC): £120,554
Date of Research: 1988 – continuing
KEYWORDS: assessment; coursework; curriculum development; General Certificate of Education; interdisciplinary approach

8/0685

20 Bedford Way, London WC1 0AL
071 387 7050
Hampshire School
Tanner Street, Winchester S023 8AD
0962 55477
Brooks, P.L. Mr; *Supervisor:* Snowling, M. Dr
Specific learning difficulties; implications for an education service
Abstract: The central aim is (1) to establish the effectiveness of current, and some novel, screening in identifying children with SLD (Specific Learning Difficulties) and (2) to see if these children respond differentially to 'traditional', and multisensory teaching methods. Part (1) involves 250 children in year 1 of junior schools in Alton. They are being followed from pre-school and correlations and predictability will be established for county screening and other indices including family history and memory/learning levels. Part (2) involves single case studies. These will initially test if SLD children respond better to multisensory, as against other, teaching methods. If this is the case, further work will aim to clarify relevant aspects of these methods and seek to further develop teaching techniques.
Source of Grant: Department of Education and Science
Date of Research: 1987 – continuing
KEYWORDS: learning difficulty; screening; teaching method

8/0686

Birkbeck College
Department of Linguistics,
43 Gordon Square, London WC1H 0PD
071 631 6117
Cheshire, J. Dr; Edwards, V. Dr
A survey of British dialect grammar
Abstract: The project aimed to give a preliminary survey of British dialect grammar, focusing on the urban centres of Britain. It was intended to point to the most frequently occurring non-standard

grammatical feature of British English and to give rise to some informed hypotheses about linguistic diffusion and change. It also aimed to produce information on dialect in Britain which might be useful to teachers. Information on dialect grammar was collected with the help of teachers and pupils throughout Britain, who took part in collaborative classroom projects on local dialect. As the end point of a language awareness course, pupils completed a questionnaire on dialect forms indicating which features occurred in their part of Britain. A dialect directory was compiled, listing available resources on dialect which teachers might use when working on dialect related topics. The directory is held by the economic and social research council.
Published Material: EDWARDS, V. & CHESHIRE, J. (1989). 'The survey of British dialect grammar'. In: Cheshire, J. et al (Eds). Dialect and education. Clevedon: Multilingual Matters.; CHESHIRE, J. et al. (1989). 'Urban British dialect grammar: the question of dialect levelling', English Worldwide, Vol 10.; CHESHIRE, J. & EDWARDS, V. (1991). 'Children as sociolinguistic researchers', In: MILROY, J. & MILROY, L. (Eds). British regional syntax. Harlow: Longman. (forthcoming).; EDWARDS, V. (1991). 'A directory of resources on British dialect grammar', In: MILROYJ. & MILROY, L. (Eds). British regional syntax. Harlow: Longman. (forthcoming).
Source of Grant: Economic and Social Research Council: £40,000
Date of Research: 1986-1989
KEYWORDS: dialect; English language; grammar

8/0687

Birkbeck College
Department of Applied Linguistics and Language Centre,
Malet Street, London WC1E 7HX
071 580 6622
London University
43 Gordon Square, London WC1H 0PD
071 631 6117
Barbe, P. Ms; *Supervisor:* Cheshire, J. Dr
Syntactic variation in Guernsey English
Abstract: A pilot study indicated the influence of Guernsey French and Guernsey English. Varieties of Guernsey French spoken in the north-east and the south-west of the island differ noticeably, which suggests that the English spoken in the two areas might also differ. The project aims to analyze syntactic variation in the spoken and written English of young people from two different areas of Guernsey; to increase our understanding of language contact and of linguistic and social constraints on syntactic variation in Guernsey English. A sample of 20 second year pupils from a school in the north-east and from a school in the south-west will be studied (10 boys and 10 girls from each school). Methods will include participant observation to facilitate recording informal speech in small groups outside lesson times; a questionnaire to assess individual geographical attachment/identity; a questionnaire to assess teacher and pupil attitude to syntactic variation. Quantitative methods will be used where appropriate.
Source of Grant: Economical and Social Research Council (ESRC): £6,250
Date of Research: 1989 – continuing
KEYWORDS: dialect; discourse analysis; English language; Guernsey; syntax;

8/0688

Birkbeck College
Department of Applied Linguistics,
43 Gordon Square, London WC1H 0PD
071 631 6117
Gardner-Chloros, P.H. Dr
Code-switching among Greek Cypriots in London: linguistic and sociolinguistic aspects
Abstract: The project concerns linguistic developments in the London Greek Cypriot community, focusing on the description of language contact/mixing phenomena such as code-switching and their implications for language shift/language change in that community. In year I (1988-1989) pilot work was carried out: interviews/observation in community centres and saturday schools, and a comparison between the dialect as spoken by 3 generations of immigrants. In year 2 (1989-1990) extensive recordings will be carried out in natural circumstances (families, shops, offices,etc.) in order to obtain a substantial corpus (approx. 100 hours of transcribed speech). This will be analysed from a linguistic and sociolinguitic point of view in year 3 (1990-1991) and is intended to give rise to a publication in book form.

Published Material: GARDNER-CHLOROS, P. & PILLAKOURI, O. (1989). 'Issues relating to language contact and code-swithching among Greek-Cypriots in London', Paper presented at the conference "Greek outside Greece" held at Birkbeck College, London, on 7-8th June 1989.; GARDNER-CHLOROS, P. (1990). Language selection and switching in Strasbourg. Oxford: Open University Press. (forthcoming)
Source of Grant: British Academy
Date of Research: 1988 – continuing
KEYWORDS: bilingualism; discourse analysis; English language; ethnic minority; Greek-Cypriot

8/0689
Birkbeck College
Department of Psychology,
Malet Street, London WC1E 7HX
071 631 6462/6209
Gregg, V. Dr; Siddons, P. Ms; *Supervisor:* Barber, P. Dr
Birkbeck human performance test battery
Abstract: The Birkbeck Human Performance Test Battery exploits the advantages of computerized testing. It consists of a set of tests which are proposed as standard measures of psychological performance and convenient to use in a wide range of circumstances. Originally developed to assess change in psychological functioning associated with natural variables (e.g. time of day) and environmental conditions (e.g. noise), the battery's usefulness in assessing training and scholastic potential is being evaluated. The research centres on unemployed adults and 10-11 year olds.
Published Material: The Birkbeck Human Performance Test Battery: User's manual, Birkbeck College 1986.
Source of Grant: Supported by departmental funds
Date of Research: 1986-1990
KEYWORDS: assessment; computer; performance; psychology of education; test

8/0690
Birkbeck College
Department of Psychology,
Birkbeck College,
Malet Street, London WC1E 7HX
071 580 6622 ext 6201
Stuart, K.M. Dr
Phonological awareness and learning to read: longitudinal and experimental work
Abstract: This research addresses the following questions: (i) is phonological awareness sufficient for reading to be learned easily, or must the child have a good knowledge of letter-sound correspondence? (ii) do phonologically aware children learn to read easily because their phonological awareness plus their knowledge of sound-letter correspondences allows them to create a primitive word-recognition system which can 'recognize' printed monosyllabic words in terms of partial information (beginning and end letters?); (iii) is ease of phonological segmentation related to phonetic class of phonemes? Is this also true of learning of sound-letter correspondences? (iv) in pre-reading children, is knowledge of sound-to-letter correspondences the same as a knowledge of letter-to-sound correspondences? (v) once the child can segment syllables into their onsets and rimes, how is the segmentation of onsets and of rimes into their constituent phonemes aquired? All of this work will involve detailed analysis of the performance of individual children. Hence the extent to which children differ from each other in the strategies they use as early readers will be directly studied. As well as carrying out these experimental studies of a new sample of pre-reading children, the researcher proposed to follow through for two more years the children already studied. This will mean that for each member of a reasonably typical group of 26 children, detailed information will be available about their linguistic capabilities before they began reading plus information about the characteristics of their reading at various points along the route to skilled reading. When these data are completely collected they will yield a complete picture of the course of reading acquisition in each child.
Published Material: STUART, K.M. (1987). Levels of Phonological Awareness, Cahiers de Psychologie Cognitive, Vol 7, No 5, pp.520-524.
Source of Grant: Economic and Social Research Council (ESRC): £30,080
Date of Research: 1986-1990
KEYWORDS: early reading; language development; phonolgy; reading

8/0691
Department of Advanced Studies in Education
Faculty of Education,
Goldsmiths' College,
University of London,
Lewisham Way, New Cross, London SE14 6NW
081 692 7171
Walter, C. Mr
Towards a theory of teaching poetry in school
Abstract: This is a school based project which sets out to initiate, develop and study a quite new approach to this area of the arts curriculum in the primary school. The project began as a years work in a London school with a class of 8/9 year olds, and seeks practical outcomes which are elements of a complete theory of poetry teaching. The teaching strategies which have been located, and which are now being developed, have a peculiar relevance to classroom work with children of any ethnic origin. In addition these strategies involve contributions by parents and other members of the community outside school. Further, in school the strategies entail the inter-locking of a wide variety of learning and teaching situations. The theory of poetry teaching which is being built is 'formal' in nature and may therefore be applied in any national context. Conclusions and publications so far have concentrated upon work with children of primary school age. The next phase of the work will seek to explore their implications for work with the 11-14 age range.
Published Material: WALTER, C. (1983). 'Form or formula? The practice of poetry teaching'. In: MEEK, M. (Ed). Opening moves. Heinemann for the University of London, Institute of Education, pp.56-71.; WALTER, C. (1986). 'The many years of telling: a tradition of failed practice of poetry teaching in the primary school', English in Education, Vol 20, No 3, 1986, pp.31-38.; WALTER, C. (1987). 'The teaching of poetry in school: formal ways to begin with teacher education,' European Journal of Teacher Education, Vol 10, No 2, 1987, pp.213-219.; WALTER, C. (1988). 'Inhabiting poetry: a formal contribution to the debate upon teaching poetry', Goldsmiths' College Monographs in Education Series, No 6.; WALTER, C. (1987). An early start to poetry. London: Macdonald.
Source of Grant: No funding apart from various institutional support
Date of Research: 1983 – continuing
KEYWORDS: poetry; primary education; theory of education

8/0692
Department of Design and Technology
Goldsmith's College,
Lewisham Way, New Cross, London SE14 6NW
081 692 7171
Kimbell, R.; Saxton, J.; *Supervisor:* Kelly, A.V.
Assessment of Performance Unit in design and technology: aimed at monitoring the performance of 15 year old pupils in design and technology
Abstract: As a result of the Assessment of Performance Unit's (APU's) discussion document 'Understanding Design and Technology', Trent Polytechnic carried out a survey of secondary schools to establish how further activities described therein were current. The outcome indicated that it would be worthwhile embarking on a test development leading to a survey in 1988/89, and in particular that many teachers were aiming to develop in their pupils competencies within a range of contexts. These will be the focus of the new APU research team in Design and Technology at Goldsmith's College. There will be three complementary types of test instruments eliciting different aspects of ability: (1) To establish criteria within the analytical APU assessment model illustrated in the previous section. These can then be used to develop test items isolating and quantifying performance under those criteria. Here many test instruments will be of the paper and pencil variety; (2) to building design project assessment devices into the monitoring with the active participation of teachers from every LEA (Local Education Authority), training two in every LEA to monitor project work in their own and neighbouring schools; (3) developing a balanced monitoring tool to focus on the procedural abilities exemplified in a CDT (Craft, Design and Technology) project but presented in an abbreviated form.
Source of Grant: Department of Education and Science, (DES); Assessment of Performance Unit: £600,000 (approximately)
Date of Research: 1985-1990
KEYWORDS: craft; design & technology; secondary education

8/0693

Department of Education
Goldsmiths College,
Lewisham Way, New Cross, London SE14 6NW
081 692 7171
Mallett, M. Ms

Non fiction in the primary school with a special focus on oral language as a means of reflecting on information in books

Abstract: This project is an attempt to apply knowledge about the learning process in children to their methods used when learning from information books. Factors associated with success, organizing prior knowledge, starting from the specific, collaboration round texts and making explicit key concepts are realised in a case study – a classroom project on squirrels. A main focus is the enabling power of spoken language in reflecting on new ideas in books. The empirical work is action research and a case study.

Source of Grant: No funding
Date of Research: 1986 – continuing
KEYWORDS: *non-fiction*

8/0694

Department of Education
Goldsmiths College,
Lewisham Way, New Cross, London SE14 6NW
081 692 7171
Hurst, V. Mrs; *Supervisor:* Kelly S.V. Prof.

Teachers' strategies of self-evaluation

Abstract: The investigation seeks to examine the processes whereby teachers evaluate the effectiveness of their teaching. It examines the collection of information about classroom, and other, educational situations, by individual teachers, and how hypotheses for future action are derived from this. The relevance of different ways of assessing children's progress in the course of self-evaluation is discussed. The investigation is through case studies. Two infant teachers, a small group of B.Ed students on teaching practice and an education lecturer constitute the participants. The results show the connection between the process of evaluation and teachers' effectiveness in meeting the needs of learners in educational situations. There is reason for concern that narrowing the focus of evaluation to predetermined goals will effectively narrow the curriculum received by pupils.

Source of Grant: No funding
Date of Research: 1986-1990
KEYWORDS: *effectiveness; evaluation; self-evaluation; teacher*

8/0695

Department of Education
Goldsmith's College,
Lewisham Way, New Cross, London SE14 6NW
081 692 7171
Mallett, M. Mrs; *Supervisor:* Kimberley, K. Mr

The role of spoken language in helping children (7-11) reflect on information in non-narrative texts

Abstract: The central question addressed is how do we support junior school children's reading of non-narrative or non-story texts? Thus the work has a strong link with preoccupations in the National Curriculum, and partly explores the implications of Attainment Target 2. A main hypothesis is that spoken language may be a powerful mediating force between child and text in the form of peer group collaboration on written materials and the teacher's oral contribution. Work has so far been carried out in a junior school classroom with a class of 8-9 year olds. The method used was participant observation. Often researcher took on role of teacher. The study emphasizes the quality of reflection achieved rather than just the acquisition of straightforward study skills. A survey of teachers' views on how children can be helped to respond to and reflect on this kind of text is planned for later this year.

Published Material: MALLETT, M. (1988). 'From 'human sense' to 'metalinguistic awareness'', English in Education. Vol 22, No 1, Spring 1988, pp. 40-45.; MALLETT, M. (1990). 'A tough nut to crack', Junior Education, Vol 14, No 1, January 1990, pp.38-39.
Source of Grant: Goldsmith's College
Date of Research: 1986 – continuing
KEYWORDS: *Engish language; nonfiction; oral work; reading; spoken language*

8/0696

Department of Education
Thomas Coram Research Unit,
41 Brunswick Square, London WC1N 1AZ
071 278 2424
Back, L. Mr.; *Supervisor:* Tizard, B. Prof.; Phoenic, A. Ms

Social identity in adolescence

Abstract: This project is concerned with the social identities of young Londoners. The researchers aim to describe the range of social groups they feel they belong to, the strength of the affiliation they feel towards each group, and what they see as the important characteristics of each group. It is also intended to describe which of these identities are most central in their lives. The social identities in which we are particularly interested are the neighbourhood, church, gender, social class, ethnic group and nationality. Interest is also being shown in the extent to which young people in schools of different ethnic composition have developed multiracial friendships, and the extent to which their skin colour is an important organizing identity in their lives. In relation to this, the researchers aim to explore their attitude to, and experience of, racial discrimination, and the extent to which their attitudes and coping strategies have been influenced by families and friends.

Source of Grant: Department of Health
Date of Research: 1988 – continuing
KEYWORDS: *adolescent; ethnic minority; group membership; identity; race relations; social interaction*

8/0697

Department of Education
Thomas Coram Research Unit,
41 Brunswick Square, London WC1N 1AZ
071 278 2424
Lloyd, E. Ms; Statham, J. Ms; *Supervisor:* Moss, P. Dr; Melhuish, E. Mr

Playgroups' study

Abstract: The first stage of this project examines the pattern of pre-school provision nationally, looking especially at the role of playgroups within it, and at the relationship between playgroups and other under-fives services. Some of the data for this stage comes from an analysis of national statistics, but the main component is a study of 25 local authorities in England, or roughly a quarter of the total. Each area has been visited, and key workers in the Education Department, Social Services Department, and the Pre-school Playgroups Association (PPA) interviewed. The second stage is a detailed study of playgroups in contrasting areas, both rural and urban. Approximately 20 playgroups will be selected in each area, taken from the local authority register so as not to confine the sample to PPA members. This stage is based on interviews with around 200 mothers; and on interviews with playgroup leaders, covering such issues as resources, training, parental involvement, methods of management, and liaison with the local authority. It is also intended during this stage to do some exploratory work on children's experiences in different playgroups, using observational methods.

Published Material: LLOYD, E. et al (1989). 'A review of research on playgroups', Early Child Development and Care, Vol 43, March 1989, pp.77-99.
Source of Grant: Department of Health
Date of Research: 1987 – continuing
KEYWORDS: *playgroup; pre-school education*

8/0698

Department of Education
Thomas Coram Research Unit,
41 Brunswick Square, London WC1N 1AZ
071 278 2424
Hennessey, E.; Martin, S. Ms; *Supervisor:* Melhuish, E. Dr; Moss, P. Mr

Day care and later development

Abstract: The day care project, which finished in 1988, was concerned with single and dual-career families over the first three years of the child's life. The current project is a follow-up of these families, which aims to answer substantial questions about the usage and effects of day care, and also parental employment over the subsequent three years. The children in the study are now attending primary school, and the implications of this for dual career families are being examined. The project also considers the implications of different types of early day care experience for the child's socio-emotional and cognitive development at the age of six. The project staff are visiting 243 families remaining in the day care project when the children are six years old. The mothers are to be interviewed, pariculary about child care and employment histories over the last three years. The children's cognitive development is assessed using standardized psychometric measure, their socio-

emotional development by questionnaires which are completed by the mother and class teacher.
Published Material: BRANNEN, J. & MOSS, P. (1988). New mothers at work: employment and childcare. London: Unwin.
Source of Grant: Department of Health
Date of Research: 1988-1990
KEYWORDS: *child care; child development; cognitive development; mother; women's employment*

8/0699
Department of Education
Thomas Coram Research Unit,
41 Brunswick Square, London WC1N 1AZ
071 278 2424
Farquhar, C. Ms
Acquired Immune Deficiency Syndrome (AIDS) related knowledge amongst young children: a feasibility study
Abstract: The perceived need for this study was based on: the emergence of anecdotal evidence of young children's concerns about Human Immunodeficiency Virus (HIV)/Acquired Immune Deficiency Syndrome (AIDS); the recommendation of the Department of Education and Science (DES) that teachers should be prepared to answer young children's questions about HIV/AIDS at school; the scarcity of research data concerning how young children think about health and illness in general, and HIV/AIDS specifically. The aims of the study were to establish the feasibility of gaining access to adults and children for research into primary school children's AIDS-related knowledge; to establish the feasibility of collecting reliable and valid information about 8-11 year olds' AIDS-related knowledge, beliefs and attitudes; and to develop a proposal for a more substantive study of young children's AIDS-related knowledge. This pilot study was based mainly in one primary school in outer London. Data has been collected in a variety of different settings and from a variety of people, including children, teachers, dinner ladies, caretakers, and other workers in the school. Although the proposed three year project was not funded, the aims were achieved.
Published Material: FARQUHAR, C. & SANDERS, P. (1989). Let's talk about AIDS. London: Franklin Watts.
Source of Grant: Economic and Social Research Council (ESRC): £35,770
Date of Research: 1988-1989
KEYWORDS: *Acquired Innune Deficiency Syndrome (AIDS); child; health education; knowledge; primary education*

8/0700
Department of Education
Thomas Coram Research Unit,
41 Brunswick Square, London WC1N 1AZ
071 278 2424
Tizard, B. Prof.
Infant school project: junior school follow-up
Abstract: This project was a follow-up, to the end of junior school, of the cohort of children who, in 1982, entered 33 multi-ethnic ILEA (Inner London Education Authority) infant schools from nursery school. This study was concerned with attainment at the end of junior school, progress during junior school, and progress throughout the primary years. Only 149 out of the starting sample of 343 children were still in their original schools by the end of juniors. In addition, pupils who had moved but stayed within the London area were tested to give a final sample of 166, 59 of whom were black (Afro-Caribbean) and 78 were white. Group reading and maths tests were used, the Suffolk reading test and the Young's 'Y' maths test. The pattern of results found during the infant school period was repeated for junior school, with girls, particularly white girls, ahead in reading, and white pupils, particularly white boys, ahead in maths. However, the mean standard scores for the sample were rather low – 90 for read and 86 for maths. The correlation for reading and maths over time were substantial.
Published Material: TIZARD, B. et al (1988). Young children at school in the inner city. Hove: Lawrence Erlbaum.
Source of Grant: Economic and Social Research Council (ESRC): £81,585
Date of Research: 1988-1989
KEYWORDS: *achievement; ethnic minority; primary education; sex difference*

8/0701
Department of Education
King's College London, Strand, London WC2R 2LS

071 836 5454
Lowe, D.P. Mrs; *Supervisor:* Cowie, E.E. Mrs
The Anglican contribution to education in the Diocese of Oxford
Abstract: The aim is to analyze the contribution of the Anglican Church to education in the Diocese of Oxford against the background of other educational provision and to compare the diocesan provision with that in the country as a whole. Hopefully, the survey will reveal every Anglican school that has existed in the Diocese since the early nineteenth century. These will be mapped at various periods in time and information about each will be examined in detail. The Log Books of a few contracting schools will be studied in detail. The contribution of the main educational agency of the Anglican Church, the National Society, will be investigated, as will the role of the voluntary school managers and parish priests. The role of Her Majesty's Inspectors and Diocesan inspectors and their relationship will be examined as will their reports, the methods and quality of teaching, the content of the curriculum and the condition of the buildings and equipment against the background of social and economic conditions. The growth in demand for secular education as well as the increase in the numbers and training of certificated teachers will be traced. Innovations in administration as a result of the Education Acts of 1870, 1897 and 1902 will be considered, together with the role of the State and attitudes towards the National Society after 1870. The results will show that the Anglican Church was responsible for the initial development of education in the Diocese and, although there has been a steady decline in the number of voluntary schools since 1870 they nevertheless still play an important part in educational provision.
Source of Grant: no funding
Date of Research: 1983 – continuing
KEYWORDS: *christian education; church; denominational school; educational provision; history of education*

8/0702
Department of Psychology
Gower Street, London WC1E 6BT
071 636 8000
Watford General Hospital
Shrodells Wing, Vicarage Road, Watford WD1 8HB
0923 244366
Millar, W.S. Dr; Weir, C. Dr
An investigation of the relationship between perinatal risk factors and contingency learning and attentive behaviour in later infancy
Abstract: The research examines the relationship between specific major categories of perinatal risk and cognitive functioning in later infancy. Attentional and contingency analysis behaviours are examined in relation to several medical risk factors because of their potential C.N.S. (central nervous system) involvement; prematurity; the effects of oxygenation/respiratory problems. Three groups of infants are established on the basis of clinical data and objective brain imaging data: (i) infants who revealed a normal brain scan and who at term were neurologically normal, i.e. no discernable C.N.S. involvement; (ii) infants whose scan analysis revealed discrete but non-threatening injury and (iii) infants whose scan revealed more complex and extensive injury. Behavioural measures on two attention/learning tasks obtained from 6-12 month old infants who previously experienced the categories of perinatal risk in order to examine the effects of early C.N.S. related risk/damage to later cognitive functioning. The findings are expected to be relevant to early educative interventive strategies for basis skills acquisition in early infancy and early childhood.
Source of Grant: No funding
Date of Research: 1985 – continuing
KEYWORDS: *cognitive development; birth; brain injury; early learning*

8/0703
Department of Undergraduate Initial Teacher Education
Goldsmith's College,
Lewisham Way, New Cross, London SE14 6NW
081 692 7171
Lewis, D.H. Mr; *Supervisor:* Spencer, M. Mrs
The role of the contemporary picture book in early literacy development
Abstract: The aim of the research has been, in the first instance, to develop a theory that can account for recent developments in the design and production of picture books for young children. Existing discourses do not facilitate an adequate analysis of illustrated text. The distinctive characteristics of certain paradigmatic

examples of the form having been determined and described the second phase of the research has involved work in school reading with young children to ascertain how they attempt to make sense of certain selected texts that call into question perceived notions of narrative discourse and thus of early literacy learning.
Source of Grant: No funding
Date of Research: 1984 – continuing
KEYWORDS: *literacy; picture book; reading*

8/0704

Goldsmiths College
Department of Mathematics and Computing,
New Cross, London SE14 6NW
081 692 7171
Southwark College
Asylum Road, London SE1 8LE
071 928 9561
Light, P. Mr; *Supervisor:* Hainline, D. Dr
Cognitive skills in novice computer programmes
Abstract: In any group of programming students there is a wide range of abilities. This phenomena cannot be adequately explained by previous academic background or pedagogic styles. This project will analyze some 100 verbal protocols in an attempt to discover the cognitive differences (if any) demonstrated between good and less able students of computer programming. The methodology and experimental design is presently being investigated.
Source of Grant: No funding
Date of Research: 1987-1990
KEYWORDS: *cognitive process; computer science; student*

8/0705

Institute of Child Health
Academic Department of Child Psychiatry,
30 Guildford Street, London WC1N 1EH
071 242 9789
The Hospital for Sick Children
Academic Department of Child Psychiatry
Great Ormond Street, London WC1
071 405 9200
Skuse, D. Dr; Wolke, D.; *Supervisor:* Graham, P. Prof.
Limits to growth: New perspectives on the environmental constraints upon physical and psychological development
Abstract: A recently completed whole population survey in a socioeconomically deprived area of inner London revealed that, at one year of age, nearly 5% of full-term caucasian singletons were failing to thrive (Dowdney et al, 1987). The aim of this community-based case comparison survey is to investigate the possible mechanisms by which so-called 'psychosocial deprivation' leads to impaired development in physical and psychological attainments. Hypotheses about causal mechanisms are being tested by the development of a number of instruments: (1) a Feeding Assessment Schedule to summarize and quantify oral-motor functioning and behaviour during feeding of infants who have no overt neurological disorder. This schedule is being used to investigate the prevalence of dysfunctional oral development among case and comparison infants. (2) A scale of rate observations of contextual factors during feeding with the aim of assessing whether the infants' needs are being adequately addressed. (3) Investigation of whether case mothers provide their infants with less social stimulation, and whether they express less positive affection during play interaction. Case infants are expected to be either temperamentally more difficult than comparisons, or apathetic and undemanding, depending on the degree of cachexia. Data collection will entail a combination of self-rating interviews, questionnaires and direct (videotaped) observations, within subjects' homes, on approximately 50 case and 50 pair-wise matched comparison infants.
Published Material: DOWDNEY, L. & SKUSE, D. et al. (1987). 'Growth retardation and developmental delay amongst inner city children', Journal of Child Psychology & Psychiatry, Vol 28, No 4, pp.529-541.; SKUSE, D. (1987). 'The psychological consequences of being small', Journal of Child Psychology & Psychiatry, Vol 28, No 5, pp.641-650.; WOLKE, D., SKUSE, D. & MATHISEN, B. 'Behavioural style in failure to thrive infants: a preliminary communication', Journal of Paediatric Psychology (submitted for publication).; MATHISEN, B., SKUSE, D. & WOLKE, D. 'Oral-motor dysfunction and growth retatdation amongst inner city children', Developmental Medicine & Child Neurology (submitted for publication).
Source of Grant: Wellcome Trust: £86,966 supplementary grants: £29,360; £6,547 Joint Research Boards: £5,980 Child Growth Foun-

dation: £2,040 Newcomen Educational Foundation: £3,000
Date of Research: 1985-1990
KEYWORDS: *backwardness; child development; deprived; mental development; development; social environment*

8/0706

Institute of Child Health
Department of Developmental Paediatrics,
The Wolfson Centre, Mecklenburgh Square,
London WC1N 2AP
081 847 7618
Huntley, R.M.C. Dr; *Supervisor:* Holt, K.S. Prof.
The revision and restandardization of the Griffiths Mental Development Scales, 0 to 2 years
Abstract: The aim of this project is to revise and restandardize the Griffiths Mental Development Scales. These were first published in 1954, and have been extensively used, but are now in need of revision. The research falls into 5 stages: (1) preparation of Revised Scales; (2) try-out on representative sample of baby population at each month, 0 to 24 months, sample size about 500; (3) analysis of results; preparation of final version of Scales following item analysis; (4) try-out on smaller representative sample (about 250), combining results from first sample modified for changes following item analysis; (5) completion of computation of results, rewriting of test form and instruction manual.
Source of Grant: Association for Research into Child Development (ARICD)
Date of Research: 1988-1990
KEYWORDS: *mental development*

8/0707

Institute of Child Health
Department of Developmental Paediatrics,
The Wolfson Centre, Mecklenburgh Square,
London WC1N 2AP
081 847 7618
Huntley, R.M.C. Dr; *Supervisor:* Holt, K.S. Prof.
The translation and restandardization of the Reynell Developmental Language Scales into Welsh
Abstract: The aim of this research is to translate and restandardize the Reynell Developmental Language Scales into Welsh, to provide a standardized test in the Welsh language for assessing and diagnosing the speech and language problems of young children whose first language is Welsh. The procedure will be to translate the Scales into Welsh, give them to a representative sample of Welsh-speaking children between 1 and 7 years (650), analyze the results, calculate means and standard deviations for each half-year of age, then give the final version to a smaller representative sample (about 350), continuing the scores from the first sample, corrected for any changes made following the item analysis, and to produce Welsh norms. A preliminary study on a small representative sample is being conducted, giving the Welsh translation of the Scales but using the English norms to score and a non-verbal performance test, which should be independent of language. If the language scores give means and distributions comparable with each other and with the English norms, then nothing more need be done. The English norms can be assumed appropriate for interpreting the Welsh language scores. If they are not comparable, then a full standardization on the large sample of Welsh-speaking children will need to be carried out.
Source of Grant: The Welsh Speech Therapists' Research Committee into Bilingualism (STRCB). The Welsh Office has granted £12,000 towards the first year of this study. Further funds have been applied for from the Leverhulme Trust
Date of Research: 1988-1990
KEYWORDS: *language development; test; Welsh language*

8/0708

Institute of Education
Department of History and Humanities,
20 Bedford Way, London WC1H OAL
071 636 1500
Bedford College of Higher Education
Polhill Avenue, Bedford MK41 9EA
0234 51671
Smart, G.R.M. Mr; *Supervisor:* Aldrich, R.E. Dr
The training and education of Froebelian teachers in England and Wales, 1889-1926
Abstract: The research is concerned with the dissemination of child-centred theories and methods of education of young children in

England and Wales between 1889 and 1926. The work is an investigation of the contribution of the Froebel movement to this process through the training and education of kindergarten teachers under the auspices of the National Froebel Union, whose previously unpublished archives form the basis of the source material. It considers the nature of the institutions concerned, the curricula followed by the students and the relationship between the Froebel movement and the maintained system.
Published Material: SMART, R. (1985). 'The diffusion of Froebelian ideas and methods in England, 1882-1914', Historia Infantiae (Budapest), Vol 2, pp.29-48.
Source of Grant: No funding
Date of Research: 1984 – continuing
KEYWORDS: history of education; nursery school; theory of education

8/0709

Institute of Education
20 Bedford Way, London WC1H OAL
071 636 1500
Bedford College of Higher Education
37 Lansdowne Road, Bedford MK40 2BZ
0234 51966
Whitehead, M. Dr; *Supervisor:* Elliott, R.K.
A study of the views of Sartre and Merleau-Ponty relating to embodiment and a consideration of the implications of these views for the justification and practice of physical education
Abstract: The thesis acknowledges the confusion that has arisen out of the various, and often extravagant, claims made to justify the inclusion of physical education in the school curriculum. It is noted that many of these are not concerned with bodily attributes but assert that physical education is instrumental in furthering a whole range of non-physical ends such as social development. The validity of these 'instrumental' claims is questioned and the profession's lack of confidence in presenting a case for the intrinsic value of its own area is identified. It is seen necessary, therefore, to consider whether such an intrinsic justification can be formulated. To this end aspects of existential and phenomenological philosophy are examined through the work of Jean-Paul Sartre and Maurice Merleau-Ponty's views on the role of the embodiment in perception. The first major focus of the thesis concludes with an argument for the inclusion of physical education alongside other aspects of education. The second major focus considers the views of Sartre concerning body modes. This examination reveals the dangers inherent in others viewing one's embodiment as an object and would seem to explain the disenchantment felt for the subject by many pupils. Recommendations for the practice of physical education are then made. The thesis concludes with a reconsideration of the aims of physical education and a reassertion of its rightful place in an education of the 'whole man'.
Published Material: WHITEHEAD, M.E. (1988). 'The danger of fun', British Journal of Physical Education, Vol 19, No 4/5, pp.155. July/Oct.; WHITEHAD, M.E. (1988). 'Health and physical education project', newsletter. (Health education authority and physical education association) No 19, November.; WHITEHEAD, M.E. (1988). 'Meaningful existence, embodiment and physical education', Journal of Philosophy of Education, Vol 23, No 1.
Date of Research: 1977-1987
KEYWORDS: aims of education; philosophy of education; physical education; value

8/0710

Institute of Education
Department of Child Development and Primary Education,
24 Woburn Square, London WC1H 0AA
071 636 1500
St James-Roberts, I. Dr; Sing, G. Mrs; Papakyriakopoulos, C. Mr
Emotional and behavioural problems in reception class children
Abstract: The first aim has been to develop instruments which enable reception class teachers to assess emotional and behavioural problems in their pupils. Contextually appropriate, reliable and valid, procedures have been developed. The researchers are now studying factors in children, families and classroom contexts which lead to such problems.
Source of Grant: Association of Commonwealth Universities London University Central Research Fund
Date of Research: 1989 – continuing
KEYWORDS: behaviour disorder; emotional disorder; primary education; problem reception class

8/0711

Institute of Education
Department of International and Comparative Education,
Bedford Way, London WC1H OAL
071 636 1500
Sandon, S. Dr; *Supervisor:* Jones, C. Mr
On site units for problem children: two case studies
Abstract: Descriptions of two on site units in an outer London borough are followed by a comparison of teachers views on their school's unit in relation to function, referral systems outcomes and opinions regarding units in general.
Source of Grant: No funding
Date of Research: 1988-1990
KEYWORDS: educational building; educational facilities; problem child

8/0712

Institute of Education
Department of International and Comparative Education,
Bedford Way, London WC1H 0AL
071 636 1500
Garner, P. Mr; *Supervisor:* Jones, C. Mr
Comparative perspectives in teaching children with emotional and behavioural difficulty in Bulgaria and United Kingdom
Abstract: The purpose of this research is to help provide cross-cultural information regarding existing practice within a given locale in relation to organization and planning for emotional and behavioural difficulty children. Secondly, comparative perspectives on referrral patterns to special education. Finally, the relationship of these alternative procedures to mainstream provision. The research is based in two schools, one in the United Kingdom, the other in Bulgaria, and it will use a number of ethnographic research instruments.
Source of Grant: West London Institute of Higher Education Research Fund: £857
Date of Research: 1990 – continuing
KEYWORDS: behaviour disorder; Bulgaria; comparative education; emotional disorder; special education

8/0713

Institute of Education
Department of International and Comparative Education,
20 Bedford Way, London WC1H OAL
071 636 1500
Little, A.W. Prof.
Primary education in Andhra Pradesh
Abstract: This project involves the establishment of a network of researchers in Andhra Pradesh, India to facilitate research in seven broad areas of relevance to the development of primary education in Andhra Pradesh. Research proposals are invited in one or more of the following broad areas: Assessment of pupil learning; curriculum; the professional development of teachers; institutional aspects of school development; socioeconomic constraints on and the impact of the development of primary education; comparative learning systems; organization and management. The research is co-ordinated from the research cell of the Andhra Pradesh Primary Education Project (APPEP) supported by the State Government of Andhra Pradesh and the British Overseas Development Administration (ODA). The research cell assists external researchers through the award of research grants and the organization of seminars for researchers; it develops and disseminates research material and conducts internal project research. One such internal project currently being undertaken is 'an exploratory investigation of the understanding of APPEP principles by APPEP teachers and APPEP professional support staff'.
Source of Grant: Overseas Development Administration: £9,000 per annum
Date of Research: 1990 – continuing
KEYWORDS: educational research; India; primary education

8/0714

Institute of Education
Department of Child Development and Primary Education,
24-27 Woburn Square, London WC1H OAA
071 636 1500
Moore, T.W. Prof.; Hindley, C.B. Prof.
Longitudinal research project: changes in general ability of normal children from infancy to adolescence
Abstract: The research began in 1949 as a collaborative project between the Institutes of Education and Child Health of London

University. There is thus a parallel research under Professor J.M. Tanner on the physical development of the same subjects. As representative a sample as possible of the London West Central 1 area was recruited from 1949 to 1952. 223 subjects were recruited, and 186 were in the sample within 18 months. For many purposes the researchers have around 110 subjects with records complete enough for general use up to 14 years; and 84 plus, up to 17 years. Subjects were seen at 8 days, 6 weeks, 3, 6, 9, 12 and 18 months, then annually from 2 to 18 years. The aim was to obtain reasonably comprehensive information, which includes: (1) Regular interviews with mothers about their child's behaviour and parental methods; (2) testing of abilities, personality, etc; (3) assessment of interests, attitudes, personal values; and (4) interviews with adolescent subjects. Data on social and family background have been obtained throughout. The researchers interests have been: (i) Comparison of child-rearing methods and early locomotion across collaborating European samples; (ii) infant sleep and the effects of anoxia at birth; (iii) effects of daily substitute care; (iv) stability and change in IQs and personality using individual curve fitting in addition to correlations, etc; (v) factors influencing development – family, social, life events, school, etc; and (vi) children's views of themselves or school, of their future, and their correspondence with outcome.
Published Material: a full list of publications can be obtained from the researchers on request.
Source of Grant: Leverhulme Trust: £60,250
Date of Research: 1949 – continuing
KEYWORDS: ability; adolescence; child development; physical development

8/0715

Institute of Education
Department of Educational Psychology and Special Educational Needs, 24-27 Woburn Square,
London WC1H OAA
071 636 1500
Cowan, R.C.J. Dr
Studies of children's development of number competence
Abstract: Four experiments were conducted to examine 98 5-6 year olds' relative number judgments of small and large number displays with and without perceptual aids. It is noted that, although one-to-one correspondence can be seen as a component of successful counting, number conservation, and relative number judgments, there is evidence of considerable discrepancies between children's competencies in these different tasks, and these discrepancies reflect differences in criteria. In Experiment I (20 Ss) Ss' relative number judgments of small and large number versions of displays with and without guidelines were studied, while Ss' judgments of displays under conditions precluding a systematic pairing of elements in two columns was explored in Experiment II (24 Ss). In Experiment III (18 Ss), the precision with which Ss recognized non-correspondence was examined, and Ss' judgments of displays where the responses suggested by a density cue and by guidelines conflicted, were investigated in Experiment IV (28 Ss). Results indicate that Ss responded to local rather than global density differences and benefited from the provision of perceptual aids on both small and large number displays with the exception of large number displays where the longer row was less numerous. (Taken from Psychological Abstracts, Vol 72, January-June 1985).
Published Material: COWAN, R.C.J. (1982). 'Children's perception of length', Educational Psychology, Vol 2, pp.73-77.; COWAN, R.C.J. (1984). 'Children's relative number judgements: one-to-one correspondence, recognition of non correspondence, and the influence of cue conflict', Journal of Experimental Child Psychology, Vol 38, pp.515-532.; COWAN, R.C.J. (1985). 'Children's understandings of number: controversies in understanding children', British Psychological Society Section Review, Vol 9, pp.36-46.; COWAN, R.C.J. (1987). 'Assessing children's understanding of one-to-one correspondence', British Journal of Developmental Psychology, Vol 5, pp.149-153.; COWAN, R.C.J. (1987). 'When do children trust counting as a basis for relative number judgements?', Journal of Experimental Child Psychology, Vol 43, pp.328-345.; COWAN, R.C.J. & AL-ZUBAIDI, A.S. (1985). 'Social context effects on children's performance of number conservation tasks: plausibility and evidence', Educational Psychology, Vol 5, pp.267-278.
Source of Grant: No funding
Date of Research: 1980 – continuing
KEYWORDS: cognitive development; numeracy; primary education

8/0716

Institute of Education
Department of Mathematics, Statistics and Computing,
20 Bedford Way, London WC1H 0AL
071 636 1500
Carshalton High School for Girls
West Street, Carshalton SM5 2QX
081 647 8294
Clayton, J.G. Mr; *Supervisor:* Kuchemann, D. Dr (Department of Mathematics, Statistics and Computing); Moon, J. Dr (London Borough of Sutton)
Estimation in schools
Abstract: Cockcroft, HMI 5-16 and the National Curriculum have all encouraged the development of estimation skills for children in schools. For the purpose of this study, estimation will be defined as follows: The skill of making an 'educated guess' of a distance, cost, size, number, etc. or arithmetic calculation. An estimate will be defined as that 'educated guess'. Findings from this test programme indicated that many children: (1) Are able to estimate within 20% of the correct answer for many tasks, but (2) experienced difficulties when metric measures were involved, and (3) had difficulties when the answers involved large magnitudes. There did not appear to be any major differences between the distribution of answers for primary versus secondary children. Individual interviews focused upon these issues and evidence was found to suggest that children continue to use the Imperial system in their everyday lives. These interviews were also used to determine the strategies that children use when estimating, but this was not as successful as many children had difficulty in expressing these. Some evidence exists to show that they do not use computational estimation techniques readily. Further study is underway to determine means to encourage estimation and develop an understanding of strategies used to rationalize a means of assessing estimated answers.
Published Material: CLAYTON, J. (1988). 'Estimation', Mathematics Teaching, No 125, pp.18-19. December.
Source of Grant: School Curriculum Development Committee: £250 London Borough of Sutton: 75% of tuition plus travelling expenses
Date of Research: 1984-1990
KEYWORDS: concept formation; mathematics; problem solving

8/0717

Institute of Education
Department of Child Development and Primary Education,
24-27 Woburn Square, London WC1H OAA
071 636 1500 ext 708
Riley, J.L. Mrs; *Supervisor:* Versey, J. Dr; Curtis, A. Mrs
The first year of school and the factors that make it an effective educational experience for the child
Abstract: This year seven reception children in each of twenty-six classrooms have been monitored by assessment at the beginning and end of their first year in school. The chosen schools were all considered to be operating in roughly the same circumstances and drew on both council and private housing estates for their intake. The schools taking part in the research project were all recommended by LEA advisers and are in the counties of Oxfordshire, Berkshire and the boroughs of Haringay, Harrow and the Inner London Education Authority. The assessment of the children consisted of: (1) the BOEHM concept development test; (2) British Picture Vocabulary Scale; (3) draw-a-man test (Goodenow); (4) a test devised by the author based on Marie Clay concepts about print; (5) Neale's analysis of Reading; (6) tests of letters (both names and sounds) of alphabet; (7) known ability to write or copy their own name; (8) the Thompson School Adjustment questionnaire was completed by the class teacher after the first term in school. The initial screening in September of 1987 enabled the researcher to assess the progress, rather than merely the attainment, of the children in July 1988. It is hoped that it will be possible to make judgements as to what extent this was attributable to the class teacher. Many interesting facts are emerging as the data are being analyzed. An initial scan of the spread and distribution indicates, as already realized, but infrequently, quantified, that there is a huge range in the functioning of children as they enter full-time school. Similarly, at the end of the year, whole groups had made varying amounts of progress. Light may be shed on the reasons for these differences when the multivariate analyses are completed. Next year it is hoped to study in greater depth ten of the class teachers from this year's project. They have been selected for their apparent greater success. The children will be monitored at the beginning and at the end of the year as in year one. In depth interviews with

the teachers are planned to determine the aims and philosophy of the reception teachers and their methods for teaching reading. Also what curriculum they cover in the first year of school and whether all the children have equal exposure to it. Issues, such as the length and type of initial and inservice training also will be addressed.
Source of Grant: London University Advanced Student Grant: £100 Central Academic Fund: £500
Date of Research: 1987-1989
KEYWORDS: achievement; assessment; primary education; reception class; teacher

8/0718

Institute of Education
Department of Music Education,
20 Bedford Way, London WC1H OAL
071 636 1500
Taylor, D.A. Mrs; *Supervisor:* Swanwick, K. Prof.
(Department of Music Education); Versey, J. Dr
(Department of Educational Psychology and Special Educational Needs)
Physical movement and music education: the nature and role of the 'Kinaesthetic' sense
Abstract: This study is concerned with the nature of the 'Kinaesthetic' sense, its manifestation in bodily movement and its role in music education at all levels. Part empirical, part philosophical, the investigation falls into 3 parts: (1) music education through movement − in which the philosophy and practice of Emile Jaques-Dalcroze is described before the testing of the hypothesis that imagery for music, promoted through bodily movement, is more effective than conventional classroom music programmes; (2) motor activity and intellectual development centres on motor learning in the context of learning theory and cognitive growth; (3) from theory into practice − the music curriculum, where the findings of the preceeding parts provide the basis for postulating a theory of music teaching which is in accordance with aesthetic and psychological principles and in which physical movement plays a significant part.
Source of Grant: No funding
Date of Research: 1979 − continuing
KEYWORDS: cognitive development; motor development; music education; physical expression

8/0719

Institute of Education
Department of Child Development and Primary Education,
20 Bedford Way, London WC1H OAL
071 636 1500
Coe, J. Mr
Induction and further training during the first two years of teaching
Abstract: The researcher's intention is to match and contrast the stated aims and content of LEA Induction and Training Schemes with the actuality of his former student's experience.
Source of Grant: No funding
Date of Research: 1987 − continuing
KEYWORDS: further education; initial training; inservice training; probationary teacher; teacher education

8/0720

Institute of Education
Department of Educational Psychology and Special Educational Needs, 20 Bedford way, London WC1 OAL
071 636 1500
Rust, J. Dr
The Rust Inventory of Schizotypal Cognitions (RISC): A psychometric measure of psychoticism in the normal population
Abstract: The Rust Inventory of Schizoid Cognitions (RISC) is a new, psychometrically constructed, cognitively based, short (26 item) questionnaire of psychoticism. It differs from previous scales in having been developed and standardized with special attention to normal distribution in the general population, using cognitive theory to generate the relevant test specification. The scale has good reliability and validity, and can clearly discriminate acute schizophrenics from normals. Although containing no obviously extreme items, its cumulative effect may be used to identify bizarre and eccentric thought patterns and as an estimate of psychotic risk in the general population. It also has a use in research into the nature of cognitive development during adolescence, particularly in relationship to the development of existential thought, religious thought and personal identity.
Published Material: RUST, J. (1987). 'The Rust Inventory of Schizoid Cognitions (RISC): A psychometric measure of psychoticism

in the normal population', British Journal of Clinical Psychology, Vol 26, No 2, pp.151-152.; RUST, J. & CHIV, H. (1988). 'Schizothpa' estimators in adolescence: the concurrent validation of the RISC', Social Behaviour and Personality, Vol 16, No 1, pp.25-31.; RUST, J., MOMEADA, A. & PAGE, B. (1988). 'Personality dimensions through the schizophrenia border line', British Journal of Medical Psychology, Vol 61, pp.163-166.; RUST, J. (1988). 'The handbook of the Rust Inventory of schizotypal cognitions (RISC)'. The Psychological Corporation: London and San Antonio.; RUST, J. (1988). 'The Rust Inventory of schizotypal cognitions', Schizotypal Bulletin, Vol 14, No 2, pp.317-322.
Source of Grant: Institute Research Fund: £200
Date of Research: 1983 − continuing
KEYWORDS: adolescent; assessment; cognition; psychotic; schizophrenia; thinking

8/0721

Institute of Education
Department of Child Development and Primary Education, 24-27 Woburn Square, London WC1H OAA
071 636 1500
Curtis, A.M. Mrs
Observational study of 4 year olds in different institutional settings, with special reference to educational provision and the curriculum
Abstract: The aim of the research is to investigate differences in curricular provision for 4 year old children in day nurseries, playgroups, nursery classes and infant classes, using observation, questionnaires and interviews.
Source of Grant: No funding
Date of Research: 1987-1989
KEYWORDS: curriculum; early childhood; education; nursery school; playgroup; pre-school education;

8/0722

Institute of Education
Department of Mathematics, Statistics and Computing,
20 Bedford Way, London WC1H OAL
071 636 1500
Sutherland, R. Ms; *Supervisor:* Hoyles, C. Prof.; Noss, R. Dr
An INSET (Inservice Education and Training of Teachers) programme developing computer based microworlds for mathematics
Abstract: Considerable resources have been spent on equipping schools with computer hardware and software. At the same time, research in a range of contexts and countries has indicated that even the very best computer software cannot stand by itself. These studies have all confirmed that the teacher assumes a critical role in children's computer based activities, and one which may differ in a number of important respects from that traditionally adopted. This project is based on a recognition that (a) there exists a considerable need on the part of mathematics teachers to learn about and apply the computer in their way, and (b) in particular roles, the computer can have a positively influential effect on the education and training of mathematics teachers. This research is aimed at investigating the educational potential for the mathematics classroom of a small number of powerful computer applications. Some of them, such as the LOGO programming language were specifically designed with education in mind. Others, such as 'spreadsheet' programs were not. In each case, the research is aimed at structuring these applications with pedagogic aims and objectives. The aims of this proposal are to develop, implement and evaluate a programme of inservice teacher education concerned with the use of some content free computer applications in mathematics. Experienced secondary mathematics teachers will be seconded for 30 days in the academic year, to gain experience of the applications, examine the educational implications of the software, and to design and test computer based educational environments for the classroom. The outcomes of the work will be: (1) a description of this computer based INSET programme and its evaluation; (2) one or two computer based microworlds which are 'built into' the school mathematics curriculum and their evaluation in terms of specific mathematical learning outcomes.
Published Material: HOYLES, C., SUTHERLAND, R. & NOSS, R. (1986). 'An INSET programme developing microworlds for secondary mathematics', ESRC, Research in Progress, May.
Source of Grant: Economic and Social Research Council (ESRC): £73,070
Date of Research: 1986-1989

KEYWORDS: computer assisted instruction; inservice education and training of teachers; mathematics; teaching

8/0723

Institute of Education
Department of Educational Psychology and Special Educational Needs, 20 Bedford Way, London WC1H OAL
071 636 1500
Brighton Polytechnic
Chelsea School of Human Movement Studies,
Trevin Towers, Gaudick Road, Eastbourne BN20 7SR
0323 21400
Allen, J. Dr; *Supervisor:* Henderson, S.E. Dr

A study of motor development in Down's Syndrome children

Abstract: The general aim of this research is the understanding of motor development in children with Down's Syndrome. More specifically, the researchers' concern is with the temporal aspects of motor control and the question of whether Down's Syndrome children have a specific problem in this area. So far, the focus of the work has been on school aged children and the methodology employed has been experimental. Twelve experiments, each with a slightly different focus, have been completed so far. Some of these have been published, the others are at various stages of analysis. In future, the intention is to expand the work to include pre-school children and to use a combination of observational and experimental techniques. The findings may be of interest to both teachers and physiotherapists.

Published Material: HENDERSON, S.E., MORRIS, J. & RAY, S. (1981). 'Performance of Down's Syndrome and other mentally retarded children on the Cratty Gross Motor Test', American Journal of Mental Deficiency, Vol 85, pp.416-424.; HENDERSON, S.E., MORRIS, J. & FRITH, U. (1981). 'The Motor Deficit in Down's Syndrome: a problem of timing?', Journal of Child Psychology and Psychiatry, Vol 22, pp.233-245.; HENDERSON, S.E. (1985). 'Motor skill development'. In: STRATFORD, B. & LANE, D. (Eds). Current approaches to Down's Syndrome, Eastbourne: Holt, Rinehart & Winston.; HENDERSON, S.E. (1986). 'Some aspects of the development of motor control in Down's Syndrome'. In: WHITING, H.T.A & WADE, M. (Eds). Motor skill acquisition – aspects of co-ordination and control, Dordrecht, The Netherlands: Martins Nijhoff Publishers B.V.

Source of Grant: Polytechnic funding for student registered for CNAA degree London University Institute of Education Research Fund: £500

Date of Research: 1986 – continuing

KEYWORDS: *Down's Syndrome; mental retardation; motor development; physical*

8/0724

Institute of Education
Department of English and Media Studies,
20 Bedford Way, London WC1H OAL
071 636 1500
Smith's College
Lewisham Way, New Cross, London SE14 6NW
081 692 7171
Gregory, E. Ms; *Supervisor:* Spencer, M.D.

Beginning reading in the multilingual classroom: The role of a joint creation of culture between teacher and child

Abstract: This study focuses on the ways in which 8 children (4 monolingual, 4 bilingual) from different social backgrounds set about learning to read upon entering infant school. The problem studied is why, in spite of apparent linguistic, social and cultural 'disadvantage', some children step quickly and easily into school literacy, whilst others do not. The study questions what may enable some children to gain success. After assessing a number of possible contributing factors, the study proposes ways in which a 'joint creation of culture' may be negotiated between teacher and child.

Published Material: GREGORY, E. (1983). 'Laying infant bricks in the secondary School?', Language Arts, Vol 60, No 8, pp.983-987.; GREGORY, E. & PENMAN, D. (1983). 'Investigating the potential of the mother tongue in school', English in Education, Spring.; GREGORY, E. (1984). 'A story, a story....', English in Education, Summer, pp.40-49.; GREGORY, E. (1984). 'Just the tea-lady, or more? the story of a women's writing group', Child Education, pp.15, October.; GREGORY, E. (1988). 'Reading with mother'. In: MILLS, C. & SPENCER, M. (Eds). New directions in literacy. Lewes: Falmer Press.

Source of Grant: Goldsmith's College plus some self financing

Date of Research: 1985 – continuing

KEYWORDS: literacy; multilingualism; primary education; reading; social origin

8/0725

Institute of Education
Department of Educational Psychology and Special Educational Needs, 20 Bedford Way, London WC1H 0AL
071 636 1500
Vaughan, T.D. Dr

An enquiry into conditions that may influence creative ability

Abstract: A questionnaire, adapted from work at the University of New Brunswick, was constructed. It examined the importance of such variables as time of day, aloneness, influence of others, influence of distraction, continuity versus simultaneous attention, and alterations of consciousness on entering and leaving sleep, on the perceived ability to develop effective lines of thought and/or work. This questionnaire was given to 54 students at a secondary school in Cambridgeshire, to 42 students at the College of the Royal Academy of Dancing in London, to 9 students following a postgraduate music teachers' course at the Institute of Education of London University, and to 20 students following a Master's course. Results indicated a definite pattern of conditions, with aloneness, time of day and social conditions significantly inter-related, among others: Analysis by chi-square and multi-dimension frequency analysis.

Source of Grant: No funding

Date of Research: 1984 – continuing

KEYWORDS: *creativity; gifted; intellectual development; intelligence; stimulus; thinking*

8/0726

Institute of Education
Department of English and Media Studies,
20 Bedford Way, London WC1H OAL
071 636 1500 ext 408
University of California
Centre for the Study of Writing,
School of Education, Berkeley, USA
McLeod, A.O. Mr; Freedman, S.W. Dr; *Supervisor:*
McLeod, A.O. Mr; Freedman, S.W. Dr

Writing exchange across the Atlantic: a study of secondary school students' writing, exchanged with peers in London and the Bay Area, California

Abstract: Following a survey of the teaching of writing in the USA and the UK (now being analyzed and published) an exchange of secondary school student writing (age 12-15) has been arranged between 5 classes in California and 5 classes in the London Area in 1986/87. The hypothesis is that an actual peer audience for student writing over a period of a whole school year, will reveal changes in the quality, interest and commitment of the student writers. The 10 classroom teachers will evaluate the outcome in the first instance. The principal researchers will collaborate on a report on the whole project.

Source of Grant: US National Writing Project: continuous grant – total unknown

Date of Research: 1986 – continuing

KEYWORDS: *cultural exchange; peer group; secondary education; United States of America; verbal communication; writing*

8/0727

Institute of Education
Education Management Unit,
20 Bedford Way, London WC1H OAL
071 636 1500
Ouston, J. Dr

The evaluation of Education 2000: The Hertfordshire Project

Abstract: The Education 2000 Hertfordshire Project, which is based in 6 secondary schools in Letchworth, is the first project funded by the Education 2000 Trust. The Trust's aim is to encourage long term planning for the country's educational needs in the 21st century. It is concerned with the development of the secondary school curriculum and with alternative patterns of INSET (Inservice Education and Training of Teachers) for teachers, making use of advances in 'new technology'. It also aims to involve parents and the wider community in the development process. The evaluation of the Project will use a variety of methods and approaches to record its implementation and the responses of pupils, including questionnaires, interviews and observations. It will continue for 1 year beyond the end of the additional resources provided by the Project, and will be able to begin to assess the extent to which the new initia-

tives become part of ordinary school practice.
Source of Grant: Department of Education and Science: £173,385
Baring Foundation: £16,000
Date of Research: 1987-1990
KEYWORDS: curriculum development; information technology; inservice education and of teachers; planning of education; secondary education

8/0728
> Institute of Education
> Department of Educational Psychology and Special
> Educational Needs, 20 Bedford Way, London WC1H OAL
> 071 636 1500
> ILEA Schools' Psychological Service
> Brixton Child Guidance Unit,
> Brixton Water Lane, London SW2
> 071 274 5459
> Corley, B.M.G. Miss; *Supervisor:* Francis, H. Prof.; Pring, L. Dr

A study of how visually impaired children in their regular school classes tackle specific cognitive tasks
Abstract: Many studies of visually impaired children have focused on the congenitally blind. This study follows on the work of Richard Lansdown and Joan Reynell. It is of partially sighted children; a very heterogeneous group. The children are of school age, worked with in school and are representative of the partially sighted population in terms of variety of eye condition and additional disability. The sample consists of 6 girls and 5 boys aged 6, through 9 years in a school for PS (partially sighted) children. The areas being studied are reading, spelling, visual memory and language. This small sample is being studied in depth over a number of years and is set against a background of an epidemiological survey of PS children of all ages in ordinary schools in 3 inner city areas of London. The method being used is to study each child over a period of time, with a series of experiments to examine aspects of visual recall and recognition, and of language development, coupled with tape recorded reading and classroom conversations. Reading and spelling are tested at intervals. Tentative results and conclusions reveal that PS children learn to read by careful and individualized phonic tuition using appropriate magnification aids and largely without the benefit of pictures. They have some difficulty at the orthographic level of spelling.
Source of Grant: No funding
Date of Research: 1984 – continuing
KEYWORDS: blind; learning strategy; reading; spelling; visually handicapped; visual perception

8/0729
> Institute of Education
> Department of Educational Psychology and Special
> Educational Needs, 20 Bedford Way, London WC1H OAL
> 071 636 1500
> Henderson, S. Dr

Further development of the Henderson Revision of the Test of Motor Impairment
Abstract: The Henderson Revision of the Test of Motor Impairment was published in 1984. Normative data on children in the UK and Canada is contained in the manual and a US Standardization is now under way. When the US data is analyzed, information on approximately 2,000 children will be available. Several reliability and validity studies have been completed and are either published or being written up. A very valuable aspect of the test from an educational viewpoint is the series of checklists which accompany the standard form of the test. They provide the teacher with a way of analyzing the problems that children who have motor difficulties have with each task. Further work on this component of the test is in progress.
Published Material: HENDERSON, S.E. (1984). 'The Henderson Revision of the Test of Motor Impairment', British Journal of Physical Education, Vol 15, pp.73-75.; SCOTT, D.H., MOYES, F.A & HENDERSON, S.E. (1985). 'Test of Motor Impairment (Henderson Revision)', The Psychological Corporation, San Antonio, Texas, USA; Toronto, Canada; and London, UK.; SCOTT, D.H., HENDERSON, S.E. & MOYES, F.A. (1986). 'The Henderson Revision of the Test of Motor Impairment: a comprehenseive approach to assessment', Adapted Physical Activity Quarterly, Vol 3, pp.204-216.; HENDERSON, S.E. (1987). 'The assessment of clumsiness in children: old and new approaches', Journal of Child Psychology and Psychiatry, Vol 28, No 4, pp.511-527, July.
Source of Grant: No funding at present. Previous funding from

National Foundation for Research into Crippling Diseases in Children 1977-80 and London University Central Research Fund
Date of Research: 1986 – continuing
KEYWORDS: motor development; physical education; physically handicapped; psychomotor test; special education

8/0730
> Institute of Education
> Department of Educational Pscycholgy and Special
> Educational Needs,
> 24-27 Woburn Square, London WC1H OAA
> 071 636 1500
> Worrall, N. Dr

Teacher-pupil relationships in the primary classroom
Abstract: This is continuing research being carried out with colleagues and research students. The sample size of a given study varies from 30 to 100. Methods have been mainly questionnaires/rating scales, increasingly supplemented by interviews. Topics explored range from child autonomy through differential curricular experiences and the development of mutual regard between children and teachers.
Published Material: INGRAM, J. & WORRALL, N. (1987). 'The negotiating classroom', Early Child Development and Care, Vol 28, pp.401-415.; WORAALL, N. & TSARNA, H. (1987). 'Teachers' reported practices towards boys and girls in science and languages', British Journal of Educational Psychology, Vol 57, pp.300-312.; WORRALL, N., WORRAL, C. & MELDRUM, C. (1988). 'Children's reciprocations of teacher evaluations', British Journal of Educational Psychology, Vol 58, pp.78-88.
Source of Grant: No funding
Date of Research: 1987 – continuing
KEYWORDS: primary education; teacher-pupil relation

8/0731
> Institute of Education
> Department of English and Media Studies,
> 20 Bedford Way, London WC1H OAL
> 071 636 1500
> College of the Bahamas
> PO Box N.8843, Nassau, Bahamas
> Wright, L.M. Mrs; *Supervisor:* McLeod, A.O. Mr

An analysis of the sociolinguistics of the Creole-standard continuum and its relationship to education in a selected sample of secondary schools in Jamaica
Abstract: This research involves 530 Grade 9 pupils aged 15 + and 54 Grade 9 teachers and the purpose of the present investigation is to: (1) determine and describe the nature of the sociolinguistic situation in a selected sample of Jamaican secondary schools by focusing on (a) the attitudes of pupils and their teachers to Jamaican Creole and Standard English, (b) pupils' perceptions of the role and status of both languages, (c) pupils' experience of, and their reactions to, criticism of Creole use at home and in school, (d) linguistic focusing and patterns of language use, (e) language variability evidenced by specimens of pupils' writing; (2) explore in some depth critical issues arising out of (1) above, e.g. the mesolect, or interlanguage; (3) assess the training levels and linguistic expertise of teachers in relation to national language goals set for this secondary sector; (4) criticize the gap between the rhetoric of avowed national goals and the realities of Grade 9 classrooms; and (5) make recommendations for language and linguistic training for teacher education, and in so doing, challenge traditionally held assumptions about language teaching and teacher education.
Source of Grant: No funding
Date of Research: 1983-1989
KEYWORDS: Jamaica; language teaching; mother tongue; secondary education; sociolinguistics; teacher education

8/0732
> Institute of Education
> Department of Educational Psychology and Special
> Educational Needs, 20 Bedford Way, London WC1H OAL
> 071 636 1500
> Earp, P. Ms; *Supervisor:* Ware, J. Dr; Norwich, B. Dr

Social interactions around microcomputers between children with severe learning difficulties
Abstract: It is known that pupils working with a microcomputer not only interact with the micro but also with each other. Pupils with severe learning difficulties are also known to interact more with each other when adults take a less dominant role. The study has already investigated the extent to which children with severe

learning difficulties spontaneously interact when using a micro without the presence of an adult. An alternating treatments design was used to compare the effectiveness of the two conditions: computer and non-computer activities for improving the social interaction of two children with severe learning difficulties. The computer condition reliably increased the task-relevant social responses of both children, whereas the non-computer condition increased responses although many of these are non-task relevant. The current experiment is a follow up study which also uses an alternating treatments design where the two conditions are: computer with an adult and computer without an adult. The two children used for this experiment are not the same as for the last, although they do have severe learning difficulties.
Source of Grant: ILEA (Inner London Education Authority): Fees paid (1987-1989)
Date of Research: 1987 – continuing
KEYWORDS: computer assisted instruction; learning difficulty; mentally handicapped; microcomputer; social interaction

8/0733

Institute of Education
Department of Music,
20 Bedford Way, London WC1H OAU
071 636 1500
Dunn, A. Mrs; *Supervisor:* Swanwick, K. Prof.
Music in adult education
Abstract: This is an analysis of the literature on adult education along with empirical work to determine an appropriate model for adults learning music in institutes of adult education. The model is derived from a study of current thought and practice in adult education and an analysis of musical experience and its development.
Source of Grant: No funding
Date of Research: 1980-1989
KEYWORDS: adult education; music education

8/0734

Institute of Education
Department of Mathematics, Statistics and Computing,
11 Woburn Square, London WC1H ONS
071 636 8000
Grey, A. Ms; Wolf, A. Mrs; *Supervisor:* Hoyles, C. Prof.
The integration of TVEI (Technical and Vocational Education Initiative) technology options with mathematics
Abstract: This project involves the Institute of Education and the London Boroughs of Harrow, Ealing, Hillingdon, Kingston, Merton and Richmond, and is funded by the Training Agency as a Joint Support Activity for TVEI (Technical and Vocational Education Initiative). The aim is to develop teaching materials which integrate mathematics with three other areas of the curriculum: design and technology, food technology, business studies/information technology. The materials are initially being developed for pupils following GCSE (General Certificate of Secondary Education) courses, but later on pupils in the 16-18 age group will be included. The project team will be responsible for: (1) the design and development of learning materials related to the mathematics requirements of the three TVEI options listed, and designed for use in mathematics and other subject classrooms; (2) Inservice teacher training, with particular emphasis on: (i) providing mathematics teachers with materials to encourage problem solving and investigation work related to the the technological world; (ii) increasing the expertise of non-mathematics specialists in developing students' ability to use mathematics in applied contexts; (iii) creating incentives, in terms of curriculum materials, for collaboration between departments and across boroughs; (3) Introduction of the modules as appropriate into schools and colleges with evaluation and modification; (4) the development of assignments which cut across subject boundaries, including GCSE coursework. The project team are therefore working with the examination boards from an early stage.
Published Material: WOLF, A. & GREY, A. (1988). 'Right for the job', Times Education Supplement, Maths Extra, 30 Sept.1988, pp.68.
Source of Grant: Training Agency: Joint Support Activities; £25,000 over 3 years
Date of Research: 1988-1990
KEYWORDS: inservice education and training of teachers; mathematics; teaching aids; Technical and Vocational Education Initiative

8/0735

Institute of Education
Department of Music,
20 Bedford Way, London WC1H OAL
071 636 1500
Martin, M. Mrs; *Supervisor:* Swanwick, K. Prof.
Music in initial teacher training
Abstract: This is a partly longitudinal study of students on courses and in the years following the course out in the teaching profession. The methodology includes an analysis of personality, career and professional profiles, attitudes and the educational and personal background of each subject.
Source of Grant: No funding
Date of Research: 1982-1990
KEYWORDS: music education; teacher education

8/0736

Institute of Education
Department of Mathematics, Statistics & Computing,
20 Bedford Way, London WC1H OAL
071 636 1500 ext 449
Sussex University
Department of Continuning and Professional Education
Falmer, Brighton BN1 9RG
0273 678039
Eraut, M.R. Prof.; Hoyles, C. Prof.
Group work with computers
Abstract: Because of the scarcity of computers, pupils using them frequently work in groups. However, the potential of groupwork is rarely exploited, and collaborative learning in such groups happens more by chance than design. There are some compelling theoretical reasons for believing that groupwork has considerable potential for the enhancement of learning. Psychologists believe that for some learning goals and tasks, groupwork is likely to be more effective than individual learning. This project will seek to provide guidance to teachers seeking to gain the maximum benefit from the use of computers. It will focus on seven questions: (1) For what types of learning goal is groupwork with computers most appropriate? (2) What is its potential contribution to the curriculum? (3) How can computer and non-computer based tasks be designed which facilitate groupwork? (4) Is it possible to identify criteria for task design, group management and their interrelationships, for effective groupwork to be established? (5) What kinds of group are best for achieving particular goals? (6) How can such groupwork best be prepared for, implemented and evaluated? (7) Is training in collaborative groupwork a significant advantage?
Published Material: ERAUT, M. & HOYLES, C. (1988). Groupwork with computers, Occasional Paper INTER/3/88. University of Lancaster, Department of Psychology: ESRC.
Source of Grant: Economic and Social Research Council: £124,983 (each centre)
Date of Research: 1988 – continuing
KEYWORDS: computer; group work; primary education

8/0737

Institute of Education
Department of English and Media Studies,
20 Bedford Way, London WC1H OAL
071 636 1500
Jones, B.M. Ms; *Supervisor:* Burgess, A.M.K. Dr
Six case studies of the writing development of 15/16 year-old students of Afro-Caribbean background: issues and dimensions
Abstract: Most of the assumptions about the achievement (or non achievement) of Afro-Caribbean students, both in their native setting and abroad, are usually made on the basis of the differences between Caribbean and standard English dialects. Consequently, investigations into students' use of language have concentrated on patterns of dialect difference and dialect interference. Within such a concentration, the focus has been on language in general, rather than on making the distinction between oral and written language. This study strives to give equal weight to linguistic and cultural issues. The students in this study, British born of Afro-Caribbean parentage, do not 'fit' within studies of any narrow assumptions about language development. Their insertion within a unique social history demands studies foregrounding their total linguistic and cultural experience. In seeking to investigate language development in multicultural classrooms and teachers' strategy in promoting this, the study examines the traditional models of language development in order to determine how language variation 'sits' within these traditions. More specifically the study focuses on the writing

development of 15-16 year old students of Afro-Caribbean background, in two London schools. The more detailed empirical work (classroom based case studies) suggests that the difficulties of the writing task may be generalizable across all 15-16 year old school children. With regard to students from working class and/or ethnic minority groups including those of Afro-Caribbean background, traditional racial/ethnic type assumptions about classroom performance and consequently achievement may still be ingrained, and so continue to mask contemporary classroom realities.
Source of Grant: Social Sciences and Humanities Research Council of Canada: CA.[12,120 average per annum (to March 1989 Only) Manitoba Teachers' Society Scholarship: CA.[2,400 total
Date of Research: 1985-1989
KEYWORDS: achievement; Afro-Caribbean youth; cultural background; language development; multicultural education; writing

8/0738
Institute of Education
Department of Child Development and Primary Education,
24-27 Woburn Square, London WC1H OAA
071 636 1500
Hurst, A.V.M. Mrs; *Supervisor:* Versey, J. Dr; Curtis, A. Mrs
The development of self confidence in nursery school children and related aspects of non-verbal behaviour
Abstract: The aim of this research is to find ways in which self confidence can be enhanced for children in nursery school. A 2 year longitudinal study, using naturalistic observation in one nursery school, has been undertaken in order to trace development of self confidence. An observation scale of 12 categories of behaviour which are thought to indicate self confidence is being used. Related aspects of non-verbal behaviour are observed, with a scale of 5 categories. The social situation is also recorded. The sample consists of 12 children, aged 3-5 years, in a cohort of 4, observed for 3 x 10 minute periods 4 times each term throughout the 2 years of their nursery attendance. A temperament scale, Barr & Plomin EAS 1984, has been used, by parents and staff. The results so far, after 1 year's observation, shows that most of the confidence categories were attained by the end of the first year, showing a general increase in amount, and sometimes a 'spurt' during the second term. Some aspects of non-verbal behaviour may be a useful measure of self confidence. The non-verbal behaviour of the adult is important, and some observations are being made in that area. The Temperament Scale shows a tendency for parents to agree with each other and nursery staff to agree with each other but not always with the parents.
Source of Grant: No funding (except £170 from an Educational Trust)
Date of Research: 1986 – continuing
KEYWORDS: confidence; non-verbal communication; pre-school child; self-esteem

8/0739
Institute of Education
Department of Curriculum Studies, 20 Bedford Way, London WC1H OAL
071 636 1500
Thames Polytechnic
Department of Primary Education
Bexley Road, London SE9 2PQ
081 789 6533
Harland, L.A. Ms; *Supervisor:* Gipps, C, Dr
Supporting teachers, supporting children with special educational needs: an exploration of the partnership between class teachers and support teachers
Abstract: The role of the Support Teacher is changing extensively. It is assumed that the move from withdrawing children with special educational needs from the classroom, towards working within the classroom, with the accompanying need to advise/consult the class teacher, has resulted in a qualitative improvement of educational provisions for these children. Questions are proposed which will explore the nature of the partnership between support teacher and class teachers. It is intended to uncover some of the tensions which accompany the work of the support teacher. So far there has been little evaluation of any possible improvement in educational provision for children with special educational needs which may have been accounted for by support teacher/class teacher collaboration.
Source of Grant: No funding
Date of Research: 1986 – continuing

KEYWORDS: class management; special education; special needs; support teacher

8/0740
Institute of Education
Department of International and Comparative Education,
20 Bedford Way, London WC1 OAL
071 636 1500
Sussex University
Department of Contiuing and Professional Education
Falmer, Brighton BN1 9RG
0273 606755 ext 2490
Lillis, K. Dr; Gardner, R. Dr; Hurst, P. Dr; Stephens, D. Dr; *Supervisor:* Hawes, H. Dr
Project to improve primary education leadership through a link between Kenyatta University and the University of London Institute of Education
Abstract: The purpose of this project is to establish a new B.Ed. programme for primary education in Kenya at Kenyatta University; to develop and write materials for that programme; to train staff for it and to monitor the whole process. The B.Ed. degree commenced in September 1985. The training, staff development and materials production phase of the programme are well under way. A series of teacher educator handbooks covering the curriculum have been produced and are being trialled and evaluated.
Published Material: A series of teacher handbooks bave been produced by the Department of Education, Communication and Technology, Kenyatta University, Kenyatta, (under direction of Professor H.O. Ayot).
Source of Grant: Overseas Development Administration
Date of Research: 1983-1989
KEYWORDS: Kenya; leadership; primary education; teacher education

8/0741
Institute of Education
Department of International and Comparative Education,
20 Bedford Way, London WC1 OAL
071 636 1500
Sussex University
Department of Continuing and Professional Education
Falmer, Brighton BN1 9RG
0273 606755
Hawes, H. Mr; Gardner, R. Mr; Stephens, D. Dr
The Cianjur Supervision Project: professional support for teachers in primary schools
Abstract: The purpose of this project was to set up a working model of a support system for primary teachers involving retraining of field supervisors and heads and the operation of a continuous inservice programme through the establishment of local teachers' groups and an in-school improvement programme. The first phase of the project, involving continuous monitoring of operations in three sub-districts and a final evaluation, operated from 1979-1984. In the current phase, the project has expanded to involve two other geographical areas and the establishment and monitoring of university-based resource centres operated as a focus for primary leadership.
Published Material: HAWES, H. (1982). Professional suport for teachers in schools: an Indonesian case study. EDC Occasional Paper No 3. London: University of London; Institute of Education.; STEPHENS, D.G. (1987). Video film: The Cianjur project – professional support for Indonesian primary school teachers. IBERD, Government of Indonesia (Copy available from Education Area, University of Sussex).
Source of Grant: Indonesian Bureau of Educational Research and Development; Government of Indonesia
Date of Research: 1979 – continuing
KEYWORDS: Indonesia; inservice education and training of teachers; primary education

8/0742
Institute of Education
20 Bedford Way, London WC1M OAL
071 636 1500
West London Institute of Higher Education
300 St Margaret's Road, Twickenham TW1 1PT
081 891 0121
Garner, P. Mr; *Supervisor:* Raynor, J. Prof.; Jones, C. Mr
Aspects of provision for 'disruptive' pupils in the United Kingdom and the United States of America: a comparative study

Abstract: The research will attempt to make a definition of 'disruptive' pupil, establishing similarities and/or differences between the UK/USA. Then an analysis will be made of characteristics of provision with particular reference to aims/objectives, organization, pedagogy and curriculum. The study will attempt comparisons of the two educational systems based upon data collected from an urban area in the UK and USA: initially a whole LEA or school board area will be surveyed by questionnaire; individual institutions will be then selected for case study. It is expected that such work should involve extended field work in both the USA and the UK.
Source of Grant: Part funded by West London Institute
Date of Research: 1988 – continuing
KEYWORDS: *comparative education; disruptive pupils; United States of America*

8/0743

Institute of Education
Department of English,
20 Bedford Way, London WC1M 0AL
071 636 1500
West Sussex Institute of Higher Education
Bishop Otter College, College Lane, Chichester,
West Sussex PO19 4PE
0243 787911
Brider, J.E. Mr; *Supervisor:* Spencer, M. Mrs

The non-teacher directed peer-group classroom talk of nine-year olds

Abstract: Observations and tape-recordings will be made of peer group non-teacher-directed talk in an opportunity sample of classrooms of nine-year-olds' in the context of whole class and group teaching strategies. Analysis will be carried out using various historical methodologies of analysis of transcripts to isolate talk which others have ignored.
Source of Grant: Fees paid by employer
Date of Research: 1984 – continuing
KEYWORDS: *peer group; primary education; verbal interaction*

8/0744

Institute of Education
Department of Mathematics, Statistics and Computing,
20 Bedford Way, London WC1H 0AL
071 636 1500
Wolf, A. Mrs; Grey, A. Ms

Mathematics and Technical and Vocational Education Initiative (TVEI)

Abstract: The project is developing and piloting materials which integrate mathematics and technology including business and food studies. A variety of topics, formats and approaches are being piloted in 7 local education authorities. The project is also investigating the feasibility of cross-curricular assessment, and of delivering National Curriculum targets through cross-curricular tasks.
Source of Grant: Training Enterprise Education Division: £130,000
Date of Research: 1988-1990
KEYWORDS: *curriculum development; mathematics; Technical and Vocational Education Initiative; technology*

8/0745

Institute of Education
Department of English and Media Studies,
20 Bedford Way, London WC1 0AL
071 636 1500
Buckingham, D.D. Mr

The development of television literacy in middle childhood and adolescence

Abstract: This research will investigate the development of children's competencies as television viewers between the ages of seven and twelve. The research will be primarily qualitative, and will concentrate particularly on the ways in which interpretations of the medium are established and negotiated in small group talk. It will also focus on the role of social class, gender and ethnic background in determining children's understanding and use of the medium. A core sample of ninety children will be interviewed both individually and in small groups on a total of eight occasions over an 18 month period. Additional interviews will be held with their teachers and parents; and control groups will be used at appropriate stages. Interviews will be transcribed and analysed using techniques derived from social semiotics and discourse analysis. Particular aspects of study will include the development of children's conceptions of television genres and narrative forms; their judgements about its

representations of the social world and its degrees of realism; and their understanding of the processes of television production. The project aims to provide an analysis of children's understanding of television which will enable broadcasters and educationalists to respond constructively to public concern about the 'effects' of the medium. In particular, it is hoped that the research will inform the development of media education within the National Curriculum.
Source of Grant: Economic and Social Research Council: £103,000
Date of Research: 1989 – continuing
KEYWORDS: *child; comprehension; media studies; television*

8/0746

Institute of Education
Department of Mathematics, Statistics and Computing,
20 Bedford Way, London WC1H 0AK
071 636 1500
Wolf, A. Mrs; Silver, R. Ms

Learning in context

Abstract: Follow-up to a large project (1985-1988) which investigated the effects of different training approaches on skill transfer. The original project established that training/teaching in varied contexts was more effective than single-context teaching in promoting skill transfer using data from exercises administered to over 1000 subjects. The current project involves further analysis of the data base with repect to: (a) the effectiveness with which future performance can be predicted within and across contexts; (b) problem-solving strategies adopted by individuals.
Source of Grant: Training Enterprise Education Division: £35,000
Date of Research: 1988-1990
KEYWORDS: *learning process; problem solving; skill; training; transfer of learning; vocational education*

8/0747

Institute of Education
Department of Mathematics Statistics and Computing,
20 Bedford Way, London WC1H 0AL
071 636 8000
Healy, L. Ms; Hoyles, C. Prof.; Sutherland, R. Dr

The role of peer group discussion in a computer environment

Abstract: The research project is concerned with an analysis of the way pupils working in pairs make generalizations and come to formalize them in mathematics. The hypothesis is that peer discussion and the distinctive nature of an interactive computer environment, a Logo programming environment, and a paper and pencil environment. The aims of the research are to: investigate the inter-relationship between the negotiation of the generalization by the pupil pair and its formal representation; investigate any effects on pupil response of the problem solving tools made available by the different environments. One research task has been designed for each of the three environments. The common element of each task is the requirement to identify and formalize relationships embedded within specific cases defined by both visual images and numbers. These tasks were given to 4 pairs of children during their mathematics lessons. All the pupils' spoken language and computer input and output was recorded during the administration of these tasks by means of a video recording.
Published Material: HEALY, S. & SUTHERLAND, R. (1988). Using spreadsheets for mathematics education: A Reader. London: London Institute of Education, University of London.; HOYLES, C. HEALY, S. & SUTHERLAND, R. (1989). 'Children talking in computer environments: New insights into the role of discussion in mathematics learning', In: DURKIN, K. (Ed). Languages and mathematics education.
Source of Grant: Leverhulme Trust: £42,550
Date of Research: 1988-1989
KEYWORDS: *cognitive process; computer assisted instruction; discussion; mathematics*

8/0748

Institute of Education
20 Bedford Way, London WC1 0AL
071 636 1500
Swanwick, K. Prof.

Teacher education and the Post-Graduate Certificate in Education (PGCE) course

Abstract: This study was a small-scale and largely qualitative probe into the positive side of student attitudes to a large Post-Graduate Certificate in Education (PGCE) course and the views of school teachers associated with it in those schools used on teaching prac-

tice. Students of this PGCE course particularly valued the contributions of the institution in giving systematic help with teaching skills, redefining curriculum subjects in relevant and inter-cultural ways, setting the social and psychological context of educational transactions, giving dependable professional and personal support and encouraging critical thinking against a background of broad and structured school experience. The 198 responses from teachers in primary and secondary schools involved with PGCE from this institution were analysed. These responses cited lack of time, the demands of pupils or lack of training and resources as reasons for what was generally a negative response, when asked if they thought they could support training of teachers in their own schools totally. One in three hardly ever helped students organize materials and almost two out of five give hardly any help with detailed lesson planning and one in four offered no help in basic ideas for lessons.
Published Material: STANWICK, K. (1989). Teacher education and Post-Graduate Certificain Education course: A research report, Institute of Education, University of London.
Source of Grant: University funds: £1500
Date of Research: 1988-1989
KEYWORDS: *post-graduate study; teacher education; teaching practice*

8/0749

>Institute of Education
>Department of English and Media Studies,
>20 Bedford Way, London WC1H 0AL
>071 636 1500
>Furlong, T. Mr; Burgess, A.M.K. Dr

Development of Standard Assessment Tasks (SATs) at the end of Key Stage 3 in the National Curriculum for English
Abstract: The work requires the development of Standard Assessment Tasks (SATs) for English. SATs will be constructed to include written and oral work, so that a pupil's performance can be set against any of the ten levels associated with the National Curriculum attainment targets. Trialling in selected Local Education Authorities will be carried out in 1989-90, a pilot exercise on a broader sample in 1991, and a full scale unreported assessment in summer 1992.
Source of Grant: School Examinations and Assessment Council (SEAC): £1,883,000
Date of Research: 1989 – continuing
KEYWORDS: *assessment; English language; secondary education; standard assessment task*

8/0750

>Institute of Education
>Department of Music,
>20 Bedford Way, London WC1H 0AL
>071 636 1500
>Swanwick, K. Prof.

A study of the Tower Hamlets string teaching project
Abstract: The research procedure of this study follows two paths. Firstly, there is to be a review of the available documentation on the project – including video recordings and material at the local education authority (LEA) music centre – will be systematically examined to determine the history, organization and philosophy of this work. Secondly, during a period of up to 8 weeks interviews will be conducted with associated personnel and there will be systematic observation of teaching and learning in the Tower Hamlets centre. The objective here is to ascertain the quality of the learning transaction and to document this unique project.
Published Material: SWANWICK, K. & JARVIS, C. (1990). The Tower Hamlets string teaching project: a research report. London: University of London, Institute of Education
Source of Grant: Baring Foundation: £13,000
Date of Research: 1989-1990
KEYWORDS: *local education authority; music education; musical intrument*

8/0751

>Institute of Education
>Department of Mathematics, Statistics and Computing,
>20 Bedford Way, London WC1H 0AL
>071 636 1500
>Goldstein, H. Prof.

Developing and disseminating multilevel models
Abstract: This project extends the work of the earlier project entitled 'Developing the use of multilevel models'. The three aims of the current project are as follows: (1) to disseminate knowledge

of multilevel modelling to the social science research community through conferences, seminars and training sessions in the use of statistical software developed for this form of analysis; (2) to extend existing methodology, especially in the area of time series and linear structural relations models; and (3) to study the practical application of the models to real data sets, especially with a view to increasing robustness and developing data diagnostic procedures. Work is in progress in many domains including the following: improving the operational efficiency of the iterative generalized least squares (IGLS) algorithm used in fitting multilevel models; comparing the IGLS algorithm theoretically and computationally with other methods that give maximum likelihood and quase-likelihood estimates of model parameters; developing the theory of multilevel analysis with latent variables; comparing various methods for treating missing data in multilevel analysis.
Published Material: GOLDSTEIN, H. (1987). Multilevel models in educational and social research. London: Griffin.
Source of Grant: Economic and Social Research Council
Date of Research: 1988-1990
KEYWORDS: *educational research; model; research technique; statistical method*

8/0752

>Institute of Education
>Department of Economic, Administrative and Policy Studies in Education, Centre for Higher Education Studies,
>59 Gordon Square, London WC1H 0NT
>071 636 8000
>Woodhall, M. Ms; Mace, J. Mr; *Supervisor:* Williams, G. Prof.

Monitoring and evaluation of new funding mechanisms in higher education
Abstract: The Education Reform Bill (1987) proposes radical changes in the method of funding higher education. In future institutions will be funded on the basis of contracts, rather then grants. The principal aims of the research will be: (i) to examine the rationale for alternative models of funding higher education within the general framework of contractual responsibilty by institutions to their funding bodies; (ii) to evaluate the operation and effects of current funding arrangements which already contain contractual obligations between higher education institutions and funding bodies; (iii) to propose ways of monitoring the effects of new funding mechanisms when they are introduced, including identifying the data requirements for measurement of output or institutional performance; (iv) to monitor the introduction of the new funding arrangements, in order to provide a basis for the full-scale evaluation of the new system, once it is fully operational. Broadly, this stage of the project will involve three activities: (a) discussions with Finance Officers and other senior administrators in universities, colleges and polytechnics to identify categories of activites subject to contractual arrangements; (b) a postal questionnaire to all higher education institutions seeking information on the extent of the activities identified and the institutional responses to them; (c) the selection of a limited number of examples, probably about 25, which would be the subject of detailed case studies to examine the educational and other implications of different funding mechanisms.
Source of Grant: Department of Education and Science: £17,806
Date of Research: 1988-1990
KEYWORDS: *economics of education; educational innovation; higher education*

8/0753

>Institute of Education
>20 Bedford Way, London WC1H 0AL
>071 636 1500
>The Hospital for Sick Children
>Department of Psychological Medicine
>Great Ormond Street, London WC1N 3JH
>071 405 9200
>Monck, E. Mrs

Sexual abuse in children and adolescents
Abstract: The aims of the study are: (i) to provide systematic information on sexually abused children and their families referred to the Department of Psychological Medicine at the Hospital for Sick Children; (ii) to assess the efficacy of two treatment programmes. A consecutive sample of approximately 150 families fulfilling the following criteria will be included: sexual abuse occuring in the previous 12 months perpetrated by a close family member or member of the household on a child of 14 or less. Separate interviews will be held with abused children, mothers and perpetrators

(where possible). Information will be collected on the following: family variables (at time of abuse and time of referral); family structure, household structure, age, sex, ethnic and employment status of all household members. Information will also be sought on (a) health and behaviour of victim in month before disclosure (informant: mother); (b) current health and behaviour (informants: mother and child); (c) behaviour at school (Rutter checklist completed by teachers), (d) mental health of parents (28 item GMQO and children (Beck Depression Inventory), (e) Measures of marital satisfaction and the marital relationship (GRIMS), (f) Self esteem of children, parents, perpetrators (Harter: Self Concept Scales). Treatment Outcome Study: approximately 100 of the families in the descriptive study will go into treatment at Great Ormond Street: 50 randomly assigned to routine treatment (individual and family work) and 50 to routine treatment plus group treatment. Families will be interviewed at the end of treatment by researchers blind to their treatment programme. Post treatment measures will include: behaviour and health of victims, current family structure, placement of child, evidence of recurrence of abuse, mental state of child, mother perpetrator, and marital ratings and self esteem.
Source of Grant: Department of Health and Social Security: £150,000
Date of Research: 1987-1989
KEYWORDS: *child; family environment; medical treatment; sexual abuse*

8/0754
Institute of Education
Department of Educational Psychology and Special
Education, 20 Bedford Way, London WC1H 0AL
071 636 1500
May, D. Mr; *Supervisor:* Worrall, N. Dr
School stress
Abstract: The research uses focused interviews of some hundred secondary school teachers. Teachers are taken through a systematic hierarchical analysis of their 'life space' so to indentify major and minor stress episodes. These episodes are analyzed for the effective, cognitive and bodily manifestations, before, during and after the episode. In addition, teachers' offered constructs and comparisons are incorporated into the analysis. Rather than aggregate across teachers, autoregressive response modelling is used to build a model of stress and coping patterns for each teacher. As a second stage, communality across teacher models can thus be examined, with a view to developing a more general picture of teacher stress-coping patterns in secondary schools.
Published Material: WORRALL, N. and MAY, D. (1988). 'Towards a person-in-situation model of teacher stress', British Journal of Educational Psychology, Vol 59, Part 2, pp.174-186.
Source of Grant: No funding
Date of Research: 1987-1990
KEYWORDS: *secondary education; stress; teacher behaviour*

8/0755
Institute of Education
20 Bedford Way, London WC1H OAL
071 636 1500
Kingston Polytechnic
Department of Education, Gipsy Hill Centre,
Kingston Hill, Kingston upon Thames KT2 7LB
081 549 1141
Bland, K. Mr; *Supervisor:* Kent, A. Mr
Curriculum planning in the primary school with particular respect to geographic work
Abstract: This is a study of the nature of geography in the primary school — research based on current surveys (HMI'S reports and unpublished surveys). Questionnaires have been sent to pilot schools (10) LEA schools (25) on the perceived nature and current role of geography. Action research will be carried out in a small number of schools in (3) and a developed model for curriculum planning.
Source of Grant: Polytechnic funds
Date of Research: 1987-1990
KEYWORDS: *curriculum development; geography; primary education*

8/0756
Institute of Education
Sociological Research Unit,
57 Gordon Square, London WC1H 0NT
071 636 1500
Hewitt, R.L. Dr
General Certificate of Secondary Education (GCSE) oral communication assessment and inter-ethnic variation
Abstract: Within the new GCSE examinations the addition of a compulsory 'Oral Communication' element to the examination of written English means that, for the first time in this country, all pupils are assessed on their oral language skills. Amongst the issues this raises is the possibility of social variation in communicative practices and in particular the question of assessment in relation to ethnic variation. The project is researching discussion amongst adolescents for whom English is their first language within groups of: (a) white majority pupils; (b) British-born pupils of South Asian origin; and (c) British-born pupils of Afro-Caribbean origin. It is seeking to discover whether there are differences, and whether or not these relate in any significant way to the English oral assessment criteria of the GCSE Examining Groups. The project will be working with adolescents in six secondary schools and six youth centres, using video and audio recordings and analyzing these for a number of features suggested both by the assessment criteria themselves and by the research literature.
Source of Grant: ESRC (Economic and Social Research Council): £82,490
Date of Research: 1988-1990
KEYWORDS: *assessment; English language; ethnic group; General Certificate of Secondary Education; verbal communication*

8/0757
King's College
Centre for Educational Studies,
552 King's Road, London SW10 OUA
071 836 5454
Rees, M.F. Ms; *Supervisor:* Rouve, S. Mrs
Reasons for the predominance of girls in modern language classes
Abstract: Concern has been expressed, since the mid-seventies, that girls outnumber boys in modern language classes by as many as 3:1 at A-level. The high drop-out of boys at the option stage (3rd year) is being examined as follows: (1) a review of background material, including examination statistics and work on sex difference in both language learning and school behaviour; (2) a survey of pupils' aptitude and attitude towards learning French at the beginning and end of the 3rd year of secondary schooling. Sample and methods: (A) An aptitude test (the York Aptitude Test) of some 200 pupils in 6 schools in South-East England at the start of their 3rd year (Autumn 1986); (B) attitude survey (by questionnaire) of the same pupils in Autumn 1986 and again in Summer 1987, establishing also their choices at option stage; (C) interviews with a sub-sample of some 300 pupils in Summer 1987. Data will be examined in relation to pupils' choice to opt in/out of French. Results to emerge so far suggest that: (i) some of the boy/girl imbalance in recent years is attributable to the growing number of girls entering for examinations in all subjects; and (ii) classroom practice strongly influences whether pupils — boys and girls — opt in/out of French, though certain factors may influence boys more strongly.
Published Material: REES, M.F. (1986). 'The wrong gender?', Times Educational Supplement 'Extra', 30.10.86.; REES, M.F. (1987). 'The wrong gender?', Modern Languages Journal, Vol 68, No 3, pp.183-187.
Source of Grant: Economic and Social Research Council (ESRC)
Date of Research: 1985-1990
KEYWORDS: *choice of studies; modern languages; secondary education; sex difference*

8/0758
Kings College
Department of Educational Studies,
552 King's Road, London SW10 OUA
071 836 5454
Fairbrother, R.W. Dr; Watson, J.R. Dr; Simon, S.A. Dr;
Jones, A. Dr; Black, P.J. Prof.
Open-ended work in science
Abstract: Open-ended work in science gives the initiative to students for finding the solution to a problem. In order to help teachers, and others, the research will: (a) produce a framework for describing and classifying open-ended work in science; (b) explore possible curriculum models which involve open-ended work in science and which are consistent with the National Curriculum; (c) clarify different models of classroom organization; (d) explore the resource implications of doing open-ended work; (e) devise methods of assessment of open-ended work which would be consistent with the schemes for national assessment. The research will produce case studies, video recordings and reports of different kinds

for use by teachers, teacher trainers and other research workers in the field.
Published Material: WATSON, J.R. et al (1989). 'The task framework', (OPENS Project: Internal research document). London: King's College.; JONES, A. et al (1989). 'A review of open-ended work in secondary science', (OPENS Project: Internal research document). London: King's College.
Source of Grant: Department of Education and Science: £300,000
Date of Research: 1988 – continuing
KEYWORDS: *curriculum development; problem solving; science education; teaching method*

8/0759
King's College
Centre for Educational Studies,
552 King's Road, London SW10 OUA
071 872 3088/3095
Lucas, A.M. Prof.
History and philosophy of science and the school curriculum
Abstract: Analysis of school curriculum documents, and their application in the classroom, is used to prepare critiques and influence curriculum materials.
Source of Grant: No funding
Date of Research: 1975 – continuing
KEYWORDS: *curriculum development; science education*

8/0760
King's College
Centre for Educational Studies,
552 King's Road, London SW10 OUA
071 872 3088/3095
Lucas, A.M. Prof.; Tulley, A. Mr
Understanding through action? Visitor interactions in an Interactive Science Centre
Abstract: Observational and experimental techniques, coupled with interviews, are used to explore the extent of understanding attained after use of interactive exhibits varying in the type of feedback they provide the user. The type of captions used changes the nature of understanding (abstractions, principles or descriptive accounts) and the proportion of visitors who are 'informed' by the exhibit.
Published Material: LUCAS, A.M. (1987). 'How do we know interactive exhibits work'?, In: RUSSELL, T. and McMANUS, P. (Eds). The nature of interactive exhibits and exhibitions. Liverpool: University of Liverpool, Department of Education.; LUCAS, A.M. (1989). Language and visitor interaction with science exhibits. Paper presented at Journee d'etude Internationale socio semiotique: 'sciences et Media', Paris, June 1989.; TULLEY, A. (1990). 'Seeing through the name? International Journal of Museum Management and Curatorship.
Source of Grant: Gatsby Charitable Foundation: £15,440
Date of Research: 1987-1990
KEYWORDS: *interaction; museum; sciences*

8/0761
King's College
Centre for Educational Studies,
552 King's Road, London SW10 OUA
071 872 3088/3095
Lucas, A.M. Prof.
Children's understanding of biological concepts
Abstract: Within the conceptual framework provided by international research traditions on science concept acquisition, students are examining a range of biological ideas, both to examine a range of concepts and to address theoretical issues within the research tradition. Techniques include interview and questionnaire methods.
Published Material: ALBALADEJO,C. & LUCAS, A.M. (1988). 'Pupils' meanings for 'Mutation', Journal of Biological Education, Vol 22, No 3, Autumn 1988, pp.215-219.
Source of Grant: No funding
Date of Research: 1985 – continuing
KEYWORDS: *biology; comprehension; concept formation; science education*

8/0762
King's College
Centre for Educational Studies,
552 King's Road, London SW10 0UA
071 836 5454
Swain, J. Dr

The development of Standard Assessment Tasks (SATs) for Key Stage 3 of the National Curriculum for science
Abstract: The National Curriculum specifies seventeen attainment targets (ATs) grouped into two profile components. The first profile component, covering attainment target 1, relates to the intellectual and practical skills which underpin the procedures of scientific exploration and investigation. Pupils will show through their responses to Standard Assessment Task (SATs) their capacity to demonstrate increasingly systematic, quantified and precise approaches to the elements of planning, implementing and evaluating. The second profile component, covering (ATs) 2-17, requires pupils to demonstrate their knowledge and understanding of a wide range of concepts and processes, including the nature of science as a human activity in which the development of scientific ideas is dependent upon the cultural, ethical and social patterns and beliefs of the time. The SATs will require pupils to demonstrate this knowledge and understanding in several modes, ranging from simple written tests to extended practical tasks in a variety of contexts. The form of the SATs will make no assumptions about approaches used in following the National Curriculum programmes of study. The SATs will be designed to cope with a variety of teaching methods delivered through a range of contexts, including those in which ATs 1 and 17 are integrated with ATs 2-16. They will only require resources that are normally available in schools, and must be easily administered, assessed and the results recorded by teachers. Development work is taking place in schools in a number of local education authorities (LEAs). Formal piloting and trialling of SATs will take place during 1990-1992.
Source of Grant: School Examinations and Assessment Council: £2,200,000
Date of Research: 1989 – continuing
KEYWORDS: *assessment; science education; secondary education; Standard Assessment Task*

8/0763
King's College
Centre for Educational studies,
552 King's Road, London SW10 0UA
071 836 5454
Ball, S. Prof.; Bowe, R. Mr
The impact of the 1988 Educational Reform Act
Abstract: The Educational Reform Act, 1988, was the outcome of educational policies generated with the minimum of consultation with the 'educational lobby'. However, the legislation requires considerable participation by the latter in the implementation. The research sets out to examine the extent to which and the ways in which the legislation and the broader political and economic context are being employed by the teachers and local authority officers and advisors in the micro-politics of educational change. The aim is to develop an empirically based, theoretical account of the capacity of the state, over time, to 'reach into' the educational arena and critically affect educational change. Equally, the capacity of schools and authorities to affect educational change is under scrutiny. Four case studies of schools, alongside case studies of the two local authorities within which the schools work, are being undertaken. These concentrate on the National Curriculum and the Local Management of Schools as key elements in the Educational Reform Act. Both place demands upon schools and authorities that they are responding to in different ways, reflecting aspects of the 'local' setting. In addition the national picture is being monitored, i.e. the government circulars, press releases, political commentary, etc. that inform the national politics of educational change. As the case study settings and the national picture develop, the research is trying to explore the form and the content of the relationships that exist between the macro and micro dimensions.
Published Material: BALL, S.J. (1988). 'Schools of Management', The English Magazine, No 20, Summer 1988.
Source of Grant: King's College research fund: £72,800
Date of Research: 1989 – continuing
KEYWORDS: *educational change; educational policy; schools;*

8/0764
King's College
Centre for Educational Studies,
552 King's Road, London SW10 0UA
071 836 5454
Ball, S. Prof.; Adey, P.S. Dr; Watson, D.M. Mrs; Moore, A. Mr; Trushell, J. Mr; *Supervisor:* Cox, M.J. Dr; Johnson, D.C. Prof.

An evaluation of the impact of information technology on children's achievements

Abstract: The project aims to evaluate the impact of information technology (IT) on pupils' learning in schools, focusing on science, mathematics, English and geography and age bands 8-10, 12-14, and 14-16. This will involve investigating: (a) the measurable effects of the use of IT on pupils' achievement of specific tasks; (b) the difference in the nature of the learning activities of pupils using IT compared with non-IT users; (c) the enrichment of pupil's learning experiences through the use of IT; (d) the effects of the level of IT provision and use, teacher intervention and organization on the learning outcomes. The research and evaluation will include four components: (1) field study involving assessments of matched pairs of classes designated as 'high' and 'low' users of IT. This will involve both some assessment of general reasoning abilities in each of the subjects and 'mini-studies'; (2) mini-studies involving assessments of specific learning outcomes in a matched pair of classrooms where the objectives are common, but the learning in the high IT classroom has been supported by the use of IT; (3) five in depth case studies of high IT use classrooms; (4) research reviews to support and extend the evaluation.
Source of Grant: Department of Education and Science: £322,000
Date of Research: 1989 – continuing
KEYWORDS: *achievement; information technology; learning; primary education; secondary education*

8/0765

King's College
Centre for Educational Studies,
552 King's Road, London SW10 0UA
071 836 5454
Watson, J.R. Dr
National Environmental Database Project

Abstract: The National Environmental Database (NED) project has set up a system which allows students in different parts of the United Kingdom to work collaboratively on real scientific investigations. The materials developed incorporate the following features: an emphasis on environmental aspects of science; the generation of both social and scientific data through studies of the local environment; the sharing of data between schools; the use of the Campus 2000 computer (formerly The Times Network System) to store national and local data; an emphasis on the relevance of science both to individuals and society as a whole; an examination of the limitations of science and the relationship between scientific facts and value judgements. The software developed allows the transfer of data between different data processing packages in different computers. the materials have been trialled in about 30 schools.
Published Material: WATSON, J.R. et al (1990). National Environmental Database Project: Teachers Manual. London: King's College National Environmental Database Project. Also topic books on acid rain, radioactivity and animal ecology.
Source of Grant: Nuclear Electricity Information Group: £160,000
Date of Research: 1988-1989
KEYWORDS: *computer assisted instruction; database; environmental study; information technology; science education*

8/0766

King's College
Centre for Educational Studies,
Educational Computing Unit,
552 Kings Road, London SW10 0UA
071 836 5454
Squires, D.; Watson, D. Mrs; *Supervisor:* Cox, M. Dr
Computers in the curriculum project

Abstract: The computers in the Curriculum project have been investigating the use of computers as an aid to learning since 1973. The aims of the project are to research into the ways in which computers are and might be used in classrooms; the influence which using computer assisted learning materials has on the learning of students; the influence on classroom organization; the role of CAL in curriculum development; the implications for teacher training; the human-machine interaction and its effects on learning and the role of software tools in the development of educational computing. This research and development work is supported strongly by educational institutions (DES) and a number of industries. The project produces published educational software, regular research papers, software tools and reports.
Published Material: List of publications available from Educational Computing Unit.

Source of Grant: Microelctronics Education Support Unit: £207,950 (1987/88) British Gas: £104,000 (1986/88) British Telecom: £104,700 (1986/88) UKAEA (United Kingdom Atomic Energy Authority): £20,000 (1987/88) Research Machines: £10,000 EEC (European Economic Community): £23,000 (1987) IBM: £20,000 (1985/87)
Date of Research: 1973 – continuing
KEYWORDS: *computer assisted instruction; curriculum development; learning;*

8/0767

King's College
Chelsea Campus,
552 Kings Road, London SW10 0UA
071 836 5454
Oxford University
Department of Educational Studies
15 Norham Gardens, Oxford OX2 6PY
0865 274024
Solomon, J. Dr
Science teachers in research

Abstract: A group of five practising science teachers are keeping teaching diaries of selected classes to whom they teach science. These accounts are being interpreted on a model based on the social/spatial theories of R. Harre. The work is validated through group discussion which is considered to be a part of the action research.
Published Material: SOLOMON, J. et al (1983). 'Pupils' view of electricity', European Journal of Science Education, Vol 7, No 3, pp.281-294.; OLDHAM, et al (1986). 'A study of pupil views on the dangers of electricity', European Journal of Science Education, Vol 8, No 2, pp.185-197.; SOLOMON, J. et al (1987). 'The pupils' view of electricity revisited', International Journal of Science Education. Vol 9, No 1, pp.13-22.
Source of Grant: Leverhulme Trust: £1,000 per annum
Date of Research: 1983-1990
KEYWORDS: *action research; science education*

8/0768

King's College London
552 King's Road, London SW10 0UA
071 872 3157
London University
Institute of Education,
20 Bedford Way, London WC1H 0AL
071 636 1500
Bliss, J.F. Dr; Ogborn, J.M. Prof.
Tools for exploratory learning programme

Abstract: The aim of this research is to examine whether or not computer tools facilitate different types of reasoning in two different modes of learning. Exploratory learning is defined as the learning that occurs when children use software tools containing representations or models of a specific domain. Expressive learning occurs when children are given the facility to represent their own ideas about the domain. Preliminaries will be a teaching session for familiarization with the computer, followed by a session to teach the children how to use the relevant software. The main study will be composed of a preliminary interview to record pupils' spontaneous reasoning in the domain area. Children will be then set an extended task in which they will use the software followed by a final interview to examine their reasoning. The tasks will be designed to call on reasoning in one of the three areas: quantitative, semi-quantitative and qualitative. The rationale of tasks will be to create 'what if' situations, that is to ask children to explore or express alternatives to reach a specific goal. Approximately, 2000 children will be sampled in the course of the study. These children will be in the age range 11 to 14 years from middle or secondary schools. During the study the children will work in same sex friendship pairs on one specific task, using one particular software tool. The interviews will be transcribed, as will any conversation between the children. These transcriptions together with observational data will form the basis of the data to be analyzed. The data will be qualitatively analyzed using systemic networks.
Published Material: BLISS, J. & OGBORN, J. (1989). 'Tools for exploratory learning', Journal of Computer Assisted Learning, Vol 5, No 1, pp.37-50.
Source of Grant: Economic and Social Research Council
Date of Research: 1988 – continuing
KEYWORDS: *computer assisted instruction; computer assisted learning*

8/0769

London School of Economics
Department of Social Psychology,
Houghton Street, London WC2A 2AE
071 405 7686
Kamel, H. Miss; *Supervisor:* Dockrell, J. Dr
The role of maternal attribution of meaning to infant behaviour in the socialization of infant facial expressions
Abstract: The study is concerned with the naturalistic investigation of mother-infant expressive interaction. It focuses on the role maternal interpretations play in the development and socialization of facial expressions of infants between 4 months to 1 year. The meaning that mothers attribute to infants facial expressions is hypothesised to be dependent on the context within which the expressions occur and the growing ability of the infant to intentionally direct communicative gestures to the mother. These interpretations therefore assume a dynamic character which accommodates to the infants growing capacities. Interaction is therefore hypothesised to be guided at each successive stage of development. Mothers and infants were filmed during play in their homes. The facial expressions of the mother and infant were coded using an anatomical coding frame. The video of the infant was shown to the mother and she was asked to comment on the infant's behaviour. These interviews were then coded and combined with the behavioural codes. The object of this was to see if there was any congruence between what mothers did and what they said about the infant's behaviour. A pilot study has shown that there appears to be marked developmental shifts between 4-6 months and 7-9 months of age. Infants are preoccupied with objects during the latter period. Maternal accounts appear to reflect this in that the reports are scanty as compared with other periods. Maternal behaviour during the middle period also reflects the infant's preoccupation with the external world. Mothers at that period spend large proportions of time observing the infant rather than attempting to engage in face to face interaction.
Source of Grant: No funding
Date of Research: 1986 – continuing
KEYWORDS: child development; facial expression; mother-child relation; non-verbal communication

8/0770

London School of Economics and Polictical Science
Department of Social Psychology,
Houghton Street, London WC1A 2AE
071 405 7686 ext 2713
Kamel, S. Miss; *Supervisor:* Dockrell, J. Dr
The role of maternal interpretation of infant facial expressions of emotions in their development and socialization between 4 months and 1 year
Abstract: The project is concerned with the socialization of the facial expressions of infants between 4 and 12 months. The development of expressions of emotion has concerned social and developmental psychologists since Darwin's book 'The Expression of Emotions in Man and Animals'. Little research, however, has been done on the mechanisms and processes that are responsible for the infant's transition from an initial state of automatic and reflexive expressions (crying, smiling) to the socially appropriate expressions that the child is capable of at the start of the second year. The present study assesses the extent to which parents influence this process through their interpretation of infant signals and their subsequent responses. Data has been collected from mother-infant pairs in play and feeding situations at home. Infants in this cross sectional sample ranged in age from 4 to 12 months. The mother-infant interactions were videotaped and the tape of the infant was shwon to the mother. The tapes will be analyzed for the facial expressions of mother and infant and the co-occurrences of expressions, frequency of expressions and behavioural sequences will be examined. Data will then be obtained this time from a longitudinal sample and the mother-infant pairs will be video taped repeatedly from infant age 4 to 12 months. It will not be possible to take accounts immediately after the filming in this case, due to the effects of repeated questioning on the behaviour of the mother. Therefore a matching cross sectional sample will be used alongside the longitudinal one, filmed only once and the maternal accounts taken immediately afterwards. These tapes will also be micro-analyzed and examined for developmental processes and behavioural sequences. It is hoped that there will be evidence in the individual histories of mother-infant pairs to show that facial expressions come to be socialized through the ability of the infant to learn the effect his or her expressions have on another person; this understanding will come through the

mother's interpretation of the baby's expressions and her response to them as if they were meaningful signals from her baby.
Source of Grant: No funding
Date of Research: 1987-1990
KEYWORDS: emotional development; infant; mother-child relation; physical expression; socialization

8/0771

London School of Economics and Political Science
Department of Social Psychology,
Houghton Street, London WC2A 2AE
071 405 7686
Dockrell, J. Dr
Compliance with Health education messages about HIV (Human Immuno Defeciency Virus)/AIDS (Acquired Immune Deficiency Syndrome)
Abstract: The present survey investigates compliance with health education messages about HIV/AIDS in young people under 24 years of age. The study uses a semi-structured interview in conjunction with a behaviour questionnaire to elicit knowledge, attitudes and specific sexual practices. The subjects comprise three groups who are likely to exhibit risk behaviour which will lead to contracting HIV – sexually active heterosexuals and homosexuals and male prostitutes. The data is analyzed within the framework of models intended to predict compliance with health education messages. Profiles of knowledge, attitudes and situational variables which lead to non-compliance are identified.
Source of Grant: Health Education Authority: £20,000
Date of Research: 1989-1990
KEYWORDS: Acquired Immune Deficiency Syndrome; compliance (psychology); health education

8/0772

London School of Economics and Political Science
Department of Statistics,
Houghton Street, London WC2A 2AE
071 405 7686
Knott, M. Dr; Albanese, T.M. Dr; *Supervisor:* Knott, M. Dr
Broad study of maximum likelihood estimation of latent variable models applied to educational testing
Abstract: The shape of the likelihood function for marginal estimation of a two parameter logistic latent variable model for binary response has been examined to check on the stability of the estimators. Bootstrap methods are used to investigate whether the asymptotic standard deviations of the parameters are satisfactory. An attempt has been made to find out when the estimates for the discrimination parameters are large.
Source of Grant: No funding
Date of Research: 1985-1990
KEYWORDS: educational test; statistical analysis

8/0773

Royal Holloway and Bedford New College
Department of Psychology,
Egham Hill, Egham TW20 OEX
0784 34455
Valentine, E.R. Dr; West, R. Dr; Mills, M. Mrs; Ashcroft, J. Mrs; *Supervisor:* Temple, C. Dr; Wilding, J.M. Dr
Studies of reading difficulties
Abstract: Several studies are continuing, examining: (a) varieties of reading difficulty; (b) cognitive correlates of reading difficulty; (c) musical ability and reading difficulty; (d) remedial methods; (e) use of computers to aid those with reading difficulty; (f) studies of word identification by normal subjects; (g) rhyming skills of surface and phonological dyslexia; (h) follow on studies of dyslexia over a 5 year period.
Published Material: a full list of publications can be obtained from the researchers on request
Source of Grant: No funding
Date of Research: 1985 – continuing
KEYWORDS: cognition; dyslexia; learning difficulty; music; reading; remedial teaching

8/0774

Royal Holloway and Bedford New College
Egham Hill, Egham TW20 OEX
0784 434455 ext 3600
French, D.J. Miss; *Supervisor:* Valentine, E.R. Dr
A psychometric investigation of Howard Gardner's theory of multiple intelligences

Abstract: Howard Gardner's theory of Multiple Intelligences (1983) presents a new way of thinking about human intelligence. This involves six independent areas of intellectual competence; linguistic; musical; spatial; logical/mathematical; bodily and personal. Emphasis is particularly placed upon these areas being domain specific resulting from the operation of computational mechanisms sensitive to only particular types of information. This research investigates the extent to which there is psychometric support for the proposed six intelligences. One hundred and seventy 10 and 11 year old children completed 32 tests, representing as nearly as possible the operations of the computational mechanisms. These variables were factor analyzed using confirmatory and exploratory techniques to assess the extent to which the six intelligences are independent and provide an explanation of the data. The confirmatory analysis showed that Gardner's model accounts for a good proportion, about two thirds, of the variance in the data. The exploratory analysis suggested specific modifications to the theory in order to improve its descriptive power. It was suggested that if the domain specific mechanisms were conceptualized as strategies for solving particular problems then at least one further intelligence was suggested by the data. This was memory, not as raw capacity but as competence at solving memory problems. It was concluded that multiple intelligence theory is a useful concept for describing individuals in an educational context but that additional models are needed to explain intellectual performance. Links were demonstrated between multiple intelligence theory and cognitive theories of intelligence to provide such an explanation.
Source of Grant: Economic and Social Research Council (ESRC): competition award 1984-1987
Date of Research: 1984-1989
KEYWORDS: *ability; intelligence; problem solving*

8/0775

Royal Holloway and Bedford New College
Department of Psychology,
Egham Hill, Egham, Surrey TW20 0EX
0784 434455
Harris, M. Dr; Barrett, M. Dr
Comprehension and production in early lexical development
Abstract: The primary aim of this research is to carry out a systematic analysis of the relation between the comprehension and production of early vocabulary. Eight children's comprehension and production of words between the ages of 6 and 24 months will be intensively examined using maternal diary records, maternal interviews, direct observation, and direct testing. The data which will be collected will be used to develop a theoretical account of early lexical development which is based not only on production data but also on comprehension data.
Source of Grant: Economic and Social Research Council (ESRC): £85,000
Date of Research: 1990 – continuing
KEYWORDS: *comprehension; language development; pre-school child; vocabulary*

8/0776

Royal Holloway and Bedford New College
Egham Hill, Egham, Surrey TW20 0EX
0784 434455
Vrije Universiteit
Department of Psychiatry
Amsterdam
Pickersgill, M.J. Dr; Arrindell, W.A. Dr
Cross-national comparative study of self-reported fears in university students and sex differences in reported fears in university students in relation to male gender – role stress and assertiveness
Abstract: A standard instrument, the Fear Survey Schedule III, has been used to assess self-reported fears; these fears can be shown to relate to five stable factors or sub-scales. Data has been collected from university students from many sources world-wide. Students are asked to complete a Personal Data sheet (including questions on educational, ethnic and religious backgrounds), the Fear Survey Schedule III, a scale for Interpersonal behaviour (assertiveness measure) and the Eysenck Personality Questionnaire (Neuroticism measure). The aim is to replicate and extend the findings of Arrindell et al (1987) with respect to cross-national differences. A second study has been carried out at Royal Holloway and Bedford New College, this investigates the finding that females scored higher than males on all five sub-scales in each of the national groups and two further measures have been administered, the BEM Sex Role Inventory and MGRS (Male Gender-Role Stress) Rating Scale.

Published Material: ARRINDELL, W.A. et al (1987). 'Self-reported fears of American, British and Dutch university students: a cross-national comparative study', Advances in Behaviour Research and Therapy, Vol 9, 1987, pp.207-245.
Source of Grant: No funding
Date of Research: 1985 – continuing
KEYWORDS: *cross-national research; fear; sex difference; student; university*

8/0777

Royal Holloway and Bedford New College
Egham Hill, Egham, Surrey TW20 0EX
0784 434455
Royal Earlswood Hospital
Redhill RH1 6JL
Wilding, J.M. Dr; Lawlor, M.M. Dr; Parmar, V. Dr; Gohil, M. Ms; Saeedi, N. Mrs
Use of microcomputers in assessment and training of subjects with special learning difficulties
Abstract: Royal Earlswood hospital has installed a BBC Econet system with outlets throughout the hospital. This is widely used by patients for playing games and learning activities. The project aims to develop methods of testing abilities through the use of games and of training in simple skills. To date a pilot study has examined performance on a version of the game 'Memory', in which 'cards' are turned up until matching pairs are found. Ability to retain information from preceding trials and to develop a systematic strategy were measured. Another research project is currently being extended to homes for mentally handicapped children in Berkshire, looking at skills requiring ordered sequences of actions such as dressing a doll or building a house.
Published Material: PARMAR, V. & LAWLOR, M. 'Use of micrcomputer network for patients in a hospital for mentally handicapped', In: WEST, R., CHRISTIE, M. & WEINMAN, J. (Eds). Psychological applications of microcomputers in health care. Chichester: Wiley.
Source of Grant: Central Research Fund, University of London: £1,300
Date of Research: 1988 – continuing
KEYWORDS: *computer assisted instruction; learning difficulty; mentally handicapped; microcomputer; special education*

8/0778

Royal Holloway and Bedford New College
Department of Psychology,
Egham Hill, Egham, Surrey TW0 0EX
0784 434455
Walsh, J. Mr; *Supervisor:* Eysenck, M.W. Prof.; Wilding, J.M. Dr
Stress in lecturers
Abstract: The project is designed to examine individual differences in perceived stress and environmental factors leading to stress in the lecturing staff at a computer training centre. A number of questionnaires covering personality measures, perceived stress at different times in the working weeks, and evaluation of working conditions have been distributed. Analysis will examine relations between personality, environment and perceived stress, with a view to reducing the latter.
Source of Grant: International Computers Ltd
Date of Research: 1988 – continuing
KEYWORDS: *stress; teaching personnel; training centre*

8/0779

Royal Holloway and Bedford New College
Department of Psychology,
Egham Hill, Egham, Surrey TW20 0EX
0784 434455
Giannoulis, K. Mrs; *Supervisor:* Wilding, J.M. Dr
Attention deficits in children assigned to nurture groups
Abstract: Initial research compared children assigned to nurture groups within the former ILEA (Inner London Education Authority) area with controls on a vigilance task (detecting repeated stimuli in a long sequence) to discover whether the nurture groups showed impaired concentration. The nurture group children performed worse but showed no greater decline in performance as task duration was increased. Some improvement occurred with increased stimulus duration, addition of colour and provision of feedback. Subsequent research investigated the effects of stimulus exposure duration on a number of tasks. Children in nurture groups demonstrated impairment on briefly exposed stimuli only. It is tentatively

concluded that these children have a defect of iconic memory.
Source of Grant: No funding
Date of Research: 1985 – continuing
KEYWORDS: attention; child development

8/0780

> Royal Holloway and Bedford New College
> Egham Hill, Egham, Surrey TW20 0EX
> 0784 434455
> Wilding, J.M. Dr

Cognitive factors in dyslexia
Abstract: The research aims to analyze the components of phonological processing which are critical for the development of adequate reading skills. Tasks are being developed to isolate such component skills and relate performance on them to reading performance.
Published Material: WILDING, J. (1989). 'Developmental dyslexics do not fit in boxes: evidence from the case studies'. European Journal of Cognitive Psychology, Vol 1, pp.105-127.; WILDING, J. (1989). 'Developmental dyslexics do not fit in boxes: evidence from six new case studies'. European Journal of Cognitive Psychology, 1989. (in press).
Source of Grant: No funding
Date of Research: 1985 – continuing
KEYWORDS: cognition; dyslexia; learning difficulty; reading

8/0781

> Royal Holloway and Bedford New College
> Department of Psychology, Egham Hill, Egham TW20 0EX
> 0784 34455
> Wilding, J.M. Dr; Valentine, E.R. Dr

Medical student learning methods
Abstract: New intakes of medical and dental students complete questionnaires covering qualifications, memory ability, work organization, study methods and learning strategy, together with early impressions of the medical/dental course. These data are correlated with examination results or dropout from the course. Data from the first cohort are being analyzed. The aim is to find criteria which will help to reduce failure rates when selecting students.
Published Material: GORDON, P., VALENTINE, E. & WILDING, J. (1984). 'One man's memory: a study of a mnemonist', British Journal of Psychology, Vol 75, Part 1, pp.1-4.; WILDING, J. & VALENTINE, E. (1985). 'One man's memory for prose, faces and names', British Journal of Psychology, Vol 76, Part 2, pp.215-219.; WILDING, J., RASHEED, W., GILMORE, D. & VALENTINE, E. (1986). 'A comparison of two mnemonic methods in learning medical information', Human Learning: Journal of Practical Research and Application, No 5, pp.211-217.; WILDING, J. & VALENTINE, E. (1990). 'Factors predicting success and failure in the first year examinations of medical and dental courses', Applied Cognitive Psychology (in press).; WILDING, J. & HAYES, S. (1990). 'Relations between approaches to studying and note-taking behaviour in lectures', Applied Cognitive Psychology (in press).
Source of Grant: Central Research Fund, University of London: £450 Pump Priming Grant, RHBNC (Royal Holloway and Bedford New College: £1,036
Date of Research: 1986 – continuing
KEYWORDS: dropout; learning strategy; medicine; study method

8/0782

> Royal Holloway & Bedford New College
> Department of Psychology, Egham Hill, Egham TW20 0EX
> 0784 34455
> Wilding, J.M. Dr

Relations between musical ability and reading ability
Abstract: Measurements of reading ability in a group of children of widely varying ability were significantly related to aspects of musical ability. The research aims to explore this finding further, and in particular to explore relations between musical ability and phonological aspects of reading and to discover whether musical ability in pre-readers is predictive of later reading performance.
Published Material: BARWICK, J., VALENTINE, E., WEST, R. & WILDING, J. (1989). 'Relations between reading and musical abilities', British Journal of Educational Psychology, Vol 59, No 2, pp.253-257, March.
Source of Grant: No funding
Date of Research: 1989 – continuing
KEYWORDS: relationship

8/0783

> Royal Holloway & Bedford New College
> Department of Psychology, Egham Hill, Egham TW20 OEX
> 0784 443709
> Christie, M.J. Dr; French, D. Dr

Psychosocial factors in childhood asthma
Abstract: The project will examine psychosocial factors including peer relationships, self esteem and coping behaviours in children with chronic asthma. It will result in the production of questionnaires and interview schedules to assess Quality of Life in children aged 4- to 16- years. The assessment of Quality of Life includes issues such as the effects of school absence, difficulties involved in taking medication to school and using it there and the consequences of chronic illness for peer relationships. The resultant questionnaires are designed specifically for use in clinical trials but have potential uses for research into the educational needs of children with chronic asthma.
Published Material: CHRISTIE, M.J., FRENCH, D., WEATHERSTONE, L. & WEST, A. 'The patients' perceptions of chronic disease and its management': 'psychosomatics', 'holism', and 'quality of life', in contemporary management of childhood asthma', Psychotherapy and Psychosomatics, (forthcoming).; WEST, A. & CHRISTIE, M.J. (Eds). Quality of life in childhood asthma. Chichester: Carden Publications. (forthcoming).; WEST, A., WEATHERSTONE, L. & CHRISTIE, M.J. Childhood asthma and quality of life 1: a short review of relevant research. Chichester: Carden Publications. (forthcoming).; WEST, A., FRENCH, D. & CHRISTIE, M.J. Childhood asthma and quality of life 2: methodological developments. Chichester: Carden Publications. (forthcoming).; CHRISTIE, M.J., WEST, A. & FRENCH, D. 'Concepts in quality of life: the relevance of childhood asthma', Proceedings of the Annual Conference of the British Psychological Society, Bournemouth, April 1991. (forthcoming).
Source of Grant: Allen and Hanburys Ltd
Date of Research: 1990 – continuing
KEYWORDS: quality of life

8/0784

> School of Oriental and African Studies
> Department of Linguistics,
> Malet Street, London WC1E 7HP
> 071 637 2388
> Ip, B.V. Mr; *Supervisor:* Kempson, R.M. Prof.

Thought, language and culture – a comparative, philosophical approach
Abstract: The research starts with an investigation into questions in philosophy of language on the basis of a comparative study between the philosophy of East and West. Its aim is to offer a philosophical interpretation of the nature of language and its relation to human minds. The second part of the research deals with the treatment of language in cognitive science from which we are going to see how it is compatible with the philosophical model. Emphases are given on the interaction between language and thought, evolution of language acquisition and practical language planning. These will have some pedagogical significance.
Source of Grant: No funding
Date of Research: 1987-1990
KEYWORDS: cognition; language sciences; philosophy

8/0785

> School of Oriental and African Studies
> Department of Linguistics,
> Malet Street, London WC1E 7HP
> 071 637 2399
> Kempson, R.M. Prof

A grammar as an input system
Abstract: Theories of linguistics invariably concentrate on characterizing a speaker's 'competence' in a language, the specialized language faculty that is discrete from all other cogntive faculties. Little or no attention has been paid to the interface processes. As a result the so called competence performance divide has seemed an unbridgeable gap. However a new theory of cognition has emerged, Relevance Theory (Sperber and Wilson Relevance: Communication and Cognition 1986), from which a rich set of consequences has emerged for linguistic theory. The aim of this research has been to investigate these consequences (finding that in all cases Relevance Theory seems to lead to correct predictions), and to construct a formal theory of competence and of performance which together provide an overall explanation of linguistic knowledge and language behaviour.

Published Material: KEMPSON, R. (1984). 'Pragmatics, anaphora and logical form'. In: SHIFFRIN, D. (Ed). Meaning, Form and Use in Context. 1-10 Georgetown. University Press.; KEMPSON, R. (1986). 'Definite NPs and context dependance'. In: MYERS, T. et al (Eds). Reasoning and discourse Processes. London: Academic Press Inc.; KEMPSON, R. (1986). 'Ambiguity and the semantics-pragmatics distinction'. In: TRAVIS, D. (Ed). Meaning and interpretation London: Blackwell.; KEMPSON, R. (1987). 'Grammar and conversational principles'. In: NEWMEYER, F. (Ed). Cambridge Linguistics Survey, Vol 2, Cambridge: Cambridge University Press.
Source of Grant: No funding
Date of Research: 1983-1990
KEYWORDS: cognitive process; grammar; language skill; linguistics

8/0786

> University College
> Department of Psychology,
> Gower Street,
> London WC1E 6BT
> 071 636 8000

8/0787

> University College
> Chandler House,
> 2 Wakefield Street,
> London WC1N 1PG
> 071 837 0113
> Snowling, M. Dr; Goulandris, N. Dr

Developmental analysis of dyslexia in childhood
Abstract: The aims of the project are to sharpen the classification of children's dyslexic difficulties by relating their individual reading and spelling profiles to their underlying language and cognitive skills. The progress of dyslexic children over time will also be monitored. At all stages of the research, dyslexics will be compared with children drawn from normal control samples so that their difficulties can be analyzed within the context of normal literacy development. Particular attention will be paid to the dyslexics' use of compensatory strategies as these will have important practical implications for the remediation of dyslexia.
Source of Grant: Medical Research Council Grant: £65,000
Date of Research: 1989 – continuing
KEYWORDS: dyslexia; phonology; reading difficulty; speech handicap

8/0788

> University College
> Department of Psychology,
> Gower Street, London WC1E 6BT
> 071 636 8000
> Hatfield Polytechnic
> Department of Education
> Wall Hall Campus,
> Aldenham, Watford WD2 8AT
> 09276 2511
> Jordan, R.R. Mrs; *Supervisor:* Frith, U. Dr

Pragmatics in the language of autistic children
Abstract: The communication problems of autistic children are a defining feature of the condition. Whatever the level of linguistic ability, problems in the communicative aspects of language (pragmatics) remain. This study aims to explore some of these pragmatic difficulties in autistic children, especially in relation to linguistic deixis. An experiment has been conducted using a group of eleven autistic children and two control groups matched for verbal age on the english picture vocabulary test; one group is of children with severe learning difficulties, the other of younger normally developing children. The experiment looked at the understanding and use of linguistic deixis of place, time and person. The results showed that the only significant difference was in the use of person deixis, in the form of the first and second pronouns for self and other reference. A further experiment is under way, looking at the use of pronominal reference in story telling, replicating a study by Karmiloff-Smith (1987) with normally developing children. Language samples of autistic children are also being collected and analyzed for presence or absence of certain pragmatic features.
Source of Grant: Hatfield Polytechnic: 75% of PhD (P.T.) Registration fees and travelling expenses
Date of Research: 1987 – continuing
KEYWORDS: autism; communication; language development

London Universtiy

8/0789

> Institute of Education
> 20 Bedford Way, London WC1H OAL
> 071 636 1500
> Kingston Polytechnic
> Department of Education
> Kingston Hill, Kingston-upon-Thames
> 081 549 1141
> Bland, K.; *Supervisor:* Kent, W.A. Mr

Curriculum planning in the primary school: geography and environmental studies
Abstract: This research assesses the current position of geography in primary schools using DES reports on individual schools since 1983. A survey has been undertaken in a large LEA in order to ascertain the current place of geography in the primary curriculum. Action research will take place during the autumn and spring term 1988/89 in a particular school.
Date of Research: 1987-1990
KEYWORDS: curriculum development; environmental study; geography; primary education

Loughborough College

8/0790

> Radmoor, Loughborough LE11 3BT
> 0509 215831
> Loughborough University of Technology
> Department of Education
> Loughborough LE11 3TU
> 0509 263171
> Toon, G.H. Mr; *Supervisor:* Armstrong, P.K. Dr

The introduction of inter-active video disks into Loughborough College as part of a computer assisted learning strategy
Abstract: This doctorate is based upon the introduction of IV (interactive video) into the Open Learning Department at Loughborough College. It records the socio/political effect of the initiative on lecturing staff, the effects on curriculum design, and chronicles the overall effect on staff and students of trying to introduce IV into the open learning/flexible curriculum part of the college's activities. Information gathering is by passive interviewing and by observation, always with an antipositivistic attitude. The establishment of this initiative is expected to take about two years, during which the basic fact-gathering will occur, after which will come the analysis, conclusion-drawing and the summing up, requiring a further 2 years.
Source of Grant: Local Education Authority Training Grant Scheme: £490 per annum
Date of Research: 1990 – continuing
KEYWORDS: computer assisted instruction; educational technology; interactive video; open learning; videodisc

Loughborough University of Technology

8/0791

> Department of Education
> Loughborough LE11 3UT
> 0509 222257
> Shepherd, D. Ms; Ayres, D.G. Mr

Survey of HIV/AIDS education in secondary schools in the East Midlands to discover its curriculum organization, incidence and teaching strategies, the problems and INSET needs of teachers and the impact of the National Curriculum
Abstract: This research will involve a survey of 150 headteachers and health education co-ordinators to discover their teaching and curriculum problems, needs and organization in HIV/AIDS (Human Immunodeficiency Virus/Acquired Immune Deficiency Syndrome), particularly in the context of DES Circular 11/87, 'Sex Education and National Curriculum Health Education' Cross Curricular Theme. Methodology will be structured questionnaires and

selected structural interviews with respondents providing basic data for subsequent analysis and report.
Source of Grant: No funding
Date of Research: 1989 – continuing
KEYWORDS: acquired immune deficiency syndrome; inservice teacher education

8/0792

Department of Education
Loughborough LE11 3TU
0509 222770
Hinton, R.A.L. Mr
Educational development of the Nomad audio-tactile device for visually impaired students
Abstract: The Nomad audio-tactile device is a computer add-on for use by blind students and which has a touch sensitive pad on which tactile diagrams and pictures can be placed for interactive use with a personal computer. It helps to overcome some of the problems of accurately linking information which would normally be in braille or tape to a clear tactile display, and of making use of the computing and data storing potential of the computer. Although this device has performed well in preliminary trials it requires educational development to enable teachers to use it effectively with blind students following a normal curriculum. The research team will be collaborating with the maths, science and geography departments of Exhall Grange school, Coventry, (initially to develop this device further and provide ancillary teaching resources).
Source of Grant: Nuffield Foundation: £19,989
Date of Research: 1990 – continuing
KEYWORDS: computer graphics

8/0793

Department of Education
Loughborough LE11 3TU
0509 222770
Hinton, R.A.L. Mr
Tactual ability and information processing in relation to tactile graphics
Abstract: This research unit has been running since January 1985. Diagrammatic methods of communication are a vital component of many contemporary study resources and it is important that effective tactile alternatives are found for blind students. The current research programme funded by this Guide Dogs for the Blind Assocation grant includes completion of a study of the development of tactual ability in young blind children, including the development of a skill enhancement curriculum component, further investigation of the influence of long term memory and previous experience on diagram interpretation, and specific curriculum development projects.
Source of Grant: Guide Dogs for the Blind Association: £58,000
Date of Research: 1990 – continuing
KEYWORDS: audiovisual aids; blind; diagram; perceptually handicapped; tactual perception

8/0794

Department of Education
Loughborough LE11 3TU
0509 222750
Cantor, L.M. Prof.
Vocational education and training in the developed world: a comparative study
Abstract: This study consists of case studies of systems of vocational education and trianing in various countries in the developed world, including the United States, Japan, Australia, West Germany, and Canada; together with articles on special institutions specialising in vocational education and training, such as the American Community College and the Japanese Special Training School.
Published Material: CANTOR, L.M. (1988). 'Staff development for further education teachers, present and future', Journal of National Association for Staff Development, No 19, pp.4-7.; CANTOR, L.M. (1989). 'The American Community Colleges: a time for reappraisal', Studies in Higher Education, Vol 14, No 3, pp.309-319.; CANTOR, L.M. (1989). 'The "Re-visioning" of vocational education in the American high school', Comparative Education', Vol 25, No 2, pp.125-132.; CANTOR, L.M. (1989). 'Public sector higher education, 1945-1986'. In: STEWART, W.A.C. (1989). Higher Education in the United Kingdom since 1945. London MacMillan.; CANTOR, L.M. (1989). Vocational education in the developed world. London: Routledge.; CANTOR, L.M.

(1990). 'Further education colleges'. In: Entwistle, N. (Ed). Handbook of Educational Ideas and Practices. London: Routledge.
Date of Research: 1986 – continuing
KEYWORDS: college of education; comparative education; labour market; teacher education; vocational education

8/0795

Department of Education
Loughborough LE11 3TU
0509 263171
Smith, A. Mr; *Supervisor:* Thomas, J.B. Mr
The psychological treatment of emotionally and behaviourally disordered children within a special school setting: a conceptual, experimental and survey analysis
Abstract: After reviewing the residential treatment of emotionally and behaviourally disturbed children, the author surveys present provision and therapy in a national sample of schools and homes, and concludes with an analysis and evaluation of family therapy in a case study of one such school.
Source of Grant: No funding
Date of Research: 1987 – continuing
KEYWORDS: emotional disturbance

8/0796

Department of Education
Loughborough LE11 3TU
0509 263171
Leeds University
Department of Education
Leeds LS2 9JT
0532 334527
Reid, I. Prof.; Wiegand, P. Mr
An investigation into the social and educational impact of project work in GCSE
Abstract: This research will involve an investigation into project work in GCSE (General Certificate of Secondary Education) subjects. The first stage involves the analysis of questionnaires completed by some 400 pupils who completed GCSEs in the summer of 1990. The second stage involves parents and teachers. The thrust of the investigation is to review the impact of project work on pupils and the extent to which factors of social background and gender affect attitudes and performance. It will also look at the overall demands and level of co-ordination of such coursework by level of ability and subject choice.
Source of Grant: Loughborough University of Technology
Date of Research: 1990 – continuing
KEYWORDS: social background

8/0797

Department of Education
Loughborough LE11 3TU
0509 222763
Busher, H.C. Mr
Change and policy making in secondary schools
Abstract: This research aims to look at the interaction between individuals and institutions and between individuals, groups of individuals in institutions, when implementing and negotiating changes in secondary schools. The research is small scale and has been carried out ethnographically. It has explored the different interpretations that participants give to the same events. It has focused on time periods when people were most likely to notice disfunctions between personal views of education and institutionally sustained views of education. The study has focused on 6 main participants, on how they perceived their work in their schools and how their colleagues perceived them working. The research has made use of tape-recorded semi-structured interviews, of classroom observation, and of enriched interviews (using video-recordings of teacher activity to trigger discussion). Some 30 interviews in all were conducted during the course of one academic year. Conclusions have yet to be drawn.
Source of Grant: No funding
Date of Research: 1987 – continuing
KEYWORDS: educational innovation; ethnology; interaction; secondary school

8/0798

Department of Education
Loughborough LE11 3TU
0509 222760
Wild, P. Dr

A study of the information technology skills used by teachers in the first two years in the profession: comparison of these skills with Information Technology content of Post Graduate Certificate of Education

Abstract: During 1989-90 a questionnaire survey was used to evaluate the effects of the post graduate certificate of education courses on student's development of the use of information technology skills in teaching. The questionnaires were used at the start and end of their courses. It will now be very useful to follow a sample of the students through their first two years of teaching to assess the impact of the teacher training course on the use of IT (information technology) within schools. The results of this survey will provide a useful contribution to the present debate on the models of IT coverage within teacher education and their relevance to the first years of teaching. It will also provide some preliminary evidence concerning the extent of IT use within the developing National Curriculum which could form the basis for further research in this area. The research will be carried out by questionnaire and follow up visits to a sample of schools in the UK. Results will be disseminated through the Information Technology in Teacher Education Group, which is an active 'grass roots' body supporting IT developments in teacher education, as well as the relevant journals.
Source of Grant: No funding
Date of Research: 1990 – continuing
KEYWORDS: *information technology; National Curriculum*

8/0799

Department of Education
Loughborough LE11 3TU
0509 263171
Litawski, R.E. Mrs; *Supervisor:* Thomas, J.B. Mr
The role of the female deputy head: an investigation into the role and profiles of female deputy heads in co-educational comprehensive schools in one local educaton authority
Abstract: This research examines sexual discrimination and/or role differentiation in comprehensive schools using a theory of micropolitics of the school, use of survey, case studies, and structured interview methodology.
Source of Grant: No funding
Date of Research: 1988 – continuing
KEYWORDS: *deputy head teacher; sex discrimination*

8/0800

Department of Education
Loughborough LE11 3TU
0509 222753
Demaine, J. Dr
Racism and multicultural education
Abstract: The research examines the arguments surrounding the notions of multicultural and antiracist education with particular reference to the pedagogic practice. The research is also concerned with the ways in which terms and categories are deployed in analyses, and discussion of differences in educational achievement between social groups whose identity is usually specified in terms of 'race' or 'ethnicity'.
Published Material: DEMAINE, J. & KADOWALA, D. (1988). 'Multicultural and antiracist education: the unnecessary divide', Curriculum, Vol 9, No 2, pp.99-102.; DEMAINE, J. (1989). 'Race, categorization and educational achievment', British Journal of Sociology of Education, Vol 10, No 2, pp.195-214.
Source of Grant: No funding
Date of Research: 1988 – continuing
KEYWORDS: *antiracism education; multicultural education*

8/0801

Department of Education
Loughborough LE11 3TU
0509 222753
Demaine, J. Dr
Problems with right wing education policy
Abstract: The research examines right wing arguments on educational provision, including the notion of a voucher scheme and the introduction of elements of a 'free market' into public sector education. It examines right wing argument on 'gradualism' as a means of securing educational reform. The research examines arguments put forward by the Right on the idea of a General Teaching Council, on the teacher labour market, and on the status of teachers.
Published Material: DEMAINE, J. (1988). 'Teachers' work, curriculum and the New Right', British Journal of Sociology of Education, Vol 9, No 3, pp.247-264.; DEMAINE, J. (1989).

'Privatisation by stealth: New Right Education Policy', ACE Bulletin, No 28, Advisory Centre for Education, pp.5-7.; DEMAINE, J. (1989). 'A General Teaching Council and the status of teachers', ACE Bulletin, No 32, Advisory Centre for Education, pp.3-5.; DEMAINE, J. (1990). 'The reform of secondary education'. In: HINDNESS, B. (Ed). Reactions to the Right. London: Routledge.
Source of Grant: No funding
Date of Research: 1987 – continuing
KEYWORDS: *education voucher*

8/0802

Department of Education
Loughborough LE11 3TU
0509 223073
Drenth, H. Mrs; *Supervisor:* Morris, A. Mrs; Tseng, G.M. Mrs
An expert system for online database selection
Abstract: This research arises out of the growth in the number of online business databases and hosts. Selection of suitable sources to meet specific information needs is becoming more difficult for the trained intermediary and almost impossible for the end-user of online retrieval services. Previous studies have shown that an expert system approach might be a way forward. The objective of the current research is to design and develop a prototype expert system to demonstrate the selection of online business databases in a specific domain, such as company information. Specific aims of the project are: to undertake a literature survey of expert systems in information retrieval; identify relevant databases for one field of business information; their coverage costing, availability etc; determine, using knowledge acquisition techniques, how experts select online business databases/hosts in this field, to embody this knowledge in an expert system shell/program and finally to evaluate the prototype.
Source of Grant: British Library, Research and Development Department: £52,150
Date of Research: 1990 – continuing
KEYWORDS: *business; expert system; online system*

8/0803

Department of Education
Loughborough LE11 3TU
0509 263171
Tyler, K.G. Mr
Experiential learning in initial teacher education
Abstract: This piece of research is an investigation into experiential learning in teacher education. The work will focus on the development of interpersonal skills within an experiential workshop setting with primary PGCE (Post Graduate Certificate of Education) students, and the relevance of such an approach to the students' overall preparation for teaching in a primary school.
Source of Grant: No funding
Date of Research: 1990 – continuing
KEYWORDS: *experiential learning; interpersonal competence*

8/0804

Department of Education
Loughborough LE11 3TU
0509 222770
Hinton, R.A.L. Mr; Wild, G.E. Dr
Communication problems of blind students in higher education
Abstract: As a result of its experience in producing tactile diagrams, this research unit has in recent years been asked to help several blind students in higher education who are pursuing courses with a high content of visually orientated material. It has become apparent that not only are more blind students seeking to study courses which have an inherent visual content but also that courses which have in the past had a predominantly verbal structure are now making increasing use of visual resources. Resources which make it possible for a blind student to access visually orientated course work may exist but they are not always easily available or may require further development. Many existing students still struggle to obtain good quality resources and some students are refused entry to the courses of their choice partly because suitable resources are not available. The present study is making detailed case studies of ten individual students pursuing a wide variety of courses with a significant visual content. Through maintaining contact with the students and their teaching and support staff over at least one complete academic year it sets out to (1) identify academic subjects where such problems occur, (2) locate the causes of the problems, (3) develop more effective teaching resources where necessary and (4)

provide for any necessary staff advice.
Source of Grant: Leverhulme Trust: £16,450
Date of Research: 1990 – continuing
KEYWORDS: blind; higher education; student; tactual perception; teaching aids

8/0805

Department of Education
Loughborough LE11 3TU
0509 63171
Thomas, J.B. Mr

Studies of teacher education in the Victorian day training college
Abstract: The project aims to describe and analyze the work of education departments in universities from 1890 to 1918. It consists of case studies of individual institutions, biographical studies and investigations of related areas, for example, the development of the academic study of education and the greater opportunities for the professional education of women.
Published Material: THOMAS, J.B. (1986). 'Amos Henderson and the Nottingham Day Training College', Journal of Educational Administration and History, Vol 18, No 2, pp.24-33.; THOMAS, J.B. (1986). 'University College, London, and the training of teachers', History of Education Society Bulletin, Vol 37, pp.44-49.; THOMAS, J.B. (1986). 'Students, staff and curriculum in a day training college (Cardiff)', Collected Original Resources in Education, Vol 10, No 3, Fiche 1 A04.; THOMAS, J.B. (1988). 'University College, Bristol: pioneering teacher training for women', History of Education, Vol 17, No 1, pp.55-70.; THOMAS, J.B. (1988). 'The beginnings of teacher training for men at University College, Bristol', History of Education Society Bulletin, Vol 41, pp.40-45.; THOMAS, J.B. (Ed). (1990). British Universities and teacher education: a century of change. London: Falmer Press.
Source of Grant: No funding
Date of Research: 1978 – continuing
KEYWORDS: history of education; teacher education; university

8/0806

Department of Education
Loughborough LE11 3TU
0509 222758
Simmons, C.V. Mr

School education and young people in Japan
Abstract: This project compares the results of two surveys, the main aim of which was to portray what young people think, feel and believe about important aspects of their lives, using as evidence their own written statements. The subjects comprised 820 15 year-olds in six schools in England in 1981 and 283 14 year-olds in two schools in Japan in 1986. The open-ended questionnaire comprised ten prompts designed to elicit responses concerning ideals and least ideals, most and least preferred companions, use of solitude, summum bonum, most and least desired outcomes to life and nascent philosophies. Two methods of analysis were used. First, references to dominant themes were totalled; second, responses were assigned to six categories according to the dominant values expressed from materialistic to altruistic. Similarities but also significant differences were found in the dominant themes and significant differences were also apparent between the values expressed by the two samples. Most marked was the tendency for the Japanese sample to place a higher valuation on education than the English but to express less regard for their parents and family.
Published Material: SIMMONS, C.V. (1987). Some comparisons between English and Japanese young people: a report on two surveys. Research Report 15. Tokyo: National Institute for Educational Research.; SIMMONS, C.V. & WADE, W. (1988). 'Contrasting attitudes to education in England and Japan', Educational Research, Vol 30, No 2, 1988, pp. 146-152
Source of Grant: Loughborough University of Technology of Technology Academic Initiative Fund:
Date of Research: 1987 – continuing
KEYWORDS: comparative research; Japan; value; youth attitude

8/0807

Department of Education
Loughborough LE11 3TU
0509 222758
Hinton, R.A.L. Mr; *Supervisor:* Cantor, L.M. Prof.

Developing tactual ability for the interpretation of diagrams
Abstract: Graphical and pictorial displays of all kinds are very important in modern education. Much progress has been made in recent years in the provision of effective tactile forms of many of

these. Previous work by the Loughborough team and others has shown that such tactile displays could be more widely used if the developmental tactual skills in young blind children was more fully understood. This research will look at blind children over a wide age range, and particularly at those who are congenitally blind, in order to discover how the necessary skills for diagram interpretation develop and how they can be enhanced. The research will include a preliminary survey of overall curriculum needs. From this, key communication areas and crucial types of diagram will be identified for closer attention. Relevant learning experiences of individual blind pupils will be examined, including their opportunities for handling concrete objects at home and in school, with a view to evaluating the significance of these opportunities. From these surveys a developing programme will be devised to help blind children use tactile material more effectively. Such a programme will need to be adaptable to different types of curriculum and teaching styles, and to respond to what is good in existing practice.
Published Material: HINTON, R.A.L. (1988). 'Tactual experience in relation to diagram use', British Journal of Visual Impairment, Vol 6, No 1, 1988, pp.11-14.; HINTON, R.A.L. (1988). New ways with diagrams: a handbook for teachers and lecturers. London: Royal National Institute for the Blind.; HINTON, R.A.L. (1988). Design and use of tactiles other than maps. Proceedings of Conference of Commission VIII of International Cartographic Society.
Source of Grant: Leverhulme Trust: £48,950
Date of Research: 1988 – continuing
KEYWORDS: blind; diagram; tactual perception

8/0808

Department of Education
Loughborough LE11 3TU
0509 222758
Cohen, L. Prof.; Blease, D. Mr

Integration of information technology into the primary school curriculum
Abstract: This project involved collaboration between teams of researchers and teachers in three European countries (Britain, France and Belgium) and one school in each country. The teachers were trained in the use of information technology and provided with support in the classroom for a period of three school terms. The final outcome of the project is a collection of accounts of how the teachers and children reacted to and worked together with a variety of computer programs.
Published Material: BLEASE, D. & COHEN, L. (1989). Coming to terms with computers. London: Paul Chapman Publishing.
Source of Grant: European Economic Community
Date of Research: 1986 – continuing
KEYWORDS: comparative research; Europe; information technology; primary education

8/0809

Department of Education
Loughborough LE11 3TU
0509 222758
Wild, P. Dr

The effectiveness of INSET in computer assisted learning and information technology
Abstract: This research outlines and analyzes the experiences of the author when working as an advisory teacher for computer assisted learning and information technology under the TVEI related inservice training (TRIST) scheme. The responses to a questionnaire sent to all schools at the start of the secondment are analyzed to find out the problems in the use of computers as seen from the teachers viewpoint. About 100 teacher returns from a possible 50 schools are available. The advisory teachers time management can be a problem with a brief covering many aspects of computer use in schools. The questionnaire returns were used in planning the overall pattern of time management, which was also affected by pressures from schools and/or teachers and the structure of the original TRIST submission. A full analysis of time management and allocation is made with an assessment of effective and ineffective activities. The results of a follow up survey by questionnaire and interview twelve to eighteen months after the courses indicate the level of effectiveness in producing change in the teachers use of computers in the classroom and integration into workschemes. This survey involved about 120 teachers from various disciplines who attended eight different courses. Initial indications are that the course and advisory teacher support play an important role but do not produce the necessary changes without major input from within the teachers own establishment.

Source of Grant: Microelectronics Education Support Unit: £400
Date of Research: 1988 – continuing
KEYWORDS: *adviser; computer assisted instruction; information technology; inservice education and training of teachers; Technical and Vocational Education Initiative; time management*

8/0810

Department of Education
Loughborough, Leicestershire LE11 3TU
0509 222776
London Univesity
King's College, Centre for Educational Studies,
552 King's Road, London SW10 0UA
071 836 5454
Nolder, R.B. Ms; *Supervisor:* Johnson, D. Prof.

Bringing teachers to the centre of the stage: a study of secondary school teachers responses to curriculum change in mathematics

Abstract: The research aims to examine the ways in which teachers respond to the changes in classroom practice demanded of them in the course of curriculum change in mathematics. The fieldwork was carried out from 1985 to 1988 during which time various changes were being introduced into the secondary mathematics curriculum in response to various publications from the Department of Education and Science and to the introduction of the General Certificate of Secondary Education. The research falls into the category of interpretivist research. It focuses on the mathematics departments of two secondary schools. Qualitative research methods are used; the main research strategy is participant observation. Data have been collected in the form of field notes, documentation and audiotaped interviews. The research is on-going, but it is anticipated that it will make a contribution to: (i) theory, with respect to teacher development, (ii) methodology, relating to the analysis of qualitative data, (iii) Inservice Training and Education of Teachers (INSET) provision, by obtaining greater insight into teacher development and a better understanding of the process of implimentation of curriculum change within the school.
Published Material: NOLDER, R.B. (1988). 'Responding to Change', In PIMM, D. (Ed), Mathematics, Teachers and Children. London: Hodder and Stoughton.; NOLDER, R.B. & TYTHERLEIGH, B. (1990). 'R2MC: a springboard to curriculum change', British Journal of Inservice Education, Vol 16, No 1, pp.14-22.; NOLDER, R.B. (1990). 'Accommodating curriculum change in mathematics: teachers' dilemmas', Proceedings of the Fourteenth Annual Conference of the International Group for the Psychology of Mathematical Education, Oaxtepec, Mexico, Vol 1, pp.167-174.
Source of Grant: No funding
Date of Research: 1985-1990
KEYWORDS: *curriculum development; educational change; educational innovation; mathematics; teacher behaviour*

8/0811

Department of Education
Loughborough LE11 3TU
0509 222752
Hough, J.R. Prof.

The financing of education

Abstract: This research studies problems in the financing of education in both developed and developing countries. The emphasis is on flows of funds, sources and uses, and on resulting inequalities and implications for educational policy.
Source of Grant: No funding
Date of Research: 1988-1990
KEYWORDS: *cost; developed country; developing country; financial resources*

8/0812

Department of Education
Loughborough LE11 3TU
0509 222752
Salih, L. Mrs; *Supervisor:* Hough, J.R. Prof.

Educational costs and finance in the Sudan

Abstract: Following detailed surveys of costs and finance in selected schools in the Sudan, this research will study the resulting patterns of inequalities and their implications for the country's educational development.
Source of Grant: No funding
Date of Research: 1988 – continuing
KEYWORDS: *cost; developing country; educational policy; equal opportunity; financial resources; Sudan*

8/0813

Department of Education
Loughborough LE11 3TU
0509 263171
Cantor, L.M. Prof.; Hough, J.R. Dr; Demaine, J. Dr

Education and work

Abstract: This is a new research group which will be developing a series of research projects relating to education and work. Particular interests will relate to: (i) flows of qualified manpower, at various levels and in various specialisms, from the education system to meet employment needs; (ii) industrial and vocational training and associated teacher-training needs; (iii) the providers of further education and training in both public and private sectors.
Source of Grant: applications for grants now pending
Date of Research: 1986-1990
KEYWORDS: *employment; further education; industrial education; manpower need; transition from school to work; vocational education*

8/0814

Department of Library and Information Studies
Library and Information Statistics Unit,
Ashby Road, Loughborough LE11 3TU
0509 223071
Mann, P.H. Dr; Cope, C.M. Miss

Library and Information Statistics Unit (LISU)

Abstract: The Library and Information Statistics Unit (LISU) is the direct successor to the Centre for Library and Information Management (CLAIM) which closed in February 1987. LISU publishes 4 regular statistical serial publications. It also works in an independent capacity in co-operation with government, public and academic bodies concerned with the collection, analysis and dissemination of all types of library statistics. When appropriate, LISU publishes its own reports but it also publishes articles in such journals as The Bookseller and Times Higher Education Supplement.
Published Material: MANN, P.H. 'Average Prices of British Academic Books' published bi-annually, January-June and July-December, giving details of the prices of 64 categories of academic books. LISU British Academic Book Prices Reports ISSN 0261-0302.; MANN, P.H. 'Average prices of USA Academic books', published bi-annually as above, giving details of the prices of 64 categories of academic books. LISU USA Academic Book Prices Reports ISSN 0951-8975.; DONOGHUE, M. & MANN, P.H. 'Public library statistics: a trend analysis', published annually, reviews key statistical data for UK public libraries over the most recent 10 years using data from CIPFA Actuals. LISU Public Library Statistics Reports ISSN 0951-8983.; MANN, P.H. 'Public library bookfund estimates', published annually, is a compilation of details of bookfunds in UK public libraries giving actual figures for the past year and estimates for the forthcoming year as details are known each early summer. LISU Public Library Bookfund Estimates ISSN 0951-8991. All the above reports are available from the Publication Section, LISU.; COPE, C. (1990). 'Performance indicator work in public libraries in the UK', Public Library Journal, Vol 5, No 4, Jul/Aug, pp.95-98.; COPE, C. & MANN, P.H. (1990). 'Book funds and book issues in public libraries', Library Association Record, Vol 92, No 6, pp.436-439.
Source of Grant: Unit grant aided by British Library Research and Development Department
Date of Research: 1987 – continuing
KEYWORDS: *book; library; information service; statistics*

8/0815

Department of Library and Information Studies
Ashby Road, Loughborough LE11 3TU
0509 223066
Smith, L.S. Mrs; *Supervisor:* Lewins, H. Ms

The transition from primary to secondary education: the role of the school library

Abstract: This research is looking further than a simple examination of transfer procedures. If children's education is to be continuous and relevant to their future lives, the skills that are taught at the primary level must be fostered and developed at their secondary level. With the current new initiatives in education, GCSE (General Certificate of Secondary Education) et al, further emphasis is being placed on information skills. The librarian/teacher-librarian has a significant role to play in promoting the effective teaching of information skills in both the primary and secondary sectors. It is this person who can co-ordinate such activities and help to ensure that independent learning 'survives' the primary-secondary

transfer. The research will not only entail the observation of successful transfer procedures, but will also provide materials which can be used in schools on a more practical level. The sample is 1 family of schools, i.e. 1 secondary school and 5 primaries, using naturalistic research methods.
Published Material: SMITH, L. (1987). 'The transition from primary to secondary education: the role of the school library', The School Librarian, Vol 35, No 3, pp.213-215.
Source of Grant: University Research Studentship basic award: £2,756 postgraduate experience allowance: £1,375
Date of Research: 1986-1990
KEYWORDS: General Certificate of Secondary Education (GCSE); information skills; school library; transition from primary to secondary school

8/0816
Department of Library and Information Studies
Ashby Road, Loughborough LE11 3TU
0509 223056
Booth, A. Dr; *Supervisor:* Meadows, A.J. Prof.
Local education authorities information systems project
Abstract: The aim of the project is to examine existing information dissemination strategies within a select group of LEAs with particular reference to information produced by M.E.S.U. (Microelectronics Education Support Unit). (This information relates to how information technology can be used to improve teaching). The purpose of the project is to produce illustrations and models of good practice of dissemination of this type of information. The methodology consists of an examination of systems used by M.E.S.U. and a limited number of co-operating LEAs using a combination of qualitative and quantitative techniques. There will be a different focus of attention in each LEA.
Source of Grant: Microelectronics Education Support Unit (M.E.S.U.): £20,255
Date of Research: 1988-1990
KEYWORDS: information dissemination; information system; information technology; local education authority

8/0817
Department of Library and Information Studies
Ashby Road, Loughborough LE11 3TU
0509 223058
Feather, J.P. Prof.
Feasibility study for an investigation of the mutual recognition of professional information qualifications in the European Community
Abstract: A feasibility study is to be carried out to investigate the implication for the library and information professions of the European Community Council directive (89/48/EEC) on the mutual recognition of higher education diplomas. The project would: (1) investigate the present structure and mechanism of education for the information professions in the member states; (2) delineate areas of comparability and difference in national or institutional practices in training and education; (3) consider the views of "competent professional associations" on the mutuality of qualifications; and (4) identify those aspects, if any, of education and training in need of modification to permit full mutual recognition.
Source of Grant: British Library; Research and Development Department: £5,500
Date of Research: 1990-1990
KEYWORDS: academic degree; equivalence; European Communities; library and information studies; qualification

8/0818
Department of Library and Information Studies
Ashby Road, Loughborough LE11 3TU
0509 223066
Lewins, H.P. Ms; Evans, M. Dr; Wilson, J.M. Dr; MacDougall, J. Mrs
Feasibility study for a national survey of school libraries
Abstract: An examination of the feasibility for a national United Kingdom survey of school libraries, undertaken by interviewing professional associations and other interested bodies concerned with school library provision and development.
Source of Grant: Loughborough University of Technology of Technology Research Fund, Department Information Studies, Management Studies, Jointly: £2,350
Date of Research: 1989-1990
KEYWORDS: school library; survey

8/0819
Department of Library and Information Studies
Ashby Road, Loughborough LE11 3TU
0509 223066
Lewins, H.P. Ms; Evans, M. Dr; Heeks, P. Mrs
Supports to learning: school library services in the United Kingdom
Abstract: This study of school library services in the United Kingdom has two aspects. One is the documentation of the current state of these services, setting out the present support that they offer schools, and identifying trends. The other aspect is the monitoring of change – and the management of change – over a two-year period. Particular emphasis will be given to change in England and Wales consequent on the requirements of the Education Reform Act 1988.
Source of Grant: British Library: second year £43,300
Date of Research: 1989 – continuing
KEYWORDS: school library; support service

8/0820
Department of Library and Information Studies
Ashby Road, Loughborough LE11 3TU
0509 223050
Meadows, A.J. Prof.; Rowland, J.F.B. Mr
Computers in Teaching Initiative Centre for library and information studies
Abstract: The object of the Computers in Teaching Initiative (CTI) is to increase the utilization of computer assisted methods in teaching in higher education in the United Kingdom. To this end, a series of 21 centres have been set up, each serving a particular academic discipline. The CTI Centre for Library and Information Studies (LIS) collects information about software and courseware that might be valuable in the teaching of LIS, and disseminates it to lecturers in LIS departments and tutor-librarians in academic libraries, by means of an electronic bulletin board, newsletters and other publications, and conferences.
Published Material: MEADOWS, A.J. (1989). 'CTI Centre for Library and Information Studies at Loughborough University of Technology of Technology of Technology', CTISS File, pp.46-47.; ROWLAND, F. & TSENG, G.M. (1990). 'Computer methods in the teaching of library and information studies', Education for Information. (in press); A complete list of publications is available from the researcher
Source of Grant: Computer Board for the Universities and Research Councils: £52,500 IBM UK Trust: £15,000
Date of Research: 1989 – continuing
KEYWORDS: computer assisted instruction; higher education; library and studies; teaching method

8/0821
Department of Physical Education and Sports Science
Loughborough LE11 3TU
0509 263171
Loughborough Technical College
Radmoor, Loughborough LE11 3BT
0509 215831
Macintyre, E. Mr; *Supervisor:* Guy, A. Mr
F.A.M. Webster: his role in the development of athletics literature and the Loughborough College School of Athletics
Abstract: F.A.M. Webster (1887-1949) wrote numerous books on athletic training theory and practice. He was also a noted coach, administrator and the first Head of Loughborough College School of Athletics. This study would examine Webster in the light of all these varied roles and in the content of his vast corpus of published material. His own writings are the primary sources. Then the archives of Loughborough University of Technology of Technol Association and the Amateur Athletics Association would be consulted. Finally, oral evidence would be gathered from members of his family and others still alive who knew him.
Source of Grant: Leicestershire County Council: fees
Date of Research: 1987-1990
KEYWORDS: athletics; coaching

8/0822
Department of Social Sciences
Loughborough LE11 3TU
0509 263171
Williams, J.A. Ms; *Supervisor:* Keil, E.T. Mrs
School-leavers' knowledge, perceptions and process of entry into the labour market, with special interest given to the construction industry

Abstract: Changing patterns of entry into the labour market have been noted for some years now, with the increase of state intervention in the transition from school to work, necessitated by high levels of widespread youth unemployment. Such intervention shows few signs of diminishing: on the contrary, we see a merging of education and training (e.g. Youth Training Scheme, (YTS); Technical and Vocational Educational Initiative, (TVEI)), which blur the distinguishing boundaries between education and employment. It is proposed to look at this process of entry into the labour market by taking particular interest in the construction industry, by considering 'ports of entry' open to youngsters, the part played by 'YTS'and the changing attitudes of employers towards school-leavers. The aim is to look through the eyes of school-leavers at the hurdles to be crossed in order to gain entry, and from the employers' side to look at the problems faced in finding enough qualified individuals to fulfil the industries' requirements in a time of falling numbers of 16-year-olds. A questionnaire will be administered to 16-year-olds (and sixth formers) in selected schools within Leicestershire, (chosen from areas of contrasting unemployment figures) in order to ascertain how many would consider the construction industry, what alternative aspirations they have, and what barriers and opportunities they see before them. Access is also secured to groups of trainees on 'YTS' in the area (approximately 200 trainees). By using questionnaires and group interviews, the aim is to ascertain their reasons for entering the construction industry.
Source of Grant: Science and Engineering Research Council (SERC): fees and maintenance
Date of Research: 1987-1990
KEYWORDS: construction industry; labour market; school leaver; transition from school to work

Luton College of Higher Education

8/0823

    Putteridge Bury Campus, Hitchin Road, Luton LU2 8LE
    0582 418339
    Coggins, P.C. Dr; Cooper, A.D. Mr
Education and training in waste management
Abstract: This research will involve the review of existing courses for professionals and technicians. Identification of the needs of these two groups, and their relationships with proposed certificates of competence and certificates of proficiency, and the existing professional courses. Preparation of outline aims and objectives, and detailed curriculum requirements identified by this survey. It is assumed that the research will take cognisance of work being undertaken under the auspices of WAMITAB (Waste Management Industry Training Board), IWTM (Institute of Waste Management), and IWEM (Institute of Water and Environmental Management). The research will cover both full-time (2) and part-time (1) modes of study, and the availability of distance learning packages.
Source of Grant: No funding
Date of Research: 1990 – continuing
KEYWORDS: waste disposal

8/0824

    Park Square, Luton LU1 3JU
    0582 34111
    Bride, R.A.; *Supervisor:* Davies, B. Prof.
Cultural influences on learning with special reference to West Indian/Afro Caribbean groups
Abstract: This research shows that the relative lack of success by the West Indian/Afro Caribbean ethnic group members of society is not attributable to biology but to social interaction. The factors operating are socio-economic and resemble those which sustain stratification in the majority white culture, but with added dimensions. However, there are additional influences in the shape of the utilitarian requirements of social competence for the effective social identity, together with the actions and beliefs of those interfacing with the ethnic minority groups. In particular, erroneously based forms of well-intentioned patronage, romanticism and provisim can create a form of entrapment and containment for this ethnic minority group's members.
Source of Grant: No funding
Date of Research: 1981 – continuing

KEYWORDS: education; ethnic minority; social interaction; social structure; socio-economic status

8/0825

    Park Square, Luton LU1 3JU
    0582 34111
    Hounslow, E. Mr; *Supervisor:* Griffin, S. Mr
A comparison between published EFL grammars and dictionaries
Abstract: This research will compare the usefulness of the major 'English as a Foreign Language' grammars and dictionaries, seeking the view of experienced EFL teachers, course designers, trainee EFL teachers, and of course EFL students. The aim is to make recommendations to EFL grammarians and lexicagraphers, and EFL publishers, regarding changes to the next generation of published material.
Source of Grant: No funding
Date of Research: 1990 – continuing
KEYWORDS: English (second language)

8/0826

    Putteridge Bury Campus, Hitchin Road, Luton LU2 8LE
    0582 34111
    Connelly, S. Ms; *Supervisor:* Hawkins, R. Mr
TTNS (The Times Network System)
Abstract: TTNS (The Times Network System) provides 2 mail facilities: (a) electronic mail; (b) information retrieval. This project is concerned with making staff in colleges aware of what TTNS can offer in the classroom, in administration and for communication between staff. A TTNS local database for the region is being set up called ANGLIA which is accessible by all TTNS subscribers. This can be used to demonstrate the use of electronic communications to students, as an incentive to students to produce work to onto the database and as a means of communication between staff. Awareness of TTNS will be increased by holding workshops both at Putteridge Bury and at interested colleges.
Source of Grant: Education Support Grant
Date of Research: 1987 – continuing
KEYWORDS: database; electronic mail

8/0827

    Park Square, Luton LU1 3JU
    0582 34111
    Coggins, P.C. Dr
Remote sensing and technician training in mapping science
Abstract: Remote sensing has become more important with the introduction of second generation resources satellites such as Landsat 4, 5 and SPOT. The emphasis to date has been on proving resource-based application. Workers in this field have usually been subject specialists with subsidiary training in remote sensing. There is a need to provide technician training in remote sensing, to work in conjunction with applications scientists. These persons will require keyboard skills, an understanding of image analysis and an appreciation of remote sensing applications. They will also be training in conventional carto-graphic skills and also digital mapping, thus providing a broad background in mapping science. The work is therefore primarily concerned with curriculum design and the preparation of teaching materials. Use of satellite remote sensing in school geography curricula has also been studied as part of this staff development.
Published Material: COGGINS, P.C. (1985). Remote sensing and technician training. Paper to EARSEL Annual Symposium, Copenhagen.; HILTON, K., COGGINS, P.C. and BOOTE, E. (1987). 'Geography from space: Landsat thermatic mapper scenes in the classroom', Teaching Geography, 1987, pp.65-68.; HILTON, K.J. (Ed). (1989). Space view U.K.: a teachers guide to Landsat TK images in the classroom (contributing author). Nottingham: Remote Sensing Society.; COGGINS, P.C. (1990). Horses for courses: education and training in geographical information systems. Mapping Awareness Annual Conference. Oxford: Miles Arnold.
Source of Grant: No funding
Date of Research: 1983 – continuing
KEYWORDS: curriculum development; geography; satellite; teaching aids; technician; vocational training

8/0828

    Park Square, Luton, Bedfordshire LU1 3JU
    0582 34111
    McGarr, S.A. Mrs
Effectiveness of teaching aids with particular attention to videos
Abstract: Highly academic subjects of an abstract nature are still

taught in very traditional ways eg. Law generally and Company Law in particular. Hence few, if any, teaching aids are available. Videos have been used in management studies for a number of years. Using visual aids in academic subjects and assessing the value in terms of knowledge and interest to the student is the main aim and the subsidiary aim is to assess those areas of study where more visual aids are required. Students whose studies include Company Law will be used by means of a questionnaire and consultative interviews. Results will be analysed. Also the methods used in the videos will be analysed.

Source of Grant: No funding
Date of Research: 1989 – continuing
KEYWORDS: law; teaching aids; video recording

8/0829

Park Square, Luton LU1 3JU
0582 34111
Wood, A.J. Dr

Pattern perception and mathematical ability

Abstract: The long term aim of this study is to find ways of helping teachers of young children (circa 5- to 9- years) to establish objective assessments of mathematical aptitude, which are easy to administer and which can be used to supplement their own personal observations. The research is predicated on the long-held belief that the key component to mathematical understanding lies in the learner's ability to perceive the pattern or structure in a situation. Conversely, that the degree to which one can perceive pattern may be used as an indicator of mathematical aptitude. Over a period of several months, an initial bank of over 100 partially-completed puzzle pictures were developed, each of which required an understanding of the underlying structure for successful completion. During successively held trials, these have been revised and refined against tests of statistical consistency. Most recently, during 1985/87 a revised bank of 80 puzzles and practice items were trialled with over 300 children in schools in Bedfordshire and West Sussex. Provisional age-related norms (ages 5 years 6 months to 10 years) have been prepared for 64 statistically consistent items. The work is continuing.

Source of Grant: The Leverhulme Foundation: £4,000
Date of Research: 1984 – continuing
KEYWORDS: aptitude; assessment; mathematics; perception; primary education

8/0830

Department of Applied Social Studies
Centre for Business Studies, Park Square, Luton LU1 3JU
0582 34111
Hughes, P.E. Mrs; *Supervisor:* Shuttlewood, A.

Science education as an influence on the workplace activities and student research projects of occupational health nursing students

Abstract: The response to science education by female students has been identified by classroom behaviour and career outcome. Entrants to nurse training are not required to have completed any science education before commencing nurse education/training although nursing is a science based study. Nurses select areas of work where clinical or interpersonal skills predominate. Applicants for occupational health nursing courses require only nursing qualifications for entry, but environmental toxicology and bio-chemistry are the major study themes. Within the work environment the occupational health nurse is increasingly required to monitor the effects of human exposure to chemical substances. Many nurses report stress and avoidance tactics when faced with these tasks and cannot interpret the results. Using educational data provided by student applicants, this study will create a profile of the science education of occupational health nurses and investigate the possible relationship between science education and workplace activities. The relationship between science education and topic selection of the student project will be tested.

Source of Grant: No funding
Date of Research: 1990 – continuing
KEYWORDS: work education relationship

8/0831

Department of Law
Park Square, Luton LU1 3JU
0582 34111
Young, M. Mr

The use of expert systems in law teaching

Abstract: The aim of this research is to investigate how effective use can be made of expert systems to help students solve problems.

An ultimate questionnaire will be used to examine students perceptions of the use of expert systems. Essay and exam marks will also be considered. The expert systems will be used in 'live classes' as part of normal teaching.

Source of Grant: No funding
Date of Research: 1989 – continuing
KEYWORDS: computer assisted instruction; law; problem solving

Manchester Polytechnic

8/0832

Elizabeth Gaskell, Hathersage Road, Manchester M13 OJA
061 247 2000
Smith, C. Dr

Student needs in the first year of higher education and institutions responses

Abstract: Students entering higher education have many needs, some of which arise from the nature of their chosen subject. This research is particularly concerned with the special problems of students entering a field which draws on many disciplines. Such students often have confidence sapping weak areas and have concurrently to adapt to new teaching methods and the disruption of leaving home. Within the first year student groups, averaging 50 mainly female students, the researchers aim to identify the problems and examine the effectiveness of measures taken to deal with them. Questionnaires, small group and individual interviews will be used as a means of achieving this.

Published Material: SMITH, C. (1988). 'Coping with a diversity of needs in the first year', New Series, No 8, pp.1-5, April. Society for Research into Higher Education International Newsletter.; SMITH, C. (1987). 'Coping with a diversity of needs in the first year', pp.84. Proceedings of the Second International Conference on the First Year Experience, Southampton University.
Source of Grant: Supported by departmental funds
Date of Research: 1988 – continuing
KEYWORDS: student needs

8/0833

Didsbury School of Education,
799 Wilmslow Road, Didsbury, Manchester M20 8RR
061 445 7871
University of East Anglia
Centre for Applied Research in Education,
Norwich NR4 7TJ
0603 56161
Ovens, P.J. Mr; *Supervisor:* Elliott, J. Prof.

A tutor's use of action research for professional development within an inservice course for teachers

Abstract: Action research occurs at two levels within the inservice course in primary school science which is being studied. The teachers are encouraged to conduct action research into the development of their teaching, whilst as the course tutor, the researcher is conducting action research into his role as enabler to and critic of their action research. In both cases, action research is seen to be the paradigm for professional development. As a result of the research course, strategies have been evolved to make considerable improvements. Three main aspects of these changes are the subject of particular attention. Firstly, the course members' developments during the course are described and analyzed, in order to characterize autonomous professional development. Secondly, experience of the tutorial role is examined with particular attention to the tension between enabling and assessing activities, as perceived by the tutor and the teachers. Thirdly, the permeation of informal, naturalistic assessments within the thinking of the tutor and course members, in all aspects of the course experience is considered in relation to the formal assessment structures of award bearing courses. The research will consider the theory of an inservice course for professional development as constituted within the practices and experiences of the course examined. It will provide a basis for hypotheses about the pedagogy, assessment and planning of inservice courses aiming for longer term autonomous professional development

Published Material: OVENS, P.J. (1989). The assessment of professional development. Paper given to the British Educational Research Association seminar on research in inservice education, September 1989 at Sunderland Polytechnic.
Source of Grant: No funding

Date of Research: 1985 – continuing
KEYWORDS: *action research; assessment; inservice education and training of teachers; professional development*

8/0834

Didsbury School of Education,
799 Wilmslow Road, Didsbury, Manchester M20 8RR
061 445 7871
Hustler, D. Mr; Goodwin, A. Mr
TVEI (Technical and Vocational Education Initiative) in initial teacher training: Manchester Polytechnic
Abstract: The project has been designed together with a consortium of three LEAs (Local Education Authorities) Manchester, Rochdale and Salford, with whom the Polytechnic has had a TVEI (Technical and Vocational Education Initiative) evaluation relationship for the last four years. With local developments in mind, and in particular the extension performance indicators for the three LEAs, the project is concerned with four key development areas. These are: (1) technology for all; (2) information technology, with special reference to self-study support; (3) schools/industry links; (4) profiling for student teachers within the teaching practice context. In addition, there is a general concern for active learning strategies relating to these four areas. The staff development model adopted involves an action research mode and takes account of the joint concern that the project should contribute directly to the work of schools as TVEI extension takes place. In the first year, a team of seven staff have been allocated some timetable release to work with specific schools, in one or other of the above development areas. In the second year, the team will work with additional teacher training colleagues on the trialling of materials, approaches and strategies, within college based elements of courses and, where appropriate, with teachers within schools. The intention is that through stafff development of teacher trainers, and associated course developments, new teachers will be better prepared to work on TVEI extension within the National Curriculum.
Source of Grant: Training Enterprise Education Division: £100,000
Date of Research: 1989 – continuing
KEYWORDS: *staff development; teacher education; Technical and Vocational Education Initiative*

8/0835

Didsbury School of Education,
799 Wilmslow Road, Manchester M20 8RR
061 445 7871
Goodwin, A.J. Mr; Hustler, D. Mr
TVEI (Technical and Vocational Education Initiative) consortium evaluation (Manchester, Rochdale and Salford)
Abstract: The School of Education has been contracted by the TVEI (Technical Vocational Education Initiative) projects in Manchester, Rochdale and Salford to provide the external evaluation. This has subsequently been developed (from September 1989 to cover the extension programme TVEI(E)). Two tutors from the School of Education are attached to each LEA (Local Education Authority) and the programme is coordinated across the consortiom by a group representative of LEA and polytechnic interests. In the first year the focus was upon the teacher's experience of TVEI pilot and reports were written based upon structured interviews with about 65 teachers across the consortium. The second year explored the students' experience of 14 year old pupils especially relating to active learning and the use of technology. This entailed observation of classroom experiences involving six pupils in each pilot school and an interview with the pupils at the end of the year. The third year followed these pupils into their final year of compulsory schooling and examined their work experience and preparation for 'the world of work'. The relationship between the teachers in the school and the evaluators has evolved to make the process of evaluation much more a cooperative venture. This provides much more immediate feed-back and involves teachers in the process of pevaluation. The involvement of a team of tutor-evaluators rather than a single full-time evaluator was deliberately used as a strategy to maximise the feedback of TVEI information back into initial teacher education programmmes.
Source of Grant: LEAs (Local Education Authorities): £66,000
Date of Research: 1986 – continuing
KEYWORDS: *evaluation; Technical and Vocational Education Initiative; transition from school to work*

8/0836

Department of Community Studies and Education
799 Wilmslow Road, Didsbury, Manchester M20 8RR

061 445 7871
Moore, J. Ms; *Supervisor:* Hogbin, J. Mr; Archer, M. Mr
The new teacher in school
Abstract: The Manchester Polytechnic BEd course is an innovative course of initial teacher training. The broad aim of the research project is to measure by a study of its graduates in their probationary year, the effectiveness of the course in meeting its own aims and the appropriateness of those aims to the needs of the teacher. Phase One is primarily a comparative study in which 59 of the courses 1988 graduates were compared, in their perceptions of their training and their experiences in school, with the 297 teachers from training institutions across the country surveyed by HMI in 1987. Phase One also provides benchmark data for the final group of graduates whose course was unaffected by 1984 criteria of the Council for the Accreditation of Teacher Education. Information was gathered by means of a questionnaire similar to that used by HMI, and by interviews with a sample of newly qualified teachers and their headteachers. The results showed similarity with those of the HMI survey, with teachers wanting a more practical bias to their courses, less specialist subject study and more time devoted to classroom strategies and the teaching of reading. However, most of the Manchester Polytechnic cohort affirmed the value of their Education Studies programme which had enabled them to analyze their teaching and to justify and moderate their teaching practices.
Published Material: The new teacher in school: intermin report (1989) Manchester: Manchester Polytechnic
Source of Grant: Manchester Polytechnic
Date of Research: 1989 – continuing
KEYWORDS: *course; effectiveness; probationary teacher; teacher education*

8/0837

Department of Community Studies and Education
799 Wilmslow Road, Manchester M20 8RR
061 445 7871
Crewe & Alsager College
Hassall Road, Alsager, Cheshire ST7 2HL
0270 882500
Hustler, D.E. Mr; Robinson, J. Mr; Jones, J. Ms
Perceptions of the 'Arts Education for a Multicultural Society' in Cheshire
Abstract: The main aim is to uncover the various participants' perceptions of the AEMS (Arts Education for a Multicultural Society) project in Cheshire. More specifically these include perceptions of what the project is about; their own roles within it; the development of the project; the impact of the project on attitudes and values. The main source of the data will be interviews with the involved schools, the artists, the Advisory Service, the project coordinator and the Arts Council. The results of the project will be used as a basis for further curriculum developments.
Source of Grant: Chesire Local Education Authority: £3,000
Date of Research: 1989-1990
KEYWORDS: *art education; artist; curriculum development; multicultural education*

8/0838

Department of Community Studies in Education
Didsbury School of Education,
799 Wilmslow Road, Manchester M20 8RR
061 445 7871
Johnson, P. Dr
The Book Art Project
Abstract: The objectives of the Book Art Project are: (a) the encouragement of language skills through the self-made book; (b) the development of design, technological and graphic skills through the book production; (c) the dissemination of the book concept and its place in learning; (d) to foster the role of book art in relation to the demands of the National Curriculum (eg. cross-curricular activities). Independant research has been conducted in ten primary schools in Greater Manchester. This has been linked to INSET (Inservice Education of Teachers) provision in collaboration with the Metropolitan Boroughs of Stockport, Oldham and Rochdale. (Manchester and Trafford presently under discussion). A series of polytechnic based inservice courses have disseminated the project further and has enabled school-based action research in over thirty additional schools. Several book art specialists are currently involved in school-based activities under the Artists' in Residence Scheme (Regional Arts Association). There are growing links with book art agencies abroad eg. Center for the Book Arts (San Francisco). A current investigation involves B. Ed. Year I (Art & Design)

students under the Government's Enterprise Initiative Scheme.
Published Material: JOHNSON, P. (1988). A book of one's own. Manchester: Manchester Polytechnic.; JOHNSON, P. (1989). Books which move. Manchester: Manchester Polytechnic.
Source of Grant: Craft Council: 1986 £450 Watersone's Booksellers: 1989 £250 Manchester Polytechnic: 1988-89 £4,000
Date of Research: 1986 – continuing
KEYWORDS: art education; book; language skill

8/0839

Department of Education
Wilmslow Road, Didsbury, Manchester M20 8RR
061 445 7871
Proctor, N. Mr
The school curriculum and teacher education
Abstract: This research covers the design and development of the school curriculum, leading to the establishment of a National Curriculum, taking in child-centred approaches, special needs, the so-called 'basics' of education, aesthetics, and vocational education. It is advocated that all these can be introduced through a curriculum framework consisting of the five 'languages', or forms of communication, of literacy, oracy, numeracy, graphicacy and physiognomacy. These are considered through a number of subjects including English, geography, art, PE, history and the humanities. Finally the question of matching this scheme to teacher education is considered with reference to course content (particularly professional studies) and partnership with schools.
Published Material: PROCTOR, N. (1987). 'Writing a special needs curriculum statement', Education Today, Vol 37, No 2, 1987, pp.10-17.; PROCTOR, N. (1988). 'Government control of the curriculum: some evidence', British Educational Research Journal, Vol 14, No 2, June 1988, pp.155-166.; PROCTOR, N. (1988). 'Developing lively enquiring minds: some considerations for curriculum planning', Education Today, Vol 38, No 3, August 1988.; PROCTOR, N. (1989). The purpose and aims of primary education today. London: Falmer Press; A complete list of publications is available from the researcher
Source of Grant: No funding
Date of Research: 1984 – continuing
KEYWORDS: basic education; curriculum development; teacher education

8/0840

Didsbury School of Education
Department of Science Education, 799 Wilmslow Road, Manchester M20 8RR
061 445 7871
Gibson, F. Mr
Collaborative action research for staff and course development in a higher education primary science course
Abstract: This is a piece of action research into practice, carried out by a team of higher education tutors collaboratively. The context was the teaching of a whole year-group of primary B. Ed. students by a team of five tutors, where each tutor had his or her "own" group within the structure, rather than working within any team-teaching situation. It was an attempt to use detailed reports of teaching sessions as data for discussion and analysis, in order both to develop theory and to improve practice. One particular feature was that it involved all five of the tutors who, between them, taught the "same" course to the whole of a year-group. It also involved an external person who acted as observer and critical friend. The tutors hoped by this means; to increase their knowledge of each others practice; to improve the coherence of the course for the students; to improve their own practice; to develop theory.
Source of Grant: Polytechnic Research and Staff Development: £400
Date of Research: 1989-1989
KEYWORDS: action research; course; higher education; staff development; teacher education

Manchester University

8/0841

Centre for Audiology,
Education of the Deaf & Speech Pathology,
Oxford Road, Manchester M13 9PL
061 275 3379/3380

Aplin, D.Y. Dr; *Supervisor:* Taylor, I.G. Prof.
Dyspraxia in hearing-impaired children
Abstract: Dyspraxia, in relationship to deaf children, has been described as a motor handicap involving the limbs and speech musculature which in addition to deafness is said to hinder the development of oral language. It is related to particular memory skills. Dyspraxic children are identified at a Dutch school for the deaf by Van Uden by specific tests and are withdrawn into a subgroup to benefit from a manual system of communication (one-handed finger spelling) in addition to speech. This research aims to investigate whether this practice is effective. A sample of 106 Manchester-born children aged 7-16 years, having a range of sensori-neural hearing losses was assessed. Results were compared with those obtained by Van Uden in a sample of profoundly deaf children. Van Uden's eupraxic/dyspraxic profile was not the main profile found for the Manchester children. It was shown that deaf children with dyspraxic profile were extremely rare if a population of hearing-impaired children was investigated and that those so identified did not appear to have the language problems consistent with his theory. The main profile to emerge for the Manchester children suggested a linguistic/non-linguistic dichotomy within the subtests.
Published Material: VAN UDEN, A.M.J. (1981). 'Early diagnosis of those multiple handicaps in prelingually profoundly deaf children which endanger an education according to the purely oral way', Journal of the British Association of Teachers of the Deaf, Vol 5, No 4, pp.112-127.; VAN UDEN, A.M.J. (1983). 'Diagnostic testing of deaf children: the syndrome of dyspraxia', Lisse: Swets and Zeitlinger.; APLIN, D.Y. (1985). 'The social and emotional adjustment of hearing-impaired children in special schools', Journal of the British Association of Teachers of the Deaf, Vol 9, No 4, pp.84-94.; APLIN, D.Y. (1987), 'Social and emotional adjustment of hearing impaired children in ordinary and special schools', Educational Research, Vol 29, No 1, pp.56-64.; APLIN, D.Y. (1987). 'Classification of dyspraxia in hearing-impaired children using the Q-technique of factor analysis', Journal of Child Psychology and Psychiatry, Vol 28, No 4, pp.581-596.
Source of Grant: North West Regional Health Authority: £16,958
Date of Research: 1982 – continuing
KEYWORDS: dyspraxia; hearing defect; language development; learning difficulty

8/0842

Hester Adrian Research Centre,
Oxford Road, Manchester M13 9PL
061 275 3334
Jupp, S. Mrs; *Supervisor:* Cunningham, C. Prof.; Sloper, T. Dr
Congenital anomaly – disclosure of diagnosis and early support
Abstract: The study looks at current practices at disclosure and consequent Health Authority support services for parents whose children have been diagnosed as having some form of congenital anomaly. The study examines the feelings, attitudes and behaviours of both the parents and professionals involved in the process. All parents of children between the age of 0-2 years who had been diagnosed as having some form of congenital anomaly within a specific Health Authority District were contacted and interviewed concerning their experiences at disclosure of the condition and aftercare services. A total sample of 238 parents were interviewed. All professional groups involved in disclosure were asked to take part in the study. Two groups in sufficient number agreed to co-operate i.e. 24 midwives and 41 health visitors. Information concerning their feelings, attitudes and behaviour at disclosure were sampled by questionnaire. All data has been collected and an analysis is in progress.
Published Material: JUPP, S. (1987). 'Breaking the news: a way of telling parents their newborn child is handicapped', Mental Handicap, March 1987, pp.8-11.; JUPP, S. (1987). 'Developing a comprehensive support service for parents whose babies are born with a congenital anomaly', International Journal of Rehabilitation Research, Vol 10, No 4, 1987, pp.450-451.
Source of Grant: No funding
Date of Research: 1985-1989
KEYWORDS: birth; counselling; handicapped; parent education

8/0843

Institute of Science and Technology,
Manchester School of Management,
PO Box 88, Manchester M60 1QD
061 236 3311
Cooper, C.L. Prof.; Travers, C. Ms
Occupational stress in teaching

Abstract: This is a three part investigation. In phase 1, a random sample of about 60 teachers were interviewed to help design a teacher stress inventory. On the basis of this phase, a nation-wide investigation of 1,800 teachers throughout the UK was undertaken. In the third phase, an in depth psycho-physiological and biochemical investigation of 60 teachers during a school term is being carried out. Comprehensive blood chemistry, blood pressure, heart rate and other measures have been taken at the beginning of the school year, and will be taken at the end of the first term. The data collection from the large scale survey of 1,800 teachers is now complete and the analysis is underway. Results are, as yet, not available. The purpose of this part of the study is to assess the extent of teacher stress in terms of mental well being, job satisfaction, intention to leave the profession and health behaviours (e.g. smoking, drinking); and then to determine which job stressors are predictive of high levels of each of the stress outcomes described (e.g. mental ill health, intention to leave).
Source of Grant: National Association of Schoolmasters/Union of Women Teachers: £12,000
Date of Research: 1989 – continuing
KEYWORDS: *occupational environment; stress; teacher behaviour*

8/0844
> Centre for Audiology,
> Education of the Deaf and Speech Pathology
> Oxford Road, Manchester M13 9PL
> 061 275 3379/3380
> Aplin, D.Y. Dr; Gallaway, C. Dr; Newton, V.E. Dr
The GMC (Greater Manchester Council) project
Abstract: The aim of the research is to provide longitudinal data on the cognitive and linguistic levels of a complete population of children with prelingual sensori-nerual hearing losses and to identify contributory factors to the child's acquisition of oral language based on aetiological, social, cognitive and interactional evidence. The research consists of all children with bilateral sensori-neural hearing loss born in Greater Manchester in the years 1977-1980 (n-133) with a hearing loss averaging a minimum of 25 dB HL in the better ear (range 25-121dB HL). In phase 1 those children without additional handicaps & from English-speaking homes were studied between the ages of 4 and 7 (n = 79). It is hoped to chart at least some of the children's progress when they have entered secondary school. Comprehensive audiological, psychological and language assessments were carried out in the departmental clinics on 2-3 occasions. A short play session was videotaped to provide mother-child interaction data in addition to the scores from standardized tests. Subsequently these scores have been analyzed. In the follow-up study, it is hoped to visit the children in their schools and obtain data leading to an assessment of their communicative skills in their teens.
Published Material: a list of publications is available from the researchers
Source of Grant: Internal centre funding and donations from the Al-Fayed Charitable Foundation
Date of Research: 1981 – continuing
KEYWORDS: *cognitive development; deaf; language development; hearing defect; oral expression*

8/0845
> Department of Adult and Higher Education
> Oxford Road, Manchester M13 9PL
> 061 275 2000
> Connolly, L.J. Ms; *Supervisor:* MacDonald, J.J. Dr
The role of primary health care in combating the spread of AIDS in rural Africa
Abstract: The aim of the research is to use a substitute AL 721 product to treat HIV (Human Immunodeficiency Virus) positive AIDS (Acquired Immune Deficiency Syndrome) patients, within a primary health care set-up for 6 months to 1 year (and hopefully longer). The research will investigate methods of educating people into taking control over their own health and well-being and that of the community in which they live.
Source of Grant: No funding
Date of Research: 1987 – continuing
KEYWORDS: *acquired Immune Deficiency Syndrome (AIDS); Africa; health education*

8/0846
> Department of Adult and Higher Education
> Oxford Road, Manchester M13 9PL
> 061 275 2000

> Ponga, A.B. Sister; *Supervisor:* Carmen, R.
Education for rural development in Zambia: implications for out of school youth
Abstract: Education has long been recognized as necessary for development. The question remaining is what type of education? The education system in Zambia has failed to bring about socio-economic development, especially in rural areas. A type of education that can play an effective role in rural areas is one that will empower the people so that they can decide on and design their own destinies. The youth in rural areas could be mobilized, made aware and used to bring about the desired development. The proposed development process will have to be under the control of the people themselves; unlike current rural projects in the country. The aim at a selected group of individuals whereas the researcher proposes an involvement of as many and of as varied a group as possible, preferably the whole village. The researcher has visited 13 rural projects in four provinces of Zambia after a year of literary research. The fieldwork involved interviews with project managers, trainees and sometimes villagers. Almost all the youth projects offered skills in wood/metal work, building, tailoring and farming based on a syllabus (direction) from the Ministry of Youth and Sport. Most projects had a European volunteer leading or playing a major role in the running of the project. In the sense of producing a number of skilled youths these training schemes could be said to be achieving something, but they are not achieving rural development which is the stated aim. Those who included farming on their syllabuses were aiming at producing emergent 'commercial farmers', who would use the villagers as cheap labour. In short the Training Skills Centres, which are meant to engineer rural development stand in the midst of rural areas which have very little to do with rural development.
Source of Grant: No funding
Date of Research: 1987-1989
KEYWORDS: *rural development; system of education; youth; Zambia*

8/0847
> Department of Education
> Oxford Road, Manchester M13 9PL
> 061 275 3407
> Phillips, J.A.N. Mrs
Closer involvement of teachers and advisers in teacher training (PGCE)
Abstract: The aim of the research is to investigate the feasibility of involving heads of departments and advisers in the initial training of a PGCE group of foreign languages students. The teachers and advisers have been involved at every stage of the course from selection to examining. The researcher is now investigating the comparative usefulness of such involvement – where it is better to have such involvement, where the involvement produces greater benefit for both the students and the teachers and advisers. Research is by experiment questionnaire and interview feedback.
Published Material: PHILLIPS, J.A.N. (1985). 'An experimental scheme for PGCE courses in modern languages', National Association of Language Advisers Journal, No 16, pp.20-22.
Source of Grant: No funding
Date of Research: 1983 – continuing
KEYWORDS: *curriculum development; post-graduate; teacher education*

8/0848
> Department of Education
> Oxford Road, Manchester M13 9PL
> 061 275 3407
> Phillips, J.A.N. Mrs
Family workshop project
Abstract: This project was to train leaders in Scotland and the north of England to work on liberation work with young people up to and including the age of 12 years. It assists the young people in retaining/reclaiming their sense of powerfulness and helping their siblings, friends and associates to do the same. The researcher organized a series of workshops for young people with their parents and other adults. These were led by T. Jackins and P. Wipfler from Palo Alto, California, USA, who worked with trainee leaders from England and Scotland.
Source of Grant: Network for Social Change: £1,000 The Re-evaluation Foundation: £2,500
Date of Research: 1987-1989
KEYWORDS: *family; guidance; parent-child relation; youth*

8/0849
Department of Education
Oxford Road, Manchester M13 9PL
061 275 3463
Antonio, J.T. Mr; *Supervisor:* Harris, J.M. Dr
The philosophy and language of African arts
Abstract: There will be an investigation of the use of imagery and symbolism, especially in folk and traditional arts. There will also be an attempt to answer the following questions: (1) Are African indigenous arts entirely 'primitive' and 'non-classical'? (2) Is there a 'civilized' art at all? If so, what are the criteria for its identification? (3) Can cultural differences affect understanding and appreciation of a work of art? (4) How has European contact affected African arts? (5) What role can modern African literature play in establishing the philosophy of 'African thought'?
Source of Grant: No funding
Date of Research: 1981 – continuing
KEYWORDS: *Africa; civilization; cultural development; folk art; literature*

8/0850
Department of Education
Oxford Road, Manchester M13 9PL
De061 275 3492
Evans, D.R. Mr; *Supervisor:* Robertson, A.B. Dr
The Stockport Sunday School 1784-1900
Abstract: It is intended to examine every facet of the work of the Stockport Sunday School during the specified dates, as well as examining the role in the life of the community it served. There will be an examination as to how the aims and objectives of the founders were met in the early days, and how these changed later on. The curriculum of the school and the methodologies used will be examined, and comparisons made with other Sunday Schools. The effects of the competition of Board and other schools will be considered, as well as the trends affecting Sunday School attendance during its history.
Source of Grant: No funding
Date of Research: 1985 – continuing
KEYWORDS: *denominational school; history of education; school-community relation*

8/0851
Department of Education
Centre of Adult and Higher Education,
Oxford Road, Manchester M13 9PL
061 275 3463
Ledwith, M. Mrs; *Supervisor:* Ruddock, R. Mr; Toye, N.H. Mr
Antonio Gramsci: the application of his theoretical concepts to working class adult education
Abstract: The British adult education context is constantly criticized for its lack of praxis. Jane Thompson in particular attacks theory as 'bland, latinate and unilluminating' and practice as too specific. The result is a divorce theory from social reality. Without a sound theoretical framework, the multiplicity of issues in the field obscures decisions and distorts perspectives. This research will analyze the writings of Gramsci in relation to working class adult education and assess their contribution to a practical theory.
Published Material: LEDWITH, M. (1984). 'Antonio Gramsci and adult education: an introduction'. University of Manchester.
Source of Grant: No funding
Date of Research: 1984 – continuing
KEYWORDS: *adult education; theory of education; working class*

8/0852
Department of Education
Oxford Road, Manchester M13 9PL
061 275 3463
Foster, R.M. Mr; *Supervisor:* Drake, K.B. Mr
The costs of knowledge production and their significance for the relationships between primary schools and their communities
Abstract: The aims and objectives of the research are as follows: (1) To develop a systems model to clarify the processes and resources utilized in the production of knowledge thought by teacher, parent or administrator, to be relevant to an understanding of the contribution of the school and its resources to the community; (2) to cost the resources employed by the participants to produce knowledge. This costing is to be attempted at two levels: (a) A direct financial cost analysis of the equipment material; and (b) an appraisal of the opportunity costs, with particular reference to the human cap-

ital resources and the utilization of time; (3) to apply the model to the activities of a small group of primary schools and their communities in an effort to identify and delimit the possible influences of the incidence of knowledge production and acquisition costs on the behaviour of individuals and groups; (4) an investigation will be undertaken of the costs of producing knowledge for the express purpose of informing (improving?) decision-making in relation to specific decisions of varying magnitude and complexity.
Source of Grant: No funding
Date of Research: 1983 – continuing
KEYWORDS: *cost of education; primary education; school-community relation*

8/0853
Department of Education
Oxford Road, Manchester M13 9PL
061 275 3516
O'Sullivan, A.M. Miss; Loughlin, A.M. Miss; *Supervisor:* Lonton, A.P. Mr
Adults with Spina Bifida: their further education, employment, daily living skills, social life and health problems
Abstract: Relatively little has been published on the problems of adults with Spina Bifida. This study is directed towards further education, employment, daily living skills, social life and the health problems of these multiply disabled adults. Information has been obtained from questionnaires sent to 157 adults, and from structured interviews with 90 adults aged 18-26 years. Results obtained have indicated a high attendance rate at FE colleges, followed by very poor employment records. Few live away from home, and few of even the more physically capable adults look after their daily needs e.g. making meals or doing their own laundry. Less than a quarter had a regular boy/girlfriend, and only 3% were married. The most common health problems were pressure sores and urinary tract complications.
Published Material: LONTON, A.P., O'SULLIVAN, A.M. & LOUGHLIN, A.M. (1983). 'Spina Bifida adults', Zeitschrift fur Kinderchirurgie, Vol 38, No 2, pp. 110-112.; LONTON, A.P., LOUGHLIN, A.M. & O'SULLIVAN, A.M. (1984). 'The employment of adults with Spina Bifida', Zeitschrift fur Kinderchirurgie, Vol 39, No 2, pp.132-134.; RICKWOOD, A.M.K., HODGSON, J., LONTON, A.P. & THOMAS, D.G. (1984). 'Medical and surgical complications in adolescent and young adult patients with Spina Bifida', Health Trends, Vol 16, pp.91-95.
Source of Grant: Richard Fund: £5,000 Special Education Needs National Advisory Council: £250
Date of Research: 1982 – continuing
KEYWORDS: *adult; employment; further education; physically handicapped; Spina Bifida*

8/0854
Department of Education
Oxford Road, Manchester M13 9PL
061 275 3440
Owen, P. Ms; Stainton, C. Miss; *Supervisor:* Beveridge, M.C. Dr; Christie, T. Mr
Development of specifications for graded tests of literacy for the 11-16 year age group
Abstract: The research proposed is to identify aspects of reading and writing (Dr Beveridge) which are developmental, educable and assessable. Current practice in the published literature will be reviewed and an informal sampling of practice in the three LEAs (Local Education Authorities) collaborating with the JMB (Joint Matriculation Board) on educational records in Salford LEA, which is collaborating with the host department and in the FE (Further Education) literacy courses accredited by Manchester Open College Federation will be used to evaluate potential means of enhancing literacy and to field test assessment materials. By the end of the first year, techniques required for the production of graded tests tailored to individual needs will have been explored (Mr Christie) and microprocessor-based screening tests, largely focused on reading produced. In the second year, seminars for teachers will be held on the assessment and development of reading and writing skills, and after implementation, the success of the screening test as a predictor of examination entry point will be evaluated, and an outline graded 'syllabus' and a specification for graded examinations with specimen materials will be drawn up.
Source of Grant: Joint Matriculation Board: £80,000
Date of Research: 1984 – continuing
KEYWORDS: *literacy; reading; secondary education; test; writing*

8/0855

Department of Education
Oxford Road, Manchester M13 9PL
061 275 3516
Lonton, A.P. Mr
Integration of Spina Bifida children into ordinary schools
Abstract: In 1975 a vigorous policy of integrating children was initiated by the author at the Sheffield Children's Hospital Combined Clinic for Spina Bifida children. The effects of this policy and the 1981 Education Act have been studied in 1986 both in Sheffield and in Manchester schools. The bulk of the Sheffield children are now successfully integrated. Both studies found parents, teachers and the children themselves to be overwhelmingly in favour of integration. Many children were transferred from special to ordinary schools, with very few being returned as a result of failed integration. The parents found substantial social and educational advantages in integration. Areas in which improvements are needed include: (1) Non-teaching support for toiletting; (2) more physiotherapy; (3) more opportunities for inservice education of teachers.
Published Material: LONTON, A.P. (1981). 'The integration (mainstreaming) of Spina Bifida children into ordinary schools', Zeitschrift fur Kinderchirurgie, Vol 34, No 4, pp.356-364.; LONTON, A.P. (1986). 'The integration of Spina Bifida children – are their needs being met?', Zeitschrift fur Kinderchirurgie, Vol 41, Supplement 1, pp.45-47.
Source of Grant: Richard Fund: £2,000 Economic and Social Research Council (ESRC): £9,000 Leverhulme Trust: £5,300
Date of Research: 1975 – continuing
KEYWORDS: integration; physically handicapped; pupil; Spina Bifida

8/0856

Department of Education
Oxford Road, Manchester M13 9PL
061 275 3463
Simpson, K.M.L. Mr; *Supervisor:* Robertson, A.B. Dr
The history of the King's School, Chester, from 1642
Abstract: The intention of this thesis is to write a comprehensive history of the King's School, Chester, from 1642, to the point at which the Cathedral's direct authority over, and responsibility for, the School were terminated. All aspects of the School's development during this time will be carefully studied. The masters, ushers, masters of choristers and other fee paying pupils will be searched out, and biographical studies will be attempted for many of them. A detailed study of the curriculum and its development over the centuries will be attempted, with a keen eye to the time and circumstances of the introduction of modern subjects, and a continuing interest in the classics and religious education. For this purpose it is hoped that evidence of some of the text books used will be found. The standards of education achieved will be gauged as far as possible. Throughout the thesis there will remain the constant theme of an attempt to write the history of the School in the context of its setting within the City of Chester, as an integral part of the Cathedral, and there will be an attempt to assess the ways in which the great historical events, issues and wars, especially the Civil War, affected the school and its members. Financial and religious implications and difficulties of the school's control by the Cathedral will constitute an important part of the research which will aim to judge whether the benefits of such a close connection were outweighed by the disadvantages. The social background of the scholars will be studied, as will the masters' qualifications, hours, holidays and religious obligations.
Source of Grant: No funding
Date of Research: 1980 – continuing
KEYWORDS: denominational study; history of education

8/0857

Department of Education
Oxford Road, Manchester M13 9PL
061 275 3463
Gleave, I.P. Mrs.; *Supervisor:* Robertson, A.B. Dr
The Manchester Education Committee: 1903 to 1930
Abstract: Aspects of influence, policy and power, as they existed in Manchester prior to the passing of the 1902 Education Act, are considered in relation to the setting up of the Education Committee, to its composition and development, and to various areas of provision up to 1930. Manchester had been a centre of educational controversy prior to 1870. In 1903, the transfer of authority from School Board and the SEEs of Manchester and Salford to the City Council was achieved with seeming ease. This suggests an intervening move towards consensus, locally rather than nationally. Between 1870 and 1903, the city's area trebled, increasing further by 50% in 1904. The Education Committee of this, the second largest County Borough outside London, was prestigious, but subject, nevertheless, in its actions to the City Council's sanction. An attempt is made to analyze the composition of this Committee throughout the period and to study the roles of ordinary members, both elective and co-optive, and of the chairmen. Attention is given to the development of the administrative structure and to the roles of the directors, especially C.H. Wyatt and Spurley Hey. Influences, especially those of local origin albeit external to the Committee, are considered as are pressure group activities. Local political parties have warranted investigation. Whilst party politics seemed relatively unimportant in policy formation, party group support could be crucial in seeing a project through Council. The relationship between the Committee and the Board of Education is considered in regard to policy and finance.
Source of Grant: No funding
Date of Research: 1983 – continuing
KEYWORDS: administration of education; educational policy; financial resources; history of education; secondary education

8/0858

Department of Education
Oxford Road, Manchester M13 9PL
061 275 3463
Fairbairn, G.J. Mr; *Supervisor:* Harris, J.M. Dr
Responsibility
Abstract: The thesis will first examine some theoretical views of responsibility. There will be a review of earlier work (Aristotle on freewill, division, voluntary and involuntary actions; H.L.A. Hart, J. Glover, J. Harrison and J. Rachels on responsibility; the existentialist position on responsibility; the emphasis on humanistic psychology on responsibility for self). There will be a critique of H.L.A. Hart's 'Varieties of Responsibility' and then an examination of casual and moral responsibility and negative responsibility. The second part of the thesis will deal with responsibility and morality and will consider the following: (1) Human action; (2) the nature of morality; (3) the importance of intention in morality; (4) responsibility, morality and self. The last part of the thesis will examine responsibility in human living, considering: (1) Education and therapy; and (2) the development of responsible (e.g. moral) persons.
Source of Grant: No funding
Date of Research: 1981 – continuing
KEYWORDS: moral development; responsibility; therapy

8/0859

Department of Education
Oxford Road, Manchester M13 9PL
061 275 3463
Bentley, D. Mrs; *Supervisor:* Griffiths, R. Mr
An examination of the development of non-verbal awareness in children aged five to eighteen years
Abstract: There are three major objectives to this piece of research: (1) To produce a comprehensive analysis of the development of the awareness of non-verbal behaviours with special reference to a classroom situation, in children aged five to eighteen. This analysis is intended to include an examination of the differences in non-verbal cueing and inference in white and West Indian children; (2) an examination of the mediating influence of non-verbal behaviours of teachers upon the response of the pupils in the classrooms; and (3) an examination of the development of teachers attitudes as a result of their interpretations of pupil non-verbal cues.
Source of Grant: no funding
Date of Research: 1982 – continuing
KEYWORDS: interaction; non-verbal communication; pupil: teacher behaviour

8/0860

Department of Education
Oxford Road, Manchester M13 9PL
061 275 3463
Farr, M.V. Mrs; *Supervisor:* Roberts, C. Miss
Pupils' views on institutional racism
Abstract: The work consists of an investigation into the attitudes of target groups of pupils from different ethnic minority groups towards institutional racism, an investigation of possible variations in group perspectives, and an exploration of a variety of methods for obtaining pupils' views of their teachers and schools to assess

the irrelative merit, particularly with regard to: (1) The elicitation of the pupils' own constructs about actual teachers rather than researcher imposed constructs about hypothetical or stereotypical teachers; (2) the structure and frequency of the constructs and their relationship with constructs reported in previous literature; (3) their effectiveness in provoking full and free discussion as getting pupils to express their views at any length about their teachers and schools, particularly in the sensitive area of racial prejudice, is regarded as a problem.
Source of Grant: No funding
Date of Research: 1983 – continuing
KEYWORDS: attitude; ethnic minority; pupil; racism; stereotype

8/0861

Department of Education
Oxford Road, Manchester M13 9PL
061 275 3440
O'Connor, A. Mrs; Greenslade, L. Mr; *Supervisor:* Christie, T. Mr; Peers, I.S. Mr
Development and dissemination of a Family Smoking Education project
Abstract: This project involves (I).The development of FSE (Family Smoking Education) materials. Review of studies on smoking prevention. Evaluation of an effective Norwegian campaign and feasibility trials in British schools. The aims of the research are to: (a) enquire whether the Norwegian programme in translation was suitable for use in British schools; and (b) if the programme holds good, at what age range of pupils should it be targeted. Commenced with sample of teachers, HEOs (Health Education Officers), pupils and parents from Scotland, England, N. Ireland and North Wales. The subjects involved were: 32 teachers, 24 parents, 2 HEOs and 36 pupils. (II). In the light of the previous study, the materials were adapted for use in British schools. The second phase of the study was to disseminate the FSE programme using a range of strategies and to monitor which strategies produced the highest level of programme use. Three target groups were assessed: (i) District Health Management teams; (ii) LEA (Local Education Authority) advisers; and (iii) headteachers.
Published Material: PEERS, I.S. (1984). 'The development of Family Smoking Education Materials', Journal of Education on Health, Vol 2, No 5, pp. 97-103.; PEERS, I.S., CHRISTIE, T. & LEDWITH, F. (1984). 'Development of the Family Smoking Education Materials', Interim reports to the Health Education Council, London, May & November.
Source of Grant: Health Education Council, London: £48,000 for two years
Date of Research: 1984 – continuing
KEYWORDS: family; health education; parent participation; prevention; smoking

8/0862

Department of Education
Oxford Road, Manchester M13 9PL
061 275 3463
Harrison, I. Mr; *Supervisor:* Christie, T. Mr
An examination of the attitudinal and motivational response of primary school children to microcomputers in the classroom
Abstract: The research is seeking to answer the following questions with particular emphasis upon the effects of software and program content on pupil motivation and attitude information: (a) To what extent are the high levels of motivation and concentration due to the Hawthorne effect, i.e. due to the impact and novelty caused by the introduction of the micro rather than by the direct effect of the machine upon pupils' motivation? (b) what can account for the apparent short term effect upon the motivation of some pupils, albeit a small minority?; (c) what is the relationship between pupils' attitudes and conceptions towards the micro and the level of motivation produced by the experience of using a micro? (d) how are these attitudes and conceptions to the micro changed and modified by the experience of working with microcomputers in the classroom? (e) what evidence is available to support Mullan's suggestion that pupils' attitudinal responses to the micro reflect their teachers' attitudes, and what is the effect of teacher attitudes upon pupils' responses? (f) to what extent is the impact and effect of the microcomputer determined by the available software? Initial motivation with the micro appears to be high for the majority of pupils; does the available software affect this motivation and if it does, what types and qualities of program enhance or retard this motivation.
Source of Grant: No funding

Date of Research: 1984 – continuing
KEYWORDS: computer assisted instruction; microcomputer; motivation primary education; software

8/0863

Department of Education
Oxford Road, Manchester M13 9PL
061 275 3463
Davies, J. Mrs; *Supervisor:* Christie, T. Mr
Staff perceptions of student learning difficulties and implications for staff development
Abstract: The objectives of the research are to examine: (1) How conscious individual staff are of student learning problems and how this varies as a function of length of experience and type and nature of training; (2) the extent to which individual staff place a greater emphasis on lecturing or learning technique and how this varies as a function of subject and level of study; (3) the extent to which their teaching strategies are consciously geared to perceived student needs. As a test of the utility of this information it will be possible to: (1) Identify individual staff who, judging from the gaps in their descriptions of student learning problems, can by an exploration of this area come to a greater understanding of their teaching problems – staff development; (2) infer the motivational patterns existing among staff, at least as a crude intrinsic-extrinsic continuum, which may be capitalized upon in staff development programmes.
Source of Grant: No funding
Date of Research: 1980 – continuing
KEYWORDS: learning difficulty; staff development; student; teaching technique

8/0864

Department of Education
Oxford Road, Manchester M13 9PL
061 275 3463
Yates, J. Mr; *Supervisor:* Elliott, C.D. Dr
The differential impact of sign acquisition on the communicative behaviour of hearing, mute, subnormal children
Abstract: The objectives of the research are as follows: I. The Sign Lexicon: (i) To generate an initial sign lexicon of approximately 100 signs based on developmental linguistic principles; (ii) to describe the origins of terms of iconicity and motor complexity; (iii) (a) to use such a description to construct an ordering of relational signs based on probable ease of acquisition; (b) to use such a description to construct parallel or equivalent lists of substantive signs so that individual topic preferences can be taken account of in the teaching programme; (iv) to compare such a lexicon with the Makator Vocabulary. II. The Analysis of Sign Acquisition: (i) To describe and contrast the pre-verbal cognitive, communicative and social behaviour of two groups of children: a severely language handicapped, sociable subnormal group and a severely language handicapped autistic subnormal group; (ii) to teach each group to imitate, understand and use the initial sign lexicon; (iii) (a) to observe the relationship between iconicity, motor complexity and speed of acquisition for individuals and groups; (b) to compare predicted ease of acquisition with actual speed; (iv) to examine the power of various pre-intervention measurements as predictors of success in sign acquisition; (v) to describe and contrast the impact of sign acquisition on the social, cognitive and communicative behaviours of the two groups.
Source of Grant: No funding
Date of Research: 1981 – continuing
KEYWORDS: communication; dumb; lexicon; mentally handicapped; sign; social behaviour

8/0865

Department of Education
Oxford Road, Manchester M13 9PL
061 275 3463
Kantab, T. Mr; *Supervisor:* Beveridge, M.C. Dr
A study of structural generality in emotionally disturbed and normal children from the point of view of a theory of construct system organization
Abstract: The broad areas of concern in this research will be studied in an attempt to: (1) Assess the use of triadic grid techniques in the diagnosis of emotional disturbance; (2) develop a functionally differential perspective for meaningfully conceptualizing the two major properties of construct structures – differentiation and organization; (3) take a further step towards a theoretically consistent integration of the areas of person perception, construct struc-

ture and modes of interpersonal constructing; (4) determine if initial construct validity for the present construction of structural generality can be established; and (5) evaluate the fruitfulness of construing interpersonal conceptual structures of emotionally disturbed children from the present point of view. It is recognised, of course, that these objectives are closely inter-related, all contributing to and influencing one another. Keeping this in mind will facilitate a more coherent evaluation of the results of this research and will enable the investigator to validate his initial and continuously developing construction of the social-cognitive behaviour in emotionally disturbed children.
Source of Grant: No funding
Date of Research: 1984 – continuing
KEYWORDS: child; emotional disorder; maladjusted; social behaviour

8/0866
Department of Education
Centre for Adult and Higher Education,
Oxford Road, Manchester M13 9PL
061 275 3487
Boreham, N.C. Dr
Cognitive components of experience in professional diagnosis and decision making, with implications for professional education
Abstract: Task analyses are being carried out of diagnosis and decision making in selected professions. Using protocol analysis techniques, computable models of the cognitive processes involved are being constructed. Comparisons between experts and novices are being made, and the results are being used to suggest improvements in current professional education and training.
Published Material: BOREHAM, N.C. (1989). 'Modelling medical decision making under uncertainty', British Journal of Educational Psychology, Vol 59, pp.187-199.; BOREHAM, N.C. (1987). 'Causal attributions by sensing and intuitive types during diagnostic problem solving', Instructional Science, Vol 16, pp.123-136.
Source of Grant: No funding
Date of Research: 1987 – continuing
KEYWORDS: cognition; decision making; problem solving; profession

8/0867
Department of Education
Oxford Road, Manchester M13 9PL
061 275 3463
Alston, D.J. Mrs; *Supervisor:* Lonton, A.P. Mr
The handwriting of Cheshire primary school children
Abstract: The objectives of the research are: (1) To establish normative samples for Cheshire seven, eight and nine year-old pupils; (2) to identify those pupils who continue to experience difficulty in handwriting at the age of ten years; (3) to examine and classify their problems; and (4) to establish and evaluate remedial measures.
Source of Grant: No funding
Date of Research: 1984 – continuing
KEYWORDS: primary education; remedial teaching; writing

8/0868
Department of Education
Oxford Road, Manchester M13 9PL
061 275 4363
McNamara, E. Mr; *Supervisor:* Elliott, C.D. Dr
Behavioural interventions with secondary aged pupils: a theoretical and clinical investigation
Abstract: The research is seeking to provide, in varying degrees, answers to the following questions: I. Applied behaviour analysis in the classroom: (i) What are the obstacles to the implementation of behaviour modification in secondary school classrooms? (ii) If the obstacles are overcome, is social reinforcement an effective reinforcer? (iii) Is there teacher resistance to the demand for change implicit in behaviour modification? II. Situational surveys: (i) What is the nature and extent of classroom problems as perceived by secondary school teachers? (ii) What are the natural rates of social reinforcement in the secondary classroom? (iii) What systems of reward and punishment exist in secondary schools? (iv) What is the pupil's perception of rewards and punishments? III. Non-classroom based behavioural interventions: (i) Are there available strategies which are not based on the teacher as contingency manager, for bringing the pupil's behaviour under teacher control and perhaps even self-control, e.g. self-monitoring procedures and behavioural contacts? (ii) Is the simplistic operant model of externally controlled behaviour modification programmes appropriate

for the school population found in secondary schools?
Source of Grant: No funding
Date of Research: 1981 – continuing
KEYWORDS: behaviour; punishment; reward; secondary education; social interaction

8/0869
Department of Education
Centre for Educational Guidance and Special Needs,
Oxford Road, Manchester M13 9PL
061 273 3333 ext 3000
Porter, E.R. Miss; *Supervisor:* Conti-Ramsden, G. Dr; Mittler, P. Prof.
Fathers and the language-impaired child
Abstract: Research of the last fifteen years has suggested that parent-child interactions play a potentially important role in the language development of a child but although extensive research has been carried out to investigate features of mothers' speech, there has been a dearth of investigations on father's contribution to the linguistic environment of the young child. The aims of this project are: (1) to pinpoint similarities and differences in rate and manner of development of the language-impaired child and its younger sibling, and to see over time how systems diverge and what consistencies there are; (2) to document the differences in maternal and paternal speech input to both their language-impaired and normally developing children. The observation method will be adopted using a mixed design of both longitudinal and cross sectional studies. The detailed longitudinal study will help validate the findings of the cross-sectional study. All families in the sample have a language-impaired child and younger normally developing siblings. Two families will be followed on a monthly basis for 2 years. Five families will participate in a cross-sectional study and control families will also be used.
Published Material: PORTER, R. & CONTI-RAMSDEN, G. (1987). 'Clarification requests and the language-impaired child', Child Language Teaching and Therapy, No 3, pp.133-150.
Source of Grant: Economic and Social Research Council (ESRC) linked studentship: £3,496 per annum
Date of Research: 1985 – continuing
KEYWORDS: family environment; interaction; language development; language impairment; sibling;

8/0870
Department of Education
Centre for Physical Education,
Oxford Road, Manchester M13 9PL
061 275 4962
Harrison, P.W. Mr; *Supervisor:* Macdonald, A.I.
Factor analysis of the environmental influences causing poor fitness response and obesity in post-adolescent children
Abstract: The medical profession has for many years been concerned with the relationship of fitness, obesity and cardiovascular disease, and the Health Education Council has, in the last decade, spent large sums of money trying to re-educate the population. We now have the firm philosophy that prevention is better than cure, which is both ethically and financially sound. Physical education from its earliest beginnings had fitness and training as major emphases in its programmes. This philosophy waned in the 60s and 70s, but a more health conscious approach is again very much to the fore. As a population, we are now taking better care of our bodies, being more concerned about our eating habits, and taking regular exercise. Although many exercise and dietary programmes are offered, there has been little research carried out into the reasons why an individual becomes over-weight or less fit. If one can, for the moment, eliminate hereditary factors and disease, any causative factors must therefore be environmental. This study proposes to examine these environmental factors to identify the major constituent causes and thus develop a programme which would result in fitter, healthier, more aware individuals.
Source of Grant: No funding
Date of Research: 1987-1990
KEYWORDS: adolescent; fitness; health education; nutrition; obesity

8/0871
Department of Education
Oxford Road, Manchester M13 9PL
061 275 3463
Jordan, J.A. Miss; *Supervisor:* Mittler, P.J. Prof.

In class support for pupils experiencing learning difficulties in high schools
Abstract: A great deal has been written about 'remedial' and special education, and more recently, about meeting 'special educational needs' within a mainstream curriculum. However, there is little research in this area. 'Support' teaching as an alternative to 'withdrawal' is still very much in its infancy as an approach and the literature to date is speculative rather than conclusive. The main purpose of this research is to investigate 'in class support' within the context of a 'whole-school' approach, as an effective means of enabling those 18% of pupils (estimated by Warnock) already attending secondary schools access to a broader curriculum. Questionnaires were designed and delivered to all Manchester high schools (January-March 1987). There was a good response – 23 of the 28 schools visited completed a total of 116 questionnaires; 43 support teachers, and 73 subject specialists responded. The information gained led to follow-up visits to schools which seemed to indicate a commitment to support teaching as a means to curriculum change. One school has been targeted for in depth study and exploration of actual practice. The focus is on the school, the class, and individual pupils experiencing learning difficulties. Currently, the emphasis is on classroom observation, with and without a support teacher present, and the learning experiences for pupils experiencing learning difficulties.
Source of Grant: Manchester LEA: fees
Date of Research: 1986-1990
KEYWORDS: ability grouping; integration; learning difficulty; secondary education; special needs; support teacher

8/0872
Department of Education
Oxford Road, Manchester M13 9PL
061 275 3463
Goodman, J.F. Ms; *Supervisor:* Taylorson, D.E. Dr; Robertson, A.B. Dr
Women and the management of education 1800-1914
Abstract: The research aims to trace the patterns of women's participation in the organization of education in Manchester and Chester in the period 1800-1914. The focus is on how women's participation in the organization of education in Manchester and Chester was related to involvement with other issues and activities of importance to women (philanthropy, enfranchisement, trade unionism, etc.) as well as its relation to the existence of friendship, marital and political networks amongst the women. How such networks affected the development of the philosophy and practice regarding the education of girls and women is a major theme of the research. The research examines general 19th Century texts concerning women and girls, as well as archival material relating specifically to Manchester and Chester. The extent and manner of women's involvement in the management of girls' and women's education, their relative involvement vis a vis men, and in co-operation with men; the effects of their work considered against the background of changes in the education of women and girls during the period; the increasing participation of middle-class women in employment and in public life, as well as in the light of the general developments in local government reform and in the provision of education.
Source of Grant: Economic and Social Research Council (ESRC) Competition Award: £5,500
Date of Research: 1986-1989
KEYWORDS: administration of education; feminism; history of education; particpation; women's education; women's movement

8/0873
Department of Education
Oxford Road, Manchester M13 9PL
061 275 3437
London University
Institute of Education,
20 Bedford Way, London WC1H OAL
071 636 1500
Hodkinson, S.R. Mr; Thomas, L.M. Ms
The Economic Awareness Teacher Training Programme (EcATT)
Abstract: The Economic Awareness Teacher Training Programme (EcATT) aims to promote and monitor the development and implementation of economic awareness programmes in schools, colleges and LEAs (Local Education Authorities).
Published Material: HODKINSON, S.R. & THOMAS, L.M. (Eds). (1988). 'What is economic awareness?', Economic Awareness Journal, Vol 1, No 1, September, pp.5-11.

Source of Grant: British Petroleum; 1987-88: £30,000 Banking Information Service: £30,000 Department of Trade and Industry: £107,000 Unilever: £10,000 Esmee Fairbairn Charitable Trust: £33,300 University Grants Committee: £60,000
Date of Research: 1986 – continuing
KEYWORDS: curriculum development; economic studies; teacher education

8/0874
Department of Education
Oxford Road, Manchester M13 9PL
061 275 3437
Davies, P.I.J. Mr; *Supervisor:* Hodkinson, S.R. Mr
The contribution of geography to economic awareness
Abstract: In the context of national statements, legislation and curriculum initiatives in Geography and Economic Awareness, the aim of this research is to investigate the work of a geography department in secondary school. This is an ethnographic study in which the work of members of the department are observed inside and outside the classroom. The observations are augmented by informal interviews, personal diaries, teacher biographies and an analysis of documents. These records will be used to describe the way in which members of the department are tackling economic awareness in their teaching, and the influences that bear on this work.
Source of Grant: No funding
Date of Research: 1986-1990
KEYWORDS: curriculum development; economic studies; geography; secondary education

8/0875
Department of Education
The English Language Centre,
Oxford Road, Manchester M13 9PL
061 275 3467
Motteram, G.J. Mr; Whitehead, J. Mr
Bilingual Learners Project – Pilot Scheme
Abstract: This research has 3 main purposes: (1) to provide information about the English language needs of multilingual children; (2) to look at the role of support teachers in the mainstream; the attitudes of teachers towards support and withdrawal; the methods used in schools; areas for INSET (Inservice Education and Training of Teachers); (3) based on (1) and (2) above – to provide ESOL (English to Speakers of Other Languages) teachers with help in the production of materials; helping them define their role; highlighting areas for further study. Data is currently being collected in 1 secondary school in Oldham. This is being done by video and sound recording classes and by interviewing teachers. This is a pilot study only. There are potentially 12 members of staff involved. The main concentration in the classroom is on a group of seven 4th year students who are now only occasionally withdrawn.
Source of Grant: Department of Education funds: £300
Date of Research: 1987 – continuing
KEYWORDS: ability grouping; bilingualism; English language; language teaching; multilingualism; support teacher

8/0876
Department of Education
Oxford Road, Manchester M13 9PL
061 275 3499
Supervisor: Mittler, P.J. Prof.
The curricular experiences of maladjusted pupils with special reference to their personal, social and moral education
Abstract: This research aims to evaluate the curricular experience and needs of pupils with social and emotional problems (the maladjusted) in 25-30 north west schools. Particular reference will be made to their personal, social and moral education. Phase I (1986-87), involves a literature search, preliminary reading and piloting of questionnaires and interview schedules for teachers and heads. Phase II (1987-88), will include, (1) a preliminary survey of 25-30 schools and units; interviewing head teachers (6-page schedules) and the issue of a 10-page questionnaire to all teachers; pupils will be interviewed using BAS Social Reasoning Scale and Word Definition Test (at least 400); (2)(a) an in depth survey of 1-2 schools; (b) carrying out a moral education programme; (3) collating and evaluating the results. Phase III (1989-90), will be the final report and the presentation of the thesis.
Source of Grant: No funding
Date of Research: 1986-1990
KEYWORDS: educational need; maladjusted; moral education; social development

8/0877

Department of Education
Centre for Physical Education,
Oxford Road,
Manchester M13 9PL
061 275 4962
Wigglesworth, N. Mr; *Supervisor:* Hardman, K. Mr;
McNair, D. Mr

A social history of rowing in England from 1715 to the present day

Abstract: A survey of social trends in the history of rowing from 1715 — the first time boat racing was institutionally organized in the Doggett's Coat and Badge Race — paying particular attention to elements of trade, commercialism, professionalism, recreationalism and amateurism in the production of the sport of rowing as it is known today. Main sources include the minute books from some 50 rowing clubs from Berwick on Tweed to Bideford and contemporary newspaper reports which together should redress the balance against non-amateur and non-Oxbridge rowing exhibited in all rowing histories. The main thesis seeks to prove that rowing in all its occupational and sporting forms pre-dates any upper class involvement and that public school and Oxbridge participation moulded the sport into its own establishment image through the rigorous application of amateurism against the will of many, and that this schism has its effects on the sport today.

Published Material: WIGGLESWORTH, N.D. (1986). 'A history of rowing in the North West of England', The British Journal of Sports History, Vol 3, No 2, pp.145-157.; WIGGLESWORTH, N.D. (1987). 'Victorian and Edwardian Boating'. London: Batsford Books.

Source of Grant: No funding
Date of Research: 1984 – continuing
KEYWORDS: history; social development; water sport

8/0878

Department of Education
Oxford Road,
Manchester M13 9PL
061 275 3467
O'Brien, T. Ms; *Supervisor:* Jordan, R.R.

A comparison of linguistic performance in continuous assessment and unseen examination writing at undergraduate level

Abstract: The research aims to discover whether there is any basis to students' intuitive feelings that their linguistic performance deteriorates in examination conditions. Continuous assessment essays and examination questions written on the same areas and within a very short space of time of each other are being analyzed in ignorance of the grades already awarded. Scope is limited to undergraduates in the Psychology Department, writing in 4 special subject areas. The results of the analysis of linguistic performance up to and including discourse level, will eventually be compared with the grades that have been awarded.

Published Material: O'BRIEN, T. (1987). 'Writing for continuous assessment or examinations: a comparison of style'. In: Proceedings of the Selmons Conference, 1985. ELT Docs. Oxford: Pergamon.

Source of Grant: No funding
Date of Research: 1982 – continuing
KEYWORDS: comparative analysis; continuious assessment; examination; linguistics; undergraduate; writing

8/0879

Department of Education
Centre for Adult and Higher Education,
Oxford Road, Manchester M13 9PL
061 275 3487/3399
Boreham, N.C. Dr; Arthur, T.A.A. Dr

Learning to diagnose faults in computer controlled production systems

Abstract: Students were trained to detect and diagnose faults in a computer-controlled production system. Three experiments were conducted on the effects of (1) lengthy practice on speed and accuracy of diagnosis; (2) lengthy practice on resistance to interference, and (3) pre-training in diagnostic heuristics on transfer to a novel problem. The results provided guidelines for industrial training, and evidence that fault diagnosis may become automatic with sufficient practice.

Source of Grant: Leverhulme Trust: £34,000
Date of Research: 1988-1990
KEYWORDS: cognition; computer engineering; diagnosis; failure; vocational training

8/0880

Department of Education
Oxford Road, Manchester M13 9PL
061 273 3333
Tomlinson, P.A. Miss; *Supervisor:* Roberts, G. Mr

Children's oral stories and reading achievements

Abstract: The aim of the research is to discover whether there is any relationship between a child's oral storytelling ability upon entry to school, and his reading achievement in the final year of the infant's school. The study will be conducted in six Clwyd schools, three infants and three primary, with 24 children from each school being asked to tell stories to the researcher in the first term of their first year in school, the second term of their second year, and the third term of their final year, when their reading achievement will be measured using standardized and informal objective tests. The stories collected, 2 per child per year, will be analyzed and scored using an analysis based on the works of Applebee (1978), Perera (1984) and Pitcher and Prelinger (1963).

Source of Grant: Full grant from Clwyd Local Education Authority
Date of Research: 1987 – continuing
KEYWORDS: oral work; primary education; story telling

8/0881

Department of Education
Oxford Road,
Manchester M13 9PL
061 275 2065
Johnson, D.F. Mr; *Supervisor:* Beveridge, M. Dr

The effectiveness of a genre based approach to academic writing for teacher training in Zimbabwe

Abstract: Most teachers of language, it appears, do not fully understand the nature of language: the difference between oral and written discourse, the development of writing, genre forms, discourse relations or contexts of communication. This research aims: (i) to make teacher trainers more aware of writing as a communicative process; (ii) to improve their methods of task setting and evaluating; (iii) to provide appropriate strategies for teacher trainees to improve their written argument and analysis. The research will be conducted at a teacher training college. Explicit and implicit understanding of language/writing of both teacher trainers and teacher trainees will be measured. This will involve the use of questionnaires, interviews, recorded group discussions and an analysis of written scripts. Two separate programmes, one with the college staff involved and another with selected students, will be implemented. The success of the programmes will be measured by how understanding and use of writing improves.

Source of Grant: Canon Collins Trust Fund (Tuition fees): £3,950
Africa Education Trust (Maintenance): £3,500
Date of Research: 1988 – continuing
KEYWORDS: language teaching; teacher education; writing; Zimbabwe

8/0882

Department of Education
Oxford Road,
Manchester M13 9PL
061 275 2000
Hoy, C. Dr

The management of adult and non-formal education in Nigeria with particular reference to Borno State

Abstract: The organization and administration of adult and non-formal education is now facing greater challenges than at any time in the history of developing countries. This is as a result of too much government intervention or lack of it with the consequences of increasing unemployment, enrolment into the formal schools, and the increasing rate of drop out etc. Attempts have been made by other countries in tackling these problems, including Nigeria. Two states have created agencies outside the usual government ministries. However, no studies have yet been undertaken about the two agencies and the applied models used to determine their effectiveness or lack of it. A questionnaire has been designed for field officers and an interview schedule for senior administrators for comparison. The result of these investigations will determine the effectiveness of these models, their deficiencies, and possible adoption with modification.

Source of Grant: Sponsorship by the Nigerian Government: (National Universities Commission)
Date of Research: 1985-1989
KEYWORDS: adult education; developing country; Nigeria; non-formal education

8/0883

Department of Education
Oxford Road, Manchester M13 9PL
061 275 2000
Isaac, R. Mr; *Supervisor:* Taylorson, D. Dr
The construction of social order in schooling
Abstract: The research aims firstly to explicate the common-sense constructs employed by teachers to obtain social order in schools, and secondly to locate these constructs within the institutional and social context of which they are part. The description of teachers' common-sense constructs draws upon interactionist studies into school practices, with the research data being obtained through qualitative research techniques, particularly the 'unstructured interview'. The explanatory hypothesis underlying the second aim is that instrumental reason structures the dominant form of thinking determining school practices: that the everyday reasoning employed by teachers is instrumental, and accordingly fails to 'count the human cost' of achieving social order in the ways that teachers do achieve order. The data will be obtained through interviews with teachers at all levels within the staffing hierarchy, including supplementary interviews to verify the researcher's accounts of respondents' constructs, and if respondents prove willing, to engage in critical reflection upon the 'moral cost' of teacher practices. The number of respondents has not yet been finalized.
Source of Grant: Costs paid by Manchester City Council (Education)
Date of Research: 1986 – continuing
KEYWORDS: *social structure; sociology of education*

8/0884

Department of Education
Oxford Road, Manchester M13 9PL
061 273 3333
Foy, C. Mr; *Supervisor:* Robertson, A. Dr
The influence of the Heywood family in Manchester in the nineteenth century
Abstract: This is an investigation of the ways in which Benjamin, James and Oliver Heywood (all members of the same family) used the money they had obtained from their banking interest to improve the lot of people in Manchester in the nineteenth century. Investigations of the following will take place: Manchester Grammar School, Mechanics Institute, Chetham's Hospital School, Owen's College (now Manchester University), hospitals, the Manchester Statistical Society, churches, the Literary and Philosophical Society, the Athaneum, parks and other amenities. Benjamin's and James' roles as M.P.'s, Abel's newspaper and publishing interest and the part he played in the municipal life of Manchester, particularly during his two mayoralties. The area covering the Victorian men who ran our great cities is a greatly neglected one and there is virtually no published material on either of these two Heywood families. Hopefully, therefore, completion of this project will go part way to answering the question 'How was the City of Manchester run in the nineteenth century and what sort of people were the Heywood family'?
Source of Grant: No funding
Date of Research: 1986-1990
KEYWORDS: *history of education*

8/0885

Department of Education
Oxford Road, Manchester M13 9PL
061 275 3510
Lonton, A.P. Mr
Conductive education
Abstract: The aim of the study is to chart the spread of the ideas and practice of conductive education in English schools, and to evaluate the efficacy of conductive education as practiced in England and in Budapest. The method involved: (a) sending questionnaires to all 109 schools for physically disabled children in England and Wales; (b) locating and sending questionnaires to parents who have sent their children to Budapest; (c) selective interviews with some of the above parents. The results indicated that the ideas of conductive education had spread rapidly among the teachers of and parents, particularly since 1985. Reports of improvements in children who attended conductive education groups in England were encouraging, and those attending the Peto Institute in Budapest even more impressive. However, the evaluations in the English schools were rarely done with scientific rigour, and the children accepted in the Peto Institute seemed to be highly selected. The absence of any large scale control groups makes it difficult
to establish the true efficacy of conductive education at present.
Published Material: LONTON, P. & RUSSELL, A. (1989). 'Conductive education: magic or myth'? Zeitschrift fur Kinderchirurgie, Vol 44, Supp. 1, pp.21-23.
Source of Grant: Richard Fund: £2,000 American Appraisal (UK Ltd): £1,000 Special Educational Needs Advisory Council: £300
Date of Research: 1988 – continuing
KEYWORDS: *conductive education; physically handicapped; special education*

8/0886

Department of Education
Humanities I Building, Oxford Road, Manchester M13 9PL
061 275 3412
Williams, J.S. Mr; Steeg, T. Mr; Wise, R. Mrs
Mechanics in action cross-curricular GCSE (General Certificate of Secondary Education) project
Abstract: This project has developed practical approaches to applied mathematics in the secondary school curriculum for pupils aged 11-18. It has involved research and development with eight North-West LEAs (local education authorities) and 13 project schools from which local networks and courses have disseminated. The project is continuing to work with funding direct from courses, consultancies and royalties. A number of inservice training packs and resource packs have been produced. The project is now extending the work to include research and development of cross-curricular and inter-disciplinary teaching in secondary school mathematics, science and technology. The project is working with the support of TVEI (Technical and Vocational Education Initiative) and LEA advisers in the North-West to stimulate, identify, evaluate and disseminate good practice in these areas.
Published Material: WILLIAMS, J.S. (1989). 'Modelling with mechanics, a cross-curricular problem solving approach to learning mathematics', In: BLUM, W. et al (Eds), Proceedings of the 1989 ICTMA conference, Roskilde, Denmark. (in press).; CHEROUVIM, N. et al. (1990). Practical projects with mathematics, Cambridge University Press: (in press).; WILLIAMS, J.S. (1990). 'Real problem-solving in mechanics: the role of practical work in teaching mathematical modelling'. In: BLUM, W. et al. Modelling applications and applied problem-solving. Chichester: Ellis Horwood. (in press).
Source of Grant: University Grants Committee
Date of Research: 1988-1990
KEYWORDS: *cross-curricular approach; mathematics; mechanics; practical work; science education; secondary education*

8/0887

Department of Education
Oxford Road, Manchester M13 9PL
061 275 3412
Leeds University
Department of Mathematics
Leeds LS2 9JT
0532 431751
Willams, J.S. Mr; Kitchen, A. Mrs; Savage, M.D. Dr; Jagger, J.M. Mrs
Mechanics in action: curriculum development in applied mathematics 16-19
Abstract: This joint project between the mechanics in action teams from the Universities of Manchester and Leeds was set up to develop a new approach to mechanics. It will be looking at curriculum development in 16-19 mathematics and working closely with the SMP (School Mathematics Project) on their new A level mechanics modules. It will also hope to have input to other A level boards as they change their syllabuses to suit the needs of students who have taken GCSE (General Certificate of Secondary Education). Its main aims are to produce A level modules for use by SMP which include practical work, projects and investigations of the real world of science and engineering; to continue the development and integration of new problem-solving materials; to trial all materials in schools in the North-West and Yorkshire; to provide suitable video materials for introducing new topics, and to develop appropriate assessment procedures and INSET (In-Service Training and Education of Teachers) materials and courses by 1991.
Published Material: SAVAGE, M.D. & WILLIAMS, J.S. (1989). Mechanics in action. Cambridge University Press. (in press).; WILLIAMS, J.S. (1989). 'Modelling with mechanics'. In: Proceedings of the Nottingham Mathematics 16-20 Conference, July 10-14, 1989. (in press).
Source of Grant: Gatsby Charitable Trust: £198,000

Date of Research: 1989 – continuing
KEYWORDS: *curriculum development; mathematics; mechanics; science education; secondary education*

8/0888

Department of Education
Oxford Road, Manchester M13 9PL
061 275 3510
Lonton, A.P. Mr

The National Curriculum for children with physical disabilities
Abstract: The aim of the research is to investigate: (a) the nature of the traditional curriculum in secondary special schools for physically disabled pupils; (b) the problems they are encountering in adapting to teach the full range of subjects in the National Curriculum; (c) attitudes and policies regarding the possibility of full or partial exemption of some pupils from the National Curriculum. Detailed questionnaires were sent to 109 schools for physically disabled children in England and Wales. Selected interviews have been carried out with a small number of experienced teachers and parents of disabled children.
Source of Grant: Richard Fund: £1,000
Date of Research: 1989 – continuing
KEYWORDS: *curriculum; physically handicapped; special school*

8/0889

Department of Education
Oxford Road, Manchester M13 9PL
061 275 3415
Nelson, R.D.

Software creation and the initial training of teachers
Abstract: In 1983-86, 50 Post Graduate Certificate in Education (PGCE) students took a 24-hour 2-term course in computer appreciation and programming. As part of the assessment, each student wrote a piece of software. The project has 3 components: (1) Analysis of the software they produced; (2) investigation, by questionnaire, of the subsequent value of the course to the students; (3) relation of (1) to (2) and conclusion.
Source of Grant: No funding
Date of Research: 1983-1989
KEYWORDS: *microcomputer; software; teacher education*

8/0890

Department of Education
Centre for Physical Education,
Oxford Road, Manchester M13 9PL
061 275 3463
Hardman, K. Mr

Cross-cultural study of teachers' and pupils' attitudes to participation in inter-school sports competition
Abstract: The idea for the investigation arose at the 1984 Maleste 4th Seminar of the International Society for Comparative Physical Education and Sport (ISCPES). Concern has been expressed by physical educationists about competition within and between schools, and the internal and external pressures to which it is being subjected. Related research literature demonstrates considerable differences in opinions on issues related to inter-school competition none more so than in the area of values and participation. The aims of the study reflect the literature survey findings and the special needs of some countries for information on various related aspects. The aims of the research are: (1) To discover whether pupils participating in inter-school competition have greater identity with school values than non-participants; (2) to establish teachers' and pupils' perceptions of the purposes of inter-school sport. The subsidiary aims are: (i) to determine the proportion of pupils involved in inter-school competition; (ii) to ascertain the number and range of activities; (iii) to determine the proportion of pupils gaining representative honours; (iv) to establish the extent of teachers' and pupils' commitment to preparation for competition; (v) to discover if competition enhances social status; (vi) to gain an estimate of parental approval; (vii) to establish the mode and effect of financing for inter-school sport. The investigation was originally limited to 3 countries – England, Greece and the USA. Further investigation will involve Brazil, Portugal, Canada, Federal Republic of Germany et al. The sample comprised random groups of equal numbers of boys and girls of 14 years of age, enrolled in similar levels of schools: England 100; Greece 132; USA 140. The methods involved: (a) literature search; (b) historical content; (c) teachers' and pupils' questionnaires; (d) range of statistical techniques in analysis.

Published Material: HARDMAN, K., KROTEE, M. & CHRISSANTHOPOULOS, A.V. (1986). 'A comparative study of inter-school competition in England, Greece and the United States', Paper presented at the 5th ISCPES Seminar, University of British Columbia, Vancouver, May 1986.
Source of Grant: No funding
Date of Research: 1984 – continuing
KEYWORDS: *attitude; comparative education; competition; cross-cultural research; participation; sport*

8/0891

Department of Education
Oxford Road, Manchester M13 9PL
061 275 3443
Peens, I.S. Mr

Evaluation of Regional smoking education programme
Abstract: The aim of this project is to evaluate effectiveness of a regional smoking prevention programme. The regional programme has 5 main elements: (1) working with mass media to help smokers who want to give up to do so; (2) working with schools to influence children and family; (3) working with corporate organizations to promote a smoke-free environment; (4) working within the NHS; (5) working with sponsorship activities when the opportunity arises. The evaluation is designed to produce useful and useable data within the life of the project. Data will not be limited to what is scientifically respectable, but will be collected by a wide variety of means so as to provide various approximations to knowledge and thus to reduce biases inherent in a single method. There will be a fidelity perspective with outcome measures but also measures of process. Process measures will be of 2 kinds: (i) Strict process accounts of how project diffused/disseminated and implemented; and (ii) intermediate proximal measures of progress. The types of measures and target groups are as follows: (a) Detailed narrative of innovations as they unfold; (b) proximal measures of attitudes, behaviour, awareness of target groups i.e. general public (4,000 baseline survey), pupils (2,000 baseline survey), teachers, non-teachers in school, health professionals; (c) survey of LEA and District Health Authority staffs' compliance with smoking policy.
Published Material: a full list of publications can be obtained from the researcher on request
Source of Grant: Health Education Council: £150,000 over 3 years
Date of Research: 1985 – continuing
KEYWORDS: *evaluation; health education; prevention; smoking*

8/0892

Department of Education
Oxford Road, Manchester M13 9PL
061 275 3415
Lonton, A.P. Mr

Education and management of children with physical disabilities
Abstract: This study examines the educational curriculum and other aspects of the management of children with physical disabilities. The general thrust of the research is directed towards those children who are integrated into ordinary schools. However, the needs of the more severely disabled children in special schools are also examined. Information will be obtained from teachers of children with disabilities, as well as from clinical and classroom studies of the children themselves.
Source of Grant: Leverhulme Trust: £5,300 Richard Fund: £500
Date of Research: 1985 – continuing
KEYWORDS: *child; curriculum; integration; physically handicapped; special*

8/0893

Department of Education
Oxford Road, Manchester M13 9PL
061 273 3333
Fielden House Productivity Centre
856 Wilmslow Road, Didsbury, Manchester
061 445 2426
Jeffcutt, P.S. Mr; *Supervisor:* Toye, M. Mr

Persistence and changes in an Organisation Culture – a longitudinal study of a retraining scheme for the female adult unemployed
Abstract: Over the past ten years a fresh research perspective into organization has evolved. This perspective seeks to understand organizations as cultures, with a focus of interest on what it means to be organized in particular settings. A researcher thus explores an organization as a network of meaning, focusing on verbal and non-verbal symbols as artefacts of a living culture. The setting of this research is unique, a government sponsored retraining

programme; most research in the field concerns industrial or commercial organizations. The design is also unique, since it concerns a longitudinal study in real time which covered the entire 'life cycle' of the organization in question – most other longitudinal studies have been of mature organizations and have relied on retrospective data collection. The research process is ethnographic and is based on participant observation and informal interviewing, throughout the 'life cycle' of the organization. The researcher seeks to record such cultural phenomena as specialized vocabularies, stories, rituals and ceremonies that are manifest in the organization. Of particular concern has been verbal imagery – (metaphor, analogy, jokes) which the organizations members use to describe what it means to be organized in particular settings and at particular times in the organizations 'life cycle'. This research programme seeks to explore and elucidate the structures of an organization culture and their change over time. Of particular concern are issues of persistence and change in meanings that describe the participants experience of being organized in the settings of a retraining programme. Other issues of special interest that have previously only been accessible retrospectively, are the exploration of those meanings associated with the organizations 'birth' and 'death'. Of subsequent interest is the comparison of meanings across organizational settings, and the exploration of 'unique' and 'common' understandings. This research programme is involved in pioneering work in the field of organization culture and change. Not only has the entire 'life cycle' of a particular organization been recorded in real-time, but this research programme also introduces organization culture research into a new field of operations – Post Compulsory Education.
Published Material: JEFFCUTT, P.S. (1983). 'Thought in Organizations', International Studies of Management and Organisation, Vol XIII, No 3, pp.35-42.; JEFFCUTT, P.S. (1985). 'Organization discourse', Centre for European Business Education Studies Journal, Vol 1, No 2, pp.34-44.
Source of Grant: No funding
Date of Research: 1983 – continuing
KEYWORDS: *communication; culture; meaning; organization*

8/0894
Department of Education
Oxford Road, Manchester M13 9PL
061 275 3516
Sheffield University
Department of Paediatrics
Sheffield S10 2TN
0742 768555
Lonton, A.P. Mr
Neuropsychological and educational studies of children with spina bifida and hydrocephalus
Abstract: Since 1973, over 2,000 children with spina bifida, hydrocephalus and related disorders have been given psychological assessments of their abilities and academic attainments. This data, together with relevant paediatric and neurological data, have been analyzed by mainframe computer in order to explore the relationships between anatomical and neurological abnormalities and psychological functioning. Among the many studies completed have been investigations of the effect of thinning of the cortex (measured originally by air ventriculography, and since the mid-1970s by computed axial tomography – CT scans) on intellectual function. Studies have also been done on the physical features present in Spina Bifida neonates and the degree to which they are predictors of subsequent intellectual and physical problems.
Published Material: a full list of publications can be obtained from the researcher on request
Source of Grant: Association for Spina Bifida and Hydrocephalus: £10,000 Richard Fund: £5,000
Date of Research: 1973 – continuing
KEYWORDS: *assessment; child psychology; hydrocephalus; integration; spina*

8/0895
Department of Education
Oxford Road, Manchester M13 9PL
061 275 3463
Edge Hill College of Higher Education
Department of English
Ormskirk L39 4QP
0695 75171
Hughes, M. Dr; *Supervisor:* Beveridge, M.C. Dr
Sensitising primary school teachers to discourse relations in children's writing
Abstract: This research attempted to familarize a group of 30 primary school teachers with information from text and discourse analysis which had particular relevance to young children's writing development. The study examined the apparent influence of this information over a period of three years upon primary school teachers' responses to specimens of children's writing. Attempts were made to identify the teachers' acceptance or dismissal of particular features of discourse information through the analysis of their responses, which were made in the shape of notes to the children and to collaborating peer teachers. The results indicated a moderate acceptance of discourse information. This was identified through increases in references to approximately 30% of the discourse features introduced to the teachers. Further information is presented concerning these apparent increases as well as a detailed report on the teachers' responses to 26 specified features of discourse organization. The results however seen to argue against seeking the influence of exposure to discourse information in teachers' responses to children's texts. Instead it is proposed that such influence might more successfully be sought in teachers' introductions to writing tasks. The results are also seen to argue for the use of a more explicitly experience-based model of teacher education in contrast to that followed in this research, which took insufficient account of the teachers' existing knowledge and expertize.
Source of Grant: No funding
Date of Research: 1982 – continuing
KEYWORDS: *primary education; teacher education; writing*

8/0896
Department of Education
Oxford Road, Manchester M13 9PL
061 275 3463
Barnes, A. Mr; *Supervisor:* Robertson, A.B. Dr
The role of the church in providing education in Wells, Somerset, from the eve of the Reformation until the closing years of the 19th Century
Abstract: This is a study of education in a unique settlement – a small market town cum Cathedral City. The role of the church is the central theme and the interplay of church and secular institutions, latterly the state, comes through strongly. The aim is to add materially to scholars' understanding of how the various participants in the development of our nation's education system competed, supported and complemented each other.
Source of Grant: Somerset County Council: tuition fees and travelling expenses
Date of Research: 1979-1990
KEYWORDS: *church; denominational school; history of education; religious organization; United Kingdom*

8/0897
Department of Education
Oxford Road, Manchester M13 9PL
061 275 4965
Sanderson, P. Mrs; *Supervisor:* Murray, C. Dr
Factors influencing attitudes of secondary school pupils to aesthetic aspects of sport and dance
Abstract: In order to investigate attitudes to aesthetic aspects of sport and dance, a survey was undertaken involving 1,670 boys and girls aged between 11 and 16 years of age, in 19 mixed high schools in different areas of England. A questionnaire was employed incorporating 7 attitude scales which had been developed in a pilot study. Independent variables were age, gender, social class, school experience, family and pupil leisure interests in arts and sports. Data was analyzed using ANOVA and Multiple Regression statistical techniques. Results show that family interests, gender and social class are major influences, wtih pupil interests playing a lesser role. Age and school experience do not appear to be important variables.
Published Material: SANDERSON, P. (1986). 'Factors influencing attitudes of secondary school pupils towards aesthetic aspects of sport and dance'. In: Proceedings of the VIII Commonwealth and International Conference on Sport, Physical Education, Dance, Recreation and Health (Dance Section).; SANDERSON, P. (1989). 'Secondary school pupils' attitudes to dance'. Proceedings of the DACI Conference, pp.224-251. London: Roehampton Institute.; SANDERSON, P. (1988). 'A methodology for measuring attitudes to dance'. Proceedings of the CORD Conference, Toronto, Canada.
Source of Grant: No funding
Date of Research: 1985 – continuing

KEYWORDS: aesthetics; attitude; dance; secondary education; sport

8/0898

Department of Education
Centre for Ethnic Studies in Education,
Oxford Road, Manchester M13 9PL
061 275 3468
Christ Church College of Higher Education
Canterbury CT1 1QU
0227 65548
Verma, G.K. Dr; Zec, P. Mr
Race relations in secondary schools
Abstract: The Swann Report (HMSO 1985) found no shortage of evidence to suggest that many obstacles lay in the path of children from certain ethnic minority groups (e.g. West Indian and Bangladeshi) and which prevented or detracted from their being able to maximize their educational potential. Among the issues were those relating to the state of inter-ethnic relations in schools and to the role of the school in equipping all children for life in a plural society. The project proposes to study in depth a group of secondary schools, in each of the three areas of England – the North (Lancashire/West Yorkshire), the Midlands and the London area. The schools will each be visited by a researcher for a period of half a term. The data to be collected will cover various aspects of race relations but its focus will be on the behaviour patterns of pupils in multi-ethnic schools – in particular, careful note will be taken of incidences of bullying and harassment by other ethnic groups on members of another – and how these are monitored and modified by the schools. An assessment will be made of the contribution of different aspects on the processes affecting good race relations.
Source of Grant: Department of Education and Science: £182,000
Date of Research: 1987-1989
KEYWORDS: ethnic minority; race relations; secondary education

8/0899

Department of Education
Oxford Road, Manchester M13 9PL
061 275 3463
Hill, S.M. Ms; Silvester, G.A. Inspector; Supervisor: Smithers, A.G. Prof
Graduates in the police service
Abstract: Over the past two decades, the police service has been actively recruiting graduates and encouraging serving officers to undertake higher education. Several schemes to increase the proportion of graduates in the Service were introduced in the 1960s, but these have not been fully assessed in the light of present conditions. This project will be an independent national evaluation of the recruitment, deployment, progress and premature voluntary resignation of graduates. Our national evaluation will utilize published sources, data provided by the Home Office and individual forces, and the personal accounts of serving and resigned officers. The issues for particular inquiry include: the numbers and distribution of graduates nationally and the reasons for variation between forces; the career aspirations of graduates and non-graduates considered in relation to deployment, promotion and wastage; the value of higher education and the need for graduates in the police service; the performance of graduates compared to non-graduates; the desirability of continuing the Graduate Entry Scheme and higher education schemes for serving officers; premature voluntary resignation of graduates and non-graduates focusing on the reasons for leaving and the destinations of resignees. The study will be of practical relevance. It will clarify the role of graduates in the police service and outline the costs and benefits of the various graduate recruitment and higher education schemes. It will also shed light on how to make best use of the skills and knowledge possessed by graduates from various disciplines and backgrounds, and how best to retain the services of expensively trained personnel. It should provide a sound basis for planning and the utilization of resources.
Source of Grant: University of Manchester Support Fund Greater Manchester Police Sir Richard Sutton's Settled Estates Home Office Grant British Aerospace
Date of Research: 1987-1989
KEYWORDS: graduate; police; recruitment

8/0900

Department of Education,
Centre for Formative Assessment Studies
Oxford Road, Manchester M13 9PL

061 273 6263
Liverpool University,
Department of Education,
PO Box 147,
Liverpool L69 3BX
051 794 2476
Christie, T. Mr
Standard tests and assessments implementation research
Abstract: The aim of the project is to refine and implement the proposals of the Task Group on Assessment and Testing for the assessment of pupils' progress through the National Curriculum at key stage one. Work is classroom-based, drawing upon the experience of five groups of 50 teachers, each group coming from defined classroom circumstances; small schools, bilingual schools, inner urban schools, rural schools and relatively well-resourced information technology schools. Each group works in parallel to develop first teacher assessment practice and subsequently standard assessment tasks. The latter are trialled and piloted on national samples of approximately 5000 seven year olds in about 200 schools. The model of assessment assumes sequential decision making within a tailored testing approach. Teacher assessment determines which sub-tasks of the standard assessment task will be attempted by each pupil. All sub-tasks are levelled. This first confirmatory phase of standard assessment task administration is followed up by a second phase, contingent upon a further set of teacher decisions about each child, in which upper and/or lower bounds are established for the child's performance. The main independent evaluation of the SAT is in terms of teacher's confidence in the evidence produced. The main analytic technique is generalisability theory modified to take account of the criterion-referenced nature of all decisions.
Source of Grant: Schools Examinations and Assessment Council (SEAC): £2,800,000
Date of Research: 1989 – continuing
KEYWORDS: assessment; primary education; standard assessment task; teacher assessment

8/0901

Department of Government
Dover Street, Manchester M13 9PL
061 275 4895
Parry, G.B. Prof.
Educational thought and political thought: history and conceptual analysis of interrelationships
Abstract: A study of the interrelationships between political thought and educational thought from the sixteenth century to the present. The aim is to examine the educational writings of such political thinkers as Locke, Rousseau, Godwin, J.S. Mill, Dewey and Oakeshott and the implications of these writings for their respective political philosophies. The approach will be both historical and analytical.
Source of Grant: No funding
Date of Research: 1989 – continuing
KEYWORDS: history; philosophy of education; political philosophy

8/0902

Department of Humanities
Oxford Road, Manchester M13 9PL
061 273 3333
Davies, J.A. Mrs; Supervisor: Roberts, G.R. Mr
The effects of the National Curriculum: a monitoring exercise in six primary schools
Abstract: The objectives of this research are to examine the premise that the introduction of a National Curriculum will raise standards in primary schools. To this end, cognitive and non-cognitive areas of development will be monitored through a series of NFER maths and reading tests, behavioural schedules and a self esteem measure. The methodology used by primary teachers to implement the National Curriculum, will also be analyzed. Time tabling arrangements in the classes will be monitored. Teachers and heads will be interviewed with regard to classroom management and organization as well as about the curriculum on offer and the ways in which it is delivered. Classroom resources will be noted. A sample of year 2 and year 6 children and teachers from 6 randomly selected primary schools in one LEA will be analyzed.
Source of Grant: No funding
Date of Research: 1988 – continuing
KEYWORDS: assessment; curriculum; primary education

8/0903
Department of Management
Institute of Science and Technology,
PO Box 88, Sackville Street, Manchester M60 1QD
061 236 3311
Manchester Polytechnic
Department of Educational Studies
Education Management Centre,
799 Wilmslow Road, Manchester M20 8RR
061 445 7871 ext 371; 061 434 2817 (24 hours)
Kelly, M.J. Mr; *Supervisor:* Cooper, C. Prof.
Occupational stress and the incidence of stress-related illness among head teachers and principals of educational institutions in the UK: identification, investigation, and management strategies
Abstract: The research began with pilot interviews among the target population of senior managers in education and a literature survey. 4500 questionnaires were circulated, of which 2638 were returned. The first analysis, using SPSSx, has been completed. A first report is in the process of being written. The second stage will involve further multi-variate analysis, with SPSSx, and the development of a stress management system, organizational group and personal strategies, with a co-related investigation of stress-related illness.
Source of Grant: National Association of Head Teachers: £1,250 for 1st stage (1987-88)
Date of Research: 1987 – continuing
KEYWORDS: administration of education; disease; head teacher; occupational environment; stress

8/0904
Department of Psychology
Oxford Road, Manchester M13 9PL
061 275 2585
Clark, J.H. Dr
Student problems encountered at universities, polytechnics and colleges and practical methods to solve them
Abstract: The research will involve discussions of students' problems in an informal seminar setting. Handouts will also be provided, giving practical methods for tackling specific problems. These handouts will eventually form the basis of a book dealing with a wide variety of problems met by students.
Source of Grant: No funding
Date of Research: 1987 – continuing
KEYWORDS: guidance; student life; student problems

8/0905
Department of Psychology
Manchester M13 9PL
061 275 2579
Lloyd, P. Dr
The development of verbal communication skills in primary school children
Abstract: A number of studies have been carried out on the ability of children (5-10 years) to exchange verbal information. A second aim has been to look at the way in which children communicate by telephone. The experimental procedure has made some departures from traditional methods by introducing a measure of realism. This has been achieved by excluding the adult investigator and having pairs of children talk by telephone. The standard task involves giving route directions with the aid of maps. As well as peer dyads, comparison studies have been done with adult and mother-child pairs. It is argued that a proper understanding of the factors giving rise to communication success and failure requires a close examination of the negotiation procedures by means of discourse analysis. A model outlining a communicative support system offers a framework for studying language in use especially in an instructional context where both adults and children may play the role of tutor. Results indicate that redundancy in communication plays an important role in facilitating understanding (it is common between adults and less so among 7 year olds). The hearer's ability to introduce new but relevant information into dialogues by way of requests for clarification is a major factor in resolving communication failure.
Published Material: LLOYD, P. (1990). 'Child communication in the school years'. In: GRIEVE, R. & HUGHES, M. (Eds). Understanding children: essays in honour of Margaret Donaldson. Oxford: Blackwell
Source of Grant: British Council/Spanish Ministry of Education/University of Barcelona: jointly £5,000
Date of Research: 1988 – continuing

KEYWORDS: discourse analysis; primary education; telephone; verbal communication

8/0906
Department of Psychology
Manchester M13 9PL
061 275 2579
Arnold, P. Dr
Working memory and the speech quality of partially hearing children
Abstract: The work originated from the observation that the speech quality of partially hearing children deteriorated when they read the more difficult passages of the Neale Reading Test. A speech spectrographic and an analysis by speech therapists will be made in various contexts of different loads on working memory.
Source of Grant: Manchester University, Faculty of Science
Date of Research: 1989 – continuing
KEYWORDS: hearing defect; memory; speech defect

8/0907
Department of Sociology
Manchester M13 9Pl
061 275 2500
Sussex University
Department of Contiuing and Professional Education
Falmer, Brighton BN1 9RG
0273 606755
Griffiths, V. Ms; *Supervisor:* Morgan, D. Dr; Kelly, A. Dr
Adolescent girls and peer relationships
Abstract: In this thesis, friendships between fifty adolescent girls (white, Afro-Caribbean, Asian) in West Yorkshire were investigated using feminist ethnographic methods. The girls were involved in the research process as far as possible, and the researcher's own experience was brought into the research at all stages. Friendships between the girls were found to be close and supportive, based on trust and loyalty. Both instrumental and expressive elements were present in the relationships, which involved reciprocity and mutual obligations. It was important for the girls to have friends to go around with both in and outside school, to establish self-identity and to enhance their feelings of self-worth. Central characteristics of the friendships included physical closeness, 'togetherness' and 'having a laugh'. Another important feature was talking – particularly confiding talk – between friends, which enabled them to share experiences and help sort out problems. Friendship groups were evident, as well as occasional interaction sets, in lessons. The intensity of friendships, particularly between 12-13 year olds, was strong, and friends often 'fell out', particularly because of jealousy of other girls or because their friends were too bossy. Most friendships were restored although there were some changes of friendships owing to the transition to adolescent interest. However, there were many ways in which the young women resisted the break-up of the their friendship groups, even when they had regular relationships with boys. In general, friends used many positive strategies to overcome or minimise constraints on their lives, either in school or in outside activities. These forms of resistance gave the friendships a political significance as well as demonstrating the strength and importance of friendships between young women.
Published Material: GRIFFITHS, V. (1987). 'Adolescent girls: transition from girlfriends to boyfriends?'. In: ALLATT, P. et al (Eds). Women and the life cycle: transitions and turning points. Conference Proceedings. Macmillan.; GRIFFITHS, V. (1988). 'Working with adolescent girls: making the research process feminist'. In: Writing feminist biography 2. University of Manchester.; GRIFFITHS, V. (1989). Adolescent girls and peer relationships. PhD Thesis. Manchester University.
Source of Grant: Economic and Social Research Council
Date of Research: 1982-1989
KEYWORDS: adolescent; friendship; girl; leisure

8/0908
Departmnet of Education
Oxford Road, Manchester M13 9PL
061 275 2000
Robinson, M.C. Mrs; *Supervisor:* Reid, D. Dr
An evaluation of the knowledge of science and scientists expressed by students entering tertiary education
Abstract: An investigation into the nature of science, its methods, criteria of validity, theories, laws, hypotheses etc. will be undertaken, using a search through the literature on the philosophy and sociology of science. A synthesis of conflicting views in this area

will be attempted to produce a model of science as practiced at the present time. It is hypothesized that pupils in the 11-16 age group are following a curricula which do not reflect the true nature of the modern practice of science. It is proposed to test this hypothesis by using a series of aptitude and attitude tests on a cohort of students entering some form of tertiary education in the Bolton/Wigan area. The following points will be addressed: (1) does the students' image of science correspond with the model evolved in the research? (2) Do the students posess the skills identified in the model as necessary for the study of science at higher levels; (3) if the students have a different image of science, how do they perceive it? (4) What effect do factors such as choice of science/arts courses at 16+, success or failure at GCSE, ethnic background etc. have on their view of science.
Source of Grant: Bolton Metropolitan Borough: GRIST (Grant-related In-Service Training)
Date of Research: 1986 – continuing
KEYWORDS: attitude scale; philosophy of education; science education; tertiary education

8/0909

> Faculty of Education
> Centre for Youth Studies, Manchester M13 9PL
> 061 273 3333
> Murray, C. Dr

Styles of life of young people
Abstract: The research focuses on the transition process from school to work to unemployment. The notions of lifestyle, employment and labour market are examined for their conceptual usefulness and are found to be wanting. Preliminary analysis of data reflecting the perceptions of school leavers provides conceptual clarification of the concepts involved, for example, moral cynicism, work ethic, independent action, occupational passivity, financial management and survival optimism.
Published Material: MURRAY, C. et al (1987). 'Youth lifestyles, employment and the labour market: concepts in need of clarification', British Journal of Education and Work, Vol 2, No 2, 1987, pp.27-46.
Source of Grant: No funding
Date of Research: 1987 – continuing
KEYWORDS: labour market; life style; school leaver; transition from school to work; youth employment

8/0910

> Hester Adrian Research Centre
> Oxford Road, Manchester M13 9PL
> 061 275 3463
> Cavet, J. Ms; *Supervisor:* Hogg, J. Dr

Occupational and leisure activities for people with profound retardation and multiple impairments
Abstract: The project is concerned with the identification and description of good practice in leisure provision for people with profound retardation and multiple impairments. It will produce a detailed review of the world literature and a series of case studies undertaken in selected EEC countries. A report will be produced and a series of dissemination conferences held in EEC countries on completion of the work.
Source of Grant: Commission of the European Communities (ECU): £45,000 MENCAP City Foundation: £4,500 The Mental Health Foundation: £12,142 Lebenshilfe (International League of Societies for Persons with Mental Handicap): US [9,000
Date of Research: 1988-1989
KEYWORDS: European Economic Community (EEC): handicapped; leisure; mentally physically handicapped

8/0911

> Hester Adrian Research Centre
> Oxford Road, Manchester M13 9PL
> 061 275 3463
> MENCAP PRMH Project
> Piper Hill School, 200 Yew Tree Lane, Northenden, Manchester M23 0FF
> 061 998 4161
> Lambe, L.J. Ms; Hogg, J.H. Dr

The Royal Society for Mentally Handicapped Children and Adults (MENCAP): profound retardation and multiple handicap project
Abstract: The project was established as a national initiative by the Royal Society for Mentally Handicapped Children and Adults (RSMCHC & A) to assist parents and carers in providing for both children and adults with profound mental handicap and additional

sensory and physical handicaps. A major national survey has been completed and has guided the development of a series of workshops on areas of special concern. These workshops have been open to both parents and care-givers and have been evaluated by the Hester Adrian Research Centre, Manchester University. Among the topics covered are: (a) feeding and communication; (b) dental care; (c) behaviour problems; (d) legal aspects of provision; (e) physical mangagement; (f) evolving approaches to leisure. The last mentioned topic is being developed in collaboration with the National Federation of Gateway Clubs and will yield a Training Pack for use by both volunteers and parents. In addition, the project is developing an information resource on these subjects available to both parents and professionals.
Published Material: LAMBE, L.J. & HOGG, J. (1985). The needs of parents and caregivers of children and adults who are profoundly retarded and multiply handicapped: A pilot study, MENCAP, London.; LAMBE, L.J. (1986). MENCAP'S PMRH Project – 'Hydrotherapy scheme helps handicapped children in a major way', 'Parents Voice, Vol 36, Summer, pp.10-11. MENCAP, London; HOGG, J., LAMBE, L.J., COWIE, J. & COXTON, J. (1988). 'Children and adults with profound retardation and multiple handicaps attending schools or social education centres: a final report on the needs of their parents, foster parents and relatives', MENCAP, London.
Source of Grant: Royal Society for Mentally Handicapped Children & Adults City Foundation John Paul Getty Jr Charitable Trust MENCAP local societies Barclays Charitable Trust The Stanley Thomas Johnson Foundation
Date of Research: 1985-1990
KEYWORDS: care; information service; mentally handicapped; parent role; handicapped

8/0912

> School of Education
> Oxford Road, Manchester M13 9PL
> 061 275 3510
> Brown, V. Mrs; *Supervisor:* Hodkinson, S. Mr

A training programme for economic awareness
Abstract: In the context of national statements and curriculum initiatives concerned with delivering the cross curriculum theme of Economic and Industrial Understanding, the research aims to evaluate training methods and to provide a programme of inservice training suitable for the introduction of Economic and Industrial Understanding and in so doing to provide a model for future developments.
Source of Grant: No funding
Date of Research: 1989 – continuing
KEYWORDS: curriculum development; economic studies; teacher education

Middlesex Polytechnic

8/0913

> The Burroughs, Hendon NW4 4BT
> 081 202 6545
> Harrow College of Higher Education
> Northwick Park, Watford Road, Harrow HA1 3TP
> 081 864 5422
> Monk, R.E. Mr; *Supervisor:* Ghobadian, A. Dr; Cowling, A. Dr

The nature of managerial work in Britain
Abstract: The first objective of this research is to identify the work of managers and their perceptions of the ways in which that work is changing and developing. This will be done by means of a postal survey of a random sample of practicing managers. The second objective is to construct and test a hypothetical model of the contemporary manager. This will be obtained from the postal survey and tested through a programme of structured interviews with a stratified sample of the respondents to the survey. The third objective is to identify the changing and developing work of managers over a period of time as observed by some of the writers and researchers of the twentieth century in the field of organization and management. Secondary source research through published works will lead to the compilation of a bibliography including writers associated with the recognized schools of management thought. The final objective is to develop a theoretical model of the work of the industrial manager of the late 1980's. Analysis of the above research

should identify those common elements which seem "core managerial function(s)" and which are likely to be found in most if not all managerial jobs.
Source of Grant: Harrow College: limited support
Date of Research: 1988 – continuing
KEYWORDS: management; management education

8/0914

    Department of Education
    Trent Park, Cockfosters Road,
    Barnet, London EN4 OPT
    081 440 5181
    Stewards School
    Parnall Road, Harlow
    0279 25141
    Smith, B. Mrs; *Supervisor:* Goodacre, E. Prof.; Jones, L. Mr
Evaluating the use of dictated stories as reading tests for poor secondary readers
Abstract: The aim of this research has been to produce a description of the process of dictating a story, using an untrained volunteer as a scribe. The dictated stories have also been analyzed in order to produce a description of the features of a dictated story to oral and written discourse and stories. Two sample groups of eleven year olds, a first phase sample of five and a second phase of six, were paired with a volunteer scribe/listener. Volunteers were trained to scribe and to listen to the composers' reading their texts. Training materials for the Phase Two were modified in the light of information gained in Phase One. In Phase One eight sessions of composing and reading were tape-recorded and the data analyzed to show significant interactions between volunteers and pupils and changes in reading behaviour in the pupils. In Phase Two reading behaviour was again recorded and the process of editing the original dictation was also recorded. The dictated stories were analyzed in order to provide a description of the discourse and the structure of the dictated story. The purpose of the research has been to illuminate the process and to describe the product of the language experience approach to reading and to describe changes in reading behaviour observed in pupils reading their own dictated stories. Areas for further research have been identified.
Published Material: SMITH, B. (1986). 'A local habitation and a name'. In: SMITH, P. (Ed). Parents and teachers together. London: MacMillan.
Source of Grant: County award for fees/travel
Date of Research: 1982-1989
KEYWORDS: language teaching; learning difficulty; reading; secondary education; storytelling; test

8/0915

    Department of Education,
    Performing Arts and Combined Studies
    Trent Park, Cockfosters Road,
    Barnet EN4 OPT
    081 368 1299 ext 4321
    Furey, P. Ms.; *Supervisor:* Whomsley, J.P. Mr
The assessment of experiential learning within students placements on teacher education courses
Abstract: The objectives of this project are: (1) to investigate the perceptions of 3 of the participant groups on placement within the teacher education framework. These are the teachers, the students and the tutors − pupil perception will not be included; (2) to investigate the perceptions of these 3 groups as to how learning by experience actually takes place. Each group will see the role of the other 2 from their own perspective whilst jointly focusing on the same practical experience; (3) to add to the growing body of knowledge of experiential learning so that practice may be informed and improved; (4) to suggest better models for the assessment of experiential learning within teacher education courses. The cohort studied was year 3 of a 4 year BEd (Hons.) Degree. Each tutor/student/teacher group formed a triad. Twelve triads were covered by visit and interview taped by research assistant. Preliminary results indicate that 2 models of interaction will be provided with themes derived from both the polarized triad models and the continuum between them. In 1989 research to be extended using questionnaires.
Source of Grant: Council for National Academic Awards (CNAA) Development Fund: £4,427
Date of Research: 1987-1989
KEYWORDS: learning; teacher education; teaching experience; teaching practice

Moray House College

8/0916

    Centre for Leisure Research,
    Holyrood Road, Edinburgh EH8 8AQ
    031 556 8455
    Arrowsmith, J.M. Mrs
Parent-teacher communication in the secondary school (curriculum and assessment): an illuminative study of good practice
Abstract: With recent legislation, communication between parents and teachers about curriculum and assessment matters has finally become a formal duty required of the school. Those involved are anxious to make that communication as effective as possible. Practical problems emerge of how those relatively inexperienced go about improving mutual understanding. The aim of the study was to offer insight into working examples of good practice; to highlight the dynamic, evolving nature of the process of building relationships of trust and honest exchange between parents and teachers. It was hoped that sharing good ideas, tried and tested in schools already, might help inform school policy, encourage schools to assess the communication system in their own school and to monitor and evaluate their own efforts, taking account of both staff and parents' viewpoints. Three schools, with very different catchment areas, but all noted for their positive attention to communication with parents, were studied. In each case, evidence was gathered from written documentation, together with interviews with management staff, guidance teachers, subject teachers and sets of parents in their own homes. From the study it is clear that school policy is never created in the abstract, but develops as the needs and understanding of the participants change. Many suggestions emerge about improving both oral and written communication, including Parents' Evenings, individual report cards and School Associations. These are summarized and presented with questions raised for those in the field.
Published Material: ARROWSMITH, J. (1989). 'Lets be honest', Times Scottish Education Supplement, 3 November, pp.26.
Source of Grant: Scottish Education Department: £5,750
Date of Research: 1988-1989
KEYWORDS: assessment; curriculum; parent-teacher relation; secondary school

8/0917

    Centre for Leisure Research,
    Holyrood Road, Edinburgh EH8 8AQ
    031 556 8455
    Diniz, F.A. Mr
The curricular implementation of the college policy on equal opportunites: disability and race
Abstract: The main aim of this research is to monitor the curricular implementation of the Policy on Equal Opportunity (Disability and Race). The curricular dimension is regarded as a major strategy for students and staff to develop ciritical perspectives on discrimination, in relation to disability and race.
Source of Grant: Moray House College
Date of Research: 1990 – continuing
KEYWORDS: college of education; curriculum development; educational policy; equal education; equal opportunity; physically handicapped; racial discrimination

8/0918

    Centre for Leisure Research,
    Holyrood Road, Edinburgh EH8 8AQ
    031 556 8455
    Carver, D. Mr
The cognitive content of student assignments
Abstract: The aims of the research are to discover how tutors and students perceive the cognitive demands of assignment tasks; examine simple assignments and characterise the cognitive operations of the product; relate perception and analysis to assessment criteria and grades obtained and reach conclusions about the formative value of assignment tasks with the cognitive domain.
Source of Grant: Moray House College
Date of Research: 1990 – continuing
KEYWORDS: assignment; cognitive process; project; student

8/0919

    Centre for Leisure Research,
    Holyrood Road, Edinburgh EH8 8AQ
    031 556 8455

Aldridge, J. Mr
The reading of non-fiction
Abstract: The aims of the research are to investigate strategies used by primary school children in reading non-fiction and extracting information from text.
Source of Grant: Moray House College
Date of Research: 1989-1990
KEYWORDS: cognitive process; non-fiction; primary education; reading

8/0920
Centre for Leisure Research,
Holyrood Road, Edinburgh EH8 8AQ
031 556 8455
Bisset, C. Mr
The impact of demography and other factors on 'Team Sports'
Abstract: The aims of the research are to provide an analysis of the relationship between demographic change and participation in 'single sex' team sports, utilize the information gained as a parameter in the strategic planning process in specific sports, and identify other variables impacting on participation.
Source of Grant: Moray House College
Date of Research: 1990 – continuing
KEYWORDS: demography; participation; sport

8/0921
Centre for Leisure Research,
Holyrood Road, Edinburgh AH8 8AQ
031 556 8455
Adams, F. Mr; Francis, E. Ms; Martin, P. Mr; Skinner, D. Mr
Enterprise awareness in teacher education: the development of a placement project for B.Ed students
Abstract: This research will aim to develop a placement scheme which will increase the awareness and understanding that B.Ed (Primary) students have in industry, commerce and enterprise.
Source of Grant: Department of Trade & Industry
Date of Research: 1990 – continuing
KEYWORDS: commerce; comprehension; enterprise; industry education relationship; industry teacher education

8/0922
Centre for Leisure Research,
Holyrood Road, Edinburgh AH8 8AQ
031 556 8455
Closs, A. Ms
Career perceptions of young adults with 'specific learning difficulties': a repeat study
Abstract: The initial study examined the perceptions of 24 young adults with specific learning difficulties of their 'careers' in primary, secondary and tertiary education. Personal perceptions were given prime importance but were triangulated by parental evidence and by educational psychologists records. Findings indicated deficits in the educational system, in particular in assessment and diagnosis of difficulties, remediation/support of difficulties, and in educational/vocational guidance. That research cohort left school between 1973 and 1985. This follow up research study will re-run parts of the research with a cohort leaving school in 1989 or 1990 to assess whether the developments in learning support and educational guidance over the last 5-10 years have improved the quality of such pupils' experiences in education. Guidelines for improved practice would be developed.
Source of Grant: Moray House College
Date of Research: 1990 – continuing
KEYWORDS: educational guidance; learning difficulty; special education; support services

8/0923
Centre for Leisure Research,
Holyrood Road, Edinburgh AH8 8AQ
031 556 8455
Conlon, T. Mr
Pupils and parallelism
Abstract: The aims of the research are to identify parallel computing tools which are appropriate for pupil use; adopt and develop new parallel tools where this seems possible and desirable and to make recommendations for future work, which relates parallel computing to the school curriculum.
Source of Grant: Moray House College
Date of Research: 1990 – continuing

KEYWORDS: computer assisted instruction; curriculum; parallel computer systems

8/0924
Centre for Leisure Research,
Holyrood Road, Edinburgh EH8 8AQ
031 556 8455
Crawford, E. Dr
Fitting into institutions
Abstract: The aims of the research are to examine the experience of students in placement schools; examine the experience of schools accepting students; identify institutional factors (as opposed to personal factors) which affect the experience of both parties; evaluate these factors with regard to beneficial and detrimental aspects of the experiences and develop induction and preparation procedures and compare with present preparation techniques.
Source of Grant: Moray House College
Date of Research: 1990 – continuing
KEYWORDS: experience; pupil placement; school

8/0925
Centre for Leisure Research,
Holyrood Road, Edinburgh EH8 8AQ
031 556 8455
Dickinson, N. Ms
The identification of the feasibility of the preparation of MA Dissertations in distance mode in developing countries
Abstract: The aims of the research are to identify the feasibility of preparing and writing MA (Master of Arts) dissertations in distance mode, and to identify the areas of difficulty in writing dissertations in distance mode in respect of: (i) resources, (ii) local supervision, (iii) external (Moray House) supervision, and (iv) time factors. The project aims to identify difficulties inherent in distance learning and in country dissertation mixing and to seek solutions.
Source of Grant: Moray House College
Date of Research: 1990 – continuing
KEYWORDS: developing country; distance study; masters degree; thesis

8/0926
Centre for Leisure Research,
Holyrood Road, Edinburgh EH8 8AQ
031 556 8455
Lawrie, R. Mr
Macintosh multi-media project
Abstract: The aims of the research are to investigate the suitability of Hypercard Applications in a Multi-media environment. Using the Van Gogh video disc, a suite of software has been redesigned to meet the needs of the Scottish Art Curricula at 'Standard' and 'Higher' grade.
Source of Grant: Moray House College
Date of Research: 1989-1990
KEYWORDS: computer assisted instruction; educational technology; multimedia approach; teaching aids; videodisc

8/0927
Centre for Leisure Research,
Holyrood Road, Edinburgh EH8 8AQ
031 556 8455
Frame, B. Ms
An investigation into techniques for the teaching of non-fiction in schools
Abstract: The aims of the research are to describe the present use of non-fiction; compare this with the suggested programmes of study for reading as set out in the Scottish Education Department English Language 5-14; describe the difficulties for teachers in planning, organizing, teaching, monitoring and evaluating the use of non-fiction; describe the reading demands/difficulties involved in the activities relating to the use of non-fiction; devise approaches which will enable teachers to teach skills, highlighted in 5-14, such as genre recognition, text categorization and style analysis which should lead to better understanding and interpretation of text; finally to combine the findings of this research project with the findings of a parallel project dealing with the use of non-fiction at the lower end of the school.
Source of Grant: Moray House College
Date of Research: 1990 – continuing
KEYWORDS: non-fiction; reading; teaching technique

8/0928
Centre for Leisure Research,
Holyrood Road, Edinburgh EH8 8AQ
031 556 8455
Francis, E. Ms
Specific learning difficulties (Dyslexia) project
Abstract: The aims of the research are to investigate the potential for developments in teacher education to meet the needs of those concerned about the education of children with specific learning difficulties associated with dyslexia.
Source of Grant: Scottish Dyslexia Trust
Date of Research: 1990 – continuing
KEYWORDS: dyslexia; learning difficulty; special education; teacher education

8/0929
Centre for Leisure Research,
Holyrood Road, Edinburgh EH8 8AQ
031 556 8455
Goodier, J. Ms
Harmonisation of curriculum from nursery to P1
Abstract: The aims of the research are to discover what would help P1 (Scottish level of Education) teachers to plan and provide a learning environment and learning experiences which effectively build on children's previous learning in nursery, with particular reference to curriculum. To help teachers thus provide optimum learning opportunities for the individual children in their class, and to assess whether this reduces difficulties for individual children.
Source of Grant: Moray House College
Date of Research: 1990 – continuing
KEYWORDS: curriculum; developmental continuity; nursery school; transitional class

8/0930
Centre for Leisure Research,
Holyrood Road, Edinburgh EH8 8AQ
031 556 8455
Grassie, M. Mr
Critical activity and its effect on the art and design curriculum
Abstract: The aims of the research are to study the effect of the new Standard Grade Critical Activity units on the Art and Design Curriculum especially in S1 and S2; to prepare slide packs, display boards and appropriate visual material as back for Critical Activity Units in Expressive and Design Areas and to enquire whether these can be adapted for use in the common course. The subsidiary or extended aim is to consider the new Higher Art and Design and the Critical Activity element proposed in relationship to present Standard Grade development.
Source of Grant: Moray House College
Date of Research: 1990 – continuing
KEYWORDS: art education; critical sense; curriculum; design education

8/0931
Centre for Leisure Research,
Holyrood Road, Edinbugh EH8 8AQ
031 556 8455
Hamilton, J. Dr
Language medium teaching
Abstract: The aims of the research are to examine the effects of language medium teaching on learner motivation and foreign language proficiency within the Scottish context.
Source of Grant: Moray House College
Date of Research: 1990 – continuing
KEYWORDS: language skill; language teaching; motivation

8/0932
Centre for Leisure Research,
Holyrood Road, Edinburgh EH8 8AQ
031 556 8455
Hosie, D. Mr; Turner, M. Ms
Comparative study of children with a hearing impairment
Abstract: The aims of the research are to present a preliminary study to assess the merits of 3 distinct models of teaching children with a hearing impairment.
Source of Grant: Moray House College
Date of Research: 1990 – continuing
KEYWORDS: child; hearing defect; teaching method

8/0933
Centre for Leisure Research,
Holyrood Road, Edinburgh EH8 8AQ
031 556 8455
Jackson, S. Dr
Implications of moving towards a more resource based approach to teaching
Abstract: The aims of the research are to examine the implications of a move towards a more resource based teaching approach. This will include looking at the implications for (i) the role of the teacher; (ii) departmental and school administration; (iii) development of materials, and assessment. One of the aims will be to see the extent to which similar or different implications can be identified in different subject areas.
Source of Grant: Moray House College
Date of Research: 1990 – continuing
KEYWORDS: resource based learning; teaching method

8/0934
Centre for Leisure Research,
Holyrood Road, Edinburgh EH8 8AQ
031 556 8455
Landon, J. Mr; McLeod, D. Mr
The roles and relationships of support systems in multilingual schools
Abstract: The aims of the research are to investigate the development of support systems within multilingual schools by identifying, (i) the different areas of focus of that support; (ii) the processes involved in identifying and responding to an area of need, and (iii) the issues involved in collaboration and the management of support systems.
Source of Grant: Moray House College
Date of Research: 1990 – continuing
KEYWORDS: multilingualism; school; support services

8/0935
Centre for Leisure Research,
Holyrood Road, Edinburgh EH8 8AQ
031 556 8455
Grant, C. Mr
Computers in nursery schools
Abstract: The aims of the research are to examine the use of computers in the context of the nursery classroom whether in a nursery school or a nursery class attached to a primary school. The specific sequence of research will be to establish the policy of Her Majesty's Inspectorate as regards the use of computers in the nursery classroom context; establish regional policy/guidelines on the use of computers in nursery school classrooms; establish the number of nursery classrooms where computers are used, and identify the type of computer used and times available; identify the degree of computer training given to teachers of nursery classess by the colleges where they originally trained; examine the amount and nature of inservice training offered by the regions and the colleges.
Source of Grant: Moray House College
Date of Research: 1989 – continuing
KEYWORDS: computer assisted instruction; further education of teachers; inservice teacher education; nursery school

8/0936
Centre for Leisure Research,
Holyrood Road, Edinburgh EH8 8AQ
031 556 8455
Lloyd, G. Ms
Problem girls
Abstract: The aim of the research is to explore the nature of school based deviance in adolescent girls and the responses of schools to such deviant behaviour.
Source of Grant: Moray House College
Date of Research: 1990 – continuing
KEYWORDS: defiant behaviour; girl; problem child; pupil

8/0937
Centre for Leisure Research,
Holyrood Road, Edinburgh EH8 8AQ
031 556 8455
Macintyre, C. Dr
Scottish dance for primary schools
Abstract: The aims of the research are to produce a book of activities, technical instructions and dances which will stimulate dance lessons based on understanding and appreciating movement pat-

terns and activities within a technical (ethnic) framework. The researchers will also produce a video showing young children dancing a selection of these activities and dances − as a teaching aid as well as a demonstration, the video would primarily concern the teaching of the dance.
Source of Grant: Moray House College
Date of Research: 1990 − continuing
KEYWORDS: *dance; primary education; teaching aids; videorecording*

8/0938
> Centre for Leisure Research,
> Holyrood Road, Edinburgh EH8 8AQ
> 031 556 8455
> Watson, J. Dr; McAree, R. Ms

Reading with young deaf children in the home
Abstract: This research will examine the reading habits of young deaf children at home at the pre-school stage, with special attention given to what happens when parents and children read together. The transition from home to school will be monitored, reading at school will be observed if possible and an attempt will be made to determine difficulties and their causes − whether a deafness or teaching and learning issue.
Source of Grant: Moray House College
Date of Research: 1988 − continuing
KEYWORDS: *deaf; home education; parent-child relation; pre-school child; reading; transitional class*

8/0939
> Centre for Leisure Research,
> Holyrood Road, Edinburgh EH8 8AQ
> 031 556 8455
> O'Neill, P. Mr

Dissemination of benefits of inservice primary courses within regions
Abstract: This research will explore the nature of the professional enhancement engendered by the Inservice BEd (Primary) and how the benefits of this enhancement can best be understood and disseminated within the profession.
Source of Grant: Moray House College
Date of Research: 1988 − continuing
KEYWORDS: *further education of teachers; inservice teacher education; primary education*

8/0940
> Centre for Leisure Research,
> Holyrood Road, Edinburgh EH8 8AQ
> 031 556 8455
> Page, C. Dr

Transition to college
Abstract: This research will provide evidence about the nature of the transition to college, as experienced by new students, which could help the college (and others) make wise decisions on future planning in the areas of teaching and learning, advising and counselling, residence, college ethos, and health education. The researcher will also address such questions as; to what extent does the new student experience homesickness? How is it related to links with home? (links e.g. letters, home events missed, vacations etc.). What preparation for the transition was experienced? In what ways does homesickness affect course work?
Source of Grant: Moray House College
Date of Research: 1990 − continuing
KEYWORDS: *college student; higher education; student adjustment; student life*

8/0941
> Centre for Leisure Research,
> Holyrood Road, Edinburgh EH8 8AQ
> 031 556 8455
> Lloyd, G. Ms

Gender and PGCE courses
Abstract: This research will investigate the recruitment, gender balance etc. of students of PGCE (Postgraduate Certificate in Education) (secondary) and explore student awareness of gender issues and the extent of permeation through the curriculum.
Source of Grant: Moray House College
Date of Research: 1990 − continuing
KEYWORDS: *admission; equal education; gender equality; postgraduate certificate in education; recruitment; sex; teacher education*

8/0942
> Centre for Leisure Research,
> Holyrood Road, Edinburgh EH8 8AQ
> 031 556 8455
> Quickfall, M. Mr

Computer based training: an analysis of the market
Abstract: This research will analyze the market size and potential for growth of computer based training in Scotland. The work will be based on an empirical study which builds upon the current literature and some of the more generalized studies which have already been carried out. The data will be collected by a combination of questionnaire and semi-structured interviewing of training managers and human resource managers.
Source of Grant: Moray House College
Date of Research: 1990 − continuing
KEYWORDS: *computer assisted instruction; economic conditions; marketing*

8/0943
> Centre for Leisure Research,
> Holyrood Road, Edinburgh EH8 8AQ
> 031 556 8455
> Thornton, R. Mr

A comparison of the internal organization of proportions within English and French discourse and its bearings on the teaching of English to native speakers of French
Abstract: This research aims to provide a basis for the production of learning activities and materials for native speakers of French learning English as a second language.
Source of Grant: Moray House College
Date of Research: 1989 − continuing
KEYWORDS: *English (second language); native speaker*

8/0944
> Centre for Leisure Research,
> Holyrood Road, Edinburgh EH8 8AQ
> 031 556 8455
> Tymms, P. Mr

Development of performance indicators
Abstract: This research aims to develop instrument(s) for the regular monitoring of client satisfaction, and consider the evaluation of teaching and learning.
Source of Grant: Moray House College
Date of Research: 1990 − continuing
KEYWORDS: *achievement; education; evaluation; performance*

8/0945
> Centre for Leisure Research,
> Holyrood Road, Edinburgh EH8 8AQ
> 031 556 8455
> Wait, A. Mr

The introduction of 'Management' to the secondary curriculum
Abstract: This research is a two year project which seeks to examine the problems associated with the introduction of the new higher grade course in 'Management and Information Studies' (commencing 1991). This is a brand new subject area in secondary education and a stand-alone higher with no equivalent standard grade. It is intended to research the preparedness and ability of Business Studies teachers to deliver the course and examine the problems associated with the learning and teaching approaches and assessment structure. The research will establish the current level of pre-service training; the requirements for inservice training and the problems associated with the introduction of the course.
Source of Grant: Moray House College
Date of Research: 1990 − continuing
KEYWORDS: *curriculum development; further education of teachers; inservice teacher education; management education; secondary education*

8/0946
> Centre for Leisure Research,
> Holyrood Road, Edinburgh EH8 8AQ
> 031 556 8455
> Gilfillian, E. Miss; Lynn, A. Mr; *Supervisor:* Maile, A. Mr

An investigation into changes in aerobic and anaerobic capacities in age-group swimmers, by blood lactate profiles and the identification of objective levels of training loads for young swimmers
Abstract: A current concern in sport is for the welfare of young children who are involved in competitive sport. Recent conferences have pointed out that there are many signs of over training in these

young athletes, with undesirable consequences in terms of performance, participation and well-being. Swimming is a sport where this is a possibility, particularly so where training programmes are not based on rationally determined training levels. The aim of the project is to provide information and data on the aerobic and anaerobic capacities of swimmers in the age group 12-14 years in order to determine optimum training loads, intensities, volume and variation. This information will be used to provide training guidelines for coaches working with age-group swimmers, and is aimed at maximizing improvement whilst preventing the stress and over training that result from ill-founded training methods and inappropriate intensities of work. Blood lactate profiles will be established on 3 groups of 12 year old swimmers and monitored over a 2 year period. Each group will follow a different training regime: Group 1 will follow an experimental aerobic-based programme; Group 2 will be subject to established training procedures; and Group 3 will act as a control group. Matters of medical sensitivity will be handled by the SASA (Scottish Amateur Swimming Association).
Source of Grant: The National Coaching Foundation (NCF): £8,000 over 5 years Scottish Swimming Association: £1,000 over 2 years
Date of Research: 1987-1989
KEYWORDS: *child; competitive sport; physical development; swimmming; training*

8/0947
Scottish Centre for Physical Education, Movement and Leisure, Holyrood Road,
Edinburgh EH4 6JD
031 556 8455
Macintyre, C. Dr
An investigation into how pupils perceive and react to stressful situations in school
Abstract: The study aims to find how young people in school identify and respond to situations which they perceive as stressful. A longitudinal study is envisaged with children from junior classes, from the transition from primary/secondary and from SIV forming the initial group. The researcher would be involved with these pupils in discussions and in observing their behaviour. By these means individual stressors would become known. In the first year, the researcher would concentrate on this identification process in a small number of schools, probably in Edinburgh. Thereafter, the task would be to design appropriate measures so that stress might be alleviated. The research focuses on children and their perceptions of stressful situations. The researcher would be required to interact with children from the different age groups and having identified stressors, conceptualize and implement measures which would allow them to be reduced. The pupils themselves would be encouraged to evaluate the new procedures.
Source of Grant: Health Promotion Trust/Economic and Social Research Council: £3,150; Student fees, maintenance, travel and general expenses: (1987-89)
Date of Research: 1987-1989
KEYWORDS: *perception; primary education; stress*

8/0948
Scottish Centre for Education Overseas,
Holyrood Road,
Edinburgh EH8 8AG
031 556 8455
Cousin, W.D. Mr; *Supervisor:* Morrison, J.W.
Computer management of a language learning resource
Abstract: An investigation of ways in which a database listing materials and suggested exploitations of materials can be used to further the control of learning in the Centre's existing Self-Directed Language Skills Course. The research has focused very much on the definition of the requirements that any database system would have to meet in matching the calls made upon it by advisers or helpers within a Self-Access or Self-Directed language learning system. Further work on this program must await decisions about work on the current system of handling the database using Rapport.
Published Material: CARVER, D. & DICKINSON, L. (Eds). (1981). Collected Papers in Self-Directed Learning in English Language Learning. SCEO. Mimeo.; COUSIN, W.D. (Ed.) (1982). Report of the workshops on the role and training of helpers for Self-Access Language Learning Systems. SCEO. Mimeo.
Source of Grant: Moray House: £80
Date of Research: 1984 – continuing
KEYWORDS: *computer assisted instruction; database; language teaching; teaching aids*

8/0949
Department of Applied Social Science
Holyrood Road,
Edinburgh EH8 8AQ
031 556 8455
Calder, J.R. Dr
A content-oriented classification
Abstract: The research rests on criticisms of the Bloom process-oriented taxonomy of objectives, and the incomplete nature of the Gagne content-oriented classification of possible learning outcomes. The method of investigation entails examining the widest possible spectrum of instructional material to analyze which types of content, with their implied objectives, are already 'ear-marked' by the categories of existing classifications of objectives; and which, on the other hand, are as yet underlineated 'alien' forms. The latter, not having been isolated, would not figure in systematically prepared achievement tests. Some new types of content have already been identified, but until a relatively complete classification can be offered as a contender, the existing strangely entrenched Bloom/Gagne schemes will continue to rule the roost despite blatant shortcomings.
Published Material: CALDER, J.R. (1983). 'In the cells of the Bloom taxonomy', Journal of Curriculum Studies, Vol 15, No 3, pp.291-302.
Source of Grant: Moray House College: £200 per annum
Date of Research: 1988 – continuing
KEYWORDS: *aims of education; classification; educational objectives; teaching aids*

8/0950
Department of Language Studies
Holyrood Road,
Edinburgh EH8 8AQ
031 556 8455
Hill, A.G. Mr
Group textual study of fiction in primary school
Abstract: The aims of the project are to explore the potential for educational development in the group discussion of children's fiction texts and to make resulting insights and developed expertise available to teachers. The project originated in a perceived need, in an area of Scotland, for the encouragement of oral work and the use of fiction as more than a Friday afternoon relaxation. It rests upon the beliefs that imagination (defined as mental operation upon the possible, as distinct from the actual) is an important aspect of intelligence, and that good children's fiction, as a product of imagination, might have an important role in fostering imagination, and responses to imaginative stimuli, in children. It is also thought that structured discussion might expand children's understanding and appreciation of what is being read by enabling them to share insights and responses, developing their ability to take literal and inferred meaning from text, enhance children's enjoyment of a text through sharing insights and responses; actively motivate less committed readers by demonstrating the wider varieties of enjoyment and response contained within a text; and promote children's language development, firstly by giving them an experience which is both common (the novel) and individually differentiated (subjective reading and responses), and secondly by presenting occasions when they need to express and articulate their own understandings and perceptions, and listen to and consider the responses and opinions of others in the group. To various extents, according to circumstances, observations by the researcher and by teachers suggest that these beliefs are valid. The resulting materials work well.
Published Material: HILL, A.G. (1985). Group textual study of fiction in the primary school. Edinburgh: Moray House.; HILL, A.G. (1985). Exemplar on, 'The lion the witch and the wardrobe'. Edinburgh: Moray House.; HILL, A.G. (1986). Exemplar on, 'Island of the blue dolphin'. Edinburgh: Moray House.; HILL, A.G. (1986). Exemplar on, 'What difference does it make Danny'? Edinburgh: Moray House.; HILL, A.G. (1988). Exemplar on, 'The battle of bubble and squeak'. Edinburgh: Moray House.; HILL, A.G. (1989). Exemplar on, 'I am David'. Edinburgh: Moray House.; HILL, A.G. (1990). Recommended titles for the group textual study of fiction in primary and middle schools. Edinburgh: Moray House.
Source of Grant: No funding
Date of Research: 1983 – continuing
KEYWORDS: *fiction; groupwork; imagination; primary education; reading*

8/0951
Department of Language Studies
Holyrood Road, Edinburgh EH8 8AQ
031 556 8455
Bogle, D. Mr
Methods of assessment – pronunciation features in the teaching of English as a foreign language
Abstract: The initial requirement will be to identify appropriate procedures and to establish criteria related to the needs of a variety of different target populations. Before assessment tools can be devised, it is important to have a clear idea of which features are to be evaluated, and priority areas here will differ depending upon the contexts and purposes for learning English. The sound system will be analyzed and decisions made concerning which aspects are most 'meaningful' and consequently constitute priorities for learning and assessment among different groups of learners. Criteria for selection therefore should reflect specific priority areas judged as being important for the transfer of meaning and successful interaction within a specified speech community. Decisions here will inevitably lead into the standards and awareness debate and consideration of learner's expectations in learning English and the desirability – or otherwise – of acquiring a specific model. Following a review of tests currently available, proposals will be made for improved tests which are judged to be more appropriate, and sample tests will be devised. As the skill of the tester is crucial, inservice recommendations will be made to ensure a degree of accuracy and validity of results. It is hoped that future trials of tests can be undertaken by course members from overseas returning to their home environment and piloting the assessment tools.
Source of Grant: Moray House College: £225
Date of Research: 1989-1990
KEYWORDS: assessment; English (second language); language teaching; oral expression; pronunciation

8/0952
Department of Leisure Studies
Scottish Centre for Physical Education, Movement and Leisure, Holyrood Road, Edinburgh EH8 8AQ
031 556 8455
Dean, A. Mr
Institution and evaluation of a community health initiative: health education around drug use
Abstract: The fellowship comprises 2 interrelated components. Initial work is directed towards examining the social basis of the use of addictive substances. This is an extension of another recent study and will be based on an ethnographic study of urban and rural subcultures. It involves in depth interviews, group discussions and participant observation. The findings of the Phase I empirical work will serve to inform the development of a community-based health education initiative. This will relate closely to young people's day-to-day understanding and use of specific addictive substances and will seek to explore, among other methods, the use of drama as a medium for health education.
Source of Grant: Health Promotion Research Grant: fellowship grant to cover salary and other costs for 3 years
Date of Research: 1986-1989
KEYWORDS: alcoholism; drama; drug addiction; health education; youth

8/0953
Department of Movement Studies
Scottish Centre for Physical Education, Movement and Leisure Studies, Holyrood Road, Edinburgh EH8 8AQ
031 556 8455
Crowther, N. Mr
Natural and man-made habitats
Abstract: REST produce resource materials for schools at low cost. This particular research and development work involves the publication of materials for classroom use on natural and man-made habitats. Five slide sets with teachers' notes are projected – (4 have been completed).
Published Material: CROWTHER, N. (1983). 'Woodlands in Scotland'. Teacher's Booklet and Slide series, REST Publications, Moray House.; CROWTHER, N. (1984). 'Seashore and coastal habitats', Teacher's Booklet and Slide series, REST Publications, Moray House.; CROWTHER, N. (1985). 'Mountains and moorlands', Teacher's Booklet and Slide series, REST Publications, Moray House.; CROWTHER, N. (1987). 'Freshwater habitats', Teacher's Booklet and Slide series, REST Publications, Moray House.
Source of Grant: No funding
Date of Research: 1982-1989
KEYWORDS: ecology; environmental study; slide; teaching aids

8/0954
Department of Professional and Curriculum Support Studies
Holyrood Road, Edinburgh EH8 8AQ
031 556 8455
Watson, J. Dr; Mackay, M. Mrs; Eales, J. Mrs
Autonomy in pupils with severe learning difficulties
Abstract: In both official policy documents and research studies there is general agreement concerning the goals of education for pupils with severe learning difficulties. The Warnock Report (1978) stated that the aim of education is 'to enable (the child) to enter the world after formal education is over, as an active participant in society and a responsible contributor to it, capable of achieving as much independence as possible'. Surveys show that teachers and parents of pupils with severe learning difficulties agree in wanting them to grow up into adults who are capable of independent thought and action and also recognize that interdependence in our society is essential. The present authors prefer the term 'autonomy' to 'independence' because 'autonomy' emphasises personal freedom, self determination, making one's own decisions and having responsibility for them. Commentators, however, have regularly noted that much of traditional special education may inadvertently reduce pupil's autonomy. Environments have sometimes been protective, highly organized, often controlling and leaving little choice and decision making to the pupil. Often they seem highly effective in teaching specific skills but may also risk inducing feelings of helplessness and dependency and low initiative in wider contexts. The report focuses on recent curricular developments in two schools for pupils with severe learning difficulties. Both have developed programmes which aim to develop autonomy in senior pupils, in very different spheres and in different ways. The first describes an orientation programme and the second 'growing up'.
Published Material: WATSON, J. (1989). Autonomy and the curriculum for pupils with severe learning difficulties: a report of two developments. Edinburgh: Moray House College.; WATSON, J. (1990). Independent travel: developments in schools for pupils with severe learning difficulties. Edinburgh: Moray House College.
Source of Grant: No funding
Date of Research: 1988-1990
KEYWORDS: autonomy; curriculum development; learning difficulty; special education

8/0955
Department of Professional and Curriculum Support Studies
Holyrood Road, Edinburgh EH8 8AQ
031 556 8455
Buultjens, M. Ms
The use of microtechnology in the curriculum and assessment of those with identified special learning needs
Abstract: The aims of the research are to identify examples of good practice in the use of microtechnology with pupils/students with identified special learning needs.
Source of Grant: Moray House College
Date of Research: 1990 – continuing
KEYWORDS: assessment; computer assisted instruction; curriculum development; educational technology; special education

8/0956
Department of Professional and Curriculum Support Studies
Holyrood Road, Edinburgh EH8 8AQ
031 556 8455
Francis, E. Ms
Discussion as a context for learning
Abstract: This project invites proposals from Central Support Groups, Curriculum Development Officers, TVEI (Technical and Vocational Education Initiative) and 16+ Co-ordinators on the development of a discussion curriculum related to particular topics. The Discussion Development Group will prepare guidelines, suggest resources and pilot small scale action research projects on discussion as a context for learning with different reference groups. The aim of the project is to apply the principles derived from two previous projects funded by the Scottish Education Department on group discussion.
Published Material: FRANCIS, E. (1985). 'Learning to Discuss'. Edinburgh: Scottish Curriculum Development Service.; FRANCIS, E. & DAVIDSON, J. (1987). Working together on discussion: a study of process innovation and dissemination. Edinburgh: Moray

House.; FRANCIS, E. (1987). 'Group processes'. In: Dillon, J. (Ed). Questioning and discussion: a multidisciplinary study. Ablex Publishing Corporation.
Source of Grant: College funding: £350
Date of Research: 1987-1989
KEYWORDS: curriculum development; discussion; group work; open learning

8/0957
Department of Social Studies
Holyrood Road, Edinburgh EH8 8AQ
031 556 8455
Price, D. Ms; *Supervisor:* Masterton, T.H. Mr
Environmental Development Unit and Resources for Environmental Studies Teaching (REST)
Abstract: This Unit has been concerned with investigation of consultancy needs in its area, and with co-ordination of provision from college to users. It has also developed a large series of teacher-oriented resources, now soon to be enlarged by pedagogical videos. These materials are the product of its approach to college/school joint classroom focused development work.
Published Material: a full list of publications can be obtained from the researchers on request
Source of Grant: College Research and Development Committee: £200 per annum
Date of Research: 1983 – continuing
KEYWORDS: environmental study; inservice training; primary education; teaching aids

8/0958
Department of Special Educational Needs
Holyrood Road, Edinburgh EH8 8AQ
031 556 8455
Edinburgh University
CALL (Communication Aids for Language and Learning) Centre, 4 Buccleuch Place, Edinburgh EH8 8AQ
031 667 1011 ext 6713
Buultjens, M. Ms; Odor, J.P. Mr
Production of raised diagrams, maps and pictures using the Apple Macintosh and the Minolta Heat Copier
Abstract: This project will provide: (1) A resource for teachers of visually impaired children throughout Scotland; and (2) research and development under the following headings: (a) investigation of the legibility of fill patterns, lines, point symbols and layout strategies which can be used in the Macintosh production method – this basic research will be necessary to provide the Toolkit; (b) investigation of strategies to enable young children to learn to use and understand raised diagrams and pictures; (c) investigation of the perception of objects and the understanding of spatial relationships developing in the young, and whether children have 2D representations which are more accessible because they are topologically transformed from sighted representational forms, or because they embody different coding schemes.
Published Material: The following public domain software and documentation is available from the project team: Raised Diagrams Tools 1; Raised Diagrams Tools 2; The Raised Diagram Toolkit: An accessory for Macintosh Computer Users creating master artwork for the Minolta Thermal Raised Diagram System.
Source of Grant: Moray House discretionary grant: £400 plus equipment
Date of Research: 1987-1990
KEYWORDS: microcomputer; perception; space perception; teaching aids; visually handicapped

8/0959
Department of Teaching Studies
Holyrood Road, Edinburgh EH8 8AQ
031 556 8455
Bain, W.H. Mr
Analysis of reports on curriculum
Abstract: The years between 1945-1990 have been a period of major change in school curriculum, assessment, and certificates as well as in advisory groups such as HMI (Her Majesty's Inspectors) and the SEB (Scottish Examination Board), SCOTVEC (Scottish Vocational Education Council), SCCC (Scottish Consultative Council on the Curriculum), and GTC (General Teaching Council). The researcher is analyzing the processes of decision making which led to specific reports and their implementation or shelving, in both primary and secondary education. In addition, the analysis considers teachers' and others' involvement in working parties and

bodies such as the GTC and SCCC, and the expanding of certification in secondary schools. A range of sources, chiefly reports and primary documents, are being studied for this work.
Published Material: BAIN, W.H. (1988). '29 steps to standard grade', Times Educational Supplement Scotland, No 1113, 4 March, pp.12.; BAIN, W.H. (1989). 'The Sera conference reports', Times Educational Supplement Scotland, 6 October, pp.5.
Source of Grant: Financial support for equipment
Date of Research: 1988 – continuing
KEYWORDS: assessment; certification; curriculum development; education policy; history of education

8/0960
Department of Teaching Studies
The Scottish Centre for Education Overseas,
Holyrood Road, Edinburgh EH8 8AQ
031 556 8455
Wilson, J.D. Dr; *Supervisor:* Cumming, C.E. Dr
Teachers as inservice tutors: Botswana
Abstract: Secondary education in Botswana is centrally directed from Gaborone. The system is experiencing a numbers explosion, and new community schools are opening at a rate equivalent to more than 1 per month. Restructuring of stages of education, and rapid curriculum development are also occurring. Staffing is characterized by high proportions of unqualified and newly trained staff, inexperienced co-ordinators (heads of department) and high turnover. Pending the introduction of a local administrative structure, the Ministry of Education (MoE) agreed an Overseas Development Administration (ODA) proposal to pilot in north-east Botswana redeployment of 6 experienced Overseas Service Aid Scheme (OSAS) teachers plus 1 Zimbabwean (2 each in English, mathematics and science, 1 in technical studies) from January 1987, as 'Professional Tutors' (PTs). The inservice remit of PTs is to improve the quality of teachers' curriculum delivery in their subject area in allocated 'circuit' schools, while maintaining a teaching commitment in their 'base' school. PTs report to Senior Education Officers (SEOs) in MoE. The main aim of the evaluation is to improve the generalization of the scheme to the remainder of the country. The cost-effectiveness of using British-aided teachers in a multiple role is a second aim of the evaluation. The pilot scheme, and its extension, are of interest to education planners beyond Botswana since the schemes may provide experience and evidence of how to plan the inservice education and training of teachers (INSET) through a novel approach.
Source of Grant: Overseas Development Administration: £32,440
Date of Research: 1986-1989
KEYWORDS: Botswana; developing country; inservice education and training of teachers; planning of education; supervision

8/0961
Departments of Applied Social Science and Primary Education, Holyrood Road, Edinburgh EH8 8AQ
031 556 8455
Draper, J. Ms; Fraser, H. Ms; Taylor, W. Mr
Students and probationers in transition
Abstract: The study aims to examine the relationship between students' experience of the course and probationers' experience of teaching, with particular reference to individual variations which arise in the process of transition to professional life. Additionally, the researchers hope to identify predictors of difficulties encountered by individuals both on the course and during the probationary period, which could then lead to appropriate differentiations in the provision made for individuals. In this longitudinal investigation, the researchers intend to follow cohorts of postgraduate teacher training students (both primary and secondary) from their initial selection for college through the college courses, and at various points in their probationary period. In the first instance the sample would be taken from the one year postgraduate courses, but this does not preclude the inclusion of other groups of students if this seems appropriate. The main method will consist of interviewing subjects at intervals both as students and probationers, seeking information on their expectations and experience of teaching and how these may change over a period of time. There will also be interviews with school staff as appropriate, and limited follow-up of those who fail to obtain teaching posts. Finally, results may offer some degree of long term course evaluation for the College.
Source of Grant: Scottish Education Department: £2,800 plus College support
Date of Research: 1987-1990

KEYWORDS: *course; evaluation; guidance; probationary teacher; teacher education*

Moray House College of Education

8/0962

Centre for Leisure Research
Cramond Road North, Edinburgh EH4 6JD
031 312 6895
Macrae, S. Ms
Pupils' perceptions of and reactions to stressful situations in school
Abstract: This study has examined pupils' perceptions of and reactions to stress in school during their second and third years of secondary education. Emphasis has been placed on analyzing how coping behaviours develop, or fail to develop, in the course of one year. Phase one of the main study was carried out in two comprehensive schools in Edinburgh and 98 pupils were interviewed in 34 small groups of their own choosing. Phase two took place exactly one year after the beginning of phase one and the same pupils who had taken part in phase one were involved. A total of 130 pupils were interviewed in small groups and individually; nine senior staff were interviewed as well as a total of 17 staff and outside agencies with responsibility for guidance, learning support services, educational welfare, educational psychology and careers education. An off-site support unit offering alternative education to pupils who have difficulty in coping in school was also visited.
Source of Grant: Health Promotion Research Trust: £18500
Date of Research: 1987-1990
KEYWORDS: *pupil; secondary education; stress*

8/0963

Centre for Leisure Research
Holyrood Road, Edinburgh EH8 8AQ
031 556 8455
McDonald, F. Ms; *Supervisor:* Carlisle, B. Mr; Adams, F. Mr
Aspects of new paradigm research and non-traditional learning: innovative approaches performance excellence in sport
Abstract: This study seeks to establish new parameters for training and performance in sport and the terms and conditions of a new paradigm research and development method in action. The project aims to: (1) offer a critique of training theory; (2) analyze performance in terms of key concepts, underlying values and performance goals; (3) develop a methodology for working within the parameters of what has come to be known as 'New Paradigm Research'; (4) establish what is non-traditional as opposed to traditional learning; (5) spot emergent training parameters and consider general applications; (6) establish the broad features of a new training system.
Source of Grant: Moray House College of Education: £1,000
Date of Research: 1988 – continuing
KEYWORDS: *performance; physical education; sport; training*

8/0964

Centre for Leisure Research
Holyrood Road, Edinburgh EH8 8AQ
031 556 8455
Wight, D. Mr; Wimbush, E. Ms; Duffield, B. Mr
Evaluation of the West Lothian Enterprise Education Programme
Abstract: The aim of the West Lothian Enterprise Education Programme (WLEEP) is to train teachers in student centred and process oriented approaches to teaching/learning which are relevant to the new Standard Grade and TVEI courses and National Certificate modules, and to develop in teachers a more change oriented or 'enterprising' outlook. The evaluation of this programme has been formative in approach, aiming to assist the WLEEP Executive to identify and overcome problems as they arise and showing how strengths might be maximized. There was also a concern that the evaluation should attempt to 'measure' any changes that could be attributed to the training programme. The evaluation methods agreed with the WLEEP Steering Group have included: (i) regular visits to the schools each term; (ii) case studies of 'enterprise' projects or lessons implemented by trainees; (iii) a 'before and after' survey of those teachers who have participated in the training programme; (iv) a survey of non-participating teachers.
Source of Grant: Standing Committee on Research (SCOR): £6,000 Scottish Development Agency/West Lothian Regional Council: jointly £10,000
Date of Research: 1987-1989
KEYWORDS: *economic studies; enterprise; evaluation; inservice education and of teachers; staff development*

8/0965

Centre for Leisure Research
Cramond Road North, Edinburgh EH4 6JD
031 312 6895
Dobie, S. Ms (Movement Studies); Lambert, P. Mr (Professional & Curriculum Support Services)
Implications of perceptual motor dysfunction and under-achievement
Abstract: It is agreed that defective development of the perceptual and motor processes which underlie the acquisition and performance of all motor receptive tasks may result in poor performances of a range of skilled acts. This research examines the relationship of motor impairment and under-achievement in association with a process model of intervention.
Source of Grant: Moray House College of Education: £850
Date of Research: 1988-1990
KEYWORDS: *learning difficulty; motor disorder; perceptual handicap; underachievement*

8/0966

Centre for Leisure Research
Cramond Road North, Edinburgh EH4 6JD
031 312 6895
Francis, E. Ms; Jarvie, M. Ms; Sinclair, A. Mr
Perceptions of enterprise within an educational context
Abstract: Interviews are being conducted with guidance teachers, students on the BA (Hons) Recreation course and school pupils visiting a chemical industrial plant with a view to ascertaining their perceptions of 'enterprise' and case studies of learning approaches to promoting enterprise are being investigated.
Source of Grant: Standing Committee on Research (SCOR) & Moray House College of Education: £6,500
Date of Research: 1988-1989
KEYWORDS: *economic studies; enterprise; perception*

8/0967

Department of Aesthetic Studies
Centre for Leisure Studies,
Holyrood Road, Edinburgh EH8 8AQ
031 556 8455
Hildred, M. Mr
Critical activity and art appreciation: development of resources for schools
Abstract: The current research relates directly to recently published work on critical activity, 'New Ways of Seeing', based on the researcher's courses with children in the 14-16 age group. These were developed and piloted over a period of 6 years in the evolving context of Standard Grade, the Scottish Examination to replace 'O' Grade (equivalent to GCSE). The present initiative involves curriculum development within the overall primary school context but especially focusing upon environmental themes appropriate to the upper primary and transition to secondary school, 10-14 age group. Two primary schools in Edinburgh are involved in the initial research. Processes so far have involved considerable staff development, identification of strategies, including the development of assignment cards and the gathering of pupil and staff responses to prototypes. The work will culminate in a report, and video production is under consideration.
Published Material: HILDRED, M. (1986). 'New ways of seeing', Report of courses in practical art appreciation and critical activity in 3 Scottish secondary schools. Edinburgh: Moray House College.; HILDRED, M. (1986). 'New ways of seeing', slide – tape – video, based on the report, presented and directed by the author. Produced by Moray House E.T.V. Unit.; HILDRED, M. (1987). 'New ways of seeing', Journal of Art and Design Education, Vol 6, No 2, pp.171-187.
Source of Grant: College Research and Development Committee: £1,000
Date of Research: 1986-1989
KEYWORDS: *aesthetic education; art education; critical sense; curriculum development*

8/0968

Department of Movement Studies
Holyrood Road, Edinburgh EH8 8AQ
031 556 8455
Crowther, N. Mr

Development of curriculum based resources

Abstract: Since 1982 a series of filmstrips for schools have been published under the collective title 'Habitats in Scotland'. Each is accompanied by a teacher's booklet. Initially the publications were made to meet the curriculum resource needs of specialist teachers of outdoor and environmental education. Increasingly in recent years the resource needs of primary teachers, identified by the PEDP (Primary Education Development Project) has been a major outlet for sales. Work continues on reprinting and updating previous titles in addition to the completion of the remaining title in the series.

Published Material: CROWTHER, N. (1983). Woodlands in Scotland. Edinburgh: Moray House.; CROWTHER, N. (1984). Seashore and coastal habitats. Edinburgh: Moray House.; CROWTHER, N. (1985). Mountains and moorlands. Edinburgh: Moray House.; CROWTHER, N. (1987). Freshwater habitats. Edinburgh: Moray House.; CROWTHER, N. (1988). Woodlands in Scotland. Edinburgh: Moray House.

Source of Grant: Moray House: £470 RESST (Resources for Environmental and social Studies Teaching): publication costs

Date of Research: 1982 – continuing

KEYWORDS: ecology; environmental study; primary education; teaching aids

8/0969

Department of Special Educational Needs
Centre for Leisure Research,
Holyrood Road, Edinburgh EH8 8AQ
031 556 8455
Edinburgh University
Communication Aids for Language and Learning Centre,
4 Buccleuch Place, Edinburgh EH8 9LW
031 667 1011 ext 6713
Buultjens, M. Ms; Aitken, S. Dr

Assessment of functional vision in children with visual and multiple impairments

Abstract: The objective is the provision of the most appropriate techniques for assessment of vision in children who, in addition to having a visual impairment, have other disabilities by: (i) determining the assessment methodologies used previously in ascribing visual impairment to a number of multiply-impaired children; (ii) establishing the relationship between form of assessment and implications for resulting intervention/remediation at either pre-school or school age level; (iii) employing with these children alternative methods of assessment of vision which, given the presence of other disabilities may be considered more appropriate (e.g. with children having additional cerebral palsy, adoption of a simplified fixation preference technique); (iv) demonstrating the implications of these assessment methods for intervention/remediation procedures. The subjects are a number of children (spread geographically throughout Scotland) identified by the project 'Meeting the Special Educational Needs of the Visually Impaired: The Process of Decision Making' (Thomson et al, 1985) as having a visual impairment as their principal impairment but having other recognizable impairments. A number of other children with multiple impairments for whom visual impairment was not considered to be their principal disability have also been identified and the alternative methods (see iii) of assessment of vision employed with these children. The final phase of the project will involve pilot studies of the assessment procedures in selected schools for use by teachers and other members of staff.

Published Material: BUULTJENS, M. & AITKEN, S. (1987). 'Assessment of vision in multiply-impaired children: a consideration of evidence', British Journal of Special Education, Vol 14, No 3, pp.112-114.; AITKEN, S. & BUULTJENS, M. 'Children with multiple impairments: a dichotomy between assessement and remediation', (Submitted to the British Journal of Opthalmology).

Source of Grant: Moray House Discretionary Grant: £2,250 (over 3 years)

Date of Research: 1986-1990

KEYWORDS: assessment; handicapped; visually handicapped

8/0970

Department of Teaching Studies
Holyrood Road, Edinburgh EH8 8AQ
031 556 8455

Cameron-Jones, M. Mrs

The Primary Placement Project

Abstract: The project aims to improve the supervision of students on professional placement, their assessment and the final reports of their competence.

Published Material: a list of publications can be obtained from the researcher on request

Source of Grant: Council for National Academic Awards (CNAA): £95,000

Date of Research: 1986-1989

KEYWORDS: assessment; performance; supervision; teacher education; teaching practice

National Association for Gifted Children

8/0971

Park Campus,
Broughton Green Road, Northampton NN2 1AL
0604 792300
Welch, J. Mr

Survey of provision for gifted and talented children in local education authorities

Abstract: After considerable discussion with the DES and the Welsh Office, followed by consultation with various Associations for Directors of Education, a questionnaire was sent out to ten Directors of Education. When the responses to this Pilot Programme had been received it was proposed to modify the questionnaire if necessary and then send it out to the remaining hundred-odd authorities in England and Wales. An analysis of the results of the questionnaires would then be carried out. All the authorities were invited to reply and 66 did so. Analysis of the results of the questionnaires is now complete.

Source of Grant: Department of Education and Science: £2,500

Date of Research: 1988-1990

KEYWORDS: educational provision; gifted; local education authority

National Children's Bureau

8/0972

8 Wakley Street, London EC1V 7QE
071 278 9441
Grimshaw, R. Dr; *Supervisor:* Berridge, D. Dr

A comparative, evaluative study of residential special schools for children with emotional and behavioural difficulties

Abstract: This is a 20 month research study to investigate the processes by which children are defined as having emotional and behavioural difficulties (EBD) and being in need of residential experience. This will be approached with particular regard to the overlap between education and social services responsibilities. The work will analyze the treatment methods, social and educational functioning and impact on children of a sample of EBD residential schools. This will be located within the context of what is known to be good practice in residential child care. The researcher will be living in the schools for significant periods, observing daily activities and interviewing adults and pupils.

Source of Grant: The Nuffield Foundation: £75,000

Date of Research: 1991 – continuing

KEYWORDS: residential school

8/0973

8 Wakley Street, London EC1V 7QE
071 278 9441
Cliffe, D. Mr; *Supervisor:* Berridge, D. Dr

Child care in Warwickshire research project

Abstract: This research project was established to examine the consequences of Warwickshire County Council's decision to close all of the Social Services Department children's homes. The use of residential care by social services departments has been in decline for many years, but Warwickshire was the first authority to close all its homes. The County reallocated money to establish specialist Children's Services Teams and the impact of these teams on child

care outcomes will be examined. At the time of the run down of the last of the children's homes, Warwickshire Education Department experienced a marked upturn in the numbers of residential special school placements being made for children identified as having EBD (educational and behavioural difficulties) previously labelled as 'maladjusted'. The research aims to establish whether the upturn in residential EBD placements can be linked to the closure of the children's homes. A variety of methods are being used. These include: analysis of historical and statistical data; detailed interviews with managers and practitioners; a longitudinal study of 250 child care cases over an 18 month period; case studies of children in five different groups (including residential EBD groups); and a postal survey of county education authorities to provide comparative data on statements completed for children with emotional and behavioural difficulties and the numbers of residential EBD placements being made.
Published Material: CLIFFE, D. & BERRIDGE, D. (1987). 'Warwickshire child care policies', Adoption and Fostering, Vol 11, No 2.
Source of Grant: Warwickshire County Council: £74,000
Date of Research: 1987-1990
KEYWORDS: child care; maladjusted; residential care; social services; special school

8/0974
8 Wakley Street, London EC1V 7QE
071 278 9441
Ames, J.C. Ms; *Supervisor:* Berridge, D. Dr
An exploratory and descriptive study of three intermediate treatment projects in the North West of England
Abstract: This was a 20-month exploratory study of three intermediate treatment centres in the North West of England, which are funded jointly by a major voluntary organization and the relevant local authorities. The research study explored work processes and outcomes in the three centres and is designed to provide information about the different methods of intervention adopted in the centres and the implications of these for the young people who participate in the programmes offered by the centres. The study began in April 1988 and a publication will be available from the National Childrens's Bureau in early 1991.
Source of Grant: Barnardo's: £37,000
Date of Research: 1988-1990
KEYWORDS: juvenile delinquencey; juvenile detention; treatment

National Council for Voluntary Youth Services

8/0975
Wellington House, 29 Albion Street, Leicester LE1 6GD
0533 471400
Cleaver, T. Ms; *Supervisor:* Cattermole, E.F. Rev.; Leat, D. Dr
Good practice in youth work; the independent voluntary sector of the youth service
Abstract: By obtaining, recording and collating information from a representative sample of local authority areas in England (using contacts with local authorities, councils for voluntary youth services and voluntary organizations), this research hopes to identify: (1) The youth work functions performed by the independent voluntary sector and to assess the key contribution this sector makes to youth service provision, with particular reference to work with young people from ethnic minorities and young people at risk in inner urban areas; (2) to consider with youth service providers at local level how the efficiency and effectiveness of the youth service, including the wider dissemination of good practice, could be assisted by closer working links between the organized youth service at local and national level and the independent sector; (3) to identify one or two areas for establishing agreed pilot arrangements for closer consultation between organized and independent sectors for a period of 12 months, and to evaluate these arrangements; (4) to report fully the collated findings of the above to the youth service unit of the Department of Education and Science and to make recommendations to the Department for further, appropriate action including any recommendations for the establishment of a long term data-base of information about the independent voluntary services.

Source of Grant: Department of Education and Science: £110,621
Date of Research: 1989 – continuing
KEYWORDS: ethnic minority; urban area; voluntary organization; youth service

National Curriculum Council

8/0976
Newcombe House, 45 Notting Hill Gate, London W11 3JB
071 229 1234
Wilson, A. Ms; *Supervisor:* Johnson, J. Mr
National oracy project
Abstract: The aims of the project are (a) to enhance the role of speech in the learning process, encouraging active learning, (b) to develop the teaching of oral communication skills, (c) to develop methods of assessment of and through speech, including assessment for public examinations at 16+, (d) to improve pupils' performance across the curriculum, (e) to enhance teachers' skills and practice, (d) to promote recognition of the value of oral work in schools and increase its use as a means of improving learning. The National Oracy Project will operate in three phases. Phase One (1987-88) will see the project team work closely with the National Writing Project in the five named local authorities. In addition there will be preparatory activities for Phase Two, including forging links with the 7 LEAs that will receive Educational Support Grants from the DES to undertake developmental work in oracy, surveying current developments in oracy, and preparing for the entry to the Project of a substantial number of LEAs in September 1988. Phase Two (1988-91) will be the main development phase, in which teachers in local authorities will work in curriculum areas and on activities which have been agreed between LEAs and the Project. Among the principal foci for investigation will be: Talk in the Primary School; Talk in Secondary English; Talk in Secondary Mathematics or Science; Talk in Secondary History or Geography. The project team will support local co-ordinators and teachers in this work. Phase Three (1991-93) will be the dissemination phase, in which the project team will seek to provide general support to LEAs in England and Wales as the Project's outcomes are disseminated. It is hoped to provide some regular communication to teachers and others interested in the work of the Project, possibly in the form of a newsletter.
Source of Grant: National Curriculum Council: £1.6 million
Date of Research: 1987 – continuing
KEYWORDS: communication; learning process; oral expression; speech; teaching method

National Foundation for Educational Research

8/0977
The Mere, Upton Park, Slough SL1 2DQ
0753 574123
Weston, P. Mrs; Jamison, J. Mr; Barrett, E. Dr; *Supervisor:* Stoney, S.M. Dr
Managing the curriculum: the implications for schools of the Education Reform Act
Abstract: The inquiry is designed as an evaluative review of how schools are coping with the management of the curriculum as the Education Reform Act takes effect. The main aims are to assist LEAs (local education authorities) and schools by discussing various approaches to curriculum management in different LEA settings, to provide regular feedback to the LEAs involved through meetings and short papers and to disseminate the more general findings to a national audience. A mixture of methods and levels of inquiry will be employed: detailed case studies in a small number of schools and LEAs, regular discussions in three regional groups involving several LEAs, and a national survey of schools. Three LEAs with differing characteristics have been selected for the case studies. Within each a 'family' of schools has been identified: a secondary school and its primary feeder schools. The case studies will involve working intensively with the secondary school and a small number of its feeder schools during the period of the research. The intention is also to maintain an overview of what is happen-

ing and how participants react within and between schools. The national questionnaire survey will be of a sample of primary and secondary schools and should provide a broad context for the case studies. During the review process short briefing papers will be produced, discussed by regional panels and circulated widely. General guidelines for schools and LEAs will probably accompany the final summative report.
Source of Grant: National Curriculum Council: £115,539
Date of Research: 1989 – continuing
KEYWORDS: administration of education; curriculum; National Curriculum

8/0978

The Mere, Upton Park, Slough SL1 2DQ
0753 574123
Baker, L.W. Mr; *Supervisor:* Bradley, J. Dr
The well governed school
Abstract: Following the Education Act (No.2) 1986 the composition of governing bodies has changed considerably, with an increase in parent governors, the addition of co-opted governors to include the representation of local community and business interests, and a decrease in LEA (local education authority) appointed governors. The project will focus on how the new partnership between the school governing body, the head and staff can be made to work effectively for the benefit of the school. The research will look beyond the simple exchange of information to mechanisms for joint co-operative decision making, identifying and documenting examples of good practice. The project will consist of three phases: Phase 1: (a) a review of recent and current work in this field; (b) an exploration of the role of governors from business and industry; (c) initial contacts with several LEAs and schools. Phase 2: a detailed analysis of some of the well-governed schools identified in Phase 1, concentrating on 10-12 case studies in at least five LEAs. Phase 3: the Phase 1 visits and the Phase 2 case studies will be drawn upon to produce training materials and an inservice trai ning pack.
Source of Grant: National Foundation for Educational Research
Date of Research: 1989-1990
KEYWORDS: administration of education; decision making; governing body; school; school governor

8/0979

The Mere, Upton Park, Slough SL1 2DQ
0753 574123
Foxman, D. Mr; Hutchison, D. Mr; Bloomfield, B. Mrs
The APU (Assessment of Performance Unit) experience
Abstract: The NFER (National Foundation for Educational Research) is co-ordinating the production of a volume documenting the expertise acquired by the APU (Assessment of Performance Unit) in all the facets of research and development with which the Unit has been concerned during its existence. Information for the writing of the document is being obtained from members of the monitoring teams and from their various reports. The document will highlight APU experience and expertise relating to general issues in the development of assessment materials and conducting large scale surveys. The main audiences for the document are seen as test developers and researchers involved in surveys of pupils' performance including those working on various aspects of the National Assessment.
Source of Grant: School Examinations and Assessment Council: £24,236
Date of Research: 1989-1989
KEYWORDS: assessment; performance; test

8/0980

The Mere, Upton Park, Slough SL1 2DQ
0753 574123
Foxman, D. Mr; Harman, J. Mr
Across the curriculum: a review
Abstract: The research is intended as an exploration of issues arising out of cross-curricular approaches in the whole curriculum, with special reference to the requirements of the National Curriculum. A framework for describing and analyzing cross-curricular issues is to be developed to review the differing meanings of 'cross-curriculum' in existing and emerging initiatives. A small number of schools are being selected for study. Schools will be sought that have already made, and are in the process of implementing plans to meet the cross-curricular requirements of the National Curriculum. The findings would be used to propose research questions for a more detailed project in this area.
Source of Grant: NFER (National Foundation for Educational

Research): £38,000
Date of Research: 1989-1990
KEYWORDS: cross-curricular approach; curriculum development; project work

8/0981

The Mere, Upton Park, Slough SL1 2DQ
0753 574123
Stoney, S.M. Dr; Dickson, P. Mr
Development of performance indicators and evaluation and methodologies for flexible learning
Abstract: The overall aim of the project was to provide an effective basis for assessing the impact of flexible learning within the Training Agency's TVEI (Technical and Vocational Education Initiative) Flexible Learning Development by: (i) Developing and testing a series of key performance indicators against which the attainment of the objectives of Flexible Learning Development can be evaluated; (ii) developing guidelines on what sort of evaluative evidence should be collected locally and nationally, and how this can be organized so that patterns and contradictions become apparent; (iii) assessing the effectiveness of central control systems and the regional network for Flexible Learning Development as appropriate, and making recommendations for the future. The project's research methods were based on a developmental approach which ensured that through wide consultation it built on current initiatives in flexible learning and was grounded in the experience of practitioners and project co-ordinators. The main research activities included a review of relevant literature and documentation, field based studies and the development of 10 generic performance indicators with a commentary on their use in different flexible learning contexts.
Published Material: MORRIS, M. & TWITCHIN, R. (1990). Evaluating flexible learning: a users' guide. Training Enterprise and Education Division and NFER.; SIMS, D. & STONEY, S.M. (1990). Development of performance indicators and evaluation methodologies for flexible learning. Final report for the Training Enterprise and Education Division and NFER.
Source of Grant: TEED (Training Enterprise Education Division): £45,351
Date of Research: 1989-1990
KEYWORDS: evaluation; flexible learning; performance indicator; Technical and Vocational Education Initiative

8/0982

The Mere, Upton Park, Slough SL1 2DQ
0753 574123
Taylor, M. Miss; Weston, P. Mrs; *Supervisor:* Stoney, S.M. Dr
Survey of Surrey young people's attitudes to post age 16 options
Abstract: This survey of young people in Surrey who are reaching minimum school leaving age focuses on their attitudes and awareness as they assess the various opportunities open to them in the sixth form, further education colleges, Youth Training Scheme employment and training openings. The main aims of the study are to: (i) examine the reasons for the choices young people make, the extent to which they understand their options (especially in relation to training) and their attitudes to these options; (ii) provide information to assist the development of provision for 16-19 year olds, so the Training Agency, LEA (local education authority) and Careers Service can improve quality and coherence, especially in the direction of their marketing and advisory efforts; (iii) establish the impact of what is already done in terms of careers education and guidelines and make recommendations for improvement where appropriate. The three types of data collected are: questionnaire data from all fifth years in 10 Surrey schools (7 state and 3 private chosen to give an LEA wide geographical spread and to include 12-16 and 12-18 schools); summaries of interviews with a 15 per cent sample of these pupils paired with a friend; contextual information from careers teachers and careers officers on educational, training and job opportunities available to Surrey school leavers and on careers guidance approaches in the 10 schools.
Published Material: TAYLOR, M.J., WESTON, P.B. & STONEY, S.M. (1990). 'Attitudes of young people in Surrey to post-age 16 options'. A report to TEED of a questionnaire interview survey of fifth formers in ten Surrey schools in 1989.; TAYLOR, M.J. (1990). Surrey fifth formers' attitudes to their options after 16. A survey in ten schools in 1989.; TAYLOR, M.J. (1991). 'Post-16 options: young people's awareness, attitudes, intentions and influences on their choice. Article being submitted to Research Papers in Education for publication.

Source of Grant: TEED (Training Enterprise Education Division):
£24,962
Date of Research: 1989-1990
KEYWORDS: *careers guidance; educational opportunities; training; transition from school to work; youth attitude*

8/0983

> The Mere, Upton Park, Slough SL1 2DQ
> 0753 574123
> National Foundation for Educational Research
> University College Swansea, Department of Education,
> Hendrefoilan, Swansea SA2 7NB
> 0792 201231
> Price, E. Dr; Powel, R. Mr; *Supervisor:* Foxman, D. Mr;
> Whetton, C. Mr

Development of Standard Assessment Tasks in Welsh for Key Stage 3 of the National Curriculum
Abstract: The Consortium of which the Foundation is a member has obtained the contract from SEAC (School Examinations and Assessment Council) for the development of Welsh Standard Assessment Tasks at Key Stage 3 of the National Curriculum. The three-year contract requires the creation of SATs (standard assessment tasks) to assess the full range of attainment from Level 1 to Level 10 on both the Welsh and Welsh Second Language programmes proposed by the Report of the Welsh Working Party. Formal trials of the SATs will be held in Summer 1990, a national Pilot in 1991, and the First Unreported Run in 1992. The project also involves the creation of INSET (Inservice Training and Education of Teachers) materials and their use in the training of teachers to administer the SATs.
Source of Grant: School Examinations and Assessment Council:
£2,584,919
Date of Research: 1989 – continuing
KEYWORDS: *assessment; language skill; secondary education; standard assessment task; Welsh language*

8/0984

> The Mere, Upton Park, Slough SL1 2DQ
> 0753 574123
> Taylor, M. Miss; *Supervisor:* Stoney, S.M. Dr; Gates, B. Dr

Religious education and the implementation of the Education Reform Act
Abstract: The Education Reform Act 1988 contained many new provisions for religious education and collective worship. A working party of The Religious Education Council, including an NFER representative, met between April 1988 and 1989 to consider and review current practices in RE and collective worship and has produced guidelines for Agreed Syllabus Conferences and Standing Advisory Councils on Religious Education on the aims and objectives of RE in the light of ERA and how they might be achieved. In conjunction with this work, in the autumn term 1988, the NFER undertook a national survey of advisers on RE to explore their interpretations of the Act and their perspectives on the implications of its implementation in local policy and practice.
Published Material: Religious Education Council of England and Wales (1989). Handbook for Agreed Syllabus Conferences, SACRES and Schools, The Report of a Working Party, Summer 1989. Available from RE-ME Enquiry Service, S. Martin's College, Lancaster, LA1 3JD.; TAYLOR, M.J. (1989). 'Religous education, values and worship: LEA advisers' perspectives on implementation of the Education Reform Act 1988. Slough: NFER/REC.
Source of Grant: National Foundation for Educational Research Religious Education Council: jointly £6,840
Date of Research: 1988-1989
KEYWORDS: *denominational school; educational policy; legislation; religious education*

8/0985

> The Mere, Upton Park, Slough SL1 2DQ
> 0753 574123
> Sainsbury, M. Dr; Christophers, U. Mrs; Ashby, J. Mr;
> Jones, G. Mrs; Clarke, J. Mrs; *Supervisor:* Whetton, C. Mr

Development of standard assessment tasks for pupils at the end of the first key stage of the National Curriculum
Abstract: A consortium consisting of the NFER, Bishop Grosseteste College, NFER-Nelson and two LEAs are developing standard assessment tasks (SATs) and associated INSET (Inservice Education and Training of Teachers) material. The SATs will provide valid, reliable assessments of attainment targets in mathematics,

English (or Welsh) language and science, appropriate to seven year-olds. Issues such as the production of evidence for moderation, bias, special educational needs and the assessment of low and high achieving children are all being addressed. INSET material is being developed in order to ensure that national assessment and SATs are fully understood. The project has now been extended to cover the production of SATs for the first two years of full national assessment, 1991 and 1992.
Source of Grant: School Examinations and Assessment Council
Date of Research: 1989 – continuing
KEYWORDS: *assessment; primary education; test; standard assessment task*

8/0986

> The Mere, Upton Park, Slough SL1 2DQ
> 0753 574123
> Sims, D. Mr; *Supervisor:* Stoney, S.M. Dr

Recruitment selection for hairdressing
Abstract: The advent of YTS (Youth Training Scheme), the introduction of a unified system of NVQ (National Vocational Qualifications) and the design of the National Preferred Scheme for hairdressing are together radically changing the recruitment and training of entrants into the hairdressing industry. Against this background, in which the potential impact of the demographic downturn has become a primary consideration, the Hairdressing Training Board sponsored the NFER to carry out a short research project to examine the effectiveness of trainee recruitment practices in the hairdressing industry. Interviews were conducted with 50 representatives of a wide range of hairdressing salons and groups, YTS Managing Agents and further education colleges in five different areas of England. The project investigated the range of recruitment methods and selection criteria used by hairdressers and identified areas of good practice. In addition, the project examined recruitment difficulties encountered by managers and explored their reactions. The project furnished the Hairdressing Training Board with a full and executive summary report which discussed the main findings of the research and provided guidelines for trainee recruitment.
Published Material: SIMS, D. (1989). At the cutting edge. Report of the NFER project on recruitment selection for hairdressing. Doncaster: Hairdressing Training Board.
Source of Grant: Hairdressing Training Board: £8,825
Date of Research: 1989-1989
KEYWORDS: *recruitment; vocational training; youth employment*

8/0987

> The Mere, Upton Park, Slough SL1 2DQ
> 0753 574123
> Sims, D. Mr; *Supervisor:* Stoney, S.M. Dr

Essex access course: evaluation of the planning period
Abstract: The Essex Access Scheme in further education colleges has two major stages. The first stage is a 10 week Planning Period (April to June) in which students, assisted by guidance and counselling, review past experience and consider future directions. In addition to sampling, students develop a range of skills through a combination of individual study and groupwork. The Planning Period culminates in the completion by students of a personal statement including education and career plans. The Access Main Course (September to June) encompasses core studies as well as to specialist subject options. A new departure is the introduction of open learning components in the Planning Period, in particular the piloting of the Open College's 'The Effective Learner' pack. The NFER has evaluated four aspects of the Access Planning Period: the management and co-ordination; education guidance and counselling provision; students' experience of open learning and their views on its relevance to their needs; and the implications of supporting open learning for staff development. The project, which has focused on five colleges, has used qualitative methods including group discussions, interviews and classroom observation. The evaluation has provided feedback for staff training activities in Essex in addition to a full report and executive summary.
Source of Grant: Essex Local Education Authority: £11,494
Date of Research: 1989-1989
KEYWORDS: *access programme; further education; open learning; planning of education*

8/0988

> The Mere, Upton Park, Slough SL1 2DQ
> 0753 574123
> Sizmur, S. Mr; Harris, S. Mrs; *Supervisor:* Ruddock, G. Dr

Primary science assessments

Abstract: Two sets of assessment materials in the area of primary science will be developed. The first of these will be incorporated into a curriculum package being written at Bishop Grosseteste College. The second will be a set of free standing assessments in science to be sold to schools and local education authorities by NFER-Nelson.
Source of Grant: NFER-Nelson Thomas Nelson U.K. Ltd
Date of Research: 1989 – continuing
KEYWORDS: *assessment; primary education; science education; technology*

8/0989

The Mere, Upton Park, Slough SL1 2DQ
0753 574123
Keys, W. Dr; Sims, D. Mr; Joffey, L. Dr; *Supervisor:* Stoney, S.M. Dr
Policy review of the REPLAN programme: commissioned study
Abstract: The evaluation, which lasted from August to December, 1989 examined the clarity and coherence of REPLAN's aims and objectives, including diversity of interpretation and changes in emphasis. REPLAN is a DES programme for the education of the unemployed. In assessing the management and organization of REPLAN's component parts, the study reviewed the implications emerging from changes in education, training and employment for its development. The research team evaluated the main outcomes and the overall impact of the various strands of the REPLAN initiative. A combination of research methods – documentary analysis, strategic interviews, group discussion and a small-scale survey – was used. The final report was submitted to the Department of Education and Science in January 1990 and is available on request from the DES's Adult Training Publications Unit.
Source of Grant: Department of Education and Science: £21,981
Date of Research: 1989-1989
KEYWORDS: *educational policy; unemployed*

8/0990

The Mere, Upton Park, Slough SL1 2DQ
0753 574123
MacNeil, M. Dr; *Supervisor:* Stoney, S.M. Dr
Evaluation of teaching about HIV (Human Immunodeficiency Virus) and AIDS (Acquired Immune Deficiency Syndrome) teaching pack
Abstract: The Health Education Authority commissioned the NFER to evaluate a pack of its teaching materials on HIV and AIDS, and its associated training programme. The pack 'Teaching about HIV and AIDS' is available free to secondary schools, and distribution is virtually complete. The purpose of the evaluation is to provide detailed feedback on how the pack is received and used in schools, how the training has been offered and received and consequent effects on knowledge levels and attitudes of young people pertaining to HIV and AIDS. Evaluation of training involves observation at two levels; at selected courses offered to trainers, and at subsequent courses offered by those who have been trained. Follow-up interviews of approximately 10% of participants are providing additional details about the training experienced. Information on training opportunities, policies and practices on a wider level is also currently being obtained from national surveys of advisers and schools. At school level, detailed case studies entailing classroom observation and assessment of students are providing evaluative information on the teaching pack and its use. A review of how schools have presented the teaching pack to school governors and parents is planned. The evaluation will provide a report to the Health Education Authority on the main findings and their implications for inservice teacher training and the future development of appropriate teaching materials.
Source of Grant: Health Education Authority: £55,451
Date of Research: 1989-1990
KEYWORDS: *Aids (Acquired Immune Deficiency Syndrome); health education; teaching aids*

8/0991

The Mere, Upton Park, Slough SL1 2DQ
0753 574123
Sharp, C. Miss; *Supervisor:* Weston, P. Mrs
Assessment, progression and purposeful learning in Europe
Abstract: Following on the work carried out under a previous EC contract (Assessment, Certification and the Needs of Young People), the Foundation has been awarded a further contract to co-ordinate five national case studies of good practice in assessment, on the lines identified in the Conference Report from the earlier project. These case studies are now being carried out by researchers in Denmark, France, Italy and Spain; the English study is being undertaken by the Foundation. Each case study is evaluating some aspect of 'good practice' in assessment for less successful pupils at school and classroom level, through observation of classroom practice and interviews or questionnaires with students, teachers and (in some cases) parents. The focus is on students around the end of compulsory education, but studies span the age range 12-16 years. An overview report, identifying issues and findings of common interest across all the case studies, is being prepared.
Source of Grant: Commission of the European Communities: £66,500
Date of Research: 1989-1989
KEYWORDS: *assessment; European Communities; learning difficulty; secondary education*

8/0992

The Mere, Upton Park, Slough SL1 2DQ
0753 574123
Keys, W. Dr; *Supervisor:* Bradley, J. Dr
Examination of LEA plans/programmes for WRNAFE (Work-Related Non-Advanced Further Education)
Abstract: The main aim of this project is to assess the progress made by LEAs towards meeting the aims and objectives of the WRNAFE Agreement. To this end, the study will compare a sample of LEA plans for 1987-90 and the associated programmes for 1987-88 with the plans for 1989-92 and programmes for 1989-90 from the same LEAs. Comparisons will focus on the following questions: (a) What evidence is there that the development of plans and programmes has improved WRNAFE procedures? (b) What evidence is there of changes in curriculum development, flexibility of provision, equal opportunities, and of account being taken of the views of employers and students? (c) What evidence is there of increasing provision of appropriate staff development? (d) What evidence is there of improvements in the identification of skill needs in local labour markets? (e) What evidence is there of improvements in the quality of the performance indicators on WRNAFE? In addition, the research will offer recommendations that will assist the collection and recording of more systematic information in future years.
Source of Grant: Training Enterprise Education Division: £20,000
Date of Research: 1989-1989
KEYWORDS: *labour market; non-advanced further education; work experience*

8/0993

The Mere, Upton Park, Slough SL1 2DQ
0753 574123
Ashforth, D. Dr; *Supervisor:* Stoney, S.M. Dr
Essex Local Education Authority: strategic quality management
Abstract: The Training Enterprise Education Division initiated a project intended to establish the strategic implications of a commitment to quality by the further education service. As one of the three LEAs involved in this project, Essex engaged the NFER to investigate the components of further education provision which bear upon the development of strategic quality management. The study was carried out between April and September 1989 against the backcloth of changes prompted by the 1988 Education Reform Act. It focused on the work of senior managers within the LEA and four of the authority's colleges and examining the decision making and planning processes, commitment to total quality and the relationships between colleges, LEAs and outside agencies. The study's findings are discussed in a final report which was used to inform the subsequent construction of a strategic quality planning programme within the authority. Copies of the report are available from the local education authority.
Source of Grant: Essex Local Education Authority: £22,000
Date of Research: 1989-1989
KEYWORDS: *administration of education; decision making; further education; planning of education; quality of education*

8/0994

The Mere, Upton Park, Slough SL1 2DQ
0753 574123
Bridgwood, A. Dr; Sims, D. Mr; Wardman, M. Mr; *Supervisor:* Keys, W. Dr
Degree/HND (Higher National Diploma) course choices of young people with maths and physics A-level qualifications
Abstract: The Government and the engineering industry are con-

cerned that places on engineering courses are not being filled and that applications for courses in higher education establishments in engineering and technology are decreasing. These shortfalls are occurring at a time when the number of places available has been growing and the demand for engineering graduates is increasing. This research is designed to identify the factors which influence the decisions of suitably qualified young people on whether or not to study engineering. Two complementary studies are being carried out. The first (consisting of group discussions) will focus on new entrants to courses in universities and polytechnics who have mathematics and physics A-levels, but who are not studying engineering. The second will be a questionnaire survey on young people in the second year of maths and physics A-level courses in schools and colleges of further education. A small number of group discussions have been carried out with students in further and higher education institutions. Further group discussions with students in universities, polytechnics, colleges and schools have taken place and more are planned. A questionnaire for A-level pupils in schools and colleges is being designed on the basis of these discussions. The questionnaire survey will take place early in the autumn term 1989.
Source of Grant: Department of Education and Science: £15,000
Date of Research: 1989-1989
KEYWORDS: choice of studies; engineering; higher education

8/0995

The Mere, Upton Park, Slough SL1 2DQ
0753 574123
Jowett, S. Mrs; Walton, I. Ms; Payne, S. Ms; *Supervisor:* Bradley, J. Dr
Evaluation of general nurse education and training
Abstract: An advisory group, which will be chaired by an NFER member of staff, is being established which will formally select the six case study demonstration districts. In the meantime, preliminary interviews have been held with local contacts (e.g. ENB (English National Board for Nursing, Midwifery and Health Visiting)) officers, nurse tutors and other researchers), key personnel at the Department of Health and Sheila Collins who conducted an enquiry into the six ENB pilot schemes. A literature search has been organized. Fieldwork is being undertaken in the six ENB pilots with a view to writing a preparatory formative paper on the problems and issues in mounting experimental programmes in nurse training. Further monitoring of the initiation of the demonstration districts will proceed once ENB approval has been awarded to the schemes and an agreement budget has been negotiated between the districts and the Department of Health.
Source of Grant: Department of Health: £385,000
Date of Research: 1989 – continuing
KEYWORDS: nurse; vocational education

8/0996

The Mere, Upton Park, Slough SL1 2DQ
0753 574123
Baginsky, M. Mrs; *Supervisor:* Bradley, J. Dr
Vocational education opportunities for students with speech and language impairments
Abstract: The aim of this research is to gather detailed information on the vocational education provided in schools and colleges of further education for young people who have speech and language impairments. The findings will be used as a basis for indicating ways in which improvements might be made in both policy and practice in this area of work. The research will be undertaken by means of a combination of qualitative and quantitative techniques. It will focus on the views and experiences of young people in their final year at special schools and on those who go on to attend vocational courses at specialist or mainstream colleges.
Source of Grant: AFASIC (Association for All Speech Impaired Children): £6,000
Date of Research: 1989-1990
KEYWORDS: educational opportunities; language impairment; speech defect; vocational education

8/0997

The Mere, Upton Park, Slough SL1 2DQ
0753 574123
Weston, P. Mrs
PETRA: a European Community action programme for the vocational training of young people and their preparation for adult and working life
Abstract: The research strand of the Action Programme on the

vocational training of young people and their preparation for adult and working life (the PETRA programme), was set up in the framework of the Council Decision of 1st December 1987. The general aim of the PETRA Programme is to support and supplement efforts of Member States aimed at ensuring that all young people who so wish receive one year's, or, if possible, two or more years', vocational training after the completion of their full-time compulsory education. The Decision provides for a number of Community level measures aimed at adding a European dimension to the actions undertaken in Member States to achieve PETRA's main aim. The Programme has three main strands: (a) the setting up and monitoring of a European Network of Training Initiatives; (b) the promotion of youth initiative projects which involve young people in their planning, organization and implementation; (c) the setting up and monitoring of a Research Strand on vocational training, providing a framework for transnational co-operation in research on aspects of training policy and provision and the evolution of vocational qualifications. The NFER has been asked to act for the UK in relation to one of the five themes within the Research Strand: the improvement of pre-vocational and special youth training programmes. It will involve the development of Research Partnerships with institutions in other EC countries selected to work on this theme. The aim is to link relevant research projects already underway in each institution through a variety of approaches, including exchange of information, visits and workshops.
Source of Grant: Commission of the European Communities: £13,200
Date of Research: 1989-1990
KEYWORDS: European Communities; pre-vocational training; post-compulsory education; vocational training; youth policy

8/0998

The Mere, Upton Park, Slough SL1 2DQ
0753 574123
Lee, B. Mrs; *Supervisor:* Bradley, J. Dr
Staff development and appraisal in further education
Abstract: The DES has funded seven colleges to set up pilot schemes on staff development and appraisal. The Foundation has been sponsored to carry out the national evaluation of these schemes with the aim of informing policy decisions on the future development of schemes for the FE (further education) sector as a whole. The evaluation will be undertaken by means of intensive case study in the seven colleges and their respective local education authorities.
Source of Grant: Department of Education and Science: £35,000
Date of Research: 1989-1990
KEYWORDS: further education; personnel evaluation; staff development

8/0999

The Mere, Upton Park, Slough SL1 2DQ
0753 574123
Bridgwood, A. Dr; Sims, D. Mr; Wardman, M. Mr; *Supervisor:* Keys, W. Dr
Non-completion of courses by engineering students on undergraduate and HND (Higher National Diploma) courses
Abstract: The high levels of student dropout from engineering courses in universities and polytechnics is a cause for concern. Estimates for the university sector suggest that wastage from some engineering courses may be as high as 20 per cent (twice the average rate for all university undergraduate courses) and it seems possible that non-completion rates for students on HND courses in engineering may be even higher. The aims of this research are to assess the overall extent and variation of engineering non-completion across the range of engineering courses, to determine the main reasons for non-completion and to suggest ways of reducing it. The research involves a mix of postal surveys, face-to-face and telephone interviews, supplemented by searches of existing databases. In March and April, the project team carried out interviews with about 30 academic and other staff in a number of higher education institutions. As a result of these interviews, two questionnaires (one for course tutors and one for students who have withdrawn from engineering courses) have been designed. In addition, an interim report based on the interviews has been submitted to the DES. A questionnaire survey of about 350 engineering departments in universities and polytechnics in England and Wales is currently being carried out. In addition, registry departments in about 20 universities and polytechnics are mailing a questionnaire on the Foundations behalf to former engineering students who had withdrawn between 1 October 1987 and 30 September 1988 from a sample of full-time and sandwich engineering courses. It is pro-

posed to follow up the postal survey of students with a small number of face-to-face interviews. A final report will be submitted to the DES in autumn 1989.
Source of Grant: Department of Education and Science: £19,000
Date of Research: 1989-1989
KEYWORDS: course; dropout; engineering; higher education

8/1000

The Mere, Upton Park, Slough SL1 2DQ
0753 574123
Saunders, L. Ms; Stradling, B. Dr; Murray, K. Ms;
Supervisor: Stoney, S.M. Dr
Evaluation of the management of the TVEI (Technical and Vocational Education Initiative) extension
Abstract: The Training Enterprise Education Division (TEED) has commissioned the NFER to evaluate the Extension phase of the Technical and Vocational Education Initiative. The investigation, which will start in July 1989 and continue until January 1991, focuses on the management, monitoring and review of organizational and curricular change within those LEAs which have now embarked on the Extension. Detailed case studies are being carried out in six LEAs, selected because they represent different stages of development and because they are employing a range of different management structures for the Initiative. A national survey will be conducted in 1990 to gauge the extensiveness of the issues identified by the case study research. The main purpose of the evaluation is to produce for TEED and LEAs a set of guidelines on the effective management of the Extension which will be firmly rooted in current practice and will offer a range of alternative strategies illustrated by examples of good practice drawn from every level of the management structure.
Source of Grant: Training Enterprise Education Division (formerly Training Agency): £149,611
Date of Research: 1989-1990
KEYWORDS: administration of education; Technical and Vocational Education Initiative (TVEI)

8/1001

The Mere, Upton Park, Slough SL1 2DQ
0753 574123
Dickson, P. Mr
Flexible learning: review of the availability of materials
Abstract: This project is one of the national projects in the Flexible Learning Development of the Training Enterprise Education Division. It aims to produce a database of learning materials in the curriculum areas of Business and Enterprise, Science and Modern Languages. The majority of these will be evaluated for their suitability for use with flexible learning strategies by a panel of expert teachers. The database is intended for use by teachers to assist in identifying potential useful resources and for assisting in adapting materials already in use. Handbooks will be produced giving advice on how to evaluate and adapt materials for flexible learning methods in the three curriculum areas. Data collected from school and college visits will be used in the writing of these handbooks. The institutions visited were selected as those known to be using flexible learning methods and innovative practice. The focus of the visits was on the materials used, how teachers adapted them, implemented their use in the classroom and improvements they would make given the resources. The handbooks will outline a prodecure for evaluating materials using well defined criteria focusing on desirable attributes for any resource encouraging or supporting flexible learning. Suggestions will be made of strategies to be used during training for individuals or groups of teachers. The database will become available from the Training Enterprise Education Division in June 1990 having been supplied in both print and disc versions.
Source of Grant: Training Enterprise Education Division: £117,000
Date of Research: 1989-1990
KEYWORDS: commercial education; data bank; database; educational material; evaluation; individualized teaching; modern languages; science education; teaching aids

8/1002

The Mere, Upton Park, Slough SL1 2DQ
0753 574123
Dickson, P. Mr; Lee, B. Ms
Evaluation of ESG (Education Support Grant) programmes of diversification of first foreign language
Abstract: The predominance of French in the secondary curriculum and its consequences for other languages have long been a con-

cern to foreign language teachers. The present policy to diversify provision has widespread support but many problems remain to be resolved. Previous research carried out at the NFER (National Foundation for Educational Research) identified, in particular, the problems of training, organization and costs to schools as well as the more fundamental question of staffing and recruitment. The aim of the project was to evaluate the programme in which ten LEAs (local education authorities) were implementing, with the help of Education Support Grants, schemes for diversifying first foreign language in schools. The evaluation encompassed questions of planning, provision, resources and training. It aimed to assist the pilot schemes by supporting local monitoring and evaluation and disseminating information among participant LEAs. The results of the evaluation will help to guide the formulation of policy, at local and national level, when diversification is implemented more widely. The project was conducted in three phases. In the first phase, the work of the local co-ordinators, in planning and launching the schemes, was examined in detail. A report on the planning stage was disseminated among participant LEAs. In the second phase, selected issues, crucially relevant to the implementation of the policy by schools and LEAs, were investigated in depth through interviews and attendance at meetings. The work in phase 3 involved a review of the data collected by the NFER evaluation and by local evaluators and the production of a summary report. Final conclusions have yet to be agreed, but the following issues will be discussed. The relationship between local and national evaluations, implications for schools in terms of policy, practice and training needs, Implications for LEAs in terms of policy and provision of resources and INSET (Inservice Education and Training of Teachers) and implications for national policy in terms of teacher supply and training, and language priorities.
Source of Grant: Department of Education and Science: £54,000
Date of Research: 1989-1990
KEYWORDS: choice of studies; Education Support Grant; evaluation; foreign languages; modern languages

8/1003

The Mere, Upton Park, Slough SL1 2DQ
0753 574123
Tomlins, B. Dr; *Supervisor:* Stoney, S.M. Dr
Reorganizing further education: the tertiary option
Abstract: Since the first tertiary college was established at Exeter in 1970, demographic changes and constraints on local authority spending have encouraged other authorities to consider reorganizing educational provision for 16-19 year olds along tertiary lines, and there are now more than 60 tertiary colleges. Much of the literature on tertiary systems is based on personal accounts of tertiary reorganization and provision. The project seeks to provide a broad based and objective assessment of the tertiary option. It aims to explore the variety of approaches to tertiary reorganization to be found in different local authorities and to provide a fund of data and set of guidelines on the the management of tertiary systems. Interviews have been conducted with senior local education authority officers and college principals in 15 tertiary authorities, and more detailed case study work carried out in 7 authorities. Approaches and experiences in all other tertiary and non-tertiary authorities are being explored by means of questionnaires. A literature review has been published and the project's major findings will be reported on and disseminated.
Source of Grant: National Foundation for Educational Research
Date of Research: 1990 – continuing
KEYWORDS: further education; post-secondary education; sixteen to nineteen education; tertiary education

8/1004

The Mere, Upton Park, Slough SL1 2DQ
0753 574123
White, J. Mrs; Brooks, G. Dr; English, F. Ms; *Supervisor:* Gorman, T. Dr
Monitoring performance in language in the schools of England, Wales and Northern Ireland: Phase II
Abstract: The APU (Assessment of Performance Unit) was set up by the DES (Department of Education and Science) in 1975 to promote the developments of assessing and monitoring the achievement of children at school and to seek to identify the incidence of under-achievement. The main aims are to develop measures to assess performance in reading and writing, listening and speaking. The first survey of 11 year old children took place in May 1979 and was followed in November 1979 by a survey among 15 year-olds. Surveys were carried out annually until 1983 and primary and

secondary surveys were undertaken in 1988. The assessment measures in reading, writing, listening and speaking are based on a functional view of language and reflect the kinds of activities that pupils are asked to carry out in the classroom and outside it and have been devised to show how pupils can read a wide range of materials. The surveys also include integrated tests which involve the use of different modes of language such as listening, reading and speaking. In the 1988 surveys a video component was included as part of the oracy study. Finally, pupils' attitudes to reading, writing and spoken language and media are studied and reported on.
Published Material: GORMAN, T. et al (1988). Language performance in schools: review of language monitoring, 1979-83. London: HMSO.; THORNTON, G. (1987). Language testing 1979-83. An independent appraisal of the findings.; A full list of publications is available from the Project Director
Source of Grant: Department of Education and Science The Welsh Office Department of Education in Northern Ireland
Date of Research: 1985-1989
KEYWORDS: achievement; assessment; language; primary education; secondary sex difference

8/1005

The Mere,
Upton Park, Slough SL1 2DQ
0753 574123
Streatfield, D. Mr
Survey of the new governing bodies
Abstract: Following the reconstitution of school governing bodies in England and Wales (October 1988) a questionnaire survey is to be conducted of 500 primary and secondary schools. Heads will be asked about their experience of reconstituting their governing bodies and about the composition and activities of the new bodies.
Published Material: JEFFERIES, G. & STREATFIELD, D. (1989). Reconstitution of school governing bodies. Slough: NFER.
Source of Grant: Department of Education and Science: £8,000
Date of Research: 1989-1989
KEYWORDS: administration of education; governing body

8/1006

The Mere,
Upton Park, Slough SL1 2DQ
0753 574123
Cleave, S. Mrs; Brown, S. Mrs; *Supervisor:* Bradley, J. Dr
The educational needs of four year olds
Abstract: This project is concerned with the growing practice of admitting 4 year- olds to school. The main aims are: (1) to identify the educational needs of 4 year-olds with particular regard to a developmentally appropriate curriculum; (2) to describe practical ways in which these needs can be met in reception classes; and (3) to provide a framework for curriculum policy with examples of good practice which would assist teachers working with 4 year-olds in infant classes and inform courses in initial and inservice training. The research is being carried out in 3 stages. The first provides a theoretical base for the study by examining the major theories which have shaped early childhood education and by taking account of recent research in this country and abroad. The second stage focuses on the needs of 4 year-olds as perceived by a range of professionals and practitioners in child development and education. The views of advisers, teacher trainers, headteachers, nursery and infant teachers, nursery nurses, parents, and leaders of playgroups and nursery centres will be explored and examples of curriculum guidelines gathered. The third stage concentrates on practice and looks at ways in which perceived needs are being successfully provided for in a number of infant/primary schools. Examples of good classroom practice and the development and implementation of selected inservice initiatives will be observed and discussed with the people concerned. The final report will offer guidance on providing appropriate experiences for children admitted early to school and will be of immediate practical relevance to reception teachers and course providers.
Published Material: 'Four year-olds in school: policy and practice', An NFER/SCDC seminar report. Slough: NFER.; CLEAVE, S. & BROWN, S. (1989). Four year-olds in school – meeting their needs. Slough: NFER.
Source of Grant: National Foundation for Educational Research: £140,000
Date of Research: 1988-1989
KEYWORDS: curriculum development; early childhood education; educational need; primary education; reception class

8/1007

The Mere, Upton Park, Slough SL1 2DQ
0753 574123
Hagues, N. Mr
Maths microprobe: computer administered diagnostic tests of addition and subtraction
Abstract: Many educational tests labelled as 'diagnostic' do little more than to indicate what a pupil can and cannot do. A diagnostic arithmetic test has been developed which actually makes use of pupils' incorrect answers to build a picture of their misconceptions about the procedures required to arrive at correct answers. When a child calculates, for example, a subtraction question incorrectly, it is often not an irrational or erratic error which is made. Children are remarkably competent procedure followers, but they are liable to arrive at incorrect answers simply by following a wrong procedure – for example, in subtraction, either by a slight error in operating the 'decomposition' algorithm, or by dispensing with decomposition and using a simpler operation instead. The test is run on a BBC microcomputer and can identify in very fine detail a total of 64 wrong procedures adopted in formal subtraction and addition problems.
Published Material: HAGUES, N. (1989). Maths microprobe: a computer administered diagnostic tests of addition and subtraction. Windsor: NFER-Nelson.
Source of Grant: National Foundation for Educational Research
Date of Research: 1984-1989
KEYWORDS: arithmetic; diagnostic test; error

8/1008

The Mere, Upton Park, Slough SL1 2DQ
0753 574123
Lee, B. Ms; *Supervisor:* Dickson, P. Mr
MODLS (Modern Languages in Schools): development of APU (Assessment of Performance Unit) assessment materials for teachers
Abstract: This project aims to develop, with foreign language teachers, materials and procedures which can be used for assessing pupils in school. The project also seeks to describe the process by which the materials and procedures are generated. In the course of the foreign language monitoring programme carried out for the APU, a wide range of assessment materials and procedures was produced in order that such a valuable resource should be exploited fully, the MODLS project was established. Some of the APU material has direct relevance to classroom assessment, whilst other aspects provide a useful starting point for teachers to begin the development of approaches which are relevant to the situation in schools. The project team worked with foreign language teachers in five LEAs: Birmingham, Buckinghamshire, Lancashire, Kent and Wiltshire. Two groups were concerned with the assessment of French, two of German and one of Spanish. The project had three main phases. The first phase involved establishing the teacher groups, discussing the purposes for which assessment is used and the aims of the development programme. Subsequent meetings identified particular areas of concern which were to provide a starting point for the development of procedures and materials. The themes selected fall into two broad categories: the regular assessment of speaking and the testing of listening and reading. The second phase of the project was covered in the academic year 1987-88, when the teachers implemented agreed procedures in the classroom, evaluating (with the help of the team) the results, and, in the light of this experience, refining their approaches and engaging in further development. A residential conference for all project teachers took place in the middle of this phase to provide an opportunity for each group to evaluate their progress, share ideas and plan and prepare further trials. The final phase involved the collection and collation of all the assessment materials produced in the course of the project and the review of all data relating to the development process. This documentation will be assembled in conjunction with the teacher groups and packaged in a way which would make it most accessible for inservice training purposes. The project aims to produce a package which will draw on the procedures carried out by the teachers and examples of the materials developed. There will also be observations on the process involved in the development work and recommendations for ways of using the materials as an inservice training resource.
Published Material: LEE, B. & DICKSON, P. (1989). Assessment in action. Slough: NFER.
Source of Grant: Department of Education and Science: £128,191
Date of Research: 1987-1989
KEYWORDS: assessment; foreign languages; performance; teaching aids

8/1009

The Mere, Upton Park, Slough SL1 2DQ
0753 574123
Keys, W. Dr; *Supervisor:* Stoney, S.M. Dr

Monitoring for short courses in public sector further and higher education

Abstract: In January 1987, the NFER was commissioned by the DES to develop a statistical monitoring system for short courses in public sector further and higher education in England and Wales. The aim of this initial 18-month study was to provide information on the extent and scope of short courses in the public sector which would be used by the DES, the National Advisory Board (NAB) and the Training Agency in the planning and funding of future provision. For example, the DES/PICKUP initiative, which is designed to support and encourage FHE (further and higher education) establishments in the development of self-financing vocational updating provision, will use the survey to monitor the extent of existing provision and identify specific areas where the needs of industry and commerce for updating and retraining are not being met. In autumn 1987 a survey of short courses which had taken place during the academic year 1986-87 was undertaken in a sample of about 200 FHE establishments in England and Wales. The results of this survey were reported to the DES and the Welsh Office in summer 1988. The project has been extended twice. In autumn 1988 the NFER undertook a survey of short courses in all 500 FHE establishments in England and Wales for the academic year 1987-88 and in autumn 1989 it is proposed to carry out a similar survey for the academic year 1988-89. The DES and Welsh Office intend eventually to take over the short course monitoring system.
Source of Grant: Department of Education and Science
Date of Research: 1987-1990
KEYWORDS: *course; educational provision; further education; higher education; planning of education; statistical analysis*

8/1010

The Mere, Upton Park, Slough SL1 2DQ
0753 574123
Maychell, K. Ms; *Supervisor:* Bradley, J. Dr

Multi-professional support for young adults with special needs

Abstract: The need for co-operation among various services involved in supporting young people with special needs has long been recognized. Yet relatively few examples may be cited of co-operative action to meet the needs of these young people in their transition from school or college to adult life. This study aims to: identify relevant models of inter-professional working; ascertain how they relate to desired objectives in terms of suppporting young people as they progress from school or college to continuing education and training; and highlight the lessons for practice elsewhere. It will also make an assessment of the type of training that would facilitate the introduction and development of co-operative working relationships. The first phase involves identifying those local authorities where co-operative working is being planned or is already in existence in order to gain information on their development and operation. On the basis of the information gathered, a number of initiatives will be selected for detailed investigation in phase two. It is envisaged that this will involve extended field visits to each location. These are likely to include a series of one-to-one interviews with key personnel, observation, attendance at meetings, and interviews and group discussions with all relevant staff. A final report will be prepared which will document the range of initiatives studied, analyze these for their relevance to the practice of co-operative working in other locations, provide information to guide future policy and practice, and offer recommendations on appropriate training initiatives at the national and local levels.
Source of Grant: National Foundation for Educational Research
Date of Research: 1988 – continuing
KEYWORDS: *co-operation; local education authority; social service; special needs; transition from school to work; youth*

8/1011

The Mere, Upton Park, Slough SL1 2DQ
0753 574123
Fletcher-Campbell, F. Ms; Hall, C. Mr; *Supervisor:* Bradley, J. Dr

The education of children in care

Abstract: There is some evidence that children in care have a low level of educational attainment but there is little information about their actual educational experiences – which may compound, or to some extent compensate for – , the disadvantages arising from the circumstances that led to placement. The study aims to collect factual information about current provision for children in care; and analyze the degree to which the children's educational needs appear to be met. The research has involved a questionnaire survey distributed to social services departments; intensive case studies of a representative sample of four local authorities (interviews with relevant individuals; examination of documentation; attendance at meetings); and the production of a written report outlining the major findings.
Published Material: FLETCHER-CAMPBELL, F. & HALL, C. (1990). Changing schools? Changing people? The education of children in care. Slough: NFER.
Source of Grant: National Foundation for Educational Research Economic and Social Research Council
Date of Research: 1988-1989
KEYWORDS: *care; child; educational provision; social service*

8/1012

The Mere, Upton Park, Slough SL1 2DQ
0753 574123
Bradley, J. Dr

The selection of candidates for initial teacher training

Abstract: The project aims to gather information on the procedures for initial and in-training selection now in operation in CDCC (Conseil de Cooperation Culturelle) countries, and on any new initiatives that are currently being tried out and evaluated. The project will be undertaken in two main phases. Phase 1 will be devoted to the collection of background information on current policy and practice in all CDCC countries. An approach will be made to the Council of Europe Secretariat and to national Ministries of Education, as appropriate, requesting (i) information on whether countries have established teacher selection criteria and procedures at the national, regional or local level; and (ii) lists of teacher training institutions within each country. The second phase will involve the development and administration of a questionnaire. In those countries where selection criteria and procedures have been established at the national level, the questionnaires will be sent to the Ministry of Education. In all other cases the questionnaires will be sent to representative samples of teacher training institutions in each country. Samples would be selected on the basis of geograhical location and the age range of pupils for who teaching students are being trained. A final report detailing the results of the two phases will be presented to the Council of Europe Secretariat at the end of the project.
Source of Grant: Council of Europe
Date of Research: 1988-1990
KEYWORDS: *Council of Europe; selection; teacher education*

8/1013

The Mere, Upton Park, Slough SL1 2DQ
0753 574123
Smith, P. Dr; Traynelis, J.F. Mrs; *Supervisor:* Whetton, C. Mr

The analysis and use of spatial ability in educational contexts

Abstract: This project aims to develop a test of spatial memory which is suitable for use as an educational research tool. Both computerized and conventional formats are being trialled. Normative information is being gathered by testing large groups of pupils aged 8, 12 and 16 to 17. The predictive validity of the test will be assessed by obtaining subsequent examination results from the older pupils.
Source of Grant: MacFarlane Smith bequest
Date of Research: 1989 – continuing
KEYWORDS: *assessment; cognitive process; space perception*

8/1014

The Mere, Upton Park, Slough SL1 2DQ
0753 574123
Foxman, D. Mr; *Supervisor:* Burstall, C. Dr

Second International Assessment of Educational Progress (IAEP2)

Abstract: In this research the Foundation is acting as the agency for the participation of England and Wales in a second IAEP (International Assessment of Educational Progress) co-ordinated by the Centre for the Assessment of Educational Progress in the United States. The first IAEP, of 13 year-olds in mathematics and science in 6 countries (12 educational systems), was carried out in February 1988. The aim of reporting within a year was successfully achieved at both international and national levels early in 1989. The reports aroused a good deal of interest and about 20 countries are expected to pariticipate in the second assessment. In IAEP2, a second age group, 9 year-olds will be involved. There will also be som e questions on geography and an exploratory administra-

tion of practical items in mathematics and science for 13 year-olds.
Source of Grant: No funding
Date of Research: 1989 – continuing
KEYWORDS: *assessment; cross-national research; geography; mathematics; science education*

8/1015

Department of Assessment and Measurement
The Mere, Upton Park, Slough SL1 2DQ
0753 574123
Hagues, N. Mr; *Supervisor:* Ruddock, G.J. Dr
Development of primary mathematics assessment for Key Stage 2 of the National Curriculum
Abstract: The National Foundation for Educational Research is developing assessment materials to assist teachers in their Teacher Assessment for Key Stage 2 of the National Curriculum. The material will cover levels 2 to 5 of the National Curriculum.
Source of Grant: NFER-Nelson
Date of Research: 1990 – continuing
KEYWORDS: *assessment; mathematics; primary education; teaching aids*

8/1016

Department of Assessment and Measurement
The Mere, Upton Park, Slough SL1 2DQ
0753 574123
Brunel University
Coopers Hill Lane, Egham TW20 OJZ
0784 431341
Ruddock, G.J. Dr; Harris, D. Prof.; *Supervisor:* Whetton, C. Mr; Foxman, D. Mr
Evaluation of National Curriculum Assessment at Key Stage 3 in mathematics, science, English and technology
Abstract: The project will evaluate the first nationwide National Curriculum assessment of fourteen year olds in science and mathematics in 1992, and in English and technology in 1993. The results of these will be surveyed and the procedures used will be evaluated. The focus of evaluation is the validity and reliability of the results. Three elements make up the study: a statistical survey of results; use studies of schools' management of the assessment process; comparison of results with those from assessment probes specially constructed by the project.
Source of Grant: School Examinations and Assessment Council: £569,000
Date of Research: 1991 – continuing
KEYWORDS: *English studies; assessment; science education; technology*

8/1017

Department of Evaluation and Policy Studies
The Mere, Upton Park, Slough SL1 2DQ
0753 574123
Macneill, M. Dr; *Supervisor:* Stoney, S.M. Dr
Evaluation of the licensed teacher route to QTS (Qualifed Teacher Status)
Abstract: The evaluation of the new licensed teacher route to QTS (Qualifed Teacher Status) aims to obtain a detailed overview of the structure and operation of this route, and to monitor its effects and implications at LEA, training institution and school level. The evaluation is conducted mainly through case study and survey methods, with some background documentary analysis. One survey is designed for the total population of licensed teachers in England, which will also cover the headteachers and mentors involved. This will run during the summer of 1991. A second survey of all LEAs using the licensed teacher route will take place the following year. The case study work focuses on interviews with the key personnel involved in the training of licensed teachers, within a wide representation of different ways of implementing the licensed teachers route. A final report will be presented to the Department of Education and Science in autumn 1992.
Source of Grant: Department of Education and Science: £116,866
Date of Research: 1990 – continuing
KEYWORDS: *evaluation; licensed teacher; teacher education*

8/1018

Department of Evaluation and Policy Studies
The Mere, Upton Park, Slough SL1 2DQ
0753 574123
Stoney, S.M. Dr; Saunders, L. Ms; Stradling, B. Dr; Murray, K. Ms; *Supervisor:* Stoney, S.M. Dr

National Evaluation of Compacts
Abstract: This research has arisen out of the Employment Department commissioning the NFER to evaluate the operation of Compact schemes in England and Wales. Compact schemes – based in Urban Programme Authority or priority areas – aim to raise the attainment of young people and to prepare them for the world of work by guaranteeing a job with training (or training leading to a job) to all young people who meet their agreed targets. The investigation will use both national and case study data to elicit any changes in student performance over time (notably in attainment and attendance) which could be associated with a 'Compact effect'. Some comparability with non-Compact students/schools is built into this part of the investigation. Additionally, the project will investigate how Compacts operate in changing labour market and educational contexts. The views of participating schools, training providers and employers on the programme's input will also be sought.
Source of Grant: Department of Employment: £548,923
Date of Research: 1990 – continuing
KEYWORDS: *evaluation; pre-vocational education; transition from school to work*

8/1019

Department of Evaluation and Policy Studies
The Mere, Upton Park, Slough SL1 2DQ
0753 574123
Sims, D. Mr; *Supervisor:* Stoney, S.M. Dr
LEAs: their roles and relationships with TECs
Abstract: Tecs (Training and Enterprise Councils) are a pivotal mechanism in the government's employment strategy for the 1990s. This policy initiative, which devolves responsibility for the organization of quality training and enterprise development to the 82 employer-led bodies, changes the balance of control for locally provided VET (Vocational Education and Training) away from the education service in favour of the industrial and business sectors. The research project explores the developing relationship between TECs and LEAs (Local Education Authorities) and examines the impact of this new relationship on VET provision, skill shortages and education-industry partnerships. The preliminary phase of the 12 month project (January-March 1991) aims to provide an annotated database on labour market and TEC-edcuation service issues (based on the collection and analysis of quantitative and qualitative data) and to prepare a critical review of the information collected. The main project phase (April-December 1991) aims to provide a national picture of the nature, extent and range of relationships which LEAs are building with their local TECs by gathering data from exploratory visits and interviews with TEC and education personnel, from a questionnaire survey of all LEAs and from a questionnaire survey of all 82 TEC directors. The main outcomes will be an annotated database on labour market and LEA-TEC information; a critical review of the database information for publication during the summer of 1991; and a final report (with executive summary) on the findings of the project.
Source of Grant: National Foundation for Educational Research: £36,000
Date of Research: 1991 – continuing
KEYWORDS: *data bank; industry education relationship; vocational education*

8/1020

Department of Evaluation and Policy Studies
The Mere, Upton Park, Slough SL1 2DQ
0753 574123
Jamison, J. Mr; Sims, D. Mr; *Supervisor:* Stoney, S.M. Dr
Training Credits pilot scheme evaluation case study: SOLOTEC
Abstract: TCs (Training Credits) are being introduced in 1991 as a means of motivating young people to participate more effectively in the training market. This government initiative is designed to increase young people's access to, and employers' participation in, training and to improve training quality. Eleven TECs (Training and Enterprise Councils) have been invited to run Training Credit pilot schemes in which LEAs (local education authorities) and the Careers Service will have key roles. These schemes offer opportunities to try out different approaches to TC management and delivery and to evaluate their impact on young people's motivation, progress and achievement. This project is a case study of the TC scheme operated by SOLOTEC (South London Polytechnic) three LEAs – Croydon, Bexley and Bromley. The aims of this research are to assess the impact of Training Credits on local Further Education Provision, TEC management, employers' training activities,

young people's motivation to train and access to training for young people, including members of ethnic minorities and those with special educational needs. The research methods used include analysis of labour market and post-16 destination data, and programmes of interviews with key staff in SOLOTEC, the LEAs, the Careers Service, further education, in addition to interviews with a sample of 120 school pupils and 50 employers. The outcome will be a series of reports covering the core aims of the TCs initiative.
Source of Grant: Department of Employment: £47,643
Date of Research: 1991 – continuing
KEYWORDS: case study; credits; further education; vocational training

8/1021

Department of Evaluation and Policy Studies
The Mere, Upton Park, Slough SL1 2DQ
0753 574123
Taylor, M. Miss; *Supervisor:* Stoney, S.M. Dr
Multicultural education after ERA: concerns and challenges for the 1990s
Abstract: The values underpinning the 1988 Education Reform Act and the structures and targets set by the implementation of the National Curriculum have raised new issues and challenges in the realization of equal opportunites and the translation of multicultural polices into practice. This project, which has just begun, seeks to be diagnostic and responsive by establishing current concerns among LEAs and identifying promising developmental strategies in relation to institutional, training and curricular issues which may be more widely disseminated. The research will have three phases – a national questionnaire, adviser/inspector interviews and LEA case studies – which will build on previous work, enabling comparisons to be made between recent and contemporary issues and developments. At this early stage when the project is collecting and identifying concerns it is not possible to specify the topics, levels of education or ethnic groups on which the research will focus. However, it is likely to include considerations such as Section 11 funding, collection of ethnic data on teachers and pupils, open enrolment, TECs (Training and Enterprise Councils) and aspects of the curriculum teacher training and community involvement. It is intended that research will take a variety of forms as appropriate for various audiences and throughout the life of the project.
Source of Grant: £154,649
Date of Research: 1991 – continuing
KEYWORDS: intercultural education; multicultural education

8/1022

Department of Professional Studies
The Mere, Upton Park, Slough SL1 2DQ
0753 574123
Fletcher-Campbell, F. Miss; *Supervisor:* Bradley, J. Dr
LEA policy and practices in supporting special education provision in schools
Abstract: The research aims to document and analyze LEAs current policies for SEN (Special Educational Needs); to examine the nature of special support as policy is realised in practice; to identify INSET (Inservice Education and Training of Teachers) needs and provision; to investigate the effect of the 1988 Education Act on SEN provision; and to consider the ways in which LEAs monitor and evaluate their SEN provision. In the initial phase, all LEAs in England and Wales were invited to submit any documentation relating to SEN. In the second phase, a small number of LEAs are being studies in depth. Issues being focused on are: structure and management of support services; assessment; monitoring and evaluation; INSET and resourcing. The research findings will be presented in journal articles and a final report will be published in 1992.
Source of Grant: National Foundation for Educational Research
Date of Research: 1990 – continuing
KEYWORDS: educational policy; further education of teachers; inservice teacher education; special education

National Institute for Careers Education and Counselling

8/1023

Sheraton House, Castle Park, Cambridge CB3 0AX

0223 460277
Hatfield Polytechnic
Hertford Campus, Balls Park, Hertford SG13 8QF
0992 558451
Killeen, J. Mr; Hawthorn, R. Ms
Advice and guidance: implementing learning outcomes
Abstract: The aims of the research are to develop an instrument which will permit the Training Agency Council and Training Agency staff to evaluate guidance provision. Specifically, to permit evaluation in terms of the learning outcomes likely to be induced in the clients of guidance. A pilot instrument will be developed by consultation with expert providers and on the basis of a review of existing (notably U.S.) evaluation studies. Field trials will be conducted in selected provider organizations. Examples of good guidance practice will be recorded and illustrative case studies of good practice will be produced for incorporation to the evaluation instrument.
Source of Grant: Training Agency: £34,800
Date of Research: 1990-1990
KEYWORDS: educational guidance; evaluation; guidance; vocational guidance

8/1024

Sheraton House, Castle Park, Cambridge CB3 0AX
0223 460277
Watts, A.G. Mr; Hawthorn, R. Ms
Guidance aspects of the enterprise in higher education programme
Abstract: The aim of the project is to examine the ways in which institutions involved in the Training Enterprise Education Division's EHE (Enterprise in Higher Education) programme can help students to establish linkages between the competencies and skills they are developing and their possible futures. The project will prepare case studies of examples of existing practice in five institutions, feed back the case studies to the institutions concerned in ways which will be likely to foster further development work, and disseminate examples of good or interesting practice to other institutions involved in the EHE initiative. The case studies will be made available in published form as part of a document including recommendations for policy and guidelines for practice.
Source of Grant: £74,716
Date of Research: 1990 – continuing
KEYWORDS: career counselling; enterprise education; higher education; occupational choice; vocational guidance

8/1025

Sheraton House, Castle Park, Cambridge CB3 0AX
0223 460277
Watts, A.G. Mr; Kidd, J.M. Dr; Knasel, E.G. Dr
Formative evaluation of the PROSPECT (HE) computer aided careers guidance system
Abstract: During the academic year 1988/89 the PROSPECT (HE) computer-aided careers guidance system was pilot tested in four universities and two polytechnics. The aim of the project was to evaluate these field trials and to identify ways in which the system might be improved. A variety of methods were used, including logged data, questionnaires, observations, interviews and group discussions.
Published Material: WATTS, A.G., KIDD, J.M. & KNASEL, E. (1989). PROSPECT (HE) pilot evaluation: first report. Cambridge: NICEC.; WATTS, A.G., KIDD, J.M. & KNASEL, E. (1989). PROSPECT (HE) pilot evaluation: second report. Cambridge: NICEC.
Source of Grant: Department of Education and Science: £30,750 plus direct costs
Date of Research: 1988-1989
KEYWORDS: careers guidance; computer; higher education; occupational choice

National Institute of Adult and Continuing Education

8/1026

19b DeMontfort Street, Leicester LE1 7GE
0533 551451
McGivney, V.K. Dr; *Supervisor:* Buffton, J. Ms
Evaluation of the Women's Education Project (Northern Ireland)
Abstract: The aims of the evaluation were to document and assess

the achievements of the project after more than five years of operation; to place the work in the changing social, economic and educational context in Northern Ireland and to evaluate its potential as a model of good practice that could inform policy and the work of other agencies. The evaluation involved a review of project records, annual reports, other documentation and published materials, background reading; documentation relating to education, social and economic issues and the position of women in Northern Ireland; documentation relating to educational evaluation, an intensive interview programme, and attendance at relevant events. The aim of the interview programme was to solicit views and perceptions on the project and the context in which it operates from as wide a group as possible. The evaluation has found that the project provides a very effective first point of contact for women in the community and assists their access to other educational opportunities. In its support of women's groups it also contributes significantly to community development and better community relations. However, a basic problem is that there is no real infrastructure for community education and no statutory education funding for voluntary projects of this kind. Thus much of the project's energies are spent on fund-raising to ensure survival, to the detriment of its purpose.
Source of Grant: Northern Ireland Voluntrary Trust: Northern Ireland Policy, Planning and Research Unit: Joseph Rowntree Charitable Trust: £15,000 Jointly
Date of Research: 1989-1990
KEYWORDS: evaluation; women's education

8/1027

    Research, Library and Information Services Division,
    19b DeMontfort Street, Leicester LE1 7GE
    0533 551451
    Charnley, A.H. Dr; McGivney, V.K. Dr; Withnall, A. Mrs;
    Supervisor: Charnley, A.H. Dr
Identification of resource materials in adult literacy and basic skills
Abstract: The aim of the research is to identify resource materials in adult basic education. This will include utilization of National Institute of Adult Continuing Education networks amongst providers of adult education and training. Resource materials are identified, registered in computer data banks and where original resources are available, transferred to Nottingham University Library for safekeeping.
Source of Grant: No funding
Date of Research: 1982 – continuing
KEYWORDS: adult education; adult literacy; basic education; communication skills; data bank; English (second language); numeracy; resource materials

8/1028

    19b DeMontfort Street, Leicester LE1 7GE
    0533 551451
    McGivney, V.K. Dr; McCafferty, J. Ms
Pilot study of feasibility of linking women's groups in the UK with women's groups in Africa
Abstract: The aim of the project was to initiate a process whereby individual women's groups with an educational focus in the Third World could develop their own special links (perhaps leading to sponsorship) with established women's groups and networks with an education/training dimension in the UK. The aims are to make initial contact with informal women's groups with an educational focus in Kenya. To explore the specific priorities and remit of these groups and the problems they face. Investigate methods of contact and recruitment in a developing country, and informal delivery systems and methodologies appropriate for women in the Third World. Finally to prepare the ground for a link-up which would bring Kenyan women's groups into contact with women's groups/organizations/networks with a similar educational focus in the UK. Methodology involved interviews with Kenyan and UK women's groups, and the organization of links and putting individual groups in contact. The project identified the many difficulties of developing a linking scheme at local level. In Kenya, there is the problem of postal delay, reliance on a 'mediator' who spoke English, and his time, interest and goodwill. It appeared that Kenyans were less interested in reciprocal communication than in receiving financial assistance for their projects. In the UK, only a small percentage of enquirers were actually willing to commit themselves to writing an initial letter. Personal enquiries did not lead to a link, and some of the British groups who did write were disconcerted by the length of time before receiving a response and on occasion by straight forward requests for money.

Published Material: McCAFFERTY, J. & McGIVNEY, V.K. (1988). Pilot project to link women's groups in the Third World to women's groups in Britain: a report of a visit to Kenya, March-April 1987. British Council/NIACE.
Source of Grant: British Council: £2,000
Date of Research: 1987-1990
KEYWORDS: communication; developing country; interaction; women's education; women's organization

8/1029

    19B DeMontfort Street, Leicester LE1 7GE
    0533 551451
    Charnley, A.H. Dr; Withnall, A. Mrs
Characteristics of students in adult basic education schemes
Abstract: The Adult Literacy and Basic Skills Unit intends to commission once every three years an in-depth survey of a representative cross-section of local education authorities provision of adult basic education, in order to produce a substantive report to the Secretaries of State. At present, there is little statistical information available about the make-up of the student body, so that the aim of this project is to investigate the characteristics of students in basic education schemes across a sample of local education authorities. A questionnaire will be sent to adult basic education organizers in 29 local education authorities requesting information about the students enrolled since September 1989, including gender, age, employment status, disabilities, length of time in scheme, reasons for drop-out. Information will be collated and a report provided to the Adult Literacy and Basic Skills Unit.
Source of Grant: Adult Literacy and Basic Skills Unit: £20,000
Date of Research: 1990-1990
KEYWORDS: adult basic education; adult education; adult students; literacy

8/1030

    Library and Information Services Division, 19b DeMontfort
    Street, Leicester LE1 7GE
    0533 551451
    Charnley, A.H. Dr
Indicators of fee levels charged to part-time adult students by local education authorities; (NIACE Fee Survey (1990-91)
Abstract: Background developments in the finance of the adult education service are investigated for those adults who are involved in part-time study. Statistics are obtained from all the local education authorities. Fees charged to part-time students, concessionary fees, fee changes, financial arrangements, methods and timing of payment, number and length of class meetings, enrolments, and accommodation are researched.
Published Material: CHARNLEY, A.H. & McGIVNEY, V.K. Indicators of fee levels charged to part-time adult students by local education authorities. (NIACE Fee Survey 1985-86). NIACE.; CHARNLEY, A.H. & McGIVNEY, V.K. Indicators of fee levels charged to part-time adult students by local education authorities. (NIACE Fee Survey 1986-87). NIACE.; CHARNLEY, A.H. & McGIVNEY, V.K. Indicators of fee levels charged to part-time adult students by local education authorities. (NIACE Fee Survey 1987-88). NIACE.; CHARNLEY, A.H. Indicators of fee levels charged to part-time adult students by local education authorities. (NIACE Fee Survey 1988-89). NIACE.; CHARNLEY, A.H. Indicators of fee levels charged to part-time adult students by local education authorities. (NIACE Fee Survey 1989-90). NIACE.
Source of Grant: No funding
Date of Research: 1990 – continuing
KEYWORDS: adult education; educational finance; fees; part-time course

8/1031

    19b DeMontfort Street, Leicester LE1 7GE
    0533 551451
    Sargant, N. Prof.
Londoners learning: an interim report of the ILEA/NIACE survey of adult learners in inner London
Abstract: As ILEA (Inner London Education Authority) hands over to the inner London Boroughs in April 1990 concern has been expressed about the ability of the new inner London education authorities to maintain the range of learning opportunities and to offer equal opportunities to working class adults, people with disabilities, black people and others from ethnic and linguistic minorities. One major purpose for ILEA in commissioning research on adult learning was to provide a map of that participation in order to help the new authorities in their work. A second reason was to

see if a relationship could be established between the level of public investment in post-school education and training opportunities, and the amount of independent study which adults undertake. This interim report summarises the first findings of a research survey of adult learning in Britain undertaken by NIACE.
Published Material: SARGANT, N. & TUCKETT, A. (1990). Londoners learning: an interim report. Leicester: NIACE.
Source of Grant: Inner London Education Authority: £27,000
Date of Research: 1989-1990
KEYWORDS: access to education; adult education; equal opportunity; ethnic minority; physically handicapped

8/1032
19b DeMontfort Street, Leicester LE1 7GE
0533 551451
Withnall, A. Mrs; Pole, E. Ms; *Supervisor:* Charnley, A.H. Dr
Data base of research resources in adult education
Abstract: This project aims to identify, locate and record details of published and unpublished research and resource materials, post 1945, concentrating on English materials, with some European, North American and Commonwealth materials, on certain major topics of concern for the education of adults. It is intended to undertake a similar exercise relating to materials produced since 1980 on adult basic education, including literacy, numeracy and materials for people with disabilities.
Published Material: Research monographs, Volume 1 to 12 are available from NIACE.
Source of Grant: Department of Education and Science Adult Literacy and Basic Skills Unit Replan National Institute of Adult and Continuing Education
Date of Research: 1982 – continuing
KEYWORDS: adult education; basic education; comparative education; data bank; physically handicapped; resource materials; unemployed; education

8/1033
19b DeMontfort Street, Leicester LE1 7GE
0533 551451
Sutcliffe, J. Ms
Continuing education for adults with learning difficulties
Abstract: This project aims: (1) to establish an interactive network of providers of education for adults with learning difficulties in England and Wales; (2) to collect examples of good educational practice with adults who have learning difficulties in the widest variety of settings and all levels of ability; (3) to research good practice in the education of the general community about the needs and potential of people with learning difficulties; (4) to disseminate the lessons of good practice in educational provision for adults with learning difficulties and related community education by the publication of a handbook and its launch at a national conference; (5) to mount a series of regional dissemination events; (6) to publish three booklets on selected topics to follow up the project handbook.
Source of Grant: Joseph Rowntree Foundation
Date of Research: 1988 – continuing
KEYWORDS: adult education; continuing education; educational provision; learning difficulty

8/1034
19b De Montfort Street, Leicester LE1 7GE
0533 551451
McGivney, V.K. Dr; *Supervisor:* Charnley, A.H. Dr
Access, non-participation and programme development in adult continuing education
Abstract: This research aims to explore the extent to which providers currently make contact and negotiate with non-participant groups about the creation of appropriate programmes for them. Information was sought from a representative sample of providers in both sectors and in different geographical areas. The data will enable the researchers to review current practice relating to programme development; to identify the contact and recruitment procedures perceived to be most effective by providers and student groups, and to explore the basic economic implications of programme development, recruitment procedures and different methods of delivery. The strategy of research is based on the principles of triangulation conducted on the tactics of synchronic induction.
Published Material: McGIVNEY, V.K. (1990). 'Non-participant adult groups: recruitment and programme development', Adults Learning, Vol 1, No 6, pp.156-158, February.; McGIVNEY, V.K.

(1990). 'Education's for other people; access to education for non-participant adults'. Leicester: National Institute for Adult Continuing Education.
Source of Grant: Economic and Social Research Council: £23,000
Date of Research: 1986-1989
KEYWORDS: adult education; participation; recruitment

8/1035
Department for the Development of Adult Continuing Education
Christopher House, 94b London Road, Leicester LE2 0QS
0533 542645
Browning, D. Mr; Mager, C. Ms; *Supervisor:* Alloway, J. Dr
Open College networks project
Abstract: The overall aim of the project is to investigate the potential and encourage the development of accreditation based Open College Networks in England and Wales. Accreditation is used as a means of building links between groups of institutions (of further, higher, adult and community education and training), employers and voluntary sector groups in order to make education and training more accessible for adults. UDACE is working with the Manchester Open College Federation, which is one of the best established networks of this kind. An account of the current state of Open College Networks is being produced. This process has enabled links to be established with interested groups and raised awareness and potential interest in accreditation based networks. The project will now seek to provide consultancy, collaborative training and development to committed and interested groups who are offering potential bases for development on an accreditation pattern. Recommendations will be produced for further development.
Source of Grant: Department of Education and Science Research Fund: £100,000
Date of Research: 1989-1990
KEYWORDS: adult education; community education; credits; further education; higher education; open learning

Newcastle upon Tyne University

8/1036
Centre for Physical Education and Sport, Kings Walk, Newcastle upon Tyne NE1 7RU
091 232 8511
Jones, B.A. Mr
An analysis of the variables affecting the change in attitudes of school children towards curriculum physical education
Abstract: A reliable and valid attitude inventory has been developed to measure children's attitude towards curriculum physical education (ATCPE). A survey of attitudes has been undertaken across four areas of England and a local longitudinal survey implements this. Three teaching interventions have been undertaken to measure the consequent effect on childrens attitude to physical education. These interventions concerned, the content of the teaching syllabus, the teaching strategy and style adopted by the leader and the effect of school based INSET (Inservice Education and Training of Teachers).
Published Material: JONES, B.A. (1988). 'A scale to measure the attitudes of school pupils towards their lessons in physical education', Educational Studies, Vol 14, No 1, pp.51-63.; JONES, B.A. (1989). 'Attitudes of school pupils to curriculum physical education', British Journal of Physical Education, Research Supplement No 3. pp.10-12.; JONES, B.A. (1990). 'Assessing the effects of a course in health related fitness in changing the stated attitudes of pupils towards curriculum physical education', British Journal of Physical Education: Research Supplement No 5.
Source of Grant: No funding
Date of Research: 1985 – continuing
KEYWORDS: attitude; physical education; pupil

8/1037
Department of Education
St Thomas Street, Newcastle upon Tyne NE1 7RU
091 232 8511
Fitz-Gibbon, C.T. Dr
The effects of peer tutoring
Abstract: Peer tutoring usually involves older pupils tutoring youn-

ger pupils in a one-to-one tutoring situation and is thus often referred to as cross-age tutoring. The kind of peer tutoring investigated here is primarily 'learning-by-tutoring' in which the tutoring projects typically, of three or four weeks' duration, are implemented primarily to improve the learning and motivation of the tutors. In more than a dozen experiments to date, tutoring has been applied to reading projects (including projects in H.M. Detention Centres), mathematics, French, humanities and science. It has been used to improve behaviour of non-exam Easter leavers and to improve the learning of O-level Physics pupils. Many potential applications (e.g. encouraging girls to tackle science and mathematics; enhancing personal and social development and parenting skills; improving inter-ethnic relationships, etc.) are yet to be examined. The results of the experiments conducted so far have shown tutoring to be as effective as, or more effective than, normal classroom instruction. These have been short experiments with careful preparation of the tutors and close supervision and while it is not suggested that these results should be generalized too widely, it is worth noting that recent meta-analyses in the U.S. found tutoring to be twice as cost-effective as computer assisted learning. (Levin Glass and Meister, 1984).
Published Material: FITZ-GIBBON, C.T. & REAY, D.G. (1982). 'Peer tutoring: brightening up FL teaching in an urban comprehensive school', British Journal of Language Teaching, Vol XX, No 1, pp.39-46.; FITZ-GIBBON, C.T. (1988). 'Peer tutoring as a teaching study', Educational Management, Vol 14, No 3.
Source of Grant: No funding (formerly funded by Social Science Research Council)
Date of Research: 1975 – continuing
KEYWORDS: intercultural education; motivation for studies; peer group teaching; transfer of learning

8/1038

Department of Education
St Thomas Street, Newcastle upon Tyne NE1 7RU
091 232 8511 ext 3561
Lister, C.M. Dr

The development of understanding of quantity in handicapped children

Abstract: In order to examine fundamental questions of sequence and structure in cognitive development, a series of investigations is being carried out with children who have visual, hearing, and language impairments, as well as with mentally retarded and nonretarded children. The research attempts to resolve empirically the conflicting conclusions about the development of conservation concepts in deaf, partially hearing and visually impaired children which arise in the literature. It extends the similar-sequence and similar-structure hypotheses of the developmental theorists in the field of mental retardation to work with children who have other handicapping conditions. It also introduces the necessary controls for organic impairment in trying to clarify issues central in the retardation literature on the developmental difference controversy; both Down's Syndrome and mentally retarded children with no known organic etiology are being studied. In designing the series of investigations, particular attention has been paid to the need for comparability as this has been a problem in interpreting much of the previous research giving rise to differing conclusions. Standard Piagetian tasks appropriately adapted for presentation to the handicapped children and consistent criteria for classifying their responses are being used throughout the studies. Detailed recordings of individual children's patterns and levels of understanding of conservation are made and scalogram and other specific analyses carried out. Results have been reported which have clear educational implications. Findings on sequence in development and on levels of understanding of conservation concepts can contribute to appropriately ordering material in the curriculum and to extending handicapped children's understanding.
Published Material: LISTER, C.M. & ATHA, G. (1986). 'The use of a Piagetian approach in work with the visually handicapped child', Early Child Development and Care, Vol 23, No 1, pp.63-74.; LISTER, C.M., CHARLTON, J., MADDEN, L. & LEACH, C. (1987). 'The development of understanding of conservation in hearing impaired children', Early Child Development and Care, Vol 27, No 4, pp.493-505.; LISTER, C. & LEACH, C. (1987). 'Implications of the developmental difference controversy for work with children who have special educational needs', British Psychological Society Education Section Review, Vol 11, No 2, pp.22-30.; LISTER, C.M., LEACH, C. & McCOOMBE, R. (1988). 'Sequence in development conservation concepts in children with language disabilities', Early Child Development and Care, Vol 34, pp.1-13.;

LISTER, C.M., LEACH, C. & WESENCRAFT, K. (1988). 'Sequence in hearing impaired children's development of concepts', British Journal of Educational Psychology, Vol 58, pp.127-133. A full list of publications is available from the researcher.
Source of Grant: No funding
Date of Research: 1983-1989
KEYWORDS: cognitive development; concept formation; physically handicapped; special education; visually handicapped

8/1039

Department of Education
St Thomas Street, Newcastle upon Tyne NE1 7RU
091 232 8511 ext 6585
Stanley, D. Mr; *Supervisor:* Davies-Jones, H. Mr

An identification, exploration and evaluation of the nature of residential care provision within a broad context of social work, education and related services

Abstract: This study proposes to trace the way in which residential care services have developed within a broad context of social work, education, and related services; to consider the critical factors which have influenced that development; and to examine the level of service which has evolved. The focus will be on areas of statutory provision, although the provision of the voluntary and private sectors will, of course, feature where relevant. There are two major components of the study: Part I will develop a composite picture of the range of residential services in a descriptive, reflective sense. This 'anatomy' of residential care will present a medium through which selected factors influencing development may be explored, and will form a substantive part of the whole study. It will also serve as an indicator of issues to be pursued in Part II. Part II will take the form of a case study of the development of representative provision within a statutory social work agency. It is anticipated that the case study will generally complement and amplify findings of Part I.
Source of Grant: Sunderland Polytechnic: fees and travel expenses
Date of Research: 1982-1989
KEYWORDS: educational provision; residential care; social work

8/1040

Department of Education
St Thomas Street, Newcastle upon Tyne NE1 7RU
091 232 8511
Hazelwood, R.D. Mr; Tymms, P. Mr; *Supervisor:* McCabe, J.J.C. Mr; Fitz-Gibbon, C.T. Dr; Atkins, M.J. Dr; Beattie, J.F.; Straker, N. Dr; Haywood, R.G. Dr

Local evaluation of Technical and Vocational Education Initiative (TVEI) pilot projects, North Eastern area

Abstract: Six colleagues work with 2 research associates to evaluate the TVEI (Technical and Vocational Education Initiative) pilot projects in 9 local authorities. Methods used include questionnaires, individual interviews, group discussions (both with students and teachers) and analysis of attitude and examination measures. At first, the evaluation was largely general, but later focused on more specific topics and areas of special concern to local authorities, especially with extension proposals in mind. A data bank covering schools in 5 authorities was established. Regular reports are provided for local authorities.
Published Material: McCABE, C. (Ed). (1986). 'TVEI, the organization of the early years of the initiative', Multlingual Matters.; BEATTIE, J.F. (1986). 'Organization and Management – some theoretical considerations'. In: McCABE, C. (Ed). TVEI, the organization of the early years.; McCABE, C. (1986). 'The negotiation and familiarization stage of TVEI local evaluation', TVEI Working Paper No 1. University of East Anglia, pp.15-25.; McCABE, C. (1986). 'How to choose your evaluator'. In: HOPKINS, D. (Ed). Evaluating TVEI, Cambridge Institute Monograph.; FITZ-GIBBON, C.F. (1986). 'The roles of the TVEI 'local ' evaluator'. In: HOPKINS, D. (Ed). Evaluating TVEI, Cambridge Institute Monography, pp.18-30.; McCABE. C. (1987). 'The external evaluator, inspector of management consultant', Evaluation and Research in Education, Vol 1, No 1, pp.1-8.; McCABE, C. (1987). 'Evaluation and TVEI, an introduction', MSC Evaluation Pack No 2.
Source of Grant: Manpower Services Commission (MSC) through 9 Local Education Authorities: £210,000 over 5 years
Date of Research: 1984 – continuing
KEYWORDS: evaluation; local education authority (LEA); secondary education; Technical and Vocational Education Initiative (TVEI)

8/1041

Department of Education
St Thomas Street,
Newcastle upon Tyne NE1 7RU
091 232 8511
Bowman, M.P. Mr; *Supervisor:* Bond, S. Dr; McCabe,
J.J.C. Mr

The examination of the role of the staff nurse/charge nurse
Abstract: The principal aim of the study is to analyze the role
of staff nurse and ward sister/charge nurse to provide an understanding of the function of nurses at this level in order to develop
relevant curricula criteria for their education and training. The
problem presented is that the role of the nurse at ward level is
complex and unclear. The main aims of the study are: (1) To discover the basis for diverse perspectives of the role of the nurse,
including the perception of this role by: (a) the patients; (b) statutory and professional bodies; (c) employers; (d) the nurses themselves. (2) To assess the level of responsibility, authority and
accountability currently included in the role of staff nurse and
ward sister/charge nurse. (3) To recommend the criteria for the
appropriate curricula for their education and training. Hypotheses
suggest; (1) that the role of the ward nurses, together with their
education and training, is not in accord with the requirements
of their job; (2) some inter-professional and intra-professional
groups exhibit different perspectives of the role of the nurses, and
the development of curricula does not exhibit appropriate consideration of all these needs. The principal methods used are questionnaires, structured interviews and observation. The study will
investigate the role of the nurse on the ward in two districts in
the Northern Regional Health Authority. Senior nurse managers
involved in the research will be interviewed, plus a 20 per cent
sample of patients and a 20 per cent sample of doctors. It is hoped
that 33 1/3 per cent of senior nurse leaders, staff nurses, enrolled
nurses and ward sister/charge nurses in each authority would be
included.
Source of Grant: No funding
Date of Research: 1984-1989
KEYWORDS: curriculum development; nurse; vocational training

8/1042

Department of Education
St Thomas Street,
Newcastle upon Tyne NE1 7RU
091 232 8511
Hogg, G.W. Mr

**The history of teacher education with special reference to North
East England**
Abstract: An investigation into the history of teacher education
in North East England with special reference to the development
of day training colleges in universities from 1890.
Source of Grant: No funding
Date of Research: 1986-1990
KEYWORDS: history of education; teacher education

8/1043

Department of Education
St Thomas Street,
Newcastle upon Tyne NE1 7RU
091 232 8511
Skelton, C. Ms

The careers of male teachers of young children
Abstract: The focus of this research emerged from an ethnographic
study of a primary PGCE (Post-Graduate Certificate in Education) course, carried out in 1985. One of the issues which arose
from this ethnograpy was that, not only do more females than
males opt for primary teaching as a career, but those males who
do enter the profession exhibit a marked preference for teaching
the older primary age-range. The aim of this study is to gain some
insight into the careers of male teachers of young children (aged
4-7 years) post the Sex Discrimination Act (1975). The techniques
adopted for this research are life history methods; specifically,
semi-structured interviews. The teachers involved in this research
are all employed in the North East of England, an area of the
country generally associated with traditional male attitudes and
values.
Source of Grant: No funding
Date of Research: 1988-1989
KEYWORDS: career; primary education; sex difference; teacher

Newcastle upon Tyne University

8/1044

Department of Education
St Thomas Street, Newcastle upon Tyne NE1 7RU
091 232 8511
Carrington, L.B. Mr; Fitz-Gibbon, C.T. Dr

Supporting urban schools
Abstract: This is an action research initiative conducted in two urban
secondary schools and their feeder primary schools to implement
and monitor a series of peer tutoring experiments. The aim of the
research is to assess the effects of peer tutoring on a range of cognitive, social and effective outcomes. Attention will be given to
achievement in science and mathematics, satisfaction with school,
ethnic relations, teachers and pupils perceptions and, the range of
applications of 'learning by tutoring' in a school setting. The methodology will combine both ethnographic and experimental techniques.
Source of Grant: Research Committee, University of Newcastle
upon Tyne: £44,000
Date of Research: 1989 – continuing
*KEYWORDS: achievement; multicultural education; peer group
teaching; tutoring; urban school*

8/1045

Department of Education
St Thomas Street, Newcastle upon Tyne NE1 7RU
091 232 8511
Newcastle upon Tyne Polytechnic
Coach Lane Campus,
Benton, Newcastle upon Tyne NE7 7XA
091 232 6002 ext 3551
Whitfield, P. Mr; *Supervisor:* Straker, N. Mr

**A review of practical activities in mathematical education with par-
ticular reference to games in the primary classroom**
Abstract: Initially, consideratin was given to reports throughout
this century and along with other important points the need for
practical work was highlighted. This suggests that there were
problems for schools in implementing a practical approach.
Teachers reactions to practical work were collated through the use
of a questionnaire. A good cross-reference of infant, junior,
primary and middle school teachers were used. Also a contrast was
made by teachers who had been on inservice courses and those who
had not. The need to provide children with practical, relevant,
enjoyable experiences was highlighted. This, plus a psychological
and philosophical review provides the backbone of the study.
Mathematical games became such an important aspect, that a full
consideration of their use was added to the research. Inservice work
and the way ahead rounded off the project.
Source of Grant: No funding
Date of Research: 1985-1989
*KEYWORDS: game; mathematics; practical work; primary edu-
cation*

8/1046

Department of Education
St Thomas Street, Newcastle upon Tyne NE1 7RU
091 232 8511
Haywood, R.G. Dr; Baxter, B. Mr

**The Low Attaining Pupils Programme (LAPP) in Newcastle Local
Education Authority (LEA)**
Abstract: The aim of this project is: (1) planning, design, implementation and institutionalization of a Low Attainers' Programme of
curriculum development as part of the 'whole school approach'
of 1 school in Newcastle LEA (Local Education Authority); and
(2) evaluation of processes and products (raised attainment) of the
programme and its links with other LEA schools through dissemination.
Source of Grant: Department of Education and Science
(DES)/Local Education Authority (LEA): £29,188 (April
1987-September 1989 plus £15,400 for extension to September 1990
Date of Research: 1987-1990
KEYWORDS: curriculum development; low attainer

8/1047

Department of Education
St Thomas Street, Newcastle upon Tyne NE1 7RU

091 232 8511 ext 2598
Routledge, R. Mr
Evaluation of the ESG (Education Support Grant) rural schools project
Abstract: The aim of the project is: (1) evaluation of the ESG (Education Support Grant) Rural Schools Project in Northumberland, involving 45 schools assigned to 9 clusters, and collecting data by interview and questionnaire; and (2) to enhance the quality and extend the range of the curriculum in these schools.
Source of Grant: Department of Education and Science (DES): £100,000 per year
Date of Research: 1986-1990
KEYWORDS: curriculum development; evaluation; rural school

8/1048
Department of Education
St Thomas Street, Newcastle upon Tyne NE1 7RU
091 232 8511 ext 6585
Bristol Polytechnic
Department of Education
Redland Hill, Bristol BS6 6UZ
0272 741251
Gerwitz, S.J. Miss; *Supervisor:* Edwards, A.D. Prof.; Whitty, G.J. Prof.
A new choice of school? The City Technology Colleges
Abstract: This research builds on the investigators' previous study of the Assisted Places Scheme. At the national level, evidence will be collected about the origins of the initiative, the declared purposes of the colleges' sponsors and the arguments generated by the initiative. Detailed studies of particular colleges will include investigation of how pupils and staff are recruited, and how curriculum and resources in the colleges are managed. The initiative will be analyzed in the context of other approaches to the educational problems of the inner cities.
Source of Grant: Economic and Social Research Council (ESRC): £36,915
Date of Research: 1988 – continuing
KEYWORDS: City Technology College; educational opportunities; inner city; private education

8/1049
Department of Education
St Thomas Street, Newcastle upon Tyne NE1 7RU
091 232 8511
National University of Lesotho
International Primary School,
PO Roma 180, Lesotho, S.E. Africa
Fitter, R. Miss Lesotho); *Supervisor:* Williamson, J.
An investigation into the skills associated with early reading of 5 year old children of different cultures at point of entry in English medium primary schools in Lesotho
Abstract: Various aspects of linguistic and cultural diversity will be examined with a view to determining whether they are relevant to success in early reading in an English language medium school.
Source of Grant: No funding
Date of Research: 1986 – continuing
KEYWORDS: bilingualism; Lesotho; primary education; reading

Newcastle Upon Tyne University

8/1050
Department of Education
St Thomas Street, Newcastle Upon Tyne NE1 7RU
091 232 8511 ext 6585
Davison, A. Mr; *Supervisor:* Davies Jones, H. Mr
Operational reality and self-determination as facets of the treatment of disturbed children in residential care
Abstract: The research centres on children admitted to the care of local authorities. Its focus is on the ways in which children make sense of their own worlds rather than on the professional interpretations placed on their behaviour. The relationship of the internal representational systems to the conceptual networks are analyzed within psycho-linguistic parameters together with the ways in which attitudinal and belief structures are developed. The methods of investigation (interview, concept/referent elicitation questionnaires and utterance sampling) are applied to a number of individual children in an attempt to understand the way in which former life experiences shape expectations in the life situations in which they find themselves. The project is now well advanced.
Source of Grant: No funding
Date of Research: 1988-1990
KEYWORDS: child care; psychotherapy; residential care

8/1051
Department of Education
St Thomas Street,
Newcastle Upon Tyne NE1 7RU
091 232 8511
Greenwood, L.A. Mrs; *Supervisor:* Davies Jones, H. Mr
Policy making and associated decision making in local authority community education provision
Abstract: The study examines the relationship between local authority education department policy and its practical outcome. Particular concerns are the mechanisms for formulating decisions and the processes by which decisions are disseminated. The substantive areas considered are community education with the unemployed and assessment in schools. Two case studies of neighbouring local authorities are being developed using a range of methods including documentary analysis, interviewing, questionnaire and direct observation. Formal and informal systems receive attention. The data collecting phase is now complete.
Source of Grant: No funding
Date of Research: 1986 – continuing
KEYWORDS: community education; decision making; educational policy; local education authority; unemployed

8/1052
Department of Speech
St Thomas Street,
Newcastle Upon Tyne NE1 7RU
091 232 8511
Newcastle upon Tyne Polytechnic
Department of Education
Coach Lane, Newcastle upon Tyne NE7 7XA
091 232 6002
Robson, C.B.; *Supervisor:* Milroy, L. Dr
The development of children's writing: a longitudinal study
Abstract: This is a case study of the writing development of three children during their last three years of junior school. The purpose of the study is to gain insight into the problems which some children encounter in achieving competence in using language in the written mode. The three subjects chosen therefore are children within the mainstream classroom experiencing more than average difficulty in their writing development. The study follows the children's development from the beginning of their second year of junior school until their departure from it. This makes it possible to investigate their progress during the years in which they could normally be expected to gain complete independence in writing and during which substantial developments in many facets of their work could be expected to occur. The three children are followed systematically for two years, their work being sampled on a regular and frequent basis and at least once a month. They are also observed within the context of the classroom to obtain a fuller picture of their writing behaviour. In addition to this specific focus on writing the study attempts to discover what other factors might have influenced the children's writing development such as their performance in spoken language, sociolinguistic features of their background, attitudes to and experience of literacy and perceptions of the writing task. These observations should enable a broad profile to be composed which will relate linguistic features of the writing such as those of syntax, semantics cohesion and discourse to a multifaceted perspective of the child's overall communicative competence. In particular it will provide valuable insights into the relationship between spoken and written language. As well as analytical measures like the T-unit and Subordinate Clause Index the study would employ such techniques as questionnaire, interview and observation. It should usefully illuminate the problems some children face in developing an adequate mastery of written language by focusing on writing within the broader context of literacy and communicative competence.
Source of Grant: Polytechnic funded: fees; £400 per annum
Date of Research: 1985-1990
KEYWORDS: language development; low attainer; primary education; spoken language; writing

New College Durham

8/1053

Neville's Cross Centre,
Darlington Road, Neville's Cross, Durham DH1 4SY
091 384 7325
Trout's Lane Special School (Headteacher)
Earl's House, Durham
0385 64911
Lishman, J.W. Miss

An investigation into the effects of training programmes upon movement leading to dance with special school children

Abstract: The study tests the capacity of ESN(S) (Educationally Subnormal (Severe)) children to respond to and learn from programmes based on the teachings of Rudolph Laban. The contribution of dance within the PE (physical education) curriculum for ESN(S) children is examined. A pilot study was carried out to establish procedures and then training programmes were designed. Each child was used as his own control on pre- and post-tasks. Tests were given to establish base lines in performance. Weekly training sessions took place over two years with 30 boys and girls aged 7-18. Tests for both exercise and body response were given. An individual analysis of each child's movement behaviour was made and the application of multiple base line operations. Executing these skills is a matter of using these rules in a certain order. This programme focuses on learning rather than product. Videotape aided the analysis of movement behaviour and individual development. Improvements of motor skills are identified as a result of mental practice, task familiarity and the maturation of the learner. Individual differences in response are not influenced significantly by age, verbal ability or sex variables. The study revealed that training programmes can lead to dance with ESN(S) children.

Published Material: Communication and Handicap. Report of EASE 80. Congress for Special Education 1980 Finland. Publisher: The Finnish Association for Special Education.; 'Movement leading to dance with ESN(S) children', pp.90-92, Durham University Research Bulletin, January, 1981. pp.1.

Source of Grant: Funding for videotape work World Health funding for write-up Mental Handicap funding for materials Ontario CLD Society and Norwegian SSS for ongoing expenses

Date of Research: 1984-1990

KEYWORDS: *dance; mentally handicapped; special education; special school*

8/1054

Department of Inservice Education, Communication and Computing, Neville's Cross Centre,
Darlington Road, Neville's Cross, Durham DH1 4SY
091 384 7325
Reece, I. Mr; Walker, S. Mr

Problem-solving in craft, design and technology in the primary school

Abstract: To investigate the relevance of problem solving in CDT (craft, design and technology) in the primary school. Several schools were used as a basis for investigation, ranging from reception class in infant school to final year junior. Small groupwork to design, make, test and evaluate the solution to a given problem using a limited range of typical primary school materials. Initial work is encouraging with pupils enjoying the activities. Teachers see the work as a useful part of project work and as an integrating aspect of the curriculum.

Published Material: WALKER, S. & REECE, I. (1987). 'Plain dailing', Junior Education, November, pp.28-29.

Source of Grant: New College

Date of Research: 1986 – continuing

KEYWORDS: *craft, design and technology; problem solving; primary education*

8/1055

Department of Special Needs
Faculty of Inservice Studies,
Neville's Cross Centre, Darlington Road, Neville's Cross, Durham DH1 4SY
091 384 7325
Beverton, S. Dr (United Kingdom Reading Association)

Family reading groups project

Abstract: The background of this research project lies in the perceived successes of several loosely affiliated initiatives concerning Family Reading Groups (FRGs). Although FRGs have often been running for several years, no monitoring or evaluations study has hitherto been conducted on a wide scale. This project attempts to rectify that situation. A Family Reading Group is a collective and collaborative gathering of parents, children, teachers and librarians whose main aim is to foster and encourage the love of books among children. This research project looks into how FRGs are best established and what factors are most indicative of their success. It considers the various roles of the group participants and how they interact. The end products of the research hopefully include a handbook for intending FRG leaders (be they parent, teacher or librarian) and a booklet for the local education authorities and governors explaining the benefits of FRGs.

Source of Grant: Department of Education and Science: £10,000

Date of Research: 1988-1990

KEYWORDS: *book; family; reading; parent participation*

Newman College

8/1056

Genners Lane, Bartley Green, Birmingham B32 3NT
021 476 1181
Exeter University
Department of Education
Heavitree Road, Exeter EX1 2LU
0392 264861
Davenport, A. Mr; *Supervisor:* Peacock, A. Dr; Desforges, C. Prof.

IT-INSET (Information Technology-Inservice Education and Training of Teachers) and the higher education tutor

Abstract: This research involves an ethnographic study of the cognitive, social, pedagogical and professional pathways taken by university and college tutors involved in IT-INSET (Information Technology – Inservice Education and Training of Teachers). There will be continuing research into the evaluative procedures used by higher education tutors during a degree-centred INSET programme.

Source of Grant: Newman College

Date of Research: 1989 – continuing

KEYWORDS: *computer assisted instruction; electronic data processing; further educaion of teachers; higher education; information technology; inservice teacher education*

8/1057

Genners Lane, Bartley Green, Birmingham B32 3NT
021 476 1181

8/1058

Genners Lane, Bartley Green, Birmingham B32 3NT
021 476 1181
Birmingham University
Department of Education
Edgbaston, Birmingham B15 2TT
021 414 3344
Moore, M. Mrs; *Supervisor:* Wade, C.B. Dr

Structure or choice: an investigation of current approaches to the teaching of reading with specific reference to children who have experienced difficulties in learning to read

Abstract: Although the use of story books in the teaching of reading has gained in popularity, structured reading schemes and traditional approaches are still current when teaching children with difficulties in reading. The whole/integrated language approach (utilizing speaking, listening, reading and writing) is also often absent for such children. The research design has been simplified into two groups: within each group there are 48 children, matched for age (7-9 years) social background and IQ (i.e. within normal range). All of the children have been designated by their schools as having difficulty with reading. One group is receiving reading tuition via the traditional approach (structured reading scheme/skills), the other is receiving tuition via a whole language approach (literature, writing etc. but within a structured framework). After one full academic year, progress will be measured by the following criteria. Reading age, comprehension (test and interview), attitudes to reading, intonation when reading, literature awareness, awareness of communicative value of reading.

Source of Grant: No funding

Date of Research: 1988 – continuing

KEYWORDS: *integrated curriculum; language teaching; reading; reading difficulty*

8/1059

Department of Educational Studies
Guildford GU2 5XH
0483 571281
Smith, F. Mr; *Supervisor:* Denicolo, P. Dr

A case study of an innovatory inservice degree course

Abstract: The purpose of this enquiry was to carry out a case study of the first year of an inservice degree course for serving teachers. The course is described as innovatory in that one of its main purposes is to encourage a new network of partnerships, in schools and within LEAs (local education authorities). These partnerships will emerge from the increased development of the participants' academic skills and professional competence. A further dimension of the notion of innovation is the latitude which it is intended students should enjoy in determining for themselves the direction of the course. There is a review of previous work in the area, in the course of which, and as a background to an account of the methodological approach which is adopted, an extensive range of literature is examined. The research adopted is described as naturalistic and ethnographic. Appropriate methods are used to obtain data to give an illuminative account of what appears to be happening. Techniques used include participant observation, questionnaires and interviews. Questions of validity and reliability are raised and steps are taken to reduce the possibility of researcher bias. The findings are discussed and various conclusions are drawn. It is apparent that the course aims are realistic, and that there are strong indications that they are, to a notable extent, being realized. Partnerships are being established, although there are at least two aspects of this process which are lacking. The question of student autonomy hangs very much in the balance.

Source of Grant: Newman College: £500
Date of Research: 1988-1989
KEYWORDS: *academic degree; further education of teachers; inservice teacher education*

Newman-Westhill Colleges

8/1060

Department of Science
Newman Campus, Bartley Green, Birmingham B32 3NT
021 476 1181
Negus, M. Dr

The presentation of science education for Christian and Muslim children in the primary school

Abstract: The project has for its objective the presentation of science for children in the primary school, based upon the National Curriculum Key Stages 1 and 2, in which Christian values and beliefs, and/or Muslim values and beliefs, are incorporated as an inseparable part of the presentation. Advice will be sought from experts in Christian and Muslim education. The project will be trialled in selected schools.

Source of Grant: College financed
Date of Research: 1991 – continuing
KEYWORDS: *muslims; religious cultural groups*

Northbrook College of Design and Technology

8/1061

Broadwater Road, Worthing BN14 8HJ
0903 31445
Surrey University
Department of Educational Studies
Guildford GU2 5XH
0483 571281
Ridge, P.C. Mr; *Supervisor:* Kilty, J. Dr

Co-operative experiential inquiry with young people in further education settings

Abstract: The issues of personal development, group work and experiential learning with young people in further education settings have up until now, received scant attention from educational researchers. Despite the fact that they are now regarded as key elements in CPVE (Certificate in Pre-Vocational Education); the TVEI (Technical and Vocational Education Initiative) and the BTEC (Business and Technical Education Certificate) courses, it remains the case that these areas have not been systematically mapped and tested out in classroom settings. This 5 year long project has attempted to do just this using a new paradigm research methodology called co-operative experiential inquiry. In essence, this teacher/reseacher has conducted the inquiry with young further education trainees on Youth Training Schemes and students on BTEC courses. Together they identify research areas of shared concern; those areas of particular personal significance which they are prepared to research in depth as a co-operative learning group in order to develop their personal skills, knowledge and attitudes. These inquiries are, for the most part, initiated, planned, experienced and evaluated as collaborative ventures so that, in practice, the roles of subject and researcher merge as do the roles of student and teacher. Inquiry topics have so far included confidence, stress, fitness, cultural awareness, discipline, gender, and alcohol. The data collected from these projects indicate the wide range of reactions to self directed learning.

Source of Grant: West Sussex County Council: £300 approx over three years Northbrook College: £400 approx over two years
Date of Research: 1985-1990
KEYWORDS: *experiential learning; further education; group work; personal research method*

8/1062

Broadwater Road, Worthing BN14 8HJ
0903 31445
Sussex University
Department of Continuing and Professional Education
Falmer, Brighton BN1 9RH
0273 606755
Angelo, M.L. Mrs; *Supervisor:* Abbs, P. Dr

Imaginal education: design and piloting of an open learning course for adult study

Abstract: This research deals with early retirement, increasing adult leisure, fascination with self and psychology and flexible attractive open learning opportunities. These suggest a receptive student base for course development in imagination. This is arguably the quintessential human ability, but culturally stereotyped as marginal, 'for children', 'artists', or 'crazies'. Psychologies of image – Jungian, archetypal or transpersonal, characteristically place a therapeutic rather than education framework around their understanding of both imagining as a personal process, and imagination as the 'as if' location of autonomous content i.e. 'the unconscious', 'the imaginal'. Hence, education is largely identified with the social engineering of children; and image work which is directed rather than spontaneous, particularly if systematically educative is often criticized as egtostic, manipulative and restrictive. This research argues for a positive re-valuing of the educational mode, enabling imaginal discipline of active imagination and guided fantasy to become valid aesthetic studies. It is suggested that a 'non-egoic' directing pattern can be found in the traditional tree of life symbol system of the renaissance polymath. Understood as the archetype of inter-relationships and using the 'art of money' techniques, intrinsic image connections open out for individual exploration. A one-year open learning course has been designed on this basis to provide an 'imaginal apprenticeship'. 24 practical sessions are on tape, guiding an imaginal journey. An accompanying 'travellers diary' is written/drawn weekly, regular personal tutorials discourage the over familiar cognitive reductions of image into symptom but explore the cultural amplifications of 'depth-aesthetics'. There will be three piloting years involving small groups meeting on a monthly basis. Qualitative, individual case studies are nearing completion.

Source of Grant: Self funded
Date of Research: 1984 – continuing
KEYWORDS: *adult education; aesthetic education; fantasy; imagination; open learning*

North Cheshire College

8/1063

Winwick Road, Warrington WA2 8QA
0925 814343

Keen, T.R. Dr
Appraisal of teacher effectiveness
Abstract: The aim of the project was to determine a means of evaluating teacher effectiveness. The study, initially as a PhD project but latterly post-doctoral, has utilized several hundred respondents. The study utilizes a personal constraint psychology methodology and is designed to provide individual teachers with a printed profile of their strengths and weaknesses as teachers. More recently the research has been extended into the field of management appraisal. The post-doctoral research has resulted in the evolution of a self administered computer package (running on MS-DOS) together with a self instructoral manual.
Published Material: A full list of publications is available from the researcher
Source of Grant: No funding
Date of Research: 1975 – continuing
KEYWORDS: *effectiveness; personality; self-evaluation; software; teacher appraisal*

8/1064
Cheshire Language Centre, Padgate Campus,
Fearnhead Lane, Fearnhead, Warrington WA2 ODB
0925 814343
Keith, G.R. Mr
Teaching english language
Abstract: Following the launching (pilot scheme, 1983, nationally, 1987) of JMB's 'A' level English Language examination, a number of teachers and examiners are now investigating the teaching of English language at 16 +. The four theoretical areas of the syllabus under investigation are: language acquisition; language varieties; language and society; language change. Of special concern are the ways in which students may come to an explicit understanding about the nature and functions of language, the need for which underlies study in all of these areas.
Published Material: KEITH, G.R. (1987). 'Variety, more than the spice of language'. In: JONES, M.R. and WEST, A., (Eds). Learning me your language. Edinburgh: Mary Glasgow.
Source of Grant: No funding
Date of Research: 1986-1989
KEYWORDS: *english language; examination; language teaching; secondary education*

Northern College

8/1065
Aberdeen Campus, Hilton Place, Aberdeen AB9 1FA
0224 482341
Simpson, M. Dr
Self evaluating school
Abstract: In the first phase of the project, a review of school self-evaluation procedures will be produced. In phase two, models of self-evaluation will be developed and piloted with support from college staff in selected secondary and primary schools in a number of educational authorities in Scotland.
Source of Grant: Scottish Education Department
Date of Research: 1989 – continuing
KEYWORDS: *evaluation; school; self-evaluation*

Northern College of Education

8/1066
Aberdeen Campus, Hilton Place, Aberdeen AB9 1FA
0224 482341 ext 231/241
Saunders, A. Dr; *Supervisor:* Simpson, M. Dr
A longitudinal study of pupils' learning experiences from late primary to early secondary school
Abstract: The general aim of the research is to monitor in a longitudinal study the developing understanding and skills of individual pupils as they progress through late primary and early secondary education and to relate this to the form and content of the instruction they receive in order to identify those factors which promote the coherence, continuity and progression of learning. This will pro-

vide a detailed picture of the way in which pupils build up knowledge structures and of the relationship between the qualities of early learning, and subsequent educational attainment; robust information will thus be provided for the developers of the proposed National Curriculum and Assessment. Decisions relating to the size and composition of the sample are yet to be finalized. The methods used in the research will include interviews with teachers to determine their expressed aims and to establish expected learning outcomes, observations of practice, and analysis of the content of resource material. Interviews and discussions with the individual pupils involved will also be conducted as well as written assessment material designed to determine what pupils know; concept maps and classification tasks will be used. Tests of reasoning, working memory and of attainment in problem solving tasks will also be administered. The emerging data on school attainment will then be compared with the teachers' assessments and National Assessements – as they become available. Two interim reports will be presented before the final report in 1992.
Source of Grant: Scottish Education Department: £140,000
Date of Research: 1988 – continuing
KEYWORDS: *assessment; knowledge level; learning process; teaching method*

8/1067
Aberdeen Campus, Hilton Place, Aberdeen AB9 1FA
0224 482341 ext 231
Simpson, M. Dr
Differentiated approaches to pupils' learning in primary school
Abstract: This study comprised three phases: a study of practices and outcomes of present attempts to provide an education which is appropriate to the individual needs of pupils; a series of action research investigations of methods of improving that provision and two brief studies of 'good practice'. Samples of task-related learning experiences of 36 pupils (in six schools) were monitored in detail over a four month period; the foci of interest were the teacher's intention in allocating a task, the nature of the task as experienced by the pupils, and the extent to which the demands of the task were appropriate to the attainments of the pupils in the specific topic domain of the task. The results revealed a significant level of mismatch between the teachers' intentions and the pupils' learning experiences. A 'compression' effect was also noted; the capabilities of 'better able' pupils were frequently underestimated, while those of 'less able' pupils were more likely to be overestimated.
Published Material: SIMPSON, M. (1988). 'Improving learning in schools – what do we know? a cognitive science perspective', Scottish Educational Review, Vol 20, No 1, pp.22-31, May.; SIMPSON, M. (1989). 'Differentiated approaches to teaching and learning: a discussion paper', Aberdeen: Northern College.; SIMPSON, M. (1989). 'Meeting the learning needs of primary pupils', SCRE Newsletter, Summer 1989.; SIMPSON, M. et al (1989). 'Differentiation in the primary school: investigations of learning and teaching', Report to the Scottish Education Department.; SIMPSON, M. (Ed). (1989). 'Differentiation in the primary school: classroom perspectives', Report to the Scottish Education Department.
Source of Grant: Scottish Education Department: £80,000
Date of Research: 1987-1989
KEYWORDS: *differentiation; primary education; teaching method*

Northern Ireland Council for Educational Research

8/1068
NICER Research Unit, Queen's University of Belfast,
52 Malone Road, Belfast BT9 5BS
0232 661111 ext 4366
D'Arcy, J.M. Mr; *Supervisor:* Wilson, J.A. Dr
Annual follow-up of newly-trained teachers
Abstract: In collaboration with the teacher training institutions in Northern Ireland, the Northern Ireland Council for Educational Research (NICER) carries out an annual survey of newly-qualified teachers. The investigation seeks to describe the newly-qualified teachers in terms of their subject specialism, sector emphasis and type of training; to identify employment status by the same characteristics; to take note of teachers' experiences in seeking teaching posts and to examine trends in teacher employment. The data are collected by means of questionnaire surveys during October and

a follow-up questionnaire the following January for those newly-qualified teachers who were in temporary employment, still seeking posts and those who had not replied to the first questionnaire.
Published Material: A list of publications is available from the NICER.
Source of Grant: Department of Education and Science: £10,380
Date of Research: 1978 – continuing
KEYWORDS: Ireland, Northern; labour market; teacher education; teacher employment

8/1069
NICER Research Unit, Queen's University of Belfast,
52 Malone Road, Belfast BT9 5BS
0232 661111 ext 4366
D'Arcy, J.M. Mr; *Supervisor:* Wilson, J.A. Dr
Register of research in education – Northern Ireland
Abstract: Five volumes of the Register of Educational Research in Education – Northern Ireland have been produced. They present information on published and unpublished research in education which was completed in the period from 1945 to 1982. The development of the Register recently has become chiefly a computer based resource. A database has been set up which holds information on projects since 1982. The database can be accessed by accredited researchers and educational institutions via the JANET computer network. Dissertations or theses for advanced and post-graduate qualifications are arranged by institution and academic department. Published books, articles and papers are included where these were written by authors resident or otherwise concerned with education in Northern Ireland. While the five published volumes contain abstracts for published work and post-graduate research, the computerized version uses the EUDISED keywording system to describe the research area.
Published Material: WILSON, J. (1979). (Ed) 'Register of Research in Education (Northern Ireland), Volume IV (1975-1978)'. Belfast: The Northern Ireland Council for Educational Research.; SUTHERLAND, A. (1984). (Ed). Register of Research in Education (Northern Ireland), Volume V (1978-1982)'. Belfast: The Northern Ireland Council for Educational Research.
Source of Grant: Department of Education and Science: £7,380
Date of Research: 1978 – continuing
KEYWORDS: database; educational research; information service; Ireland, Northern

8/1070
NICER Research Unit, Queen's University of Belfast,
52 Malone Road, Belfast BT9 5BS
0232 661111 ext 4366
Wells, I.F. Dr
The NICER (Northern Ireland Council for Educational Research) research and consultancy service
Abstract: The NICER Research and Consultancy Service was established as a means of involving the Northern Ireland Education and Library Board and other responsible sectors of the education service in collaborative research activities. The work to date has included the following projects: (1) A review of some of the published evidence on disruptive behaviour among school children; (2) an analysis of the views of principal teachers on the level of school financing in 1982 and the effects of change in recent years; (3) the views of teachers on the need for inservice education and the best means of provision; (4) an examination of the work and aspirations of primary school principals, the problems they encounter and the help they need: (5) a report on schools' use of locally-produced television programmes, their suggestions for improvements to programmes, and levels of equipment in schools for receiving programmes; (6) an account of the views of full-time youth workers in Northern Ireland on the principal aspects of their duties; (7) an enquiry among teachers involved in nursery education on levels of provision and the needs for nursery schooling; and (8) an appraisal of the work of an education-industry liaison officer; (9) the development of a language and literacy curriculum in Belfast primary schools; (10) views on school design, as expressed by teachers of children with severe learning difficulties; (11) the development and use of Records of Achievement in schools in Northern Ireland; (12) the placement of pupils with moderate learning difficulties in a college of further education.
Published Material: a full list of publications can be obtained from the researcher on request.
Source of Grant: No funding
Date of Research: 1982 – continuing

KEYWORDS: administration of education; co-operation; educational research; Ireland, Northern

8/1071
Queen's University of Belfast
52 Malone Road, Belfast BT9 5BS
0232 661111 ext 4366
D'Arcy, J.M. Mr; *Supervisor:* Wilson, J.A. Dr
Stress in teaching
Abstract: At the request of the teachers' organizations in Northern Ireland, NICER (Northern Ireland Council for Educational Research) agreed to carry out a literature review on teacher stress to ascertain whether or not research into teacher stress should be implemented in the province. The literature review was discussed at an invitational seminar organized by NICER during which it was suggested by delegates that research on teacher stress in Northern Ireland would be welcome. As a result of the seminar the Northern Ireland Council commissioned NICER to prepare a research proposal on its behalf so that funding for a research study into teacher stress in Northern Ireland might be sought. The proposed research involves a year-long study of a number of teachers in a variety of schools. Data will be collected using detailed interviews and using structured diaries.
Published Material: D'ARCY, J.M. (1989). Stress in Teaching: the research evidence. (NICER Occasional Paper No 1). Belfast: Northern Ireland Council for Educational Research.
Source of Grant: Grant-in-aid and Northern Ireland Teachers' Council: £2500
Date of Research: 1988-1989
KEYWORDS: Ireland, Northern; stress; teacher behaviour

8/1072
Queen's University of Belfast
52 Malone Road, Belfast BT9 5BS
0232 661111
Sutherland, A.E. Miss; Sloan, V.L. Dr
Teachers seconded for curriculum development
Abstract: Increasing use is being made in Northern Ireland of teacher secondments to assist with curriculum development. In 1988-89 some 180 teachers were employed in this way and the number will increase as schools prepare for the new curriculum. As secondments on this scale represent a considerable investment, NICER (Northern Ireland Council for Educational Research) was asked by the Department of Education, N.I. (Northern Ireland) to undertake a short-term investigation into the organization of secondments, concentrating on the following topics: the initial appointment, induction into the new role, management and continuing support, post-secondment careers, the preferred length of secondments and the possibility of such alternatives as fixed-term contracts. There were three groups of informants. All known secondees since 1980 were sent a questionnaire. This survey, which had 229 respondents (a 76% response rate) was complemented by interviews with 52 past and present secondee. The second group. which was interviewed, comprised those with responsibility for seconded teachers and included Board advisers and education officers in the museums. The third group, contacted through a telephone survey, was a sample of over 40 principals with teachers out on secondment.
Source of Grant: Department of Education for Northern Ireland: £21125
Date of Research: 1989-1989
KEYWORDS: curriculum development; secondment; teacher

North London Polytechnic

8/1073
Department of Teaching Studies
Prince of Wales Road, Kentish Town, London NW5 3LB
071 607 2789
Garton, M. Mrs; *Supervisor:* Brown, M. Dr; Mansell, T. Dr
History of mathematics teaching in London elementary schools (1830-1900)
Abstract: There is very little in the literature about the history of mathematics teaching in the elementary sector during the nineteenth century, and this research project is intended to rectify this omission, with special reference to the mathematics curriculum in London schools, between 1830 and 1900. It has been found necessary to consult original documents, notably London Board of Edu-

cation minutes, Committee of Council reports and Inspectors' reports. A broad approach has been taken initially to consider the preparation of elementary school teachers in teacher training colleges, as well as infant departments and elementary schools. Mathematical content being researched currently, includes mechanics, science and drawing in addition to the usual topics (algebra, trigonometry, etc). Future work is to include the perusal of school log books, and the research may be later confined to a particular aspect of mathematics, say arithmetic, or a particular age-range, e.g. infants/pre-standard.
Published Material: 'Teaching mathematics in 1886 – or cherries, cups and knitters', (1986). South East Region Mathematics Council Bulletin, Autumn.; 'Teacher training 1840s style: some questions from the past', (1987). South East Region Mathematics Council Bulletin, Autumn.
Source of Grant: North London Polytechnic: Fees
Date of Research: 1985 – continuing
KEYWORDS: history of education; mathematics; teacher education

North Riding College

8/1074
　　Filey Road,
　　Scarborough YO11 3AZ
　　0723 362392
　　University of Western Australia
　　Murdoch Campus,
　　Murdoch,
　　Australia WA6150
　　Davis, R.V. Dr; *Supervisor:* Marsh, C. Dr; Bolam, R. Dr
The planning and dissemination of inservice innovations in Britain and Australia
Abstract: The study portrays how teachers create and exploit inservice training opportunities for planning and disseminating curriculum innovations in the teachers' centre setting. Centres are viewed as a culture originating in the British national setting during the early 1960s. Through critical reflection and inquiry the study examines the extent to which the concept is transferable to the Australian national setting. The approach is through complementary case studies set in each national context to portray key conceptual and substantive issues identified from the literature. Australian, British and American literature is reviewed under two headings. First are the substantive issues of variety in provision of centres, the professional services offered to clients, how teachers actually use the centres, and how they are organized and managed. Six conceptual issues are then considered. These include interpersonal interactions in the teachers' centre setting, how centre users behave in the centre environment, how teachers learn through voluntary participation in centre-focused inservice training programmes, how curriculum innovations diffuse or are disseminated from their points of origin, and how the teachers' centre institution relates to schools as organizations. The final section of the study summarises trends portrayed by the case studies. Theoretical frame factors are viewed through ideological, epistemological, psychological and sociological perspectives and the findings are related to contemporary issues in each national setting.
Published Material: DAVIS, R.V. (1979). 'How to involve teachers in their own inservice training', British Journal of Inservice Education, Vol 5, No 2, pp.30-38.; DAVIS, R.V. (1980). 'Creating opportunities for low-cost teacher development through school – community interaction', Australia School's Commission, Fremantle Education Centre Publications.; DAVIS, R.V. (1981). 'Academic respectability: some political and organizational perspectives for education centres'; Conference Papers for 2nd National Conference, Adelaide.; DAVIS, R.V. & TREAGUST, D.F. (1981). 'Education centres as a focus for curriculum dissemination'; Conference Papers for CONASTA XXX National Conference, State College of Victoria (Toorak), Melbourne.; TREAGUST, D.F. & DAVIS, R.V. (1981). 'The role of education centres in science teaching in Western Australia', Conference Papers for 7th Annual Science Education Conference, Perth.
Source of Grant: No funding
Date of Research: 1985-1989
KEYWORDS: Australia; curriculum development; educational innovation; inservice education and training of teachers; teachers centre

Northumberland Education Department

8/1075
　　County Hall, Morpeth NE61 2EF
　　0670 514343
　　Matthews, A.P. Dr
Evaluation of the Northumberland self study project
Abstract: In initiating a major curriculum change in Post-16 approaches to learning, Northumberland will track each stage through a systematic programme of action research and evaluation. This will involve a baseline survey of 16 + take-up, option guidance, learning styles and performance indicators, a comparative evaluation of various models for production units; an assessment of training needs and programmes for project staff; evaluation of the process of course development and the effectiveness of development teams; and research into the impact of supported self-study approaches and materials on management and learning in schools and colleges. Experience shows the value of intrinsic evaluation. Each project team member will therefore be an evaluator, thus enabling aspects of the development and delivery processes to reflect immediate feedback from evaluation. There will be a role for external consultants, particularly in the research methodology, and appropriate aspects of the evaluation will be commissioned.
Published Material: MATTHEWS, A.P. (1989). Sixth form education in Northumberland. Morpeth: Northumberland County Council, Education Department.; MATTHEWS, A.P. (1989). Evaluation of the supported self study unit. Morpeth: Northumberland County Council, Education Department.
Source of Grant: Department of Education and Science: £150,000
Date of Research: 1988 – continuing
KEYWORDS: curriculum development; secondary education; self instruction; study method

Nottingham District Health Authority

8/1076
　　Community Unit, Memorial House, Standard Hill,
　　Nottingham NG1 6FX
　　0602 481800
　　Perkins, E.R. Dr
Introducing parents to the school health service
Abstract: This is a study of what parents like and dislike about the school health service, and specifically, examinations of school entrants. Particular attention is paid to the extent to which the entrant examination helps parents to understand how the system works. Structured interviews will be conducted with parents at entrant medicals, and at an experimental series of entrant nurse appraisals involving parents. Approximately 60 parents will be interviewed in all. It is possible that the report will be used to develop a second phase of the project, in constructing a consumer satisfaction questionnaire which school staff can use themselves. Whether or not this second phase materialises, the results will be used to inform the process of rethinking entrant examinations locally.
Source of Grant: District Health Authority: £5,000 approximately
Date of Research: 1990 – continuing
KEYWORDS: school health service

8/1077
　　Community Unit, Memorial House, Standard Hill,
　　Nottingham NG1 6FX
　　0602 481800
　　Perkins, E.R. Dr
Parents' information needs on the school health service
Abstract: The study was developed from the conference of a regional health authority campaign to 'personalize the service' and a district policy of reviewing the aims and workings of specific services and their relationship to consumer demand. The intention was to find out what, if anything, parents knew about the school health service and what they would like to know, and how they would like to be informed. A convenience sample of over 100 parents were contacted at schools, clinics and day nurseries, chosen to cover different social classes and different levels of health service provi-

sion. Semi-structured interviews revealed widespread bafflement about the workings and purposes of the school health service, and produced clear ideas about what information would be welcome and how it could be conveyed. The ensuing research report was discussed extensively with managers and staff, and the researcher was commissioned to produce, with the help of a multidisciplinary advisory group of professionals, leaflets and other materials to inform both parents and teachers about the service. The project ended with an evaluation report to the Health Authority and the preparation of articles for the medical and nursing press.
Published Material: PERKINS, E.R. (1988). 'School health services – why are parents so poorly informed?', Health at School, Vol 4, No 3, pp.85-88.; PERKINS, E.R. (1989). 'The school health service through parents' eyes', Archives of Disease in Childhood, No 64, pp.1088-91.
Source of Grant: Nottingham District Health Authority
Date of Research: 1986-1989
KEYWORDS: health education; information need; parent education; school health service

Nottingham Polytechnic

8/1078
Department of Education
Clifton Hall,
Clifton, Nottingham NG11 8NS
0602 418248
Bassey, M. Prof.
Planning and assessment procedures for teachers in the National Curriculum
Abstract: The aim is to devise planning and assessment procedures for teachers which facilitate work with the National Curriculum and use as little time as practical. In planning procedures the emphasis is on integrated work for primary schools. The assessment procedures developed so far are FISTA (Formative Informal System for Teacher Assessment) and SISTA (Summative Informal System for Teacher Assessment).
Published Material: BASSEY. M. (1989). 'Trent planning guide for National Curriculum in primary schools', (3 volumes). London: LEAP (Local Education Authority Publications).; BASSEY, M. (1990). 'Trent assessment guide for primary schools, National Curriculum, Key Stage One. London: LEAP (Local Education Authority Publications).
Source of Grant: No external funding
Date of Research: 1989 – continuing
KEYWORDS: assessment; curriculum; primary school

8/1079
Department of Education
Clifton Hall,
Clifton, Nottingham NG11 8NS
0602 418418
Bloomfield, A. Dr
History in action at Clifton Hall
Abstract: This is a history in action project involving the performance arts for primary children. The history in action at Clifton Hall focuses on dance, drama, music and visual art as cultural and aesthetic experiences linking the past with the present in terms of creative and interpretive expressions by utilizing Clifton Hall as an educational resource. The project enables students, teachers, parents and children to visit the Hall and work together in different parts of the house to make history come alive. Three historical 'patches' have been selected, and costumes for these periods – the Carolian, Georgian and Victorian – have been produced for a whole class of primary school children. Role-play and dance, of the civil war period, take place in the Payes' room, while domestic drama and country dance are performed in an elegant Georgian parlour designed by Carr of York. A Victorian kitchen is used by servants as they prepare for the celebrations of the master's weekend houseparty. One room has been restored as a nursery. A teachers handbook, Prima for Action, is being prepared along with video and sound tapes, suggesting a wide range of school-based activities in history and the arts.
Source of Grant: Nottingham Poytechnic Research Initiative Fund: £1,500
Date of Research: 1988-1990
KEYWORDS: aesthetic education; art activity; history

8/1080
Department of Education
Clifton Hall, Clifton, Nottingham NG11 8NS
0602 418418
Bell, G.H. Prof.
Networks and networking
Abstract: The project aimed to estabish computerized information retrieval and storage systems to link groups of teacher researchers. One network was established to study problems and issues of the management of change. Four consecutive networks were organized to maximize transfer of practical professional knowledge and experience between practitioners in the field of special educational needs. A suite of microcomputer databases has been developed and evaluated in relation to the underlying processes of professional development. A feasibility study has been commissioned with a view to extending the model networking process evolved through the various phases of this project.
Published Material: BELL, G.H. (1985). 'Sir and teacher based research: a pilot evaluation', British Library Research and Development Department, Report 5829.; BELL, G.H. (1985). 'Sir and teacher based research: a pilot evaluation', CORE (Collected Original Resources in Engineering), Vol 9, No 1.; BELL, G.H. (1988). 'Networking and the management of change', CORE, Vol 12, No 3, October.; BELL, G.H. (1988). 'Information technology and teacher based research'. In: SMITH, E.D. (Ed). New technologies and professional communications in education. London: Council for Educational Technology; BELL, G.H. (1989). 'Why networks'? Classroom Action Research Bulletin, Vol 9B, Summer.
Source of Grant: Humberside Local Education Authority Sheffield Local Education Authority: jointly £18,500
Date of Research: 1984 – continuing
KEYWORDS: computer network; database; information retrieval; researcher; education

8/1081
Department of Education
Clifton Hall, Clifton, Nottingham NG11 8NS
0602 418418
Yeomans, B. Mr; Howkins, S. Ms
National Curriculum: cross-curricular business studies
Abstract: Elements of Business Studies feature in a number of the foundation subjects in the National Curriculum. This project seeks to ensure that cross-curricular links between these can be made from the perspective of Business Studies.
Source of Grant: No funding
Date of Research: 1989 – continuing
KEYWORDS: business education; interdisciplinary approach

8/1082
Department of Education
Clifton Hall, Clifton, Nottingham NG11 8NS
0602 418418
Spavin, S. Mr; Johnson, J. Mr; Johnson, E. Mrs; Hayes, M. Ms
National Curriculum: microcomputers in the primary classroom
Abstract: Investigations within this research project are, the use of concept keyboards in the development of literacy in infants; the use of databases in topic work for developing skills such as selection and hypothesising; the use of computer simulation with nursery and infant children to study language skills, and the influence of the use of computers in society.
Source of Grant: No funding
Date of Research: 1989 – continuing
KEYWORDS: microcomputer

8/1083
Department of Education
Clifton Hall,
Clifton, Nottingham NG11 8NS
0602 418248
Bloomfield, A. Dr
National Curriculum: history in action
Abstract: This is a pilot project in experiential learning in which drama, dance and music as well as cultural life-styles will be experienced by children through use of costume, properties and artefacts in role-play situations. The work will lead to teaching packs and aids, and video cassettes: it will involve direct links with schools. Ultimately the results of the experiment will be published.
Source of Grant: Polytechnic Research Committee: £1,000
Date of Research: 1988 – continuing

KEYWORDS: *experiential learning; history; primary education; teaching method*

8/1084

Department of Education
Centre for Inservice Education,
Clifton Hall, Clifton, Nottingham NG11 8NS
0602 418248 ext 3117
Morris, A. Dr; Smith, B. Mrs

Evaluation of the Nottinghamshire TVEI Project

Abstract: The aims of the project are to inform the LEA of (i) the development of the Nottinghamshire TVEI project; and (ii) of the experiences gained in running the project. The issues for evaluation will be identified by the LEA, and an annual programme of work will be agreed by the LEA and the Polytechnic. It will include: time spent per issue; methods used; evaluators; and nature/form and frequency of reports.

Source of Grant: Nottinghamshire County Council: £7,500 per annum
Date of Research: 1987 – continuing
KEYWORDS: *evaluation; Technical and Vocational Education Initiative (TVEI)*

8/1085

Department of Education
Clifton Hall, Clifton, Nottingham NG11 8NS
0602 418248
Hadfield, M.P. Mr; *Supervisor:* Antouris, G. Dr; Bassey, M. Prof.

The development of an equality of opportunity perspective in primary schools via the use of concept based social enquiry

Abstract: The research has arisen from two areas of concern. (1) The lack of work covering social enquiry or topic work within schools which means that conceptual and intellectual skills are not developed. (2) The lack of a permeator for equality of opportunity work throughout the curriculum which is not based on a conceptual understanding of related issues such as racism, sexism and classism. The aims of the research are to identify the present level of conceptual understanding held by local education authorities in the area of equality of opportunity via a theoretical analysis of policy documents issued by LEA's in England and Wales. A conceptual framework for use by teachers and pupils will be developed for the analysis of factors and the mechanisms which promote discrimination between groups, however defined. A training programme will also be developed which will enable teachers to approach more effectively the area of equality of opportunity in their topic work. The effectiveness of the training programme and conceptual framework will be evaluated by running inservice training courses in 3 LEA's and this will be followed up by an evaluation of the teaching process and content over a year in approximately 50 schools.

Source of Grant: Polytechnic research assistant/demonstrator
Date of Research: 1988 – continuing
KEYWORDS: *educational policy; equal opportunity; multicultural education; primary education*

8/1086

Department of Education
Burton Street, Nottingham NG1 4BU
0602 418248
Pearce, A. Mr; *Supervisor:* Fox, D.H. Mr

Transfer of study skills from one subject context to another: promoting and inhibiting factors in a group of 13-14 year old pupils

Abstract: The study seeks to identify the factors which promote and inhibit the transfer of certain kinds of study skills from one subject context to another. The study skills are those which are developed and identified through the use by pupils of supported self study packages which are used with class-sized groups of pupils in the second and third years of secondary school. Data is obtained eclectically through observation, interviews, diaries as well as the actual performance of the pupils in the self study packages.

Source of Grant: No funding
Date of Research: 1988 – continuing
KEYWORDS: *curriculum subject; independent study; study skills*

8/1087

Department of Education
Clifton Hall,
Clifton Village, Clifton, Nottingham NG11 8NS
0602 418248

Williamson, D.C. Mr

Wheelchair exerciser project

Abstract: This project was aimed at developing a wheelchair exercise appropriate to youngsters so that motivation could be developed to facilitate 'active' sports orientated exercise. One prototype device was built but further development was halted as a commercially available one was found to be more appropriate. This was field tested with young disabled participants.

Source of Grant: Sports Council: £427 Polytechnic Research Fund: £38.36 Central Council for Physical Recreation; Colson Trust: £427
Date of Research: 1984 – continuing
KEYWORDS: *equipment; physical education; physically handicapped*

8/1088

Department of Education
Clifton Hall, Clifton, Nottingham NG11 8NS
0602 418248
Antonouris, G. Dr; Wilson, J.B. Mr

The inter-cultural European dimension in teacher training

Abstract: This research starts with a review of books, articles and active learning materials for both teachers and others in initial or inservice professional training. New and existing materials will be used to develop packs which involve participants in relevant learning and problem solving activities. Pilot studies on selected groups of trainees and professionals will be followed by the design and testing of packs intended to develop multi-cultural and anti-racist awareness, knowledge and skills.

Source of Grant: No funding
Date of Research: 1987-1990
KEYWORDS: *Inservice Education and Training of Teachers; multicultural education; race relations; teacher education; teaching aids*

8/1089

Department of Education
Centre for European Education,
Clifton Hall, Clifton, Nottingham NG11 8NS
0602 418248
Bell, G.H. Prof.

Europe in the primary school

Abstract: This project is the second phase of a study first established in 1982. Phase One was concerned with establishing action research units in member states of the EEC to investigate problems and issues in teaching about Europe in primary schools. Phase Two was established to investigate the extent to which teaching materials produced in one member state can be adopted in another. Case studies recording the outcomes of phase one are currently being published from the units designed to facilitate collaborative research and development.

Published Material: BELL, G.H. (1983). 'Teaching about Europe in the primary school: an outline of an Educational Action Research Project', Teaching about Europe, Vol 10, No 3, Summer, pp.1-5.; BELL, G.H. (1987). 'Developing inter cultural understanding: an action research approach', School Organization, Vol 7, No 3, pp.273-279.; BELL, G.H. (1989). 'Europe in the primary school', British Journal of Inservice Education, Vol 15, No 2,; BELL, G.H. (1989). 'Una Ricerca per L'Europa', Vita e Pensiero, 6/1989, pp.426-434.; BELL, G.H. (1989). 'Pedagogia Interculturale: Alcune Riflessioni sul Metodo', Dirigenti Scuola, pp.10-19.; BELL, G.H. (1989). 'Europe in the primary school in England: a case study'. PAVIC Publications.

Source of Grant: European Economic Community: £11,500
Date of Research: 1987 – continuing
KEYWORDS: *action research; Europe; primary education*

8/1090

Department of Education
Clifton Hall, Clifton, Nottingham NG11 8NS
0602 418248
Hayes, M. Ms

Re-analysis of the Stott Moyes Henderson Test of Motor Impairment

Abstract: This study is a follow-up to a report which outlined the nature of motor difficulties in children, and considered the issues relating to the assessment of the school-aged child. The previous report analyzed data prepared in England by Stott Moyes & Henderson and the present study is an analysis of parallel data from Canada, also provided by Stott Moyes & Henderson. The previous study considered the discrimination of the test as a whole and individual scores for age, sex and socio-economic groups and for

individuals. It used univariate anova, multivariate anova and factor analysis. The study considered implications of test use for normative measure, clinical exploration and as a measure of the capacity for improvement, all related to the 1981 Education Act. The study raised questions of critical periods at 7 years and 11 years and proposed a link between age norms and developmental stage theories via childrens motor strategies. The present study hopes to throw more light on these questions via a new sample of approximately the same size and composition − 360 children (60 per age band) from a wide, representative socio-economic range, from one area of South East England and one area of Canada.
Source of Grant: No funding
Date of Research: 1987-1990
KEYWORDS: cross-cultural research; motor disorder; test;

8/1091
Department of Educational Studies
Clifton Hall, Clifton, Nottingham NG11 8NS
0602 418248
Richards, J.K. Mr; Antonouris, G. Dr
The concept and proper incidence of community education
Abstract: This project looks at the development of community education with special reference to educational reform and multicultural and anti-racist approaches to the curriculum in schools and institutions of higher education.
Published Material: RICHARDS, J.K., PAINE, J. and CARTER, A. (1984). Teachers for a Multicultural Society, Schools Council, December 1984.; RICHARDS, J.K. & PAINE, J. (1985). Curriculum development: case studies in multiculturalism and anti-racism in schools. Commission for Racial Equality, February, 1985.; ANTONOURIS, G. (1986). 'Research report on the racial assumptions of staff and students in one department of teacher education', Multicultural Teaching, Vol 4, No 2, Spring.; ANTONOURIS, G. (1986). 'The race issue in education', Multicultural Education Review, No 6, Summer.
Source of Grant: No funding
Date of Research: 1981 − continuing
KEYWORDS: community education; curriculum development; multicultural education; reform of education

8/1092
Department of Educational Studies
Clifton Hall, Clifton, Nottingham NG11 8NS
0602 418248
Calthrop, K.E. Mr; Ede, J. Miss
Pedagogy of poetry teaching in the infant school
Abstract: A detailed study of poetry teaching in selected infant schools in Nottinghamshire and Derbyshire is to be carried out in order to identify successful practice as judged by experienced teachers. Both the reading and writing of poetry are to be included. The investigation will cover: (i) teachers' perceptions about poetry; (ii) teachers' methodology, including the use of resource materials and (iii) identification of appropriate resources. The outcome of the survey is to be a second report on poetry teaching which it is envisaged will be distributed to all infant schools in the two counties.
Published Material: CALTHROP, K. and EDE, J. (1984). Not Daffodils Again! Teaching Poetry 9-11. Harlow: Longman. For the Schools Council.
Source of Grant: Nottinghamshire LEA and Derbyshire LEA: travel expenses School Curriculum Development Committee: £400
Date of Research: 1985-1989
KEYWORDS: poetry; primary education

8/1093
Department of Educational Studies
Clifton Hall, Clifton, Nottingham NG11 8NS
0602 418248
Wright, A. Mr; *Supervisor:* Rothera, M.S.; Stephens, M.D. Prof.
A conceptual and empirical investigation of the critical thinking ability of adolescent students in several educational establishments in Nottinghamshire
Abstract: The project has three specific aims: (i) to show that the student's level of cognitive complexity, positioned on a continuum between critical thinking and reproductive-repetitive thinking, determine his or her success in problem solving skills; (ii) to modify existing measures of cognitive complexity (repertory grid related and other projective measures) for assessing critical thinking skills. Empirical work will allow: (a) comparisons to be made of the methodological effectiveness of revised tests and (b) measurement of cognitive complexity in a wide range of vocational and non-vocational students; (iii) to determine whether the critical thinking ability of students can be improved by experience in problem solving situations.
Source of Grant: No funding
Date of Research: 1986-1990
KEYWORDS: cognitive process; critical sense; student

8/1094
Department of Educational Studies
Clifton Hall, Clifton, Nottingham NG11 8NS
0602 418248
Weston, V. Mrs; Bunn, C. Mr; Howe, A. Mr; Bostock, P. Mr
The self-evaluation of practical teaching in local colleges by video and computer analysis
Abstract: The aim of this project is to provide an objective, systematic yet flexible means of assisting practising teachers in the post-compulsory education service to evaluate their own teaching and learning strategies by computer aided analysis of their video recordings taken in a variety of teaching settings and analyzed in context. The pilot stage has provided the basis for the computer analysis with further development and application to a wider range of skills, attitudes and competencies. It is envisaged that users will have the option to construct a personal profile and evolve action plans.
Source of Grant: No funding
Date of Research: 1987 − continuing
KEYWORDS: computer; further education; self evaluation; teacher; video recording

8/1095
Department of Physical Education
Clifton Hall, Clifton, Nottingham NG11 8NS
0602 418248
Williamson, D.C. Mr
Adapted sport and recreation equipment for handicapped youngsters with disabilities
Abstract: This project aims to consider via literature survey, observation and research, a number of potential equipment adaptions and special equipment for helping the severely handicapped to participate in recreation and sports. Staff, technicians and students will make contributions to the development of the prototype and field testing in schools and centres and outside groups will be involved in producing between 6 and 12 of the special models. A competition/exhibition of the equipment will be put on with supporting guidelines and literature. The majority of the items have now been produced. Guidelines for their use are being drawn up so that the items can be demonstrated to specific school groups and then presented to them.
Source of Grant: Nottinghamshire County Council
Date of Research: 1984 − continuing
KEYWORDS: equipment; handicapped; physical education; sport

8/1096
Department of Primary Education
Clifton Hall, Clifton, Nottingham
0602 418418
Hadfield, M.P. Mr; *Supervisor:* Wilson, J.; Antonouris, G.
Equal opportunites work in childrens topic work
Abstract: The research is concerned with the difficulties teachers have in using concepts to plan their topic work and developing their understanding of the processes involved by using concepts which are present within issues of equal opportunities. The aim being to develop teachers ability to permeate equal opportunities into all their topic planning. The project is initially based in five schools in Nottinghamshire and based upon action research methodology in which teachers contribute to the production of curriculum development theory.
Source of Grant: Nottingham Polytechnic: £30000
Date of Research: 1988 − continuing
KEYWORDS: action research; curriculum development; equal opportunity; primary education; project method

8/1097
Department of Primary Education
Clifton Hall, Clifton, Nottingham NG11 8NJ
0602 418418
Delaney, K.C. Mr; Sparrow, R.L. Mr
National Curriculum: manipulatives in primary school mathematics
Abstract: Manipulative or structural apparatus can enable children

to internalize images that are of great importance in developing a mental facility with numbers. This project is an exploration of current practice and future potential and is being carried out in Nottinghamshire schools and in Spanish schools in co-operation with Professor Adela Jaime of the University of Valencia.
Source of Grant: British Council: £780 Nottingham Polytechnic: £600
Date of Research: 1989 – continuing
KEYWORDS: comparative education; manipulative material; mathematics; primary Spain; teaching aids

8/1098
Department of Primary Education
Clifton Hall, Clifton, Nottingham NG11 8NS
0602 418418
Lewis, G.E. Dr
Young childrens perception and use of text features in the process of reading
Abstract: The study explores those aspects of text which are used by young children in the process of reading. A triangular model (process model: text analysis: readers' response) is used to refine information in each area mentioned. The reader's response is appraised by protocol analysis. The texts are those of ecological validity i.e. they are written for children to enjoy in their own right. The project consistently uses small group samples, in which information is qualitative and retained at the individual level. The outcome is in terms of 1. An exposition of text features which have procedural validity, rather than logical adequacy. 2. An exploration of stategies which may account for aspects of reading complex, authentic texts.
Published Material: LEWIS, G.E. (1982). 'Text structure, text processing and testing reading', Midland Association of Linguistic Studies, Vol 7, 1982, pp.43-69; LEWIS, G.E. (1983). 'Childrens perception of dynamics in narrative prose', Midland Association of Linguistic Studies, Vol 8, 1983, pp31-48.; LEWIS, G.E. (1985). 'Reading effective communication through text'. In: CLARK, M. (Ed). New directions in the study of reading. Lewes: Falmer Press.; LEWIS, G.E. (1987). Young childrens perception and use of text features in the process of reading narrative text. Thesis (PhD) Birmingham. 1987
Source of Grant: No funding
Date of Research: 1984-1990
KEYWORDS: early reading; learning strategy; perception; reading; reader response; reader text relationship; text structure

Nottingham University

8/1099
University Park, Nottingham NG7 2RD
0602 484848
Thomas, J.E. Prof.
An analysis of Japanese industrial education
Abstract: The aim of the research is to discover the relationship of industrial education in Japan to the practice of work. The researcher is examining the assumptions underlying the curriculum and methods of training, and to that end he has spent some time in Japan visiting the training units in several big companies. The preliminary conclusion is that training for management is confined to a limited group (for example men) and that it is derived from singular Japanese social mores.
Source of Grant: Nottingham University Research Funds: £2,000
Date of Research: 1987-1990
KEYWORDS: industrial training; Japan; management education

8/1100
Shell Centre for Mathematical Education, University Park, Nottingham NG7 2RD
0602 484848
Brekke, G. Mr; *Supervisor:* Bell, A.W. Dr
Notions on multiplication and division
Abstract: A substantial amount of research into children's understanding of mathematical concepts has been carried out. Until recently this has focused on early number concepts and skills, but within the last decade there has been a marked increase in attention towards learning in the early years of the secondary school. So far, less work has been done on the development of the multiplication and division concepts. From a theoretical standpoint it

would be important to fill this gap, and also from the point of view of developing more helpful and relevant teaching material. A major area of interest in the investigation is to be able to describe the acquisition of various aspects of the concepts, to identify major obstacles in development and to develop and test relevant teaching material to overcome some of the obstacles. So far this study has consisted of: (a) exploratory interviews with children 7 to 11 years old solving word problems, individually and in groups, both in England and Norway; (b) structured interviews and a written test for one fourth year primary school class, used as a pre- and post-test to a teaching experiment. Some conclusions are: (1) most children seem to recognize the structure of the two aspects of division; (2) proportion problems involving discrete numbers are solved by a 'building-up' strategy; (3) a very strong wrong additive strategy in ratio problems involving measure; (4) Cartesian product problems were solved by a larger proportion than anticipated; (5) a great variation in calculation methods, many very inefficient, were observed; (6) the necessity for the teaching to be intensive.
Source of Grant: Norwegian Research Council for Science and Humanities
Date of Research: 1987 – continuing
KEYWORDS: concept formation; mathematics; number concept

8/1101
Shell Centre for Mathematical Education, University Park, Nottingham NG7 2RD
0602 484848
Burkhardt, H. Prof; Swan, M.B. Mr; Fraser, R.E. Ms; Ridgway, J. Dr
Testing strategic skills
Abstract: The aim is to look for more effective methods of promoting planned curriculum change, using changes in public examinations linked to the development of supportive curriculum materials and distance-learning inservice training. Research methods are used throughout, some of them new, including developments in structural classroom observations: they inform both the successive refinement of materials and the basic understanding of the dynamics involved. Sample size grows from 4 classrooms with 'volunteer' teachers through the final trials in about 50 randomly chosen schools to detailed sample feedback on implementation in about 2000 schools. The methods are empirical but broadly based, taking a 'systems' approach. The outcomes are still provisional but suggest that effective methods of promoting qualitative changes in curriculum and teaching style of randomly chosen teachers are emerging through this approach; there is more to be done on the dynamics of large scale implementation.
Published Material: BEEBY, T., BURKHARDT, H. & FRASER, R. (1980). SCAN – systematic classroom analysis notation for mathematics. Nottingham: Shell Centre for Mathematical Education.; FRASER, R. (1982). Design and development of programs as teaching material. London: Centre for Educational Technology.; The language of functions and graphs. (1985). Nottingham: Shell Centre for Mathematical Education, Joint Matriculation Board.; BURKHARDT, H. (1984). Curriculum development planning; ambition and realism. Nottingham: Shell Centre for Mathematical Education.; Problems with patterns and numbers. (1984). Nottingham: Shell Centre for Mathematical Education, Joint Matriculation Board.
Source of Grant: Shell UK Ltd: £100,000 Joint Matriculation Board: £250,000 University of Chicago, University of Nottingham, Midlands Examining Group and others.
Date of Research: 1980-1989
KEYWORDS: assessment; curriculum development; distance study; examination; education and training of teachers; teaching aids

8/1102
Centre for Legal Studies
University Park, Nottingham NG7 2RD
0602 484848
Mackie, K.J. Dr
Legal skills research
Abstract: The legal skills research group is a project managed from the Institute of Advanced Legal Studies in the University of London. A team of national experts are reviewing the practice of legal skills education at all levels of education with the aim of developing awareness of appropriate methodologies and competencies in legal skills education.
Source of Grant: No funding
Date of Research: 1989 – continuing
KEYWORDS: higher education; law; legal education

8/1103
> Department of Adult Education
> Centre for Research into the Education of Adults,
> Cherry Tree Buildings, Nottingham NG7 4RD
> 0602 484848
> Morgan, W.J. Mr

Aspects of workers' adult education in Britain since 1900
Abstract: The investigation seeks to identify, describe and comment on specific, little known aspects of workers' adult education in Britain since 1900. A particular emphasis is placed upon the political and ideological nature of such education and its independent voluntarist nature.
Published Material: MORGAN, W.J. (1988). 'Some political origins of workers' education in Britain', Educational Philosophy and Theory, Vol 2, No 1, 1988, pp.27-36.; MORGAN, W.J. (1988). 'The burning question of workers' education: Ruskin College and the plebs' league', Educational Research and Perspectives, Vol 14, No 2, 1988, pp.38-48.; MORGAN, W.J. 91988). 'Hugh Gaitskell, democratic scoialism and adult educators'. In: MORGAN, W.J. (eds) Politics and consensus in modern Britain. London: Macmillan.; MORGAN, W.J. (1989). 'The political education of adults in Great Britain: history, theory, practice', Adult Education, Public Information and Ideology, Nottingham: Department of Adult Education.
Source of Grant: No funding
Date of Research: 1988-1990
KEYWORDS: adult education; workers' education

8/1104
> Department of Adult Education
> Centre for Research into the Education of Adults,
> Cherry Tree Buildings, Nottingham NG7 2RD
> 0602 484848
> Morgan, W.J. Mr

Political education, voluntary associations and civil society in state socialist countries
Abstract: The research seeks to identify and analyse the relationship of adult political education and voluntary associations to the emergence of civil society in state socialist countries. The key concepts will be defined theoretically and examined empirically through a series of related historical and sociological studies. Three countries will be considered initially, the Soviet Union, Hungary and the German Democratic Republic.
Published Material: MORGAN, W.R. (1989). 'Homo Sovieticus – political education and civil society in the Soviet Union'. In: MORGAN, W.P. (Eds) Proceedings of the standing conference of university teachings and research into the education of adults. Nottingham.; MORGAN, W.P. (1989). 'Workers adult education in the Soviet Union', Bulletin of the International Congress of University Adult Education, Vol 2, No 1, Spring 1989.
Source of Grant: British Council Travel Grant
Date of Research: 1989 – continuing
KEYWORDS: adult education; German Democratic Republic; Hungary; political education; socialism; USSR

8/1105
> Department of Adult Education
> Centre for Research into the Education of Adults,
> Cherry Tree Buildings, University Park,
> Nottingham NG7 2RD
> 0602 484848
> Stock, A.K. Prof.

International documentation of policy issues in adult continuing education
Abstract: The research is intended to identify, collect and analyse international documentation relating to policy issues in adult continuing education. A data base is to be established and occasional papers are intended.
Source of Grant: No funding
Date of Research: 1989 – continuing
KEYWORDS: adult education; continuing education; educational policy

8/1106
> Department of Adult Education
> Centre for Research into the Education of Adults,
> Cherry Tree Buildings, University Park,
> Nottingham NG7 2RD
> 0602 484848
> Morgan, W.J. Mr; Bayliss, F.J. Prof

Policy issues in training for employment including international comparisons
Abstract: The research is intended to identify and analyse policy issues in the development of employment training together with international comparisons. These are considered in an open seminar through a series of case studies. Seminar discussions are published and are supplemented with further work. Funding is being sought for the international comparisons to be undertaken.
Published Material: MORGAN, W.J. (1988). 'Future trends in graduate employment', Education and Training, Vol 30, No 6, 1988, pp.12-13.; MORGAN, W.J. (1989). 'A report on the training for employment seminar'. In: NAYLISS, F.J. (Eds) CREA (Centre for Research into the Education of Adults), Occasional Paper 2, Nottingham, 1989, pp43.
Source of Grant: No funding
Date of Research: 1988 – continuing
KEYWORDS: Adult education; educational policy; vocational training

8/1107
> Department of Adult Education
> 14-22 Shakespeare Street,
> Nottingham NG1 4FJ
> 0602 483838
> Sutton, I.D. Dr

The value of field residential courses in the teaching of earth sciences
Abstract: The research is intended to investigate the value of field studies in the teaching of adults in the area of earth sciences. The study involves the investigation of the way field activities can be integrated into the teaching of earth sciences to adults with special reference to teaching methods, day, weekend, longer residential and foreign study tours. The value of pre-course preparation for the field study is an important aspect of the research.
Source of Grant: No funding
Date of Research: 1986 – continuing
KEYWORDS: adult education; earth sciences; field study

8/1108
> Department of Adult Education
> 14-22 Shakespeare Street,
> Nottingham NG1 4FJ
> 0602 483838
> Jotham, R.W. Dr; Ellis, M.M. Mrs

Aspects of educational practice in the physical sciences and information technology
Abstract: The aim of this project is to evaluate, comment upon and improve educational practice in science and information technology. The methodology involves direct experimentation work with student groups, followed by discussion with students and tutors. The research also includes extensive studies of statistical information on the extent, diversity and logistics of provision of adult education in this general area.
Published Material: Alist of publications is available from the researcher
Source of Grant: No funding
Date of Research: 1970 – continuing
KEYWORDS: information technology; physical sciences; science eduvcation; teaching method

8/1109
> Department of Adult Education
> 14-22 Shakespeare Street,
> Nottingham NG1 4JF
> 0602 483838
> Wood, A. Mr; *Supervisor:* Jotham, R. Dr

The role of information technology in the education of socially handicapped children
Abstract: Particular topics in numeracy and literacy areas are taught to groups of children in a special school for maladjusted children in formats which (a) do not use information technology; (b) use information technology extensively. Observers who are normally present in classes record characteristics such as attention span systematically for individual children to establish primary data for comparison.
Source of Grant: Derbyshire Local Education Authority: registration/tuition and travel expenses
Date of Research: 1989 – continuing
KEYWORDS: computer-assisted instruction; maladjusted; socially handicapped; special education

8/1110

Department of Adult Education
14-22 Shakespeare Street, Nottingham NG1 4FJ
0602 483838
Derby College of Further Education,
Wilmorton Site, Derby DE2 8UG
0332 73012
Cooper, A. Mr; *Supervisor:* Jotham, R.W. Dr
Evaluation of special educational support centre located in a college of further education
Abstract: The purpose of the project is to evaluate the effectiveness of an educational support centre for special needs students located within Derby college of further education. Methodology involves regular consultation with the centre staff, students and management staff.
Source of Grant: Derbyshire County Council: tuition fees
Date of Research: 1987 – continuing
KEYWORDS: further education; special needs; support service

8/1111

Department of Adult Education
14-22 Shakespeare Street, Nottingham NG1 4FJ
0602 483838
Sherman, I. Mr; *Supervisor:* Jotham, R.W. Dr
The potential of computer-mediated-communication for developing social and educational oppportunites for adults with physical and sensory difficulties
Abstract: The aim is to establish a communication network for training and related activities between disabled centres and individual users in the East Midlands with links through the Joint Academic Network and the Packet Swith system to researchers, practitioners and other disabled people in the United Kingdom and worldwide. The efficient use of the network will be evaluated by monitoring traffic and by consultation with disabled users and professionals working with them.
Published Material: A list of publications is available from the researchers
Source of Grant: Leverhulme Trust: £55,000 over three years
Date of Research: 1989 – continuing
KEYWORDS: adult education; communication; computer network; physically handicapped; special needs

8/1112

Department of Adult Education
University Park, Nottingham NG7 2RD
0602 484848
Jones, D.J. Dr; Wallis, J.V. Dr
Adult education in China – an enquiry into reasons for attending
Abstract: The project aims to discover reasons why adults attend courses in the People's Republic of China. 1600 questionnaires were administered in Shandung Province to those attending adult education courses. Not all attenders, it was discovered, relate their training to improved economic performance, which is the official reasons for mounting these courses.
Source of Grant: No funding
Date of Research: 1989-1989
KEYWORDS: adult education; China; motivation

8/1113

Department of Adult Education
University Park, Nottingham NG7 2RD
0602 484848 ext 3558
Stephens, M.D. Prof.
The training of adult education leaders in China
Abstract: Four Chinese university lecturers have been brought to England to absorb British theoretical and practical approaches to management and leadership in adult education. They are undergoing a three year carefully monitored programme. This has a focus of working for a higher degree and around this is built a series of visits, a research project, interviews and other relevant experience to gather information on British provision, ideas and debates on adult education. Each year is evaluated with various assessments being made by the researchers and the students themselves as to a variety of criteria of change. This is reported to the Leverhulme Trust. The research has become mainly qualitative. *Source of Grant:* Leverhulme Trust: £63,000
Date of Research: 1988 – continuing
KEYWORDS: adult education; China: leadership; teacher education

8/1114

Department of Adult Education
Cherry Tree Buildings, Nottingham NG7 2RD
0602 484848 ext 2582
Zhang, X. Mr; *Supervisor:* Jones, D. Dr; Fielden, D. Mr
Comparative study of organizations and structure of provision of adult education in the People's Republic of China and the United Kingdom
Abstract: This is a comparative study of organizations and structure of provision of adult literacy education in China and the United Kingdom. The study is mainly based on literature available and its aim is to find out by comparison and contrast what factors are relatively more important in influencing both the shaping and functioning of adult literacy education in the two countries. The results to be derived from the study are expected to be of relevance and significance to the practice of adult literacy education for China in the 1990's. It is true that China has made great achievements in its literacy education already in the past forty years, but with still such a high percentage of illiterates and the urgent needs for economic development, literacy education is among the immediate concerns of the country's policies for the decade to come.
Source of Grant: The Leverhulme Education Foundation
Date of Research: 1989 – continuing
KEYWORDS: adult education; China; comparative education; literacy; United Kingdom

8/1115

Department of Adult Education
Cherry Tree Buildings, Nottingham NG7 2RD
0602 484848
Bin, L. Ms; *Supervisor:* Morgan, W.J. Mr; Lawson, K.H. Dr
A comparison of the main concepts in the philosophy of education used in Britain and China
Abstract: The main concepts used in the philosophy of education in Britain and China will be defined, analysed and compared with a view to establishing both universals and those that are bound within a cultural context.
Source of Grant: No funding
Date of Research: 1989-1990
KEYWORDS: China; philosophy of education; United Kingdom

8/1116

Department of Adult Education
Cherry Tree Buildings, University Park,
Nottingham NG7 2RD
0602 484848
Wong, K.K. Mr; *Supervisor:* Morgan, W.J. Mr; Shipstone, D.M. Dr
Evaluation of the process of curriculum design of technical and vocational education in Hong Kong
Abstract: An evaluation of the process of curriculum design in technical and vocational education in Hong Kong will be undertaken. Special reference will be made to the interaction amongst education, training, employment and economic outcomes. It is also intended to identify present and likely difficulties, and to suggest ways of linking technical and vocational education with the general education system in order to ensure an adequate supply of competent technical personnel for the 1990's and beyond 1997.
Source of Grant: No funding
Date of Research: 1989 – continuing
KEYWORDS: curriculum development; Hong Kong; technical education; vocational education

8/1117

Department of Adult Education
14-22 Shakespeare Street, Nottingham NG1 4FJ
0602 483838
The Acorn Centre,
Dalkeith Terrace, Hyson Green, Nottingham
0602 483838
Neale, A.R. Mrs; Hole, R. Mr; Sherman, I. Mr; Turner, R. Mrs; Green, P. Mrs; Bentley, T. Mr; *Supervisor:* Jotham, R.W. Dr
The logistics of provision of vocational training in information technology for adult students with physical and sensory disabilities
Abstract: The aim is to establish and evaluate a model for the delivery of IT (information technology) training to disabled adults by direct experimentation. A key feature of the arrangement is that training operates in parallel with a workshop managed by disabled people with IT skills. The methodology involves regular consulta-

tion between staff, trainers and associated practitioners. The group of disabled people involved numbers approximately 70.
Published Material: A list of publications is available from the researchers
Source of Grant: Nottingham Task Force European Social Fund Nottinghamshire County Council: jointly £210000
Date of Research: 1988 – continuing
KEYWORDS: adult education; computer; information technlolgy; physically special needs; vocational training

8/1118

Department of Adult Education
Nottingham NG1 4FJ
0602 483838
Neale, A.R. Mrs; Phillips, R.B. Mr; Lamerton, P. Mrs; Quinton, E. Mrs; Cooke, B.J. Dr; *Supervisor:* Jotham, R.W. Dr

The Logistics of provision of courses in Information Technology for Adult students with physical and sensory disabilities
Abstract: Centres with good disabled access have been equipped with computers and software for the provision of computer courses for disabled students and mixed groups of disabled and able-bodied students. As well as continually reviewing the logistics of such provision, including the need for special hardware aids, student progress is monitored and compared with progress of able-bodied adults attending similar computer courses at other centres. The number of disabled students involved in this educational programme is approximately 300.
Published Material: A list of publications is available from the researchers
Source of Grant: Leverhulme Trust Nottinghamshire County Council Lincolnshire County Council Derbyshire County Council: jointly £59000
Date of Research: 1985 – continuing
KEYWORDS: adult education; computer; information technology; physically special needs

8/1119

Department of Adult Education
14-22 Shakespeare Street, Nottingham NG1 4FJ
0602 483838
Neale, A.R. Mrs; Leicester, D. Mr; Busby, M. Mrs; Morgan, M. Mrs; Clay, J. Mr; Turner, R. Mrs; Green, P. Miss; *Supervisor:* Jotham, R.W. Dr

The use of information technology in adult basic education of students with physical and sensory handicaps
Abstract: Against a backcloth of computer courses for disabled adults in the University Adult Centre, students whose educational needs lie primarily in the area of adult basic education are worked with individually and/or in very small groups. Various teaching methods and materials are compared and contrasted, but the principle methodology is regular review of students' progress with tutors and Centre staff. The group of students under study numbers approximately 50.
Published Material: A complete list of publications is available from the researchers
Source of Grant: Leverhulme Trust Nottinghamshire County Council Lincolnshire County Council Derbyshire County Council: Jointly £59000
Date of Research: 1987 – continuing
KEYWORDS: adult education; basic education; computer-assisted instruction; technology; physically handicapped; special needs

8/1120

Department of Adult Education
Centre for Research into the Education of Adults,
Cherry Tree Buildings (Block B), University Park,
Nottingham NG7 2RD
0602 484848
Holland, D. Mrs; *Supervisor:* Eldson, K.T. Mr; Stephens, M. Prof.

Assessment of learning progress in adult literacy (ALPAL)
Abstract: The research project is a response to the need expressed by those working in the field, for models of assessment which are student-centred and helpful to planning and which will enable the organization to monitor and express its effectiveness in a meaningful way. In recent years increasing concern with the aims and outcomes of assessment and evaluation and their relationship to curriculum development has stimulated many new initiatives in assessment. It is intended that this two year research project should explore

these new developments in use in education generally and design models which make best use of such developments and are appropriate to adult literacy. The project sees assessment as a continuing process, integral to a student centred approach to learning which is concerned with encouraging and enabling the individual to take responsibility for his/her own learning. It is intended that the models developed should help students and their tutors to assess the progress made and should be useful in determining curriculum and methodology for future work. To this end the project recognizes that: the student should be directly involved in the process of assessment and, that any information gained should be useful in subsequent learning/teaching situtations; also that the form of assessment outcomes should be useful to programmes in expressing the effectiveness. The emphasis in the project is on progress and it is hoped that this project can devise models which are sufficiently flexible to be useful to individuals but which are also valuable to those who need to plan and evaluate provision.
Source of Grant: Adult Literacy and Basic Skills Unit: £50,000
Date of Research: 1987-1989
KEYWORDS: achievement measurement; adult education; literacy

8/1121

Department of Adult Education
University Park, Nottingham NG7 2RD
0602 484848 ext 2289/2291
Marks, H.E.S. Mr; Elsdon, K.T. Mr

Adults in the colleges of further education
Abstract: Although a large proportion of the education and training of adults, of every kind, is carried out by and in colleges of further education, this provision has never been studied systematically, nor have its implications for college organization and staffing or for policy-making generally. The project sought to fill this gap by means of intensive case studies of a representative sample of 16 colleges, a survey of a further 16 colleges, and a wider trawl of information from a variety of sources. The main topics dealt with are: contexts and external factors, collaboration in planning and provision, the pattern of course provision (including growing and interesting areas of work), other aspects of good practice, and the influence of structure, finance and organization, and evaluation.
Published Material: ELSDON, K.T. (1989). 'Adults in colleges – what staff development?', Journal of the National Association for Staff Development, No 21, June, pp.13-16.; ELSDON, K.T. 'Adults in the colleges of FE – some findings on the influence of structure, finance, organization and evaluation on the quality of provision', (forthcoming).; MARKS, H.E.S. & ELSDON, K.T. 'Adults in the colleges of FE', (forthcoming).
Source of Grant: Further Education Unit: £14,000
Date of Research: 1986-1989
KEYWORDS: adult education; college of further education; educational policy

8/1122

Department of Adult Education
University Park, Nottingham NG7 2RD
0602 484848
Allman, P. Dr

Adult development and the implications of theory and research for an andragogical approach to adult education
Abstract: Andragogy as defined by this project is an approach to adult education which enables learners to be the initiators and controllers of their own learning. The formulation and guiding principles of this approach derive from the work of Paulo Freire. The research involves the continuous evaluation, by the learners involved, of their learning whilst engaged in the approach. In any one year this involves about 25 people. Some of the criteria used in the evaluation are linked to the emerging theory and research in adult developmental psychology, viz the development of dialectic thinking and the development of more complex theories of knowledge, learning and action.
Source of Grant: No funding
Date of Research: 1984 – continuing
KEYWORDS: adult education; andragogy; cognitive development

8/1123

Department of Adult Education
University Park, Nottingham NG7 2RD
0602 484848
Stephens, M.D. Prof.

Comparison of American and English Nineteenth Century educational initiatives

Abstract: The research arose out of work done over 15 years on the educational response in Britain to the Industrial Revolution (e.g. 'Education and Industry in the Nineteenth Century', Longman, 1978). Was the American educational reaction to early industrialisation similar to that of pioneering Britain? Some notable differences have been found so far. The archive and similar resources were explored in Massachusetts in the Summer of 1980. In 1981 the autumn term was spent at Harvard by a visiting professor within the Department of the History of Science. The material generated by these periods in America has been used for subsequent writing. Further trips are planned.
Published Material: RODERICK, G.W. & STEPHENS, M.D. (1984). Post-school education in Nineteenth Century America and England. London: Croom Helm.; STEPHENS, M.D. (1983). 'Fashioning Americans: the role of education in the development of the United States', International Journal of Lifelong Education, Vol 2, No 3, pp.245-271.
Source of Grant: Leverhulme Trust: £500 Fulbright
Date of Research: 1979 – continuing
KEYWORDS: *comparative education; history of education; industrialization; United of America*

8/1124

Department of Adult Education
Centre for Research into the Education of Adults, University Park, Nottingham NG7 2RD
0602 484848
Bayliss, F.J. Prof.; Morgan, W.J. Mr
Company training policies and open learning – a comparison of Jaguar plc and Daimler Benz AG
Abstract: The purpose of the research is to compare the company training policies adopted by two manufacturers of quality motor cars, one in the UK, one in the Federal Republic of Germany. The core of the training policy appears to rest upon the open learning principle. The effectiveness of this principle in meeting the requirements of the perspective employers and the aspirations of employees will be compared and assessed through the use of questionnaire and in depth interview. An attempt will be made to elaborate the theory of open learning within this framework of industrial education practice.
Source of Grant: The Anglo-German Foundation for the Study of Industrial Society: approx. £20,000
Date of Research: 1989-1990
KEYWORDS: *industrial education; industry; open learning; training method*

8/1125

Department of Adult Education
University Park, Nottingham NG7 2RD
0602 484848
Kinder School
Bassetlaw Hospital, Worksop S81 ODD
0909 472831 ext 290
Watts, G. Mr; *Supervisor:* Jotham, R. Dr
Computer assisted learning for children with profound and multiple learning difficulties
Abstract: This research is based in a unit for children with profound and multiple learning difficulties. Twentyfive children have been involved, aged 1 to 19 years. The way that computer equipment, software and peripheral hardware can be used to enhance their learning is being investigated by means of an 'action research' model, dating from when a computer was first used in the unit in 1982. A very structured method of working with the children is combined with careful monitoring of progress, re-assessment of needs and the development of new programmes and specific items of hardware. Tentative conclusions indicate that the effectiveness of learning depends on the appropriateness of the 'setting events' around the child – the precise type of visual displays, sound effects, single touch switches, adult behaviour, body position, development targets, etc. The computer programmes are used in over 400 schools worldwide, and tested in a sample of 30 units.
Published Material: WATTS, G. (1984). 'Making the right connections', Learning to Cope, No 3, pp. 60-62.; WATTS, G. (1985). 'Computer assisted work with the multiply handicapped', Journal of the Association of Paediatric Chartered Physiotherapists.; WATTS, G. (1985). 'Computers in a special needs unit', British Journal of Special Education, Vol 13, No 3, pp.96.; WATTS, G. et al (1987). Computer assisted learning for children with profound and multiple learning difficulties. TGW Software Developments.; WATTS, G. (1987). 'Gershwin or gunfire, granny or golden silence:

Microelectronics, sound and a special needs unit', Journal for the Hearing Impaired, No 7, 1987, pp.4-12.
Source of Grant: Nottinghamshire Local Education Authority: Registration/Tuition and travel expenses
Date of Research: 1982-1990
KEYWORDS: *computer assisted instruction; learning difficulty*

8/1126

Department of Adult Education
University Park, Nottingham NG7 2RD
0602 484848 ext 3558
Stephens, M.D. Prof.; *Supervisor:* Thomas, J.E. Prof.; Daines, J. Dr; Fielden, R.D.S. Mr; Jones, D. Mr; Graham, B. Mr
Leadership training in Chinese adult education
Abstract: The Department of Adult Education at Nottingham University is helping to establish China's first institute of research and training in adult education at Jinan. Three members of staff have been seconded to Nottingham from Jinan for three years to train for leadership roles in Chinese adult education. They will read for Ph.D. degrees in adult education, review policy and practice throughout the United Kingdom, and the programme will be assessed in the final year of the research funding. This project is part of an interconnecting programme of initiatives.
Source of Grant: Leverhulme Trust: £70,000
Date of Research: 1988 – continuing
KEYWORDS: *adult education; China; leadership*

8/1127

Department of Adult Education
Centre for Research into the Education of Adults, University Park, Nottingham NG7 2RD
0602 484848
Scott, N.T. Mr; *Supervisor:* Morgan, W.J. Mr
Gateway to export programme
Abstract: Based upon the recommendations of an FEU (Further Education Unit) Report (RP 358) – published December 1987, an attempt is being made to derive a model for short post-graduate vocationally orientated courses including an element of professional preparation (initially the Institute of Export Pt. I Exams and Royal Society of Arts commercial languages). From experience thus gained a general pattern for such courses may arise. This particular field could attract EC (European Community) funding (the Social Fund). Additionally the material used in teaching may be used as the basis for distance learning packs for graduates. The National Extension College at Cambridge is interested in this aspect.
Source of Grant: The Training Enterprise Education Division: £22,000
Date of Research: 1988-1989
KEYWORDS: *distance study; exports; post-graduate study; vocational training*

8/1128

Department of Adult Education
University Park, Nottingham NG7 2RD
0602 484848 ext 3127/3669
Cox, D.L. Mr; *Supervisor:* Brotherton, C. Mr; Towers, B. Mr
The mass media and the social construction of memory
Abstract: The research will explore the ways in which many parts of people's memories are socially derived and will especially focus on those parts that are dependent on vicarious experience, learned about via the mass media (although the research will not ignore the importance of inter-personal vicarious experience). Using a case study approach, the research will attempt to locate mass media influence in an historicized context. This is necessary because of (a) the way we interpret present events will be affected by what we remember from the past and (b) how we remember events from the past will be qualified by how new events are reported. As what we remember will also be filtered through the ideological positions of different people, then socially constructed memory has also to be seen in terms of ideological memory. The case studies chosen for the research will examine the reporting of various types of industrial relations issues in national daily newspapers, but will not use conventional content analysis techniques alone. There will be an attempt to refine other qualitative measures. The research will also consider issues in the education of adults, especially how students' memory resources can be channelled, and how they have to be critically questioned and interpreted, rather than being simply accepted as evidence.

Source of Grant: No funding
Date of Research: 1988 – continuing
KEYWORDS: adult education; ideology; mass media; memory

8/1129

Department of Adult Education
14-22 Shakespeare Street, Nottingham NG1 4FT
0602 473022
Thomas, J.E. Prof.
An analysis of the relationship between language, politics, religion, and adult education in Wales
Abstract: The object of this research is to re-examine a number of generally held assumptions about the interrelationships of language, religion, politics and education in Wales. It is held that language and religion radicalized politics and that adult education has been an important formative element. An analysis of historical process will show, however that langauge and religion, with the collusion of adult education, have been reactionary forces, and that nationalism has been an inhibitory factor in culture development.
Source of Grant: No funding
Date of Research: 1986-1989
KEYWORDS: adult education; cultural development; language; politics; religin; Wales

8/1130

Department of Adult Education & Continuing Education
University Park, Nottingham NG7 2RD
0602 484848
Daines, J. Dr; Graham, B. Mr
Look after yourself tutor training
Abstract: The aim is to evaluate tutor training and to advise and consult on subsequent training and allied activities.
Published Material: DAINES, J. & GRAHAM, B. (1989). LAY report: innovations and outcomes 1978-1986. University of Nottingham; Department of Adult Education.; DAINES, J. & GRAHAM, B. (1989). Adult learning; adult teaching; a manual. University of Nottingham; Department of Adult Education.
Source of Grant: Health Education Authority: £100,000
Date of Research: 1982-1989
KEYWORDS: health education; teacher education; tutor

8/1131

Department of Education
University Park, Nottingham NG7 2RD
0602 484848
Griffiths, M. Dr
Self esteem and educational practice
Abstract: This research is a philosophical examination, which draws on psychological and feminist sources. The research is considering the central concepts of achievement and belonging and their role in fostering self esteem. Current influential theories emphasise the dependence of self esteem on personal achievement, though others focus on belonging. The internal and mutual coherence of the two are being investigated. The theories are being considered in the light of philosophical theories of personal identity, and of feminist theories of identity politics. The implications for educational practice will be drawn out, with special reference to equal opportunities.
Source of Grant: No funding
Date of Research: 1990 – continuing
KEYWORDS: achievement; equal education; equal opportunity; philosophy of education; self esteem

8/1132

Department of Education
University Park, Nottingham NG7 2RD
0602 484848
Tolley, B.H. Dr
The history of the University of Nottingham
Abstract: Nottingham University received its full charter in 1948. This study was oral evidence to supplement traditional archives. Interviews are being conducted with a wide range of personnel involved in every aspect of post-war development. The outcome of this research will be a new official history.
Source of Grant: University of Nottingham: £32,000 Wellcome Trust: £3,000 approximately
Date of Research: 1988 – continuing
KEYWORDS: history of education; United Kingdom; university

8/1133

Department of Education
University Park, Nottingham NG7 2RD
0602 484848 ext 3456
Parker-Jenkins, M. Dr
What do Muslim children need from the education system?
Abstract: This case study of the Muslim Girls' High School, Leicester will provide an insight into an unexplored area which has recently provoked educational debate here and abroad: the lack of understanding between the state educational system and the Muslim community. Adopting an ethnographic approach, the aim of the study is to consider the extent to which the maintained school sector is able to accommodate Muslim pupils. The two year project will comprise of four stages of work. Firstly, initial research of the Muslim Girls' High School Leicester, visits to other Muslim schools in Britain to provide comparative analysis, and in depth interviewing of interested parties: educationalists; clergy; academics; and community leaders. Finally, the production of a report, study guide and articles for publication, offering practical solutions to the problems of educating Muslim children within state schools and in accordance with parents' religous convictions. The education system is presently being criticised by 'Muslims' who see an incompatability between values taught at home and those at school. Although voluntary aided status may be granted to Muslim schools in the future, there will still be a large element of Muslim children who remain in regular maintained schools. Accommodating their educational needs will continue to be a pressing concern for educationalists and this research will provide a direct contribution to knowledge in the field of cultural activity.
Published Material: PARKER-JENKINS, M. (1990). 'Muslim needs won't disappear', New Era in Education, Vol 17, No 1, April.; PARKER-JENKINS, M. (1990). 'Muslim educational needs', Multicultural Education Journal, Autumn.; PARKER-JENKINS, M. (1990). 'Multiculturalism in British schools: lessons for Canada', Canadian School Executive, Vol 10, No 5, November.
Source of Grant: Funding applied for
Date of Research: 1991 – continuing
KEYWORDS: multicultural education; muslim

8/1134

Department of Education
University Park, Nottingham NG7 2RD
0602 484848
Griffiths, M. Dr; McBride, R. Dr; Weiner, G. Ms
Equal opportunities and socal justice
Abstract: This research is a theoretical and philosophical examination of the central concepts and their relationship to teacher development in the 1990s. The work as a whole will include an investigation of the concept of justice and social justice, to inequality with reference to race, class, sexuality, etc. Key themes will include the importance of focusing on both individuals and groups as a unit of analysis; the significance of metaphors of balance and harmony and their possible inappropriateness in a dynamic society; and changing meanings of the notion of justice in across time and place. These themes will be used to illuminate evidence about inequalities in modern British society. The implications for policy will be drawn out and formulated in terms of an education agenda for the 90s.
Source of Grant: No funding
Date of Research: 1990 – continuing
KEYWORDS: justice; teacher development

8/1135

Department of Education
University Park, Nottingham NG7 2RD
0602 484848
Strong, H. Mr; Supervisor: Muckle, J.Y. Dr; Harrison, C. Dr
The imperative for educational reform in the USA in the 1980s
Abstract: This research will examine official resources to the The National Commission on Excellence in Education report in 1983 from a number of states in the Union. There is to be particular concentration on one case study, the state of New Hampshire, and of the school district of Keene within it. It is intended to draw conclusions about the various agencies of educational change and the constraints upon them which dictate the pace and extent of such change.
Source of Grant: No funding
Date of Research: 1988 – continuing
KEYWORDS: educational change

8/1136
Department of Education
University Park, Nottingham NG7 2RD
0602 484848
Tolley, H. Mr; Boyett, I. Ms; *Supervisor:* Day, C. Dr;
Murphy, R. Prof.
The accreditation of work based learning in higher education
Abstract: The research aims to investigate ways in which work
achieved through prior experience and current learning on the job
in industry may be accredited towards awards offered by higher
education. The project is undertaken by the Universities of Nottingham and Sheffield in partnership with Rolls Royce plc and other
industry. The project works with three cohorts of design engineers,
trainers and managers. Through action research, the development
of worker-learner profiling systems and supervisor training, it is
intended to build case studies of practice which will enable other
industrial concerns and higher education institutions to develop
schemes for the accreditation of work based learning. The results
will be disseminated through a number of conferences and
documentation.
Source of Grant: Training Enterprise Education Division: £100,000
Date of Research: 1990 – continuing
KEYWORDS: accreditation; industry education relationship

8/1137
Department of Education
University Park, Nottingham NG7 2RD
0602 484848
Reading University
Department of Education
London Road, Reading RG1 5AQ
0734 875234 ext 217
Wright, J.E. Mrs; *Supervisor:* Brown, G. Dr; Youngman,
M.B. Dr
The submission rates of PhD students
Abstract: The research will consider (a) the criteria for the selection of PhD students, (b) the students expectation of studying for
a PhD, (c) how the research skills they acquired in their previous
full time learning environment compare to the thesis related skills,
(d) if it is possible to create a research skills profile of the PhD
student, (e) how the students acquire the skills they require for the
thesis. Very little is known about the effects of different supervisory approaches and selection criteria on academic success at PhD
level. Until it is known which students succeed or fail to submit,
it will not be possible to identify better predictors of success than
those implicit in current selection methods. This study is investigating the selection and supervision of research students and the process
of doctoral research from the perspectives of both student and
supervisor. A study of the pattern of supervision in the University
of Reading has been carried out, and of the supervisors and the
higher degree students as they start their PhD. Questionnaires have
been sent to students and supervisors, and a series of taped interviews has been carried out with the supervisor of every student who
has completed a questionnaire. A comparison will then be made
between the scores of the student and supervisors questionnaires
to arrive at an individual Research Skills Profile for each student.
A follow up questionnaire has been devised. A study is also being
made of the learning process of the PhD student.
Source of Grant: Economic and Social Research Council: £20,000
over three years
Date of Research: 1985 – continuing
*KEYWORDS: doctorate; post-graduate; selection; study skills;
supervision; thesis*

8/1138
Department of Education
University Park, Nottingham NG7 2RD
0602 484848
Watts, R.E. Mrs
**An investigation of the variety of GCSE (General Certificate of
Secondary Education) syllabuses in humanities, with differing aims
and assessment objectives, to see if each has a distinctive pedagogy**
Abstract: Three GCSE syllabuses have been chosen from the broad
spectrum of syllabuses in geography and Integrated Humanities.
The amount of coursework assessment in these syllabuses varies
from 100% to 25%. The aims of the research are, (i) analysis and
classification of the syllabuses, (ii) assessment of the constraints
which operate in the schools teaching each syllabus and how the
content of the published syllabus is modified, (iii) observation and
analysis of classroom transactions to see if there is a distinctive
pedagogy associated with each of the three syllabuses. The sample
will probably cover the work of about 750 pupils.
Source of Grant: No funding
Date of Research: 1987-1990
*KEYWORDS: curriculum subject; General Certicicate of Secon-
dary Education; geography; humanities; secondary education*

8/1139
Department of Education
University Park,
Nottingham NG7 2RD
0602 484848
Thomas, J.E. Prof.
Industrial education in Japan
Abstract: The purpose is to analyze the nature of industrial educa-
tion in Japan. In particular, to examine the curriculum, the extent
of such education, and its relationships with recruitment and pro-
motion. During this research there will be in depth interviews and
discussions with the major companies engaged in such work in
Japan.
Source of Grant: Nottingham University Research Funds: £4,000
Date of Research: 1988-1989
KEYWORDS: industrial education; Japan

8/1140
Department of Education
Cherry Tree Buildings,
Nottingham NG2 7AP
0602 484848
Preston, P.J.D. Mr
Literature in adult education
Abstract: This is partly in-post research about the demand for literature in adult education. It involves regular contact with part-time
tutors, students, WEA (Workers' Educational Association)
branches and local arts/literature groups and organizations. A
specific contribution to the debate about the role of literature in
adult education will be published probably in 1991. This is a collection of essays by full and part-time tutors. Further work on the
history of literature in adult education is planned.
Published Material: PRESTON, P.J.D. (forthcoming). Literature
in the adult class: tradition and challenge. Nottingham University;
Department of Adult Education.
Source of Grant: No funding
Date of Research: 1986 – continuing
KEYWORDS: adult education; literature

8/1141
Department of Education
University Park,
Nottingham NG7 2RD
0602 484848
Bilbow, G.T. Mr; *Supervisor:* Muckle, J. Dr; Morgan, W.J.
Mr
**Educational reform and innovation in the Czechoslovak Socialist
Republic**
Abstract: Educational reform in Czechoslovakia since the takeover
of power by the Communist Party in 1948 has brought with it
changes which belie the albeit short-lived liberal traditions which
were established during the First Republic. Lay education, one of
the foundations of liberal education, has given way to moral and
ideological training; collective effort has succeeded individual effort;
in-school activities and out-of-school activities, such as youth
brigades and political rallies, have become inextricably linked; the
polytechnical principle has taken over from the Czechs' once proud
academic tradition. The purpose of this research is to determine
the means by which this process of educational reform was achieved,
and to distinguish the extent to which it can be termed to have been
successful. It is the researcher's contention that education and training in Czechoslovakia currently face a number of problems, at least
some of which arise from the discrepancy between the lofty political aims of a communist upbringing and the 'bourgeois' aspirations of many Czechoslovak parents. It remains to be seen whether
the dramatic changes inherent in perestroika and glasnost will have
much impact on Czechoslovak education.
Source of Grant: GRIST (Grant Related Inservice Training) Henley
College, Bell Green, Coventry CV2 1ED: fees
Date of Research: 1988 – continuing
*KEYWORDS: Czechoslovakia; educational innovation; reform of
education*

8/1142

Department of Education
University Park, Nottingham NG7 2RD
0602 484848
Nottingham School of Nursing
Queen's Medical Centre, Nottingham NG7 2UH
Bradley, J. Mrs; *Supervisor:* Brown, G. Dr; Daines, J. Dr
Assessing the clinical progress of student nurses
Abstract: This current research has four main aims: (1) to identify
the tools used for the assessment of clinical progress of student
nurses; (2) to discover how students and assessors perceive the use
of a particular type of progress assessment form; (3) to establish
what preparation trained staff receive for their role as assessors;
(4) to devise and evaluate a handbook to assist assessors. An initial questionnaire was sent to 50 schools of nursing in order to establish their method of assessment, exploratory interviews were carried
out locally with assessors and students to identify problem areas.
From the resulting topic clusters 2 questionnaires were devised —
one for assessors and one for students. The questionnaires were
sent to 4 schools and a sample of 259 students and 167 assessors
responses was obtained. The data was processed with the aid of
a computer and chi-square and Kendall's TAVC statistical tests
applied to ascertain if there were any differences in the perceptions
of students and assessors regarding progress assessment. Some
differences were highlighted and these were used as the basis for
a handbook to assist assessors in the clinical area. The current situation is that the handbook is being used. Assessors attending an
assessors preparation course have been sent a pre-course questionnaire to establish what are their particular worries about assessment and what is their attitude to certain aspects identified in the
previous questionnaire and which form part of the handbook.
Course members are divided into control and experimental groups.
The experimental group will use the handbook for three months.
The control group will not receive a handbook. At the end of three
months both groups will be interviewed using a structured schedule which will incorporate some of the pre-course questionnaire
items. It is hoped that the usefulness of the handbook will be
reflected by a more positive attitude towards assessment and by
a greater confidence expressed in the ability of the assessors in the
experimental group. There are 24 assessors in each of the control
and experimental groups.
Published Material: BRADLEY, J. (1987). 'Is clinical progress
assessment fair?', Senior Nurse, Vol 7, No 5, November 1987,
pp.14-16.
Source of Grant: Kings Fund Centre for Health Service Development: £200 per annum
Date of Research: 1986-1990
KEYWORDS: assessment; nurse education; progress report

8/1143

Department of Education
University Park, Nottingham NG7 2RD
0602 484848
Tse Shek-kam, B. Mr; *Supervisor:* Dolan, T. Mr; Saunders,
M.A. Mr
The composing processes of Hong Kong children in primary schools
Abstract: In Hong Kong, most of the children speak in Cantonese;
a Chinese dialect. They do not speak English at home. They also
have little chance to speak English in class as the number of students in each class is about 45. In general, there is no suitable
environment for children to learn to write English. However,
English is considered the most important school subject in this British colony. There is a common saying: 'English with tears', which
means that children learn English with difficulty. The present
research attempts to study the mental processes of Chinese children when writing English and to find out the extent of the intra
and interlanguage interference within and between, Chinese and
English, which is responsible for the difficulties Hong Kong children encounter when learning to write. In this research, the case
study approach and thinking aloud protocols are applied. Two
pupils will be selected from primary 3, 4 and 5 Chinese schools
respectively. They will be followed for 2 years. Each year they will
be asked to write 2 modes of composition in Chinese and English
respectively. A comparative study between the two composing
processes of the two languages will be made. During the experiments, the subjects will compose aloud before the writing. A video
camera will be used to record the writing activities of the subjects.
The writing behaviour question guide and the background interview will be used to obtain more information of their writing
behaviour. Data will be collected for analysis.

Source of Grant: No funding
Date of Research: 1988 – continuing
*KEYWORDS: Chinese language; composition; English language;
Hong Kong; learning difficulty; writing*

8/1144

Department of Education
University Park, Nottingham NG7 2RD
0602 484848
The Society of Homes for the Hamdicapped
Level 204, Shopping Block, Lai Yiu Estate, Kwai Chung,
New Territories, Hong Kong
3-7454214
Chan, S.S.Y. Mr; *Supervisor:* Stratford, B. Dr; Dolan, T. Mr
**Development of services for adults with severe mental handicap
in Hong Kong**
Abstract: Examining the effectiveness of educational, training,
social and medical provision for severely mentally handicapped
adults in Hong Kong requires reviewing the progress made since
the 1977 White Paper on Rehabilitation together with a number
of other sources of evidence. This data will be analyzed with several
aims in mind: (1) to assess the relative successes, failures and shortcomings of progress towards satisfactory provision for the severely
mentally handicapped in Hong Kong society; (2) to offer some comment on whether the previous resource input, financial and human,
has been adequate to the task; (3) to draw up plans and proposals
for future developments and innovations; (4) to evaluate the work
of the Society of Homes for the Handicapped against other voluntary agencies in the field and to see whether the model upon which
it bases its activities is suitable for extension to cover the whole
of Hong Kong; (5) to set short-term priorities for future actions
and articulate a clear set of aims and objectives for the services
for the severely mentally handicapped. There is considerable uncertainty about what might happen in Hong Kong in the years following its restoration to China in 1997, but it seems likely that it
will be imperative that Government rather than voluntary inspired
provision for the severly mentally handicapped will need to pre-
vail. It is hoped that the present study will make some contribution to the services for the mentally handicapped in Hong Kong,
and that its implication will carry relevance for a wider audience,
particularly in China.
Published Material: CHAN, S.S.Y. (1986). How to assist persons
with severe learning difficulties. Hong Kong. The Society of Homes
for the Handicapped Annual Report 1985/86.; CHAN, S.S.Y. &
LAM, S.W. (1987). Mentally handicapped adults – a preliminary
study of their physical condition and functional abilities. Annual
Report 1986/87. Hong Kong: The Society of Homes for the Handicapped.; TSE, J., CHAN, S.S.Y. & CHU, M.L. (1987). Working with siblings of persons with mental retardation. 8th Asian
Conference on Mental Retardation, November 14-19, 1987, Singapore.; CHAN, S.S.Y. (1988). Historical review of services for
persons with mental handicap prior to 1978 Rehabilitation
Programme Plan. Hong Kong: The Society of Homes for the Han-
dicapped 10th anniversary Brochure.; CHAN, S.S.Y. (1988). Tem-
porary residential care programme. Hong Kong. The Society of
Homes for the Handicapped.; GOW, L. et al (1988). Report on
the Survey of the Needs of Elderly People with Mental Handicaps.
Hong Kong Council of Social Services.
Source of Grant: Sir Robert Black Trust Fund Scholarship: £24,000
Hong Kong Dollars
Date of Research: 1986-1990
KEYWORDS: adult; Hong Kong; mentally handicapped

8/1145

Department of Education
University Park,
Nottingham NG7 2RD
0602 484848
Kennewell, S.E. Mr; *Supervisor:* Phillips, R.; Bell, A.
Mathematical problem solving and computer assisted learning
Abstract: Secondary schools are encouraged to teach pupils the use
of generic computer software packages such as 'databases' and
'spreadsheets'. In the business world these are used to help solve
problems and model processes, often with a mathematical content.
This research aims to explore ways in which such computer packages can help pupils to learn problem-solving techniques; to apply
such techniques to the solution of 'real-life' problems; and to work
together in groups. The research will also consider how pupils can
most effectively learn how to use such packages and how best to
organize access to equipment. Materials are being developed and

their use observed in a variety of schools by different age/ability groups.
Source of Grant: No funding
Date of Research: 1987 – continuing
KEYWORDS: *computer assisted instruction; mathematics; problem solving; secondary education; software*

8/1146

Department of Education
University Park, Nottingham NG7 2RD
0602 484848 ext 2423
Day, C.W. Dr
An evaluation of the management of delegated INSET finance (under LEA Training Grants Scheme) by primary schools in an East Midlands LEA
Abstract: A proportion of finance under LEATGS has been delegated to six primary schools who will make decisions concerning expenditure during the year in relation to INSET needs identified within their staff development plans. The purpose of the investigation is to ascertain the impact of this upon the management of the schools and the degrees to which staff development and training is enhanced by this measure. The results will inform LEA policy of financial delegation over the next few years. The evaluation will be divergent and will be carried out through interview, non-participant observation and questionnaire. The results will be reported to the commissioning LEA.
Source of Grant: Local Education Authority: £8,000
Date of Research: 1988-1989
KEYWORDS: *administration of education; expenditures; inservice education and training of teachers; local education authority; primary education; staff development*

8/1147

Department of Education
University Park, Nottingham NG7 2RD
0602 484848
Masterman, L. Dr
Critical responses to recent developments in advertising & marketing
Abstract: This research will attempt to: (1) describe the most up-to-date techniques used in marketing, especially via the mass media, e.g. product placement; political marketing; public relations; manufacturers and privatization of information; (2) explore the central issues and questions raised by these developments, especially in relation to work in schools (traditionally, teachers of English and media studies have taught about advertizing as it is more narrowly defined); (3) provide materials for use in schools – especially at GCSE & A levels, and in media studies.
Published Material: MASTERMAN, L. (1985). Teaching the media. London: Routledge (formerly Comedia).
Source of Grant: No funding
Date of Research: 1987-1989
KEYWORDS: *advertising; marketing; mass media; media studies; teaching aids*

8/1148

Department of Education
University Park, Nottingham NG7 2RD
0602 484848
Ascher, M.A. Mr; *Supervisor:* Thomas, K.C. Dr
Integration of statemented pupils with special educational needs into main-stream schools
Abstract: This research focuses on the working of section 2 of the Education Act, 1981 and how local education authorities and schools satisfy the three conditions for integration: firstly, that the child who is the subject of a statement of special educational need perceives the special educational provision he requires; secondly, that the education of the children with whom he will be educated is 'efficient'; and thirdly, that resources are used efficiently. The implicit motives of the act and the unintended consequences are discussed. Policies and practices of LEAs representative of differing sizes and local conditions will be examined and opinions of officer, school staff, children and parents elicited. Methods for integration of pupils with special needs are compared as are variations in what is normal provision and support services in different LEAs. It is hoped that the conclusions will be of use to LEAs when monitoring and modifying their practices.
Source of Grant: No funding
Date of Research: 1988 – continuing
KEYWORDS: *educational policy; integration; local education authority; special needs*

8/1149

Department of Education
University Park, Nottingham NG7 2RD
0602 484848
Miller, M. Ms; *Supervisor:* Thomas, J.E. Prof.; Gammage, P. Prof.
The role of education in professional career change
Abstract: Increasing numbers of professionals are returning to school to take another degree or certificate in order to change to a different occupational field. In times of economic uncertainty, increasing competition for jobs, and shifting values and life-styles, it is becoming more commonplace for people to pursue a second professional career. This study seeks to identify different ways in which professionals using higher education change careers; examine the role that education plays in facilitating or hindering career change; distinguish professional career changers from others with whom they may be compared eg. mature students; and examine how professionals learn while they are changing careers, in particular, the relevance of theory and practice. Data will be collected by means of interviews and case studies. Respondents will be accessed from a sample of professional programs at the University of Calgary (Alberta, Canada) and may be found taking second degrees, graduate degrees or continuing professional education certificates. An additional number who have completed the change in the past 3 years will also be included in the study.
Published Material: MILLER, M. (1989). 'Career change and continuing management education: some new insights', Canadian Journal of University Continuing Education.
Source of Grant: No funding
Date of Research: 1987-1989
KEYWORDS: *adult education; career change; higher education; professional personnel*

8/1150

Department of Education
University Park, Nottingham NG7 2RD
0602 484848
Hunter, S. Mrs; *Supervisor:* Strong, M. Mrs; Bagguley, P. Mr
A study of the Christian education of adults in the Church of England with particular reference to the role of the clergy and accredited lay ministry
Abstract: The research originated in a proposal from the Advisory Council for the Church's Ministry. It aims to identify the level of involvement and effectiveness of the Church of England's accredited ministers in the task of educating adults in the Christian faith. Models have been developed to help identify perceptions of Ministry and Christian growth/development among laity and accredited ministers and the subsequent effects of these perceptions on how the educational task itself is perceived. The inquiry will rely upon questionnaire and interview in order: (a) to test the perception outlined above; (b) to identify the use of the accredited Ministry in the present provision of adult Christian education in two dioceses in the Church of England. It may be possible as a result to make recommendations concerning the role of the accredited minsters in the Christian education of adults in the dioceses concerned and other dioceses may benefit. It needs to be stressed, however, that because of the autonomous nature of the dioceses in the Church of England the representative nature of the sample is limited and it would be unwise and undesirable to draw conclusions concerning other dioceses solely on the evidence contained in the samples.
Source of Grant: All Saint's Educational Trust: £1,000 per year plus fees
Date of Research: 1986-1990
KEYWORDS: *adult education; Christian education; church*

8/1151

Department of Education
University Park, Nottingham NG7 2RD
0602 484848
Hall, E. Dr
Outcomes of experimental training for teachers in personal and social education
Abstract: This research aims to evaluate the effects of one-week intensive courses on the behaviour of teachers and their students in schools. Four courses of 90 teachers have been followed up to six months after the courses. Questionnaire data showed changes in attitude from custodial to humanistic and from competitive to co-operative. Diary data revealed changes in the behaviour of both teachers and students which reflected a greater personal control

of behaviour. Small group training was seen to be the most effective form of training.
Source of Grant: No funding
Date of Research: 1983 – continuing
KEYWORDS: inservice education and training of teachers; course; teacher behaviour

8/1152

Department of Education
University Park, Nottingham NG7 2RD
0602 484848

Tsiane, B.R.D. Mr; *Supervisor:* Fielden, R.D.S. Mr; Graham, B. Mr

Adult education participation in rural development: case studies of village communities in Botswana

Abstract: Background research from many developing countries shows that 'top down' development policies tend to show poor returns in village communities. Active participation and continuance of projects are highlighted as problems. This research aims to focus on these two by using a participant observation and ethnographic interview to generate data for 3 case studies of different projects in different communities. The primary focus is on understanding influences on the learning process in informal education settings. The policy outcomes will be concerned with the training of intervention agents.
Source of Grant: British Council Overseas Development Agency
Date of Research: 1986-1990
KEYWORDS: adult education; Botswana; development policy

8/1153

Department of Education
University Park, Nottingham NG7 2RD
0602 484848

Beck, A.W. Dr

Abstracts of philosophy of education higher degree theses

Abstract: Compilation of abstracts of philosophy of education higher-degree theses from 1975. Main index used is BETI (British Educational Theses Index) A first volume of abstracts from research theses 1975-80 is now complete.
Source of Grant: No funding
Date of Research: 1985-1990
KEYWORDS: abstract; higher education; philosophy of education; thesis

8/1154

Department of Education
University Park, Nottingham NG7 2RD
0602 484848

Gibbons, M.J. Mr; *Supervisor:* Tolley, H. Mr

The analysis of geography examination syllabuses and question papers in the U.K. at sixteen plus

Abstract: In 1988 the geography examination at sixteen plus in England and Wales will be the new GCSE (General Certificate of Secondary Education) type and should be more uniform than its predecessors. The aim of this research is to develop a technique for analyzing these examination papers and syllabuses so that quantifiable comparison can be made between the different papers and between these papers and the former GCE (General Certificate of Education) and CSE (Certificate of Secondary Education) which were ended in 1987. The research has revealed that these examinations provide a picture or insight into the nature of the subject. Much work has been done on the Geography Curriculum and there are many attempts to define it or what it should be. But this study of the examination provides a different viewpoint of the nature of school geography on Britain revealed by the actual examination 16 year olds took in 1985 and 1988.
Source of Grant: Derbyshire County Council: fees and travel expenses
Date of Research: 1986-1989
KEYWORDS: curriculum development; examination; General Certificate of Secondary Education; geography; secondary education

8/1155

Department of Education
University Park, Nottingham NG7 2RD
0602 484848

Hunter, S. Mrs; *Supervisor:* Strong, M. Mrs; Bagguley, P. Mr

A study of the education of adults in the Church of England with particular reference to the role of the accredited ministry

Abstract: The research originated in a proposal form from the Advisory Council for the Church's Ministry. It aims to identify the level of involvement and effectiveness of the Church of England's accredited ministers in the task of educating adults in the Christian faith. Models have been developed to help identify perceptions of ministry and Christian growth/developement among laity and accredited ministers and the subsequent effects of these perceptions on how the educational task itself is perceived. The inquiry will rely upon questionnaire and interview in order (a) to test the perception outlined above (b) to identify the use of the accredited ministry in the present provision of adult education in two dioceses in the Church of England. It may be possible as a result to make recommendations concerning the role of the accredited ministers in the Christian education of adults, from dioceses concerned. Other dioceses may also benefit. It needs to be stressed, however, that because of the autonomous nature of dioceses in the Church of England the representative nature of the sample is limited and it would be unwise and undesirable to draw conclusions concerning other dioceses solely on the evidence contained in the samples.
Source of Grant: University Fees plus £1,000 per year
Date of Research: 1986-1990
KEYWORDS: adult education; christian education; church; religious education

8/1156

Department of Education
University Park, Nottingham NG7 2RD
0602 484848

Lotinga, C. Mr; *Supervisor:* Smith, D.M. Mr

Dehierarchicisation

Abstract: The aim is to understand how learning might be dispersed and the processes that are involved in such changes – both at the interactive and structural level. The theoretical element draws upon hermeneutic techniques (and deconstruction) to challenge the models of change-management currently in vogue. A version of Gidden's structuration theory, which uses the notion of duality of structure is deployed, since this is the best concrete attempt to come to grips with synthesis required as the upshot of the recent reflexive accent currently imported from the Continent and America under the general title of postmodernism. One of the benefits of this approach is that it is, syncretistic and eclectic, yet resists the temptation to simply project the methods onto the social world without seeing all approaches as essentially limited. Thus the research will be tailored to meet the demands of each section: ethnographic/narrative; structural/organizational; hermeneutic/deconstrutive; critical theoretical; and genealogical. In so far as there is a thesis, it is that management models have a need to be deconstructed if they are to effectively contribute to the active realization of educational management change in the current contingently historical context, the juncture of which we now find ourselves facing.
Source of Grant: Derbyshire County Council/LEA: fees (part-time)
Date of Research: 1986 – continuing
KEYWORDS: administration of education; educational innovation; structural analysis

8/1157

Department of Education
University Park, Nottingham NG7 2RD
0602 484848

Robinson, W. Mr; *Supervisor:* Stratford, B. Dr; Alman, P. Dr

Education and the mentally handicapped adult

Abstract: In response to the trend towards community based experiments in lifestyle situations for mentally handicapped people, this piece of research has been designed to test the rate of gain in terms of social skill acquisition on mentally handicapped people in varying living situations. Six groups were studied over two distinct twelve month periods and comparisons were made on the basis of gains and losses using standardized measures. Methods used including case studies of (I.Q.) Social Index Scores over the test periods results could be interpreted in relation to the environmental situation of the various sample groups. Initial results indicate that the social acquisition rate is increased in those people who live closest to normal social networks of communal activity.
Source of Grant: Nottingham Education Authority: expenses
Date of Research: 1984-1989
KEYWORDS: community education; integration; mentally handicapped; social skills

8/1158
Department of Education
University Park,
Nottingham NG7 2RD
0602 484848
Young, D.A. Mr; *Supervisor:* Bastiani, J. Dr; Saunders, M. Mr
Pupils, teachers and a changing English Curriculum 14-16
Abstract: The research is an exploration of how pupils perceive English 14-16 with a focus on how both pupils and teachers perceive and adapt to change in the curriculum. The aim of this research is to examine: (1) pupil perceptions of the English curriculum 14-16, with particular reference to their self-image as writers, their commitment to the subject, and their identification of the gains and benefits they have received from English courses during the last 2 years of compulsory schooling; (2) the versions of English which teachers make available to pupils and to investigate teacher perceptions, concerns and interests at a time when the public examination system is undergoing radical change. The approach is broadly ethnographic, and the sample is drawn from 3 Derbyshire secondary schools. To date, some 170 pupils have responded to a questionnaire, with a second data collection of a similar size planned. Early results indicate that pupils identify gain in 1 of 4 ways, with acquisition of skills seen as the major gain by most respondents.
Source of Grant: Derbyshire Local Education Authority (LEA): fees
Date of Research: 1986-1990
KEYWORDS: English language; curriculum; pupil; secondary education; teacher perception

8/1159
Department of Education
University Park,
Nottingham NG7 2RD
0602 484848
Lewis, D. Mr; *Supervisor:* Youngman, M.B. Dr; Day, C.W. Dr
Teacher appraisal: teachers' opinions on issues and schemes
Abstract: The aim of the research is to record teacher opinions about existing staff evaluations and appraisal schemes and the issues which emerge. The investigation is in two sections; (1) by postal questionnaire to schools which had been visited and whose staff were interviewed to establish the details of the questionnaire and (2) by case studies in six schools which provided different examples of types of staff evaluations and appraisal schemes. The questionnaire was sent to approximately 20 schools and more than 400 teachers replied. It was analyzed statistically to determine whether opinion was linked to any of the biographic detail provided. At this early stage, interesting links between opinions and the salary scale of the respondents were emerging. The case study schools provided an opportunity to assess the category into which the schools' scheme could be classified and to check opinions of a range of staff from the school. It is hoped to establish links between the two sections of the research which link opinions not only to the biographic detail from the questionnaire but also to the types of schemes studied in section two. The questionnaire will be improved and could be offered to institutions and bodies as an evaluation of opinion package.
Source of Grant: Local Education Authority
Date of Research: 1986-1990
KEYWORDS: evaluation; opinion; performance; teacher; teacher behaviour

8/1160
Department of Education
University Park,
Nottingham NG7 2RD
0602 484848
Selkirk, K.E. Dr
Pupil's appraisal of post-graduate certificate student-teachers
Abstract: The aim of this research is to study how well pupils in secondary schools can appraise their teachers, (in this case student teachers). Questionnaires will be used, with free-response section. The study consists of approximately 20 teachers and 400 pupils.
Published Material: 'Marks out of ten for the teacher', Times Educational Supplement, 15 November 1985, pp.23.
Source of Grant: No funding outside department
Date of Research: 1985-1989
KEYWORDS: assessment; pupil; secondary education; student teacher; teacher-pupil relation

8/1161
Department of Education
University Park, Nottingham NG7 2RD
0602 484848
James, I.K. Mr; *Supervisor:* Elsdon, K. Mr
Achieving and maintaining equilibrium in the system: the marketing of continuing education in Staffordshire
Abstract: This is an attempt to link personal efforts to promote and develop Lichfield College with an investigation to discover the most effective way for an LEA such as Staffordshire County Council to change its traditional provision to accommodate the variety of needs expressed within a system of 'lifelong' education and training, and to see if there is an alternative approach within the long neglected area of adult education; (1) Consideration of theories of marketing and their application to continuing education; (2) discussion and critical analysis of the variety of post-16 provision in Staffordshire: (a) looking at the 9 districts in the county (population/migration employers, existing post-16 provision, costs, student destinations etc.); (b) with continuing reference to existing organizations, a review of alternative means of provision which perhaps takes greater account of the lifelong nature of education could be investigated and evaluated; (3) it is likely that changes may be required to bring about more effective use of resources and this requires a marketing strategy which could be recommended to the Local Education Authority.
Source of Grant: Staffordshire County Council: tuition fees and travelling expenses
Date of Research: 1987 – continuing
KEYWORDS: adult education; continuing education; life-long education; local education authority; marketing

8/1162
Department of Education
University Park, Nottingham NG7 2RD
0602 484848
Steele, J. Mr; *Supervisor:* Stratford, B. Dr
Investigation into the prevalence of Down's syndrome
Abstract: Before establishing specialist provision (either educational, medical or social service) for any group, an accurate description of that population is needed. Hence this study aims: (i) to establish the number of people with D.S.(Down's syndrome) living in Great Britain, together with an age and sex breakdown of that population, and where possible a description of residence and educational/day service provision; (ii) to examine the population for any trends or clustering in either time or geographical location; (iii) to explain the biological nature of D.S. and examine factors that may affect the D.S. poulation; making some estimation of how this population may be affected in the future; (iv) to compare the situation in Britain with that reported from other cultures. 120 social service or health authority registers will be contacted throughout Britain, and information will be gathered from those that list D.S. separately, the method and operation of registers will be considered, and results will be statistically analyzed.
Published Material: STRATFORD, B. & STEELE, J. (1985). 'Incidence and Prevalence of Down's syndrome – A Discussion and Report', Journal of Mental Deficiency Research, Vol 29, pp.95-107.; STRATFORD, B., STEELE, J. & ALBERTINI, G. (1988). 'Down's syndrome and ionizing radiation – possible effects of ionizing radiation on the incidence and prevalence of Down's syndrome', Rivista di Neuroscience Pediatriche (Journal of Pediative Neuroscience), Vol 4, pp.129-143.
Source of Grant: Derbyshire County Council: tuition fees (approx. £400 per annum) plus travelling expenses
Date of Research: 1985-1989
KEYWORDS: Down's syndrome; educational provision; population; social service

8/1163
Department of Education
University Park, Nottingham NG7 2RD
0602 484848
Howard, E.M. Ms; *Supervisor:* Stratford, B. Dr
A functional assessment of visual perception for pre-school children
Abstract: The project aims to design a visual perception assessment for pre-school children (aged 3-4 years old). Twenty one short subtests utilize three-dimensional play materials where possible to maintain the interest and involvement of young children. Requirements for comprehension of verbal instructions are minimised, as is the necessity for accurate movement response. Normative data is being obtained on 100 children, and 20 non-English speakers. Reliabil-

ity studies to date appear satisfactory. Validation was established by comparison with existing measures of visual perception.
Source of Grant: Lancashire County Council; part payment of university fees: £80 National Council for Special Education: equipment
Date of Research: 1983-1989
KEYWORDS: assessment; pre-school child; visual perception

8/1164
Department of Education
University Park, Nottingham NG7 2RD
0602 484848
Bell, S. Ms; Roussou, M. Dr; *Supervisor:* Gammage, P. Prof.
Linguistic diversity in the primary school
Abstract: The aim of the project has been to develop the initial and inservice education of primary school teachers in the field of linguistic diversity. Over the past three years, the project, together with five LEAs, has organized a number of pilot courses which explored strategies for supporting linguistic development and awareness. Consideration was given to both classroom approaches and to the current debate on linguistic diversity. This phase of the project has now been completed and evaluated and reports are available from the Project Office. The fourth year has a dual purpose. Firstly, it aims to look at a small number of the schools which were involved with the pilot courses in the different LEAs and undertake a systematic follow-up study. This study will focus particularly on the factors which facilitate or constrain change at both an individual and institutional level. Secondly, using the experience and evaluation of previous courses, new courses will be prepared in collaboration with five different LEAs. These courses will take account of the changing context of the educational system, in particular that of the Education Reform Act and the National Curriculum. Thirdly, in conjunction with Northampton LEA, a video tape and materials on linguistic diversity is being prepared, entitled 'Dissertation through Northamptonshire LEA'.
Published Material: A list of publications is available from the project office.
Source of Grant: European Commission: £87,000
Date of Research: 1986 – continuing
KEYWORDS: bi-lingualism; inservice education and training of teachers; language; multicultural education; primary education; teacher education

8/1165
Department of Psychology
University Park, Nottingham NG7 2RD
0602 506101
Newson, E.A. Dr
Research into autism
Abstract: The interventions to be studied are those which are explicitly provided for children perceived as autistic. They will include pre-school programmes of any kind, whether described in terms of behaviour, social development, languages, play etc; school-age programmes, whether provided in classroom, residential unit or home; and programmes for young adults, wherever or of whatever type may be found. Both privately and publicly funded facilities will be included and special provision in mainstream settings will be looked at.
Source of Grant: Department of Education & Science/Department of Health & Social Security: £50000
Date of Research: 1987-1989
KEYWORDS: autism; special education

8/1166
Department of Psychology
University Park, Nottingham NG7 2RD
0602 484848
Underwood, G. Dr
Cognitive processes in reading and spelling
Abstract: The aim of the project is to identify the cognitive processes which enable us to read and spell – those processes through which written information must be transformed by the competent reader to reach understanding. Dependent measures of reading speed and accuracy are observed as a function of controlled variables. Measures are used to observe eye movements also. Experiments have been performed on skilled adult readers, young readers and the latter with reading difficulties. Recognition of isolated words and the comprehension of coherent text have been investigated. The

role of attention in recognition concerning isolated words has been studied and also the role of alternative processing routes (graphemic/phonological) by manipulating the orthographic regularity of the words presented. The role of regularity in spelling has also been investigated. Findings suggest that for children of 10+ and adults, attention is not essential for isolated word recognition but is for measuring of sentences. Good and poor readers do not differ in their ability to recognize the meanings of isolated words so much as in their ability to use word meanings after recognition. Individual differences in reading ability are more associated with post-recognition processes such as those involved in the use of working memory than with initial encoding. One of the researchers' interests is in the patterns of eye movements (saccades, regressive saccades and fixation durations) made by skilled readers who are comprehending sentences, with specific interest in the cognitive mechanisms of eye guidance.
Published Material: a list of publications is available from the researchers on request
Source of Grant: (1979-82) Medical Research Council: £22,724 (1982-84) Science and Engineering Research Council: £34,459 (1986-87) Medical Research Council
Date of Research: 1979 – continuing
KEYWORDS: cognitive process; comprehension; reading; spelling; word recognition

8/1167
Department of Psychology
University Park, Nottingham NG7 2RD
0602 484848
Dodds, A.G. Mr; Beggs, A.W.D. Mr; Gaskell, A.; Hellawell, D.; *Supervisor:* Howarth, C.I. Prof.
The mobility of blind and visually impaired persons
Abstract: The Unit publishes its work in the national and international journals. Principal interests are investigation of the assessment of visual handicap and how trainers are taught to teach mobility of visually impaired people. Work has been done on electronic aids for the blind and also on the use of (tactile) maps.
Published Material: CLARK-CARTER, D., HEYES, A.D. & HOWARTH, C.I. (1986). 'The efficiency and walking speed of visually impaired people', Ergonomics, Vol 29, No 6, pp.779-789.; BEGGS, W.D.A. (1986). 'Mobile training today – I: dealing with the real world', British Journal of Visual Impairment, Vol 4, No 3, pp.87-89.; HEYES, A.D. (1984). 'The Sonic Pathfinder – a new electronic travel aid', Journal of Visual Impairment and Blindness, Vol 78, No 5, pp.200-202. A complete list of publications is available from the B.M.R.U.
Source of Grant: Department of Health and Social Security: £100,000 per annum approximately
Date of Research: 1960 – continuing
KEYWORDS: blind; trainer; training method; visual handicap

8/1168
Department of Sociology
University Park, Nottingham NG7 2RD
0602 484848
Evetts, J. Mrs
Women in primary teaching
Abstract: How the detail of individuals life histories and career biographies can contribute to educational understanding about women primary teachers and to sociological understanding about women and career. Using career history interviews from a sample of twenty-five married women primary and infant headteachers, the research has considered what were for the women themselves, the external structural conditions and the characteristics of the labour market for primary teachers. The research has also considered what strategies women have devised to manage and negotiate such contexts. The research has enabled me to argue and demonstrate that career histories can illustrate both structural conditions in particular labour markets and the strategies of individuals developing careers.
Published Material: EVETTS, J. 'Primary teachers careers: the contexts of expansion and contraction', Cambridge Journal of Education'. (forthcoming); EVETTS, J. (1989b). 'Married Women and Career', International Journal of Qualitative Studies in Education, Vol 2, No 2, pp.89-105.; A complete list of publications is available from the researcher.
Source of Grant: No funding
Date of Research: 1985-1990
KEYWORDS: career ladders; primary education; woman teacher; women's employment

8/1169
Department of Sociology
University Park,
Nottingham NG7 2RD
0602 484848
Harris, S. Miss; *Supervisor:* Lawrence, D. Dr
The work and roles of careers officers and careers teachers in a Midlands area
Abstract: An examination of the occupational roles of careers officers and careers teachers and the changing pattern of careers work and careers education in two contrasting areas of a Midlands county. A major consideration will be the impact of high youth unemployment and the development of alternatives to unemployment on both groups. A variety of research methods are being employed including: unstructured and semi-structured interviews with key careers officers in the service concerned; structured interviews with all careers officers in the selected areas; observations of the interaction between selected teams of careers officers and the associated careers teachers; unstructured and semi-structured interviews with those responsible for providing careers education in the selected schools and structured interviews with the careers teachers.
Source of Grant: Nottingham University Research Fund: £8,516
Date of Research: 1985-1990
KEYWORDS: *careers guidance; careers service; occupational choice; youth unemployment*

8/1170
School of Education
Department of Adult Education,
University Park,
Nottingham NG7 2RD
0602 484848
Watanabe, Y. Mrs; *Supervisor:* Elsdon, K.T. Mr
The training of adult educators in the U.K. (United Kingdom) and its implications for policy development in Japan
Abstract: This research is part of a project based at the University of Ochanomizu, Tokyo. The context of the UK-based part of the project is the Japanese Government's intention to make considerable changes in the present structure of adult and continuing education, including potential developments in the education and training of part and full-time staff engaged in it. The project is intended to make a study of in-service and (as far as it exists) pre-service training for such staff in the UK (including both fieldwork and the study and analysis of relevant literature), to produce a critical description and to identify any implications which British experience may have for future policy in Japan.
Source of Grant: No funding
Date of Research: 1989-1990
KEYWORDS: *adult education; Japan; teacher education*

8/1171
School of Education
University Park,
Nottingham NG7 2RD
0602 484848 ext 3639
Youngman, M.B. Dr
Role expectations of research supervisors and students
Abstract: The research aims to produce a detailed picture of the actual practices of research supervisors and students in the social sciences. It employs a checklist survey approach which has already been successfully used for teachers, engineers and nurses. A national sample will be approached covering most areas of social science research degree work in universities. The outcome will be a detailed specification of actual experiences of the sample members. In addition to simple frequency counts, the analysis will use cluster analysis to define research activities. Differences in the incidences of these activities will be related to sample characteristics such as role, subject area, experience and departmental size. Since this is largely an exploratory study, we anticipate developing it later on a wider scale, and incorporating interviews and visits to elaborate issues emerging. Once the formal report is complete general publications in the form of articles will br produced.
Source of Grant: ESRC (Economic and Social Research Council): £5871
Date of Research: 1989-1989
KEYWORDS: *academic degree; post graduate study; research; social sciences*

8/1172
School of Education
University Park, Nottingham NG7 2RD
0602 484848
Hay. D, Dr
Religious experience and education project
Abstract: The aim of the programme is to research and develop an educationally responsible method of helping pupils to understand the experiential dimension of religion. The end product is a handbook for teachers, to be published in March 1990. The materials have been developed and tested in a large number of primary schools in the East Midlands and North East England, with the aid of teacher volunteers.
Published Material: HAY, D. (1985). 'Suspicion of the spiritual: teaching religious education in a world of secular experience', British Journal of Religious Education, Vol 7, No 3, Summer, pp.140-147.; HAY, D. (1990). 'The bearing of empirical studies of religious experience on education', Research Papers in Education, Vol 5, No 1 March 1990, pp.3-29.; HAMMOND, J. & HAY, D. et al (1990). New methods in religious education teaching: an experiential approach. London: Oliver & Boyd/Longmans.; HAY, D. (1990). Religious experience today: studying the facts. London: Mowbray.
Source of Grant: Dulverton Trust Halley Stewart Trust John Paul Trust Hibbert Trust Alister Hardy Research Centre, Oxford: jointly £100,000
Date of Research: 1985-1990
KEYWORDS: *primary education; religious education*

8/1173
School of Education
University Park, Nottingham NG7 2RD
0602 484848
Gammage, P. Prof.
Comparative study of early childhood education in Alberta and British Columbia
Abstract: An attempt to examine the context of movements towards more individualized learning in the provision of schooling (up to age nine) in Western Canada. This includes the movements away from BASAL Readers (primers) and the disenchantment with school achievement tests. The opinions of a small sample of principals, researchers and teacher trainers is sought from selected places in Alberta and British Columbia, together with some discussion with members of the Teacher Associations. This latter to include some elements of expected changes in inservice provision for teachers as the Provinces begin to emerge from a long period of fairly centralised and prescribed curricula. It is hoped to place this alongside some of the changes in British primary curricula in order to highlight what appear to be changing and possibly opposite emerging ideologies.
Source of Grant: No funding
Date of Research: 1990 – continuing
KEYWORDS: *Canada; curriculum development; early childhood education; primary education*

8/1174
School of Education
University Park, Nottingham NG7 2RD
0602 484848
Coles, M.J. Mr; *Supervisor:* Gammage, P. Prof.
Teaching effective thinking through dialogical enquiry in the primary classroom
Abstract: This research will attempt to develop a model of dialogical inquiry appropriate for primary schools, which has the possibility of encouraging in young children a disposition as well as an ability to think critically. the model will be built from a critical appraisal of British 'teaching thinking' programmes as they occur in primary schools, an examination of appropriate theories and concepts, and an assessment of critical discussion in primary schools using the approach of 'illuminative evaluation'.
Published Material: COLES, M.J. (1986). 'Teaching children to think', Primary Education Review, No 27.; COLES, M.J. (1987). 'No talking in class', The Journal of the National Association of Primary Education, Spring.; COLES, M.J. (1987). 'Critical children: philosophy for the young', Cognito, Vol 1, No 2.; COLES, M.J. & ROBINSON, W. (Eds). (1989). Teaching and thinking: a survey of programmes, Bristol: Bristol Classical Press (in press).
Source of Grant: No funding
Date of Research: 1989 – continuing

KEYWORDS: *dialogue; primary school; teaching technique; thinking*

8/1175

School of Education
University Park,
Nottingham NG7 2RD
0602 484848
Shipstone, D.M. Dr

TVEI (Technical and Vocational Education Initiative) in initial teacher training

Abstract: This research and development project has a substantial staff development component and focuses upon developments that have taken place within education in the 14-18 age range through the impetus provided by the TVEI (Technical and Vocational Education Initiative). Many school of education lecturers will engage in research studies within 5 broad themes: new technology learning; personal and social education, guidance and profiting; industry links and work experience; equal opportunities. Publications will take the form of workshop materials and case studies to be used on initial and in-service training courses, research papers and monographs dealing with aspects of education which have been particularly influenced by TVEI.
Source of Grant: The Training Agency: £100000
Date of Research: 1989 – continuing
KEYWORDS: *secondary education; teacher education; Technical and Vocational Education Initiative*

8/1176

School of Education
University Park,
Nottingham NG7 2RD
0602 484848
Harrison, C. Dr; Hay, D. Dr

An improved method of identifying technical literacy in potential employees

Abstract: The aim of the project is to pilot and produce a standardized computer assisted technical literacy profile which will provide a more valid method of developing and predicting technical literacy than non-computer-based methods currently available. The profile will be developed with the use of Hypercard software for the Apple-Mackintosh computer.
Source of Grant: Nottingham University Research Fund: £7,837
Date of Research: 1989 – continuing
KEYWORDS: *computer-assisted instruction; literacy; profile; technical education*

8/1177

School of Education
University Park,
Nottingham NG7 2RD
0602 623773 ext 2267
Smith, D.M. Mr

Management of scientific and technological education. 1940' and 1980's

Abstract: The study is a comparative analysis of power relations between agencies managing science and technological education during two periods of significant developments – 1940's and 1980's. It is a socio-historical examination based on current published material and records available at the public records office. The purpose of the study is to reveal how power relations between agencies are an outcome of conditions, intentions and contingencies.
Published Material: SMITH, D.M. (1981). 'The management of state bursaries for science education 1941-1947: a case study of centre government management in education', In: RIBBINS, P. & THOMAS, h. (Eds). Research in Educational Management and Administration, Birmingham: British Educational Management and Administration Society.; SMITH, D.M. (1989). 'Unintended transformations of control over education: a process of structuring', British Journal of Sociology of Education, Vol 10, No 2, 1989, pp.175-193.; SMITH, D.M. (1989). 'Policy making. unintended consequences and transformative change in education', In; SARAN, N.R. & TRAFFORD, V. (Eds). Research in Education Management and Policy. Lewes: Falmer Press.
Source of Grant: Leverhulme Trust: £1000
Date of Research: 1982 – continuing
KEYWORDS: *administration of education; educational policy; history of education; science education; technology*

8/1178

School of Education
University Park, Nottingham NG7 2RD
0602 484848
Yapp, B.G. Mr; *Supervisor:* Beck, A.W. Dr

Utilitarianism and education

Abstract: Philosophical investigation into Utilitarianism and education, taking in both nineteenth-century philosophers and twentieth-century philosophers of education (principally Robin Barrow)
Published Material: YAPP, B.G. (1989). 'Descriptions and evaluations', Journal of Philosophy of Education, (forthcoming).
Source of Grant: No funding
Date of Research: 1986-1990
KEYWORDS: *history of education; philosopy; philosophy of education*

8/1179

School of Education
University Park
Nottingham NG7 2RD
Southwood House School,
Portway, Holbrook, Derby DE5 0TE
0332 880208
Wood, G.A. Mr; *Supervisor:* Jotham, R. Dr; Dolan, T. Mr

Information technology and the learning needs of emotionally and behaviourally disturbed children

Abstract: The research will test the hypothesis that the learning inhibiting behaviours (classroom conformity, task orientation, acceptance of authority, peer relationships, emotional control, self worth, self responsibility and problem solving) emitted by the emotionally disturbed child can be significantly reduced by the use of CAL/IT (computer-assisted learning information technology) providing the opportunity for a significant improvement in learning. It will be necessary: (1) to measure and record the child's learning inhibiting behaviours in the presence and absence of CAL/IT; (2) to measure and record the child's attainments and progress in the presence and absence of CAL/IT; (3) to ascertain reasons for this progress/lack of progress in terms of the child's academic abilities, personality and attitude to CAL/IT, of the presentation model of the learning task, and of the learning environment of the hardware.
Source of Grant: Derbyshire County Council expenses 1989/90 only
Date of Research: 1988 – continuing
KEYWORDS: *computer-assisted instruction; emotional disorder; information technology; learning difficulty*

8/1180

School of Education
University Park, Nottingham NG7 2RD
0602 484848 ext 2423
Day, C.W. Dr

Evaluating inservice: effects of different models on teachers' thinking and practice

Abstract: This is a research project which aims to determine how teachers' professional development is affected through different planned inservice events. Methods of data collection include interview, documentary analysis, non-participant observation. The work is to be carried out in four primary schools in Derbyshire. The results will be a report for the sponsoring body and paper for conference on teachers' thinking and practice.
Source of Grant: Derbyshire County Council: £20000
Date of Research: 1989-1990
KEYWORDS: *inservice education and training of teachers; primary education; professional development; teacher behaviour*

8/1181

School of Education
Department of Adult Education,
University Park, Nottingham NG7 2RD
0602 484848 ext 2289
Elsdon, K.T. Prof.

The educational impact of local voluntary organizations on their catchment areas

Abstract: The importance of local voluntary organizations to the quality of life of local communities is generally acknowledged, but lacks the support of systematic research evidence. The project aims to undertake a series of case studies to investigate the nature, the means and the effects of the impact made, particularly in adult education, by what is intended to build up to a representative sample

of local voluntary organizations. It is hoped thus to make a start on producing a corpus of evidence from which conclusions may be drawn to support both theory and practice. The project is expected to continue over a number of years.
Published Material: ELSDON, K.T. (1989). 'Confusion confounded: or, adult education and ideas of community'. In: HAKE, B.J. & MORGAN, W.J. (Eds). Adult education, public information and ideology. Nottingham: Nottingham University, Department of Adult Education.
Source of Grant: No funding
Date of Research: 1989 – continuing
KEYWORDS: adult education; community development; voluntary organization

Open University

8/1182
Institute of Educational Technology,
Walton Hall, Milton Keynes MK7 6AA
0908 274066
Field, J.G. Dr
Tuition and counselling adults: a system for staff development
Abstract: A tuition and counselling system involving 5000 staff for adults with mixed or no qualifications enrolled in distance education, was devised in the seventies. Since then types of course, of students and of communication have proliferated. Using survey, other data and qualitative information to decide what functions need to be sustained, enhanced, integrated, pruned or devised according to different priorities.
Source of Grant: No funding
Date of Research: 1989-1990
KEYWORDS: adult education; counselling; distance study; educationl guidance; Open University; staff development

8/1183
Institute of Educational Technology,
Walton hall, Milton Keynes MK7 6AA
0908 274066
Kirkup, G. Ms; Kirkwood, A. Mr; Jones, A. Dr
An evaluation of home computers in adult distance education
Abstract: An investigation of the effects of compulsory use of a personal computer by students studying particular courses in the undergraduate programme of the Open University. Students studying are sampled during their studies in 1989-1989-1990. Issues of interest: access and availability of equipment; costs; the effect of introducing home based computing on study habits, content difficulty; impact on family of computer in home. Teaching staff are also researched to discover how their contact with students is affected and their teaching load. Research methods included survey questionnaires at points in the year; interviews; self completion journals. Each survey involves – 250 students (500-750 per course per year); interviews – 20 per course per year.
Published Material: KIRKWOOD, A. (1988). 'Computers in distance education: student access and issues of openness', Open Learning, Vol 3, No 3, November.; KIRKUP, G. (1989). 'Equal opportunities and computing at the Open University', Open Learning, Vol 4, No 1, February. A complete list of publications is available from the researcher.
Source of Grant: Open University
Date of Research: 1988 – continuing
KEYWORDS: computer uses in education; microcomputers; Open University

8/1184
Institute of Educational Technology,
Walton Hall, Milton Keynes MK7 6AA
0908 274066
Kirkup, G. Ms
The effect on women students of the use of computers in distance education
Abstract: The Open University has begun a programme where many courses will require a student to have access to a personal computer. The research has been monitoring the different effects this is having on male and female students. From 1988 a large sample of students has been surveyed 700+, 1000+ will be surveyed in 1989 and similar for 1990. A small number have been interviewed and some keep journals. The data suggests that women have differ-

ent preferred learning styles from men, and their styles as well as their insecurity with the equipment make their learning problems greater. Domestic arrangements also make it more difficult for them to use equipment at home. The research hopes to suggest strategies which will be appropriate to women students in particular.
Published Material: KIRKUP, K. (1989). 'Equal opportunities and computing in the Open University', Open Learning, February 1989.
Source of Grant: No funding
Date of Research: 1986 – continuing
KEYWORDS: computer; distance study; gender equality; higher education; learning strategy; Open University; sex difference

8/1185
Institute of Educational Technology,
Walton Hall, Milton Keynes MK7 6AA
0908 274066
Nicodemus, R.B. Dr
Team building and group relations
Abstract: Reasearch on the experience of working in groups in the Open University was initiated in the Open University IET (Institute of Educational Technology) in 1978 with a one year contract with consultants from the Tavistock Institute of Human Relations. Dr R. Nicodemus, a member of IET, subsequently undertook training appropriate to the Tavistock approach to consultancy or group relations training which is based on a psychodynamic model. This internal capacity for consultancy has been in continuous development since 1981 with Dr Nicodemus' work with many different groups of academic staff as well as individuals. In additon to a parallel programme of workshops and seminars based in IET, consultancy on group processes has been extended to clients outside the Open University such as a mental health team and a mental handicap team in the National Health Service.
Published Material: NICODEMUS, R.B. (1985). 'Externalized anxieties in summer schools and what they reflect about institutional integration', Sociological Review, Vol 33, No 1, pp.91-105.; NICODEMUS, R.B. (1984). 'Lessons from a course team', Teaching at a Distance, Vol 25, pp.33-39.; NICODEMUS. R.B. (1983). 'Geologists map course production', Journal of Geography in Higher Education, Vol 7, No 2, pp.201-203.; LAWRENCE, W.G. (1979). The Open University. TIHR Doc. 2T-271
Source of Grant: No funding
Date of Research: 1979 – continuing
KEYWORDS: group behaviour; group dynamics; interpersonal relations; teamwork; training

8/1186
Institute of Educational Technology,
Walton Hall, Milton Keynes MK7 6AA
0908 274066
Woodley, A. Mr
Dormant students: Open University undergraduates who appear not to be returning to complete a Degree
Abstract: The aim is to find aout why many O.U. (Open University) undergraduates gain a number of credits and then cease studying. Is it because they have met their aims, because they have been prevented from continuing, or because they have transferred elsewhere? A pilot study involving 2400 dormant students will test out the appropriate methodology for surveying a group which are notoriously difficult to locate.
Source of Grant: Open University
Date of Research: 1989-1990
KEYWORDS: adult student; dropout; dropout research; Open University; student; student wastage; wastage

8/1187
Institute of Educational Technology,
Walton Hall, Milton Keynes MK7 6AA
0908 274066
Peberdy, A.S. Ms; *Supervisor:* Calder, J. Dr; Brechin, A. Ms
Evaluation of the Open University course, mental handicap: patterns for living
Abstract: In 1986 the Open University in collaboration with MENCAP launched a new, distance-learning, course designed for anyone who has direct contact with people with learning difficulties due to a mental handicap. Its main aim was to promote positive change in the lives of people with learning difficulties by reaching and influencing large numbers of care staff, parents and volunteers. To provide those involved in the training of people in the front-line of community care policies information and insight into the operation and outcomes of the course. The two-year enquiry

has combined both qualitative and quantitative methods, including a postal survey of over 1,000 students, in depth interviews and group observation. Within its first two years, the course was used by over 16,000: about 50 per cent were care staff; 20 per cent parents; and 15 per cent volunteers. The main gains reported by the students were increased insight into the needs and feelings of people with a mental handicap, their families and others working in this field. They also spoke of discovering an ability to study, increased self-confidence and a greater readiness to listen to people with a mental handicap.
Published Material: PEBERDY, A. (1989). Evaluation of the Open University course, mental handicap: patterns for living. London: Health Education Authority.
Source of Grant: Health Education Authority: £41,000
Date of Research: 1986-1989
KEYWORDS: distance study; Health Service personnel; mentally handicapped; Open University; special education; support staff

8/1188

Institute of Educational Technology,
Walton Hall, Milton Keynes MK7 6AA
0908 274066
Womphrey, R. Mr; Calder, J. Dr
Annual survey of new Open University courses
Abstract: The Open University, being a distance-teaching institution, mailed self-completion surveys which are essential to acquaint the university with the reactions of students to course materials and services. A survey of all undergraduate courses in first presentation is carried out at the end of the courses. The samples vary from 200-800 undergraduates who all receive a mailed self-completion survey report form, followed by two reminders. The survey results assist the allocation of resources to courses, and the improvement of the design of courses.
Source of Grant: No funding
Date of Research: 1989-1990
KEYWORDS: course evaluation; distance study; evaluation; Open University; student reaction; survey

8/1189

Institute of Educational Technology,
Walton Hall, Milton Keynes MK7 6AA
0908 274066
Lockwood, F.G. Mr; *Supervisor:* Laurillard, D. Dr; Morgan, A. Dr
Activities in distance learning texts
Abstract: Survey items in a routine evaluation of an O.U.(Open University) course revealed that students did not do the activities in the text but they found them very helpful. The present study was mounted to investigate these provisional findings. Small scale qualitative research, based on individual interviews, was conducted with an increasing number of O.U. students and O.U. authors. Investigation centred upon one O.U. course and those authors and students associated with it. The investigation focused on one O.U. teaching text, involved four O.U. authors and 64 students who studied that text. The sample of students was representative of the course population. The initial phases of the investgation used unstructured/focused interviews. Later phases combined replies on self recorded audio tape and traditional questionnaires. Final data provided by 23 interviews, 16 self recorded tapes, 25 questionnaires. The findings revealed a mismatch between authors assumptions and expectations and student perception and use of activities in distance learning texts. Students were able to identify the potential benefits of activities but had to balance these against the costs that their study incurred. A major cost was consumed study time. Others were identified along three continua with poles described as deference – confidence, degradation – completion, effective and efficient – guilt and inadequacy. It is believed that the findings have significance for the authors of distance learning texts.
Source of Grant: Institute of Educational Technology
Date of Research: 1983-1990
KEYWORDS: autoinstructional aid; distance study; evaluation; Open University; programmed text; textbook evaluation

8/1190

Walton Hall, Milton Keynes MK7 6AA
0908 274066
Grant, J. Dr; Gale, R. Dr
Development of guidelines for change in postgraduate and continuing medical education
Abstract: Change in postgraduate and continuing medical educa-

tion has been the subject of recommendations but these have met only with sporadic and unpredicatable implementation. Such recommendations have never been accompanied by a strategy for implementation of the new order. The aim of the research project is to review the experience of change in post-basic medical education and meld this with other experience and theories of change management to produce guidelines for change in medical education. The method involves semi-structured interviews with initiators and implementers of change in medical education at national, regional, district and local levels in hospitals and community setting. Content analysis reveals active categories of behaviour, cultural factors and tactical options. A model of change is devised and annotated with notes for its use.
Published Material: GRANT, J. & GALE, R. (1989). 'Changing medical education', Medical Education, No 23, pp.252-257.; GRANT, J. & GALE, R. (1990). 'Leading educational change', Journal of Course Organisers, in press.
Source of Grant: Leverhulme Trust: £26,000
Date of Research: 1989-1990
KEYWORDS: education; Health Service personnel; life-long education; medical education; post-graduate study

8/1191

Walton Hall, Milton Keynes MK7 6AA
0908 274066
Grant, J. Dr; Marsden, P. Dr
A study of service commitments of Senior House Officers in South East Thames Regional Health Authority: The integration of a programme of postgraduate training
Abstract: A previous survey in South East Thames Regional Health Authority had shown that junior hospital doctors (Senior House Officers) in medicine and related subspecialties had little training, either formal or informal. The study made a series of recommendations for improvement. The present study is aimed at assessing the service conditions of Senior House Officers in medicine and accident and emergency and designing a formal training programme, along the lines of the recommendations, within the limits of service and within current budgets. Hypothetical training schemes will be developed in two contrasting locations: firstly in a relatively well-staffed hospital; and secondly in a relatively poorly staffed hospital. The hypothetical training schemes will be assessed for their feasibility in all departments of medicine and accident and emergency in the Region.
Source of Grant: Department of Health
Date of Research: 1989-1990
KEYWORDS: doctor; education; Health Service personnel; hospital; medical education; training programme

8/1192

Institute of Educational Technology,
Walton Hall, Milton Keynes MK7 6AA
0908 274066
Chambers, E.A. Ms; Durbridge, N. Ms
Distance education and the Humanities
Abstract: Investigation of all aspects of adult students' encounters with distance courses in the Humanities. To date most research has been done into beginning students (i.e. those taking an interdisciplinary Foundation course) and those studying philosophy and music. The research covers: students' expectations of and attitudes to studying; difficulty encountered in studying text, TV, radio, audio-cassette; students' acquisition of study skills; the particular problems facing students new to the study of philosophy (and, in 1990, literature, art history, music and history). The methods used are: survey questionnaires, large and small samples; interviews, small samples; institutional data (e.g. drop out, exam pass rates etc.).
Published Material: CHAMBERS, E.A. (1984). 'A project component in architectural history'. In: HENDERSON, E. & NATHENSON, M. (Eds) Independent learning in higher education. Englewood Cliffs, New Jersey: Prentice-Hall Inc.; CHAMBERS, E.A. & DURBRIDGE, N. (1987). 'Preparing for the examination', A102 An Arts Foundation Course, Units 31-32, Open University Press.; A complete list of publications is available from the researcher
Source of Grant: Open University
Date of Research: 1975 – continuing
KEYWORDS: adult education; distance study; Humanities; Open University

8/1193

Institute of Educational Technology,
Walton Hall, Milton Keynes MK7 6AA
0908 274066
Burt, G.J. Mr

The curriculum as culture and ideology

Abstract: According to common-sense view, education is about individual people "learning" ideas and skills. It is an apolitical activity, which meets the needs of individuals and of society as a whole. The aim of the curriculum as culture and ideology project is to challenge this view. Education is not about people learning ideas and skills: it is about cultural ideas and practices taking possession of people. Education then is simply one of a number of arenas in which different cultures and ideologies with differential powers seek to promote themselves, and hence come into conflict. Cultures seek to promote themselves in every sphere of society. Hence cultures demand education about every social sphere. The aim of the research project is to study educational provision with a view to identifying the cultural and ideological promotions involved. Currently under study are the areas of educational technology, educational computing, mathematics and technology education, management education and community education. Teaching materials in these areas involve cultural and ideological promotion relating to issues of gender, class, ethnicity, individualism, technicism and militarism. Proposals for how education might be redesigned to take account of this critique are also being developed.
Published Material: BURT, G.J. (1988). 'Education as challenge and emancipation', Open Learning, Vol 3, No 2, pp.51-52.; A complete list of publications is available from the researcher
Source of Grant: No funding
Date of Research: 1988 – continuing
KEYWORDS: *cultural influences; culture; ideology; philosophy of education; sociology of education*

8/1194

Institute of Educational Technology,
Walton Hall, Milton Keynes MK7 6AA
0908 274066
Whalley, P. Dr

Developing measures of argument integration for the evaluation of hyper-text: the cued recall method

Abstract: The general pupose of this study is to develop a methodology suited to the study of the memory processes of organization and reconstruction that will take place when studying with the hypertext medium. A significant problem that has to be overcome in any such study of text comprehension, is that of developing a non-intrusive measure of conceptual understanding and relatedness. The methodology should also be able to evaluate the role of the active learner making relational inferences between topics, as opposed to merely logical inferences within topics. A further unresolved issue in this area of study is that it is often not possible to determine whether the measured effects are 'input' or an 'output' phenomena; whether they occur as a consequence of the way that the students impose some organization on the material as they study, or because of the way that they subsequently obtain access to the concepts as they write an essay or answer questions. It appears reasonable that methodologies such as the 'cued-recall' paradigm, which requires no planned thought by the subject, are likley to prove the least intrusive of measures. Results thus far indicate that the cued-recall methodology can provide an effective measure of concept relatedness at the level of topic and arugument understanding. This methodology appears to have immediate practical significance in the evaluation of the educational worth of the hypertext media.
Source of Grant: No funding
Date of Research: 1987 – continuing
KEYWORDS: *autoinstructional aid; automatic teaching; computer assisted instruction; educational technology; learning process; teaching machine*

8/1195

Institute of Educational Technology,
Walton Hall, Milton Keynes MK7 6AA
0908 274066
Zand, H. Dr; Burt, G.J. Mr

Affects and learning mathematics

Abstract: Learners of mathematics experience a variety of emotions such as anxiety, raised/lowered self image, depression, elation, etc. In this project, the researchers have been studying the emotional experiences of mathematics learners and their influence on their ability to learn. The researchers are also interested in questions such as how affects exert their influence and the implications for teaching mathematics; how affects influence memory and mathematical insight.
Published Material: ZAND, H. & BURT, G.J. (1989). Social and emotional aspects of learning mathematics, Educational and Training Technology International, Vol 26, No 1.
Source of Grant: No funding
Date of Research: 1986 – continuing
KEYWORDS: *affectivity; emotion; emotional response; learning psychology; mathematics; mathematics education; teaching*

8/1196

Institute for Educational Technology,
Walton Hall, Milton Keynes MK7 6AA
0908 274066
Loughborough University
Hussat Research Centre, Loughborough LE11 3TU
0509 263171
Whalley, P. Dr

Problems of structuring arguments in hypertext formats

Abstract: The purpose of this research proposal is to side step the technology-driven momentum being developed, and to examine the theoretical problems of locating hypertext within a general theory of discourse and reader-text relations. The historical record of over-hasty adoption and consequent misuse of earlier technologies in the educational and information science disciplines points to the dangers of this level of research not being supported at a sufficiently early stage. There are three main areas to be investigated. Firstly, rhetorical and linguistic issues: descriptive problems of identifying 'linguistic' features of hypertext displays and problems of structuring arguments in topic-frame format, also, graphic issues: diagrammatic representations of content and rhetorical structure and development of icons/metaphors for new text features/events. Finally cognitive issues: problems of fugitive information structures; catering for sequencing effects in traversing knowledge nets and the active role of the reader.
Source of Grant: No funding
Date of Research: 1987 – continuing
KEYWORDS: *educational technology; electronic data processing; information technology; programmed text*

8/1197

Institute for Educational Technology,
Walton Hall, Milton Keynes MK7 6AA
0908 274066
Bento, S. Mr

Intelligent computer aided instruction in an industrial setting

Abstract: This research is concerned with the comprehensive evaluation of Innovated Computer Based Learning Systems (ICBLs). These include most CBT type systems and systems incorporating Artificial Intelligence (AI). Some of the evaluation methods include video-analysis, performance testing, hermeneutics, cost-analysis and the administration of various types of rating scales. The current context of the research involves the evaluation of computer based simulations used to assist in the teaching of Newtonian Mechanics to 9-10 year olds in a middle school. The outcomes of the research should indicate to what extent it is viable to computerise the teaching of the British National Curriculum pertaining to Attainment Target 10. The fruits of the research, have, and should benefit education as well as industry and commerce.
Source of Grant: Open University
Date of Research: 1989 – continuing
KEYWORDS: *autoinstructional aid; automatic teaching; commercial training; computer assisted instruction; educational technology; industrial training; teaching machine*

8/1198

Institute for Educational Technology,
Walton Hall, Milton Keynes MK7 6AA
0908 274066
Imperial Cancer Research Fund
PO Box 123, Lincoln's Inn Fields,
London WC2A 3PX
071 242 0200
Alpay, L. Mr; O'Neill, M. Dr

An intelligent tutoring system for medical diagnosis

Abstract: This research is concerned with the development of an intelligent medical tutor to teach medical diagnosis, particularly the student modelling aspect. A literature review demonstrated that

an alternative approach for a teaching system should be proposed which should have an understanding for the clinical reasoning of the student from their point of view, not the expert physicians. A new type of user model defined as developmental is suggested. The student is regarded as a 'progressive and dynamic entity' and goes through a process of development in medical diagnostic skill. The model will maintain a representation of the current state of the student from their viewpoint by incorporating the clinical reasoning process of the student. The model will also introduce the question of strategy change over time, and how this can be modelled and computationally implemented. The medical domain, back pain was chosen for the tutor.
Source of Grant: Open University
Date of Research: 1987-1990
KEYWORDS: *autoinstructional aid; automatic teaching; clinical diagnosis; computer assisted instruction; diagnosis; educational technology; medical treatment; teaching machine*

8/1199

Institute of Educational Technology,
Walton Hall, Milton Keynes MK7 6AA
0908 274066
Devi, R. Mr; Joiner, R. Mr; O'Malley, C. Ms; O'Shea, T. Mr; Scanlon, E. Ms

Co-operative problem solving in physics
Abstract: This reasearch will aim to design computer based support for the individual and co-operative problem solving skills in physics and mathematics for the classroom and distance education. One of the contexts to which research is being applied is the Open University where students find problem solving extremely hard. The research will investigate how students actually solve problems to enable us to examine the Open University physics 'practice makes perfect' approach, compared to the mathematicians desire to teach problem solving as a 'learnable skill'. We will also investigate the hypothesis that group work is more effective in fostering problem solving skills. Eventually aiming to understand the kind of computer based support that is most suitable for distance learning. Research is by questionnaire and observational studies on videotape.
Source of Grant: Open University computer assisted learning group
Date of Research: 1987 – continuing
KEYWORDS: *computer assisted instruction; co-operative learning; distance study; group learning; mathematics; physics; problem solving*

8/1200

Institute for Educational Technology,
Walton Hall, Milton Keynes MK7 6AA
0908 274066
Whalley, P. Dr

Hypertechnic – an object orientated control language for children
Abstract: A computer language with a micro-world of Lego and cardboard models rather than the screen based and abstract ones usually provided. An introduction to object orientated programming, it will appeal to children who view problems in terms of relationships between multiple agents, rather than one active agent responding to a multiplicity of conditions. It is based on the notion of actors responding to each others scripts. A 'dramatic metaphor' where children put on a play. Programs are written using role play to develop scripts for each object in the system. Each actor is represented by an icon on the screen which may be opened up to examine or change the script. The icons control, or are controlled by, objects in the Lego world, and are animated. The system has been implemented with the graphic orientated Hypercard programming environment and can be modified easily. Teacher's manuals are available for set of basic microworlds covering National Curriculum requirements. A generalized 'construction set' version developed in conjunction with Resource will be available in early 1991.
Source of Grant: Equipment support from: Apple UK, Fischer Technik, Lego and Resource
Date of Research: 1987 – continuing
KEYWORDS: *autoinstructional aid; automatic teaching; child; computer assisted instruction; computer microworlds; programming languages; teaching machine*

8/1201

Institute of Educational Technology,
Walton Hall, Milton Keynes MK7 6AA
0908 274066
Vincent, T. Dr

Developing models of assessment for blind people who use information technology
Abstract: This project is seeking to identify an appropriate assessment strategy for blind people. It is being conducted in collaboration with Exhall Grange School for the Visually Handicapped. Exhall Grange school makes extensive use of an information technology for pupils with visual handicaps. In collaboration with Exhall Grange, a number of individual case studies will be undertaken involving pupils from within the UK. The 'CALL Centre case study approach' will be adopted which involves initial assessment, identification of local support, training of pupils and staff, and the monitoring of progress over approximately one year. The proposed case studies (between 6 and 10 dependent on resources) should provide information on suitable strategies for the introduction of information technology for pupils with visual handicaps and for the provision of on-going support. The project has been extended to include two further schools where there are children with visual disabilities, (Priestley Smith School, Birmingham and Smestow School, Wolverhampton). The theme of 'access to text' was adopted. This has involved the provision and evaluation of high quality computer workstations to produce laser printed materials in fonts and font sizes to meet individual needs; personal, portable electronic magnifiers; braille transcription workstations; and a computer workstation with high quality definition (colour) display.
Source of Grant: DTI (Department of Trade & Industry): £16,000
Date of Research: 1989 – continuing
KEYWORDS: *assessment; autoinstructional aid; blind; computer assisted instruction; electronic data processing; information technology; visually handicapped*

8/1202

Institute of Educational Technology,
Walton Hall, Milton Keynes MK7 6AA
0908 274066
Elsom-Cook, M. Mr

Tutorial dialogue mechanisms
Abstract: This work follows on from some earlier research on the implementation of goal and focus directed architectures for teaching interactions. It combines analysis of dialogues, proposals for architectures and theoretical underpinnings of the field. The collected dialogues are of a human teacher teaching Prolog to a student via back to back terminals 400 miles apart. These transcripts are being analyzed in terms of goal structures (dialogue games) focus spaces and educational goals. The architecture being proposed is to think of dialogue as a combination of top-down planning and situated actions, resulting in an opportunistic planning mechanism. The planner is multiple agent and engages in real-time monitoring. A spreading activation model of focus is included.
Date of Research: 1987 – continuing
KEYWORDS: *autoinstructional aid; automatic teaching; computer assisted instruction; educational technology; teaching machine*

8/1203

Institute of Educational Technology,
Walton Hall, Milton Keynes MK7 6AA
0908 274066
Devi, R.

The application of machine learning to tutoring systems
Abstract: This research is in studying machine learning for tutoring systems. The researchers will model the student's conception of the domain and not the expert's representation. An area of research for this is the program's ability to change its representation language. It is also intended to progress towards modelling the student's learning process, not only at any one time, but also over a period, by identifying the way in which knowledge is acquired. This will be done firstly by the system applying a learning algorithm to the concept being taught in order to imitate the way the student might be learning it. This would allow the system to make predictions about how the student acquired a concept. A system could have several learning algorithms, applying each one to the concept being learned and comparing the results of their learning with that of the students. If a learning algorithm's result matches that of the student's, then it is a good approximation of the student's learning mechanisms. This would also enable the tutoring system to make more informed predictions about teaching strategies, and could be applied for making decisions about what teaching action to take next. With further research the system could reason about the strategies and derive its own.
Source of Grant: Rank Xerox Open University

Date of Research: 1987-1990
KEYWORDS: autoinstructional aid; automatic teaching; computer
assisted educational technology; learning process; teaching machine

8/1204

Institute of Educational Technology,
Walton Hall, Milton Keynes MK7 6AA
0908 274066
Moyse, R. Mr

Multiple viewpoints for the intelligent tutoring systems

Abstract: Intelligent Tutoring systems need multiple viewpoints
upon their domain. Stevens, Collins and Goldin concluded that
WHY (tutoring rainfall) required 'functional' knowledge of
processes as well as scriptal knowledge of conditions. 'Representations' are distinct from 'viewpoints'. The clause 'the happy baby
is eating the tarantula' may be represented as a semantic net or
as clauses in a predicate calculus. Conversely, a single representation such as the quantitative circuit model of SOPHIE 1 (Brown
and Burton, 1975) may be used by a number of procedural
specialists to answer 'what if' questions or to evaluate student
hypotheses. Viewpoints are seen as goal oriented and model based.
The model is seen as a set of structural primitives. Different operators may be applied to the same model to infer different information. A top level algorithm builds function into a viewpoint,
making it goal oriented by deciding when a particular model is
applicable to a particular problem. Viewpoints are distinct from
'mental models' in that they propose some mechanism for deciding when the model is applicable, and they propose specific mechanisms for making inferences from the model and for choosing
amongst these mechanisms. Therefore a viewpoint is seen as a
mental model. The research aims to show that the description of
viewpoints in terms of goals, models and operators is reasonable
and that different inferences are made and decisions reached when
different models are used. The Viewpoint study investigates the
differences of inference, control and prediction betrween groups
applying functional and structural models to a simulated nuclear
power station. The second phase will consider the implication of
ITS design and attempt to implement a system exploring some of
them in particular domains. Salient issues include the need to integrate different 'kinds' of knowledge (qualitative or quantitative)
and the issue of 'control' knowledge, or knowing when to apply
different viewpoints to produce different problem spaces.
Published Material: BROWN, J.S. & BURTON, R.R. (1975). 'Multiple representations of knowledge for tutorial reasoning'. In:
BOBROW, D. & COLLINS, A. (Eds). Representation and understanding: studies in cognitive science. New York: Academic Press.;
di SESSAL, A.A. (1986). 'Models of computation'. In: NORMAN,
D.A. & DRAPER, S.W. (Eds). User Centred System Design. Hills-
dale, New Jersey & London: Lawrence Erlbaum Associates.;
KIERAS, D.E. & BOVAIR, S. (1984). 'The role of mental models
in learning to operate a device', Cognitive Science, No 8,
pp.255-273.; STEVENS, A.L., COLLINS, A. & GOLDIN, S.
(1982). 'Misconceptions in students' understanding'. In: SLEEMAN
& BROWN, (Eds). Intelligent tutoring systems. New York: Academic Press.
Source of Grant: SERC (Science and Engineering Research Council)
Date of Research: 1987-1990
KEYWORDS: autoinstructional aid; automatic teaching; computer
assisted instruction; educational technology; teaching machine

8/1205

Institute of Education,
Walton Hall, Milton Keynes MK7 6AA
0908 274066
Elsom-Cook, M. Mr; Spensley, F. Ms

Dominie: a tutor for procedural skills

Abstract: DOMINIE teaches procedural skills which are carried
out at a computer interface. It features multiple teaching strategies. Knowledge is represented by a set of basic interface actions
(e.g. select) which are grouped into purpose for interface tasks.
These in turn form the action parts of planning procedures which
are combined by a strips-like planner to generate a mechanism for
reading a particular goal. The procedures are also linked to a
declarative representation of important concepts in the domain
being taught. Teaching strategies include cognitive apprenticeship
and Socratic diagnosis. The 'trainer' interface guides the domain
expert through the provisional knowledge with a series of questions. It divides the task into action, these are shown to the author
and more detailed descriptions of the actions are elicited. The system
then asks the author to name the highest goal of the activity and

its immediate sub-goals. Finally, the system elicits the concepts
associated with each planning procedure, gets the author to describe
the links between concepts and associates the text with them. It
then assigns segments of the action sequence to individual sub-goals.
This is repeated recursively until the plan has been defined.
Source of Grant: ESPRIT: £300,000
Date of Research: 1987-1989
KEYWORDS: autoinstructional aid; automatic teaching; computer
assisted instruction; educational technology; teaching machine;
teaching method

8/1206

Institute of Educational Technology,
Walton Hall, Milton Keynes MK7 6AA
0908 274066
Vincent, T. Dr; Child, D. Mr

Alternatives to print for visually disabled students

Abstract: This research will be to see whether improved access to
textual material could be provided to visually disabled students
through use of new information technology. This project concerns
investigation of three formats for material which could be produced
easily with the aid of new technology. They are enlarged print,
braille and synthetic speech. The final result will be sets of guidelines relating to each of these possibilities indicating how best they
can be exploited. This research has been extended in 1990 to include
an investigation into the use of compact dish technology (CD-ROM)
together with hypertext retrieval systems and synthetic speech
environments to give interactive access to text on an electronic form.
Source of Grant: The Mercers' Company: Clothworkers' Foundation: £9,500 jointly
Date of Research: 1989 – continuing
KEYWORDS: autoinstructional aid; computer assisted instruction;
educational electronic data processing; information technology;
programmed text; visually handicapped

8/1207

Institute of Educational Technology,
Walton Hall, Milton Keynes MK7 6AA
0908 274066
Sibbitt, R. Ms

Lexical and non-lexical processes in non-word spelling

Abstract: This research examines spelling from two different directions. Firstly, the non-phonetic spellings of children with spelling
difficulties are examined in terms of the phoneme-grapheme grammars they possess. Secondly, the dual-route model of spelling is
expanded to incorporate interaction between the lexical and non-
lexical spelling routes, in order to account for non-phonetic spellings. Both these investigations are carried out using nonwork
stimuli. It is shown that children use phoneme-grapheme mappings
to spell words they have not seen before, and that these mappings
can be derived from mis-spelt words in the lexicon. Using nonword
spellings, faulty phoneme-grapheme mappings can be identified for
remediation. This research also shows that morphemes, such as the
past-participle marker 'ed', can be used in nonword spelling. It is
suggested that the dual-route model should therefore allow interaction between the lexical and non-lexical routes, and that categorization of children's spelling errors as phonetic or non-phonetic does
not allow for this interaction.
Source of Grant: Rank Xerox Open University
Date of Research: 1987-1990
KEYWORDS: cognitive processes; learning difficulty; literacy;
reading; spelling

8/1208

Institute of Educational Technology,
Walton Hall, Milton Keynes MK7 6AA
0908 274066
Baker, M. Mr

**An architecture of an intelligent tutoring system for musical struc-
ture and interpretation**

Abstract: Research began by looking at musical interpretation and
its relationship to musical structure in co-ordination with the existing
intelligent computer aided instruction in the arts project at the Open
University. The work explored problems which would arise for intelligent tutoring in an area where existing knowledge is largely intuitive, incomplete or uncertain. The result is an overall design of an
architecture for an intelligent tutoring system. The three main foci
of research is firstly the development of a new cognitive model for
perception of musical structure in tonal melodies. Secondly, a
guided discovery environment to enable novice musicians to create

interpretations of melodies, based around a graphic editing tool linked to a music synthesizer, and finally a model of tutorial dialogue, for tutoring in incomplete and uncertain knowledge domains, based on generating critical arguments (instantiated in the domain of musical structures derived from the music parser analysis of input melodies).

Published Material: BAKER, M.J. (1987). 'Psychological modelling and pianoroll machines', AISB Quarterly, No 61, Spring.; BAKER, M.J. (1988). 'A computational model for perception of musical grouping structures', Contemporary Music Review, Winter Special issue on Music and the Cognitive Sciences.; BAKER, M.J. (1988). 'Tutoring with incomplete and uncertain knowledge', International Journal of Educational Research, October.; BAKER, M.J. (1988). An architecture of an intelligent tutoring system for musical structure and interpretation. Proceedings of the First International Workshop on Artificial Intelligence and Music. AAAI, St Paul, Minnesota.; BAKER, M.J. (1989). 'An artificial intelligence approach to musical grouping analysis', Contemporary Music Review, Spring, special issue on science and music.; Report number 51 (September 1988). Arguing with the tutor: a model for tutorial dialogue in uncertain knowledge domains. To be published in Guided Discovery Tutoring (a book edited by M. Elsom-Cook).
Source of Grant: SERC (Science and Engineering Research Council)
Date of Research: 1987-1989
KEYWORDS: autoinstructional aid; automatic teaching; computer assisted instruction; educational technology; music; music theory; teaching machine

8/1209

Institute of Educational Technology,
Walton Hall, Milton Keynes MK7 6AA
0908 274066
Jones, A. Dr
An empirical study of novices programming
Abstract: This research is concerned with the difficulties that people have in learning to program when they have no previous experience, and with the problems they encounter in using self-instructional or distance learning materials which have been specially designed for novices. One of the major problems facing novices is how to link the new information which they encounter with their existing knowledge. Both Piagetian and artificial intelligence models of learning emphasise that knowledge must be structured in order to be meaningful and accessible. In order to learn, new information needs to be assimilated into the existing structure. One way of helping novices to bridge the gap between their existing knowledge and new information is to use a conceptual model, which serves to explain the new information in familiar terms. An important role of the conceptual model is to help the user understand what is going on inside the machine, at an appropriate level. The user needs to understand the effects of the commands she is learning to use. The difficulties which novices have when learning to program with the help of a conceptual model were investigated, i.e. what happens under good, if not ideal, conditions. When designers have thought about and provided a conceptual model, what kind of mental model does the learner develop? The curricula and conceptual models of four programming languages designed to teach novices were analyzed. The problems that learners have when learning their first programming language, in forming mental models, making adjustments to these models, and in transferring these models to a new language were investigated by carrying out empirical studies.
Source of Grant: No funding
Date of Research: 1980-1990
KEYWORDS: autoinstructional aid; automatic teaching; computer assisted instruction; computer programming; computer science; distance study; educational technology; teaching machine

8/1210

Institute of Educational Technology,
Walton Hall, Milton Keynes MK7 6AA
0908 274066
University of Indonesia
POB 295, JL Salemba, Jakarta, Indonesia
Jakarta 882955
Elsom-Cook, M. Mr; Stainton-Ellis, K. Ms; O'Malley, C. Ms
Extended computer assisted learning
Abstract: This project is an experiment in minimalism in tutoring systems or a bridging of the gap between intelligent tutoring systems and traditional CAL (Computer Assisted Learning). It tackles the problem of supporting courses which are more flexible and adaptive to the learner whilst simplifying the authorising process

and relating the design of computer based teaching materials more closely to the design of other forms of course. A number of developments from work on artificial intelligence in education will be used and which are well known and combine these ideas with a frame-based approach to produce a more powerful system. This is called ECAL (Extended Computer Assisted Learning). It embodies a course design model based upon the specification of intended learning outcomes and the relationship between these. An artificial intelligence model of interaction between student and system, based on regarding the interaction as a focus based dialogue and taking execution time decisions about suitable changes in focus. A model of the student based upon numeric overlay techniques using complex updating algorithms to tackle the credit assignment problem. Finally a definition of the interface between this system and simulation or problem generation packages.
Source of Grant: World Bank Department of Employment Training Agency
Date of Research: 1988 – continuing
KEYWORDS: autoinstructional aid; automatic teaching; computer assisted computer assisted learning; teaching machine

8/1211

Institute of Educational Technology,
Walton Hall, Milton Keynes MK7 6AA
0908 274066
Elsom-Cook, M. Mr
Data-driven tutoring
Abstract: This project investigated the nature of knowledge representations in tutoring systems with specific reference to the implicit educational assumptions involved in any given representation. A number of existing tutoring systems will be constructed in a single system to compare their differences. These systems use a semantic network as a common representation, but the way in which the network is constructed varies. for example in the system 'Scholar' there are two types of link: 'superpart' and 'superconcept' with attribute/value pairs associated with nodes. In the system 'Trill' there are no attributes associated with nodes, but the links are associated with specific forms of teaching strategy. Following this re-implementation, a graphical design tool for educational knowledge representation (using semantic nets) is being constructed. It makes use of ideas from curriculum design to specify an educationally meaningful set of constraints upon the representation. The networks are unusual in that the links are multiply typed. Each link has a domain dependent and a domain independent (educational) type. Both can be operated on by the system teaching strategies.
Published Material: 01 11
Source of Grant: SERC (Science and Engineering Research Council): £70,000
Date of Research: 1987-1990
KEYWORDS: autoinstructional aid; automatic teaching; computer assisted instruction; educational technology; teaching machine

8/1212

Institute of Educational Technology,
Walton Hall, Milton Keynes MK7 6AA
0908 274066
Tata Institute for Fundamental Research
National Centre for Software Technology,
Bombay, India
Elsom-Cook, M. Mr
Simultaneous equations tutor
Abstract: The simultaneous equations tutor is a system to support high school students in learning to solve simultaneous equations. Students can provide some equations and a complete or partial solution. The tutor can critique and annotate the solution. It can also offer advice on what to do next in partial solutions, and can introduce new methods of solving equations to the students. It operates from a set of chunked production rule models of correct behaviour in solving simultaneous equations. It essentially engages in model tracing from these rules until such time as it finds a mismatch between the student behaviour and the predicted behaviour. At this point it decomposes the production into constituent rules and attempts to find the exact point of divergence. It can then use domain knowledge about the description language of the rule interpreter to attempt to generate malrule descriptions for the student. This generation is heuristically guided. The heuristics are linked to a conceptual knowledge base which is intended to provide the student with explanations about the misconceptions underlying their behaviour.

Source of Grant: United Nations Development Programme British Council
Date of Research: 1987 – continuing
KEYWORDS: autoinstructional aid; automatic teaching; computer assisted educational technology; equations (mathematics); mathematics; teaching machine

8/1213
Institute of Educational Technology,
Walton Hall, Milton Keynes MK7 6AA
0908 274066
Evertsz, R. Mr; Floyd, A. Ms; Fox, M. Mr; Hennessy, S. Ms; O'Shea, T. Mr
An intelligent computer tutor for arithmetic
Abstract: Research is being carried out towards an adaptive computer tutor for arithmetic calculation and for the principles underlying that skill. Further research is being carried out to help children develop an extensive repertoire of informal techniques for performing arithmetic in everyday situations and learning to formulate shortcuts to problem solving. Artificial intelligence techniques are being applied in the construction of computer based activities which foster certain arithmetic principles and which aid the researchers in diagnosing important misunderstandings in relation to those principles, these are then used in the development of student models for the computer tutor. In this system the computer is an intelligent participant in activities involving small groups of children. The tutor builds up experience enabling it to make sensible judgements, and also keeps a chronological record of individual progression, observed difficulties, and it provides immediate feedback. The project reflects the increased prominence of the calculator and reduced use of algorithms. A program entitled 'shopping on Mars' is aimed at 8-12 year olds who are presented with a series of calculation tasks, and these can be solved with one of a range of technologies. It will make children aware of the variety of tools for calculation and choose between the more and less efficient.
Source of Grant: The Alvey Directorate: £500,000
Date of Research: 1987 – continuing
KEYWORDS: arithmetic; autoinstructional aid; automatic teaching; computer assisted instruction; educational technology; mathematics; teaching machine

8/1214
Institute of Educational Studies,
Walton Hall, Milton Keynes MK7 6AA
0908 274066
Vincent, T. Dr
New technology, disability and special educational needs: state of the art and case studies in further education
Abstract: The aim of this research is to produce a 'state of the art' publication which will identify initiatives concerning the introduction and application of technology for students with disabilities and special educational needs in further education and the current level of activity. A further aim is to produce a range of case studies of students who have use of new technology to access the curriculum, particularly those involved in transitions between school and further education, further education and employment, training or other education, and between special and mainstream provision. Finally to reinforce the network of people involved. The method used will be written articles. Thirteen will focus on individual colleges, and common base-line information sought will include students involved, courses, staffing assessment, and staff/student training. Case studies will be compiled on students who have used the new technology for at least two years to meet their individual needs in relation to the curriculum. The eventual outcome of research will be two publications and an associated national conference in 1989.
Published Material: VINCENT, T. (1990). New technology, disability and special educational needs: some case studies. Empathy (Hereward College) Coventry.
Source of Grant: Department of Education and Science Further Education Unit: £10,000
Date of Research: 1988-1990
KEYWORDS: autoinstructional aid; automatic teaching; computer assisted instruction; educational technology; further education; handicapped; special education; teaching machine

8/1215
Institute of Educational Technology,
Walton Hall, Milton Keynes MK7 6AA
0908 274066
Joiner, R. Mr
Understanding why two heads are better than one
Abstract: Recently there has been a lot of research on designing computer systems that support learning in a co-operative context. There are also theoretical reasons for believing that problem solving facilitates learning. Vygotsky and Piaget have both proposed that joint problem solving promotes cognitive development. Research in cognitive science on constructive interaction suggests that joint problem solving facilitates learning. One reason for the faciliatory effects of peer interaction are the differences in point of view between participants. One problem is that it is not clear how differences in point of view lead to cognitive change. In co-operative problem solving dialogical processes are very important, because it is through dialogue that it is carried out. The aim of this project is to investigate how changes in point of view are mediated by language. A study by the author has already been carried out which shows peer interaction facilitates learning. This was video-taped and will be analyzed to build up some understanding of how differences in point of view lead to cognitive change. The aim is to build a detailed computer model of the processes using AI theories of dialogue which will be then capable of giving guidelines for designing computer supported co-operative learning.
Source of Grant: Science and Engineering Research Council
Date of Research: 1987-1989
KEYWORDS: autoinstructional aid; automatic teaching; cognitive development; computer assisted instruction; co-operative learning; educational technology; teaching machine

8/1216
Institute for Educational Technology,
Walton Hall, Milton Keynes MK7 6AA
0908 274066
Kirkup, G. Ms
The effects of gender on the use of computers in distance education
Abstract: The Open University has always provided teaching with and through computers. A policy of student provided computing equipment has been adopted on some courses. The Open University is innovatory with respect to this policy, and its effects are therefore being evaluated. The effects are different for men and women. This research explores the positive and negative effects on women students of integrating obligatory computer use onto distance education courses. The work is used as information helpful in designing special initiatives for women or disadvantaged students.
Published Material: KIRKUP, G. (1989). 'Equal opportunities and computing at the Open University', Open Learning, Vol 4, No 1, February, pp.3-9.; KIRKUP, G. et al (1990). 'Home based computing for woment students'. In: KIRKUP, G. Women in computing. Selected Papers 1988-1990. Springer-Verlag Workshop Series.; Reports of the Centre for Information Technology in Education (CITE), Institute of Educational Technology, Open University. Report numbers 65, 69, 80, 83, 95.
Source of Grant: No funding
Date of Research: 1988 – continuing
KEYWORDS: computer assisted instruction; distance education; gender equality; women's education

8/1217
Walton Hall, Milton Keynes MK7 6AA
0908 274066
Brook, C. Dr
Regional difference in Open University student progress
Abstract: The research stresses the importance of cross regional comparisons and the fact that Open University students face difficult circumstances, and perform differently in each of the University's 13 regions. This research stresses the importance of cross regional comparisons and the fact that O.U. students face difficult circumstances and perform differently in each of the University's 13 regions.
Published Material: BROOK, C. (1985). 'Something strange in our regions', Teaching at a Distance, Vol 25, pp.77-83. Milton Keynes: Open University
Source of Grant: Open University Research Committee
Date of Research: 1986 – continuing
KEYWORDS: comparative achievement; distance study; geographic location; open university; performance

8/1218
Walton Hall, Milton Keynes MK7 6AA
0908 274066
Woods, P. Mr; Supervisor: Mackay, H. Dr
Consumerist perspectives on education

Abstract: A study of the development of institutionalized forms of home-school links in secondary schools with particular reference to parent governors and parent teacher associations (PTAs). These links are contextualized in notions of consumerism, which is considered in terms of its displacing the hitherto dominant approaches to the area of labourism and socialism.
Source of Grant: No funding
Date of Research: 1988 – continuing
KEYWORDS: parent-school relation; secondary education

8/1219

Department of Education
Walton Hall, Milton Keynes MK7 6AA
0908 274066
Flintoff, A. Ms; *Supervisor:* Deem, R. Dr
Breaking the mould? An analysis of the professional socialization of physical education teachers with reference to gender relations
Abstract: Despite a flourishing feminist critique of the way in which schools reproduce gender relation, it is only recently that there has been any attempt to consider gender equality in physical education (eg Leaman 1984, Scraton 1986, Carrington and Leaman 1986). Similarly, although there have been a few studies that have looked at inservice work on gender relations with teachers (eg the GIST (girls into science and technology) project), there have been few corresponding studies of ITT (initial teacher training) and, in particular, studies on ITT in PE (physical education). This study will aim to consider the ways in which teacher training institutions construct, confirm or contest gender identities in PE. Information will be collected from a number of sources: documentary evidence on the history of PE and specific colleges and institutions, DES (Department of Education and Science) regulations regarding ITT and education generally, and PE journals and material from professional groups such as the Physical Education Association and the Standing Conference on Physical Education in Teacher Education. The main part of the study, however, will consist of an ethnographic case study of two institutions with different historical backgrounds. Information will also be collected by semi-structured interviews with those members of staff who have had major control over decision making an policy implementation.
Source of Grant: Open University: £126,000
Date of Research: 1989 – continuing
KEYWORDS: colleges of education; gender equality; physical education; sex difference; teacher education

8/1220

Department of Education
Centre for Human Learning and Development,
Walton Hall, Milton Keynes MK7 6AA
0908 652601
Hatfield Polytechnic
Department of Psychology
Hatfield AL10 9LB
07072 79000
Light, P. Prof.; Messer, D. Dr; Littleton, K. Ms; Joiner, R. Mr
Collaboration and feedback in children's computer based problem solving
Abstract: The present study seeks to investigate why information in the form of feedback or help by the computer is so often apparently ineffective in supporting children's learning and problem solving and why the support provided by a working partner is, by contrast, apparently so effective. The two issues will be addressed by taking them together and exploring their interactions.
Source of Grant: Leverhulme Trust: £100,000 approximately
Date of Research: 1990 – continuing
KEYWORDS: computer assisted instruction; feedback; interaction; learning; problem solving

8/1221

Department of Education
Centre for Educational Policy & Management,
Walton Hall, Milton Keynes MK7 6AA
0908 274066
Glatter, R. Prof.; Woods, P. Mr; *Supervisor:* Glatter, R. Prof.
Parental and institutional choice: effects of more open enrolment and local management of schools (LMS)
Abstract: This is an exploratory study of the interaction between parental choice and school decision-making. Various provisions of the Education Reform Act 1988 (ERA), particularly those relating to Local Management of Schools (under which a school's funding is based largely on the numbers and ages of its pupils) and more open enrolment, are aimed at creating a climate of heightened competition between schools for pupils, and the present study will be conducted within this new context. A number of researchers have investigated parents' expectations, preferences and choices with regard to their children's schooling. This study will focus in addition on the responses made by schools, examining issues such as how they obtain, interpret and act upon 'clues' regarding the preferences of parents of potential pupils, and what factors constrain them in understanding and reacting to such information. The project will prepare the conceptual and methodological basis for a longer term enquiry into such issues and test it in one or more pilot studies. This is one of a number of studies within the Centre examining the implementation of aspects of ERA, under the general heading of the 'CHARGE' (Challenge and Response in the Government of Education) Project.
Source of Grant: Economic and Social Research Council
Date of Research: 1990 – continuing
KEYWORDS: Education Reform Act (1988); parent choice; school based management

8/1222

Department of Education
Centre for Educational Policy and Management,
Walton Hall, Milton Keynes MK7 6AA
0908 274066
Bush, T. Mr
The management of grant-maintained schools
Abstract: This is a study of two of the first grant-maintained schools. Methodology will include interviews with four parallel postholders at each school; analysis of all relevant documents and observation of governing body meetings. Conclusions reached include that there are advantages for schools in 'opting-out', principally in terms of finance and managerial autonomy.
Published Material: BUSH, T. (1990). 'Going it alone – managing grant-maintained schools', Educational Management and Administration, Vol 18, No 4, pp.10-28.
Source of Grant: No funding
Date of Research: 1989 – continuing
KEYWORDS: school management

8/1223

Department of Education
PO Box 49, Milton Keynes MK7 6AA
0908 274066
Russell, C.W. Mr; *Supervisor:* Glaister, R.T.D. Dr; Jonathon, R. Dr
Inspectorate reports on primary schools and their effect upon parental choice
Abstract: The researcher's concern with the decision to publish reports on primary schools by the Inspectorate followed on from his MEd. (Master of Education) dissertation to the University of Edinburgh. In that work, it was contended that truly educational choices could only be made in a truly education conscious society and environment. It was concluded that this was not the case. It would seem then that publication of reports might help to improve the educational consciousness of the public, and hence lead to better informed decision taking. To establish if this will come to pass, the researcher has embarked on a research programme, which is currently shaping thus: Inspection (a) the concept; (b) the historical and contemporary application of the concept including an empirical investigation in the Borders region of Scotland. Inspectors – guardians of the concept. Reporting – the broader audience including an empirical study of range and manner of impact. Reaction – the manner in which the new audience makes use of the information, with particular reference to placement requests under the Education (Scotland) Act 1981. The hypothesis is that the criteria of judgement of the Inspectorate differs from those of the parents. Reaction will be discernable, unless methods of bridging the gap are employed.
Source of Grant: No funding
Date of Research: 1985-1990
KEYWORDS: attitude; inspection; parent-school relation; parental decision making; primary education

8/1224

Department of Education
Centre for Human Development and Learning,
Walton Hall, Milton Keynes MK7 6AA

0908 274066
Light, P. Prof.
Social interaction and cognitive development in school aged children
Abstract: An extensive programme of research (mostly in the form of small experimental projects) has addressed social aspects of children's cognitive development. Topics have encompassed social perspective taking, spatial perspective taking and drawing, conservation and logical reasoning. Current work is focused on the role of pragmatic scherias in deductive reasoning and the role of peer interaction in problem-solving, using computers.
Published Material: RICHARDS, M. & LIGHT, P. (Eds). (1986). Children of social worlds. Oxford: Polity Press.; LIGHT, P., FOOT, T., COLBOURN, C. & McCLELLAND, I. (1987). 'Collaborative interactions at the microcomputer keyboard; Educational Psychology', Vol 17, No 1, 1987, pp.13-21.; LIGHT, P. & PERRET-CLERMONT, A.N. (1989). 'Social context effects in reasoning and testing'. In: GELLATLY, A. et al (Eds). Cognition and Social Worlds. Oxford: Clarendon Press.
Source of Grant: Economic and Social Research Council Foundation Fyssen (Paris) Open University Leverhulme Trust
Date of Research: 1979 – continuing
KEYWORDS: cognitive development; problem solving; social interaction

8/1225

Department of Education
Walton Hall, Milton Keynes MK7 6AA
0908 274066
London University
Birkbeck College, Malet Street, London WC1E 7HX
071 580 6622
Bell, R.E. Dr; Tight, M. Dr
The history of distance higher education in the United Kingdom
Abstract: This is an investigation of all forms of higher education developed in the United Kingdom, where the student was assumed always to be at a distance from the source of instruction or the degree awarding institution. It is principally concerned with the development of the London External Degree and the Royal University of Ireland as well as with the L.L.A. of St Andrews and the various agencies teaching their students. It explores also the role played by the Oxford and Cambridge extension movements and the various experiments and proposals that led to the establishment of the Open University. A key issue is the extent to which such distance study was regarded as equal in status to face to face instruction in a conventional university setting.
Source of Grant: No funding
Date of Research: 1987 – continuing
KEYWORDS: distance study; higher education; history of education

8/1226

Department of Educational Technology
Walton Hall, Milton Keynes MK7 6AA
0908 274066
Scanlon, E. Ms; O'Shea, T. Prof.; Driver, R. Dr; Draper, S. Dr
Conceptual change in science
Abstract: The research aims to clarify and describe the process of change in learners' conceptual understandings of natural phenomena. It will begin by reviewing the literature on models of conceptual change and on children's conceptions on a number of selected topic areas in science. Strategies for exploring and developing children's ideas in these areas will also be explored and developed, and computer software which could be useful in exploring children's reasoning and promoting conceptual change will be identified. From this review, two or three topic areas will be selected, where progress in understanding requires different types of conceptual change. For each area, the prior conceptions of a number of children will be explored in some detail with a range of phenomena and will be documented using think-aloud protocols. A range of intervention strategies will be developed to promote conceptual change, focusing on the use of computer based methods and approaches based on ARK-like and STELLA-like software. Detailed protocols of these interventions will be produced from a video and audio tape record. The extent of conceptual change will be assessed by re-administration of the original tasks; and the protocols of the intervention strategies will be analyzed too, to develop a theoretical description of the change process. The analyses from all the selected topic domains will be used to develop a more general description of the processes involved in conceptual change, and

hypotheses arising from this work will be tested with other groups of children through experimental studies.
Source of Grant: Economic and Social Research Council: £255,000
Date of Research: 1988 – continuing
KEYWORDS: concept formation; learning; science education

8/1227

Institute of Educational Technology
Walton Hall, Milton Keynes MK7 6AA
0908 274066
Mason, R. Dr; *Supervisor:* Laurillard, D. Dr
The use of computer conferencing in mass distance education
Abstract: The aim of this research is to study the first large scale use of computer conferencing in education. The Open University used the CoSy (conferencing system) for the first time in 1988 as a tutorial support medium for 1300 students on a second level course in information technology. The case study method was used to give a holistic approach based on qualitative data – interviews, participant observation, conferencing messages. Quantitative data – computer generated statistics, survey questionnaires etc. were used to give validity and reliability. The results show that computer conferencing can be used in mass distance education as a tutorial medium. However, using the medium as a very small component of a course is not recommended.
Published Material: MASON, R. & KAYE, A.R. (1989). (Eds). Mindweave: communication computers and distance education. Oxford: Pergamon.
Source of Grant: No funding
Date of Research: 1987-1990
KEYWORDS: distance study; Open University; telecommunication; teleconferencing

8/1228

School of Ecuation
Walton Hall, Milton Keynes MK7 6AA
0908 274066
Treasure, I.C. Mr; *Supervisor:* Bell, R. Dr; Robertson, A. Dr
Conflict and compromise in religious issues and Liberal Party educational policies 1906-14
Abstract: The study follows the religious and educational issues which formed the background to the education bills of the Liberal Government in the period 1906-08. It seeks to establish the role of the Established Church in the provision of elementary education in the 19th Century showing that the voluntary agencies were incapable of supplying an educational need. The impact of the Education Act of 1870 and its implications for the voluntary schools is considered. The position of the voluntary agencies and in particular the position of the Church of England is considered alongside the provisions of the Edcuation Act of 1902. The claims and grievances of the Nonconformists are reviewed and the impact of the churches upon the lives of people is considered. The political consequences of the Conservative Government's defeat and the return of power of the Liberal Government in 1906 is outlined together with a review of that Election. The work of the Archbishop of Canterbury as the chief negotiator on behalf of the Established Church is closely followed to draw the distinction between those working at the highest level of negotiation and those at grass roots level. The Liberal Government's social reforms and the decline in popularity of the Liberal Party as a vehicle for political Nonconformism is considered. This is reviewed alongside the stalemate in educational legislation affecting religious issues. The growth of Government interventions in the field of social welfare affecting the lives of ordinary people and its subsequent consequences upon the lessening impact of religion in the overall life of the nation is also reviewed.
Source of Grant: No funding
Date of Research: 1986 – continuing
KEYWORDS: educational legislation; history of education; politics education relationship; religion and education; voluntary organization; voluntary schools

8/1229

School of Education
Walton Hall, Milton Keynes MK7 6AA
0908 274066
Parker, D.H. Mr; *Supervisor:* Bell, R.E. Dr; Sutherland, G. Dr
Elementary education, society and politics in Hertfordshire 1918-1939
Abstract: This research follows a Master of Philosophy thesis enti-

tled "The impact of the First World War upon elementary education in Hertfordshire". Both studies examine the provision of elementary education locally in the light of national thought and trends. The primary research mainly involved source material in the Hertfordshire Record Office (county council papers, parish files and school files), the Public Record Office (Board of Education files), the British Library, Colindale (county newspapers and national journals), the Census Office, private collections and local museums. Oral evidence was taken from local residents. The PhD thesis will analyze the impact of new and rapid residential and industrial development upon local society and public affairs, and the effect of national economic and political thought and trends upon education. The factors influencing curriculum change will be highlighted, in particular to shed light upon the growing vocational aspect of education for older elementary children (not least the attention given to technical and rural education in the county), the equivocal attitude towards the role of the central schools and the concern to determine an "appropriate" expansion of secondary education. The impact of the three Hadow reports, especially that of 1926, will be examined, with its major implication for local reorganization, parental attitudes, school meals, transport, the future of Dual Control and the role of the denominational schools. Research has been undertaken into the county's attempts to identify and provide for children suspected of mental deficiency and backwardness, and into the ambivalent attitudes towards the education of elementary schoolchildren after the age of eleven.
Source of Grant: 1988-1989 Hertfordshire County Council: £6,000 1989-1991 No funding
Date of Research: 1988 – continuing
KEYWORDS: backwardness; curriculum development; economic conditions; history of politics education relationship; special education; war

8/1230

School of Education
Walton Hall,
Milton Keynes MK7 6AA
0908 274066
Deem, R. Dr; Brehony, K.J. Dr

Reforming school governing bodies: a sociological investigation
Abstract: School governing bodies in England and Wales were reshaped in the Autumn of 1988 as a result of the 1986 (No. 2) Education Act, with greater parental representation and more co-opted governors (including those from the business community). The 1986 Act and the 1988 Education Act have also given governors more power over schools than previously. The project will focus on an indepth study of ten school governing bodies (five primary and five secondary) in two local education authorities. A pilot study has already traced the progress of these new bodies and seven others since October 1988. The research will monitor what coping strategies governing bodies are using to deal with the tasks and responsibilities given to them by the new educational legislation and will also focus on the identification of power relations (including gender and race/ethnicity), decision making processes and networks of influence operating in the eight governing bodies. The project will, in addition, seek to discover whether co-opted governors and parent governors (widely described as 'consumer') come to predominate over those sometimes termed 'producer' governors (teacher and local education authority representative) and headteachers. The ork will be done through observation of formal, informal and sub-committee meetings, attendance at governor training sessions, questionnaires and interviews. Through these means the researchers hope to generate legislation (including local management of schools) on governors and their schools and make a contribution to the future education and support of school governors.
Published Material: BREHONY, K.J.B. (1990). 'Neither rhyme nor reason – primary schooling and the National Curriculum. In: FLUDE, M. & HAMMER, M. (Eds). The 1988 Education Act. London: Falmer Press.; DEEM, R. (1990). 'The reform of school governing bodies – the power of the consumer over the producer?'. In: FLUDE, M. & HAMMER, M. (Eds). The 1988 Education Act. London: Falmer Press.; DEEM, R. (1991). 'Governing by gender – the new school governing bodies'. In: ABBOTT, P. & WALKER, C. (Eds). Gender, sexuality and power. London: Macmillan.; BREHONY, K.J.B. & DEEM, R. 'Charging for free education; an exploration of a debate in school governing bodies', Journal of Education Policy, November.; DEEM, R. & BREHONY, K. (1990). 'The long and the short of it', Times Educa-

tional Supplement, 13 July.; HEMMINGS, S. (1990). 'Determined to see it through', Times Educational Supplement, 21 July. Earlier titles are available from the researchers.
Source of Grant: ESRC (Economic and Social Research Council): £56,720
Date of Research: 1990 – continuing
KEYWORDS: parent participation; school based management; school governors; school governing bodies

8/1231

School of Education
Walton Hall,
Milton Keynes MK7 6AA
0908 274066
Small, N.J. Mr; *Supervisor:* Bell, R.E. Dr; Bown, L.J. Prof.

The role of education for citizenship with reference to Zambia
Abstract: The research explores the informal area of education from which and by which adults develop a sense of identity at a national level. More positive is the idea and work of 'nation building' which can also arise from educational provision. The context is what counts as citizenship in states formed in the last century in former British colonial territories in east and central Africa. This offers a comparative background to the main focus on Zambia. Zambia was administered by a chartered company for about a quarter of a century; was the responsibility of the British Colonial Office for forty years as Northern Rhodesia; and has been an independent state in the Commonwealth for a quarter of a century. In that last period, it has faced particular external difficulties, relecting circumstances in Southern Rhodesia, now Zimbabwe; and from its position economically with regard to South Africa. Internally, copper mining has been the major supplier of exports and of foreign exchange; but a decline in demand and a fall in price have seriously affected the robustness of the economy to finance expansion of desired infrastructure, and social, health and educational development. The researcher hopes to review the role of education among adults, and indicate if and how it contributes to a commitment to a sense of identity with the state; and whether the adult as citizen is a concept that is consciously pursued by agencies formal and informal.
Date of Research: 1985 – continuing
KEYWORDS: adult education; Africa; citizenship education; colonialism; community education; informal education; nationalism; Zambia

8/1232

School of Education
Walton Hall,
Milton Keynes MK7 6AA
0908 274066
Open University Library,
Walton Hall,
Milton Keynes MK7 6AA
0908 652674
Dale, S.M. Miss; *Supervisor:* Bell, R.E. Dr

Adult learners, educational change and libraries in England and Wales and the Netherlands: a comparison
Abstract: To examine the reaction (or lack of reaction) of libraries/librarians to the opening up, in the period 1969 onwards, of educational opportunities for adults in England and Wales and the Netherlands. The emphasis will be on libraries in relation to educational change rather than educational change per se, with the prime focus on non-traditional students. In the Western world the last twenty to thirty years have seen far-reaching changes with regard to education for adults, with more emphasis on flexibility, independence and autonomous learning, has resulted in changes of methodology and the introduction of non-traditional patterns such as open and distance learning. Political factors and economic pressures have also played their part. Lifelong learning also carries with it the ideal of a comprehensive system of education for adults. Public libraries in England and Wales and in the Netherlands had originally, at least in part, an educational role. One might suppose, therefore, that the changes outlined above, which have occurred in both countries, will have impinged upon public as well as academic libraries.
Source of Grant: No funding
Date of Research: 1988 – continuing
KEYWORDS: adult education; comparative education; library; library role; life-long education; Netherlands; non formal education; United Kingdom

Oxford Polytechnic

8/1233
Department of Education
Wheatley Campus, Oxford OX9 1HX
0865 819000
Howson, J.O. Mr
Headteacher vacancies in England and Wales
Abstract: Longitudinal study into vacancies for head teachers in primary and secondary schools in England and Wales. Data set is based upon nationally advertised posts and is arranged in local authority and date order. Posts readvertised are specifically identified. Annual Surveys and periodic reviews of the database are published. During 1989 it is hoped to extend the database to include deputy headteachers.
Source of Grant: Polytechnic research grant
Date of Research: 1988 – continuing
KEYWORDS: head teacher; labour market

Oxfordshire Programme for Training, Instruction and Supervision

8/1234
Cricket Road Centre, Cowley, Oxford OX4 3DW
0865 716000
Bristol Polytechnic
Coldharbour Lane, Frenchay, Bristol BS16 1QY
0272 656261
Drowley, B.W. Mr; Burnham, M. Mr; *Supervisor:* Drowley, B.W. Mr; Burnham, M. Mr; Jones, B.; Thrower, B. Mrs
A method of training school teachers supporting pupils with special educational needs
Abstract: OPTIS (Oxfordshire Programme for Training, Instruction and Supervision) wish to research, develop, test and evaluate the provision of a training course for mainstream teachers in primary and secondary schools, which will (a) enhance their knowledge regarding pupils with special educational needs and (b) develop teaching skills to this client group. The course will be in Open Learning text format, will be piloted in three education authorities and will be aimed at CNAA (Council for National Academic Awards) recognition. Pilot students will register at Bristol Polytechnic, will be expected to complete assignments and if successful will be awarded a certificate or credit towards a higher award. A total of 45 teachers will be recruited for the pilot and will complete evaluation and final course reports. OPTIS will report the results to the Department of Education and Science.
Published Material: BURNHAM, M., DEANS, M. & BRAYTON, H. (1989). 'Working together', Open Learning Pack for Special Needs Assistants in Schools. (Pack consists of 5 modules of Open Learning format). Oxford: OPTIS.
Source of Grant: Department of Education and Science: £22,637.50
Date of Research: 1990 – continuing
KEYWORDS: further education of teachers; inservice teacher education; mainstreaming; open learning; special education; training course

Oxford University

8/1235
Department of Educational Studies
15 Norham Gardens, Oxford OX2 6PY
0865 274024
Williams, V. Dr
Monitoring and evaluation of local education authority Training Grants Scheme INSET provision
Abstract: Department of Education and Science uncertainty over variable practices revealed in local education authority monitoring and evaluation of accurate targeting of training provision in connection with the LEA Training Grants Scheme, prompted Oxfordshire LEA to undertake a circulation of the then current years programmes which were already being implemented by the LEA under restricted time and funding arrangements. Consequently, the evaluation research was reviewed as an ad hoc 'dipstick' exercise. The research had three basic objectives. Firstly, to establish the effectiveness of staff development provision. Secondly, to examine how the processes through which INSET development had been organized and experienced. Finally, to consider the perception of teachers involved about the relevance of INSET activities, and their responsbilities for planning and organizing school determined professional development.
Source of Grant: Two LEA's: researchers' expenses
Date of Research: 1989 – continuing
KEYWORDS: evaluation; financing; inservice teacher education; inservice training; teacher

8/1236
Department of Educational Studies
15 Norham Gardens, Oxford OX2 6PY
0865 274024
Flanders, R.M. Miss; *Supervisor:* White, C. Dr; Phillips, D. Dr
The educational role of museums and art galleries: a comparative study
Abstract: The research is concerned with the role of museums and art galleries as both curatorial and educational institutions. This involves an historical study and a comparative analysis of present developments. The research pays particular attention to the Victorian model. Museum archives provide primary source material and the study will include government and independent advisory body policy, as generated by the Office of Arts and Libraries and the International Council of Museums (particularly its Education and Cultural Action Committee initiatives). The Museums Association, British Council and the Arts Council will also be considered. Having established this background, case studies of national museums will be undertaken, drawing parallels with national institutions in Australia, which were established, and have developed, on the same Victorian social and educational base. The approach taken is both historical and an analysis of the current role played by curators and by educational staff specifically employed to assist in interpretation of the collections. The establishment by museums of educational programmes is an innovation which demands attention. Research to date has shown that important developments are occurring across the full range of the museum field. Much of this is taking place on an independent basis and there appears to have been little framework for the cross-fertilization of ideas. The lack of co-ordinated exchange of information betweem museums has been noted, and a comparison with nineteenth century practice is being undertaken.
Source of Grant: No funding
Date of Research: 1988 – continuing
KEYWORDS: aesthetic education; art; art education; comparative education; museum

8/1237
Department of Educational Studies
15 Norham Gardens, Oxford OX2 6PY
0865 274024
Kouvou, O. Miss; *Supervisor:* Harre, R. Mr; Wilson, J. Mr
Visual and verbal acts and their relationship to the art teacher's vocabulary
Abstract: This investigation will try to delimit the function of language in the process of aesthetic perception of paintings, as one specifying the intellectual concerns of this process, and therefore as giving further insight into the role and tasks of the art teacher. The sources of the study are mainly theoretical, including relevant bibliography on linguistic, perceptual and educational matters. In this investigation, the researchers experience as an art teacher plays a crucial role in testing theoretical hypotheses. In terms of methodology, theories of metaphor with their underlying theories of meaning will be examined and secondly how these can be seen as affecting our natural capacity of a more indirect perception of paintings. This analysis will hopefully lead to some constructive hypotheses concerning the function and educational potentialities of the language used in the art classroom.
Source of Grant: Greek State
Date of Research: 1987-1990
KEYWORDS: aesthetic education; art appreciation; art education; language; painting; vocabulary

8/1238

Department of Educational Studies
15 Norham Gardens, Oxford OX2 6PY
0865 274024
Toh, K.A. Mr; *Supervisor:* Woolnough, B.E. Mr

A study of the factors affecting students' performance in laboratory investigational work

Abstract: The research explored the extent to which performance in laboratory investigations is affected by affective and cognitive factors, as well as by instruction. It also examined the nature of the constituent processes that make up laboratory investigations; in particular the discreteness of these processes, and the extent to which these processes are generalizable frrom one situation to another. The field work involved 296 thirteen-year-old students from two schools in Singapore. The findings of the study show that: teaching and practice, both individually and collectively, contribute significantly towards student success in laboratory investigations. Performance in the processes of preliminary trials, planning and communication is significantly better with explicit instruction. Tacit knowledge is adequate for performance in the processes of performing and interpreting. The factors of attitude to school, attitude to science, academic self-concept and prior knowledge show a strong positive correlation with performance in laboratory investigation. Four factors, attitude to school, attitude to science, academic self-concept and prior knowledge account for 68% of the variability in performance in laboratory investigations. No sex-related differences are found with regard to performing of laboratory investigations as a whole. Boys and girls, but especially girls, perform better with content familiarity. The constituent processes of laboratory investigations are discrete. The ability to perform laboratory investigations as a whole appears to be generalizable. Preliminary trials and planning are two constituent processes which appear to be generalizable. The constituent process of interpreting appears to be context dependent.

Published Material: TOH, K.A. & WOOLNOUGH, B.E. (1990). 'Assessing through reporting, the outcomes of scientific investigation', Educational Research, Vol 32, No 1, Spring.; TOH, K.A. (1990). 'Insights from research: factors affecting success in science investigations'. In: WOOLNOUGH, B.E. (Ed). Practical Science. Buckingham: Open University Press.; WOOLNOUGH, B.E. & TOH, K.A. (1990). 'Alternative approaches to assessment of practical work in science', School Science Review, Vol 71, No 256, March.; TOH, K.A. (1989). 'Investigative work: can students do it?', Scientas, Singapore: Science Teachers Association of Singapore, Vol 23, pp.5-8.

Source of Grant: Institute of Education Singapore
Date of Research: 1987-1990
KEYWORDS: *laboratory work; performance; performance factors; pupil*

8/1239

Department of Educational Studies
15 Norham Gardens, Oxford OX2 6PY
0865 274024
Filmer-Sankey, C.F. Mrs; *Supervisor:* Phillips, D.G. Dr

Attitudes towards first foreign languages in the early stages of secondary school: an investigation into French, German and Spanish

Abstract: This study is being undertaken within the framework of the OXPROD (Oxford Project on Diversification of First Foreign Language Teaching) and draws on information from the same sample of six 11-18 schools and c. 1,100 pupils used in the main project. The study aims to investigate pupils' attitudes towards French, German and Spanish where they are taught as first foreign languages. It is focused on how much pupils enjoy the various languages, how difficult they perceive them to be, how useful they think they are and how motivated they are to go to the foreign country. Information is being gathered by means of questionnaires and interviews. Analyses are being carried out to compare pupils' attitudes towards the three different languages, boys' and girls' attitudes and the attitudes of pupils of different abilities. Results so far show pupils to be at least as positively motivated towards German and Spanish as they are towards French. All the evidence gathered will be set within the context of the pupils' learning with detailed accounts of schemes of work, use of course books, teaching styles and composition of groups. Results from questionnaires administered to first-year pupils are published as OXPROD Occasional Paper 3.

Published Material: FILMER-SANKEY, C. (1988). 'Diversification: The OXPROD Project'. In: Coloquio 40: Proceedings of the colloquium on the teaching of Spanish, December 1987, Associa-

tion of teachers of Spanish and Portuguese.; FILMER-SANKEY, C. (1989). 'The basis of choice'. In: PHILLIPS, D. (Ed.) Which language? Diversification and the National Curriculum. London: Hodder & Stoughton.; PHILLIPS, D. & FILMER-SANKEY, C. (1989). 'Vive la difference? Some problems in investigating diversification of first foreign language provision in schools', British Educational Research Journal, Vol 15, No 3.; FILMER-SANKEY, C. (1989). 'A study of first-year pupils' attitudes towards French, German and Spanish', OXPROD Occasional Paper 3. University of Oxford, Department of Educational Studies.

Source of Grant: Oxford University: 1985-1986: £2,600 1987 No funding
Date of Research: 1985 – continuing
KEYWORDS: *foreign languages; modern languages; motivation for studies; pupil secondary education*

8/1240

Department of Educational Studies
15 Norham Gardens, Oxford OX2 6PY
0865 274024
Monteiro, B.F. Ms; *Supervisor:* Backhouse, J.K.

Factors affecting mathematics teachers' use of computers and software in secondary schools

Abstract: The aim of this research is to investigate the multidimensional and social and psychological factors affecting mathematics teachers' use of computers in secondary schools. Data is being collected from 101 mathematics teachers in 32 secondary comprehensive schools in two stages: (a) questionnaires including attitude scales (Likert Type); (b) interviews in mathematics department in some schools. Non inferential statistical methods are being used in the questionnaires analysis. Qualitative approaches were preferred for the interviews. All data-gathering is being carried out in Oxfordshire.

Source of Grant: Capes/Brazilian Government
Date of Research: 1987 – continuing
KEYWORDS: *computer; mathematics; secondary school; teacher attitude; teacher behaviour*

8/1241

Department of Educational Studies
15 Norham Gardens, Oxford OX2 6PY
0865 274024
Wilson, J. Mr

Moral education

Abstract: Theoretical basis and practice of moral education personal and social education pastoral care. Philosophical analysis of relevant concepts, an empirical enquiry into teachers and others perceptions (from random samples) and interviews determining whether teachers' perceptions can be altered socratically.

Published Material: WILSON, J. (1986). What philosophy can do. London: Macmillan; WILSON, J. (1987). Preface to morality. London: Macmillan; A complete list of publications is available from the researcher
Source of Grant: Privately funded
Date of Research: 1987 – continuing
KEYWORDS: *moral education; pastoral care*

8/1242

Department of Educational Studies
15 Norham Gardens, Oxford OX2 6PY
0865 274024
Pring, R.A. Prof.

Technology through home economics (TTHE): evaluation

Abstract: Evaluation of the way in which TTHE (technology through home economics) is affecting practice within the pilot authority schools (7 South-West LEA's), particularly in the way in which home economics delivers TTHE and yet maintain its distinctive identity. Different ways of gathering data from participating schools are brought together in a tentative annual report as the basis for further discussion.

Source of Grant: Training Agency (now Training Enterprise Education Division (TEED)): £3,000
Date of Research: 1989-1990
KEYWORDS: *design education; evaluation; home economics; technology; technology education*

8/1243

Department of Educational Studies
15 Norham Gardens, Oxford OX2 6PY
0865 274024

Mpepo, V.M. Mr; *Supervisor:* Miller, A. Ms; Phillips, D. Dr
A study of functional/communicative teaching of oral English in some Zambian schools
Abstract: Accepting the view put forward by several authors, (Hymes 1972, Saville-Troike 1982), that the concept of communicative competence, or what it means to know a language for communication purposes has to be embedded in the socio-cultural context, the introduction of a functional/communicative question of what patterns and characteristics will have to be used during the teaching and learning process. Considering that Zambia is traditionally a country with a multiplicity of socio-cultural and linguistic characteristics, the study is interested in establishing which characteristics are used in the teaching of communcation skills in English. Since Zambia can technically be called an ESL (English as a second language) situation, the problem also becomes that of establishing whether Zambian or British socio-cultural patterns are encouraged during the learning process. Broadly speaking, however, the study aims to illustrate what the teaching of oral English using the functional/communicative methodology amounts to in the Zambian context. The study offers a unique opportunity to look at the translation of theory into practice in a radically different environment from where it was developed.
Source of Grant: Rhodes Trust Overseas Research Scholarship
Date of Research: 1987-1990
KEYWORDS: communication skills; communicative competence; English (second language teaching; oral work; spoken language; verbal communication; Zambia

8/1244

Department of Educational Studies
15 Norham Gardens, Oxford OX2 6PY
0865 274024
Wilson, J. Mr
Religious Education and the new Act
Abstract: Theoretical basis and practice of religious education. A philosophical analysis and empirical enquiry into teachers and others perceptions (from random samples), and interviews determining whether teachers' perceptions can be altered socratically.
Published Material: WILSON, J. (1986). What philosophy can do. London: Macmillan.; WILSON, J. (1987). Preface to morality. London: Macmillan.; A complete list of publications is available from the researcher
Source of Grant: Privately funded
Date of Research: 1987 – continuing
KEYWORDS: Religious education

8/1245

Department of Educational Studies
15 Norham Gardens, Oxford OX2 6PY
0865 274024
West, D. Mr; *Supervisor:* Pring, R.A. Prof.
Technical and Vocational Iniative (TVEI) evaluation: Dorset
Abstract: The final year of Dorset TVEI (Technical and Educational Initiative) is being closely observed by a retired head teacher who, through interviews with key staff and through observation and through participation in meetings, is able to identify key issues that need to be addressed by the project. Results are reported annually to the TVEI team.
Source of Grant: Training Agency (now Training Enterprise Education Division (TEED)): £4,000
Date of Research: 1986-1990
KEYWORDS: evaluation; technical education; vocational education

8/1246

Department of Educational Studies
15 Norham Gardens, Oxford OX2 6PY
0865 274024
Wilson, J. Mr
Philosophy in schools
Abstract: Teaching of philosophy in schools and elsewhere. A philosophical analysis, and empirical enquiry into teachers' and others perceptions (from random samples) and interviews determining whether teachers' perceptions can be altered socratically.
Published Material: WILSON. J. (1986). What philosophy can do. London: Macmillan.; WILSON. J. (1987). Preface to morality. London: Macmillan.
Source of Grant: Privately funded
Date of Research: 1987 – continuing
KEYWORDS: philosophy; schools

8/1247

Department of Educational Studies
15 Norham Gardens, Oxford OX2 6PY
0865 274024
Williams, V. Dr
Appraisal for LEA (Local Education Authority) staff
Abstract: The problem of perception of reviewer and reviewed is central to performance appraisal. If it is improved through a focused dialogue about performance at individual and relevant organizational levels, its sharing is itself a developmental process owned by at least two individuals with the prize that both recognize the importance of the mutuality of the process and their interdependence in the search for improved collective performance. Oranizational development arises from individual development, and a central management task is to ensure the improved performance of employees through the development of appropriate skills. Equally important is the encouragement of loyalty and commitment to organizational objectives through the creation of a 'climate' which has these characteristics as central values permeating performance appraisal procedures. We show the core value of mutuality, and consequently our appraisal system is entitled 'mutual review and development'.
Source of Grant: Local Education Authorities: expenses
Date of Research: 1987-1990
KEYWORDS: assessment; performance; personnel; personnel evaluation

8/1248

Department of Educational Studies
15 Norham Gardens, Oxford OX2 6PY
0865 274024
Miller, J.F. Mrs; *Supervisor:* McIntyre, D. Mr
The behaviour of bright disruptive children in the classroom
Abstract: The aim of the research is to discover whether or not there are distinctions to be made, in terms of classroom behaviour and related cognitive processes, between disruptive pupils who have high academic potential (HAP) and other disruptive pupils. The nature of any such distinctions are to be investigated. The study consists of two phases. The first phase, already completed, established that the research questions were valid and that the phenomenon of disruptive behaviour by 'HAP' pupils was distinct from disruptive behaviour by other pupils. Techniques used here included construct elicitation and repertory grid work with teachers and informal observation in the classroom. The second phase consists of a triangulation process which attempts to obtain the perspectives of teachers, disruptive 'HAP' pupils, disruptive non-'HAP' pupils and an outside observer. The techniques being used are systematic observation, semi-structured interviews and questionnaire work.
Source of Grant: Private Trust Funds
Date of Research: 1988 – continuing
KEYWORDS: disruptive pupil

8/1249

Department of Educational Studies
15 Norham Gardens, Oxford OX2 6PY
0865 274024
Westminster College
Harcourt Hill, North Hinskey, Oxford OX2 9AT
0865 247644
Atkinson, S. Ms; *Supervisor:* McIntyre, D. Mr
Strategies of school-based teacher development in relation to primary maths teaching
Abstract: The project is an action research investigation, undertaken from the position of Deputy Headteacher/Teacher with responsibility for mathematics, designed at one level to develop the use of an investigative approach to mathematics teaching without threatening or 'deskilling' collegues; and at a more theoretical level, designed to implement and to test principles formulated by Patrick Easen for the effective professional development of teachers.
Source of Grant: No funding
Date of Research: 1987 – continuing
KEYWORDS: mathematics; primary education; teacher

8/1250

Department of Educational Studies
15 Norham Gardens, Oxford OX2 6PY
0865 274024
Corney, G.J. Mr
Geography, schools and industry project (GSIP)

Abstract: GSIP (Geography, schools and industry project) is a curriculum development and research project with two aims: (1) to identify the contribution of geography teachers in helping pupils aged 11-16 to increase their economic understanding; (2) to involve geography teachers and the Geographical Association together with persons from industry and commerce in the development, dissemination and evaluation of activities designed to promote such understanding. Its process of curriculum development involves a partnership between local (LEA) groups and a central team. The role of the local groups consists of development, evaluation and dissemination; the role of the central team consists of support, research and dissemination. GSIP has involved groups of teachers in 25 LEA's Given the context of GSIP, the aims of the research are; (1) to record the innovations carried out by teachers; (2) to investigate the factors which influence teachers as they innovate. A survey approach through case studies of teachers in the context of their own schools and LEA groups. The sample consists of teachers in each of at least 5 LEA groups. The methods used are: (1) record of teachers' schemes of work; (2) questionnaire to all project participants; (3) semi-structured interviews with teachers om sample LEA's.
Published Material: CORNEY, G.J. (Eds). (1985). Geography, schools and industry. Sheffield: Geographical Association.; CORNEY, G.J., BEVAN, D., & KELLY, J. (1986). 'The geography, schools and industry project', Teaching Geography, Vol 11, No 1, pp.106-117, April; CORNEY, G.J. (1988). 'What influences school centred curriculum development'. Proceedings of 1988 Symposium on Geographical Education. International Graphical Union: Brisbane, Australia.; CORNEY, G.J. (Eds). (1991). 'Teaching economic understanding through geography: the experience of GSIP. Sheffield: Geographical Association.; RAWLING, E. (1990). 'Geography: working with the community to study a local issue', Economic Awareness, Vol 2, No 3.; RAWLING, E. & CORNEY, G.J. (1991). 'Geography and economic understanding in the National Curriculum. Harlow: Longman Group Ltd.
Source of Grant: Banking Information Service British Petroleum Building Societies Association British Telecom plc Department of Trade & Industry Training Agency The Nestle Company: jointly £220,000
Date of Research: 1984 – continuing
KEYWORDS: curriculum development; educational innovation; geography; industry; relation; secondary education

8/1251
Department of Educational Studies
15 Norham Gardens, Oxford OX2 6PY
0865 274024
Filmer-Sankey, C.F. Mrs; Clark, G.A. Dr; Geatches, H. Miss; *Supervisor:* Phillips, D.G. Dr
Oxford project on diversification of first foreign language teaching (OXPROD)
Abstract: Although it is now government policy to encourage diversification of first foreign language (FL1) teaching, French continues to predominate as the sole FL1 taught in British schools. OXPROD aims to investigate and compare pupils' experience of learning French and languages other than French (LOTF). The research hypothesis is that there is nothing in the nature of German, Spanish and Italian as subjects in the school curriculum that makes these languages unsuitable as FL1s for the whole ability range. It aims to describe in detail pupils' experience of learning French, German, Spanish and Italian where they are taught as first foreign languages, focusing on two main areas: pupil attitude to learning and difficulties encountered in each language. The project will also shed light on organizational problems for schools. The main investigative work is taking place in six 11-18 comprehensive schools in which LOTF are taught in parallel or together with French as FL1s. A further number of 'associated schools' will provide information on organizational problems and policy issues. Pupils' and teachers' attitudes to the languages will be assessed once a year by attitude questionnaires and interviews. School attainment test scores will be collected. Evidence gathered will be set within the context of the pupils' learning with a detailed account of schemes of work, use of course books, teaching styles, timetabling and composition of groups. A series of occasional papers will be published as the research progresses, a report will be written at the end of December 1990, and a final report at the end of December 1992.
Published Material: PHILLIPS, D. (1989). (Eds). Which language? diversification and the National Curriculum. London: Hodder & Stoughton.; PHILLIPS, D. & FILMER-SANKEY, C. (1989). 'Some problems in investigating diversification of first foreign lan-

guage provision in schools', British Educational Research Journal, Vol 15, No 3. A full list of publications is available from the researcher.
Source of Grant: The Leverhulme Trust; 2 grants: £84,250 & £73,700 The Goethe Institut: £4,200 The Italian Cultural Institute: £150 The Spanish Institute: £2,500 Oxford University General Board: £16,000
Date of Research: 1987 – continuing
KEYWORDS: curriculum development; educational policy; first foreign language; teaching

8/1252
Department of Educational Studies
15 Norham Gardens, Oxford OX2 6PY
0865 274024
Palacio, D. Dr; Kruger, C.J. Mr; *Supervisor:* Summers, M.K. Mr
Primary school teachers and science (PSTS) Project
Abstract: The Primary School Teachers and Science Project is investigating primary school teachers' understanding of science concepts in the light of the National Curriculum and its requirement that primary pupils should develop an understanding of specified science concepts. In the first phase of the research, in depth interviews of an opportunity sample of 20 primary teachers were used to investigate the teachers' understanding of forces, changes in materials and energy. The findings showed that nearly all the teachers interviewed held views of science concepts that are not in accord with the generally accepted scientific viewpoint. The work moved on to establish the prevalance of particular misconceptions in a large number of primary teachers (about 450) using a questionnaire based on the interview findings. In the light of the results, inservice training materials are being produced to help improve understanding in areas identified as most problematical.
Published Material: KRUGER, C. (1990). 'Some primary teachers ideas about energy', Physics Education, Vol 25, No 2, pp.86-91, March; KRUGER, C., PALACIO, D. & SUMMERS, M. (1990a). 'A survey of primary school teachers' conceptions of force and motion', Educational Research, Vol 32, No 2, pp.83-95.; KRUGER, C., PALACIO, D. & SUMMERS, M. (1990b). 'Adding forces – a target for primary science INSET', British Journal of Inservice Education, Vol 16, No 1, pp.45-52.; KRUGER, C. & SUMMERS, M. (1988). 'Primary school teachers' understanding of science concepts', Journal of Education for Teaching, Vol 14, No 3, pp.259-265.; KRUGER, C. & SUMMERS, M. (1989). 'An investigation of some primary teachers' understanding of changes in materials', School Science Review, Vol 71, No 255, pp.17-27. December.; KRUGER, C., PALACIO, D. & SUMMERS, M. (1990). Primary school teachers and science project: Forces, INSET pack. Oxford: Oxford University Department of Educational Studies/Westminster College, Oxford.; KRUGER, C., PALACIO, D. & SUMMERS, M. (1990). Primary school teachers and science project: Energy, INSET pack. Oxford: University Department of Educational Studies/Westminster College, Oxford.; a full list of publications is available from the researcher
Source of Grant: Leverhulme Trust: £58,850 (1989 & 1990)
Date of Research: 1987-1990
KEYWORDS: comprehension; concept formation; inservice education and training of teachers; primary education; science education; teacher

8/1253
Department of Educational Studies
15 Norham Gardens, Oxford OX2 6PY
0865 274024
Solomon, J. Dr
Discussion of issues in school science
Abstract: This project is a part of the linked research programme organized by the Science Policy Research Group on the public understanding of science. It aims to explore how 17 year old school students who are taking a course in Science Technology and Society discuss science-based social issues presented to them by the showing of a video. In each of the two school years 1988-89 and 1989-90 some 10 schools are taking part in different parts of the country. The size of the classes involved varies from 5 to 25. Each discussion group contains only 3 to 4 students who tape record their own discussions. There are six different videos which are shown in order during the year. The tapes are transcribed and studied by content and by individual contribution. Pre- and post-questionnaires are also administered and compared with those completed by control groups in each school. Results obtained so far show how the stu-

dents use their knowledge, their personal experiences, their value systems and their attributions of bias in coming to opinions about the issues.
Published Material: SOLOMON, J. & SWIFT, J. (1989). 'Talking about kidney transplants', Journal of Biological Education, Vol 24, No 1, pp.27-31.; SOLOMON, J. (1989). 'Discussing nuclear power', Physics Education, Vol 24, No 6, pp.344-347, November.; SOLOMON, J. (1990). 'The discussion of social issues in the science classroom', Studies in Science Education, No 18, pp.105-126.; SOLOMON, J. & HARRISON, K. (1990). 'Arguing about industrial wastes', Education in Chemistry, Vol 27, No 6, pp.160-162.
Source of Grant: Economic and Social Research Council: £68,000
Date of Research: 1988 – continuing
KEYWORDS: discussion; influence; mass media; science education; secondary education; social environment

8/1254
Department of Experimental Psychology
South Parks Road, Oxford OX1 3UD
0865 274024
Henry, L.A. Dr; *Supervisor:* Millar, S. Dr
The development of memory in children
Abstract: The aim of this research was to determine why memory span improves with age. Memory span involves remembering sequences of discrete items, and is an important skill which is often assumed to underpin intellectual development. Three hypotheses, and the evidence for them were reviewed and tested. The rehearsal hypothesis, which suggested children learn a strategy of repeating items covertly in order to improve recall, was not supported with children aged five to seven years, and only very limited evidence was found to support it in the age range of seven to nine years. This was important, as much previous work had assumed a central role for rehearsal in this age range. The identification time hypothesis suggested that an increase in the familiarity of words with age could explain the development of memory span. However, although word familiarity clearly increased between the ages of 5 and 7 years, this factor could not on its own explain span development. The articulation time hypothesis argued that children become faster at rehearsing items with age and that this improves recall. The key factor was speech rate (from the working memory model), and the use of rehearsal at all ages was assumed. This model was modified, because little evidence for rehearsal had been found. The modified version assumed that speed of recalling items was the critical factor rather than speed of rehearsing them. Some support was found for this model, but there were certain important qualifications. It was concluded that the development of memory span is complex, involving several factors including familiarity with the materials and speech rate. Accounts which focus almost exclusively on rehearsal, either as the main factor or as an assumed process are not adequate.
Published Material: HENRY, L.A. (1991). 'Word length and phonemic similarity effects in young children's short-term memory', Quarterly Journal of Experimental Psychology, (forthcoming).; HENRY, L.A. (1991). 'The development of auditory memory span: the role of rehearsal', British Journal of Developmental Psychology, (forthcoming).
Source of Grant: Economic and Social Research Council
Date of Research: 1986-1989
KEYWORDS: rehearsal

8/1255
Department of Social and Administrative Studies
Barnett House, Wellington Square, Oxford OX1 2ER
0865 52041/5
Aldgate, J. Dr; Heath, A.F. Dr
The educational progress of children in care
Abstract: This research aims to identify factors contributing to the educational success or difficulties of children in care. To this end the researchers aim is to study young children in care, together with their parents and careers, and to compare their social and educational experiences with those of young children living with their own families but known to social services department and receiving social work help (probably under Section 1, 1980 Child Care Act). In order to draw causal inferences about the educational consequences of being in care, a longitudinal research design is required. It is therefore proposed to follow up children over a two-year period, measuring their educational progress over this time. This would enable the research staff to tackle important questions such as whether children entering care are already lagging behind educa-

tionally and whether, once in care, they make as much progress as the control group living with their own families.
Source of Grant: Economic and Social Research Council: £56,830
Date of Research: 1987 – continuing
KEYWORDS: achievement; child care; comparative achievement; social work

Peterborough Regional College

8/1256
Park Cresent, Peterborough PE1 4DZ
0733 67366
Surrey University
Department of Educational Studies
Guildford GU2 5XH
0483 571281
Edey, D. Mrs; *Supervisor:* Haffenden, I. Dr
Developing the competency based curriculum in further education for National Vocational Qualifications
Abstract: The research is still in its early stages. It is intended to use a variety of departments and qualifications to review developments, questionnaire and concept map staff, in order to gain a more informed understanding of the concepts underpinning the development of competence based qualifications at the level of college lecturer.
Source of Grant: Peterborough Regional College
Date of Research: 1988 – continuing
KEYWORDS: competency based education; curriculum development; further education; vocational education

Polytechnic of East London

8/1257
Centre for Institutional Studies,
Manbey Park Road, London E15 1EY
081 590 7722
Locke, M. Mr; Gallagher, A. Ms; *Supervisor:* Locke, M. Mr
Government and management of colleges of further education before the implementation of the Education Reform Act 1988
Abstract: The research is to establish a base-case of college government and management before the Education Reform Act so that future research can assess the changes consequent upon the Act. Methods include documentary analysis of government, questionnaire survey of principals on their experiences and views, collection of data on college income; collection of data on attendance at governors' meetings and a questionnaire survey of governors from industry and commerce on their experiences and views.
Source of Grant: Department of Education and Science: £15,682
Welsh Office: £1,716
Date of Research: 1990-1990
KEYWORDS: college administration; college of further education; governance; education; post-compulsory education

8/1258
Centre for Institutional Studies,
Manbey Park Road, London E15 1EY
081 590 7722
Locke, M. Mr
College government
Abstract: The study is monitoring the impact of present systems of college government and proposing solutions to current problems. One part of this work during 1986-87 was to advise the Committee of Directors of Polytechnics on corporate status for polytechnics. The study is using documentary analysis (including instruments and articles of government) and interviews.
Published Material: LOCKE, M., PRATT, J., SILVERMAN, S. & TRAVERS, T. (1987). 'Polytechnic Government', Committee of Directors of Polytechnics.; LOCKE, M. (1987). 'The instruments and articles of government of polytechnics', Centre for Institutional Studies Commentary, NELPCO, North East London Polytechnic.
Source of Grant: Committee of Directors of Polytechnics (in part)/internal Polytechnic funding

Date of Research: 1984 – continuing
KEYWORDS: administration of education; further education; governing body; higher education; polytechnic

8/1259
Department of Business Studies
Longbridge Road,
Dagenham RM8 2AS
081 590 7722
London University, Department of Economic,
Administrative and Policy Studies in Education,
Institute of Education, 20 Bedford Way,
London WC1H OAL,
London Borough of Waltham Forest,
School Psychological Service,
Summerfield Centre, Leyton Green Road,
London E10 6DB
071 636 1500 (London University);
081 556 9951 (London Borough of Waltham Forest)
Gersch, I.S.; *Supervisor:* McKenna, E. Prof.; Young, P. Dr
School organization and management and pupil behaviour
Abstract: The aim of this research is to investigate aspects of school management and systems and pupil behaviour in a number of secondary schools.
Published Material: GERSCH, I.S. (1984). 'Behaviour modification and systems analysis in a secondary school: combining two approaches', Behavioural Approaches with Children, The quarterly journal of the Association for Behavioural Approaches with Children, Vol 8, No 3, pp.83-91.
Source of Grant: London Borough of Waltham Forest and personal funding
Date of Research: 1984-1990
KEYWORDS: administration of education; behaviour; pupil; secondary education; system of education

Polytechnic of Wales

8/1260
Llantwit Road,
Treforest, Pontypridd,
Mid Glamorgan CF37 2AB
0443 480480
Beynon, J. Dr; Mackay, H. Dr
Information technology into education
Abstract: The research starts from the position that information technology (IT) has been introduced into schools with few questions being asked. Unlike previous educational technologies and innovations, questions about the relationship of IT to teaching and learning have not featured prominently in the agenda. 'More' is seen as inherently better, as perceived economic needs become translated into educational practices. Hard and software therefore remain the emphasis, and problems and limitations are addressed insufficiently. The study is concerned to apply ethnographic, classroom based research approach to IT in education, within an interactionist perspective. Field work is underway in three LEAs, in primary and secondary sectors, and focusing on the teaching of literacy and computer literacy. The work locates IT in education in its broader social, historical and cultural context; dismantles the technoromantic rhetoric which surrounds the subject, and develops a range of critical and analytical concepts to inform both a theoretical understanding of IT in education and teacher practice in this area. The work will continue post-1991 with an ethnographic analysis of technology-in-use in teaching and learning in selected contexts in both primary and secondary schools.
Published Material: MACKAY, H., YOUNG, M. & BEYNON, J. (1991). Computers in classrooms: more questions than answers, Volume 1. London: Falmer Press. (forthcoming).; BEYNON, J. & MACKAY, H. (1991). Computers in classrooms: more questions than answers, Volume 2. London: Falmer Press. (forthcoming).; BEYNON, J. & MACKAY, H. (1991). Computers in classrooms: more questions than answers, Volume 3. London: Falmer Press. (forthcoming).
Source of Grant: No funding
Date of Research: 1987-1989
KEYWORDS: computer; educational innovation; educational policy; information technology

8/1261
Department of Behavioural and Communication Studies
Room T9, Pontypridd CF37 1DL
0443 480480 ext 2597
Francis, L. Mr; *Supervisor:* Granfield, A.J. Dr
Pre-vocational education and the transfer from school to work
Abstract: The project has grown out of previous research into friendship cliques in the classroom and academic performance. The project is concerned with the transfer from school to work at the age of 16 +. It is examining the perceived needs of industry in terms of the qualities and skills they require of young employees, it is investigating the actual qualities and skills of young employees in relation to their success in adapting to the world of work, and it is looking at the attempts of the educational establishment to create a more vocational curriculum. Two schemes have recently been instituted to help overcome what is seen as a lack of secondary education: the Technical and Vocational Education Initiative (TVEI) and the Certificate of Pre-vocational Education (CPVE). Part of the research involves an evaluation of TVEI/CPVE training, and other similar initiatives of particular interest is the extent to which such courses have involved industry in their preparation, and the extent to which courses actually being taught reflect the aims of the planning groups. Two surveys have already been completed, and preliminary results published.
Published Material: GRANFIELD, A.J. & JONES, T.C. (1986). 'Government forces education to see the writing on the wall', The Teacher, Vol 8, 6th April.; GRANFIELD, A.J. & JONES, T.C. (1987). Education and industry links in South East Wales. The Polytechnic of Wales, Recruitment and Training Research Unit.
Source of Grant: No funding
Date of Research: 1985 – continuing
KEYWORDS: curriculum development; industry; transition from school to work; vocational education; youth employment

Polytechnic South West

8/1262
Drake Circus, Plymouth, Devon PL4 8AA
0752 60600
Graham, E. Mr; *Supervisor:* Berry, J. Dr; Burghes, D.N. Prof.
The use of video in teaching mechanics
Abstract: This project has concentrated on two areas, the evaluation of video for teaching mechanics and student understanding of mechanics. An experiment designed to determine whether video can improve student understanding of mechanics is being undertaken. The first stage of this was the preparation of a review of the existing video resources for mechanics. From this a teaching programme was developed in consultation with the teaching staff involved. Tests have been developed to measure student understanding. These have been trialled in local schools and modified to provide an effective means of assessing understanding. The data that has been collected from the experiment to date has revealed that there is no significant difference between the performance of the control and experimental groups on the tests. However, student reactions to the videos, recorded on questionnaires, have provided much useful information. From this it has been possible to suggest the best way to use video in mechanics. This approach has been used in the production of two videos, which will be evaluated as the project continues. From the responses given by the students on the experiment's pre-test it has been possible to identify the students initial, intuitive ideas about mechanics concepts. The post-test responses have been used to formulate a model of conceptual development, based on a set of hierarchies, for the concept of force. The project is continuing with a large scale survey to validate the model described above and with the extension of the video experiment.
Published Material: GRAHAM, E. & BERRY, J. (1989). 'Video resources for the teaching of mechanics', Mathematics in school, Vol 18, No 2, March.; GRAHAM, E. (1989). 'A review of the video materials available for the teaching of mechanics at A-level'. Exeter University
Source of Grant: Polytechnic funded
Date of Research: 1988 – continuing
KEYWORDS: comprehension; concept formation; mechanics; teaching aids; video recording

8/1263

Drake Circus,
Plymouth P14 8AA
0752 600600
Prideaux, A. Mr; *Supervisor:* Winders, R. Mr; Moreby,
D. Prof.

Evaluation of support systems for open distance learning

Abstract: The research aims to: (1) compare the effectiveness of existing open/distance learning support systems; (2) to develop, pilot and apply a modified support system to produce improved success rates for open/distance learners. The intended method involves producing, piloting and distributing questionnaires designed to obtain information on the effectiveness of a number of tutoring strategies in selected open/distance learning schemes. Interviews will then be conducted with a sample of students that have completed or dropped out of these schemes. Samples will be obtained using the records of the collaborating delivery systems, at present there are: Total Training, Exeter; Eastek, Ipswich; Flexible Learning Unit, Slough; Manchester Open Learning. Others are under negotiation. The information gained will be used to identify the constraining and enabling variables in the support systems under investigation. From this information theoretical constructs and support models will be identified. From appropriate models the data will be analyzed and a theoretical support model will be constructed and tested. The models developed will be introduced in collaborating organizations and their effectiveness analyzed. These models will then be examined to determine their more general applicability to other open/distance learning situations.

Source of Grant: No funding
Date of Research: 1988 – continuing
KEYWORDS: distance study; open learning; support services

8/1264

Rolle Faculty of Education
Centre for International Studies,
Exmouth EX8 2AT
0395 264902
Morgan, R. Mr; Dunlop, J. Mr; Zwaga, K.; Godwin, N.
Ms; Dreyer, I. Ms

Environment, development and migration project

Abstract: This research project involves three phases: materials collation; strategy development; piloting and dissemination. In phase 1, five third world locations were visited to examine environment problems, development policy which addresses these and resultant migration. Action research teams are drawn from Eire, Netherlands (Nd), United Kingdom (UK), Federal Republic of Germany (FRG) and Denmark (DK). The second phase involves detailed development and piloting of teaching strategies at primary and secondary levels for implementation in participating countries. The third phase involves a process of dissemination in each country. Central evaluation is carried out by: (1) Dr. Hans Hooghoff, CEVNO, The Netherlands. (2) Professor Ingrid Classen-Bauer, Hochshule Luneberg, FRG. (3) Dr Roy Williams, School of Education, University of Sussex, Brighton. (4) Dr Jurgen Jansen, Institute fur Politische Wissenschaft, Aachen, (FRG).

Source of Grant: Foundation for International Education Commission of European Communities Danish Broadcasting Christian Aid German Foundation: jointly £140,000
Date of Research: 1986-1989
KEYWORDS: developing country; development policy; environmental study; teaching method

Poole General Hospital

8/1265

Maternity Unit,
Longfleet Road,
Poole BH15 2JB
0202 675100
Surrey University
Department of Educational Studies
Guildford GU2 5XH
0483 571281
Emmons, E. Mrs; *Supervisor:* Jarvis, P. Dr

The values, beliefs and knowledge base in midwifery – in search of commonalities

Abstract: This study examines the relationship of theory and practice in midwifery. The initial explanatory phase of the research suggests that there is a gap between theory and practice that involves more than mere technical skills and procedures. There appeared to be a differing set of values, beliefs and a knowledge base adopted by the clinicians and educators of midwifery. By using a naturalistic research methodology, it is hoped that the research will generate some hypotheses and a theory.

Source of Grant: No funding
Date of Research: 1989 – continuing
KEYWORDS: midwifery; theory practice relationship

Queen Margaret College

8/1266

Department of Occupational Therapy
Clerwood Terrace,
Edinburgh EH12 8TS
031 339 8111
Strathclyde University
Department of Psychology
Turnbull Building,
155 George Street,
Glasgow G1 1RD
041 552 4400
Nicol, M. M. Ms; *Supervisor:* Anderson, A. Dr

Use of computers with mentally handicapped people

Abstract: The design of this research project permits comparisons to be made among a computer assisted learning group of mentally handicapped adults, a more traditional intervention group and a normal control group in an adult training centre. In particular the areas of numeracy skills, literacy skills and community living skills will be investigated in some detail.

Source of Grant: No funding
Date of Research: 1987 – continuing
KEYWORDS: adult education; computer assisted instruction; life skills; literacy education; mentally handicapped; numeracy

Queen's College

8/1267

1 Park Drive,
Glasgow G3 6LP
041 337 4000
McCormack, A.E. Dr; Gardner, A.P.W. Mr

Power and Action: students with special needs in higher education

Abstract: This research arises out of recent figures (British Psychological Society 1989) which suggest that up to one in six people in the general population have special needs. These special needs may be described as physical, sensory or mental impairment caused by a congenital condition, birth trauma or acquisition through accident or disease. Within education, students with special needs may be those identifed above, but, it is argued that students returning to education after long term unemployment or absence for domestic reasons, should also be included, since they often display similar characteristics, e.g. a lack of self confidence and self esteem, associated with students with a disability. This research aims to estimate the proportion of students with special needs who have chosen to be in further and higher education; canvass their opinions on access to education in their own institution and to education in general, and investigate the policy status of institutions, i.e. do they have a policy on students with special needs, and does the policy match the perception of the students in its implementation.

Published Material: McCORMACK, A.E. & GARDNER, A.P.W. (1991). 'Students with special needs in higher education'. Proceedings of Standing Conference on Educational Development Annual Conference. May 1990. Gateshead, Newcastle upon Tyne: Newcastle upon Tyne Polytechnic.
Source of Grant: Internal college and staff development funding
Date of Research: 1990 – continuing
KEYWORDS: further education

8/1268

> 1 Park Drive, Glasgow G3 6LP
> 041 334 8141
> McCormack, A.E. Dr; Gardner, A.P. W. Mr

Power and action: looking at life

Abstract: This research concerns the learning package 'Looking at Life' which was developed to fill a need in the provision of learning materials to facilitate students self-awareness and promote consideration of his/her lifestyle. Whilst other packages are available for use on a group basis, no other package is suitable for use on an individual study plan. The package currently consists of six basic units, but it is envisaged that other units will be added in the near future. The basic package was used and evaluated by staff and students at a Scottish centre for students with disabilities who were entering higher education. Small numbers in this group preclude statistical analysis, but feedback sessions indicate a strong positive acceptance of the value of this approach. The aims of 'Looking at Life' relate to the development of self awareness and the promotion of life skills. This package is suitable for all age groups and levels of ability and is especially useful for individuals with special needs. Further work in the use and evaluation of this package with students with disability is urgently required. The 'Power and Action' project based in The Queen's College, Glasgow seeks to facilitate this development. Individuals interested in trying the package out as part of an extended pilot study should contact the project directors. Other content areas need to be developed to extend this package. Ideas for future collaboration and module development are invited.

Source of Grant: No funding
Date of Research: 1988 – continuing
KEYWORDS: life skills

8/1269

> Department of Health Studies
> 1 Park Drive,
> Glasgow G3 6LP
> 041 334 8141
> Gardner, A. Mr; Myles, S. Ms

An investigation into the attitudes of students

Abstract: The 1987/88 cohort of applicants for entry to BSc (Physiotherapy) completed various attitudinal and personality measures. Analysis of the results will compare successful with unsuccessful applicants. Students selected for the course will be monitored for a three year period. Implications for procedures in the selection of students will be examined. Attitudinal profiles of students will be compared to establish professional profiles in specialist areas in physiotherapy. The assumption of professional roles is a central feature.

Source of Grant: Queen's College
Date of Research: 1987 – continuing
KEYWORDS: attitude; higher education; selection; student

8/1270

> Department of Physiotherapy
> 1 Park Drive,
> Glasgow G3 6LP
> 041 334 8141
> Donaghy, H.A. Miss; *Supervisor:* Bell, F. Dr; McCormack, A. Dr; Garven, F. Mrs

Critical evaluation of the assessment of clinical education in the BSc physiotherapy, The Queens College, Glasgow

Abstract: Physiotherapy students are required by the Chartered Society of Physiotherapy to complete 1000 hours on clinical site. They do this under the guidance and supervision of qualified physiotherapists and their level of competence on each placement is assessed. Centres responsible for the education of physiotherapists devise their own clinical assessment methodology. At The Queen's College, Glasgow there has been growing concern over the validity and reliability of the assessment procedure. This project has arisen from a need to investigate the concern. The main aims of the project are to identify and investigate problems with the present clinical assessment procedure and to examine the process of changing it. The first part of the study concentrates on the current method and considers the devising of the system, its content validity, how it is used, problems with its use and an investigation of identified problems. Methodology includes questionnaires, interviews, observation on clinical site, tests of inter-rater reliability, student self-rating and an analysis of former student clinical grades. Results from this part of the study will be used to inform the review of clinical education assessment. Proposed changes will be evaluated

and their introduction monitored. In addition the retrospective views of former graduates will be surveyed and reported to the Department of Physiotherapy.
Source of Grant: The Queens College: £3500
Date of Research: 1988 – continuing
KEYWORDS: assessment; health service personnel; physiotherapy; training

Queen's University of Belfast

8/1271

> Department of Psychology
> University Road, Belfast BT7 1NN
> 0232 245133
> McCann, M.T. Miss; *Supervisor:* Greer, B. Dr

Children's production of word problems fitting calculations involving multiplication and division of integers, fractions and decimals

Abstract: Children's understanding of applications of muliplication and division of integers, decimals and fractions were tested using a method which involved making up stories to fit given calculations. In general the child's ability to write stories has not been widely researched. Three different tests were administered to a total of 480 children (245 girls, 235 boys). Their ages ranged from 9-15 years. The first test involved only integers, the second involved integers and decimals, and the third test involved integers and fractions. Each child worked through nine calculations, 3 muliplication and 6 division. Two stories were constructed for each calculation. Results indicate that the levels of story-writing proficiency vary depending on the numbers and the different calculation combinations present. Writing word problems from calculations that contained either decimals or fractions proved a more difficult task than writing word problems that embodied whole numbers. A classification of the mathematical structures and contexts revealed among other things that equal groups is the most popular model for multiplication, while for division, partition dominates over quotition in the integers test and in the decimals and fractions tests when the divisor is greater than one, but when the divisor is less than one the quotition appears to be the dominant structure in both the decimal and fractions test.

Source of Grant: Department of Education for Northern Ireland: £372,400 per annum
Date of Research: 1989 – continuing
KEYWORDS: composition; mathematics; word problems (mathematics)

Reading University

8/1272

> Bulmershe Court,
> Woodlands Avenue, Earley, Reading RG6 1HY
> 0734 663387
> Theale Green School
> Theale, Reading RG7 5DA
> 0734 302741
> Kempe, A.J. Mr; Holroyd, R. Mr

Drama in the English National Curriculum

Abstract: The end product of the research will be two books for use in top primary/lower secondary classrooms. A pupil book will contain a range of resources on three separate topics. Literature, visual material, realia and research or creative tasks will be bound together by a linking narrative for each of the three topics. An accompanying teacher's book will outline how each individual resource may be used as part of an enactive learning programme and suggest various strategies by which the resources may be combined into dramatic structures. Within the whole project, there will be opportunities to meet the stated attainment targets of English in the National Curriculum document and some reference will also be made to the history, science, and craft, design and technology documents. Most of the material is being trialled at a comprehensive school in Reading. Other elements are being used on Inservice Education of Teachers and a programme of primary school sessions. The final publications are hoped to provide the basis for a more extensive and refined publishing programme aimed at meeting the needs of the National Curriculum without destroying current good practice.

Published Material: KEMPE, A. & HOLROYD, R. (1986). 'Team teaching', 2D, Vol 6, No 1.
Source of Grant: No funding
Date of Research: 1988 – continuing
KEYWORDS: drama; literature

8/1273

Bulmershe Court,
Woodlands Avenue, Earley, Reading RG6 1HY
0734 663387
The Avenue School
Basingstoke Road, Reading RG2 OEN
0734 871032
Kempe, A.J. Mr; *Supervisor:* Weller, M. Mr
Drama and special needs
Abstract: The research syndicate will be made up of three teachers in a special school, two university lecturers and a small number of PGCE (Post Graduate Certificate of Education) drama students. The project will aim to find ways of enabling young people with a variety of special educational needs to engage with drama as an expressive and performing art. The practical work will be trialled with one group of 11- to 12-year olds with moderate learning difficulties and one group of 15- to 17-year olds with various physical and learning difficulties. A report documenting all of the practical project and referring it to the available theory in the field will be produced. A shorter article will be distilled from this and submitted for publication to a national Drama in Education journal.
Source of Grant: Technical Vocational Education Initiative (TVEI) syndicate: £1,500
Date of Research: 1990 – continuing
KEYWORDS: drama; special education

8/1274

London Road, Reading RG1 5AQ
0734 875123
Kunji, F.M.S. Mrs; *Supervisor:* Sheridan, W. Mr
Bahrain primary education reform: a study of social change
Abstract: Focusing on this perspective, the study intends to evaluate the primary education reform project of 1983 in Bahrain as a communication process. It tries to find out the intentions of the reform in relation to the policy makers, the different personnel involved in its implementation – in the Ministry of Education and members of the education department in the University of Bahrain – and the practicing teachers. The empirical part intends to find out the similarity and differences in the opinions about the reform objectives and compare these with what is happening at the school level using three methods of data collection – interviews, questionnaires and observation.
Source of Grant: No funding
Date of Research: 1986-1989
KEYWORDS: Bahrain: educational policy; primary education; reform of education

8/1275

London Road, Reading RG1 5AQ
0734 318846
Malvern, D.D. Mr
Primary mathematics language project
Abstract: The first phase involved the enhancement of performance in mathematics among 6- to 8-year olds by extra small group teaching concentrating on mathematical language and the encouragement of discussion. Phase two generalized the methods to explore activities and organization, and to allow such an approach to become possible within the normal classroom without extra teaching resources. The present phase is consolidating this and exploring the kinds of language which needs stressing in early teaching in order to facilitate children's ability to discuss mathematics.
Published Material: MALVERN, D.D. & BENTLEY, C. (1982). The Reading University/ Berkshire Local Education Authority Mathematics/Language Project evaluation report. Berkshire LEA.; ENSOR, B. & MALVERN, D.D. (1988). Children talking mathematics. Berkshire Local Education Authority.
Source of Grant: Berkshire Local Education Authority (1981-1986)
Blue Circle Cememt plc: (1986-1988)
Date of Research: 1981 – continuing
KEYWORDS: discussion; language development; mathematics; primary education

8/1276

London Road, Reading RG1 5AQ
0734 875123
Watson, J.K.P. Dr
Analysis of local education authorities for multicultural education
Abstract: The purpose of the research is to ascertain, in the light of the Swann Report recommendations, how many local education authorities have introduced multicultural education documents and how many have appointed specialist advisors. It will also examine and compare the similarities and differences; assessing if there is any real impact at school level.
Source of Grant: University Grants Committee
Date of Research: 1987 – continuing
KEYWORDS: educational policy; local education authority; multicultural education

8/1277

London Road, Reading RG1 5AQ
0734 875123 ext 7851
Richards, B. Dr
Environmental predictors of auxiliary and copula verb growth in young children
Abstract: Several studies have found that the frequency of Yes/No questions addressed to young children predicts the rate of which they learn auxiliary verbs. A possible reason is that one category of Yes/Nos highlights the auxiliary by placing it at the beginning of the sentence where it is more likely to be stressed and phonologically non reduced. The problem with this explanation is that researchers who have sub-catergorized Yes/Nos have not generally found such an effect with those which invert the auxiliary. The proposed research will investigate copula and auxiliary verb development to test the hypotheses about the processes of acquiring form classes. Utterances addressed to children will be coded according to the features of the auxiliary or copula which are displayed. Effects of Yes/No inversions, sentence-final ellipsis and tag questions will be examined, as well as the contributions of contracted and non-contracted verb forms in medial positive in declarative utterances. Care in matching children and in calculating child gain scores will circumvent methodological pitfalls for which other research of this type has frequently been criticized. Data will be obtained from existing transcripts of 33 children in the younger cohort of the British Longitudinal Study of Language development. Child language measures will be taken from two recordings (T1 and T2) 9 months apart, and gain scores calculated. Measures of input frequency at T1 will be correlated with the gain scores.
Published Material: RICHARDS, B.J. (1987). 'Individual differences and the development of the auxiliary verb system in young children', Unpublished PhD Dissertation, University of Bristol.; RICHARDS, B.J. (1986). 'Yes/No questions in input and their relationship with rate of auxiliary verb development in young children'. In: Proceedings of the Child Language Seminar, University of Durham.; RICHARDS, B.J. Language development and individual differences: a study of auxilliary verb learning. Cambridge: Cambridge University Press. (in press).
Source of Grant: Economic and Social Research Council: £27,817
Date of Research: 1988-1990
KEYWORDS: child development; language development; language sciences; syntax

8/1278

Agricultural Extension and Rural Development Department
London Road, Reading RG1 5AQ
0734 875123
Further Education Unit
Information Centre, Grove House, 2-6 Orange Street, London WC2H 7WE
071 321 0433
Mackenzie, V.L. Mrs; *Supervisor:* White, J. Dr
Adapting to change: further education and the rural economy – implications for staff development (FEU/Pickup Project RP 578)
Abstract: A changing rural economy is creating a need for new and more flexible training opportunities. Uptake of training is lower in rural areas. Employment patterns are changing, with a growth in rural enterprise and colleges themselves are adapting to local management, and new forms of income generation. In this climate there is a need to see what opportunities are available for staff development and how college lecturers and instructors are updating themselves. The project aims to investigate staff development needs in Further Education, particularly in agricul-

tural colleges in England and Wales. It is intended to make appropriate recommendations concerning these needs, with particular relevance to the provision of more effective, relevant and flexible learning opportunities for manpower development within a changing rural economy. It also aims to identify good practice, focus on the role of agricultural colleges in a future rural economy, and the type and amount of continuing professional development that should be undertaken by their staff. There will be three phases to the project. The first will be an extensive review of literature and research findings. The second stage will involve the collection of data by means of postal questionnaire, in depth interviews and observation techniques in all colleges and centres of agricultural education in the UK and Wales. A sample of these will be selected for an in depth study. Finally, the analysis, interpretation and presentation of results. A report will be produced containing advice on collaborarive procedures for analyzing needs in order to design learning programmes, advice on procedures and techniques for market research and evaluation, case studies of curriculum-led institution development in action at college level, analysis of staff development needs, guidance on how these might be met and evaluation models applicable to staff development programmes.
Source of Grant: Further Education Unit Pickup: jointly £25,911
Date of Research: 1989-1990
KEYWORDS: *agricultural college; economic conditions; further education; further of teachers; inservice teacher education; rural area*

8/1279

Department of Arts and Humanities in Education
Bulmershe Court, Woodlands Avenue,
Earley, Reading RG6 1HY
0734 663387
Woolland, B. Mr; Taylor, E. Ms
Drama, theatre and performance in the primary school
Abstract: The aim is to examine ways of developing drama and theatre in primary schools to enhance the provisions of the National Curriculum, enabling teachers to perceive and use drama and performance as a continuum ranging from small group work in classrooms to large school plays for an external audience; to develop the notion that drama is simultaneously an important subject in its own right and an essential learning medium.
Source of Grant: GRIST (Grant Related Inservice Training): £1,390
Date of Research: 1989-1989
KEYWORDS: *drama; primary school; theatre*

8/1280

Department of Arts and Humanities in Education
Bulmershe Court, Woodlands Avenue,
Earley, Reading RG6 1HY
0734 663387
Richards, B. Dr; Chambers, F. Dr
Oral assessment in modern languages
Abstract: The project will investigate the reliability of oral assessment criteria currently in use at GCSE (General Certificate of Secondary Education) level in Modern Languages. Using a cross section of the criteria used by the Examining groups, 30 French teachers will assess the performance of 30-40 candidates entered for the oral test in GCSE French. Inter- and intra-marker agreement will be examined. Ratings will be compared with more objective analyses of tape recordings and transcripts of the children's performance. Attempts will be made to derive descriptives criteria more closely related to candidates' levels of performance than is currently the case, and the ability of French children to perform similar tasks will be investigated in a sample of 40 sixteen year olds attending schools in France. Finally, the effects of training in oral assessment will be investigated using a group of 25 postgraduate modern linguists currently training to be teachers.
Source of Grant: Reading University; Research Endowment Fund: £30,000
Date of Research: 1990 – continuing
KEYWORDS: *comparative education; France; french language; modern languages; oral examination; teacher education*

8/1281

Department of Educational Studies and Management
Bulmershe Court, Woodlands Avenue,
Earley, Reading RG6 1HY
0734 663387
Cowan, B.J. Mr; *Supervisor:* Watson, K. Prof.

Marketing state schools: the wider issues
Abstract: The principal purpose of this study is to examine in what ways state schools have responded to recent pressures, emanating from changes in educational legislation, management, funding and the falling rolls siutation, to develop marketing strategies. The writer posits that these strategies are often founded on ignorance and misconception and are little more than short-term survivalist tactics. This study seeks to present a wider perspective of marketing which not only has the potential to redefine basic school processes and systems but offers schools a substantial model for future growth. In order to offer and support a wider view of marketing for state schools, one which embraces the idea of schools educating their public, developing closer relationships with parents and adopting more creative attitudes towards evaluation and accountability, the study contains an examination of the practices, attitudes and potential of marketing found in a variety of settings; industry, colleges of further education, independent schools, local education authorities and state schools themselves. In these organizations the writer undertook surveys (by questionnaire) into marketing commercial organizations (ranging in size from 12 to 350,000 personnel), 60 colleges, 60 independent schools, and 60 local authorities. The examination of marketing in state schools is currently underway. The study will conclude by offering both a model of marketing for state shcools which will take heed of the wider issues explored throughout the thesis and ideas for further research and investigation.
Source of Grant: No funding
Date of Research: 1986-1990
KEYWORDS: *marketing*

8/1282

Department of Education and Community Studies
Council for Environmental Education,
London Road, Reading RG1 5AQ
0734 318921
Gayford, C.G. Dr
INSET programmes in environmental education
Abstract: This project involves the production of inservice teaching approaches suitable for use by local authorities, schools or colleges. The emphasis is on interactive methods both for educating teachers and giving suggestions for ways in which environmental education can be integrated into the curriculum. Extensive trialling will occur in several invited local authorities on a partnership basis. Modules for inservice use are available from the researcher.
Source of Grant: Central Electricity Generating Board: £50,000
Date of Research: 1988 – continuing
KEYWORDS: *environmental edcuation; inservice education and training of teachers*

8/1283

Department of Linguistic Science
Whitknights, Reading RG6 2AA
0734 875123
Kerseill, P.E. Dr; Williams, A. Dr
A new dialect in a new city: childrens' and adults' speech in Milton Keynes
Abstract: The research aims to examine the processes behind the formation of a new dialect in a city where the majority of the population originates from different parts of the country and to enquire how children develop 'sociolinguistic competence' – awareness of different accents and dialects in their community, and of their apparent use. A range of sociolinguistic methods are used in the study of 48 children aged 4, 8 and 12.
Source of Grant: Economic and Social Research Council: £51,550
Date of Research: 1990 – continuing
KEYWORDS: *child; dialect; sociolinguistics; spoken language; United Kingdom*

8/1284

Department of Psychology
Whiteknights, Reading RG6 2AL
0734 875123 ext 7539
Henry, L.A. Dr; Norman, T. Miss; *Supervisor:* Henry, L.A. Dr
The development of visual memory strategies in children
Abstract: The aim of this research was to chart the development of verbal memory strategies in children. Previous research had suggested that children progress from visual to verbal strategies of memory coding with age. However, this claim has not been

adequately tested. The first stage of the present research has been to test this claim with a wide age range (5, 7, 9, and 11 year olds). Children recalled sequences of pictures which were either visually similar (they looked the same) or phonemically similar (they sounded the same). Recall for these types of pictures was contrasted with recall for control pictures which were neither visually nor phonemically similar. The results showed that all age groups were poorer at remembering phonemically similar pictures, suggesting that they all used verbal memory strategies. There was very little evidence for the use of visual memory strategies in any group. Further work with 4 year olds found that they did not appear to use any distinct strategy for remembering pictures. These findings conflicted with previous research which showed that five year olds used visual coding, and ongoing research is testing the competing claim of various hypotheses concerning the development of picture memory in children.
Source of Grant: University of Reading Endowment: £21,000 over three years, (T. Norman). Dr Hendrys' research is not funded
Date of Research: 1990 – continuing
KEYWORDS: phonemics; verbal development; visual perception

8/1285

Department of Psychology
Whiteknights, Reading RG6 2AL
0734 875123
Lewis, C. Dr
Young children's understanding of testing and training: explorations in semantic, social-cognitive and memory development
Abstract: Research on cognitive development has focused increasingly upon the interactions between experimenters and young children. This series of experiments attempts to examine how children construe a variety of cognitive tasks, with the aim of formalizing their approaches. Three experiments have investigated the apparent confusion shown by infant school children in understanding polar adjectives denoting size, like 'big'. By testing children more thoroughly than previous researchers and examining their error patterns, these investigations suggest that the decrement in performance between three and five years is caused by a combination of semantic and non linguistic factors. Five year olds are more sensitive than three year olds to the variety of uses to which we put language and the nature of adult-child interaction in educational contexts. Two studies explore the reasons why three year olds fail to make inferences about others' beliefs. It is currently assumed that such findings reflect serious social-cognitive limitations which are overcome in the fourth and fifth years. This work examines whether three year olds can demonstrate social cognitive abilities when the nature of their task is made explicit. A study training six year olds to rehearse when memorizing has found not only improvements in recall, but also gains in a test of wider metamnemonic awareness. This latter result has been interpreted in terms of the experimenter-child interaction, in preference to a simple explanation that specific training gives rise to widespread cognitive gains.
Source of Grant: No funding
Date of Research: 1987 – continuing
KEYWORDS: cognitive development; infant; memorizing; semantics; social learning

8/1286

Department of Psychology
Earley Gate, Whiteknights, Reading RG6 2AL
0734 875123
Bellin, W. Dr
Social areas and educational changes in Wales
Abstract: Educational changes are monitored by means of local authority data in Gwynedd, North Wales. Schools are compared for the relation between in-migration of children without Welsh, and the percentage of children whose attainment would allow them to proceed with Welsh medium secondary edcuation. Location of the effects in social areas as revealed by the Census is attempted.
Source of Grant: University funds
Date of Research: 1988 – continuing
KEYWORDS: bilingualism; change; Wales

8/1287

Department of Science and Technology Education
Bulmershe Court, Woodlands Avenue,
Earley, Reading RG6 1HY
0734 663387
Archer, D.F. Mr; *Supervisor:* Malvern, D.D. Mr

Chemically related inservice primary science project (CRISP)
Abstract: The National Curriculum for Science for England and Wales and that for Northern Ireland contains topics which are of a chemical nature. There is both statistical and anecdotal evidence to suggest that very few teachers of pupils at Key Stages 1 and 2 have more than a vague knowledge of chemistry. There are also signs that those parts of the curriculum which are of a more chemical nature are being less well interpreted than are those of biology and physics. The Royal Society of Chemistry has decided to help teachers of primary age pupils to gain confidence in the field of chemistry by offering them a distance learning publication. It is currently envisaged that the publication will offer help at up to four interest levels over a range of twelve science curriculum topics such as chemical aspects of materials and environmental chemistry. It is anticipated that the material will be copyright free within a school; that each section will probably be complete within itself and that there will be cross references to the curriculum documents for science for England and Wales and Northern Ireland.
Source of Grant: Royal Society of Chemistry
Date of Research: 1990 – continuing
KEYWORDS: inservice teacher education; National Curriculum

8/1288

Faculty of Education amd Community Studies
Bulmershe Court, Woodlands Avenue,
Earley, Reading RG6 1HY
0734 663387
Oxford University
Department of Educational Studies
15 Norham Gardens, Oxford OX2 6PY
0865 274000
Postlethwaite, K.C. Dr; McIntyre, D. Mr
Attending to individual differences
Abstract: The study is mainly concerned with a review of two broad fields: (i) research relevant to understanding the differences between children which affect their learning, and to instructional strategies designed to take account of these (e.g. research on mastery learning, aptitude treatment interaction, mixed ability teaching, special needs, cognitive modifiability), (ii) research relevant to ways in which teachers do perceive differences between pupils, how they take account of these, and what effects this action has on pupils. The study will review and synthesize findings in these two broad fields. It will consider a range of suggested practical solutions to the question of how to attend to individual differences against the theoretical framework thus developed. It will lead to the formulation of a research proposal for a funded investigation of ways in which the theoretical insights can be used by tutors, student teachers and experienced teachers to improve teacher education and classroom practice in this area.
Source of Grant: No funding
Date of Research: 1987 – continuing
KEYWORDS: ability; individuality; secondary education; special needs; teaching method

8/1289

Faculty of Education and Community Studies
Bulmershe Court, Woodlands Avenue,
Earley, Reading RG6 1HX
0734 663387
Richards, B. Dr
Environmental predictors of auxiliary and copula verb growth in young children
Abstract: Several studies have found that the frequency of y/ns (yes/no questions) addressed to young children predicts subsequent rate of auxiliary verb learning. A possible reason is that one category of y/ns highlights the auxiliary by placing it at the beginning of the utterance where it is more likely to be stressed and less likely to be phonologically reduced. However, research which has subcategorized y/ns has not usually found any effect associated with those which invert the auxiliary. The research focuses on the development of auxiliary and copula verbs in order to test hypotheses about the role of input in the acquisition of form classes. Utterances addressed to children have been coded according to the features of the auxiliary or copula which are displayed. The contribution of inversions, sentence-final ellipsis, and tag questions are being analyzed, as well as the effects of contracted and noncontracted verb forms in medial position in declarative utterances. The methodology of previous studies has been improved by carefully matching the sample of children for their stage of

language development at the beginning of the study, and by statistically adjusting gain scores for any remaining variation in initial status. A subsample of 33 children, matched for language development and age was selected from the younger cohort of the Bristol study of language development. Child language measures from recordings 9 months apart were obtained and gain scores calculated. These are being correlated with input frequences taken from the first recording.
Published Material: RICHARDS, B.J. (1986). 'Yes/no questions in input and their relationship with rate of auxiliary verb development in young children'. In: Proceedings of the child language seminar. University of Durham.; RICHARDS, B.J. (1987). Individual differences and the development of the auxiliary verb system in young children. Unpublished Phd dissertation, University of Bristol.; RICHARDS, B.J. (1990). Language development and individual differences: a study of auxiliary verb learning. Cambridge: Cambridge University Press.; RICHARDS, B.J. (1990). 'Environmental predictors of copula verb development'. In: FORRESTER, M., SMITH, L. & SHIRE, B. (Eds). Proceedings of the 1990 Child Language Seminar. Canterbury: University of Kent.; RICHARDS, B.J. 'Access to the agenda: some observations on language development research and its relevance for the practitioner', Australian Journal of Remedial Education, No 22, pp.16-20. (in press).; RICHARDS, B.J. (1990). 'Predictors of auxilliary and copula verb growth', Paper presented to the Fifth International Congress for the Study of Child Language, Budapest, July 1990.; RICHARDS, B.J. 'Investigating relationships between maternal input and rate of children's language development: a reanalysis of Yoder', Journal of Speech and Hearing Research. (in press).
Source of Grant: Economic and Social Research Council: £27,400
Date of Research: 1988-1990
KEYWORDS: child language; language; language acquisition; syntax

8/1290
Faculty of Education and Community Studies
Bulmershe Court, Woodlands Avenue,
Earley, Reading RG6 1HX
0734 663387
Redfern, A. Ms
Literacy in the early years in Barbados
Abstract: The research aims to provide an up to date account of factors affecting literacy acquisition in primary education in Barbados. The researcher interviewed staff of the University of the West Indies, Erdiston Training College, head teachers, ex-head teachers, teachers, parents and children of various primary schools, the president of the Association of Teachers of English. Methods used included classroom observation interviews, photographs, evaluation of resources.
Source of Grant: No funding
Date of Research: 1989-1990
KEYWORDS: Barbados; literacy; primary education

8/1291
Faculty of Education and Community Studies
Bulmershe Court, Woodlands Avenue,
Earley, Reading RG6 1HY
0734 663387
Bedford College of Higher Education
Cauldwell Street, Bedford MK24 9AH
0234 351671
Lyons, H. Ms; Keiner, J. Ms; Grugeon, A. Mrs
Evaluation of National Oracy Project 1988-1992
Abstract: The National Oracy Project was established by the then Secretary of State to promote good practice in oral work across the curriculum and to develop appropriate modes of assessment for pupils aged 3- to 18-years. The evaluation of the National Oracy Project aims to explore the extent to which the project's work fulfills its stated aims. A case study approach has been adopted, drawing on a selection of seven local authority consortia of teacher based groups involved in the project, in conjunction with studies of the National Project Team, its relationship with National Curriculum Council and other national educational policy bodies, and of publications and other data emerging from the project. Methods used include analysis of published materials and other documents; field visits and interviews and participant observation. Results and conclusions will be published in a final report.
Source of Grant: National Curriculum Council: £22,000
Date of Research: 1990 – continuing

KEYWORDS: communication; learning process; oral expression; speech; teaching method

8/1292
Faculty of Education and Community Studies
Council for Environmental Education,
London Road, Reading RG1 5AQ
0734 318921
Field Studies Council
Central Services, Preston Montford, Montford Bridge, Shrewsbury SY4 1HW
0743 850674
Hindon, J. Dr; Hale, M. Ms
Charging for out of classroom activities in schools
Abstract: The aim of the research is to discover the impact of the charging aspects of the Education Reform Act on out of school activities, in particular, fieldwork related to geography and science. There were a number of stages to the investigation. In 1989/90 a questionnaire was sent to approximately 400 Field Study Centres to assess the impact of charging. In 1990/91 there will be a repeat of the 1989/90 survey and a questionnaire will also be sent to all schools in 8 selected local education authorities. The sample size of the centres survey was 160. However, the response rate is not yet known for the schools survey. The research has concluded that the initial impact of the charging legislation appears to be mixed, with most centres fearing a far greater effect in 1990/91 when local management of schools is implemented in many schools. The data from schools is currently being analyzed.
Source of Grant: Field Studies Council Council for Environmental Education (CEE) Department of Education and Science (DES): £1,500
Date of Research: 1989 – continuing
KEYWORDS: Education Reform Act (1988); field study; financing; out of school

8/1293
Faculty of Education and Community Studies
Bulmershe Court, Woodlands Avenue,
Earley, Reading RG6 1HY
0734 663387
Wells, C. Mr; *Supervisor:* Kemp, A.E. Dr; Hopper, G. Mrs
The effects of information technology on the sequencing and development of concept acquisition, particularly in open ended, creative situations
Abstract: A preliminary study has been completed over a period of one year in one primary school with very good access to computer facilities. Work in creative areas, particularly in creative writing, and in art, was monitored throughout the year – both with and without the use of the computer. Children from ages 5 to 11 were involved, though more detailed observations were made of a group of 30 9- to 10-year olds. This data is still being analyzed, but will enable the focusing on particular sequencing and developmental trends in the main research.
Source of Grant: No funding
Date of Research: 1990 – continuing
KEYWORDS: information technology

8/1294
Faculty of Education and Community Studies
Bulmershe Court, Woodlands Avenue,
Earley, Reading RG6 1HY
0734 663387
Cowan, B.J. Mr; Wright, N. Mr
Management of staff and school development
Abstract: This report into the use and management of school INSET (Inservice Education and Training) and 'Baker day' provision was designed to be a follow-up to that carried out in 1989) and published in Education, Vol 175, No 5, 2 February 1990) which examined the organization and management of 110 'Baker days'. The purpose of this study was to determine the current management of school and staff development, in a number of state schools, in order to offer recommendations for better future practice. Information was collected in a number of ways. Sixty four heads and teachers were surveyed by questionnaire and interview. Other perspectives were gained from students in schools, teacher unions and from an unpublished study into the role and function of 30 INSET (Inservice Education and Training of Teachers) coordinators. Since the writers reside in different parts of the country the sample conveniently reflects a north/south mix. Emerging from the research were issues related to the organization and plan-

ning of both staff and school development initiatives. Clearly not enough care is taken to ensure that the needs of both individual and organization are reflected in the training programmes. A principal recommendation stresses the need for schools to develop 'school development plans' in which are clearly stated, the short, medium and long term objectives for both staff and school development. The need to involve staff in planning and evaluating all development programmes is strongly argued as well as a more assiduous approach to the use of external consultants for school training days. We read constantly that levels of teacher morale and motivation are diminishing fast. The writers conclude by advocating then, that a more committed and creative approach to staff and school development, by all parties, will lead to the generation of new ideas, skills and attitudes among teachers which will ultimately result in better learning opportunities for our children.
Published Material: COWAN, B.J. & WRIGHT, N. (1990). Managing for school and staff development. Sheffield Papers in Education, No 88. Sheffield: Sheffield City Polytechnic, Centre for Education Management and Administration.
Source of Grant: No funding
Date of Research: 1990-1990
KEYWORDS: educational development; inservice teacher education

8/1295
Faculty of Education and Community Studies
Bulmershe Court, Woodlands Avenue,
Earley, Reading RG6 1HY
0734 663387
Beck College
43 Gordon Square, London WC1H OPD
071 580 6622
Fuller, M.I. Dr; Redfern, A. Mrs; Edwards, V.K. Dr
Policy and practice in multicultural education in Ontario and Great Britain
Abstract: This research will analyze British and Canadian multicultural education policies and practices, particularly the development of policy which is responsive to the needs of a multilingual, multicultural school population, strategies for providing language support for children in the process of acquiring English and, the planning and management of multicultural, multilingual classroom resources. The study will be a mixture of observation of classroom practices, interviews with teachers, principals and policymakers and administrators. Methodology included semi-structured interviews; less formal observation; analysis of published policy papers. The sample consisted of principals and staff in two elementary and two high schools: trustees, superintendents and other administrators in one Ontario Board of Education and staff at York University and OISE (Ontario Institute for Studies in Education).
Source of Grant: Canadian Government; Department of External Affairs: £5,500
Date of Research: 1990 – continuing
KEYWORDS: multicultural education

8/1296
Faculty of Education and Community Studies
Bulmershe Court, Woodlands Avenue,
Earley, Reading RG6 1HY
0734 663387
Middleton, R.L. Mr; *Supervisor:* Raban, B. Dr
Teaching non-fiction in the secondary school
Abstract: This research will examine the question of why teachers use non-fiction. Is it for language development, reading and writing cross-fertilization, or helping pupils refine their knowledge of the world and themselves? What kinds of linguistic, intellectual and cultural demands do non-fiction texts make on pupils? Is non-fiction literature taught in the same way as fiction literature or does the case for using non-fiction rest partly on its difference from fiction? What kinds of teaching strategies are appropriate and is a specialist critical vocabulary necessary? Research methodology will include case studies/surveys of practice – lesson observation and interviewing of teachers and pupils. A survey of pupils voluntary non-fiction reading. This will involve the co-operation of Berkshire's education library service, and possible contributions of linguistic and literary theory.
Source of Grant: No funding
Date of Research: 1990 – continuing
KEYWORDS: non-fiction

8/1297
Faculty of Education and Community Studies
Bulmershe Court, Woodlands Avenue,
Earley, Reading RG6 1HY
0734 663387
Council for Environmental Education
London Road, Reading RG1 5AQ
0734 318921
Gayford, C.G. Dr
The monitoring and profiling in environmental education in the National Curriculum
Abstract: This project involves monitoring the ways in which schools are delivering environmental education in the National Curriculum. Models for achieving integration of cross-curricular elements in the whole curriculum will be investigated and approaches to profiling pupils performance developed. Training materials suitable for providing appropriate INSET (Inservice Education and Training of Teachers) will be produced.
Source of Grant: World Wide Fund for Nature National Westminster Bank: jointly £600,000
Date of Research: 1991 – continuing
KEYWORDS: inservice teacher education; National Curriculum

8/1298
Faculty of Education and Community Studies
Bulmershe Court, Woodlands Avenue,
Reading RG6 1HY
0734 663387
Fuller, K.D. Mr; *Supervisor:* Malvern, D.D.
Curriculum renewal and the Nuffield science projects
Abstract: Through a study of the history of the Nuffield Science Projects and associated developments, the processes of curriculum renewal will be examined. Key areas include changes in the ways in which curriculum development is funded, notably the institutionalization of funding, the response of the curriculum development system to changing educational conditions and an analysis of what changes: content, pedagogy, the model of science, etc. The Nuffield Science Projects and Nuffield Physics courses in particular provide an example of courses and texts which have presented a particular approach to education but have been reviewed and rewritten. The research addresses the questions, what prompted the revisions and what is responsible for the timimg of the revisions.
Published Material: FULLER, K.D. & MALVERN, D.D. (1986). 'One don, one beak – university pressure and curriculum development in the first Nuffield 'A' level physics project', British Journal of Educational Studies, Vol 32, No 1, pp.220-234.
Source of Grant: No funding
Date of Research: 1986-1990
KEYWORDS: curriculum development; history of education; science education

8/1299
Faculty of Education and Community Studies
Bulmershe Court, Earley,
Reading RG6 1HY
0734 663387
Goodwyn, A.C. Mr
The relationship between the use and understanding of narrative structures and general language development
Abstract: The project will investigate the links between children's general language competence and their ability to comprehend and use narrative structures. This will involve the study of children's reading and writing habits and the pedagogical implications for the way narratives are used in schools. The project will be chiefly of interest to teachers of language in primary and to teachers of English in secondary schools. In the early stages research will involve small scale studies of narrative work with children at primary and secondary level. These early studies will be used as the basis for more detailed work with a small number of children, mainly at secondry level. It is hoped that the study will produce results that can help teachers and children to improve both their work with language and on narrative. Particular areas would include: the suitability of stories for specific age groups or development groups; the appropriateness of certain forms of narrative structure for particular age groups; the identification of staging points in pupil's development; the development of pedagogical strategies for improving children's engagement with narratives; identifying relationships between children's reading level and writing level; children's comprehension of visual narratives and their relationships to other forms.

Date of Research: 1989 – continuing
KEYWORDS: language skill; language teaching; narration; reading; writing

8/1300

Faculty of Education and Community Studies
Bulmershe Court, Woodlands Road,
Earley, Reading RG6 1HY
0734 663387
Gothard, W.P. Dr

Adult guidance in careers service
Abstract: Adult guidance in the careers service has been developing for some years. Its future development is of great importance for both the individuals and the service. This study seeks to monitor its development and the likely progress within each local authority.
Source of Grant: No funding
Date of Research: 1987-1989
KEYWORDS: adult; careers guidance; careers service

8/1301

Faculty of Education and Community Studies
Music Education Information and Research Centre,
Bulmershe Court, Woodlands Avenue,
Reading RG6 1HY
0734 663387
Pimley, B. Mr; *Supervisor:* Kemp, A.E. Dr

Keyboards in primary school
Abstract: The project focuses on the use of electronic keyboards in primary schools, both as a stimulus and also as an aid to developing skills in creative music making. The research will also investigate the use of ancillary equipment such as sound mixers and headphone listening stations as a means to the effective use of the keyboards by both pupils and teacher. In its initial stages the researchers will visit several primary schools in which keyboards are already in everyday use. Through extended observation several case studies of good practice will be documented. Collaborative work with these teachers will allow the development of worksheets and other teaching materials. Selected middle and secondary schools will also be visited in order to establish in what ways this activity with keyboards in primary schools relates to later stages of the music curriculum. The second stage will involve producing draft support materials and carrying out trials of these in several primary schools. These support materials will encompass aspects of classroom management and organization. The third stage will comprise re-drafting of materials in the light of the trials together with the production of video material featuring examples of good practice. The video recordings, together with the written materials, will comprise a teacher-support and lesson pack which will eventually be published and distributed by the funding body.
Source of Grant: Microelectronics Education Support Unit (MESU): £30,000
Date of Research: 1988-1989
KEYWORDS: music education; primary education; teaching aids

8/1302

Faculty of Education and Community Studies
Bulmershe Court, Woodlands Avenue,
Earley, Reading RG6 1HY
0734 663387
Spear, M. Dr; Singh, A. Dr; *Supervisor:* Singh, A. Dr

A local authority based demonstration trial of 'good practice' in road safety education
Abstract: The primary aim of the project is to develop, implement and evaluate policies of 'good practice' in road safety education for children aged 5-16. The initial phase of the project is being spent developing guidelines for the management and coordination of road safety education both at local authority and at school level in collaboration with educational advisers, teachers, road safety officers, health education officers and the police, and in conducting a pilot trial in one local authority. During the second phase of the research, the revised policy document will be implemented through inservice training in all the primary and secondary schools (about 130 schools) within the selected areas of the two trial authorities. The third phase of the research will be concerned with monitoring the implemented programmes closely in 20 primary and 10 secondary schools in order to assess the impact on educational outcomes over a given period of time, for example in pupils' knowledge, skills, attitudes, behaviour and future intentions regarding road safety. The research design will be quasi-

experimental. The input, process and evaluation data will be obtained through visits, interviews, questionnaires, telephone calls, observation of lessons and unobtrusive observation of actual behaviour on the roads. The cost effectiveness of programmes including measures of changes in casualty rate will also be assessed. The final phase of the research will comprise feedback to the participants, dissemination of the findings and the production of a report designed to assist local authorities and schools in implementing such policy(ies) effectively and economically.
Source of Grant: Department of Transport; Transport and Road Research Laboratory: £407,303
Date of Research: 1988 – continuing
KEYWORDS: educational policy; road safety education

8/1303

Faculty of Education and Community Studies
Music Education Information and Research Centre,
London Road, Reading RG6 1HY
0734 663387
Meaney, P. Mr; *Supervisor:* Kemp, A.E. Dr

Microtechnological support in multicultural music making in the classroom
Abstract: The purpose of this project is to provide teachers with a range of ideas in approaching listening, performing and composing activities which involve multicultural aspects of music with the support of microtechnology. Central issues such as authenticity of sounds and playing techniques will be considered in relation to approaches, strategies and activities suitable for different age ranges (primary and secondary), and ways of integrating them into the wider curriculum. The project will initially identify musical elements for the purpose of developing a variety of specific and progressive activities. These will in turn provide the basis for a number of further listening, performing and composing activities by combining both common and diverse features or concepts. Finally, a series of compositional approaches will be identified which represent a diversity of styles in world music and which offer possibilities of various cross-cultural transformations.
Source of Grant: Microelectronics Education Support Unit (MESU): £30,000
Date of Research: 1988-1989
KEYWORDS: computer assisted instruction; multicultural education; music education

8/1304

Faculty of Education and Community Studies
Bulmershe Court, Woodlands Avenue,
Earley, Reading RG6 1HY
0734 663387
Free University
1081 BT Amsterdam
020-548 0958
Straughan, R.R. Dr; Spiecker, B. Prof.

Freedom and indoctrination in education
Abstract: Freedom and indoctrination are topics that have long dominated pedagogical and educational discourse in the European countries. On the national level, there have always been considerable differences in the way these topics are discussed. Now that the inner-borders of the European countries are disappearing, supranational structures will gradually change pedagogical ideologies and the demands on national educational systems and institutions. As a result, freedom and indoctrination will become even more topical subjects for debate. It is hoped to produce a book and an informal seminar is planned.
Date of Research: 1988 – continuing
KEYWORDS: Europe; freedom; indoctrination; system of education

8/1305

Faculty of Education and Community Studies
Bulmershe Court, Woodlands Avenue,
Earley, Reading RG6 1HY
0734 663387
Malvern, D.D. Mr

Science in primary teacher education (SPRITE)
Abstract: The research will look at the implications for teacher education of the proposals for the National Curriculum, and develop material and courses for teacher trainers. The National Curriculum proposes the introduction of programmes of study in science and technology for the primary phase. The notions of science and technology, and the progression to be followed are

layed down, alongside a series of assessments conforming to a national pattern. Inevitably, such an innovation requires considerable INSET (Inservice Education of Teachers) and also alters the demands of initial training courses. This project seeks to clarify those requirements and provide appropriate activities and training for teacher education. The next phase looks at the character of education required by primary teachers through an analysis of teachers' notions of selected topics in science both before and after inservice courses.
Published Material: HARLEN, W. (et al). (1990). Progress in primary science. London: Routledge.
Source of Grant: University Funding Council: £32,000
Date of Research: 1988 – continuing
KEYWORDS: curriculum development; teacher inservice education; primary education; science education; technology

8/1306
Faculty of Education and Community Studies
Bulmershe Court, Woodlands Avenue,
Earley, Reading RG6 1HY
0734 663387
Wright, J. Mrs
Appraisal and staff development
Abstract: The objectives of the project would be as follows: (a) to evaluate the experimental appraisal scheme which all universities have to introduce in the course of this academic year, and to compare it with the model of appraisal adopted by IBM; (b) to underline comparative research regarding management development in the university and in IBM which would enable the content of courses to be developed; (c) to assess the real cost to universities of a comprehensive staff development and appraisal programme; (d) to jointly recommend to the CVCP (Committee of Vice-Chancellors & Principals) how a national strategy might be devised for appraisal and staff development in all universities. At a time when universities have had the idea of staff development and appraisal foisted on to them from outside, with no time to plan before starting to operate and the need to fund this new initiative from ever-decreasing resources, it becomes a paramount necessity to undertake comparative research with a company with the expertise of IBM, lest we impose an inappropriate model of management on higher educational institutions.
Source of Grant: No funding
Date of Research: 1989-1990
KEYWORDS: comparative research; higher education; industry; personnel evaluation; staff development

8/1307
Faculty of Education and Community Studies
Agricultural Extension and Rural Development Department,
London Road, Reading RG1 5AQ
0734 318877
Oakley, P. Dr
The practice of participation in rural development in the Third World
Abstract: The research is based upon a substantial review of the practice of participation in rural development projects funded both by United Nations Agencies (Food and Agriculture Organization and World Health Organization) and major non-government organizations (Oxfam, Ainstram Aid). The research concentrates upon the methodology of this process.
Published Material: OAKLEY, P. (1990). Projects with people: the practice of participation in rural development. (forthcoming). Geneva: International Labour Office.
Source of Grant: Research support grant provided by a group of U.N. agencies
Date of Research: 1988 – continuing
KEYWORDS: developing country; non-formal education; participation; rural development; United Nations

8/1308
Faculty of Education and Community Studies
AIMER Project, Bulmershe Court, Woodlands Avenue,
Earley, Reading RG6 1HY
0734 663387
Collis, S. Mrs; *Supervisor:* Adelman, C. Prof.
Access to information on multi-cultural education resources (AIMER)
Abstract: The aim of this project is to provide teachers and other educationalists with information about resources being produced by LEAs and other small scale organizations. Resources are indexed

and listed in a computer database. Users of the enquiry service indicate their interests in terms of curriculum area, age range etc. and are supplied with a printout of possible resources. Long term aims include the identification of resource needs with a view to commissioning new materials.
Source of Grant: Department of Education and Science (DES): £50,000
Date of Research: 1987 – continuing
KEYWORDS: database; information service; multicultural education; teaching aids

8/1309
Music Education Information and Research Centre
Bulmershe Court, Woodlands Avenue,
Earley, Reading RG6 1HY
0734 663387
Woodward, E. Miss; *Supervisor:* Kemp, A.E. Dr
National programme of Inservice Training for music curriculum leaders in primary schools
Abstract: The purpose of the project is to provide a programme of inservice training for primary school music teachers who wish to develop consultancy skills. This training will be offered on a national basis, organized in various locations throughout the country, and will consist of four-week phased courses of the kind which have been held at the University of Reading Music Education Centre since 1982. These courses offer teachers an updated view of recent developments in the primary music curriculum and training in the processes of consultancy work amongst colleagues. They also offer conferences for primary headteachers within their structure. A second important facet of the project will be the development of regional groups of music consultants to encourage ongoing professional interchange and aftercare.
Published Material: SMITH, J. (1987). Music consultancy in Berkshire Primary Schools. Reading: Royal County of Berkshire Music Department.
Source of Grant: Music Industries Association: £75,000 Caloustie Gulbenkian Foundation: £15,000
Date of Research: 1988 – continuing
KEYWORDS: consultancy; curriculum development; inservice education and training teachers; music education; primary education

8/1310
Music Education Information and Research Centre
Bulmershe Court, Woodlands Avenue,
Earley, Reading RG6 1HY
0734 875855
Wells, C. Mr; *Supervisor:* Tabberer, R. Mr (Microelectronic Education Support Unit (MESU); Kemp, A. Dr (Music Education Centre)
Microtechnology in music education – research and development of packs of material for teachers
Abstract: This project involves classroom research, leading to the development of six packs of materials as follows. Each will consist of support material for the teacher and classroom activity ideas, and also have an inter-linked training pack including video case studies. (1) Resource/training pack for creative music from 5 to 16; this pack will support a wide range of music activities and approaches for primary and secondary pupils of all abilities. (2) Resource/training pack for using a music computer system across the music curriculum 11/16; this pack will link with curriculum guidelines and provide a structured progression of ideas in a wide range aspects of composing, listening and performing, for all abilities. (3) Resource/training pack on use and and integration of electronic music keyboards in the primary music classroom; this pack will include structured material on a wide range of musical activities linked with the primary music curriculum. (4) Resource/training pack for supporting the multicultural music curriculum, a pack providing a range of ideas illustrating the contribution of microtechnology to many aspects of multicultural music in primary and secondary schools with pupils of all abilities. (5) Resource/training pack for supporting the use of microtechnology by physically handicapped pupils in music, materials and ideas for both primary and secondary, and covering a range of abilities and approaches. (6) Resource/training pack on uses of non-keyboard input devices, in particular the microphone, for creative music activities, practical ideas for primary and secondary pupils of all abilities making use of the musical freedoms provided by non-keyboard interface devices.
Source of Grant: MESU (Microelectronic Education Support Unit): £213,644

Date of Research: 1987-1990
KEYWORDS: microcomputer; music education; teaching aids

8/1311

Music Education Information and Research Centre
Bulmershe Court, Woodlands Avenue,
Earley, Reading RG6 1HY
0734 663387
Cox. G. Mr; *Supervisor:* Kemp, A.E. Dr; Wilson, R. Prof.

Music in the multicultural curriculum

Abstract: The study will set out to formulate a rationale for a multicultural curriculum in music. At the same time it will investigate the aims and purposes of multicultural education. An important part of the research will be the monitoring of an inservice project for teachers, 'Music in the multicultural curriculum'. Certain strategies form the foundation of this project, and teachers will be monitored continuously and systematically in terms of: (i) Analyzing current practice – considering the extent to which it is dominated by one particular musical style; (ii) applying the theory of multicultural education – seeking explanations of current practice within the wider framework of understanding; (iii) developing new musical techniques and skills – enhancing the general musicianship of the teacher by widening aural and improvisatory skills in particular which may be associated with unfamiliar musical styles; (iv) applying these techniques to the classroom – providing children with additional skills and techniques which will enhance the quality of their musical activities; (v) evaluating the effectiveness of such classroom work – judging what has proved effective in terms of the children's achievement; (vi) developing a multicultural curriculum in music – making innovations and modifying current practice; and (vii) communicating ideas to other music teachers – persuading them of the value of a multicultural approach. Such issues will be considered by a teachers' working group, which will meet on a regular basis to discuss and develop work in the classroom based on multicultural innovation. It is hoped that the study will clarify the contribution music can make to the multicultural curriculum, and will also have something of importance to say about the process of curriculum innovation and the inservice education of music teachers.
Published Material: COX, G. 'Broadening horizons'. Times Educational Supplement 17.02.84.; COX, G. (1986). 'Music in the multicultural curriculum: the working party in action', British Journal of Inservice Education, No 12, pp.86-91.
Source of Grant: No funding
Date of Research: 1984-1990
KEYWORDS: curriculum development; inservice education and training of teachers; multicultural education; music education

8/1312

Music Education Information and Research Centre
Bulmershe Court, Woodlands Avenue,
Earley, Reading RG6 1HY
0734 663387
Woodward, E. Miss; *Supervisor:* Kemp, A.E. Dr

National programme of training for primary school music consultants

Abstract: The purpose of the project is to provide a programme of inservice training for primary school music teachers who wish to develop consultancy skills. This training is offered on a national basis, organized in various locations throughout the country, and consists of four-week phased courses of the kind held at the University of Reading Music Education Centre since 1982. These courses offer teachers an updated view of recent developments in the primary music curriculum and training in the processes of consultancy work amongst colleagues. They also offer conferences for primary headteachers within their structure. A second important facet of the project will be the development of regional groups of music consultants to encourage on-going professional interchange and aftercare.
Published Material: SMITH, J. (1987). Music consultancy in Berkshire primary schools. Reading: Royal County of Berkshire Music Department.; KEMP, A.E. (1988). 'Towards national adoption of music consultancy in primary schools'. In: BARTON, M. amd STEWART, A. (eds). British music education yearbook 1988/89. London: Rhinehold.; KEMP, A.E. & WOOTTON FREEMAN, S. (1988). 'New tasks for music in primary schools and teacher training', International Journal of Music Education, No 11, 1988, pp. 21-24.
Source of Grant: Music Industries Association: £75,000 Calouste Gulbenkian Foundation: £15,000

Date of Research: 1988 – continuing
KEYWORDS: consultancy; inservice education and training of teachers; music primary education

8/1313

Music Education information and Research Centre
Bulmershe Court, Woodlands Avenue,
Earley, Reading RG6 1HY
0734 663387
Cox, G.S.A. Mr; *Supervisor:* Kemp, A.E. Dr; Straughan, R. Dr

From 'singing' to 'music': a history of music education in England 1870-1927 with particular reference to the role of the Music Inspectorate

Abstract: The study will focus on the music curriculum during a period in which there was a steady advance away from the often irksome and uncongenial traditions associated with the revised code towards the cultivation of taste rather than the acquirement of technical proficiency. This broadening of scope was symbolized in the change of nomenclature in 1927 – from 'singing' to 'music'. The central concern of the study will be to assess the significance of the music inspectorate as agents of curriculum change and to investigate their original contributions to the development of the subject. The study is organized in three parts: (1) 'Disendowed if not disestablished': John Hullah and the decline of music in schools 1872 – 1883; (2) 'An economical inspiration': the utilitarian era of Stainer 1883 – 1901; (3) 'The cultivation of the taste': the liberalization of the music curriculum and the contribution of Arthur Sopperwell 1901-1927. The research draws upon a considerable amount of unpublished materials, oral evidence, and texts of the period. It should provide a detailed study of curriculum change and conflict which should lead to a greater knowledge of the process involved in 'becoming a subject'.
Source of Grant: No funding
Date of Research: 1988 – continuing
KEYWORDS: curriculum development; history of education; inspectorate; music education

Robert Gordon's Institue of Technology

8/1314

School of Librarianship and Information Studies,
Hilton Place, Aberdeen AB9 1FP
0224 482211
Johnson, I.M. Mr; Hannabuss, C.S. Mr; Wildgoose, D. Mr

A review of management education for librarians

Abstract: The review arises out of the recent general interest in the extent and quality of management education and training, and particular concern about the nature of management training for librarians. The aim of the study is to investigate the need for the provision of management education for mid-career professional librarians in all types of library. The study would concentrate on middle and senior management levels. The objectives are to identify management competencies and skills necessary at different career levels, relating these to existing and likely future job needs; review existing provision – examine what is available and what can be provided by external agencies, e.g. MBA, DMS programmes, local government unit, industrial society etc; study the profession's perceptions of provision, and the pattern of uptake; identify gaps in existing provision; make recommendations as to future provision, and propose a development plan. A review of existing and planned courses in Scottish institutions leading to management qualifications, and short courses in Scotland in management topics will be undertaken. In addition a survey of provision of short courses in management for librarians will be undertaken. Identification of management competencies required would be achieved through consultation, using as its basis, the Occupational Standards for Managers. The enquiry would also elicit the profession's perception of provision and the pattern of uptake, information on resources available for staff development, and the relative priorities attached to management development. The enquiry will be a telephone survey based on a representative sample of 50 of the libraries and information centres in Scotland.

Source of Grant: Library and Information Services Committee (Scotland): £6,500
Date of Research: 1990 – continuing
KEYWORDS: librarian; management education

Robert Gordon's Institute of Technology

8/1315
School of Librarianship and Information Studies,
Hilton Place,
Aberdeen AB9 1FP
0224 482211
University College of Wales
Department of Information and Library Studies
Aberystwyth,
Dyfed SY23 2AX
0970 3177
Johnson, I.M. Mr; *Supervisor:* Edwards, R.J. Mr

The development of education programmes for library technicians
Abstract: In most occupations an increase in the responsibility or complexity of the tasks undertaken by the senior personnel results in delegation of the more routine duties to junior staff, initially supported by inservice training, but after subsequently by educational programmes leading to formal qualifications at an appropriate level. Despite the apparent merits of these programmes in the field of librarianship, relatively few have been established in Britain. A variety of largely unexplained factors inhibit developments in this field. The purpose of this research is to review the factors involved in operating programmes at this level. The objectives of the study are firstly, to define the role of the library technician, examine the origins of educational programmes for library technicians and identify clearly the underlying causes, review the methods of developing established programmes and identify the factors contributing to their retention, investigate the causes of failure of these programmes, and to evaluate the relative significance of the various criteria identified. The study will provide a model strategy for the successful initiation, development and maintenance of educational programmes for library technicians in developed and developing countries. Past and present practices and attitudes will be documented in a series of case studies of library technician programmes in a number of countries, based on the literature and on overseas field trips. British experience in establishing sub-professional educational programmes in librarianship and information work will also be compared with other occupations in Britain. A survey will be undertaken to assess the relative significance of factors identified in the earlier parts of the study.
Published Material: JOHNSON, I.M. (1981). Library technicians in the USA. Education Resources Information Center.; JOHNSON, I.M. (1984). 'Education and training of library technicians in Czechoslovakia', International Library Review, Vol 16, No 3, July, pp.247-270.; JOHNSON, I.M. (1990). 'The development of library technicians – a review of experience in selected countries', Paper presented at the International Federation of Library Associations conference, Stockholm, August 1990.
Source of Grant: No funding
Date of Research: 1986 – continuing
KEYWORDS: comparative education; library; library technician; para professional personnel; personnel; training programme

Roehampton Institute

8/1316
Froebel Institute College,
Grove House, Roehampton Lane,
London SW15 5PJ
081 876 2242
Jones, L. Ms; *Supervisor:* Evans, R. Dr

Assessment and record keeping
Abstract: Important elements in this research are supported self study combined with individual tutoring in the work situation in order to enhance participants professional development, and the assessment and reporting of development in schools through school based projects. Key elements of the innovation have included; the regular collaboration with Roehampton Institute (planning, publicity, other support); the emphasis on an action research method of development, and the opportunity for teachers from all schools phases to work together and to enhance their qualifications through action research; the opportunity for individual choice demonstrated in the wide ranging topics being addressed through projects; the systematic evaluation, session by session, conducted by a team of teachers acting as independent evaluators, and the influence the evaluations have had in forward planning; the personal and professional development of the evaluation team through their evaluation experience (with one evaluator intending to submit a report for certificate purposes); the potential for publication of project reports through Roehampton Institute local education authority.
Source of Grant: Local Education Authority Advisory teaching team
Date of Research: 1990 – continuing
KEYWORDS: inservice teacher education

Royal Association for Disability and Rehabilitation

8/1317
25 Mortimer Street,
London W1N 8AB
071 637 5400
Simpson, P. Mr

The employment of disabled teaching staff
Abstract: This research aims to update a previous RADAR (Royal Association for Disability and Rehabilitation) survey, KETTLE, M. (1985). which interviewed disabled members of the teaching profession. This national quantitative survey assesses data provided by 51 LEAs (local education authorities) in the UK on their recruitment/retention policies/practices regarding disabled teachers. The postal questionniare provides addresses, numbers of disabled teachers employed in the primary, secondary and tertiary sectors; support services for disabled staff (including newly disabled people); facilities; and measures to recruit disabled staff.
Source of Grant: No funding
Date of Research: 1990 – continuing
KEYWORDS: employment; physically handicapped; teacher

Royal National Institute for the Deaf

8/1318
105 Gower Street
London WC1E 6AH
Daniels, S.D. Miss; Corlett, E.S. Miss

Access to higher education for deaf students
Abstract: The RNID (Royal National Institute for the Deaf) is concerned about the small proportion of deaf people involved in higher education. As part of explanatory access it was necessary to have some statistics of the present position. The aim is to use this information to campaign to improve access through increasing available support, providing funding for this support and thus increasing numbers of deaf students. Research was conducted through two questionnaires sent out to 233 higher education institutions. They covered equal opportunities policies, available support, funding and admissions. The research concluded that there was very little communication for deaf students, within higher education. It was patchy and often dependent on sympathetic local education authorities. Also many students are expected to provide and fund their own communication support. Few institutions have equal opportunities policies relating to deaf students, or a staff member to coordinate support and many respondents admitted low awareness of deaf issues.
Source of Grant: No funding
Date of Research: 1988-1990
KEYWORDS: access to education; deaf; equal opportunity; higher education

Ruskin College

8/1319

Ruskin Hall,
Old Headington, Oxford OX1 2HE
0865 63437
William Temple Foundation
Manchester
061 273 8228
Bryant, R. Mr; Addy, T. Rev.
Communities in crisis: an adult education and resource programme for local groups and community leaders
Abstract: The project has two aims: (1) to provide local activists/volunteers with the opportunity to reflect on their experiences and share ideas across different localities, towns, regions. Programme seeks to link groups in the north-west with groups in the southern regions; (2) undertake project based learning which, (a) will be of value to the participants, (e.g. confidence, writing skills etc.), and (b) will yield socially useful knowledge for local groups, e.g. data for jobs and applications. Research/Evaluation is concerned with: (a) recording the organization of the programme. (b) monitoring the experiences of the participants; (c) evaluating the use of the project material by local groups.
Published Material: ADDY, T. & BRYANT, R. et al (1985). Communities in Crisis. Ruskin College/William Temple Foundation.; BRYANT, R. (1989). Learning from experience: project work with community groups. Ruskin College/William Temple Foundation.
Source of Grant: No funding
Date of Research: 1983 – continuing
KEYWORDS: *adult education; intergroup relations; local community; project method*

Salford Local Education Authority

8/1320

Chapel Street,
Manchester M3 5LT
061 832 9751
The College of Ripon and York St John
Lord Mayor's Walk,
York YO3 7EX
0904 56771
Anning, A. Ms; *Supervisor:* Ashton, P.M.E. Dr
To devise a framework within which teachers might explore how children learn
Abstract: The project developed from inservice activities in Salford LEA (Local Education Authority) primary and secondary schools using the Open University Curriculum in Action materials and from a school-based staff development programme based on classroom observations in a Salford first school. The purpose of the project is to design inservice material which will provide a framework within which teachers might explore how children learn. Three infant and three junior school teachers were asked to select 3 groups of pupils from their classes working on 3 different tasks. The teachers were asked to record their expectations of the children's learning behaviour on the task. The group task sessions were recorded on videotape. Each teacher and the researcher used the recordings to analyze the sessions for: (a) evidence of pupil learning; and (b) strategies employed by the teacher in response to this evidence. In a structured post-task interview the teachers were asked to generalize from the specific insights gained by the analysis of the tapes to general issues about how children learn in their classrooms. Finally, a Kelly grid exercise was used to elicit the constructs the teachers had about the learners in the groups. The data will be analyzed to provide insights into the teachers' perceptions of how the children in their classrooms learn. Using this information as a base-line, inservice material will be designed and piloted to provide a framework within which teachers might explore how children learn.
Source of Grant: LEA (Local Education Authority)/College Association for the Study of the Curriculum
Date of Research: 1987 – continuing
KEYWORDS: *inservice education and training of teachers; learning strategy*

Scottish Council for Research in Education

8/1321

15 St John Street, Edinburgh EH8 8JR
031 557 2944
Mellor, A. Mr
Bullying in schools
Abstract: The project aims to investigate the incidence of bullying in a number of Scottish secondary schools and to investigate and describe successful coping strategies. The research will take place in ten secondary schools drawn from two regions. A questionnaire for pupils will be administered and interviews will be held with management and guidance teachers.
Source of Grant: Scottish Education Department: £5000
Date of Research: 1988-1989
KEYWORDS: *behaviour problems; bullying; secondary school*

8/1322

15 St John Street, Edinburgh EH8 8JR
031 557 2944
Munn, P. Mrs
The needs of mature entrants to higher and further education
Abstract: The research focuses on the identification and effectiveness of innovative approaches in supporting the needs of mature entrants in higher and further education and on ways of attracting potential adult returners back into education and training. It builds on our previous work in these areas, concentrating on case study approaches in higher and further education institutions to complement our larger scale survey work. The case studies would concentrate on areas where there has traditionally been difficulty in attracting mature students, engineering, electronics, maths and sciences. A telephone survey of potential returners would supplement the case study work.
Source of Grant: Scottish Education Department: £55,000
Date of Research: 1990 – continuing
KEYWORDS: *adult education; further education; higher education; mature students; re-entry students*

8/1323

15 St John Street, Edinburgh EH8 8JR
031 557 2944
Munn, P. Mrs
Provision and take up of School Board training
Abstract: The research concentrates on four main areas: (1) Board members' views on the information and training available to them; (2) their preferences for particular forms of training; (3) the factors affecting the take-up and selection of forms of training provision; (4) gaps in available provision. The research design combines depth with breadth and is in three strands. Strand One consists of a telephone survey of 100 Boards. Strand Two involves case studies of 15 Boards. Strand Three involves a survey of 1,000 Board members.
Source of Grant: Scottish Education Department: £55,000
Date of Research: 1990 – continuing
KEYWORDS: *board of governors; parents; school boards; school governors; training*

8/1324

15 St John Street, Edinburgh EH8 8JR
031 557 2944
Munn, P. Mrs
Returners to teaching
Abstract: The research aims to explore the factors affecting the career choice of different groups of non-practising teachers and to assess whether there are practical measures to encourage these groups to return to teaching. A two stage research design is proposed. Stage One consists of face-to-face interviews with over 40 teachers about the factors affecting their non-return. Stage Two involves telephone interviews with 500 non-practising teachers using the information from stage one to construct the telephone interview schedule.
Source of Grant: Scottish Education Department: £34,000
Date of Research: 1989 – continuing
KEYWORDS: *career change; demand for teachers; occupational choice; occupational mobility; teacher mobility; teacher supply and demand; teacher transfer*

8/1325

15 St John Street,
Edinburgh EH8 8JR
031 557 2944
Black, H.D. Mr; Malcolm, H.M.C. Mrs; Blair, A. Ms;
Latta, J. Ms; Zaklukiewicz, S. Mr; *Supervisor:* Black, H.D.
Mr

Teaching and learning strategies in the Extension of TVEI in Scotland

Abstract: This research seeks to evaluate the changes in and impact of teaching and learning strategies in the TVEI (Technical and Vocational Education Initiative) extension in Scotland. Five questions will be addressed: (i) what strategies for teaching, learning and assessment are used in schools and colleges to deliver TVEI in selected areas of the curriculum? How effectively is assessment integrated with teaching and learning? (ii) what claims are made for these teaching, learning and assessment strategies, particularly in relation to their preparing young people for adult and working life? (iii) to what extent are these strategies supportive of the aspirations of TVEI? (iv) what impact do they have on student achievements which will be of value to them in adult and working life, both in terms of formal qualifications and other characteristics? (v) How does 'what is taught' and 'how it is taught' articulate with other aspects of the management of the curriculum in Scottish education? The research will identify examples of interesting and effective practice in five Round Two and Round Three TVEI projects through a series of related stages leading through progressive focusing to a small set of case studies. There are five stages. One and two will provide an overview of practice, Stage 1 through a documentary analysis and Stage 2 through interviews with key individuals. Stage 3 will involve a questionnaire analysis of the nature and extent of practice identified in the first two stages. Stage 4 will comprise visits to and interviews with the key staff of a short list of possible units for case study, while Stage 5 will provide the most substantial set of data through intensive case studies of practice using interviews, observation of classroom and other relevant work, and questionnaires.

Source of Grant: Training Agency (now Training Enterprise Education Divison (TEED)): £152,153

Date of Research: 1989 – continuing

KEYWORDS: achievement; assessment; curriculum; learning strategy; teaching method; technical education; vocational education

8/1326

15 St John Street,
Edinburgh EH8 8JR
031 557 2944
Black, H.D. Mr; Hall, J. Dr; Martin, S. Dr

Advanced courses development programme

Abstract: The main aim of the project is to evaluate the Advanced Courses Development Programme with regard to its overall effectiveness. It will examine the actual process of developing the higher national units used in advanced courses and will also concern the product of this process, and the actual units and courses themselves. Each of these two concerns will focus on aspects such as criteria for good practice, strengths and weaknesses, and articulation with other qualifications.

Source of Grant: Scottish Education Department

Date of Research: 1990 – continuing

KEYWORDS: further education

8/1327

15 St John Street,
Edinburgh EH8 8JR
031 557 2944
Black, H.D. Mr; Turner, E. Mrs; Devine, M. Mrs; Schlapp,
U. Ms

A diagnostic resource for technology

Abstract: The outcome of the project will be a diagnostic resource which can be used in classroom assessment by teachers of technology within a range of subject areas across the curriculum. The assessment instruments result from collaborative work with practising teachers and relate to central and fundamental aspects of technology learning. They will be appropriate for use in standard grade courses, short courses, National Certificate modules and General Certificate of Secondary Education.

Published Material: TURNER, E., BLACK, H. & DEVINE, M. (1989). Technology in home economics. Edinburgh: SARSU/SCRE.; TURNER, E., BLACK, H. & DEVINE, M.

(1990). 'Technology: an annotated bibliography'. Edinburgh: SARSU/SCRE for the Training Enterprise Education Division.

Source of Grant: Training Enterprise Education Division

Date of Research: 1989 – continuing

KEYWORDS: assessment; diagnostic test

8/1328

15 St John Street, Edinburgh EH8 8JR
031 557 2944
Black, H.D. Mr; Devine, M. Mrs; Turner, E. Mrs; Schlapp,
E. Ms

Schools Assessment Research and Support Unit (SARSU)

Abstract: SARSU carries out a rolling programme of action research and exploratory studies in assessment. It also encourages the dissemination of research findings and provides a support service for local authorities' inservice staff development programmes in assessment.

Published Material: BLACK, H.D., DEVINE, M. & TURNER, E. (1990). Geography: settlement studies. Edinburgh: SCRE/SARSU.; TURNER, E., BLACK, H.D. & DEVINE, M. (1990). Technology: an annotated bibliography. Edinburgh: SCRE/SARSU.; TURNER, E., BLACK, H.D., HALL, J. & DEVINE, M. (1989). Technology in Home Economics. Edinburgh: SCRE/SARSU.; BLACK, H.D., DEVINE, M. & TURNER, E. (1989). Aspects of assessment: a primary perspective. Edinburgh: SCRE/SARSU.; BLACK, H.D., DEVINE, M., TURNER, E. & HARRISON, C. (1988). Standard Grade Assessment: a support package for schools. Edinburgh: SCRE/SARSU, in collaboration with the Scottish Education Department.; BLACK, H.D. & DEVINE, M. (1988). Mathematics checkpoint 7: assessment materials for primary 7 pupils. Edinburgh: SCRE/SARSU. A full list of publications is available from the researcher.

Source of Grant: Local Authorities Scottish Education Department Scottish Council for Research in Education (SCRE)

Date of Research: 1983 – continuing

KEYWORDS: inservice teacher education

8/1329

15 St John Street, Edinburgh EH8 8JR
031 557 2944
Black, H.D. Mr; Zaklukiewicz, S. Mr; Visocchi, P. Ms

Evaluation of the Fife TVEI aware work experience scheme

Abstract: The study is looking at the experience of one school in implementing the TVEI aware scheme. The views of pupils, teachers and employers are being canvassed.

Source of Grant: Fife Region

Date of Research: 1990-1990

KEYWORDS: work experience

8/1330

15 St John Street, Edinburgh EH8 8JR
031 557 2944
Munn, P. Mrs

Teaching and learning in continuing education

Abstract: This project will explore the kinds of teaching methods used by a variety of providers of education for adults. It aims to discover why these methods are used and to gather perceptions of their effectiveness. More specifically the general aims of the research are: to assess whether the needs of mature students differ from those of young students and to look at any implications of this possible difference for the selection of the most appropriate teaching methods; to look at the problems, learning needs and motivations of mature students and the ways in which these needs are catered for by different providers of continuing education; to determine which are the most effective teaching approaches for mature students; and to provide notes of guidance or a checklist of possible questions for course organizers. A series of five pairs of case studies of different kinds of providers of adult education will be undertaken. These case studies will concentrate on the views of adult learners and their teachers about the teaching methods employed. The selection of case studies will allow a limited degree of variability in terms of the level at which subjects are taught and the type of providing agency or institution. As well as providing a checklist of questions for providers of education about their teaching methods, it is envisaged that, in addition to a final project report, a number of subject based reports will be produced during the course of the research.

Source of Grant: Scottish Education Department

Date of Research: 1987-1989

KEYWORDS: adult education; teaching method

8/1331

15 St John Street, Edinburgh EH8 8JR
031 557 2944
Macdonald, C. Ms; Lowden, K. Mr; *Supervisor:* Munn, P. Mrs

Opportunities for adult students

Abstract: The aim of this project is to investigate the perceptions of adults in Scotland towards returning to education and training. It is undertaken in the context of changing opportunities for adult students and of increasing demands for an adaptable and flexible workforce. The project has three main strands. The first strand concerns a survey of the adult population in Scotland; investigating attitudes towards and perceptions of returning to education and training. It will be supplemented by a number of case studies which will examine in greater depth, reasons for non-participation. In addition, the case studies will explore strategies which may promote interest and, where feasible implement such strategies. The second strand involves a survey of identified 'returners' and 'potential returners' (those who have expressed an interest in returning) and the provision made for them. As in strand one, this survey will be supplemented by a number of case studies. The aim of these will be to explore the factors which encourage and inhibit 'returners' and 'potential returners' and will include the perspectives of both providers of education and training and employers. The third main strand of the research will be a series of interview studies with a variety of employers. The project hopes to provide a useful working definition of adult returners and, in the early stage at least, will take a broad definition of training and education.

Published Material: MUNN, P. (1988). 'Adult participation in education and training', Practitioner Mini Paper 4, Edinburgh: SCRE.; LOWDEN, K., MUNN, P. & MACDONALD, C. 'Adult returners to education and training: a review of the literature', Practitioner Mini Paper, Edinburgh: SCRE (forthcoming).; MACDONALD, C., LOWDEN, K. & MUNN, P. (1989). Providing for adults: the views and policies of providers of education and training. SCRE Practitioner Mini Paper 7. Edinburgh: SCRE; MUNN, P. & MACDONALD, C. (1988). 'Participation in adult education and training in Scotland: what effects return to learning?, Adult Education, Vol 6, No 3, pp.220-226.; LOWDEN, K. (1989). 'Employers and adult training: attitudes and practices', Spotlight 15. Edinburgh: SCRE.; LOWDEN, K., MUNN, P. & MACDONALD, C. (1990). Attitudes and access to adult education, SCRE Project Report Series.
Source of Grant: Scottish Education Department
Date of Research: 1986-1989
KEYWORDS: adult education; educational opportunities; employment opportunities; perception of others; Scotland; training

8/1332

15 St John Street, Edinburgh EH8 8JR
031 557 2944
Munn, P. Mrs

Discipline in Scottish schools

Abstract: The aim of the research is to look at classroom discipline and at whole-school discipline in a way which will be of direct, practical benefit to teachers. The research focuses not on assessing the amount or type of indiscipline in school or classroom, but rather on what constitutes "effective discipline" as opposed to effective teaching. The research hopes to uncover what pupils and teachers see as effective discipline in a range of different contexts. It will concentrate on the kinds of strategies that bring about effective discipline in these situations. The researchers hope to move beyond a common-sense list of managerial or organizational routines into an understanding of how effective discipline comes into operation in the school and classroom. Work will take place in eight schools: four secondary and four primary schools in two education authorities. Two years will be devoted to case study work in schools and classrooms. In the third and final year of the investigation, the research will focus on putting into action in one or two schools some of the earlier findings on effective discipline strategies. Findings will be reported as the research progresses, and as the researchers feel that there is something to say about how good pratice operates. Reports will take the form of workshops and seminars as well as short papers and fuller reports.

Published Material: JOHNSTONE, M. and MUNN, P. (1987). 'Discipline in schools: a review of 'causes' and 'cures'', Edinburgh: Scottish Council for Research in Education.; JOHNSTONE, M. & MUNN, P. (1987). 'Discipline: a pilot study', (SCRE Project Report Series), Edinburgh: Scottish Council for Research in Education.; MUNN, P., JOHNSTONE, M. & HOLLIGAN, C. (1990).

'Pupils' perceptions of effective disciplinarians', British Educational Research Journal, Vol 16, No 2, pp.191-198.
Source of Grant: Scottish Education Department
Date of Research: 1987-1990
KEYWORDS: class management; discipline; Scotland

8/1333

15 St John Street, Edinburgh EH8 8JR
031 557 2944
Thorpe, G. Mr; Watson, G. Mr

Central Support Unit: the assessment of achievement programme

Abstract: The Central Support Unit (CSU) has been funded by the Scottish Education Department to provide the technical support and infra-structure for its Assessment of Achievement Programme (AAP). The AAP is a systematic programme, designed to monitor pupil attainment. To date it has conducted major studies in Mathematics (1983), English (1984) and Science (1987), Primary 7 and Secondary 2 levels. (Cycle of studies again in 1988). Individual teams with knowledge and expertise in the particular subject under study are established to have responsibility for the content-specific part of the projects. The CSU provides technical support to all projects across the subject spectrum. This support includes: advice on experimental design; sampling; liaison with schools; collation, distribution and collection of test materials; computing the desired analyses and advising on the statistics of these. Part of the general support of the Assessment of Achievement Programme will incorporate the development and continuous updating of a set of guidelines for AAP projects. These guidelines will assist the project teams in the efficient design of their assessment programmes, will offer a repertoire of analytic approaches designed to enable the teams to extract different kinds of information from their data, and will make practical suggestions which will help to overcome anticipated difficulties.

Source of Grant: Scottish Education Department
Date of Research: 1987 – continuing
KEYWORDS: achievement measurement; assessment; pupil; Scotland; technical assistance

8/1334

15 St John Street, Edinburgh EH8 8JR
031 557 2944
Brown, S. Dr; Visocchi, P. Ms

Media education in Scotland: a study of curriculum, school policy and management

Abstract: The primary aim of this project is to gain an understanding of the concepts of 'media education' which inform school policies; to investigate the influence of school policies on the control and articulation of the curriculum context and progression of media education; to identify the important management issues which impinge on the introduction of media education. The secondary aims are to analyze the effects on teachers and pupils involved; to identify implications for future developments; to make a start on the generation of various models for development and associated school policies. The research will be undertaken in the 8 schools (4 primary and 4 secondary) which are involved in the media education initiative by the Scottish Film Council. Interviews of a semi-structured kind will be undertaken with school managers, class teachers and the SFC support team. Observation of team meetings, between-school liaison groups and some classroom activity will be undertaken. Because the developments are at an early stage the research will be relatively open and inductive in nature.

Published Material: VISOCCHI, P. & BROWN, S. (1989). 'Media education in Scottish schools: development and research', Educational Media International, Vol 26, No 4.
Source of Grant: ESRC (Economic and Social Research Council)
Date of Research: 1988 – continuing
KEYWORDS: curriculum development; educational policy; media studies; Scotland

8/1335

15 St John Street, Edinburgh EH8 8JR
031 557 2944
Beck, L.L. Mrs; *Supervisor:* Black, H.D. Mr

Evaluation of Lothian TVEI (Technical and Vocational Education Initiative)

Abstract: The Technical and Vocational Education Initiative (TVEI) is a pilot project devised and managed by the local education authority, within criteria established by the Manpower Services Commission (MSC), and funded by MSC. The project is looking at methods of organizing, managing and delivering education for

14-18 year olds, in ways which will further widen and enrich the curriculum to prepare young people for life beyond school. It aims to make the curriculum more relevant and to establish closer collaboration between education and industry. Each local authority's project has an evaluator attached to it, and in the case of Lothian Region, SCRE (Scottish Council for Research in Education), is undertaking the evaluation function. The role of evaluation is seen as a supportive one in relation to the implementation and development of TVEI. Through evaluation, useful information can be provided to assist local decision makers, officials and professionals. SCRE has undertaken a number of evaluation studies of Lothian Region's TVEI project. Evaluation is intended to have a formative impact on the project and already there are signs that the project has tackled/is tackling some of the issues which these evaluation studies have revealed.

Published Material: BECK, L.L. & BLACK, H.D. (1987). What is good practice in TVEI. SCRE Project Report Series. Edinburgh: Scottish Council for Research in Education.; BECK, L.L. & BLACK, H.D. (1988). The proof of the pudding. SCRE Project Report Series. Edinburgh: Scottish Council for Research in Education.; BECK, L.L. (1988). 'Evaluation of TVEI in Lothian'. In: Broadcast, Newsletter of the Curriculum Advice Support Team, pp.5-7.; BECK, L.L. & BLACK, H.D. (1989). The vocational assignment: a study of its use in S5 in the Lothian TVEI pilot. SCRE Project Report Series. Edinburgh: SCRE.

Source of Grant: Training Agency (now Training Enterprise Education Division) – Lothian Region

Date of Research: 1986-1990

KEYWORDS: curriculum development; evaluation; local education authority; Scotland; Technical and Vocational Education Initiative (TVEI)

8/1336

15 St John Street,
Edinburgh EH8 8JR
031 557 2944
Black, H.D. Mr

National TVEI (Technical and Vocational Education Initiative) Curriculum Database

Abstract: The Technical and Vocational Education Initiative (TVEI), initially a five-year pilot scheme in selected Scottish Authorities, has now been extended to other authorities over a ten-year period. Its broad overall aim is to encourage technical and vocational education for 14 to 18 year olds. The Manpower Services Commission (MSC) is concerned to gather as much information as possible on how this innovation is faring in practice. Formative feedback to each scheme comes from independent local evaluators, and a large-scale national evaluation is examining issues over all the schemes. The Curriculum Database is a further aspect of the information gathering process. Its primary aim is to gather statistical data on the curricula of all TVEI projects in Scotland. This information is then stored in a database and is organized so that various analyses can be run. The Database will thus hold a description of the curriculum in each TVEI school (e.g. how many subjects are taught, and for how many periods in each week, and whether they have or have not chosen to be part of TVEI in that school), and will be able to provide each school with a description in graph form, for example of the uptake of subjects in the school. Each school has access to its own data only, but will be able to make comparisons between its own curriculum and those of the TVEI schools in its region (or nationally) as the curricula can be put together in a set of regional or national graphs.

Source of Grant: Manpower Services Commission (now Training Enterprise Education Division)

Date of Research: 1986-1990

KEYWORDS: curriculum development; database; evaluation; Scotland; Technical and Educational Education Initiative (TVEI)

8/1337

15 St John Street,
Edinburgh EH8 8JR
031 557 2944
Black, H.D. Mr

TVEI (Technical and Vocational Education Initiative) Students /Teachers Database

Abstract: The Student/Teacher Database is a simple statistical record of the number of young people involved in TVEI courses in each of the Scottish projects and of the number of teachers involved. Apart from being a straightforward statistical record however, the database also allows analysis of a number of fundamental issues. For example, a central aim of the initiative is that it should not be seen as an option solely for low achievers. The evidence available to us suggests that although there are some Regional differences, teachers' estimates of the likely final attainments of pupils indicate that TVEI is attracting young people from the whole range of potential. The national data for 1985/86 indicated that there was a slight imbalance in the extent to which the initiative is proving more attractive to boys than to girls. In fact, however, more detailed analysis suggests that this imbalance was attributed almost exclusively to two of the six projects, the others not being significantly biased either way. The information from the database is fed back to the coordinators of each of the projects as well as to the TVEI adviser in Scotland. It provides a useful objective base of comparison both for policymakers and for evaluation of the underlying reasons for any problems highlighted.

Published Material: THORPE, G. & BLACK, H.D. (1987). TVEI students and studies two years on: first report of the student/teacher database for Scotland. Edinburgh: SCRE.; THORPE, G. & BLACK, H.D. (1988). TVEI students at the end of S4: second report. Edinburgh: SCRE.; THORPE, G. & BLACK, H.D. (1988). TVEI students and studies four years on: third report. Edinburgh: SCRE.

Source of Grant: Manpower Services Commission (MSC) (now Training Enterprise Education Division) Lothian Region

Date of Research: 1986-1989

KEYWORDS: database; educational policy; low attainer; Scotland; sex difference; Technical and Vocational Education Initiative (TVEI)

8/1338

15 St John Street,
Edinburgh EH8 8JR
031 557 2944
Black, H.D. Mr

National TVEI (Technical and Vocational Education Initiative) Evaluation

Abstract: The Technical and Vocational Education Initiative (TVEI) represents a substantial investment of resources in the educational system. In consequence, to ensure that maximum benefit is obtained, a programme of local and national evaluation has been established. Local evaluations tend to centre on local issues, and feedback is given directly to the projects to which the evaluators are attached. The National Evaluation is concerned with obtaining an overview of all the TVEI schemes operating in Scotland, and to focus research attention more closely wherever the information gathered suggests that there are issues likely to be of interest. The findings are expected to be of value to the individual projects themselves, but they will also offer a broader picture of TVEI in Scotland, which should be of use to policy makers at local and national levels. The evaluation will be carried out through three distinct strands. In the first strand the aim is to build up a profile of the curriculum of each TVEI scheme running in Scotland, by talking, in the first instance to some of the key people involved in making each one work. The second strand will use this curriculum profile to identify a number of issues which are emerging as important in all of the TVEI projects. Four studies are planned for the third strand (focused studies): management, change and resources, pupil choice in TVEI and attainment (an area so potentially complex that it will need two studies). Widespread sets of data will be gathered through interviews and questionnaires involving parents, pupils and teachers.

Published Material: BLACK, H.D., MALCOLM, H.M. & ZAKLUKIEWIZC, S. (1988). The TVEI Curriculum in Scotland: a profile 1986/87. Sheffield: Manpower Services Commission.; BLACK, H.D. MALCOLM, H.M. & ZAKLUKIEWICZ, S. (1988). The gift horse: a study of management, change and resources in seven TVEI pilot projects in Scotland. Sheffield: Manpower Services Commission.; BLACK, H.D., MALCOLM, H.M. & ZAKLUKIEWICZ, S. (1989). The classes of '88: a report on the curriculum in Round Five TVEI projects, school session 1987-88. Sheffield: Training Enterprise Education Division.; BLACK, D., MALCOLM, H. & ZAKLUKIEWWICZ, S. (1990). An accepted part of the landscape: a report on the curriculum in Round Two and Round Three pilot projects, school session 1988-89. Sheffield: Training Enterprise Education Division.

Source of Grant: Manpower Services Commission (now Training Enterprise Education Division)

Date of Research: 1986-1990

KEYWORDS: educational policy; evaluation; Scotland; Technical and Vocational Education Initiative (TVEI)

Scottish Human–Computer Interaction Centre

8/1339

36 North Hanover Street, Glasgow G1 2AD
041 552 1576
Strathclyde University
Department of Psychology
Alexander Turnbull Building,
155 George Street, Glasgow G1 1RD
041 552 4400
Kibby, M.R. Dr; Mayes, J.T. Dr; Anderson, A. Dr

Evaluation of HyperCard and StrathTutor, two novel learning environments for the Macintosh

Abstract: The project examines whether recent developments in microcomputer interface promote learning with computers in schools. Two novel learning environments for the Macintosh are being evaluated. The first is HyperCard, which combines hypertext, database, and programming facilities within a stack-of-filecards presentation metaphor. The second is StrathTutor, a new type of reactive learning environment based on a browsing paradigm with intelligent links between frames. The major focus of the research is the evaluation of HyperCard, and evaluation of both learning aspects (in teachers and pupils) and authoring by teachers will be undertaken. As well as attempting to evaluate the software, the project provides the opportunity for a number of teachers in several subject areas to gain experience with the software, and hardware and with the researchers evaluation methods, and to contribute to further development of the learning environments.

Published Material: KIBBY, M.R., MAYES, J.T., KNUSSEN, C. (1989). 'Hypertext as a medium for interactive learning', Proceedings of the 6th Canadian Symposium on Instructional Technology, Halifax, Nova Scotia, May 1989, pp.321-324.
Source of Grant: Microelectronics in Education Committee, Scottish Council for Educational Technology: £35,601
Date of Research: 1988-1990
KEYWORDS: computer assisted instruction; computer assisted learning; educational software; educational technology; evaluation; further education of teachers

Sheffield City Education Department

8/1340

PO Box 67, Leopold Street, Sheffield S1 1RJ
0742 26341
Steven, B.R.

Primary information technology project

Abstract: The project is exploring with 6 junior schools the significance of Information Technology for the curriculum. The approach is computer orientated, but is based on environmental studies and information skills contributions. This work yielded valuable experience and ideas. Work is commencing in producing modular materials for use with all schools.

Source of Grant: Local Education Authority (LEA)
Date of Research: 1982 – continuing
KEYWORDS: environmental study; information skills; information technology; primary education

8/1341

PO Box 67, Leopold Street, Sheffield S1 1RJ
0742 26341
Garforth, J.M. Ms

Analysis of external examination results

Abstract: The Authority monitors annual performance in external examination results. Results for GCE (General Certificate of Education), CSE (Certificate of Secondary Education) and 16+ joint examination are analyzed by school, subject and by sex of pupils.

Published Material: Analysis of external examination results. Annual report, Sheffield Education Department.
Source of Grant: LEA funded
Date of Research: 1973 – continuing
KEYWORDS: comparative analysis; evaluation; examination

8/1342

PO Box 67, Leopold Street, Sheffield S1 1RJ
0742 26341
Steven, B.R.

Library/Resource Centre computerisation

Abstract: One secondary school received LEA (Local Education Authority) support to explore the use of a microcomputer for stock control, load recording and resource centre database evolvement. Preliminary work was very successful and several secondary schools are now involved. A bar code system has been developed and programming has commenced on the general catalogues. The work has been extended to the primary level and 6 schools are involved. The whole project is now on a co-operative basis with the Schools Library Section of Sheffield City Libraries. The bar coding work is in co-operation with the Microelectronic Education Programme (MEP) bar code project at Newcastle.

Source of Grant: Local Education Authority (LEA)
Date of Research: 1982 – continuing
KEYWORDS: library; microcomputer; resource centre

8/1343

PO Box 67, Leopold Street, Sheffield S1 1RJ
0742 26341
Lindsay, G.A. Dr; Pennock, J. Miss

Monitoring children's learning

Abstract: To develop in primary and nursery teachers an understanding of the methods of and the rationales for monitoring children's learning. This has been an inservice approach which has been largely school-based and school-focused. It inter-relates with the Infant Rating Scale Project, and with ongoing research by Dr G.A. Lindsay on early identification of learning difficulties. Large numbers of Sheffield primary schools (100 approximately) with pupils 3-12 years have been involved.

Published Material: LINDSAY, G.A. & PEARSON, L.S. (1981). 'Identification and intervention: school-based approaches'. TRC Publishing.; LINDSAY, G.A. (Ed). 'Screening for children with special needs'. London: Croom Helm.
Source of Grant: Schools Council Open University 'Curriculum in Action'
Date of Research: 1975 – continuing
KEYWORDS: assessment; learning; learning difficulty; pre-school education; education

8/1344

PO Box 67, Leopold Road, Sheffield S1 1RJ
0742 26341
Lindsay, G.A. Dr

Evaluation of special nursery units

Abstract: Three units attached to mainstream schools, providing for children with communication difficulties, are being evaluated with particular reference to integration. In addition, an INSET (Inservice Education and Training of Teachers) programme has been conducted with the staff of the nurseries and other interested colleagues.

Published Material: LINDSAY, G. & DESFORGES, M. (1986). 'Integrated nurseries for children with special educational needs', British Journal of Special Education, Vol 13, No 2, June, pp.63-66.; DESFORGES, M. & LINDSAY, G. 'Integrated nurseries for children with special educational needs', In: LINDSAY, G. (Ed). Integration: practice, possibilities and problems, educational and child pshychology. British Psychological Society.
Source of Grant: No funding
Date of Research: 1981 – continuing
KEYWORDS: communication; inservice education and training of teachers; integration; nursery school; special needs

8/1345

Psychological Service
9 Newbould Lane, Sheffield S10 2PJ
0742 684665
Lindsay, G. Dr; Desforges, M. Dr

Evaluation of integrated resources in primary schools

Abstract: The project follows on from the evaluation of three integrated nursery resources in Sheffield. It is concerned with integrated resources for children with special needs at primary level. Six schools are involved: one first (age range 5-8 years); one middle (8-12 years); one first and middle (5-12 years); and three junior and infant (5-11 years). The schools may admit up to five (schools A and B) or ten (C to F) children with Statements of their special educational needs. These children are integrated into mainstream

classrooms, supported by a teacher and a non-teaching assistant. The aims of this project are to evaluate the resources and to support the in-service development of the staff, including the feedback of research findings.
Published Material: LINDSAY, G. 'Evaluating Integration'. In: Educational Psychology in Practice, Vol 5, No 1, April 1989, pp.7-16.
Source of Grant: No funding
Date of Research: 1986 – continuing
KEYWORDS: integration; primary education; special needs

Sheffield City Polytechnic

8/1346
Department for Education Management and Administration
36 Collegiate Crescent,
Sheffield S10 2BP
0742 532323
Kedney, R.J. Mr; *Supervisor:* Watson, L.E. Prof.
The efficient and effective use of space in further education colleges
Abstract: This research consists of analysis and field testing of methodologies relating to aspects of the efficient and effective use of college buildings as the basis for preparing a manual of guidance for senior staff. Working papers, standard definitions and details of methodologies relating to the measurement of capacity and occupancy will be prepared, with supporting documentation. A classification of space types, covering both teaching and support areas will be required. Case studies will be used to test the manual of guidance and investigation into strategies for management action will be undertaken. Examples of measurement instruments will be collected and disseminated as part of the preparation of a draft Manual of Guidance.
Source of Grant: Department of Education and Science: £13,250
Date of Research: 1988-1989
KEYWORDS: college of further education; space arrangement

Sheffield University

8/1347
Educational Research Centre,
Qualitative and Quantitative Research Group,
Arts Tower, Floor 9, Sheffield S10 2TN
0742 768555
Gray, J. Prof.; Jesson, D. Mr
Performance indicators project
Abstract: Over the past year more than one in ten of the country's LEAs (local education authorities) have requested specific help in the areas of shaping and implementing policy initiatives, particularly in the area of the evaluation of pupil and school performance. In one LEA a thorough review of secondary school examination performance has been undertaken, whilst elsewhere advisers and inspectors have sought assistance in developing comprehensive indicators of institutional performance. An increasing number of professional bodies (such as the National Association of Inspectors and Advisers and the Association of Metropolitan Authorities) have turned to the group for advice and assistance.
Published Material: GRAY, J. & JESSON, D. (1990). 'The negotiation and construction of performance indicators', Evaluation and Research in Education, (forthcoming).; GRAY, J., JESSON, D. & SIMS, N. (1990). 'Estimating differences in the examination performances of secondary schools in six LEAs: a multi-level approach to school effectiveness', Oxford Review of Education, (forthcoming).; GRAY, J. (1990). 'Performance indicators and the social organisation of evaluation: some proposals for change'. In: FITZ-GIBBON, C.T. (Ed). Performance indicators. Clevedon: Multilingual Matters for British Educational Research Association.
Source of Grant: Local Education Authorities: £16,000
Date of Research: 1989 – continuing
KEYWORDS: achievement measurement; examination; performance; performance indicator; pupil

8/1348
Educational Research Centre,
Qualitative and Quantitative Studies in Education Group,

Arts Tower, Floor 9, Sheffield S10 2TN
0742 768555
Gray, J. Prof.
Youth cohort study: essay analysis of pupils' comments
Abstract: To provide a source of information on the attitudes and views of young people about their Vocational Education Training experiences post-age 16 drawn from comments written by young people in reply to the major Youth Cohort Study of 16-19 year olds in England and Wales. After pilot work undertaken in Sheffield and Bradford during 1984 the national surveys, which are administered by the Social Community Planning Research group began in 1985. The Youth Cohort Study of England and Wales has been in receipt of continuous funding from its sponsors (the Training Enterprise Education Division, The Department of Education and Science and the Department of Employment who all have major responsibilities for the provision of education, training and employment opportunites for the 16-19 age group). Undertaken in collaboration with Social and Community Planning Research, the study of 16-19 year olds is one of the largest of its kind ever undertaken in this country. To date three cohorts of 16 year-olds have been followed-up on three occasions as they make their way through the structure of education and training opportunities for the 16-19 age-group. Young people complete detailed questionnaires on their experiences of education, training, work and unemployment as well as providing information on their qualifications and social backgrounds. The first national cohort to be surveyed had reached minimum school leaving age by the summer of 1984; they were first followed up during 1985 and again in 1986 and 1987 (Sweeps 1, 2, and 3 respectively). Similar surveys have been conducted of those reaching minimum school leaving age by the summer of 1985 (the second cohort) 1986 (the third cohort) and 1988 (the fourth cohort). Sample sizes are large (20,000 +), nationally respresentative; response rates are good and drawn from all types of school. work on following up a fourth chohort has commenced whilst there si also interest in funding pioneering work on how respondents might be followed up into their mid-twenties.
Source of Grant: Training Enterprise Education Division: £5,000
Date of Research: 1990-1990
KEYWORDS: post-compulsory education; training; vocational education; vocational training; youth attitude

8/1349
Educational Research Centre,
Qualitative and Quantitative Studies in Education Group,
Arts Tower, Floor 9, Sheffield S10 2TN
0742 768555
Gray, J. Prof.
Youth cohort study: study of black 16-19 year olds
Abstract: To examine Youth Cohort Study data on ethnic minority young people with reference to educational experience/attainment, experiences in education and training and the experiences of those moving into the labour market. After pilot work undertaken in Sheffield and Bradford during 1984 the national surveys, which are administered by the Social and Community Planning Research group began in 1985. The Youth Cohort Study of England and Wales has been in receipt of continuous funding from its sponsors (the Training Enterprise Education Division, The Department of Education and Science and the Department of Employment who all have major responsibilities for the provision of education, training and employment opportunities for the 16-19 age group). Undertaken in collaboration with Social and Community Planning Research, the study of 16-19 year olds is one of the largest of its kind ever undertaken in this country. To date, three cohorts of 16 year olds have been followed up on three occasions as they make their way through the structure of education and training opportunites for the 16-19 age group. Young people complete detailed questionnaires on their experiences of education, training, work and unemployment as well as providing information on their qualifications and social backgrounds. The first national cohort to be surveyed had reached minimum school leaving age by the summer of 1984; they were first followed up during 1985 and again in 1986 and 1987 (Sweeps 1, 2 and 3 respectively). Similar surveys have been conducted of those reaching minimum school leaving age by the summer of 1985 (the second cohort), 1986 (the third cohort) and 1988 (the fourth cohort). Sample sizes are large (20,000 +), nationally representative; response rates are good and drawn from all types of school. Work on following up a fourth cohort has commenced whilst there is also interest in funding pioneering work on how respondents might be followed up into their mid-twenties.
Published Material: DREW, D. & GRAY, J. (1990). 'The black-

white gap in exam achievement: a statistical critique of a decade's research'. In: MARSH, C. (Ed). Social Divisions and Social Change. (forthcoming) London: Routledge.; DREW, D. & GRAY, J. (1990). 'The fifth-year examination achievements of black young people in England and Wales', Educational Research, (forthcoming).

Source of Grant: Training Enterprise Education Division: £14,500
Date of Research: 1989-1990
KEYWORDS: *achievement; ethnic minority; labour market; transition from school to work; youth employment*

8/1350

Educational Research Centre,
Qualitative and Quantitative Studies in Education Group,
Arts Tower, Floor 9, Sheffield S10 2TN
0742 768555
Gillborn, D. Dr; Rudduck, J. Prof.; Nixon, J. Dr

Positive approaches to discipline in inner city schools
Abstract: Inner city schools are likely, for a number of familiar reasons, to present the greatest challenge to the building and sustaining of a supportive and orderly environment for working. Carefully contextualized accounts of good practice in schools which have different pasts, localities, characters and problems, can powerfully demonstrate the possibilities that are open to all schools staffs. It is now more than a decade since Her Majesty's Inspectors (HMI) published 'Ten good schools' (1977). In the USA, Lightfoot's 'The good high school' (1983) has made a considerable impact on people's perceptions of schools and their achievements. This study will build on these models by using detailed studies of 6 inner city schools to identify and explore what HMI have called 'The complex and difficult task of achieving and maintaining high standards of behaviour and discipline'.

Source of Grant: Department of Education and Science: £44,755
Date of Research: 1990 – continuing
KEYWORDS: *behaviour; discipline; inner city; quality of education; urban school*

8/1351

Department of Psychology
Sheffield S10 2TN
0742 768555
Smith, P.K. Dr; Boulton, M.J. Dr; Cowie, H.A. Dr

Prejudice, isolation and bullying: intervention in ethnically mixed classes
Abstract: Research has shown that racial prejudice, social isolation, and bullying are far from uncommon during the middle school period. The first aim of the project is to document the extent and inter-relationship of these problems on a large sample of classes. At present, for example, we do not know whether racial prejudice and bullying are related, and if so, whether in some cases the former may be a cause of the latter. In a previous one year ESRC (Ecomomic and Social Research Council) funded project, the research team found that prejudice could be ameliorated to some extent, and liking of peers increased, in classes where teachers were trained in and used CGW (cooperative group work). The central feature of this approach is the opportunity to learn through the expression and exploration of diverse ideas and the cooperative solution of problems, in groups formed across ethnic and gender barriers. In our present project, the CGW curriculum will be refined and more focused in some respects, based on our previous experience. The second aim of the project is that it should provide a more definitive test of the efficacy of this form of school-based intervention program. The extent to which the preliminary results from the one year project can be replicated will be assessed on a larger sample and over a longer time period. Periodic assessments, both quantitative and qualitative, will be made of the nature of social relationships in the participating classes.

Source of Grant: Economic and Social Research Council: £82496
Date of Research: 1990 – continuing
KEYWORDS: *bullying; middle school; racial discrimination; racism; social isolation*

8/1352

Department of Psychology
Sheffield S10 2TN
0742 768555
Smith, P.K. Dr; Ahmad, Y. Ms

Piloting a survey service to schools on bully/victim problems
Abstract: The aim of this project was to pilot a survey service for schools which would inform them of the nature and extent of

bully/victim problems. During the grant period the researchers prepared a package which was suitable for teachers to understand so that administration of questionnaires was easy and efficient. This questionnaire, to be filled out by the headteacher, required information about size, location, and population of school, to determine (in later surveys), whether these factors affected the level of bullying in schools. A portfolio was then sent back to the school to give detailed information about the level of bullying, where the bullying occurred and which class had a high level of bullying. This was felt to be importent so that teachers were aware of which classes required attention; as time and provision is not always available to target every class in the school. An information sheet was also included in the portfolio, giving some ideas on how to tackle the problem of bullying and further references to resources and books on the topic. Three schools (all in South Yorkshire) took part in the pilot survey: 2 middle schools and 1 secondary school. All were different in racial mix, location (rural/urban) and size, to provide variety of experience with the questionnaire. Also, at their request, a fourth secondary school in London is being included.

Source of Grant: Gulbenkian Foundation: £2000
Date of Research: 1989-1990
KEYWORDS: *bullying; survey*

8/1353

Department of Psychology
Medical Research Council/Economic and Social Research Council, Sheffield S10 2TN
0742 756600
Roker, D. Ms; *Supervisor:* Banks, M.H. Dr

The political socialization of young people: the experience of private education
Abstract: The research project is linked to the ESRC 16-19 Initiative; a sample longitudinal study of school leavers in Britain. The initiative sample is drawn from local authority schools only; thus socialization processes and outcomes of those from independent schools (approximately 7% of the school age population) is not explored. The author's research therefore focuses on the political socialization of young women in private schools. The theoretical framework is multi-disciplinary, utilizing concepts from political science, sociology, education, and psychology. The research highlights omissions in earlier work by taking females and schooling (rather than the home and family), as the focus for exploring political socialization in youth. The effect of education on political socialization is explored by sampling from a local authority school and an independent school in the same, economically advantaged area; this method is designed to control for the effects of family background. Two age cohorts within the 15-18 range were selected from each school, the total sample numbering 150. Questionnaires were administered exploring attitudes to work, training and education, and were followed by individual structured interviews. These investigated political knowledge, attitudes and values. Analysis of the data is currently underway. The results are considered to affect understanding of the socialization process, political development and education, and the effects of education on attitudes and values.

Source of Grant: Medical Research Council: two-year studentship
Date of Research: 1987-1989
KEYWORDS: *girl; independent school; political socialization; youth*

8/1354

Department of Psychology
Sheffield S10 2TN
0742 768555
Smith P.K. Dr; Boulton, M. Mr

Ethnic relations and sociometric status in middle school: an intervention study
Abstract: This project forms part of the research initiative 'The Educational Needs of a Multiracial Society'. It has three main aims. The first aim is to document the inter-relationships amongst children's ethnic identity and preference, self-esteem, and sociometric (friendship) status in the classroom. How extensive is ethnic preference? Do more prejudiced children differ in their popularity and self-esteem? The second aims is to see how the above measures change over the course of a school year. Does ethnic preference increase, or decline? How do such changes relate to friendship changes? The third aim is to pilot out the effectiveness of a co-operative group work curriculum as a means of enhancing interracial co-operation and attitudes to other ethnic groups. This has found to be effective in the USA. The research is being carried out in three middle-schools within the Sheffield LEA. In each school,

two classes will be monitored through the year; one of these classes will in addition experience an enhanced co-operative group work intervention.

Source of Grant: Economic and Social Research Council: £20,710
Date of Research: 1988-1989
KEYWORDS: ethnic relations; group work; middle school; sociometry

8/1355
Department of Psychology
Medical Research Council/Economic and Social Research Council, Sheffield S10 2TN
0742 756600
Banks, H.M. Dr; Parkinson, B. Dr
Work socialization of youth (WOSY): a cross-national study
Abstract: This is a collaborative cross-national research approach that seeks to describe and explain work role development of youth in ten countries, through a common theoretical and methodological framework. A minimum of two samples are drawn in each country, representing jobs selected to emphasize work with either 'data' or 'things'. The samples will comprise 200 young people beginning jobs with information systems such as word processors, and 200 machine operators in manufacturing companies. Interviews will be carried out on three occasions: within six months of starting the job or training scheme, nine to twelve months later, and two years after the first interview. Interviews will gather information about education, early career, and job characteristics. Motivational variables include employment commitment, job attitudes, and information about the personal meanings of work. Young people's perceptions of the personal impact on their job and their colleagues and the match between prior expectations and later circumstances, will also be assessed. In addition, several indices of career advancement and satisfaction will be obtained. The aim is to determine individual, organizational and societal factors which underlie successful entry into the labour market. Changes across time will be identified, and these will be examined in relation to previously gathered data. Cross-national comparisons will permit evaluation of characteristic educational and training arrangements within each country.
Source of Grant: Medical Research Council sponsors British Fieldwork
Date of Research: 1988 – continuing
KEYWORDS: comparative analysis; motivation; socialization; youth employment

8/1356
Department of Psychology
Medical Research Council/Economic and Social Research Council, Sheffield S10 2TN
0742 756600
Mean, L. Ms; *Supervisor:* Evans, S.T. Dr
Psychological aspects of high unemployment and compulsory YTS: a study of youth
Abstract: This research aims to establish whether there are young people who have accepted the inevitability of unemployment (in the light of the extended period of high unemployment levels and the consequent high probability of experiencing unemployment either personally or through their social network). It is hoped to re-establish whether, and if so why, these young people have chosen not to attend YTS, and have adopted attitudes, activities and a way of life which maintains or results in a healthy level of psychological well-being during unemployment. An attempt will be made to determine what features of their activities and attitudes provide positive reinforcment as an alternative to training or paid employment. A further aim is to observe any effects occurring as a reaction to the policy of enforced attendace on YTS of all young people eligible and unemployed. The research will comprise two studies: (1) a longitudinal and quantitatively based study of 1987 and 1988 school leavers who have either been continuously unemployed since leaving school or leave YTS early (moving into unemployment). There will be three data collection points, at three month intervals, using postal questionnaires, plus interviews with the first and last data collections where appropriate. First data collection point is October 1988; (2) an ethnographical study of a women's group run for the young and unemployed at a local youth centre.
Source of Grant: Economic and Social Research Council: Three-year studentship
Date of Research: 1987-1990
KEYWORDS: psychology; Youth Training Scheme; youth unemployment

8/1357
Department of Psychology
Sheffield S10 2TN
0742 768555
Fawcett, A. Mrs; *Supervisor:* Martlew, M.
Developmental dyslexia, performance and strategies of subgroups in cognitive processes underlying the acquisition of literacy
Abstract: This research takes a multivariate approach to the analysis of heterogeneity in developmental dyslexia. Subgroups show different patterns of comparative strengths and weaknessess in the cognitive processes underlying the acquisition of literacy. These reflect a range of relatively intact or impaired perceptual, motor and memory processes. Recognition of these differences facilitates the provision of appropriate remediation geared specifically to the individual needs of the child. In preliminary research, thirty-six dyslexic children were tested on non-reading tasks designed to differentiate between subgroups. These children were matched with control groups for chronological and reading age. This ensures that differences between subjects and controls do not simply reflect lower reading ages in dyslexic children. Four significant differences were found between groups whose difficulties were predominantly visual or auditory, coupled with significant interactions between group membership and performance. A second study investigated the status of developmental dyslexia as maturational lag or cognitive deficit. Children who had overcome their reading difficulties and were therefore designated "remediated" continued to experience substantial difficulties in five areas. In three sequencing tasks, showing greater difficulty than controls two years younger. This suggests that a maturational delay model may be appropriate for reading, while a deficit model is more appropriate for the cognitive skills underlying literacy. Further research in these two areas will examine the performance and strategies of dyslexic children, following up the original sample longitudinally, and enlarging the scope and sample size. Future areas will include recognition of faces, naming difficulties, and semantic errors, predicting differences between subgroups.
Source of Grant: University scholarship
Date of Research: 1986-1989
KEYWORDS: cognitive process; dyslexia; learning difficulty; literacy; remedial teaching; special needs

8/1358
Department of Psychology
Sheffield S10 2TN
0742 76855
Tapton Mount School
20 Manchester Road, Sheffield S10 5DG
0742 667151
Spencer, C.P. Dr; Blades, M. Dr; Ungar, S. Mr
Evaluation of mobility education for young blind children
Abstract: The researchers' previous research on the education for mobility of the visually handicapped has included: (1) development of spatial concepts; (2) the hierarchy of skills underlying successful mobility; (3) the evaluation of experimental programmes to improve aspects of training; and (4) the evaluation of tactile maps in learning a novel area. One such project – on the parental approach to independence – and mobility skills for children prior to school – has led the researchers on to embarking upon the present project, which will study children through the years prior to entry to blind school, and their first few years of formal mobility training within the school. Research will be conducted in conjunction with Tapton Mount, the special school for the visually handicapped in Yorkshire and surrounding counties. The aim is to plan and test mobility training programmes designed to develop the child's techniques for: (i) acquiring and storing knowledge of spatial layout; (ii) updating one's position within a locale; and (3) applying systems of spatial concepts to plan routes.
Published Material: SPENCER, C.P. & TRAVIS, J. (1985). 'Learning a new area with and without the use of tactile maps', British Journal of Visual Impairment, Vol 3, pp.5-7.; DRYHURST, B., SPENCER, C.P. & BAYBUTT, K. (1985). 'Evaluation of a training programme in articulation skills', British Journal of Visual Impairment, Vol 3, pp.41-44.; HILL, A., SPENCER, C.P. & BAYBUTT, K. (1985). 'Predicting efficiency of travel', Journal of Visual Impairment, Vol 79, pp.297-300.; MORSLEY, K. & SPENCER, C.P. (1988). 'Use of maps and models in the training of mobility', Proceedings of the 2nd International Symposium on Cartography for the Blind. International Cartographic Association.; MORSLEY, K. & SPENCER, C.P. (1988). 'Maps, models and long white caves', The Psychologist, Vol 1, pp.215.; SPENCER, C.P., BLADES, M.

& MORSLEY, K. (1989). The child in the physical environment. Chichester: Wiley.
Source of Grant: Economic and Social Research Council
Date of Research: 1990 – continuing
KEYWORDS: mobility; space perception; special education; teaching aids; visually handicapped

8/1359
> Division of Education
> Arts Tower, Floor 3, Sheffield S10 2TN
> 0742 768555
> Hannon, P.W. Dr

Working with parents to promote early literacy development
Abstract: The project is the United Kingdom contribution to the European Communities' Action Research Programme on the Prevention and Combatting of Illiteracy and is linked to 16 others in the member states. It aims to develop methods of working with parents of pre-school chldren to promote literacy development in the early stages. The focus is on children's learning at home, but both home-based and school-based methods are being explored through a set of 14 case studies of families. The project team has adopted an emergent literacy perspective and has attempted to share it with parents, some in distinctly disadvantaged circumstances. The outcomes will be descriptions of methods to be shared with other workers, and a qualitative evaluation of their feasibility and impact which may lead to future experimental studies.
Published Material: HANNON, P. (1990). 'Parental involvement in pre-school literacy development'. In: WRAY, D. (Ed). Emerging partnerships: current research in language and literacy. BERA (British Educational Research Association) Dialogues in Education, 4. Clevedon, Avon: Multilingual Matters.; WEINBERGER, J., HANNON, P. & NUTBROWN, C. (1990). Ways of working with parents to promote early literacy development. USDE (University of Sheffield, Division of Education) Papers in Education, 14. Sheffield: University of Sheffield, Division of Education.
Source of Grant: European Commission Department of Education and Science
Date of Research: 1988 – continuing
KEYWORDS: EEC; literacy; parent participation; parent-teacher relation; education

8/1360
> Division of Education
> Arts Tower, Floor 9, Sheffield S10 2TN
> 0742 768555 ext 4733
> Pullin, R. Mr; Poppleton, P. Dr

Teacher perspectives on educational change in England and the USSR
Abstract: A study of teacher perceptions of educational change is proposed that would inform debate within the UK and be part of a cross-cultural investigation with the USSR. The study focuses upon teacher perspectives as crucial variables in the mediation of national objectives and as particularly important in times of rapid educational change in which new and, arguably, greater responsibilities are attached to teachers' roles. The aims of the study are to examine how, and to what extent, teacher frameworks mediate the implementation of centrally determined objectives at the level of schools' programmes of development. To explore how teachers perceive their roles in the management of the changes in curriculum and pedagogy that follow from recent educational initiatives such as the introduction of the National Curriculum, TVEI (Technical and Vocational Education Initiative), LMS, (Local Management of Schools), the delegation of inservice development to schools and teacher appraisal. Through exploring teachers' perceptions of their resource and training needs in relation to these developments, to examine the roles that higher education institutions can play in meeting their needs. To consider these questions and their implications for the management of change in the two educational systems of the UK and USSR as each introduces elements of a market economy into education and adopts different strategies for centralizing or de-centralizing education. Finally, to consider how these matters may inform the activities of central government agencies in monitoring and furthering educational change in the two countries.
Published Material: GERSHUNKSY, B. & PULLIN, R. (1990). 'Current dilemmas for Soviet secondary education: an Anglo-Soviet analysis', Comparative Education, Vo 26, No 2/3, pp.307-318.
Source of Grant: Sheffield University: £1,554 British Council: £3,020
Date of Research: 1989 – continuing

KEYWORDS: comparative education; cross-cultural research; educational change; attitude; teacher behaviour; United Kingdom; USSR

8/1361
> Division of Education
> Arts Tower, Floor 9, Sheffield S10 2TN
> 0742 768555 ext 4618
> Quicke, J. Dr

Special needs awareness project (SNAP): teaching about mental handicap in school
Abstract: The project involves research and development of a 'whole school' approach to mental handicap awareness in the secondary school. A survey carried out by the Project Director in local schools suggested a need for 'good practice' guidelines in this area. The project is in two phases. The first phase involved one secondary school in which an educational programme was piloted. In the second phase two secondary schools representing different organizational forms and curriculum practices attempted to integrate their own 'awareness' programmes into existing curriculum structures. In all schools the project focused on second year pupils. The programme was evaluated using a mixture of methods – a before and after questionnaire for pupils, structured interviews with pupils and teachers and participant observation. The research concluded that the dominant image of mental handicap at time one (before the programme) and time two (after the programme) was similar, but certain changes were noted in pupils' knowledge of mental handicap and views about affectionate behaviour and normality. Pupils remained ambivalent about integration but sex differences were noted with boys being more pessimistic on this point than girls. Some progress was evident in responses to the question about personality and mental handicap and feelings towards a person so labelled. In all schools, the aim that teachers should 'own' the project was only partially realized. Likewise, the aim that the project should be integral to curriculum development was achieved in some aspects but not in others. Despite the ambivalent findings, the researcher was encouraged by the degree of moral commitment amongst pupils and teachers. Further work will involve a more in depth investigation of the nature of prejudice towards special needs pupils.
Published Material: QUICKE, J.C. (1987). 'The disability curriculum', Pastoral Care in Education, Vol 5, No 2, pp.114-123.; QUICKE, J.C. (1987). 'Teaching about mental handicap in secondary schools', International Journal of Rehabilitation Research, Vol 10, No 2, pp.39-40.; QUICKE, J.C. (1989). 'Pupils' knowledge of mental handicap', International Journal of Rehabilitation Research, Vol 12, No 1, pp.17-26.; BEASLEY, K. & QUICKE, J.C. (1989). 'A curriculum approach to mental handicap in a comprehensive school', Pastoral Care in Education, Vol 7, No 1, pp.13-17.; QUICKE, J.C. (1989). 'Mental handicap awareness and gender relations in a comprehensive school'. In: ROAF, C. & BINES, H. Needs, rights and opportunities: developing approaches to special education. Lewes: Falmer Press.; QUICKE, J.C., BEASLEY, K. & MORRISON, C. (1990). Challenging prejudice through education: the story of a mental handicap awareness curriculum project. Lewes: Falmer Press.
Source of Grant: MENCAP City Foundation: £5,000 Mental Health Foundation: £15,000
Date of Research: 1985 – continuing
KEYWORDS: attitude; integration; mental handicap; secondary school; special

8/1362
> Division of Education
> Arts Tower, Floor 9, Sheffield S10 2TN
> 0742 768555 est 4733
> Poppleton, P.K. Dr

Secondary teachers' job satisfaction: a comparative study (UK, USA, Singapore, Japan, West Germany)
Abstract: This research aims to establish an international database for cross-cultural analysis of the work perceptions of secondary school teachers in three countries about the tasks and conditions of teaching, their teaching roles and responsibilities in the 1980s. The research will also evaluate the possible effects on secondary teachers within each of these countries regarding changes in educational policies in recruitment, training and professional status in so far as these can be related to identities and non-identities in the working environments and practices of different cultures and educational systems. Methods will include the statistical comparative analysis of responses to a common questionnaire, 'Job Satisfaction in

Teaching' by representative samples of secondary teachers in the countries concerned. By the beginning of this project the questionnaire had already been administered to such samples in all the countries concerned as part of a cross-cultural study that began in 1984 and included the ESRC (Economic and Social Research Council) sponsored British study 'Teacher professional satisfaction: its implications for secondary education and teacher education', (Poppleton, 1988). An interpretative collaboration with colleagues in the other countries concerned in the processes of data preparation, analysis and interpretation will also take place. The samples are, UK.: 686 teachers from 20 secondary comprehensive schools in 6 local authorities in the north of England, (60% of the target sample); USA.: 888 teachers from public secondary schools in 60 school districts randomly selected from 20 intermediate school districts in the state of Michigan, (63% of the target sample); Singapore: 930 teachers from government and government-aided junior colleges and pre-university centres in Singapore, (96% of the target sample); Japan: 1,308 teachers from public high schools and junior high schools randomly selected from each of Japan's 47 prefectures, (40% of the target sample); West Germany: 693 teachers from Gesamtschule in the state of Hessen (24% of the target sample). *Published Material:* MENLO, A. & POPPLETON, P. (1990). 'A five country study of the work perceptions of secondary teachers in America, England, Japan, Singapore and West Germany (1986-1988)', Comparative Education, Vol 26, No 2/3, pp.173-182.; POPPLETON, P. (1990). 'The survey data', Comparative Education, Vol 26, No 2/3, pp.183-210.; POPPLETON, P. & RISEBOROUGH, G. (1990). 'A profession in transition: educational policy and secondary school teaching in England in the 1980s', Comparative Education, Vol 26, No 2/3, pp.211-226. *Source of Grant:* Economic and Social Research Council: £12,240 *Date of Research:* 1988-1990 *KEYWORDS: comparative education; cross-cultural research; occupational satisfaction; secondary school; teacher role; teacher status*

8/1363
Division of Education
Arts Tower, Floor 9, Sheffield S10 2TN
0742 768555 ext 4868
Wellington, J.J. Dr
Information technology in education and employment
Abstract: This research carries on from the previous research project 'Skills for the Future' project. The research has arisen from the increase in the use of microcomputers in both education and industry. In consequence, greater attention has been paid to the need for specific 'information technology skills' – skills which need to be taught in schools, colleges and training schemes to meet the needs of industry. This project draws on interviews with a sample of employers, questionnaire responses, in depth interviews and case studies. By also considering previous research in the area, the project gives a detailed investigation into present provision, aims, and policy in training related to 'IT' (Information Technology) and discusses how this provision relates to employers' needs and requirements. The final publication gives a clear and accessible overview of the connection between IT and industry's needs.
Published Material: WELLINGTON, J.J. (1989). Education for employment: the place of information technology. Windsor: NFER-Nelson.
Source of Grant: Training Enterprise Education Division; 1986 only: £31,000
Date of Research: 1986-1989
KEYWORDS: information technology; microcomputer

8/1364
Division of Education
Educational Research Centre,
Arts Tower, Floor 9, Sheffield S10 2TN
0742 768555 ext 4724
York University
Department of Economics & Related Studies
York YO1 5DD
0904 433761
Mayston, D. Prof.; Jesson, D. Mr
Developing models of educational accountability
Abstract: The research attempts to model the outputs of the secondary educational system using techniques drawn from the theory of production functions in economics. A major concern is to accommodate a wide variety of 'outputs', which, whilst including examination results, are capable of embracing other 'performance indicators'. The initial thrust has been to contrast the interpretations of previous studies using regression analysis with those obtained using data envelope analysis applied to inter-LEA studies. The phase now opening explores the potential at the intra-LEA level. *Published Material:* JESSON, D., MAYSTON, D. & SMITH, P. (1987). 'Performance assessment in the education sector: educational and economic perspectives', Oxford Review of Education, Vol 13. No 3, 1987, pp.249-266.; JESSON, D. & HAYSTON, D. (1988). 'Developing models of educational accountability', Oxford Review of Education, Vol 14, No 3, 1988, pp. 321-339. *Source of Grant:* University of Sheffield Research Fund: small grant *Date of Research:* 1987 – continuing *KEYWORDS: accountability; examination results; model; performance indicator; secondary education*

8/1365
Division of Education
Arts Tower, Floor 9, Sheffield S10 2TN
0742 768555
York University
Language Teaching Centre, Heslington, York YO1 5DD
0904 430000
Pullin, R.T. Mr; Rix, D.J. Mr
The York-Sheffield Russian Project
Abstract: The project aims to: (1) support a network of teacher-based teaching materials groups which will produce new materials to meet the changing needs of Russian at GCSE level and for 11 + beginners' courses; (2) to promote models of teacher development through exchange of ideas and experience, participation in the production of collaborative materials and a series of national and regional inservice courses and (3) to monitor, evaluate and publicize new developments and initiatives for the consolidation and extension of Russian teaching in British Secondary schools.
Published Material: Times Educational Supplement; Modern Languages Extra, November 25th 1988.
Source of Grant: Nuffield Foundation: £15,000
Date of Research: 1988-1990
KEYWORDS: inservice education and training of teachers; language teaching; Russian language; teaching aids

8/1366
Division of Education
Educational Research Centre,
Arts Tower, Floor 9, Sheffield S10 2TN
0742 768555
Gillborn, D.A. Dr
Responding to change in the late 1980's
Abstract: The late 1980s are a time of fundamental change in the state-funded education sector. Yet the calls for change have come at a time when levels of resourcing and morale are relatively low. Given this situation we need to know how teachers perceive the changes and thereby highlight the processes which lead some school-based innovations to succeed while others fail. The project explores the meaning and experience of change in educational settings via ethnographic case study approaches. The research focuses upon three comprehensive schools in a northern education authority which face calls for change from several quarters, for example; (1) the Education Reform Act 1988, (2) locally based industry-school initiatives and (3) the desire for school-based curriculum innovation encouraged by a series of teacher secondments in each institution. The work examines how headteachers, senior colleagues and classroom teachers sought to make sense of the changes and manage innovation at a time of low morale, contracting pupil rolls and cuts in the local education budget.
Source of Grant: Sheffield University: Educational Research Centre *Date of Research:* 1988-1990
KEYWORDS: educational innovation; financial resources; morale; teacher attitude

8/1367
Division of Education
Arts Tower, Floor 9, Sheffield S10 2TN
0742 768555
Poppleton, P.K. Dr
Secondary teachers' job satisfaction: a comparative study (UK, USA, Singapore, Japan)
Abstract: The purpose of the study is to relate secondary school teachers' perceptions of the tasks and conditions of teaching to identities and non-identities in the working practices and environments of different cultures and educational systems. The aim in doing

so is to evaluate the effects on secondary teachers of changes in educational policies, and to spell out the implications of those policies for professional recruitment, training and status in each of the countries studied. A theoretical aim is to test the general application of theories of job satisfaction among teachers which have been developed on a unicultural basis, often from samples of people in many different occupations. The research represents the second stage of cross-national collaborative studies undertaken by colleagues working in education in a number of countries. The three countries directly involved are those which have already used a common survey instrument to derive data on teachers' perceptions of their work. This is a questionnaire which incorporates aspects of working conditions, roles and responsibilities, classroom practices and demographic information. The British study, which was supported by the ESRC, was completed in 1988 and, with others, will contribute to the building up of an international database on secondary school teachers.

Source of Grant: Economic and Social Research Council: £11,620
Date of Research: 1988-1990
KEYWORDS: *comparative research; educational innovation; educational policy; occupational satisfaction; secondary education; teacher*

8/1368

Division of Education
Arts Tower, Floof 9, Sheffield S10 2TN
0742 768555
Jones, D. Mr; Gilroy, D.P. Mr; *Supervisor:* Rudduck, J. Prof.

Professional knowledge and the initial training of teachers
Abstract: The project has been designed to investigate some of the more important ways in which PGCE (Post-graduate Certificate of Education) students on their courses identify and deal with problems concerning the search for, and the organization, presentation and criticisms of knowledge and information. This area of interest is a development of Jean Rudduck's previous work for the British Library, when the context was the use of libraries and books by sixth form teachers and pupils and the particular views of knowledge that were transmitted by different practices. The new project, however, is faced with an interesting additional dimension in that 'knowledge' in the context of the PGCE course covers at least two areas; the practical knowledge of teaching skills and the academic knowledge of the subject being taught. Because relatively little attention is often given, explicitly, to such issues in the crowded schedule of a PGCE course, the study is very much an exploratory one. The central feature of the field work will be interviews with students and tutors in order to identify their experiences and perceptions of the mix of experiential and theoretical 'knowledges' which have to be assimilated during the one-year PGCE course. The interviewer, following the conventions of condensed field work, would usually spend between five and ten (but no more than fifteen) working days in the department, timed to allow the exploration of students' perceptions of teaching practice/school experience as well as university-based work. Four students are interviewed from each of the following areas: English, social studies (if offered), biology, history and mathematics. Interviews will also be conducted with the head of the PGCE course, with appropriate method tutors and with the education librarian.
Source of Grant: British Library: £30,000
Date of Research: 1987 – continuing
KEYWORDS: *knowledge; teacher education*

8/1369

Division of Education
Arts Tower, Floor 9, Sheffield S10 2TN
0742 768555 ext 4612
Social and Communty Planning Research
35 Northampton Square, London EC1V OAX
071 250 1866
Gray, J. Dr; Jesson, D. Mr; Courtenay, G. Ms; Hedges, B. Mr

Pathways 16-19: the youth cohort study of England and Wales
Abstract: The Youth Cohort Study is surveying nationally representative samples from three cohorts of young people in England and Wales. Each respondent is contacted on three occasions, at ages 16+ and 18+ years, by means of a postal questionnaire. Data from the surveys will provide a comprehensive framework of information to illuminate the processes of transition from school to work. The intention is that those responsible for policy on education, training and employment provision for young people over 16 years of age will have, for the first time, a common database to inform aspects of their decision-making and planning. A basic concern of the study is to learn more about the 'routes' young people take through the framework of 16-19 provision. At the same time, another major aim of the monitoring exercise is to produce detailed data which are sufficiently flexible, not merely to test hypotheses formulated at the outset of the project, but to address a range of issues and questions which may occur as the project proceeds. The study will, for example, enable the evaluation of the various routes for transition from school to further education, training and employment; the relevance of education and qualifications to subsequent training and occupations (and progress within these occupations), and the extent and nature of training and its usefulness across a variety of job types.
Published Material: GRAY, J. & PATTIE, C. (1987). The Youth Cohort Study: an introduction and codebook for Cohort 1 Sweep 1. Sheffield University.; CLOUGH, E., GRAY, J. & JONES, B. (1987). 'Those who say no to YTS', British Journal of Education and Work, Vol 1, No 2, pp.79-89.; CLOUGH, E., GRAY, J. & JONES, B. (1988). 'Routes through YTS'. Sheffield: Manpower Services Commission Research and Development Series, No 42.; CLOUGH, E., GRAY, J. & JONES, B. (1988). 'Curricular patterns in post-compulsory education', Research Papers in Education, Vol 13, No 1, pp.27-41.; COURTENAY, G. (1986). England and Wales Youth Cohort Study: preliminary results from the 1985 survey. London: Social and Community Planning Research. A full list of publications may be obtained from the researcher on request.
Source of Grant: Training Agency, Department of Education and Science Department of Employment: jointly £1,000,000 approximately
Date of Research: 1985 – continuing
KEYWORDS: *further education; national planning; survey; transition from school work; youth; youth employment*

8/1370

ical Research Council and ESRC Social and Applied Psychology Unit
Sheffield S10 2TN
0742 768555
Banks, M. Dr; Evans, S. Dr; Gray, J. Dr; Bates, I. Dr; Quicke, J. Dr; Riseborough, G. Mr

Economic and Social Research Council 16-19 initiative: the Sheffield Project
Abstract: The main purpose of the 16-19 Initiative is the development of explanations of the processes and outcomes of economic and political socialization, using frameworks and categories drawn largely from psychological and sociological traditions. Using, as organizing principals, perspectives from recent work in social psychology we seek to understand more fully such things as: the socialization of young people as producers and consumers, taking into account the changing complexity of relationships and self-perceptions within institutional (education and employment) and non-institutional (family and peer group) settings; and the political socialization of young people, including influences, attribution, identity and agency. Key mediating variables in the socialization process are young people's career paths and status transitions. This proposal also justifies the inclusion of an ethnographic component to the research, allowing us to expose and explore the richness and variety of the 16-19 arena, and to complement the quantitative design of the Initiative as a whole. Postal questionnaires were sent to a 1 in 10 sample of fifth formers, and to a similar sample who are two years older. Further follow-ups of these two cohorts in Sheffield will be made in 1988 and 1989. The questionnaires included items on early career (older cohort), attitudes to education and training (YTS), educational achievement, economic life and values, attitudes to employment, leisure, self-concept, political views and family life. Interspersed with the questionnaires are two waves of in depth interviewing with a selected sub-sample of both cohorts, chosen to represent the possible range of early careers and experiences. In total, the Sheffield proposal incorporates a range of methodological and theoretical approaches, which previously have not been brought together.
Published Material: BANKS, M.H. et al (1987). Education, training and labour market orientations in 16-19 Year Olds. British Educational Research Association Conference, Manchester, September.; BANKS, M.H. (1988). 'Education, training and employment in Sheffield: the ESRC 16-19 Initiative', Cambridge Journal of Education, Vol 18, No 3, pp.365-375.; BANKS, M.H. (1988). 'Half of children think they gain little from schooling', The Times, November 7.

Source of Grant: Economic and Social Research Council (ESRC): £120,942
Date of Research: 1986 – continuing
KEYWORDS: career; political socialization; socialization; youth; youth attitude

S. Martin's College of Higher Education

8/1371
    Institute for Research and Development in Primary Eduction, Lancaster LA1 3JD
    0524 63446
    Edwards, A. Dr
Meeting the needs: parents and professionals working with the under fives
Abstract: The aim of the study is to examine the evolution of a combined family centre from its origins as a traditional day nursery. The expectations and perceived needs of both clients and staff will be studied through a framework of identity theory developed with adolescents by Honess and Edwards (1987) and with mothers of young children by Edwards and Creed (1986). Data is being gathered in a variety of ways. Policy documentation is being analyzed, centre staff and senior administrators in both social services and education are being interviewed. Data is also being collected from parents. Some observational data will also be gathered. Detailed content analysis of the interview and observation data should reveal issues of relevance at a local level to the inservice development of professionals. At a more general level the study should allow the development of an accessible framework within which both professional and client needs can be examined.
Published Material: EDWARDS, A. and CREED, R. (1985). The coping strategies of young mothers in an area of social isolation (Unpub. report).; HONESS, T. and EDWARDS, A. (1987). 'qualitative and case study research with adolescents'. IN: HONESS, T. and YARDLEY, K. (1987). (eds) Self and identity: perspectives across the lifespan. London: Routledge and Kegan Paul.
Source of Grant: Association for Child Psychology and Psychiatry: £1,000
Date of Research: 1988-1989
KEYWORDS: identity; need; nursery school; parents; pre-school child

8/1372
    Bowerham Road, Lancaster LA1 3JD
    0524 63446 ext 235
    Hughes, E. Mr
CREATE (Curriculum Religious Education and Teacher Education)
Abstract: The project is distinctive in that it is a collaborative venture involving voluntary aided schools, Church of England and Roman Catholic and local authority primary schools. This participation emphasises that all schools share the common educational task of preparing their pupils to live in a rapidly changing world. The ecumenical dimension of the project also roots Roman-Anglican dialogue solidly in a shared practical endeavour. On the basis of in school experience and changes effected CREATE (Curriculum Religious Education and Teacher Education) would seek to respond to these questions: (1) what are significant current factors affecting R.E. development in primary schools across the dual system? (2) can Church of England, Roman Catholic and county primary schools work together to develop Religious Education practice? (3) what skills, expertise, and support structures are necessary for confident staff based R.E. curriculum development? (4) how is the school as an institution affected by an R.E. curriculum development exercise?
Published Material: The Times Educational Supplement, 12th December 1986, Act of Faith pp.30.
Source of Grant: All Saints Educational Trust: £125,000 Lancaster Roman Catholic Diocese: £17,000 Lancashire Education Authority: seconded teacher and travelling expenses
Date of Research: 1986 – continuing
KEYWORDS: curriculum development; primary education; religious education; education

8/1373
    Bowerham Road, Lancaster LA1 3JD
    0526 63446
    Edwards, A. Dr
The coping strategies of professionals and clients at two family centres
Abstract: The expectations and perceived needs of both staff and clients at two family centres are studied through an identity theory framework developed by Honess and Edwards (1987). This allows an exploration of personal identity in terms of personal powers and liabilities and environmental affordances and constraints. Data include in depth staff, 24 to date, and similar client interviews, 8 to date, and documentation from both the education and social services departments of the local authority. Detailed content analysis of this should reveal issues of relevance to the inservice development of professionals, the specific work of each centre studied and should allow the construction of an accessible framework within which both client and professional needs may be examined.
Published Material: HONESS, T. & EDWARDS, A. (1987). 'Qualitative and case study research with adolescents'. In: HONESS, T. & YARDLEY, K. (Eds). Self and identity: perspectives across the life-span. London: Routledge & Kegan Paul.
Source of Grant: Association for Child Psychology and Psychiatry
Date of Research: 1988-1990
KEYWORDS: childcare occupations; day care centre; day-nursery; nursery nurse

Southampton University

8/1374
    The School Mathematics Project,
    Southampton SO9 5NH
    0703 559122 ext 3680
    Little, C.T. Mr
The School Mathematics Project – SMP 11-16
Abstract: The School Mathematics Project is a charitable trust charged with the improvement of mathematics education in schools. The Project is a teacher-based organization. The work of the project is overseen by a Board of Trustees. The chairman is Professor Geoffrey Houwson. The Executive Officer is Mr Chris Little. The principal current initiatives of the project are SMP 11-16 and SMP Mathematics 16-19. The SMP 11-16 project started in 1976 with the aim of constructing a secondary mathematics curriculum which is motivating, understandable and relevant to the needs of children with a wide range of ability in mathematics. Inservice courses are run both nationally and locally, with the help of the three SMP 11-16 Development Officers, Mr Graham Goodall, Mr Tony Burghall and Miss Diana Sharvill. Work is now in hand to ensure that the curriculum materials fully support implementation of the National Curriculum in mathematics for secondary schools.
Published Material: A full list of SMP 11-16 materials is available from Cambridge University Press.
Source of Grant: Curriculum project (charitable trust)
Date of Research: 1983 – continuing
KEYWORDS: curriculum development; mathematics; microcomputer; secondary education; teaching aids

8/1375
    The School Mathematics Project, Southampton SO9 5NH
    0703 559122 ext 3680
    Dolan, S.W. Dr
The School Mathematics Project 16-19
Abstract: The SMP Mathematics 16-19 Project (director Dr Stan Dolan) started in 1987. The aim of the project is reform of the teaching and learning of mathematics at sixth form level, by the provision of a syllabus, curriculum and assessment materials which encourage active learning and understanding of concepts. In addition to these major projects, SMP is constantly revising and updating syllabuses and materials from previous projects. Examples of work of this kind recently published are SMP New Books, Revised Advanced Mathematics (New Edition) and the new SMP Further Mathematics series, all published by Cambridge University Press. SMP's work on the content of the mathematics curriculum has had considerable influence worldwide, and has acted as a stimulus to curriculum development work throughout the world.
Published Material: The SMP mathematics materials are published by Cambridge University Press.

Source of Grant: No funding
Date of Research: 1987 – continuing
KEYWORDS: curriculum development; mathematics; secondary education; sixth form; teaching aids

8/1376

Department of Adult Education
Southampton SO9 5NH
0703 595000
University of Pertanian Malaysia
Department of Education
Serdang, Selangor,
Malaysia
Nawawi, H. Mrs; *Supervisor:* Fordham, P. Prof.

Adult education and rural women: an analysis of participation in adult education and its relevance to rural development in Malaysia

Abstract: Adult education (AE) for women in Malaysia has been carried out for more than 10 years and there has been no systematic analysis on its relevance to the needs of the community. The study sets out to examine the availablity and access to adult education for rural women in the settlement schemes of the Federal Land Development Authority in West Malaysia. It is also to assess the role of adult education in promoting women's participation in rural development programmes. The study uses a mixture of quantitative and qualitative methods. It involves the use of questionnaires as well as interviews. The questionnaire and the interviews were conducted in the National Language and were later translated into English. Data obtained included socio-economic background, the nature of adult education activities currently promoted and the impact they have achieved. Interviews were used to obtain data, the underlying factors affecting participation and non-participation in adult education and rural development activities. There were 459 respondents involved in the study. At the time of this report, the research results and conclusions have not been completed.

Source of Grant: British Council award
Date of Research: 1985-1989
KEYWORDS: adult education; Malaysia; participation; rural area; women's education

8/1377

Department of Physical Education
Highfield,
Southampton SO9 5NH
0703 595000
Evans, J. Dr

A study of health education initiatives in physical education

Abstract: The aim of this research is to study the impact of health education initiatives in PE (physical education) on curriculum and teaching of PE in secondary schools. The study focuses on curriculum and teaching of PE in one large co-educational comprehensive school. The study is adopting a qualitative methodology (largely employing interview and observation techniques) and is sociological in theoretical orientation.

Source of Grant: University of Southampton Research Fund
Date of Research: 1989 – continuing
KEYWORDS: curriculum; health education; physical education; secondary school

8/1378

Department of Physical Education
Highfield,
Southampton SO9 5NH
0703 595000 ext 2819
Evans, J. Dr; Penney, D. Miss; *Supervisor:* Evans, J. Dr

The impact of the National Curriculum and LMS (Local Management of Schools) on the provision of sport and physical education in schools

Abstract: The research will be conducted over a three year period to monitor the impact of the National Curriculum and Local Management of Schools on the provision of sport and physical education in schools in England and Wales. The research will be conducted in two phases. The first will employ a qualitative methodology to survey the impact of LMS on the levels and nature of (PE) physical education and sport provision in schools. The second will use a qualitative methodology to monitor the effects of LMS and a National Curriculum for PE on processes of teaching and learning in PE and sport in schools.

Source of Grant: The Sports Council
Date of Research: 1990 – continuing
KEYWORDS: physical education; sport

8/1379

Department of Physical Education
Southampton SO9 5NH
0703 595000
Asquith, A.; *Supervisor:* Evans, J. Dr

Games teaching in the primary school: a participant observation study of an innovatory teaching programme

Abstract: This study explores the nature and meaning of games teaching in the primary school. Much of the study is based on the findings of work conducted with secondary school children and is an attempt to see if the conclusions reached by the researchers with that age group could be transferred to junior age range. Initially two observational studies were embarked upon (involving 70 + children) to ascertain if this area was a worthwhile area of investigation, and to confirm (or otherwise) other work in this field. A full teaching programme was embarked upon using a games making approach. The programmes, together with monitoring and evaluation is fully recorded. The study concludes with an analysis of the findings, comments by national figures in the field of physical education and with some tentative suggestions on possible future developments.

Published Material: WILLIAMS, A. (Ed). (1989). Issues in physical edcuation for the primary years. London: Falmer Press.; ASQUITH, A. (1989). 'Primary games: an appraisal of the games making approach', The British Journal of Physical Education, Vol 20, No 4, pp.183-186, Winter.
Source of Grant: No funding
Date of Research: 1984-1989
KEYWORDS: games; physical education; primary school

8/1380

Department of Psychology
Southampton SO9 5NH
0703 595000
Cameron, R.J. Dr

Parents, professionals and pre-school children with special needs: towards a partnership model of problem solving

Abstract: This study re-examines the problems faced by families who have a young child with moderate or severe handicapping conditions, and support services received. Major deficits in these services are highlighted and traditional views of these families are questioned. The problem centred approach to evaluation is offered as an alternative to applied research and service development. This procedure is used to evaluate the Portage Home Teaching approach, which uses parents as the major change agents for their handicapped children. Comparisons are made between the frequency of child, parent and family problem indicators by families experiencing a Portage Service, and general surveys of this client group carried out in the United Kingdom. The data indicated similarities between all three groups on endigenous child variables such as handicap, physical health, hospitalization and death rate. However, parent variables (such as physical and mental health) and family variables (such as divorce, sibling disturbance, separation) clear differences emerged, those families receiving a Portage Home Teaching Service having a lower problem incidence than families in the comparison samples. Examination of service outcome data suggests that some external variables, such as frequency of child deaths, are related to high service demand, although no social class or home teacher effects could be established. It was noted that a small group of high service demand families requiring intense levels of support existed. Data collected on everday problems of all the Portage families were examined. In the case of educational, family, Portage Service, agency and inter-agency probems, qualitative differences in terms of the person who was the focus of the problem and an agreed strategy for change emerged. This was used to generate a new advanced training curriculum for home teachers, and an inservice training programme for Portage personnel future research includes, at service level, the possibility of using systematic problem solving procedure as a means for empowering parents.

Source of Grant: No funding
Date of Research: 1985-1990
KEYWORDS: handicapped; home education; parent participation; parent-teacher relation; pre-school child

8/1381

Department of Psychology
Room 235, Murray Building, Southampton SO9 5NH
0703 595000 ext 2588
Cameron, R.J. Mr; *Supervisor:* Gale, A. Prof.; Burden, R. Dr; Van Der Eyken, W. Dr

Helping families who have a pre-school child with special needs, to manage with family problems

Abstract: In this study, data collected on the Winchester Portage Home Teaching Service from 1976 to 1986 will be examined and an attempt will be made to clarify the non-educational problems faced by parents who have a severely handicapped pre-schooler as well as some of the approaches which supporting professionals can adopt when helping such parents to develop strategies for reducing and overcoming some of the everyday problems which they face.
Published Material: CAMERON, R.J. (1985). 'A problem centred approach to family problems'. In: DALY, B. et al. Portage: the importance of parents. Windsor: NFER-Nelson.; CAMERON, R.J. (1986). 'Extending Portage: helping families with family problems', Educational and Child Psychology, No 3, 1986, pp. 79-86.; CAMERON, R.J. (1987). 'Helping parents to help children', Physiotherapy, Vol 73, No 4, 1987, pp.172-175.; CAMERON, R.J. (1989). 'Teaching parents to teach children: the Portage approach to special needs'. In: JONES, N. (ed) Special needs: No 1. Basingstoke: Falmer.
Source of Grant: No funding
Date of Research: 1984-1989
KEYWORDS: family environment; mentally handicapped; parent role; pre-school child; special needs

8/1382

Department of Psychology
Southampton SO9 5NH
0703 559122 ext 2626
Goodman, J. Miss; Hewitt, J. Mr; *Supervisor:* Remington, B. Dr

Communication training via manual signing for non-speaking mentally handicapped children

Abstract: This is an ongoing research programme which aims to investigate the factors responsible for the development of effective communication in non-speaking children. Initially, the work focused both on children with a mental handicap and autistic children, but are now concerned primarily with mental handicap. Methods usually involve single-subject experimental designs. The role of receptive speech on expressive signing and the developments of novel sign combinations through specialized training methods have been investigated. The current interests of the research staff are in the communicative function of signing, and the investigation of transfer between requesting and naming functions.
Published Material: REMINGTON, B., LIGHT, P. & PORTER, D. (1982). 'A comparison of two methods of training symbol-object matching skills in non-speaking severely mentally retarded children', Behaviour Research of Severe Developmental Disabilities, No 2, pp.157-174.; LIGHT, P., REMINGTON, B. & PORTER, D. (1982). 'Substitutes for speech? non-vocal approaches to communication'. In: BEVERIDGE, M. (Ed). Children thinking through language. London: Edward Arnold.; REMINGTON, B. & CLARKE, S. (1983). 'Acquisition of expressive signing by autistic children: an evaluation of the relative effects of simultaneous communication and sign-alone training', Journal of Applied Behaviour Analysis, No 16, pp.315-328.; CLARKE, S., REMINGTON, B. & LIGHT, P. (1986). 'An evaluation of the relationship between receptive skills and expressive signing', Journal of Applied Behaviour Analysis, No 19, pp.231-239.; REMINGTON, B. (1987). 'Teaching non-oral children to use signs communicatively', Bulletin of the British Psychological Society, 40, A56(Abs).; CLARKE, S., REMINGTON, B. & LIGHT. P. (1988). 'The role of referential speech in sign learning by mentally retarded children', Journal of Applied Behaviour Analysis, No 21.
Source of Grant: Economic and Social Research Council Grant 1978-1980. ESRC Linked Studentship Award 1983-present. Current funding is for one ESRC Post Graduate Student
Date of Research: 1978 – continuing
KEYWORDS: communication; dumb; mentally handicapped; non-verbal communication; sign

8/1383

Department of Social Studies
Highfield, Southampton SO0 5NH
0703 559122
Pritchard, C. Prof.

Drug misuse and its relationship to truancy in 934 secondary school children and their knowledge of HIV and drug misuse

Abstract: In May 1989 the researchers repeated a modified prevalence study of drug misuse and its relation to truancy following surveys in 1985 and 1986. Using groups of normal fourth and fifth year comprehensive school students in a supervised classroom situation, they responded to a self-completion questionnaire. The validity and reliability of the instrument has been demonstrated through the three studies, in particular, resolving the problem of bravado false reporting. To mask the primary interest in drugs the researchers explored a range of illegal and problematic behaviours and found that drug experimenting students were also significantly more likely to be under-aged drinkers, be more than casual smokers, fight more frequently, vandalize and be solvent sniffers. The relationship to truancy was particularly noticeable. The social characteristics of the drug experimenters were that they were more likely to come from broken homes, an unemployed father, in receipt of free school dinners, larger families and relative overcrowding. In 1985/1986/1989 the experimental rate was 19%, 18% and 16% of the sample involved in a whole range of drug misuse, but most were triers/experimenters. Between 4% and 5% had experimented with hallucinogens (hard) drugs and a core 3% with some frequency. A logistical regression analysis showed that persistent truancy and more than casual smoking were key features. The 1989 study also explored 934 students' knowledge of HIV infections and its relationship to a range of behaviour, and AIDS was seen as very dangerous, and students appreciated that it was not singlularly a sex, male related disease, but also had a drug misuse link.
Published Material: PRITCHARD, C., DIAMOND, I., COX, M. and CHOWDHURY, N. (1987). 'The relationship of truancy and drug and solvent abuse in secondary school children', Maladjustment and Therapeutic Education, No 53, pp.2-13.; DIAMOND, I., PRITCHARD, C., FIELDING, M. & COX, M. (1988). 'Incidence of drug and solvent abuse in normal school children: a repeat study 1985-6', Public Health, No 102, pp.107-114.
Source of Grant: Dorset Drug Advisory Service: £2,000
Date of Research: 1988-1990
KEYWORDS: Acquired Immune Deficiency Syndrome (AIDS); behaviour disorder; drug addiction; secondary education; truancy

8/1384

Department of Sociology and Social Policy
New Technology Research Group, 143 University Road, Southampton SO9 5NH
0703 595000
Halliday, M. Mr; *Supervisor:* Causer, G. Mr

Information technology labour power and higher education: the articulation of skill shortages and the policy response

Abstract: The research aims to answer two broad questions. Firstly, how was the problem of information technology skill shortages articulated? What were the dimensions of the problem and what type of evidence was being used to back up skill shortage claims? Who were making those claims? What did they believe were the causes of the shortages and what were the implications of the shortages? The second question is concerned with the nature of the policy response. What was the nature of the policy response? How did it fit with the skill shortage claims and was it successful in acheiving the policy goals? What were the factors that shaped the policy response? The resultant thesis is limited to looking at graduate skill shortages. It relies on documentary methods.
Source of Grant: SERC (Science and Engineering Research Council) studentship
Date of Research: 1987 – continuing
KEYWORDS: graduate employment; higher education; information technology; labour shortage

8/1385

School of Education
Highfield, Southampton SO9 5NH
0703 595000 ext 3470
Figueroa, P. Dr

Evaluation of the Wiltshire Education Support Grant Project, 'Education for All'

Abstract: Following the publication of the Swann Report, 'Education for All' (DES 1985), Wiltshire County Council established an Education Support Grant Project entitled 'Education for All' in Salisbury. The aim of this was to further the development of 'multicultural education' in the area. The present project is concerned with both the formative and summative evaluation of this work. Methods include interviews with the Project staff, visits to three schools mainly to observe (in a participant-observer mode) the work the Project team are sponsoring in those schools, participation in Steering Committee meetings, analysis of all available documentation, and informal interviews with some of the staff in the schools visited.

Published Material: Wiltshire Education Support Grant Project, 'Education for All' Evaluation Report, 10 November 1989.
Source of Grant: Wiltshire County Council: £1,187
Date of Research: 1988-1989
KEYWORDS: *antiracism education; evaluation; intercultural education; multicultural education*

8/1386

School of Education
Highfield, Southampton SO9 5NH
0703 595000
Greig, S. Mrs; *Supervisor:* Brumfit, C.J. Prof.
Spelling: teachers' perceptions, attitudes and expectations
Abstract: This research will investigate that teachers misunderstand the spelling system and how it is learned and used by writers. If the important features could be explained to them and they could be offered clear and easily followed advice on teaching, spelling, correcting poor spelling and the marking of written work, their practice would improve and, with it, their attitudes to their pupils and to the spelling skill. Higher expectations would follow and would spread to pupils with benefits all round. The method will be to investigate these questions by interview and/or questionnaire with teachers in schools and student teachers and teacher trainers and perhaps try to introduce them to the practices mentioned above and observe the outcome of that.
Source of Grant: No funding
Date of Research: 1989-1990
KEYWORDS: *learning difficulty; spelling; teacher attitude; teacher behaviour; teacher expectation; teacher response*

8/1387

School of Education
Assessment and Evaluation Unit,
Highfield, Southampton SO9 5NH
0703 595000
Morris, B. Mr; *Supervisor:* Torrance, H. Dr
Evaluation of Inner London Education Authority Records of Achievement programme
Abstract: The aim of this research is to consider the effect of recording achievement on the overall curriculum and organization of secondary schools and to pay specific attention to the relationship between records of achievement and other comparable initiatives. Specific attention is also being focused on the dissemination of the development from pilot schools to others in the authority and to consider the relationship between records of achievement and equal opportunities within school.
Source of Grant: ILEA (Inner London Education Authority): £12,500
Date of Research: 1988-1990
KEYWORDS: *academic records; achievement; equal opportunity; evaluation; pupil profile; student record*

8/1388

School of Education
Assessment and Evaluation Unit,
Highfield, Southampton SO9 5NH
0703 595000
Hogan, A.P. Ms; *Supervisor:* Clift, P. Mr
The role of teacher assessment in the National Curriculum
Abstract: The aims of this research are to: (i) identify from teachers what they perceive to be their professional INSET (Inservice Education and Training of Teachers) requirements for the development of assessment skills appropriate to the successful delivery of the National Curriculum; (ii) to develop resource materials to meet the above requirements and attempt to establish a model of inset which teachers find useful; (iii) to evaluate any proposed resource materials. By the end of the project, the researcher would hope to see the following targets attained: (a) the resource materials refined and edited in the light of feedback from teachers; (b) the production of a trialled set of resource materials on the role of teacher assessment; (c) a model or models of INSET to accompany the materials; (d) a formal report giving an overview of the project and a summary of the research completed on teachers' own assessment of the National Curriculum attainment targets.
Source of Grant: University Grants Committee: £24,000
Date of Research: 1989-1990
KEYWORDS: *evaluation; further education of teachers; resource materials; teacher; teacher appraisal; teacher inservice education*

8/1389

School of Education
Highfield, Southampton SO9 5NH
0703 595000
Campbell, G.F. Mr
Development of a health education curriculum for older people
Abstract: This research aims to identify models of good practice in the education and training of those involved in the health promotion of older people. While it is currently focusing on the pre-retirement phase, it intends to embrace younger age groups including children. Early models have drawn heavily upon pioneer work in the USA. Later work will relate to Europe.
Source of Grant: No funding
Date of Research: 1988 – continuing
KEYWORDS: *agency co-operation; elderly person; health education; old age*

8/1390

School of Education
Highfield, Southampton SO9 5NH
0703 595000
Campbell, G.F. Mr
Staff development in schools in the independent sector
Abstract: Independent schools, especially those with a high proportion of boarders are having to adjust to many of the changes experienced by schools in the maintained system. This work, which is adopting a case study approach, is attempting to identify staff training needs and priorities especially in the area of personal, social and health education.
Source of Grant: No funding
Date of Research: 1988 – continuing
KEYWORDS: *community education; further education of teachers; health education; inservice teacher education; inservice training; life skills; private school; teacher*

8/1391

School of Education
Highfield, Southampton SO9 5NH
0703 595000
Campbell, G.F. Mr
Inter-agency co-operation towards effective community health education
Abstract: Progress in community health education depends upon the various agencies involved, principally community health services, local education authorities and higher education institutions co-operating closely to ensure that client needs and priorities are being clearly identified and met through the provision of appropriate learning activities. Ongoing research seeks to identify models of good practice emerging from jointly planned work especially in non-award bearing courses.
Published Material: CAMPBELL, G. (1987). et al (Eds). Health education, youth and community: a review of research and developments. Sussex: Falmer Press.
Source of Grant: No funding
Date of Research: 1983 – continuing
KEYWORDS: *agency co-operation; community health services; co-operation; health education; higher education*

8/1392

School of Education
Highfield, Southampton SO9 5NH
0703 595000
Benton, M.G. Dr
The sister arts: enquiries into the perceived relationship between literature and painting as evidence in the responses of secondary school pupils
Abstract: Teacher-researcher investigations by three teachers in different schools working with GCSE (General Certificate of Secondary Education) pupils. Paired paintings and poems were used to investigate the processes of reading paintings and poetry. Methodologically, attention focused on the effects of different means of monitoring responses. Substantively, the elements of response that emerged most strongly in both arts were narrative, formal composition, viewpoint/stance, significant detail, feeling/thought. Pedagogically, teaching approaches have been devised which are utilised in the publication entitled Double Vision. How the constructs of augustan/romantic periods are created through the literature and visual arts of the 18th and 19th century.
Published Material: BENTON, M. & BENTON, P. (1990). Double vision; reading paintings reading poems. London: Hodder and

Stoughton.; BENTON, M. On literature and learning. Buckingham: Open University Press. (forthcoming).
Source of Grant: No funding
Date of Research: 1989 – continuing
KEYWORDS: aesthetic education; art; literature; painting; pupil reaction; relationship

8/1393
School of Education
Assessment and Evaluation Unit,
Highfield, Southampton SO9 5NH
0703 595000
Dann, R.C. Ms; *Supervisor:* Mitchell, R. Dr
Pupil assessment in the primary school
Abstract: The research aims to explore whether recent developments in pupil assessment have taken account of the proclivities of primary schooling, examine the adequacy of these advances in the light of emerging national requirements for assessing a national curriculum; gain critical purchase on the interrelationships of assessment, learning and teaching; suggest possible approaches to developing and promoting school-based assessment policies bearing in mind vital and differing contextual factors and contribute towards the integration of theory, policy and practice in pupil assessment. The methodology draws on an analysis of recent assessment literature, scrutiny of emerging national assessment frameworks, a case study of one local education authorities approach to advancing assessment practices and three primary school case studies focusing on merging school based assessment initiatives with national assessment requirements.
Published Material: EMERY, H., SAUNDERS, N., DANN, R. & MURPHY, R. Topics in Assessment. York: Longman. (forthcoming).
Source of Grant: Economic & Social Research Council (ESRC): £3,800 p.a.
Date of Research: 1987-1990
KEYWORDS: assessment; primary school; pupil; pupil evaluation; school based assessment

8/1394
School of Education
Highfield, Southampton SO9 5NH
0703 595000
Chappell, D.M.A. Miss; *Supervisor:* Mitchell, R. Dr
Native and non-native use of English
Abstract: This is an empirically based study focusing on the structure, nature and use of English by native and non-native speakers in the specific discourse type of information exchange. Data will be gathered from public arenas where transactions between: (i) native/native, (ii) native/non-native, (iii) non-native/non-native speakers take place and, in addition, from within the language learning classroom where activities of a like nature have been set up. The naturally-occurring events and classroom tasks will then be analyzed at an interactional level and characteristic features of each identified. The use of a psycholinguistic analysis endeavours not only to identify the reasons for participants' interpretive choice during interaction, but also to uncover any underlying relationships between use of thse choices and their effect on the language learning process. In this way it is hoped that such descriptions may inform our understanding of, firstly, particular points through and by which language learning takes place, secondly, the elements that facilitate such learning, and finally, the conditions under which those elements are best served. The pedagogical implications related to any of the aforementioned aspects include a re-examination of teachers' own choices concerning aims, methodology and materials which may ultimately lead to a re-assessment of the evaluation process at all subsequent levels.
Source of Grant: Economic and Social Research Council: £5,285
Date of Research: 1989 – continuing
KEYWORDS: communication research; discourse analysis; English language; English (second language); language research; language teaching; native speakers

8/1395
School of Education
Highfield, Southampton SO9 5NH
0703 595000
Bidgood, S.J. Dr; *Supervisor:* Weare, S.K. Ms
The role of chiropractors in health education
Abstract: This research explores the role of chiropractors in health education. It aims to answer whether chiropractors should educate

as well as treat their patients and if chiropractors do educate their patients in practise. The research hopes to suggest strategies for better initial and inservice training.
Published Material: BIDGOOD, S.J. (1988). 'A study to discover the health status of students at a college of chiropractic', Faculty of Educational Studies, University of Southampton.
Source of Grant: Foundation for Chiropractic Education and Research
Date of Research: 1989 – continuing
KEYWORDS: health service; health service personnel; physical therapy; physiotherapy

8/1396
School of Education
Highfield, Southampton SO9 5NH
0703 595000
Southampton General Hospital
Southampton School of Radiography,
D8 West Wing, Southampton General Hospital,
Tremona Road, Southampton SO9 4XY
0703 772444
Castle, A. Mr; *Supervisor:* Weare, K. Ms; Hayes, M. Ms
Assertiveness training for student radiographers
Abstract: Some studies have suggested that ATC's (assertiveness training courses) may be an effective tool to strengthen and enhance both personal and professional effectiveness. The perceived need for ATC's for radiographers can be identified in terms of the paramedical, gender and student contexts. The three main aims of the research are to develop and implement appropriate ATC's for student radiographers, assess assertive behaviour skills and finally to evaluate the effectiveness of the ATC's. The pilot study consisted of research design along the lines of a quasi-experiment with control, experimental and follow-up groups. The results of the pilot study were encouraging and by building upon this, new ATC's assessment and evaluation procedures will be developed. It is anticipated that once the quantitative results (in terms of changes in assertive behaviour) and qualitative results (in terms of effectiveness) have been analyzed, recommendations will be made about the inclusion of ATC's in the academic curriculum of student radiographers.
Source of Grant: No funding
Date of Research: 1989 – continuing
KEYWORDS: assertiveness; communication; health service personnel; inservice training; interpersonal relations

8/1397
School of Education
Highfield, Southampton SO9 5NH
0703 595000
Bilton, L. Miss; *Supervisor:* Mitchell, R.F. Dr
Adaptation in lecturing styles to English L2 audiences
Abstract: The background and aims of this research is lecturing to audiences in an overseas context where English as a foreign language is expanding as new universities adopt English as the medium of instruction for science and technology. Expatriate lecturers are on the whole unprepared for their undergraduates' low level of English and much of their effort in planning and delivering lectures is wasted. The aim is to find out what goes on during lectures and where foreign students have particular difficulties in order to be able to make recommendations about adapting lecturing to audience needs.
Source of Grant: No funding
Date of Research: 1989 – continuing
KEYWORDS: English (second language); foreign country; higher education; language of instruction; lecture; science education; technology education; university teaching

8/1398
School of Education
Health Education Unit,
Highfield, Southampton SO9 5NH
0703 595000
Hill, F. Mrs; *Supervisor:* Kelly, P. Prof.
Health Education Authority 16-19 HIV (Human Immunodefeciency Virus)/AIDS (Acquired Immune Deficiency Syndrome) project
Abstract: This project has three main aims: to provide staff development courses concerning HIV/AIDS education and young people, 16-19, (these will be organized on a regional basis, involving local education authorities from the nine further education regions of England); to investigate by the use of questionnaires the provision

of HIV/AIDS education in further education colleges; to review current educational materials in this area.
Source of Grant: Health Education Authority: £64,115
Date of Research: 1989-1990
KEYWORDS: *Acquired Immune Deficiency Syndrome; disease; further education; further education of teachers; inservice teacher education; sexual behaviour*

8/1399

School of Education
Highfield, Southampton SO9 5NH
0703 595000
Ghebrehiwet, T. Mr; *Supervisor:* Weare, K. Ms
The determinants of health promoting behaviour in the family
Abstract: According to most health education literature, barriers to positive health behaviour are located in the belief system of individuals. This behavioural approach tends to isolate individuals from their social, economic and physical environment. The emphasis on personal behaviour neglects crucial influences such as family life, socioeconomic resources and cultural forces. The aim of this research is, therefore, to analyze the extent to which environmental and personal/family characteristics reciprocate to influence health-promoting behaviour. Using health-promoting behaviour as a dependent variable, and environmental/family characteristics as independent variables; the study aims at delineating those factors which may singly or additively predict or explain the occurrence of health-promoting behaviour within the family. The study will be a survey method in design, and a representative sample of families will be randomly selected from electoral registers. Data will be collected using self administered questionnaires designed to elicit information on the study variables.
Source of Grant: Committee of Vice Chancellors and Principles: £2,410
Date of Research: 1989 – continuing
KEYWORDS: *family influence; family life; health; health activities; health promotion; socioeconomic influence*

8/1400

School of Education
Highfield, Southampton SO9 5HN
0703 593473
Merilion, L. Ms; *Supervisor:* Box, V. Ms; Weare, K. Mrs
To investigate the relationship between career choice and gender with reference to young people
Abstract: This research is part of a larger 4 year project examining the relationship between career, job and academic choice of young people. A basic assumption which the project will attempt to address is the gender specific nature of certain occupations and courses which prevent young people from following their own personal skills. The project will begin with a library search to investigate current arguments and debates in this area and to identify any current research which would be useful to the investigation. Following this library search, the appropriate methods of investigation will be used to assess what influences young people in deciding what job, career or academic course to follow. From these investigations it will be possible to devise teaching materials to be used with parents, staff and students to begin to challenge the assumptions of following a certain career.
Source of Grant: No funding
Date of Research: 1990 – continuing
KEYWORDS: *choice of studies; occupational choice; sex; stereotype*

8/1401

School of Education
Highfield, Southampton SO9 5NH
0703 559122
Evans, J. Dr.
The application of ethnographic research methods to the study of teaching and learning in physical education and sport
Abstract: The aim of this research programme is to promote the application of qualitative ethnographic research methods to the study of physical education and sport. This is an ongoing project which places emphasis upon teacher based research. To date, research has focused on the physical education departments in two large comprehensive schools. In one, the research has concentrated on the routine of teaching and learning in the PE (physical education) curriculum; in the other, on the nature of 'dissent' in schoolboy and junior football. In both schools the research has pointed to the complexity of the social processes involved in the contribu-

tion of the teachers' and pupils' social and educational identity.
Published Material: EVANS, J. & COOK, S. (1985). 'Teacher strategies and pupil identities: the physical education curriculum'. Paper presented to the ICHPER (International Council on Health, Physical Education and Recreation) World Congress, 3rd August (available from the Department of Physical Education, University of Southampton)
Source of Grant: No funding
Date of Research: 1980 – continuing
KEYWORDS: *physical education; secondary education; sport; teaching method*

8/1402

School of Education
Highfield, Southampton SO9 5NH
0703 595000
Ochs, T. Mr; *Supervisor:* Figueroa, P. Dr
Explicit and implicit culture in the international school: an ethnographic study of cultural diversity and its implications
Abstract: The purpose of this cross-cultural research is to articulate the complex factors, both implicit and explicit, that are present within the multicultural environment of an international school in Japan and to discern how these cultural subtleties interrelate to create an exceptional learning atmosphere. An identification of the cultural dynamics inherent within a school comprised of thirty-five nationalities provides a model for comprehending and enhancing the educational opportunities existent in related cross-cultural institutions. In particular the research focuses on the coexistence and ramifications of diverse languages, value assumptions, and social norms within a pluralistic context, and the ways in which these and other elements affect the educational process. The research considers how international schools can use their singularity to initiate new academic programmes that are specifically designed for international students rather than relying on the common practice of adopting existing national education formats for implementation in a foreign setting. The study employs a multimodal design in which interviews, questionnaires, and participant observation techniques form the basic means of data collection.
Source of Grant: No funding
Date of Research: 1987-1990
KEYWORDS: *cross-cultural research; cultural pluralism; curriculum development; educational opportunities; international school*

8/1403

School of Education
Highfield, Southampton SO9 5NH
0703 595000
Mitchell, R. Dr
Teachers' understanding of language and the role of knowledge about language in language development
Abstract: This project explores teachers' views on the place of explicit discussion of language in language teaching, and the contribution such discussion may make to children's language development. The impetus for the project derived from current language education policy initiatives which stress the development of explicit knowledge about language (KAL) for both teachers and pupils. In order to understand better the likely impact of such initiatives, it was decied to explore; (a) the current state of teachers' own KAL; (b) current classroom practices regarding the development and application of KAL in developing their pupils' practical language proficiency. In autumn 1988 semi-structured interviews were conducted with 46 teachers in local primary and secondary schools. All had special responsibility for language, either as primary school language consultants, or as secondary school heads of English/modern languages. Preliminary analysis of the interview data suggests that the three groups of language specialists involved maintain somewhat distinct perspectives on KAL and its value in language development. Thus for example, secondary English teachers seem to value sociolinguistic KAL highest and to be best informed about it, while secondary MLs teachers seem to have greater concern for syntactic knowledge, and primary language consultants for the technicalities of the writing system. KAL is however generally seen as marginal in first language development, and levels of KAL among teachers themselves seem low, with a 'parts of speech/clause analysis' interpretation of KAL appearing prevalent.
Source of Grant: University of Southampton: £4,000
Date of Research: 1988-1989
KEYWORDS: *knowledge; language development; language teaching; teacher attitude; teaching method*

8/1404
School of Education
Highfield, Southampton SO9 5NH
0703 595000
Massey, I.D. Mr; *Supervisor:* Figueroa, P. Prof.

A consideration of attempts to develop an awareness of and positive attitudes towards cultural diversity through first hand experience

Abstract: This is an evaluation of a Hampshire Education Support Grant project which involves 6 mainly all-white primary schools 'twinning' with multi-ethnic schools. The projects aims and objectives are; to develop positive attitudes towards diversity through first hand experience; to foster curriculum development; to give pupils opportunities to work collaboratively; to examine critically bias, stereotyping and racial prejudice; to provide opportunities for pupils to form inter-cultural friendships; to promote parental support and participation. The evaluation is ethnographic in style and includes observation of exchanges, interviews with children about their experiences, teachers and projects.
Source of Grant: Hampshire Local Education Authority: fees
Date of Research: 1988-1990
KEYWORDS: attitude change; cultural pluralism; curriculum development; multicultural education; primary education

8/1405
School of Education
Highfield, Southampton SO9 5NH
0703 595000
Chambers, F. Dr; *Supervisor:* Mitchell, R. Dr

Evaluation of Hampshire Modern Languages Skills Development Project

Abstract: The Hampshire Modern Languages Skills Development Project is a local education authority sponsored materials development project, designed to facilitate the implementation of communicative language teaching methods in the teaching of French, German and Spanish in Hampshire schools. Materials for teaching and assessment have been developed by local teacher groups and are currently being piloted in 20 schools. This research project aims to evaluate the impact of the new materials on classroom practice. It is concerned with the extent to which principles of communicative language teaching are being implemented in the classroom, and in particular with the extent to which the use of the target language is being promoted as a medium of classroom communication. Case studies are being conducted of project implementation in three pilot schools. The main research techniques being employed are classroom observation and semi-structured interviews with participating teachers. Findings are not yet available but a report will be submitted to the local education authority end 1989.
Source of Grant: Hampshire County Council: seconded teacher fellow
Date of Research: 1988-1989
KEYWORDS: communication; language skill; modern languages; teaching aids; teaching method

8/1406
School of Education
Highfield, Southampton SO9 5NH
0703 595000
Omu, F. Mrs; *Supervisor:* Weare, K. Ms

The attitudes and beliefs of 10 and 11 year olds about sexuality

Abstract: This research, which is still in its early stages, will investigate the knowledge and attitudes of 10 and 11 year olds about sexuality, and compare these with the children's teachers' beliefs about where the children are on this issue. The hypothesis is that children's knowledge and attitudes are more sophisticated than their teachers suspect. The methodology is still being worked out; it will include tape recording discussions with children and a game.
Source of Grant: Commonwealth Institute: Overseas Student Fellowship
Date of Research: 1988 – continuing
KEYWORDS: attitude; belief; child; sexuality

8/1407
School of Education
Centre for Language in Education, Southampton SO9 5NH
0703 595000
Zotou, V. Ms; *Supervisor:* Mitchell, R. Dr

Effective teaching in EFL (English as a Foreign Language): a Greek case study

Abstract: Given the dearth of descriptive studies of EFL (English as a Foreign Language) teaching in Greece, the aim of the researcher is to discover the extent to which classroom practice of teachers, judged 'effective' by their fellow professionals and superiors, conforms to a 'normative' model of effective teaching (conceptualized as 'communicative' language teaching) and what the factors are which have shaped their classroom behaviour. Eight main case studies will be conducted in different parts of Greece. Classroom observation will be the main element of each case study. A systematic observation instrument developed for the study of communicative language teaching will be employed as the main classroom data gathering procedure. The observations will be supplemented with teacher interviews seeking; (a) their views on the nature of effective teaching and the contextual factors promoting/inhibiting it; (b) accounts of practice and (c) accounts of major influences on their own professional development. In addition, contextual data will be collected from pupils and institutions (including student achievement data). It can be expected that a group of teachers selected in this way will vary considerbly in degree of conformity to a normative model of communicative EFL teaching. If so, within-group comparisons will be necessary, in trying to establish what the typical classroom practices are of the most 'effective' sub-group, and what professional influences and contextual factors have contributed substantially to greater and lesser degrees of 'effectiveness'. Finally, it is hoped to draw conclusions relevant to teacher training and the upgrading of more teachers to 'effective' levels of practice.
Source of Grant: Greek Ministry of Education: Sabbatical leave of absence; £350 monthly plus annual fees (£1,800)
Date of Research: 1988 – continuing
KEYWORDS: Greece; English (second language); teaching method

8/1408
School of Education
Southampton SO9 5NH
0703 595000
Hart, A.P. Dr

Media education in Hampshire schools and colleges

Abstract: In September 1987, Hampshire LEA conducted a survey by postal questionnaire of all schools and colleges in Hampshire. The researchers were commissioned to analyze and report back on this survey for Hampshire. This was done in November 1988. Since then, the research has been extended to include structured interviews with secondary school and sixth form college teachers and lecturers. These interviews explore the personal histories of involvement in media education of these teachers and relate this to curriculum change. An analysis of them will provide a basis for a second report in 1990.
Source of Grant: University Grants Committee: £525
Date of Research: 1988-1990
KEYWORDS: media studies; secondary education

8/1409
School of Education
Highfield, Southampton SO9 5NH
0703 595000
Turner, G. Mr; *Supervisor:* Williams, T. Mr; Clift, P.S. Mr

National evaluation of the education support grant drug education co-ordinators initiative

Abstract: This project was funded by the Department of Education and Science to evaluate the impact of the Education Support Grant Initiative which set up Drug Education Co-ordinators in Local Education Authorities. Their task is to stimulate the development of drug education in schools, the youth service and other relevant agencies. The evaluation was carried out mainly by means of case studies of eleven divergent LEAs. A questionnaire was also sent to all of the Drug Education Co-ordinators throughout England (approximately 100 on average, per LEA). The evaluation has examined the approach to preventative education adopted by co-ordinators, their local context, liaison with other agencies, the provision of inservice training, setting up initiatives and other aspects of their role. The purpose of the report to LEAs is to offer advice and suggestions for the continuation of drug education when the Education support grant ceases. An active dissemination of this report will follow its publication.
Published Material: TURNER, G.R. (1988). The ESG funded drug education co-ordinators initiative: a national evaluation, Interim Report, Southampton University (Mimeo).; TURNER, G.R., MURPHY, R. & WILLIAMS, D.T. (1989). 'Education and misuse of drugs: a national evaluation of the Drug Education Co-ordinators

Initiative'. A report to LEA's: Published by the Department of Education & Science.
Source of Grant: Department of Education and Science: £42,381
Date of Research: 1987-1990
KEYWORDS: drug addiction; health education; local education authority; narcotic

8/1410
School of Education
Assessment and Examination Unit,
Highfield, Southampton SO9 5NH
0703 592642
McArdle, S. Mr; Inkson, G. Mrs; Stapylton, K. Mr; Izzard, E. Mr; Pack, M. Ms; Saunders, N. Mr; Emery, H. Mr; *Supervisor:* Murphy, R.J.L. Dr
Primary school pupil assessment project
Abstract: The project has been conducted through three phases. The first involved a survey of assessment policies and practices in a sample of fifty Hampshire primary schools. The second phase involved much more detailed case studies of assessment practices in four individual case study schools. The third phase has involved active dissemination of ideas arising from the earlier phases of the project, the development of trialling INSET (Inservice Education and Training of Teachers) materials related to different aspects of assessment. There has also been a development of the project's original plan to incorporate developments currently arising in relation to National Curriculum assessments at 7 and 11 years of age, and the possible introduction of Records of Achievement in Primary Schools.
Published Material: A list of published papers is available from the above address
Source of Grant: Hampshire Local Education Authority: £48,000 plus 7 one year teacher secondments (jointly, Hampshire LEA and ESRC support for a linked research studentship)
Date of Research: 1986-1989
KEYWORDS: assessment; criterion referencing; primary education; student record

8/1411
School of Education
Highfield, Southampton SO9 5NH
0703 595000
Evans, J. Dr; Davies, B. Prof.
A study of new vocational initiatives in the secondary school curriculum
Abstract: The research is focused upon the introduction of new vocational initiatives into the curriculum of four large secondary schools. It is a study of 'unsponsored TVEI', the secondary schools failed in their bid to secure MSC (Manpower Services Commission) funding. Methodologically the study is employing case study techniques, largely involving interviews and observations of teachers and pupils, to explore the perspectives and actions of individuals involved in the initiatives. Broadly stated, the aim is to examine the implications of TVEI for the educational opportunities, identities and careers of teachers and pupils.
Published Material: EVANS, J. and DAVIES, B. (1986). 'Fixing to mix in Vocational Initiatives'. Paper presented to the International Sociology of Education Conference. Birmingham (January 1986). Available from the Department of Physical Education, University of Southampton.; EVANS, J. & DAVIES, B. (1986). 'The rise and fall ov Vocational Education', Paper presented to the conference, Education and training 14-18. St Hilda's College Oxford, Available from the Department of Physical Education, University of Southampton.
Source of Grant: No funding
Date of Research: 1983 – continuing
KEYWORDS: curriculum development; secondary education; Technical and Vocational Education Initiative (TVEI);

8/1412
School of Education
Highfield, Southampton SO9 5NH
0703 595000
Weare, K. Ms; *Supervisor:* Kelly, P.J. Prof.; Waters, E.J. Prof.
Developing health promotion in the undergraduate medical education
Abstract: This research is being carried out within the medical faculty at the University of Southampton. Its aim is to discover ways in which health promotion and health education can be best

developed within a medical curriculum and to develop appropriate initiatives. In 1986 the curriculum was reviewed by interviewing 50 co-ordinators of courses, identified barriers to and opportunities for development and implemented several curriculum innovations across the curriculum, included within clinical teaching. Two conferences were held in March 1987 and March 1989, the first, a British, the second a European one, which discussed what was already happening in medical schools and how it should be developed.
Published Material: WEARE, K. (1986). 'What do medical teachers understand by health promotion?', Health Education Journal, Vol 45, No 4, pp.235-238.; WEARE, K. (1988). (Ed.) 'Developing health promotion in undergraduate medical education: report of national workshop', Health Education Authority.; WEARE, K. & KELLY, P. (1989). (Eds). 'Health education in medical education': a report of a World Health Organization Consultation at the University of Perugia, Italy. World Health Organization.; WEARE, K. (Ed). 'Health eduction in medical education': a supplementary report of papers to a report of a World Health Organization Consultation at the University of Perugia, Italy. World Health Organization.
Source of Grant: No funding
Date of Research: 1985 – continuing
KEYWORDS: health education; medicine; undergraduate study

8/1413
School of Education
Highfield, Southampton SO9 5NH
0703 559122
Irons, P.C. Mrs; *Supervisor:* Mitchell, R. Dr
Factors influencing the aquisition of children's second language reading skills
Abstract: The aim of this study is to investigate the acquisition of reading skills by children, who speak English as their second language. The investigation will be based on detailed case studies of twenty children aged 10+ who come from four Asian cultures. Qualitative and quantitative methods of assessment will be analyzed in relation to cognitive abilities, attitudes, culture and oral proficiency. Results will be analyzed with reference to the pertinent literature. Conclusions will be drawn and recommendations for further research will be indicated.
Source of Grant: No funding
Date of Research: 1986-1990
KEYWORDS: bilingualism; ethnic minority; first foreign language; reading

8/1414
School of Education
Highfield, Southampton SO9 5NH
0703 559122
Pinel, A.J. Mr; *Supervisor:* Briggs, B.I. Ms
Embedded teacher development: an examination of the processes whereby teachers develop perceptions of their task while continuing as classroom practitioners
Abstract: The central interest 'embedded teacher development' refers to processes through which teachers develop perceptions of their task, while continuing as classroom practitioners. The major concerns are how they learn more about the capabilities and powers of their pupils and how they attempt to provide more opportunities for the release of these powers through reflecting on and restructuring their approaches to them and to their teaching material. The medium is (mainly) mathematics. The teachers are primary teachers.
Source of Grant: No funding
Date of Research: 1987 – continuing
KEYWORDS: mathematics; perception; primary education; teacher behaviour; teacher-pupil relation

8/1415
School of Education
Highfield, Southampton SO9 5NH
0703 595000
Kapinga, M.K. Mr; *Supervisor:* Brumfit, C.J. Prof.
A proposal for a self-instructional (language) learning scheme for post-primary education with reference to the educational system of Tanzania
Abstract: In Tanzania, at present, well over 95% of the children completing primary education (at 14+) do not get a place in secondary schools (Government and private). Even by the year 2000, it is projected that 85% of them will leave school at primary VII.

The need for adolescent-adult education i.e. the pressure to provide some opportunities for learning for school leavers poses a great challenge. On one hand a self-instructional learning scheme is proposed. The illustration for its use is drawn from language learning working of the proposed scheme will be 'tested' for results and conclusions for its potential application. A background discussion is attempted on the place of self-instruction in the Tanzanian educational system, on the place of this approach in general learning, and on the patterns of its use elsewhere in Africa and the world. Design, including the size and composition of the sample will consist of groups of learners who will use materials and resources prepared for the scheme, with the researcher participating as a helper for about a three to four month learning period. The sample will be drawn from a rural setting in Tanzania. (The materials may also be given to learners in 'institutions' with teachers as helpers, to investigate their wider potential use). The learning experience of these learners will be investigated. A multi-method approach is envisaged, with the use of such techniques as: interviews, questionnaire, tests, diaries (participant researcher).
Source of Grant: The Commonwealth Scholarship Commission in the United Kingdom
Date of Research: 1987-1990
KEYWORDS: adolescent; languages; post-compulsory education; self instruction; Tanzania

South Bank Polytechnic

8/1416
83 New Kent Road, London SE1 6RD
071 407 8191
Insley, K.E. Mrs; *Supervisor:* Cooper, K. Dr; Ritterman, J. Dr; Parker, S. Dr
A study of the perceptions and expectations primary teachers may have of music and music teaching and a comparison with the teaching of music education to prospective primary school teachers in the London area
Abstract: The aims of this project are: (1a) to clarify what is assumed by the non-specialist primary teacher about music in the primary school curriculum; (1b) to explore and examine the criteria used by non-specialist primary teachers to determine the content and methodology of their music teaching; considering in particular how these criteria are selected and what their relationship is to school, local authority and national policies; (2) to examine the practices of teaching music within the context of the school curriculum identifying the areas of content and methodology; (3) to examine the implicit hypotheses and generate others about change in the practice of music teaching by the classteacher in the school. The study will be organized within two phases. Phase 1 will use a sample consisting of cluster samples of primary, nursery, infant and junior schools in ILEA division 8, so working across the whole range 3 to 11 years. Work in this phase will involve unstructured interviewing of teachers, music postholders and headteachers, ethnographic observation of teachers working with their classes and identification of strategies employed by teachers within music. Phase 2 will be a sample consisting of Polytechnics and Colleges of Education in the London area which undertake initial teacher training. Work in this phase will involve a critical examination of inservice work, an identification of the implementation of policy in terms of change, a critical examination of work in initial teacher training in music education and a comparison of results with phase 1. The study will investigate not only the factors which have historically contributed to change but those that operate at present, and will seek to highlight the areas which offer the greatest potential for development. Investigations will be made into the relationship between change and policy.
Source of Grant: No funding
Date of Research: 1987-1989
KEYWORDS: curriculum development; educational policy; music education; primary education; teacher education

8/1417
Borough Road, London SE1 OAA
071 928 8989
Edwards, R. Ms; *Supervisor:* David, M. Dr
Mature mother-student returners to education
Abstract: The research aims to look at mother-students returning to education. It will take a life history approach, looking at the

women's experiences of the education system prior to their return to education, on their return, and after they have completed their studies. The effect of 'education' upon their personal lives (family, domestic duties, friendships etc.) will be a focus of the research, as will race and class. Exact sampling details have not yet been finalized.
Source of Grant: Inner London Education Authority
Date of Research: 1988 – continuing
KEYWORDS: family life; mature student; mother; women's education

8/1418
Department of Education and Home Economics
83 New Kent Road, London SE1 6RD
071 407 8191
Wenman, S. Ms; *Supervisor:* David, M. Dr; Parker, S. Dr
Mature students in teacher training
Abstract: The project is to investigate and monitor the motivation, percpetions and progress of mature women returning to higher education on a BEd Honours course leading to a professional qualification. Self-selected groups have group and individual interviews (ongoing) at strategic points through the course. Previous experience, home relations, changes in personal circumstances are monitored. Individual experiences are set within the context of ideological, cultural and economic factors of the Teacher Education system. Evaluation of various dimensions of course provision are an integral part of study.
Source of Grant: No funding
Date of Research: 1987 – continuing
KEYWORDS: higher education; mature student; motivation for studies; teacher education; women's education

8/1419
Department of Mathematics and Computing
Borough Road, London SE1
071 928 8989
Shearer, G. Ms; *Supervisor:* Scott-Hodgetts, R. Mr
Investigating further education lecturers beliefs, attitudes and views relating to mathematics and mathematics education
Abstract: A bank of six activities was designed to investigate lecturers' ideas about a range of aspects of mathematics and mathematics education. The areas covered include philosophical views relating to the nature of mathematics, the student qualities perceived as necessary for success in mathematics, and the subject's ease for learning. The results of administering these activites to staff teaching mathematics in one ILEA college for further education were discussed and compared with some results of classroom observation. Possibilities for cross-referencing and checking results between tasks were indicated and the value of the bank of activities for building up a multi-faceted picture, as profile, of lecturer's thinking was discussed. The work is exploratory in nature and continues.
Source of Grant: No funding
Date of Research: 1986 – continuing
KEYWORDS: attitude; further education; mathematics; teacher behaviour

8/1420
Department of Social Sciences
103 Borough Road, London SE1 OAA
071 928 8989 ext 2929
David, M.E. Dr
Parents and educational policy
Abstract: This study aims to evaluate the implementation of the GERBIL (Government Educational Reform Bill) with respect to the changing role of parents both as parent govenors and in choice of type of school. The focus will be on how parents decide, in a sample of LEAs, about schools and whether of not to 'opt out' to 'grant-maintained' schools. In this study, the researcher will look at what parents 'want' from education both for themselves and for their children. This will be done by discussing, with a sample of parents, what they think about the schools which their children attend and what they would like to see which is not at present provided.
Source of Grant: Inner London Education Authority
Date of Research: 1988 – continuing
KEYWORDS: educational policy; government policy; legislation; parent participation

8/1421

Department of Social Sciences
HELM (Higher Education and the Labour Market),
Borough Road, London SE1 OAA
071 928 8989
McGeevor, P.A. Dr; Murray, K.; *Supervisor:* Brennan, J.L.;
Lyon, E.S.

Graduate panel study: higher education and career development
Abstract: The HELM survey examines the early employment experiences of a sample of 1982 and 1985 graduates. The target sample, of CNAA and University Graduates (as well as a comparison group of BTEC – Business and Technical Education Council HND – Higher National Diploma) are drawn from 29 universities, 30 polytechnics and 47 colleges of higher education. There are 24 course types and a target sample of 8,000. The aim of the project is to inform policy making about the links between higher education and the labour market. It examines the contribution their courses have made to their career development, as well as aspects of personal change and development associated with the experience of higher education.
Published Material: A complete list of publications is available from the project office.
Source of Grant: CNAA Development Fund: £129,554
Date of Research: 1986-1989
KEYWORDS: *career; educational policy; graduate; higher education; labour market*

South Glamorgan Institute of Higher Education

8/1422

Language and Reading Centre
Cyncoed Road, Cardiff CF2 6XD
0222 551111
University of Wales College of Cardiff,
Cathays Park, Cardiff CF1 1XL
0222 874000
Baird, A. Mrs; *Supervisor:* Harris, J. Dr; Davies, W.B. Prof.

The implications of second language acquisition for ethnic minority children in Cardiff primary schools
Abstract: This study examined the primary classrooms of children who learn ESL (English as a second language). In order to interpret the language learning opportunities that these children encounter, linguistic interactions are considered from the perspective of three levels of organization; the school, the classroom and the lesson. Each level of organization is located within a particular tier of the study. It is suggested that, within each level, there are visible and invisible contexts and that these inter-dependent contexts affect the linguistic interactions that take place between the teacher and her ESL pupils. The first tier of the study described the school level of organization by means of the results of a questionnaire. Various linguistic groups of ESL children are identified. The second tier of the study focused on the intentions and perceptions of the teachers who are responsible for organizing many of the language learning opportunities that ESL children encounter within the classroom context. Three identified teaching styles are linked to the organization of language learning situations and how such situations are interpreted by the teachers. For the third tier of the study, a sub-group of the interviewed teachers presented audio recordings of linguistic interactions that occurred within their own classrooms. Quantitative and qualitative analyses of these transcriptional data suggested that ESL children are, at least, as interactive as their English speaking peers, but that often neither group has the opportunity to initiate or sustain dialogue. However, a number of the audio recordings indicated much more variable situations. Different levels of ESL pupil participation are linked to teachers' intentions and to the broader contexts of the interaction. A number of practical suggestions are made, associated with encouraging ESL participation. It is suggested that pupil participation is a first stage in reciprocal interaction.
Published Material: BAIRD, A. & HARRIS, J.C. (1984). 'Second language acquisition among Cardiff primary school children', Education for Development, Vol 8, No 1, pp.3-27.; HARRIS, J.C. & BAIRD, A. (1984). Constructing the social ecology of the classroom: a perspective on second language learning. Paper presented

at the British Psychological Development Section Annual Conference, University of Lancaster.
Source of Grant: Economic and Social Research Council
Date of Research: 1983-1990
KEYWORDS: *English (second language); English language; ethnic minority; foreign languages; second language*

Spastics Society

8/1423

Centre for Studies on Integration in Education,
16 Fitzroy Square, London WIP 5HQ
071 607 1013
Vaughan, M.; Wallis, E. Mrs

Register of schools and colleges in England and Wales to identify where children with special needs are being educated side by side with ordinary children/students
Abstract: The 1981 Education Act promoted for the first time in implemented legislation the education of children with special needs in ordinary schools, alongside children without such needs, rather than in separated and segregated special schools and units. The duties to integrate into ordinary schools, and once in the school, within its normal activities, apply to all children whatever their particular disability and however severe it may be. But there are conditions which must be satisfied. In order to ascertain the degree to which the integration principle is being implemented in ordinary schools, a questionnaire is being sent to every school and college in the country, nearly 30,000 in all. Questions are asked on the name, address and type of institution, degree of integration, resources, personnel, support, aids and equipment and exclusions. Another questionnaire is being sent to the 104 LEAs (Local Education Authorities) in England and Wales seeking information on statistics of special needs children, statementing under the Act and where the education of special needs children is taking place. From this information a database will be compiled, maintained and updated. It will be available for general enquiries.
Source of Grant: The Spastics Society
Date of Research: 1983 – continuing
KEYWORDS: *database; integration; special education; special needs*

Staff College

8/1424

Resources Intelligence Unit,
Coombe Lodge,
Blagdon, Bristol BS18 6RG
0761 62503
Spencer, A. Dr

Course costing for Dudley colleges
Abstract: The aim of this research is to design, develop, test, validate and embed a system of course and unit costing for use in all the colleges in the Dudley Metropolitan Borough. The system should be: as simple as possible and as far as possible based on data which is readily available; analyze the course and unit costs to identify costs by the major heads of expenditure – academic staff, technician staff, administrative and clerical staff, supplies and services etc; and capable of amendment over time to come into line with the method recommended by Coopers and Lybrand and accepted for general application in NAFE (Non-advanced Further Education) by the Joint Efficiency Study. The costing method was designed and developed in September 1988 and then used to cost courses in either Halesowen or Stourbridge colleges. In January 1989, the results of this were presented and discussed with all colleges in the LEA and the method refined and amended as necessary. In collaboration with college staff, all courses in Dudley colleges were costed (February-June 1989). Finally, the results will be presented, the documentation prepared and the system begun to be embedded (July-August 1989).
Source of Grant: Dudley Metropolitan Borough: £10,653
Date of Research: 1988-1990
KEYWORDS: *college of further education; cost; course; economics of education; information system*

8/1425

Resources Intelligence Unit, Coombe Lodge, Blagdon, Bristol BS18 6RG
0761 62503
Spencer, A. Dr

Resource allocation and control: an action learning and training scheme
Abstract: The intention is for The Staff College to work in partnership with Hampshire: (i) in the context of the Education Reform Bill, to explore the issues and problems presented by the new planning resource allocation and control processes and procedures in the pilot schemes, and to identify solutions; (ii) to ensure that the recommendations of the Joint Efficiency Study Group with regard to performance appraisal, costing and budgeting are taken into account and integrated into the systems design; (iii) to prepare a 'management budgeting' manual; (iv) to design, develop and test an appropriate training programme in Hampshire; and (v) as a result of the above to design and develop appropriate training programmes with supporting materials for other LEAs; and to otherwise disseminate the outcomes. The following outcomes are expected: (i) greater understanding of the technical and managerial issues and problems involved in implementing the recommendations of the Joint Efficiency Study Group, the National Evaluation Group and the Education Reform Bill with regard to strategic planning, budgeting and the appraisal of institutional performance; (ii) as a result of (1) a clearer specification of systems design, processes and procedures; (iii) as a result of (ii) a smoother implementation of the new regime; (iv) in pursuit of (iii) the preparation of a budgeting manual and the design, development and testing of a training programme initially for use in Hampshire and subsequently for use by other authorities; (v) reports of the outcomes of all of the above to be published in the COOMBE LODGE REPORT series and incorporated in resource management courses at The Staff College.
Published Material: BIRCH, D., LATCHAM, J. & SPENCER, A. (1990). Financial delegation for Further Education colleges: a case study. Coombe Lodge Report, Vol 21, No 8.
Source of Grant: Mutual Development Fund, Training Agency: £81,600
Date of Research: 1989-1990
KEYWORDS: *administration of education; budgetary control; financial resources; planning of education; training*

8/1426

Coombe Lodge, Blagdon, Bristol BS18 6RG
0761 62503
Pardey, D. Mr

Forecasting student enrolments for further education colleges
Abstract: This research is an analysis of forecasting methodologies used in deriving enrolment projections for furthr education plans at college and local education authority level.
Source of Grant: The Staff College
Date of Research: 1990 – continuing
KEYWORDS: *enrolment projection; forecasting; further education; registration*

8/1427

Coombe Lodge, Blagdon, Bristol BS18 6RG
0761 62503
Atkinson, D. Mr

English local education authorities schemes of local financial management
Abstract: This research is a comparative analysis of English local education authority funding schemes (schemes of local financial management) for maintained further education colleges which have been prepared in accordance with the Education Reform Act 1988 and the Department of Education and Science Circular 9/88.
Source of Grant: The Staff College
Date of Research: 1990 – continuing
KEYWORDS: *college of further education*

8/1428

Coombe Lodge, Blagon, Bristol BS18 6RG
0761 62503
Civil, J. Mrs; *Supervisor:* Fineman, S. Dr

Effects of emotion and sexuality in the organizational processes of management
Abstract: This research will look at the effect of emotions and sexuality in the organizational processes of management. Particularly, appraisal, management, structures, interviews promotions and divisions of labour.

Source of Grant: The Staff College
Date of Research: 1990 – continuing
KEYWORDS: *organization*

8/1429

Coombe Lodge, Blagdon, Bristol BS18 6RG
0761 62503
Gray, L.S. Mr

Marketing service industries: a comparative study of education and banking
Abstract: This research will involve a comparative study of the education service and banking with reference to the organization of the marketing function, the preparation and use of marketing plans and the relevance of marketing to the development of intangible services.
Published Material: GRAY, L.S. (1991). Marketing education. Buckingham: Open University Press.
Source of Grant: No funding
Date of Research: 1991 – continuing
KEYWORDS: *banking; marketing*

8/1430

Coombe Lodge, Blagdon, Bristol BS18 6RG
0761 62503
Graystone, J.A. Mr

The new governing bodies for further education colleges
Abstract: This research will involve an investigation of instruments and articles of government of further education colleges in England and Wales, and an analysis of the development needs of the new governors.
Published Material: GRAYSTONE, J.A. & WILLIAMS, D. (1990). Development programmes for further education governors: a guide for providers. Bristol: Further Education Unit.
Source of Grant: Further Education Unit The Staff College
Date of Research: 1990 – continuing
KEYWORDS: *college of further education; further education*

8/1431

Coombe Lodge, Blagdon, Bristol BS18 6RG
0761 62503
Gray, L.S.; Warrender, A-M. Mrs; Latcham, J. Mr

Reviewing post-16 provision in four occupational sectors
Abstract: This research will involve a review of current and future demand for post-16 provision of education and training in the sectors of agriculture and horticulture, art and design, caring and the motor vehicle industry.
Source of Grant: Gloucestershire Local Education Authority: £40,000
Date of Research: 1990 – continuing
KEYWORDS: *further education; sixteen to nineteen education*

8/1432

Coombe Lodge, Blagdon, Bristol BS18 6RG
0761 62503
Supervisor: Spencer, A. Dr

Distribution of a total college budget
Abstract: The project will formulate a method of distributing the whole of the funds available to Dudley College of Technology under the conditions that will appertain after the implementation of the Education Reform Act. The project will utilize the active and sophisticated Management Information System within the institution to generate a framework for the dissemination of all the monies available to the Governing Body after the implementation of the Education Reform Act. It is intended that a methodology be drawn up which will act as a source of reference to those facing such a task in the future.
Source of Grant: Dudley College of Technology: £2,800
Date of Research: 1989-1990
KEYWORDS: *administration of education; budgetary control; college of further education; financial resources; information system; management*

8/1433

Coombe Lodge, Blagdon, Bristol BS18 6RG
0761 62503
Spencer, A. Dr

Evaluation of the Merton and Carshalton colleges' project to develop the use of Management Information Systems
Abstract: The development of a Management Information System by Carshalton College of Further Education and Merton College

is to be evaluated. The researcher will: (i) work with the systems analyst, to inform her/him about the further scene as it is likely to develop subsequent to the Education Reform Act (1988); (ii) liaise with EMIS Ltd so that the systems analyst is fully aware of the potential of the FEMIS software, and also aware of how the software will be further developed; (iii) work with the systems analyst to prepare her/his plan of action and to monitor progress with the implementation of the plan; (iv) to prepare and present a report evaluating the project.
Source of Grant: London Boroughs of Merton and Sutton: £5,000
Date of Research: 1989-1989
KEYWORDS: administration of education; college of further education; information system; management; software

Staffordshire Polytechnic

8/1434
> Computers in Economics Unit,
> Leek Road, Stoke on Trent ST4 2DF
> 0782 412515
> Hurd, S.J. Mr

Second national survey of computer use in economics and business studies in secondary education
Abstract: The aim is to find out about current hardware and software, and their levels of use in the context of courses with an economics or business education element. A number of hypotheses explored in the first survey will be re-examined. An attempt will be made to identify the characteristics of both users and non-users of computers among economics and business education teachers. Sample size = 6000, comprising members of the Economic Association and the Society of Teachers in Business Education, and using a postal questionnaire.
Source of Grant: Banking Information Service in collaboration with Economics Associations and Society of Teachers in Business Education: £3,000 approx.
Date of Research: 1988-1989
KEYWORDS: business education; computer assisted instruction; economics; secondary education

8/1435
> Department of Computing
> Blackheath Lane, Stafford ST18 OAD
> 0785 53511
> Iddles, C.M. Ms; *Supervisor:* Bradley, P.J. Mr; Byrne, J.A. Mr; Dagger, G.W. Dr; Self, J.A. Dr

An intelligent tutor using causal knowledge
Abstract: This project is developing an intelligent computer based tutor that can diagnose student misunderstandings in the teaching of metamorphism in geology. The tutor is an expert system which incorporates a causal model. The expert system need not perform at a level which would be useful to a professional geologist, but it contains skills appropriate to the teaching of undergraduate geology students. It is a mixed expert system which contains both shallow rules, and a causal model for reasoning from first principles. Hitherto unknown problems are reasoned from first principles using the causal module, then new rules are generated and added to the rule base. An Anderson type tutoring system is employed incorporating ideal and buggy rule sets. Ideal rules consist of paths which will help the student solve the problem, while buggy rules consist of paths arising from poor understanding of the teaching material, which the student should not follow.
Published Material: Full details of Computing Department Technical Reports are available from Dr J.D. Wilcock, Reader in Computing, at Staffordshire Polytechnic.
Source of Grant: Science and Engineering Research Council
Date of Research: 1985 – continuing
KEYWORDS: computer assisted instruction; geology; higher education; tutoring

8/1436
> Department of Computing
> Blackheath Lane, Stafford ST18 OAD
> 0785 53511
> Frondigoun, M.E. Mrs

Management satisfaction metrics' in computer based training
Abstract: This project concerns the application of computer based training to the chemical industry, with particular regard to produc-

tion and control operatives, examining in detail software used, target groups and learning modes. This is an attempt to develop a method of artifical intelligence for measuring training experience from a learners vantage point, and of examining methods by which managements quantify the nature of of an individuals learning experience. Selected firms have been visited for data collection and interviews.
Published Material: Full details of Computing Department Technical Reports are available from Dr J.D. Wilcock, Computer Reader at Staffordshire Polytechnic.
Source of Grant: Department of computing funds
Date of Research: 1987 – continuing
KEYWORDS: artificial intelligence; computer assisted instruction; evaluation; vocational training

8/1437
> Department of Computing
> Blackheath Lane, Stafford ST18 OAD
> 0785 53511
> Hussain, T.S. Mr; *Supervisor:* Zambarding, R.A. Dr; Bradley, P.J. Mr; Wilcock, J.D. Dr; Byrne, J.A. Mr; Ford, L. Dr (University of Exeter)

The development of a computer programming language tutor system using artifical intelligence
Abstract: This project has designed and implemented a computer based tutor system for teaching the PROLOG programming language. It has four modules: a control module, a student modelling module, a teaching strategy module and a teaching expertize module. The system has several files which contain the expert information, the problems to be set to students, and the teaching/response history of each student. These files are used to choose appropriate teaching material for each student, presenting the teaching materials at varying levels of difficulty according to the students strengths and weaknesses. The system has the ability to improve its teaching strategy by artifical intelligence methods and by human expert guidance.
Published Material: HUSSAIN, T.S. (1987). 'Some aspects of computer tutoring systems', Computing Department Technical Reports. CDTR 87-6, December 1987.; HUSSAIN, T.S. (1987). 'Computer tutor systems, with in-built improving capabilities', Computing Department Technical Reports, CDTR 87-7, December 1987.
Source of Grant: Government of Iraq
Date of Research: 1985-1989
KEYWORDS: computer assisted instruction; programming language; tutoring

8/1438
> Department of Sociology
> Brindley Building, Leek Road, Stoke on Trent ST4 2DF
> 0782 412515
> Jary, D. Mr; Newton, D. Mr; Chapman, A. Dr; Zacune, J. Mr; Gatley, D. Mr

Higher education and the labour market: secondary analysis of sample survey data in relation to CNAA graduates
Abstract: Secondary analysis of panel surveys of CNAA (Council for National Academic Awards) graduates (approximate size of study: 4,000 – postal questionnaire – 3 annual waves, to be followed by further surveys). Particular focus is on the influence of social class and gender, on career destination, and involves the analysis of attitudinal data in relation to course of study, career choice, etc., in the light of alternative 'models' of the effects and functions of higher education.
Published Material: JARY, D. (1985). Higher education and the labour market: the social sciences – the first year after graduation. London: Council for National Academic Awards.; CHAPMAN, A. (1986). Men and women graduates in the labour market. London: Council for National Academic Awards.; ZACUNE, J., GATLEY, D. & JARY, D. (1986). CNAA graduates two years after graduation. London: Council for National Academic Awards.
Source of Grant: Council for National Academic Awards (CNAA): £6500 approx. North Staffordshire Polytechnic: funding for Research Assistant over 2-3 years
Date of Research: 1984-1990
KEYWORDS: graduate; occupational choice; sex difference; social class; work

8/1439
> Department of Sociology
> Leek Road, Stoke on Trent ST4 2DF
> 0782 412515 ext 4013

Gatley, D.A. Dr; McAuley, J.W. Mr; McNare, G. Mr; Jory, D.W. Prof.; *Supervisor:* Chapman, A.D. Dr

Staffordshire Polytechnic graduates in the labour market

Abstract: The research aims to compare the occupational destinations on graduation and later in careers of three cohorts of graduates from Staffordshire Polytechnic (1982, 1984, 1986). Twelve degree and two HND (Higher National Diploma) courses were selcted for analysis to reflect a broad spread of degree types. Two aspects of research have been identified: a questionnaire survey for each cohort and qualitative interviews to establish the reasons why some graduates are more successful than others in the labour market. The research hopes to identify the extent to which graduates from different disciplines are moving into new types of employment as the labour market changes according to the needs of the economy. The survey is not led by an interest in employers needs so much as an interest in discrimination against certain graduates. Particular attention will be paid to the age, race/ethnicity, sex and class background of graduates in the analysis.

Source of Grant: National Advisory Body: £12,000

Date of Research: 1988-1989

KEYWORDS: discrimination; graduate; labour market; occupational choice

Standing Conference on Schools' Science and Technology (SCSST)

8/1440

1 Birdcage Walk, London SW1H 9JJ

071 222 7899

National Project Office

Colerne CE School, Colerne, Chippenham SN14 8DU

0225 743133

Davenport, G. Miss; O'Shea, K. Mr; *Supervisor:* Sellwood, P.M. Mr

National project: practical problem solving 5-13

Abstract: The main aim of the project is to develop practical problem solving as an approach to learning throughout the curriculum but with special emphasis on science/technology, practical mathematics, art and design. The main objectives are: (a) to encourage a problem solving approach to learning; (b) to establish a framework for progression in skills, concepts and attitudes; (c) to develop an effective means of recording, assessing and evaluating practical work; (d) produce guidelines for organization and management of practical activities. The project will begin by focusing on six LEAs and Kingston Polytechnic where it will concentrate its efforts on two or three primary schools and their catchment secondary schools. The project team will offer inservice courses, workshops and lectures for other LEAs as time allows. Two residential conferences will be organized each year for staff from the project LEAs and advisers, lecturers, and teachers from other LEAs. The team will provide an input to undergraduate courses at institutes of higher education based within the main project areas. One initial training course based on project guidelines is presently in the planning stage.

Source of Grant: Department of Trade and Industry: £100,000 per annum

Date of Research: 1987-1990

KEYWORDS: learning strategy; primary education; practical work; problem solving; science education

St Andrew's College of Education

8/1441

Duntocher Road, Bearsden, Glasgow G61 4QA

041 943 1424

Craigie College of Education

Craigie Way, Ayr KA8 OSR

0292 260321

Hanlon, M. Mrs; *Supervisor:* Sweeney, D. Dr; Forbes, D.

Post-programme evaluation of inservice activities

Abstract: The project originated as part of the St Andrew's College attempt to follow-up the findings of the INCISE Project (Inter-College Inservice Evaluation Project, March 1986) funded by the Scottish Education Department. Since Craigie had been involved in the former it was agreed that a collaborative venture with St Andrew's in the lead role would be appropriate (the intention was to involve also Jordanhill College of Education, but INCISE Project staff there became involved in a major national project and had to withdraw.) The aims of the project are to examine the importance of dialogue and interaction with teachers themselves in the evaluation of inservice activities and the value of simultaneous planning of the inservice activity and its subsequent education. The methodology would involve the use of an interview schedule with teachers and headteachers who had been involved in school-focused programmes which had involved St Andrew's and Craigie College staff respectively.

Source of Grant: Standing Committee on Research: £6,000

Date of Research: 1988-1989

KEYWORDS: evaluation; inservice education and training of teachers

8/1442

Duntocher Road, Bearsden, Glasgow G61 4QA

041 943 1424

Joyce, S. Mr; *Supervisor:* Naylor, A. Dr

Citizenship and values education

Abstract: This project is a joint development programme. The base for the development work is St Andrew's College, Glasgow and the funding comes from the Gordon Cook Foundation, Aberdeen. Phase I was a pilot project which was the result of a seminar on values education held at the College in September 1987. The pilot project aimed at introducing citizenship and values education materials to a group of student teachers. There was also a nine week school-based assessment of the materials. The resource materials being used were from the Gordon Cook Plan on Citizenship and Values Education. This educational plan provides teachers with a set of carefully structured materials to help in the teaching of basic, non-controversial values. Some of the main areas covered in the plan are: basic moral values, personal relationships, health education, social skills. Key research areas in Phase I were trying to assess the impact of the materials in school and how best they could be utilized by teachers. Phase II of the joint development programme started in June 1988. A College Advisory Committee has been set up to monitor and support the progress of the second phase of the project. A key investigation in this phase will be how teachers can best use a selection of materials on values education in the transition stages of primary 7 and secondary I. The development programme will also structure a 'specialist study' for student teachers at the college.

Published Material: JOYCE, S. (1987). Pilot project on values education. Glasgow: St Andrew's College/Gordon Cook Foundation.

Source of Grant: Gordon Cook Foundation

Date of Research: 1987 – continuing

KEYWORDS: citizenship education; moral education; teaching aids; value

8/1443

Duntocher Road, Bearsden, Glasgow G61 4QA

041 943 1424

Gibson, D. Mr; McQueen, I. Mrs

Evaluation of interactive video-tape (Take five system)

Abstract: The project is designed to assess the educational implications and applicability of a tape-based system of interactive video. The scope for production of original material is restricted by cost and equipment availablity in terms of interactive video-disc. Tape-based systems offer schools and colleges the opportunity to produce material tailored to local needs but on a more limited level of sophistication. The project attempts to evaluate their advantages and disadvantages.

Source of Grant: No funding

Date of Research: 1987 – continuing

KEYWORDS: educational technology; interactive video; teaching aids; videotape

8/1444

Courthill, Bearsden, Glasgow G61 4QA

041 943 1424

Franklin, I.M. Mrs; Proudfoot, A. Miss

History through drama

Abstract: The project was conceived to satisfy the lack of appropriate drama resources with an historical background. The aim is to make teachers view the possibilities of approaching/appreciating historical events through children experiencing the thoughts and feelings of the people of the time. Four resource packs are proposed which will be piloted in schools.
Date of Research: 1988 – continuing
KEYWORDS: drama; history; teaching aids

8/1445
Department of Language and Literature
Duntocher Road, Bearsden, Glasgow G61 4QA
041 943 1424
Philp, A.M. Mr
The assessment of group discussion at S3/S4 levels
Abstract: The first stage of this project was an action research investigation relating to the assessment of group discussion in Scottish secondary English classes at S3 and S4 (years 10 and 11 in England/Wales. This was set in the context of the development of standard grade English and involved the use and evaluation of a checklist of functional discussion skills by eleven teachers throughout a school session. The report on this work (which is now available from the college, price £3.00) contains (a) the background articles listed below, (b) the comments of the teachers, (c) a coded transcript showing the functional categories applied to an S3 discussion, (d) some suggestions on how to link the approach to summative assessment in standard grade English. The work is also relevant to GCSE (General Certificate of Secondary Education) English and to the development of group discussion and its assessment in the upper primary and lower secondary stages. At present the second stage is being completed, viz the coding of the utterances of some of the project transcripts in terms of the functional catergories used in stage one, i.e. how far they provide an adequate framework for analyzing how pupils actually use language in discussions, and how far the original categories need to be supplemented by further categories if we are to provide an adequate description. This work, although limited, is likely to provide teachers with some useful, and fairly accessible information on how group discussions work.
Published Material: COLLINS, F. & BLOOD, B. (1984). 'Assessing talk', Lantern (Lanarkshire English Magazine), Summer 1984.; PHILP, A.M. (1984). 'Group discussion: its importance and its assessment', Teaching English, Autumn, (Scottish Curriculum Development Service, Edinburgh Centre).; McGONIGAL, J. (1985). 'Sketching the silences: an approach to assessing group discussion', Teaching English, Summer.; PHILP, A.M. (1989). The assessment of group discussion at S3/S4 levels: report on the action research stage of the project. Published by St Andrews College. October 1989.
Source of Grant: College internal funding: £700
Date of Research: 1983-1989
KEYWORDS: assessment; discussion; English language; group discussion; group learning; group work; secondary school

8/1446
Department of Music
Duntocher Road, Bearsden, Glasgow G61 4QA
041 943 1424
McGregor, J. Mrs; *Supervisor:* Pitcathley, J. Mr
Music's role in a curriculum for children with complex learning difficulties and multiple handicap
Abstract: The project began with a dual remit: (i) inservice training of non-specialist teachers; (ii) An investigation into ways in which music can help develop areas of the curriculum. It involved staff workshop sessions and work with staff and children in individual classrooms. In the initial stages considerable time was spent observing how programmes of work were implemented to meet individual needs and to identify where they might effectively contribute. Seven different groups were involved. Materials were then designed to be used in a variety of activities, either to help realise special objectives related to work programmes, or to promote specific skills. Areas highlighted were motor skills, language/communication, socialization, cognitive skills, sensory/play and self help skills. Various approaches in the presentation of materials were experimented with, keeping in mind that any approaches or materials found to be effective should be such that they could be used by non-specialist staff. Discussions with staff thereby centred on the usefulness of materials and the degree of confidence with which they could deliver them, with consideration being given to possible adaptations or necessary re-writing. Material

devised for use with groups or individuals, was worked through with staff and children in class, reinforced at staff training sessions and, where appropriate, placed on audio tape. The materials now require to be written up in a structured format and to receive further piloting. Thereafter, in the light of feedback and evaluation, further writing may be required.
Source of Grant: No funding 87/88 College internal funding 88/89: £286 No funding at present
Date of Research: 1987-1990
KEYWORDS: curriculum development; music education; inservice training; special teacher

St Andrew's University

8/1447
Department of Psychology
St Andrews, Fife KY16 9JN
0334 76161 ext 7217
Victoria University of Wellington
PO Box 600, Wellington 1, New Zealand
Wellington 721-000
Johnston, R. Dr; Holligan, C. Dr; Thompson, G.B. Dr
A cross-national study of cognitive processes during reading development in the primary school
Abstract: The aim of this project is to assess the extent to which the use of a phonological approach to reading is due to internal cognitive changes within the child, or is due to the explicit teaching of phonics. In order to do this, 8 year old New Zealand children (who learn to read using a 'book experience approach') were compared with 8 year old Scottish children (who learn to read using a phonics approach). All of the children were asked to judge whether items such as 'poast', 'loast' and 'snow' were real words or not. The Scottish children were significantly more likely to classify items such as 'poast' as words than items such as 'loast', whereas the New Zealand children were not. This indicated that phonological information was being generated and utilized by the former group but not the latter. This work is currently being extended to compare 8 and 11 year olds on reading for meaning tasks in order to investigate this issue further.
Published Material: JOHNSON, R.S. & THOMPSON, G.B. (1989). 'Is dependence on phonological information in children's reading a product of instructional approach?' Journal of Experimental Child Psychology, Vol 48, pp.131-145.
Source of Grant: No external funding
Date of Research: 1988 – continuing
KEYWORDS: cognitive process; phonology; reading; teaching method; cross-national research; New Zealand; Scotland

8/1448
Department of Psychology
St Andrews, Fife KY16 9JU
0334 76161 ext 7217
Johnson, R.S. Dr
Segmentation and word recognition skills in poor readers
Abstract: One of the aims of this research is to investigate visual and auditory segmentation difficulties in average intelligence poor readers in order to examine what impact these problems have on their word recognition ability. A further aim is to investigate whether poor readers of below average intelligence also have impaired visual and auditory skills, in order to establish whether remedial programmes designed to improve segmentation ability are appropriate for all poor readers regardless of their general intelligence.
Source of Grant: Medical Research Council: £47,279
Date of Research: 1989 – continuing
KEYWORDS: dyslexia; learning difficulty; reading; word recognition

8/1449
Department of Psychology
St Andrews, Fife KY16 9AT
0334 76161
Duncan, L. Ms; *Supervisor:* Johnson, R.S. Dr
Cognitive and perceptual impairments in poor readers
Abstract: It is assumed that readers can read aloud by transforming the orthographic representation of a letter string into a phonological form without the involvement of semantic processing. The

level of segmentation that normal and poor readers invoke during this process is the subject of this research. This issue is relevant to current cognitive models of normal reading and its development while extending our understanding of the problems experienced by the poor reader.
Source of Grant: Medical Research Council research studentship
Date of Research: 1987-1990
KEYWORDS: *cognitive process; dyslexia; learning difficulty; reading*

Stirling Univeristy

8/1450

Department of Psychology
Stirling FK9 4LA
0786 73171
Butterworth, G.E. Prof.
The geometry of pre-verbal communication
Abstract: The aim of the research is to learn about changes in cognitive development of babies that enable them to comprehend and produce manual pointing. Pointing is a species of human means of making definite reference and is thought to be a precursor of naming. Babies aged between 6 and 21 months are being studied in social interaction with an adult (usually the mother). The accuracy with which the baby can locate a target designated by the line of gaze or line of pointing of the mother is assessed. The aim is to establish whether the infant uses 'triangulation' between its own position and that of the adult to locate the referent and to determine the accuracy of this geometry. Production of pointing by the infant is measured in studies where a radio controlled car enters the laboratory. This has been very successful in eliciting pointing and vocalization in babies as young as 8 months. The posture of the hand, patterns of deployment of attention by the baby, spatial position of the target when pointing occurs are being measured.
Published Material: WEISKRANTZ, L. (Ed). (1988). Thought without langauge: Symposium proceedings. Oxford: Oxford University Press.
Source of Grant: Economic and Social Research Council (ESRC): £50,000
Date of Research: 1986-1989
KEYWORDS: *cognitive development; infant; non-verbal communication*

Stirling University

8/1451

Department of Education
Stirling FK9 4LA
0786 73171
Scottish Council for Educational Technology
Dowanhill, 74 Victoria Crescent Road, Glasgow G12 9JN
041 334 9134
Drever, E.L. Mr
Software reviews: what do teachers need to know?
Abstract: The ways in which teachers gain information and form expectations about 12 to 15 widely used software packages will be studied. The research covers packages used in primary and secondary schools and assesses the extent to which expectations are borne out. Postal questionnaires, interviews and informal classroom observation will be used. Special attention will be given to teachers' views and practices in integrating the packages into the curriculum at classroom level.
Source of Grant: Scottish Council for Educational Technology: £32,809
Date of Research: 1989 – continuing
KEYWORDS: *computer software reviews; educational software; educational technology; teacher*

8/1452

Department of Education
Stirling FK9 4LA
0786 73171
Weeden, E. Mrs; *Supervisor:* Drever, E.L. Mr
Language and primary maths
Abstract: This is an investigation into the language used in primary mathematics texts and the interaction between teachers and pupils, with the emphasis on the pupils' perspective. An initial focus will be on the materials from the Scottish Primary Maths Group, and possibly from the Schools Maths Project.
Source of Grant: No funding
Date of Research: 1988 – continuing
KEYWORDS: *language; mathematics; primary education; textbook*

8/1453

Department of Education
Stirling FK9 4LA
0786 73171
Comrie, A. Mr; *Supervisor:* Waterhouse, S. Dr
Beginning teachers classroom strategies
Abstract: This research project is into the use of teaching strategies in beginning teachers – with particular reference to the implementation of 'venture' strategies. A classroom observation study.
Source of Grant: No funding
Date of Research: 1987-1990
KEYWORDS: *probationary teacher, teaching method*

8/1454

Department of Education
Stirling FK9 4LA
0786 73171
Northern College
Hilton Place, Aberdeen AB9 1FA
0224 482341
Northcroft, D.J. Mr; *Supervisor:* Peacock, C. Mr; Lloyd, J. Mr
A critical history of secondary school English teaching in Scotland, 1940-1990
Abstract: This study will investigate both the principals and practice that have determined and made up the English teaching curriculum in secondary schools in Scotland since the Second World War. Research is to be based upon a study of materials produced by the Scottish Education Department, the Central Committee and the Scottish Examination Board. Investigation will also be made into the literature of the subject in so far as it exists. The working hypothesis has been adopted that there exists a gap between the rhetoric and the reality of English teaching in Scotland and that this disparity is one that is being caused and perpetuated by the failure of those who work to develop the Scottish curriculum to appreciate the variety of perceptual standpoints by which those involved in both practising and advising have viewed English teaching. Consequently there has been a national failure to negotiate a shared working ideology, one which addresses itself, not only to aims and ideals, but also to practical circumstances and to solving cognitive challenges and professional and institutional difficulties that arise from working assumptions that have guided the actual practice of post war English teaching. The result is that despite forty years of official exhortation that English teaching should move towards the adoption of a 'personal/experiential child-centred philosophy' the traditional Scottish teacher-centred/academic curriculum still exerts a powerful and constraining effect – a fact that can be seen if we examine actual teaching and learning materials against the key question of what is the experience of English that is being offered to our pupils?
Source of Grant: Northern College: fees and travel expenses
Date of Research: 1986-1990
KEYWORDS: *curriculum development; english language; history of education; Scotland; secondary education*

8/1455

Department of Education
Stirling FK9 4LA
0786 73171
Drever, E.L. Mr; McKay, M. Ms
Teachers' use of GRC (Grade related criteria)
Abstract: Teachers find difficulty in applying grade related criteria in assessment for Scottish standard grade. Microcomputer programmes have been developed to assist the process, in English, Science, French and Craft and Design, from original versions for technological studies. These allow teachers to build in different criteria and rules for aggregation, and also allow the researchers to study teachers' decision making and the areas of difficulty which they experience.
Source of Grant: Scottish Education Department: £4,770

Date of Research: 1987-1989
KEYWORDS: assessment; criterion referencing; decision making; microcomputer

8/1456
Department of Education
Stirling FK9 4LA
0789 73171
Vasiliou, G. Mr; *Supervisor:* Drever, E.L. Mr
Assessment in the Greek primary school
Abstract: The work investigates teachers views and practices in assessment in the Greek primary school, and relates these to national policy trends and the needs of the teacher education system.
Source of Grant: No funding
Date of Research: 1983-1990
KEYWORDS: assessment; educational policy; Greece; primary education; teacher education

St. Mary's College of Education

8/1457
191 Falls Road, Belfast BT12 6FE
0232 327678
Stranmillis College
Stranmillis Road, Belfast BT9 5DY
0232 381271
Farren, S. Mr; *Supervisor:* Finn, P. Mr; Kirk, T. Mr
Students together – but how close? A comparative study of teacher education institutions in a divided community
Abstract: The research is set in the context of the debate on integrated education in Northern Ireland. The aim of the investigation is to examine the impact on students of their experiences in different teacher training institutions. The method of investigation is to develop profiles of students for the three relevant institutions at the stage where they are entering their training. These profiles will be examined on two further occasions in the course of their studies to determine if attitudes/values/aspirations have changed over time. Stranmillis College is a state sponsored institution where the vast majority of students come from the Protestant community, St Mary's College is a Catholic College where all students come from the catholic community, whilst the University of Ulster Education Department has a religious mix of students. The researchers will use questionnaire derived data to consider the similarities and differences between student profiles on the basis of (1) institutions and (2) religion.
Source of Grant: Ireland Fund: £4,000 (IR)
Date of Research: 1987-1990
KEYWORDS: integration; Ireland, Northern; religious affiliation; teacher education

St. Mary's College of Higher Education

8/1458
Department of Theology and Religious Studies
Waldegrave Road, Strawberry Hill, Twickenham TW1 4SX
081 892 0051
St Joseph's College
Beulah Hill, London SE19 3HL
081 761 1426
Conroy, J. Mr
Religious education in a Catholic school – an ethnomethodological study of the collective consciousness of a religious education department and the effects of this on teaching
Abstract: This research involves an ethnomethodological study of a religious studies department in a large comprehensive school in South London. Its aim is to explore how the members of the department, individually and collectively, perceive and conceive their task; what the influences on such perceptions and conceptions are, and how they influence pedagogic style. It is also designed to explore whether or not there is any disparity between purported aims and

actual practice. If goal displacement does exist an analysis of such will figure prominently in this research. Sub-headings for this exploration might well include the following: (a) purposes of R.E.; (b) the importance of a multifaith approach; (c) ecumenical approaches; (d) underlying rationale for content choice; (e) relationship between the R.E. department and various agencies including Roman Catholic ecclesial bodies, local authority and other departments.
Source of Grant: College Staff and Research Development Committee: £250 plus secretarial support as necessary
Date of Research: 1988-1989
KEYWORDS: aims of education; religious education; teacher role

Strathclyde University

8/1459
Scottish Human Computer Interaction Centre,
36 North Hanover Street, Glasgow G1 2AD
041 552 1577
Scottish Council for Educational Technology
Dowanhill, 74 Victoria Crescent Road,
Glasgow G12 9JN
041 334 9314
Kibby, M. Dr
School based evaluation of tutorial design for a reactive learning environment
Abstract: The project is intended to explore the potential use in schools of StrathTutor, a new type of reactive learning environment based on the mouse-window-menu interface of the Macintosh computer. The project provides the opportunity for a number of teachers to gain experience with the system and to contribute suggestions for its further development. StrathTutor encourages the student to exercise choice in progressing from one frame to the next along a non-predetermined route in a lesson. The lesson holds subject knowledge in addition to frames, to guide the system shell when reacting to the student. Tutorial design is different from conventional authoring but it only requires that teachers are able to design frames and to translate knowledge into the required form with the tools provided. The object is to test whether teachers are able to devise their own tutorials successfully with the system.
Source of Grant: Scottish Council for Educational Technology: £40,000
Date of Research: 1988 – continuing
KEYWORDS: autoinstructional aid; computer assisted instruction; evaluation; teaching machine

8/1460
Department of Psychology
George Street, Glasgow G1 1RD
041 552 4400
Warden, D. Dr; Esperet, E. Dr; de Goes, C. Dr
The development of planning and control processes in childrens writing
Abstract: The aim of this research is to make a contribution to the understanding of children's written language development by conducting cross-linguistic studies of the development of planning and control processes, and of the structures and coherence of children's writing in two languages. Children at two age levels, 8 years and 11 years, will be asked to provide two written texts, one on a narrative theme, the other descriptive. During this period of development, novice writers begin to gain in their ability to plan, structure and revise their texts. Our aims are to study the development of these processes, in particular the development of control over reference and sequencing, viz. the ability to refer unambiguously and to construct coherent texts, and the capacity for revision; and to compare such development in French and English. The analysis of the texts will be based upon and developed from a method used by Warden in studies of expository and descriptive writing, which affords examination of both the linguistic connectivity of the texts, and the cohesion and relevance of the content.
Published Material: de GOES, C. & WARDEN, D. Developmental trends in childrens written production of descriptive and expository texts. (forthcoming).; de GOES, C. & WARDEN, D. Differences between childrens oral and written narratives. (forthcoming).
Date of Research: 1988 – continuing
KEYWORDS: child; French language; language development; written expression; written language

8/1461

Department of Psychology
155 George street,
Glasgow G1 1RD
041 552 4400
Anderson, A. Dr; Howe, C. Dr; Mayes, J.T. Dr

The nature of constructive interaction: dialogues in group problem solving

Abstract: This research examines small-group learning of physics concepts, using computer implemented problems in dynamics (experiment 1) and kinematics (experiment 2). Previous research in this area has suggested that the best group performance (in terms of fostering generalized conceptual development) occurs when the participants' initial knowledge states differ. In these experiments therefore subjects are individually pre-tested, and paired according to whether they exhibit similar or different levels of performance on a set of problems. Three pairs then work together to solve computer presented versions of the problems (for instance, in experiment 1, predicting the path of objects falling freely under horizontal motion). These sessions are recorded on videotape. Subsequently subjects are post-tested to ascertain what learning gains have occurred. An important focus of the research is the examination of patterns of dialogue that occur within the groups, and the relationship of these to change between pre- and post-test, with the object of isolating the properties of interaction which facilitate conceptual development.

Source of Grant: Economic and Social Research Council: £45,176
Date of Research: 1988-1990
KEYWORDS: computer assisted instruction; group learning; physics

8/1462

Department of Psychology
George street,
Glasgow G1 1RD
041 552 4400
Glasgow University
Department of Psychology
Adam Smith Building,
Glasgow G12 8QQ
041 339 8855
Warden, D. Dr; Gillies, J. Dr; Mayes, G. Dr

Evaluation of child safety training programmes

Abstract: A number of primary schools in the Glasgow area are currently planning to introduce personal safety training programmes ('Kidscape' or 'Safety Net') into the curriculum. The present proposal is aimed at carrying out an evaluation of the effectiveness of such programmes, in particular, the persistence of learning generated by the training and the extent to which such learning generalises to other types of personal safety situation. The study will involve two groups ('experimental' and 'control') drawn from two age groups (primary 2 and primary 6) in schools matched for location, social class composition, etc. The 'experimental' group (children receiving 'Kidscape'/'Safety Net' training) will be presented with a series of drawings and accompanying short narratives representing increasingly remote variations on the four principal themes of the training programme (bullying; approach by a stranger; inappropriate intimate behaviour; disclosing 'bad' secrets) and will be asked to make judgements of the relative degree of threat which such situations represent and of the appropriate action which a child in such a situation should take. Children's reasons for their judgements will also be explored. This picture/story method has proved worthwhile in a preliminary study of the 'Kidscape' programme in Glasgow schools (Mayes, Gillies & Brown, 1989). It appears to be well accepted by young children and children's responses will be obtained in individual interviews and tape-recorded for later transcription and analysis. Children's responses will be rated for appropriateness by an independent panel of expert professionals concerned with the area of child abuse and its prevention (psychologists, educationists, etc.). A key feature of the proposed research will be the re-testing of both 'experimental' and 'control' children around four months after the initial testing. Previous research on the effectiveness of such safety training/abuse prevention programmes has tended to use only very short follow-up periods (seldom more than one week) and little is known about the longer term effectiveness of training.

Source of Grant: Economic and Social Research Council: £14,000
Scottish Education Department: £13,000
Date of Research: 1989-1990
KEYWORDS: evaluation; primary school; safety education

8/1463

Department of Psychology
Turnbull Building,
155 George Street,
Glasgow G1 1RD
041 552 4400
McAteer, E. Dr; Anderson, A. Dr; O'Hagan, F.J. Dr

The efficacy of computer assisted learning in promoting constructive interaction

Abstract: This research project will investigate the efficacy of computer assisted learning in promoting constructive interaction among secondary school pupils who are experiencing learning difficulties. Through the use of detailed dialogue analyses it is intended to ascertain: (1) differences between pupil-pupil dyads and teacher-pupil dyads working at the microcomputer interface; (2) the features of educational software associated with successful learning in the mathematics and language domains; and (3) the ways in which open-ended educational programs in both mathematics and language influence constructive interaction as compared with software which is closed and guided within the context of learning. The techniques used to collect data for analyses will include the simultaneous videorecording of both pupil-pupil and teacher-pupil dyads and of the visual display unit. In this way the researchers will be able to pay careful scrutiny to the quality of constructive interaction and to the learning ountcomes of the participants.

Published Material: ANDERSON, A. & O'HAGAN, F.J. (1989). 'The efficiency of computer assisted learning in promoting constructive interaction', Software Bulletin, No 22, contained in: ESRC Data Archive Bulletin, No 42, January 1989.
Source of Grant: Economic and Social Research Council: £45,560
Date of Research: 1989 – continuing
KEYWORDS: computer assisted instruction; computer assisted learning; educational software; group learning; interaction; process analysis

8/1464

Department of Psychology
155 George Street,
Glasgow G1 1RD
041 552 4400
Howe, C. Dr

Children's understanding in physics

Abstract: The project is concerned with the understanding children aged five to fourteen have, of events involving changes in pressure, force, substance and temperature. The motivation for the project is threefold. Formal teaching of the relevant subject matter is at present unusual with the age group of interest. Under the National Curriculum for science this should change. Teaching must acknowledge the understanding children evolve from informal sources. By a combination of literature reviews and empirical studies, the project aims to chart informal understanding in detail. Particular attention will be paid to the variation between children across and within age groups and the variation between apparently equivalent problems across and within children.

Source of Grant: Nuffield Foundation: £16,292
Date of Research: 1990 – continuing
KEYWORDS: comprehension; concept formation; physics; science education; teaching method

8/1465

Department of Psychology
Turnbull Building, 155 George Street,
Glasgow G1 1RD
041 552 4400
Schaffer, H.R. Prof.

The organization of learning experiences of young children

Abstract: The study focuses on the provision of those experiences that are relevant to the fostering of early literacy and numeracy skills. It takes place in a day nursery context and is thus concerned with children from the more deprived sector of the community. The study is taking place in 2 phases. The first is of a descriptive nature and aims to document in detail what is already happening in nurseries that is relevant to the acquisition of literacy and numeracy skills. The second constitutes an action research programme designed to promote a variety of different schemes of preparing children for acquiring such skills.

Source of Grant: Strathclyde Regional Council; Education Department: £70,000
Date of Research: 1989 – continuing
KEYWORDS: day care centre; numeracy

8/1466

Department of Psychology
Turnbull Building, 155 George Street, Glasgow G1 1RD
041 552 4400
Schaffer, H.R. Prof.; Ogilvy, C. Dr

Staff-child interaction in multi-ethnic preschool settings

Abstract: The main focus of the project is the analysis of staff-child interaction styles in nursery schools. Two contexts will accordingly be examined: (1) a series of key situations set up to highlight certain specific, educationally important aspects of teacher-child interaction; (2) the general routine activities of the nursery, with respect to both free play and group activities. The first context refers to three situations: a teaching task, a one-to-one conversation and a group play situation; analysis of video recordings of these will yield data at a fine-grained level that will enable us to make statements about relatively subtle expressions of discriminatory behaviour. The second will provide a more general, representative picture; data will be obtained by systematic observational techniques and yield findings about both the rate and the type of interaction occurring with white and black children respectively. The descriptive material obtained from these two kinds of context will show to what extent and in what way children in nursery school are treated differently according to ethnicity and are thus given varying access to educationally useful experiences. It will also be possible to determine whether particular situations or domains of early learning can be identified where differential behaviour is most likely to occur. In addition a number of factors that may be related to differential treatment will be examined. Accordingly the researchers will: (i) conduct interviews with staff in order to ascertain their attitudes and perceptions with regard to ethnic minority children, as well as investigate the declared policy of the school. (ii) Assess children's cognitive status by means of standardized tests (drawn from the British Abilities Scale and the Reynell Scales) and their behavioural characteristics (using the Preschool Behaviour Checklist). (iii) Collect the data in two types of nursery differing in ethnic mix, i.e. those with a relatively high and those with a relatively low proportion of ethnic minority children. (iv) Include some observations of black teachers' interactions with children in order to ascertain in what way differential behaviour is related to staff ethnicity.

Source of Grant: Economic and Research Council: £54,771
Date of Research: 1988-1990
KEYWORDS: *interaction; multicultural education; pre-school education; teacher-pupil relation*

8/1467

Department of Psychology
155 George Street, Glasgow G1 1RD
041 552 4400
Warden, D. Dr; Bull, R. Prof.

Children as ear-witnesses: reporting conversations and arguments

Abstract: Although research on witness reporting is growing, it has focused almost exclusively on eyewitness reports of identity and events. Memory for verbal events, in the context of witnessing a conversation or an argument, has received limited attention. This ongoing research explores the abilities of adults and children (7-10 years) to report conversations that they have witnessed. The specific foci of the research are (a) the effect of emotional arousal and personal involvement in the verbal events to be reported; (b) the method of eliciting recall; (c) typical errors of ommission and commission; and (d) the ability to recognize voices. Preliminary work has produced the following findings which require substantiation, elaboration and clarification: (i) children only report what they understand or percieve to be relevant; (ii) more accurate verbatim recall for arousing material was obtained from children after a delay of several days; (iii) children's errors of commission were based upon familiarity with speaker's style, cues from visual memory, and attempts to produce a coherent dialogue, and (iv) adults were more prone than children to report inferred meanings.

Published Material: WARDEN, D. (1987). "Children as ear-witnesses", Paper presented to Child Langauge Seminar, University of York.
Source of Grant: No funding
Date of Research: 1989 – continuing
KEYWORDS: *conversation; memory; verbal communication; witness*

8/1468

Department of Psychology
Alexander Turnbull Building,
155 George Street, Glasgow G1 1RD

041 552 4400
O'Hagan, F. Dr; Anderson, A. Dr

The effects of peer tutoring and computer assisted learning: interactional and software variables

Abstract: Previous research has demonstrated that computer assisted learning (CAL) can have beneficial effects, particularly with learning-disadvantaged children. There is some evidence to suggest that tutoring by an older peer plus computer assisted learning is particularly efficacious. The present study is an attempt to examine in detail the interaction between the learners (both same-age peers in a cooperative learning situation and also cross-age peers in a peer tutoring situation) during CAL sessions, using videotape records. These records will be analyzed to ascertain (i) which features of the dialogue between the learners are associated with successful learning outcomes, and (ii) which features of the CAL software are particularly beneficial. A variety of software programs designed to teach elementary mathematics (arithmetic and logic) will initially be employed.

Source of Grant: Work sponsored by Department of Psychology
Date of Research: 1987-1989
KEYWORDS: *computer assisted instruction; interaction; peer group; tutoring*

8/1469

Department of Psychology
155 George Street, Glasgow G1 1RD
041 552 4400
Mwaba, S. Mr; *Supervisor:* Warden, D. Dr

Father-son interaction and son's academic performance

Abstract: By means of observation, questionnaire and experimental manipulation, aspects of fathers' interactions with their 7-9 year-old sons during the performance of cognitive tasks were assessed. The same father-son pairs were studied over a period of two years. The children's academic performance at school was assessed by means of standardized tests and teachers' ratings. The aim of the research is to look for patterns, relationships between modes of interaction in the home and academic (e.g. reading) and academic-related (e.g. self-discipline, communication skills) behaviours in school.

Source of Grant: Government of Zambia
Date of Research: 1985-1989
KEYWORDS: *cognitive development; father-child relation; interaction; performance; son*

8/1470

Department of Psychology
155 George Street, Glasgow G1 1RD
041 552 4400
Warden, D. Dr

Development of group conversational skills in the primary classroom

Abstract: Group-orientated learning has been encouraged in a number of recent education reports from Plowden (1967) onwards. This project aims to explore (i) the extent to which primary age children can learn from and participate in the group situation and (ii) how good communication skills can be developed in group work.

Source of Grant: Scottish Education Department
Date of Research: 1986 – continuing
KEYWORDS: *communication; group work; primary education*

8/1471

Department of Psychology
155 George Street, Glasgow G1 1RD
041 552 4400
Yelland, A.E. Ms

Microcomputer use in schools

Abstract: The study looks at the use of computers in secondary and primary schools. The investigation is at three levels: (i) policy level (ii) involvement of teachers (iii) the work of pupils.

Source of Grant: No funding
Date of Research: 1985 – continuing
KEYWORDS: *educational policy; microcomputer; primary education; secondary education*

8/1472

Department of Psychology
Turnbull Building, 155 George Street, Glasgow G1 1RD
041 552 4400
Coggans, N. Mr; *Supervisor:* Davies, J.B. Dr; O'Hagan, F.J. Dr

The evaluation of drug education
Abstract: In this research project an evaluation of drug education in Scotland is currently being undertaken. The evaluation exercise has three main aims covering different aspects of drug education. The first of these is to carry out an assessment of drug-related educational provision. This feature will include both types of inservice courses which have been attended by professionals and the uptake between training programmes with differing theoretical and educational perspectives. The second aim is to examine the impact of the ideas and knowledge disseminated through inservice training on school staff and on broader school policies. The nature of drug education programmes, links with outside agencies including the police, and the extent of parental involvement will also be investigated. The third aim will focus on factors related to the acquisition of new knowledge about drugs. Under this aim pupils' knowledge and perceptions concerning drug education, drug use and drug users will be examined in relation to features of the drug education which is provided. Additionally the validity and reliability of the subjects' answers concerning drug problems, reported drug abuse, and socio-economic factors will be topics for investigation.
Source of Grant: Scottish Education Department: £87,831
Date of Research: 1987-1989
KEYWORDS: drug addiction; evaluation; health education

8/1473
Department of Sociology
Livingstone Tower, 26 Richmond Street, Glasgow G1 1XH
041 552 4400
Kay, I. Ms; Struthers, J.S. Mr
The 'Partnership in Education' project
Abstract: The 'Partnership in Education' Project aims to devise and disseminate ways of working with parents of young children (0-8), professionals and community groups in order to support the educational and social development of the children. Its approach is based on theories of cognitive development, experiential and participative learning programmes which develop partnerships in learning between children and parents, groups of parents, parents and professionals, professionals in different services. In Phase I and II such programmes were developed and piloted in two neighbourhoods in Glasgow. In Phase III, through professional inservice training programmes and setting up of parent networks, a neighbourhood approach to inter-professional and professional-parent partnerships is being followed in several areas in Strathclyde Region. The evaluation of this action research has both formative and summative aspects. Formative evaluation has included guiding project workers on monitoring their own programmes and providing feedback on programmes, inservice sessions and project documents produced to disseminate the work. The summative evaluation has a time series of interviews with co-operating professionals, two samples with over 200 parents in each and language and literacy tests for two age cohorts of children in one neighbourhood. Evaluation findings suggest that: professionals in different services can co-operate in ongoing programmes in partnership with parents; a majority of parents in deprived areas, given the opportunity, are willing and able to work co-operatively with professionals; children's language and literary skills are positively affected when their parents have help in supporting their educational development.
Published Material: 'The Partnership in Education Project' – a public report (1988), Strathclyde Regional Council.; 'What is the 'Partnership in Education' Project?', (1987). Strathclyde Regional Council.
Source of Grant: Bernard van Leer Foundation 1983-86: £56,000; 1986-93: £79,800
Date of Research: 1983 – continuing
KEYWORDS: child development; co-operation; deprived; inner city; parent participation; social service

Sunderland Polytechnic

8/1474
Department of Education
Hammerton Hall, Gray Road, Sunderland SR2 7EE
0783 76231
Mercer, D. Mr; *Supervisor:* Constable, H. Dr
Job satisfaction in teaching
Abstract: The research will involve a survey of the literature aimed

at identifying lines of enquiry, followed by an attempt to adapt models of job satisfaction from the industrial context in education. There has been some work done along these lines but only a beginning has been made in the development of these models to an educational setting. Initially, it is proposed to adapt a model of job satisfaction developed by March and Simon in which they identified conformity of job to self image, predictability of job relationships and compatibility of job and other roles as key determinants of job satisfaction. Allied to this approach is work which has been done on teacher stress. However this is only one aspect of job dissatisfaction and we must not allow the current emphasis on teacher stress to skew the overall picture. Determining the validity of the models developed will be through questionnaire and in depth interviews of a representative sample of teachers from the secondary sector in the north of England. The use of a questionnaire will require the creation of an instrument aimed at eliciting information on teacher attitudes with regard to their jobs. The research will attempt to apply findings in an attempt to create a synthesis. It is anticipated that this will have practical outcomes in terms of a foundation for the development of programmes within secondary schools aimed at increasing job satisfaction, thereby reducing wastage from the profession.
Source of Grant: No funding
Date of Research: 1990 – continuing
KEYWORDS: occupational satisfaction; teacher; teaching

8/1475
Department of Education
Hammerton Hall, Gray Road, Sunderland SR2 7EE
091 515 2000
Abbott, I.D. Mr; *Supervisor:* Constable, H. Dr; Edwards, T. Prof.
The City Technology College initiative with particular reference to the establishment of a City Technology College on Teesside
Abstract: The study aims to assess the effectiveness and impact of a city technology college on the educational system of a deprived urban area, particularly the effect the college will have on the local education authority schools within the locality. The means of collectng data will include in depth interviews, observation and the use of questionnaires and surveys. Specifically extensive contacts have been made with the institutions and individuals involved in this process. It is expected that a wide range of issues will be identified including the role of the industrial sponsors, the position of the local authority, the effect on schools and colleges, the response of teachers and the impact on parents, pupils and staff involved in the college. The study will be looking at a rapidly developing area and it is expected that it will provide data which will be of use in determining future policy decisions.
Published Material: ABBOTT, I.D. (1991). 'British and American approaches to science and technology', Education and Training, Vol 33, No 1, pp.5-7.; ABBOTT, I.D. (1991). 'School industry links: an American perspective', Head Teachers Review. (forthcoming).
Source of Grant: No funding
Date of Research: 1989 – continuing
KEYWORDS: city technology college; industry education relationship

8/1476
Department of Education
Hammerton Hall, Gray Road, Sunderland SR2 7EE
0783 76231
Biott, C.
Experiential and co-operative learning in the primary school
Abstract: The aim of Phase I was to study processes of pupil interaction in small, self-directed, co-operative groups and to study the ways in which pupils take responsibility for quality of work in leaderless groups. Eight teachers formed a working group for the analysis of tapes and transcripts of pupils at work in their own classrooms. The report on Phase I includes sections on the characteristics of self-directed groups, sharing responsibility for quality, judging the performance of pupils and devising and improving group tasks. The aim of Phase II is to explore learning patterns in enquiry-based teaching activities with particular reference to: (i) Co-operative learning; (ii) experiential learning; (iii) pupils' understanding of their own progress. Data will be collected by audio/videotape recording of lessons, pupil and teacher interviews, diaries and pupils' work tasks. Substantial data analysis will be conducted in a collaborative teaching group (2 Local Education Authority advisers and 12 teachers plus project leader).

Published Material: BIOTT, C. & CLOUGH, M. (1983). 'Co-operative group work in primary classrooms: action research and professional support', Education, Vol 3, No 13, Autumn, pp.33-36.; BIOTT, C. (1984). 'Getting on without the teacher: primary school pupils in co-operative groups', Sunderland Polytechnic/Schools Council.
Source of Grant: Phase I – Schools Council: £500 Phase II – Polytechnic sponsored
Date of Research: 1984 – continuing
KEYWORDS: co-operation; group work; interaction; learning; primary education

8/1477
Department of Education
Hammerton Hall, Gray Road, Sunderland SR2 &ER
0783 76231
Kennard, R. Mr; Adamson, F. Mr
A study of mature entrants to the teaching profession
Abstract: Given their extensive experience of industry, commerce and life in general, it is popularly assumed that mature students have much to offer the teaching profession. To what extent is this belief rooted in reality?. Using both qualitative and quantitative approaches for the collection of data from mature entrants, other school staff and LEA advisers, the research will attempt to identify and evaluate the qualities that mature entrants bring to teaching and the problems they face in training and in school during the early years of their teaching career. The research team hope to provide recommendations for institutions with responsibility for the recruitment and training of mature students and for 'good practice' regarding the support of mature probationary teachers in school.
Source of Grant: Department of Education and Science: £17,600
Date of Research: 1989 – continuing
KEYWORDS: mature student; probationary teacher; teacher education

8/1478
Department of Education
Hammerton Hall, Gray Road, Sunderland SR2 7ER
0783 76231
Mercer, D. Mr
Democratic approaches to initial teacher education
Abstract: This is a study of a variety of student-centred approaches in initial teacher education. These include a democratic learning approach, partnership supervision in the teaching practice and student profiling.
Published Material: MERCER, D. & ABBOTT, I. (1989). 'Democratic learning in initial teacher education: a comparative study', Educational Review, Vol 41, No 1, pp.3-8.; MERCER, D. & ABBOTT, I. (1989). 'Democratic learning in initial teacher education: partnership supervision in the teaching practice', Journal of Education for Teaching, Vol 15, No 2, pp.141-148.
Source of Grant: No funding
Date of Research: 1988 – continuing
KEYWORDS: learning strategy; teacher education

8/1479
Department of Education
Hammerton Hall, Gray Road, Sunderland SR2 7EE
0983 76231
Abbott, I.D. Mr; Troyna, B.S. Mr
The educational and vocational aspirations and experiences of female and male students
Abstract: The purpose of this research is to explore gender differences in the educational and vocational experiences of students in the context of high unemployment. The researchers are working with a local school to follow the progress of the present fifth year.
Source of Grant: No funding
Date of Research: 1987 – continuing
KEYWORDS: educational opportunites; labour market; sex difference; youth employment

8/1480
Department of Physical Education and Creative Studies
Hammerton Hall, Gray Road, Sunderland SR2 7EE
0783 76231
Williams, T. Dr
Integration of sensorially and physically disabled young people in school physical education
Abstract: The project will examine the extent of integration of han-

dicapped pupils in the North-East and the adaptions of organization; curriculum and pedagogy which have been made. It will then consider the implementation and evaluation of integrative strategies.
Source of Grant: Sports Council 1987-88: £29,000
Date of Research: 1987-1990
KEYWORDS: integration; physical education; physically handicappped

Surrey University

8/1481
Department of Educational Studies
Guildford GU2 5XH
0483 571281 ext 2681
Middlehurst, R.M. Ms; *Supervisor:* Pope, M. Dr
Leadership development: requirements and programmes for senior university staff
Abstract: This research project is based on an earlier evaluation study of a series of leadership courses for heads of academic departments in British universities. Building on the earlier investigation of leadership and management development provision for middle management in universities, the current project is focused upon the learning requirements and development opportunities available to senior university staff – as individuals and as management teams. The analysis will be based firmly on a study of current roles and responsibilities within university senior management teams and perceptions of these roles. This analysis will feed an appraisal of current development provision. Methods of data collection will include in depth interviews with senior staff and a cross section of university personnel. Questionnaire surveys, the study of documentary evidence and direct observation of staff development provision will also be undertaken. Comparisons will be made with opportunities at a comparable level in other sectors and via documentary evidence in two overseas locations. It is anticipated that the findings will assist in the evaluation and development of training policy for the new national unit for university management and staff development set up by the Committee of Vice-Chancellors and Principals in the Autumn of 1988.
Published Material: MIDDLEHURST, R. (1988). 'Leadership training and development for university academics'. In: Conference Preeceedings, British Educational Management and Administration Society Conference, Cardiff, (12-14 April 1988).; MIDDLEHURST, R. (1988). 'Management and leadership development in universities: what's happening and where are we going?'. In: Eggins, H. (Ed). Restructuring higher education. Society for Research into Higher Education and Open University Press.; MIDDLEHURST, R. (1989). 'Leadership and Universities', Higher Education, 17 January 1989.
Source of Grant: Department of Education and Science: £77,360
Date of Research: 1989 – continuing
KEYWORDS: administration of education; management education; university

8/1482
Department of Educational Studies
Guildford GU2 5XH
0483 571281
Evans, K. Dr; Brown, A. Mr
Technical and training mastery in the workplace
Abstract: This research aims to explore the issues involved in the implementation of attempts to develop people who combine both technical and training mastery in the workplace and to make recommendations on the development of a strategy which addresses delivery as well as policy issues. It is intended that the research findings should be of interest to both practitioners and policy makers in the run up to the implementation of the Single European Market, 1992. The researchers will investigate attempts to promote the development of 'keyworkers' – people who combine both technical and training mastery in the workplace. (This will cover both individual company initatives and the attempt by CGLI (City and Guilds of London Institute) to develop a national system for accreditation of skilled 'masters'). It is also intended to identify factors significant in the success or failure of such initiatives with reference to selected international comparisons.
Source of Grant: Leverhulme Trust: £37,650
Date of Research: 1991 – continuing

KEYWORDS: Europe; industrial training; technical ability; training personnel

8/1483

Department of Educational Studies
Guildford GU2 5XH
0483 571281 ext 3136
Haffenden, I. Dr; Brown, A. Mr; Blackman, S. Dr;
Supervisor: Haffenden, I. Dr; Brown, A. Mr

Implications of the implementation of competence-based curricula

Abstract: The aim of this research is to assist the further education system by providing advice and guidance regarding the design and implementation (including assessment) of competence-led curricula leading to competence-based vocational qualifications. The methods used have been varied but have sought to analyze and synthesize information emerging from six college and seven occupational sector projects set up nationally.

Published Material: HAFFENDEN, I. & BROWN, A. (1989). A study of new vocational qualifications: interim findings and implications for teacher education, Journal of Further and Higher Education, Vol 13, No 3, pp.46-58.; HAFFENDEN, I. & BROWN, A. (1989). 'Implications of the competence-based curricula. London: FEU.; HAFFENDEN, I. & BROWN, A. (1989). 'Towards the implementation of competence-based curricula in colleges of further education'. In: Burke, J. (Ed). Competency-based education and training. Lewes: Falmer Press.; HAFFENDEN, I. (1990). 'Preparing for competence-led curriculum in further education,' Competence & Assessment, No 10, Spring. Training Enterprise Education Division.; HAFFENDEN, I., BLACKMAN, S. & BROWN, A. (1990). 'Research Partnership and an Issues Framework: a review of the methodology of an overarching project on competence'. Paper presented to the British Educational Research Association's Annual Conference, Roehampton Institute.; BLACKMAN, S., BROWN, A. & HAFFENDEN, I. (1990). 'Resource allocation: the brake on innovation; National Vocational Qualifications in England and Wales. Paper presented to the International Association for Education Assessment, Maastricht, The Netherlands.

Source of Grant: Training Enterprise Education Division (TEED)/Further Education Unit: £66,227
Date of Research: 1989 – continuing
KEYWORDS: assessment; competency-based education; curriculum design; curriculum development; further education; vocational education

8/1484

Department of Educational Studies
Guildford GU2 5XH
0483 571281
Shields, D. Mr; *Supervisor:* Denicolo, P. Dr

A case study of a staff development project involving a whole school team in the special education area

Abstract: The aims of this research are to develop and implement a model of staff development as a continuous ongoing concern in a small special boarding school. As a teacher, the researcher has encouraged others to advance their understanding of the world in which they live, promoted continuous self-development and contested that learning (including academic and professional) should be ongoing. The background to this study is an attempt at professional self-development as a teacher/childcarer, and to simultaneously draw in colleagues as in headteacher/staff developer. The researcher will be seeking a participative, collaborative approach which will involve reflection and action, hopefully delivered in a way which is enjoyable and professionally valuable for the researcher and colleagues individually and collectively. Ultimately the study will aim to provide a model for staff development which will have direct significance for the quality of teaching and learning in such small community settings. Taking a paradigm 2 orientation, this case study will involve eight teachers and ten childcarers, utilizing a personal construct psychology and action research methodology. The tools will include in depth interviews, repertory grids, observation, concept mapping and critical incident analysis and a diary of introspection will also be kept. The plan is to examine: (i) general issues of professionalism and practice; (ii) the technological, administrative and socio-interactive components; (iii) participants views of their pupils. The focus changes from the general to the specific and personal, the theoretical to the practical. The results/conclusions will consider the reflective value of such an exercise and the consequent actions, leading to a multi-level guide for staff development in small schools/communities.

Source of Grant: No funding

Date of Research: 1988 – continuing
KEYWORDS: action research; boarding school; futher education of teachers; inservice teacher education; personal construct theory; special education; special school

8/1485

Department of Educational Studies
Guildford GU2 5XH
0483 571281
Memon, M. Dr; *Supervisor:* Denicolo, P. Dr; Hobrough, J. Dr

An illuminative study of curriculum changes in English language teaching and learning in Pakistan

Abstract: Pakistan's curriculum change mechanism is based on a bureaucratic model in which teachers are 'humble servants' of the system. The study is concerned with understanding the teachers' and students' perspective on innovations developed externally to the schools in the realms of teaching and learning English as an additional compulsory language. Further, it explores alternative curriculum development models, grounded in the learning context, which may improve the existing situation. Schwab's (1973) 'deliberative approach' and Kelly's (1955) 'theory of personal construct psychology' provided the theoretical underpinnings to a naturalistic approach to the inquiry. A modified form of Parlett and Dearden's (1977) illuminative evaluation method allowed for an emergent research design model which included both the survey and case studies as complementary methods. The former provided information for generating 'working hypotheses' while the latter allowed for in depth probing in the natural setting. The case studies indicated that teachers were faced with a conflict of demands between the desired goals of innovation and the current examination system. They were not familiar with the innovation and they lacked a support mechanism to guide their classroom actions. Consequently, they fell back on various survival strategies. The main sources of the practical problems were identified: governing factors (teachers' personal theories), frame factors (instructional milieu) and social factors (learning milieu). Mismatch between teachers' teaching styles and students' preferred learning strategies also produced problems. This detail accords with the general sources of the failure of curriculum innovation attempts in both developed and developing countries as identified in the literature. The proposed alternative model contains five main dimensions as a basis for formulating coherent curriculum change policy: curriculum negotiations; curriculum materials; professional development; reflective teaching; supportive mechanisms. The feasibility of this model is discussed in the light of the research findings and relevant literature. Some conclusions are drawn with the implications for further research described.

Source of Grant: Government of Pakistan; Ministry of Education
Date of Research: 1985-1989
KEYWORDS: classroom research; curriculum development; English language; English (second language); Pakistan; teaching

8/1486

Department of Educational Studies
Guildford GU2 5XH
0483 571281
McCann, J. Dr; *Supervisor:* Evans, K. Dr; Hobrough, J. Dr

The management of TVEI (Technical and Vocational Education Initiative) within post-16 institutions of Hampshire

Abstract: The reseacher, Dr J. McCann is currently employed as a TVEI (Technical and Vocational Educational Initiative) Co-ordinator. The research programme is designed to analyze the perceptions of TVEI co-ordinators in relation to management structures adopted within post-16 institutions. A general/institutional summary is obtained using interviews, documented by a verified-reporting technique. Perceptions of senior managers and TVEI coordinators are obtained using repertaory grids, concept maps (after Novak) and information models (after Kontainen and Hobrough). Comparisons between 11-18 schools, sixth form colleges, technical colleges and tertiary colleges will be made. Some comparison between Hampshire and 'distant' case studies will also be completed.

Source of Grant: Hampshire Local Education Authority: £1,400
Date of Research: 1988 – continuing
KEYWORDS: co-ordinator; educational administrator; further education; management; technical education; vocational education

8/1487

Department of Educational Studies
Guildford GU2 5XH
0483 571281
Dovaston, V.M. Miss; *Supervisor:* Evans, K. Dr

Needs and provision for ethnic minority groups in youth training schemes in Surrey

Abstract: The background and aims of this research is the Training Agency 'local quality initiative' designed to increase participation by ethnic minority young people in Surrey based Youth Training Schemes. The design and scope will be action research focused on community and individual needs for information, English language provision and counselling and advice. Research methodology will be mostly by interview. The eventual outcome will be recommendations focused on developing networks and provision.

Published Material: EVANS, K. & DOVASTON, V.M. (1990). 'Needs and provision for ethnic minority groups in Youth Training Schemes'. Report submitted to the Training Agency.
Source of Grant: Training Agency of Department of Employment: £11,935
Date of Research: 1988-1989
KEYWORDS: *ethnic minority; training programme; work experience programme; youth employment*

8/1488

Department of Educational Studies
Guildford GU2 5XH
0483 571281
James, D.E. Prof.; Dovaston, V.M. Ms

Performance indicators for adult and continuing education in universities

Abstract: The aim of this project is to produce a guide to assist planners and administrators, to review the current provision and identify the way forward in providing appropriate adult and continuing education in their universities. American experience was used initially and a draft United Kingdom document constructed by the researchers based on the American literature. This was then discussed with appropriate colleagues mainly from the United Kingdom scene including administrators and academics, both involved and not involved in adult education. A further draft was produced and sent to 14 institutions and a final document is now being prepared for publication.

Published Material: JAMES, D.E. & DOVASTON, V.M. (1989). 'Adult participation in universities'. Available from Surrey University,Department of Educational Studies.
Source of Grant: Department of Education and Science: £15,000
Date of Research: 1987-1989
KEYWORDS: *adult education; comparative education; continuing education; life-long education; performance; university*

8/1489

Department of Educational Studies
Guildford GU2 5XH
0483 571281
Riggs, A. Mrs; *Supervisor:* Brownhill, R. Dr

The interaction of values and beliefs in the development and teaching of modern technology with particular reference to biotechnology

Abstract: The growth of science and technology in recent years is reflected in two connected issues: (a) discussion of the consequences of technological and scientific developments by public and private bodies and (b) the increased time allocated to technology education in schools and colleges. Technological developments only happen if there are perceived benefits. Benefits and consequences are terms which are value laden. Science and technology cannot be viewed as value free; consideration must be given not only to the potential effects of developments on individuals, cultures and on the environment, but also to the values inherent in the developments. Values which may not be overtly stated but which are themselves determined by cultural, ethical and moral factors. The inclusion of social issues in scientific education in schools has gradually increased. This increasing interest is continued in the National Curriculum Science and Design and Technology standing orders. These require teachers to discuss the relationship of values and beliefs in scientific and technological developments. It is indicated that such issues should be discussed across the school curriculum. At the time of writing, little information and teaching material is available to teachers on these issues. The research aims to investigate the values and beliefs in modern technology, particularly biotechnology, the understanding of such issues by teachers and

students and will attempt to indicate the type of material which could be produced for schools.
Source of Grant: No funding
Date of Research: 1989 – continuing
KEYWORDS: *biotechnology; philosophy of science; science education; social problems; teaching method; technological change; technology education*

8/1490

Department of Educational Studies
Human Potential Resource Group, Guildford GU2 5XH
0483 571281
Mulligan, J. Mr; Bond, M. Ms

Personal and interpersonal effectiveness

Abstract: This project is an ongoing action research and co-operative inquiry into various approaches to personal development, interpersonal skills, and effective group participation. Research results refine or extend various methods tested through workshop presentation. These are then built into workshop design and learning methods or used to devise new ones.

Published Material: MULLIGAN, J. (1988). The personal management handbook. London: Sphere
Source of Grant: No funding
Date of Research: 1988 – continuing
KEYWORDS: *action research; group membership; interpersonal competence; interpersonal relations; personality development*

8/1491

Department of Educational Studies
Human Potential Resource Group, Guildford GU2 5XH
0483 571281
Mulligan, J. Mr; Heron, J. Mr

Interpersonal skills training

Abstract: This research entails ongoing development and extension of a model of skilled intervention for helpers of all kinds, though they are mostly professional teachers, trainers, doctors counsellors etc. The action research approach is used to test and refine the model with the express purpose of developing 'the intentional practitioner' among the various professional groups. Six Catergory Interventional Analysis is both a method for analyzing interventions and a tool for training purposes.

Published Material: HERON, J. (1989). Six category intervention analysis, 3rd edition. Surrey: Surrey University, Human Potential Resource Group.; HERON, J. (1990). Helping the client. London: Sage Publications Ltd.
Source of Grant: No funding
Date of Research: 1975 – continuing
KEYWORDS: *action research; inservice training; interaction; interpersonal relations; intervention*

8/1492

Department of Educational Studies
Human Potential Resource Group
Guildford GU2 5XH
Mulligan, J. Mr; Heron, J. Mr

Group facilitation

Abstract: This research is the ongoing development and refinement of a model of group facilitation devised for the facilitation of experiential learning in groups. Action research approaches are used by workshop facilitators who use the model in facilitating groups and in training group facilitators.

Published Material: HERON, J. (1989). The facilitators handbook. London: Kogan Page
Source of Grant: No funding
Date of Research: 1977 – continuing
KEYWORDS: *action research; experiential learning; group learning; leadership training*

8/1493

Department of Educational Studies
Guildford GU2 5XH
0483 571281
Denicolo, P. Dr; Hobrough, J. Dr; Pope, M. Dr; Turner, C. Mr

Staff development using a variety of techniques: face-to-face, self instructional material and distance learning techniques

Abstract: This is an action research programme in which teaching staff, including academic and industry-based trainers both at home and abroad, collaborate with education researchers, who are also programme providers, to evaluate the programmes for staff

development with which they are involved. Some of the particular foci for attention are: fitness to context (professional, institutional and cultural) of the programmes; how they fit into a scheme of continuing education for staff; how they contribute to personal development; strengths and limitations of modes of delivery. Methods of investigation include questionnaires, interviews, concept maps and repertory grids which combine in an iterative and reflexive process to illuminate the issues under investigation and which, in themselves, contribute to awareness raising and development.
Source of Grant: No funding
Date of Research: 1988 – continuing
KEYWORDS: *academic staff development; distance study; further education of teachers; inservice teacher education; inservice training; self-instruction; teaching personnel*

8/1494

Department of Educational Studies
Guildford GU2 5XH
0483 571281
Tjok-A-Tam, S. Ms; *Supervisor:* Denicolo, P. Dr
Towards a collaborative strategy in management development
Abstract: This research is in management development. It is initially concerned with national initiatives and developments in the area. Open interviews were conducted with national awarding bodies, professional institutes and colleges concerned with management development. Interview findings indicated a need for a proactive approach to management education provision. APL (assessment of prior learning) could be a process to develop greater collaboration between employers, education providers and management students in order to establish flexible and work-related learning for managers. Linking with MCI (Management Consultancy Institute) in qualitative research to ascertain motivation and development needs of the experienced manager. The aim of this research is to substantiate the need for APL to be implemented in order to provide the quantity and quality of management skills in the future. Due to demographic changes; global competitiveness and 1992; technological and social changes intend to prove a need for APL in order to develop potential managers. A major issue could be the development of wider equal opportunities in order to develop future managers.
Source of Grant: Croydon College
Date of Research: 1988 – continuing
KEYWORDS: *co-operative programmes; experiential learning; inservice training; management development; management education*

8/1495

Department of Educational Studies
Guildford GU2 5XH
0483 571281
Thorne, B. Mr; *Supervisor:* Denicolo, P. Dr
How do teachers view appraisal purpose, planning and implementation?
Abstract: The subject of this research is teacher appraisal. Questions underpinning the research will be; what do teachers really think and feel about appraisal? what constructs do they have, and could it be surmised that such constructs are inhibiting or illuminative? Ought such constructs be used to influence the design and presentation of models for appraisal schemes? Is there a consensus between various teacher groups? Finally, what changes may be needed to be made for successful schemes to be implemented? As a result, qualitative methodology has been adopted to reflect the changes in educational epistemology and method; to view the real world in a naturalistic setting from a holistic viewpoint and to produce illuminative responses to a complex whole i.e. appraisal. Personal construct psychology (Kelly 1955) has been selected which utilises semi-structured interview, repertory grid and open ended questionnaire. This will reflect the real world of teachers and the interactive nature of teaching within the model proposed by Pope and Denicolo (1986). As yet, more clarification is needed to identify the groups of teachers for this research, but in broad terms they may be secondary based and teach in mixed, urban comprehensive schools.
Published Material: KELLY, G.A. (1955). 'The psychology of personal constructs', Vol 1 & 2, New York: W.W.Norton & Co. Inc.; POPE, M. & DENICOLO, P. (1986). 'Initiative theories – a researcher's dilemma: some practical methodological implications', British Educational Research Journal, Vol 12, No 2, pp.153-165.
Source of Grant: St Mary's College Twickenham: £1,000 per annum

Date of Research: 1989 – continuing
KEYWORDS: *evaluation; performance; personal construct theory; teacher; teacher evaluation; teaching*

8/1496

Department of Educational Studies
Guildford GU2 5XH
0483 571281
Evans, K. Dr; Roberts, K. Prof.; Heinz, W. Prof.; Hurrelmann, K. Prof.; *Supervisor:* Bynner, J. Prof.
Becoming adult in the 1990s
Abstract: The research provides, perhaps, a unique opportunity to gain insights into young people's situations and transition problems in the FRG (Federal Republic of Germany) and the United Kingdom and to find policy solutions. In the earlier study for the Foundation on Vocational Preparation in the two countries, 160 young people aged 16-19 from each of two FRG cities, Bremen and Paderborn, were matched with their counterparts, pursuing broadly the same occupational career routes, in two UK cities, Liverpool and Swindon. Bremen and Liverpool were chosen to represent contracting labour markets and Bielefeld and Swindon, expanding labour markets. From the 640 young people involved in the project, samples of up to 40 from the older group in each city will be followed up at age 21 and interviewed. The researchers will also interview some of the key people in their lives such as employers and teachers. The interviewing will be carried out by bilingual research assistants working as much as funding permits in the opposite country. An initial stage of the work being funded by the European Commission includes mapping the range of institutional support services available to young people in the four towns, gaining a preliminary view of their appraisal of them, and developing the interviewing and other data collection approaches for the main enquiry. Interviewing will focus on the quality of experience in the different areas of life including employment, education, family and leisure. The young people will be questioned about the choices they have made or intend to make, the knowledge and resources available to them, the critical influences upon them and the value of institutional and community support. The other informants will be questioned about the context of the young people's experience, especially education, training and support services provision. The data collected will be added to the existing data set enabling the researchers to chart the respondents' progress from their situation at age 18 to their current 'young adult' locations in prosperous as opposed to economically depressed areas. It will then be possible to extend the detailed work comparing career routes in the two countries and to find out whether the striking cross-national differences in training experiences and attitudes persist at this later stage of development. Finally, it is hoped to be able to examine in detail the values of young people in the different career routes in the two countries and link these to local and national circumstances and the new international conditions. How, for example, is German reunification perceived and what changes in the preparation for adult citizenship are implied by it?
Source of Grant: Anglo-German Foundation: £70,000
Date of Research: 1991 – continuing
KEYWORDS: *career monograph; cross-national research; Germany FR; occupational choice; transition from school to work; United Kingdom; vocational guidance; youth*

8/1497

Department of Educational Studies
Guildford GU2 5XH
0483 571281
Collins, S.M. Dr; *Supervisor:* Jarvis, P. Dr
Curriculum innovation in response to 'The Future Pattern of Basic General Student Nurse Training/Education' – English Nursing Board 1984
Abstract: The focus of the research is on the process of implementing curriculum innovation in 6 English nursing schools, chosen by the statutory body, the ENB (English Nursing Board), following the invitation, in September 1984, for collaboration between nursing schools and institutions of higher, or advanced further education. After a review of the previous attempts to reform nursing education, content analysis of the six submissions reveals different approaches to innovation. The researcher made annual visits to each pilot scheme during the past 3 years study, for open interviews, some of which were taped, to elicit the views of teachers of nursing, ward sisters, staff nurses, mentors, lecturers and nurse managers about the plans and preparation for change, and the implementation of plans. Five schemes offered supernumerary

status for students – for periods of 6 months to 2 years; and altered the social milieu, the context for learning. Two of these linked nursing schools with polytechnics, one with a college of education, one with a tertiary college, and one nursing school made no links with an educational institution. The sixth scheme, where supernumerary status was precluded, and the social context unchanged, made major changes in curriculum content, learning strategies and assessment, in collaboration with lecturers from the extra mural department of a university. Factors influencing the educational and organizational changes are discussed and issues raised in the six schemes include: the time scale for adoption of plans, for preparing everyone involved for changing roles, and time spent travelling between sites; developing the infrastructures and communication system; workload for innovators and implementors, maintaining support networks and the complexity with large, or frequent, intakes of students. The evidence points to the need for assessment and evaluation to be an integral part of the planning procedure within parameters agreed by the statutory bodies. The issues raised are relevant to those planning nursing courses for Project 2000.
Published Material: COLLINS, S.M. (1988). 'Changing the curriculum', Nursing Times, Vol 84, No 7, pp.67-70. February.; COLLINS, S.M. (1989). 'Paving the way for Project 2000: the pilot schemes', Nursing Standard, Vol 4, No 6, pp.28-31. November.; COLLINS, S.M. (1990). 'The ENB pilot schemes: how plans have become reality', Nursing Times, Occasional Paper, Vol 86, No 31, pp.30-33. August.
Source of Grant: No funding
Date of Research: 1986-1989
KEYWORDS: curriculum development; education; educational innovation; nurse

8/1498

Department of Educational Studies
Guildford GU2 5XH
0483 571281
Meaden, C.A. Mrs; *Supervisor:* Hobrough, J.E. Dr
Production of a curriculum following the development of a method of assessing and categorising people with a disability for sport – The Profile System
Abstract: This research will investigate the establishment of The Profile System which is a 2-dimensional classification system which caters for all people with a disability and covers a wide range of competitive sports. The system includes a written definition for each profile using medical terms which describe the person's locomotor, sensory or mental impairment. It also uses illustrations which enable everyone to visualize the nature of the functional ability. The curriculum includes theory, a practical session, video material and a training manual which can be used as a distance learning package. The course is run as a one day workshop but could be expanded to a 2 day course if funding were available. Research methods were used to produce a standard assessment procedure, find a base line score for each profile, and to analyze the results of experimental competitions. Further research has addressed enquiries into the content of a teaching package on assessment of locomotor impairment, and monitoring that employment of the standard assessment. The system has been implemented during 1989/90 within 6 national competitions in the following sports – airguns, athletics, bowls, swimming, snooker and table tennis. The curriculum has been used and evaluated at 5 workshops. Action research was considered to be an important part of this project, because an untried theoretical system could not have tested the practical application which was required for competition within sport for disabled people.
Source of Grant: British Sports Association for the Disabled
Date of Research: 1988 – continuing
KEYWORDS: profile

8/1499

Department of Educational Studies
Guildford GU2 5XH
0483 571281
Fricker, M. Ms; *Supervisor:* Tivers, J. Dr
Using workshop methods in women's education is an effective method of changing their attitudes and helping them overcome the problems of gender stratification in women's employment
Abstract: Using workshop methods in women's education is an effective method of helping change their attitudes which contribute to the gender stratification in employment. Gender stratification still occurs widely in spite of legislation and will only change

if women themselves change their attitudes and achieve more positions of power in top jobs. Workshops give confidence to women at all levels, whether as school girls, housewives, undergraduates or women returners or those already in employment. By creating a 'safe' environment, a learning situation and a substitute for the old boy network. They are useful in women's phase specific life/work patterns and should help women take advantage of the 'demographic window of opportunity', before it closes again. The method used is that of illuminative evaluation and is both qualitative and quantitative, exploring the literature and history of women's education and employment and using interviews and questionnaires with workshop users and facilitators. It also looks at the theoretical background of workshop design.
Source of Grant: No funding
Date of Research: 1987 – continuing
KEYWORDS: workshop

8/1500

Department of Educational Studies
Guildford GU2 5XH
0483 571281
Denicolo, P.M. Dr; Pope, M. Dr
Towards an enterprise culture: innovative techniques using personal construct and action research approaches to professional development in education
Abstract: Rapid developments in communication, knowledge and technology have produced consequent pressures on learners, with teachers being urged to develop their roles to emphasise process skills/independent 'active' learning facilitation. Such devolution of control over the process requires teachers to reconstrue their role and traditional activities. Such examination of preconeptions in relation to current relevance is not without potential threat and hostility and this research investigates, with teacher participants, innovative methods which encourage them to view and review their personal theorising and practice regarding teaching and learning. These methods treat the teacher as being a self-directed learner, cultivating personal transferable skills.
Source of Grant: No funding
Date of Research: 1990 – continuing
KEYWORDS: inservice teacher education; personal construct theory; professional development

8/1501

Department of Educational Studies
Guildford GU2 5XH
0483 5712811
Pope, M. Dr; Denicolo, P. Dr
The implications of personal construct psychology for practice and research in education
Abstract: The constructivist perspective of George Kelly has considerable influence on this activity. Current research areas include: epistemologies assumed in teaching and learning situations, together with negotiations of knowledge taking place; teachers' thinking and professional practice; developing the concepts of enterprise in education; the interaction between educational establishments and the surrounding communities. The work is conducted at a variety of levels within the system; secondary, tertiary, further, continuing education and industrial training, and in many discipline areas. The participants are teachers of varying experience and status, students/pupils and other staff integral to the education process. The methodology used is within a qualitative paradigm and includes many innovatory research instruments as well as case studies employing interviews, observations and repertory grids.
Published Material: a full list of publications can be obtained from the researcher on request including details of current MPhil/Ph.D student studies.
Source of Grant: No funding
Date of Research: 1987 – continuing
KEYWORDS: psychology of education; research method

8/1502

Department of Educational Studies
Guildford GU2 5XH
0483 571281
Hobrough, J. Dr; Pope, M. Dr
The implications of personal conceptions for the design and conduct of science education
Abstract: The research programme originated as an enquiry into the meanings of words used in science, as understood by students. It evolved into the development of techniques for the classroom

evolution of these conceptions and a consideration of their implications for curriculum designed for assessment. This work was strongly influenced by personal construct psychology and made extensive use of ethnographic techniques. Subsequently the approach was broadened again, with the introduction of distance learning techniques, to provide a constructivist approach to science teacher education through the Diploma/M.Sc. (Master of Science) in the practice of science education (jointly with Roehampton Institute). The initial work in science education (under the previous direction of Professor John Cilbert now at Reading University) has been expanded to include work on the learning of science by adult students and the development of techniques for eliciting adults understanding of scientific concepts (particularly ENERGY) using 'concept mapping' and CAl packages. The programme has done some work in conunction with the entry under 'The implications of personal construct psychology for practice and research in education', Dr Maureen Pope, being the principal researcher.
Published Material: a full list of publications can be obtained from the researcher on request.
Source of Grant: Department of Education and Science innovative award and personal research
Date of Research: 1979 – continuing
KEYWORDS: *adult education; concept analysis; psychology of education; science education; teacher education*

8/1503
Department of Educational Studies
Guildford GU2 5XH
0483 571281
Germon, S. Mrs; *Supervisor:* Evans, K. Dr
TVEI (Technical and Vocational Education Initiative) local evaluation
Abstract: In setting up the TVEI (Technical and Vocational Education Initiative), the MSC (Manpower Services Commission) stipulated that each LEA operating a pilot scheme should make arrangements for it to be evaluated by an independent local evaluator. The purpose of the local evaluation has been to undertake research into a key aspect of the pilot schemes in operation and feed back the results to those involved at managerial level, in order to aid future planning. Local evaluation also gives an independent unbiased viewpoint at 'grasroots' level. Methods have been mainly questionnaire survey and in depth interview. Topics for research have varied, responding to local needs, and include: (1) pupils perceptions at varying stages during their progress through TVEI schemes; (2) the employment dimension, in which the value and use of TVEI to former pupils now in employment, and employers' knowledge and perspectives on TVEI were investigated; (3) impact on TVEI schools and colleges, which explored the outcomes of TVEI in comparison with anticipation, achievements, barriers to change and areas for future development, as perceived by key participants. These studies, in particular, informed not only the pilot schemes but also those consortia engaged in developing TVEI extension plans, by highlighting the lessons learned.
Source of Grant: Surrey, Kingston, Sutton, Berkshire LEAs: £20,000 West Sussex LEA: £25,000
Date of Research: 1984 – continuing
KEYWORDS: *evaluation; Technical and Vocational Education Initiative*

8/1504
Department of Educational Studies
Guildford GU2 5XH
0483 571281
Boyden, A.J. Mr; *Supervisor:* Evans, K. Dr; Shipman, M. Dr
The effects of the introduction of a GCSE modular curriculum scheme by Kingston Technical and Vocational Initiative Project on teaching and learning methods in schools
Abstract: In the first annual review of its progress in 1986, Kingston Technical and Vocational Initiative Project concluded that its curricular aims for students in the 14-16 age range would be better served by the introduction of a modular scheme. Such a scheme, though validated through GCSE, would maintain the desired prevocational flavour of the programme by delaying specific vocational option choice. It would allow the integration of 'core skills', most especially information technology. It would, it was argued, prevent gender stereo-typing in option choice. It was also important that it should encourage the employment of a range of teaching and learning strategies in the schools which adopted the modular scheme. The introduction of the scheme raised a number of fundamental questions concerning planning, teacher professional

development and the necessary conditions for facilitating the scheme in the various institutions involved. The major focus of this piece of research is the effect the introduction of the scheme has had on teacher attitudes and approaches and looks at how far the hopes of its authors have been fulfilled. Through student questionnaires and interviews, teacher interviews and observation of classroom practice it examines whether that practice is significantly different from that in more traditional TVEI courses in Kingston or, indeed, non-TVEI courses.
Source of Grant: Royal Borough of Kingston upon Thames: £900
Date of Research: 1987-1990
KEYWORDS: *curriculum development; learning strategy; modular course; teaching method; Technical and Vocational Education Inititative*

8/1505
Department of Educational Studies
Guildford GU2 5XH
0483 571281
Pope, M. Dr; *Supervisor:* Evans, K. Dr; Stone, M. Dr
Development education in the youth service
Abstract: There have been calls for development education in the youth service in the Thompson Report and other publications. Not much is done in the youth service other than international youth exchanges. One aim of this project is to encourage the local authority to have a policy on development education. The research has focused on visits by young people to Third World countries as part of an exchange programme. A pilot study was undertaken of a group to India on which the researcher was a participant observer. From this it was possible to refine the tools of enquiry, which were questionnaires and interviews with individuals and groups. The pilot sample was twelve 15/25 year olds. The hypothesis of the main study was whether young people's expectations and prejudices are reinforced by a visit to a Third World country. The main research includes young people from three separate outward visits of an exchange programme with two separate enquiries, one immediately after their return and the other six months later. The size of the sample is expected to be about 40. In addition there will be other interviews of people who have gone to a Third World country as ordinary visitors and not as part of an exchange. Other developmental issues within the Youth Service will be used contextually.
Source of Grant: Buckinghamshire County Council Education Department; Youth Community Service
Date of Research: 1987 – continuing
KEYWORDS: *developing country; development education; exchange programme; youth service*

8/1506
Department of Educational Studies
Guildford GU2 5XH
0483 571281
Reed, B. Mr; *Supervisor:* Denicolo, P. Dr; Pope, M. Dr
The influence of personal values, perceptions and prior learning of learners participating in return-to-study
Abstract: This research aims to investigate the influence of personal and social values on the perceptions of adults on return-to-study and access courses in further education. The main focus of the research is centred on the course as a 'locus of values', but it also embraces subjects' perceptions of and views concerning their previous learning experiences.
Source of Grant: No funding
Date of Research: 1987 – continuing
KEYWORDS: *access programme; adult education; prior learning; value*

8/1507
Department of Educational Studies
Guildford GU2 5XH
0483 571281
Liverpool University
Department of Sociology
Eleanor Rathbone Building, Myrtle Street, P.O. Box 147, Liverpool L69 3BX
051 709 6022
Evans, K.M. Dr; Robert, K. Prof.; Heinz, W. Prof.; Hurrelman, K. Prof.; Pope, M. Dr; Breakwell, G. Dr; *Supervisor:* Bynner, J. Prof.
The vocational preparation of 16-19 year olds: an Anglo-German study in contrasting labour markets

Abstract: The study is comparing young people in transition from school to work in British and German labour markets encountering similar economic trends. First Bremen and Liverpool will be compared, which, through the collapse of shipbuilding and associated maritime industries, demonstrate economic decline. In contrast, two other towns, Paderborn and Swindon, have both benefited from major new technology developments and represent buoyant and expanding labour markets. The purpose of the study is to investigate the experiences of young people progressing along different career paths with the focus on their outcomes in terms of economic prospects, work competence, enterprise, work related values and personal wellbeing. The aim is to uncover the processes by which education and training in the two countries shape these outcomes, how choices are made by young people within them and between them and how the local labour market structures both the process of development and its outcomes. There will be important policy consequences from the work. It will be possible to identify which career trajectories need changing or enhancing in a given labour market. The research will also identify the improvements needed in the advice and counselling services for young people, and on the appropriate curriculum content for vocational preparation in each country. Data collection will be by self completion questionnaire and structured interview with a core of common questions employed in each city. In the interview there will also be scope for more extended investigation of the young people's post-school careers.
Source of Grant: Anglo-German Foundation: £20,000
Date of Research: 1988-1990
KEYWORDS: *comparative analysis; Germany, Federal Republic; labour market; transition from school to work; vocational education; youth employment*

8/1508

Department of Educational Studies
Guildford GU2 5XH
0483 571281 ext 3132
Roehampton Insitute,
Southlands College, Wimbledon Parkside,
London SW19 5NN
01 946 2234
Evans, K. Dr; Yates, J. Dr
The evaluation of TRIST (TVEI-related inservice training) in England and Wales
Abstract: In funding TRIST, the Training Agency required participants to monitor and evaluate their programmes at a local level. In addition the TA identified the need for an overall evaluation of TRIST and envisaged that the evaluation would be achieved in three fixed stages. (The present project covers the first two years of the stages, with a view to a subsequent three-year stage. The TA suggested the following terms of reference for the evaluation: to assess the extent to which TRIST is promoting more systematic approaches to INSET planning and delivery across the curriculum of the kind envisaged by the principles of TVEI (Technical and Vocational Education Initiative). In stage 1, documentary analysis and direct contact at LEA level are major features of the evaluation. Analysis of LEAs TRIST plans and other relevant documentation will be amplified through discussion with LEAs appointed TRIST co-ordinators or other officers, TA appointed TRIST regional advisers and managers and those involved in local evaluations of TRIST schemes. The broad 'types' of LEA schemes will be discussed with the TA's TRIST Central Unit, regional advisers and others leading to criteria for the selection of around 15 LEAs for stage 2 of the evaluation. Approximately 15 LEAs have been selected for stage 2, which is the more detailed part of the study. Data will be compiled through questionnaire, interview, feedback sheets and self-assessment schedules, as well as through debriefing of others with evaluative roles.
Published Material: BATTLE, S. et al (1988). An evaluation of TRIST management. Sheffield: Training Agency.
Source of Grant: Training Agency: £85,000
Date of Research: 1986-1989
KEYWORDS: *evaluation; inservice education and training of teachers; Technical and Vocational Education Initiative*

8/1509

Department of Educational Studies
Guildford GU2 5XH
0483 571281
West Lambeth Health Authority
Education Centre, Tooting Bec Hospital, London SW17 8BL

081 672 9933
Lemmer, B. Mr; *Supervisor:* Denicolo, P. Dr; Pope, M. Dr
Research education, and action in community training (REACT): an experimental pedagogy is used to discover the relation between knowing existing knowledge and producing new knowledge
Abstract: This study applies a method of third millenium educational research to the problems of teaching and learning in mental health care. The context for this study is the relocation of long-stay mental hospital patients, and their staff, to community based care in South London. The philosophy of participatory research (eg. Shor & Freire 1987 – A pedagogy for liberation: dialogues for transforming education) and methodology (eg. Dhar, Tandon and Pandey 1987 – Training of trainers: a manual for participatory training methodology in development) is used with direct-care staff and former patients in three community houses and two curriculum/course groups. The assumption being tested is that equal opportunity to collaborate in research and share personal knowledge is of educational and practical significance. The main data collecting tool is video-taped recordings, and these are self-assessed by participants. The recognition of their individual contribution is expected to be empowering to patients and staff who, in the past, have been considered either incapable of equal opportunity in adult education or less valued as a result of their social experience in hospital. The aim of the study is to identify learning experiences of clients and staff. In the process, the study aims to address learning difficulties by using a methodology which values personal knowledge. The first two years of the study have been used to develop a core for the English National Board of Nursing Course 812 curriculum – the qualifiying course for community psychiatric nursing. Curriculum development for a multi-disciplinary course is residential and day care is also part of the study to be completed in 1991.
Source of Grant: West Lambeth Health Authority
Date of Research: 1988 – continuing
KEYWORDS: *care; community; knowledge; mental illness; training*

8/1510

Department of Educational Studies
Guildford GU2 5XH
0483 571281
Cattermole, B.P. Ms; *Supervisor:* Evans, K. Dr; Stone, M. Dr
Researching girls' experiences of equal opportunities initiatives in schools
Abstract: Using both quantitative and qualitative methods, the aim is to research the nature of equal opportunities initiatives, whether 'top-down' (such as those resulting from the TVEI (Technical and Vocational Education Initiative criterion), or 'bottom-up' (such as grassroots teachers' strategies), as experienced by girls at the option choice stage. After a pilot study this year, conducted in 2 TVEI schools in the south (one mixed, one girls' school), the researcher will be setting up a national survey and case studies next year in 8 schools representing the north/south, TVEI or grassroots, single-sex or mixed variables. Using the cultural reproduction of gender theory to frame the inquiry, a prime area of interest will be the inter-relation between the contribution of schooling to the construction of gender codes, and the active engagement/struggle with these codes as experienced by adolescent girls. The aim is to identify personal constructs as articulations of negotiated gender identities. It may then be possible to identify cultural groups of personal constructs, or 'group constructs', as a collective site of struggle. Successful equal opportunities initiatives would be ones where schools work with these struggles, not against them.
Source of Grant: No funding
Date of Research: 1987-1990
KEYWORDS: *choice of studies; equal opportunity; girl; sex difference*

8/1511

Department of Educational Studies
Guildford GU2 5XH
0483 571281
Peden, K.M. Mrs; *Supervisor:* Denicolo, P. Dr; Pope, M. Dr
Promoting understanding of statistics in psychology courses
Abstract: The research is concerned with the teaching and learning of statistics on psychology courses. Students appear to have problems understanding some of the fundamental concepts of statistics and many teachers feel this results from inappropriate teaching. Therefore, the aims are to identify the problems, to discover some of their causes and to develop teaching methods to alleviate them.

Source of Grant: No funding
Date of Research: 1986-1990
KEYWORDS: psychology; statistics; teaching method

8/1512
Department of Educational Studies
Guildford GU2 5XH
0483 571281
Baker, K. Ms; Supervisor: Denicolo, P. Dr; Pope, M. Dr
An investigation of course teams in education
Abstract: This research seeks to investigate the effectiveness of course team management in the delivery of new initiatives in education. The research aims to explore various aspects of team building such as issues surrounding recruitment and selection and commitment to both the course and team through a comparative study of teams in industry.
Source of Grant: No funding
Date of Research: 1986-1990
KEYWORDS: administration of education; course; industry; recruitment; selection; team teaching

8/1513
Department of Educational Studies
Block AA, Guildford GU2 5XH
0483 571282 ext 3173
Denicolo, P.M. Dr; Pope, M.L. Dr
Teachers perspectives on their profession and its practice
Abstract: This research uses innovative methods based in the qualitative paradigm to both promote and access reflective approaches to the development of professional practice. Methods used include in depth interviews and a variety of techniques used to elicit relevant autobiographical data with pertinance to professional role performance. The participants are mature teachers with a variety of length of service in the profession, many of them being novice teachers in a professional field (e.g. health service, youth and community work) which has been their sphere of practice for some years previous to teacher training. Interim results demonstrate that a variety of life experiences have considerable effects on style of practice, not least being the perceived attitudes and approaches in their own educational experience. The most notable finding is that teachers attach great value to the method of enquiry which facilitates their own personal confrontation of why they perform as teachers in a certain way, as well as focusing on how they achieve intended aims. Thus, guided reflection enables them to contemplate development and change in a motivated and self-directed way.
Published Material: DENICOLO, P. & POPE, M. (1990). 'Adults learning – teachers thinking'. In: DAY, C., POPE, M. & DENICOLO, P. (Eds). Insights into teachers' thinking and practice. Lewes: Falmer press.
Source of Grant: No funding
Date of Research: 1986 – continuing
KEYWORDS: profession; professional status; teacher behaviour; teacher role

8/1514
Department of Educational Studies
Guildford GU2 5XM
0483 571281
Cunningham, E. Mr; Supervisor: Evans, K.M. Dr; Chadwick, A.F. Dr
Inservice certification provision for further education teachers and their career development: a case study in one local education authority
Abstract: The research seeks to identify the significance of one part-time inservice Certificate in Education (FE) course, as perceived by some 200 teachers in one LEA a minimum of three years after completing it, with particular references to their subsequent teaching career and/or personal education. Illuminative evaluation, using questionnaire and follow-up interview, is the principal investigative methodology.
Source of Grant: Portsmouth Polytechnic Staff Research Fund: £350 (1984-85)
Date of Research: 1984-1989
KEYWORDS: career; further education; inservice education and training of teachers (INSET); staff development; teacher education

8/1515
Department of Educational Studies
Guildford GU2 5XH
0483 571281

Breakwell, G.M. Dr; Dale, A. Dr; Evans, K. Dr
16-19 Identity formation: social and political aspects
Abstract: The Education and Human Development Committee has recently launched a co-ordinated programme of research on social and psychological development during late adolescence and young adulthood. The research is based in 4 areas (Kirkaldy, Liverpool, Sheffield and Swindon – see also research projects based at Universities of Sheffield, Dundee and Liverpool. The University of Surrey is conducting the study based on the Swindon area. The purpose of the research is to study adolescent political and economic socialization. It explores social psychological processes such as identity formation, social representation and self-efficacy in relation to educational and employment status. The research involves the collection and analysis of data from representative samples of teenagers in each area together with a detailed case study of selected features of economic and political socialization in the context of the local labour market and education system. The 'core' study comprises data collected at 3 levels: (1) a short questionnaire to establish demographic charateristics of the sampling frame for two cohorts (15-16 and 17-18 year olds); (2) three, yearly questionnaire sweeps of an initial sample of 600 in each cohort stratified by educational and occupational status; (3) two interviews (separated by two years) of subsamples of 40 from each cohort. The attempt will be made to construct a typology of 'Career Patterns' for 16-19 year olds.
Published Material: BYNNER, J. & EVANS, K. (1990). 'Does prevocational education work?', Research Papers in Education, Vol 5, No 3, pp.183-201.; EVANS. K. (1989). 'Post-16 education, training and employment: provision and outcomes in two contrasting areas', British Journal of Education and Work, Vol 3, No 2, pp.41-59.; A list of thirty 'Occasional Papers' published by Social Statistics Research Unit, City University, (1988-1991).
Source of Grant: Economic and Social Research Council: £82,130
Date of Research: 1986-1990
KEYWORDS: labour market; personality development; political socialization; socialization; social psychology; youth

8/1516
Department of Educational Studies
Guildford GU2 5XH
0483 571281
Kingston Polytechnic
Department of Education
Gipsy Hill Centre, Kingston Hill,
Kingston upon Thames KT2 7LB
081 549 1141
Jones, B.L. Mr; Supervisor: Denicolo, P. Dr; Pope, M. Dr
An investigation into the development of practical teaching skills in Post Graduate Certificate of Education (secondary) training
Abstract: This is a collaborative research involving teachers and college tutors – the researcher being one of the latter – which seeks to illuminate the practice of teaching practice supervision. In essence, the objective is to find ways and means of enabling student teachers to turn experience into learning. Structurally, the first task was to set up a network of role relationships forming a team of supervisors and thereafter focusing on the actual counselling skills involved in supervision. The latter forms the bulk of the research. This action research may be distinctive in that the researcher is integrally involved in developing his skills as opposed to using other participants as data providers, as well as co-ordinating the quest to develop supervisory skills. The research is a time collaborative enterprise seeking to improve practice by joint evaluation of each persons skills. In this way it promotes reflective teaching by enabling students to turn experience into learning and ipso facto to develop personal theories of learning and teaching and to be able to articulate them and develop them as they progress.
Published Material: JONES, B.L. (1989). 'In conversation with myself: becoming an action researcher', British Education Research Association dialogues, No 1, Management of Change.
Source of Grant: No funding
Date of Research: 1987 – continuing
KEYWORDS: supervision; teacher education; teaching practice

8/1517
Department of Psychology
Guildford GU2 5XM
0483 571281 ext 9175
Lyons, E. Dr; Supervisor: Breakwell, G. Dr
Evaluation of the Enterprise programme – University of Surrey
Abstract: As part of a national initiative, funded by the Training Enterprise Education Division, the University of Surrey has con-

tracted to develop its courses to focus on the development of personal transferrable skills for all students. This activity will be developed as a partnership with students and employers. Essential to every initiative, there will be a local evaluation of progress made and staff in the psychology department have contracted to carry out this evaluation. This will be done by questionnaires and by structured and semi-structured interviews, to students, staff and employers. The evaluation will be specifically directed at 9 departments in the university with a sample of students and staff from each.
Source of Grant: Confidential
Date of Research: 1990 – continuing
KEYWORDS: enterprise education

Sussex University

8/1518

Institute of Manpower Studies,
Mantell Building, Falmer, Brighton BN1 2HD
0273 686751
Pearson, R. Mr; Pike, G. Mr; Gordon, A. Mr; Weyman, C. Ms

How many graduates in year 2000? the choice is yours
Abstract: The purpose of this research is to detail the flows of students into higher education, analyzing particpation rates and underrepresentation. Demand for higher education is investigated and put in the context of the demographic changes facing higher education and the labour market. Trends in student numbers by institution, gender, age and subject are detailed together with the corresponding output from first degrees. The transition from higher education to a labour market is investigated showing changes in employment, training and early careers of graduates. The current situation of graduate shortages and demand escalating is highlighted with Institute of Manpower Studies projected scenarios and generating projections of the future supply into and out of higher education.
Source of Grant: The Leverhulme Trust Shell, BP Council for Industry & Higher Education: jointly funded
Date of Research: 1988-1989
KEYWORDS: demand for education; demography; employment; forecasting; graduate; education; labour market; student; trend

8/1519

Institute of Cognitive and Computing Sciences,
Falmer, Brighton BN1 9GH
0273 606755
Du Boulay, J.B.H. Dr

Explanation facilities for Prolog: towards more versatile intelligent tutoring systems
Abstract: The purpose of this research is to undertake empirical work on skilled human explanations of Prolog programmes, in particular to investigate the range and versatility of the explanations offered. To educate different existing trace mechanisms for Prolog, in particular, the visual TPM versus a technical tracer. Also, to investigate the implementation of TPM-like features in Poplog and to implement a versatile tracer which focuses on data and variable bindings rather than flow of control. Finally, it is hoped to explore the possibilities of and implement an explanation facility for elementary (and initially correct) Prolog programmes which focuses on the problem domain of the programme.
Source of Grant: Joint Research Council Initiative in Congitive Science Human Computer Interaction: £120,000 jointly
Date of Research: 1989 – continuing
KEYWORDS: autoinstructional aid; computer assisted instruction; educational teaching machine

8/1520

Institute of Continuing and Professional Education,
Education Development Building,
Falmer, Brighton BN1 9RG
0273 606755
Eraut, M. Prof.; Hewton, E. Dr; Jolley, M. Mr; Garner, R. Mr

Making time for staff development
Abstract: New funding arrangements have encouraged an already changing INSET (Inservice Education and Training of Teachers) scene. According to an HMI (Her Majesty's Inspectorate of Schools and Colleges) survey in 1989 there is now a more careful analysis of the development needs of schools and their teachers, and an increasing range of staff development activities taking place. Courses are still offered by traditional providers, but increasingly staff development has come to imply activities which take place within schools including, for instance, classroom observation, job enrichment and rotation of tasks, and visits to other schools. The provision of five non-teaching days per year is clearly not sufficient to meet all staff development needs, and supply cover, and even if possible, can be disruptive to pupils' education. A number of ideas (some controversial) have been tried or referred to in reports or articles. They include for instance: the more effective use of five non-teaching days; the implications of directed time in planning staff development; twilight, weekend or vacation activities; the possibilities and consequences of paying teachers for engaging in staff development out of school time; meetings as a form of staff development; more effective use of supply cover; enhanced staffing for staff development; the use of student teachers to release other members of staff for short periods; LEA (local education authority) support in schools provided through advisory teachers, area INSET or staff development teams; timetabling specifically to facilitate staff development; school federations promoting group staff development policies; instructional materials for individual or group learning exercises; or more generally, the creation of staff development opportunities in the day to day life of the school. Which of the above are likely to be feasible, appropriate and worthwhile? What other possibilities are there? This project seeks to answer these questions by undertaking a number of case studies. The researchers will be looking beyond the activity itself to its effects and broader potential. They will also be concerned with the extent to which LEAs encourage and facilitate such activities through budgetary or other support. A booklet will eventually be prepared setting out ideas and incorporating evaluative comments. Using the booklet as background material, workshops or conferences will then be organized in order to create a better understanding of the possibilities of making time for staff development.
Source of Grant: Department of Education and Science (DES): £57,000
Date of Research: 1990 – continuing
KEYWORDS: arrangement of school time: further education of teachers; inservice teacher education; staff development; time management

8/1521

Institute of Continuing Education,
Education Development Building,
Falmer, Brighton BN1 9RG
0273 678039
Taubman, D.R. Mr; *Supervisor:* Yates, P. Dr

Cultural action for pluralism: the phenomenological praxis of myth in education
Abstract: This thesis examines possibilities of enhancing pluralist- and self-development through the school use of global mythology. Firstly the theory is derived using the action oriented philosophies of Husserl (phenomenology) and Heidegger (hermeneutics). The former enables development of a (transcended) pluralist ethic and perspective, the latter establishes an interpretive focus on language as action. The combination of these two philosophies comprises a synthesis which may be characterised as 'holistic'. This holism is suited to work with today's audio-visual (mythic) media, which are posited as vital tools of cultural action for pluralism. Religious education meets media studies. Using these as the theoretical pillars for analysis and ethnographic practice, a child-centred pedagogy is developed involving adaption of the ideas of Brazilian educator Paulo Freire for UK use. His political emphasis is replaced by a pragmatic one while retaining the broader humanist essence of his work. Cultural, not 'political', action is seen as the key to pluralist 'revolution', which will derive more from human consciousness than from external structural forces. Ethnographic theory and pedagogy are tested in urban and provincial school settings. The two fieldwork projects show the ideas in practice. The data from each site are subjected to further comparative analysis. The thesis concludes with a global survey of current developments congruent with this thesis, highlighting the historical congruity of the exercise and aims.
Source of Grant: ESRC (Economic and Social Research Council)
Date of Research: 1986-1989
KEYWORDS: intercultural education; philosophy of education; religious education

8/1522

Institute of Continuing and Professional Education,
Education Development Building,
Falmer, Brighton BN1 9RG
0273 678039
O'Neill, J. Ms; *Supervisor:* Lacey, C. Prof.

Athletics in secondary schools: a consumer perspective

Abstract: An examination of pupil perspectives in seeking to establish how and to what extent they assist in clarification of effective teaching of athletics and the inclusion of this activity within the physical education curriculum in secondary schools. This is a cohort study over years 1-3 of the secondary school. Semi-structured interviews with pupils will seek to examine two aspects: what do they understand by the term 'athletics' and how do pupils respond to what they see as effective/ineffective teaching? Participant observation of lessons will seek to identify and examine interactive processes and behaviour.

Source of Grant: No funding
Date of Research: 1989 – continuing
KEYWORDS: athletics; physical education; secondary education

8/1523

Institute of Continuing and Professional Education,
Education Development Building,
Falmer, Brighton BN1 9RG
0273 678039
Gilroy, A. Ms; *Supervisor:* Lewis, M.

Art therapists and their art

Abstract: This is a questionnaire and interview based study considering the occupational motivation of art therapists, the influence of post-graduate professional education, and experiential work in particular on students' art and the subsequent influence of clinical practice and further education on art therapists' art.

Source of Grant: No funding
Date of Research: 1983 – continuing
KEYWORDS: art therapy; motivation; occupational aspiration; therapist

8/1524

Institute of Continuing and Professional Education,
Education Development Building,
Falmer, Brighton BN1 9RG
0273 678039
Buttle, J.W.; *Supervisor:* Cooper, B. Dr

Educational projects: theory, practice and curriculum

Abstract: The educational projects for Nuffield A-level biology and Cambridge A-level technology are located socio-historically from the point of view of the pro-active curriculum; and studied ethnographically in terms of the enacted curriculum: for the purpose of illuminating issues of the relationship between theory and practice. The work incorporates a hegemonic dimension – more specifically, by exploring the influence of aristocratic and bourgeois hegemonies – in the evolution of a school subject.

Source of Grant: No funding
Date of Research: 1980-1990
KEYWORDS: biology; curriculum; project method; technology; theory practice relationship

8/1525

Institute of Continuing and Professional Education,
Educaton Development Building,
Falmer, Brighton BN1 9RG
0273 678039
Ross, A. Mr; *Supervisor:* Lewin, K. Dr

Science performance and science teaching in primary school teachers in Papua New Guinea

Abstract: The intention is to profile the science backgrounds of community primary school teachers in Papua New Guinea through an analysis of secondary science curricula, school certificate examination in science, and surveys of college student opinion on the quality of their school science backgrounds. A curriculum analysis of the primary science curriuclm will also be conducted to identify science performance expectations in teachers. Data so obtained will be used to generate a diagnostic science performance profile test which will be administered to all college students and an opportunity sample of primary school teachers. The second part of the study will consist of a series of case studies of teachers in selected primary schools in Papua New Guinea in order to analyze science teaching performance in terms of science performance.

Source of Grant: Ministry of Overseas Development; 1989-90

Date of Research: 1989 – continuing
KEYWORDS: curriculum; Papua New Guinea; primary school; science education; teacher education

8/1526

Institute of Continuing and Professional Education,
Education Development Building,
Falmer, Brighton BN1 9RG
0273 678039
Stainwright, D.A. Mr; *Supervisor:* Burrell, D. Mr

Access to and development of secondary and technical education in Brighton in the late 19th and early 20th centuries

Abstract: An outline of the growth of technical and secondary education in Brighton in the late 19th and early 20th centuries with special consideration to access by gender and class. Access to technical and secondary education is considered in terms of membership of education committees, entry to relevant institutions and to type of knowledge.

Source of Grant: No funding
Date of Research: 1985-1990
KEYWORDS: access to education; equal opportunity; history of education; secondary education; sex difference; social class; technical education

8/1527

Institute of Continuing and Professional Education,
Education Development Building,
Falmer, Brighton BN1 9RG
0273 678039
Larcombe, A. Mr; *Supervisor:* Torrance, H. Dr

The impact of the requirement to assess her own pupils upon the classroom rapport established between teacher and pupils in the infant classroom

Abstract: As a result of the introduction of the National Curriculum, teachers of children at Key Stage 1 must become involved in assessment of their own pupils both in the teacher assessment and in the SATs (Standard Education Tasks). Being involved with one of the consortia designing SATs will enable observation at first hand of the teachers in many infant classrooms as they become involved in this new task. This research aims to look at the extent to which observable changes arise in the interaction between teacher and pupil in the infant classroom. Particularly, it is hoped to establish some systematic way of describing rapport and then seeking evidence of change in the dynamics associated with this rapport.

Source of Grant: No funding
Date of Research: 1990 – continuing
KEYWORDS: assessment; infant; interaction; teacher-pupil relation

8/1528

Institute of Continuing and Professional Education,
Education Development Building,
Falmer, Brighton BN1 9RG
0273 678039
Peterson, J.L. Mr; *Supervisor:* Burrell, D. Mr; Binns, A. Mr

The English secondary school as a third world country: an evaluation of GCSE (General Certificate of Secondary Education) implementation

Abstract: This is a case study research of an east Sussex secondary school and the evaluation of GCSE there. Methods of observation will be participant observation, questionnaires, interviews, attitude assessment through personal construct theory, document analysis, using the interpretive perspective. Based on data collected, the aim is to develop a model which can be used to analyze future education innovations. The putative model is 'The English secondary school as a third world country', but its future depends on the data collected and its analysis.

Source of Grant: No funding
Date of Research: 1987 – continuing
KEYWORDS: case study; evaluation; examination; General Certificate of Secondary Education; secondary school; United Kingdom

8/1529

Institute of Continuing and Professional Education,
Education Development Building,
Falmer, Brighton BN1 9RG
0273 678039
Harkin, J. Mr; *Supervisor:* Eraut, M. Prof.

The place and purpose of english and communication in further education

Abstract: The research has entailed both literature-based and empir-

ical enquiries, covering areas that include the framework of ideas in which further education operates, the institutional framework in which further education curricula are generated, the needs of 16-18 year old students on vocational courses, the perception of the needs of employers, and the history and typology of English and communication.
Source of Grant: West Sussex Local Education Authority Oxford Polytechnic
Date of Research: 1985-1990
KEYWORDS: communication; english language; english literature; further vocational education; vocational training

8/1530
Institute of Continuing and Professional Education,
Education Develpment Building,
Falmer, Brighton BN1 9RG
0273 678039
Goddard, W.D. Mr; *Supervisor:* Cooper, B. Dr
Re-definitions and reconstructions of technical education in secondary schools in England and Wales
Abstract: This is a socio-historical study of the development of technical education in secondary schools in England and Wales, between the Butler and Baker Education Acts. It examines the development which have taken place in the subject area in terms of curriculum development and of external influences. There is a focus on the Schools Council research projects. There will be an analysis of subject development in the schools of the tripartite system and of the comprehensive era, and latterly on the development of TVEI (Technical and Vocational Education Initiative) and the National Curriculum. A particular interest has been taken in the influence of subject associations on the development of subject area.
Source of Grant: No funding
Date of Research: 1985-1990
KEYWORDS: craft design technology; curriculum development; history of education; secondary education; technical education

8/1531
Institute of Continuing and Professional Education,
Education Development Building,
Falmer, Brighton BN1 9RG
0273 678039
Sigurgeirsson, I. Mr; *Supervisor:* Eraut, M. Prof.
Inquiring about curriculum materials in Icelandic schools (Grades IV-VI)
Abstract: The purpose of this project was to explore how Icelandic primary school teachers (of grades IV to VI) used curriculum materials and other instructional materials. Inquiry was made through classroom observation in twenty classrooms in twelve schools in different parts of Iceland (two weeks of observation in each classroom). Data was also collected through interviews with teachers (semi-structured interviews with 23 class teachers) and pupils (structured interviews with a sample of 120 pupils); questionnaires (random samples of 100 sixth grade teachers); and collection of documents and curriculum analysis materials. The major research questions are: How do teachers select and use curriculum materials? Which patterns of use can be identified? What is the role of the materials in the classrooms? How do different materials affect classroom procedures? Which are the major problems encountered or concerns perceived by teachers regarding curriculum materials? What are teachers' and pupils' attitudes towards the different materials used? What is the role of teachers' guides and audio-visual materials?. Tentative analysis of the data suggests that curriculum materials are the major determinants of instruction in most of the classrooms observed. 60% to 80% of instructional time is spent on direct work with published curriculum materials. The findings indicate that the pupil textbook plays a key role in the classroom proceedings. Other sources and media are only used to a limited extent. Efforts made by the Icelandic Educational Authorities to bring about curriculum change through innovative curriculum material programmes in which stress has been put on inductive learning, independent work and the use of various sources, seem to have been successful.
Source of Grant: Icelandic Institute of Education (partly)
Date of Research: 1986 – continuing
KEYWORDS: curriculum; education materials; Iceland; teaching aids

8/1532
Institute of Continuing and Professional Education,
Education Development Building,

Falmer, Brighton BN1 9RG
0273 678039
Kahn, H. Mr; *Supervisor:* Eraut, M. Prof.
The primary school and the microcomputer: case studies of an innovation in process
Abstract: The research aims to examine the background to the decision to introduce microcomputers to the primary classroom, i.e. how the decision making processes functioned. This will include examining the social and political background against which micros have reached the primary school. Factors such as the setting up of the MEP (Microelectronics Education Programme) by the DES; the Department of Industry's subsidy to schools purchasing microcomputers; the effects of falling rolls in primary schools; the prospects for employment in a world with an exceptional rate of increase of IT (Information Technology); the rapid expansion of micros in the home and the genuine educational value to the learning process, will all form part of the backcloth of the research. The research will also examine the 'foreground' of the innovation process, i.e. what in fact has taken place at LEA, school and classroom levels. It will include a close look at how the innovation reached the schools via the LEA etc, and how the case study schools coped with the challenge; what backup they received from outside support agencies. It will include a study of the inservice education provided for the teachers, its adequacy or otherwise. The actual type of use made of the micro in the schools will be examined both from the educational point of view – skill and drill, database and group use etc, and from the physical angle – located in a 'computer room' or in the classroom, free standing or Econet system etc. Teachers' perceptions concerning the effect of microcomputers on their role and the effects this has on the education of children will also be investigated. An attempt will be made to assess the influence of all these factors on the success of the work. Finally, the research aims to relate factors outlined above to the theories of innovation, and where appropriate to make recommendations both relating specifically to the introduction of microcomputers to the educational system (primary) and more generally concerning innovation theory as highlighted by the examples of the research.
Source of Grant: No funding
Date of Research: 1985 – continuing
KEYWORDS: case study; computer; educational innovation; primary school

8/1533
Institute of Continuing and Professional Education,
Education Development Building,
Falmer, Brighton BN1 9RG
0273 678039
Robinson, C.A. Ms; *Supervisor:* Yates, P. Dr
Ideological and cultural change and schooling
Abstract: This research aims to look at 'culture' as a process of transmission and isolate the factors which contribute towards the transmission of culture within the comprehensive school. It is intended to consider the relationship between ideological and cultural change. It is anticipated that the study will involve two comprehensive schools. A comparative study of the two schools will be made, with particular reference to; the organization of the school's social processes, the extent to which class culture differs and determines elements within the school's social processes and the relationship between the pupils' social class and their self concept, the stability of friendship patterns, the pupils' likely occupational aspirations, and the pupils' perception of their family setting. Findings from the research will be compared with research carried out in the 1960s-70s, in order to analyze the ideological and cultural changes.
Source of Grant: No funding
Date of Research: 1989 – continuing
KEYWORDS: comprehensive secondary school; culture; social environment; socio-cultural activities

8/1534
Institute of Manpower Studies,
Mantell Building,
Falmer, Brighton BN1 9RF
0273 686751
Seccombe, I.J. Dr; Pike, G. Mr
Manpower planning of school management staff
Abstract: The main purpose of the feasibility stage in the proposed study is to pilot and design a manpower planning system which will enable local education authorities in England and Wales to monitor trends in the supply of school management staff (heads,

deputies and department/section heads) and to forecast their recruitment needs. The study will include discussions with, and data collection in, a sample of LEAs. It will also involve the use of existing computer based manpower planning models. The study will provide an indication of the data and resources which need to be committed to work of this kind.
Source of Grant: Department of Education and Science (DES): £10,465
Date of Research: 1990-1990
KEYWORDS: administration of education; department head; deputy head; head teacher; local education authority; manpower planning; middle management; recruitment; school management

8/1535
Institute of Continuing and Professional Education,
Education Development Building,
Falmer, Brighton BN1 9RH
0273 678039
Eraut, M. Prof.; Steadman, S.D. Mr
The effectiveness of different forms of INSET
Abstract: This project will investigate the effectiveness of different forms of INSET (Inservice Education and Training of Teachers) in primary and secondary schools. It will study what combinations of training make for the most effective cumulative impact of INSET within a school or department, or for individual teachers. A second question is: in what school management contexts, particularly those planning within a staff cycle, is INSET moset effective? The study will also investigate how the true costs of INSET may be assessed. Small samples of primary and secondary schools in two contrasting local education authorities will be the focus of the work, which will use performance indicators, jointly agreed with the schools, teachers and providers.
Source of Grant: Department of Education and Science: £96,107
Date of Research: 1990 – continuing
KEYWORDS: evaluation; further education of teachers; inservice teacher education

8/1536
Institute of Continuing and Professional Education,
Education Development Building,
Falmer, Brighton BN1 9RG
0273 678039
Lewin, K. Dr
The implementation of 9-year compulsory education in North East China
Abstract: This project is concerned with the implementation of a policy of 9-year compulsory education in three areas of North East China. There will be an investigation of this from a number of different perspectives starting with the accumulation of base-line data grounded from field research. Indicators of achievement and school quality will be investigated, to see what progress is being made in different conditions and gain some insight into the circumstances which lead to full and partial implementation of the policy.
Source of Grant: United Nations International Children's Emergency Fund (UNICEF): £15,000 (US)
Date of Research: 1990 – continuing
KEYWORDS: basic education; China; compulsory education; educational policy

8/1537
Institute of Continuing and Professional Education,
Education Development Building,
Falmer, Brighton BN1 9RG
0273 678039
Towner, E. Ms
Development and evaluation of environmental education in the Seychelles
Abstract: The project will develop environmental issues in the Seychelles. Seychellois B.Ed (Bachelor of Education) students, and possibly members of the teaching team, will be involved in producing and trialling the materials for use in the Seychelles. It is hoped that the materials will be published for more widespread use.
Source of Grant: World Wide Fund for Nature: £4,000
Date of Research: 1990 – continuing
KEYWORDS: environmental study; evaluation; Seychelles

8/1538
Institute of Continuing and Professional Education,
Education Development Building,

Falmer, Brighton BN1 9RG
0273 678039
West, N. Mr
Management development opportunities for staff in primary/middle schools
Abstract: This research uses a model of skills, competences and arts to promote the development of staff. Most work has been done in relation to deputy heads and participants have written accounts of their experience. The model has been developed with heads and deputies on management development programmes.
Source of Grant: No funding
Date of Research: 1987 – continuing
KEYWORDS: inservice teacher education; staff development

8/1539
Institute of Continuing and Professional Education,
Education Development Building,
Falmer, Brighton BN1 9RG
0273 606755 ext 2521
Willson, M. Mr; *Supervisor:* Lewin, K. Dr
The effectiveness of primary science inset programmes on teaching styles and the learning process in the classroom
Abstract: The research will investigate the role of the primary science co-ordinator as change agent, particularly with respect to the introduction of the National Curriculum in Science in schools. It will evaluate the effectiveness of primary science INSET programmes in assisting co-ordinators in this role and the effect they have on children's learning in science, both in the co-ordinator and teachers classroom. The investigation will centre on twelve schools initially, and home in on 4 or 5 schools for detailed case studies at a later date. Methods used will be part questionnaire, part participant observation. The results of the studies will be made available to LEAs (local education authorities).
Source of Grant: No funding
Date of Research: 1990 – continuing
KEYWORDS: change agent; co-ordinator; inservice teacher education

8/1540
Institute of Continuing and Professional Education,
Education Development Building,
Falmer, Brighton BN1 9RG
0273 678039
Lewin, K. Dr; Caillods, F. Ms
Planning science education in developing countries
Abstract: This project is part of the five year programme planned IIEP (International Institute for Educational Planning). It is concerned with different planning aspects of science education in developing countries. In 1991 it will involve one or more detailed case studies in selected countries to explore the relative impact of different policy options, different institutional mechanisms for delivering science education, and information on the achievement of students under different conditions.
Source of Grant: UNESCO; IIEP (International Institute for Educational Planning): £20,000
Date of Research: 1990 – continuing
KEYWORDS: achievement; developing country; educational policy; planning of education; science education

8/1541
Institute of Continuing and Professional Education,
Education Development Building,
Falmer, Brighton BN1 9RG
0273 678039
Eraut, M. Prof.; Cole, G. Mr
Mapping policy options in 16-19 provision in schools
Abstract: The aims of the project are to; review what has been learned from TVEI (Technical and Vocational Education Initiative) that is relevant to the current policy debate and how TVEI might itself respond and contribute to that debate; review and further clarify different versions and interpretations of curriculum principles and common learning outcomes for 16-19 provision, their possible modes of delivery, and associated implementation problems; map out policy options for schools and sixth form colleges (and possibly tertiary colleges), drawing attention to a range of good practice. The main focus of the project will be on provision for the first two years of post-compulsory education and training in England and Wales in schools, sixth form colleges and tertiary colleges.
Source of Grant: Training Enterprise Education Division: £63,000

Date of Research: 1990 – continuing
KEYWORDS: further education; learner centred curriculum; sixteen to nineteen education

8/1542

Institute of Manpower Studies,
Mantell Building,
Falmer, Brighton BN1 9RF
0273 686751
Seccombe, I.J. Dr; Vaz, E. Miss

Manpower planning of school management staff
Abstract: This research follows a small scale IMS (Institute of Manpower Studies) feasibility study in 1990, which reviewed the use of manpower planning techniques in five local education authorities in England and Wales. The present study continues that work by developing a detailed case study of one LEA and focusing on secondary school management staff (heads, deputies and department heads). The research is making use of existing data from the authority's personnel information system to examine manpower systems; key manpower indicators (age/length of service analysis); career progression; staff turnover; replacement policies; equal opportunites issues; the use of supply and demand forecasting models. The case study will be used to illustrate a general management guide to manpower planning in education.
Source of Grant: Department of Education and Science: £20,664
Date of Research: 1990 – continuing
KEYWORDS: manpower planning; school management

8/1543

Falmer, Brighton BN1 9RH
0273 606755
Gretton, R. Mr; *Supervisor:* Ivey, G. Mr

Admissions to higher education project
Abstract: The aim of this research is to explore the use of non-traditional selection criteria when considering students for higher education. The admissions policies and selection criteria of universities, polytechnics and colleges of higher education are being explored as is the extent to which they consider non-traditional information in student applications. The Project team included representatives of Brighton Polytechnic, Sussex University and Roehampton Institute of Higher Education as well as representatives of local education authorities and the Training Enterprise Education Division. Among several aims the most important outcome will be the establishment of a model for using alternative selection criteria for admissions to higher education.
Source of Grant: Training Enterprise Education Division: £150,000
Date of Research: 1990 – continuing
KEYWORDS: admission requirements; higher education; selection criterion

8/1544

Education Development Building,
Falmer, Brighton BN1 9RH
0273 606755
West Sussex Institue of Higher Education
Bishop Otter College,
College Lane, Chichester DO1 4PE
0243 787911
Paton, R.A.E.; *Supervisor:* Dateman, T. Dr; Harvey, J. Prof.

The nature and function of musical knowledge; improvisation, strategies for musical learning
Abstract: The research aims to investigate the emotional and social functions of music and the nature of musical knowledge. Two strands of investigation are in operation, the one philosophical, the other pragmatic (applied). Various projects in music improvization are being undertaken with three sample groups: (1) children age 9-10; (2) pupils age 13-14; (3) adults. All practical sessions are being recorded and analyzed to ascertain the type of learning that results and the nature of the music produced. These results are then compared with the abstract model of musical knowledge constructed in the philosophical strand.
Source of Grant: West Sussex Institute of Higher Education: fees
Date of Research: 1986-1989
KEYWORDS: improvisation; learning strategy; music education

8/1545

Education Development Building,
Falmer, Brighton BN1 9RH
0273 606755

Crozier, G.A. Ms; *Supervisor:* Lacey, C. Prof.; Cooper, B. Dr

Teachers' interpretations and practice of multicultural education
Abstract: An ethnographic study of teachers' interpretations and practice of multicultural education in two secondary schools, in two local education authorities. Participant observation and interviews, both semi-structured and unstructured were used to gather data. The field work lasted for a period of six terms. The researcher is analyzing the practice of multicultural education, the constraints upon its development and answering the possibility of further developments. Also being taken into account is the structural and ideological influences upon the interpretation and practice of multicultural education.
Published Material: CROZIER, G.A. (1988). 'Some unintended consequences of multicultural education'. In: BANTON, L. and WALKER, S. (Eds). Power, Politics and Education. Buckingham: Open University Press.
Source of Grant: Originally funded by the Economic and Social Research Fund but grant has now expired
Date of Research: 1987 – continuing
KEYWORDS: multicultural education; secondary education; teacher role

8/1546

Department of Cognitive and Computing Sciences
Falmer, Brighton BN1 9QH
0273 606755
Noble, R.A. Mr; *Supervisor:* Du Boulay, B. Dr

An investigation into the use of exemplars by novice Prolog programmers
Abstract: This research is looking at the ways in which exemplars such as demonstrations and code examples, can be used to facilitate the learning of the Prolog computer language by novice programmers. The research will empirically investigate the knowledge of experts as a starting point for examining the development of expertise by novices. The major empirical work will concern the ways in which novices use or misuse demonstration material. If the results are appropriate, a production system will be designed to model aspects of the learning process.
Source of Grant: SERC (Science and Engineering Research Council)
Date of Research: 1989 – continuing
KEYWORDS: computer programming; computer science; electronic data processing; programming languages

8/1547

Department of Cognitive and Computing Sciences
Falmer, Brighton BN1 9RF
0273 606755
Sharples, M. Dr

The radiology tutor: computer based tuition in the interpretation of medical images
Abstract: The aim of this project is to design a computer based system that can teach the skills of medical image interpretation and visual categorization. The initial area of investigation is cardiac radiology, though the principles can be generalized. A prototype radiology tutor has been implemented on a Sun 3 workstation. It can carry out three types of task: to allow the student to browse through a database of digitized radiographic images; to form a teaching strategy that will give a sequence of exemplar images for tutoring; and to tutor about each radiographic image in a subset of English, indicating relevant features on the displayed image. The researchers have investigated a uniform method of representing knowledge about images, pathologies and the student's understanding, in the form of a multi-dimensional 'feature space'.
Published Material: SHARPLES, M. & DuBOULAY, B. (1988). 'Knowledge representation for a concept tutoring system'. In: Proceedings of European Conference on Artificial Intelligence, Munich 1988. (Munich University, Institute of Technical Information).; SHARPLES, M. (1989). 'The radiology tutor: computer based teaching of visual categorization'. In: BIERMAND., BRUKER, J. & SANDBERG, J. (Eds). Proceedings of 4th International Conference on Artificial Intelligence and Education. Amsterdam: IOS.; SHARPLES, M. (1991). 'Computer based tutoring of visual concepts: from novice to expert', Journal of Computer Assisted Learning. (forthcoming).
Source of Grant: Hunsett Trust: 1 year personal research fellowship for Dr Sharples April 1987 – April 1988 Renaissance Trust: £15,000 for equipment
Date of Research: 1987 – continuing

KEYWORDS: *artificial intelligence; computer assisted instruction; health service personnel; medical education*

8/1548

Department of Cognitive and Computing Sciences
Falmer, Brighton BN1 9RF
0273 606755
Wood, S. Dr; *Supervisor:* du Boulay, J.B.H. Dr; Pateman, T. Dr

Expert systems in teacher education: trainee teacher support system
Abstract: This project has been concerned with formalising the knowledge of experienced teachers regarding their classroom practice, as a basis for advising trainee teachers on various aspects of their own classroom practice. Underlying the approach taken in this project is a regard for the professional status of teaching expertise. The skills of the experienced teacher are considered to be a reflection of the professional knowledge of teachers regarding their knowledge and understanding of classrooms and how to teach in the classroom setting, which are acquired through study and practice. The project has been concerned with identifying the teacher's professional knowledge in use in the classroom and rendering this implicit knowledge explicit, so that it may be passed on directly to trainees in order to complement the knowledge they acquire through teaching practice. A model has been developed of classroom processes which teachers perceive, either directly or indirectly, to underlie classroom events. A prototype computer based advisory system has been implemented. This is currently being used to explore, in consultation with experienced teachers and teacher educators, the accuracy of the model in explaining classroom events and its role in advising trainee teachers on their classroom practice. Some interesting observations regarding experienced teachers' knowledge of classroom practice have been made which serve to increase our understanding of this important area.
Published Material: WOOD, S. (1986). 'Artificial Intelligence and Theories of Social Situation'. In: GILL, K.S. (Ed). Artificial Intelligence for Society. Chichester: John Wiley; WOOD, S. (1986). 'Expert systems for theoretically ill-formulated domains'. In: BRAMER, M. (Ed). Expert systems 86. Cambridge: Cambridge University Press.; WOOD, S. (1988). 'Expert systems and understanding teacher education and practice'. In: CALDERHEAD, J. (Ed). Teachers' professional learning. Lewes: Falmer Press.; WOOD, S. (1988). 'The trainee teacher support system; an expert system for advising trainee teachers on their classroom practice', Expert Systems, Vol 5, No 4, pp.282-289.; WOOD, S. (1990). 'A model of classroom processes; towards the formalisation of experienced teachers' professional knowledge'. In: GOODYEAR, P. (Ed). Teaching knowledge and intelligent tutoring. Norwood, N.J.,: Ablex Publishing Corporation. A full list of publications can be obtained on request.
Source of Grant: The Renaissance Trust: £60,000 over three years
Date of Research: 1984-1990
KEYWORDS: *artificial intelligence; guidance; information system; student teacher; teacher education; teaching practice*

8/1549

Department of Experimental Psychology
Falmer, Brighton BN1 9RF
0273 606755
Perner, J. Dr; Leakam, S. Dr

Autistic children's theory of mind
Abstract: Autistic children are contrasted with normal, Down's syndrome and language delayed children in their ability to impute mental states (beliefs, intentions, emotions) to themselves and others. The results are to decide between several alternative hypotheses about autistic children's deficiency, i.e. whether they cannot understand (1) social interaction, (2) internal states, (3) emotions, (4) representational states (in particular beliefs).
Source of Grant: No funding
Date of Research: 1988-1989
KEYWORDS: *autism; cognitive development; mental development*

8/1550

Department of Social Sciences
Falmer, Brighton BN1 9RH
0273 606755
Sheffield University
Department of Management
Sheffield S10 2TN
0742 768555
McCormick, K.J. Dr; Mccormick, B.J. Prof.

Multinationals, education and training: some education and training implications of direct inward investment
Abstract: This research examines how multinationals cope with the training problems which can arise from differences between the education and training systems of home and host countries. For example do companies change production processes? Do they invest in general education? Do they get help from local authorities or other agencies in the provision of education? Pilot studies will examine the experiences of Japanese manufacturing companies in Britain.
Source of Grant: Sheffield University Sussex University
Date of Research: 1989 – continuing
KEYWORDS: *corporate education; industrial training; study abroad*

8/1551

Department of Social Sciences
Falmer, Brighton BN1 9QN
0273 606755 ext 2435
McCormick, K.J. Dr

A comparative study of the education, training and employment of graduate engineers in Britain and Japan
Abstract: The central purpose of this project is to examine company perspectives on the education, training and continuing professional development of engineering and scientific staff in Britain and Japan. How much difference does the Japanese 'lifetime employment' pattern actually make? How much divergence or convergence is there in the way that companies encourage their technical manpower to cope with rapidly changing technologies, business environments and skill requirements? Answers to these questions are sought through interviews with managers in 15 Japanese and 9 British companies, interviews with engineering and science professors, and interviews with researchers in human resource development.
Published Material: McCORMICK, K.J. (1988). 'Vocationalism and the Japanese educational system', Comparative Education, Vol 24, No 1, Spring 1988, pp. 37-51.; McCORMICK, K.J. (1988). 'Small firms, new technology and the division of labour in Japan, New Technology, Work and Employment', Vol 3, No 2, Autumn 1988, pp. 134-142.; McCORMICK, K.J. (1988). 'Engineering education in Britain and Japan: some reflections on the use of 'best practice' models in international comparisons', Sociology, Vol 22, No 4, November 1988, pp. 583-605.
Source of Grant: University of Sussex: Unit for comparative research on industrial relations
Date of Research: 1983-1989
KEYWORDS: *comparative education; engineer; Japan; post-compulsory education; vocational education*

8/1552

Department of Social Sciences
Psychology Division, Arts Building E,
Falmer, Brighton BN1 9QN
0273 606755
Semin, G.R. Dr

The transmission and formation of AIDS related representations in adolescents
Abstract: The twofold aim of the research project is to (a) examine the formation and transformation of AIDS-related representations in the media during the period 1981-1987. This consists of an analysis of an exhaustive coverage of AIDS-related reports in 6 national dailies; (b) a longitudinal study over two points in time, with an interval of a year, on adolescents' representations of AIDS and of their risk-related practices, as well as their parents' representations of AIDS and parents' socialization practices relevant to the adolescents' risk behaviour. This is an extensive questionnaire-based study of linked interviews with adolescents and parents. The study is being replicated in France, Italy, FRG, and in all likelihood Greece, Spain and the USA.
Source of Grant: ESRC (Economic and Social Research Council): £136,980
Date of Research: 1987 – continuing
KEYWORDS: *Acquired Immune Deficiency Syndrome (AIDS); adolescent; behaviour; mass media; perception*

8/1553

Department of Social Sciences
Falmer, Brighton BN1 9QN
0273 606755 ext 2435
McCormick, K.J. Dr

Science education, independent schools and the Industrial Fund for the Advancement of Science Education in Schools (1956-1963)
Abstract: This project examines the origins, operations and impact of the Industrial Fund for the Advancement of Science Education in Schools (1956-1963). The Industrial Fund channelled 3.25m to independent and direct grant grammar schools in order to improve laboratory and apparatus provision. Underlying the Industrial Fund was a perceived need to boost the potential supply of scientific and engineering manpower for industrial research and development
Published Material: McCORMICK, K.J. (1989). 'Scientific education, girls' schools and the Industrial Fund', British Journal of Sociology of Education, Vol 10, N0 1, March, pp. 53-66.
Source of Grant: University of Sussex/Institute of Manpower Studies Joint Research Fund: £500
Date of Research: 1983-1989
KEYWORDS: *grant; independent school; school-industry relation; science education*

8/1554

> Department of Social Sciences
> Falmer, Brighton BN1 9QN
> 0273 606755 ext 2435
> McCormick, K.J. Dr

Engineers and scientists in British, American, German and Japanese industry: a survey of industrial careers and training in research and development
Abstract: The central purpose of the project is to examine industrial research and development workers' experience of education, training and continuing professional development. How much difference does the Japanese 'lifetime employment' pattern actually make? How much divergence or convergence is there in the way scientists and engineers cope with rapidly changing technologies, business environments and skill requirements? These questions are being examined through a postal questionnaire with responses from 555 respondents in six Japanese companies and 242 respondents in five British companies. Co-operating companies were drawn from the electronics and chemical fields. Respondents were graduate scientists or engineers, aged 25-45, and working in research and development.
Source of Grant: Great Britain-Sasakawa Foundation: £12,000 University of Sussex/Institute of Manpower Studies Joint Research Fund: £6,892
Date of Research: 1986-1990
KEYWORDS: *comparative education; engineer; Japan; post-compulsory education; personnel; vocational education*

8/1555

> Institute of Continuing & Professional Education
> Education Development Building,
> Falmer, Brighton BN1 9RH
> 0273 606755
> Dyhouse, C. Ms

Women and higher education
Abstract: The aim of this research is to explore sexual divisions in the history of British universities, focusing on the social, educational and occupational experiences of women teachers and students between 1870 and 1939. In the first instance the focus will be on London and the provincial universities, since more research has been done on the historical experiences of women in Oxford and Cambridge. The researchers main interest is in women's experiences in relation to the changing role of universities themselves in generating research and scholarship, in providing a 'liberal' education, and in preparing students for employment. Did female students and teachers have differing expectations in these areas?. The position of women as scholars will also be investigated and the extent to which they can be said to have made distinctive impact upon definitions of 'academic knowledge' and the 'culture of disciplines'.
Source of Grant: No funding
Date of Research: 1991 – continuing
KEYWORDS: *higher education; history of education; university; woman teacher; women's education*

8/1556

> Institute of Continuing & Professional Education
> Education Development Building,
> Falmer, Brighton BN1 9RH
> 0273 606755
> Sheridan, V. Ms; *Supervisor:* Kutnick, P. Dr

The Montessori method: links between theory and practice

Abstract: The study concentrates upon the links between theory and practice in Montessori schools based in the London area. It aims to investigate the interpretations of the Montessori approach as an educational method. Three basic areas have been identified concerning the practical aspects of a Montessori system: the materials; the social environment; and the teachers' role in class. The variety of approaches to these areas has been established by means of a questionnaire, which provided access to the views of a wide range of teachers. Analysis of the results has given a picture of the types of attitudes and interpretations prevalent among Montessori teachers today. In order to investigate further how these areas are approached in practice, and the different emphases and diversity therein, questionnaires will be followed by periods of classroom observation in a selection of schools, enriched and clarified by interviews with the teachers. The questionnaire results were analyzed using SSPSX software.
Source of Grant: No funding
Date of Research: 1987 – continuing
KEYWORDS: *early childhood education; Montessori method; pre-school education*

8/1557

> Institute of Continuing & Professional Education
> Education Development Building,
> Falmer, Brighton BN1 9RH
> 0273 606755
> Kutnick, P. Dr

Effects of preschool and type of preschool on social and academic performance in primary schools in Trinidad
Abstract: The role of pre-schools, particularly their ability to compensate for educational disadvantage, and the effectiveness of type of pre-school, has been the subject of much debate and research. Only recently, though, has information been published as to the long-term educational effects. This recent research has found that pre-school attendance has enhanced social and cognitive performance through primary schooling (although initial benefit may not be so apparent). In the current study, the effect of type of pre-school has been assessed on social and cognitive aspects of primary school performance at various stages of primary school. Data was collected in Trinidad. This research in a developing country will be compared to current 'developed' country results, and fed back into the Trinidadian system, which places great reliance on the role of pre-schools.
Source of Grant: Leverhulme Trust: £3,800
Date of Research: 1988 – continuing
KEYWORDS: *cognitive development; comparative education; developing country; pre-school education; Trinidad and Tobago*

8/1558

> Institute of Continuing & Professional Education
> Centre for International Education,
> Education Development Building,
> Falmer, Brighton BN1 9RH
> 0273 606755
> Lewin, K. Dr

Policy analysis and science and technology educational planning
Abstract: This research will explore different aspects of the planning of science and technology education in ways that contribute to national development. The research explores connections between different development strategies and science and technology policy as they impinge on education systems. It has produced a review of different planning approaches to accommodate the changes which are taking place as a result of the introduction of new technology. The work has also involved assistance with establishing a policy analysis and research division in the National Institute of Education in Sri Lanka. A study of some aspects of science education development in China has been completed and it is planned to develop several related studies.
Published Material: LEWIN, K., JONES, R. (1985). Out of school learning in science and technology in Commonwealth countries, London: Commonwealth Secretariat.; LEWIN, K. (1987). Research and policy analysis in the National Institute of Education, Sri Lanka, Phase 1. Technical Report. Paris: UNDP/UNESCO.; LEWIN, K. & LITTLE, A. (1987). Science education and teacher training, China Research Report No 4. Falmer: University of Sussex, Institute of Development Studies.; LEWIN, K. (1987). 'Science education in China: transformation and change in the 1980s', Comparative Education Review, Vol 32, No 2.; LEWIN, K. (1988). Policy analysis and educational development research, National Institute of Education, Colombo, Sri Lanka, Phase 2.

Technical Report Paris: UNDP/UNESCO.; LEWIN, K. (1989).
'Educational planning for scientific and technological development'.
In: International Encyclopaedia of Education. Oxford: Pergamon
Press. (In press).; LEWIN, K. (1989). A preliminary agenda for
research on science and technology education. Paris: IIEP,
UNESCO.
Source of Grant: No funding
Date of Research: 1985 – continuing
KEYWORDS: *development policy; educational policy; planning
of education; science education; Sri Lanka*

8/1559

    Institute of Continuing & Professional Education
    Education Development Building,
    Falmer, Brighton BN1 9RH
    0273 606755
    Eraut, M. Prof.; Cole, G. Dr
National Business Education Teacher Development Network
Abstract: The purpose of this project is to provide evaluation and
consultancy support to the activities of the National Education
Studies Teacher Development Network. The main aims of the evaluation are: (1) to provide periodic feedback to the Network on its
progress towards achieving its objectives, together with some analysis of problems encountered; (2) to investigate particular strategies, issues or concerns identified as important for the Network;
(3) to provide a summative evaluation of the network's achievement and impact over the three-year period of funding, with special attention to the Network concept itself as a novel innovation
strategy of potential relevance for future Training Enterprise Education Division initiatives. The five main foci for evaluation are:
networks; change strategies; needs assessment; local evaluation; and
materials evaluation.
Source of Grant: The Training Enterprise Education Division:
£75,000 jointly with the Business Education Handbook Project
Date of Research: 1988-1990
KEYWORDS: *business education; teacher education*

8/1560

    Institute of Continuing & Professional Education
    Centre for International Education,
    Education Development Building,
    Falmer, Brighton BN1 9RH
    0273 606755
    Lewin, K. Dr
Educational planning in response to austerity
Abstract: The purpose of the research has been to explore the nature
and extent of the financial crisis which has affected many developing
countries and resulted in reductions in expenditure on education
systems. This has been a particular problem in sub-Saharan Africa
and in some Asian and Latin America countries. The work has
involved considerable secondary analysis of data internationally
and the development of models and planning techniques to assist
systems to adjust to new conditions. A major feature of the development of this work is to examine the problems and possibilities of
using various kinds of cost recovery schemes to assist in the financing of education systems.
Published Material: LEWIN, K., COLCLOUGH, C.L. & OXEN-
HAM, J.C.P. (1985). 'Donor agency support for primary education', International Journal of Educational Development, Vol 3,
No 1.; LEWIN, K. (1986). 'Educational finance in recession', Lead
paper for special issue, Prospects, Vol 16, No 2.; LEWIN, K.
(1987). Education in austerity: options for planners. Monograph,
Fundamentals of Educational Planning Series. Paris: UNESCO:
IIEP.; LEWIN, K. (1988). 'The organizational response to par-
simony', Compare, Vol 18, No 1, April.; LEWIN, K. (1988). 'Perspectives on planning; new initiatives for the nineties', Educational
Review, Vol 40, No 2, July.; LEWIN, K. & BERTSTECHER, D.
(1989). 'The cost of recovery: are user fees the answer?' IDS Bulletin, Vol 20, No 1, January.; LEWIN, K. (1989). Recovering costs:
panacea or pathology? International Advisory Group on Education and the Impact of the Recession. Paris: UNESCO (March).
Source of Grant: UNESCO: International Institute for Educational
Planning
Date of Research: 1986-1990
KEYWORDS: *developing country; financial resources; planning
of education; poverty; system of education*

8/1561

    Institute of Continuing & Professional Education
    Education Development Building,

Falmer, Brighton BN1 9RH
0273 606755
Burke, J. Dr
National Vocational Qualifications (NVQs) and institutional change
Abstract: The aims and objectives of this research are: (1) to advise
NCVQ how it might further raise awareness of the model of NVQs,
and the impact the introductions of NVQs will have on education
and training; (2) to look at the institutional and attitudinal changes
which will be required in further and higher education establishments; (3) to examine methods of promoting training within indus-
tries and organizations which have little tradition of training.
Published Material: BURKE, J. (Ed). (1989). Competency based
learning. London: Falmer Press.; BURKE, J. (1989). 'Attitudinal
change in FE in response to the introduction of NVQs'. In: BURKE,
J. (Ed). Competency based education and training. London: Falmer
Press.; BURKE, J. (1990). NVQs – the challenge of the 90s.
London: Falmer Press. (forthcoming).; BURKE, J. (1989).
'Research in competency-based education and training', Compe-
tence and Assessment, Vol 8, pp.12-13.; BURKE, J. (1991). Struc-
tural impediments to the introduction of NVQs in Further
Education. An NCVQ Research and Development Report. (forth-
coming).
Source of Grant: NCVQ (National Council for Vocational Qualifi-
cations): £22,061
Date of Research: 1988-1990
KEYWORDS: *further education; higher education; qualification;
vocational education*

8/1562

    Institute of Continuing & Professional Education
    Education Development Building,
    Falmer, Brighton BN1 9RH
    0273 606755
    Lacey, C. Prof.
Andhra Pradesh primary education project
Abstract: The project aims to improve the quality of primary education by implementing a child centred approach to learning in all
primary schools. This approach is based on six principles: activity
based learning, practical work, group work, recognition of
individual differences, use of the local environment, display of
learners' and teachers' work. It has involved a massive training
programme and building of new primary schools. The next phase
of the project (main phase) will involve applying the lessons learnt
in the pilot study to the whole Andhra Pradesh system. The budget
for the next five years is £33,000,000. Colin Lacey's role in the pilot
stage has been to evaluate the project and eventually write a project
evaluation report. The success of this first phase has enabled the
main phase to go ahead.
Source of Grant: Overseas Development Administration: £10,000
per year for 5 years British Council: £2,000
Date of Research: 1986-1990
KEYWORDS: *evaluation; India; primary education*

8/1563

    Institute of Continuing & Professional Education
    Education Development Building,
    Falmer, Brighton BN1 9RH
    0273 606755
    Kutnick, P. Dr
Children's perception of their teacher
Abstract: A large scale study has been undertaken in which 2000
children have been asked to write an essay on a 'good teacher'.
Data is currently being analyzed with regard to development of children (aged 8-18), relation to achievement in school, and stratification issues. The study is based upon/replicates previous research
on perception of teachers, but does so in a large-scale and representative mannner, and based in a developing country. It continues
and extends previous research by the author which has been published in article and book form.
Source of Grant: No funding
Date of Research: 1988 – continuing
KEYWORDS: *pupil attitude; teacher-pupil relation; teaching
quality*

8/1564

    Institute of Continuing & Professional Education
    Education Development Building,
    Falmer, Brighton BN1 9RH
    0273 606755
    Kutnick, P. Dr

Effects of collaborative and cooperative groups in promoting science and cognitive development in schools

Abstract: Based on two approaches from psychological and educational literature, methods and uses of co-operation in the classroom have been explored: from the co-operative learning literature the effects of size and structure of pupil groupings on learning, and from recent research in cognitive development, the use of dyadic pairings to enhance thought. Both approaches provide greater understanding of the social dynamics of classroom learning.

Published Material: KUTNICK, P. (1982). 'The development of co-operation: explorations in cognitive and moral competence and social authority', British Journal of Educational Psychology, Vol 52, pp.361-365.; KUTNICK, P. (1988). Relationships in the primary school classroom, London: Chapman.; KUTNICK, P. (1988). 'A social critique of cognitively based science curricula'. In: ADEY, P. (Ed). Adolescent development and school science. London: Falmer Press; KUTNICK, P. The role of co-operation in enhancing cognitive development in the classroom. Paper given at the British Educational Research Association conference, Norwich.
Source of Grant: No funding
Date of Research: 1988 – continuing
KEYWORDS: cognitive development; co-operation; group work; learning strategy; primary education

8/1565

Institute of Continuing & Professional Education
Education Development Building,
Falmer, Brighton BN1 9RH
0273 606755
Becher, R.A. Prof.

Research organization and graduate education: British component of a five-country study

Abstract: The study forms the British component of an extensive cross-national enquiry into the relationship between research organizations and the education of advanced students, carried out simultaneously in Britain, France, West Germany, Japan and the USA. The exercise involves a general portrayal of each national system of post-graduate provision, together with a more detailed focus on three contrasting disciplinary areas: economics, history and physics. Postgraduate training and research in professional fields such as medicine, engineering and education will be taken into account but will not form a central part of the investigation. The prime concern is to identify the ways in which the demands of research and scholarship interact with those of advanced education and training, and how both are linked to the availability of material and human resources.

Source of Grant: Spencer Foundation, through University of California: £15,500
Date of Research: 1987-1989
KEYWORDS: comparative research; cross-national research; organization of research; post-graduate study

8/1566

Institute of Continuing & Professional Education
Education Development Building,
Falmer, Brighton BN1 9RH
0273 606755
Kutnick, P. Dr

Demographic, biographic and process influences on school achievement in developing countries

Abstract: Information from various educational studies in Trinidad and Tobago (undertaken by the author and colleagues) have been analyzed to show stratification by parental occupation, gender and type of school attended. Initial focus in these studies has been within the science curriculum, and found that girls generally perform better in the classroom at all levels of schooling. Other stratified results were found as well. Resulting from the initial study, comprehensive data for all curriculum areas has been analyzed: type of school attended (whether managed by government, church, privately), gender, location of school, etc. Preliminary results attest to stratification in post-colonial schools and critically appraise government concerns to extend quantity and quality of education in a developing country.

Published Material: KUTNICK, P. (1988). 'Antecedents affecting science achievement scores in classrooms in Trinidad and Tobago', International Journal of Educational Development, No 8.
Source of Grant: No funding
Date of Research: 1988 – continuing
KEYWORDS: achievement; developing country; science education; Trinidad and Tobago

8/1567

Institute of Continuing & Professional Education
Education Development Building,
Falmer, Brighton BN1 9RH
0273 606755
Kutnick, P. Dr

Moral education in primary schools

Abstract: Previous work on moral education has included theoretical explanations for the development of morals in young children, programmes to enhance moral behaviour, and surveys of teachers' attitudes to moral education in the primary school. Present research is working towards an understanding and implementation of a moral education curriculum through natural and (teacher) structured interactions with children in the classroom.

Published Material: KUTNICK, P. (1982). 'The development of cooperation: explorations in cognitive and moral competence and social authority', British Journal of Educational Psychology, Vol 52, pp.361-365.; KUTNICK. P. (1982). 'Moral incursions into constraint'. In: WEINREICH-HASTE, H. & LOCKE, D. (Eds). The making of morality. Chichester: Wiley.; KUTNICK, P. (1986). 'The relationship of moral judgement and moral action: Kohlberg's theory, criticisms and revision'. In: MODGIL, S. & MODGIL, C. (Eds). Kohlberg: consensus and controversy. London: Falmer Press.; KUTNICK, P. (1988). 'I'll teach you: primary school teachers' attitudes to and use of moral education in the curriculum', Journal of Moral Education, Vol 17, pp.40-51.
Source of Grant: No funding
Date of Research: 1988 – continuing
KEYWORDS: moral education; primary education

8/1568

Institute of Continuing & Professional Education
Education Development Building,
Falmer, Brighton BN1 9RH
0273 606755
Cooper, B. Dr

Ethnography, education and policy

Abstract: This project follows a group of thirteen mathematics students on a school-based PGCE (Post-Graduate Certificate in Education) course during the academic year 1988-89. The group has a very varied membership. Some are maths graduates, some are not. Some of the former have had a positive experience as maths undergraduates, some have not. Some of the students have previously worked in industry and commerce, some have not. The students also received their own experience of school maths in distinct periods of time. They therefore have differential experience of both school organizational forms and maths curricula. All the students were interviewed at least once in the autumn term, with a second round of interviews in the spring term. There will also be some classroom observation of their teaching during the spring term. The study will, however, remain largely interview-based. The intention is to explore these students' different reactions to the current move away from textbook based teaching approaches and towards 'investigations' and 'problem solving' in secondary school maths. An attempt will be made to make sense of these differences in terms of the students' particular mix of prior experiences of maths, schooling, higher education and work, as well as their experience of the PGCE year.

Date of Research: 1988 – continuing
KEYWORDS: mathematics; post-graduate study; teacher education; teaching method

8/1569

Institute of Continuing & Professional Education
Education Development Building,
Falmer, Brighton BN1 9RH
0273 606755
Eraut, M. Prof.; Nash, C. Mr

Effective management of flexible learning in schools

Abstract: The aim of the project is to support the management of the introduction and development of flexible learning systems for the 14-18 age group within TVEI (Technical and Vocational Education Initiative) aims and criteria, and in the context of current educational reforms. The objectives for the year April 1989 to April 1990 are to develop and feed into the Training Enterprise Education Division's Flexible Learning Programme the following resources: (1) a set of case studies on different approaches to flexible learning, accompanied by an analysis of problems encountered during their implementation; (2) an analysis of the management knowledge and skills needed to operate an effective system of flex-

ible learning, at school level and at classroom level; (3) an analysis, based on case studies and wider consultation, of the 'management of change' issues which arise during the introduction of flexible learning systems.
Source of Grant: Training Enterprise Education Division
Date of Research: 1989-1990
KEYWORDS: *educational innovation; open learning; Technical and Vocational Education Initiative; flexible learning*

8/1570

Institute of Continuing & Professional Education
Education Development Building,
Falmer, Brighton BN1 9RH
0273 606755
Eraut, M. Prof.; Steadman, S.D. Mr; Pearce, J. Mr
Whole school development in information technology
Abstract: The place of IT (Information Technology) in the school curriculum has evolved from the single-discipline approach of computer studies to recognition of its value across the curriculum. 'IT' is recognized as a cross-curricular theme in the National Curriculum. The evolution of 'IT' in schools has reached the stage where it is important to develop whole school policies. A policy would not only state aims but also provide plans and targets for action. The main aim of this project is to develop and disseminate INSET strategies and materials of proven effectiveness in the following areas: (1) whole school policies for IT; (2) school management of IT; (3) school focused staff development in IT. A school policy for IT would cover: the curriculum; school administration, resource management; finance, and staff development. The Project team will work closely with fifteen schools − three in each of five LEAs − to assist in the development, implementation and documenting of a whole school policy. The Project will work in three overlapping phases; policy development and implementation; the production of INSET strategies and materials for developing IT; and dissemination.
Published Material: The following working papers are now available: (1) The meaning of policy − this sets out in broad terms the areas that policy for IT should cover. (2) IT in the National Curriculum − this summarizes the requirements for IT in Maths, Science, English, and Design and Technology. (3) A digest of Curriculum Matters No 15: IT from 5-16. (4) Frameworks − this offers approaches to conducting audits of the curriculum, staff skills and resources in IT. At the moment this is still in draft. (5) An analysis of IT 'profiles' of the 16 schools which are working with the Project. (6) Checklist − provides a list of ingredients that might be considered in detail when formulating an IT policy.
Source of Grant: Training Enterprise Education Division: £250,000
Date of Research: 1988 − continuing
KEYWORDS: *curriculum development; educational policy; information technology; inservice education and training of teachers*

8/1571

Institute of Continuing & Professional Education
Education Development Building,
Falmer, Brighton BN1 9RH
0273 606755
Eraut, M. Prof.; Cole, G. Dr; Wright, A. Mr; Ryba, R. Mr
Business Education Handbook
Abstract: The University of Sussex has been funded by the Training Enterprise Education Division to prepare a Handbook of Policy Options in Business Education. The Handbook includes a number of case-studies of 'good practice' in business education from selected schools in England and Wales. The Handbook is aimed primarily at headteachers, advisers and others concerned with curriculum policy development in schools, but will also be of interest to teachers, parents, business people and governors. The Handbook attempts to map out the main policy options available to schools, pointing out the implications of each in terms of timetabling, resourcing, staffing and staff development. The case-studies of 'good practice' are used to illustrate how the various combinations of business education can be managed by schools. The analysis is pursued in the context of wide-ranging curriculum changes in schools in the light of TVE Extension, the National Curriculum, GCSE and other influential movements. The Handbook provides examples to show how, in the context of the National Curriculum, business education may be delivered as a specialist option for 14-16 year olds, through supported work experience and/or mini-enterprises and through a cross-curricular approach to economic awareness. The forthcoming publication on this research is to be distributed to schools in England and Wales during October

/November 1990.
Published Material: ERAUT, M. (1990). Business education − a handbook for schools. Sheffield: Training Enterprise Education Division.
Source of Grant: Training Enterprise Education Division
Date of Research: 1989-1990
KEYWORDS: *business education; curriculum development; educational policy; enterprise education*

8/1572

Institute of Continuing & Professional Education
Education Development Building,
Falmer, Brighton BN1 9RH
0273 606755
Seychelles Polytechnic
PO Box 77, Republic of Seychelles
Pennycuick, D.B. Dr; Stuart, J. Dr; Lacey, C. Prof.; Stephens, D. Dr
Monitoring inservice and research programme (Seychelles B.Ed Project)
Abstract: The Government of the Seychelles has embarked on a programme of collaboration with the University of Sussex to establish a split Bachelor of Education degree course which is being followed by Seychelles trainee teachers to equip them to teach primarily in the Seychelles NYS (National Youth Service). This new course is to be supported by a programme of monitoring, inservice and research, which will include visits to the Seychelles by Sussex University staff. A main objective of the research is to evaluate the effect of the training programme on the quality of education in NYS. The research will be collaborative and responsive; it will focus on a range of aspects of NYS education and encompass a variety of research styles. One component of the research programme is concerned with mathematics education in the Seychelles, and fieldwork was conducted in October to December 1989 by David Pennycuick and Yasmin Coopoosamy, using multi-site case study at NYS and primary levels. The aims of this component are to provide data for further development of the mathematics element of the B.Ed course and to make suggestions to the Seychelles Ministry of Education for the improvement of the quality of mathematics education. Another area of research concerns an on-going evaluation of the Sussex part of the B.Ed programme focusing particular attention on the development of the course, student perceptions of the training programme, and related issues. This is being carried out by Janet Stuart and David Stephens. The third component of the research programme currently in progress is a study of teaching styles, teacher support and school organization at NYS by Colin Lacey and Makrookh Pardiwalla.
Published Material: PENNYCUICK, D. & COOPOOSAMY, Y. (1990). Mathematics education the Seychelles. A report for the Seychelles Ministry of Education.
Source of Grant: Overseas Development Agency: £101,000
Date of Research: 1988 − continuing
KEYWORDS: *academic degree; exchange programme; Seychelles; teacher education*

8/1573

Institute of Continuing & Professional Education
Centre for International Education,
Education Development building,
Brighton BN1 9RH
0273 606755
Lewin, K. Dr; Little, D. Dr; Hui, X.; Zheng, J.W.
The implementation of the 1985 educational reforms in China
Abstract: The research is concerned with analyzing the implementation of different aspects of the 1985 Education Reforms announced by the Central Committee of the Chinese Communist Party. The researchers are examining the progress that has been made in 3 areas within China in different aspects of the Reform. These include: universal compulsory primary schooling to grade 9; science education reform; the development of technical and vocational schools at the upper secondary level; the changes in administration and organization of higher education; and changes in assessment and examining. The research is based on the analysis of policy, empirical field work, and has a comparative dimension in so far as some links are being made on progress with the reforms with experience in other Asian countries.
Published Material: LEWIN, K., ERAUT, M. & LITTLE, A. (1987). Teaching and learning in Chinese schools: training, research and practice. China Research Report No 5. Falmer: University of Sussex, Institute of Development Studies.; LEWIN, K. (1987).

'Science education in China; transformation and change in the 1980s', Comparative Education Review, Vol 32, No 2.; LEWIN, K. (1989). China's educational reform policies in practice; evidence from the field. China Research Report No 7. Falmer: University of Sussex, Institute of Development Studies.; LEWIN, K. & HUI, X. (1989). 'Rethinking revolution: reflections on China's 1985 educational reforms', Comparative Education, Vol 25, No 1. May.; LEWIN, K. & LU, W. (1990). 'University entrance examination in China: a quiet revolution', In: BROADFOOT, P. et al (Eds) Changing educational assessment: International perspectives on youth, development and education. London: Croom Helm.
Source of Grant: British Council: £65,000
Date of Research: 1988 – continuing
KEYWORDS: China; educational policy; reform of education

8/1574

Institute of Continuing & Professional Education
Education Development Building,
Falmer, Brighton BN1 9RH
0273 606755
Brunel University
Department of Government
Uxbridge, Middlesex UB8 9PH
0895 56461
Becher, R.A. Prof.; Kogan, M. Prof.
A synoptic model of higher education
Abstract: This research aims to extend and bring up to date a study conducted by Tony Becher and Maurice Kogan during the late 1970s (and reported in Process and Structure in Higher Education, Heinemann 1980). Over the last decade major changes have taken place in the structure of higher education and in the interconnection between its main components. The exploratory model earlier put forward to help clarify the workings of the enterprise will be revised in the light of recent developments, comments from other scholars, and subsequent research done by the principal investigators. Particular attention will be given to the changing relationships of higher education to the wider social and political context.
Source of Grant: Economic and Social Research Council: £8,995
Date of Research: 1988-1990
KEYWORDS: higher education; structural analysis

8/1575

Institute of Continuing & Professional Education
Education Development Building,
Falmer, Brighton BN1 9RH
0273 606755
Lewis, M. Ms
Developing writing in the primary school
Abstract: This is a curriculum development project aimed at establishing and evaluating recently developed theory concerning children's development and progress as writers. The project involves the participating teachers in action research and the teacher-as-researcher activities, thus adding a staff development dimension to the project.
Source of Grant: No funding
Date of Research: 1988 – continuing
KEYWORDS: curriculum development; primary education; writing

8/1576

Institute of Continuing & Professional Education
Falmer, Brighton BN1 9RH
0273 606755
Lorac, C. Ms; Quinn, G. Mr
Televisual literacy: adult education in a new era
Abstract: The project's aim was to understand the nature of audio-visual language and its various uses, as a contribution to teaching and training in this field. A range of practical training courses in video production was set up, and used as a basis for research into teaching approaches and media literacy. The courses were experimental workshops in video production, which trained and encouraged students to explore creatively the potential of audio-visual language to make video poetry, video-essays, video reports, notebooks, diaries, letters. The project was innovative in developing a formal understanding of pictorial structure and meaning and their role in audio-visual communication. The workshop courses produced impressive video materials. The study packs demonstrate how theory and practice in media may be approached as a unified study combining criticism with composition. As public access to video increases, and as television output increases through cable and satellite networks, there is a growing need to develop a more

critical understanding of audio-visual media: this project was seen as establishing a basis for such development. A project report is in preparation. It will make use of visual 'quotations', and will include a graded sequence of teaching material. The report also develops the theory of an audio-visual language, and argues for the value of an education in televisual literacy which equips people to produce as well as to view communications in recorded sound and images.
Published Material: Study packs on video with accompanying printed materials: 'Translating dramatic text and theatrical form into television presentation' (in collaboration with TVS). (forthcoming).; Looking at visual form and meaning – and understanding the visual arts in media (in collaboration with South East Arts).(forthcoming); Video poetry: explorations of poetic forms of video and television languages based in the arts (in collaboration with Channel 4) (forthcoming).
Source of Grant: Department of Education and Science
Date of Research: 1987-1989
KEYWORDS: adult education; audio-visual education; video recording

8/1577

Institute of Continuing & Professional Education
Education Development Building,
Falmer, Brighton BN1 9RH
0273 606755
Yates, P. Dr
Ethnography of religious communities
Abstract: The essential links between the religious life and the life of the community have become tenuous with the growing privatization and marginalization of religion. This significantly contributes to the cognitive distance between pupils and the study of religion. The aim is to construct ethnographic accounts of the religious/communal life of some of the major faith communities as basic data for an anthropological approach to Religious Studies.
Source of Grant: Nuffield Trust: £1,860
Date of Research: 1989 – continuing
KEYWORDS: community development; ethnography; religion; religious education

8/1578

Institute of Continuing & Professional Education
Education Development Building,
Falmer, Brighton BN1 9RH
0273 606755 ext 3584
Lacey, C. Prof.; Williams, R. Mr
Education Network for Education and Development Project
Abstract: The Education Network for Education and Development Project based at the University of Sussex was established to infuse a sense of urgency and confidence amongst people and institutions who are involved in the education of future generations. It seeks to do this by promoting a critical understanding of some of the major issues and concerns of the world in which we live. The project has two main purposes: to build a network for collating information and analyzing global change in the context of environmental and developmental systems and processes; and to change the provision of education so that it takes account of the importance of environment and development issues and implements through curricular programmes appropriate knowledge, skills and values. Education, through its formal and non-formal arrangements for teaching and learning, uses a range of media and organizations to dispense knowledge and establish values. Through these means it assists and governs our understanding of the world and helps to formulate out attitudes towards it. The ENED Project is an attempt to engage with persons, agencies and organizations that examine and analyze the present state of the world; in particular, its ecological well-being and its processes of global development. As part of this engagement, the project aims to harness the expertise, energy, understanding and vision of those who broadly share its aims and purposes. The process for achieving its objectives is the stimulation of continuous and public debate, wherein new and creative ideas and critical thinking are brought to bear upon the impact of those systems and forces which shape the human predicament. Through a programme of research, through a series of seminars, and through the publication of a newsletter, occasional papers and books, the project intends to introduce into the debate forms of knowledge and radical perspectives as the means to renew educational approaches to global problems.
Published Material: LACEY, C. & WILLIAMS, R. (Eds). (1987). Education, ecology and development: the case for an education

network. London: Kogan Page/World Wildlife Fund.; LACEY, C. (Ed). (1987). British charities and education. ENP Occasional Paper No 1.; LACEY, C. (1989). The world bank and the environment. ENP Occasional Paper No 2.; ABRAHAM, J., LACEY, C. & WILLIAMS, R. (Eds) (1990). Deception, demonstration and debate. London: Kogan Page/World Wildlife Fund.; BOARDMAN, J. (1990). Soil erosion in Britain. ENED Social Audit Papers, No 1.
Source of Grant: World Wide Fund for Nature: £66,175 then £65,000 per year for 3 years
Date of Research: 1987 – continuing
KEYWORDS: development policy; ecology; educational policy; environmental study; global approach; value system

8/1579

Institute of Continuing & Professional Education
Education Development Building,
Falmer, Brighton BN1 9RH
0273 606755
Lewis, M. Ms
Apprenticeship approaches to the teaching of reading
Abstract: This is a curriculum development project aimed at supporting and developing the teaching of reading. The project involves the participating teachers in action research and the teacher as-researcher activities, thus adding a staff development dimension.
Source of Grant: No funding
Date of Research: 1988 – continuing
KEYWORDS: curriculum development; language teaching; reading

8/1580

Institute of Continuing & Professional Education
Education Development Building,
Falmer, Brighton BN1 9RH
0273 606755
Miller, C. Dr
Facilitator training of youth workers in evaluation
Abstract: Arising from the ILEA (Inner London Education Authority) Youth Service Evaluation Project completed in 1986 with the publication of Miller (et al) 1986, work is continuing with the associated ILEA Inspector on evaluation and the development of methods which professionals can use to evaluate their own work. A second handbook will be produced for youth workers who will act as facilitators to train other youth service personnel in evaluation techniques.
Published Material: MILLER, C., SEXTON, T. & KELLY, D. (1986). The youth workers' evaluation handbook. London: ILEA.
Source of Grant: No funding
Date of Research: 1986 – continuing
KEYWORDS: self-evaluation; training; youth service

8/1581

Institute of Continuing & Professional Education
Education Development Building,
Falmer, Brighton BN1 9RH
0273 606755
Relf, S.J. Mr; *Supervisor:* Pennycuick, D. Dr
Primary/secondary continuity in mathematics education
Abstract: The aim is to discover those factors which make primary/secondary transfer a success (where it is successful) and those which militate against successful transfer (where it is not successful). Dimensions considered include perceptions of the nature of mathematics, teaching styles, classroom organization, usage of published schemes, methods of assessment and recording, and teacher attitudes and self-image. The approach is largely through case study with the additional use of attitude scaling techniques.
Source of Grant: No funding
Date of Research: 1988 – continuing
KEYWORDS: continuity; mathematics; primary education; secondary education; transfer

8/1582

Institute of Continuing & Professional Education
Education Development Building,
Falmer, Brighton BN1 9RH
0273 606755
Cant, S.J. Ms; Longman, D. Mr
Computer based music tools in the infant classroom
Abstract: This project was set up to explore the potential of the microcomputer as a musical resource in the infant classroom by developing computer based materials to extend the music curriculum. Creative music-making with infant age children can be inhibited by their lack of skill with the normal range of classroom instruments. This tends to limit the possibilities of music making for largely non-musical reasons. The researchers are in the process of developing structured computer materials enabling even the youngest children to be musically creative whilst reflecting on musical ideas such as high and low, loud and soft, fast and slow, etc, which are the basis of music education at this stage.
Published Material: CANT, S. & LONGMAN, D. (1986). 'Musical micros', Child Education, Vol 6, No 9, September, pp.26-27.
Source of Grant: Calouste Gulbenkian Foundation: £1,600
Date of Research: 1985 – continuing
KEYWORDS: computer; music education; primary education; program

8/1583

Institute of Continuing & Professional Education
Education Development Building,
Falmer, Brighton BN1 9RH
0273 606755
Gray, F. Dr; Jerrome, D. Dr; Ryle, M. Mr
Access provision in the south east region
Abstract: The major aim of the project is to examine and promote Access course provision in the south east region. (Access courses help people without orthodox educational qualifications to gain access to higher education). The project operates within what is best described as an action research mode. In reviewing and assessing Access course provision within both further and higher education it has addressed issues such as the range of management, administrative and curricular structures, and the degree of intra and inter-institutional co-operation and competition around Access. Subsidiary research themes include an examination of government policy over the entry of non-traditional mature students to higher education; funding mechanisms; and student profiles, needs and demands. Distinct although related dimensions of the project are to develop appropriate structures and relationships both within the University of Sussex and with other institutions regionally.
Source of Grant: Sussex University Development Fund: £28,000
Date of Research: 1989 – continuing
KEYWORDS: mature student; nontraditional education

TACADE

8/1584

3rd Floor, Furness House, Trafford Road, Salford M5 2XJ
061 848 0351
Schickler, P. Ms
Co-ordination of alcohol education – resources and training
Abstract: Over the last 20 years there has been an increased need and demand for alcohol education. This has been matched by the spread and development of organizations, resources, research and information concerned with alcohol and alcohol education. Thus there seems to have arisen a need for co-ordination of what is available and what is being produced, both to avoid duplication and to provide the professionals or young people with up-to-date information on what is available in the field of alcohol and drug education. The project has been running for 2 years and has contacted many agencies who undertake alcohol education. It now has information on database and on file, about 369 agencies which work in alcohol education, over 900 addresses and contacts in the field, over 440 alcohol education resources, and 475 training courses which have been run or will be run in the future. This information will be updated and disseminated in 1990. Four manuals will be produced with all the information and will be available from January 1990. These will be: (1) all addresses and contacts in alcohol education; (2) details of agencies involved in alcohol education; (3) alcohol education resources and (4) training in alcohol education.
Source of Grant: No funding
Date of Research: 1983 – continuing
KEYWORDS: alcoholism; database; drug addiction; health education; teaching aids; training

8/1585

3rd Floor, Furness House, Trafford Road, Salford M5 2XJ
061 848 0351
Wright. L. Mrs; *Supervisor:* Lee, J.T. Mr
Alcohol education and the Youth Service

Abstract: The aim of this research is to identify the alcohol education needs of youth workers. The study will seek to identify youth workers perceptions of alcohol related problems and their needs in terms of materials, training, policy and support in order to address alcohol issues. The study will also investigate youth workers perceptions of the barriers, advantages and disadvantages of addressing the issue of alcohol in youth work settings. The study will involve consultation with youth workers across the full range of statutory and voluntary provision, including full time, part-time and voluntary workers, and in a variety of settings. Consultation will be via on-site meetings, semi-structured interviews, structured group work and self-completion questionnaire. A review of the literature on alcohol and youth work will be conducted.
Source of Grant: Alcohol Education and Research Council: £26,250
Date of Research: 1989-1990
KEYWORDS: *alcoholism; educational need; Youth Service*

8/1586

3rd floor, Furness House, Trafford Road, Salford M5 2XJ
061 848 0351
South Bank Polytechnic
103 Borough Road, London SE1 0AA
071 928 8989
Schickler, P. Ms; *Supervisor:* Lee, J. Mr; Slavin, H. Ms

Feasibility study on how best to obtain effective, efficient and ethical data concerning young peoples attitudes and behaviour

Abstract: The study will aim to develop appropriate materials or instruments for obtaining data concerning young people's drinking behaviour; their attitudes towards alcohol use and misuse; their perceptions of the causes of alcohol misuse and their remedies for solving the problem. Interactive approaches to obtaining research data and other effective reliable and ethical methods will be investigated. These will be, if possible, youth centred, high-tech and user-friendly. The outcomes of the study will be a detailed recommendation for a thorough study of young people's drinking attitudes and behaviour using the most effective method which emerges from the research; a preliminary report of findings regarding young people's drinking behaviour arising from the study; negotiated agreements from, for example youth clubs, licensed premises, football supporters clubs etc to participate in the study using the research tools available; and a potential list of collaborators in the production of suitable interactive/software computer materials.
Source of Grant: Courage Breweries: £20,000
Date of Research: 1990-1990
KEYWORDS: *alcoholism; drinking; youth attitude*

Teesside Polytechnic

8/1587

Interactive Systems Research Group,
Borough Road, Middlesborough, Cleveland TS1 3BA
0642 218121
Barker, P.G. Dr

Data base support for multi media CAL

Abstract: The multi-media approach to computer assisted learning necessitates the use of human-computer interaction environments that are capable of supporting highly parallel, mixed-mode dialogue. An environment that is able to meet these requirements is often referred to as multi-media workstation. Multi-media CAL workstations provide sophisticated interaction environments for a learner or trainee. These environments usually contain a wide range of interaction peripherals, including a light pen, a keyboard, a bar code reader, one or more concept keyboards, a digitizer, a touch screen, an image scanner, and so on. In addition to these interaction devices; the workstation might also contain a cluster of local storage peripherals. The feasibility study that is being proposed here is therefore intended to investigate the potential utility of data base technology as a support aid within a multi-media workstation environment. Both conventional and intelligent data base software resources would be examined. A major objective of the study would be to find appropriate means of simplifying both the use and control of a sophisticated workstation that is attached (as an active device) to a distributed wide area computer network system. Such a workstation would be able to act both as a means of facilitating distributed courseware authoring and as a method for the effective realization of distributed distance learning. In the latter context, it is important to realise that many of the resources used for instruction might reside at remote host installations or they may be available locally. The database support facilities embedded within the workstation will therefore need to keep track of those resources which are held locally and those which must be accessed through remote sites. Obviously, intelligence in the data base will enable the workstation to be connected to the most appropriate host — where a selection exists.
Published Material: BARKER, P.G. & YEATES, H. (1985). Introducing computer assisted learning. Hemel Hempstead: Prentice-Hall.; BARKER, P.G. (1987). Author languages for CAL. London: Macmillan Press.; BARKER, P.G. (1987). 'A practical introduction to authoring for computer assisted instruction, Part 8: Multi-media CAL', British Journal of Educational Technology, Vol 18, No 1, pp.20-36.
Source of Grant: No funding
Date of Research: 1986-1989
KEYWORDS: *computer assisted instruction; computer science; database; distance study; interaction*

8/1588

Interactive Systems Research Group,
Borough Road, Middlesborough, Cleveland TS1 3BA
0642 218121
Barker, P.G. Dr; Woodhouse, D. Dr

Application of knowledge engineering to interviewing techniques

Abstract: The specific objectives of this current research project are divided into two basic groups. Firstly an initial feasibility study (steps 1, 2, and 3 below). Secondly a development study (step 4 below). (1) To develop a formal model of the process of interviewing; (2) to establish a knowledge based computer model of the interviewing process; (3) to create a computer based model of the way in which an expert interviewer conducts an interview; (4) to develop an intelligent knowledge transfer system capable of utilizing the model derived from phase 1 to facilitate the transfer of interviewing skills from an expert to a novice.
Source of Grant: £24,000
Date of Research: 1986-1989
KEYWORDS: *computer assisted instruction; computer science; interview; knowledge; model*

8/1589

Interactive Systems Research Group,
Borough Road, Middlesborough, Cleveland TS1 3BA
0642 218121
Barker, P.G. Dr

WORM and CDROM utility within a CAL workstation environment

Abstract: Distance learning is concerned with the provision of learning facilities and resources at centres or sites that are remote from those at which these resources are produced. Distributed computer networks provide one mechanism by which distance learning may be realised. However, there are currrently many severe limitations associated with the presently available telecommunications facilities with respect to the services available for high speed transmission of large volumes of text, sound and picture material. In due course (with the advent of ISDN (Integrated Service Digital Network), these limitations are likely to be overcome. However, common access to ISDN over geographically large areas is likely to be some decades away. This feasibility study is therefore concerned with how Write-Once-Read-Many (WORM) and Compact Disc Read Only Memory (CDROM) discs might be used to help realise some of the goals of distance learning. In particular, it is intended to study how such discs might be used within a CAL workstation environment to facilitate the storage of large volumes of textual information and digitised sound and pictorial material. Some of the aspects of optical disc technology (1,2,3) that we would consider in this feasibility study would therefore be the use of: (1) pre-mastered discs (such as conventional dictionaries, reference works, enclyclopeadias, picture libraries, etc.) within CAL courseware; and (2) the use of discs created locally (containing image data, sound resources and so on). The first of these studies would involve the fabrication of a multi-media workstation to which is connected one or more CDROM units. The second study would require the workstation to be enhanced through the addition of appropriate image/sound input peripherals, suitable digitization equipment and, of course, a WORM unit. To support this work an investigation into interfaces and standards would also be necessary.
Published Material: BARKER, P.G. (1985). 'Programming a Video Disc', Microprocessing and Microprogramming, No 15, pp.263-276.; BARKER, P.G. (1986). 'Video discs in libraries', The

Electronic Library, Vol 4, No 3, pp.166-176.; BARKER, P.G. (1987). 'Video discs in education'. (forthcoming).
Source of Grant: No funding
Date of Research: 1986-1989
KEYWORDS: computer assisted instruction; computer science; distance study; videodisc

8/1590
> Department of Computing and Mathematics
> Interactive Systems Research Group,
> Middlesborough, Cleveland TS1 3BA
> 0642 221329
> Barker, P. Dr

Design guidelines for electronic books
Abstract: Electronic books based upon the use of digital optical storage (CDROM) technology are capable of providing many new and novel approaches to the problems of disseminating knowledge and information. They are particularly useful for implementing a wide variety of different types of learning and training activity. Unfortunately, few guidelines currently exist to enable authors of such books to create effective page and book structures. This work is therefore intended to investigate this problem with a view to formulating a set of design guidelines and a collection of fabrication procedures. Three basic optical storage technologies are being studied: basic CDROM; CD-I (compact disc interactive); and DVI (digital video interactive). Six different categories of electronic book are currently being studied: text books; static picture books; moving picture books; multi-media books; intelligent electronic books; and tele-conferencing books. Authoring tools to enable authors to produce these different types of electronic book are also being investigated. To date a number of books have been designed and fabricated. The groups most recent book template is called SPBAN (static picture books with audio narrations). The potential of this category of electronic book as a tool for promoting foreign language learning is currently being investigated.
Published Material: BARKER, P.G. & MANJI, K.A. (1989). 'Designing electronic books', Journal of Artificial Intelligence in Eduation, Vol 1, No 2, pp.31-42.; BARKER, P.G. (1990). 'Designing, authoring and fabricating electronic books', Proceedings of the Seventh International Conference on Technology and Education, Brussels, Belgium, 20-22 March 1990, pp.291-293; BARKER, P.G. (1990). 'Intelligent electronic books', Journal of Artificial Intelligence in Education, (forthcoming).; BARKER, P.G., GILLER, S. & MANJI, K.A. (1990). Electronic books for foreign language learning. Paper submitted to European Hypertext Conference, Paris, France, 1990, (forthcoming).
Source of Grant: Training Enterprise Education Division: £64,000
Date of Research: 1990 – continuing
KEYWORDS: computer assisted instruction; educational technology

8/1591
> Department of Information Engineering
> Middlesbrough, Cleveland TS1 3BA
> 0642 218121
> Barker, P.G. Dr

The evaluation and design of courseware authoring tools and the application of distributed computing to the problems of disseminating educational resources
Abstract: Author languages provide one solution to the problem of generating instructional programs by those who are unskilled in computer programming techniques. In this project, the work has critically analyzed the facilities that such tools provide – attaching particular importance to the support they offer for multi-media instruction. To date, the researchers have investigated IPS (Instructional Programming System), PILOT (Programmed Inquiry, Learning or Teaching) and MICROTEXT (computer language). Currently being investigated are, STAF (Science Teachers' Author Facility) and the researchers hope soon to investigate PHILVAS (Philips' Laser Vision Author System) and ALLVA (Author Language for Laser Vision Applications). Development of the researchers own multi-media authoring system (MUMEDALA) has been discontinued as a result of the recent availablity of commercial products. However, research and investigation is continuing into the development of: (1) user-friendly authoring facilities for producing teletext overlays for interactive video applications; (2) digital animation injection techniques for CAL (Computer Assisted Learning) workstations; (3) speech synthesis techniques for use in conjunction with (2); and (4) the use of computer networking for the provision of access to open learning systems.

Published Material: BARKER, P.G. & SINGH, R. (1982). 'Author languages for computer based learning', British Journal of Educational Technology, Vol 13, No 3, pp.167-196.; BARKER, P.G. & STEELE, J.W. (1983). 'A practical introduction to authoring for computer assisted instruction, Part I: IPS', British Journal of Educational Technology, Vol 14, No 1, pp.26-45.; BARKER, P.G. & SINGH, R. (1983). 'A practical introduction to authoring for computer assisted instruction, Part II: PILOT', British Journal of Educational Technology, Vol 14, No 3, pp.15-41.; BARKER, P.G. & SINGH, R. (1984). 'A practical introduction to authoring for computer assisted technology, Part III: MICROTEXT', British Journal of Educational Technology, Vol 15, No 2, pp.82-106.; BARKER, P.G. (1984). 'MUMEDALA – An approach to multi-media authoring', British Journal of Educational Technology, Vol 15, No 1, pp.4-13.; BARKER, P.G. & YEATES, H. (1985). Introducing computer assisted learning, Hemel Hempstead: Prentice-Hall.; BARKER, P.G. (1987). Author languages for CAL. London: Macmillan Press.
Source of Grant: Teesside Polytechnic British Council
Date of Research: 1981-1990
KEYWORDS: computer assisted instruction; open learning; program; teaching aids

8/1592
> Department of Information Engineering
> Division of Applied Computing and Information Technology, Borough Road, Middlesbrough,
> Cleveland TS1 3BA
> 0642 218121
> Barker, P.G. Dr

Knowledge based computer assisted learning
Abstract: In the past, most of the conventional approaches to the creation of software for computer assisted learning (CAL) have suffered from a number of significant limitations. One of the most serious of these has been the need to embed the knowledge and skills (that are to be transferred to the student) within particular and discrete items of software. Embedding instructional material within courseware itself can be a source of many difficulties. For example, it leads to a very inflexible approach to the effective utilization of instructional resources particularly with respect to the creation of software that is adaptable to the particular learning and training needs of individual students. In view of this, the research advocates that a better design principle would involve the creation of a computer resident, shared knowledge-base that acts as a central repository for all the instructional material within a given teaching domain. The knowledge base is then used to service different types of 'presentation software' that does not embed any specific domain knowledge. Such an approach to the design of courseware could cater for multiple views of knowledge, and hence, the production of effective and adaptable courseware. This research is primarily concerned with an investigation into the potential utility of knowledge-based CAL and the development of appropriate knowledge engineering techniques to support this approach to the development of courseware for use in sophisticated interactive learning systems.
Published Material: BARKER, P.G. (1986) 'Knowledge-based CAL', 137-143, In: Proceedings of the Fifth Canadian Symposium on Instructional Technology, Ottawa, Canada, 5th-7th May.; BARKER, P.G. & PROUD, A. (1987). 'A practical introduction to authoring for computer assisted instruction, Part 10: knowledge based CAL', British Journal of Educational Technology, Vol 18, No 2, pp.140-160. MAy.; BARKER, P.G. (1988). 'Knowledge engineering for CAL', Computers in Education, pp.529-535. Proceedings of the IFIP European Conference on Computers in Education, 25th-30th July, Lausanne, Switzerland, Edited by LOVES & TAGG, E.D. North Holland, Amsterdam.
Source of Grant: No funding
Date of Research: 1986-1989
KEYWORDS: computer assisted instruction; interactive learning; knowledge; software; teaching aids

Thames Polytechnic

8/1593
> Department of Primary Education
> Bexley Road, London SE9 2HP
> 081 316 8000

Harland, L.A. Ms; Taylor, P.
Reflective teaching and learning
Abstract: The project's broad aim is to have practical consequences throughout Thames Polytechnic in the improvement of teaching techniques in seminars, and the development of teaching skills which will encourage and promote independent learning among students. Methodology will include pairs of tutors working together, monitoring and evaluating seminar leadership, using an action research, collaborative model, involving observation, student interviews, and post seminar joint evaluation.
Source of Grant: Thames Polytechnic: £4,000
Date of Research: 1990 – continuing
KEYWORDS: polytechnic

8/1594
Department of Primary Education
Avery Hill Campus,
Bexley Road, Eltham,
London SE9 2PQ
081 850 0081
Draper, M. Mr
The use of video as a medium for teaching and learning
Abstract: The use of video as an educational tool is currently receiving a lot of 'press'. IV, IVIS, TVI are acronyms the informed dare not understand! The satellite broadcasting explosion might, it is surmized, be about to offer further opportunities to realise the educational 'global village'. Where are the real benefits to be found? Is there evidence that the medium (video) is being utilized effectively and efficiently? This report is the result of looking at published material about contemporary uses of video for teaching, visits to production departments and conversations with users (potential and real). There has been no attempt to re-write (nor further investigate) the field of media research. This history of media research methodology will be well understood by those in education and training, even by those with only a passing interest in uses of audio visual methods. The thrust of research of the 1945-65 era 'is this medium more effective than this (often a particular delivery device), given controlled experimental conditions' was displaced by a later period of emphasis on what is to be learned by whom under what conditions and which is therefore the most appropriate medium to use. The latter was much more empathetic with a range of concerns across the whole field of learning not least with the needs of each individual learner. Increased emphasis on the characteristics of the medium rather than the delivery device was welcomed. By this is meant the emphasis on choosing between a moving or still image for example rather than whether to use an overhead projector of slide projector. Rather, this modest investigation has sought to make contact with ongoing projects and practice in order to gauge measures of success. It has also sought to identify some practical benefits which might emerge from particular systems.
Source of Grant: No funding; 100 staff hours allowed
Date of Research: 1987-1989
KEYWORDS: further education; higher education; interactive video; teaching aids; video equipment

8/1595
Department of Primary Education
Avery Hill Campus,
Bexley Road, Eltham,
London SE9 2PQ
081 316 8000
Hart, S. Ms; *Supervisor:* Oliver, M. Dr; Dalton, T. Dr
Learning collaboratively in the primary school
Abstract: The social, cognitive and organizational benefits of encouraging collaboration between pupils have been a recurring feature of the literature over the past three decades. Yet little specific advice and/or practical training/support opportunities exist for teachers wishing to encourage collaborative methods of working in their classrooms. This may, at least in part, account for the continued predominance of individualized teaching styles identified in numerous recent observational studies of primary practice. The purpose of the project is to investigate the role in learning and the role of the teacher in creating a learning environment which fosters collaboration between pupils. These will be used as a basis for producing a set of resources to support teachers and trainee teachers wishing to explore the potential of collaborative learning methods. The research is being conducted collaboratively between lecturers representing different subject disciplines and teachers already experienced in collaborative methods of working across the whole

primary age range. Methods include classroom observation, interviews with teachers and pupils, preparation and analysis of audio tape and video tape recordings of pupils working together and teachers interacting with individuals and groups. Outcomes of the research include a resource bank of classroom materials, edited tape and video recordings and accompanying workshop activities designed to promote collaboration; and mutual support between teachers or trainee teachers who as part of their studies at college are exploring the processes of collaborative learning in particular subject areas or across the curriculum.
Published Material: HART, S. (1988). 'Why encourage children to work collaboratively?', 2 page mimeo reference listing.; HART, S. (1989). 'Collaborative learning, group work and the spaces in between', 26 page report, Thames polytechnic, School of Primary Education.
Source of Grant: Polytechnic funding
Date of Research: 1988-1989
KEYWORDS: co-operation; groupwork; learning strategy; primary education; teaching aids

8/1596
Department of Social Sciences
Wellington Street,
Woolwich, London SE18 6PF
081 854 2030
Acton, T.A. Dr; Kenrick, D.S. Dr; Douglas Home, G. Ms; *Supervisor:* Liegeois, J-P. Prof.
Education of travelling children in the U.K.
Abstract: The report will give details and analysis of the developments of education for gypsy/traveller children in all parts of the UK, and will give some comparison with other EEC countries.
Published Material: LIEGEOIS, J-P. (1987). School provision for gypsy and traveller children – synthesis report. Commission of the European Communities.; ACTON, T. & KENRICK, D.S. (1990). 'From summer voluntary schools to European community bureaucracy: The development of special provision for traveller education in the United Kingdom since 1967', European Journal of Inter-cultural Studies, Vol 1, No 3.
Source of Grant: European Economic Community; Social Commission: £1,700 approx.
Date of Research: 1989-1989
KEYWORDS: comparative research; gypsy

The Northern Ireland Council for Educational Research

8/1597
52 Malone Road, Belfast BT9 5BS
0232 661111 ext 4366
D'Arcy, J. Mr; *Supervisor:* Wilson, J. Dr
A Northern Ireland educational research and development input to EUDISED
Abstract: In February 1984 the Northern Ireland Council for Educational Research (NICER) agreed at the request of the Department of Education for Northern Ireland (DENI) to act as a national agency for collecting educational research information and submitting this information to the Council of Europe's European Documentation and Information System for Education (EUDISED). The objectives of this undertaking are as follows: to make available to the Council of Europe details on selected educational and research developments in Northern Ireland; to ensure that research and development work in Northern Ireland is properly documented in a European context; to ensure that the EUDISED information system is brought to the attention of the potential users in Northern Ireland. NICER submits details on such projects as: ongoing or recently completed research projects in education; curriculum and other planned and monitored development projects in education; recently completed doctoral theses which relate to education and other research and/or development work which, not strictly educational, nevertheless touches on education.
Published Material: Entries in the EUDISED R & D Bulletin
Source of Grant: Department of Education for Northern Ireland: £3,425
Date of Research: 1984 – continuing
KEYWORDS: educational research; EUDISED; information service; Ireland, Northern

Touche Ross Management Consultants

8/1598

Hill House, 1 Little New Street, London EC4A 3TR
071 936 3000
Department of Education and Science
Room 15/2, Elizabeth House, York Road, London SE1 7PH
071 934 0759
Fuller, P.M. Mr

Study of the feasibility and desirability of introducing local management for special schools

Abstract: The study aims to report on the feasibility and desirability of extending LMS (Local Management of Schools) to special schools. It follows requests from some LEAs (local education authorities) to the Department of Education and Science that they should be allowed to make such an extension. Four LEAs and eight special schools will be visited, and semi-structured interviews held with LEA staff, heads and governors. Experts in the field will be consulted as to the interview findings. The LEAs are selected to provide a sample of one London, one metropolitan, and two shire counties, spread around England. The school sample will cover most types of special need. Semi-structured interviews will also be conducted with health authorities connected with each LEA, and with one non-maintained special school. Recommendations will cover whether or not delegated management and/or formula funding could be applied to special schools. If formula funding is recommended, guidance and examples of possible formulae will be included.

Published Material: FULLER, P.M. (1990). 'Extending local management to special schools'. A feasibility study for the Department of Education and Science.

Source of Grant: Department of Education and Science: £40,000 plus expenses

Date of Research: 1990-1990

KEYWORDS: special school

Training Enterprise Education Division

8/1599

Evaluation and Research Branch,
Moorfoot, Sheffield S1 4PQ
0742 704863
Carroll, V.J. Ms

Evaluation of the experimental programme in high technology

Abstract: The Experimental Programme provided pump priming for 2 years to post-graduate courses, designed and developed with a view to meeting existing and future national skill shortages. The purpose of the evaluation were to ascertain whether the aims and objectives of the programme had been met; to assess how effective the programme had been; to establish the overall impact of the programme, and to assess the quantity and quality of dissemination undertaken by HEIs (Higher Education Institutions). Methods included audits, in depth interviews with relevant HEI staff and employers, surveys of graduates and current trainees, and of employers. The research found that the programme was very effective in terms of the quality of courses; the ability to attract graduates of a high calibre; the employability of its post-graduates and success in relevant employment and in meeting employers' needs. Dissemination had not been widespread, however, because of perceived competition for finding.

Published Material: CARROLL, V.J. (1990). 'Evaluation of the experimental head office programme', A Training Enterprise Education Division Report. January.

Source of Grant: Training Enterprise Education Division

Date of Research: 1989-1989

KEYWORDS: computer science; course evaluation; labour market; post-graduate study; skill shortage; technology

8/1600

Evaluation and Research Branch,
Moorfoot, Sheffield S1 4PQ
0742 704863

Tavistock Institute
Tavistock Centre, Belsize Lane, London NW3 5BA
071 435 7111
Carroll, V.J. Ms

Evaluation of Enterprise in Higher Education (EHE) Initiative

Abstract: The Enterprise in Higher Education project sought to 'encourage the development of qualities of enterprise amongst those seeking higher education qualifications'. It builds on the curriculum innovations in the 14-18 sector such as TVEI (Technical and Vocational Education Initiative) and YTS (Youth Training Scheme). It will aim to promote change in higher education. Faster, more enterprising students, develop their personal transferable skills, make them more realistic about employment opportunities, and more prepared to take responsibility in their professional and working lives. This will be achieved through facilitating change and integrating innovation within the present organizational and curriculum structure of the institution. These innovations will include student centred learning, involving employers as partners in validating syllabuses, assessing students, encouraging a sense of ownership of EHE amongst staff, and creating a programme of staff development. Two separate evaluations were carried out. In the first year (1988-89) by the Tavistock Institute and in the second year by the National Foundation for Educational Research. At the time of the first year evaluation, 11 higher education institutions across the binary divide were involved, and in the 2nd year, 26. In the first year the evaluation was based on a case study approach, and in the 2nd year a combination of case studies and questionnaire surveys of students and staff and employers involved. Both evaluations were formative rather than summative, and an interim and final report will be produced.

Source of Grant: Training Enterprise Education Division

Date of Research: 1988-1989

KEYWORDS: curriculum development; enterprise education; evaluation; higher education

Trent Polytechnic

8/1601

Department of Primary Education
Clifton Hall, Clifton Village, Nottingham NG11 8NS
0602 418248
Smith, D. Mr; *Supervisor:* Bassey, M. Dr; Johnson, J. Mr

Strategies for negotiation in the primary classroom

Abstract: The research aims to look at the nature of the language employed by teachers and children in the primary school as a vehicle for the negotiation of meaning, and particularly at the strategies implicit in the language.

Date of Research: 1987 – continuing

KEYWORDS: language, meaning; primary education

Trinity and All Saints' College

8/1602

Brownberrie Lane, Horsforth, Leeds LS18 5HD
0532 584341
Rees, M.A. Dr

The provision of special schools for gifted children

Abstract: The aim of this research is to study the schools in the UK offering separate education to children with special gifts (music, dance, drama, athletics, academic subjects) and to attempt to assess the advantages and disadvantages of this type of schooling.

Source of Grant: No funding

Date of Research: 1986 – continuing

KEYWORDS: gifted; special education

8/1603

Brownberrie Lane, Horsforth, Leeds LS18 5HD
0532 584341
Walton, J. Ms; Metcalfe, R. Dr

Curriculum resources for teaching social studies in mixed ability classrooms (3-13) years

Abstract: The project aims (1) to identify and evaluate currently available resources and approaches, and (2) to develop alternative resources and approaches to teaching Social Studies in mixed abil-

ity classrooms 3-13 years. The approach adopted involves (1) analysis and evaluation of current provision, based (a) on literature and related search, and (b) INSET (Inservice Education and Training of Teachers) and IT INSET courses, and (2) development and evaluation of alternative approaches, based (a) on INSET and IT INSET courses, and (b) complemented by trial use in schools.
Source of Grant: No funding
Date of Research: 1986 – continuing
KEYWORDS: ability grouping; primary education; social studies; teaching aid; teaching method

Trinity College

8/1604
Carmarthen, Dyfed SA31 3EP
0267 237971
Francis, L.J. Dr
Personality and religion among primary and secondary school pupils
Abstract: This project is locating religious development within the context of Eysenck's dimensional model of personality. An interrelated set of databases has been established using various different versions of the Eysenck personality indices alongside a Likert scale of attitude towards Christianity.
Published Material: PEARSON, P.R. (1989). 'The dual nature of the Eysenckian lie scales: are religious adolescents more truthful?', Personality and Individual Differences, Vol 10, pp.1,041-1,048.; FRANCIS, L.J., LANKSHEAR, D.W. & PEARSON, P.R. (1989). 'The relationship between religiosity and the short form JEPQ (JEPQ-S) indices of E, N, L and P among eleven year olds', Personality and Individual Differences, Vol 10, pp.763-769.
Source of Grant: No funding
Date of Research: 1989 – continuing
KEYWORDS: personality development; primary school; pupil; religion; secondary school

8/1605
Carmarthen, Dyfed SA31 3EP
0267 237971
Francis, L.J. Dr
Roman Catholic secondary schools and pupil attitudes towards Christianity
Abstract: This project has drawn together data from Catholic secondary schools in England, Scotland and Northern Ireland to explore the development of pupils' attitudes towards Christianity between the ages of 11 and 16 years. The project involves the completion of a twenty-four item Likert attitude scale and an exploration of the psychometric properties of this scale in the three differing cultural contexts.
Published Material: FRANCIS, L.J. (1987). 'Measuring attitudes towards Christianity among 12- to 18-year old pupils in Catholic schools', Educational Research, Vol 29, No 3, pp.230-233.; GIBSON, H.M. & FRANCIS, L.J. (1989). 'Measuring attitudes towards Christianity among 11- to 16-year old pupils in Catholic schools in Scotland', Educational Research, Vol 31, No 1, pp.65-69.; GREER, J.E. & FRANCIS, L.J. (1991). 'Measuring attitudes towards Christianity among pupils in Catholic secondary schools in Northern Ireland', Educational Research, (forthcoming).
Source of Grant: No funding
Date of Research: 1987-1990
KEYWORDS: attitude; catholic school; catholicism; christianity; denominational school; pupil; religion

8/1606
Carmarthen, Dyfed SA31 3EP
0267 237971
Francis, L.J. Dr
Small schools and pupil attitudes
Abstract: This project is re-analyzing data collected from the fourth year junior pupils attending 82% of the state maintained primary schools in a shire county, in order to explore the relationship between school size and pupil attitude towards school and towards certain key subjects, including English, maths, music, physical education and religious education. Attitudes were measured by means of semantic differential grids.
Source of Grant: No funding
Date of Research: 1989 – continuing

KEYWORDS: attitude; primary school; pupil; rural school; small school

8/1607
Carmarthen, Dyfed SA31 3EP
0267 237971
Francis, L.J. Dr
Church of England schools and village church life
Abstract: This project is re-analyzing data collected from over 7,000 Anglican churches to explore the impact of rural church schools on a range of features of rural church life. The presence of a church school is shown to augment slightly the village church's usual Sunday contact with 6- to 9-year olds and with adults. The presence of a church school is also shown to have a small positive influence on the number of infant baptisms, the number of 6- to 13-year olds in the village church choir and the number of young confirmands under the age of 14 years.
Published Material: FRANCIS, L.J. & LANKSHEAR, D.W. (1990). 'The impact of church schools on village church life', Journal of Educational Studies, Vol 16, pp.117-129.
Source of Grant: No funding
Date of Research: 1989-1990
KEYWORDS: denominational school; religion and education; religious behaviour; rural school

8/1608
Carmarthen, Dyfed SA31 3EP
0267 237971
Francis, L.J. Dr
Secondary school pupils' attitudes towards science and religion
Abstract: This project is analyzing data collected from 5,000 secondary pupils in England to explore the relationships between attitudes to science, religion, creationism and scientism. Attitudes are measured by Likert scales.
Published Material: FRANCIS, L.J., GIBSON, H.M. & FULLJAMES, P. (1990). 'Attitudes towards Christianity, creationism, scientism and interest in science', British Journal of Religious Education. (forthcoming).
Source of Grant: No funding
Date of Research: 1989 – continuing
KEYWORDS: attitude; pupil; religion; sciences; secondary school

8/1609
Carmarthen, Dyfed SA31 3EP
0269 237971
Pontyberem County Primary School
Pontyberem, Dyfed
0269 870306
Eynon, A. Mr; Evans, G. Dr; *Supervisor:* Evans, G. Dr
Planning for differentiation in the primary classroom
Abstract: This research will explore strategies for planning for differentiated work. It is intended for children in primary schools to match their abilities and needs.
Source of Grant: Curriculum Council for Wales
Date of Research: 1990 – continuing
KEYWORDS: planning

Ulster University

8/1610
Jordanstown, Newtownabbey BT37 0QB
0232 365131
Eason, G. Miss; *Supervisor:* Connolly, M. Prof.; Cromie, S. Dr
Aspirations
Abstract: The research objectives are as follows: (1) to quantify the number of women teachers at various levels in further/secondary and primary education; (2) to quantify (by means of representative sampling) the career aspirations of women teachers as compared to male teachers. There will be an assessment of what percentage of women teachers are interested in promotion; how much promotion they are interested in achieving and there will also be an analysis of the reasons underlying their aspirations. The teaching profession will be compared with a limited number of other professionals (e.g. social workers, accountants etc). These criterion groups will be compared to teachers to see how similar or different they are. A number of sample groups will be selected in the

UK. (e.g. one English, one Scottish and one Welsh) and a comparative study carried out to see if there are any significant regional differences in the Northern Ireland group. A non-professional group of men and women will be chosen to see if there are significant similarities or differences in their career aspirations as compared with teachers. An in depth study among women teachers in senior posts will be carried out. This investigation would attempt to tease out how and why they come to be in a senior post and what professional and personal difficulties they encountered on their way. It is hoped that this study would unearth a number of variables that seem important in the pursuit of promotion and would provide the basis for a set of recommendations to any 'aspiring' teacher.
Source of Grant: Stranmillis College Belfast: fees
Date of Research: 1987 – continuing
KEYWORDS: career aspiration; Ireland, Northern; sex difference; woman teacher

8/1611
Department of Education
Magee College,
Northland Road,
Londonderry BT48 7JI
0504 265621
North, R.F.J. Dr
Managing information technology policy into classroom practice
Abstract: This is an investigation into the processes by which local authority policy is translated into classroom practice. The focus of the study is on the role of the school Information Technology Co-ordinator in managing change within the school. The major purpose of the research is the production of management training materials suitable for use by local education authorities in their inservice training programmes for Information Technology Co-ordinators. The research itself follows a naturalistic mode of enquiry and is grounded in the activities taking place within eleven secondary schools and two Education and Library Boards in Northern Ireland.
Source of Grant: MESU (Microelectronics Education Support Unit): £9,500
Date of Research: 1988-1989
KEYWORDS: curriculum development; educational innovation; educational policy; information technology; inservice education and training of teachers; management

8/1612
Department of Education
Newtownabbey BT37 OQB
0232 365131
Newtonabbey College of Further Education
400 Shore Road,
Newtownabbey BT37 9RS
0232 864331
Green, D.J. Mr; *Supervisor:* Wilkinson, C. Dr
Power and effectiveness in the middle manager's role
Abstract: This present research is an extension of previous research on the effectiveness of a further education head of department. This research aims to establish the relationship between power and effectiveness in the jobs of middle managers in the public and private sectors, in particular their jobs as: man managers, administrators, professional leaders, members of senior management teams. The research methodology will include questionnaires, interviews and references to managerial research, if any, in the area of middle managerial effectiveness.
Source of Grant: Self-financing
Date of Research: 1988 – continuing
KEYWORDS: effectiveness; leadership; middle management; power; success

8/1613
Department of Education
Coleraine,
County Londonderry BT52 1SA
0265 44141
Rae, G. Dr; Austin, R. Dr
Children's ability to handle evidence
Abstract: The present study attempts to identify the factors that influence children's ability to handle evidence on both 'neutral' and controversial topics and to determine what steps might be taken to assist children in acquiring these skills. The main study will involve the administration of test material dealing with fictional incidents on two separate occasions to approximately 4500 post-

primary children throughout Northern Ireland. Supplementary studies will also be carried out in other selected schools to determine the role of other potentially important variables (e.g. teaching style, role of discussion). It is hoped that the findings will be of assistance to those engaged in the task of producing learning resources for schools.
Source of Grant: No funding
Date of Research: 1986-1989
KEYWORDS: history; intellectual development; secondary education; teaching aids

8/1614
Department of Psychology
Cromore Road,
Coleraine,
County Londonderry BT52 8SA
0265 44141
Chambers, M.G.A. Mrs; *Supervisor:* McGarvey, B. Dr
Learning psychiatric nursing skills: the contribution of the ward environment
Abstract: Much has been written about student nurse learning within the context of general nursing, for example Fretwell (1982) and Orton (1981). However, to date the research in relation to psychiatric student nurses has been limited. The aim of this study is to ascertain those factors within the ward environment which facilitate student psychiatric nurses in the learning of psychiatric nursing skills. The study is exploratory, descriptive and analytical in nature incorporating several methods of data collection including the Delphi technique, interview and participant observation. The study population consists of approximately 300 student psychiatric nurses (the total population), all tutorial staff and a sample of ward sisters/charge nurses. Data has been collected for the intitial phase of the study and is currently being analyzed. This will be ready for discussion and publication by December 1990.
Published Material: FRETWELL, J.E. (1982). Ward teaching and learning: Sister and the learning environment. London: Royal College of Nursing.; ORTON, H.D. (1981). Ward learning climate: a study of the role of the ward sister in relation to student nurse learning on the ward. London: Royal College of Nursing.
Source of Grant: No funding
Date of Research: 1987 – continuing
KEYWORDS: learning conditions; nurse education; psychiatric service

Understanding British Industry

8/1615
Rank Xerox Ltd,
Parkway,
Marlow SL7 1YL
0628 893415
Melton, L.J. Mrs; *Supervisor:* Howell, R. Mrs
Evaluation of effectiveness of the national education programmes unit's workshops and identification of future training needs
Abstract: The UBI-RX National Education Programmes Unit (formerly the UBI-Rank Xerox Partnership) provides training opportunities with an industrial perspective for senior managers in education. One major element of provision is the 'Management of Change' series of workshops for headteachers of secondary schools throughout the UK. The purpose of this research is threefold. (1) to collect and present evidence of change in practice in delegates institutions which has lead to improved teaching and learning; (2) to design and trial follow-up support for those who have attended workshops; (3) To identify future management training needs of headteachers and senior staff. The evidence is being collected by means of a postal questionnaire, personal interviews with LEA groups of head-teachers of secondary schools in Great Britain. The results will be used to develop the current practice of the unit and to contribute to the future planning of management training – development in education.
Source of Grant: Department of Education and Science: £5,000
Date of Research: 1988-1989
KEYWORDS: administration of education; head teacher; industry; management education

University College of North Wales

8/1616

Deparment of Education
Top College, Bangor, Gwynedd LL57 2DG
0248 351151
Baker, C.R. Dr

Attitudes to the Welsh language and bilingualism

Abstract: The Welsh language has rapidly declined this century. At the turn of the century, some half of the population in Wales spoke Welsh. The Census of 1981 revealed that this figure had dropped to one in five residents in Wales. Attitude to the Welsh language is an important barometer of likely future language trends in Wales. In particular, previous research has indicated that attitudes to Welsh tend to decline during the early and middle teens. The research aims to investigate the reasons for change in attitude to the Welsh language amongst 13 to 16 year olds. An attitude survey of first, second and third year secondary pupils in 1988 will be repeated with the same pupils in 1990. Change in the attitude to Welsh of some 800 pupils will be examined in terms of youth culture, use of mass media, identification models, language background of the home as well as the school and neighbourhood, type of school attended, self concept, achievement level, gender and age. In addition the research will examine attitude to bilingualism as a concept importantly different from attitude to Welsh.
Source of Grant: Economic and Social Research Council: £2,340
Date of Research: 1988 – continuing
KEYWORDS: attitude; bilingualism; Welsh

8/1617

Department of Education
Top College, Bangor, Gwynedd LL57 2DG
0248 351151
Owen, M. Mr; *Supervisor:* Williams, I.W. Prof.

Teacher development in IT (Information Technology) in science teaching

Abstract: This project aims to look for innovative strategies to encourage the use of IT (Information Technology) in science education within the context of TVEI (Technical and Vocational Educational Initiative). Particular contexts that apply to this project are the bilingual communities served by schools in the area and the fact that teachers working in rural areas are often islolated by distances from meetings and courses. To this end the current focus of the project is to develop materials to disseminate good practice based on case studies within selected pilot schools. The research emphasis will concentrate on three science departments in the first instance and by means of close involvement with the teachers elucidate their preferred strategies and motivation for acquiring new skills. The projects publication will be a mix of publication for teachers and an empirical and theoretical consideration on the nature of the experience of inservice training in information technology.
Source of Grant: Training Enterprise Education Division: £299,980
Date of Research: 1989 – continuing
KEYWORDS: bilingualism; further education teachers; information technology; inservice teacher education; rural school; science education; technical education; vocational education

8/1618

Department of Education
Top College, Bangor, Gwynedd LL57 2EP
0248 351151
Jones, M.G. Dr

Attitudes to the European dimension in education in initial teacher training and in secondary schools in North Wales

Abstract: Initially a survey will be made of attitudes to Europe of students in teacher training, teachers in post, and school pupils in North Wales. The pilot will concentrate on approximately 90 students, and one class of pupils in each school where a modern languages student is doing teaching practice (involving between 200 and 300 pupils). The staff of one or two schools (including one Welsh-meduim) would be asked to participate. A comparative element will be introduced as far as pupils are concerned. The teaching English as a second/foreign language, students do one teaching practice in Spain. Again the questionnaires will be given to approximately 200-300 pupils in Valencia. Questionnaires for students in training and teachers are very similar, focusing on the interpreta-
tion of Europe, the relevance of school subjects to Europe, the extent to which European dimension can permeate the secondary school curriculum, and the feelings of participants if asked to provide a European dimension to their teaching. Pupil questionnaires will seek to determine attitude and extent of knowledge.
Source of Grant: No funding
Date of Research: 1989-1990
KEYWORDS: attitude; Europe; pupil; secondary school; student teacher

8/1619

Department of Education
Top College, Bangor, Gwynedd LL57 2DG
0248 351151
Williams, P. Prof.

The special education handbook

Abstract: The project aims to compile a comprehensive reference source for the special education. The database used for the investigator's glossary of special education has been updated for this purpose. The new publication (the handbook) is more technical, more discursive and less descriptive, and refers the reader to appropriate source material.
Published Material: WILLIAMS, P. (1990). The special education handbook. Buckingham: Open University Press (forthcoming).
Source of Grant: Leverhulme Emeritus Fellowship: £4,000
Date of Research: 1986-1990
KEYWORDS: reference book; special education

8/1620

Department of Education
Linguistics Section, Bangor, Gwynedd LL57 2DG
0248 351151
Malele, M.L. Mr; *Supervisor:* James, C. Dr

Contrastive analysis of English, French and Kikongo interrogatives

Abstract: The aim of this work is to investigate the extent to which it is possible to predict and explain learners' errors and the relative difficulty of learning particular aspects of a construction by Contrastive Study. This work is particularly concerned with interrogative structures in English, French and Kikongo (a language spoken in Zaire). This investigation involves the description of these structures. This is done within the framework of a contemporary model of syntax: X-bar Syntax, in the version outlined in Chomsky's Remarks on Nominalization (1970) and in Radford's Transformational Grammar (1988). These interrogative structures are described in terms of the movements, ie. I-movement WH-movement and V-movement they involve. This allows us to point out similarities and differences among these languages as to how and when these movements take place. From these similarities and differences we can predict and explain certain difficulties encountered by Kikongo/French speaking students learning English interrogative structures. This work also presents the results of the investigations carried out in Zaire on this field to see if the predictions are in fact confirmed, using a variety of elicitation techniques on two levels of learners. This study is so useful that these results will be of great help to teachers of English as a second or foreign language and to material designers in the way they can improve the design and classroom techniques in the language teaching/learning process.
Source of Grant: British Council
Date of Research: 1987-1990
KEYWORDS: English (second language); language teaching; Zaire

8/1621

Department of Education
Top College, Bangor, Gwynedd LL57 1DZ
0248 51151
Ellis, T.R. Mr; *Supervisor:* Williams, I.W. Prof.

An evaluation of inservice BEd courses and the professional development of teachers

Abstract: The aim of the study was to evaluate the contribution of the Normal College's BEd. Inservice courses to the professional development of course members. Professional development was defined with reference to the Trait Theory. Consequently a number of criteria relevant to teaching were identified and an attempt was made to ascertain how and to what extent the course had contributed to their traits. Furthermore, a supplementary study was undertaken to ascertain whether factors such as teaching experience, professional status, gender and previous experience of INSET)Inservice Education and Training of Teachers) had influenced course members' responses and perceptions. Course members' views were also investigated as to the different teaching approaches adopted within the course. A three-fold approach was adopted to study the problem: (1) documentary evidence – extended essays were analyzed to ascertain how research had contributed to the 'research' criterion; (2) a questionnaire was administered to ascertain how the course had contributed to the relevant criteria; (3) a representative sample of course members were questioned by means of a semi-structured interview to extend on information received through stages (1) and (2). Results revealed that the course had succeeded in extending course members' previous perceptions with regard to teaching, had reduced bias versus theory and had enlightened innovation as well as encouraging them to read more professional literature. Research information was gathered concerning tutoring. It was ascertained that only half of course members had succeeded in perceiving an acknowledged problem to research. Teacher researchers were worried by a shortage of time and by teacher versus researcher role conflict. The course succeeded in strengthening course members' professional development as well as encouraging them to trial more progressive teaching approaches. The supplementary study revealed that the previously mentioned factors – especially professional status and the type of school taught in had influenced course members' responses. Finally, limitations of the research and its implications were discussed, recommendations were also made in further research.

Source of Grant: Normal College: tuition fees
Date of Research: 1983-1990
KEYWORDS: academic degree; evaluation; inservice education and training of teachers; teacher education

8/1622

Department of Education
Top College,
Bangor, Gwynedd LL57 1DZ
0248 51151
Yatim, A.M. Mr; Baker, C.R. Dr
Attitudes to bilingualism and bilingual education
Abstract: The research uses 5 samples of Malaysian students to test the cross cultural replicability of Gardner's instrumental and integrative motivation theory (and measurement scales). It has so far indicated by use of factor analysis that integrative and instrumental motivation in becoming bilingual are not the pivotal motives in Malaysia. Thus the universality of the dominant theory of language motivation is being called into question.
Date of Research: 1986-1989
KEYWORDS: attitude; bilingualism; motivation

8/1623

Department of Education
Top College,
Bangor, Gwynedd LL57 2DG
0248 351151
Swansea Drug Project
8 Calvert Street, Swansea SA1 6AR
Rees, W.D.C. Dr
Evaluation of Swansea drugs project
Abstract: This is an evaluation of a two-year training programme aimed at volunteer counsellors. An attempt is made to assess the aims, objectives and outcome by interview and questionnaire, of tutors and students and by appraising the content of methodology of the course.
Source of Grant: Mental Health Foundation: £2,000
Date of Research: 1988-1989
KEYWORDS: drug addiction; guidance officer; training

8/1624

Department of English & Linguistics
Linguistics Section,
Top College, Bangor, Gwynedd LL57 2DG
0248 55151
El Sakran, T.M. Mr; *Supervisor:* James, C. Dr
Footnotes in academic written discourse: a formal and functional analysis
Abstract: The aim of the study is to investigate the structures of footnotes, their different types and their utility to the reader in understanding the texts they accompany and their disruptive effect on reading comprehension.
Source of Grant: Egyptian Government Scholarship
Date of Research: 1987 – continuing
KEYWORDS: comprehension; document; linguistics; morphology

8/1625

Department of English & Linguistics
Linguistics Section,
Top College, Bangor, Gwynedd LL57 2DG
0248 351151
Scholfield, P.J. Mr; Vougiouklis, P.; Davies, D.R.
Lexical learning and communication strategies
Abstract: This project aims to explore how speakers, especially learners of English, learn vocabulary, and how they manage when they lack it. Thus it covers: learning strategies adopted to try to memorize new vocabulary; inferencing and dictionary use when reading; transfer; circumlocution, dictionary use etc. in the production process. So far a major survey of learning strategies adopted by Sudanese school children and university learners of English, analyzed with Cluster Analysis, shows three distinct profiles of use of such strategies by good learners – loosely the co-operative, bilingual and monolingual approaches. Ongoing test-based work on Greek learners of English is illuminating the differences in success in guessing the meaning of unknown words made of Greek versus Latin elements, and the relationship between objective success (i.e. correctness) and subjective success (ie. confidence). It appears so far that Greeks are likely to be overconfident on words they recognize as Greek.
Published Material: SCHOLFIELD, P. (1987). 'Communication strategies – the researcher outmanoeuvred?', Applied Linguistics, Vol 8, No 3, pp.219-232.; SCHOLFIELD, P. 'Using the English dictionary for comprehension', TESOL, (Teachers of English to Speakers of Other Languages), Quarterly 16.; SCHOLFIELD, P. (1987). 'Vocabulary problems in communication: what determines the learner's choice of strategy?', Bangor Teaching Resource Materials in Linguistics.
Source of Grant: No funding
Date of Research: 1985 – continuing
KEYWORDS: communication; English language; foreign languages; language teaching; learning strategy; vocabulary

8/1626

Department of Linguistics
School of English and Linguistics,
Top College, Bangor, Gwynedd LL57 2DG
0248 351151 ext 2264
James, C. Dr; Garrett, P. Mr
The effects of the use of the mother tongue in the preparation for writing
Abstract: The aim of this research is to identify and measure the effects of the use of the mother tongue on one aspect of bilingual pupils' performance in their second language, namely writing; to identify and measure the effects of the use of the mother tongue on pupils' motivation and attitudes; to make comparisons between two different bilingual situations within multi-cultural Britain; to identify problems with writing English that may be specific to particular groups of non-native speakers; to contribute to theories of bilingualism; cognitive functioning, affect in learning and language transfer. This is a longitudinal study involving bilingual experimental and control groups at primary school level. The introduction of the mother tongue for teaching Level 2 writing is an independent variable, potentially inducing changes in the dependent variables of attitudes and Level 2 English writing competence.
Source of Grant: ESRC (Economic and Social Research Council): £29,250
Date of Research: 1989-1990
KEYWORDS: assessment; attitude; bilingualism; first foreign language; mother tongue; pupil; writing

8/1627

Department of Physical Education
Bangor LL57 1DZ
0248 351151
Erskine, J. Mr; Edge, A. Mr; Hooper, D. Dr; Fazey, D.M.A. Mrs; *Supervisor:* Fazey, J. Dr; Hardy, L. Dr.
A schema model for motor learning
Abstract: The aim of the project is to investigate the predictions of Fazey's (1985) reformation of a schema model for the initiation, guidance and development of skilful human motor behaviour. These predictions are mainly concerned with: (1) the effects of variability of practice conditions on transfer; (2) the efficient development of a recognition capacity for detecting and correcting errors by invoking control strategies appropriate for the current level of expertise; (3) the development of recognition capacity (of Jagacinsky, Miller and Burke, 1979) for prediction and pre-selection

of parameter settings appropriate to specific situations. Recent work has also suggested that several of the 'Laws of KR (Knowledge of Results)' may not in fact be correct (Lee and Magill, 1983; Hardy and Ringland, 1984; Hardy, 1985). Using a transfer paradigm, it is proposed to investigate further the interference in learning which seems to occur as a result of certain KR manipulations (Hardy, 1985). In particular, the following predictions of Fazey's (1985) model will be tested: (1) error-labelling is not necessary if the movement is 'good'; (2) error-labelling occurs only when a movement is 'bad'; (3) a labelled error is needed (KR) when the subject is unsure about outcomes, or detects an error; (4) a signalled error is necessary when the subject is confident, but 'wrong'. The project should have important applications in relation to the acquisition of general movement skills, sports skills and industrial workforce flexibility.
Published Material: HARDY, L. & RINGLAND, A. (1984). 'Mental rehearsal and the Inner Game', Human Learning, Vol 3, pp.203-7.
Source of Grant: Northern Ireland Education Board research studentship: £7,800 National Coaching Foundation: £3,000
Date of Research: 1982-1989
KEYWORDS: *motor development; teaching aids; teaching method*

8/1628
Department of Psychology
Top College, Bangor, Gwynedd LL57 2DG
0248 351151
Miles, T.R. Prof.
Dyslexia and mathematics
Abstract: It is hypothesised that the mathematical difficulties of dyslexics are a consequence of the same anomaly of development which affects their literary skills. It has been shown (Pritchard et al. 1989) that 15 dyslexic boys aged 12 to 14 had fewer 'number facts' available than a suitably matched control. Work is now in progress on the time needed by dyslexics and matched control to carry out different types of mathematical operations. Data on the mathematical performance of over 12,000 10 year olds (clinical health and education study), including some dyslexics, are in the process of being analyzed.
Published Material: MILES, T.R. (1989). 'Dyslexia and mathematics', Ace Reports, No 16, pp.16-20.; PRITCHARD, P.A., MILES, T.R., CHINN, S.J. & TAGGART, A.T. (1989). 'Dyslexia and knowledge of number facts', Links, Vol 14, No 3, pp. 17-20.
Source of Grant: No funding
Date of Research: 1988 – continuing
KEYWORDS: *dyslexia; learning difficulty; mathematics*

University College of Swansea

8/1629
Centre for Applied Linguistic Studies,
Singleton Park, Swansea SA2 8PP
0792 205678
Meara, P. Dr
Lexical behaviour in a second language
Abstract: This project is actually a group of linked studies aimed at improving our understanding of vocabulary acquisition in a second language. The project comprises: (a) a large scale bibliographical study; (b) studies of the effects of first language orthography on word handling skills in a second language; (c) lexical avoidance; (d) lexical errors.
Published Material: A list of publications is available from the researcher
Source of Grant: Eurocentres: £6,600 Oxford Examinations Delegacy: £6,600 Longman Group: £3,000
Date of Research: 1981 – continuing
KEYWORDS: *language skill; modern languages; second language; vocabulary*

8/1630
Singleton Park, Swansea SA2 8PP
0792 205678
Stray, C.A. Mr; *Supervisor:* Parker, A.J. Mr; Shannon, R. Prof.
The redefinition of classical education in England and Wales 1870-1930
Abstract: The object of the research is to provide a historical sociol-ogy of classical education and scholarship in England within the specified period. It will attempt to relate the content, structure and institutional form of the teaching and learning of Classics to major features of contemporary culture and society: for example, class, the division of labour and state intervention. Primary source material has been collected from libraries and archives in universities and public schools, as well as from papers held in private hands. Most of this relates to secondary schooling, but the professionalization of classical scholarship is also a subject for analysis. The primary empirical focus is on the debates on curriculum which followed the passage of the 1902 Education Act. In particular, subject groupings (Classical Association, Association for Reform of Latin Teaching) are investigated and their relationship with the Board of Education explored.
Published Material: STRAY, C.A. (1985). 'From monopoly to marginality: Classics in English education since 1800'. In: GOODSON, I. (Ed). Social histories of the secondary curriculum. London: Falmer Press.; STRAY, C.A. (1986). '1902 and all that: the defence of Classics in the early 20th century', JACT Review, No 5, pp.6-9.; STRAY, C.A. (1986). 'Culture or discipline? The redefinition of classical education'. In: PRICE, M.H. (Ed). The development of the secondary curriculum. Beckenham: Croom Helm.; STRAY, C.A. (1988). 'England, culture and the 19th century', Liverpool Classical Monthly, Vol 13, No 6, June 1988, pp.85-90.; STRAY, C.A. (1989). 'Paradigms of social order: the politics of Latin grammar in 19th century England', Henry Sweet Society Newsletter, No 13, November 1989, pp.13-23.; STRAY, C.A. (1990). 'A cellarful of ghosts?', The Educational Division of South Kensington Museum. Paradigm No 2, April 1990.
Source of Grant: No funding
Date of Research: 1985-1990
KEYWORDS: *classics; history of education*

8/1631
Department of Education
Hendrefoilan, Swansea SA2 7NB
0792 201231
Banks, F.R.J. Mr
An evaluation of distance learning INSET (Inservice Education and Training of Teachers) in Wales
Abstract: The problems of geographical isolation and the small number of teachers requiring INSET (Inservice Education and Training of Teachers) in some curriculum areas make distance-learning an attractive option for many Welsh LEAs (local education authorities). The study seeks to illuminate both effective course design and good practice in LEA management of teacher support. Teachers in Wales, from all LEAs, involved in (initially) one distance-learning INSET programme have been interviewed about their perceived progress and satisfaction with the course, its delivery, and the extent to which they think the course will alter their practice. An attempt will be made to design an evaluation method which will include a longitudinal study of how teachers change over time following an INSET experience. They were asked to give factual details of patterns of study and use of the materials. The INSET co-ordinators from the corresponding LEAs have been asked to supply details of the support they are prepared to give to the teachers in terms of fees, expenses, free time etc., and have been interviewed to gather their opinion of the effectiveness of the programmes.
Source of Grant: University of Wales, Faculty of Education: £3,400
Date of Research: 1989-1990
KEYWORDS: *distance study; evaluation; further education of teachers; inservice teacher education*

8/1632
Department of Education
Hendrefoilan, Swansea SA2 7NB
0792 201231
Daugherty, R. A. Mr; Thomas, B. Mrs
GCSE (General Certificate of Secondary Education) in Wales
Abstract: The project is investigating the response of maintained secondary schools in Wales to the curriculum and assessment demands of the GCSE (General Certificate of General Education). It focuses on the subject areas of Welsh, History and Geography. From a survey of all maintained secondary schools in Wales and a more intensive study of a sample of 15 schools, the study is seeking to establish how the GCSE national framework is being implemented. Five major themes are highlighted: – the GCSE curriculum in Wales, styles of teaching and learning, teachers assessment of pupils, differentiation, teacher support systems.
Source of Grant: Welsh Office: £93,000

Date of Research: 1989-1990
KEYWORDS: General Certificate of Secondary Education; response; secondary school

8/1633

Department of Education
Hendrefoilan, Swansea SA2 7NB
0792 201231
Tanner, H.F.R. Mr

The use of information technology in mathematics education
Abstract: The aims of the project are to establish the extent of IT (information technology) in British secondary schools, determine the restrictions percieved to exist by teachers in terms of training, access to equipment suitability of software and educational philosophy, determine the extent to which IT should be taught in mathematics, and to develop techniques which would make such teaching possible for the average teacher. Also to suggest introductory ideas for problem solving using IT. Schools known to use IT to support problem solving have been visited and lessons observed. Informal interviews have taken place and a questionnaire designed and trialled. The questionnaire has been sent to a random sample of schools. Experimental lessons will take place with teachers lacking experience in IT use, and ideas developed.
Source of Grant: No funding
Date of Research: 1989-1990
KEYWORDS: computer assisted instruction; electronic data processing; information science; information technology; mathematics

8/1634

Department of Education
Hendrefoilan, Swansea SA2 7NB
0792 201231
Jones, G.E. Prof.

History of education in Wales since 1780
Abstract: The research has investigated the means by which central government has controlled school education in Wales during the 20th Century. It examines the confrontations between local authorities in Wales and central government in 1902-06, 1932 and after the 1944 Education Act. It concludes with a survey of education in Wales in recent decades and the nature of present controlling influences, especially that of the Welsh Office.
Published Material: JONES, G.E. (1990). Which nation's schools? Direction and devolution in Welsh education in the Twentieth Century. University of Wales Press.
Source of Grant: No funding
Date of Research: 1980-1990
KEYWORDS: educational policy; government policy; history of education; United Kingdom

8/1635

Department of Education
Hendrefoilan, Swansea SA2 7NB
0792 201231
Hughes, C. Mr; *Supervisor:* Jones, G.E. Dr

A case study of the relationship between education and industrial society: Glamorgan 1833-1944
Abstract: To look at the inter-relationship between elementary, secondary, technical, adult and higher education and the evolution of an industrial society in the most dramatically changing of all counties in Wales in the nineteenth and twentieth centuries.
Source of Grant: No funding
Date of Research: 1986 – continuing
KEYWORDS: history of education; industrialization; Wales

8/1636

Department of Education
Hendrefolian, Swansea SA2 7NB
0792 201231
Rogers, P.J. Mr; *Supervisor:* Rothera, H. Mr

An evaluative study of alternative strategies of curriculum planning in selected primary schools
Abstract: An initial survey of curriculum planning procedures in a sample of some 30 primary schools in Mid- and West-Wales will be followed by an in depth investigation of decision-making and curriculum priorities in half of them. The aim is to develop a model of curriculum planning for the primary school from existing good practice.
Source of Grant: No funding
Date of Research: 1986 – continuing

KEYWORDS: curriculum development; planning of education; primary education

8/1637

Department of Education
Hendrefoilan, Swansea SA2 7NB
0792 201231
Al-Saifi, R. Mr; *Supervisor:* Littlewood, W.T. Mr

A comparative study of attitudes and approaches to the teaching of mother-tongue grammar in Iraqi and British secondary schools
Abstract: There is currently considerable controversy, both in Iraq and in the United Kingdom, concerning the role that grammar teaching should perform in a child's mother-tongue education at secondary school. This project will consider the background and causes of the controversy in both countries. Through consulting relevant sources, observing lessons and conducting interviews with educators, the researchers will examine and compare current attitudes and approaches to the teaching of grammar in Iraq and the UK. On the basis of the results and an evaluation of them, the researcher will make proposals relating to future attitudes and approaches in Iraqi secondary schools.
Source of Grant: Iraqi Ministry of Higher Education
Date of Research: 1987-1990
KEYWORDS: comparative education; grammar; Iraq; mother tongue; secondary education

8/1638

Department of Education
Hendrefoilan, Swansea SA2 7NB
0792 201231
Mohammad, S. Mrs; *Supervisor:* Laing, A.F. Dr; Cox, T. Dr

A study of Kindergartens in Qatar with particular reference to teacher-child interaction
Abstract: The research has two main aims: (1) to survey the Kindergartens in Qatar using specially devised questionnaires for principals and teachers. Information will be gathered on staffing; organization; staff views on aims and purposes of pre-school education; curriculum; parental involvement; proposed developments; (2) to carry out an interactional analysis in one third of the Kindergartens, paying particular attention to staff interactions with girls as compared to boys.
Source of Grant: Student supported (3 years) by Ministry of Education in Qatar
Date of Research: 1986-1989
KEYWORDS: nursery school; pre-school education; Qatar; sex difference; teacher-pupil relation

8/1639

Department of Education
Hendrefoilan, Swansea SA2 7NB
0792 201231
Philips, E.D. Mr; *Supervisor:* Rothera, H. Mr

The development of the technical and vocational education initiative in Wales (1982-1990) and its contribution to curriculum change
Abstract: The aim is to examine all the TVEI Curriculum Programmes developed in schools and colleges in Wales in order to identify the nature of their enhanced and expanded curricula; to pin-point the most important developments; to compare TVEI-initiated curriculum change in different parts of Wales with that in England in Wales as a whole and to seek to identify curriculum trends.
Source of Grant: No funding
Date of Research: 1987 – continuing
KEYWORDS: curriculum development; Technical and Vocational Education Initiative (TVEI); Wales

8/1640

Department of Education
Hendrefoilan, Swansea SA2 7NB
0792 201231
Cox, T. Dr

Microcomputer systems and small group discussions amongst primary school children
Abstract: It is claimed that the introduction of the microcomputer into the classroom facilitates small group collaborative work and discussion amongst primary school children. Assessing this claim requires the close monitoring of the linguistic and social interaction of children working in groups around a microcomputer. In the present exploratory study both infant and junior aged groups are being observed working together on selected programmes and

their talk tape recorded and transcribed. A suitable framework for analysis of the transcriptions is being developed, with the aim of identifying both productive and less productive verbal interaction strategies which the children use in their discussions. The provisional analyses carried out so far support the view that the use of suitable microcomputer programmes can generate productive thinking and collaboration amongst primary school children as young as seven years, provided that the teacher is willing to spend time in setting up, monitoring and, where necessary, intervening in the discussions.
Published Material: COX, T. (1989). 'Granny's Garden Revisited', Education 3-13, Vol 17, No 1, March.
Source of Grant: University of Wales; Faculty of Education: £750
Date of Research: 1986 – continuing
KEYWORDS: *discussion; microcomputer; primary education; small group; verbal interaction*

8/1641
Department of Education
Hendrefoilan, Swansea SA2 7NB
0792 205678
Ahmed, M.A. Mr; *Supervisor:* Littlewood, W. Mr
An experimental study of the reading comprehension ability of sixth-grade Iraqi primary school children
Abstract: The level of learning Arabic as a mother tongue in Iraqi schools need to be improved. The present study focuses on reading comprehension in primary schools for two main reasons: the extent of the poor performance in reading comprehension and the importance of the primary school in preparing students for the later stages of education. The study has two main aims: to identify and evaluate the objectives in teaching reading which have been set up by the Iraqi Ministry of Education, and to identify the main skills of reading comprehension, students main weaknesses in reading comprehension and the main problems in the teaching of reading. Attempts will be made to discover any correlations between students' opinions about reading and their performance, whether environment and sex affect reading ability, whether parents influence their children's reading ability, and to assess the readability level of the reading textbook used at school. The study will use the following procedures: official documents; tests (cloze tests, comprehension questions, pronunciation tests) and questionnaires to students, teachers and parents. The sample will be chosen from the Baghdad area, as follows: 100 female pupils and 100 male pupils from urban and rural areas; 50 female and 50 male teachers in urban and rural schools and 20% of the parents of the pupils living in rural and urban areas. According to the results obtained from the tests and questionnaires the writer will make recommendations at the end of the investigation.
Published Material: AHMED, H.A. (1988). 'A critical evaluation of the specific objectives of teaching Arabic in Iraqi intermediate schools', M.Ed thesis, University College Cardiff.
Source of Grant: Iraqi Government; Ministry of Education
Date of Research: 1988 – continuing
KEYWORDS: *Arabic; Iraq; language teaching; mother tongue; primary school; reading*

8/1642
Department of Education
Hendrefoilan, Swansea SA2 7NB
0792 201231
Tanner, H. Mr
The use of the (SMP) School Mathematics Project (11-16) curriculum development project in the first two years of secondary school
Abstract: The aim is to examine different methods of (a) classroom management, (b) pupil assessment, (c) teaching strategy and (d) pupil grouping, currently in use in schools using Schools Mathematics Project (11-16) booklets in West Glamorgan schools in years one and two. The aim is also to develop teaching and management skills in the team of teacher researchers, and to develop any necessary supplementary materials. Methodology consists of participant observation of classrooms by a small team of teacher researchers.
Source of Grant: University of Wales
Date of Research: 1988-1990
KEYWORDS: *curriculum development; mathematics; secondary education; teaching aids; teaching method*

8/1643
Department of Psychology
Singleton Park, Swansea SA2 8PP

0792 205678
Gruneberg, M.M.
Application of mnemonical techniques to foreign language learning
Abstract: The aim of the research is to apply mnemonic aids to the learning of foreign languages with the aim of enhancing school performance of below and average children. Two classes of pupils from Bishop Vaughan school in Swansea are being taught using the Linkword method, and evaluation will be possible in 2 years time.
Source of Grant: No funding
Date of Research: 1982 – continuing
KEYWORDS: *foreign languages; language teaching; mnemonics*

8/1644
Department of Psychology
Singleton Park, Swansea SA2 8PP
0792 295599
Benton, D. Dr
The influence of diet on childrens' behaviour
Abstract: The study of childrens behaviour is one of a range of studies examining the relationship between diet and behaviour. To date, using double-blind and placebo designs, the impact of increasing blood glucose and the giving of vitamin/mineral supplements has been examined. In 6/7 year-old children the giving of a glucose drink, late in the school day, improved attention and decreased evidence of frustration when faced with a difficult task. When 90 twelve year-old children were given a vitamin/mineral supplement for 8 months, non-verbal but not verbal IQ increased significantly (P< .001). The finding was discussed in terms of possible dietary deficiencies.
Published Material: BENTON, D., BRETT. V. & BRAIN, P.F. (1987). 'Glucose improves attention and reaction to frustration in children', Biological Psychology, 24, 1987, pp.95-100.; BENTON, D. & ROBERTS G. (1988). 'Effect of vitamin and mineral supplementation on intelligence of a sample of schoolchildren', The Lancet, 23 January, 1988, pp.140-143.
Date of Research: 1985 – continuing
KEYWORDS: *diet; pupil behaviour*

8/1645
Department of Psychology
Singleton Park, Swansea SA2 8PP
0792 295599
Beaumont, J.G. Prof.
Expert systems support for diagnostic assessment of arithmetic skills
Abstract: The research arises out of a series of procedures, developed by Dr Neil Hagues in the NFER Test Development Unit, for the computer assisted diagnosis of the errors committed by children in performing addition and subtraction of pairs of three figure numbers. These procedures are well validated and permit the identification of up to 32 errors in either addition or subtraction. The current implementation is within a procedural system which applies an elementary algorithmic search for the various error types. The research aims to implement these fundamental procedures within a rule-based programming environment: the 'intelligent environment' of Crystal. The first stage will be to replicate the procedures already established, but with some gains in efficiency and flexibility. However, the subsequent stage will be to explore the power of this environment to perform further induction upon the object-values presented to the system, to demonstrate the potential added power which this type of system can confer in an assessment context.
Source of Grant: No funding
Date of Research: 1988-1989
KEYWORDS: *arithmetic; assessment; diagnostic test; error*

8/1646
Department of Sociology and Anthropology
Singleton Park, Swansea SA2 8PP
0792 205678
Adams, S. Ms; *Supervisor:* Jenkins, R. Dr
Mature students in higher education
Abstract: The research aims to look into the possible source of insight mature students (especially women) may offer into changing gender relations in the family and in society. There is also the question of why the numbers of mature women students is rising. This can be partly explained by the fact that due to demographic changes more mature women are needed in the labour market and access to university is now being made easier for them. It can also be partly explained by women now having more control over their fertility and by changes in womens employment patterns and eco-

nomic participation rates. But the rising numbers may also be partly explained by a change in womens self-perceptions due partially to two decades of activity by the Womens Movement. The researcher is interested in how mature women, particularly those who have experienced a change in self perception get on in university. Does higher education deal equitably with the needs of mature male and female studends? The researcher intends to look at changes in life courses and whether mens life courses affect womens to a far greater extent than vice-versa. Also to investigate how women experience directly the pressures imposed on them to be good wives, mothers, daughters etc. How they negotiate their own social and sociological reality in this situation, and how they negotiate this reality as mature students, what changes of what types, may occur. Related to this is an analysis of the way in which women are inscribed in unequal, passive and subordinate relations by the State, the law and all the other spheres which have the ability to shape the subjects lives for them.
Source of Grant: No funding
Date of Research: 1989 – continuing
KEYWORDS: *adult education; higher education; mature student; sex role; women's education*

8/1647

Department of Sociology and Anthropology
Singleton Park, Swansea SA2 8PP
0792 205678
Hutson, S. Dr
Saturday jobs – part-time working by young people 16-18 years in full-time education
Abstract: The aims of the research was to find out more about the part-time working, by young people 16-19 years in two tertiary colleges and two sixth forms in South Wales and London (Bromley). Half were studying A level; half were studying B. Tech National. Four hundred and forty self-fill questionnaires were collected and 30 interviews were conducted. Saturday job working was extensive but invisible to economists and educationists; 77% of the girls were working in South Wales, 51% of the boys were working in South Wales, and 76% of the whole sample were working in London. This follows high rates of working (67%) before 16 (paper rounds etc.). Earnings in South Wales were: 82% earn over £30 in the week in the holidays. 28% earn over £30 in the term, and 13% earn over £80 in the holidays. With these earnings, the monetary rewards of staying on in education after 16 are high. Wage rates are often higher than the Youth Training Scheme allowance. Parents keep Child Allowance and those at school do not pay 'board money'. Only with a change in benefit regulations can school leavers use Saturday jobs as a step into full-time work. Many of these young earners are educational achievers from affluent homes. They are working for independent money. Parents, children and schools tend to see this work positively. A few young people are financing themselves through the sixth form. These earnings, and money from parents, underpin a similarity of life-style across class and gender. Homework, hobbies, savings, holidays, presents, step-families are also mentioned.
Source of Grant: Economic and Social Science Research Council
Date of Research: 1989-1990
KEYWORDS: *further education students; part-time work; pupil; sixth form students*

University College of Swansea

8/1648

Department of Education
Hendrefoilan, Swansea SA2 7NB
0792 201231
Cox, T. Dr; Sanders, S. Ms
A study of the early impact of the National Curriculum on the education of five year old children
Abstract: This study is designed to obtain the views of a representative sample of teachers in primary schools in a South Wales LEA (local education authority) on the impact of the introduction of the National Curriculum in September 1989 on their work. A sample of twenty eight infant/primary schools has been drawn up and the headteachers and class teachers of five year old pupils are currently being interviewed using structured interview questionnaires. These

will yield information concerning the schools' preparation for the introduction of the new curriculum and the teachers' judgements about its likely influence on their work during the first year of its implementation including the resources needed and problems anticipated. Particular attention is being paid to the way in which the teachers' assessment procedures are being developed to meet the requirements of the National Curriculum. A short attitude scale included in the questionnaires taps the teachers' views about the likely benefits or otherwise of the new curriculum. The interviews will be repeated in the summer term 1990 with adaptations to the questionnaire to allow a review by the teachers of the operation of the curriculum during the first year and a prospective view of its further development in the year 1990-91 leading to the standardized assessment of the children's attainments in the core subjects.
Source of Grant: University of Wales: £6,600
Date of Research: 1989-1990
KEYWORDS: *National Curriculum; primary school; pupil; United Kingdom*

University College of Wales, Aberystwyth

8/1649

Department of Education
Aberystwyth SY23 2AX
0970 623111
Morris Jones, R.
Child language
Abstract: The research is based on a corpus of the recorded spontaneous conversations of children in the nursery age range 3-7 years old. The corpus includes material in Welsh and English, i.e. Welsh speakers and English speakers. The general aim is to describe the sentence-grammar and the discourse of the language. There is also a collection of background information about the children giving socio-economic, educational and linguistic facts as well as school type. Linguistic analyses of children can thus be correlated with extra-linguistic factors. Both sets of data are stored on computer in the college.
Source of Grant: No funding
Date of Research: 1979 – continuing
KEYWORDS: *child development; language development; verbal communication*

University of Wales

8/1650

Department of Education
42 Park Place, Cardiff CF1 3BB
0222 872000
Weston-Super-Mare Colleve of Further Education
Knightstone Road, Weston-Super-Mare BS23 2AL
0934 621301
Carter, E. Mr; *Supervisor:* Hopkin, A.G. Dr
Curriculum innovation, international education in a college of futher education: a case study
Abstract: The aim of the project is to observe the reception of the formal incorporation of international studies into an English language syllabus, which had taken place, previously, on an informal basis. The investigation will be undertaken in two colleges of further education. All students taking English language in the two colleges were asked to complete pre-course questionnaires designed to appraise student attitudes and knowledge; similar post-course questionnaires will be issued at the end of the course. Differences in the attitudes and knowledge of the students who were taught on the course will be compared with those who were not. Basically, illuminative evaluation will be the method used to assess students' reception of the project. Senior staff from both institutions have been requested to complete questionnaires; further, to participate in a series of interviews, in order to gauge the reception of international studies in both colleges. The research will take place over two years ending in 1991. The results will be written-up as a PhD thesis to be completed in 1992.

Source of Grant: Avon County Council: £475 per annum
Date of Research: 1989 – continuing
KEYWORDS: curriculum; English language; international studies

8/1651

Department of Education
42 Park Place, Cardiff CF1 3BB
0222 874000
Kandeh, F.B. Mr; Supervisor: Sutton, R.A. Dr

Teaching, learning and educational technology: a case study of a sample of secondary schools in Sierra Leone

Abstract: Under achievement in final secondary school examinations, a high drop out rate together with a high rate of repeats have become characteristic of the secondary school system in Sierra Leone. The study will involve a survey of current teaching methods and the level of use of educational technology, both in terms of hardware and philosophy. The outcome is intended to provide a plan of action to improve the system. The sample contains a representative selection of secondary schools. The investigation uses standard survey techniques.
Source of Grant: No funding
Date of Research: 1989 – continuing
KEYWORDS: educational technology; final examination; secondary school; Sierra Leone; underachievement

8/1652

Department of Education
42 Park Place, Cardiff CF1 3BB
0222 874000
Refaa, S. Mr; Supervisor: Sutton, R.A. Dr

Practical work in science in Saudi Arabian intermediate schools

Abstract: This research aims to answer the following questions. What are the types of practical work currently in use? How much practical work is included in the curriculum? What are the aims of practical work as perceived by teachers and by staff supervisors? What is the attitude of teachers towards practical work? Data is to be collected from a representative sample of intermediate schools in Saudi Arabia using standard survey techniques.
Source of Grant: Saudi Arabian Government; Department of Education
Date of Research: 1989 – continuing
KEYWORDS: middle school; practical work; Saudi Arabia; science education; teacher behaviour

University of Wales College of Cardiff

8/1653

Department of Education
PO Box 68, Cardiff CF1 3XA
0222 874000
Akhtar, S. Mr; Supervisor: Durojaye, S. Dr

Multicultural education and policy implementation

Abstract: The United Kingdom is a multicultural and multiracial society but society, i.e. white people, ignores this concept. Consequently the immigrants feel that their lives and belongings are not safe. This concept is transferred to youngsters and they are caught between two worlds. The aim of this research is to discover the problems of Pakistani children in Cardiff, and to see what the South Glamorgan authority is doing to solve these problems in response to the Swann Report and to Government directives. Methods used include interviewing, participant observation, observation and questionnaires.
Published Material: AKHTAR, S. and STRONACH, I. (1986). 'They call me Blacky', Times Educational Supplement, 19th September.
Source of Grant: No funding
Date of Research: 1988-1990
KEYWORDS: educational policy; ethnic minority; multicultural education; race relations; Wales; youth

8/1654

Department of Education
PO Box 68, Cardiff CF1 3XA
0222 874000
Oxfam Education (Wales)

33 Whitchurch Road, Cardiff
Heard, A. Ms; Evans, T.E. Rev.; Supervisor: Hopkin, A.G. Dr

Promoting developmental education in the curriculum

Abstract: The principal aim is to use academic MEd courses as a means of getting Developmental Education promoted in schools. The normal pattern has been for students to do their MEd dissertations in this field. A common method has been for students to devise a teaching unit of 8 weeks to a term, implement it, evaluate it and write it up as a dissertation. To date about 30 have been complemented in following areas: primary, secondary and tertiary and in various subject areas including history, home economics, geography, French, science, integrated subjects, R.E. and in teacher education. It has been established that this dimension can have a considerable impact on an attitudinal development particularly at the primary and lower secondary levels. A fellowship has been sponsored for 2 years 1983-1985.
Published Material: HEARD, A.C. (1985). A/O level, World Development: Teachers Guide and Handbook. Cardiff, Faculty of Education.; HOPKIN, A.G. 'Development education in the curriculum', Education for Development, Vol 10, No 2.
Source of Grant: Some Local Education Authority sponsorship
Date of Research: 1979 – continuing
KEYWORDS: curriculum development; development education

8/1655

Department of Education
PO Box 68, Cardiff CF1 3XA
0222 874000
Evans, T.E. Rev; Supervisor: Hopkin, A.G. Dr

Attitudes of public and voluntary agency workers (Christian Aid and Catholic Fund for Overseas Development) to developmental issues

Abstract: The research arose because of the researcher's concern that in his capacity as Christian Aid Education Officer, those who worked for Christian Aid on a voluntary and professional basis were often not aware of the developmental issues involved in the aid work. The principal aim will be to determine the extent to which contributory members of the public and voluntary workers for Christian Aid and Oxfam in South East Wales are aware of the issues underlying the need for aid. Voluntary workers will fill in questionnaires and be interviewed. During World Week in May 1988 donating members (about 100) of the public will be interviewed after contributing. The data will be processed and the findings will be used as a basis for the further education of voluntary aid workers in South East Wales, particularly those with Christian Aid.
Source of Grant: Christian Aid
Date of Research: 1987-1989
KEYWORDS: development aid; development education; developmental policy; public opinion

8/1656

Department of Education
Senghenydd Road, Cardiff CF2 4AG
0222 874459
Al-Mosibeeh, S. Mr; Supervisor: Harris, J. Dr

A cross-national, psychometric study of Saudi university students personality traits using the Eysenck Personality Questionnaire

Abstract: The influence of cultural background on test performance has been an important issue in educational and psychological testing. A test which has been developed and has been successfully used in a certain culture may not be suitable for another culture with a different background. H.J. Eysenck is a psychologist who has a positive attitude towards a universal and cultural view of the cross-cultural personality. Research into individual differences has led him to believe in the universal basis of personality, which affects people's behaviour and attitudes cross-culturally. He has suggested that the three-dimensional model of personality has a high degree of universal validity, in the sense that the same three dimensions emerge from many different studies, using different item pools and samples from many countries (Eysenck 1986). Therefore, the aims of this study will include; a full translation of the Eysenck Personality Questionnaire to the native language of the subjects according to the highest standard of translation methods; examining the Factor structure of the instrument as a means of assessing its factor validity, assessing the reliability of the Scale using internal consistency reliability; examining each of the test items to find out the relationships among the four scales, E,N,P and L, a comparison of the results obtained in the Saudi culture with the original research in England using college students only. After an adaption of E.P.Q

to Saudi University students, the researcher will attempt to look at the relationship between certain Personality traits, subjects studied, and age. 1000 students will be selected from the biggest and oldest University in Saudi Arabia.
Source of Grant: Saudi Arabian National Guard
Date of Research: 1987-1989
KEYWORDS: cross-cultural research; cultural background; personality assessment; psychological testing; Saudi Arabia

8/1657
Department of Education
Senghenydd Road, Cardiff CF2 4AG
0222 874459
Harris, J. Dr
Language teaching and language learning in special schools
Abstract: While it is clearly recognized that language development and language teaching are important aspects of the school curriculum for children with severe language difficulties, there remains considerable uncertainty regarding (a) what are the most effective school based activities for promoting language learning; and (b) how teachers in schools can be helped to introduce innovative ideas for curriculum change. In order to answer both of these questions it is necessary for researchers to have a much clearer idea about what teachers are seeking to achieve in terms of language assessment and lanaguage teaching, and secondly, the opportunities for language learning which are made available to pupils during the course of the school day. A survey by postal questionnaire was employed to determine the aims and methods employed by schools for language assessment and language teaching. Secondly, a small number of teachers were interviewed to further explore how they perceive the role of language in the special school curriculum. Thirdly, children and teachers were recorded during classroom based language activities. The result of the questionnaire survey indicated that teachers recognize the importance of grammar and vocabulary but give little prominence to functional and conversational skills. There is relatively little awareness of the role of unstructured play activities in creating language learning opportunites. It is anticipated that the analysis of the interviews and the language samples of classroom activities will provide a more detailed picture of the relationship between teachers views of language learning, the activities which they establish in the classroom and the opportunites for language learning which these activities provide.
Published Material: HARRIS, J. (1988). Language development in schools for children with severe learning difficulties. London: Croom Helm.
Source of Grant: University of Wales: £1,500
Date of Research: 1984-1989
KEYWORDS: language development; language teaching; learning difficulty; special school

8/1658
Department of Education
Senghenydd Road, Cardiff CF2 4AG
0222 874459
South Glamorgan County Council
Schools Psychological Services,
Gabalfa House, North Road, Cardiff
Harris, J. Dr; Tyre, C. Mr
Children with behaviour problems in ordinary primary schools
Abstract: While there is an increasing awareness that a significant minority of children in primary schools demonstrate problematic behaviour, little is known about the prevalence of such problems, the form they take or the most effective ways of dealing with them. This study sets out to determine the prevalence of behaviour problems among children aged between 6-11 years in South Wales primary schools. Following completion of an initial screening questionnaire, teachers will be invited to fill in a Child Behaviour Checklist (Achenbach and Edelbrock 1986) for each pupil identified as experiencing behavioural and/or emotional difficulties (N= approx 900). Teachers will also complete Checklists on a sample of randomly chosen pupils for the purposes of comparison. Assessments of the target group and the comparison group will be repeated after one year when most of the children will be in different classes. The Checklist can be scored on a number of related scales which can be interpreted both quantitively and qualitatively. This data will be used to determine the extent and nature of behaviour problems for children of different ages and the stability of behavioural difficulties over time. It will also be possible to cross validate CBCL scores with teachers initial responses to the screening instrument. It is anticipated that this study will provide the basis for the develop-

ment and monitoring of in-school support for teachers working with problematic children.
Source of Grant: South Glamorgan County Council University College Cardiff; Department of Education
Date of Research: 1988-1990
KEYWORDS: behaviour disorder; emotional disorder; primary education

8/1659
Department of Education
Senghennydd Road, Cardiff CF2 4AG
0222 874000
King Saud University
Riyadh, Saudi Arabia
Aldkheel, M. Mr; *Supervisor:* Donald, G.A.H. Dr
An evaluation study of teaching training programmes for adult education in Saudi Arabia
Abstract: The aims of this research are to work within the framework of National Objectives to evaluate the effectiveness of teacher training for adult education. Research will include: methods and content of current provision, views of teachers, planners and students and investigation of progress (problems) of teachers in becoming qualified.
Source of Grant: Saudi Arabia Government Scholarship
Date of Research: 1987-1989
KEYWORDS: adult education; Saudi Arabia; teacher education

8/1660
Department of Education
42 Park Place, Cardiff CF1 3BB
0222 874000
Hopkin, A.G. Dr
Development education and teacher education in Wales
Abstract: The principal aim of the project is to explore the feasibility of promoting development education through pre-service teacher education in Wales. This will be done through attempting to promote interface between non-government organizations and pre-service teacher institutions in Wales. The status and perception of development education and the non-government organizations will be established through the use of questionnaires and interviews. Questionnaires have been issued to all Post-Graduate Certificate of Education and fourth year BEd students in the ten teacher education institutions in Wales (about 1,100 students). Questionnaires have been sent to five staff in each. Structured interviews will be conducted with four students and two staff in each institution. An inventory of resources will be returned by seven nongovernmental organizations and development education centres and an interview will be conducted with one officer from each. All ten teacher education institutions in Wales have agreed to participate. Preliminary findings will form the basis of a seminar for participating educational institutions and non-governmental organizations to be held in the Michaelmas Term 1990/1991. The findings, proceedings and decisions made will form the basis of the final report.
Source of Grant: Christian Aid Development Education Funding Committee for Wales: £3,000 Joseph Rowntree Charitable Trust: £13,000
Date of Research: 1989 – continuing
KEYWORDS: development education; teacher education

8/1661
Department of Education
Senghenydd Road, Cardiff CF2 4AG
0222 874459
South Glamorgan Institute of Higher Education
Speech Therapy Section, Western Avenue, Cardiff CF5 2YB
0222 551111 ext 4214
Duckworth, M.S. Mr; *Supervisor:* Harris, J. Dr
Stuttering and fluency in conversational speech
Abstract: There is relatively little research into the conversational behaviour of people with speech handicaps. This study examines the aspects of the interaction between people who stutter (S) and their non stuttering conversational partners (NS) which influence the occurrence of stuttering in conversation. For example, the types of turn initiation, the way in which turn allocation is structured, and the manipulation of conversational repair strategies may be covertly negotiated by the conversational partners to facilitate the greatest amount of non-stuttered speech during an interaction. Some people who stutter will therefore experience a repeated confirmation of the need to produce fluent speech; a need which, when cons-

ciously exercised, frequently produces less fluent speech. The conversational interactions between S and NS will be video recorded and subjected to conversational analysis. The analysis will employ, in part, a coding scheme derived from a pilot study of 3 interactions. The pilot study showed a strong relationship between the pragmatic force of NS's utterances which immediately preceded S's turn. The more S was constrained to respond, the more likely stuttering was to occur. The next phase of the research will (a) examine the predictive strength of the observations already made and (b) look at the interactions over time to discover the strategies S and NS employ to enhance the amount of fluency in the conversation. The effect of this evidence on theoretical models of stuttering in adults and hence upon therapy for stuttering, will be considered.

Published Material: DUCKWORTH, M. (1988). Stuttering and linguistics. In: BALL, M. (ed). Theoretical linguistics and disordered language. London: Croom Helm.
Source of Grant: South Glamorgan County Council: part of fees
Date of Research: 1984 – continuing
KEYWORDS: adult; conversation; speech handicapped; speech therapy; stuttering

8/1662

School of Education
Senghenydd Road, Cardiff CF2 4AG
0222 974459
Ramasut, A. Ms; *Supervisor:* Harris, J. Dr
Teacher training and special educational needs
Abstract: The study examines the attitudes of two cohorts of postgraduate student teachers towards pupils with special educational needs in mainstream secondary schools. The aims of the study are: (i) To establish whether attitudes change during the professional training year and, if so, for what reason. (ii) To find out whether attitudes held at the end of the first year of teaching are in any way different from those reported earlier. (iii) To examine the views of students and newly qualified teachers on integration. (iv) To find out whether newly qualified teachers feel that their training course adequately prepares them to meet special educational needs in secondary schools. The sample consisted of two cohorts of post-graduate students (n = 105 & 108) at a university department of education preparing to teach a wide variety of subjects at secondary level. A questionnaire was administered at the beginning and end of the training course and again towards the end of the probationary year. A sub-sample of students who had obtained posts in South Wales was followed up and interviewed in school. A day was spent with each newly qualified teacher and they were all observed teaching a variety of classes. Data collection took place between 1985 and 1988 and is currently being analyzed. Early impressions indicate that students complete their training year with a positive attitude towards pupils with special educational needs but that they feel different qualities are needed to teach these pupils to those needed to teach their subect to other pupils.
Source of Grant: No funding
Date of Research: 1985 – continuing
KEYWORDS: attitude change; probationary teacher; special needs; student teacher

8/1663

School of Social and Administrative Studies
62 Park Place, Cardiff CF1 1XL
0222 874000
South Glamorgan Institute of Higher Education,
Cyncoed, Cardiff CF2 6XD
0222 551111
Treadwell, P. Mr; *Supervisor:* Lodge, P. Dr
Sports coach and physical education in Great Britain – a sociocultural analysis of occupations striving towards the ideal of a profession via professionalization, and the shaping factors which have affected development
Abstract: The research would examine the development of organized physical education and sports coaching in Gt.Britain, from the period when sport became formalized in the 1850's and expecially after 1914 when the position of salaried chief coach to the Amateur Athletic Association was first offered, through to the emergence of the National Coaching Foundation, first established by the Sports Council in 1983, and the development of their National Coaching 'network' in 1987. It would seek to describe and analyse the routes that individuals, and the occupation as a whole has taken in attempting to reach the levels of knowledge and dedication to service that society considers necessary for a profession to emerge. In particu-

lar, it would analyse the recent work by the National Coaching Foundation and the British Association of National Coaches along with individual institutions and organizations in Scotland and Northern Ireland in striving towards the ideal of a profession via the process of professionalization and assess whether the diplomats from those agencies, have obtained professional recognition.
Published Material: TREADWELL, P. (1987). Coach education. London: E & FN Spon Ltd.
Source of Grant: No funding
Date of Research: 1989 – continuing
KEYWORDS: athletics coach; history of education; physical education

Wakefield District College

8/1664

Margaret Street, Wakefield, West Yorkshire WF1 2DH
0924 370501
Further Education Unit
2-6 Orange Street, London WC2H 7WE
071 321 0433
Hegarty, M. Mr; Wood, S. Ms; *Supervisor:* Marshall, D.E. Mr
The accreditation of staff development (RP 606)
Abstract: This research has arisen out of the development of links between Wakefield District College and a number of establishments on 'Credit Accumulation Transfer Schemes'. Inservice training was targetted early for accreditation as the college allocates a great deal of money to staff training and is obviously concerned that this should produce effective learning. The development of a mechanism of accreditation should afford greater ownership of the curriculum for staff. As appraisal and the profiling of staff develops in college there is an increasing need to be able to negotiate their own goals and training needs. Before this, it is necessary to map out the extent of cashing provision. This will target colleges and consortia that can serve as useful models/contracts/partners and provide an overview of the current situation. The research will establish an overall picture of accreditation and recording of Inservice Training in Further Education in England and Wales. A significant dimension will be to ascertain the views and emphasis on accreditation procedures in staff training by practitioners. Research methods will involve questionnaire distribution. This will enable a number of case studies to be made of institutions involved. A Steering Committee will also give direction and support. A report will be produced which will be designed to inform the continuing work of the FEU in this area.
Source of Grant: Further Education Unit
Date of Research: 1990-1990
KEYWORDS: accreditation (courses); further education; further education of teachers; inservice teacher education; inservice training

Warwickshire College of Agriculture

8/1665

Moreton Hall, Moreton Morrell, Warwick CV35 9BL
0926 651367
Further Education Unit
Grove House, 2-6 Orange Street, London WC2H 7WE
071 321 0433
Hoyte, N. Mrs; *Supervisor:* Gaynor, N. Mr (Warwickshire College of Agriculture)
Developing training strategies for rural employers
Abstract: This research arises out of demographic trends, government initiatives and legislation necessitating rural employers to collaborate in order for their interests to be represented. They often find it difficult to find time to implement staff training, and their locations do not naturally relate to urban based technical colleges. The projects aim to form a Warwickshire training consortium that will develop a training strategy for rural employers. It will aim to secure a trained workforce for industry from schools, government training schemes and other sources. This will be achieved through collaborative action (Warwickshire College of Agriculture and

industry), visiting schools throughout the country and via its Youth Training Scheme, and Education Training Programmes. A standard of workmanship will be maintained through regular training and updating skills for the existing workforce, and the consortium's interest will be represented in any new forum such as the Training and Enterprise Councils. There will be four phases to the project; firstly the formation of a consortium, and needs analysis among rural employers, such as agricultural contractors and agricultural engineers. The second phase will consist of researching, designing and planning training programmes in conjunction with employers to meet their needs and national standards. Thirdly, the delivery of training programmes with collaborating employers and monitoring of progress and feedback. Finally, a review and evaluation of the work carried out. A steering committee will monitor the progress of the project and will include representatives from industry, training agencies and the local Training and Enterprise Council. The project aims to achieve a better understanding of problems faced by small rural employers in providing training, provision of training programmes tailored to individual employer needs, and a report will be produced on the methodology and special problems of servicing this client group.
Source of Grant: Further Education Unit
Date of Research: 1989-1990
KEYWORDS: consortia; employment; rural area; training

Warwick University

8/1666
Centre for Education and Industry,
Coventry CN4 7AL
0203 523523
Mubanga, R. Mr; *Supervisor:* Woolhouse, J. Prof.;
Richardson, W. Mr; Finegold, D. Mr
Education/industry partnerships in the UK: the policies and practice of major companies
Abstract: The aim of the research is to examine how companies' education policies are formulated; how policies are turned into programmes of action; how company staff are involved and what such policies and programmes are thought to achieve. Ten to fifteen leading United Kingdom companies will be investigated. The research will also examine the congruence of companies education policies and the practice in the education service in working with companies.
Source of Grant: Department of Education and Science Training Enterprise Education Division British Petroleum: £125,000 jointly
Date of Research: 1989 – continuing
KEYWORDS: cooperation; education; industrial training; industry; industry relationship

8/1667
Centre for Educational Development, Appraisal and Research, Coventry CV4 7AL
0203 523523
Galloway, S. Ms; *Supervisor:* Burgess, R. Prof.
An evaluation of inservice training and professional development
Abstract: Warwickshire Local Education Authority, wishing to investigate how the LEATGS (Local Education Authority Training Grant Scheme) is operating in the Authority, funded this project over one year on a half-time basis. The research proposal specifies three broad areas for study: institution-focused inservice work (including professional development days); the link between inservice work and classroom practice; and the effectiveness of inservice training including the ways in which schools evaluate. Qualitative methods provided interview and observational data from primary and secondary schools, to be set alongside documentary material. Preliminary interviews with sixteen INSET (Inservice Education and Training of Teachers) co-ordinators led into more detailed case studies in the primary phase, particularly in clusters of small rural schools. Here, the research examined key processes in collaborative forms of INSET both within schools and between schools. The final report includes case studies of four schools' training programmes on information technology, art, science and assessment. The project was reported in August 1990, following interim reports in December 1989, and March and June 1990.
Source of Grant: Warwickshire Local Education Authority: £20,440
Date of Research: 1989-1990

KEYWORDS: further education of teachers; inservice teacher education; inservice training; teacher

8/1668
Centre for Educational Development, Appraisal and Research, Coventry CV4 7AL
0203 523523
Burgess, R. Prof.; Phtiaka, H. Dr
Library use, information skills and GCSE (General Certificate of Secondary Education)
Abstract: The project will examine library use and the teaching of information skills to pupils preparing GCSE (General Certificate of Secondary Education) course work. The project will focus on four co-educational comprehensive schools where library use and information skills will be examined through different subject areas. Emphasis will be placed on a case study method of investigation. A significant development in GCSE is the introduction of course work that is assessed by teachers during the candidate's period of study. Course work involves pupils developing knowledge, understanding and concepts based upon their use of information skills including information handling, knowledge building and its relationship to other area of the curriculum. This project focuses on the ways in which information skills are transmitted and used by pupils in preparing coursework for GCSE. The project aims to examine the role of the library in the school, identify the way in which library resources have been established in schools in relation to the GCSE, identify the information skills that are transmitted to pupils, and examine the ways in which pupils use information skills in preparing GCSE course work. The project will involve focusing on fourth year pupils engaged in GCSE and their teachers. Four case studies of co-educational comprehensive schools will be conducted where all GCSE courses are taken with one examining group. The researcher will be involved in using case study methods involving documentary evidence, observation, participant observation and in depth interviews with pupils and teachers. It is hoped that the findings will finally be disseminated through discussions, presentations to courses and conferences, and through published work.
Source of Grant: British Library Research and Development Department
Date of Research: 1989 – continuing
KEYWORDS: General Certificate of Secondary Education; information skills; school library

8/1669
Centre for Educational Development, Appraisal and Research, Coventry CV4 7AL
0203 523523
Morrison, M. Ms; *Supervisor:* Burgess, R. Prof.
School development plans
Abstract: Research is focused on ways in which the LEA (local education authority), schools. teachers and interested bodies, like governors, perceive the role and funtion of school development plans, specifically in relation to immediate and medium-term needs of the school, links between SDPs (school development plans) and staff development policies, links between SDPs and curriculum practice. Methodology and interviews is through documentation analysis and course and school-based observation. A case study will be carried out and a report submitted to the LEA.
Source of Grant: Warwickshire Education Authority
Date of Research: 1989-1990
KEYWORDS: educational development; plan; planning of education; school

8/1670
Centre for Race and Ethnic Relations, Coventry CV4 7AL
0203 523523
Vincent, B. Mr; *Supervisor:* Ball, W. Ms; Troyna, B. Mr
Parental participation in the management of multi racial primary schools
Abstract: Parental participation is a major part of government policy to increase the autonomy of the market and influence of consumers. However a number of factors could be problematic. Parents are not a homogenous group, but divided by differences in race, class and gender, which may well affect their perception of their role in their childs' formal education. Teachers may see the increase in parental influence as an attack on their autonomy. The research will focus primarily on one new urban left authority in London, created by the abolition of the ILEA (Inner London Education Authority). The authority, although opposed in general

terms to central government education and social policy, welcomes the opportunity to increase parental and community involvement. It is to be expected that this range of divergent perceptions concerning the correct role for parents is likely to produce a variety of outcomes. Consequently the study will be primarily school-based, providing insights into the way in which schools as individual institutions mediate these competing influences. The research will involve extended periods of participant observation within four to six institutions. This will be accompanied by a series of informal and semi-structured interviews with the various other actors involved in the running of a school, such as local councillors, education officers, heads, teachers, union representatives, and members of governing bodies, as well as community groups and parents themselves.
Source of Grant: Economic and Rearch Council Research Training Award: £5,000
Date of Research: 1989 – continuing
KEYWORDS: *intercultural education; multicultural education; parent participation; parent-school relation; parent-teacher relation*

8/1671
 Centre for English Language Teaching,
 Coventry CV4 7AL
 0203 523523
 Idris, N. Mr; Nesi, H. Ms; *Supervisor:* Nesi, H. Ms
An investigation into patterns of lexical difficulty in economics textbooks
Abstract: This study is concerned with academic english vocabulary, and in particular the lexis of economics at undergraduate level in Malaysia. It aims primarily to identify those vocabulary items which the Malaysian undergraduate will have greatest difficulty with – those words outside the scope of the high school syllabus, but which the textbook writer assumes that the student already knows. This vocabulary will be identified by: (a) examining undergraduate economics textbooks with the aid of a concordancing program, to find those words which are not commonly taught in Malaysian schools but which are not defined within the textbooks themselves; (b) interviewing staff and students at the National Islamic University, Kuala Lumpur, to establish the vocabulary requirements of the undergraduate economics course, and the lexis students have greatest difficulty comprehending; (c) testing the lexical knowledge of undergraduate entrants to the economics department, and comparing students' actual knowledge with the requirements of the course, as reflected in the findings from (a) and (b). The second stage of the study will involve the preparation of glossaries for the use of readers of economics textbooks at the National Islamic University, Kuala Lumpur, and the monitoring of their usefulness.
Source of Grant: No funding
Date of Research: 1990 – continuing
KEYWORDS: *English (second language); lexis*

8/1672
 Centre for English Language Teaching,
 Coventry CV4 7AL
 0203 523200
 Gillett, A.J. Mr; *Supervisor:* Bloor, M.
Applied linguistics: models of listening comprehension for english language teaching
Abstract: The objective of the research is to come up with a model of the listening process which would help teachers of English as a foreign or second langauge. The procedure involves the following stages: To investigate the existing advice that exists for teachers who are teaching listening comprehension in the classroom; look into the background of this advice and see on what research it is based, and check the validity of this research. Investigate the psychological and educational research into comprehension and see to what extent it is relevant to listening. Can we agree with Widdowson when he says that there exists a 'general discourse processing strategy' which is therefore also relevant for listening? Try some experiments to test the theories from a listening point of view. Look at the specific problems that non-native speakers have. For example, it is important to consider to what extent discourse processing strategies are universal and hence transferrable across cultures. The objective of this is to use this research to come up with a model of the listening process which would make it clear to teachers exactly what is involved in listening. This would enable them to base their teaching on a stronger theoretical background which ought to help the learners.
Source of Grant: No funding

Date of Research: 1988 – continuing
KEYWORDS: *English (second language)*

8/1673
 Centre for Educational Development, Appraisal and Research (CEDAR), Coventry CV4 7AL
 0203 523806
 Hockey, J. Dr; Pole, C. Dr; *Supervisor:* Burgess, R.G. Prof.
Becoming a postgraduate student: the social organization of postgraduate training
Abstract: This research will be a two year study involving examining the first year of doctoral study undertaken by students in the disciplines of sociology, economics and business studies. This involves field research (interviewing and observation) in three contrasting sites for each discipline. The case study method is being used, so that institutional and disciplinary case studies will be compiled. The research is part of a wider initiative funded by the ESRC on research training in the social sciences.
Source of Grant: Economic and Social Research Council
Date of Research: 1990-1990
KEYWORDS: *academic degree; postgraduate study; social sciences; student sociology*

8/1674
 Centre for Educational Development, Appraisal and Research, Coventry CV4 7AL
 0203 523806 (direct dial); 0203 523523 ext 2912
 Priestley, C. Ms; Pole, C. Mr; *Supervisor:* Burgess, R.G. Prof.
Action research project on Records of Achievement in Warwickshire schools
Abstract: The project is to run for two years and will involve action research within schools which will involve further development work with teachers. The study will concern itself with the introduction and development of ROA (Records of Achievement) schemes in the north and eastern areas of the education authority. From these areas, four case study schools will be identified, whilst there will also be a survey of practice across all institutions. In relation to the four schools case study methodology will be used. At present it is envisaged that this will include observation, participant observation, in depth interviews and the collection of documentary materials. The aim is to identify how the current materials, already produced by the education authority, are being introduced, extended and developed by the schools. From the research findings, criteria relating to the successful implementation and development of ROA schemes will be identified. These criteria would then form the basis for future developmental work within the authority. Specifically this would involve the dissemination of the case study findings, which would be linked to the inservice training of teachers. Issues to be explored will include teacher time; the role and perceptions of pupils, teachers, parents and other users; how teaching and learning styles have been modified and also the role of information technology in respect of the administration of ROA schemes. These issues and indeed the research strategies themselves are subject to change and modification as the research project proceeds. Throughout the study interim reports will be produced, with a final report in September 1990.
Source of Grant: Warwickshire County Council: £54,301 over two years
Date of Research: 1988-1990
KEYWORDS: *achievement; profile; student record*

8/1675
 Centre for Educational Development Appraisal and Research, Coventry CV4 7AL
 0203 523523
 Pole, C.J. Mr; *Supervisor:* Burgess, R.G. Prof.
An evaluation of Records of Achievement in further education and the Youth Training Scheme in Coventry
Abstract: The evaluation which will take a case study approach, being based in one further education college in the City of Coventry, will seek to address the following key tasks: (i) to explore the relationship between Records of Achievement in schools and profiles currently used in futher education and the Y.T.S.; (ii) to develop common principles and practices of recording achievement in colleges and the Y.T.S.; (iii) to investigate the implementation of Records of Achievement in further education and the Y.T.S. Further issues will be identified as the evaluation progresses and will relate in particular to student and teacher/lecturer perceptions of Records of Achievement. Further themes will also be developed

in order to facilitate meta-evaluation and cross comparison by those engaged in the national evaluation of Records of Achievement.
Source of Grant: Coventry Education Department (Education Support Grant): £14,000
Date of Research: 1988-1990
KEYWORDS: achievement; further education; profile; student record; Youth Training Scheme

8/1676
Centre for Educational Development, Appraisal and Research, Coventry CV4 7AL
0203 523806
Newton, M. Mr; *Supervisor:* Burgess, R.G. Prof.
The evaluation of school focused inservice training
Abstract: Current arrangements for inservice education and training under LEATGS (The Local Education Authority Training Grants Scheme) require local authorities to establish procedures for the monitoring and evaluation of their inservice provision. The primary aim of this project is to develop within an authority a number of models and strategies to assist the process of evaluation at institutional level in terms of the effectiveness of inservice training for teachers. A secondary aim is to lay some foundations for future work in the authority concerning the impact of teachers' inservice training on students' learning. A study by semi-structured interview of current thinking and practice on evaluation in some of the authority's secondary schools will be conducted.
Source of Grant: Local education authority: (seconded Head-teacher)
Date of Research: 1988-1989
KEYWORDS: evaluation; local education authority; inservice education and training of teachers

8/1677
Centre for Educational Development, Appraisal and Research, Coventry CV4 7AL
0203 523806
Sanday, A.P. Mr; *Supervisor:* Burgess, R.G. Prof.
Making schools more effective
Abstract: A review and re-analysis of the literature on effective schools and school improvement (CEDAR Occasional Paper No 2) led to the hypothesis that an important reason why purposeful leadership does not always result in an effective school is the strong homeostatic forces generated by the group structure of school organization. Funding is being sought to research this hypothesis. The review also indicated the need for an attitude inventory as a performance indicator for secondary schools. This is being developed. Another research project is being formulated on the effectiveness of inspections in bringing about school improvement.
Source of Grant: No funding
Date of Research: 1988 – continuing
KEYWORDS: local education authority; school effectiveness

8/1678
Centre for Educational Development, Appraisal and Research, Coventry CV4 7AL
0203 523806/523523
Scott, D.A.D. Mr; *Supervisor:* Burgess, R.G. Prof.
The effects of the assessment of coursework on students following a curriculum based entirely on the Midland Examining Group GCSE syllabuses
Abstract: Six case studies have been made. Their primary focus was on the demands made by the Midlands Examining Group GCSE syllabuses on students who are assessed by coursework in different areas. Six areas were looked at: (1) what actually is asked of students by Examination Boards; (2) how the syllabus requirements are interpreted by the teachers; (3) how pupils actually interpret those instructions; (4) how pupils go about those tasks; (5) how those performances match up to the expectations of the Examination Board in the first place; (6) how those performances match up to the expectations of teachers. In addition it explored other theoretical issues such as the reliability and validity of coursework and the effects of coursework on pupil/teacher relationships.
Published Material: SCOTT, D.A.D. (1989). The GCSE: an annotated bibliography and an introductory essay. Warwick: CEDAR, University of Warwick.
Source of Grant: Midland Examining Group: £50,000
Date of Research: 1988-1989
KEYWORDS: assessment; coursework; General Certificate of Secondary Education; performance

8/1679
Centre for Education and Industry,
Westwood, Coventry CV4 7AL
0203 523523
Richardson, W. Mr
Industrial company's approaches to participation and funding in education
Abstract: The work is intended to investigate the attitude of leading UK companies to their involvement in the education system, particularly in schooling up to the age of 18. A survey will be made of major company involvement in education/industry work and a sample of 20/30 leading companies will be examined more closely to ascertain, through structured interviews with senior employees, the likely future pattern of company involvement.
Source of Grant: British Petroleum: £100,000
Date of Research: 1989 – continuing
KEYWORDS: financial resources; industry; labour market; participation; secondary education

8/1680
Coventry CV4 7AL
0203 523844
Byrd, B. Dr; Duke, C. Prof.; Tight, M. Dr
The progress of part-time higher education students
Abstract: This research will monitor the progress of students engaged on Warwick University's part-time degree programme. It will look at their expectations and experience over time, the reactions of staff and the impact on family circumstances. The research will be longitudinal. In addition, case studies will be conducted of part-time students at five other British higher education institutions, across the binary divide.
Source of Grant: Universities Funding Council
Date of Research: 1987 – continuing
KEYWORDS: academic degree; family life; higher education; part-time course

8/1681
Centre for English Language Teaching,
Coventry CV4 7AL
0203 523523
Halilou, I. Mr; *Supervisor:* Lawrence, L. Dr
An evaluation of the English language curriculum in Niger: the mismatch between curriculum planning and production of teaching learning materials
Abstract: A formative evaluation will be carried out in Niger to investigate the reform of the English language curriculum at secondary level. The research study will examine the design of a syllabus and analyze teaching materials. A classroom study will be carried out to determine the implementation of the syllabus. The research will be qualitative and interpretative based on interviews, questionnaires and classroom observation. It will determine the harmony between design and implementation of the English language curriculum.
Source of Grant: British Council Scholarship
Date of Research: 1990 – continuing
KEYWORDS: English (second language)

8/1682
Department of Arts Education
Westwood, Coventry CV4 7AL
0203 523523 ext 2807
Alcock, J. Mr
Sensitive social issues: a developing role for theatre-in-education
Abstract: This research continues earlier work on diversification of Theatre in-Education beyond school curriculum-based emphases, looking especially at community based learning needs in the areas of health and social education. It will involve individual reading and field research with Theatre-in-Education (TIE) companies in Great Britain, Canada and USA. There will be a practical application to field-test postulation – e.g. artistic director, Acting for Health, national theatre-in-health-education festival and conference, Birmingham, September 1988, sponsored by South Birmingham Area Health Authority. Dissemination of the findings will be through journal articles, practical training programmes, contribution to management of Theatre in Health Education (THE) Trust.
Published Material: ALCOCK, J. (1984). 'Nothing short of revolutionary – Theatre-in-Education for the handicapped', West Midlands Arts Report, June. ; ALCOCK, J. (1989). 'Sensitive social issues: a developing role for TIE', Journal of National Associa-

tion for Pastoral Care in Education, (NAPCE), Vol 7, No 1, pp.18-22.
Source of Grant: No funding
Date of Research: 1987-1990
KEYWORDS: community education; drama; health education; theatre

8/1683

Department of Arts Education
Westwood, Coventry CV4 7AL
0203 523523
Swallow, T. Mr

The political dimensions of curriculum development in foreign language teaching in the United Kingdom
Abstract: The post-war period has seen considerable changes in the Foreign languages curriculum of UK schools. Some of these developments have clearly been influenced by developments abroad, particularly in France. Few of these developments have been adequately researched and documented so that no body of knowledge is accumulating in relation to some of the most important developments in FL teaching to have occurred this century. Virtually no writing on the development of the foreign language curriculum in the UK has had the political dimension as its focus. At the same time, it is clear that FLs are possibly the most politically charged component of the school curriculum. The project traces from a political rather than a historical angle, the initiatives that were taken, at national and international level to improve the quality and the range of FL provision in schools. At the international level this will include the role of Unesco throughout the period in question, via the Ceylon Seminar and regional conferences as well as by less formal means, the relationship of the deliberations of the European Ministers of Education to national pronouncements about FL curriculum policy and steps to implement policy as well as the possible impact of developments in the USA on government and elite group thinking. In the UK, attention centres on the role of the Nuffield Foundation in the start-up of the Primary French Pilot Project, on pressure group activity, particularly in professional organizations, which developed around new conceptions of the purposes of FL teaching, and on intiatives to increase the range of FLs offered in UK schools (the Scarbrough, Annan and Hayter reports for instance). Methodology is by: (i) documentary analysis of secondary literature and of primary sources; (ii) structured and semi-strucutred elite interviewing.
Source of Grant: Warwick University; Research and Innovations Fund: £500
Date of Research: 1987 – continuing
KEYWORDS: curriculum development; educational policy; foreign languages; politics

8/1684

Department of Arts Education
Westwood, Coventry CV4 7AL
0203 523523
Green Lanes Primary School
Chelmesley Wood, Birmingham,
Smiths Wood Secondary School,
Chelmesley Wood, Birmingham
Alcock, J.A. Mr ; *Supervisor:* Jenkins, D. Prof.

The evaluation and dissemination of the National Curriculum Council's 'Pupil Autonomy in Learning' at Green Lanes Primary school, Chelmesley Wood, Birmingham
Abstract: The aim of this research is to evaluate by field observation, data gathering and written report analysis the National Curriculum Council approved project 'Pupil Autonomy in Learning' (PAL) at Green Lanes School, Chelmesley Wood, Birmingham. It is intended to develop and promote pupil autonomy in learning and to identify teaching strategies to encourage pupils to take part in systematic self-analysis. The findings of the project will be shown through written report, articles, a commissioned video and a conference/forum.
Source of Grant: National Curriculum Council: £2,500
Date of Research: 1987-1989
KEYWORDS: autonomy; learning strategy; self evaluation; teaching method

8/1685

Department of Arts Education
Coventry CV4 7AL
0203 523523

Jenkins, D. Prof. ; Yeomans, R. Dr ; *Supervisor:* Gibson, N.A.M. Mr

Art, design and reading: connections and developments in higher order abilities in the upper primary school
Abstract: The research takes its starting point from an area of curriculum development which was initiated in Scotland in 1978. The field of investigation is concerned with the relationships between the higher order skills and abilities in visual art in reading, as they emerge and develop in the upper primary school. There are two major elements in the research. The first is a study of the literature on art, design, and reading in education since 1945, complemented by a review of recent, relevant literature in the field of psychology. The second, underpinned by the academic study, is action research in schools. This will be carried out in collaboration with teacher colleagues in the schools concerned. The potential outcomes are contributions to learning theory or to models of teaching.
Source of Grant: No funding
Date of Research: 1988 – continuing
KEYWORDS: art; primary education; reading; skill

8/1686

Department of Arts Education
Coventry CV4 7AL
0203 523523 ext 2579/2873
Jackson, R. Mr ; *Supervisor:* Nesbitt, E.M. Ms

Punjabi Hindu nurture in Coventry
Abstract: The Punjabi Hindu Nurture in Coventry project arose from the Hindu Nurture in Coventry project (1986-1988). The aim is to discover details of the religious/cultural lives of Coventry children between the ages of eight and thirteen whose families belong to two distinct communities, the Balmikis and the Ravidasis. Each community has a Coventry place of worship and each is 'untouchable' in Indian caste terms. Through participant observation and photographing in their temples and homes and through tape recorded interviews data will be collected. This material will be used in articles for social scientists, religious studies specialists and educationalists. It will also supplement material used in the training of teachers.
Source of Grant: The Leverhulme Trust: £25,900
Date of Research: 1988-1989
KEYWORDS: child; cultural environment; religious minority

8/1687

Department of Continuing Education
Coventry CV4 7AL
0203 523835
Duke, C. Prof.

The development of continuing education within higher education in Britain
Abstract: This research consists of policy studies and action research, both longitudinal and related to and tested through activities in leading a new university department of continuing education. There has been an exploration of different facets and strategies of promoting continuing education in higher education, including: regional and transbinary collaboration; funding finance and rewarding systems; staff development for continuing education; economic and equity objectives/ the vocational – liberal dichotomy; performance measurement and evaluation; staff development for continuing education and the 'mainstreaming' of continuing education within higher education; specific areas of interest include; access; part-time degrees; self-financing (Pickup) and subvention (RB) issues.
Published Material: BILLHAM, T. (Ed). et al (1988). Various working documents available from researcher and 'Government funding policies' in the Pickup Papers. DES, pp.1-24.
Source of Grant: Universities Funding Council
Date of Research: 1986 – continuing
KEYWORDS: continuing education; educational policy; higher education

8/1688

Department of Continuing Education
Coventry CV4 7AL
0203 523835
Duke, C. Prof.

Adult education for third world development and the training of adult educators
Abstract: Studies of the relationships between Adult Educational

Development in the Third World, including the meaning of 'development', and the training of adult educators.
Published Material: DUKE, C. (1985). Combating poverty through adult education. London: Croom Helm. ; DUKE, C. (1986). Adult education: international perspectives from China. London: Croom Helm. ; DUKE, C. (1987). 'Adult education, poverty and development', Journal of Lifelong Education, Vol 6, No 4, pp.319-330.
Source of Grant: No funding
Date of Research: 1982 – continuing
KEYWORDS: adult education; developing country; training

8/1689
Department of Continuing Education
Westwood, Coventry CV4 7AL
0203 523523
Field, J. Mr (Department of Continuing Education) ; Smith, C. Mr (West Midlands Advisory Council for Further Education and Training) ; *Supervisor:* Stock, Y. Ms
Adults and the General Certificate of Secondary Education
Abstract: As with the examinations it replaced, GCSE is an important means for adults to gain an educational qualification. It represents a means of access and progression to other educational, training or employment opportunities; GCSE courses are also, for many, a rewarding form of learning regardless of their final grade. After representations made by teachers of adults in early 1988, the West Midlands Advisory Council and the Department of Continuing Education, University of Warwick, embarked on an enquiry into the implications of the new examination for adult learners. The project is being conducted with the co-operation of the Midlands Examining Group. The aims of this project will be to (a) map the extent of adult participation in GCSE; (b) identify patterns of adult participation and performance; (c) identify the educational and socio-economic characteristics of adult participations in GCSE; (d) investigate adult participants' motivation, experiences and perceptions of the new system, and their preferred modes of study; (e) investigate their teachers' experiences and perceptions of the new system; (f) establish the organizational and financial basis upon which GCSE operates as a part of adult general education; and (g) summarize current policy thinking in the field. The outcomes of the project will be used as the basis for (a) dissemination, including staff development activities; (b) policy discussion, directed towards LEAs, DES and others with an interest in general qualifying education for adults; and (c) identification of issues for consideration and action by examining bodies.
Source of Grant: This project is being conducted with the co-operation of the Midlands Examining Group
Date of Research: 1985-1990
KEYWORDS: adult education; educational opportunities; General Certificate of Secondary Education; participation; qualification

8/1690
Department of Education
Westwood, Coventry CV4 7AL
0203 523523
Oxford University
Department of Educational Studies
15 Norham Gardens, Oxford OX2 6PY
0865 274024
Sylva, K. Prof.
The High/Scope curriculum in Britain
Abstract: Observational studies were carried out in three pre-school settings, two in LEA (local education authority) nurseries and one in a voluntary family centre. Twelve children were observed in each setting (N = 36) during the planning phase of the High/Scope curriculum and during a free play session. Differences between the two kinds of play are discussed in terms of amount and quality of structure in pre-school curriculum.
Source of Grant: Dr.Bernardo's 1987-1988
Date of Research: 1987-1989
KEYWORDS: curriculum; early childhood education; nursery school curriculum; play; pre-school education

8/1691
Department of Education
Westwood, Coventry CV4 7AL
0203 523523
Wiggins, G.A. Mr ; *Supervisor:* Sikes, P. Dr ; Merson, M. Mr
Career perceptions and expeiences of advisory teachers in one local education authority

Abstract: This research project aims to examine the career perceptions and experiences of a number of advisory teachers employed by one local education authority. The majority of these advisory teachers are seconded for a limited period (normally two years) from teaching posts in school. Taking an ethnographic approach, and relying principally on interviews, the research will explore advisory teachers' perceptions of the job, how they feel their role as providers of inservice training can best be carried out, and their relationships with teachers and with advisors/inspectors. It will examine their reasons for wanting to become an advisory teacher, and their longer term career plans, and will attempt to establish to what extent advisory teachers' perspectives are affected by their background. It will seek to identify any occupational culture or cultures which may exist among advisory teachers and how new members are socialised into the culture.
Source of Grant: No funding
Date of Research: 1989 – continuing
KEYWORDS: advisor; career development; employment expectations; educational guidance; guidance officer; inservice training; role perception

8/1692
Department of Education
Coventry CV4 7AL
0203 523523
Blair, M. Ms ; *Supervisor:* Troyna, B. Mr
Multi-cultural/anti-racist education
Abstract: The aim of this research is to investigate the obstacles to the educational success of Afro-Caribbean pupils whilst simultaneously attempting to remove or reduce such obstacles by working with the school on policies of anti-racism and equality of opportunity. The focus will be the education perspectives of the Afro-Caribbean pupils themselves and their families. The research is therefore participative and action-orientated. The researcher will engage critically with the pupils and their families on issues of concern to them in an attempt to create a conaciousness of the collective power they have to influence direct the decisions, attitudes and behaviours which affect the education of their children. There are 20 out of 550 Afro-Caribbean pupils from the ages of 11 to 16. The bulk of the research will be in the form of individual or group interviews of pupils, their parents and staff members. It may be necessary to interview pupils in their final year of the feeder junior school and to use documentary research to trace the destinies of former pupils from the school. Questionnaires will be used to elicit responses to social and sexual harrassment and bullying. These responses to their educational experiences will form the basis of the consciousness raising of parents and the background to more effective dialogue between the school and the community.
Source of Grant: Cambridgeshire County Council: £483
Date of Research: 1989 – continuing
KEYWORDS: Afro Caribbean youth; educational discrimination; equal education; equal opportunity; ethnic minority; race relations; racism

8/1693
Department of Education
Westwood, Coventry CV4 7AL
0203 523523
Bell, L.A. Dr
The development of a newly formed comprehensive school
Abstract: This study provides a description of the closure of three comprehensive schools, their amalgamation into one new school, and the strategies used by those within the school to cope with this process. It goes on to examine the initial impact of the Education Reform Act on the school. The research uses interviews, observation and documentary sources.
Source of Grant: The Nuffield Foundation: £3,000
Date of Research: 1988 – continuing
KEYWORDS: administration structure; closures; educational legislation; mergers; school

8/1694
Department of Education
Coventry CV4 7AL
0203 523523
Troyna, B.S. Mr ; Hatcher, R. Mr ; Berridge, D. Dr
Race relations in the primary school
Abstract: Race relations in the primary school is the subject of a new two year project to be carried out by the National Children's Bureau in collaboration with Warwick University. The research,

funded by the Economic and Social Research Council, will look at how older pupils' views develop on race and race related matters in a small number of primary schools. The researcher, who is an experienced teacher, will observe classroom behaviour as well as interviewing teachers, pupils, policy makers and parents in an LEA (local education authority) where there are few but nonetheless significant numbers of ethnic minority pupils. For much of the time the researcher will be based in the upper forms of primary schools talking to pupils, observing their patterns of contact and exploring their views on race and related matters. The researchers hope to be able to identify some common factors in the way racial incidents in schools are sparked off. As a result, it would be possible to recommend strategies which either pre-empt these incidents or, at least, enable them to be dealt with in an appropriate and effective manner by teachers and parents.
Source of Grant: Economic and Research Council
Date of Research: 1989-1990
KEYWORDS: primary school; race relation; racial attitude; racism

8/1695

Department of Education
Coventry CV4 7AL
0203 523523
Open University
Department of Technology
Walton Hall, Milton Keynes Mk7 6AA
0908 274066
Savory, C. Mrs ; *Supervisor:* Sylva, K. Prof.
A systematic approach to training junior aged children in group-process social skills
Abstract: A controlled experiment was carried out to test the efficacy of a systematic training programme for junior aged children. The training programme, based on management courses in industry, helped children develop skills at listening to others, defining group tasks and means, acting supportively, and evaluating group efforts. Outcome measures included effective groupwork, task achievement, process skills, parental views, and student evaluation of their own performance.
Source of Grant: ESRC (Economic and Social Research Council)
Date of Research: 1986-1990
KEYWORDS: group work; interpersonal relations; listening; listening skills; pupil; self-evaluation; social skills

8/1696

Department of Education
Westwood, Coventry CV4 7AL
0203 523523
Siraj-Blatchford, I. Ms
The experiences of black students in initial teacher education
Abstract: The Swann report commented on the need for black teachers in mainstream schooling and on the problems of recruiting those teachers. The researchers cite racism in schools and the clearly evident restricted career opportunities open to black teachers (Education for All. Swann 1985 pp.609/10). More recent research from the Bradford and Ilkley Community College has shown how only 4% of a sample of 140 young Asian sixth-formers decided on a teaching degree. This research also points to poor promotion opportunities and racism as the main deterrents (Asian and White Perceptions of the Teaching Profession. Ramindar Singh. Bradford and Ilkley Community College 1988). While a small proportion of black students enter teacher education these students positive perceptions of teaching and career motivations are systematically if unintentionally undermined by the institutions. Factors as diverse as accommodation, curricula, counselling and other social influences conspire to colour the experiences of the students and lead to underachievement and disillusionment. Efforts to change these perceptions of the profession are doomed to failure if students are to be further discouraged on entering training institutions. The proposed research project will extend the work of the commission for Racial Equality publication 'Learning in Terror' and the finding of the survey on ethnic minority teachers. It is also intended to provide further evidence and concrete proposals for change in institutions of teacher education. This research, a national survey of the experience of Asian and Afro-caribbean students including a number of in depth interviews, will identify those aspects of organization and curricula which initial teacher education institutions must review if they are to respond to the needs of society, and promote, multi-ethnic recruitment.

Source of Grant: Commission for Racial Equality: £200
Date of Research: 1989-1990
KEYWORDS: black teachers; equal opportunity; ethnic minority; minority group teachers; racism; supply of teachers; teacher education; teacher recruitment

8/1697

Department of Education
Westwood, Coventry CV4 7AL
0203 523523
Sikes, P. Dr ; Troyna, B. Mr
Life history and initial teacher education
Abstract: Research evidence suggests that many teachers continue, consciously or otherwise, to make important decisions about the organization, orientation and delivery of the formal and informal curricula on grounds which are racist, sexist and discriminatory in a range of other ways. Should we therefore succumb to a system of teacher education/training in which these practices could well be reproduced systematically? Or should we, instead, develop pre-service courses geared towards the development of a teaching force which reflects in a critical manner on taken-for-granted assumptions, which can articulate reasons for co-testing some of the conventional wisdoms about pupils, their interests and abilities, and which, ultimately, might influence future cohorts? In contrast to recent calls for the dismemberment of ITE (initial teacher education) course, as they are presently constituted, the researchers argue for the introduction of life history methods as a strategy for facilitating the transition from pupil to teacher status. The research draws on the past experiences of using this strategy with a group of first year students following an ITE course.
Published Material: TROYNA, B. & SIKES, P. (1989). 'Putting the 'why' back into teacher education', Forum, Vol 32, No 1.
Source of Grant: No funding
Date of Research: 1988 – continuing
KEYWORDS: teacher background; teacher education

8/1698

Department of Education
Policy Analysis Unit, Coventry CV4 7AL
0203 523523 ext 2968
Campbell, R.J. Mr ; Neill, S. St.J. Dr
The use of teachers' time
Abstract: The aim of the project is to analyze the time that teachers spend on work, using five broad categories, viz. teaching, preparation, inservice training, administration, and other activities. The analysis is related to education policy, including the delivery of the National Curriculum. 95 teachers in Key Stage One, and 300 teachers in secondary schools are participating by completing a daily time diary and questionnaire. Analysis is by a specially written program. A sub-sample of 40 Key State 1 teachers is being followed up in interview.
Published Material: CAMPBELL, R.J. & NEILL, S. ST.J. '1330 days: final report of a pilot study of teacher time in Key Stage 1'. London: Assistant Masters and Mistresses Association.
Source of Grant: Assistant Masters and Mistresses Association: £15,000
Date of Research: 1990 – continuing
KEYWORDS: time management

8/1699

Department of Education
Coventry CV4 7AL
0203 523523
Birke, L. Dr
Women and scientific literacy
Abstract: This research project is mapping the extent of understanding in science and science policy among women (with particular attention to ways in which women may have some scientific knowledge but do not identify it as such); and is identifying those issues within science which are of particular interest − actual and potential − to women who have no previous experience of higher education. Outcomes are oriented towards the development of policy and practice, and will be tested through a number of pilot courses.
Source of Grant: No funding
Date of Research: 1990 – continuing
KEYWORDS: adult education; comprehension; higher education; sciences; science policy; women's education

8/1700
> Department of Education
> Westwood, Coventry CV4 7AL
> 0203 523523
> Bell, L.A. Dr

An analysis of the impact of policy changes on the management of a comprehensive school
Abstract: The school in this study was formed in 1985 as a result of the merger of 3 schools. It had a new headteacher appointed in 1987 and is now feeling the loss of its 6th form. It also has to cope with the changes embodied in the Education Act 1988. This study will monitor the impact of these changes through a series of interviews with and observations of the staff of the school over a two year period.
Source of Grant: The Nuffield Foundation: £2,271
Date of Research: 1988-1990
KEYWORDS: administration of education; comprehensive school; educational policy; reform of education

8/1701
> Department of Education
> Coventry CV4 7Al
> 0203 523848
> Eggleston, S.J. Prof.; Lashley, H.

Improving access to education for young black adults
Abstract: The general aim of this research project is to prepare a directory of projects with details of their curriculum arrangements and a short term evaluation focusing on quality of training, placement of trainees, content and organization of curriculum, access criteria and opportunity for further advanced training, and jobs obtained. The research work will be organized in a Northern and a Southern Region divided by the Midlands, Coventry being the northern limit of the Southern Region and Birmingham/Leicester the southern end of the Northern Region. A base for each regional research associate will be provided in London (Southern Region) and Manchester (Northern Region) at the relevant Replan offices. The Directorate and Administration of the project will be based at Warwick University.
Source of Grant: Further Education Unit (DES): £37,848
Date of Research: 1987-1989
KEYWORDS: curriculum; ethnic minority; evaluation; training; unemployed

8/1702
> Department of Education
> Coventry CV4 7AL
> 0203 523523
> Swalcliffe Park School Trust
> Swalcliffe, Banbury, Oxon
> Cooling, M. Mr; *Supervisor:* Lloyd-Smith, M. Mr; Heward, C. Dr

An examination of some of the factors influencing the re-adjustment of special needs children with emotional and behavioural difficulties in a residential school
Abstract: An examination of the factors influencing the readjustment of special needs children with emotional and behavioural problems in a residential school. Use will be made of both qualitative and quantative information gathered from survey, follow-ups of past pupils, case file data and personal interviews making use of pupil perception of their educational experience. All of this to be viewed in a historical perspective taking cognizance of such influences as Underwood, Warnock and the various social and psychological theories which have influenced this area of education. Size of observed group being used will be up to 100.
Source of Grant: No funding
Date of Research: 1988 – continuing
KEYWORDS: adjustment; behaviour disorder; emotional disorder; maladjusted; residential school; special needs

8/1703
> Department of Education
> Coventry CV4 7AL
> 0203 523523
> Westminster College
> North Hinksey, Oxford OX9 2AT
> 0865 247644
> *Supervisor:* Gardner, P.

Moral education
Abstract: The research is philosophical. It is an inquiry into: the possibility of objectivity in moral judgement, the nature of reasoning in morality, the role of knowledge and reason in the development of moral character.
Source of Grant: Westminster College
Date of Research: 1987 – continuing
KEYWORDS: community education; moral development; moral education

8/1704
> Department of Education
> Coventry CV4 7AL
> 0203 523523
> The Meadows School
> Hawthorn Lane, Tile Hill, Coventry CV9 4PB
> Heward, C. Dr; Lloyd-Smith, M. Mr; *Supervisor:* Silvester, P.D. Mr

An examination of the relation between family background and emotional, behavioural and learning difficulties in two special schools
Abstract: This research investigates the referral process and the type of pupil referred to two special schools. The core of the research is the inter-
relationship between learning difficulty, emotional and behavioural problems and pupils' family background. The evidence consists of pupil files for the period 1973-86, interview transcripts, and documentary material. The analysis takes the form of a three stage statistical survey and content analysis against a backcloth of archive evidence. The results so far suggest that: (1) educational establishments may be fulfilling social functions, (2) referral and assessment processes may well be influenced by factors other than pupils' educational needs.
Published Material: SILVESTER, P.D. (1987). 'A study of the boys referred to a new residential school for the maladjusted (1973-1986)'. M.Ed Dissertation, University of Warwick.
Source of Grant: Local Education Authority: c.£450 per annum
Date of Research: 1986 – continuing
KEYWORDS: family environment; learning difficulty; maladjusted; residential school; special education

8/1705
> Department of Education
> Westwood, Coventry CV4 7AL
> 0203 523523
> Campbell, R.J. Mr; David, P. Ms

Evaluation of intercultural support services in South Warwickshire
Abstract: The aim of this research is to evaluate an ESG (Education Support Grant) funded programme of training teachers in intercultural education. Qualitative methods were used in 11 pilot schools; 8 primary and 3 secondary in an 'all-white' area. The role of 2 advisory teachers in supporting the programme was also examined. It was concluded that there had been substantial and significant curriculum change; that mathematics and science subjects had been difficult for teachers to incorporate multi-cultural perspectives into and that the project had been unable to help the school tackle racism adequately.
Published Material: DAVID, P. & CAMPBELL, R.J. (1988). Inter-Cultural Curriculum Support Service Project – Interim Report. Warwickshire County Council. ; DAVID, P. & CAMPBELL, R.J. (1990). Inter-Cultural Curriculum Support Service Project, Final Report. Warwickshire County Council.
Source of Grant: Warwickshire County Council: £10,000
Date of Research: 1988-1990
KEYWORDS: curriculum development; ethnic relations; evaluation; multicultural education

8/1706
> Department of Education
> Coventry CV4 7AL
> 0203 523850
> Campbell, R.J. Mr; David, P. Ms

Evaluation of primary teachers use of first hand experience programme
Abstract: The aim of this research is to evaluate a training programme for primary teachers in the use of first hand experience. Qualitative methods were used. 26 schools were involved, selected by the local education authority on the basis of their good practice. The role of the five advisory teachers in supporting the programme is examined.
Published Material: Reports are available from R. Campbell, Department of Education, Warwick University.
Source of Grant: Warwickshire Local Education Authority: £20,000

Date of Research: 1988-1990
KEYWORDS: *inservice education and training of teachers; learning process; primary education; teaching aptitude*

8/1707

Department of Education
Westwood, Coventry CV4 7AL
0203 523821
Tomlinson, J.R.G. Prof.

Hereford & Worcester LEA: 6 small rural high schools – an evaluation

Abstract: The object of the research is to see how far a small secondary school in a rural setting may be educationally viable and to what extent it is supported by and contributes to its local community. The work specifically relates to 6 small schools nominated by the LEA.

Published Material: TOMLINSON, J.R.G. (1990). Small rural and effective: a study of six small secondary schools in a remote are of England. Warwick University, Institute of Education.
Source of Grant: Hereford & Worcestershire Local Education Authority: £52,500 over 3 years
Date of Research: 1988-1990
KEYWORDS: *rural school; school-community relation; secondary education; small school*

8/1708

Department of Psychology
Coventry CV4 7AL
0203 523158
Lewis, V.A. Dr; Boucher, J.M. Dr

The assessment of symbolic play in young children

Abstract: The aim of this research is to develop a test which assesses symbolic play. A prototype test has been developed based on pilot work with over 140 children aged between one and seven years, including small numbers of disabled children. The test assesses children's ability to let either themselves, a teddy or a non-representational object such as a piece of material or a small cube of wood stand for another object; to attribute a property to themselves or a teddy; or to refer to an absent object used either by themselves or by a teddy. Play may be modelled, instructed or elicited (when the child is encouraged to produce examples of her or his own). Test instructions may be conveyed non-verbally by gestures, signs and modelling, or verbally, depending on the age and ability of the child and the condition in which play is being assessed. Funding is being sought for standardization and validation of the test. However, from the work to date, it is thought that this test provides an alternative way of looking at the communicative and cognitive competences of children up to the developmental age of six years.

Source of Grant: National Autistic Society: £2,000 Nuffield Foundation: £3,000
Date of Research: 1989 – continuing
KEYWORDS: *pretend play*

8/1709

Department of Science Education
Coventry CV4 7AL
0203 523211
Gray, E.M. Mr

Childrens' strategies for arithmetical number problems

Abstract: Detailed case studies, will be compiled, with the help of a Schoolteacher Fellow, of the strategies adopted by individual lower ability children aged 7-11 in Dorset and Warwickshire, and a comparison with selected average ability and high ability children. The strategies are those adopted in response to numerical addition and subtraction sums and range from different kinds of counting methods to direct recall. The outcomes include an extension of 1972 classification used by Carpenter and Moser, a more detailed classification of strategies coming under the general heading of 'derived facts', and conclusions on how the level of sophistication changes over time with different children. The consequences of the adoption of too low a level of sophistication are clearly demonstrated.

Source of Grant: Warwickshire Local Education Authority; (Teacher Fellow) University Research Fund: £6,000
Date of Research: 1987-1990
KEYWORDS: *arithmetic; learning strategy; primary education*

8/1710

Department of Science Education
Coventry CV4 7AL
0203 523213/523218
Schwarzenberger, R.L.E. Prof.; *Supervisor:* Pirie, S.E.B. Dr; Newman, C. Ms; Pratt, K. Ms

Discussion in the mathematics classroom

Abstract: This research consists of case studies in five different schools concerning the mathematical discussion among pupils who are taught by teachers who encourage such activity. Small groups of pupils working together are tape recorded, and transcripts analyzed. Classification of discussion episodes is assisted by the notes of a classroom observer. Results of the research include information on successful and unsuccessful strategies for starting discussion, the relationship between mathematical discussion and the development of mathematical understanding, the importance of incoherent exchanges within discussion episodes, and the role of 'social chat' within purely mathematical discussion.

Published Material: PIRIE, S.E.B. (1988). 'Understanding – instrumental, relational, formal, intuitive... how can we know?', For the Learning of Mathematics, Vol 8.; PIRIE, S.E.B. & SCHWARZENBERGER, R.L.E. (1988). 'Mathematical discussion and mathematical understanding', Educational Studies in Mathematics, Vol 19.; PIRIE, S.E.B. & SCHWARZENBERGER, R.L.E. (1988). 'Mathematical discussion: it's what you say AND what you do', Mathematics Teaching, No 123, pp.58-60, June.
Source of Grant: Leverhulme Trust: £66,578
Date of Research: 1986 – continuing
KEYWORDS: *comprehension; discussion; group work; mathematics*

8/1711

Department of Science Education
Coventry CV4 7AL
0203 523867
Tall, D.O. Dr; *Supervisor:* Thomas, M.O.J.; Blackett, N.

Versatile learning in mathematics using computer technology

Abstract: The project has involved two PhD students in comparative work in mathematics classrooms of a comprehensive school. The researcher has developed a theoretical model of advance organizers in the formation of mathematical concepts which is being tested (i) by M.O.J. Thomas with regard to the learning of algebra, and (ii) by N. Blackett, and also by Dr Tall himself, with regard to calculus. The results show clear benefits in using microcomputer software which has been written to provide appropriate advance organizers. The benefits appear to be greater for pupils whose visualization skills are greater than their verbal and numerical skills.

Published Material: THOMAS, M.O.J. (1988). A conceptual approach to the early learning of algebra using a computer. University of Warwick, PhD thesis.; BLACKETT, N. (1987). Computer graphics and children's understanding of linear and locally linear graphs. University of Warwick, MSc thesis.; TALL, D.O. (1987). 'Graphical packages for mathematics teaching and learning'. In: JOHNSON, D.C. & LOVIS, F. (Eds). Informatics and the teaching of mathematics, pp.39-47. Amsterdam: Elsevier Science Publishers.; TALL, D.O. & WEST, B. (1986). 'Graphic insight into calculus and differential equations'. In: HOWSON, G. & KAHANE, J.P. (Eds). The influence of computers and informatics on mathematics and its teaching, pp.107-199. Cambridge: Cambridge University Press.
Source of Grant: School Mathematics Project
Date of Research: 1985-1990
KEYWORDS: *computer assisted instruction; concept formulation; learning strategy; mathematics; microcomputer*

8/1712

Department of Science Education
Coventry CV4 7AL
0203 523523
Harwood, D.L. Mr

The nature of teacher-student interaction in 'active learning' approaches to teaching

Abstract: 'Active Learning' is one of a number of recent curriculum initiatives, which encourage students to be more personally and independently involved in their own learning. This research aims to study the nature of teacher-student classroom interaction in lessons, identified as 'active' by the teachers themselves. The sample of teachers is differentiated, according to the source of their training in 'active' methods, e.g. Active Tutorial Work etc. The methods involve the observation and interaction analysis of tape-

recorded lessons, as well as interviews with students and teachers. The results of the first report on Active Tutorial Work concluded that, although there is greater use of co-operative groupwork, the teacher remains at the centre of interaction, whenever present in the group. Comparison is made with a similar analysis of transcripts from the Humanities Curriculum Project.
Published Material: HARWOOD, D.L. (1986). 'Evaluation of personal and social education within the Coventry TVEI project; Part One: Active Learning', University of Warwick.; HARWOOD, D.L. (1989). 'The nature of teacher-pupil interaction in the Active Tutorial Work approach: using interaction analysis to evaluate student-centred approaches', British Educational Research Journal, Vol 15, No 2, pp.177-194.
Source of Grant: Warwick University: £300 Coventry Local Education Authority
Date of Research: 1985-1990
KEYWORDS: curriculum development; learning strategy; teacher-pupil relation; method

8/1713
　　　　Department of Science Education
　　　　Coventry CV4 7AL
　　　　0203 523845
　　　　Schwarzenberger, R.L.E. Prof.; *Supervisor:* Ainley, J.M. Ms
Questioning in the mathematics classroom
Abstract: Use of videotaped extracts for primary school mathematics lessons to compare the perceptions of (i) pupils and (ii) teachers as to the purpose of teachers' questions during mathematics lessons. The research uses a case study approach, contrasting different groups of children and different groups of teachers.
Published Material: AINLEY, J.M. (1987). 'Telling questions', Mathematics Teaching, No 118, pp.24-26.; AINLEY, J.M. (1988). 'Perceptions of teachers' questioning styles', Proceedings of the 12th Annual Conference of the International Group for the Psychology of Mathematics Education, Veszpre,, Hungary, pp.92-99.
Source of Grant: University Research Fund: £500
Date of Research: 1986 – continuing
KEYWORDS: mathematics; perception; primary education; questioning

West Cumbria College

8/1714
　　　　Park Lane, Workington, Cumbria CA14 2RW
　　　　0900 64331
　　　　Further Education Unit
　　　　Grove House, 2-6 Orange Street, London WC2H 7WE
　　　　071 321 0433
　　　　Wakefield, J. Mr
Mathematics learning for engineering students
Abstract: This research arises out of the failure of traditional teaching methods in mathematics to equip engineering students with the necessary skills to progress to higher education. Similar experiences through the levels of BTEC (Business and Technician Education Council) indicate that mathematics has not found its place in the 'integration' process of a multi-disciplinary approach. It aims to develop practical techniques and methods for the effective teaching and learning of mathematics to engineering students, and prepare them for progression to the next level. It will also investigate the implications for traditional structures and attitudes within mathematics and engineering departments, and also address the staff development issues which would arise from the introduction of these methods. The techniques and methods will be developed on the BTEC engineering courses, including First Diploma in Engineering, National Diploma in Engineering and the Mathematics Unit for 4th year engineering apprentices hoping to study for HND's (Higher National Diploma) or degrees. Techniques and methods will include practical activities, investigations, computer based activities, integrative assignments, consolidation and practice, discussion and communication of ideas, and student centred learning material. A report to the FEU will be produced describing the project methodology and recommending practical techniques and methods for effective teaching and learning of relevant mathematics in FE (further education) programmes, comments on the implications of this for college structure and staff attitudes and suggests appropriate staff development.

Source of Grant: Further Education Unit
Date of Research: 1990-1990
KEYWORDS: engineering; further education; mathematics; student; teaching method

West London Institute of Higher Education

8/1715
　　　　300 St Margaret's Road, Twickenham TW1 1PT
　　　　081 891 0121
　　　　Garner, P. Mr; *Supervisor:* Jones, C. Mr (London University)
Disruptive behaviour in United Kingdom and United States schools: a comparative study
Abstract: This research uses 'pupil reality' to investigate disruptive behaviour in the UK and USA. Such a response is at the heart of a paradigm which might be best described as 'ecological', where the pupil is viewed as central to the microsystem. The research focuses upon two case studies (one each in the US and UK). Pupils and their teachers are interviewed (unstructured) and other instruments include critical biographies, diaries, and gathering formal documentary evidence. The research hopes to point to cross-cultural differences in the responses of disruptive pupils to their schooling.
Source of Grant: West London Institue of Higher Education, Staff Development Fund: £354
Date of Research: 1988 – continuing
KEYWORDS: behaviour disorder; comparative education; disruptive behaviour; misconduct; USA

8/1716
　　　　Lancaster House,
　　　　Borough Road, Isleworth, Middlesex TW7 5DU
　　　　081 568 8741
　　　　Musty, E. Mrs; *Supervisor:* Marratt, H.W. Prof.
Religious education for children with special needs
Abstract: The aim is to research into the concepts, experiences, values and attitudes relevant to the spiritual development of children with learning difficulties. It is also hoped to adapt and initiate relevant religious education resource materials, and to provide advice, consultation and inservice training in order to disseminate development and record finding.
Source of Grant: All Saints Trust: £19,500 per year for 3 years
Date of Research: 1988 – continuing
KEYWORDS: inservice education and training of teachers; learning difficulty; religious education; special needs; teaching aids

8/1717
　　　　Lancaster House,
　　　　Borough Road, Iselworth, Middlesex TW7 5DU
　　　　081 568 8741
　　　　Manchester Polytechnic
　　　　799 Wilmslow Road, Didsbury, Manchester M20 8RR
　　　　061 445 7871
　　　　Blake, C.R.L. Mr; *Supervisor:* Marratt, H.W. Prof.; Hogbin, J.W.G. Mr (Manchester Polytechnic)
An investigation into the identification and assessment of the affective domain of religious studies, with particular reference to General Certificate of Secondary Education (GCSE) examinations
Abstract: This project will investigate the nature of GCSE religious studies, and in particular the assessment of pupils' attainments of affective objectives in religious studies. Use will be made of documentary analysis and action research techniques, focused upon the classroom practices of GCSE religious studies classes. Investigation will also be made of affective objectives upon assessment processes. Methods used include action research in two phases, involving 10 schools. Researcher and teachers will co-operate in designing learning programmes and assessment instruments in relation to affective objectives. The sample used will be a school of denominational and non-denominational status, using religious studies examination syllabuses of textual, ethnical and multi-faith nature.
Published Material: BLAKE, C.R.L. (1986). 'GCSE under starter's order: a review of the syllabuses', R.E. Today, Autumn 1986.; BLAKE, C.R.L. (1987). 'Assessment of the affective domain: a

British venture into the unknown', Religious Education Journal of Australia, Vol 3, No 1.
Source of Grant: British and Foreign School Society
Date of Research: 1985-1990
KEYWORDS: assessment; curriculum development; examination; General Certificate of Secondary Education; religious education

Westminster College

8/1718
        North Hinksey, Oxford OX2 9AT
        0865 247644
        Bigger, S.F. Dr
World religions in the school curriculum: theory and practice
Abstract: The purpose of this research has been to develop the information about religions into a form that pupils can find relevant and meaningful. It has therefore involved developmental work in school, discussion with teachers and religious educationalists, and interviews with members of a range of faiths. The research has throughout, addressed itself to a 5-18 age range. The conclusions are that religious education must involve more than giving pupils information, but must build conceptual frameworks and foundations so that the information can be appropriately understood. 'How the pupil learns' should be as important as 'what the pupil learns', and bias should be an issue constantly on the agenda of both teachers and pupils.
Published Material: BIGGER, S.F. (1987). 'Multifaith education in the Shires: two projects in primary RE'. Westminster Studies in Education, Vol 10, pp.37-51.; BIGGER, S.F. (1989). 'Teaching about God: building a framework', Journal of Beliefs and Values, Vol 10.; BIGGER, S.F. (1989). 'Religious education: issues from the 1980's', Journal of Beliefs and Values, Vol 10.; BIGGER, S.F. (1990). 'Exclusive brethren?: and education dilemma', Journal of Beliefs and Values, Vol 11.; BIGGER, S.F. (1990). 'RE and TVEI', Journal of Beliefs and Values, Vol 11.; BIGGER, S.F. (Ed). (1989). Creating the old testament: the emergence of the Hebrew bible. Oxford: Basil Blackwell.
Source of Grant: Technical and Vocational Education Initiative
Date of Research: 1983-1989
KEYWORDS: intercultural education; primary education; religious cultural group; religious education; scripture; Technical and Vocational Education Initiatve; world studies

8/1719
        North Hinksey, Oxford OX2 9AT
        0865 644247
        Prosser, J. Dr
Evaluation of the voice of the child in care's independent representative scheme
Abstract: This research will be a case study of four institutions with secure units for children in care. This will involve semi-structured interviews of staff, those in care, and independent representatives. Early data suggests the scheme is successful and only refinements are required.
Source of Grant: Voice of the Child in Care
Date of Research: 1990 – continuing
KEYWORDS: secure unit

West Sussex Institute of Higher Education

8/1720
        The Dome, Upper Bognor Road, Bognor Regis PO21 1NR
        0243 787911
        London University
        Department of Educational Psychology
        Institute of Education,
        20 Bedford Way, London WC1H OAL
        071 636 1500
        Hamblett, J.M. Mrs; *Supervisor:* May, D. Mr; Worral, N. Dr
Organizational climate: perspectives on a problematic concept
Abstract: The study investigates the veridical nature of the construct, organizational climate by addressing its conceptual and methodological problems. Typically, the construct has been represented as a set of linear dimensions to take account of assumptions of its differentially perceived global nature. Perceptual measurement techniques however, in averaging individual responses, are uncertain as to whether climate is an individual or an organizational attribute. Phenomenological approaches too, have been few and unsystematic. Neither approach has considered the role of symbolic processes nor subjective feelings. The study reinterprets organizational climate as an intersubjective construct in which roles, and tacit rules as individual meanings and feelings of organizational interaction, are linked as an organization-wide, or hierarchical level force, to investigate the extent to which teachers in secondary school organizations consider the construct as an individual or an organizational attribute. Unstructured interview data concerning issues of school organizational interaction by the headteachers, 37 teachers and 23 teachers respectively from each of two secondary schools, are categorized by systematic network analysis and their salient features compared and contrasted to elicit the construct's emergent organizational-force properties. Qualitative interpretation is supported by the quantitative data of 18 INSET (Inservice Education of Teachers) teachers and 37 headteachers from 55 different secondary schools. The hermeneutic significance of the data challenges traditional perspectives of the construct and has implications for management practice. To teachers, the construct represents their personal reactions and feelings as recipients of headteachers' management processes and it differs from their meanings of ethos and school climate. To headteachers, the terms are synonyms.
Source of Grant: Social Science Research Council: 1978-1980 West Sussex Institute of Higher Education: 1982-1987
Date of Research: 1986-1990
KEYWORDS: educational development; organizational theory; school management

8/1721
        The Mathematics Centre,
        Upper Bognpor Road, Bognor Regis PO21 1HR
        0243 861704
        Craig, B. Mrs; Eden, J. Mr; Jackson, P. Mr; Lacey, P. Mr; *Supervisor:* Ahmed, A. Mr (West Sussex Institute of Higher Education); Williams, H. Ms (West Sussex Institute of Higher Education)
Raising achievement in mathematics project (RAMP)
Abstract: The main aim of the project is to raise achievement in mathematics for all pupils involved and has two main emphases. Firstly, a broadening of the Low Attainers in Mathematics Project 1983-1986 findings to encompass work with pupils across the age and ability ranges, and also the replication of their work in other regions of the country. RAMP set out to explore reasons for underachievement, identify and communicate what constitutes raised achievement in mathematics, proposed strategies for raising pupil's achievement and investigates methods of disseminating the projects findings. The project has demonstrated how pupils of all abilities and aptitudes are able to achieve better test and examination results, along with increased motivation, confidence and interest through using and applying mathematics. The key issues we have identified and addressed were associated mainly with people's belief in what constitutes the basic building blocks of mathematics, how it is learnt, how it should be taught and how best to assess it. Thus the route to raising pupils' achievement and developing effective classroom practice is through encouraging teachers' confidence in their own professionalism. RAMP has offered a cost effective and least disruptive model for qualitatively improving pupils' mathematical experiences and achievements. RAMP operates through a network office and regional centres and has adopted an action research method of investigation. This work is being carried out at a number of educational institutions.
Published Material: A full list of publications is available from the researchers.
Source of Grant: Department of Education and Science: £538,725 Various local education authorities: £396,000
Date of Research: 1986-1990
KEYWORDS: mathematics; underachievement

8/1722
        The Mathematics Centre,
        Upper Bognor Road, Bognor Regis PO21 1HR
        0243 861704
        Ahmed, A. Mr; Oldknow, A. Mr; Williams, H. Ms; *Supervisor:* Ahmed, A. Mr

Flexible learning approaches in sixth form mathematics
Abstract: This project has identified an urgent need to seek ways of establishing long term productive links with industry and commerce that are self-sustaining, and focus on what education and industry have to offer each other in the context of mathematics. In order that the efforts and resources committed by industry, commerce and education accrue maximum benefit, industry must become an integral resource for schools and vice-versa. The central aim is to broaden teachers', students' and society's perception of what constitutes the effective learning of a crucial subject such as mathematics and to enable young people, particularly in the 16-19 age range, to gain maximum benefit from their education and training. In particular the strategies and publications developed are designed to motivate students by offering them access to mathematics being used in both abstract and real contexts; encapsulate 'real-world' situations to encourage the natural interest of students; encourage teachers and students to use resources more effectively, including a wide range of technological devices, databases etc; act as a catalyst for changing classroom approaches to using and applying mathematics; offer students opportunities to encounter mathematics; through challenging tasks; support teachers and students in diagnosis, self-evaluation and record keeping; encourage teachers to become discerning users of support materials; provide opportunites for exploiting the connections that already exist between mathematics and other subject areas and provide a basis and resource for staff development in order to involve a wider group of teachers in sustained professional development programmes. During the first year of the Project, structures, approaches and mechanisms have been developed which can contribute to the improvement in students' creative and analytical skills, innovative flair and problem solving attitudes and approaches.
Published Material: AHMED, A., OLDKNOW, A.F. & WILLIAMS, H. (1990). Sixth form mathematics. Bognor: West Sussex Institute of Higher Education, Mathematics Centre.; AHMED, A., OLDKNOW, A.F. & WILLIAMS, H. (1990). Mathematics in context. Bognor: West Sussex Institute of Higher Education, Mathematics Centre.; AHMED, A., OLDKNOW, A.F. & WILLIAMS, H. (1990). Using resources. Bognor: West Sussex Institute of Higher Education, Mathemactics Centre.; AHMED, A., OLDKNOW, A.F. & WILLIAMS, H. (1990). Using a microcomputer in sixth form mathematics classrooms. Bognor: West Sussex Institute of Higher Education, Mathematics Centre.; AHMED, A., OLDKNOW, A.F. & WILLIAMS, H. (1990). Using graphics calculators. Bognor: West Sussex Institute of Higher Education, Mathematics Centre.; AHMED, A., OLDKNOW, A.F. & WILLIAMS, H. (1990). A report of the first phase of the research. West Sussex Institute of Higher Education, Mathematics Centre.
Source of Grant: Training Enterprise Education Division; February 1989-April 1990: £72,200 Training Enterprise Education Division; April 1990-March 1991: £118,610
Date of Research: 1989 – continuing
KEYWORDS: industry-education relationship; sixth form education

8/1723

The Dome,
Upper Bognor Road, Bognor Regis PO21 1NR
0243 787911
London University
Institute of Education,
20 Bedford Way, London WC1H OAL
071 636 1500
Gaine, C. Mr; *Supervisor:* Ball, S. Prof. (London University)
Antecedents and effectiveness in anti-racist initiatives in all white secondary schools
Abstract: The research aims to develop a model of the factors which promote or prevent an initiative about 'race' in largely white secondary schools. This will be based upon existing records and accounts and some interview material. The second part will look at school factors which enable (or prevent) the initiative to continue or develop, and finally focus on curriculum content and teaching approach. Several schools will be involved here, but the close analysis of pedagogy wil be in one or two schools.
Published Material: GAINE, C. (1987). No problem here. London: Hutchinson Publishing Co.; GAINE, C. (1989). 'On getting equal opportunities policies'. In: COLE, M. (Ed). Education for equality. Basingstoke: Falmer Press.
Source of Grant: West Sussex Institute of Higher Education
Date of Research: 1980 – continuing
KEYWORDS: anti-racism education

8/1724

The Dome,
Upper Bognor Road, Bognor Regis PO21 1NR
0243 787911
London University
Department of Education
Goldsmiths College,
Lewisham Way, New Cross, London SE14 6NW
071 692 7171
Whitty, G. Prof.
A comparative study of school based, school focused and college based approaches to teacher education
Abstract: This research aims to examine and evaluate contemporary developments in teacher education, and to explore the possibilities of developing a left radical analysis of teacher education policy, using a model of the critical reflective practitioner and teacher educator as 'transformative intellectual'. The main objectives of this study are: to ascertain and evaluate the nature of a variety of routes to teacher education; critique radical left, radical right and liberal perspectives on teacher education and schooling; elicit novice teachers' reactions to key elements and issues in their training programmes; identify elements and approaches that facilitate the development of critical reflective approaches to teacher education and schooling; assist in the development of radical left policies for teacher education.
Published Material: HILL, D. (1990). Something old, something new, something borrowed, something blue: teacher education, schooling and the radical right in Britain and the USA. London: Tufnel Press.; HILL, D. (1990). 'Thatcherism, teacher education and the suppression of critical thought', Liberal Education, Issue 64, Winter 1989/90.; HILL, D., COLE, M. & CLAY, J. (1990). 'Black achievement in initial teacher education: how do we proceed into the 1990's', Multicultural Teaching, Vol 8, No 3, pp.31-35, Summer.; HILL, D. (1990). 'Local management of schools', New Socialist, September. (forthcoming).; HILL, D. (1990). 'Developing a socialist education system: the Hillcole Group', Forum, January 1991. (forthcoming).; HILL, D. (1991). 'The citizen as individual and nationalist or social and internationalist: what is the role of education'? Critical Social Policy (forthcoming).
Source of Grant: West Sussex Institute of Higher Education: fees
Date of Research: 1990 – continuing
KEYWORDS: politics education relationship

8/1725

Upper Bognor Road, Bognor Regis PO21 1HR
0243 865581
Chambers, F. Mr; *Supervisor:* Lewis, P.J. Dr
The evaluation of the management of English language teaching aid projects
Abstract: Using Soft Systems methodology, the investigation develops a consensus model of the purpose of ELT (English language teaching) aid which is then used to provide a source for a bank of evaluation questions.
Source of Grant: West Sussex Institute of Higher Education
Date of Research: 1989 – continuing
KEYWORDS: development aid; English language; evaluation; teaching

8/1726

Bognor Regis College
Upper Bognor Road, Bognor Regis PO21 1HR
0243 865581
Seale, G.M. Mr
Teacher's work: a case study of teacher education
Abstract: This enquiry aims to enhance the understanding of work in higher education. Processes of course development, evaluation and appraisal are being analyzed and theorized. This study is located against the following background: a recent 'series' of ethnographic portraits of educational institutions in Britain; a rise or 'movement' of teachers-as-researchers; a post-modern collapse of confidence in the ability of scientific discourse to deliver anything other than truth-effects; and a lively political debate about teachers, schools and education. The design of the investigation is a case study. In space and time its scope is one educational institution's practices from 1983-1988 and the prevailing national politics of education within the context of one teacher/tutor's work. The size and composition of the sample varies from an in depth study of a group comprising six student teachers (secondary), their tutor and several comprehensive school history teachers, to a survey of several courses involving around 150 people. The research strategy has involved

these methods; participant observation, social theorizing, and writing. Results have not yet been collated and presented. They combine the empirical with the theoretical. The fore-shadowed conclusion is that educational enquiry and evaluation seem problematic in practice and in theory yet most of us slide over this in our work as teachers and administrators.
Source of Grant: College pays annual fees for supervision
Date of Research: 1985-1990
KEYWORDS: educational research; evaluation; higher education; teacher education; teaching

Worcester College of Higher Education

8/1727

GRIST Evaluation Project,
Henwick Grove, Worcester WR2 6AJ
0905 428080
Ghaye, A.L. Dr; Hudson, G. Dr; Pascal, C. Dr
An evaluation of the implementation and experience of GRIST (Grant-Related Inservice Training) within one local education authroity
Abstract: The proposed evaluation project is a collaborative venture which seeks to examine the processes and experience of GRIST (Grant-Related Inservice Training within one authority, 1989-1992. The principal intention is to show how aspects of GRIST are working in practice, how it is viewed by the participants and planners and how its operation might be developed and improved. More specifically the project focuses on two areas of interest. One area is broader and requires the monitoring of the relationship between GRIST activities and the quality of teacher-student interaction over time. The other is more specific and short-term and focuses upon the evaluation of particular local authority initiatives. In consultation with local authority representatives the project will evaluate up to four such initiatives, 1989-1992. The project will develop an appropriate methodology that includes survey techniques, interviews, document analysis and written accounts in order to establish the dynamics of personal experience and perception. Each year a report will be published.
Source of Grant: Local Education Authority
Date of Research: 1989 – continuing
KEYWORDS: evaluation; grant; inservice education and training of teachers; local education authority

York University

8/1728

Language Teaching Centre,
Heslington, York YO1 5DD
0904 430000
Universtitat Munchen
Lehrstuhl fur die Didaktik der Englischen Sprache und Literatur, Schellingstrasse 3, D-8000 Munchen 40, Germany
2180 2995
Green, S. Mr; Hecht, K. Prof.
Learners' language
Abstract: This is an on-going project to investigate learners' language and compare it at all stages with the language of native peers. The project involves German school learners of English and English school pupils in performing three communicative tasks in English, and assessment by native and non-native teachers: (1) a letter-writing task; (2) an oral narrative and (3) oral transaction. To date there are 2490 pupil productions from Germany and England. The productions are analyzed from the following standpoints: (1) linguistic form; (2) content; (3) communicative effectiveness; (4) strategies; (5) self-correction/monitoring; (6) grammatical and lexical competence and performance; (7) the development of communicative competence; (8) assessment/reactions by natives and non-natives. Conclusions are very varied.
Published Material: GREEN, P.S. & HECHT, K.H. (1987). 'The influence of accuracy on communicative effectiveness', British Journal of Language Teaching, Vol 25, No 2, 1987, pp.79-84.; GREEN, P.S. & HECHT, K.L. (1988). 'The sympathetic native speaker –

a GCSE role-play for the teacher', Modern Languages, Vol 69, No 1 1988, pp.3-10.
Source of Grant: British Council Academic Linking Scheme: approx. £600 European Commission: approx. £1,400 EC Erasmus: £1,400 on-going departmental funding
Date of Research: 1980 – continuing
KEYWORDS: English (second language); Germany, Federal Republic; language skill; teaching; learning strategy;

8/1729

Department of Education
Heslington, York YO1 5DD
0904 430000
Normington, J. Mrs; *Supervisor:* Kyriacou, C. Dr
Exclusion from high schools and inter-disciplinary interventions
Abstract: The aim of this research is to investigate the procedure and identify issues of major concern to schools and local education authorities (LEAs) in connection with pupil expulsion from school, following the implementation of the 1986 Education (No 2 Act). Officers responsible for exclusions and secondary headteachers from seven LEAs were interviewed and five major issues were identified. Officers feared that the right of permanent exclusion would lead to an increasing number of difficult fifth year pupils requiring education out of their schools. Schools wished to develop alternatives to exclusion involving inservice training, time-out facilities, links with special needs departments, parents, and support agencies. Local management of schools was not considered to be likely to be supportive of such aims. The need for careful recording and reporting of disruption and exclusions was emphasised by both groups, accurate information being essential in effective planning. The use of the 1981 Education (Special Needs) Statementing procedures for disruptive children was apparently unhelpful. The quantity and quality of inter-departmental co-operation was another common concern. It is proposed to investigate the matter of interdepartmental co-operation using case studies in which the extensive documentation will be reviewed, those members of the various involved agencies interviewed, and the decision making process observed in more than one LEA. The aim is to examine the effectiveness of multi-disciplinary interventions and seek to identify ways in which understanding and co-operation may be improved so as to benefit everyone concerned.
Source of Grant: Local Education Authority: university fees
Date of Research: 1988 – continuing
KEYWORDS: dsicipline; disruptive pupil; expulsion; misconduct

8/1730

Department of Educational Studies
Helsington, York YO1 5DD
0904 430000
Putsoa, B. Mrs; *Supervisor:* Campbell, R.M. Dr
Assessing the ability of school leavers in Swaziland to use process skills
Abstract: The study is motivated by the fact that only a minority of school leavers proceed into institutions of higher education at the end of high school. The more fortunate among the remaining majority are either absorbed into professional training institutions or move straight into the adult world of work. The less fortunate join the mainstream of the unemployed. The study aims to find out about the extent to which school science may be of use to school leavers in coping cognitively with the experiences they will encounter in the future. Would they rely on the concepts and objective processes that characterize the sciences to interpret the events and situations that arise?. The assessment attempts to account for the time and effort spent in teaching and learning science by showing the extent to which it is likely to be used by those who have spent time on it. Paper and pencil tests were used in the assessment. A total of 45 questions were designed with the specific purpose of re-enacting the experiences of junior secondary school science and converting them to portray everyday events and experiences in the Swazi environment. Each of the 45 questions were distributed among school leavers in sample schools such that each participating school leaver received 10 questions containing the 10 processes being assessed. The sample consisted of all 5th formers in the 20 schools which were selected to represent all regions and types of schools in the country. This sample represented 40% of the target group at the time when the study began, which was 1,088 school leavers. Pupils' responses have been recently analyzed. The current status of the research has reached the stage of writing, after which conclusions will be drawn.
Source of Grant: British Council Technical Assistance to Swaziland

Date of Research: 1988 – continuing
KEYWORDS: cognitive ability; school leaver; science education; Swaziland

8/1731

Department of Educational Studies
Heslington, York YO1 5DD
0904 430000
Metcalfe, C. Mr; *Supervisor:* Lazonby, J. Mr

Case study of staff development in a large comprehensive school
Abstract: The objective of the research is to make a major case study of staff development in a large, purpose built comprehensive school with a particuluar focus on the emergence of a scheme of peer counselling as a means of individual and institutional development. At this stage the main instrument in the research is the qualitative interview but it is possible that other methods (e.g. questionnaires) may be used at a later stage. The research is still in an early and fairly open phase.
Source of Grant: Local Education Authority
Date of Research: 1987 – continuing
KEYWORDS: comprehensive school; self-education; staff development; teacher

8/1732

Department of Educational Studies
Heslington, York YO1 5DD
0904 430000
Davies, I. Mr; *Supervisor:* Lister, I. Prof.

Guidelines for political education
Abstract: There will be 3 main sections to this research. Firstly, a combination of narrative and analysis which shows the early call for guidelines, the West German example, DES and LEA guidelines. The researcher will be seeking to illuminate the nature of different guidelines, considering to what extent they address aims, content, methods, evaluation and to suggest how they relate to the recommendations made by key political educators. Secondly, the research will examine the perceptions of guidelines by the producers, by the political educators, by teachers and by gatekeepers who may include heads, governors, LEA officers and a sample of politicians. Finally, the research seeks to enquire how the guidelines help practice and focus on the relation between reality and theory in a number of LEAs.
Published Material: DAVIES, I. (1988). 'Guidelines for political education', Social Science Teacher, October.
Source of Grant: Hampshire Education Authority: costs and travel expenses
Date of Research: 1987 – continuing
KEYWORDS: educational policy; political education

8/1733

Department of Educational Studies
Heslington, York YO1 5DD
0904 430000
Grainger, N. Mr; *Supervisor:* Lister, I. Prof.

Welfare rights, health and education: a consideration of welfare rights and environmental health in courses on housing education
Abstract: The aims of the project are to: (a) examine components of housing education in polytechnic/university courses, (b) in particular assess importance of welfare rights and environmental health in housing curricula, (c) changes to housing functions in public sector, including housing associations; to consider proposals to develop housing education and the impact on the teaching of welfare rights and health issues, (d) assess effectiveness of different models of housing education and their strenghts and weaknesses. Design and Scope of the investigation so far undertaken: (i) Principles of Housing Education. An examination of the 'literature' on the models of housing curricula and the nature of housing education, (ii) A study of Undergraduate housing degrees in terms of course design in the United Kingdom, (iii) A study of Postgraduate housing diplomas in terms of course design in the United Kingdom, (iv) What are 'Welfare Rights'? What is 'Public/ Environmental Health'? A study of the historical development of these areas, the critics and related problems; and the place of welfare rights and environmental health in Legislation and in International Declarations and Conventions. What are the linkages with housing education? It is intended that the study will proceed to a survey at several institutions where housing education courses are operated.
Source of Grant: Sheffield City Polytechnic, annual fees and some travelling expenses: £650 per annum.

Date of Research: 1987 – continuing
KEYWORDS: environment; health education; higher education; housing

8/1734

Department of Language and Linguistic Science
York YO1 5DD
0904 432666
Verma, M.K. Mr; Bayer, J. Dr (India); *Supervisor:* Verma, M.K. Mr

Language maintenance and shift: the Tamil community in London
Abstract: This is a collaborative research pilot study which aims to examine the sociolinguistic behaviour of the Tamil community in London, and the impact of migration on language choice and language attitudes, language maintenance and shift: English and mother tongue (Tamil) interviews and a questionnaire. There will also be an analysis of the views of teachers, parents and community leaders.
Source of Grant: No funding
Date of Research: 1988-1989
KEYWORDS: bilingualism; ethnic minority; first foreign language; mother tongue; Sri Lanka; Tamil; United Kingdom

8/1735

Department of Language and Linguistic Science
Heslington, York YO1 5DD
0904 423666
Verma, M.K. Mr; Mukherjee, A. Dr (Hyderabad); *Supervisor:* Verma, M.K. Mr

Language maintenance and shift: the Bengali (Bangladeshis) community in Leeds
Abstract: This is a collaborative research project to examine the attitudes of the Bangladeshi community in Leeds towards their mother tongue, the place of Bengali in the school curriculum and the use of English and Bengali in various domains. A questionnaire was administered and members of the community interviewed.
Source of Grant: No funding
Date of Research: 1987-1990
KEYWORDS: Bangladeshi; Bengali; English (second language); ethnic minority; first foreign language; mother tongue; United Kingdom

8/1736

Department of Language and Lingusitic Science
Heslington, York YO1 5DD
0904 432666
Verma, M.K. Mr; Khanna, A.L. Dr (New Delhi); *Supervisor:* Verma, M.K. Mr

Attitudes and motivations of adult ESL learners in Great Britain
Abstract: This is a collaborative research programme to examine the attitudes and motivations of adults learning English as second language (ESL) in Great Britain. It will involve designing, pre-piloting, and finalising the questionnaire for the pilot study which was administered to approximately 200 adults learning English as a second language at approximately thirteen ESL centres in England, Scotland and Wales. Teachers and learners will be interviewed for in depth analysis of their teaching and learning strategies, their attitudes and motivations, their views on important issues such as the use of the mother tongues of the learners and the role of the bilingual teachers in the classroom.
Source of Grant: No funding
Date of Research: 1989-1990
KEYWORDS: adult education; English (second language); first foreign language; language teaching

8/1737

Department of Lanuage and Linguistic Science
Heslington, York YO1 5DD
0904 410822
Warner, A.R. Dr; Russell, J.C. Dr; Verma, M. Mr; Christie, P. Dr (UWI Jamaica); Devonish, D. Dr (UWI Jamaica); *Supervisor:* Le Page, R.B. Prof. (Department of Language and Linguistic Science); Tabouret-Keller, A. Prof. (Universite Louis Pasteur, Strasbourg); Carrington, L. Dr (University of the West Indies)

International group for the study of language standardization and the vernacularization of literacy
Abstract: Biennial workshops bring together research workers concerned with the language related educational problems of developing countries, particularly with former colonies of France and Britain,

in order to monitor progress with these problems while at the same time using them to refine linguistic sociolinguistic and psycholinguistic insights, theory and stereotypes generally. At each workshop short presentations are made on the application of points in a position paper, and circulated beforehand, to the particular area of each participant. Most of the participants are concerned in some way with teacher training, the formulation of policy and the preparation of descriptions of vernaculars and of teaching materials in the vernaculars. The 1986 York workshop was concerned with the stereotypes concerning 'standardization', and the volume of abstracts and transcription of discussions was concerned with English, French, German, Italian, Greek, Hindi, Punjabi, Chinese, Swahili, Malay, Bislama, Creole English, Creole French and Sango. The 1988 workshop was concerned with literacy and orthographies for these same language communities with the exception of Italian. The 1990 York workshop was concerned with evaluations of historical progress in literacy. In each case the history of the older 'standard languages' will be compared with linguistic evolution in the developing countries in order to illuminate stereotypes about both. The 1992 Workshop to be held at Sevres will be concerned with the preparation of chapters for a book seeking to find possible ways forward from the various disasters which have overtaken many of the UNESCO initiatives since publication in 1953 of Monograph VIII 'The use of vernacular languages in education'.
Published Material: LE PAGE, R.B. (Ed.). (1986). 'Abstract of the proceedings of the April 1986 York Workshop of the International group for the study of Language Standardization and the Vernacularization of Literacy'. Department of Language and Linguistic Science, University of York, Mimeo, pp.139. Idem (1988). pp.154. Idem (1990), pp.136.; LE PAGE, R.B. & TABOURET-KELLER, A. (1985). Acts of Identity. Cambridge: Cambridge University Press.
Source of Grant: Economic and Social Research Council: £3,000 Nuffield Foundation: £1,000 Department of Language & Linguistics Science, University of York: £600 British Academy: £2,000
Date of Research: 1986 – continuing
KEYWORDS: developing country; educational policy; language teaching; literacy; tongue; standard; vernaculars

8/1738

Department of Psychology
Heslington, York YO1 5DD
0904 433190
Hulme, C. Dr (Department of Psychology); Rack, J.P. Dr (Department of Psychology); Allinson, N.M. Mr (Department of Electronics); Cohen, A. Mr (Department of Psychology); Snowling, M.J. Dr (National Hospitals College of Speech Sciences, London)
A connectionist model of the development of visual word recognition
Abstract: The project will develop and evaluate a model of the processes involved in learning a sight vocabulary in the early stages of learning to read. The model will be evaluated and refined on the basis of data from studies of children's reading errors and will provide an explicit theoretical account of why good phonological skills aid the rapid learning of a sight vocabulary and how such learning may be impeded in dyslexic children. The research, which depends crucially on collaboration between different disciplines, will also contribute to the development of connectionist modelling techniques by advancing understanding of how to build a prior knowledge into such models, and in applying ideas taken from the study of self-organizing neural maps to the modelling of higher level cognitive processes.
Source of Grant: Economic and Social Research Council, Medical Research Council, Science and Engineering Research Council-Cognitive Science/Human Computer Interaction Initiative: £134,672
Date of Research: 1990 – continuing
KEYWORDS: sight vocabulary

8/1739

Department of Psychology
Heslington, York YO1 5DD
0904 430000
Eames, C.M.A. Ms; *Supervisor:* Cox, M.V. Dr
Graphic and perceptual development in autistic children and autistic savants
Abstract: The development of depth representation in the drawings of normal children is now beginning to be understood. This research project was carried out to see whether the development

of depth portrayal in the drawings of autistic children follows a 'normal' path. Comparing autistic children with Down's Syndrome children and normal children, matched on non-verbal mental age, it was found that autistic children are developmentally delayed in their depth representation rather than showing anomalous strategies of depth portrayal. Work in progress is now focusing upon the strategies of depth representation by autistic children who are gifted in the visual arts.
Source of Grant: Medical Research Council: £4,560 per annum
Date of Research: 1989 – continuing
KEYWORDS: autistic; Down's Syndrome; drawing; graphic literacy; visual arts

8/1740

Department of Psychology
Heslington, York YO1 5DD
0904 430000
McDougall, S. Ms; *Supervisor:* Ellis, A. Prof.; Hulme, C. Dr; Monk, A. Dr
Extent and correalates of variability among different groups of readers
Abstract: The study has two principle aims. The first aim is to investigate whether different groups of readers matched on reading age show the same or different patterns of reading performance when latency as well as accuracy, and variability, as well as central tendency are taken into consideration. This should resolve current controversy over the extent to which dyslexic reading performance follows simply from their reading age or includes a differential deficit in, for example, phonological processing. The groups concerned will be; dyslexic children (high IQ) with specific and unexpected reading retardation, poor readers (low IQ) with nonspecific learning difficulties, precocious readers (high IQ) whose reading age is ahead of their chronological age and normal readers. If reading age is the sole determinant of group reading patterns, then these four groups should not differ from one another. The second aim is to discover whether different reading patterns related to different patterns of strength and weakness in performance on tasks which do not involve reading per se, but tap aspects of cognition which may be relevant to the acquisition of reading. Different patterns of strength and weakness in basic visual and phonological processes. A broader subsidiary aim of this project is to evaluate the extent to which information-processing accounts of a skill like reading can also provide the dimensions for characterising individual differences in cognitive ability.
Source of Grant: Economic and Social Research Council: £56,966
Date of Research: 1990 – continuing
KEYWORDS: cognition; dyslexia; individual characteristics; reading

8/1741

Department of Psychology
York YO1 5DD
0904 430000
Littleton, K. Ms; *Supervisor:* Cox, M.V. Dr
Perspective drawing in young children
Abstract: In order to draw an object in perspective, the artist must represent the projected shape of the object rather than its actual shape. Adults as well as children have difficulty in seeing the apparent shape, let alone in drawing it. Even trained artists may need special aids such as the 'perspective frame', or 'Leonardo window' to enable them to draw what they see. This research project investigates the use of such aids with 7 year-old children.
Source of Grant: No funding
Date of Research: 1987 – continuing
KEYWORDS: drawing; art education; teaching aids

8/1742

Department of Psychology
York YO1 5DD
0904 430000
Hatcher, P. Mr; *Supervisor:* Ellis, A. Prof.; Hulme, C. Dr
Individual differences among poor readers and their implications for remediation
Abstract: A battery of cognitive tests will be administered in order to discover the strengths and weaknesses of each of a sample of seven year old poor readers. Different remedial approaches will then be tried with different subgroups to discover whether the approaches differ in their overall effectiveness, and whether par-

ticular types of poor readers respond differently to different remediation procedures.

Source of Grant: self-financing
Date of Research: 1988 – continuing
KEYWORDS: reading; remedial teaching; teaching method

8/1743

Department of Psychology
Heslington, York YO1 5DD
0904 59861
Cox, M.V. Dr

The development of children's pictorial representation

Abstract: Young children seem to draw stereotyped pictures which include more features of an object or scene than can be seen from a particular viewpoint. Thus children draw what they know, not what they see. This research project comprises of a number of experiments designed to show under what circumstances children do draw stereotyped pictures and those in which they will draw the object how it actually is seen. Tasks include the drawing of the object behind and partially hidden by another and 3-D objects such as cubes.

Published Material: COX, M.V. (1981). 'One thing behind another: problems of representation in children's drawings', Educational Psychology, No 1, pp.275-287.; COX, M.V. (1986). 'Cubes are difficult things to draw', British Journal of Developmental Psychology, No 4, pp.341-345.; COX, M.V. (1985). 'One object behind another: young children's use of array-specific or view-specific representations'. In: FREEMAN, N.H. & COX, M.V. (Eds). Visual order: the nature and development of pictorial representation. Cambridbge: Cambridge University Press.; FREEMAN, N.H. & COX, M.V. (Eds). (1985). Visual order: the nature and development of pictoral representation. Cambridge: Cambridge University Press.; COX, M.V. (1986). The child's point of view: the development of cognition and language. Brighton: Harvester Press.; COX, M.V. (1987). The child's point of view: the development of cognition and language. Brighton: Harvester Press.

Source of Grant: No funding
Date of Research: 1987 – continuing
KEYWORDS: art; child; drawing; picture

8/1744

Department of Psychology
Heslington, York YO1 5DD
0904 430000
Roger, D.B. Dr; Cox, M.V. Dr

The construction and validation of a test battery for assessing aptitude, ability and interests

Abstract: The project is aimed at constructing and validating a comprehensive battery of vocational guidance tests. In contrast with existing tests, this battery is designed to include measures of ability, aptitude and interests, and can be administered and scored by careers teachers themselves in secondary schools. A further advantage of the new test battery is that it can be completed within a timetabled double school period.

Source of Grant: Funded by small sums (less than £500) awarded by bodies within the University
Date of Research: 1985-1989
KEYWORDS: ability; aptitude test; secondary education; test; vocational guidance

Youthscan

8/1745

International Centre for Child Studies, Ashley Down House, 16 Cotham Park, Bristol BS6 6BU
0272 429961
Adult Literacy and Basic Skills Unit
229/231 High Holborn, London WC1V 7DA
071 405 4017
Butler, N. Prof.; *Supervisor:* Brain, S. Mr (Adult Literacy and Basic Skills Unit)

An investigation of the origins and effects of literacy problems in children and young adults

Abstract: It has been estimated by the ALBSU (Adult Literacy and Basic Skills Unit) in 1978 that 6,000,000 adults in Britain have some difficulties with basic skills and or numeracy skills. It has been estimated by the Training Enterprise Education Division in 1989 that there will be a fall-off in available 16-19 year olds in the labour market between 1989-94. The fundamental aim of the research will be to predict the kind of literacy skills required, together with training needs, in the next decade to meet the problems raised by the drop in school leavers and the growing skill shortage. The research will be based on a longitudinal analysis investigating origins and predispositions factors that lead to literacy problems in early childhood. This will be implemented by the delivery of an interview based questionnaire on a sample group of 10,000 aged 20-21. These will be drawn from within 12-16 education authorities. A further sub-sample will engage in a series of tests which have a practical location (time-tables, instructions, accessing information etc). These tests will be standardized. Results and conclusions will be published by the Adult Literacy and Basic Skills Unit.

Source of Grant: Adult Literacy and Basic Skills Unit: £65,000 Paul Hamlyn Foundation: £35,000
Date of Research: 1990 – continuing
KEYWORDS: basic education; labour market; labour shortage; literacy; numeracy; leaver; skill

Author Index

Subject Index

8/0608 curriculum development; Japan; multicultural education
8/0609 assessment; higher education
8/0611 aesthetics; critical sense; curriculum development
8/0837 artist; curriculum development; multicultural education
8/0838 book; language skill
8/0930 critical sense; curriculum; design education
8/0967 aesthetic education; critical sense; curriculum development
8/1236 aesthetic education; art; comparative education; museum
8/1237 aesthetic education; art appreciation; language; painting; vocabulary
8/1741 drawing; teaching aids

ARTIFICIAL INTELLIGENCE
8/0361 autoinstructional aid; automatic teaching; computer assisted instruction; dialogue (language); explanation; teaching machine
8/0362 computer assisted instruction; computer science; microcomputer
8/0448 autoinstructional aid; computer assisted instruction; teaching machine
8/1436 computer assisted instruction; evaluation; vocational training
8/1547 computer assisted instruction; health service personnel; medical education
8/1548 guidance; information system; student teacher; teacher education; teaching practice

ARTIST
8/0837 art education; curriculum development; multicultural education

ART THERAPY
8/1523 motivation; occupational aspiration; therapist

ASIA
8/0026 dance; evaluation

ASSERTIVENESS
8/1396 communication; health service personnel; inservice training; interpersonal relations

ASSESSMENT
8/0017 child; cognitive process; maladjusted; social behaviour
8/0073 higher education; quality of education
8/0130 curriculum; educational change; primary education; reform of education
8/0138 evaluation; profile; record of achievement; student record
8/0150 ability; mathematics; undergraduate; Malaysia
8/0156 examination; profession; vocational education
8/0157 curriculum development; examination; mathematics; performance
8/0172 achievement; evaluation; profile; student record
8/0175 physically handicapped; special education; standardized test
8/0219 learning strategy; management education
8/0264 doctor; examination; professional association
8/0268 centralization; curriculum; educational policy
8/0317 attention; gifted; hyperactivity; performance
8/0328 behaviour rating scales; comprehension tests; learning
8/0332 English language; language development; oral expression
8/0333 primary education; science education; video recording
8/0346 communication; educational technology; handicapped; teaching aids; speech handicapped
8/0347 parent choice; performance; school effectiveness; secondary education
8/0348 English language; primary education; profile; teaching
8/0366 Scotland; higher education; technology; performance

8/0367 achievement; English language
8/0368 communication; further education; personality development; skill
8/0374 achievement; English language; primary education; Scotland; secondary education
8/0390 curriculum development; examination; mathematics; secondary education
8/0393 computer assisted instruction; database; performance; pupil; software
8/0430 higher education; work experience
8/0456 practical work; science education
8/0468 nurse; profile; vocational education; work experience
8/0472 achievement measurement; science education
8/0497 aptitutde; employer; management education; student
8/0545 behaviour disorder; emotional disorder; special needs
8/0559 achievement; board of examiners; record of achievement
8/0571 science education; secondary education
8/0605 access programme; higher education; information system; mature student; performance
8/0609 art education; higher education
8/0627 learning test; primary education; project method; study skills; teaching aids
8/0645 aesthetic education; creativity; primary education
8/0653 humanities; primary education
8/0684 coursework; curriculum development; General Certificate of Education; interdisciplinary approach
8/0689 computer; performance; psychology of education; test
8/0717 achievement; primary education; reception class; teacher
8/0720 adolescent; cognition; psychotic; schizophrenia; thinking
8/0749 English language; secondary education; standard assessment task
8/0756 English language; ethnic group; General Certificate of Secondary Education; verbal communication
8/0762 science education; secondary education; Standard Assessment Task
8/0829 aptitude; mathematics; perception; primary education
8/0833 action research; inservice education and training of teachers; professional development
8/0894 child psychology; hydrocephalus; integration; spina
8/0900 primary education; standard assessment task; teacher assessment
8/0902 curriculum; primary education
8/0916 curriculum; parent-teacher relation; secondary school
8/0951 English (second language); language teaching; oral expression; pronunciation
8/0955 computer assisted instruction; curriculum development; educational technology; special education
8/0959 certification; curriculum development; education policy; history of education
8/0969 handicapped; visually handicapped
8/0970 performance; supervision; teacher education; teaching practice
8/0979 performance; test
8/0983 language skill; secondary education; standard assessment task; Welsh language
8/0985 primary education; test; standard assessment task
8/0988 primary education; science education; technology
8/0991 European Communities; learning difficulty; secondary education
8/1004 achievement; language; primary education; secondary sex difference
8/1008 foreign languages; performance; teaching aids
8/1013 cognitive process; space perception
8/1014 cross-national research; geography; mathematics; science education
8/1015 mathematics; primary education; teaching aids
8/1016 English studies; science education; technology
8/1066 knowledge level; learning process;

teaching method
8/1078 curriculum; primary school
8/1101 curriculum development; distance study; examination; education and training of teachers; teaching aids
8/1142 nurse education; progress report
8/1160 pupil; secondary education; student teacher; teacher-pupil relation
8/1163 pre-school child; visual perception
8/1201 autoinstructional aid; blind; computer assisted instruction; electronic data processing; information technology; visually handicapped
8/1247 performance; personnel; personnel evaluation
8/1270 health service personnel; physiotherapy; training
8/1325 achievement; curriculum; learning strategy; teaching method; technical education; vocational education
8/1327 diagnostic test
8/1333 achievement measurement; pupil; Scotland; technical assistance
8/1343 learning; learning difficulty; pre-school education; education
8/1393 primary school; pupil; pupil evaluation; school based assessment
8/1410 criterion referencing; primary education; student record
8/1445 discussion; English language; group discussion; group learning; group work; secondary school
8/1455 criterion referencing; decision making; microcomputer
8/1456 educational policy; Greece; primary education; teacher education
8/1483 competency-based education; curriculum design; curriculum development; further education; vocational education
8/1527 infant; interaction; teacher-pupil relation
8/1626 attitude; bilingualism; first foreign language; mother tongue; pupil; writing
8/1645 arithmetic; diagnostic test; error
8/1678 coursework; General Certificate of Secondary Education; performance
8/1717 curriculum development; examination; General Certificate of Secondary Education; religious education

ASSIGNMENT
8/0918 cognitive process; project; student

ASSISTANT
8/0519 class management; integration; primary education; special needs

ATHLETICS
8/0482 foreign student; recruitment; United States of America; university
8/0821 coaching
8/1522 physical education; secondary education

ATHLETICS COACH
8/1663 history of education; physical education

ATTENDANCE
8/0487 absenteeism; law; social control

ATTENTION
8/0317 assessment; gifted; hyperactivity; performance
8/0779 child development

ATTENTION DEFICIT DISORDER
8/0336 cognition; creativity; hyperactivity; learning difficulty

ATTITUDE
8/0015 discipline; disruptive behaviour; misconduct; pupil
8/0054 achievement; career; student; teacher education
8/0085 achievement; co-education; girls' education; secondary education; sex difference; single sex schools
8/0279 interpersonal relations; participation; political social interaction; youth
8/0436 further education; teacher education; technology

8/0260 commercial education; computer assisted instruction; evaluation; game

CALCULATOR
8/0170 arithmetic; curriculum development; number; primary education

CANADA
8/0601 comparative education; continuing education
8/1173 curriculum development; early childhood education; primary education

CARE
8/0134 curriculum; guidance; secondary education; social inequality
8/0911 information service; mentally handicapped; parent role; handicapped
8/1011 child; educational provision; social service
8/1509 community; knowledge; mental illness; training

CAREER
8/0054 achievement; attitude; student; teacher education
8/0118 employment; graduate; labour market; women's employment
8/1043 primary education; sex difference; teacher
8/1370 political socialization; socialization; youth; youth attitude
8/1421 educational policy; graduate; higher education; labour market
8/1514 further education; inservice education and training of teachers (INSET); staff development; teacher education

CAREER ASPIRATION
8/0301 employment; hotel and catering education
8/1610 Ireland, Northern; sex difference; woman teacher

CAREER CHANGE
8/1149 adult education; higher education; professional personnel
8/1324 demand for teachers; occupational choice; occupational mobility; teacher mobility; teacher supply and demand; teacher transfer

CAREER COUNSELLING
8/1024 enterprise education; higher education; occupational choice; vocational guidance

CAREER DEVELOPMENT
8/1691 advisor; employment expectations; educational guidance; guidance officer; inservice training; role perception

CAREER EDUCATION
8/0555 flexible learning; individualized teaching; open learning; resource materials; vocational guidance

CAREER LADDER
8/0030 comparative education; EEC; labour shortage; women's profession; women's employment
8/1168 primary education; woman teacher; women's employment

CAREER MONOGRAPH
8/1496 cross-national research; Germany FR; occupational choice; transition from school to work; United Kingdom; vocational guidance; youth

CAREERS GUIDANCE
8/0067 Careers Service; employment opportunities; transition from school to work
8/0251 questionnaire
8/0982 educational opportunities; training; transition from school to work; youth attitude
8/1025 computer; higher education; occupational choice
8/1169 careers service; occupational choice; youth unemployment

8/1300 adult; careers service

CAREERS SERVICE
8/0067 careers guidance; employment opportunities; transition from school to work
8/1169 careers guidance; occupational choice; youth unemployment
8/1300 adult; careers guidance

CASE STUDY
8/0149 deviance; physically handicapped; social adjustment; special school
8/1020 credits; further education; vocational training
8/1528 evaluation; examination; General Certificate of Secondary Education; secondary school; United Kingdom
8/1532 computer; educational innovation; primary school

CASEWORK
8/0271 childcare; decision making; social work

CATCHMENT AREAS
8/0351 geographic location; information system; school distribution

CATHOLICISM
8/0435 liberal education; theology
8/1605 attitude; catholic school; christianity; denominational school; pupil; religion

CATHOLIC SCHOOL
8/1605 attitude; catholicism; christianity; denominational school; pupil; religion

CENTRALIZATION
8/0268 assessment; curriculum; educational policy

CEREBRAL PALSY
8/0036 driver education; motor disorder; physical handicap
8/0096 conductive education; motor disorder; special education

CERTIFICATE
8/0257 course; evaluation; inservice training

CERTIFICATION
8/0959 assessment; curriculum development; education policy; history of education

CHANGE
8/1286 bilingualism; Wales

CHANGE AGENT
8/1539 co-ordinator; inservice teacher education

CHEMISTRY
8/0525 higher education; open learning
8/0579 comprehension; Nigeria; secondary education

CHILD
8/0011 interaction; leisure; socialization
8/0013 achievement; leisure; play; sex difference; social class
8/0017 assessment; cognitive process; maladjusted; social behaviour
8/0059 game; play; social development
8/0087 communication; language development; meaning; verbal communication
8/0206 phonology; reading; spelling
8/0370 achievement; motivation; Nigeria; social environment
8/0389 fitness; heart disease; prevention
8/0437 exercise; health
8/0491 cognition; earth sciences; science education
8/0699 Acquired Innune Deficiency Syndrome (AIDS); health education; knowledge; primary education
8/0745 comprehension; media studies; television
8/0753 family environment; medical treatment; sexual abuse
8/0865 emotional disorder; maladjusted; social behaviour
8/0892 curriculum; integration; physically handicapped; special

8/0932 hearing defect; teaching method
8/0946 competitive sport; physical development; swimmming; training
8/1011 care; educational provision; social service
8/1200 autoinstructional aid; automatic teaching; computer assisted instruction; computer microworlds; programming languages; teaching machine
8/1283 dialect; sociolinguistics; spoken language; United Kingdom
8/1406 attitude; belief; sexuality
8/1460 French language; language development; written expression; written language
8/1686 cultural environment; religious minority
8/1743 art; drawing; picture

CHILD CARE
8/0271 casework; decision making; social work
8/0698 child development; cognitive development; mother; women's employment
8/0973 maladjusted; residential care; social services; special school
8/1050 psychotherapy; residential care
8/1255 achievement; comparative achievement; social work

CHILD CARE OCCUPATIONS
8/1373 day care centre; day-nursery; nursery nurse

CHILD DEVELOPMENT
8/0187 learning difficulty; pre-school child; vision
8/0214 social structure
8/0281 special education; teacher behaviour
8/0552 history; primary education
8/0632 birth; intellectual development; motor disorder
8/0698 child care; cognitive development; mother; women's employment
8/0705 backwardness; deprived; mental development; development; social environment
8/0714 ability; adolescence; physical development
8/0769 facial expression; mother-child relation; non-verbal communication
8/0779 attention
8/1277 language development; language sciences; syntax
8/1473 co-operation; deprived; inner city; parent participation; social service
8/1649 language development; verbal communication

CHILD LANGUAGE
8/1289 language; language acquisition; syntax

CHILD PSYCHOLOGY
8/0069 survey
8/0894 assessment; hydrocephalus; integration; spina

CHILD REARING
8/0319 Egypt; moral education; parent role

CHILDREN'S LITEATURE
8/0181 fairy tale; literary criticism; style; translation

CHINA
8/0414 youth; sociology
8/1112 adult education; motivation
8/1114 adult education; comparative education; literacy; United Kingdom
8/1115 philosophy of education; United Kingdom
8/1126 adult education; leadership
8/1536 basic education; compulsory education; educational policy
8/1573 educational policy; reform of education

CHINA: LEADERSHIP
8/1113 adult education; teacher education

CHINESE LANGUAGE
8/1143 composition; English language; Hong Kong; learning difficulty; writing

COLONIALISM
8/1231 adult education; Africa; citizenship education; community education; informal education; nationalism; Zambia

COMMERCE
8/0921 comprehension; enterprise; industry education relationship; industry teacher education

COMMERCIAL EDUCATION
8/0259 business management; computer assisted information system; instruction; simulation
8/0260 business management; computer assisted instruction; evaluation; game
8/0459 economics; microcomputer; secondary education; software
8/0676 curriculum development; inservice education and training of teachers; teaching aids
8/1001 data bank; database; educational material; evaluation; individualized teaching; modern languages; science education; teaching aids

COMMERCIAL TRAINING
8/1197 autoinstructional aid; automatic teaching; computer assisted instruction; educational technology; industrial training; teaching machine

COMMUNICATION
8/0087 child; language development; meaning; verbal communication
8/0122 audio-visual method; language development; social skills
8/0136 comprehension; primary education
8/0237 deaf; movement; physcial education; socialization
8/0262 computer; conversation; physically disabled; speech handicapped
8/0273 computer assisted instruction; conversation; physically handicapped
8/0346 assessment; educational technology; handicapped; teaching aids; speech handicapped
8/0368 assessment; further education; personality development; skill
8/0371 curriculum development; educational technology; handicapped; teaching aids
8/0502 achievement; cognition; listening; reading; television
8/0551 comparative research; foreign languages; language teaching; modern languages
8/0577 English (second language); language development; primary education
8/0596 deaf; hearing defect; special school
8/0788 autism; language development
8/0864 dumb; lexicon; mentally handicapped; sign; social behaviour
8/0893 culture; meaning; organization
8/0976 learning process; oral expression; speech; teaching method
8/1028 developing country; interaction; women's education; women's organization
8/1111 adult education; computer network; physically handicapped; special needs
8/1291 learning process; oral expression; speech; teaching method
8/1344 inservice education and training of teachers; integration; nursery school; special needs
8/1382 dumb; mentally handicapped; non-verbal communication; sign
8/1396 assertiveness; health service personnel; inservice training; interpersonal relations
8/1405 language skill; modern languages; teaching aids; teaching method
8/1470 group work; primary education
8/1529 english language; english literature; further vocational education; vocational training
8/1625 English language; foreign languages; language teaching; learning strategy; vocabulary

COMMUNICATION RESEARCH
8/1394 discourse analysis; English language; English (second language); language research; language teaching; native speakers

COMMUNICATION SKILLS
8/1027 adult education; adult literacy; basic education; data bank; English (second language); numeracy; resource materials
8/1243 communicative competence; English (second language teaching; oral work; spoken language; verbal communication; Zambia

COMMUNICATION STUDIES
8/0230 Europe; exchange visit; higher education; industry; undergraduate

COMMUNICATIVE COMPETENCE
8/1243 communication skills; English (second language teaching; oral work; spoken language; verbal communication; Zambia

COMMUNITY
8/0376 further education; higher education; system of education; States of America
8/0378 learning conditions; nurse; practical work; vocational education
8/0530 adult; literacy
8/1509 care; knowledge; mental illness; training

COMMUNITY DEVELOPMENT
8/0318 Ireland; youth organization
8/1181 adult education; voluntary organization
8/1577 ethnography; religion; religious education

COMMUNITY EDUCATION
8/0163 socialization; youth welfare
8/0394 biography; maladjusted; philosophy of education; school
8/0460 employment; youth service
8/1035 adult education; credits; further education; higher education; open learning
8/1051 decision making; educational policy; local education authority; unemployed
8/1091 curriculum development; multicultural education; reform of education
8/1157 integration; mentally handicapped; social skills
8/1231 adult education; Africa; citizenship education; colonialism; informal education; nationalism; Zambia
8/1390 further education of teachers; health education; inservice teacher education; inservice training; life skills; private school; teacher
8/1682 drama; health education; theatre
8/1703 moral development; moral education

COMMUNITY HEALTH SERVICES
8/1391 agency co-operation; co-operation; health education; higher education

COMPARATIVE ACHIEVEMENT
8/1217 distance study; geographic location; open university; performance
8/1255 achievement; child care; social work

COMPARATIVE ANALYSIS
8/0878 continuous assessment; examination; linguistics; undergraduate; writing
8/1341 evaluation; examination
8/1355 motivation; socialization; youth employment
8/1507 Germany, Federal Republic; labour market; transition from school to work; vocational education; youth employment

COMPARATIVE EDUCATION
8/0030 career ladder; EEC; labour shortage; women's profession; women's employment
8/0031 education; EEC; Europe; labour market; qualification; skill; technological change; training
8/0032 family life; France; higher education; United Kingdom; women's education; women's employment
8/0043 experiential learning; industry education work experience
8/0120 leisure education; physical education
8/0137 educational policy; reform of education; education
8/0287 Hong Kong; Japan; Singapore
8/0601 Canada; continuing education

8/0621 computer assisted instruction; microcomputer; Turkey
8/0661 school-industry relation; United States of America
8/0712 behaviour disorder; Bulgaria; emotional disorder; special education
8/0742 disruptive pupils; United States of America
8/0794 college of education; labour market; teacher education; vocational education
8/0890 attitude; competition; cross-cultural research; participation; sport
8/1032 adult education; basic education; data bank; physically handicapped; resource materials; unemployed; education
8/1097 manipulative material; mathematics; primary Spain; teaching aids
8/1114 adult education; China; literacy; United Kingdom
8/1123 history of education; industrialization; United of America
8/1232 adult education; library; library role; life-long education, Netherlands; non formal education; United Kingdom
8/1236 aesthetic education; art; art education; museum
8/1280 France; french language; modern languages; oral examination; teacher education
8/1315 library; library technician; para professional personnel; personnel; training programme
8/1360 cross-cultural research; educational change; attitude; teacher behaviour; United Kingdom; USSR
8/1362 cross-cultural research; occupational satisfaction; secondary school; teacher role; teacher status
8/1488 adult education; continuing education; life-long education; performance; university
8/1551 engineer; Japan; post-compulsory education; vocational education
8/1554 engineer; Japan; post-compulsory education; personnel; vocational education
8/1557 cognitive development; developing country; pre-school education; Trinidad and Tobago
8/1637 grammar; Iraq; mother tongue; secondary education
8/1715 behaviour disorder; disruptive behaviour; misconduct; USA

COMPARATIVE RESEARCH
8/0551 communication; foreign languages; language teaching; modern languages
8/0806 Japan; value; youth attitude
8/0808 Europe; information technology; primary education
8/1306 higher education; industry; personnel evaluation; staff development
8/1367 educational innovation; educational policy; occupational satisfaction; secondary education; teacher
8/1565 cross-national research; organization of research; post-graduate study
8/1596 gypsy

COMPETENCY BASED EDUCATION
8/0401 curriculum; further education; vocational education
8/1256 curriculum development; further education; vocational education
8/1483 assessment; curriculum design; curriculum development; further education; vocational education

COMPETITION
8/0890 attitude; comparative education; cross-cultural research; participation; sport

COMPETITIVE SPORT
8/0946 child; physical development; swimmming; training

COMPLIANCE (PSYCHOLOGY)
8/0771 Acquired Immune Deficiency Syndrome; health education

COMPOSER
8/0442 education; music

COMPOSITION
8/0431 argumentation; narration; writing; written expression
8/1143 Chinese language; English language; Hong Kong; learning difficulty; writing
8/1271 mathematics; word problems (mathematics)

COMPREHENSION
8/0136 communication; primary education
8/0180 meaning; reading; reading skills; word study skills
8/0320 Brazil; cognition; reading
8/0327 Brazil; cognition; metacognition; primary school; reading
8/0379 meaning; word
8/0384 cognitive process; reading
8/0391 computer assisted instruction; group work; interaction; program
8/0562 concept formation; science education; teaching aids
8/0563 mathematics; mechanics; secondary education
8/0570 learning strategy; science education; secondary education
8/0579 chemistry; Nigeria; secondary education
8/0584 algebra; cognitive process
8/0590 mechanics
8/0600 acceleration; higher education; mathematics; mechanics; secondary education
8/0745 child; media studies; television
8/0761 biology; concept formation; science education
8/0775 language development; pre-school child; vocabulary
8/0921 commerce; enterprise; industry education relationship; industry teacher education
8/1166 cognitive process; reading; spelling; word recognition
8/1252 concept formation; inservice education and training of teachers; primary education; science education; teacher
8/1262 concept formation; mechanics; teaching aids; video recording
8/1464 concept formation; physics; science education; teaching method
8/1624 document; linguistics; morphology
8/1699 adult education; higher education; sciences; science policy; women's education
8/1710 discussion; group work; mathematics

COMPREHENSION TESTS
8/0328 assessment; behaviour rating scales; learning

COMPREHENSIVE SCHOOL
8/0282 ability grouping; european studies; evaluation; GCSE (General Certificate of Secondary Education); special education
8/0299 education policy; equal opportunity; political party
8/1533 culture; social environment; socio-cultural activities
8/1700 administration of education; educational policy; reform of education
8/1731 self-education; staff development; teacher

COMPULSORY EDUCATION
8/1536 basic education; China; educational policy

COMPUTER
8/0018 author; computer assisted instruction; interactive video; knowledge; teaching aids
8/0220 administration of education; computer uses in education; school organization
8/0262 communication; conversation; physically disabled; speech handicapped
8/0409 design; higher education; teaching technique
8/0445 doctor; information technology; management; professional status; skill
8/0506 attitude; sex difference
8/0689 assessment; performance; psychology of education; test
8/0736 group work; primary education

8/1025 careers guidance; higher education; occupational choice
8/1094 further education; self evaluation; teacher; video recording
8/1117 adult education; information technlolgy; physically special needs; vocational training
8/1118 adult education; information technology; physically special needs
8/1184 distance study; gender equality; higher education; learning strategy; Open University; sex difference
8/1240 mathematics; secondary school; teacher attitude; teacher behaviour
8/1260 educational innovation; educational policy; information technology
8/1532 case study; educational innovation; primary school
8/1582 music education; primary education; program

COMPUTER ASSISTED EDUCATIONAL TECHNOLOGY
8/1203 autoinstructional aid; automatic teaching; learning process; teaching machine
8/1212 autoinstructional aid; automatic teaching; equations (mathematics); mathematics; teaching machine

COMPUTER ASSISTED INFORMATION SYSTEM
8/0259 business management; commercial education; instruction; simulation

COMPUTER ASSISTED INSTRUCTION
8/0002 french language; language teaching; teaching aids; translation
8/0016 french language; language teaching; translation
8/0018 author; computer; interactive video; knowledge; teaching aids
8/0094 blind; microcomputer; software; teaching aids; visually handicapped
8/0108 learning strategy; learning test; verbal learning; visual learning
8/0119 adult eduction; learning strategy; word processing
8/0191 computer network; educational software; learning process; local area network; primary school; teaching method
8/0200 reading
8/0224 higher education; information technology; language teaching; translation
8/0231 autoinstructional aid; programmed text
8/0254 database; higher education; history; information retrieval; information skills
8/0260 business management; commercial education; evaluation; game
8/0273 communication; conversation; physically handicapped
8/0275 mental retardation; microcomputer; special needs
8/0298 computer network; co-operation; higher education; primary education
8/0324 independent work; microcomputer; development; teaching method
8/0330 classroom; group work; teacher role; verbal communication
8/0338 educational technology; language teaching; second foreign language
8/0349 database; microcomputer; model
8/0360 belief; cognition; learning process; science education
8/0361 artificial intelligence; autoinstructional aid; automatic teaching; dialogue (language); explanation; teaching machine
8/0362 artificial intelligence; computer science; microcomputer
8/0363 language development; special education
8/0386 class management; educational technology; interactive video; teacher education
8/0391 comprehension; group work; interaction; program
8/0393 assessment; database; performance; pupil; software
8/0412 dyslexia; learning difficulty; teacher education; teaching aids
8/0443 cognitive development; educational technology; information technology; special education

8/0444 evaluation; software; teaching aids
8/0448 artificial intelligence; autoinstructional aid; teaching machine
8/0452 microcomputer; music education; primary education
8/0458 art education; creativity
8/0461 microcomputer; social studies; software
8/0470 discussion; group learning; group work; microcomputers; teaching method
8/0500 decision-making; interactive video; mentally handicapped
8/0523 further education; teaching aids
8/0528 higher education; history; simulation; software
8/0533 distance study; educational technology; interactive video; management education
8/0549 software; teaching aids
8/0582 concept formation; science education; secondary education
8/0594 history; simulation; teaching aids
8/0604 anatomy; autoinstructional aid; automatic teaching; neuroanatomy; neurology
8/0621 comparative education; microcomputer; Turkey
8/0634 concept formation; microcomputer science education; teaching aids
8/0669 computer microworld; expert system; information technology
8/0722 inservice education and training of teachers; mathematics; teaching
8/0732 learning difficulty; mentally handicapped; microcomputer; social interaction
8/0747 cognitive process; discussion; mathematics
8/0765 database; environmental study; information technology; science education
8/0766 curriculum development; learning
8/0768 computer assisted learning
8/0777 learning difficulty; mentally handicapped; microcomputer; special education
8/0790 educational technology; interactive video; open learning; videodisc
8/0809 adviser; information technology; inservice education and training of teachers; Technical and Vocational Education Initiative; time management
8/0820 higher education; library and studies; teaching method
8/0831 law; problem solving
8/0862 microcomputer; motivation primary education; software
8/0923 curriculum; parallel computer systems
8/0926 educational technology; multimedia approach; teaching aids; videodisc
8/0935 further education of teachers; inservice teacher education; nursery school
8/0942 economic conditions; marketing
8/0948 database; language teaching; teaching aids
8/0955 assessment; curriculum development; educational technology; special education
8/1056 electronic data processing; further educaion of teachers; higher education; information technology; inservice teacher education
8/1125 learning difficulty
8/1145 mathematics; problem solving; secondary education; software
8/1176 literacy; profile; technical education
8/1179 emotional disorder; information technology; learning difficulty
8/1194 autoinstructional aid; automatic teaching; educational technology; learning process; teaching machine
8/1197 autoinstructional aid; automatic teaching; commercial training; educational technology; industrial training; teaching machine
8/1198 autoinstructional aid; automatic teaching; clinical diagnosis; diagnosis; educational technology; medical treatment; teaching machine
8/1199 co-operative learning; distance study; group learning; mathematics; physics; problem solving
8/1200 autoinstructional aid; automatic teaching; child; computer microworlds;

programming languages; teaching machine
8/1201 assessment; autoinstructional aid; blind; electronic data processing; information technology; visually handicapped
8/1202 autoinstructional aid; automatic teaching; educational technology; teaching machine
8/1204 autoinstructional aid; automatic teaching; educational technology; teaching machine
8/1205 autoinstructional aid; automatic teaching; educational technology; teaching machine; teaching method
8/1206 autoinstructional aid; educational electronic data processing; information technology; programmed text; visually handicapped
8/1208 autoinstructional aid; automatic teaching; educational technology; music; music theory; teaching machine
8/1209 autoinstructional aid; automatic teaching; computer programming; computer science; distance study; educational technology; teaching machine
8/1211 autoinstructional aid; automatic teaching; educational technology; teaching machine
8/1213 arithmetic; autoinstructional aid; automatic teaching; educational technology; mathematics; teaching machine
8/1214 autoinstructional aid; automatic teaching; educational technology; further education; handicapped; special education; teaching machine
8/1215 autoinstructional aid; automatic teaching; cognitive development; co-operative learning; educational technology; teaching machine
8/1216 distance education; gender equality; women's education
8/1220 feedback; interaction; learning; problem solving
8/1266 adult education; life skills; literacy education; mentally handicapped; numeracy
8/1303 multicultural education; music education
8/1339 computer assisted learning; educational software; educational technology; evaluation; further education of teachers
8/1434 business education; economics; secondary education
8/1435 geology; higher education; tutoring
8/1436 artificial intelligence; evaluation; vocational training
8/1437 programming language; tutoring
8/1459 autoinstructional aid; evaluation; teaching machine
8/1461 group learning; physics
8/1463 computer assisted learning; educational software; group learning; interaction; process analysis
8/1468 interaction; peer group; tutoring
8/1519 autoinstructional aid; educational teaching machine
8/1547 artificial intelligence; health service personnel; medical education
8/1587 computer science; database; distance study; interaction
8/1588 computer science; interview; knowledge; model
8/1589 computer science; distance study; videodisc
8/1590 educational technology
8/1591 open learning; program; teaching aids
8/1592 interactive learning; knowledge; software; teaching aids
8/1633 electronic data processing; information science; information technology; mathematics
8/1711 concept formulation; learning strategy; mathematics; microcomputer

COMPUTER ASSISTED LEARNING
8/0768 computer assisted instruction
8/1210 autoinstructional aid; automatic teaching; teaching machine
8/1339 computer assisted instruction; educational software; educational technology; evaluation; further education of teachers
8/1463 computer assisted instruction;

educational software; group learning; interaction; process analysis

COMPUTER ENGINEERING
8/0196 curriculum; further education; higher education; information science
8/0879 cognition; diagnosis; failure; vocational training

COMPUTER GRAPHICS
8/0792

COMPUTER MICROWORLD
8/0518 computer programming; learning
8/0669 computer assisted instruction; expert system; information technology
8/1200 autoinstructional aid; automatic teaching; child; computer assisted instruction; programming languages; teaching machine

COMPUTER NETWORK
8/0191 computer assisted instruction; educational software; learning process; local area network; primary school; teaching method
8/0298 computer assisted instruction; co-operation; higher education; primary education
8/1080 database; information retrieval; researcher; education
8/1111 adult education; communication; physically handicapped; special needs

COMPUTER PROGRAMMING
8/0518 computer microworld; learning
8/0680 learning strategy; microcomputer
8/1209 autoinstructional aid; automatic teaching; computer assisted instruction; computer science; distance study; educational technology; teaching machine
8/1546 computer science; electronic data processing; programming languages

COMPUTER SCIENCE
8/0362 artificial intelligence; computer assisted instruction; microcomputer
8/0704 cognitive process; student
8/1209 autoinstructional aid; automatic teaching; computer assisted instruction; computer programming; distance study; educational technology; teaching machine
8/1546 computer programming; electronic data processing; programming languages
8/1587 computer assisted instruction; database; distance study; interaction
8/1588 computer assisted instruction; interview; knowledge; model
8/1589 computer assisted instruction; distance study; videodisc
8/1599 course evaluation; labour market; post-graduate study; skill shortage; technology

COMPUTER SOFTWARE REVIEWS
8/1451 educational software; educational technology; teacher

COMPUTER USES IN EDUCATION
8/0220 administration of education; computer; school organization
8/0397 electronic data processing; further education; records of achievement; student record
8/1183 microcomputers; Open University

CONCEPT ANALYSIS
8/0186 cognition; concept formulation; early learning; learning process
8/1502 adult education; psychology of education; science education; teacher education

CONCEPT FORMATION
8/0186 cognition; concept analysis; early learning; learning process
8/0197 adult; cross-cultural research; earth sciences; fuel; misconception; scientific concepts
8/0240 environmental study; primary education
8/0329 mathematics; test construction

8/0562 comprehension; science education; teaching aids
8/0582 computer assisted instruction; science education; secondary education
8/0634 computer assisted instruction; microcomputer science education; teaching aids
8/0659 primary education; science education
8/0716 mathematics; problem solving
8/0761 biology; comprehension; science education
8/1038 cognitive development; physically handicapped; special education; visually handicapped
8/1100 mathematics; number concept
8/1226 learning; science education
8/1252 comprehension; inservice education and training of teachers; primary education; science education; teacher
8/1262 comprehension; mechanics; teaching aids; video recording
8/1464 comprehension; physics; science education; teaching method
8/1711 computer assisted instruction; learning strategy; mathematics; microcomputer

CONDUCTIVE EDUCATION
8/0079 motor disorder; special education
8/0096 cerebral palsy; motor disorder; special education
8/0474 learning difficulty; special education
8/0885 physically handicapped; special education

CONFIDENCE
8/0738 non-verbal communication; pre-school child; self-esteem

CONSORTIA
8/1665 employment; rural area; training

CONSTRUCTION
8/0335 construction set; model technology; primary education; science education; sex difference

CONSTRUCTION INDUSTRY
8/0822 labour market; school leaver; transition from school to work

CONSTRUCTION SET
8/0335 construction; model technology; primary education; science education; sex difference

CONSULTANCY
8/1309 curriculum development; inservice education and training teachers; music education; primary education
8/1312 inservice education and training of teachers; music primary education

CONSULTANT
8/0637 educational innovation; primary education; teacher appraisal

CONSULTATION
8/0155 course; doctor; inservice training; trainer

CONTENT ANALYSIS
8/0619 narration; primary education; teacher

CONTINUING EDUCATION
8/0116 access to education; higher education; mature student
8/0265 distance study; doctor
8/0266 doctor; management education; time
8/0501 doctor; medicine
8/0526 access programme; higher education; mature student; part-time course
8/0601 comparative education; Canada
8/1033 adult education; educational provision; learning difficulty
8/1105 adult education; educational policy
8/1161 adult education; life-long education; local education authority; marketing
8/1488 adult education; comparative education; life-long education; performance; university
8/1687 educational policy; higher education

8/1372 primary education; religious education; education
8/1374 mathematics; microcomputer; secondary education; teaching aids
8/1375 mathematics; secondary education; sixth form; teaching aids
8/1402 cross-cultural research; cultural pluralism; educational opportunities; international school
8/1404 attitude change; cultural pluralism; multicultural education; primary education
8/1411 secondary education; Technical and Vocational Education Initiative (TVEI)
8/1416 educational policy; music education; primary education; teacher education
8/1446 music education; inservice training; special teacher
8/1454 english language; history of education; Scotland; secondary education
8/1483 assessment; competency-based education; curriculum design; further education; vocational education
8/1485 classroom research; English language; English (second language); Pakistan; teaching
8/1497 education; educational innovation; nurse
8/1504 learning strategy; modular course; teaching method; Technical and Vocational Education Inititative
8/1530 craft design technology; history of education; secondary education; technical education
8/1570 educational policy; information technology; inservice education and training of teachers
8/1571 business education; educational policy; enterprise education
8/1575 primary education; writing
8/1579 language teaching; reading
8/1600 enterprise education; evaluation; higher education
8/1611 educational innovation; educational policy; information technology; inservice education and training of teachers; management
8/1636 planning of education; primary education
8/1639 Technical and Vocational Education Initiative (TVEI); Wales
8/1642 mathematics; secondary education; teaching aids; teaching method
8/1654 development education
8/1683 educational policy; foreign languages; politics
8/1705 ethnic relations; evaluation; multicultural education
8/1712 learning strategy; teacher-pupil relation; method
8/1717 assessment; examination; General Certificate of Secondary Education; religious education

CURRICULUM SUBJECT
8/0417 curriculum development; primary education; specialization
8/0656 aesthetic education; philosophy of education; physical education; moral education; religious education
8/1086 independent study; study skills
8/1138 General Certicicate of Secondary Education; geography; humanities; secondary education

CURRICULUM TECHNOLOGY
8/0567 primary education

CZECHOSLOVAKIA
8/1141 educational innovation; reform of education

DANCE
8/0025 educational provision; youth
8/0026 Asia; evaluation
8/0061 interactive video; secondary education
8/0607 participation; race; sex difference; social class
8/0897 aesthetics; attitude; secondary education; sport
8/0937 primary education; teaching aids; videorecording

8/1053 mentally handicapped; special education; special school

DATABASES
8/0012 information retrieval; photograph; picture; videodisc
8/0132 course; information technology; training
8/0151 audiovisual aids; information retrieval; information service; teaching aids
8/0254 computer assisted instruction; higher education; history; information retrieval; information skills
8/0280 attitude change; microcomputer; pupil; sex difference
8/0349 computer assisted instruction; microcomputer; model
8/0393 assessment; computer assisted instruction; performance; pupil; software
8/0765 computer assisted instruction; environmental study; information technology; science education
8/0826 electronic mail
8/0948 computer assisted instruction; language teaching; teaching aids
8/1001 commercial education; data bank; educational material; evaluation; individualized teaching; modern languages; science education; teaching aids
8/1019 industry education relationship; vocational education
8/1027 adult education; adult literacy; basic education; communication skills; English (second language); numeracy; resource materials
8/1032 adult education; basic education; comparative education; physically handicapped; resource materials; unemployed; educatio
8/1069 educational research; information service; Ireland, Northern
8/1080 computer network; information retrieval; researcher; education
8/1308 information service; multicultural education; teaching aids
8/1336 curriculum development; evaluation; Scotland; Technical and Educational Education Initiative (TVEI)
8/1337 educational policy; low attainer; Scotland; sex difference; Technical and Vocational Education Initiative (TVEI)
8/1423 integration; special education; special needs
8/1584 alcoholism; drug addiction; health education; teaching aids; training
8/1587 computer assisted instruction; computer science; distance study; interaction

DAY CARE CENTRES
8/1373 childcare occupations; day-nursery; nursery nurse
8/1465 numeracy

DEAF
8/0237 communication; movement; physcial education; socialization
8/0419 memory; visual perception
8/0596 communication; hearing defect; special school
8/0844 cognitive development; language development; hearing defect; oral expression
8/0938 home education; parent-child relation; pre-school child; reading; transitional class
8/1318 access to education; equal opportunity; higher education

DEATH
8/0263 educational need; health service personnel; teaching method

DECENTRALIZATION
8/0337 budgetary control; financial resources

DECISION MAKING
8/0271 casework; childcare; social work
8/0500 computer assisted instruction; interactive video; mentally handicapped
8/0866 cognition; problem solving; profession
8/0978 administration of education; governing body; school; school governor

8/0993 administration of education; further education; planning of education; quality of education
8/1051 community education; educational policy; local education authority; unemployed
8/1455 assessment; criterion referencing; microcomputer

DEFIANT BEHAVIOUR
8/0936 girl; problem child; pupil

DELINQUENCY
8/0248 adolescence; behaviour disorder; occupational pupil; secondary school; transition from school to work; life skills

DEMAND FOR EDUCATION
8/1518 demography; employment; forecasting; graduate; education; labour market; student; trend

DEMAND FOR TEACHERS
8/1324 career change; occupational choice; occupational mobility; teacher mobility; teacher supply and demand; teacher transfer

DEMOCRATIC LEARNING
8/0100 teacher education; teaching method

DEMOGRAPHY
8/0099 economic conditions; history of education; sociology of education
8/0920 participation; sport
8/1518 demand for education; employment; forecasting; graduate; education; labour market; student; trend

DENOMINATIONAL SCHOOL
8/0701 christian education; church; educational provision; history of education
8/0850 history of education; school-community relation
8/0896 church; history of education; religious organization; United Kingdom
8/0984 educational policy; legislation; religious education
8/1605 attitude; catholic school; catholicism; christianity; pupil; religion
8/1607 religion and education; religious behaviour; rural school

DENOMINATIONAL STUDY
8/0856 history of education

DEPARTMENT HEAD
8/1534 administration of education; deputy head; head teacher; local education authority; manpower planning; middle management; recruitment; school management

DEPRIVED
8/0358 achievement; secondary education; youth
8/0705 backwardness; child development; mental development; development; social environment
8/1473 child development; co-operation; inner city; parent participation; social service

DEPUTY HEAD TEACHER
8/0799 sex discrimination
8/1534 administration of education; department head; head teacher; local education authority; manpower planning; middle management; recruitment; school management

DESCHOOLING
8/0005

DESIGN
8/0409 computer; higher education; teaching technique
8/0505 teaching aids; textbook; typography; visual perception
8/0517 management education; problem solving; teacher education; technology

8/1220 computer assisted instruction;
interaction; learning; problem solving

FEES
8/1030 adult education; educational finance;
part-time course

FEMINISM
8/0194
8/0872 administration of education; history of
education; particpation; women's education;
women's movement

FICTION
8/0950 groupwork; imagination; primary
education; reading

FIELD STUDY
8/1107 adult education; earth sciences
8/1292 Education Reform Act (1988);
financing; out of school

FINAL EXAMINATION
8/1651 educational technology; secondary
school; Sierra Leone; underachievement

FINANCIAL RESOURCES
8/0033 administration of education; higher
education; history of education; university
8/0090 budgetary control; school
8/0106 administration of education; local
education authority; resource allocation;
school
8/0337 budgetary control; decentralization
8/0811 cost; developed country; developing
country
8/0812 cost; developing country; educational
policy; equal opportunity; Sudan
8/0857 administration of education; educational
policy; history of education; secondary
education
8/1366 educational innovation; morale; teacher
attitude
8/1425 administration of education; budgetary
control; planning of education; training
8/1432 administration of education; budgetary
control; college of further education;
information system; management
8/1560 developing country; planning of
education; poverty; system of education
8/1679 industry; labour market; participation;
secondary education

FINANCING
8/0058 budgetary control; resource allocation;
school; socially handicapped; special
education
8/0190 curriculum development; educational
policy; further education; government policy
8/1235 evaluation; inservice teacher education;
inservice training; teacher
8/1292 Education Reform Act (1988); field
study; out of school

FIRST FOREIGN LANGUAGE
8/0565 class size; English (second language);
teaching
8/1251 curriculum development; educational
policy; teaching
8/1413 bilingualism; ethnic minority; reading
8/1626 assessment; attitude; bilingualism;
mother tongue; pupil; writing
8/1734 bilingualism; ethnic minority; mother
tongue; Sri Lanka; Tamil; United Kingdom
8/1735 Bangladeshi; Bengali; English (second
language); ethnic minority; mother tongue;
United Kingdom
8/1736 adult education; English (second
language); language teaching

FITNESS
8/0238 motivation; physical education
8/0389 child; heart disease; prevention
8/0870 adolescent; health education; nutrition;
obesity

FLEXIBLE LEARNING
8/0555 career education; individualized
teaching; open learning; resource materials;
vocational guidance

8/0981 evaluation; performance indicator;
Technical and Vocational Education
Initiative
8/1569 educational innovation; open learning;
Technical and Vocational Education Initiative

FOLK ART
8/0849 Africa; civilization; cultural
development; literature

FORECASTING
8/0070 number of pupils; school
8/1426 enrolment projection; further education;
registration
8/1518 demand for education; demography;
employment; graduate; education; labour
market; student; trend

FOREIGN COUNTRY
8/1397 English (second language); higher
education; language of instruction; lecture;
science education; technology education;
university teaching

FOREIGN LANGUAGES
8/0034 France; Japan; language teaching;
mother tongue; United Kingdom
8/0405 performance; mother tongue; reading
8/0551 communication; comparative research;
language teaching; modern languages
8/1002 choice of studies; Education Support
Grant; evaluation; modern languages
8/1008 assessment; performance; teaching aids
8/1239 modern languages; motivation for
studies; pupil secondary education
8/1422 English (second language); English
language; ethnic minority; second language
8/1625 communication; English language;
language teaching; learning strategy;
vocabulary
8/1643 language teaching; mnemonics
8/1683 curriculum development; educational
policy; politics

FOREIGN STUDENT
8/0482 athletics; recruitment; United States of
America; university
8/0511 guidance; university

FORMAL EDUCATION
8/0291 informal education; primary education;
teaching method

FRANCE
8/0032 comparative education; family life;
higher education; United Kingdom; women's
education; women's employment
8/0034 foreign languages; Japan; language
teaching; mother tongue; United Kingdom
8/0513 Australia; student unrest; Western
Europe
8/0657 international exchange; system of
education; theory of education
8/1280 comparative education; french language;
modern languages; oral examination; teacher
education

FREEDOM
8/1304 Europe; indoctrination; system of
education

FRENCH LANGUAGE
8/0002 computer assisted instruction; language
teaching; teaching aids; translation
8/0016 computer assisted instruction; language
teaching; translation
8/0499 aims of education; language teaching
8/1280 comparative education; France; modern
languages; oral examination; teacher
education
8/1460 child; language development; written
expression; written language

FRIENDSHIP
8/0907 adolescent; girl; leisure

FUEL
8/0197 adult; concept formation; cross-cultural
research; earth sciences; misconception;
scientific concepts

FURTHER EDUCATION
8/0077 curriculum; multicultural education
8/0190 curriculum development; educational
policy; financing; government policy
8/0196 computer engineering; curriculum;
higher education; information science
8/0217
8/0302 ethnic minority; learning strategy;
multicultural education; teaching method
8/0305 librarian; management education;
vocational education
8/0368 assessment; communication; personality
development; skill
8/0376 community; higher education; system of
education; States of America
8/0395 employment opportunities; labour
market; physically handicapped; special
education; vocational training
8/0396 course; evaluation; quality of education;
validation
8/0397 computer uses in education; electronic
data processing; records of achievement;
student record
8/0398 core skill; post-compulsory education;
sixteen to nineteen education; vocational
education
8/0399 curriculum development; industrial
education; resource materials; training
8/0400 National Vocational Qualification;
special education; vocational education
8/0401 competency based education;
curriculum; vocational education
8/0402
8/0403 curriculum development; handicapped;
integration; learning difficulty; special needs
8/0428 engineering; morale; teacher
8/0436 attitude; teacher education; technology
8/0466 adviser; distance study; teacher
education
8/0520 higher education; language skills;
language teaching; modern languages
8/0522 attitude; higher education; planning of
education; social class; student
8/0523 computer assisted instruction; teaching
aids
8/0524 adult education; credits; higher
education; integration; part-time course
8/0588 course; economics of education
8/0719 initial training; inservice training;
probationary teacher; teacher education
8/0813 employment; industrial education;
manpower need; transition from school to
work; vocational education
8/0853 adult; employment; physically
handicapped; Spina Bifida
8/0987 access programme; open learning;
planning of education
8/0993 administration of education; decision
making; planning of education; quality of
education
8/0998 personnel evaluation; staff development
8/1003 post-secondary education; sixteen to
nineteen education; tertiary education
8/1009 course; educational provision; higher
education; planning of education; statistical
analysis
8/1020 case study; credits; vocational training
8/1035 adult education; community education;
credits; higher education; open learning
8/1056 computer assisted instruction; electronic
data processing; higher education;
information technology; inservice teacher
education
8/1061 experiential learning; group work;
personal research method
8/1094 computer; self evaluation; teacher; video
recording
8/1110 special needs; support service
8/1214 autoinstructional aid; automatic
teaching; computer assisted instruction;
educational technology; handicapped; special
education; teaching machine
8/1256 competency based education; curriculum
development; vocational education
8/1258 administration of education; governing
body; higher education; polytechnic
8/1267
8/1278 agricultural college; economic
conditions; further of teachers; inservice
teacher education; rural area

GOVERNANCE
8/1257 college administration; college of further education; education; post-compulsory education

GOVERNING BODY
8/0117 administration of education; college of further education; employer; participation
8/0471 administration of education; primary education; school-community relation; Scotland
8/0978 administration of education; decision making; school; school governor
8/1005 administration of education
8/1258 administration of education; further education; higher education; polytechnic

GOVERNMENT POLICY
8/0101 Africa; politics; system of education
8/0190 curriculum development; educational policy; financing; further education
8/1420 educational policy; legislation; parent participation
8/1634 educational policy; history of education; United Kingdom

GRADUATE
8/0118 career; employment; labour market; women's employment
8/0210 primary education; professional development; teacher education; teacher socialization
8/0424 employment; interview; selection criterion
8/0512 Europe; higher education; politics
8/0899 police; recruitment
8/1421 career; educational policy; higher education; labour market
8/1438 occupational choice; sex difference; social class; work
8/1439 discrimination; labour market; occupational choice
8/1518 demand for education; demography; employment; forecasting; education; labour market; student; trend

GRADUATE EMPLOYMENT
8/1384 higher education; information technology; labour shortage

GRADUATE STUDY
8/0160 educational policy; higher education; recruitment; United Kingdom

GRAMMAR
8/0686 dialect; English language
8/0785 cognitive process; language skill; linguistics
8/1637 comparative education; Iraq; mother tongue; secondary education

GRANT
8/1553 independent school; school-industry relation; science education
8/1727 evaluation; inservice education and training of teachers; local education authority

GRAPHIC ARTS
8/0293 craft design and technology; curriculum development; non-verbal communication; secondary education
8/0613 curriculum development; design; Sudan

GRAPHIC LITERACY
8/1739 autistic; Down's Syndrome; drawing; visual arts

GREECE
8/0537 mathematics; secondary education
8/0583 learning strategy; mathematics; teaching method
8/0625 mathematics; primary education
8/1407 English (second language); teaching method
8/1456 assessment; educational policy; primary education; teacher education

GREEK-CYPRIOT
8/0688 bilingualism; discourse analysis; English language; ethnic minority

GROUP BEHAVIOUR
8/1185 group dynamics; interpersonal relations; teamwork; training

GROUP DISCUSSION
8/1445 assessment; discussion; English language; group learning; group work; secondary school

GROUP DYNAMICS
8/1185 group behaviour; interpersonal relations; teamwork; training

GROUP LEARNING
8/0470 computer assisted instruction; discussion; group work; microcomputers; teaching method
8/0671 music education; musical instrument; primary education
8/1199 computer assisted instruction; co-operative learning; distance study; mathematics; physics; problem solving
8/1445 assessment; discussion; English language; group discussion; group work; secondary school
8/1461 computer assisted instruction; physics
8/1463 computer assisted instruction; computer assisted learning; educational software; interaction; process analysis
8/1492 action research; experiential learning; leadership training

GROUP MEMBERSHIP
8/0696 adolescent; ethnic minority; identity; race relations; social interaction
8/1490 action research; interpersonal competence; interpersonal relations; personality development

GROUP WORK
8/0330 classroom; computer assisted instruction; teacher role; verbal communication
8/0391 computer assisted instruction; comprehension; interaction; program
8/0420 individual work performance; microcomputer; primary education; problem solving
8/0423 feedback; individual work; microcomputer; problem solving; behaviour
8/0470 computer assisted instruction; discussion; group learning; microcomputers; teaching method
8/0486 learning process; verbal interaction
8/0498 interaction; Malaysia; practical work; science education
8/0736 computer; primary education
8/0950 fiction; imagination; primary education; reading
8/0956 curriculum development; discussion; open learning
8/1061 experiential learning; further education; personal research method
8/1354 ethnic relations; middle school; sociometry
8/1445 assessment; discussion; English language; group discussion; group learning; secondary school
8/1470 communication; primary education
8/1476 co-operation; interaction; learning; primary education
8/1564 cognitive development; co-operation; learning strategy; primary education

GROUPWORK
8/1595 co-operation; learning strategy; primary education; teaching aids

GROUP WORK
8/1695 interpersonal relations; listening; listening skills; pupil; self-evaluation; social skills
8/1710 comprehension; discussion; mathematics

GUERNSEY
8/0687 dialect; discourse analysis; English language; syntax

GUIDANCE
8/0134 care; curriculum; secondary education; social inequality
8/0467 curriculum; information system; Scotland
8/0481 adult education; higher education
8/0511 foreign student; university
8/0848 family; parent-child relation; youth
8/0904 student life; student problems
8/0961 course; evaluation; probationary teacher; teacher education
8/1023 educational guidance; evaluation; vocational guidance
8/1548 artificial intelligence; information system; student teacher; teacher education; teaching practice

GUIDANCE OFFICER
8/1623 drug addiction; training
8/1691 advisor; career development; employment expectations; educational guidance; inservice training; role perception

GYMNASTICS
8/0064 interactive video; physical education

GYPSY
8/1596 comparative research

HANDICAPPED
8/0010 integration; learning difficulty; special education
8/0346 assessment; communication; educational technology; teaching aids; speech handicapped
8/0371 communication; curriculum development; educational technology; teaching aids
8/0373 special needs; transition from school to work; youth
8/0403 curriculum development; further education; integration; learning difficulty; special needs
8/0515 learning difficulty; microcomputer; software; visually
8/0842 birth; counselling; parent education
8/0911 care; information service; mentally handicapped; parent role
8/0969 assessment; visually handicapped
8/1095 equipment; physical education; sport
8/1214 autoinstructional aid; automatic teaching; computer assisted instruction; educational technology; further education; special education; teaching machine
8/1380 home education; parent participation; parent-teacher relation; pre-school child

HEAD OF DEPARTMENT
8/0631 effectiveness; mathematics; middle management; teacher appraisal

HEAD TEACHER
8/0062 physical education; stress; teacher behaviour
8/0164 evaluation; teacher appraisal
8/0541 administration of education; leadership; quality of education
8/0664 history of education
8/0903 administration of education; disease; occupational environment; stress
8/1233 labour market
8/1534 administration of education; department head; deputy head; local education authority; manpower planning; middle management; recruitment; school management
8/1615 administration of education; industry; management education

HEALTH
8/0437 child; exercise
8/1399 family influence; family life; health activities; health promotion; socioeconomic influence

HEALTH ACTIVITIES
8/1399 family influence; family life; health; health promotion; socioeconomic influence

8/0813 employment; further education; manpower need; transition from school to work; vocational education
8/1124 industry; open learning; training method
8/1139 Japan

INDUSTRIALIZATION
8/1123 comparative education; history of education; United of America
8/1635 history of education; Wales

INDUSTRIAL TRAINING
8/1099 Japan; management education
8/1197 autoinstructional aid; automatic teaching; commercial training; computer assisted instruction; educational technology; teaching machine
8/1482 Europe; technical ability; training personnel
8/1550 corporate education; study abroad
8/1666 cooperation; education; industry; industry relationship

INDUSTRY
8/0046 mathematics; simulation; teacher response; teaching aids
8/0052 mathematics; simulation; teacher response; teaching aids
8/0055 teacher education
8/0148 co-operation; information dissemination; training
8/0230 communication studies; Europe; exchange visit; higher education; undergraduate
8/0246 school-community relation; teacher behaviour
8/1124 industrial education; open learning; training method
8/1250 curriculum development; educational innovation; geography; relation; secondary education
8/1261 curriculum development; transition from school to work; vocational education; youth employment
8/1306 comparative research; higher education; personnel evaluation; staff development
8/1512 administration of education; course; recruitment; selection; team teaching
8/1615 administration of education; head teacher; management education
8/1666 cooperation; education; industrial training; industry relationship
8/1679 financial resources; labour market; participation; secondary education

INDUSTRY EDUCATION RELATIONSHIP
8/0921 commerce; comprehension; enterprise; industry teacher education
8/1019 data bank; vocational education
8/1136 accreditation
8/1475 city technology college
8/1666 cooperation; education; industrial training; industry
8/1722 sixth form education

INDUSTRY EDUCATION WORK EXPERIENCE
8/0043 comparative education; experiential learning

INDUSTRY FURTHER EDUCATION RELATIONSHIP
8/0006 college of further education; marketing; student need

INDUSTRY TEACHER EDUCATION
8/0921 commerce; comprehension; enterprise; industry education relationship

INFANT
8/0770 emotional development; mother-child relation; physical expression; socialization
8/1285 cognitive development; memorizing; semantics; social learning
8/1450 cognitive development; non-verbal communication
8/1527 assessment; interaction; teacher-pupil relation

INFLUENCE
8/0161 curriculum development; educational policy; local education authority; teaching method
8/0542 course; inservice education and training of teachers; teaching method
8/1253 discussion; mass media; science education; secondary education; social environment

INFORMAL EDUCATION
8/0291 formal education; primary education; teaching method
8/1231 adult education; Africa; citizenship education; colonialism; community education; nationalism; Zambia

INFORMATION DISSEMINATION
8/0148 co-operation; industry; training
8/0816 information system; information technology; local education authority

INFORMATION NEED
8/1077 health education; parent education; school health service

INFORMATION PROCESSING
8/0093 blind; learning pace; performance; visually

INFORMATION RETRIEVAL
8/0012 database; photograph; picture; videodisc
8/0151 audiovisual aids; database; information service; teaching aids
8/0254 computer assisted instruction; database; higher education; history; information skills
8/1080 computer network; database; researcher; education

INFORMATION SCIENCE
8/0196 computer engineering; curriculum; further education; higher education
8/1633 computer assisted instruction; electronic data processing; information technology; mathematics

INFORMATION SERVICE
8/0151 audiovisual aids; database; information retrieval; teaching aids
8/0814 book; library; statistics
8/0911 care; mentally handicapped; parent role; handicapped
8/1069 database; educational research; Ireland, Northern
8/1308 database; multicultural education; teaching aids
8/1597 educational research; EUDISED; Ireland, Northern

INFORMATION SKILLS
8/0024 library; teacher education
8/0171 General Certificate of Secondary Education; librarian; role
8/0177 curriculum development; librarian; library role; professional development; school library
8/0254 computer assisted instruction; database; higher education; history; information retrieval
8/0815 General Certificate of Secondary Education (GCSE); school library; transition from primary to secondary school
8/1340 environmental study; information technology; primary education
8/1668 General Certificate of Secondary Education; school library

INFORMATION SYSTEM
8/0351 catchment areas; geographic location; school distribution
8/0467 curriculum; guidance; Scotland
8/0605 access programme; assessment; higher education; mature student; performance
8/0816 information dissemination; information technology; local education authority
8/1424 college of further education; cost; course; economics of education
8/1432 administration of education; budgetary control; college of further education; financial resources; management

8/1433 administration of education; college of further education; management; software
8/1548 artificial intelligence; guidance; student teacher; teacher education; teaching practice

INFORMATION TECHNOLOGY
8/0132 course; database; training
8/0224 computer assisted instruction; higher education; language teaching; translation
8/0322 educational policy; research
8/0426 sex difference; Youth Training Scheme
8/0443 cognitive development; computer assisted instruction; educational technology; special education
8/0445 computer; doctor; management; professional status; skill
8/0617 curriculum development; primary education
8/0633 administration of education; Records of Achievement
8/0669 computer assisted instruction; computer microworld; expert system
8/0727 curriculum development; inservice education and of teachers; planning of education; secondary education
8/0764 achievement; learning; primary education; secondary education
8/0765 computer assisted instruction; database; environmental study; science education
8/0798 National Curriculum
8/0808 comparative research; Europe; primary education
8/0809 adviser; computer assisted instruction; inservice education and training of teachers; Technical and Vocational Education Initiative; time management
8/0816 information dissemination; information system; local education authority
8/1056 computer assisted instruction; electronic data processing; further educaion of teachers; higher education; inservice teacher education
8/1108 physical sciences; science eduvcation; teaching method
8/1117 adult education; computer; physically special needs; vocational training
8/1118 adult education; computer; physically special needs
8/1179 computer-assisted instruction; emotional disorder; learning difficulty
8/1196 educational technology; electronic data processing; programmed text
8/1201 assessment; autoinstructional aid; blind; computer assisted instruction; electronic data processing; visually handicapped
8/1206 autoinstructional aid; computer assisted instruction; educational electronic data processing; programmed text; visually handicapped
8/1260 computer; educational innovation; educational policy
8/1293
8/1340 environmental study; information skills; primary education
8/1363 microcomputer
8/1384 graduate employment; higher education; labour shortage
8/1570 curriculum development; educational policy; inservice education and training of teachers
8/1611 curriculum development; educational innovation; educational policy; inservice education and training of teachers; management
8/1617 bilingualism; further education teachers; inservice teacher education; rural school; science education; technical education; vocational education
8/1633 computer assisted instruction; electronic data processing; information science; mathematics

INITIAL TRAINING
8/0719 further education; inservice training; probationary teacher; teacher education

INNER CITY
8/1048 City Technology College; educational opportunities; private education

8/1345 primary education; special needs
8/1361 attitude; mental handicap; secondary school; special
8/1423 database; special education; special needs
8/1457 Ireland, Northern; religious affiliation; teacher education
8/1480 physical education; physically handicappped

INTELLECTUAL DEVELOPMENT
8/0632 birth; child development; motor disorder
8/0725 creativity; gifted; intelligence; stimulus; thinking
8/1613 history; secondary education; teaching aids

INTELLIGENCE
8/0677 ability; cognition; gifted; memory; mental retardation
8/0725 creativity; gifted; intellectual development; stimulus; thinking
8/0774 ability; problem solving

INTELLIGENCE QUOTIENT
8/0272 dietetics; intelligence test; non-verbal test; nutrition; reasoning

INTELLIGENCE TEST
8/0272 dietetics; intelligence quotient; non-verbal test; nutrition; reasoning
8/0666 history of education; psychology

INTERACTION
8/0011 child; leisure; socialization
8/0391 computer assisted instruction; comprehension; group work; program
8/0404 language development; verbal communication
8/0406 language skill; oral expression; spoken language
8/0498 group work; Malaysia; practical work; science education
8/0760 museum; sciences
8/0797 educational innovation; ethnology; secondary school
8/0859 non-verbal communication; pupil: teacher behaviour
8/0869 family environment; language development; language impairment; sibling
8/1028 communication; developing country; women's education; women's organization
8/1220 computer assisted instruction; feedback; learning; problem solving
8/1463 computer assisted instruction; computer assisted learning; educational software; group learning; process analysis
8/1466 multicultural education; pre-school education; teacher-pupil relation
8/1468 computer assisted instruction; peer group; tutoring
8/1469 cognitive development; father-child relation; performance; son
8/1476 co-operation; group work; learning; primary education
8/1491 action research; inservice training; interpersonal relations; intervention
8/1527 assessment; infant; teacher-pupil relation
8/1587 computer assisted instruction; computer science; database; distance study

INTERACTIVE LEARNING
8/1592 computer assisted instruction; knowledge; software; teaching aids

INTERACTIVE VIDEO
8/0018 author; computer; computer assisted instruction; knowledge; teaching aids
8/0061 dance; secondary education
8/0064 gymnastics; physical education
8/0123 audiovisual aids; business education; educational technology; inservice education and training of teachers
8/0179 inservice education and training of teachers; primary education; teacher education
8/0386 class management; computer assisted instruction; educational technology; teacher education
8/0500 computer assisted instruction; decision-making; mentally handicapped
8/0533 computer assisted instruction; distance study; educational technology; management education
8/0790 computer assisted instruction; educational technology; open learning; videodisc
8/1443 educational technology; teaching aids; videotape
8/1594 further education; higher education; teaching aids; video equipment

INTERCULTURAL EDUCATION
8/0585 adult education; Germany, Federal Republic
8/1021 multicultural education
8/1037 motivation for studies; peer group teaching; transfer of learning
8/1385 antiracism education; evaluation; multicultural education
8/1521 philosophy of education; religious education
8/1670 multicultural education; parent participation; parent-school relation; parent-teacher relation
8/1718 primary education; religious cultural group; religious education; scripture; Technical and Vocational Education Initiatve; world studies

INTERDISCIPLINARY APPROACH
8/0566
8/0684 assessment; coursework; curriculum development; General Certificate of Education
8/1081 business education

INTERGROUP RELATIONS
8/1319 adult education; local community; project method

INTERNATIONAL EXCHANGE
8/0657 France; system of education; theory of education
8/0660 curriculum development; electronic mail

INTERNATIONAL SCHOOL
8/0154 curriculum; system of education
8/1402 cross-cultural research; cultural pluralism; curriculum development; educational opportunities

INTERNATIONAL STUDIES
8/0193 teacher education
8/1650 curriculum; English language

INTERPERSONAL COMPETENCE
8/0803 experiential learning
8/1490 action research; group membership; interpersonal relations; personality development

INTERPERSONAL RELATIONS
8/0166 curriculum development; primary education
8/0279 attitude; participation; political social interaction; youth
8/0308 problem solving; socialization; teacher-pupil relation
8/1185 group behaviour; group dynamics; teamwork; training
8/1396 assertiveness; communication; health service personnel; inservice training
8/1490 action research; group membership; interpersonal competence; personality development
8/1491 action research; inservice training; interaction; intervention
8/1695 group work; listening; listening skills; pupil; self-evaluation; social skills

INTERVENTION
8/0603 aggression; mass media effects; television; violence
8/1491 action research; inservice training; interaction; interpersonal relations

INTERVIEW
8/0424 employment; graduate; selection criterion

8/1588 computer assisted instruction; computer science; knowledge; model

IRAQ
8/0510 developing country; educational policy; educational television
8/1637 comparative education; grammar; mother tongue; secondary education
8/1641 Arabic; language teaching; mother tongue; primary school; reading

IRELAND
8/0318 community development; youth organization

IRELAND, NORTHERN
8/1068 labour market; teacher education; teacher employment
8/1069 database; educational research; information service
8/1070 administration of education; co-operation; educational research
8/1071 stress; teacher behaviour
8/1457 integration; religious affiliation; teacher education
8/1597 educational research; EUDISED; information service
8/1610 career aspiration; sex difference; woman teacher

ITALIAN LANGUAGE
8/0225 language teaching; polytechnic; teaching aids

JAMAICA
8/0731 language teaching; mother tongue; secondary education; sociolinguistics; teacher education

JAPAN
8/0034 foreign languages; France; language teaching; mother tongue; United Kingdom
8/0287 comparative education; Hong Kong; Singapore
8/0608 art education; curriculum development; multicultural education
8/0806 comparative research; value; youth attitude
8/1099 industrial training; management education
8/1139 industrial education
8/1170 adult education; teacher education
8/1551 comparative education; engineer; post-compulsory education; vocational education
8/1554 comparative education; engineer; post-compulsory education; personnel; vocational education

JUNIOR SCHOOL
8/0040 curriculum; project work

JUSTICE
8/1134 teacher development

JUVENILE DELINQUENCY
8/0974 juvenile detention; treatment

JUVENILE DETENTION
8/0974 juvenile delinquencey; treatment

KENYA
8/0740 leadership; primary education; teacher education

KNOWLEDGE
8/0018 author; computer; computer assisted instruction; interactive video; teaching aids
8/0699 Acquired Innune Deficiency Syndrome (AIDS); child; health education; primary education
8/1368 teacher education
8/1403 language development; language teaching; teacher attitude; teaching method
8/1509 care; community; mental illness; training
8/1588 computer assisted instruction; computer science; interview; model
8/1592 computer assisted instruction; interactive learning; software; teaching aids

8/1394 communication research; discourse analysis; English language; English (second language); language research; native speakers
8/1403 knowledge; language development; teacher attitude; teaching method
8/1579 curriculum development; reading
8/1620 English (second language); Zaire
8/1625 communication; English language; foreign languages; learning strategy; vocabulary
8/1641 Arabic; Iraq; mother tongue; primary school; reading
8/1643 foreign languages; mnemonics
8/1657 language development; learning difficulty; special school
8/1736 adult education; English (second language); first foreign language
8/1737 developing country; educational policy; literacy; tongue; standard; vernaculars

LATERALITY
8/0235 abiltiy; dyslexia; learning difficulty; left-handed; reading

LAW
8/0487 absenteeism; attendance; social control
8/0828 teaching aids; video recording
8/0831 computer assisted instruction; problem solving
8/1102 higher education; legal education

LEADERSHIP
8/0541 administration of education; head teacher; quality of education
8/0650 administration of education; theory of education
8/0740 Kenya; primary education; teacher education
8/1126 adult education; China
8/1612 effectiveness; middle management; power; success

LEADERSHIP TRAINING
8/1492 action research; experiential learning; group learning

LEARNER CENTRED CURRICULUM
8/1541 further education; sixteen to nineteen education

LEARNING
8/0022 classroom; culture; mathematics
8/0328 assessment; behaviour rating scales; comprehension tests
8/0388 primary education; reception class
8/0518 computer microworld; computer programming
8/0597 cognitive process; mathematics
8/0599 skill; teacher education; teaching
8/0764 achievement; information technology; primary education; secondary education
8/0766 computer assisted instruction; curriculum development
8/0915 teacher education; teaching experience; teaching practice
8/1220 computer assisted instruction; feedback; interaction; problem solving
8/1226 concept formation; science education
8/1343 assessment; learning difficulty; pre-school education; education
8/1476 co-operation; group work; interaction; primary education

LEARNING CONDITIONS
8/0041 higher education; management education; self-instruction
8/0378 community; nurse; practical work; vocational education
8/1614 nurse education; psychiatric service

LEARNING DIFFICULTY
8/0010 handicapped; integration; special education
8/0167 special education; teaching
8/0187 child development; pre-school child; vision
8/0208 language development; literacy; oral expression; reading; special education; spelling; writing

8/0235 abiltiy; dyslexia; laterality; left- handed; reading
8/0274 health education; mental retardation; sex education; social skills; special school
8/0336 attention deficit disorder; cognition; creativity; hyperactivity
8/0403 curriculum development; further education; handicapped; integration; special needs
8/0412 computer assisted instruction; dyslexia; teacher education; teaching aids
8/0474 conductive education; special education
8/0515 handicapped; microcomputer; software; visually
8/0550 Brazil; evaluation; integration; methodology; special education
8/0616 literacy; special education; special needs; teaching method
8/0685 screening; teaching method
8/0732 computer assisted instruction; mentally handicapped; microcomputer; social interaction
8/0773 cognition; dyslexia; music; reading; remedial teaching
8/0777 computer assisted instruction; mentally handicapped; microcomputer; special education
8/0780 cognition; dyslexia; reading
8/0841 dyspraxia; hearing defect; language development
8/0863 staff development; student; teaching technique
8/0871 ability grouping; integration; secondary education; special needs; support teacher
8/0914 language teaching; reading; secondary education; storytelling; test
8/0922 educational guidance; special education; support services
8/0928 dyslexia; special education; teacher education
8/0954 autonomy; curriculum development; special education
8/0965 motor disorder; perceptual handicap; underachievement
8/0991 assessment; European Communities; secondary education
8/1033 adult education; continuing education; educational provision
8/1125 computer assisted instruction
8/1143 Chinese language; composition; English language; Hong Kong; writing
8/1179 computer-assisted instruction; emotional disorder; information technology
8/1207 cognitive processes; literacy; reading; spelling
8/1343 assessment; learning; pre-school education; education
8/1357 cognitive process; dyslexia; literacy; remedial teaching; special needs
8/1386 spelling; teacher attitude; teacher behaviour; teacher expectation; teacher response
8/1448 dyslexia; reading; word recognition
8/1449 cognitive process; dyslexia; reading
8/1628 dyslexia; mathematics
8/1657 language development; language teaching; special school
8/1704 family environment; maladjusted; residential school; special education
8/1716 inservice education and training of teachers; religious education; special needs; teaching aids

LEARNING PACE
8/0093 blind; information processing; performance; visually

LEARNING PROCESS
8/0045 enterprise education; experiential learning
8/0056 professional development; teacher education
8/0162 cognitive process; higher education
8/0186 cognition; concept analysis; concept formulation; early learning
8/0191 computer assisted instruction; computer network; educational software; local area network; primary school; teaching method
8/0286 bilingualism; language teaching; teaching method

8/0360 belief; cognition; computer assisted instruction; science education
8/0486 group work; verbal interaction
8/0589 college of further education; stress; teacher behaviour; teaching personnel
8/0746 problem solving; skill; training; transfer of learning; vocational education
8/0976 communication; oral expression; speech; teaching method
8/1066 assessment; knowledge level; teaching method
8/1194 autoinstructional aid; automatic teaching; computer assisted instruction; educational technology; teaching machine
8/1203 autoinstructional aid; automatic teaching; computer assisted educational technology; teaching machine
8/1291 communication; oral expression; speech; teaching method
8/1706 inservice education and training of teachers; primary education; teaching aptitude

LEARNING RESOURCES
8/0014 administration of education; educational policy; higher education

LEARNING STRATEGY
8/0108 computer assisted instruction; learning test; verbal learning; visual learning
8/0109 curriculum development; secondary education; teaching method; tutorial
8/0119 adult eduction; computer assisted instruction; word processing
8/0133 primary education; social environment
8/0219 assessment; management education
8/0247 primary education; small school; rural school
8/0261 achievement; aims of education; problem solving; method
8/0302 ethnic minority; further education; multicultural education; teaching method
8/0312 primary education; problem solving; teaching method
8/0364 higher education; student; teaching method
8/0463 academic degree; attitude; motivation for studies; student teacher
8/0570 comprehension; science education; secondary education
8/0583 Greece; mathematics; teaching method
8/0680 computer programming; microcomputer
8/0728 blind; reading; spelling; visually handicapped; visual perception
8/0781 dropout; medicine; study method
8/1098 early reading; perception; reading; reader response; reader text relationship; text structure
8/1184 computer; distance study; gender equality; higher education; Open University; sex difference
8/1195 affectivity; emotion; emotional response; mathematics; mathematics education; teachin
8/1320 inservice education and training of teachers
8/1325 achievement; assessment; curriculum; teaching method; technical education; vocational education
8/1440 primary education; practical work; problem solving; science education
8/1478 teacher education
8/1504 curriculum development; modular course; teaching method; Technical and Vocational Education Inititative
8/1544 improvisation; music education
8/1564 cognitive development; co-operation; group work; primary education
8/1595 co-operation; groupwork; primary education; teaching aids
8/1625 communication; English language; foreign languages; language teaching; vocabulary
8/1684 autonomy; self evaluation; teaching method
8/1709 arithmetic; primary education
8/1711 computer assisted instruction; concept formulation; mathematics; microcomputer
8/1712 curriculum development; teacher-pupil relation; method

8/1051 community education; decision making; educational policy; unemployed

8/1146 administration of education; expenditures; inservice education and training of teachers; primary education; staff development

8/1148 educational policy; integration; special needs

8/1161 adult education; continuing education; life-long education; marketing

8/1276 educational policy; multicultural education

8/1335 curriculum development; evaluation; Scotland; Technical and Vocational Education Initiative (TVEI)

8/1409 drug addiction; health education; narcotic

8/1534 administration of education; department head; deputy head; head teacher; manpower planning; middle management; recruitment; school management

8/1676 evaluation; inservice education and training of teachers

8/1677 school effectiveness

8/1727 evaluation; grant; inservice education and training of teachers

8/1040 evaluation; secondary education; Technical and Vocational Education Initiative (TVEI)

LOCAL STUDIES
8/0313 curriculum development; history; reference material

LOW ATTAINER
8/0639 curriculum development; educational innovation; secondary

8/1046 curriculum development

8/1052 language development; primary education; spoken language; writing

8/1337 database; educational policy; Scotland; sex difference; Technical and Vocational Education Initiative (TVEI)

LOW ATTAINMENT
8/0309 classroom communication

MAINSTREAMING
8/0168 further education of teachers; inservice teacher education; special education; teacher development

8/1234 further education of teachers; inservice teacher education; open learning; special education; training course

MAIN SUBJECT
8/0066 administration of education; number of pupils; secondary education; sixth form

MALADJUSTED
8/0017 assessment; child; cognitive process; social behaviour

8/0394 biography; community education; philosophy of education; school

8/0865 child; emotional disorder; social behaviour

8/0876 educational need; moral education; social development

8/0973 child care; residential care; social services; special school

8/1109 computer-assisted instruction; socially handicapped; special education

8/1702 adjustment; behaviour disorder; emotional disorder; residential school; special needs

8/1704 family environment; learning difficulty; residential school; special education

8/0009 leisure education; school-community relation; teacher-pupil relation; youth

MALAYSIA
8/0150 ability; assessment; mathematics; undergraduate

8/0323 curriculum development; environmental study; primary education

8/0498 group work; interaction; practical work; science education

8/1376 adult education; participation; rural area; women's education

MANAGEMENT
8/0369 administration of education; inservice training; perception; staff development; teacher behaviour

8/0445 computer; doctor; information technology; professional status; skill

8/0913 management education

8/1432 administration of education; budgetary control; college of further education; financial resources; information system

8/1433 administration of education; college of further education; information system; software

8/1486 co-ordinator; educational administrator; further education; technical education; vocational education

8/1611 curriculum development; educational innovation; educational policy; information technology; inservice education and training of teachers

MANAGEMENT DEVELOPMENT
8/0143 administration of education; co-operation; curriculum; local education authority; Technical and Vocational Education Initiative

8/0169 distance study; further education of teachers; inservice teacher education; technical education; vocational education

8/0587 distance study; evaluation; open learning

8/1494 co-operative programmes; experiential learning; inservice training; management education

MANAGEMENT EDUCATION
8/0028 distance study; video recording

8/0041 higher education; learning conditions; self-instruction

8/0219 assessment; learning strategy

8/0242 administration of education; profile

8/0243 administration of education; learning style

8/0266 continuing education; doctor; time

8/0305 further education; librarian; vocational education

8/0497 aptitutde; assessment; employer; student

8/0517 design; problem solving; teacher education; technology

8/0533 computer assisted instruction; distance study; educational technology; interactive video

8/0553 personnel management

8/0913 management

8/0945 curriculum development; further education of teachers; inservice teacher education; secondary education

8/1099 industrial training; Japan

8/1314 librarian

8/1481 administration of education; university

8/1494 co-operative programmes; experiential learning; inservice training; management development

8/1615 administration of education; head teacher; industry

MANAGEMENT OF EDUCATION
8/0114 higher education; teaching materials

MANIPULATIVE MATERIAL
8/1097 comparative education; mathematics; primary Spain; teaching aids

MANPOWER NEED
8/0425 employment; tourism; vocational training

8/0813 employment; further education; industrial education; transition from school to work; vocational education

MANPOWER PLANNING
8/1534 administration of education; department head; deputy head; head teacher; local education authority; middle management; recruitment; school management

8/1542 school management

MAP
8/0233 cognitive process; geography; sex difference

MARKETING
8/0006 college of further education; industry further education relationship; student need

8/0539 advertising; secondary education

8/0942 computer assisted instruction; economic conditions

8/1147 advertising; mass media; media studies; teaching aids

8/1161 adult education; continuing education; life-long education; local education authority

8/1281

8/1429 banking

MARXISM
8/0606 philosophy of education; sociology of education

MASS MEDIA
8/0205 primary school; television

8/1128 adult education; ideology; memory

8/1147 advertising; marketing; media studies; teaching aids

8/1253 discussion; influence; science education; secondary education; social environment

8/1552 Acquired Immune Deficiency Syndrome (AIDS); adolescent; behaviour; perception

MASS MEDIA EFFECTS
8/0603 aggression; intervention; television; violence

MASTERS DEGREE
8/0925 developing country; distance study; thesis

MATHEMATICS
8/0022 classroom; culture; learning

8/0046 industry; simulation; teacher response; teaching aids

8/0052 industry; simulation; teacher response; teaching aids

8/0060 English (second language); language development; play; primary education

8/0082 achievements; teacher behaviour; teaching technique

8/0150 ability; assessment; undergraduate; Malaysia

8/0157 assessment; curriculum development; examination; performance

8/0294 game; teaching aids

8/0297 curriculum development; microcomputer; secondary education; sixth form; teaching method

8/0329 concept formation; test construction

8/0390 assessment; curriculum development; examination; secondary education

8/0449 peer group teaching; science education; teaching method

8/0475 diagnostic test; primary education

8/0514 estimation (mathematics); primary education

8/0537 Greece; secondary education

8/0563 comprehension; mechanics; secondary education

8/0564 diagram; space perception; teaching technique

8/0583 Greece; learning strategy; teaching method

8/0591 arithemetic; error; teacher education; teaching method

8/0597 cognitive process; learning

8/0600 acceleration; comprehension; higher education; mechanics; secondary education

8/0625 Greece; primary education

8/0631 effectiveness; head of department; middle management; teacher appraisal

8/0683 equal opportunity; girl; sex difference

8/0716 concept formation; problem solving

8/0722 computer assisted instruction; inservice education and training of teachers; teaching

8/0734 inservice education and training of teachers; teaching aids; Technical and Vocational Education Initiative

8/0744 curriculum development; Technical and Vocational Education Initiative; technology

8/0747 cognitive process; computer assisted instruction; discussion

8/0810 curriculum development; educational change; educational innovation; teacher behaviour

8/0515 handicapped; learning difficulty; software; visually
8/0621 comparative education; computer assisted instruction; Turkey
8/0680 computer programming; learning strategy
8/0732 computer assisted instruction; learning difficulty; mentally handicapped; social interaction
8/0777 computer assisted instruction; learning difficulty; mentally handicapped; special education
8/0862 computer assisted instruction; motivation primary education; software
8/0889 software; teacher education
8/0958 perception; space perception; teaching aids; visually handicapped
8/1082
8/1310 music education; teaching aids
8/1342 library; resource centre
8/1363 information technology
8/1374 curriculum development; mathematics; secondary education; teaching aids
8/1455 assessment; criterion referencing; decision making
8/1471 educational policy; primary education; secondary education
8/1640 discussion; primary education; small group; verbal interaction
8/1711 computer assisted instruction; concept formulation; learning strategy; mathematics
8/0470 computer assisted instruction; discussion; group learning; group work; teaching method
8/0504 expert systems; rehabilitation; robotics; training; severe learning difficulties
8/1183 computer uses in education; Open University
8/0634 computer assisted instruction; concept formation; teaching aids

MIDDLE MANAGEMENT
8/0631 effectiveness; head of department; mathematics; teacher appraisal
8/1534 administration of education; department head; deputy head; head teacher; local education authority; manpower planning; recruitment; school management
8/1612 effectiveness; leadership; power; success

MIDDLE SCHOOL
8/1351 bullying; racial discrimination; racism; social isolation
8/1354 ethnic relations; group work; sociometry
8/1652 practical work; Saudi Arabia; science education; teacher behaviour

MIDWIFERY
8/1265 theory practice relationship

MINORITY GROUP TEACHERS
8/1696 black teachers; equal opportunity; ethnic minority; racism; supply of teachers; teacher education; teacher recruitment

MISCONCEPTION
8/0197 adult; concept formation; cross-cultural research; earth sciences; fuel; scientific concepts

MISCONDUCT
8/0015 attitude; discipline; disruptive behaviour; pupil
8/0084 class management; inservice education and training of teachers; teacher behaviour
8/1715 behaviour disorder; comparative education; disruptive behaviour; USA
8/1729 dsicipline; disruptive pupil; expulsion

MISTAKE
8/0416 early reading; reading aloud; teacher-pupil relation; teaching technique

MNEMONICS
8/1643 foreign languages; language teaching

MOBILITY
8/1358 space perception; special education; teaching aids; visually handicapped

MODELS
8/0349 computer assisted instruction; database; microcomputer
8/0353 achievement; performance; school effectiveness; survey
8/0751 educational research; research technique; statistical method
8/1364 accountability; examination results; performance indicator; secondary education
8/1588 computer assisted instruction; computer science; interview; knowledge
8/0335 construction; construction set; primary education; science education; sex difference

MODERN LANGUAGES
8/0520 further education; higher education; language skills; language teaching
8/0551 communication; comparative research; foreign languages; language teaching
8/0757 choice of studies; secondary education; sex difference
8/1001 commercial education; data bank; database; educational material; evaluation; individualized teaching; science education; teaching aids
8/1002 choice of studies; Education Support Grant; evaluation; foreign languages
8/1239 foreign languages; motivation for studies; pupil secondary education
8/1280 comparative education; France; french language; oral examination; teacher education
8/1405 communication; language skill; teaching aids; teaching method
8/1629 language skill; second language; vocabulary

MODULAR COURSE
8/1504 curriculum development; learning strategy; teaching method; Technical and Vocational Education Inititative

MONTESSORI METHOD
8/1556 early childhood education; pre-school education

MORAL DEVELOPMENT
8/0858 responsibility; therapy
8/1703 community education; moral education

MORALE
8/0428 engineering; further education; teacher
8/1366 educational innovation; financial resources; teacher attitude

MORAL EDUCATION
8/0285 language; religious education; spoken language
8/0319 child rearing; Egypt; parent role
8/0614 priority; secondary education; value system
8/0656 aesthetic education; philosophy of education; curriculum subject; physical education; religious education
8/0876 educational need; maladjusted; social development
8/1241 pastoral care
8/1442 citizenship education; teaching aids; value
8/1567 primary education
8/1703 community education; moral development

MORPHOLOGY
8/0183 discourse analysis; lexicology; word recognition
8/1624 comprehension; document; linguistics

MOTHER
8/0698 child care; child development; cognitive development; women's employment
8/1417 family life; mature student; women's education

MOTHER CHILD RELATIONSHIP
8/0769 child development; facial expression; non-verbal communication
8/0770 emotional development; infant; physical expression; socialization

MOTHER TONGUE
8/0034 foreign languages; France; Japan; language teaching; United Kingdom
8/0405 foreign languages; performance; reading
8/0731 Jamaica; language teaching; secondary education; sociolinguistics; teacher education
8/1626 assessment; attitude; bilingualism; first foreign language; pupil; writing
8/1637 comparative education; grammar; Iraq; secondary education
8/1641 Arabic; Iraq; language teaching; primary school; reading
8/1734 bilingualism; ethnic minority; first foreign language; Sri Lanka; Tamil; United Kingdom
8/1735 Bangladeshi; Bengali; English (second language); ethnic minority; first foreign language; United Kingdom

MOTIVATION
8/0063 achievement; adolescent; dropout; sport
8/0238 fitness; physical education
8/0370 achievement; child; Nigeria; social environment
8/0432 higher education; religious education; student behaviour; theology
8/0548 achievement; failure; primary education; success
8/0931 language skill; language teaching
8/1112 adult education; China
8/1355 comparative analysis; socialization; youth employment
8/1523 art therapy; occupational aspiration; therapist
8/1622 attitude; bilingualism
8/0463 academic degree; attitude; learning strategy; student teacher
8/1037 intercultural education; peer group teaching; transfer of learning
8/1239 foreign languages; modern languages; pupil secondary education
8/1418 higher education; mature student; teacher education; women's education
8/0862 computer assisted instruction; microcomputer; software

MOTOR DEVELOPMENT
8/0509 measurement
8/0718 cognitive development; music education; physical expression
8/0723 Down's Syndrome; mental retardation; physical
8/0729 physical education; physically handicapped; psychomotor test; special education
8/1627 teaching aids; teaching method

MOTOR DISORDER
8/0036 cerebral palsy; driver education; physical handicap
8/0079 conductive education; special education
8/0096 cerebral palsy; conductive education; special education
8/0632 birth; child development; intellectual development
8/0965 learning difficulty; perceptual handicap; underachievement
8/1090 cross-cultural research; test

MOVEMENT
8/0237 communication; deaf; physcial education; socialization

MOVEMENT EDUCATION
8/0204

MULTICULTURAL EDUCATION
8/0077 curriculum; further education
8/0081 audio-visual aids; primary education; religious education; teaching aids
8/0105 early childhood education; religious education; teaching aids
8/0127 educational innovation; educational policy; primary education; race relations
8/0153 antiracism education
8/0302 ethnic minority; further education; learning strategy; teaching method
8/0608 art education; curriculum development; Japan
8/0618 ethnic minority; primary education

8/1027 adult education; adult literacy; basic education; communication skills; data bank; English (second language); resource materials

8/1266 adult education; computer assisted instruction; life skills; literacy education; mentally handicapped

8/1465 day care centre

8/1745 basic education; labour market; labour shortage; literacy; leaver; skill

NURSES
8/0378 community; learning conditions; practical work; vocational education

8/0427 vocational education

8/0468 assessment; profile; vocational education; work experience

8/0575 achievement test; selection; student; validity

8/0576 recruitment; selection; student

8/0995 vocational education

8/1041 curriculum development; vocational training

8/1497 curriculum development; education; educational innovation

NURSE EDUCATION
8/1142 assessment; progress report

8/1614 learning conditions; psychiatric service

NURSERY NURSES
8/1373 childcare occupations; day care centre; day-nursery

NURSERY SCHOOLS
8/0008 early childhood education; pre-school education

8/0239 auditory perception; music education; pre-school child

8/0267 bureaucracy; culture; ethnology; sciences of education; social structure

8/0295 ethnic group; social interaction

8/0708 history of education; theory of education

8/0721 curriculum; early childhood; education; playgroup; pre-school education

8/0929 curriculum; developmental continuity; transitional class

8/0935 computer assisted instruction; further education of teachers; inservice teacher education

8/1344 communication; inservice education and training of teachers; integration; special needs

8/1371 identity; need; parents; pre-school child

8/1638 pre-school education; Qatar; sex difference; teacher-pupil relation

NURSERY SCHOOL CURRICULUM
8/1690 curriculum; early childhood education; play; pre-school education

NUTRITION
8/0272 dietetics; intelligence quotient; intelligence test; non-verbal test; reasoning

8/0870 adolescent; fitness; health education; obesity

OBESITY
8/0870 adolescent; fitness; health education; nutrition

OBSERVATION
8/0649 research technique; sample; time

OCCUPATIONAL ASPIRATION
8/1523 art therapy; motivation; therapist

OCCUPATIONAL CHOICE
8/0139 action planning; planning; transition from school to work; youth

8/1024 career counselling; enterprise education; higher education; vocational guidance

8/1025 careers guidance; computer; higher education

8/1169 careers guidance; careers service; youth unemployment

8/1324 career change; demand for teachers; occupational mobility; teacher mobility; teacher supply and demand; teacher transfer

8/1400 choice of studies; sex; stereotype

8/1438 graduate; sex difference; social class; work

8/1439 discrimination; graduate; labour market

8/1496 career monograph; cross-national research; Germany FR; transition from school to work; United Kingdom; vocational guidance; youth

OCCUPATIONAL ENVIRONMENT
8/0843 stress; teacher behaviour

8/0903 administration of education; disease; head teacher; stress

OCCUPATIONAL MOBILITY
8/1324 career change; demand for teachers; occupational choice; teacher mobility; teacher supply and demand; teacher transfer

OCCUPATIONAL SATISFACTION
8/1362 comparative education; cross-cultural research; secondary school; teacher role; teacher status

8/1367 comparative research; educational innovation; educational policy; secondary education; teacher

8/1474 teacher; teaching

OCCUPATIONAL SUCCESS
8/0447 family life; personality development; private school; pupil; social class

OLD AGE
8/1389 agency co-operation; elderly person; health education

ONLINE SYSTEMS
8/0802 business; expert system

OPEN LEARNING
8/0048 developing country; distance study; higher education; Sudan

8/0222 cost

8/0429 educational policy; higher education

8/0525 chemistry; higher education

8/0555 career education; flexible learning; individualized teaching; resource materials; vocational guidance

8/0587 distance study; evaluation; management development

8/0790 computer assisted instruction; educational technology; interactive video; videodisc

8/0956 curriculum development; discussion; group work

8/0987 access programme; further education; planning of education

8/1035 adult education; community education; credits; further education; higher education

8/1062 adult education; aesthetic education; fantasy; imagination

8/1124 industrial education; industry; training method

8/1234 further education of teachers; inservice teacher education; mainstreaming; special education; training course

8/1263 distance study; support services

8/1569 educational innovation; Technical and Vocational Education Initiative; flexible learning

8/1591 computer assisted instruction; program; teaching aids

OPEN UNIVERSITY
8/1182 adult education; counselling; distance study; educationl guidance; staff development

8/1183 computer uses in education; microcomputers

8/1184 computer; distance study; gender equality; higher education; learning strategy; sex difference

8/1186 adult student; dropout; dropout research; student; student wastage; wastage

8/1187 distance study; Health Service personnel; mentally handicapped; special education; support staff

8/1188 course evaluation; distance study; evaluation; student reaction; survey

8/1189 autoinstructional aid; distance study; evaluation; programmed text; textbook evaluation

8/1192 adult education; distance study; Humanities

8/1217 comparative achievement; distance study; geographic location; performance

8/1227 distance study; telecommunication; teleconferencing

OPINION
8/1159 evaluation; performance; teacher; teacher behaviour

ORAL EXAMINATION
8/1280 comparative education; France; french language; modern languages; teacher education

ORAL EXPRESSION
8/0208 language development; learning difficulty; literacy; reading; special education; spelling; writing

8/0332 assessment; English language; language development

8/0406 interaction; language skill; spoken language

8/0538 curriculum development; language development; secondary education

8/0598 language development; language skil; memory; primary education; writing

8/0844 cognitive development; deaf; language development; hearing defect

8/0951 assessment; English (second language); language teaching; pronunciation

8/0976 communication; learning process; speech; teaching method

8/1291 communication; learning process; speech; teaching method

ORAL WORK
8/0695 Engish language; nonfiction; reading; spoken language

8/0880 primary education; story telling

8/1243 communication skills; communicative competence; English (second language teaching; spoken language; verbal communication; Zambia

ORGANIZATION
8/0893 communication; culture; meaning
8/1428

ORGANIZATIONAL THEORY
8/1720 educational development; school management

ORGANIZATION OF RESEARCH
8/1565 comparative research; cross-national research; post-graduate study

ORIENTEERING
8/0662 navigation; outdoor pursuits

ORTHOGRAPHIC SYMBOLS
8/0185 letters (alphabet)

OUTCOMES OF EDUCATION
8/0355 performance indicators; school effectiveness; secondary education

OUTDOOR PURSUITS
8/0662 navigation; orienteering

PAINTING
8/1237 aesthetic education; art appreciation; art education; language; vocabulary

8/1392 aesthetic education; art; literature; pupil reaction; relationship

PAKISTAN
8/1485 classroom research; curriculum development; English language; English (second language); teaching

PAPUA NEW GUINEA
8/1525 curriculum; primary school; science education; teacher education

PARALLEL COMPUTER SYSTEMS
8/0923 computer assisted instruction; curriculum

PROJECT WORK
8/0040 curriculum; junior school
8/0595 ability; secondary education; technology
8/0918 assignment; cognitive process; student
8/0980 cross-curricular approach; curriculum development

PRONUNCIATION
8/0951 assessment; English (second language); language teaching; oral expression

PSYCHIATRIC SERVICES
8/1614 learning conditions; nurse education

PSYCHOLINGUISTICS
8/0125 literacy; parent participation; reading
8/0184 cognition; language development

PSYCHOLOGICAL TESTING
8/1656 cross-cultural research; cultural background; personality assessment; Saudi Arabia

PSYCHOLOGY
8/0643 aesthetics; attitude
8/0666 history of education; intelligence test
8/1356 Youth Training Scheme; youth unemployment
8/1511 statistics; teaching method

PSYCHOLOGY OF EDUCATION
8/0088 teacher education; teaching practice; theory of education
8/0689 assessment; computer; performance; test
8/1501 research method
8/1502 adult education; concept analysis; science education; teacher education

PSYCHOTHERAPY
8/1050 child care; residential care

PSYCHOSIS
8/0720 adolescent; assessment; cognition; schizophrenia; thinking

PUBLIC OPINION
8/1655 development aid; development education; developmental policy

PUNISHMENT
8/0868 behaviour; reward; secondary education; social interaction

PUPILS
8/0015 attitude; discipline; disruptive behaviour; misconduct
8/0103 disruptive behaviour; inservice education and training of teachers; secondary education
8/0280 attitude change; database; microcomputer; sex difference
8/0326 evaluation; textbook
8/0393 assessment; computer assisted instruction; database; performance; software
8/0447 family life; occupational success; personality development; private school; social class
8/0592 ability; technology
8/0855 integration; physically handicapped; Spina Bifida
8/0860 attitude; ethnic minority; racism; stereotype
8/0936 defiant behaviour; girl; problem child
8/0962 secondary education; stress
8/1036 attitude; physical education
8/1158 English language; curriculum; secondary education; teacher perception
8/1160 assessment; secondary education; student teacher; teacher-pupil relation
8/1238 laboratory work; performance; performance factors
8/1259 administration of education; behaviour; secondary education; system of education
8/1333 achievement measurement; assessment; Scotland; technical assistance
8/1347 achievement measurement; examination; performance; performance indicator
8/1393 assessment; primary school; pupil evaluation; school based assessment
8/1604 personality development; primary school; religion; secondary school

8/1605 attitude; catholic school; catholicism; christianity; denominational school; religion
8/1606 attitude; primary school; rural school; small school
8/1608 attitude; religion; sciences; secondary school
8/1618 attitude; Europe; secondary school; student teacher
8/1626 assessment; attitude; bilingualism; first foreign language; mother tongue; writing
8/1647 further education students; part-time work; sixth form students
8/1648 National Curriculum; primary school; United Kingdom
8/1695 group work; interpersonal relations; listening; listening skills; self-evaluation; social skills

PUPIL ATTITUDES
8/1563 teacher-pupil relation; teaching quality

PUPIL BEHAVIOUR
8/1644 diet

PUPIL EVALUATION
8/1393 assessment; primary school; pupil; school based assessment

PUPIL PLACEMENT
8/0924 experience; school

PUPIL PROFILES
8/1387 academic records; achievement; equal opportunity; evaluation; student record

PUPIL REACTION
8/1392 aesthetic education; art; literature; painting; relationship

QATAR
8/1638 nursery school; pre-school education; sex difference; teacher-pupil relation

QUALIFICATIONS
8/0031 comparative education; education; EEC; Europe; labour market; skill; technological change; training
8/0195 EEC; insurance
8/0817 academic degree; equivalence; European Communities; library and information studies
8/1561 further education; higher education; vocational education
8/1689 adult education; educational opportunities; General Certificate of Secondary Education; participation

QUALITY OF EDUCATION
8/0073 assessment; higher education
8/0396 course; evaluation; further education; validation
8/0541 administration of education; head teacher; leadership
8/0993 administration of education; decision making; further education; planning of education
8/1350 behaviour; discipline; inner city; urban school

QUALITY OF LIFE
8/0783

QUESTIONNAIRES
8/0215 pre-school child; sexual behaviour
8/0251 careers guidance

RACE
8/0607 dance; participation; sex difference; social class
8/1694 primary school; racial attitude; racism

RACE RELATIONS
8/0127 educational innovation; educational policy; multicultural education; primary education
8/0696 adolescent; ethnic minority; group membership; identity; social interaction
8/0898 ethnic minority; secondary education
8/1088 Inservice Education and Training of Teachers; multicultural education; teacher

education; teaching aids
8/1653 educational policy; ethnic minority; multicultural education; Wales; youth
8/1692 Afro Caribbean youth; educational discrimination; equal education; equal opportunity; ethnic minority; racism
8/1694 primary school; racial attitude; racism

RACIAL ATTITUDES
8/1694 primary school; race relation; racism

RACIAL DISCRIMINATION
8/0917 college of education; curriculum development; educational policy; equal education; equal opportunity; physically handicapped
8/1351 bullying; middle school; racism; social isolation

RACISM
8/0860 attitude; ethnic minority; pupil; stereotype
8/1351 bullying; middle school; racial discrimination; social isolation
8/1692 Afro Caribbean youth; educational discrimination; equal education; equal opportunity; ethnic minority; race relations
8/1694 primary school; race relation; racial attitude
8/1696 black teachers; equal opportunity; ethnic minority; minority group teachers; supply of teachers; teacher education; teacher recruitment

READER RESPONSE
8/1098 early reading; learning strategy; perception; reading; reader text relationship; text structure

READER TEXT RELATIONSHIP
8/1098 early reading; learning strategy; perception; reading; reader response; text structure

READING
8/0035 English language; literacy; spelling
8/0092 Braille; blind; visually handicapped
8/0125 literacy; parent participation; psycholinguistics
8/0180 comprehension; meaning; reading skills; word study skills
8/0200 computer assisted instruction
8/0206 child; phonology; spelling
8/0208 language development; learning difficulty; literacy; oral expression; special education; spelling; writing
8/0235 abiltiy; dyslexia; laterality; learning difficulty; left- handed
8/0320 Brazil; cognition; comprehension
8/0327 Brazil; cognition; comprehension; metacognition; primary school
8/0384 cognitive process; comprehension
8/0405 foreign languages; performance; mother tongue
8/0422 primary education; silent reading
8/0502 achievement; cognition; communication; listening; television
8/0638 English (second language); language teaching; primary education
8/0690 early reading; language development; phonology
8/0695 Engish language; nonfiction; oral work; spoken language
8/0703 literacy; picture book
8/0724 literacy; multilingualism; primary education; social origin
8/0728 blind; learning strategy; spelling; visually handicapped; visual perception
8/0773 cognition; dyslexia; learning difficulty; music; remedial teaching
8/0780 cognition; dyslexia; learning difficulty
8/0854 literacy; secondary education; test; writing
8/0914 language teaching; learning difficulty; secondary education; storytelling; test
8/0919 cognitive process; non-fiction; primary education
8/0927 non-fiction; teaching technique
8/0938 deaf; home education; parent-child relation; pre-school child; transitional class

8/0280 attitude change; database; microcomputer; pupil
8/0335 construction; construction set; model technology; primary education; science education
8/0426 information technology; Youth Training Scheme
8/0503 cognitive development; epilepsy; pre-school child
8/0506 attitude; computer
8/0556 boy; equal opportunity; physical education
8/0581 secondary education; science education; participation; curriculum development
8/0607 dance; participation; race; social class
8/0644 leisure; perception; work attitude
8/0683 equal opportunity; girl; mathematics
8/0700 achievement; ethnic minority; primary education
8/0757 choice of studies; modern languages; secondary education
8/0776 cross-national research; fear; student; university
8/1043 career; primary education; teacher
8/1184 computer; distance study; gender equality; higher education; learning strategy; Open University
8/1219 colleges of education; gender equality; physical education; teacher education
8/1337 database; educational policy; low attainer; Scotland; Technical and Vocational Education Initiative (TVEI)
8/1438 graduate; occupational choice; social class; work
8/1479 educational opportunites; labour market; youth employment
8/1510 choice of studies; equal opportunity; girl
8/1526 access to education; equal opportunity; history of education; secondary education; social class; technical education
8/1610 career aspiration; Ireland, Northern; woman teacher
8/1638 nursery school; pre-school education; Qatar; teacher-pupil relation

SEX DISCRIMINATION
8/0799 deputy head teacher

SEX EDUCATION
8/0274 health education; learning difficulty; mental retardation; social skills; special school

SEX ROLE
8/0038 sex difference; stereotype; youth training scheme
8/1646 adult education; higher education; mature student; women's education

SEXUAL ABUSE
8/0753 child; family environment; medical treatment

SEXUAL BEHAVIOUR
8/0215 pre-school child; questionnaire
8/0682 Acquired Immune Deficiency Syndrome (AIDS); health education; woman
8/1398 Acquired Immune Deficiency Syndrome; disease; further education; further education of teachers; inservice teacher education

SEXUALITY
8/1406 attitude; belief; child

SEYCHELLES
8/1537 environmental study; evaluation
8/1572 academic degree; exchange programme; teacher education

SIBLING
8/0869 family environment; interaction; language development; language impairment

SIERRA LEONE
8/1651 educational technology; final examination; secondary school; underachievement

SIGHT VOCABULARY
8/1738

SIGN
8/0864 communication; dumb; lexicon; mentally handicapped; social behaviour
8/1382 communication; dumb; mentally handicapped; non-verbal communication

SILENT READING
8/0422 primary education; reading

SIMULATION
8/0046 industry; mathematics; teacher response; teaching aids
8/0052 industry; mathematics; teacher response; teaching aids
8/0259 business management; commercial education; computer assisted information system; instruction
8/0528 computer assisted instruction; higher education; history; software
8/0594 computer assisted instruction; history; teaching aids

SINGAPORE
8/0287 comparative education; Hong Kong; Japan

SINGLE SEX SCHOOLS
8/0085 achievement; attitude; co-education; girls' education; secondary education; sex difference

SIXTEEN TO NINETEEN EDUCATION
8/0037 education audit; tertiary education
8/0398 core skill; further education; post-compulsory education; vocational education
8/1003 further education; post-secondary education; tertiary education
8/1431 further education
8/1541 further education; learner centred curriculum

SIXTH FORM
8/0039 Buddhism; Christian education; Christianity; General Certificate of Secondary Education; secondary education; teaching aids
8/0066 administration of education; main subject; number of pupils; secondary education
8/0297 curriculum development; mathematics; microcomputer; secondary education; teaching method
8/1375 curriculum development; mathematics; secondary education; teaching aids

SIXTH FORM EDUCATION
8/1722 industry-education relationship

SIXTH FORM STUDENTS
8/1647 further education students; part-time work; pupil

SKILL
8/0031 comparative education; education; EEC; Europe; labour market; qualification; technological change; training
8/0368 assessment; communication; further education; personality development
8/0445 computer; doctor; information technology; management; professional status
8/0599 learning; teacher education; teaching
8/0746 learning process; problem solving; training; transfer of learning; vocational education
8/1685 art; primary education; reading
8/1745 basic education; labour market; labour shortage; literacy; numeracy; leaver

SKILLS SHORTAGE
8/1599 computer science; course evaluation; labour market; post-graduate study; technology

SLIDE
8/0953 ecology; environmental study; teaching aids

SMALL BUSINESSES
8/0192 business education; success; training

SMALL GROUPS
8/1640 discussion; microcomputer; primary education; verbal interaction

SMALL SCHOOLS
8/0247 learning strategy; primary education; rural school
8/0311 primary education; rural school
8/0630 educational provision; rural school
8/0646 evaluation; primary education; rural school
8/1606 attitude; primary school; pupil; rural school
8/1707 rural school; school-community relation; secondary education

SMOKING
8/0381 adolescent; drinking; health education; self-concept; behaviour
8/0387 health education; teaching aids; teaching technique
8/0861 family; health education; parent participation; prevention
8/0891 evaluation; health education; prevention

SOCIAL ADJUSTMENT
8/0149 case study; deviance; physically handicapped; special school

SOCIAL BACKGROUND
8/0796

SOCIAL BEHAVIOUR
8/0017 assessment; child; cognitive process; maladjusted
8/0864 communication; dumb; lexicon; mentally handicapped; sign
8/0865 child; emotional disorder; maladjusted

SOCIAL CHANGE
8/0228 Europe; higher education; literature; politics; teaching aids; undergraduate study

SOCIAL CLASS
8/0013 achievement; child; leisure; play; sex difference
8/0447 family life; occupational success; personality development; private school; pupil
8/0522 attitude; further education; higher education; planning of education; student
8/0607 dance; participation; race; sex difference
8/1438 graduate; occupational choice; sex difference; work
8/1526 access to education; equal opportunity; history of education; secondary education; sex difference; technical education

SOCIAL CONTROL
8/0487 absenteeism; attendance; law

SOCIAL DEVELOPMENT
8/0059 child; game; play
8/0126 peace studies; school life; student behaviour
8/0876 educational need; maladjusted; moral education
8/0877 history; water sport

SOCIAL ENVIRONMENT
8/0133 learning strategy; primary education
8/0188 achievement test; cognitive development; economic conditions; ethnic minority; family environment
8/0314 history of education; student; university
8/0370 achievement; child; motivation; Nigeria
8/0705 backwardness; child development; deprived; mental development; development
8/1253 discussion; influence; mass media; science education; secondary education
8/1533 comprehensive secondary school; culture; socio-cultural activities

SOCIAL HANDICAP
8/0058 budgetary control; financing; resource allocation; school; special education
8/0152 physically handicapped; social status
8/1109 computer assisted instruction; maladjusted; special education

8/1520 arrangement of school time: further education of teachers; inservice teacher education; time management
8/1538 inservice teacher education
8/1731 comprehensive school; self-education; teacher

STANDARD
8/0027 evaluation; examination; measurement technique
8/1737 developing country; educational policy; language teaching; literacy; tongue; vernaculars

STANDARD ASSESSMENT TASK
8/0749 assessment; English language; secondary education
8/0762 assessment; science education; secondary education
8/0900 assessment; primary education; teacher assessment
8/0983 assessment; language skill; secondary education; Welsh language
8/0985 assessment; primary education; test

STANDARDISED TEST
8/0175 assessment; physically handicapped; special education

STATISTICAL ANALYSIS
8/0751 educational research; model; research technique
8/0772 educational test
8/1009 course; educational provision; further education; higher education; planning of education

STATISTICS
8/0211 teaching method
8/0814 book; library; information service
8/1511 psychology; teaching method

STEREOTYPE
8/0038 sex difference; sex role; youth training scheme
8/0860 attitude; ethnic minority; pupil; racism
8/1400 choice of studies; occupational choice; sex

STIMULUS
8/0725 creativity; gifted; intellectual development; intelligence; thinking

STORY TELLING
8/0880 oral work; primary education
8/0914 language teaching; learning difficulty; reading; secondary education; test

STRESS
8/0062 head teacher; physical education; teacher behaviour
8/0589 college of further education; learning process; teacher behaviour; teaching personnel
8/0754 secondary education; teacher behaviour
8/0778 teaching personnel; training centre
8/0843 occupational environment; teacher behaviour
8/0903 administration of education; disease; head teacher; occupational environment
8/0947 perception; primary education
8/0962 pupil; secondary education
8/1071 Ireland, Northern; teacher behaviour

STRUCTURAL ANALYSIS
8/1156 administration of education; educational innovation
8/1574 higher education

STUDENTS
8/0054 achievement; attitude; career; teacher education
8/0201 expectancy; higher education; perception
8/0250 expenditures; income; undergraduate
8/0314 history of education; social environment; university
8/0364 higher education; learning strategy; teaching method
8/0497 aptitutde; assessment; employer; management education

8/0522 attitude; further education; higher education; planning of education; social class
8/0575 achievement test; nurse; selection; validity
8/0576 nurse; recruitment; selection
8/0612 design education; personality
8/0704 cognitive process; computer science
8/0776 cross-national research; fear; sex difference; university
8/0804 blind; higher education; tactual perception; teaching aids
8/0863 learning difficulty; staff development; teaching technique
8/0918 assignment; cognitive process; project
8/1093 cognitive process; critical sense
8/1186 adult student; dropout; dropout research; Open University; student wastage; wastage
8/1269 attitude; higher education; selection
8/1518 demand for education; demography; employment; forecasting; graduate; education; labour market; trend
8/1714 engineering; further education; mathematics; teaching method

STUDENT ADJUSTMENT
8/0940 college student; higher education; student life

STUDENT BEHAVIOUR
8/0126 peace studies; school life; social development
8/0432 higher education; motivation; religious education; theology

STUDENT LIFE
8/0904 guidance; student problems
8/0940 college student; higher education; student adjustment

STUDENT NEEDS
8/0006 college of further eduation; industry further education relationship; marketing
8/0203 lesbianism
8/0832

STUDENT PROBLEMS
8/0904 guidance; student life

STUDENT REACTION
8/1188 course evaluation; distance study; evaluation; Open University; survey

STUDENT RECORDS
8/0138 assessment; evaluation; profile; record of achievement
8/0172 achievement; assessment; evaluation; profile
8/0397 computer uses in education; electronic data processing; further education; records of achievement
8/0534 achievement; educational policy
8/1387 academic records; achievement; equal opportunity; evaluation; pupil profile
8/1410 assessment; criterion referencing; primary education
8/1674 achievement; profile
8/1675 achievement; further education; profile; Youth Training Scheme

STUDENT TEACHERS
8/0042 primary education; professional development; teacher education
8/0115 attitude change; teacher behaviour; teacher role; teaching practice; work attitude
8/0316 probationary teacher; teacher education
8/0453 inservice education and training of teachers; teacher education; teaching practice
8/0463 academic degree; attitude; learning strategy; motivation for studies
8/0543 probationary teacher; professional development; teacher education
8/1160 assessment; pupil; secondary education; teacher-pupil relation
8/1548 artificial intelligence; guidance; information system; teacher education; teaching practice
8/1618 attitude; Europe; pupil; secondary school

8/1662 attitude change; probationary teacher; special needs

STUDENT UNREST
8/0513 Australia; France; Western Europe

STUDENT WASTAGE
8/1186 adult student; dropout; dropout research; Open University; student; wastage

STUDY ABROAD
8/1550 corporate education; industrial training

STUDY SKILLS
8/0303 academic degree; culture; ethnography; languages; language teaching; undergraduate study
8/0627 assessment; learning test; primary education; project method; teaching aids
8/0781 dropout; learning strategy; medicine
8/1075 curriculum development; secondary education; self instruction
8/1086 curriculum subject; independent study
8/1137 doctorate; post-graduate; selection; supervision; thesis

STUTTERING
8/1661 adult; conversation; speech handicapped; speech therapy

SUBCULTURE
8/0446 personal narrative

SUCCESS
8/0192 business education; small business; training
8/0489 evaluation; performance; school effectiveness
8/0548 achievement; failure; motivation; primary education
8/1612 effectiveness; leadership; middle management; power

SUDAN
8/0048 developing country; distance study; higher education; open learning
8/0613 curriculum development; design; graphic arts
8/0812 cost; developing country; educational policy; equal opportunity; financial resources

SUPERVISION
8/0140 higher education; post-graduate; research; social sciences; staff development
8/0960 Botswana; developing country; inservice education and training of teachers; planning of education
8/0970 assessment; performance; teacher education; teaching practice
8/1137 doctorate; post-graduate; selection; study skills; thesis
8/1516 teacher education; teaching practice

SUPPORT SERVICES
8/0819 school library
8/0922 educational guidance; learning difficulty; special education
8/0934 multilingualism; school
8/1110 further education; special needs
8/1263 distance study; open learning

SUPPORT STAFF
8/1187 distance study; Health Service personnel; mentally handicapped; Open University; special education

SUPPORT TEACHERS
8/0739 class management; special education; special needs
8/0871 ability grouping; integration; learning difficulty; secondary education; special needs
8/0875 ability grouping; bilingualism; English language; language teaching; multilingualism

SURVEYS
8/0069 child psychology
8/0345 school leaver; Scotland; secondary education; transition from school to work; youth

383

TEACHING APTITUDE

TEACHING EXPERIENCE

TEACHING MACHINES

TEACHING MATERIALS

TEACHING METHODS

8/1242 design education; evaluation; home economics; technology education

8/1305 curriculum development; teacher inservice education; primary education; science education

8/1524 biology; curriculum; project method; theory practice relationship

8/1599 computer science; course evaluation; labour market; post-graduate study; skill shortage

TECHNOLOGY EDUCATION

8/1242 design education; evaluation; home economics; technology

8/1397 English (second language); foreign country; higher education; language of instruction; lecture; science education; university teaching

8/1489 biotechnology; philosophy of science; science education; social problems; teaching method; technological change

TELECOMMUNICATIONS

8/1227 distance study; Open University; teleconferencing

TELECONFERENCING

8/1227 distance study; Open University; telecommunication

TELEPHONE

8/0905 discourse analysis; primary education; verbal communication

TELEVISION

8/0205 mass media; primary school

8/0502 achievement; cognition; communication; listening; reading

8/0603 aggression; intervention; mass media effects; violence

8/0642 advertising; cognitive process; memory

8/0745 child; comprehension; media studies

TERTIARY EDUCATION

8/0037 education audit; sixteen to nineteen education

8/0908 attitude scale; philosophy of education; science education

8/1003 further education; post-secondary education; sixteen to nineteen education

TESTS

8/0689 assessment; computer; performance; psychology of education

8/0707 language development; Welsh language

8/0854 literacy; reading; secondary education; writing

8/0914 language teaching; learning difficulty; reading; secondary education; storytelling

8/0979 assessment; performance

8/0985 assessment; primary education; standard assessment task

8/1090 cross-cultural research; motor disorder

8/1744 ability; aptitude test; secondary education; vocational guidance

TEST CONSTRUCTION

8/0329 concept formation; mathematics

TEXTBOOK

8/0029 history; secondary education

8/0326 evaluation; pupil

8/0505 design; teaching aids; typography; visual perception

8/1452 language; mathematics; primary education

TEXTBOOK EVALUATION

8/1189 autoinstructional aid; distance study; evaluation; Open University; programmed text

TEXT STRUCTURE

8/1098 early reading; learning strategy; perception; reading; reader response; reader text relationship

THEATRE

8/1279 drama; primary school

8/1682 community education; drama; health education

THEOLOGY

8/0300 religion; religious education

8/0432 higher education; motivation; religious education; student behaviour

8/0435 catholicism; liberal education

THEORY OF EDUCATION

8/0053 educational research; philosophy of education; professional development

8/0088 psychology of education; teacher education; teaching practice

8/0485 history of education

8/0650 administration of education; leadership

8/0657 France; international exchange; system of education

8/0691 poetry; primary education

8/0708 history of education; nursery school

8/0851 adult education; working class

THEORY PRACTICE RELATIONSHIP

8/0044 teacher education

8/1265 midwifery

8/1524 biology; curriculum; project method; technology

THERAPIST

8/1523 art therapy; motivation; occupational aspiration

THERAPY

8/0681 art

8/0858 moral development; responsibility

THESIS

8/0925 developing country; distance study; masters degree

8/1137 doctorate; post-graduate; selection; study skills; supervision

8/1153 abstract; higher education; philosophy of education

THINKING

8/0003 cognitive development; problem solving; teaching method

8/0340 philosophy; secondary education; teaching

8/0720 adolescent; assessment; cognition; psychotic; schizophrenia

8/0725 creativity; gifted; intellectual development; intelligence; stimulus

8/1174 dialogue; primary school; teaching technique

TIME

8/0266 continuing education; doctor; management education

8/0649 observation; research technique; sample

TIME MANAGEMENT

8/0809 adviser; computer assisted instruction; information technology; inservice education and training of teachers; Technical and Vocational Education Initiative

8/1520 arrangement of school time: further education of teachers; inservice teacher education; staff development

8/1698

TONGUE

8/1737 developing country; educational policy; language teaching; literacy; standard; vernaculars

TOURISM

8/0425 employment; manpower need; vocational training

TRAINER

8/0155 consultation; course; doctor; inservice training

8/0454 evaluation; inservice education and training of teachers

8/1167 blind; training method; visual handicap

TRAINING

8/0031 comparative education; education; EEC; Europe; labour market; qualification; skill; technological change

8/0132 course; database; information technology

8/0148 co-operation; industry; information dissemination

8/0192 business education; small business; success

8/0334 curriculum development; police; probation period; vocational education

8/0399 curriculum development; further education; industrial education; resource materials

8/0465 profession; vocational education

8/0504 microcomputers; expert systems; rehabilitation; robotics; severe learning difficulties

8/0547 history of education; labour market; women's education; women's employment

8/0622 administration of education; school governor

8/0746 learning process; problem solving; skill; transfer of learning; vocational education

8/0946 child; competitive sport; physical development; swimmming

8/0963 performance; physical education; sport

8/0982 careers guidance; educational opportunities; transition from school to work; youth attitude

8/1185 group behaviour; group dynamics; interpersonal relations; teamwork

8/1270 assessment; health service personnel; physiotherapy

8/1323 board of governors; parents; school boards; school governors

8/1331 adult education; educational opportunities; employment opportunities; perception of others; Scotland

8/1348 post-compulsory education; vocational education; vocational training; youth attitude

8/1425 administration of education; budgetary control; financial resources; planning of education

8/1509 care; community; knowledge; mental illness

8/1580 self-evaluation; youth service

8/1584 alcoholism; database; drug addiction; health education; teaching aids

8/1623 drug addiction; guidance officer

8/1665 consortia; employment; rural area

8/1688 adult education; developing country

8/1701 curriculum; ethnic minority; evaluation; unemployed

TRAINING CENTRE

8/0778 stress; teaching personnel

TRAINING COURSE

8/1234 further education of teachers; inservice teacher education; mainstreaming; open learning; special education

TRAINING METHOD

8/1124 industrial education; industry; open learning

8/1167 blind; trainer; visual handicap

TRAINING PERSONNEL

8/1482 Europe; industrial training; technical ability

TRAINING PROGRAMME

8/1191 doctor; education; Health Service personnel; hospital; medical education

8/1315 comparative education; library; library technician; para professional personnel; personnel

8/1487 ethnic minority; work experience programme; youth employment

TRANSFER

8/1581 continuity; mathematics; primary education; secondary education

TRANSFER OF LEARNING

8/0746 learning process; problem solving; skill; training; vocational education

8/1037 intercultural education; motivation for studies; peer group teaching

TRANSITIONAL CLASS

8/0929 curriculum; developmental continuity; nursery school

8/0938 deaf; home education; parent-child relation; pre-school child; reading

TRANSITION FROM PRIMARY TO SECONDARY SCHOOL
8/0815 General Certificate of Secondary Education (GCSE); information skills; school library

TRANSITION FROM SCHOOL TO WORK
8/0019 access to education; course; vocational education; youth
8/0067 careers guidance; Careers Service; employment opportunities
8/0139 action planning; occupational choice; planning; youth
8/0248 adolescence; behaviour disorder; delinquency; occupational pupil; secondary school; life skills
8/0345 school leaver; Scotland; secondary education; survey; youth
8/0350 Scotland; survey; Technical and Vocational Education Initiative; vocational education; youth employment
8/0354 Scotland, survey, Technical and Vocational Education Initiative; vocational education; youth employment
8/0356 Scotland; survey; Technical and Vocational Initiative; vocational education; youth employment
8/0357 school leaver; Scotland; secondary education; survey; youth
8/0359 labour market; Scotland; youth employment
8/0373 handicapped; special needs; youth
8/0478 attitude; employment opportunities; school leaver; youth employment
8/0667 socialization; youth employment; youth unemployment
8/0675 educational policy; labour market; youth unemployment
8/0813 employment; further education; industrial education; manpower need; vocational education
8/0822 construction industry; labour market; school leaver
8/0835 evaluation; Technical and Vocational Education Initiative
8/0909 labour market; life style; school leaver; youth employment
8/0982 careers guidance; educational opportunities; training; youth attitude
8/1010 co-operation; local education authority; social service; special needs; youth
8/1018 evaluation; pre-vocational education
8/1261 curriculum development; industry; vocational education; youth employment
8/1349 achievement; ethnic minority; labour market; youth employment
8/1369 further education; national planning; survey; youth; youth employment
8/1496 career monograph; cross-national research; Germany FR; occupational choice; United Kingdom; vocational guidance; youth
8/1507 comparative analysis; Germany, Federal Republic; labour market; vocational education; youth employment

TRANSLATION
8/0002 computer assisted instruction; french language; language teaching; teaching aids
8/0016 computer assisted instruction; french language; language teaching
8/0181 children's liteature; fairy tale; literary criticism; style
8/0224 computer assisted instruction; higher education; information technology; language teaching

TREATMENT
8/0974 juvenile delinquencey; juvenile detention

TREND
8/1518 demand for education; demography; employment; forecasting; graduate; education; labour market; student

TRINIDAD AND TOBAGO
8/1557 cognitive development; comparative education; developing country; pre-school education

8/1566 achievement; developing country; science education

TRUANCY
8/1383 Acquired Immune Deficiency Syndrome (AIDS); behaviour disorder; drug addiction; secondary education

TURKEY
8/0621 comparative education; computer assisted instruction; microcomputer

TUTOR
8/0290 educational innovation; primary education; teacher education
8/1130 health education; teacher education

TUTORIAL
8/0109 curriculum development; learning strategy; secondary education; teaching method
8/0413 higher education; part-time student

TUTORING
8/0277 pre-school education; problem solving
8/1044 achievement; multicultural education; peer group teaching; urban school
8/1435 computer assisted instruction; geology; higher education
8/1437 computer assisted instruction; programming language
8/1468 computer assisted instruction; interaction; peer group

TWENTIETH CENTURY HISTORY
8/0089 history of education; sociology of education; university; woman teacher

TYPOGRAPHY
8/0505 design; teaching aids; textbook; visual perception

UNDERACHIEVEMENT
8/0965 learning difficulty; motor disorder; perceptual handicap
8/1651 educational technology; final examination; secondary school; Sierra Leone
8/1721 mathematics

UNDERGRADUATE
8/0150 ability; assessment; mathematics; Malaysia
8/0230 communication studies; Europe; exchange visit; higher education; industry
8/0250 expenditures; income; student
8/0304 English (second language); language teaching; writing
8/0647 mature student; special needs
8/0878 comparative analysis; continuious assessment; examination; linguistics; writing

UNDERGRADUATE STUDY
8/0228 Europe; higher education; literature; politics; social change; teaching aids
8/0303 academic degree; culture; ethnography; languages; language teaching; study method
8/1412 health education; medicine

UNEMPLOYED
8/0407 adult education; dropout; educational provision; performance indicator
8/0989 educational policy
8/1032 adult education; basic education; comparative education; data bank; physically handicapped; resource materials; education
8/1051 community education; decision making; educational policy; local education authority
8/1701 curriculum; ethnic minority; evaluation; training

UNITED KINGDOM
8/0032 comparative education; family life; France; higher education; women's education; women's employment
8/0034 foreign languages; France; Japan; language teaching; mother tongue
8/0160 educational policy; graduate study; higher education; recruitment
8/0198 college of education; history of

education; teacher education
8/0896 church; denominational school; history of education; religious organization
8/1114 adult education; China; comparative education; literacy
8/1115 China; philosophy of education
8/1132 history of education; university
8/1232 adult education; comparative education; library; library role; life-long education; Netherlands; non formal education
8/1283 child; dialect; sociolinguistics; spoken language
8/1360 comparative education; cross-cultural research; educational change; attitude; teacher behaviour; USSR
8/1496 career monograph; cross-national research; Germany FR; occupational choice; transition from school to work; vocational guidance; youth
8/1528 case study; evaluation; examination; General Certificate of Secondary Education; secondary school
8/1634 educational policy; government policy; history of education
8/1648 National Curriculum; primary school; pupil
8/1734 bilingualism; ethnic minority; first foreign language; mother tongue; Sri Lanka; Tamil
8/1735 Bangladeshi; Bengali; English (second language); ethnic minority; first foreign language; mother tongue

UNITED NATIONS
8/1307 developing country; non-formal education; participation; rural development

UNITED STATES OF AMERICA
8/0376 community; further education; higher education; system of education
8/0482 athletics; foreign student; recruitment; university
8/0655 inservice education and training of teachers; primary education; science education
8/0658 administration of education; Europe; parent-teacher participation; parent-teacher relation
8/0661 comparative education; school-industry relation
8/0726 cultural exchange; peer group; secondary education; verbal communication; writing
8/0742 comparative education; disruptive pupils
8/1123 comparative education; history of education; industrialization

UNIVERSITY
8/0033 administration of education; financial resources; higher education; history of education
8/0089 history of education; sociology of education; twentieth century history; woman teacher
8/0314 history of education; social environment; student
8/0457 history of education; ideology; sport
8/0482 athletics; foreign student; recruitment; United States of America
8/0511 foreign student; guidance
8/0628 teacher education; teacher role; teaching personnel
8/0651 history of education
8/0776 cross-national research; fear; sex difference; student
8/0805 history of education; teacher education
8/1132 history of education; United Kingdom
8/1481 administration of education; management education
8/1488 adult education; comparative education; continuing education; life-long education; performance
8/1555 higher education; history of education; woman teacher; women's education

UNIVERSITY TEACHING
8/1397 English (second language); foreign country; higher education; language of instruction; lecture; science education; technology education

URBAN AREA
8/0975 ethnic minority; voluntary organization; youth service

URBAN SCHOOL
8/1044 achievement; multicultural education; peer group teaching; tutoring
8/1350 behaviour; discipline; inner city; quality of education

USA
8/1715 behaviour disorder; comparative education; disruptive behaviour; misconduct

USSR
8/1104 adult education; German Democratic Republic; Hungary; political education; socialism
8/1360 comparative education; cross-cultural research; educational change; attitude; teacher behaviour; United Kingdom

VALIDATION
8/0396 course; evaluation; further education; quality of education

VALIDITY
8/0575 achievement test; nurse; selection; student

VALUES
8/0408 adolescence; ambition; family life; role; youth attitude
8/0614 moral education; priority; secondary education
8/0709 aims of education; philosophy of education; physical education
8/0806 comparative research; Japan; youth attitude
8/1442 citizenship education; moral education; teaching aids
8/1506 access programme; adult education; prior learning
8/1578 development policy; ecology; educational policy; environmental study; global approach

VALUES EDUCATION
8/0047 action research; educational research; individual development; philosophy of education

VERBAL COMMUNICATION
8/0087 child; communication; language development; meaning
8/0330 classroom; computer assisted instruction; group work; teacher role
8/0404 interaction; language development
8/0726 cultural exchange; peer group; secondary education; United States of America; writing
8/0756 assessment; English language; ethnic group; General Certificate of Secondary Education
8/0905 discourse analysis; primary education; telephone
8/1243 communication skills; communicative competence; English (second language teaching; oral work; spoken language; Zambia
8/1467 conversation; memory; witness
8/1649 child development; language development

VERBAL DEVELOPMENT
8/1284 phonemics; visual perception

VERBAL INTERACTION
8/0086 discussion; language development; primary education
8/0434 Bahrain; history; secondary education; teaching method
8/0486 group work; learning process
8/0743 peer group; primary education
8/1640 discussion; microcomputer; primary education; small group

VERBAL LEARNING
8/0108 computer assisted instruction; learning strategy; learning test; visual learning

VERNACULARS
8/1737 developing country; educational policy; language teaching; literacy; tongue; standard

VIDEODISC
8/0012 database; information retrieval; photograph; picture
8/0790 computer assisted instruction; educational technology; interactive video; open learning
8/0926 computer assisted instruction; educational technology; multimedia approach; teaching aids
8/1589 computer assisted instruction; computer science; distance study

VIDEO EQUIPMENT
8/1594 further education; higher education; interactive video; teaching aids

VIDEO RECORDING
8/0028 distance study; management education
8/0333 assessment; primary education; science education
8/0828 law; teaching aids
8/0937 dance; primary education; teaching aids
8/1094 computer; further education; self evaluation; teacher
8/1262 comprehension; concept formation; mechanics; teaching aids
8/1576 adult education; audio-visual education

VIDEOTAPE
8/1443 educational technology; interactive video; teaching aids

VIOLENCE
8/0603 aggression; intervention; mass media effects; television

VISION
8/0187 child development; learning difficulty; pre-school child

VISUAL ARTS
8/1739 autistic; Down's Syndrome; drawing; graphic literacy

VISUAL IMPAIRMENTS
8/0092 Braille; blind; reading
8/0093 blind; information processing; learning pace; performance
8/0094 blind; computer assisted instruction; microcomputer; software; teaching aids
8/0107 audio visual aids; blind; religious education; special education; teaching aids
8/0515 handicapped; learning difficulty; microcomputer; software
8/0728 blind; learning strategy; reading; spelling; visual perception
8/0958 microcomputer; perception; space perception; teaching aids
8/0969 assessment; handicapped
8/1038 cognitive development; concept formation; physically handicapped; special education
8/1167 blind; trainer; training method
8/1201 assessment; autoinstructional aid; blind; computer assisted instruction; electronic data processing; information technology
8/1206 autoinstructional aid; computer assisted instruction; educational electronic data processing; information technology; programmed text
8/1358 mobility; space perception; special education; teaching aids

VISUAL LEARNING
8/0108 compter assisted instruction; learning strategy; learning test; verbal learning

VISUAL PERCEPTION
8/0419 deaf; memory
8/0505 design; teaching aids; textbook; typography
8/0728 blind; learning strategy; reading; spelling; visually handicapped
8/1163 assessment; pre-school child
8/1284 phonemics; verbal development

VOCABULARY
8/0775 comprehension; language development; pre-school child
8/1237 aesthetic education; art appreciation; art education; language; painting
8/1625 communication; English language; foreign languages; language teaching; learning strategy
8/1629 language skill; modern languages; second language

VOCATIONAL EDUCATION
8/0019 access to education; course; transition from school to work; youth
8/0156 assessment; examination; profession
8/0169 distance study; further education of teachers; inservice teacher education; management development; technical education
8/0207 ethnography; sociology of education
8/0249 engineering; evaluation; higher education
8/0305 further education; librarian; management education
8/0334 curriculum development; police; probation period; training
8/0350 Scotland; survey; Technical and Vocational Education Initiative; transition from school to work; youth employment
8/0354 Scotland, survey, Technical and Vocational Education Initiative; transition from school to work; youth employment
8/0356 Scotland; survey; Technical and Vocational Initiative; transition from school to work; youth employment
8/0378 community; learning conditions; nurse; practical work
8/0398 core skill; further education; post-compulsory education; sixteen to nineteen education
8/0400 further education; National Vocational Qualification; special education
8/0401 competency based education; curriculum; further education
8/0427 nurse
8/0465 profession; training
8/0468 assessment; nurse; profile; work experience
8/0678 apprenticeship; curriculum development; inservice training; work experience
8/0746 learning process; problem solving; skill; training; transfer of learning
8/0794 college of education; comparative education; labour market; teacher education
8/0813 employment; further education; industrial education; manpower need; transition from school to work
8/0995 nurse
8/0996 educational opportunities; language impairment; speech defect
8/1019 data bank; industry education relationship
8/1116 curriculum development; Hong Kong; technical education
8/1245 evaluation; technical education
8/1256 competency based education; curriculum development; further education
8/1261 curriculum development; industry; transition from school to work; youth employment
8/1325 achievement; assessment; curriculum; learning strategy; teaching method; technical education
8/1348 post-compulsory education; training; vocational training; youth attitude
8/1483 assessment; competency-based education; curriculum design; curriculum development; further education
8/1486 co-ordinator; educational administrator; further education; management; technical education
8/1507 comparative analysis; Germany, Federal Republic; labour market; transition from school to work; youth employment
8/1551 comparative education; engineer; Japan; post-compulsory education
8/1554 comparative education; engineer; Japan; post-compulsory education; personnel
8/1561 further education; higher education; qualification